TOPICAL
BIBLE INDEX

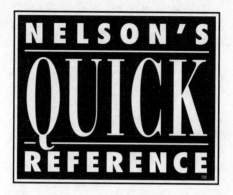

TOPICAL
BIBLE INDEX

© 1979, 1995 by Thomas Nelson, Inc.

Published in Nashville, Tennessee, by Thomas Nelson, Inc.

Library of Congress Cataloging-in-Publication Data

Nelson's quick reference topical Bible index.
    p. cm.
  ISBN 0-7852-1124-1
  1. Bible—Indexes.   I. Thomas Nelson Publishers.
BS432.N37 1996
220.5′2033—dc20
                      95-19149
                      CIP

Printed in the United States of America
1 2 3 4 5 6 7 8 9 10 11 12 — 00 99 98 97 96

TOPICAL
BIBLE INDEX

How to Use the Nelson's Quick Reference™ Topical Bible Index

Nelson's Quick Reference™ Topical Bible Index is a special kind of subject index that combines the best features of a concordance, a topical index, the usable study features of a syllabus, and other related study aids into one unique, quick, easy-to-use form. The Index offers advantages for personal Bible study that not even a combination of the above study helps would provide. With over 8,000 subjects, names, places, things, concepts, events, and doctrines of the Bible, the *Topical Bible Index* is truly a valuable key to Bible study.

An example will illustrate how to use the Index. Suppose you need to prepare or study a lesson on "The Peace of Jesus." Follow three easy steps.

Peace

A. *Kinds of:*
International . . 1 Sam. 7:14
National . . . . 1 Kin. 4:24
Civil . . . . Rom. 14:19
Domestic . . . . . . 1 Cor. 7:15
Individual . . . . . Luke 8:48
False . . . . 1 Thess. 5:3
Hypocritical . . . . James 2:16
Spiritual . . . . Rom. 5:1

B. *Source of:*
God . . . . Phil. 4:7
Christ . . . . John 14:27
Holy Spirit . . . . . Gal. 5:22

C. *Of Christ:*
Predicted . . . . Is. 9:6, 7
Promised . . . . . Hag. 2:9
Announced . . . . Is. 52:7

D. *Lord's relation to, He:*
Reveals . . . . Jer. 33:6
Gives . . . . Ps. 29:11
Establishes . . . . . Is. 26:12

E. *Among the wicked:*
Not known
by . . . . Is. 59:8

1. **Look up the Subject Heading PEACE.**

2. **Next, find the sub-heading "Of Christ."**

3. **Now you see the various Scripture references dealing with the Peace of Jesus.**

The *Topical Bible Index* has provided two important sources of information for you. First, you have the scriptural material needed to prepare or study your lesson. Second, you have this material in order as it appears in the Bible, so you have a ready-made outline for your personal use.

Topical Index to the Bible

A

Aaron—*bright*

A. *Ancestry and family of:*
Descendant of
Levi.........Ex. 6:16-20
Son of Amram and
Jochebed......Ex. 6:20
Moses' older
brother ....Ex. 7:1, 7
Brother of
Miriam........Ex. 15:20
Husband of
Elisheba......Ex. 6:23
Father of Nadab, Abihu,
Eleazar, and
Ithamar......Ex. 6:23

B. *Position of:*
Moses'
helper.........Ex. 4:13-31
Becomes "prophet" to
Moses........Ex. 7:1, 2
God inspired...Ex. 12:1
Commissioned, with Moses to
deliver Israelites from
Egypt.........Ex. 6:13, 26
  Josh. 24:5
Inferior to that of Mel-
chizedek.....Heb. 7:11-19

C. *Special privileges of:*
Appears before
Pharaoh ......Ex. 5:1-4
Performs ⎰Ex. 7:9, 10, 19,
miracles......⎱   20
Supports Moses'
hands.........Ex. 17:10-12
Ascends Mt. ⎰Ex. 19:24
Sinai.........⎱Ex. 24:1, 9
Sees God's
glory.........Ex. 24:9, 10
Judges Israel in Moses'
absence ......Ex. 24:14
Allowed inside the
veil ....Lev. 16:15
Blesses the
people ....Lev. 9:22
Intercedes for
Miriam....Num. 12:10-12

D. *Sins of:*
Tolerates
idolatry ....Ex. 32:1-4

Permits evil....Ex. 32:21-25
Conspires against
Moses.......Num. 12:1-16
With Moses, fails at
Meribah......Num. 20:1-13, 24

E. *Character of:*
A good
speaker ....Ex. 4:14
Weak in
crises ....Ex. 32:1-24
Subject to
jealousy......Num. 12:1, 2
Conscious of
guilt ....Num. 12:11
Submissive ....Lev. 10:1-7
A saint ....Ps. 106:16

F. *Priesthood of:*
Chosen by
God...........Ex. 28:1
Sons, in
office........Lev. 8:1-36
Anointed with
oil ....Ex. 30:25, 30
Duties given...Ex. 30:7-10
Garments
prescribed....Ex. 39:1-31
Ordained to
teach ....Lev. 10:8, 11
Set apart to
offer ⎰Lev. 9:1-24
sacrifices.....⎱Heb. 5:1-4
Alone enters
within the ⎰Ex. 30:10
holy place...⎱Heb. 9:7, 25
Intercedes for
others.........Num. 16:46-48
Confirmed by ⎰Num. 17:8-10
God.........⎱Heb. 9:4
Hereditary....Num. 20:23-28
For lifetime....Heb. 7:23
Inferior to Mel-
chizedek's.....Heb. 7:11-19

G. *Death and descendants of:*
Lives 123
years..........Num. 33:39
Death ....Num. 20:23-29
Eleazar,
son of, ⎰Num. 20:25-28
successor ....⎱Deut. 10:6

Aaronites—*descendants of Aaron*

Fights with
David............1 Chr. 12:27
Under Zadok......1 Chr. 27:17

Ab—*fifth month of the Jewish year*

Aaron died in .....Num. 33:38

See Jewish calendar

Ab—*father*

A part of many Hebrew names
(e.g., Abinadab, Abner,
Abijah)............1 Sam. 7:1

Abaddon—*a Hebrew word translated
"destruction"*

Designates ruin
in ....Job 31:12
Parallel with Sheol
in ....Job 26:6
Refers to death....Job 28:22
Personified........Rev. 9:11

Abagtha

A eunuch under King
Ahasuerus.........Esth. 1:10

Abanah—*a river flowing through
Damascus*

Spoken of highly by
Naaman...........2 Kin. 5:12

Abandon—*desert*

A. Required for:
Safety ....Gen. 19:12-26
                Acts 27:41-44
Salvation ......Phil. 3:7-10
Service ....Matt. 10:37-39
Sanctifi-
cation........2 Cor. 6:14-18
Spiritual
success ......Heb. 11:24-27

B. Aspects of:
Land, com-
manded.......Gen. 12:1-5
Idolatry,
admonished...Ex. 32:1-10
One's ministry,
rebuked.......1 Kin. 19:3-18
Family,
regretted......1 Sam. 30:1-6
The tabernacle, remem-
bered ....Jer. 7:12
Jerusalem,
lamented......Matt. 23:37, 38

C. Of men to judgment because of:
Sin ....Gen. 6:5-7
Rebellion ......1 Sam. 15:16-26
Unbelief ....Matt. 23:37-39
Rejecting
God...........Rom. 1:21-32
Sexual
Immorality....1 Cor. 5:1-5
Apostasy ......Heb. 10:26-29

Abarim—*regions beyond*

Moses sees the promised land
from ....Num. 27:12

Abasement—*degradation; humiliation*

A. As a judgment for:
Stubborn-
ness...........2 Kin. 14:8-14
Defaming
God...........2 Chr. 32:1-22
Pride ....Is. 14:12-17
Hating Jews ...Esth. 7:4-10
Arrogance .....Dan. 4:33, 37
                Acts 12:20-23

B. As a virtue, seen in:
Nineveh's   {Jon. 3:1-10
repentance... {Matt. 12:41
A publican's unworthi-
ness...........Luke 18:13, 14
Paul's life......1 Cor. 9:19-23
Christ's
humiliation ...Phil. 2:5-8

C. Rewards of, seen in:
Healing........2 Kin. 5:11-14
Elevation ......Matt. 23:12
Restoration ....Luke 15:11-24
Renewed
service ....1 Cor. 15:9, 10

Abate—*diminish, desist*

Flood waters......Gen. 8:8, 11
Moses' natural force
not...............Deut. 34:7
Anger of
Ephraim..........Judg. 8:3

Abba—*an Aramaic word meaning
"father"*

Used by Christ....Mark 14:36
Expressive of
sonship...........Rom. 8:15

Abda—*servant* (of God)

1. The father of
   Adoniram .....1 Kin. 4:6
2. A Levite, son of
   Shammua .....Neh. 11:17

Called
Obadiah.......1 Chr. 9:16

Abdeel—*servant of God*

The father of
Shelemiah.......Jer. 36:26

Abdi—*servant of Yahweh*

1. The grandfather of
Ethan.........1 Chr. 6:44
2. A Levite.......2 Chr. 29:12
3. A Jew who divorced his foreign
wife.........Ezra 10:26

Abdiel—*servant of God*

A Gadite residing in
Gilead.......1 Chr. 5:15, 16

Abdon—*servile*

1. A minor
judge.........Judg. 12:13-15
2. A Benjamite living in
Jerusalem.....1 Chr. 8:23, 28
3. A son of
Jeiel.........1 Chr. 8:30; 9:36
4. A courtier of King
Josiah.......2 Chr. 34:20
5. A Levitical { Josh. 21:30
city { 1 Chr. 6:74

Abed-Nego—*servant of Nego*

Name given to Azariah, a Hebrew
captive...........Dan. 1:7
Appointed by Nebuchad-
nezzar.........Dan. 2:49
Accused of
disobedience......Dan. 3:12
Cast into furnace but
delivered.........Dan. 3:13-27
Promoted by Nebuchad-
nezzar...........Dan. 3:28-30

Abel—*breath*

Adam's second
son...............Gen. 4:2
The first
shepherd.........Gen. 4:2
Offering of,
accepted.........Gen. 4:4
Hated and slain by
Cain..............Gen. 4:8
Christ's blood superior
to................Heb. 12:24
Place of, filled by
Seth..............Gen. 4:25
First martyr......Matt. 23:35
Righteous.........Matt. 23:35

Sacrificed to God by
faith.............Heb. 11:4

Abel—*meadow*

1. A city involved in Sheba's
rebellion......2 Sam. 20:14, 15,
18
2. Translated as "great stone of
Abel" in.......1 Sam. 6:18
3. Elsewhere in place names (see
below)

Abel Acacia Grove—*meadow of acacias*

A place in Moab ..Num. 33:49

Abel Beth Maachah—*meadow of the
house of oppression*

A town in North { 2 Sam. 20:14, 15
Palestine { 1 Kin. 15:20
Captured by
Tiglath-Pileser....2 Kin. 15:29
Refuge of Sheba; saved from
destruction......2 Sam. 20:14-22
Seized by
Ben-Hadad.......1 Kin. 15:20

Abel Maim—*meadow of waters*

Another name for Abel Beth
Maacah.........2 Chr. 16:4

Abel Meholah—*meadow of dancing*

Midianites
flee to...........Judg. 7:22
A few miles east of
Jabesh Gilead....1 Kin. 4:12
Elisha's native
city..............1 Kin. 19:16

Abel Mizraim—*meadow of Egypt*

A place, east of Jordan, where
Israelites mourned for
Jacob...........Gen. 50:10, 11

Abez—*whiteness*

A town of
Issachar.........Josh. 19:20

Abhor—*to detest; loathe; hate*

A. *Descriptive of:*
Disliking God's
laws.........Lev. 26:15
Prejudice toward non-
Israelites......Deut. 23:7
Right attitude toward
idolatry.......Deut. 7:25, 26
Self-rejection ..Job 42:6

Israel abhorred by
Rezon........1 Kin. 11:23-25
Israel's rejection by
God..........Ps. 89:38, 39
Rejection by former
friends.......Job 19:19
Loss of
appetite......Job 33:20
Rejecting false
description ....Prov. 24:24

B. *Expressive of God's loathing of:*
Israel's
idolatry......Ps. 78:58, 59
Customs of other
nations.......Lev. 20:23
Men of
bloodshed.....Ps. 5:6

C. *Expressive of Israel's rejection
of God's:*
Judgments.....Lev. 26:15
Statutes ....Lev. 26:43
Ceremonies....1 Sam. 2:17

D. *Expressive of the believer's
hatred of:*
Lying.........Ps. 119:163
Evil..........Rom. 12:9

Abi—*an old form of father of*

King Hezekiah's
mother...........2 Kin. 18:2
Also called
Abijah............2 Chr. 29:1

Abi-Albon

An Arbathite......2 Sam. 23:31

See Abiel

Abiasaph—*the father gathers*

A descendant of Levi through
Korah............Ex. 6:24
Called Ebiasaph...1 Chr. 6:23, 37
Descendants of, act as
doorkeepers ......1 Chr. 9:19

Abiathar—*father of preeminence*

A priest who escapes Saul at
Nob..............1 Sam. 22:20-23
Becomes high priest under
David ....1 Sam. 23:6,
9-12
Shares high priesthood with
Zadok.............2 Sam. 19:11
Remains faithful to
David ....2 Sam. 15:24-29
Informs David about
Ahithophel ....2 Sam. 15:34-36

Supports Adonijah's
usurpation ....1 Kin. 1:7, 9, 25
Deposed by   { 1 Kin. 2:26, 27,
Solomon ....{   35
Eli's line ends .....1 Sam. 2:31-35
Referred to by
Christ...........Mark 2:26

Abib—*an ear of corn*

First month in Hebrew
year.............Ex. 12:1, 2
Commemorative of the
Passover ....Ex. 12:1-28
Called Nisan in postexilic
times............Neh. 2:1

Abida, Abidah—*the father knows*

A son of Midian; grandson of
Abraham and
Keturah ....Gen. 25:4

Abidan—*the father is judge*

Represents tribe of
Benjamin.........Num. 1:11
Brings offering ....Num. 7:60, 65
Leads
Benjamites ....Num. 10:24

Abide, abiding—*continuing in a
permanent state*

A. *Applied to:*
Earth's
existence......Ps. 119:90
Three graces...1 Cor. 13:13
God's Word....1 Pet. 1:23
Believer's
eternity......1 John 2:17

B. *Sphere of, in the Christian's life:*
Christ ....John 15:4-6
Christ's
words.........John 15:7
Christ's love ...John 15:10
Christ's
doctrine.......2 John 9
The Holy
Spirit ....John 14:16
God's Word....1 John 2:14, 24
The truth.......2 John 2

C. *Descriptive of the believer's:*
Protection .....Ps. 91:1
Fruitfulness....John 15:4, 5
Prayer life ....John 15:7
Assurance .....1 John 2:28

Abiel—*God is father*

1. The grandfather of Saul and
Abner.........1 Sam. 9:1, 2

2. David's mighty
   man .... 1 Chr. 11:32
   Also called
   Abi-Albon..... 2 Sam. 23:31

Abiezer—*the father is help*

1. A descendant of
   Joseph .... Josh. 17:1, 2
   Called Jeezer .. Num. 26:30
   Family settles at
   Ophrah .... Judg. 6:24
   Gideon belongs
   to............. Judg. 6:11, 12
   Family rallies to Gideon's
   call .... Judg. 6:34
2. A mighty man and commander
   in David's
   army .... 2 Sam. 23:27

Abiezrite

A member of the family of
   Abiezer......... Judg. 6:11
                   Judg. 6:24, 34

Abigail—*the father is joyful*

1. Nabal's beautiful and wise
   wife........... 1 Sam. 25:3
   Appeases David's
   anger .... 1 Sam. 25:14-35
   Becomes David's
   wife .... 1 Sam. 25:36-42
   Captured and
   rescued .... 1 Sam. 30:5, 18
   Mother of
   Chileab .... 2 Sam. 3:3
2. A stepsister of
   David .... 1 Chr. 2:16, 17

Abihail—*the father is might*

1. A Levite head of the house of
   Merari .... Num. 3:35
2. Abishur's
   wife........... 1 Chr. 2:29
3. A Gadite chief in
   Bashan........ 1 Chr. 5:14
4. Wife of King
   Rehoboam .... 2 Chr. 11:18
5. Father of Queen
   Esther .... Esth. 2:15

Abihu—*he is father*

Second of Aaron's four
   sons............... Ex. 6:23
Ascends Mt.
   Sinai .... Ex. 24:1, 9
Chosen as priest .. Ex. 28:1
Offers, with Nadab, strange
   fire............... Lev. 10:1-7

Dies in the presence of the
   Lord .... Num. 3:4
Dies without
   heirs .... 1 Chr. 24:2

Abihud—*the father is majesty*

A Benjamite ...... 1 Chr. 8:3

Abijah—*Yahweh is Father*

1. Wife of
   Hezron........ 1 Chr. 2:24
2. Son of
   Becher........ 1 Chr. 7:8
3. Samuel's second son; follows
   corrupt
   ways.......... 1 Sam. 8:2, 3
4. Descendant of Aaron; head of
   an office of
   priests .... 1 Chr. 24:3, 10
   Zechariah belongs
   to............. Luke 1:5
5. Son of
   Jeroboam I.... 1 Kin. 14:1-18
6. Another name for King
   Abijam........ 2 Chr. 11:20
7. The mother of
   Hezekiah...... 2 Chr. 29:1
   Called Abi ..... 2 Kin. 18:2
8. A priest who signs the
   document ..... Neh. 10:7
9. A priest returning from Babylon
   with Zerub-
   babel.......... Neh. 12:1, 4, 17

Abijam—*another form of Abijah*

King of Judah..... 1 Kin. 14:31
Son and successor of King
   Rehoboam....... 1 Kin. 15:1-7
Follows in his father's
   sins .... 1 Kin. 15:3, 4
Wars against King
   Jeroboam ..... 1 Kin. 15:6, 7
Also called
   Abijah........... 1 Chr. 3:10
Slays 500,000
   Israelites .... 2 Chr. 13:13-20
Fathers 38 children by 14
   wives........... 2 Chr. 13:21

Abilene—*grassy place*

A province or tetrarchy of
   Syria .... Luke 3:1

Ability—*power to perform*

A. *Descriptive of:*
   Material
   prosperity..... Deut. 16:17

Emotional
strength ......Num. 11:14
Military
power........Num. 13:31 / 1 Kin. 9:21
Physical
strength ......Ex. 18:18, 23
Mental
power........Gen. 15:5
Moral power...1 Cor. 3:2
Spiritual
power........James 3:2

B. *Of God's power to:*
Deliver........1 Cor. 10:13
Humble men..Dan. 4:37
Create life...Matt. 3:9
Destroy.......Matt. 10:28
Preserve
believers......John 10:28
Keep His
promise......Rom. 4:21
Establish us....Rom. 16:25
Supply grace...2 Cor. 9:8
Exceed our
petitions ......Eph. 3:20
Supply
ability.........1 Pet. 4:11
Comfort
others.........2 Cor. 1:4
Keep what we have committed
to Him........2 Tim. 1:12
Save from
death ....Heb. 5:7
Resurrect
men...........Heb. 11:19
Keep from
stumbling .....Jude 24, 25

C. *Of Christ's power to:*
Heal...........Matt. 9:28, 29
Subdue all
things.........Phil. 3:21
Help His
own...........Heb. 2:18
Have
compassion ...Heb. 4:15, 16
Save
completely ....Heb. 7:25

D. *Of the Christian's power to:*
Speak for the
Lord..........Luke 21:15
Admonish .....Rom. 15:14
Survive
testings ....1 Cor. 3:13-15
Withstand
Satan ....Eph. 6:11, 13
Convict
opposition.....Titus 1:9

Bridle the whole
body ....James 3:2

Abimael—*God is Father*

A son of Joktan...Gen. 10:28

Abimelech—*the father is king*

1. A Philistine king of
   Gerar ....Gen. 20:1-18
   Makes treaty with
   Abraham......Gen. 21:22-34
2. A second king of
   Gerar ....Gen. 26:1-11
   Tells Isaac to go
   home ....Gen. 26:12-16
   Makes a treaty with Isaac
   concerning certain
   wells..........Gen. 26:17-33
3. A son of Gideon by a
   concubine.....Judg. 8:31
   Conspires to become
   king...........Judg. 9:1-4
   Slays his 70
   brothers.......Judg. 9:5
   Made king of
   Shechem......Judg. 9:6
   Rebuked by Jotham, lone
   survivor.......Judg. 9:7-21
   Conspired against by
   Gaal ....Judg. 9:22-29
   Captures Shechem and
   Thebez........Judg. 9:41-50
   Death of ......Judg. 9:51-57
4. A son of Abiathar the
   priest ....1 Chr. 18:16
   Also called
   Ahimelech ....1 Chr. 24:6

Abinadab—*the father is generous*

1. A man of Kirjath Jearim whose
   house tabernacles
   the ark of the
   Lord ....1 Sam. 7:1, 2
2. The second of Jesse's eight
   sons ....1 Sam. 16:8
   A soldier in Saul's
   army..........1 Sam. 17:13
3. A son of Saul slain at Mt.
   Gilboa ....1 Sam. 31:1-8
   Bones of, buried by men of
   Jabesh ....1 Chr. 10:1-12

Abinoam—*the father is pleasantness*

Father of Barak ...Judg. 4:6

Abiram—*the father is exalted*

1. Reubenite who conspired against Moses........Num. 16:1-50
2. The firstborn son of Hiel... {1 Kin. 16:34 / Josh. 6:26

Abishag—*the father wanders*

A Shunammite employed as David's nurse...1 Kin. 1:1-4, 15
Witnessed David's choice of Solomon as successor........1 Kin. 1:15-31
Adonijah slain for desiring to marry her.......1 Kin. 2:13-25

Abishai—*father of a gift*

A son of Zeruiah, David's sister............2 Sam. 2:18
Brother of Joab and Asahel ....1 Chr. 2:16
Rebuked by David ....1 Sam. 26:5-9
Serves under Joab in David's army.........2 Sam. 2:17, 18
Joins Joab in blood-revenge against Abner........2 Sam. 2:18-24
Co-commander of David's army.......2 Sam. 10:9, 10
Loyal to David during Absalom's uprising ....2 Sam. 16:9-12
Sternly rebuked by David ....2 Sam. 19:21-23
Loyal to David during Sheba's rebellion........2 Sam. 20:1-6, 10
Slays 300 Philistines........2 Sam. 23:18
Slays 18,000 Edomites........1 Chr. 18:12, 13
Saves David by killing a giant... {2 Sam. 21:16, / 17

Abishalom—*father of peace*

A variant form of Absalom........1 Kin. 15:2, 10

Abishua—*the father is salvation*

1. A Benjamite...1 Chr. 8:3, 4
2. Phinehas' son ....1 Chr. 6:4, 5, 50

Abishur—*the father is a wall*

A Jerahmeelite....1 Chr. 2:28, 29

Abital—*the father is dew*

Wife of David.....2 Sam. 3:2, 4

Abitub—*the father is goodness*

A Benjamite ......1 Chr. 8:8-11

Abiud—*Greek form of Abihud*

Ancestor of Jesus............Matt. 1:13

Ablution—*ceremonial washing*

Of priests ....Ex. 30:18-21
Ex. 40:30, 31
Of ceremonially unclean {Lev. 14:7-9 / Lev. 15:5-10
Of a house ....Lev. 14:52
By Pharisees ......Mark 7:1-5

Abner—*the father is a lamp*

Commands Saul's army .... {1 Sam. 14:50, 51
Introduces David to Saul.............1 Sam. 17:55-58
Rebuked by David {1 Sam. 26:5, 14-16
Saul's cousin......1 Sam. 14:50, 51
Supports Ishbosheth as Saul's successor........2 Sam. 2:8-10
Defeated by David's men.........2 Sam. 2:12-17
Kills Asahel in self-defense.......2 Sam. 2:18-23
Pursued by Joab ..2 Sam. 2:24-32
Slain by Joab .....2 Sam. 3:8-27
Death of, condemned by David ....2 Sam. 3:28-39

Abolish—*to do away with*

A. Of evil things:
Idolatry........Is. 2:18
Man-made ordinances ....Col. 2:20-22
Death ....1 Cor. 15:26
Evil works.....Ezek. 6:6
Enmity ....Eph. 2:15

B. Of things good for a while:
Old covenant ..2 Cor. 3:13
Present world ....Heb. 1:10-12
Temporal rule ....1 Cor. 15:24
Partial things ..1 Cor. 13:10

C. Of things not to be abolished:
God's righteous-ness...........Is. 51:6
God's Word....Matt. 5:18

Abominations—*things utterly repulsive*

A. *Descriptive of:*
Egyptians eating with
Hebrews ...... Gen. 43:32
Undesirable social
relations ...... Ex. 8:26
Spiritist
practices ...... Deut. 18:9-12
Heathen
idolatry ...... Deut. 7:25, 26
Child-
sacrifice ...... Deut. 12:31
Pagan gods .... 2 Kin. 23:13

B. *Applied to perverse sexual relations:*
Unnatural
acts .... Lev. 18:19-29
Wrong
clothing ...... Deut. 22:5
Prostitution and
sodomy ...... Deut. 23:17, 18
Reclaiming a defiled
woman .... Deut. 24:4
Racial inter-
marriage ...... Ezra 9:1-14

C. *In ceremonial matters, applied to:*
Unclean   {Lev. 11:10-23,
animals ...... { 41-43
Deformed
animals ...... Deut. 17:1
Heathen practices in God's
house .... 2 Chr. 36:14

D. *Sinfulness of, seen in:*
Being
enticed .... 1 Kin. 11:5, 7
Delighting in .. Is. 66:3
Rejecting admonitions
against .... Jer. 44:4, 5
Polluting God's
house .... Jer. 7:30
Being   {Ezek. 20:7,
defiled ...... { 30-32

E. *Judgments upon, manifested in:*
Stoning to
death .... Deut. 17:2-5
Destroying a
city .... Deut. 13:13-17
Diminished by God's
vengeance .... Ezek. 5:11-13
Experiencing God's
fury .... Ezek. 20:7, 8

F. *Things especially classed as:*
Silver or gold from graven
images .... Deut. 7:25

Perverse
man .... Prov. 3:32
Seven sins ..... Prov. 6:16-19
False balance .. Prov. 11:1
Lying lips ...... Prov. 12:22
Sacrifices of the
wicked .... Prov. 15:8, 9
Proud in
heart .... Prov. 16:5
Justifying the
wicked .... Prov. 17:15
Scoffer .... Prov. 24:9
Prayer of one who turns away
his ear .... Prov. 28:9
False
worship .... Is. 1:13
Scant
measures ...... Mic. 6:10
Self-righteous-
ness .... Luke 16:15

Abomination of desolation

Predicted by
Daniel .... Dan. 9:27; 11:31;
                   12:11
Cited by Christ .... Matt. 24:15

Abortion—*accidental or planned miscarriage*

Laws
concerning ...... Ex. 21:22-25
Pronounced as a
judgment .... Hos. 9:14
Sought to relieve
misery .... Job 3:16
Of animals, by
thunder .... Ps. 29:9
Figurative of abrupt
conversion ...... 1 Cor. 15:8

Abound—*to increase greatly*

A. *Of good things:*
God's grace .... Rom. 5:15, 20
Hope .... Rom. 15:13
God's work .... 1 Cor. 15:58
Suffering of
Christ .... 2 Cor. 1:5
Joy in
suffering ...... 2 Cor. 8:2
Gracious
works .... 2 Cor. 8:7
Good works ... 2 Cor. 9:8
Love .... Phil. 1:9
Fruitfulness .... Phil. 4:17, 18
Faith .... Col. 2:7
Pleasing God .. 1 Thess. 4:1
Christian
qualities ...... 2 Pet. 1:5-8
Blessings ...... Prov. 28:20

B. *Source of, in good things:*
From God .....2 Cor. 9:8
From Christian
generosity.....2 Cor. 8:2, 3
Faithfulness ...Prov. 28:20
Generosity.....Phil. 4:14-18

C. *Of evil things:*
Transgres-
sions..........Prov. 29:22
Lawlessness ...Matt. 24:12
Increasing
sins..........Rom. 5:20

Abraham—*the father of a multitude*

A. *Ancestry and family:*
Descendant of
Shem ....1 Chr. 1:24-27
Son of Terah ..Gen. 11:26
First named
Abram ....Gen. 11:27
A native of
Ur ....Gen. 11:28, 31
Pagan
ancestors .....Josh. 24:2
Weds Sarai ....Gen. 11:29

B. *Wanderings of:*
Goes to
Haran.........Gen. 11:31
Receives ⎧Gen. 12:1-3
God's call ....⎩Acts 7:2-4
Prompted by
faith ....Heb. 11:8
Enters
Canaan ....Gen. 12:4-6
Canaan promised to, by
God...........Gen. 12:1, 7
Pitched his tent near
Bethel........Gen. 12:8
Famine sends him to
Egypt........Gen. 12:10-20
Returns to Canaan
enriched ......Gen. 13:1-5
Chooses Hebron rather than
strife.........Gen. 13:6-12

C. *Testing and victory of:*
Separates from
Lot ....Gen. 13:8-12
Rescues captured
Lot ....Gen. 14:14-16
Receives Melchizedek's
blessing ......Gen. 14:18-20
Covenant renewed; a son
promised to ...Gen. 15:1-21
Justified by ⎧Gen. 15:6
faith ....⎩Rom. 4:3

Takes Hagar as
concubine.....Gen. 16:1-4
Ishmael born ..Gen. 16:5-16
Covenant renewed; named
Abraham......Gen. 17:1-8
Household of,
circum-   ⎧Gen. 17:9-14, 23-
cised.........⎩27
Promised a
son ....Gen. 17:15-19
Covenant in   ⎧Gen. 17:20-22
Isaac, not   ⎨
Ishmael......⎩Gal. 4:22-31
Receives
messengers ...Gen. 18:1-15
Intercedes concerning
Sodom........Gen. 18:16-33
Witnesses Sodom's
doom ....Gen. 19:27, 28
His intercession saves
Lot ....Gen. 19:29
Sojourns at Gerar; deceives
Abimelech ....Gen. 20:1-18
Isaac born to, and
circumcised ...Gen. 21:1-8
Sends Hagar and Ishmael
away..........Gen. 21:9-21
Makes covenant with
Abimelech ....Gen. 21:22-34
Testing of, in offering
Isaac.........Gen. 22:1-19
Receives news about
Nahor.........Gen. 22:20-24
Buys burial place for
Sarah ....Gen. 23:1-20
Obtains wife for
Isaac..........Gen. 24:1-67
Marries Keturah; fathers other
children;
dies ....Gen. 25:1-10

D. *Characteristics of:*
Friend of
God...........2 Chr. 20:7
Obedient......Gen. 22:1-18
Giving........Gen. 14:20
              Heb. 7:1, 2, 4
Generous .....Gen. 13:8, 9
Courageous...Gen. 14:13-16
Independent ...Gen. 14:21-23
Man of
prayer ....Gen. 18:23-33
Man of faith ...Gen. 15:6
Rich man......Gen. 13:2
Mighty
prince.........Gen. 23:5, 6
Good
provider......Gen. 25:5, 6

E. *References to, in the New
    Testament:*
In the line of
  faith ....Heb. 11:8-10
Christ the true seed
  of.............Matt. 1:1
Foresees Christ's
  day ....John 8:56
Hears the Gospel
  preached......Gal. 3:8
Justified by
  faith ....Rom. 4:1-12
Faith of, seen in
  works........James 2:21-23
Father of   ⎰Matt. 8:11
  true   ⎰Rom. 4:11-25
  believers .....⎱Gal. 3:7, 29
Sees the   ⎰Heb. 11:8-10, 13-
  eternal city...⎱ 16
Covenant
  with, still   ⎰Luke 1:73
  valid ....⎱Acts 3:25
Sons of, illustrate
  covenants.....Gal. 4:22-31
Tithing of, has deeper
  meaning ......Heb. 7:9, 10
Headship of, in
  marriage ......1 Pet. 3:5-7
Eternal home of, in
  heaven........Luke 16:19-25

Abraham's bosom

Expressive of heavenly
status ....Luke 16:22, 23

Abram (see Abraham)

Abronah—*passage*

Israelite
encampment .....Num. 33:34

Absalom—*the father of peace*

Son of David......2 Sam. 3:3
A handsome
  man.............2 Sam. 14:25
Receives Tamar after her rape by
  Amnon...........2 Sam. 13:20
Slays Amnon for raping
  Tamar............2 Sam. 13:22-33
Flees from
  David ....2 Sam. 13:34-39
Returns through Joab's
  intrigue ....2 Sam. 14:1-24
Fathers children...2 Sam. 14:27
Reconciled to
  David ....2 Sam. 14:28-33

Alienates the people from
  David ....2 Sam. 15:1-6
Conspires against
  David ....2 Sam. 15:7-12
Takes Jerusalem ..2 Sam. 15:13-29
Receives Hushai ..2 Sam. 15:31-37
Hears Ahithophel's
  counsel...........2 Sam. 16:20-23
Prefers Hushai's
  counsel...........2 Sam. 17:5-14
Strategy of, revealed to
  David ....2 Sam. 17:15-22
Masses his army against
  David ....2 Sam. 17:24-26
Caught and slain by
  Joab..............2 Sam. 18:9-18
Death of, brings sorrow to
  David ....2 Sam. 18:19-33
Joab rebukes David for mourning
  over.............2 Sam. 19:1-8
Death of, unites Israel again to
  David ....2 Sam. 19:9-15

Absence

A. *Of physical relations:*
A child from its
  father.........Gen. 37:32-35
Israel's ark ....1 Sam. 4:21, 22
Israel from her
  land...........2 Chr. 36:17-21
Believers from one
  another ....Phil. 1:25-27
Believers from
  Christ.........2 Cor. 5:6-9

B. *Of God's Spirit as:*
Judgment on the
  world ....Gen. 6:3
Judgment on an
  individual .....1 Sam. 16:14
Unable to
  flee ....Ps. 139:7-12

C. *Of graces:*
Holy Spirit.....Jude 19
Faith ....2 Thess. 3:2
Love...........2 Tim. 3:2
Holiness ....Rev. 22:11
Righteous-
  ness..........Rev. 22:11

Absenteeism—*habitual absence from*

Work,
  condemned......2 Thess. 3:6-14
Church, rebuked ..Heb. 10:25

Abstain—*to refrain from*

A. *From moral evil:*
Vindictive-
ness...........2 Sam. 16:5-14
Idolatry.........Acts 15:20, 29
Sexual
immorality.....Acts 15:20
Sexual sins....1 Thess. 4:3
Fleshly lusts...1 Pet. 2:11
Every form of
evil..........1 Thess. 5:22

B. *From things:*
Food.............2 Sam. 12:16, 23
Married {Ex. 19:15
relations.....{1 Cor. 7:5
Meats..........Rom. 14:1-23
              1 Cor. 8:1-13

C. *From unauthorized commands:*
Forbidding to
marry.........1 Tim. 4:3
Requiring man-made
ceremonies....Col. 2:20-23
Abstaining from
foods.........1 Tim. 4:3

Abstinence—*to refrain from*

Blood.............Acts 15:20
Evil..............1 Thess. 5:22
Eating............Acts 27:21
Sexual {Acts 15:20
immorality.....{1 Thess. 4:3
Idolatry..........Acts 15:20
Intoxicants.......Prov. 23:31
Lust..............1 Pet. 2:11
Things offered to
idols............Acts 15:29
Meats
contaminated.....Acts 15:20

Abstinence—*to refrain from strong
drink*

A. *Required of:*
Priests.........Lev. 10:9
Kings...........Prov. 31:4
Nazirites.......Num. 6:1-4

B. *Failure of, a cause of:*
Sudden
death..........1 Sam. 25:36-38
Delirium
tremens........Prov. 23:31-35
Insensibility {Is. 5:11, 12, 22,
to justice.....{ 23
Error in
judgment.......Is. 28:7
Moral
callousness....Is. 56:12

Revelry.........Dan. 5:2-4
Debauchery....Hab. 2:15, 16
A weaker brother's
stumble.......Rom. 14:20, 21
Excess.........Eph. 5:18

C. *Examples of:*
Manoah's
wife..........Judg. 13:3, 4, 7
Samson.........Judg. 16:17
Hannah.........1 Sam. 1:15
Rechabites.....Jer. 35:1-19
Daniel.........Dan. 1:8
John the
Baptist.......Luke 1:13-15

Abundance—*plentiful supply*

A. *Of material things:*
Spices.........1 Kin. 10:10
Rain...........1 Kin. 18:41
Metals.........1 Chr. 22:3, 14
Trees..........1 Chr. 22:4
              Neh. 9:25
Sacrifices.....1 Chr. 29:21
Camels.........2 Chr. 14:15
Great
numbers.......2 Chr. 15:9
Flocks and {2 Chr. 18:2
herds........{2 Chr. 32:29
Money..........2 Chr. 24:11
Weapons........2 Chr. 32:5
Riches.........Ps. 52:7
Milk...........Is. 7:22
Wine...........Is. 56:12
Horses.........Ezek. 26:10
Labors.........2 Cor. 11:23

B. *Of God's spiritual blessings:*
Goodness.......Ex. 34:6
Pardon.........Is. 55:7
Peace and
truth.........Jer. 33:6
Answers to our
prayers.......Eph. 3:20
Grace..........1 Tim. 1:14
Mercy..........1 Pet. 1:3

C. *Of spiritual things:*
Predicted for Gospel
times.........Is. 35:2
Realized in the
Messiah.......Ps. 72:7
Given to the
gentle........Ps. 37:11
Through
Christ........Rom. 5:17, 18, 20
By grace.......Eph. 1:3-6

D. *Of good things for Christians:*
Greater
usefulness....Matt. 13:11-13

Greater
reward........Matt. 25:29
Spiritual life ...John 10:10
Grace.........Rom. 5:17
Christian
service........1 Cor. 15:10
Joy...........2 Cor. 8:2
Thanks-   ⎰2 Cor. 4:15
giving........⎱2 Cor. 9:12
Rejoicing ......Phil. 1:26
Holy Spirit.....Titus 3:5, 6
Entrance in God's
kingdom ....2 Pet. 1:11

E. *Of undesirable things:*
Witchcraft ....Is. 47:9
Idleness .. ...Ezek. 16:49

F. *Characteristics of:*
Given to the
obedient ......Lev. 26:3-13
Useful in God's
work..........2 Chr. 24:11
Cannot satisfy
fully ....Eccl. 5:10-12
Not to be
trusted........Ps. 52:7
Subject to   ⎰Mal. 3:10-12
conditions....⎱Matt. 6:32, 33
Can be taken
away.........Luke 12:13-21
Not a sign of real
worth.........Luke 12:15

G. *Obtained by:*
Putting away
sin............2 Chr. 15:8, 9
Following God's
commands ....2 Chr. 17:3-5
Given by
God.........Job 36:31
Through
Christ.........John 10:10

Abuse—*application to a wrong purpose*

A. *Of physical things:*
Sexual perver- ⎰Gen. 19:5-9,
sions..........⎱   31-38
Torture........Judg. 16:21

B. *Of spiritual things:*
Misuse of   ⎰Num. 20:10-13
authority.....⎱1 Cor. 9:18
Using the world
wrongly.......1 Cor. 7:31
Perverting the
truth..........2 Pet. 2:10-22
Corrupting God's
ordinances ....1 Sam. 2:12-17
1 Cor. 11:17-22

C. *Manifested by:*
Unbelieving....Mark 15:29-32

Abyss

Translated:
"bottomless   ⎰Rev. 9:1, 2, 11
pit" ....⎱Rev. 17:8

Acacia Grove

1. Israel's last camp before
crossing the
Jordan ....Josh. 3:1
Scene of Baalam's attempted
curse.........Num. 22–24
Sin of Baal of Peor
here ....Num. 25:1-18
Site of Joshua's
commission ...Num. 27:12-23
War with Midianites
here ....Num. 31:1-54
Reuben and Gad receive
inheritance
here ....Num. 32:1-42
Scene of Moses' final
address ......Deut. 1–34
Spies sent
from ....Josh. 2:1
2. Valley blessed by the
Lord ....Joel 3:18

Acacia wood

Used in:

Making the ark ...Ex. 25:10, 13
Table of
showbread ....Ex. 37:10
Altar of incense ...Ex. 30:1
Altar of burnt
offering ....Ex. 38:1, 6
Tabernacle
boards...........Ex. 26:15-37

Accad—*a city in the land of Shinar*

City in Shinar.....Gen. 10:10

Acceptance—*the reception of one's
person or service*

A. *Objects of, before God:*
Righteousness and
justice ....Prov. 21:3
Our words and
meditations ...Ps. 19:14
Our
dedication.....Rom. 12:1, 2
Service ....Rom. 14:18
Giving.........Rom. 15:16, 27
Offerings ......Phil. 4:18

Intercession ...1 Tim. 2:1-3
Helping
parents ......1 Tim. 5:4
Spiritual
sacrifices......1 Pet. 2:5

B. *Qualifications of, seen in:*
Coming at   (Is. 49:8
God's time ... (2 Cor. 6:2
Meeting God's require-
ments........Job 42:8, 9
Receiving divine
sign..........Judg. 6:9-21
Noting God's (1 Sam. 7:8-10
response .....(John 12:28-30
Responding to God's
renewal ......Ezek. 20:40-44
Manifesting spiritual
rectitude......Mic. 6:6-8

C. *Persons disqualified for, such
as:*
Blemished
sacrifices......Mal. 1:8, 10, 13
Man's person ..Gal. 2:6
Those who swear
deceitfully ....Ps. 24:3-6

Access to God

A. *By means of:*
Christ ....John 14:6
Christ's
blood ....Eph. 2:13
Holy Spirit.....Eph. 2:18
Faith ....Rom. 5:2
Clean hands ...Ps. 24:3-5
God's grace....Eph. 1:6
Prayer ....Matt. 6:6

B. *Characteristics of:*
On God's
choosing ......Ps. 65:4
Sinners
commanded   (Is. 55:6, 7
to seek.......(James 4:8
With
confidence ....Heb. 4:16
Boldness.......Eph. 3:12
Results from reconcili-
ation..........Col. 1:21, 22
Open to
Gentiles.......Acts 14:27
Experienced in Christ's
priesthood ....Heb. 7:19-25
Sought by God's
people ....Ps. 27:4
Bold in
prayer ....Heb. 4:16

A blessing to be
chosen........Ps. 65:4

Accident—*event not foreseen*

A. *Caused by:*
An animal .....Num. 22:25
A fall..........2 Sam. 4:4

B. *Explanation of:*
Known to   (Deut. 29:29
God..........(Prov. 16:9, 33
Misunderstood by
men..........Luke 13:4, 5
Subject to God's
providence....Rom. 8:28

Acco—*a seaport 8 miles north of Mt.
Carmel (modern Acre)*

Assigned to
Asher ....Judg. 1:31
Called Ptolemais in the New
Testament........Acts 21:7

Accommodation—*adaptation caused
by human limitations*

A. *Physically, caused by:*
Age............Gen. 33:13-15
Strength and
size ....1 Sam. 17:38-40
Inability to
repay ....Luke 7:41, 42

B. *Spiritually, caused by:*
Man's
blindness......Matt. 13:10-14
Absence of the
Spirit ....John 16:12, 13
Carnality......1 Cor. 3:1, 2
Spiritual
immaturity....Rom. 14:1-23
Man's present
limitations ....1 Cor. 2:7-16
Degrees of
light ....Heb. 9:7-15

Accomplish—*to fulfill*

A. *Of God's Word concerning:*
Judah's
captivity ......Dan. 9:2
Judah's
return........2 Chr. 36:22, 23
God's sovereign
plan.........Is. 55:11
Christ's
suffering .....Luke 18:31
Christ's
death ....John 19:28-30

B. *Of human things:*
Food ....1 Kin. 5:9

Accord—*united agreement*

A. *Descriptive of:*
A spontaneous
response ......Acts 12:10
United in
spirit..........Acts 12:20
Voluntary
action..........2 Cor. 8:17
Single-
mindedness ...Josh. 9:2
Spiritual
unity..........Acts 1:14

B. *Manifested in:*
Fellowship.....Acts 2:46
Prayer.........Acts 4:24
Opposition....Acts 7:57
Response ......Acts 8:6
Decisions .....Acts 15:25
Mind ....Phil. 2:2

Accountability—*responsibility for own acts*

A. *Kinds of:*
Universal .....Rom. 14:12
Personal.......2 Sam. 12:1-15
Personal and
family..........Josh. 7:1-26
Personal and
national........2 Sam. 24:1-17
Delayed but
exacted ....2 Sam. 21:1-14
Final ....Rom. 2:1-12

B. *Determined by:*
Federal ⎰Gen. 3:1-24
headship.....⎱Rom. 5:12-21
Personal responsi-
bility..........Ezek. 18:1-32
Faithfulness ...Matt. 25:14-30
Knowledge ....Luke 12:47, 48
Conscience ....Rom. 2:12-16
Greater light...Rom. 2:17-29
Maturity of
judgment .....1 Cor. 8:1-13

Accursed—*under a curse, doomed*

A. *Caused by:*
Hanging on a
tree............Deut. 21:23
Sin among God's
people ....Josh. 7:12
Possessing a banned
thing..........Josh. 6:18
Preaching contrary to the
Gospel ....Gal. 1:8, 9

Blaspheming
Christ ....1 Cor. 12:3

B. *Objects of being:*
A city ....Josh. 6:17
A forbidden
thing..........Josh. 22:20
An old sinner ..Is. 65:20
Christ haters or non-
believers ......1 Cor. 16:22
Paul (for the sake of
Israel) ....Rom. 9:3

Accusations—*to charge; speak against*

A. *Kinds of:*
Pagan ....Dan. 3:8
Personal.......Dan. 6:24
Public ....John 18:29

B. *Sources of, in:*
The devil ......Job 1:6-12
..............Rev. 12:9, 10
Enemies ....Ezra 4:6
Man's
conscience ....John 8:9
God's Word...John 5:45
Hypocritical ...John 8:6, 10, 11
The last days ..2 Tim. 3:1, 3
Apostates......2 Pet. 2:10, 11

C. *Forbidden:*
Against
servants.......Prov. 30:10
Falsely.........Luke 3:14
Among
slanderers.....Titus 2:3

D. *False, examples of, against:*
Jacob..........Gen. 31:26-30
Joseph.........Gen. 39:10-21
Ahimelech ....1 Sam. 22:11-16
David..........2 Sam. 10:3
Job............Job 2:3-5
Jeremiah ......Jer. 26:8-11
Amos..........Amos 7:10, 11
Joshua........Zech. 3:1-5
Christ ....Matt. 26:59-66
Stephen ....Acts 6:11-14
Paul and
Silas ....Acts 16:19-21
Paul ....Acts 21:27-29
Christians .....1 Pet. 2:12

Achaia—*a region of Greece*

Visited by Paul...Acts 18:1, 12
Gallio proconsul..Acts 18:12
Apollos preaches
in ....Acts 18:24-28
Christians of, very
generous ....Rom. 15:26

Saints in all of ....2 Cor. 1:1
Paul commends
Christians of .....2 Cor. 11:10
Gospel proclaimed
throughout.......1 Thess. 1:7, 8

Achaicus—belonging to Achaia

A Corinthian Christian who visited
Paul.............1 Cor. 16:17, 18

Achan, Achar—trouble

A son of Carmi....Josh. 7:1
Sin of, caused Israel's
defeat ....Josh. 7:1-15
Stoned to death ...Josh. 7:16-25
Sin of, recalled ...Josh. 22:20
Also called
Achar ....1 Chr. 2:7

Achbor—mouse

1. Father of Edomite
   king ....Gen. 36:36, 38
2. A courtier under
   Josiah.........2 Kin. 22:12, 14
   Called Abdon ..2 Chr. 34:20

Achim—short form of Jehoiachim

Ancestor of
Jesus.............Matt. 1:14

Achish—serpent-charmer

A king of Gath....1 Sam. 21:10-15
David seeks
refuge............1 Sam. 27:1-12
Forced to expel David by Philistine
lords ....1 Sam. 29:1-11
Receives Shimei's
servants..........1 Kin. 2:39, 40

Achmetha—capital of Media
(same as Ecbatana)

Site of Persian
archives..........Ezra 6:2

Achor, valley of—trouble

Site of Achan's
stoning...........Josh. 7:24-26
On Judah's
boundary.........Josh. 15:7
Promises
concerning ....Is. 65:10

Achsah—anklet

A daughter of
Caleb.............1 Chr. 2:49
Given to Othniel ..Josh. 15:16-19

Given springs of
water ....Judg. 1:12-15

Achshaph—dedicated

A royal city of
Canaan...........Josh. 11:1
Captured by
Joshua ....Josh. 12:7, 20
Assigned to
Asher ....Josh. 19:24, 25

Achzib—a lie

1. City of
   Judah.........Josh. 15:44
   Also called
   Chezib.........Gen. 38:5
2. Town of
   Asher ....Josh. 19:29

Acknowledge—to recognize

A. Evil objects of:
  Sin ....Ps. 32:5
  Transgres-
  sions...........Ps. 51:3
  Iniquity........Jer. 3:13
  Wickedness....Jer. 14:20

B. Good objects of:
  God ....Prov. 3:6
  God's might ...Is. 33:13
  God's people...Is. 61:9
  God's
  mystery.......Col. 2:2
  God's truth ...2 Tim. 2:25
  The apostles ...1 Cor. 14:37
  Christian
  leaders........1 Cor. 16:18

Acquaintance—personal knowledge

With God, gives
peace............Job 22:21
Of God, with man's
ways ....Ps. 139:3

Acquaintances

Deserted by ....Ps. 31:11
Made an
abomination......Ps. 88:8, 18
Jesus sought
among ....Luke 2:44
Stand afar off from
Christ ....Luke 23:49

Acquit—to declare to be innocent;
pardon

Not possible with the
wicked ....Nah. 1:3

Sought by the
righteous........Job 7:21
Difficulty of
obtaining........Job 9:28-31

Acre—a land measurement

Plowing of, by a yoke of
oxen ....1 Sam. 14:14
Descriptive of
barrenness ....Is. 5:10

Acrostic

A literary device using the Hebrew
alphabet; illustrated best in
(Hebrew)..........Ps. 119:1-176

Acts of the Apostles—book of New Testament

Written by ⎰ Luke 1:1-4
Luke ....⎱ Acts 1:1, 2
Parts of, written by
eyewitness ....Acts 27:1, 2

Adadah—holiday

A city of Judah ...Josh. 15:22

Adah—ornament

1. One of Lamech's
   wives ....Gen. 4:19
2. One of Esau's ⎰ Gen. 36:2, 4,
   wives ....⎱ 10, 12
   Also called
   Basemath .....Gen. 26:34

Adaiah—Yahweh has adorned

1. The maternal grandfather
   of Josiah ......2 Kin. 22:1
2. A Levite.......1 Chr. 6:41
3. Son of
   Shimhi.......1 Chr. 8:21
   Called
   Shema ....1 Chr. 8:13
4. Aaronite
   priest ....1 Chr. 9:10-12
5. The father of
   Maaseiah .....2 Chr. 23:1
6. A son of
   Bani ....Ezra 10:29
7. Another of a different family of
   Bani ....Ezra 10:34, 39
8. A descendant of
   Judah........Neh. 11:4, 5

Adalia

Haman's son .....Esth. 9:8, 10

Adam—red earth

A. *Creation of:*
   In God's
   image.........Gen. 1:26, 27
   By God's
   breath ....Gen. 2:7
   A living soul...1 Cor. 15:45
   From dust .....Gen. 2:7
   Before Eve.....1 Tim. 2:13
   Upright.......Eccl. 7:29
   Intelligent
   being ....Gen. 2:19, 20

B. *Position of, first:*
   Worker........Gen. 2:8, 15
   To receive God's
   law ....Gen. 2:16, 17
   Husband.......Gen. 2:18-25
   Man to sin....Gen. 3:6-12
   To receive promise of
   Messiah......Gen. 3:15
   Father........Gen. 4:1
   Head of race...Rom. 5:12-14

C. *Sin of:*
   Instigated by
   Satan ....Gen. 3:1-5
   Prompted by
   Eve ....Gen. 3:6
   Done
   knowingly ....1 Tim. 2:14
   Resulted in broken
   fellowship.....Gen. 3:8
   Brought God's
   curse.........Gen. 3:14-19

D. *Descendants of, are all:*
   Sinners ....Rom. 5:12
   Subject to
   death ....Rom. 5:12-14
   Scattered over the
   earth.........Deut. 32:8
   In need of
   salvation.....John 3:16

Adam—a city near Zaretan

Site of backing up Jordan's waters
to let Israel pass
over..............Josh. 3:16

Adam, Last—an attribution of Christ

Prefigured in
Adam ....Rom. 5:14
Gift of, abound to
many............Rom. 5:15
A life-giving
spirit ....1 Cor. 15:45
Spiritual and
heavenly ....1 Cor. 15:46-48

Adamah—*red ground*

City of Naphtali...Josh. 19:35, 36

Adami Nekeb—*earthy*

In Naphtali ......Josh. 19:33

Adam, Second

Expressive of   ⎰ 1 Cor. 15:20-24
Christ ....⎱ 1 Cor. 15:45

Adar—*dark or cloudy*

A town of Judah ..Josh. 15:1, 3

Adar—*the twelfth month of the Hebrew year*

Date set by Haman for massacre of
Jews ....Esth. 3:7, 13
Date adopted for ⎰ Esth. 9:19, 21,
Purim ....⎱ 26-28
Date of completion of
Temple..........Ezra 6:15

Adbeel—*disciplined of God*

A son of
Ishmael ....Gen. 25:13

Add—*to increase the sum of*

A. *Of material things:*
Another
child ....Gen. 30:24
A population...2 Sam. 24:3
Heavy
burdens ......1 Kin. 12:11, 14
Years to life ...Prov. 3:2
Kingly
majesty ....Dan. 4:36
Stature ....Matt. 6:27

B. *Of good things:*
No sorrow .....Prov. 10:22
Inspired
words.........Jer. 36:32
Learning.......Prov. 16:23
Spiritual
blessings .....Matt. 6:33
Converts to
Christ.........Acts 2:41, 47
A covenant ....Gal. 3:15
The Law......Gal. 3:19

C. *Of evil things:*
Additions to God's
Word ....Deut. 4:2
National sins ..1 Sam. 12:19
Iniquity........Ps. 69:27
Sin to sin ......Is. 30:1

Grief to
sorrow ....Jer. 45:3
Personal sin ...Luke 3:19, 20
Afflictions .....Phil. 1:16

Addan—*strong*

A place in Babylonia whose
returnees fail to prove Israelite
ancestry..........Ezra 2:59

Addar—*wide, open place*

A Benjamite ......1 Chr. 8:3
Also called Ard....Num. 26:40

Addi—*my witness*

Ancestor of
Jesus.............Luke 3:23, 28

Additions to the church

A. *Manner and number of:*
"The Lord
added"........Acts 2:47
"Believers ... added to the
Lord" ....Acts 5:14
"Disciples ...
multiplied"....Acts 6:1
"A great company of
priests" ....Acts 6:7
"Churches ... were
multiplied"....Acts 9:31
"A great number
believed"......Acts 11:21
"Much people
added"........Acts 11:24
"Churches ... increased in
number"......Acts 16:5

B. *By means of:*
Word
preached.....Acts 2:14-41
The Spirit's convicting
power........John 16:7-11
The Gospel as God's
power........Rom. 1:16
Responding
faith ....Acts 14:1

Addon (see Addan)

Address—*a public message*

A. *In Old Testament:*
Moses'   ⎰ Deut. 1:1-
expository....⎱ 4:40
Moses'   ⎰ Deut. 4:44-
second.......⎱ 26:19
Moses'   ⎰ Deut. 27:1-
third ....⎱ 30:20

Moses'
fourth........Deut. 32:1-43
Moses' final....Deut. 33:1-29
Joshua's
exhortation ...Josh. 23:2-16
Joshua's
farewell.......Josh. 24:1-25
Solomon's to
God...........1 Kin. 3:6-9
Ezra's
expository ....Neh. 8:1-8
Jeremiah's Temple
sermon........Jer. 7:1-10:25

B. *Of Paul:*
First...........Acts 9:20-22
Second ....Acts 13:16-41
To Peter.......Gal. 2:14-21
To women .....Acts 16:13
With Silas .....Acts 16:29-32
At Athens .....Acts 17:22-31
At Troas.......Acts 20:6, 7
To elders ......Acts 20:17-35
To the crowd ..Acts 22:1-21
Before Felix ...Acts 24:10-21
Before
Agrippa ......Acts 26:1-29
On the ship....Acts 27:21-26
Final
recorded .....Acts 28:25-28

C. *Of Peter:*
In upper
room.........Acts 1:13-22
Pentecost......Acts 2:14-40
At Temple ....Acts 3:12-26
In house of
Cornelius .....Acts 10:34-43
At Jerusalem
council........Acts 15:7-11

D. *Of Others:*
Stephen ....Acts 7:2-60
Herod ....Acts 12:21, 22
James ....Acts 15:13-21
Tertullus.......Acts 24:1-8

Adiel—*ornament of God*

1. A Simeonite
prince.........1 Chr. 4:24, 36
2. Aaronite
priest ....1 Chr. 9:12, 13
3. Father of
Azmaveth.....1 Chr. 27:25

Adin—*effeminate*

1. A man whose descendants
return with
Zerubbabel....Ezra 2:2, 15

2. A man whose descendants
return with
Ezra ....Ezra 8:1, 6
3. Sealer of the
covenant......Neh. 10:1, 16

Adina—*delicate*

A Reubenite captain under
David ....1 Chr. 11:42

Adino—*slender*

A mighty man under
David,...........2 Sam. 23:8
Compare parallel passage
in ....1 Chr. 11:11

Adithaim—*double ornaments*

A city of Judah ...Josh. 15:21, 36

Adjuration—*earnest advising; to charge as if under an oath*

Joshua's, to
Jericho..........Josh. 6:26
Saul's, to those breaking a
fast ....1 Sam. 14:24-28
Ahab's, to the prophet
Micaiah ....1 Kin. 22:16
Caiaphas', by
God..............Matt. 26:63
Demon's, by
God..............Mark 5:7
Exorcists', by
Jesus............Acts 19:13
Paul's charge, by the
Lord ....1 Thess. 5:27

Adlai—*Yahweh is just*

Father of
Shaphat..........1 Chr. 27:29

Admah—*red earth*

A city near
Sodom ....Gen. 10:19
Joins other cities against
Chedorlaomer ....Gen. 14:1-4, 8
Destroyed with Sodom and
Gomorrah ....Gen. 19:24-28

Admatha—*God-given*

One of Ahasuerus'
chamberlains .....Esth. 1:13-15

Administer—*serve; execute; manage*

Applied to:

Judgment.........1 Kin. 3:28
Vengeance........Jer. 21:12
Justice............2 Sam. 8:15

Administration—*the management or disposition of affairs*

Of gifts to Jerusalem
saints ....2 Cor. 8:19, 20
Of spiritual   (1 Cor. 12:5
gifts.............(2 Cor. 9:12

Admiration—*exceptional esteem*

Reserved for
saints ....2 Thess. 1:10
Flattering, shown by false
teachers.........Jude 16

Admonition—*wise words spoken against evil acts; warning*

A. *Performed by:*
God ....Heb. 8:5
Earthly
fathers........Eph. 6:4
Leaders........1 Thess. 5:12
Christians .....Rom. 15:14

B. *Directed against:*
A remnant.....Jer. 42:19
Elders ....Acts 20:28-35
Those who will not
work.........2 Thess. 3:10, 15
Divisive man ..Titus 3:10

C. *Sources of in:*
Scriptures ....1 Cor. 10:11
Wise words....Eccl. 12:11, 12
Spiritual
knowledge ....Col. 3:16

Adna—*pleasure*

1. Jew who divorced his foreign
wife...........Ezra 10:18, 30
2. Postexilic
priest ....Neh. 12:12, 15

Adnah—*pleasure*

1. Captain of
Saul ....1 Chr. 12:20
2. Chief Captain of
Jehoshaphat ..2 Chr. 17:14

Adonai—*Lord*

The Hebrew title for God (translated "Lord") expressing lordship (found in the following five compound words)

Adoni-Bezek—*lord of Bezek*

A king of Bezek...Judg. 1:3-7

Adonijah—*my Lord is Yahweh*

1. David's fourth
son ....2 Sam. 3:2, 4
Attempts to usurp
throne ....1 Kin. 1:5-53
Desires Abishag as
wife...........1 Kin. 2:13-18
Executed by
Solomon ......1 Kin. 2:19-25
2. A teacher......2 Chr. 17:8, 9
3. A Jew who signed the
document ......Neh. 9:38; 10:16
Probably the same as Adonikam
in ....Ezra 2:13

Adonikam—*my Lord has risen*

Descendants of, return from
exile.............Ezra 2:13

Adoniram, Adoram—*my Lord is exalted*

A son of Abda ....1 Kin. 4:6
Official
under David,   (2 Sam. 20:24
Solomon, and   {1 Kin. 5:14
Rehoboam.......(1 Kin. 12:18
Stoned by angry
Israelites.........1 Kin. 12:18
Called Hadoram..2 Chr. 10:18

Adoni-Zedek—*my Lord is righteous*

An Amorite king of
Jerusalem ....Josh. 10:1-5
Defeated and slain by
Joshua ....Josh. 10:6-27

Adoption—*the legal act of investing with sonship*

A. *Used naturally of:*
Eliezer under
Abraham......Gen. 15:2-4
Joseph's sons
under   (Gen. 48:5, 14,
Jacob ....(16
Moses under
Pharaoh's   (Ex. 2:10
daughter .....(Acts 7:21
Esther under
Mordecai......Esth. 2:7

B. *Used spiritually of Israel as:*
Elected by   (Deut. 14:1, 2
God..........(Rom. 11:1-32
Blessed by
God..........Rom. 9:4
Realized in
history........Ex. 4:22, 23

C. *Used spiritually of the Gentiles as:*

Predicted in the
prophets . . . . . . Is. 65:1
Confirmed by
faith . . . . Rom. 10:20
Realized in
the new   {Eph. 2:12
covenant . . . . . {Eph. 3:1-6

D. *The time of:*

Past, predestined
to . . . . Rom. 8:29
Present,
regarded as   {John 1:12, 13
sons . . . . {John 3:1-11
Future,
glorified as   {Rom. 8:19, 23
sons . . . . {1 John 3:2

E. *The source of:*

By God's
grace . . . . Rom. 4:16, 17
By faith . . . . Gal. 3:7, 26
Through
Christ . . . . Gal. 4:4, 5

F. *Assurances of, by:*

Spirit's
witness . . . . . . Rom. 8:16
Spirit's
leading . . . . Rom. 8:14
"Abba,
Father" . . . . Rom. 8:15
Changed life . . 1 John 3:9-17
Father's   {Prov. 3:11, 12
chastening . . . {Heb. 12:5-11

G. *The blessings of:*

A new
nature . . . . 2 Cor. 5:17
A new   {Is. 62:2, 12
name . . . . {Rev. 3:12
Access to
God . . . . Eph. 2:18
Fatherly love . . 1 John 3:1
Help in
prayer . . . . Matt. 6:5-15
Spiritual   {John 17:11, 21
unity . . . . {Eph. 2:18-22
A glorious   {John 14:1-3
inheritance . . {Rom. 8:17, 18

Adoraim—*double honor*

A city fortified by
Rehoboam . . . . 2 Chr. 11:5, 9

Adoram—*the Lord is exalted*

An official over   {2 Sam. 20:24
forced labor . . . . . {1 Kin. 12:18

See Adoniram

Adoration—*reverential praise*

A. *Rendered falsely to:*

Idols . . . . Is. 44:15, 17, 19
An image . . . . . . Dan. 3:5-7
Heavenly
hosts . . . . 2 Kin. 17:16
Satan . . . . Luke 4:6-8
Men . . . . Acts 10:25, 26
Angels . . . . Col. 2:18, 23

B. *Rendered properly to God:*

Illustrated . . . . . Is. 6:1-5
Taught . . . . Ps. 95-100
Proclaimed . . . . Rev. 4:8-11

C. *Rendered properly to Christ as God by:*

Wise men . . . . . . Matt. 2:1, 11
Leper . . . . Matt. 8:2
Ruler . . . . Matt. 9:18
Disciples . . . . . . Matt. 14:22, 33
Woman . . . . Matt. 15:25
Mother . . . . Matt. 20:20
Blind man . . . . John 9:1, 38
Every
creature . . . . . . Phil. 2:10, 11

See also Worship

Adornment

A. *Used literally of:*

A harlot . . . . . . Rev. 17:3, 4
A woman . . . . . . {Is. 3:16-24
                {1 Tim. 2:9
A building . . . . . Luke 21:5
A bride . . . . Rev. 21:2

B. *Used spiritually of:*

Believer as
justified . . . . . Is. 61:10
Believer as
sanctified . . . . Titus 2:10
Israel
restored . . . . . . Jer. 31:4
Saintly
woman . . . . 1 Tim. 2:9

C. *Guidelines for:*

In modesty . . . . 1 Tim. 2:9
Not external . . . 1 Pet. 3:3-5

Adrammelech—*Adar is king*

1. A god worshiped
by the
Samarians . . . . 2 Kin. 17:31
2. Killed Senna-   {2 Kin. 19:36, 37
cherib . . . . {Is. 37:38

Adramyttium—*a seaport of Mysia in Asia Minor*

Travels of Paul . . . . Acts 27:2-6

Adriatic Sea

A part or the whole of the Adriatic
Sea named after Adria, a city of
Italy ....Acts 27:27

Adriel—*my help is God*

Marries Saul's eldest
daughter ....1 Sam. 18:19
Sons of, slain to atone Saul's
crime.............2 Sam. 21:8, 9

Adullam—*refuge*

A town of
Canaan............Gen. 38:1, 12, 20
Conquered by
Joshua...........Josh. 12:7, 15
Assigned to
Judah ....Josh. 15:20, 35
Fortified by
Rehoboam........2 Chr. 11:5-7
Symbol of Israel's
glory ....Mic. 1:15
Reoccupied ....Neh. 11:25, 30
David seeks refuge in
caves of ....1 Sam. 22:1, 2
Exploits of mighty men while
there ....2 Sam. 23:13-17

Adullamite—*a citizen of Adullam*

Judah's friend.....Gen. 38:1, 12, 20

Adulterer—*a man who commits
adultery*

Punishment of ....Lev. 20:10
Waits for the
twilight ....Job 24:15
Offspring of ....Is. 57:3
Land is full of.....Jer. 23:10
Shall not inherit the kingdom
of God ....1 Cor. 6:9
God will judge ....Heb. 13:4

Adulteress—*a woman guilty of
adultery; seductress*

A. *Sin of:*
Punished by
death ....Lev. 20:10
Ensnares the
simple ....Prov. 7:6-23
Brings a man to
poverty ....Prov. 6:26
Leads to
death ....Prov. 2:16-19
Increases trans-
gressors........Prov. 23:27, 28

Defined by
Christ..........Matt. 5:32
Forgiven by
Christ..........John 8:1-11
Mentioned by
Paul ....Rom. 7:3

B. *Examples of:*
Tamar ....Gen. 38:13-24
Potiphar's wife
(attempted) ...Gen. 39:7-20
Midianite
women........Num. 25:6-8
Rahab ....Josh. 2:1
Bathsheba .....2 Sam. 11:4, 5
Herodias.......Matt. 14:3, 4
Unnamed
woman........John 8:1-11

See Harlot

Adultery—*sexual intercourse outside
marriage*

A. *Defined:*
In God's Law ..Ex. 20:14
By Christ ......Matt. 5:28, 32
In mental
attitude.......Matt. 5:28
As a work of the
flesh ....Gal. 5:19

B. *Sin of:*
Breaks God's
Law............Deut. 5:18
Punishable by
death ....Lev. 20:10-12
Brings death ...Prov. 2:18, 19
Makes one
poor ....Prov. 29:3
Produces moral
insensi- ⎰Prov. 30:20
bility........⎱2 Cor. 12:21
Corrupts a
land...........Hos. 4:1-3
Justifies
divorce........Matt. 19:7-9
Excludes from Christian
fellowship.....1 Cor. 5:1-13
Excludes from God's
kingdom ....1 Cor. 6:9, 10
Merits God's
judgments ....Heb. 13:4
Ends in hell ⎰Prov. 7:27
(Sheol).......⎱Rev. 21:8

C. *Forgiveness of, by:*
Man ....Judg. 19:1-4
Christ ....John 8:10, 11
Repentance....2 Sam. 12:7-14
Regener-
ation...........1 Cor. 6:9-11

D. *Examples of:*
Lot ....Gen. 19:31-38
Shechem ......Gen. 34:2
Judah........Gen. 38:1-24
Eli's sons .....1 Sam. 2:22
David.........2 Sam. 11:1-5
Amnon ....2 Sam. 13:1-20
The Samaritan
woman........John 4:17, 18

Adultery, spiritual

Seen in Israel's
idolatry ....Judg. 2:11, 17
Described
graphically ......Ezek. 16
Symbolized in Hosea's
marriage ....Hos. 1:1-3
Figurative of friendship with
the world........James 4:4
Figurative of { Rev. 2:14, 15, 20-
false teaching { 22

Adummim—*red spots*

A hill between Jerusalem and
Jericho ....Josh. 15:5, 7, 8
The probable site of Good
Samaritan
parable in ....Luke 10:30-37

Advancement—*progression*

A. *Promotion to a higher office:*
Moses and Aaron, by the
Lord ....1 Sam. 12:6
Promised to
Balaam ......Num. 22:16, 17
Joseph, by true interpre-
tation ....Gen. 41:38-46
Levites, for
loyalty ....Ex. 32:26-28
Phinehas, by decisive
action........Num. 25:7-13
Haman, by
intrigue ......Esth. 3:1, 2
Mordecai, by
ability........Esth. 10:2
Daniel, by
fidelity.......Dan. 2:48
Deacons, by
faithfulness ...1 Tim. 3:10, 13

B. *Conditions of, seen in:*
Humility......Matt. 18:4
Faithfulness ...Matt. 25:14-30
Skilled in
work.........Prov. 22:29
Service to
others.........Luke 22:24-30

C. *Hindrances to, occasioned by:*
Self-glory .....Is. 14:12-15
1 Cor. 4:6-9
Pride ....Ezek. 28:11-19
1 Pet. 5:5, 6

Advantage—*superior circumstance or ability*

A. *In God's kingdom, none by:*
Birth ....Matt. 3:8, 9
Race..........Gal. 2:14-16
Position ......John 3:1-6
Works........Matt. 5:20
Wealth ....Luke 9:25

B. *In God's kingdom, some by:*
Industry.......1 Cor. 15:10
Faithfulness ...Matt. 25:14-30
Kindred
spirit..........Phil. 2:19-23
Works.........1 Cor. 3:11-15
Dedication.....Rev. 14:1-5

Advent of Christ, the First

A. *Announced in the Old
Testament by:*
Moses ....Deut. 18:18, 19
Samuel........Acts 3:24
David.........Ps. 40:6-8
Heb. 10:5-8
Prophets......Luke 24:26, 27

B. *Prophecies fulfilled by his:*
Birth ....Is. 7:14
Matt. 1:23
Forerunner ...Mal. 3:1, 2
Matt. 3:1-3
Incarnation ...Is. 9:6
Time of   { Dan. 9:24, 25
arrival ....{ Mark 1:15
Rejection .....Is. 53:1-4
Rom. 10:16-21
Crucifixion ....Ps. 2:1, 2
Acts 4:24-28
Atonement ...Is. 53:1-12
1 Pet. 1:18-21
Resurrection...Ps. 16:8-11
Acts 2:25-31
Priesthood ....Ps. 110:4, 5
Heb. 5:5, 6

C. *His first coming:*
Introduces Gospel
age ....Acts 3:24
Establishes
new   { Jer. 31:31-34
covenant.....{ Heb. 8:6-13

Fulfills
prophecy......Luke 24:44, 45
Nullifies the ceremonial
system........Heb. 9
Brings
Gentiles in ....Acts 15:13-18

Advent of Christ, the Second (see
Second Coming of Christ)

Advents of Christ, compared

A. *First Advent:*
Prophesied.....Deut. 18:18, 19
Is. 7:14
Came as
man ....Phil. 2:5-8
Announced ....Luke 2:10-14
Time
predicted......Dan. 9:25
To save the
lost ....Matt. 18:11
Subject to
government...Matt. 17:24-27

B. *Second Advent:*
Prophesied.....John 14:1-3
1 Thess. 4:16
Come as God ..1 Thess. 4:16
As a thief......1 Thess. 5:2
At a time
unknown .....Matt. 24:36
To judge the
lost ....Matt. 25:31-33,
41-46
Source of
govern-   (Rev. 20:4-6
ment.........(Rev. 22:3-5

Adversaries—*those who actively oppose*

A. *Descriptive of:*
Satan.........1 Pet. 5:8
Gospel's
enemies.......1 Cor. 16:9
Israel's
enemies.......Josh. 5:13
An enemy .....Esth. 7:6
A rival........1 Sam. 1:6
God's agent....1 Kin. 11:14, 23
God's angel....Num. 22:22

B. *Believer's attitude toward:*
Pray for ....Matt. 5:43, 44
Use God's weapons
against.......Luke 21:15
Not to be
terrified by ...Phil. 1:28
Not to give
opportunity
to.............1 Tim. 5:14

Remember God's judgment
on ....Heb. 10:27

Adversity—*adverse circumstances*

A. *Caused by:*
Man's sin ......Gen. 3:16-19
Disobedience to God's
Law...........Lev. 26:14-20

B. *Purposes of, to:*
Punish for
sin ....2 Sam. 12:9-12
Humble us.....2 Chr. 33:12
Lead us to God's
Word ....Deut. 8:2, 3
Chasten and
correct........Heb. 12:5-11
Test our
faith ....1 Pet. 1:5-8
Give us final
rest ....Ps. 94:12, 13

C. *Reactions to:*
Rebellious ....Ex. 14:4-8
Job 2:9
Distrustful....Ex. 6:8, 9
Complaining...Ruth 1:20, 21
Questioning....Jer. 20:7-10
Fainting ......Prov. 24:10
Arrogant ......Ps. 10:6
Hopeful........Lam. 3:31-40
Submissive ...Job 5:17-22
Joyful ....James 1:2-4

D. *God's relation to, He:*
Troubles nations
with ....2 Chr. 15:5, 6
Knows the soul
in ....Ps. 31:7
Saves out of ...1 Sam. 10:19
Redeems out
of.............2 Sam. 4:9

E. *Helps under:*
By prayer.....Jon. 2:1-7
By understanding
God's   (Lam. 3:31-39
purpose ......(Rom. 5:3

Advertise—*to make known publicly*

Messiah's
advent ....Num. 24:14-19
A piece of
property........Ruth 4:4

Advice—*one's judgment or counsel*

A. *Sought by:*
A king.........Esth. 1:13-15
Another
ruler ....Acts 25:13-27

A usurper......2 Sam. 16:20-23
Five men ......2 Kin. 22:12-20

B. *Sought from:*
The ephod.....1 Sam. 23:9-12
A prophet .....Jer. 42:1-6
A dead
prophet ....1 Sam. 28:7-20
A council......Acts 15:1-22
A grieving
husband ......Judg. 20:4-7

C. *Kinds of:*
Helpful ....Ex. 18:12-25
Rejected.......1 Kin. 12:6-8
Timely........1 Sam. 25:32-34
Good ....2 Kin. 5:13, 14
God-
inspired ....2 Sam. 17:6-14
Foolish ....Job 2:9
Humiliating....Esth. 6:6-11
Fatal ....Esth. 5:14
                 Esth. 7:9, 10
Ominous.......Matt. 27:19
Accepted ......Acts 5:34-41

D. *Sought from:*
Congregation of
Israel ....Judg. 20:7

Advocate, Christ our

A. *His interest in believers, by
right of:*
Election ....John 15:16
Redemption....Eph. 1:7
Regenera-
tion...........Col. 1:27
Imputed
righteous-
ness...........{ 2 Cor. 5:21
                { Phil. 3:9

B. *His defense of believers by:*
Prayer.........Luke 22:31-34
Protection .....Heb. 13:6
Provision .....Ps. 23:1
                John 10:28
Persever-
ance ....2 Tim. 4:17, 18

C. *His blessings upon believers:*
Another
Helper ....John 14:16, 17
New command-
ment..........John 13:34, 35
New nature....2 Cor. 5:17
New name.....Rev. 2:17
New life ......John 4:14
New
relationship ...John 15:15

D. *Our duties prescribed by Him:*
Our mission—world evange-
lization ....Matt. 28:16-20
Our means—the Holy
Spirit ....Acts 1:8
Our might—the
Gospel ....Rom. 1:16
Our motivation—the love of
Christ.........2 Cor. 5:14, 15

Aeneas—*praise*

A paralytic healed by
Peter.............Acts 9:32-35

Aenon—*springs*

A place near Salim where John the
Baptist baptized ..John 3:22, 23

Afar off—*at a far distance*

A. *Applied physically to:*
Distance.......Gen. 22:4
A journey .....Num. 9:10
Sound of joy...Ezra 3:13
Ostracism......Luke 17:12

B. *Applied spiritually to:*
God's
knowledge ....Ps. 139:2
Unworthi-
ness...........Luke 18:13
Eternal
separation.....Luke 16:23
Gentiles ....Acts 2:39
God's
promises......Heb. 11:13

Affability—*a personality overflowing
with benign sociability*

A. *Manifested in:*
Cordiality......Gen. 18:1-8
Compassion ...Luke 10:33-37
Generosity.....Phil. 4:10, 14-18
Unantagonizing
speech ....1 Sam. 25:23-31

B. *Examples of:*
Jonathan ......1 Sam. 18:1-4
Titus ....2 Cor. 8:16-18
Timothy ....Phil. 2:17-20
Gaius..........3 John 1-6
Demetrius .....3 John 12

Affectation—*a studied pretense*

Parade of
egotism ....Esth. 6:6-9
Boast of the
power............Dan. 4:28-30
Sign of
hypocrisy........Matt. 6:1, 2, 16
Outbreak of false
teachers.........2 Pet. 2:18, 19

Sign of
antichrist........2 Thess. 2:4, 9
Proof of spiritual
decay ....1 Cor. 4:6-8

Affection—*an inner feeling or emotion*

A. *Kinds of:*
Natural........Rom. 1:31
Paternal ......Luke 15:20
Maternal ......1 Kin. 3:16-27
Fraternal ......Gen. 43:30-34
Filial...........Gen. 49:29, 30
National......Ps. 137:1-6
Racial ....Rom. 9:1-3
For wife ......Eph. 5:25-33
For husband...Titus 2:4
Christian ......Rom. 12:10
Heavenly ......Col. 3:1, 2

B. *Good, characteristics of:*
Loyal,
intense........Ruth 1:14-18
Memorable ....2 Sam. 1:17-27
Natural,
normal........2 Sam. 13:37-39
Tested, tried ...Gen. 22:1-19
Emotional ......John 11:33-36
Grateful ......Luke 7:36-50
Joyous.........Ps. 126:1-6
Christ-
centered ......Matt. 10:37-42

C. *Evil, characteristics of:*
Unnatural ......Rom. 1:18-32
Pretended .....Matt. 26:47-49
Abnormal......2 Tim. 3:3
Fleshly ....Rom. 13:13, 14
Worldly........2 Tim. 4:10
Defiling,
degrading .....2 Pet. 2:10-12
Agonizing, in
Hades........Luke 16:23-28

Afflictions—*hardships; trials;*
tribulations

A. *Visited upon:*
Israel in
Egypt.........Gen. 15:13
Samson by   ⎧ Judg. 16:5, 6,
Philistines....⎨ 19-21
David by
God..........Ps. 88:7
Judah by
God...........Lam. 3:33
Israel by the
world ....Ps. 129:1, 2
The just by   ⎧ Amos 5:12
the wicked...⎨ Heb. 11:37
Christians by the
world ....2 Cor. 1:6

B. *Design of, to:*
Show God's
mercy........Is. 63:9
Make us seek
God...........Hos. 5:15
Bring us back to
God...........Ps. 119:67
Humble us.....2 Chr. 33:12
Test us ....Is. 48:10

C. *In the Christian's life:*
A means of
testing ....Mark 4:17
A part of life...Matt. 24:9
To be
endured.......2 Tim. 4:5
Part of
Gospel ....1 Thess. 1:6
Must not be shaken
by ....1 Thess. 3:3
Commendable
examples of...2 Tim. 3:11
Momentary ....2 Cor. 4:17
Cannot separate from
God...........Rom. 8:35-39
Deliverance from,
promised......Ps. 34:19
Terminated at Christ's
return.........2 Thess. 1:4-7

See also Trials

Afraid—*overcome with fear*

A. *Caused by:*
Nakedness.....Gen. 3:10
Unusual
dream.........Gen. 28:16, 17
God's
presence ......Ex. 3:6
Moses'
approach......Ex. 34:30
A burning
mountain .....Deut. 5:5
Giant's   ⎧ 1 Sam. 17:11,
raging........⎨ 24
A prophet's
words.........1 Sam. 28:20
Angel's
sword.........1 Chr. 21:30
God's deeds...Ps. 65:8
Gabriel's
presence ......Dan. 8:17
A terrifying
storm ....Jon. 1:5, 10
Peter's
sinking........Matt. 14:30
Changed
person ....Mark 5:15
Heavenly
hosts..........Luke 2:9

B. *Overcome by:*
The Lord's
presence ......Ps. 3:5, 6
Trusting God .. Ps. 27:1-3
God's
protection.....Ps. 91:4, 5
Stability of
heart..........Ps. 112:7, 8
God's coming
judgment .....Is. 10:24-26
The Messiah's
advent ....Is. 40:9-11
God's sovereign
power........Is. 51:12, 13
Christ's comforting
words........Matt. 14:27

Afternoon—*part of the day following noon*

Called cool of the
day...............Gen. 3:8

Afterthought—*a later reflection*

Of Esau ......Heb. 12:16, 17
Of the Israelites...Num. 14:40-45
Of one of two
sons........Matt. 21:28-30
Of the prodigal
son..............Luke 15:17
Of the unjust
steward ....Luke 16:1-8
Of the rich man in
hell..........Luke 16:23-31
Of Judas ....Matt. 27:3-5

Afterward(s)

Your hands
shall be...........Judg. 7:11
Those who are
invited ....1 Sam. 9:13
David's conscience
bothered him.....1 Sam. 24:5
His mouth will ....Prov. 20:17
Jesus findeth
him ....John 5:14

Agabus—*he loved*

A Christian prophet who foretells a
famine and   (Acts 11:27, 28
warns Paul ......(Acts 21:10, 11

Agag—*flaming or violent*

1. A King of Amalek in Balaam's
prophecy......Num. 24:7
2. Amalekite king
spared by Saul,

but slain by   (1 Sam. 15:8, 9,
Samuel......(20-24, 32, 33

Agagite—*descendant of Agag*

A title applied to the father of
Haman, enemy of the
Jews ....Esth. 3:1, 10

Agape—*Greek word rendered "love"*

Descriptive of
God ....1 John 4:8
Demanded toward
God ....Matt. 22:37
Demanded toward
neighbors ....Matt. 22:39
Fulfills Law ......Matt. 22:40
Activity of
described.........1 Cor. 13:1-13

Agate—*a stone of translucent quartz*

Worn by the high (Ex. 28:19
priest............(Ex. 39:12
Sold by Syrians ...Ezek. 27:16

Age—*time counted by years*

A. *Handicaps of, seen in:*
Physical
infirmities.....Gen. 48:10
Unwillingness to
adventure....2 Sam. 19:31-39
Declining
strength ......Ps. 71:9
Deterioration of
body ....Eccl. 12:1-7

B. *Glories of, manifested in:*
Wisdom ....Job 12:12
Maturity.......Job 5:26
Spiritual
beauty ....Prov. 16:31
Fruitfulness....Ps. 92:12-15
Judgment......1 Kin. 12:6-8
Strong faith ...Josh. 24:15, 29

C. *Attitude of others toward:*
Respect.........Lev. 19:32
Disrespect .....2 Chr. 36:17
Insolence......Is. 3:5

D. *Unusual things connected with:*
Retaining physical
vigor..........Deut. 34:7
Becoming a   (Gen. 18:9-15
father........(Luke 1:18, 36
Living to see
Christ.........Luke 2:25-32
Knowing kind of
death in.......John 21:18, 19

E. *Attaining unto, by:*
Honoring parents ...... { Ex. 20:12 / Eph. 6:2, 3
Keeping God's law ....Prov. 3:1, 2
Following wisdom ......Prov. 3:13, 16
The fear of the Lord ....Ps. 128:1, 6
Keeping from evil ....Ps. 34:11-14
God's promise ......Gen. 15:15

F. *Those of Bible times who lived beyond age of 100:*
Methuselah ....Gen. 5:27
Jared ....Gen. 5:20
Noah ....Gen. 9:29
Adam..........Gen. 5:5
Seth ....Gen. 5:8
Cainan ....Gen. 5:14
Enosh ....Gen. 5:11
Mahalaleel....Gen. 5:17
Lamech........Gen. 5:31
Enoch ....Gen. 5:23
Terah..........Gen. 11:32
Isaac ....Gen. 35:28
Abraham ......Gen. 25:7
Jacob..........Gen. 47:28
Ishmael........Gen. 25:17
Jehoiada......2 Chr. 24:15
Sarah..........Gen. 23:1
Aaron ....Num. 33:39
Moses ....Deut. 34:7
Joseph.........Gen. 50:26
Joshua........Josh. 24:29

Agee—*fugitive*

Shammah's father ....2 Sam. 23:11

Ages—*extended periods of time*

Descriptive of the times before Christ ....Eph. 3:5
Descriptive of eternity ....Eph. 2:7

Agitation—*a disturbance*

A. *Physically of:*
Mountain......Ex. 19:16-18
The earth......Matt. 27:51-53
The world ....Ps. 46:2-6
End-time events ....Luke 21:25-27
World's end....2 Pet. 3:7-12

B. *Emotionally of:*
Extreme grief ....2 Sam. 19:1-4

Remorse......Matt. 27:3, 4
Fear ....Matt. 28:1-4

C. *Figuratively of:*
Messiah's advent ....Hag. 2:6, 7
Enraged people ....Acts 4:25-28
The wicked ....Is. 57:20
The drunkard......Prov. 23:29-35

Agony—*extreme suffering*

Descriptive of:
Christ in Gethsemane ....Luke 22:44
Christ on the cross............Mark 15:34-37
Paul's sufferings .....2 Cor. 1:8, 9
The Christians' race............1 Cor. 9:24, 25

Agree, agreement

A. *Forbidden between:*
Israel and pagans........Ex. 34:12-16
God and Baal ....1 Kin. 18:21-40
Believers, demons ......1 Cor. 10:21
Truth, error....1 John 4:1-6

B. *Necessary between:*
Prophecy, fulfillment....Acts 15:15
Doctrine, life...James 2:14-21
Words, performance ......2 Cor. 10:9-11
Believers in prayer ......Matt. 18:19
Adversaries....Matt. 5:24, 25
Christian workers......Gal. 2:7-9

C. *Examples of:*
Laban and Jacob ....Gen. 31:43-53
God and Israel ....Ex. 19:3-8
David and Jonathan......1 Sam. 18:1-4
The wicked and Sheol......Is. 28:15, 18
Employer and employees.....Matt. 20:10-13
Judas and the Sanhedrin....Matt. 26:14-16
Witnesses......Mark 14:56, 59

Husband and
wife. . . . . .Acts 5:9
The Jews and
Gamaliel . . . . . .Acts 5:34-40
Conspiring
Jews . . . . .Acts 23:20
The people of
antichrist . . . . .Rev. 17:17

Agriculture—*the cultivation of the soil*

A. *Terms and implements
involved:*
Binding . . . . .Gen. 37:7
Cultivating . . . . .Luke 13:6-9
Gleaning. . . . . . .Ruth 2:3
Grafting . . . . . . .Rom. 11:17-19
Harrowing . . . . .Is. 28:24
Harvesting . . . . .Matt. 13:30
Mowing . . . . . . .Amos 7:1
Planting . . . . . . .Prov. 31:16
Plowing . . . . . . .Job 1:14
Pruning. . . . . . . .Is. 5:6
Reaping . . . . . . .Is. 17:5
Removing
stones. . . . . . . .Is. 5:2
Sowing . . . . .Matt. 13:3
Stacking. . . . . . .Ex. 22:6
Threshing . . . . .Judg. 6:11
Treading . . . . . .Neh. 13:15
Watering . . . . . .1 Cor. 3:6-8
Weeding . . . . . .Matt. 13:28, 29
Winnowing . . . . .Ruth 3:2

B. *Virtues required in:*
Wisdom . . . . . . .Is. 28:24-29
Diligence . . . . . .Prov. 27:23-27
Labor. . . . . .2 Tim. 2:6
Patience . . . . . .James 5:7
Industry . . . . . . .Prov. 28:19
Faith . . . . .Hab. 3:17-19
Bountiful-
ness. . . . . .2 Cor. 9:6, 7
Hopefulness . . .1 Cor. 9:10

C. *Enemies of:*
War . . . . .Jer. 50:16
Pestilence. . . . . .Joel 1:9-12
Fire. . . . . .Joel 1:19
Animals . . . . . . .Song 2:15
Dry seasons . . .Jer. 14:1, 4

D. *Restrictions involving:*
Coveting another's
field. . . . . .Deut. 5:21
Removing
boundaries . . . .Deut. 19:14
Roaming
cattle . . . . .Ex. 22:5
Spreading
fire. . . . . .Ex. 22:6

Military
service . . . . .Deut. 20:5, 6
Working on the
Sabbath. . . . . . .Ex. 34:21
Complete
harvest . . . . . . .Lev. 19:9, 10

E. *God's part in:*
Began in
Eden . . . . .Gen. 2:15
Sin's penalty. . .Gen. 3:17
Providence of,
impartial . . . . . .Matt. 5:45
Goodness of,
recognized . . . .Acts 14:16, 17
Judgments against,
cited . . . . .Hag. 1:10, 11

F. *Figurative of:*
Gospel seed. . . .Matt. 13:1-9
Gospel
dispen-
sation . . . .{ Matt. 13:24-30,
36-43
God's
workers . . . . . . .John 4:36-38
God's Word. . . .Is. 55:10, 11
Spiritual
barrenness . . . .Heb. 6:7, 8
Spiritual bountiful-
ness. . . . . .2 Cor. 9:9, 10
Final harvest . .Mark 4:28, 29

Aground—*stranded in shallow water*

Ship carrying
Paul. . . . . .Acts 27:41

Agur—*collector*

Writer of
proverbs. . . . . .Prov. 30:1-33

Ahab—*father's brother*

1. A wicked king of
Israel . . . . .1 Kin. 16:29
Marries
Jezebel. . . . . . .1 Kin. 16:31
Introduces Baal
worship . . . . . . .1 Kin. 16:31-33
Denounced by
Elijah . . . . .1 Kin. 17:1
Gathers prophets of
Baal . . . . .1 Kin. 18:17-46
Wars against Ben-
hadad. . . . . .1 Kin. 20:1-43
Covets Naboth's
vineyard . . . . . .1 Kin. 21:1-16
Death of,
predicted. . . . . .1 Kin. 21:17-26
Repentance of, delays
judgment . . . . .1 Kin. 21:27-29

Joins Jehoshaphat against
Syrians . . . . . . .1 Kin. 22:1-4
Rejects Micaiah's
warning. . . . . . .1 Kin. 22:5-33
Slain in
battle. . . . . .1 Kin. 22:34-37
Seventy sons of,
slain . . . . .2 Kin. 10:1-11
Prophecies concerning,
fulfilled . . . . . . .1 Kin. 22:38
2. Lying
prophet . . . . . .Jer. 29:21-23

Aharah—*after his brother*

1. Son of
Benjamin . . . . .1 Chr. 8:1
2. Called
Ahiram . . . . . .Num. 26:38
3. Called Ehi . . . . .Gen. 46:21

Aharhel—*brother of Rachel*

A descendant of
Judah . . . . .1 Chr. 4:8

Ahasbai—*blooming; shining*

The father of
Eliphelet . . . . .2 Sam. 23:34

Ahasuerus—*king*

1. The father of Darius the
Mede . . . . .Dan. 9:1
2. Persian king . . .Esth. 1:1
Makes Esther
queen. . . . . . . .Esth. 2:16, 17
Follows Haman's
intrigue . . . . . . .Esth. 3:1, 8-12
Orders Jews
annihilated. . . .Esth. 3:13-15
Responds to Esther's
plea. . . . . .Esth. 7:1-8
Orders Haman
hanged. . . . . . .Esth. 7:9, 10
Promotes
Mordecai. . . . . .Esth. 8:1, 2
Reverses Haman's
plot. . . . . .Esth. 8:3-17
Exalts
Mordecai. . . . . .Esth. 10:1-3
3. A king of Persia;
probably Xerxes,
486–465 B.C. . .Ezra 4:6

Ahava—*a town and a river in Babylonia*

Jewish exiles gather
here. . . . . .Ezra 8:15-31

Ahaz—*he has grasped*

1. A king of Judah; son of
Jotham . . . . . . .2 Kin. 16:1, 2
Pursues evil
ways. . . . . .2 Kin. 16:3, 4
Defends Jerusalem against
Rezin and
Pekah . . . . .2 Kin. 16:5, 6
Refuses a divine
sign. . . . . .Is. 7:1-16
Defeated with great
loss . . . . .2 Chr. 28:5-15
Becomes subject to
Assyria . . . . . . .2 Kin. 16:7-9
Makes Jerusalem a pagan
city . . . . .2 Kin. 16:10-18
Erects
sundial. . . . . . .2 Kin. 20:11
Death of. . . . . . .2 Kin. 16:19, 20
2. A descendant
of   {1 Chr. 8:35, 36
Jonathan. . . . .{1 Chr. 9:40-42
3. Ancestor of
Jesus. . . . . .Matt. 1:9

Ahaziah—*Yahweh has grasped*

1. A king of Israel; son of Ahab
and Jezebel . . .1 Kin. 22:40, 51
Worships
Baal . . . . .1 Kin. 22:52, 53
Seeks alliance with Jehosh-
aphat . . . . .1 Kin. 22:48, 49
Falls through lattice; sends to
Baal-Zebub, the god of Ekron
for help . . . . . . .2 Kin. 1:2-16
Dies according to Elijah's
word. . . . . .2 Kin. 1:17, 18
2. A king of Judah; son of
Jehoram and
Athaliah . . . . . .2 Kin. 8:25, 26
Made king by Jerusalem
inhabitants. . . .2 Chr. 22:1, 2
Taught evil by his
mother. . . . . . .2 Chr. 22:2, 3
Follows Ahab's
wickedness. . . .2 Chr. 22:4
Joins Joram against the
Syrians . . . . . . .2 Kin. 8:28
Visits wounded
Joram. . . . . . . .2 Kin. 9:16
Slain by
Jehu . . . . .2 Kin. 9:27, 28
Called
Jehoahaz. . . . . .2 Chr. 21:17
Called
Azariah . . . . . .2 Chr. 22:6

Ahban—*brother of intelligence*

A son of
Abishur .... 1 Chr. 2:29

Aher—*another*

A Benjamite ...... 1 Chr. 7:12

Ahi—*brother*

1. Gadite chief ... 1 Chr. 5:15
2. Asherite
   chief .... 1 Chr. 7:34

Ahiam—*mother's brother*

One of David's mighty
men .... 2 Sam. 23:33

Ahian—*fraternal*

A Manassite ...... 1 Chr. 7:19

Ahiezer—*brother is help*

1. Head of the tribe of
   Dan .... Num. 1:12
2. Benjamite chief, joined David at
   Ziklag .... 1 Chr. 12:3

Ahihud—*brother is majesty*

1. Asherite leader, helped Moses
   divide
   Canaan .... Num. 34:27
2. A Benjamite ... 1 Chr. 8:6, 7

Ahijah—*brother of Yahweh*

1. A great-grandson of
   Judah .... 1 Chr. 2:25
2. One of David's
   warriors .... 1 Chr. 11:36
3. A Levite treasurer in David's
   reign .... 1 Chr. 26:20
4. A prophet of Shiloh who
   foretells division of Solomon's
   kingdom ...... 1 Kin. 11:29-39
   Foretells elimination of
   Jeroboam's
   line .... 1 Kin. 14:1-18
   A writer of
   prophecy ...... 2 Chr. 9:29
5. The father of
   Baasha .... 1 Kin. 15:27, 33
6. A Jew who seals Nehemiah's
   covenant ...... Neh. 10:26
7. A secretary of
   Solomon ...... 1 Kin. 4:3
8. A Benjamite ... 1 Chr. 8:7
9. A priest during Saul's
   reign .... 1 Sam. 14:3, 18

Ahikam—*my brother has arisen*

A son of Shaphan the
scribe .... 2 Kin. 22:12
Sent in Josiah's mission to
Huldah .... 2 Kin. 22:12-14
Protects
Jeremiah .... Jer. 26:24
The father of Gedaliah,
governor under
Nebuchad-   ⎰ 2 Kin. 25:22
nezzar .... ⎱ Jer. 39:14

Ahilud—*a child's brother*

1. The father of Jehoshaphat, the
   recorder under David and
   Solomon ...... 2 Sam. 8:16
2. The father of Baana, a
   commissionary
   official .... 1 Kin. 4:7, 12

Ahimaaz—*brother of anger*

1. The father of Ahinoam, wife of
   King Saul ..... 1 Sam. 14:50
2. A son of Zadok the high
   priest .... 1 Chr. 6:8, 9
   Warns David of Absalom's
   plans .... 2 Sam. 15:27, 36
   Good man ..... 2 Sam. 18:27
   First to tell David of Absalom's
   defeat .... 2 Sam. 18:19-30
3. Solomon's son-in-law and
   commissioner in
   Naphtali ...... 1 Kin. 4:15
   May be the same as 2.

Ahiman—*my brother is a gift*

1. A giant son of Anak seen by
   Israelite
   spies .... Num. 13:22, 33
   Driven out of Hebron by
   Caleb .... Josh. 15:13, 14
   Slain by tribe of
   Judah .... Judg. 1:10
2. A Levite
   gatekeeper .... 1 Chr. 9:17

Ahimelech—*my brother is king*

1. The high priest at Nob during
   Saul's reign ... 1 Sam. 21:1
   Feeds David the
   showbread .... 1 Sam. 21:2-6
   Gives Goliath's sword to
   David .... 1 Sam. 21:8, 9
   Betrayed by
   Doeg .... 1 Sam. 22:9-16
   Slain by Doeg at Saul's
   command ..... 1 Sam. 22:17-19

Abiathar, son of,
escapes ....1 Sam. 22:20
David wrote
concerning...Ps. 52 (title)
2. Abiathar's
son ....2 Sam. 8:17
Co-priest with
Zadok ....1 Chr. 24:3, 6, 31
3. David's Hittite
warrior .....1 Sam. 26:6

Ahimoth—*my brother is death*

A Kohathite
Levite............1 Chr. 6:25

Ahinadab—*my brother is noble*

One of Solomon's
officers ....1 Kin. 4:14

Ahinoam—*my brother is delight*

1. Wife of Saul ...1 Sam. 14:50
2. David's wife ...1 Sam. 25:43
Lived with David at
Gath...........1 Sam. 27:3
Captured by Amalekites at
Ziklag ....1 Sam. 30:5
Rescued by
David.........1 Sam. 30:18
Lives with David in
Hebron ....2 Sam. 2:1, 2
Mother of
Amnon ....2 Sam. 3:2

Ahio—*brotherly*

1. Abinadab's
son ....2 Sam. 6:3
2. A Benjamite ...1 Chr. 8:14
3. A son of   ⎰1 Chr. 8:31
Jehiel ....⎱1 Chr. 9:37

Ahira—*my brother is evil*

A tribal leader ....Num. 1:15

Ahisamach—*my brother supports*

A Danite.........Ex. 31:6

Ahishahar—*brother of dawn*

A Benjamite ......1 Chr. 7:10

Ahishar—*my brother has sung*

A manager of Solomon's
household ....1 Kin. 4:6

Ahithophel—*brother of folly*

David's
counselor........2 Sam. 15:12
Joins Absalom's
insurrection ...2 Sam. 15:31
Plans of, prepared against by
David ....2 Sam. 15:31-34
Counsels
Absalom.........2 Sam. 16:20-22
Reputed wise ...2 Sam. 16:23
Counsel of, rejected by
Absalom.......2 Sam. 17:1-22
Commits suicide ..2 Sam. 17:23

Ahitub—*my brother is goodness*

1. Phinehas'
son ....1 Sam. 14:3
2. The father of Zadok the
priest ....2 Sam. 8:17
3. The father of another
Zadok ....1 Chr. 6:11, 12

Ahlab—*fruitful*

A city of Asher....Judg. 1:31

Ahlai—*O would that!*

1. Father of a warrior of
David........1 Chr. 11:41
2. Woman who married an
Egyptian
servant ....1 Chr. 2:31-35

Ahoah—*brotherly*

A son of Bela .....1 Chr. 8:4

Ahohite—*a descendant of Ahoah*

Applied to Dodo,
Zalmon, and   ⎰2 Sam. 23:9, 28
Ilai..............⎱1 Chr. 11:29

Aholiab—*a father's tent*

Son of
Ahisamach ......Ex. 31:6

Ahumai—*heated by Yahweh*

A descendant of
Judah ....1 Chr. 4:2

Ahuzzam—*possessor*

A man of Judah ...1 Chr. 4:6

Ahuzzath—*possession*

A friend of
Abimelech........Gen. 26:26

Ahzai—*Yahweh has grasped*

A postexilic
priest............Neh. 11:13

Also called
Jahzerah ....1 Chr. 9:12

Ai—*ruin*

1. A city east of Bethel in central
   Palestine......Josh. 7:2
   Abraham camps
   near ....Gen. 12:8
   A royal city of
   Canaan ......Josh. 10:1
   Israel
   defeated at....Josh. 7:2-5
   Israel destroys
   completely ....Josh. 8:1-28
   Occupied after
   exile ....Ezra 2:28
2. An Ammonite city near
   Heshbon ......Jer. 49:3

Aiah—*falcon*

The father of Rizpah, Saul's
concubine ....2 Sam. 3:7

Aijalon—*place of gazelles*

1. A town assigned to
   Dan..........Josh. 19:42
   Amorites not driven
   from ....Judg. 1:35
   Miracle there ..Josh. 10:12, 13
   Assigned to Kohathite
   Levites........Josh. 21:24
   City of
   refuge........1 Chr. 6:66-69
   Included in Benjamin's
   territory ......1 Chr. 8:13
   Fortified by
   Rehoboam ....2 Chr. 11:5, 10
   Captured by
   Philistines.....2 Chr. 28:18
2. The burial place of Elon, a
   judge ....Judg. 12:12

Ain—*spring*

1. A town near
   Riblah ......Num. 34:11
2. Town of
   Judah........Josh. 15:32
   Transferred to
   Simeon ......Josh. 19:7
   Later assigned to the
   priests ....Josh. 21:16
   Called Ashan ..1 Chr. 6:59
3. Letter of the Hebrew
   alphabet ......Ps. 119:121-128

Air—*the atmosphere around the earth*

Man given dominion
over.............Gen. 1:26-30

Man names
birds of..........Gen. 2:19, 20
God destroys
birds of..........Gen. 6:7
Mystery of
eagle in ....Prov. 30:19
Satan, prince of ...Eph. 2:2
Believers meet
Jesus in ....1 Thess. 4:17
God's wrath poured
out in ....Rev. 9:2
Figurative of
emptiness ....1 Cor. 9:26

Ajah—*falcon*

A Horite ....Gen. 36:24

Akel Dama

Field called "Field of
Blood" ....Acts 1:19

Akkub—*cunning*

1. Elioenai's
   son ....1 Chr. 3:24
2. A Levite head of a family of
   porters........1 Chr. 9:17
3. A family of
   Nethinim......Ezra 2:45
4. A Levite
   interpreter ....Neh. 8:7

Akrabbim—*scorpions*

An "ascent" on the south of the
Dead Sea........Num. 34:4
One border of
Judah ....Josh. 15:3

Alabaster—*container made of fine
textured, usually white and
translucent, material*

Used by woman anointing
Jesus.............Matt. 26:7

Alameth (see Alemeth)

Alammelech—*oak of a king*

Village of Asher...Josh. 19:26

Alamoth—*virgins*

A musical term probably indicating
a women's
choir ....1 Chr. 15:20

Alarm—*sudden and fearful surprise*

A. Caused physically by:
   Sudden
   attack.........Judg. 7:20-23

Death plague . . Ex. 12:29-33
A mysterious manifesta-
tion . . . . 1 Sam. 28:11-14
Prodigies of
nature . . . . Matt. 27:50-54

B. *Caused spiritually by:*
Sin . . . . 1 Sam. 12:17-19
Remorse . . . . Gen. 27:34-40
Conscience . . . Acts 24:24, 25
Hopelessness in
hell . . . . Luke 16:22-31

C. *Shout of jubilee or warning:*
Instruction to
Israel . . . . Num. 10:9
Causes
anguish . . . . . . Jer. 4:19
Prophecy of
judgment . . . . Jer. 49:2

See Agitation

Alas—*an intense emotional outcry*

A. *Emotional outcry caused by:*
Israel's
defeat . . . . Josh. 7:7-9
An angel's
appearance . . . . Judg. 6:22
A vow's
realization . . . . Judg. 11:34, 35
Army without
water . . . . 2 Kin. 3:9, 10
Loss of
an ax head . . . . 2 Kin. 6:5
Servant's
fear . . . . 2 Kin. 6:14, 15

B. *Prophetic outcry caused by:*
Israel's
future . . . . Num. 24:23, 24
Israel's
punishment . . . Amos 5:16-20
Jacob's
trouble . . . . Jer. 30:7-9
Babylon's fall . . Rev. 18:10-19

Alemeth—*hidden*

1. A Benjamite . . 1 Chr. 7:8
2. A descendant of
Saul . . . . 1 Chr. 8:36
3. A Levitical
city . . . . 1 Chr. 6:60

Aleph

The first letter in the Hebrew
alphabet . . . . Ps. 119:1-8

Alert—*watchful*

In battle . . . . Judg. 7:15-22

In personal
safety . . . . 1 Sam. 19:9, 10
In readiness for
attack . . . . Neh. 4:9-23
In prayer . . . . Matt. 26:41
In spiritual
combat . . . . Eph. 6:18
In waiting for Christ's
return . . . . Matt. 24:42-51
Daily living . . . . . . 1 Cor. 16:13
Times of testing . . . Luke 21:34-36
Against false
teachers . . . . Acts 20:29-31

Alexander—*man-defending*

1. A son of Simon of
Cyrene . . . . Mark 15:21
2. A member of the high-priestly
family . . . . Acts 4:6
3. A Jew in
Ephesus . . . . Acts 19:33, 34
4. An apostate condemned by
Paul . . . . 1 Tim. 1:19, 20

Alexander the Great—*Alexander III of
Macedonia (356–323 B.C.)*

A. *Not named in the Bible, but
referred to as:*
The four-headed
leopard . . . . Dan. 7:6
The goat with a great
horn . . . . Dan. 8:5-9, 21
A mighty
king . . . . Dan. 11:3

B. *Rule of, described:*
His invasion of
Palestine . . . . . . Zech. 9:1-8
His kingdom being
divided . . . . Dan. 7:6

Alexandria—*a city of Egypt founded by
Alexander the Great (332 B.C.)*

Men of, persecute
Stephen . . . . Acts 6:9
Apollos, native
of . . . . Acts 18:24
Paul sails in
ship . . . . Acts 27:6

Algum, almug—*a tree* (probably the red
sandalwood)

Imported from Ophir by Hiram's
navy . . . . 1 Kin. 10:11, 12
Used in constructing the
temple . . . . 2 Chr. 9:10, 11
Also imported from
Lebanon . . . . 2 Chr. 2:8

Alienation—*a withdrawing or separation*

Descriptive of Israel's
apostasy.........Ezek. 23:17, 18,
                        22, 28
Spiritual
deadness ....Eph. 4:18

Aliens—*citizens of a foreign country; strangers*

A. *Descriptive, naturally, of:*
Israel in the Egyptian
bondage ....Gen. 15:13
Abraham in
Canaan ......Gen. 23:4
Moses in
Egypt.........Ex. 18:2, 3
Israel in
Babylon.......Ps. 137:4

B. *Descriptive, spiritually, of:*
Estrangement from
friends ....Job 19:15
The condition of the
Gentiles.......Eph. 2:12

Alive—*the opposite of being dead*

A. *Descriptive of:*
Natural life ....Gen. 43:7, 27, 28
Spiritual life ...Luke 15:24, 32
Restored physical
life.............Acts 9:41
Christ's resurrected
life.............Acts 1:3
The believer's glorified
life.............1 Cor. 15:22
Korah, Dathan, and Abiram's
descent into
Sheol ....Num. 16:27, 33

B. *The power of keeping:*
Belongs to
God.........Deut. 32:39
Not in man's
power.........Ps. 22:29
Promised to the
godly ....Ps. 33:18, 19
Gratefully acknowl-
edged ....Josh. 14:10
Transformed by Christ's
return.........1 Thess. 4:15, 16

Allegory—*an extended figure of speech using symbols*

A. *Of natural things:*
A king's
doom ....Judg. 9:8-20
Old age........Eccl. 12:1-7

Israel as a transplanted
vine...........Ps. 80:8-19

B. *Of spiritual things:*
Christian as
sheep ....John 10:1-16
Two
covenants.....Gal. 4:21-31
Israel and the
Gentiles.......Rom. 11:15-24
Christ and His
Church ....Eph. 5:22-33
The Christian's
armor.........Eph. 6:11-17

Alleluia—*praise ye the Lord*

The Greek form of the Hebrew
Hallelujah ....Rev. 19:1-6

Alliances—*treaties between nations or individuals*

A. *In the time of the patriarchs:*
Abraham with Canaanite
chiefs ....Gen. 14:13
Abraham with
Abimelech ....Gen. 21:22-34
Isaac with
Abimelech ....Gen. 26:26-33
Jacob with
Laban.........Gen. 31:44-54

B. *In the time of the wilderness:*
Israel with
Moab ....Num. 25:1-3

C. *In the time of the conquest:*
Israel with
Gibeonites ....Josh. 9:3-27

D. *In the time of David:*
David with
Achish ....1 Sam. 27:2-12

E. *In the time of Solomon:*
Solomon with
Hiram.........1 Kin. 5:12-18
Solomon with
Egypt.........1 Kin. 3:1

F. *In the time of the divided kingdom:*
Asa with Ben-
Hadad ....1 Kin. 15:18-20
Ahab with Ben-
Hadad ....1 Kin. 20:31-34
Israel with
Assyria ....2 Kin. 16:5-9
Hoshea with
Egypt.........2 Kin. 17:1-6

G. *In the time of Judah's sole kingdom:*

Hezekiah with
Egypt . . . . 2 Kin. 18:19-24
Jehoiakim with
Egypt . . . . 2 Kin. 23:31-35

Alliance with evil

A. *Forbidden to:*
Israel . . . . Ex. 34:11-16
Christians . . . . . Rom. 13:12
Christ . . . . Matt. 4:1-11

B. *Forbidden because:*
Leads to
idolatry . . . . . . Ex. 23:32, 33
Deceives . . . . . Num. 25:1-3, 18
Enslaves . . . . . . 2 Pet. 2:18, 19
Defiles . . . . Ezra 9:1, 2
Brings God's
anger . . . . Ezra 9:13-15
Corrupts . . . . . 1 Cor. 15:33
Incompatible with
Christ . . . . 2 Cor. 6:14-16
Defiles . . . . Jude 23

C. *The believer should:*
Avoid . . . . Prov. 1:10-15
Hate . . . . Ps. 26:4, 5
Confess . . . . Ezra 10:9-11
Separate
from . . . . 2 Cor. 6:17

D. *Examples of:*
Solomon . . . . . . 1 Kin. 11:1-11
Jeroboam . . . . . 1 Kin. 12:25-33
Jehoshaphat . . 2 Chr. 20:35-37
Judas
Iscariot . . . . . . Matt. 26:14-16
Heretics . . . . . . Rev. 2:14, 15, 20

See Association

All in all—*complete*

Descriptive of:
God . . . . 1 Cor. 15:28
Christ . . . . Eph. 1:23

Allon—*oak*

A Simeonite
prince . . . . 1 Chr. 4:37

Allon Bachuth—*oak of weeping*

A tree marking Deborah's
grave . . . . Gen. 35:8

Allowance—*a stipulated amount*

Daily to   ⎰ 2 Kin. 25:27-30
Jehoiachin . . . . . . ⎱ Jer. 52:34

Almighty—*a title of God*

Applied to   ⎰ Gen. 17:1, 2
God . . . . ⎱ 2 Cor. 6:18
Applied to
Christ . . . . Rev. 1:8

Almodad—*the beloved*

Eldest son of
Joktan . . . . Gen. 10:26

Almond—*a small tree bearing fruit*

Sent as a present to
Pharaoh . . . . Gen. 43:11
Used in the
tabernacle . . . . . Ex. 25:33, 34
Aaron's rod
produces . . . . Num. 17:2, 3, 8
Used figuratively of old
age . . . . Eccl. 12:5
Used by Jacob . . . Gen. 30:37

Almon Diblathaim—*Almon of the double cake of figs*

An Israelite
encampment . . . . Num. 33:46, 47

Alms, almsgiving—*gifts prompted by love to help the needy*

A. *Design of, to:*
Help the
poor . . . . Lev. 25:35
Receive a
blessing . . . . . . Deut. 15:10, 11

B. *Manner of bestowing with:*
A willing
spirit . . . . Deut. 15:7-11
Simplicity . . . . . Matt. 6:1-4
Cheerfulness . . . 2 Cor. 9:7
True love . . . . . . 1 Cor. 13:3
Fairness to
all . . . . Acts 4:32-35
Regularity . . . . . Acts 11:29, 30
Law of
reciprocity . . . . Rom. 15:25-27

C. *Cautions concerning:*
Not for man's
honor . . . . Matt. 6:1-4
Not for lazy . . . 2 Thess. 3:10
Needful for the
rich . . . . 1 Tim. 6:17, 18

D. *Rewarded:*
Now . . . . Deut. 14:28, 29
2 Cor. 9:9, 10
In heaven . . . . . Matt. 19:21

E. *Examples of:*
Zacchaeus . . . . . Luke 19:8
Dorcas . . . . Acts 9:36

Cornelius......Acts 10:2
The early
Christians.....Acts 4:34-37

Aloes—*a perfume-bearing tree*

A. *Used on:*
Beds..........Prov. 7:17
-The dead......John 19:39

B. *Figurative of:*
Israel.........Num. 24:5, 6

Aloth—*ascents, steeps*

A town in Asher..1 Kin. 4:16

Alpha and Omega—*first and last letters of the Greek alphabet ("A to Z")*

Expressive of God
and Christ's⎰Rev. 1:8, 17, 18
eternity ....⎱Rev. 21:6, 7

Alphabet—*the letters of a language*

The Hebrew, seen
in ....Ps. 119

Alphaeus—*leader, chief*

1. The father of Levi
(Matthew) ....Mark 2:14
2. The father of
James........Matt. 10:3

Altar—*an elevated structure*

A. *Uses of:*
Sacrifice ......Gen. 8:20
Incense........Ex. 30:1, 7, 8
Luke 1:10, 11
National
unity..........Deut. 12:5, 6
A memorial....Ex. 17:15, 16
Protection ....Ex. 21:13, 14

B. *Made of:*
Earth..........Ex. 20:24
Unhewn
stone........Ex. 20:25
Stones........Deut. 27:5, 6
Natural rock..Judg. 6:19-21
Bronze........Ex. 27:1-6

C. *Built worthily by:*
Noah ....Gen. 8:20
Abraham ......Gen. 12:7, 8
Isaac ....Gen. 26:25
Jacob ....Gen. 33:18, 20
Moses ....Ex. 17:15
Joshua..........Deut. 27:4-7
Eastern
tribes ....Josh. 22:10, 34
Gideon ....Judg. 6:26, 27

Manoah ....Judg. 13:19, 20
Israelites ......Judg. 21:4
Samuel ....1 Sam. 7:17
Saul ....1 Sam. 14:35
David..........2 Sam. 24:18-25
Elijah..........1 Kin. 18:31, 32

D. *Built unworthily (for idolatry)
by:*
Gideon's
father........Judg. 6:25-32
King
Jeroboam .....1 Kin. 12:32, 33
King Ahab.....1 Kin. 16:30-32
King Ahaz.....2 Chr. 28:1, 3, 5
Israelite
people ....Is. 65:3
Athenians .....Acts 17:23

E. *Pagan altars destroyed by:*
Gideon ....Judg. 6:25-29
King Asa ......2 Chr. 14:2, 3
Jehoiada.......2 Kin. 11:17, 18
King
Hezekiah......2 Kin. 18:22
King Josiah....2 Kin. 23:12, 16,
17

F. *Burnt offering:*

1. *Of the tabernacle, features
concerning:*
Specifi-
cations........Ex. 27:1-8
Bezaleel, builder
of.............Ex. 31:1-6, 9
Place of, outside
tabernacle ....Ex. 40:6, 29
Only priests
allowed at.....Num. 18:3, 7
The defective not acceptable
on ....Lev. 22:22
The putting on of
blood ....Ex. 29:12
2. *Of Solomon's Temple:*
Described......1 Kin. 8:63, 64
Renewed by
King Asa......2 Chr. 15:8
Cleansed by King
Hezekiah......2 Chr. 29:18-24
Repaired by King
Manasseh.....2 Chr. 33:16-18
Vessels of, carried to
Babylon.......2 Kin. 25:14
3. *Of the postexilic (Zerubbabel's)
temple:*
Described......Ezra 3:1-6
Polluted ....Mal. 1:7, 8
4. *Of Ezekiel's vision:*
Described......Ezek. 43:13-27

G. *Incense:*
In the tabernacle,
described......Ex. 30:1-10
Location of...Ex. 30:6
Anointed
with oil.....Ex. 30:26, 27
Annual atonement
made at.......Ex. 30:10
In Solomon's
Temple........1 Kin. 7:48
In John's
vision.........Rev. 8:3

H. *New covenant:*
A place of spiritual
sacrifices.....Rom. 12:1, 2
Christ, our
pattern........Heb. 13:10-16

Altruism—*living for the good of others*

A. *Manifested in:*
Service........Matt. 20:26-28
Doing good....Acts 10:38
Seeking the welfare of
others.........Gal. 6:1, 2, 10
Helping the
weak.........Acts 20:35

B. *Examples of:*
Moses.........Ex. 32:30-30
Samuel........1 Sam. 12:1-5
Jonathan......1 Sam. 18:1-4
Christ.........John 13:4-17
Paul..........1 Cor. 9:19-22

Alush—*wild place*

An Israelite
encampment.....Num. 33:13, 14

Alvah—*high; tall*

An Edomite
chief.............Gen. 36:40
Also called Aliah..1 Chr. 1:51

Alvan—*tall*

A son of Shobal the
Horite.............Gen. 36:23
Also called Alian..1 Chr. 1:40

Always—*continually, forever*

A. *Of God's:*
Care........Deut. 11:12
Covenant......1 Chr. 16:15
Striving........Ps. 103:9

B. *Of Christ's:*
Determi-
nation ......Ps. 16:8-11
Acts 2:25-28

Rejoicing.....Prov. 8:30-31
Presence.......Matt. 28:20
Obedience.....John 8:29
Prayer.........John 11:42

C. *Of the believer's:*
Prayer.........Luke 21:36
Peace.........2 Thess. 3:16
Obedience.....Phil. 2:12
Work..........1 Cor. 15:58
Defense......1 Pet. 3:15
Rejoicing.....Phil. 4:4
Thanks-
giving.........1 Thess. 1:2
Victory.......2 Cor. 2:14
Conscience....Acts 24:16
Confidence....2 Cor. 5:6
Sufficiency.....2 Cor. 9:8

D. *Of the unbeliever's:*
Probation.....Gen. 6:3
Turmoil.......Mark 5:5
Rebellion......Acts 7:51
Lying.........Titus 1:12

Amad—*people of duration*

A city of Asher....Josh. 19:26

Amal—*toil*

Asher's
descendant.......1 Chr. 7:35

Amalek—*warlike*

A son of Eliphaz..1 Chr. 1:36
Grandson of
Esau.............Gen. 36:11, 12
A chief of Edom...Gen. 36:16
First among
nations...........Num. 24:20

Amalekites—*a nation hostile to Israel*

A. *Defeated by:*
Chedor-
laomer........Gen. 14:5-7
Joshua.........Ex. 17:8, 13
Gideon.......Judg. 7:12-25
Saul...........1 Sam. 14:47, 48
David.........1 Sam. 27:8, 9
Simeonites.....1 Chr. 4:42, 43

B. *Overcame Israel during:*
Wilderness.....Num. 14:39-45
Judges........Judg. 3:13

C. *Destruction of:*
Predicted......Ex. 17:14
Reaffirmed....Deut. 25:17-19
Fulfilled in
part by   {1 Sam. 27:8, 9
David........{2 Sam. 1:1-16

Fulfilled by the
Simeonites ....1 Chr. 4:42, 43

Amam—*gathering place*

A city of Judah ...Josh. 15:26

Amana—*permanent*

A summit in the Anti-Lebanon
mountain range ..Song 4:8

Amaranthine—*like the amaranth
flower: unfading, perennial*

This Greek word is used to
describe our
inheritance and ⎰1 Pet. 1:4
our glory ....⎱1 Pet. 5:4

Amariah—*Yahweh said*

1. The grandfather of Zadok the
   priest ....1 Chr. 6:7, 8, 52
2. A priest.........1 Chr. 6:11
3. Levite in David's
   time ....1 Chr. 23:19
4. A high priest ..2 Chr. 19:11
5. A Levite in Hezekiah's
   reign.........2 Chr. 31:14, 15
6. Son of King
   Hezekiah......Zeph. 1:1
7. One who divorced his foreign
   wife...........Ezra 10:42, 44
8. A signer of Nehemiah's
   document .....Neh. 10:3
9. A postexilic chief
   priest ....Neh. 12:1, 2, 7

Amasa—*burden-bearer*

1. The son of Jithra; David's
   nephew ....2 Sam. 17:25
   Commands Absalom's
   rebels ....2 Sam. 17:25
   Made David's
   commander ...2 Sam. 19:13
   Treacherously killed by
   Joab ....2 Sam. 20:9-12
   Death
   avenged.......1 Kin. 2:28-34
2. An Ephraimite
   leader.........2 Chr. 28:9-12

Amasai—*Yahweh has borne*

1. A Kohathite
   Levite.........1 Chr. 6:25, 35
2. David's
   officer.........1 Chr. 12:18
3. A priestly trumpeter in David's
   time ....1 Chr. 15:24
4. A Kohathite
   Levite.........2 Chr. 29:12

Amashai—*carrying spoil*

A priest...........Neh. 11:13

Amasiah—*Yahweh bears*

One of Jehoshaphat's
commanders......2 Chr. 17:16

Amazement—*an intense emotional
shock*

A. *Caused by:*
   Christ's   ⎰Matt. 12:22, 23
   miracles.....⎱Luke 5:25, 26
   Christ's
   teaching .....Matt. 19:25
   God's power ...Luke 9:42, 43
   Apostolic
   miracle........Acts 3:7-10

B. *Manifested by:*
   Christ's
   parents ......Luke 2:48
   Christ's
   disciples......Matt. 19:25
   The Jews ......Mark 9:15
   The early
   Christians.....Acts 9:19-21

Amaziah—*Yahweh is strong*

1. King of
   Judah.........2 Kin. 14:1-4
   Kills his father's assassi-
   nators.........2 Kin. 14:5, 6
   Raises a large
   army..........2 Chr. 25:5
   Employs troops from
   Israel ....2 Chr. 25:6
   Rebuked by a man of
   God...........2 Chr. 25:7-10
   Defeats
   Edomites......2 Kin. 14:7
   Worships Edomite
   gods..........2 Chr. 25:14
   Rebuked by a
   prophet ....2 Chr. 25:15, 16
   Defeated by
   Israel ....2 Kin. 14:8-14
   Killed by con-
   spirators ......2 Chr. 25:25-28
2. A priest of
   Bethel.........Amos 7:10-17
3. A Simeonite ...1 Chr. 4:34,
                        42, 43
4. A Merarite
   Levite.........1 Chr. 6:45

Ambassador—*an official sent to deal
with a foreign government or
sovereign*

A. *Some purposes of, to:*
Grant safe
passage ....Num. 20:14-21
Settle
disputes.......Judg. 11:12-28
Arrange
business.......1 Kin. 5:1-12
Stir up
trouble.........1 Kin. 20:1-12
Issue an
ultimatum ....2 Kin. 19:9-14
Spy.............2 Kin. 20:12-19
Learn God's
will ....Jer. 37:3-10

B. *Some examples of:*
Judah to
Egypt.........Is. 30:1-4
Babylonians to
Judah.........2 Chr. 32:31
Necho to
Josiah.........2 Chr. 35:20, 21

C. *Used figuratively of:*
Christ's
ministers......2 Cor. 5:20
Paul in
particular .....Eph. 6:19, 20

Amber—*a yellow, fossilized resin*

Descriptive of the divine
glory ....Ezek. 1:4, 27

Ambidextrous—*equally skilled with
either hand*

True of some of David's
warriors..........1 Chr. 12:1, 2

Ambition, Christian

A. *Good, if for:*
The best
gifts ....1 Cor. 12:31
Spiritual
goals..........Phil. 3:12-14
The Gospel's
extension .....Rom. 15:17-20
Acceptance before
God...........2 Cor. 5:9, 10
Quietness......1 Thess. 4:11

B. *Evil, if it leads to:*
Strife ....Matt. 20:20-28
Sinful
superiority ....Matt. 18:1-6
A Pharisaical
spirit..........Mark 12:38-40
Contention about
gifts ....1 Cor. 3:3-8

Selfish
ambition ......Phil. 1:14-17

Ambition, worldly

A. *Inspired by:*
Satan...........Gen. 3:1-6
                Luke 4:5-8
Pride ....Is. 14:12-15
                1 Tim. 3:1, 6
Jealousy ....Num. 12:2

B. *Leads to:*
Sin ....Acts 8:18-24
Strife ....James 4:1, 2
Suicide ....2 Sam. 17:23
Self-glory .....Hab. 2:4, 5

C. *Examples of:*
Builders of
Babel ....Gen. 11:4
Korah's
company.....Num. 16:3-35
Abimelech....Judg. 9:1-6
Absalom.......2 Sam. 15:1-13
Adonijah .....1 Kin. 1:5-7
Haman ....Esth. 5:9-14
Nebuchad-
nezzar ......Dan. 3:1-7
James and
John ....Mark 10:35-37
The
antichrist .....2 Thess. 2:3, 4
Diotrephes.....3 John 9, 10

Ambush—*strategic concealment for
surprise attack*

Joshua at Ai ......Josh. 8:1-24
Abimelech against
Shechem ....Judg. 9:31-40
Israel at Gibeah ...Judg. 20:29-48
David against the
Philistines ....2 Sam. 5:23-25
Jehoshaphat against his
enemies ....2 Chr. 20:22-25

Amen—*a strong assent to a prayer* (also
translated *"assuredly"*)

A. *Used in the Old Testament to:*
Confirm a
statement .....Num. 5:22
Close a
doxology......1 Chr. 16:36
Confirm an
oath ....Neh. 5:13
Give assent to
laws ....Deut. 27:15-26

B. *Used in the New Testament to:*
Close a
doxology......Rom. 9:5
Close epistle...Rom. 16:27
Describe God's
promises......2 Cor. 1:20
Close prayer...1 Cor. 14:16
Give assent....Rev. 1:7
Emphasize a truth (translated
"most
assuredly")....John 3:3, 5, 11

Amethyst—*a form of quartz purple to blue-violet*

Worn by the high { Ex. 39:12
priest............ { Ex. 28:19
In the New
Jerusalem......Rev. 21:20

Ami

Head of a family of Solomon's
servants..........Ezra 2:57
Called Amon......Neh. 7:59

Amittai—*true*

The father of Jonah the
prophet ....Jon. 1:1

Ammah—*mother or beginning*

A hill near Giah...2 Sam. 2:24

Ammiel—*my kinsman is God*

1. A spy representing the tribe of
Dan............Num. 13:12
2. The father of
Machir........2 Sam. 9:4, 5
3. The father of Bathshua
(Bathsheba), one of David's
wives..........1 Chr. 3:5
Called Eliam...2 Sam. 11:3
4. A son of Obed-
Edom.........1 Chr. 26:4, 5

Ammihud—*my kinsman is glorious*

1. An
Ephraimite....Num. 1:10
2. A Simeonite, father of
Shemuel ......Num. 34:20
3. A Naphtalite...Num. 34:28
4. The father of king of
Geshur........2 Sam. 13:37
5. A Judahite....1 Chr. 9:4

Amminadab—*my kinsman is noble*

1. Man of
Judah..........1 Chr. 2:10·

The father of
Nashon ....Num. 1:7
Aaron's father-in-
law ....Ex. 6:23
An ancestor of
David.........Ruth 4:19, 20
An ancestor of
Christ.........Matt. 1:4
2. Chief of a Levitical
house ....1 Chr. 15:10, 11
3. Son of
Kohath ......1 Chr. 6:22

Ammishaddai—*my kinsman is the Almighty*

A captain representing the
Danites..........Num. 1:12

Ammizabad—*my kinsman has endowed*

A son of
Benaiah ....1 Chr. 27:6

Ammon—*a people*

A nation fathered by
Lot...............Gen. 19:36, 38

Ammonites—*descendants of Ben-Ammi*

A. *Characterized by:*
Cruelty ....Amos 1:13
Pride ....Zeph. 2:9, 10
Callousness....Ezek. 25:3, 6
Idolatry........1 Kin. 11:7, 33

B. *Hostility toward Israel, seen in:*
Not aiding
Israel ....Deut. 23:3, 4
Helping the
Amalekites....Judg. 3:13
Proposing a cruel
treaty.........1 Sam. 11:1-3
Abusing David's ambassa-
dors...........2 Sam. 10:1-4
Hiring Syrians against
David.........2 Sam. 10:6
Assisting the
Chaldeans.....2 Kin. 24:2
Harassing postexilic
Jews ....Neh. 4:3, 7, 8

C. *Defeated by:*
Jephthah ......Judg. 11:4-33
Saul ....1 Sam. 11:11
David..........2 Sam. 10:7-14
Jehoshaphat ...2 Chr. 20:1-25
Jotham ....2 Chr. 27:5, 6

D. *Prohibitions concerning:*
Exclusion from
worship.......Deut. 23:3-6

No intermarriage
with ....Ezra 9:1-3

E. *Prophecies concerning their:*
Captivity ......Amos 1:13-15
Subjection .....Jer. 25:9-21
Destruction....Ps. 83:1-18

Ammonitess—*a female Ammonite*

Naamah ....1 Kin. 14:21, 31
Shimeath ....2 Chr. 24:26

Amnesty—*a pardon granted to political offenders*

To Shimei........2 Sam. 19:16-23
To Amasa........2 Sam. 17:25
                        2 Sam. 19:13

Amnon—*faithful*

1. A son of
   David........2 Sam. 3:2
   Rapes his half
   sister.........2 Sam. 13:1-18
   Killed by
   Absalom ......2 Sam. 13:19-29
2. Son of
   Shimon ....1 Chr. 4:19-33

Amok—*deep, inscrutable*

A chief priest .....Neh. 12:7, 20

Amon—*master workman*

1. King of
   Judah.........2 Kin. 21:18, 19
   Follows evil...2 Chr. 33:22, 23
   Killed by
   conspiracy ....2 Kin. 21:23, 24
2. A governor of
   Samaria.......1 Kin. 22:10, 26

Amorites—*mountain dwellers*

A. *Described as:*
Descendants of
Canaan ....Gen. 10:15, 16
Original inhabitants of
Palestine .....Ezek. 16:3
One of seven
nations.........Gen. 15:19-21
A confed-
eration........Josh. 10:1-5
Ruled by great
kings ....Ps. 136:17-19
Of great size...Amos 2:9
Very wicked...Gen. 15:16
Worshipers of
idols ....Judg. 6:10

B. *Contacts of, with Israel:*
Their defeat by
Joshua........Josh. 10:1-43
Their not being
destroyed .....Judg. 1:34-36
Peace with....1 Sam. 7:14
Solomon uses for forced
labor..........1 Kin. 9:20, 21
Intermarriage
with ....Judg. 3:5, 6

Amos—*burden-bearer*

1. A prophet of
   Israel ....Amos 1:1
   Pronounces judgment against
   nations........Amos 1:1-3, 15
   Denounces Israel's
   sins...........Amos 4:1-7:9
   Condemns Amaziah, the priest
   of Bethel......Amos 7:10-17
   Predicts Israel's
   downfall ......Amos 9:1-10
   Foretells great
   blessings .....Amos 9:11-15
2. An ancestor of
   Christ.........Luke 3:25

Amoz—*strong*

The father of Isaiah the
prophet ....Is. 1:1

Amphipolis—*a city in Macedonia*

Visited by Paul....Acts 17:1

Amplias

Christian at
Rome ....Rom. 16:8

Amram—*a people exalted*

1. Son of
   Kohath ....Num. 3:17-19
   The father of
   Aaron, Moses (Ex. 6:18-20
   and Miriam ..(1 Chr. 6:3
2. Jew who divorced his foreign
   wife...........Ezra 10:34

Amramites—*descendants of Amram*

A subdivision of the
Levites ....Num. 3:27

Amraphel—*powerful people*

A king of Shinar who invaded
Canaan during Abraham's time;
identified by some as the
Hammurabi of the
monuments ......Gen. 14:1, 9

Amulet—*charm worn to protect against evil*

Condemned . . . . Is. 3:18-23

Amusements—*entertainment*

A. *Found in:*
   Dancing . . . . Ex. 32:18, 19, 25
   Music. . . . . 1 Sam. 18:6, 7
   Earthly
   pleasures. . . . . . Eccl. 2:1-8
   Drunken- ⎰ Amos 6:1-6
   ness. . . . . ⎱ 1 Pet. 4:3
   Feasting . . . . . . Mark 6:21, 22
   Games. . . . . Luke 7:32
   Gossip . . . . Acts 17:21

B. *Productive of:*
   Sorrow . . . . Prov. 14:13
   Poverty. . . . . . . Prov. 21:17
   Vanity. . . . . Eccl. 2:1-11
   Immorality . . . . 1 Cor. 10:6-8
   Spiritual
   deadness . . . . . . 1 Tim. 5:6

C. *Prevalence of:*
   In the last
   days . . . . 2 Tim. 3:1, 4
   In Babylon . . . . Rev. 18:21-24
   At Christ's
   return. . . . . Matt. 24:36-39

Amzi—*strong one*

1. A Merarite
   Levite. . . . . 1 Chr. 6:46
2. A priest. . . . . . . Neh. 11:12

Anab—*grapes*

A town of Judah . . Josh. 11:21

Anah—*answer*

1. Father of ⎰ Gen. 36:2, 14,
   Esau's wife... ⎱ 18
2. A Horite
   chief . . . . Gen. 36:20, 29
3. Son of
   Zibeon . . . . Gen. 36:24

Anaharath—*narrow way*

A city in the valley of
Jezreel . . . . Josh. 19:19

Anaiah—*Yahweh has answered*

1. A Levite
   assistant . . . . . Neh. 8:4
2. One who sealed the new
   covenant. . . . . . Neh. 10:22

Anak—*long-necked*

Descendant of
Arba . . . . Josh. 15:13
Father of three
sons. . . . . Num. 13:22

Anakim—*descendants of Anak; a race of giants*

A. *Described as:*
   Giants . . . . Num. 13:28-33
   Very strong. . . . Deut. 2:10, 11, 21

B. *Defeated by:*
   Joshua. . . . . Josh. 10:36-39;
                              11:21
   Caleb. . . . . Josh. 14:6-15

C. *A remnant left:*
   Among the
   Philistines. . . . . Josh. 11:22
   Possibly in
   Gath . . . . 1 Sam. 17:4-7

Anamim—*rockmen*

A tribe or people listed among
Mizraim's (Egypt's)
descendants . . . . . Gen. 10:13

Anammelech—*Anu is king*

A god worshiped at
Samaria . . . . 2 Kin. 17:24, 31

Anan—*cloud*

A signer of Nehemiah's
document . . . . Neh. 10:26

Anani—*my cloud*

Son of Elioenai. . . . 1 Chr. 3:24

Ananiah—*Yahweh has covered*

1. The father of
   Maaseiah . . . . . Neh. 3:23
2. A town inhabited by Benjamite
   returnees . . . . . Neh. 11:32

Ananias—*Yahweh has been gracious*

1. Disciple at Jerusalem slain for
   lying to God . . Acts 5:1-11
2. A Christian
   disciple at ⎰ Acts 9:10-19
   Damascus. . . . ⎱ Acts 22:12-16
3. A Jewish high
   priest . . . . Acts 23:1-5

Anarchy—*a reign of lawlessness in society*

A. *Manifested in:*
Moral looseness......Ex. 32:1-8, 25
Idolatry........Judg. 17:1-13
Religious syncretism....2 Kin. 17:27-41
A reign of terror........Jer. 40:13-16
Perversion of justice........Hab. 1:1-4

B. *Instances of:*
At Kadesh.....Num. 14:1-10
During the judges........Judg. 18:1-31
In the northern kingdom......1 Kin. 12:26-33
At the crucifixion....Matt. 27:15-31
At Stephen's death........Acts 7:54, 57, 58
At Ephesus....Acts 19:28-34
In the time of antichrist.....2 Thess. 2:3-12

Anath—*answer*

Father of Shamgar........Judg. 3:31

Anathoth—*answers*

1. A Benjamite, son of Becher........1 Chr. 7:8
2. A leader who signed the document.....Neh. 10:19
3. A Levitical city in Benjamin........Josh. 21:18
Birthplace of Jeremiah........Jer. 1:1
Citizens of, hate Jeremiah......Jer. 11:21, 23
Jeremiah bought property there........Jer. 32:6-15
Home of famous mighty man........2 Sam. 23:27
Home of Abiathar, the high priest........1 Kin. 2:26
Reoccupied after exile........Ezra 2:1, 23
To be invaded by Assyria.......Is. 10:30
Reproved Jeremiah of........Jer. 29:27

Anathothite—*a native of Anathoth*

Abiezer thus called............2 Sam. 23:27

Anchor—*a weight used to hold a ship in place*

Literally, of Paul's ship.............Acts 27:29, 30, 40
Figuratively of the believer's hope.............Heb. 6:19

Ancient—*that which is old*

Applied to the beginning (eternity)........Is. 45:21
Applied to something very old.............Prov. 22:28
Applied to old men (elders)..... $\begin{cases} \text{Ps. 119:100} \\ \text{1 Sam. 24:13} \end{cases}$

Ancient of Days

Title applied to God.............Dan. 7:9, 13, 22

Andrew—*manly*

A fisherman......Matt. 4:18
A disciple of John the Baptist.........John 1:40
Brought Peter to Christ.............John 1:40-42
Called to Christ's discipleship.......Matt. 4:18, 19
Enrolled among the Twelve.............Matt. 10:2
Told Jesus about a lad's lunch.............John 6:8, 9
Carried a request to Jesus.............John 12:20-22
Sought further light on Jesus' words.............Mark 13:3, 4
Met in the upper room.............Acts 1:13

Andronicus—*conqueror of men*

A notable Christian at Rome.............Rom. 16:7

Anem—*double fountain*

Levitical city......1 Chr. 6:73

Aner—*waterfall*

1. Amorite chief.........Gen. 14:13, 24
2. A Levitical city.............1 Chr. 6:70

Angels—*heavenly beings created by God*

A. *Described as:*
Spiritual beings........Heb. 1:13, 14

Created........Ps. 148:2, 5
              Col. 1:16
Immortal......Luke 20:36
Holy..........Matt. 25:31
Innumerable...Heb. 12:22
Wise..........2 Sam. 14:17, 20
Powerful......Ps. 103:20
Elect.........1 Tim. 5:21
Respectful of
  authority....Jude 9
Sexless.......Matt. 22:30
Invisible.....Num. 22:22-31
Obedient......Ps. 103:20
Possessing
  emotions....Luke 15:10
Concerned in human
  things.......1 Pet. 1:12
Incarnate in human form at
  times........Gen. 18:2-8
Not perfect...Job 4:18
Organized in
  ranks or   {Is. 6:1-3
  orders.......{1 Thess. 4:16

B. *Ministry of, toward believers:*
Guide.........Gen. 24:7, 40
Provide for...1 Kin. 19:5-8
Protect.......Ps. 34:7
Deliver.......Dan. 6:22
              Acts 12:7-11
Gather........Matt. 24:31
Direct
  activities....Acts 8:26
Comfort.......Acts 27:23, 24
Minister to...Heb. 1:14

C. *Ministry of, toward unbelievers:*
A destruc-
  tion.........Gen. 19:1, 13
A curse.......Judg. 5:23
A pestilence...2 Sam. 24:15-17
Sudden
  death........Acts 12:23
Persecution...Ps. 35:5, 6

D. *Ministry of, in Christ's life, to:*
Announce His
  conception....Matt. 1:20, 21
Herald His
  birth........Luke 2:10-12
Sustain Him...Matt. 4:11
Witness His
  resurrection...1 Tim. 3:16
Proclaim His
  resurrection...Matt. 28:5-7
Accompany Him to
  heaven.......Acts 1:9-11

E. *Ministry of, on special
  occasions, at:*

The world's
  creation......Job 38:7
Sinai.........Acts 7:38, 53
Satan's
  binding......Rev. 20:1-3
Christ's   {Matt. 13:41, 49
  return.......{1 Thess. 4:16

F. *Appearance of, during the Old
  Testament, to:*
Abraham......Gen. 18:2-15
Hagar........Gen. 16:7-14
Lot..........Gen. 19:1-22
Jacob........Gen. 28:10-12
Moses........Ex. 3:1, 2
Balaam.......Num. 22:31-35
Joshua.......Josh. 5:13-15
All Israel....Judg. 2:1-4
Gideon.......Judg. 6:11-24
Manoah.......Judg. 13:6-21
David........2 Sam. 24:16, 17
Elijah.......1 Kin. 19:2-8
Daniel.......Dan. 6:21, 22
Zechariah....Zech. 2:3

G. *Appearances of, during the New
  Testament, to:*
Zechariah....Luke 1:11-20
The virgin
  Mary.........Luke 1:26-38
Joseph.......Matt. 1:20-25
Shepherds....Luke 2:8-15
Certain
  women.......Matt. 28:1-7
Mary
  Magdalene...John 20:11-13
The apostles...Acts 1:10, 11
Peter........Acts 5:19, 20
Philip.......Acts 8:26
Cornelius....Acts 10:3-32
Paul.........Acts 27:23, 24
John.........Rev. 1:1
Seven
  churches.....Rev. 1:20

Angels, fallen

Fall of, by pride...Is. 14:12-15
                   Jude 6
Seen by Christ....Luke 10:18
Make war on
  saints............Rev. 12:7-17
Imprisoned........2 Pet. 2:4
Everlasting fire prepared
  for...............Matt. 25:41

Angel of God, the—*distinct
  manifestation of God*

A. *Names of:*
Angel of God...Gen. 21:17

Angel of the
Lord . . . . Gen. 22:11
Captain of the army of the
Lord . . . . Josh. 5:14

B. *Appearances of, to:*
Hagar . . . . Gen. 16:7, 8
               Gen. 21:17
Abraham . . . . . . Gen. 22:11, 15
               Gen. 18:1-33
Jacob. . . . . Gen. 31:11-13
               Gen. 32:24-30
Moses . . . . Ex. 3:1, 2
Children of { Ex. 13:21, 22
Israel   { Ex. 14:19
Balaam . . . . Num. 22:22-35
Joshua. . . . . Judg. 2:1
David. . . . . 1 Chr. 21:16-18

C. *Divine characteristics:*
Deliver Israel . . 2 Kin. 19:14-20,
                 35, 36
Extend
blessings . . . . . . Gen. 16:7-12
Pardon sin . . . . . Ex. 23:20-22

Angels' food

Eaten by men . . . . . Ps. 78:25
Eaten by Elijah . . 1 Kin. 19:5-8

Anger of God

A. *Caused by man's:*
Sin . . . . Num. 32:10-15
Unbelief . . . . Ps. 78:21, 22
Error . . . . 2 Sam. 6:7
Disobedi-
ence . . . . Josh. 7:1, 11, 12
Idolatry. . . . . . . Judg. 2:11-14

B. *Described as:*
Sometimes
delayed . . . . 2 Kin. 23:25-27
Slow. . . . . Neh. 9:17
Brief. . . . . Ps. 30:5
Restrained . . . . . Ps. 78:38
Fierceness . . . . . Ps. 78:49, 50
Consuming . . . . . Ps. 90:7
Powerful. . . . . . . Ps. 90:11
Not forever. . . . . Mic. 7:18
To be feared . . . Ps. 76:7

C. *Visitation of, upon:*
Miriam and
Aaron. . . . . Num. 12:9-15
Israelites . . . . . . Num. 11:4-10
Balaam . . . . Num. 22:21, 22
Moses . . . . Deut. 4:21, 22
Israel . . . . Deut. 9:8
Aaron . . . . Deut. 9:20

Wicked cities . . Deut. 29:23
A land. . . . . Deut. 29:24-28
A king. . . . . 2 Chr. 25:15, 16

D. *Deliverance from, by:*
Intercessory (Num. 11:1, 2
prayer . . . . . . { Deut. 9:19, 20
Decisive
action. . . . . Num. 25:3-12
Obedience . . . . . Deut. 13:16-18
Executing the
guilty . . . . Josh. 7:1, 10-26

See Wrath of God

Anger of Jesus

Provoked by
unbelievers . . . . Mark 3:1-6
In the Temple. . . . Matt. 21:12
               Mark 11:15

Anger of man

A. *Caused by:*
A brother's
deception . . . . . Gen. 27:42-45
A wife's
complaint . . . . . Gen. 30:1, 2
Rape . . . . Gen. 34:1-7
Inhuman
crimes . . . . Gen. 49:6, 7
A leader's
indignation. . . . Ex. 11:8
A people's
idolatry . . . . . . Ex. 32:19, 22
Disobedi-
ence . . . . Num. 31:14-18
The Spirit's
arousal. . . . . . . 1 Sam. 11:6
A brother's (1 Sam. 17:28
jealousy. . . . . . { Luke 15:25-28
A king's
jealousy. . . . . . 1 Sam. 20:30
Righteous
indignation. . . 1 Sam. 20:34
Priestly
rebuke . . . . 2 Chr. 26:18, 19
Unrighteous
dealings. . . . . . Neh. 5:6, 7
Wife's disobedi-
ence . . . . Esth. 1:12
Lack of
respect. . . . . . . Esth. 3:5
Failure of
astrologers . . . . Dan. 2:2, 10, 12
Flesh . . . . Gal. 5:19, 20
Harsh
treatment . . . . . Eph. 6:4

B. *Justifiable, seen in:*

Jacob	Gen. 31:36
Moses	Ex. 32:19
Samson	Judg. 14:1, 19
Saul	1 Sam. 11:6
Samuel	1 Sam. 15:16-31
Jonathan	1 Sam. 20:34
Christ	Mark 3:5

C. *Unjustifiable, seen in:*

Cain	Gen. 4:5, 6
Simeon and Levi	Gen. 49:5-7
Potiphar	Gen. 39:1, 19
Moses	Num. 20:10-12
Balaam	Num. 22:27, 28
Saul	1 Sam. 20:30
Naaman	2 Kin. 5:11, 12
Asa	2 Chr. 16:10
Uzziah	2 Chr. 26:19
Ahasuerus	Esth. 1:9, 12
Haman	Esth. 3:5
Nebuchad- nezzar	Dan. 3:12, 13
Jonah	Jon. 4:1-11
Herod	Matt. 2:16
The Jews	Luke 4:28
Jewish officialdom	Acts 5:17

D. *The Christian attitude toward:*

To be slow in	Prov. 14:17
Not to sin in	Eph. 4:26
To put away	Eph. 4:31

E. *Effects of, seen in:*

Attempted assassi- nation	Esth. 2:21
Punishment	Prov. 19:19
Mob action	Acts 19:28, 29

F. *Pacified by:*

Kindly suggestion	2 Kin. 5:10-14
Righteous execution	Esth. 7:10
Gentle answer	Prov. 15:1

Anguish—*extreme pain*

A. *Caused by:*

Physical hardships	Ex. 6:9
Physical pain	2 Sam. 1:9
Impending destruction	Deut. 2:25
Conflict of soul	Job 7:11
National distress	Is. 8:21, 22
Childbirth	John 16:21

A spiritual problem	2 Cor. 2:4

B. *Reserved for:*

People who refuse wisdom	Prov. 1:20-27
The wicked	Job 15:20, 24
Those in Hades	Luke 16:23, 24

Aniam—*lament of the people*

A Manassite	1 Chr. 7:19

Anim—*springs*

A city in south Judah	Josh. 15:50

Animals

A. *Described as:*

Domesticated and wild	2 Sam. 12:3
Clean and unclean	{ Lev. 11:1-31 Deut. 14:1-20
For sacrifices	Lev. 16:3, 5 Ex. 12:3-14

B. *List of, in the Bible:*

Antelope	Deut. 14:5
Ape	1 Kin. 10:22
Badger	Ex. 25:5
Bat	Deut. 14:18
Bear	1 Sam. 17:34
Boar	Ps. 80:13
Bull	Jer. 52:20
Calf	Gen. 18:7
Camel	Gen. 12:16
Cattle	Gen. 1:25
Chameleon	Lev. 11:30
Cobra	Is. 11:8
Colt	Zech. 9:9
Cow	Gen. 32:15
Deer	Deut. 14:5
Dog	Ex. 22:31
Donkey	Gen. 22:3
Elephant ("ivory")	1 Kin. 10:22
Ewe lamb	Gen. 21:30
Fox	Judg. 15:4
Frog	Ex. 8:2-14
Gazelle	Deut. 14:5
Gecko	Lev. 11:30
Goat	Gen. 27:9
Greyhound	Prov. 30:31
Hare	Deut. 14:7
Heifer	Gen. 15:9
Hind	Hab. 3:19
Horse	Gen. 47:17
Hyena	Is. 13:22
Hyrax	Lev. 11:5
Jackal	Is. 13:22

Lamb.............Ex. 29:39
Leopard ....Rev. 13:2
Lion............1 Sam. 17:34
Lizard ....Lev. 11:29, 30
Mole...........Is. 2:20
Monkey ....1 Kin. 10:22
Mouse.........Lev. 11:29
Mule ....2 Sam. 13:29
Ox.............Ex. 21:28
Porcupine .....Is. 14:23
Ram...........Gen. 15:9
Roe deer.......Deut. 14:5
Scorpion.......Deut. 8:15
Serpent........Matt. 10:16
Sheep.........Gen. 4:2
Spider ....Prov. 30:28
Swine ....Is. 65:2-4
Whale (great sea
  creatures).....Gen. 1:21
Wolf..........Is. 11:6

C. *Used figuratively of:*
Human traits ..Gen. 49:9-14, 21
Universal
  peace ....Is. 11:6-9
Man's innate
  nature ....Jer. 13:23
World
  empires ....Dan. 7:2-8
Satanic
  powers........Rev. 12:4, 9
Christ's
  sacrifice... ..1 Pet. 1:18-20

Anise—*a plant for seasoning; the dill*

Tithed by the
  Jews ....Matt. 23:23

Ankle—*joint connecting foot and leg*

Lame man's
  healed...........Acts 3:7

Anklet—*an ornament worn by women
on the ankles*

Included in Isaiah's
  denunciation .....Is. 3:16, 18

Anna—*grace*

Aged prophetess ..Luke 2:36-38

Annas—*gracious*

A Jewish high
  priest............Luke 3:2
Christ appeared
  before...........John 18:12-24
Peter and John appeared
  before............Acts 4:6

Anointing—*pouring oil upon*

A. *Performed upon:*
The
  patriarchs.....1 Chr. 16:15-17,
                        21, 22
Priest..........Ex. 29:1, 7
Prophets.......1 Kin. 19:16
Israel's kings ..1 Sam. 10:1
Foreign
  kings ....1 Kin. 19:15
The messianic
  King ....Ps. 2:2
Sacred
  objects........Ex. 30:26-28

B. *Ordinary, purposes of, for:*
Adornment ....Ruth 3:3
Invigoration ..2 Sam. 12:20
Hospitality....Luke 7:38, 46
Battle.........Is. 21:5
Burial.........Matt. 26:12
Sanctifying ...Ex. 30:29

C. *Medicinal, purposes of, for:*
Wound ....Luke 10:34
Healing........Mark 6:13
                        James 5:14

D. *Sacred, purposes of, to:*
Memorialize an
  event ....Gen. 28:18
Confirm a
  covenant......Gen. 35:14
Set apart ......Ex. 30:22-29
Institute into
  office..........1 Sam. 16:12, 13

E. *Absence of:*
Sign of
  judgment .....Deut. 28:40
Fasting ....2 Sam. 12:16, 20
Mourning .....2 Sam. 14:2

F. *Of Christ the Messiah "the
Anointed One," as:*
Predicted ......Ps. 45:7
                        Is. 61:1
Fulfilled ....Luke 4:18
                        Heb. 1:9
Interpreted ....Acts 4:27
Symbolized in His name
  ("the   {Matt. 16:16, 20
  Christ").......{Acts 9:22
Typical of the believer's
  anointing .....1 John 2:27

G. *Significance of, as indicating:*
Divine appoint-
  ment..........2 Chr. 22:7
Special
  honor.........1 Sam. 24:6, 10

Special
privilege ......Ps. 105:15
God's
blessing ....Ps. 23:5

Anointing of the Holy Spirit

A. *Of Christ:*
Predicted .....Is. 61:1
Fulfilled ......John 1:32-34
Explained.....Luke 4:18

B. *Of Christians:*
Predicted .....Ezek. 47:1-12
Foretold by
Christ........John 7:38, 39
Fulfilled at
Pentecost .....Acts 2:1-41
Fulfilled at   { 2 Cor. 1:21, 22
conversion .... { 1 John 2:20, 27

Answer—*a reply*

A. *Good:*
Soft ....Prov. 15:1
Confident.....Dan. 3:16-18
Convicting ....Dan. 5:17-28
Astonished ...Luke 2:47
Unan-
swerable .....Luke 20:3-8
Spontaneous...Luke 21:14, 15
Spirit-
directed......Luke 12:11, 12
Ready ....1 Pet. 3:15

B. *Evil:*
Unwise ....1 Kin. 12:12-15
Incrim-
inating.......2 Sam. 1:5-16
Insolent ......2 Kin. 18:27-36
Humiliating...Esth. 6:6-11
Satanic ....Job 1:8-11

Ant—*a small insect*

An example of   { Prov. 6:6-8
industry ....{ Prov. 30:24

Antagonism—*unceasing opposition*

A. *Of men, against:*
God's people..Ex. 5:1-19
Deut. 2:26-33
The prophets ..Amos 7:10-17
Zech. 1:2-6
The light .....John 3:19, 20
The truth.....John 8:12-47
Acts 7:54-60
Christians .....Acts 16:16-24

B. *Of Satan, against:*
Job ....Job 1:9-12

Christ ....Luke 4:1-13
Peter ....Luke 22:31-34
Paul...........1 Thess. 2:18
Christians .....Eph. 6:11-18

Antediluvians—*those who lived before the flood*

A. *Described as:*
Long-lived....Gen. 5:3-32
Very wicked...Gen. 6:5
A mixed race ..Gen. 6:1-4
Jude 6, 7
Of great size..Gen. 6:4

B. *Warnings against, made by:*
Enoch ....Jude 14, 15
Noah ....2 Pet. 2:5
Christ ....1 Pet. 3:19, 20

C. *Destruction of:*
Only Noah's family
escaped ......Gen. 7:21-23
Predicted ......Gen. 6:5-7
Comparable
to Christ's   { Matt. 24:37-39
return........ { Luke 17:26, 27
Comparable to the world's
end ....2 Pet. 3:3-7

Antelope

Listed as
unclean ....Deut. 14:5

Anthropomorphisms—*applying human attributes to God*

A. *Physical likenesses, such as:*
Feet ....Ex. 24:10
Hands ....Ex. 24:11
Face...........Num. 12:7, 8
Eyes...........Hab. 1:13
Arms ....Ex. 6:6

B. *Non-physical characteristics, such as:*
Memory ......Gen. 9:16
Anger ....Ex. 22:24
Jealousy.......Ps. 78:58
Repentance....Jon. 3:10

Antichrist—*Satan's final opponent of Christ and Christians*

A. *Called:*
Man of sin.....2 Thess. 2:3
Son of
perdition ......2 Thess. 2:3
Lawless one ...2 Thess. 2:8
Antichrist......1 John 2:18, 22
Beast ....Rev. 11:7

B. *Described as:*

Lawless........2 Thess. 2:3-12

Opposing
God...........2 Thess. 2:4

Working
wonders ......2 Thess. 2:9

Deceiving the   {2 John 7
world ....   {Rev. 19:20

Persecuting
Christians.....Rev. 13:7

Satan-
inspired.......2 Thess. 2:9

Denying Christ's
incarnation ...1 John 4:3
                2 John 7

A person and a
system........2 Thess. 2:3, 7

Seeking man's
worship.......2 Thess. 2:4

One and
many ....1 John 2:18-22

C. *Coming of:*

Foretold.......2 Thess. 2:5

In the last
time ....1 John 2:18

Now
restrained.....2 Thess. 2:6

Follows removal of
hindrance.....2 Thess. 2:7, 8

Before Christ's
return........2 Thess. 2:3, 8

By Satan's
deception .....2 Thess. 2:9, 10

D. *Destruction of:*

At Christ's   {2 Thess. 2:8
return........ {Rev. 19:20

Eternal in lake of
fire...........Rev. 20:10

Antidote—*a remedy given to counteract poison*

A: *Literal:*

A tree ....Ex. 15:23-25

Meal..........2 Kin. 4:38-41

B. *Figurative and spiritual, for:*

Sin, Christ....Num. 21:8, 9
               John 3:14, 15

Christ's absence, the Holy
Spirit ....John 14:16-18

Sorrow, joy....John 16:20-22

Satan's lies, God's
truth..........1 John 4:1-6

Earth's trials,
faith ....1 Pet. 1:6-8

Testings,   {1 Cor. 10:13
God's grace .. {2 Cor. 12:7-9

Suffering, heaven's
glory.........Rom. 8:18
              2 Cor. 5:1-10

Antinomianism—*the idea that Christian liberty exempts one from the moral law*

A. *Prevalence of, among:*

Christians .....Rom. 6:1-23

False   {2 Pet. 2:19
Teachers..... {Jude 4

B. *Based on error, that:*

Grace allows
sin............Rom. 6:1, 2

Moral law is
abolished.....Rom. 7:1-14

Liberty has no
bounds........1 Cor. 10:23-33

C. *Corrected by remembering, that liberty is:*

Not a license to
sin ....Rom. 6:1-23

Limited by moral
law ....Rom. 8:1-4

Controlled by Holy
Spirit ....Rom. 8:5-14

Not to be a
stumbling   {Rom. 14:1-23
block ....{1 Cor. 8:1-13

Motivated by
love...........Gal. 5:13-15

Antioch—*a city of Syria*

Home of Nicolas ..Acts 6:5

Haven of persecuted
Christians........Acts 11:19

Home of first gentile
church..........Acts 11:20, 21

Name "Christian" originated
in ....Acts 11:26

Barnabas ministered
here..........Acts 11:22-24

Barnabas and Paul minister in
church of........Acts 11:25-30

Paul
commissioned by {Acts 13:1-4
church of........{Acts 15:35-41

Paul reports to ....Acts 14:26-28

Church of,
troubled by   {Acts 15:1-4
Judaizers........{Gal. 2:11-21

Antioch—*a city of Pisidia*

Jewish
synagogue........Acts 13:14

Paul visits......Acts 13:14, 42

Jews of, reject the
Gospel ....Acts 13:45-51

Paul revisits.......Acts 14:21
Paul recalls
persecution at ....2 Tim. 3:11

Antipas

A Christian martyr of
Pergamum ....Rev. 2:13

Antipatris—*belonging to Antipater*

A city between Jerusalem and
Caesarea ....Acts 23:31

Antitype—*the fulfillment of a type*

The ark,
baptism ....1 Pet. 3:21
The Greek word
translated "copies"
in ....Heb. 9:24
Generally, a fulfillment of an Old
Testament type...Matt. 12:39, 40
John 1:29

Antonia, Tower of—*fortress built by
Herod the Great; not mentioned by
name in Scripture*

Called "the
barracks" ....Acts 21:30-40
Possible site of Jesus' trial, called
"the Pavement" ..John 19:13

Antothijah—*answers of Yahweh*

A Benjamite ......1 Chr. 8:24

Antothite, Anathothite—*a native of
Anathoth*

Home of famous (1 Chr. 11:28
soldiers..........(1 Chr. 12:3

Anub—*strong*

A man of Judah...1 Chr. 4:8

Anvil—*a block for forging hot metals*

Used figuratively
in ....Is. 41:7

Anxiety—*a disturbed state of mind
produced by real or imaginary fears*

A. *Caused by:*
Brother's
hatred ....Gen. 32:6-12
Son's
rebellion ......2 Sam. 18:24-33
King's decree ..Esth. 4:1-17
Child's
absence ....Luke 2:48
Son's
sickness.......John 4:46-49
Friend's
delay.........2 Cor. 2:12, 13

B. *Overcome by:*
Trust ....Ps. 37:1-5
Reliance upon the Holy
Spirit ....Mark 13:11
God's
provision......Luke 12:22-30
Upward look...Luke 21:25-28
Assurance of God's
sovereignty ...Rom. 8:28
Angel's word ..Acts 27:21-25
Prayer.........Phil. 4:6
God's care .....1 Pet. 5:6, 7

See Cares, worldly

Ape—*a monkey*

Article of trade....1 Kin. 10:22

Apelles

A Christian in
Rome ....Rom. 16:10

Apharsathchites

Assyrian colonists in Samaria
opposing Zerubbabel's
work ....Ezra 4:9

Aphek—*strength, fortress*

1. A town in Plain of
Sharon........Josh. 12:18
Site of
Philistine   (1 Sam. 4:1
camp.........(1 Sam. 29:1
2. A city assigned to
Asher ....Josh. 19:30
3. Border city .....Josh. 13:4
4. A city in
Jezreel........1 Kin. 20:26-30
Syria's defeat prophesied
here ....2 Kin. 13:14-19

Aphekah—*fortress*

A city of Judah ...Josh. 15:53

Aphiah—*striving*

An ancestor of King
Saul..............1 Sam. 9:1

Aphik—*strength, fortress*

Spared by Asher ..Judg. 1:31

See Aphek 2

Aphrah—*house of dust*

A Philistine city; symbolic of
doom.............Mic. 1:10

Apocalypse—*an unveiling of something
unknown*

The Greek word usually
translated   (Rom. 16:25
"revelation" .....   \Gal. 1:12

Apocrypha—*hidden things*

Writings in Greek written during
the period between the
Testaments; rejected by
Protestants as uninspired

Apollonia—*pertaining to Apollo*

A town between Amphipolis and
Thessalonica .....Acts 17:1

Apollos—*a short or pet name for
Apollonios*

An Alexandrian Jew mighty in the
Scriptures ....Acts 18:24, 25
Receives further
instruction ......Acts 18:26
Sent to preach in
Achaia ....Acts 18:27, 28
A minister in   (1 Cor. 1:12
Corinth.........\1 Cor. 3:4, 22
Cited by Paul .....1 Cor. 4:6
Urged to revisit
Corinth ....1 Cor. 16:12
Journey of, noted by
Paul..............Titus 3:13

Apollyon—*the destroyer*

Angel of the bottomless
pit................Rev. 9:11

Apostasy—*a falling away from God's
truth*

A. *Kinds of:*
   National.......1 Kin. 12:26-33
   Individual .....2 Kin. 21:1-9
                           Heb. 3:12
   Satanic ....Rev. 12:7-9
   Angelic........2 Pet. 2:4
   General........2 Tim. 3:1-5
   Imputed ......Acts 21:21
   Final ....2 Thess. 2:3
   Irremedial .....Heb. 6:1-8

B. *Caused by:*
   Satan..........Luke 22:31
   False
   teachers ......Acts 20:29, 30
   Perversion of
   Scripture......2 Tim. 4:3, 4
   Persecution....Matt. 13:21
   Unbelief ......Heb. 4:9-11
   Love of
   world ....2 Tim. 4:10

Hardened
heart.........Acts 7:54, 57
Spiritual
blindness.....Acts 28:25-27

C. *Manifested in:*
   Resisting
   truth.........2 Tim. 3:7, 8
   Resorting to
   deception .....2 Cor. 11:13-15
   Reverting to   (2 Pet. 2:14,
   immorality ...\   19-22

D. *Safeguards against, found in:*
   God's Word....Ps. 119:11
                           2 Tim. 3:13-17
   Spiritual
   growth........2 Pet. 1:5-11
   Indoc-
   trination ......Acts 20:29-31
   Faithfulness ...Matt. 24:42-51
   Spiritual
   perception ....1 John 4:1-6
   Being grounded in the
   truth ....Eph. 4:13-16
   Using God's
   armor.........Eph. 6:10-20
   Preaching the
   Word ....2 Tim. 4:2, 5

E. *Examples of, seen in:*
   Israelites .....Ex. 32:1-35
   Saul ....1 Sam. 15:11
   Solomon.......1 Kin. 11:1-10
   Amaziah......2 Chr. 25:14-16
   Judas.........Matt. 26:14-16
   Hymenaeus and
   Philetus......2 Tim. 2:17, 18
   Demas........2 Tim. 4:10
   Certain men ...Jude 4

Apostles—*men divinely commissioned
to represent Christ*

A. *Descriptive of:*
   Christ ....Heb. 3:1
   The twelve ....Matt. 10:2
   Others (Barnabas, James,
   etc.) ....Acts 14:14
                           Gal. 1:19
   Messengers....2 Cor. 8:23
   False
   teachers ......2 Cor. 11:13
   Simon Peter ...Matt. 10:2
   Andrew.......Matt. 10:2
   James, son of
   Zebedee......Matt. 10:2
   John..........Matt. 10:2
   Philip.........Matt. 10:3
   Bartholomew
   (Na-   (Matt. 10:3
   thanael).....\John 1:45

Thomas..........Matt. 10:3
Matthew ....{Matt. 10:3
(Levi)..........{Luke 5:27
James, son of
Alphaeus.......Matt. 10:3
Thaddaeus ....{Matt. 10:3
(Judas).........{John 14:22
Simon the
Zealot ....Luke 6:15
Judas
Iscariot ....Matt. 10:4
Matthias........Acts 1:26
Paul............2 Cor. 1:1
Barnabas ......Acts 14:14
James, the Lord's
brother ....Gal. 1:19
Silvanus and .....{1 Thess. 1:1
Timothy .....{1 Thess. 2:9
Andronicus and
Junia ....Rom. 16:7

B. *Mission of, to:*
Perform
miracles.......Matt. 10:1, 8
Preach
Gospel........Matt. 28:19, 20
Witness Christ's
resur-.........{Acts 1:22
rection........{Acts 10:40-42
Write
Scripture......Eph. 3:5
Establish the
Church........Eph. 2:20

C. *Limitations of, before
Pentecost:*
Lowly in
position.......Matt. 4:18
Unlearned .....Acts 4:13
Subject to
disputes.......Matt. 20:20-28
Faith often
obscure ....Matt. 16:21-23
Need of
instruction ....Matt. 17:4, 9-13

D. *Position of, after Pentecost:*
Interpreted
prophecy......Acts 2:14-36
Defended
truth..........Phil. 1:7, 17
Exposed
heretics ....Gal. 1:6-9
Upheld
discipline......2 Cor. 13:1-6
Established
churches......Rom. 15:17-20

Appaim—*nostrils*

A man of Judah...1 Chr. 2:30, 31

Apparel—*clothing*

A. *Kinds of:*
Harlot's.........Gen. 38:14, 15
Virgin's........2 Sam. 13:18
Mourner's .....2 Sam. 12:19, 20
Gorgeous .....Luke 7:25
Rich..........Ezek. 27:24
Worldly......1 Pet. 3:3
Showy.........Luke 16:19
Official.........1 Kin. 10:5
Royal..........Esth. 6:8
Priestly ....Ezra 3:10
Angelic........Acts 1:10
Heavenly .....Rev. 19:8

B. *Attitude toward:*
Not to covet ..Acts 20:33
Without
show..........1 Pet. 3:3, 4
Be modest in ..1 Tim. 2:9, 10

C. *Figurative of:*
Christ's
blood ....Is. 63:1-3
Christ's righteous-
ness...........Zech. 3:1-5
The Church's
purity.........Ps. 45:13, 14

Apparition—*appearance of ghost or
disembodied spirit*

Samuel ....1 Sam. 28:12-14
Christ mistaken {Matt. 14:26
for ....{Luke 24:37, 39

Appeal—*petition for higher judgment*

To Christ ....Luke 12:13, 14
Of Paul, ...{Acts 25:11,
to ....{25-27
Caesar ....{Acts 26:32

Appearance, outward

A. *Can conceal:*
Deception .....James 1:10, 11
Josh. 9:3-16
Hypocrisy .....Matt. 23:25-28
Rottenness ....Acts 12:21-23
Rebellion ......2 Sam. 15:7-13
False
apostles.......2 Cor. 11:13-15
Inner glory ....Is. 53:1-3
Matt. 17:1, 2

B. *Can be:*
Misunder-
stood ....Josh. 22:10-31
Mistaken ......1 Sam. 1:12-18
Misleading.....2 Cor. 10:7-11
Misjudged .....John 7:24

Misinter-
preted........Matt. 11:16-19

Appearances, divine

A. *Of the Lord in the Old
   Testament:*
   To Abraham...Gen. 12:7
   To Isaac......Gen. 26:1, 2, 24
   To Jacob......Gen. 35:1, 9
   To Moses......Ex. 3:1, 2, 16
   To Israel.....Ex. 16:10
   In mercy
   seat..........Lev. 16:2
   In tabernacle..Num. 14:10
   To Gideon....Judg. 6:11, 12
   To Manoah...Judg. 13:2, 3, 10,
                            21
   To Samuel...1 Sam. 3:21
   To David.....2 Chr. 3:1
   To Solomon...1 Kin. 3:5

B. *Of Christ's first advent, in:*
   Nativity.......2 Tim. 1:10
   Transfig-
   uration.......Luke 9:29-31
   Resurrected
   form..........Luke 24:34
   Priestly
   intercession...Heb. 9:24
   Return........Col. 3:4

C. *Of Christ resurrected, to, at:*
   Mary
   Magdalene....John 20:11-18
   Other
   women........Matt. 28:9, 10
   Disciples on road to
   Emmaus......Luke 24:13-35
   Ten disciples...John 20:19-25
   Thomas.......John 20:26-31
   Sea of
   Galilee.......John 21:1-25
   Give great
   commission...Matt. 28:16-20
   Five hundred
   brethren......1 Cor. 15:6
   His
   ascension.....Acts 1:4-11
   Paul..........Acts 9:3-6
   John..........Rev. 1:10-18

D. *Of Christ's second advent, a
   time of:*
   Salvation......Heb. 9:28
   Confidence....1 John 2:28
   Judgment.....2 Tim. 4:1
   Reward........2 Tim. 4:8
   Blessedness....Titus 2:13

Joy...........1 Pet. 1:7, 8
Rulership......1 Tim. 6:14, 15

See Theophany

Appeasement—*means used to reconcile
two parties*

A. *Kinds of, between:*
   Brothers......Gen. 32:20
   Nations......1 Kin. 20:31-34
   Tribes........Josh. 22:10-34
   Jews and
   Gentiles......Eph. 2:11-17

B. *Means of, by:*
   Gifts..........Gen. 43:11-16
   Special
   pleading......1 Sam. 25:17-35
   Correcting an
   abuse.........Acts 6:1-6
   Slowness to
   anger.........Prov. 15:18
   Wisdom......Prov. 16:14

C. *None allowed between:*
   Righteousness,
   evil..........2 Cor. 6:14-17
   Truth, error...Gal. 1:7-9
   Faith, works..Gal. 5:1-10
   Flesh, Spirit..Gal. 5:16-26
   Christ, Satan..Matt. 4:1-11
   Heaven,
   Sheol.........Is. 28:18

D. *Of God's wrath, by:*
   Righteous
   action........Num. 16:44-50
   Repentance....2 Sam. 12:10-14
   Atoning for an
   evil..........2 Sam. 21:1-14
   Christ's
   death........Is. 53:1-7
   Christ's
   righteous-   {Zech. 3:1-5
   ness..........{2 Cor. 5:18-21

Appetite—*desire to fulfill some basic
need*

A. *Kinds of:*
   Physical......1 Sam. 14:31-33
   Sexual........1 Cor. 7:1-9
   Lustful.......Matt. 5:28
   Insatiable....Prov. 27:20
   Spiritual.....Ps. 119:20, 131

B. *Perversion of, by:*
   Gluttony......Prov. 23:1, 2
   Adultery......Prov. 6:24-29
                          Ezek. 23:1-49
   Impurity......Rom. 1:24-32

C. *Loss of, by:*
Age.............2 Sam. 19:35
Trouble........1 Sam. 28:21-23
Visions ....Dan. 10:3-16
Deep
concern......John 4:31-34

D. *Spiritual, characteristics of:*
Satisfying......Is. 55:1, 2
Sufficient .....Matt. 5:6
Spontaneous...John 7:37-39
Sanctifying ....1 Pet. 2:2
Sublime ....Col. 3:1-3

See Gluttony; Hunger; Temperance

Apphia

Christian lady of
Colosse ....Philem. 2

Appii Forum—*a town about 40 miles south of Rome*

Paul meets Christians
here..............Acts 28:15

Applause—*a visible expression of public approval*

Men seek after....Matt. 6:1-5

"Apple of the eye"—*a figurative expression for something very valuable*

A. *Translated as:*
"The apple of His
eye" ....Zech. 2:8

B. *Figurative of:*
God's care .....Deut. 32:10
God's Law .....Prov. 7:2
The saint's
security.......Ps. 17:8

Apples of gold—*something of great value*

A word fitly
spoken ....Prov. 25:11

Appoint—*to set in an official position or relationship*

A. *Descriptive of ordination, to:*
Priesthood.....Num. 3:10
Prophetic
office.........Heb. 3:2
Ruler ....2 Sam. 6:21
Apostleship....Luke 10:1
Deacon's
office..........Acts 6:3
Christ as high
priest ....Heb. 5:1
Paul as a
preacher ......1 Tim. 2:7

Elders ....Titus 1:5
Royal officer...Dan. 2:24

B. *Descriptive of God's rule, over:*
Earth..........Ps. 104:19, 20
World
history.......Acts 17:26
Israel's
history.......2 Chr. 33:8
Nations........Jer. 47:7
Man's life.....Job 14:5
Death ....Heb. 9:27
Final
judgment .....Acts 17:31
Man's
destiny.......Matt. 24:51

C. *Descriptive of the believer's life:*
Trials..........1 Thess. 3:3
Service ....Acts 22:10
Salvation ......1 Thess. 5:9
Government ...Rom. 13:1
Salvation ......Acts 13:48

Appreciation—*favorable recognition of blessings*

Sought for among
men..............Ps. 107:8-21
Of favors,
rebuffed..........2 Sam. 10:1-5
Of blessings,
unnoticed ....Acts 14:15-18

Apprehension—*the ability to understand*

God................Job 11:7
God's Word......Acts 17:11
Prophecy ....1 Pet. 1:10-12
Parables ....Matt. 13:10-17
Spiritual truths...1 Cor. 2:7-16
Christ............Phil. 3:12-14

Appropriation—*possessing for one's use*

God's promises..Heb. 11:8-16
God's Word......Ps. 119:11
Salvation ....Acts 16:30-34

Approval—*favorable acceptance*

A. *Means of, by:*
God ....Acts 2:22
The Lord ......2 Cor. 10:18
The Jews ......Rom. 2:17, 18
A church ......1 Cor. 16:3
Men ....Rom. 14:18

B. *Obtained by:*
Endurance.....2 Cor. 6:4-10
Innocence .....2 Cor. 7:11
Spiritual exami-
nation ....2 Cor. 13:5-8

Spiritual
judgment .....Phil. 1:9, 10
Diligence ......2 Tim. 2:15

Aprons—*articles of clothing*

Item of miraculous
healing...........Acts 19:12

Aquila—*eagle*

Jewish
tentmaker........Acts 18:2, 3
Paul stays with ...Acts 18:1-3
Visits Syria ......Acts 18:18
Resides in
Ephesus ....Acts 18:19
Instructs
Apollos........Acts 18:24-26
Esteemed by
Paul.............Rom. 16:3, 4

Ar—*city*

A chief Moabite
city ....Num. 21:15
On Israel's route ..Deut. 2:18
Destroyed by
Sihon ....Num. 21:28
Destroyed by
God ....Is. 15:1

Ara—*strong*

A descendant of
Asher ....1 Chr. 7:38

Arab—*a court*

A mountain city of
Judah ....Josh. 15:52

Arabia—*steppe*

A. *Place of:*
Mt. Sinai ......Gal. 4:25
Gold mines ....2 Chr. 9:14
Paul visited....Gal. 1:17

B. *People of:*
Nomadic........Is. 13:20
Paid tribute to
Solomon ......1 Kin. 10:14, 15
Plundered
Jerusalem.....2 Chr. 21:16, 17
Defeated by
Uzziah ....2 Chr. 26:1, 7
Sold sheep and goats to
Tyre ....Ezek. 27:1, 2, 21
Opposed
Nehemiah.....Neh. 2:19
Denounced by
prophets ......Is. 21:13-17
Visited Jerusalem at
Pentecost .....Acts 2:11

Arad—*fugitive*

1. A Benjamite...1 Chr. 8:15
2. A city south of
Hebron ....Num. 21:1-3
Defeated by
Joshua........Josh. 12:14
Kenites settled
near ....Judg. 1:16

Arah—*wayfarer*

1. A descendant of
Asher ....1 Chr. 7:39
2. A family of
returnees .....Ezra 2:5

Aram—*high; exalted*

1. A son of
Shem ....Gen. 10:22, 23
2. A grandson of
Nahor.........Gen. 22:21
3. A descendant of
Asher.........1 Chr. 7:34

Aramaic—*a Semitic language*

Used by the
Syrians...........2 Kin. 18:26
The language of the postexilic
period ....Ezra 4:7
Dan. 2:4
Portions of the ⎰Dan. 2:4-7:28
Bible written in,⎱Ezra 4:8-6:18
include ....Ezra 7:12-26
The same as "Hebrew"
in ....John 19:20
Words and ⎰Matt. 27:46
phrases of, found⎱Mark 5:41
in ....Mark 7:34

Aran—*wild goat*

Esau's
descendant ......Gen. 36:28

Ararat—*a high mountain range in
eastern Armenia*

Site of ark's
landing...........Gen. 8:4
Assassins flee ⎰2 Kin. 19:37
to ....⎱Is. 37:38

Aratus—*a Greek poet living about 270
B.C.*

Paul quotes from his
Phaenomena .....Acts 17:28

Araunah—*Yahweh is firm*

A Jebusite ....2 Sam. 24:15-25
His threshing floor bought by
David ....2 Sam. 24:18-25

Became site of
Temple..........2 Chr. 3:1
Also called
Ornan...........1 Chr. 21:18-28

Arba—*four*

The father of the
Anakim ....Josh. 14:15

Arbathite—*a native of Beth Arabah*

Two of David's mighty
men..............2 Sam. 23:31

Arbite—*a native of Arab*

In Judah ....2 Sam. 23:35

Arbitrator—*one authorized to settle
disputes*

A. *Exercised by:*
Judges..........Ex. 18:18-27
Priests.........Deut. 17:8-13
Kings...........1 Kin. 3:9, 16-28
Christ..........Matt. 22:17-33
Apostles ....Acts 6:1-6
Church..........Acts 15:1-29

B. *Purposes of:*
Determine
the Lord's   {Lev. 24:11-16, 23
will   {Num. 15:32-36
Settle
disputes.......Josh. 22:9-34
Settle labor   {Matt. 18:23-35
disputes.......{Matt. 20:1-16

Archaeology—*the science of digging up
ancient civilizations*

Truth springs out of the
earth ....Ps. 85:11
The stones cry
out...............Luke 19:40

See article on Greatest Archaeological
Discoveries

Archangel—*a chief angel*

Contends with
Satan ....Jude 9
Will herald the Lord's
return............1 Thess. 4:16

Archelaus—*leader of the people*

Son of Herod the
Great............Matt. 2:22

Archers—*experts with the bow and
arrow*

A. *Descriptive of:*
Ishmael.........Gen. 21:20
Jonathan ....1 Sam. 20:34-39
Sons of Ulam ...2 Chr. 8:40

B. *Instrumental in the death of:*
Saul ....1 Sam. 31:3
Uriah the
Hittite ....2 Sam. 11:24
Josiah ....2 Chr. 35:23, 24

C. *Figurative of:*
Invincibility ...Gen. 49:23, 24
The Lord's chastise-
ments..........Job 16:13
Loss of glory...Is. 21:17
Divine
judgment .....Jer. 50:29

Archippus—*master of the horse*

A church
worker ....Col. 4:17

Archite—*the long*

Canaanite tribe ...Josh. 16:2
David's friend.....2 Sam. 15:32

Architect—*one who draws plans for a
building*

Plan of, given to
Noah...........Gen. 6:14-16
Plan of, shown to
Moses............Ex. 25:8, 9, 40
Bezaleel, an
inspired ....Ex. 35:30-35
Plan of, given to
Solomon ....1 Chr. 28:11-21
Seen in Ezekiel's
vision ....Ezek. 40-42

Archives—*storage place for public and
historical documents*

The book of the law
found in ....2 Kin. 22:8
Jeremiah's roll
placed in ....Jer. 36:20, 21
Record book
kept in ....Ezra 4:15
Genealogies
kept in ....Neh. 7:5, 64

Ard—*humpbacked*

A son of
Benjamin.........Gen. 46:21
Progenitor of the
Ardites ....Num. 26:40
Also called
Addar ....1 Chr. 8:3

Ardon—*descendant*

A son of Caleb....1 Chr. 2:18

Areli—*valiant, heroic*

A son of Gad......Gen. 46:16

Areopagite—*a member of the court*

A convert.........Acts 17:34

Areopagus—*a rocky hill at Athens; also the name of a court*

Paul preached.....Acts 17:18-34

Aretas—*pleasing*

The title borne by four Nabataean rulers, the last of whom Paul mentions (Aretas IV, Philopatris, 9 B.C.–A.D. 40) ......2 Cor. 11:32, 33

Argob—*mound or region of clods*

1. District of Bashan with 60 fortified cities.......... { Deut. 3:4 / 1 Kin. 4:13 }
2. Guard killed by Pekah........2 Kin. 15:25

Aridai

A son of Haman ..Esth. 9:9

Aridatha

A son of Haman ..Esth. 9:8

Arieh—*lion*

Guard killed by Pekah.............2 Kin. 15:25

Ariel—*lion of God*

1. Ezra's friend...Ezra 8:15-17
2. Name applied to Jerusalem ......Is. 29:1, 2, 7

Arimathea—*a height*

Joseph's native city ....John 19:38

Arioch—*lion-like*

1. King of Ellasar ....Gen. 14:1, 9
2. Captain of Nebuchadnezzar ....Dan. 2:14, 15

Arisai

A son of Haman ..Esth. 9:9

Arise—*to stand up*

A. *Descriptive of:*
Natural events ....Eccl. 1:5
Standing up ...1 Sam. 28:23
Regeneration ..Luke 15:18, 20
Resurrection....Matt. 9:24, 25
A miracle....Luke 4:38, 39

B. *Descriptive of prophetic events:*
World kingdoms .....Dan. 2:39
The Messiah's advent ....Is. 60:1-3
Persecution....Mark 4:16, 17
False Christs...Matt. 24:24

Aristarchus—*the best ruler*

A Macedonian Christian ....Acts 19:29
Accompanied Paul.............Acts 20:1, 4
Imprisoned with Paul.............Col. 4:10

Aristobulus—*the best counselor*

A Christian at Rome ....Rom. 16:10

Ark of bulrushes—*a basket made of reeds* (papyrus)

Moses placed in ...Ex. 2:1-6
Made by faith .....Heb. 11:23

Ark of Noah

Construction......Gen. 6:14-16
Cargo.............Gen. 6:19-21
Ready for the flood ....Matt. 24:38, 39
Rested on Mt. Ararat.............Gen. 8:1-16
A type of baptism ....1 Pet. 3:20, 21

Ark of the Covenant—*a small box containing the tablets of the Law*

A. *Called:*
Ark of the covenant......Num. 10:33
Ark of the testimony .....Ex. 30:6
Ark of the Lord........Josh. 4:11
Ark of God ...1 Sam. 3:3
Ark of God's strength ......2 Chr. 6:41

B. *Construction of:*
Described.....Ex. 25:10-22
Executed ......Ex. 37:1-5

C. *Contained:*
The Ten Command-
ments........Deut. 10:4, 5
Aaron's {Num. 17:10
rod............{Heb. 9:4
Pot of
manna ....Ex. 16:33, 34

D. *Conveyed:*
By Levites .....Num. 3:30, 31
Before Israel ..Josh. 3:3-17
Into battle ....1 Sam. 4:4, 5
On a cart ......1 Sam. 6:7-15

E. *Purposes of:*
Symbol of God's
Law...........Ex. 25:16, 21
Memorial of God's
provision......Ex. 16:33, 34
Place to know {Ex. 25:22
God's will ....{Ex. 30:6, 36
Place of
entreaty ......Josh. 7:6-15
Symbol of
God's {1 Sam. 6:19
holiness......{2 Sam. 6:6, 7
Place of
atonement ....Lev. 16:2, 14-17
Symbol of
heaven........Rev. 11:19

F. *History of:*
Carried across
Jordan ....Josh. 3:14-17
Caused Jordan's
stoppage .....Josh. 4:5-11, 18
Carried around
Jericho........Josh. 6:6-20
At Mt. Ebal
ceremony .....Josh. 8:30-33
Set up at
Shiloh........Josh. 18:1
Moved to house of
God.........Judg. 20:26, 27
Returned to
Shiloh.........1 Sam. 1:3
Carried into
battle ....1 Sam. 4:3-22
Captured ......1 Sam. 4:10-22
Caused Dagon's
fall............1 Sam. 5:1-4
Brought a
plague ....1 Sam. 5:6-12
Returned to
Israel ....1 Sam. 6:1-21
Set in Abinadab's
house........1 Sam. 7:1, 2

In Obed-Edom's
house ....2 Sam. 6:10-12
Established in
Jerusalem....2 Sam. 6:12-17
During Absalom's
rebellion ......2 Sam. 15:24-29
Placed in
Temple........1 Kin. 8:1-11
Restored by
Josiah.........2 Chr. 35:3
Carried to
Babylon.......2 Chr. 36:6, 18
Prophetic {Jer. 3:16, 17
fulfillment....{Acts 15:13-18

Arkite—*belonging to Arka*

Canaan's {Gen. 10:17
descendants {1 Chr. 1:15

Arm of God

A. *Described as:*
Stretched
out ....Deut. 4:34
Everlasting ....Deut. 33:27
Strong,
mighty........Ps. 89:10, 13
Holy...........Ps. 98:1
Glorious ....Is. 63:12

B. *Descriptive of, God's:*
Redeeming ....Ex. 6:6
Saving.........Ps. 44:3
Victorious .....Ps. 98:1
Ruling.........Is. 40:10
Strength-
ening ....Ps. 89:21
Protecting .....Deut. 7:19
Destroying.....Is. 30:30

Arm of the wicked—*expression for molestation*

Shall be broken ..Ps. 10:15

Armageddon—*Mount Megiddo; site of*

Historic wars.....Judg. 5:19
Notable deaths....1 Sam. 31:8
Final battle ......Rev. 16:16

Armholes

Armpits, protected with
rags.............Jer. 38:12

Armoni—*belonging to the palace*

A son of Saul .....2 Sam. 21:8-11

Armor—*a protective article of warfare*

A. *As a protective weapon:*
Shield ....1 Sam. 17:7, 41
Helmet ....1 Sam. 17:38

Scale-armor....1 Sam. 17:5, 38
                       1 Kin. 22:34
Greaves ....1 Sam. 17:6
Body armor...2 Chr. 26:14
                       Jer. 46:4

B. *As an aggressive weapon:*
Rod ....Ps. 2:9
Sling ....1 Sam. 17:40
Bow and
  arrow ....2 Sam. 1:18
Spear..........Is. 2:4
Sword ....1 Sam. 17:51

Armorbearer—*man who bears the arms of another*

Assists kings in
  battle ....Judg. 9:54
David serves Saul
  as ....1 Sam. 16:21
Jonathan's, a man of
  courage ....1 Sam. 14:7, 12
Saul's, dies with
  him ....1 Sam. 31:4-6
Goliath's, precedes
  him ....1 Sam. 17:7, 41

Armor, spiritual

The Christian's, (Eph. 6:11-17
  complete ....(1 Thess. 5:8
Of light ....Rom. 13:12
Of righteousness ..2 Cor. 6:7
The Bible, the
  sword ....Eph. 6:17
Not of flesh ......2 Cor. 10:4, 5

Armory—*an arsenal*

Armor
  stored in ....Neh. 3:19
God's, opened for
  war ....Jer. 50:25
David's, well
  stocked..........Song 4:4

Army—*men organized and disciplined for battle*

A. *Consisted of:*
Men over 20 ...Num. 1:3
Infantrymen ..2 Chr. 25:5
Archers ....1 Chr. 5:18
Sling stones ..2 Chr. 26:14
Chariots ....1 Kin. 4:26
Foreigners .....2 Sam. 15:18
Choice men....2 Sam. 10:7-9

B. *Led by:*
God ....Josh. 5:13-15
Judges..........Judg. 11:1, 5, 6,
                       32

Commander ..2 Sam. 2:8
Kings..........2 Sam. 12:28, 29

C. *Commands regarding:*
Use of
  chariots.......Deut. 17:16
Deferred
  certain   (Num. 2:33
  classes ....(Deut. 20:1-9
Division of
  spoil ....1 Sam. 30:21-25
Fearfulness ....Deut. 20:1

D. *Units of:*
Fifties ....2 Kin. 1:9
Hundreds.....Num. 31:14, 48
Legions........Matt. 26:53
Bands ....Acts 21:31
Guards ....Acts 28:16
Squads ....Acts 12:4
Thousands....Num. 31:14, 48

E. *Of Israel, conquered:*
Egyptians......Ex. 14:19-31
Jericho ....Josh. 6:1-25
Midianites .....Judg. 7:1-23
Philistines .....1 Sam. 14:14-23
Syrians ....2 Kin. 7:1-15
Assyrians ......2 Kin. 19:35, 36

Army, Christian

A. *Warfare against:*
The world .....James 4:4
                       1 John 2:15-17
The flesh ......Gal. 5:17-21
Satan..........1 Pet. 5:8, 9
Evil men......2 Tim. 3:8
False
  teachers ......Jude 3, 4
Spiritual
  wickedness....Eph. 6:12
Worldly "vain
  babblings" ....1 Tim. 6:20

B. *Equipment for:*
Sufficient for   (Eph. 6:12-17
  total war......(1 Thess. 5:8
Spiritual in
  nature ....2 Cor. 10:3, 4
Sharper than any
  sword ....Heb. 4:12

C. *The soldier in, must:*
Enlist..........Matt. 28:18-20
Obey ....2 Cor. 10:5, 6
Please
  captain........2 Tim. 2:4
Use
  self-control....1 Cor. 9:25-27
Stand firm .....Eph. 6:13-17

Endure
hardship ..... 2 Tim. 2:3
Show
courage ..... 2 Tim. 4:7-18
Fight hard .... 1 Tim. 6:12
Be pure .... 1 Pet. 2:11, 12
Be alert .... 1 Pet. 5:8
Be faithful ..... 1 Tim. 1:18-20

D. *Jesus Christ, the Captain of, is:*
Perfect .... Heb. 2:10
Undefiled ...... Heb. 7:26
Powerful .... 2 Thess. 2:8

Arnan—*strong*

A descendant of
David .... 1 Chr. 3:1, 21

Arnon—*a river*

Boundary between Moab and
Ammon .... Num. 21:13, 26
Border of
Reuben.......... Deut. 3:12, 16
Ammonites
reminded of ..... Judg. 11:18-26

Arod—*hunchbacked*

A son of Gad..... Num. 26:17
Called Arodi ...... Gen. 46:16

Aroer—*naked*

1. A town in east
   Jordan .... Deut. 2:36
   An Amorite boundary
   city .... Josh. 13:9, 10, 16
   Sihon ruled .... Josh. 12:2
   Assigned to
   Reuben .... Deut. 3:12
   Rebuilt by
   Gadites .... Num. 32:34
   Beginning of David's
   census .... 2 Sam. 24:1, 5
   Taken by
   Hazael .... 2 Kin. 10:32, 33
   Possessed by
   Moab .... Jer. 48:19
2. A city of
   Judah .... 1 Sam. 30:28
3. A city of
   Gad............ Josh. 13:25

Aroma—*a pleasant smell*

Of sacrifices....... Lev. 26:31
Figurative of
gifts............. Phil. 4:18

Arpad—*a couch, resting place*

A town in
Samaria .... 2 Kin. 18:34
End of,
predicted .... Jer. 49:23

Arphaxad

A son of Shem .... Gen. 10:22, 24
Born two years after the
flood .... Gen. 11:10-13
An ancestor of
Christ .... Luke 3:36

Arrogance—*overbearing pride*

Mentioned with other
evils............ Prov. 8:13
To be punished by
God .... Is. 13:11
Seen in
haughtiness ...... Jer. 48:29

Arrows—*sharp instruments hurled by a bow*

A. *Uses of:*
Hunting ..... Gen. 27:3
Send
message....... 1 Sam. 20:20-22
Divination .... Ezek. 21:21
Prophecy ...... 2 Kin. 13:14-19
War .... 2 Kin. 19:32

B. *Described as:*
Deadly......... Prov. 26:18
Sharp.......... Ps. 120:4
Bright .... Jer. 51:11
Like
lightning..... Zech. 9:14

C. *Figurative of:*
God's
judgments .... Deut. 32:23, 42
Intense
affliction ...... Job 6:4
Wicked
intentions..... Ps. 11:2
Messiah's
mission ...... Ps. 45:5
Bitter words ... Ps. 64:3
God's power ... Ps. 76:3
Daily
hazards .... Ps. 91:5
Children ...... Ps. 127:4
A false
witness .... Prov. 25:18
A deceitful
tongue........ Jer. 9:8

Arson—*setting fire to property maliciously*

A. *Features concerning:*

A law
forbidding.....Ex. 22:6
A means of
revenge.......Judg. 12:1

B. *Instances of, by:*

Samson........Judg. 15:4, 5
Danites........Judg. 18:26, 27
Absalom.......2 Sam. 14:30
Enemies ....Ps. 74:7, 8

Art

Ointment after
the...............Ex. 30:25
Stones
graven by ....Acts 17:29

Artaxerxes—*great king*

Artaxerxes I, king of Persia
(465–425 B.C.), authorizes Ezra's
mission to
Jerusalem ....Ezra 7:1-28
Temporarily halts rebuilding
program at
Jerusalem ....Ezra 4:7-23
Commissions Nehemiah's
mission...........Neh. 2:1-10
Permits Nehemiah to
return...........Neh. 13:6

Artemas—*gift of Artemis*

Paul's companion at
Nicopolis ....Titus 3:12

Artemis—*the mother-goddess of Asia Minor* (known as Cybele)

Worship of, at Ephesus, creates
uproar...........Acts 19:23-41

Artificers—*skilled workmen; craftsmen*

Tubal-Cain, the
earliest ....Gen. 4:22
Employed in temple
construction.....1 Chr. 29:5
Removed in
judgment........Is. 3:1-3

Arts and crafts in the Bible

Armorer ....1 Sam. 8:12
Baker.............Gen. 40:1
Barber...........Ezek. 5:1
Blacksmith.......1 Sam. 13:19
Brickmaker.......Ex. 5:7
Carpenter........Mark 6:3
Carver...........Ex. 31:5
Caulker.........Ezek. 27:9
Cook.............1 Sam. 8:13

Coppersmith ......2 Tim. 4:14
Draftsman ....Ezek. 4:1
Dyer.............Ex. 25:1-5
Embalmer........Gen. 50:2, 3
Engraver.........Ex. 28:11
Farmer...........Gen. 4:2
Fisherman........Matt. 4:18
Gardener.........John 20:15
Gatekeeper ....2 Sam. 18:26
Goldsmith........Is. 40:19
Jeweler..........Ex. 28:17-21
Lapidary.........Ex. 35:33
Launderer........Mark 9:3
Mason ....2 Sam. 5:11
Moulder..........Ex. 32:4
Musician ....2 Sam. 6:5
Oarsmen ....Ezek. 27:8, 9
Painting ....Jer. 22:14
Perfumer.........Ex. 30:25, 35
Potter...........Jer. 18:3
Refiner..........Mal. 3:2, 3
Ropemaker ....Judg. 16:11
Sewing...........Ezek. 13:18
Ship building ....1 Kin. 9:26
Silversmith.......Acts 19:24
Smelter ....Job 28:1, 2
Spinner..........Prov. 31:19
Stonecutter ......Ex. 31:5
Tailor...........Ex. 28:3, 4
Tanner...........Acts 10:6
Tapestry maker ...Ex. 35:35
Tentmaking.......Acts 18:3
Watchman........2 Sam. 18:26
Weaver ....Ex. 35:35
Winemaker ....Neh. 13:15
Worker in   { Gen. 4:22
metal...........{ Ex. 31:3, 4
Writer...........Judg. 5:14

Arubboth—*the lattices*

A town in one of Solomon's
districts ....1 Kin. 4:10

Arumah—*height*

A village near Shechem;
Abimelech's
refuge............Judg. 9:41

Arvad—*wandering*

A Phoenician city built on an
island north of
Tyre..............Ezek. 27:8, 11

Arvadites—*inhabitants of Arvad*

Of Canaanite   { Gen. 10:18
ancestry.........{ 1 Chr. 1:16

Arza—*earth*

King Elah's steward in
Tirzah............1 Kin. 16:9

Asa—*physician*

1. Third king of
Judah.........1 Kin. 15:8-10
Reigns 10 years in
peace ....2 Chr. 14:1
Overthrows
idolatry ....2 Chr. 14:2-5
Removes his
mother........1 Kin. 15:13
Fortifies
Judah.........2 Chr. 14:6-8
Defeats the
Ethiopians ...2 Chr. 14:9-15
Leads in national
revival ....2 Chr. 15:1-15
Hires Ben-Hadad against
Baasha........2 Chr. 16:1-6
Reproved by a
prophet ....2 Chr. 16:7-10
Diseased, seeks physicians
rather than the
Lord ....2 Chr. 16:12
Buried in
Jerusalem.....2 Chr. 16:13, 14
An ancestor of
Christ....Matt. 1:7
2. A Levite among
returnees .....1 Chr. 9:16

Asahel—*God has made*

1. A son of Zeruiah, David's
sister..........1 Chr. 2:16
Noted for ⎰ 2 Sam. 2:18
valor.........⎱ 2 Sam. 23:24
Pursues
Abner.........2 Sam. 2:19
Killed by
Abner.........2 Sam. 2:23
Avenged by
Joab ....2 Sam. 3:27, 30
Made a captain in David's
army..........1 Chr. 27:7
2. A Levite
teacher ....2 Chr. 17:8
3. A collector of
tithes ....2 Chr. 31:12, 13
4. A priest who opposes Ezra's
reforms ....Ezra 10:15

Asaiah—*Yahweh has made*

1. A Simeonite
chief..........1 Chr. 4:36

2. A Levite during David's
reign..........1 Chr. 6:30
Helps restore ark to
Jerusalem.....1 Chr. 15:6, 11
3. An officer sent to
Huldah........2 Chr. 34:20-22
2 Kin. 22:12-14
4. The firstborn of the
Shilonites .....1 Chr. 9:5
Probably called
Maaseiah .....Neh. 11:5

Asaph—*collector*

1. A Gershonite Levite choir
leader in the
time of David ⎧ 1 Chr. 15:16-19
and ⎨ 1 Chr. 16:1-7
Solomon .....⎩ 2 Chr. 5:6, 12
Called a seer...2 Chr. 29:30
Sons of, made
musicians .....1 Chr. 25:1-9
Twelve Psalms ⎰ Ps. 50–83
assigned to...⎱ 2 Chr. 29:30
Descendants of,
among ⎰ Ezra 2:41
returnees.....⎱ Neh. 7:44
In dedication
ceremony .....Ezra 3:10
2. The father of Hezekiah's
recorder.......2 Kin. 18:18, 37
3. A chief forester whom
Artaxerxes commands to
supply timber to
Nehemiah.....Neh. 2:8
4. A Korhite
Levite.........1 Chr. 26:1
Also called
Ebiasaph......1 Chr. 9:19

Asarel—*God has bound*

A son of
Jehaleleel.........1 Chr. 4:16

Asarelah—*Yahweh is joined*

A son of Asaph in David's
time..............1 Chr. 25:2
Called
Jesharelah........1 Chr. 25:14

Ascension—*rising to a higher place*

A. Descriptive of:
Physical rising ⎰ Ex. 19:18
of smoke.....⎱ Josh. 8:20, 21
Going up hill .. Luke 19:28

Rising to
heaven........Ps. 139:8
Christ's
ascension .....John 6:62
Sinful
ambition .....Is. 14:13, 14

B. *Of saints:*
Enoch,
translation   {Gen. 5:24
of............{Heb. 11:5
Elijah,
translation   {2 Kin. 2:11
of............{Matt. 17:1-9
Christians, at
Christ's   {1 Thess. 4:13-18
return........{1 Cor. 15:51, 52

C. *Of Christ:*
Foretold in
the Old   {Ps. 68:18
Testament ...{Eph. 4:8-10
Announced by
Christ........John 20:17
Forty days after
His resur-   {Luke 24:48-51
rection......{Acts 1:1-12
Enters heaven by
redemp-   {Heb. 6:19, 20
tion.........{Heb. 9:12, 24
Crowned with glory and
honor.........Heb. 2:9
Rules from David's
throne ....Acts 2:29-36
Sits at the
Father's   {Eph. 1:20
side ....{Heb. 1:3
Intercedes for the
saints ....Rom. 8:34
Preparing place for His
people ....John 14:2
Highly   {Acts 5:31
exalted.......{Phil. 2:9
Reigns tri-   {1 Cor. 15:24-28
umphantly ...{Heb. 10:12, 13
Exercises priestly
ministry......Heb. 4:14-16
Heb. 8:1, 2

Ascent of Akrabbim—*steep*

Ascent south of the Dead
Sea ....Josh. 15:3

Asceticism—*stern restraint upon bodily
appetites*

A. *Forms of, seen in:*
Nazirite, vow ..Num. 6:1-21
Manoah's
wife..........Judg. 13:3-14

Samson........Judg. 16:16, 17
Elijah's life ....1 Kin. 19:1-9
The
Rechabites ....Jer. 35:1-19
John the   {Matt. 3:4
Baptist.......{Matt. 11:18
Jesus Christ ...Matt. 4:2
Paul ....1 Cor. 9:27

B. *Teaching concerning:*
Extreme,
repudiated ....Luke 7:33-36
False,   {Col. 2:20-23
rejected......{1 Tim. 4:3, 4
Some,   {1 Cor. 9:26, 27
necessary ....{2 Tim. 2:3, 4
Temporary,   {Ezra 8:21-23
helpful.......{1 Cor. 7:3-9
Figurative of complete
consecra-   {Matt. 19:12
tion..........{Rev. 14:1-5

Asenath—*belonging to the goddess
Neith*

Daughter of Poti-Pherah and wife
of Joseph......Gen. 41:45
Mother of Manasseh and
Ephraim........Gen. 41:50-52
Gen. 46:20

Ashamed—*shame instilled by evil doing*

A. *Caused by:*
Mistreat-
ment..........2 Sam. 10:4, 5
Sad tidings ....2 Kin. 8:7-13
Trans-
gression.......Ps. 25:3
Inconsistent
action.........Ezra 8:22
Idolatry......Is. 44:9-17
Rebellion against
God...........Ps. 45:24
Lewdness......Ezek. 16:27
False
prophecy......Zech. 13:3, 4
Rejecting God's
mercy.........Is. 65:13
Unbelief ......Mark 8:38
Unpre-
paredness.....2 Cor. 9:4

B. *Avoidance of, by:*
Waiting for   {Ps. 34:5
the Lord .....{Is. 49:23
Regarding God's
commands ....Ps. 119:6
Sound in
statutes.......Ps. 119:80
Trusting God ..Ps. 25:20

Believing in
Christ........ {Rom. 9:33 / Rom. 10:11
Christian
diligence......2 Tim. 2:15
Assurance of
faith ....2 Tim. 1:12
Abiding in
Christ........1 John 2:28

C. *Possible objects of, in the
Christian's life:*
Life's plans ....Phil. 1:20
God's
message.......2 Tim. 1:8
The Gospel ....Rom. 1:16
The old life ....Rom. 6:20, 21
One's faith.....1 Pet. 4:16

Ashan—*smoke*

A city of Judah ..Josh. 15:42
Later allotted to
Judah ....Josh. 19:7
Assigned to the
Levites ....1 Chr. 6:59

Ashbea—*let me call as witness*

A descendant of
Shelah ....1 Chr. 4:21

Ashbel—*having a long upper lip*

A son of
Benjamin....... {Gen. 46:21 / 1 Chr. 8:1
Progenitor of the
Ashbelites ......Num. 26:38

Ashchenaz

A nation associated with Ararat,
Minni ....Jer. 51:27

Ashdod—*stronghold; fortress*

One of five Philistine
cities ....Josh. 13:3
Anakim refuge....Josh. 11:22
Assigned to
Judah ....Josh. 15:46, 47
Seat of Dagon
worship ....1 Sam. 5:1-8
Captured by
Tartan ....Is. 20:1
Opposed
Nehemiah ....Neh. 4:7
Women of, marry
Jews ....Neh. 13:23, 24
Called Azotus .....Acts 8:40

Asher—*happy*

1. Jacob's second son by
Zilpah ....Gen. 30:12, 13

Goes to Egypt with
Jacob ....Gen. 46:8, 17
Father of five
children.......Gen. 46:17
Blessed by
Jacob ....Gen. 49:20
2. The tribe fathered by Asher,
Jacob's son....Deut. 33:24
Census
of............. {Num. 1:41 / Num. 26:47
Tolerant of
Canaanites....Judg. 1:31, 32
Failure of, in national
crisis..........Judg. 5:17
Among
Gideon's .... {Judg. 6:35 / Judg. 7:23
army..........
A godly remnant
among ....2 Chr. 30:11
Anna, descendant
of..............Luke 2:36-38
3. A town in
Manasseh .....Josh. 17:7

Asherah—*a goddess of the Phoenicians
and Arameans*

1. The female
counterpart { Judg. 3:7
of Baal....... 1 Kin. 18:19
Asa's mother
worships ......1 Kin. 15:13
Image of, erected by Manasseh
in the
temple ....2 Kin. 21:7
Vessels of, destroyed by
Josiah..........2 Kin. 23:4

2. Translated
"wooden { Ex. 34:13
images," idols Deut. 12:3
used in the { Deut. 16:21
worship of { 1 Kin. 16:32, 33
Asherah...... 2 Kin. 23:6, 7

Ashes—*the powdery residue of burned
material*

A. *Used for:*
A miracle......Ex. 9:8-10
Purification....Num. 19:1-10
Heb. 9:13

B. *Symbolic of:*
Mourning......2 Sam. 13:19
Esth. 4:1, 3
Dejection ......Job 2:8
Repentance....Job 42:6
Matt. 11:21
Dan. 9:3

C. *Figurative of:*

Frailty........Gen. 18:27
Destruction....Ezek. 28:18
Victory.........Mal. 4:3
Worthless-
ness..........Job 13:12
Trans-
formation.....Is. 61:3
Deceit.........Is. 44:20
Afflictions.....Ps. 102:9
Destruction....Jer. 6:26

Ashhur—*blackness*

A descendant of ⎧ 1 Chr. 2:24
Judah..........⎨ 1 Chr. 4:5-7

Ashima—*heaven*

A god or idol worshiped by
Assyrian colonists at
Samaria..........2 Kin. 17:30

Ashkelon—*holm-oak*

One of five ⎧ Josh. 13:3
Philistine cities..⎨ Jer. 47:5, 7
Captured by
Judah...........Judg. 1:18
Men of, killed by
Samson........Judg. 14:19, 20
Repossessed by ⎧ 1 Sam. 6:17
Philistines.....⎨ 2 Sam. 1:20
Doom of, ⎧ Jer. 47:5, 7
pronounced ⎪ Amos 1:8
by the ⎨ Zeph. 2:4, 7
prophets........⎩ Zech. 9:5

Ashkenaz

A descendant of
Noah through ⎧ Gen. 10:3
Japheth..........⎨ 1 Chr. 1:6

Ashnah—*hard, firm*

1. A village of Judah near
Zorah.........Josh. 15:33
2. Another village of
Judah.........Josh. 15:43

Ashpenaz

The chief of Nebuchadnezzar's
eunuchs..........Dan. 1:3

Ashtaroth, Astaroth—*plural of*
Ashtoreth

1. A city in Bashan;
residence of ⎧ Deut. 1:4
King Og.....⎨ Josh. 12:4

Captured by
Israel.........Josh. 9:10
Assigned to
Manasseh.....Josh. 13:31
Made a Levitical city
("Be
Eshterah")....Josh. 21:27
Uzzia, a
native of.....1 Chr. 11:44
2. A general designation
of the
Canaanite
female ⎧ 1 Sam. 7:3, 4
deities........⎨ 1 Sam. 31:10

Ashteroth Karnaim—*twin peaks near*
Ashtaroth

A fortified city in Gilead
occupied by the
Rephaims........Gen. 14:5

Ashtoreth—*the name given by Hebrews*
to the goddess Ashtart (Astarte)

A. *A mother goddess of love,*
fertility and war worshiped by:
Philistines.....1 Sam. 31:10
Sidonians.....1 Kin. 11:5, 33
Hebrews (see below)

B. *Israel's relation to:*
Ensnared by...Judg. 2:13
Judg. 10:6
Worship of, by
Solomon.....1 Kin. 11:5, 33
Destroyed by
Josiah........2 Kin. 23:13

See Ashtaroth

Ashurites

A people belonging to Ishbosheth's
kingdom.........2 Sam. 2:8, 9

Ashvath—*made*

An Asherite.......1 Chr. 7:33

Asia—*in New Testament times, the*
Roman province of proconsular Asia

People from, at
Pentecost........Acts 2:9, 10
Paul forbidden to
preach in........Acts 16:6
Paul's later
ministry in.......Acts 19:1-26
Paul plans to
pass by..........Acts 20:16, 17

Paul's great
conflict in . . . . 2 Cor. 1:8
Peter writes to
saints of . . . . 1 Pet. 1:1
Seven
churches of . . . . Rev. 1:4, 11

Asiel—*God has made*

A Simeonite . . . . 1 Chr. 4:35

Asking in prayer

A. *Based upon:*
God's fore-
knowledge . . . . Matt. 6:8
God's
willingness . . . . Luke 11:11-13
God's love . . . . . John 16:23-27
Abiding in
Christ . . . . John 15:7

B. *Receiving of answer, based upon:*
Having faith . . . James 1:5, 6
Keeping God's
commands . . . . 1 John 3:22
Regarding God's
will . . . . 1 John 5:14, 15
Believing
trust . . . . Matt. 21:22
Unselfish-
ness . . . . James 4:2, 3
In Christ's   (John 14:13, 14
name . . . . \John 15:16

Asnah—*thornbush*

The head of a family of
Nethinims . . . . Ezra 2:50

Asnapper, Osnapper—probably the
Aramaean name for *Ashurbanipal*, an
Assyrian king

Called "the great and
noble" . . . . Ezra 4:10

Asp—*a deadly snake*

Figurative of
man's evil   (Ps. 140:3
nature . . . . \Rom. 3:13

Aspatha—*horse-given*

A son of Haman . . Esth. 9:7

Asphalt

In Babel's tower . . Gen. 11:3
In Moses' ark . . . . . Ex. 2:3
Kings fall in . . . . Gen. 14:10

Aspiration—*exalted desire combined
with holy zeal*

A. *Centered in:*
God Himself . . . . Ps. 42:1, 2
God's
kingdom . . . . . Matt. 6:33
The high
calling . . . . . . Phil. 3:8-14
Heaven . . . . Col. 3:1, 2
Acceptableness with
Christ . . . . 2 Tim. 2:4

B. *Inspired by:*
Christ's love . . 2 Cor. 5:14-16
Work yet to   (Rom. 15:18-20
be done . . . . . . \2 Cor. 10:13-18
Christ's
grace . . . . 2 Cor. 12:9-15
The reward . . . . 2 Tim. 4:7, 8
The Lord's   (Matt. 24:42-47
return . . . . \1 John 3:1-3
World's end . . 2 Pet. 3:11-14

Asriel—*God has filled with joy*

A descendant of
Manasseh and   (Num. 26:31
progenitor of the \Josh. 17:2
Asrielites . . . . . . \1 Chr. 7:14

Assassination—*killing by secret and
sudden assault*

A. *Actual cases of:*
Eglon by   (Judg. 3:17, 20,
Ehud . . . . \21
Sisera by
Jael . . . . Judg. 4:17-21
Abner by
Joab . . . . 2 Sam. 3:27
Ishbosheth by sons of
Rimmon . . . . . 2 Sam. 4:5-8
Amnon by   (2 Sam. 13:28,
Absalom . . . . . \29
Absalom by
Joab . . . . 2 Sam. 18:14
Amasa by
Joab . . . . 2 Sam. 20:10
Elah by
Zimri . . . . 1 Kin. 16:8-10
Ben-Hadad by
Hazael . . . . 2 Kin. 8:7, 8, 15
Jehoram by
Jehu . . . . 2 Kin. 9:24
Ahaziah by
Jehu . . . . 2 Kin. 9:27
Jezebel by
Jehu . . . . 2 Kin. 9:30-37
Joash by
servants . . . . . . 2 Kin. 12:20, 21

Zecharikah by
Shallum......2 Kin. 15:8-10
Shallum by
Menahem....2 Kin. 15:14
Pekahiah by
Pekah.........2 Kin. 15:25
Pekah by
Hoshea.......2 Kin. 15:30
Amon by
servants......2 Kin. 21:23
Gedaliah by
Ishmael......2 Kin. 25:25
Sennacherib by his
sons.........2 Kin. 19:36, 37

B. *Attempted cases of:*
Jacob by
Esau.........Gen. 27:41-45
Joseph by his
brothers......Gen. 37:18-22
David by
Saul.........1 Sam. 19:10-18
David by
Absalom......2 Sam. 15:10-14
Joash by
Athaliah.....2 Kin. 11:1-3
Ahasuerus by
servants......Esth. 2:21-23
Jesus by the (Luke 4:14, 28-30
Jews.........(John 7:1
Paul by the (Acts 9:23-25
Jews.........(Acts 23:12-31

C. *Crime of:*
Against God's image in
man.........Gen. 9:6
Punishable by (Ex. 21:12-15
death.........(Num. 35:33
Not to be
condoned.....Deut. 19:11-13
Puts the guilty under a
curse..........Deut. 27:24
Abhorred by the
righteous.....2 Sam. 4:4-12

Assembly—*a large gathering for official business*

A. *Descriptive of:*
Israel as a
people.......Num. 10:2-8
Israel as a (Judg. 20:1, 2
nation.......(2 Chr. 30:23
God's elect
people.......Ps. 111:1
A civil court...Acts 19:32-41
A church
gathering.....James 2:2-4

B. *Purposes of:*
Proclaim (Judg. 10:17, 18
war..........(1 Sam. 14:20
Establish the ark in
Zion.........1 Kin. 8:1-6
Institute (Ezra 9:4-15
reforms.......(Neh. 9:1, 2
Celebrate
victory.......Esth. 9:17, 18
Condemn (Matt. 26:3, 4,
Christ........(57
Worship (Acts 4:31
God..........(Heb. 10:25

C. *Significant ones, at:*
Sinai........Ex. 19:1-19
Joshua's (Josh. 23:1-16
farewell......(Josh. 24:1-28
David's
coronation....2 Sam. 5:1-3
The Temple's
dedication....2 Chr. 5:1-14
Josiah's (2 Kin. 23:1-3,
reforma-
tion..........(21-23
Ezra's reading the
Law.........Neh. 8:1-18
Jesus' trial....Matt. 27:11-26
Pentecost....Acts 2:1-21
The Jerusalem
Council......Acts 15:5-21

Assent—*agreeing to the truth of a statement or fact*

A. *Concerning good things:*
Accepting God's
covenant......Ex. 19:7, 8
Agreeing to (1 Sam. 7:3, 4
reforms......(Ezra 10:1-12, 19
Accepting a scriptural
decision......Acts 15:13-22
Receiving Christ as
Savior.......Rom. 10:9, 10

B. *Concerning evil things:*
Tolerating
idolatry......Jer. 44:15-19
Condemning Christ to
death.........Matt. 27:17-25
Putting Stephen to
death........Acts 7:51-60
Refusing to hear the
Gospel........Acts 13:44-51

Asshur—*level plain*

1. One of the sons of Shem;
progenitor of
the (Gen. 10:22
Assyrians....(1 Chr. 1:17

2. The chief god of the Assyrians;
   seen in names like
   Ashurbanipal
   (Osnapper)....Ezra 4:10
3. A city in Assyria or the nation
   of Assyria.....Num. 24:22, 24

Asshurim—*mighty ones*

Descendants of Abraham by
Keturah..........Gen. 25:3

Assir—*prisoner*

1. A son of   (Ex. 6:24
   Korah   (1 Chr. 6:22
2. A son of
   Ebiasaph......1 Chr. 6:23, 37
3. A son of King
   Jeconiah......1 Chr. 3:17

Assistance, divine

A. *Offered, in:*
   Battle..........2 Chr. 20:5-17
   Trouble........Ps. 50:15
   Crises ....Luke 21:14, 15
   Prayer ....Rom. 8:16-27
   Testimony .....2 Tim. 4:17
   Wisdom ....James 1:5-8

B. *Given:*
   Internally......Phil. 2:13
                  Heb. 13:21
   By God......1 John 4:9, 10
                  2 Cor. 8:9
   By Christ......Phil. 4:13
   By the Spirit...Zech. 4:6
   By God's
   Word ....1 Thess. 2:13
   By grace.......1 Cor. 15:10
   By prayer......James 5:15-18
   By trusting
   God...........Ps. 37:3-7
   By God's
   providence....Rom. 8:28

Association—*joining together for
mutually beneficial purposes*

A. *Among believers, hindered by:*
   Sin ....Acts 5:1-11
   Friction........Acts 6:1-6
   Inconsis-
   tency ....Gal. 2:11-14
   Disagree-
   ment..........Acts 15:36-40
   Selfishness....3 John 9-11
   Ambition .....Matt. 20:20-24
   Error ....2 John 7-11
   Partiality .....James 2:1-5

B. *Among believers, helped by:*
   Common
   faith ....Acts 2:42-47
   Mutual
   helpfulness....Gal. 6:1-5
   United
   prayer ....Matt. 18:19, 20
   Impending
   dangers ......Neh. 4:1-23
   Grateful
   praise ....Acts 4:23-33

See Alliance with evil; Fellowship

Assos—*a seaport of Mysia in Asia
Minor*

Paul walks to, from
Troas.............Acts 20:13, 14

Assurance—*the security of knowing
that one's name is written in heaven*

A. *Objects of, one's:*
   Election ....1 Thess. 1:4
   Adoption .....Eph. 1:4, 5
   Union with
   Christ.........1 Cor. 6:15
   Possession of (John 5:24
   eternal life ...(1 John 5:13
   Peace..........Rom. 5:1

B. *Steps in:*
   Believing God's
   Word ....1 Thess. 2:13
   Accepting Christ as
   Savior ....Rom. 10:9, 10
   Standing upon the
   promises .....John 10:28-30
   Desiring spiritual
   things.........1 Pet. 2:2
   Growing in
   grace ....2 Pet. 1:5-11
   Knowing life   (2 Cor. 5:17
   is changed ...(1 John 3:14-22
   Having inner
   peace and   (Rom. 15:12, 13
   joy...........(Phil. 4:7
   Victorious
   living ....1 John 5:4, 5
   The Spirit's
   testimony .....Rom. 8:15, 16
   Absolute   (Rom. 8:33-39
   assurance ....(2 Tim. 1:12

C. *Compatible with:*
   A nature still
   subject to   (1 John 1:8-10
   sin............(1 John 2:1

Imperfection of life............Gal. 6:1
Limited knowledge....1 Cor. 13:9-12
Fatherly chastisement..........Heb. 12:5-11

Assyria—*the nation ruled from Asshur (first) and Nineveh (later)*

A. *Significant facts regarding:*
Of remote antiquity......Gen. 2:14
Of Shem's ancestry ......Gen. 10:22
Founded by (Gen. 10:8-12
Nimrod ......(Mic. 5:6
Nineveh, chief city of............Gen. 10:11
Hiddekel (Tigris) River flows through......Gen. 2:14
Proud nation ..Is. 10:5-15
A cruel military power........Nah. 3:1-19
Agent of God's (Is. 7:17-20
purposes .....(Is. 10:5, 6

B. *Contacts of, with Israel:*
Pul (Tiglath-Pileser III, 745-727 B.C.) captures Damascus.....Is. 8:4
Puts Menahem under tribute ....2 Kin. 15:19, 20
Occasions Isaiah's prophesy......Is. 7-8
Puts Pekah under tribute ....2 Kin. 15:29
Shalmaneser (727-722 B.C.) besieges Samaria.......2 Kin. 17:3-5
Sargon II (722-705 B.C.) captures Israel ....2 Kin. 17:6-41

C. *Contacts of, with Judah:*
Sargon's general takes Ashdod (in Philistia)..Is. 20:1-6
Sennacherib (704-681 B.C.) invades Judah........2 Kin. 18:13
Puts Hezekiah under tribute ....2 Kin. 18:14-16
Threatens Hezekiah through Rabshakeh....2 Kin. 18:17-37
Army of, miraculously slain ....2 Kin. 19:35
Assassination of, by his sons ....2 Kin. 19:37

D. *Prophecies concerning:*
Destruction of, anciently foretold ......Num. 24:22-24
Israel captive (Hos. 10:6
in land of ....(Hos. 11:5
Doom of,   (Is. 10:12, 19
mentioned ...(Is. 14:24, 25
End eulogized .....Nah. 3:1-19
Shares, figuratively, in Gospel blessings ......Is. 19:23-25

Astonishment—*an emotion of perplexed amazement*

A. *Caused by:*
God's   (1 Kin. 9:8, 9
judgments ...(Jer. 18:16
Racial intermarriage ......Ezra 9:2-4
Urgent message......Ezek. 3:14, 15
A miracle......Dan. 3:24
An unexplained vision......Dan. 8:27
Christ's knowledge ....Luke 2:47
Christ's teaching ......Luke 4:32
Christ's   (Mark 5:42
miracles......(Luke 5:9
Gentile conversions ...Acts 10:45
Miracles ......Acts 12:5-7, 13-16
           Acts 13:6-12

B. *Applied figuratively to:*
God ....Jer. 14:9
Babylon ......Jer. 51:37, 41
Jerusalem......Ezek. 5:5, 15
Priests.......Jer. 4:9

Astrologers—*those who search the heavens for supposed revelations*

Cannot save Babylon ....Is. 47:1, 12-15
Cannot interpret (Dan. 2:2, 10-13
dreams ....(Dan. 4:7
Cannot decipher handwriting ......Dan. 5:7, 8
Daniel surpasses ..Dan. 1:20
Daniel made master of........Dan. 5:11
God does not speak through ....Dan. 2:27, 28

Asylum—*protection, refuge*

Afforded by   (1 Kin. 1:50-53
altar............(1 Kin. 2:28

Cities of refuge....Ex. 21:12-14
                    Deut. 19:1-13

Asyncritus—*incomparable*

A Christian at
Rome ....Rom. 16:14

Atad—*thorn*

A mourning site east of
Jordan ....Gen. 50:9-13

Atarah—*crown*

A wife of
Jerahmeel........1 Chr. 2:26

Ataroth—*crowns*

1. Town of Gad ..Num. 32:3, 34
2. A town of
   Ephraim ......Josh. 16:7
3. A town between Ephraim and
   Benjamin .....Josh. 16:2
   Probably the same as
   Ataroth   (Josh. 16:5
   Addar.........(Josh. 18:13
4. A village near Beth-
   lehem.........1 Chr. 2:54

Ataroth Addar—*crowns of Addar*

A frontier town of
Ephraim..........Josh. 16:5

See Ataroth 3

Ater—*crippled one*

1. The ancestor of
   a family of   (Ezra 2:16
   returnees.....(Neh. 7:21
2. The ancestor of
   a family of   (Ezra 2:42
   porters.......(Neh. 7:45
3. A signer of Nehemiah's
   document.....Neh. 10:17

Athach—*lodging, inn*

A town in south
Judah ....1 Sam. 30:30

Athaiah—*Yahweh is helper*

A Judahite in Nehemiah's
time.............Neh. 11:4

Athaliah—*Yahweh is exalted*

1. The daughter
   of Ahab and   (2 Kin. 8:18, 26
   Jezebel.......(2 Chr. 22:2, 3

Destroys all the royal
seed except   (2 Kin. 11:1, 2
Joash ....(2 Chr. 22:10, 11
Usurps throne for six
years..........2 Kin. 11:3
Killed by
priestly   (2 Kin. 11:4-16
uprising.......(2 Chr. 23:1-21
Called
wicked.........2 Chr. 24:7
2. A Benjamite ...1 Chr. 8:26, 27
3. The father of
   Jeshaiah ......Ezra 8:7

Atharim—*spys*

Israel attacked
there.............Num. 21:1

Atheism—*the denial of God's existence*

A. *Defined as:*
   The fool's   (Ps. 14:1
   philosophy ...(Ps. 53:1
   Living
   without   (Rom. 1:20-32
   God..........(Eph. 2:12

B. *Manifestations of, seen in:*
   Defiance of   (Ex. 5:2
   God..........(2 Kin. 18:19-35
   Irreligion ......Titus 1:16
   Corrupt   (Rom. 13:12, 13
   morals ....(1 Pet. 4:3

C. *Evidences against, seen in:*
   Man's inner
   conscience ....Rom. 2:14, 15
   Design in   (Job 38:1-41
   nature ....(Job 39:1-30
   God's works ...Ps. 19:1-6
   God's   (Ps. 104:1-35
   providence ...(Acts 14:17
   Clear
   evidence ......Rom. 1:19, 20
   The testimony of
   pagans ....Dan. 4:24-37
   Fulfillment of (Is. 41:20-23
   prophecy.....(Is. 46:8-11

Athens—*a Greek city named after the goddess Athena*

Paul preaches in ..Acts 17:15-34
Paul resides in ....1 Thess. 3:1

Athlai—*Yahweh is strong*

A Jew who divorced his foreign
wife.............Ezra 10:28

Athletes

Discipline	1 Cor. 9:24-27
Removal of weights	Heb. 12:1
Prize	Phil. 3:14

Atonement—*reconciliation of the guilty by divine sacrifice*

A. *Elements involved in, seen in:*

Man's sin	Ex. 32:30
	Ps. 51:3, 4
The blood sacrificed	Lev. 16:11, 14-20
	Heb. 9:13-22
Guilt transferred	Lev. 1:3, 4
	2 Cor. 5:21
Guilt removed	Lev. 16:21
	1 Cor. 6:11
Forgiveness granted	Lev. 5:10, 11
	Rom. 4:6, 7
Righteousness given	Rom. 10:3, 4
	Phil. 3:9

B. *Fulfilled by Christ:*

Predicted	Is. 53:10-12
	Dan. 9:24-26
Symbolized	Is. 63:1-9
	Zech. 3:3-9
Realized	Rom. 3:23-26
	1 Pet. 1:18-21

Atonement, Day of

A. *Features regarding:*

Time specified	Lev. 23:26, 27
The ritual involved in	Lev. 16:3, 5-15
A time of humiliation	Lev. 16:29, 31
Exclusive ministry of the high priest in	Lev. 16:2, 3
	Heb. 9:7

B. *Benefits of, for:*

The holy place	Lev. 16:15, 16
The people	Lev. 16:17, 24
The high priest	Lev. 16:11
	Heb. 9:7

C. *Result of, seen in:*

Atonement for sin	Rom. 3:24-26
Removal of sin	Heb. 9:7-28
	Heb. 13:10-13

Atonement of Christ

A. *Typified by:*

The paschal lamb	Ex. 12:5, 11, 14
	John 1:29
	1 Cor. 5:7
The Day of Atonement	Lev. 16:30, 34
	Heb. 9:7-28

B. *What man is:*

A sinner	Rom. 5:8
Alienated in mind	Col. 1:21
Strangers	Eph. 2:12

C. *What God does:*

Loves us	John 3:16
Demonstrates His love toward us	Rom. 5:8
Sends Christ to save us	Gal. 4:4, 5
Spared not His own Son	Rom. 8:32

D. *What Christ does:*

Becomes a man	Heb. 2:14
Becomes our ransom	Matt. 20:28
Dies in our place	1 Pet. 3:18
Dies for our sins	1 Pet. 2:24
Dies as a sacrifice	Eph. 5:2
Dies willingly	John 10:18
Reconciles us to God	Rom. 5:10
Brings us to God	1 Pet. 3:18
Restores our fellowship	1 Thess. 5:10

See Blood of Christ

E. *What the believer receives:*

Forgiveness	Eph. 1:7
Peace	Rom. 5:1
Reconciliation	2 Cor. 5:19
Righteousness	2 Cor. 5:21
Justification	Rom. 3:24-26
Access to God	Eph. 2:18
Cleansing	1 John 1:7
Liberty	Gal. 5:1
Freedom from the devil's power	Heb. 2:14
Christ's intercession	Heb. 2:17, 18

Atroth Beth Joab

A village near
Bethlehem ....1 Chr. 2:54

Atroth Shophan

A city built by the
Gadites ....Num. 32:34, 35

Attai—*timely*

1. A half-Egyptian
Judahite ......1 Chr. 2:35, 36
2. A Gadite in David's
army..........1 Chr. 12:11
3. Rehoboam's
son ....2 Chr. 11:18-20

Attalia—*a seaport town of Pamphylia
named after Attalus II*

Paul sails from, to
Antioch ....Acts 14:25, 26

Attend

To care for ....Esth. 4:5

Attendance, church

Taught by   ⎰Acts 11:25, 26
example........ ⎱Acts 14:19, 20,
                    26, 27
Not to be
neglected.........Heb. 10:25

Attitude—*the state of mind toward
something*

A. *Of Christians toward Christ,
must:*
Confess........Rom. 10:9, 10
Obey ....John 14:15, 23
Follow.........Matt. 16:24
Imitate ....1 Pet. 2:21

B. *Of Christians toward the world,
not to:*
Conform to....Rom. 12:2
Abuse ....1 Cor. 7:29-31
Love...........1 John 2:15
Be friend of...James 4:4
Be entangled
with ....2 Tim. 2:4
Be defiled
with ....Jude 23

C. *Of Christians toward sinners:*
Seek their
salvation......1 Cor. 9:22
Pray for ....Rom. 9:1-3
Plead with ....Acts 17:22-31
Rebuke........Titus 1:10-13
Persuade ......2 Cor. 5:11

Audience—*an assembly of hearers*

Disturbed ....Neh. 13:1-3
Attentive ....Luke 7:1
Hostile...........Luke 4:28-30
Receptive ....Acts 2:1-41
Menacing ....Acts 7:54-60
Rejecting ....Acts 13:44-51
Critical..........Acts 17:22-34
Sympathetic .....Acts 20:17-38
Vast ....Rev. 5:9
                  Rev. 7:9, 10

See Assembly

Auditorium—*a room for assembly*

Hearing ....Acts 25:23

Augustus' regiment—*a battalion of
Roman soldiers*

Paul placed in
custody of.....Acts 27:1

Author—*creator; originator; writer*

God of peace......1 Cor. 14:33
Christ of
salvation ....Heb. 5:9
Christ of faith.....Heb. 12:2
Solomon of many proverbs and
songs.............1 Kin. 4:32

Authority—*the lawful right to enforce
obedience, power*

A. *As rulers:*
Governor ......Acts 23:24, 26
                  Matt. 10:18

B. *Delegated to, man as:*
Created........Gen. 1:26-31
A legal state ...Esth. 9:29
                  Luke 22:25
Agent of the   ⎰Matt. 8:9
state .... ⎱Rom. 13:1-6
Husband.......1 Cor. 14:35
Agent of religious
leaders........Acts 26:10, 12

C. *Christ's, seen in His power:*
Over demons ..Mark 1:27
In teaching ....Matt. 7:29
To forgive .....Luke 5:24
To judge.......John 5:22, 27
To rule ....Matt. 2:6
                  1 Cor. 15:24
                  1 Pet. 3:22
To commis-
sion..........Matt. 28:18-20

D. *Purpose:*
Protection .....Heb. 13:17
Instruction ....1 Pet. 5:2, 3

Example of Christ's
power........Matt. 8:5-13
Testimony to {1 Pet. 3:13-15
unbelievers...{1 Tim. 6:1

E. *Of Christians, given to:*
Apostles.......2 Cor. 10:8
Ministers......Titus 2:15
The
righteous.....Prov. 29:2

Ava—*a region or city in Assyria*

Colonists from, brought to Samaria
by Sargon........2 Kin. 17:24
Worshipers of Nibhaz and
Tartak...........2 Kin. 17:31

Avarice—*covetousness; greed*

A. *Productive of:*
Defeat.........Josh. 7:11, 21
Death.........1 Kin. 21:5-16
Discontent.....James 4:1-4

B. *Examples of:*
Balaam........2 Pet. 2:15
Achan.........Josh. 7:20, 21
Ahab..........1 Kin. 21:1-4
Judas
Iscariot......Matt. 26:14-16
Ananias and
Sapphira.....Acts 5:1-10
Rich men.....Luke 12:16-21
James 5:1-6

Aven—*wickedness*

1. The city of On in
Egypt near
Cairo;
known as {Gen. 41:45
Heliopolis.{Ezek. 30:17
2. A name contemptuously applied
to Bethel......Hos. 10:5, 8
3. Valley in
Syria..........Amos 1:5

Avenge—*to retaliate for an evil done*

A. *Kinds of:*
Commanded by
God...........Num. 31:1, 2
Given strength
for............Judg. 16:28-30
Sought
maliciously...1 Sam. 18:25
Possible but not
done..........1 Sam. 24:12
Attempted but
hindered......1 Sam. 25:26-33
Obtained in
self-defense...Esth. 8:12, 13

B. *Sought because of:*
A murdered {Num. 35:12
neighbor {Josh. 20:5
A wife's mistreat-
ment..........Judg. 15:6-8
Judah's sins....Jer. 5:9
Mistreat-
ment..........Acts 7:24, 25
Impurity......1 Thess. 4:5-7

C. *Performed by:*
God Himself...Lev. 26:25
Luke 18:7, 8
Wicked men...2 Sam. 4:8-12
Impetuous {2 Sam. 18:18, 19,
general.......{ 31
An anointed
king..........2 Kin. 9:6, 7
A judge.......Luke 18:3, 5
God...........Rev. 19:2

D. *Restrictions on:*
Personal,
prohibited.....Lev. 19:17, 18
Christians
prohibited.....Rom. 12:19

Avenger of blood (literally, "*redeemer
of blood*")

An ancient
practice..........Gen. 4:14
Seen in kinsman
as "redeemer" of {Lev. 25:25,
enslaved {47-49
relative..........{Ruth 4:1-10
Seen also in kinsman as "avenger"
of a murdered
relative..........Num. 35:11-34
Avenger alone must kill
murderer........Deut. 19:6,
11-13
Practice of, set aside by
David.............2 Sam. 14:4-11
Same word translated
"kinsman" and {Ruth 4:1
"redeemer".....{Job 19:25
Figurative of a violent
person............Ps. 8:2

Avim, Avims, Avites—*villagers*

1. A tribe of early Canaanites
living near Gaza; absorbed by
the Caphtorim
(Philistines)...Deut. 2:23
2. A city of Benjamin near
Bethel.........Josh. 18:23
3. Colonists brought from Ava in
Assyria.......2 Kin. 17:24, 31

Avith—*ruin*

An Edomite city...Gen. 36:35

Awakening, spiritual

A. *Produced by:*
Returning to
Bethel........Gen. 35:1-7
Discovering God's
Word ....2 Kin. 22:8-13
Reading God's
Word ....Neh. 8:2-18
Confessing
sin ....Ezra 10:1-17
Receiving the (John 7:38, 39
Spirit ....(Acts 2:1-47

B. *Old Testament examples of,
under:*
Joshua........Josh. 24:1-31
Samuel ....1 Sam. 7:3-6
Elijah..........1 Kin. 18:21-40
Hezekiah ......2 Chr. 30:1-27
                2 Chr. 31:1
Josiah ....2 Kin. 23:1-25
Ezra ....Ezra 10:1-17

C. *New Testament examples of:*
John the
Baptist........Luke 3:2-14
Jesus in
Samaria......John 4:28-42
Philip in
Samaria......Acts 8:5-12
Peter at
Lydda.........Acts 9:32-35
Peter with
Cornelius .....Acts 10:34-48
Paul at Antioch in
Pisidia ....Acts 13:14-52
Paul at
Thes-   (Acts 17:11, 12
salonica......(1 Thess. 1:1-10
Paul at
Corinth ....2 Cor. 7:1-16

Awe—*fear mingled with reverence*

Proper attitude toward
God ....Ps. 33:8
Also toward God's
Word ....Ps. 119:161

Awl—*a sharp tool for piercing*

Used on the ear as a symbol of
perpetual   (Ex. 21:6
obedience ......(Deut. 15:17

Ax—*a sharp instrument for cutting
wood*

A. *Used in:*
Cutting
timber ....Judg. 9:48
War ....1 Chr. 20:3
Malicious
destruction...Ps. 74:5-7
A miracle; floated in
water ....2 Kin. 6:5, 6

B. *As a figure of:*
Judgment......Matt. 3:10
God's
sovereignty ...Is. 10:15

Ayyah

Ephraimite town ..1 Chr. 7:28

Azal, Azel

1. A descendant of
Jonathan......1 Chr. 8:37, 38
2. A place near
Jerusalem.....Zech. 14:5

Azaliah—*Yahweh has set aside*

Father of
Shaphan ....2 Kin. 22:3

Azaniah—*Yahweh has heard*

A Levite who signs the
document ....Neh. 10:9

Azarel, Azareel—*God has helped*

1. A Levite in David's army at
Ziklag ....1 Chr. 12:6
2. A musician in David's
time ....1 Chr. 25:18
3. A prince of Dan under
David ....1 Chr. 27:22
4. A Jew who divorced his
foreign wife...Ezra 10:41
5. A postexilic
priest ....Neh. 11:13
6. A musician in dedication
service........Neh. 12:36

Azariah—*Yahweh has helped*

1. Man of
Judah.........1 Chr. 2:8
2. A Kohathite
Levite.........1 Chr. 6:36
3. A son of Zadok the high
priest ....1 Kin. 4:2
4. A son of
Ahimaaz......1 Chr. 6:9
5. A great-grandson of
Ahimaaz......1 Chr. 6:9-10

6. Son of
   Nathan ...... 1 Kin. 4:5
7. A son of Jehu, with Egyptian
   ancestry ... 1 Chr. 2:34-38
8. A prophet who encourages
   King Asa ...... 2 Chr. 15:1-8
9. Son of King Jehosh-
   aphat .... 2 Chr. 21:2
10. A captain under
    Jehoiada ...... 2 Chr. 23:1
11. Another under
    Jehoiada ...... 2 Chr. 23:1
12. A head of
    Ephraim ...... 2 Chr. 28:12
13. King of
    Judah .... 2 Kin. 15:1
14. A high priest who rebukes King
    Uzziah .... 2 Chr. 26:16-20
15. Kohathite, father of
    Joel .... 2 Chr. 29:12
16. A reforming
    Levite .... 2 Chr. 29:12
17. Chief priest in time of
    Hezekiah ...... 2 Chr. 31:9, 10
18. A high priest, son of
    Hilkiah .... 1 Chr. 6:13, 14
19. Ancestor of
    Ezra .... Ezra 7:1-3
20. An opponent of
    Jeremiah ...... Jer. 43:2
21. The Hebrew name of Abed-
    Nego .... Dan. 1:7
22. Postexilic
    Jew .... Neh. 7:6, 7
23. A workman under
    Nehemiah ..... Neh. 3:23, 24
24. A prince of
    Judah .... Neh. 12:32, 33
25. An expounder of the
    law .... Neh. 8:7
26. A signer of the
    covenant ...... Neh. 10:1, 2
27. A descendant of
    Hilkiah .... 1 Chr. 9:11

Azaz—*strong*

A Reubenite ... 1 Chr. 5:8

Azaziah—*Yahweh is strong*

1. A musician .... 1 Chr. 15:21
2. Father of
   Hoshea .... 1 Chr. 27:20
3. A temple
   overseer ...... 2 Chr. 31:13

Azbuk—*pardon*

Father of a certain Nehemiah; but
not the celebrated
one .... Neh. 3:16

Azekah—*tilled*

Great stones
cast upon .... Josh. 10:11
Camp of Goliath .. 1 Sam. 17:1, 4,
                                        17
Fortified by
Rehoboam .... 2 Chr. 11:5, 9
Reoccupied after
exile .... Neh. 11:30
Besieged by Nebuchad-
nezzar .... Jer. 34:7

Azem, Ezem—*bone*

A town of Judah .. Josh. 15:29
Allotted to
Simeon .... Josh. 19:3
Also called
Ezem .... 1 Chr. 4:29

Azgad—*fate is hard*

Head of exile   ⎰ Ezra 2:12
family ....⎱ Ezra 8:12
Among document
signers .... Neh. 10:15

Aziel—*God strengthens*

A Levite
musician .... 1 Chr. 15:20
Called Jaaziel ..... 1 Chr. 15:18

Aziza—*strong*

Divorced foreign
wife .... Ezra 10:27

Azmaveth—*death is strong*

1. One of David's mighty
   men .... 2 Sam. 23:31
2. A Benjamite ... 1 Chr. 12:3
3. David's
   treasurer ...... 1 Chr. 27:25
4. A son of
   Jehoaddah .... 1 Chr. 8:36
5. A village near
   Jerusalem ..... Neh. 12:29
   Also called Beth
   Azmaveth ..... Neh. 7:28

Azmon—*strong*

A place in south
Canaan .... Num. 34:4, 5

Aznoth Tabor—*peaks of Tabor*

Place in
Naphtali .... Josh. 19:34

Azor—*helper*

Ancestor of
Christ ....Matt. 1:13, 14

Azotus—*fortress*

Philip went
there............Acts 8:40
Same as Ashdod ..1 Sam. 6:17

Azriel—*God is a help*

1. A chief of
   Manasseh .....1 Chr. 5:24
2. Father of
   Jerimoth ......1 Chr. 27:19
3. Father of
   Seraiah ....Jer. 36:26

Azrikam—*my help has arisen*

1. Son of
   Neariah ......1 Chr. 3:23
2. A son of
   Azel ....1 Chr. 8:38
3. A Merarite
   Levite.........1 Chr. 9:14
4. Official under King
   Ahaz.........2 Chr. 28:7

Azubah—*forsaken*

1. Wife of
   Caleb ....1 Chr. 2:18, 19
2. Mother of Jehosh-
   aphat ....1 Kin. 22:42

Azur, Azzur—*helpful*

1. Father of
   Hananiah .....Jer. 28:1
2. Father of
   Jaazaniah.....Ezek. 11:1
3. A covenant
   signer........Neh. 10:17

Azzan—*strong*

Father of Paltiel...Num. 34:26

B

Baal—*lord, possessor, husband*

A. *The nature of:*
   The male god of the
   Phoenicians and Canaanites;
   the counterpart of the female
   Ashtaroth.....2 Kin. 23:5
   Connected
   with   ⎧Num. 25:1, 3, 5
   immorality ...⎩Hos. 9:10

Incense
burned to .....Jer. 7:9
Kissing the   ⎧1 Kin. 19:18
image of .....⎩Hos. 13:1, 2
Dervish rites by
priests of.....1 Kin. 18:26, 28
Children burned in
fire of ....Jer. 19:5
Eating
sacrifices......Ps. 106:28

B. *History of:*
   Among Moabites in Moses'
   time ....Num. 22:41
   Altars built to, during
   time of   ⎧Judg. 2:11-14
   judges ....⎩Judg. 6:28-32
   Jezebel introduces into
   Israel ....1 Kin. 16:31, 32
   Elijah's overthrow of, on Mt.
   Carmel.......1 Kin. 18:17-40
   Athaliah
   encourages it ⎧2 Kin. 11:14-20
   into Judah ...⎩2 Chr. 22:2-4
   Revived again in
   Israel and   ⎧Hos. 2:8
   Judah ....⎩Amos 5:26
   Manasseh
   worships ......2 Kin. 21:3
   Altars
   everywhere ...Jer. 11:13
   Overthrown by
   Josiah.........2 Kin. 23:4, 5
   Denounced by ⎧Jer. 19:4-6
   prophets .....⎧Ezek. 16:1, 2,
                   20, 21
   Historic
   retrospect.....Rom. 11:4

Baal—*master; possessor*

1. A Benjamite, from
   Gibeon........1 Chr. 8:30
2. A descendant of
   Reuben ....1 Chr. 5:5, 6
3. A village of
   Simeon ....1 Chr. 4:33
   Also called Baalath
   Beer ....Josh. 19:8

Baalah—*mistress*

1. A town also known as Kirjath
   Jearim ....Josh. 15:9, 10
2. A hill in
   Judah.........Josh. 15:11
3. A town in South
   Judah.........Josh. 15:29
   Probably the same as
   Bilhah ....1 Chr. 4:29

May be the same as
Balah ....Josh. 19:3

Baalath—*mistress*

A village of Dan ..Josh. 19:44
Fortified by
Solomon ....1 Kin. 9:18

Baalath Beer—*mistress of the well*

A border town of
Simeon............Josh. 19:8
Called Ramah of the
south............Josh. 19:8
Also called Baal ..1 Chr. 4:33

Baal-Berith—*lord of covenant*

A god (Baal) of ⎰Judg. 8:33
Shechem ....⎱Judg. 9:4
Also called
Berith ....Judg. 9:46

Baale—*Judah*

A town of Judah ..2 Sam. 6:2
Also called Baalah and
Kirjath Jearim....Josh. 15:9, 10

Baal Gad—*lord of good fortune*

A place in the valley of
Lebanon..........Josh. 11:17

Baal Hamon—*lord of a multitude*

Site of Solomon's
vineyard..........Song 8:11

Baal-Hanan—*lord of grace*

1. Edomite king ..Gen. 36:38
2. David's
   gardener ......1 Chr. 27:28

Baal Hazor—*lord of a village*

A place near
Ephraim..........2 Sam. 13:23

Baal Hermon—*lord of Hermon*

A mountain east of
Jordan ....Judg. 3:3

Baals—*lords* (plural of Baal)

Deities of Canaanite
polytheism ......Judg. 10:10-14
Ensnared ⎰Judg. 2:11-14
Israelites ....⎱Judg. 3:7
Rejected in Samuel's
time..............1 Sam. 7:4

Historic
reminder ....1 Sam. 12:10
Ahaz makes images
to ....2 Chr. 28:1-4

Baalis

An Ammonite
king............Jer. 40:14

Baal Meon—*lord of Menon* (habitation)

An Amorite city on the Moabite
boundary........Ezek. 25:9
Rebuilt by ⎰Num. 32:38
Reubenites ......⎱Josh. 13:15, 17

Baal Peor, Baal of Peor—*lord of Peor*

A Moabite god ....Num. 25:1-5
Infected Israel; 24,000
died..............Num. 25:1-9
Vengeance
taken on ....Num. 31:1-18
Sin ⎧Deut. 4:3, 4
long ⎨Josh. 22:17
remembered......⎩Ps. 106:28, 29
Historic
reminder ....1 Cor. 10:1-8

Baal Perazim—*lord of breaking through*

Where David defeated the
Philistines........2 Sam. 5:18-20
Same as
Perazim ....Is. 28:21

Baal Shalisha—*lord of Shalisha*

A place from which Elisha received
food..............2 Kin. 4:42-44

Baal Tamar—*lord of the palm*

A place in
Benjamin........Judg. 20:33

Baal-Zebub—*lord of flies*

A Philistine god at
Ekron ....2 Kin. 1:2
Ahaziah
inquired of ......2 Kin. 1:2, 6, 16
Also called ⎰Matt. 10:25
Beelzebub ......⎱Matt. 12:24

Baal Zephon—*lord of darkness*

Israelite camp ⎰Ex. 14:2, 9
site..............⎱Num. 33:7

Baana—*affliction*

1. Supply
   officer........1 Kin. 4:12
2. Zadok's
   father........Neh. 3:4

Baanah—*affliction*

1. A murderer of Ish-
   bosheth ...... 2 Sam. 4:1-12
2. Heled's
   father .... 1 Chr. 11:30
3. A returning   (Ezra 2:2
   exile .... \Neh. 7:7
   Signs
   document ..... Neh. 10:27
4. Supply
   officer .... 1 Kin. 4:16

Baara—*foolish*

Shaharaim's
wife .... 1 Chr. 8:8

Baaseiah—*work of Yahweh*

A Levite ancestor of
Asaph .... 1 Chr. 6:40

Baasha—*boldness*

Gains throne by
murder .... 1 Kin. 15:27, 28
Kills Jeroboam's
household .... 1 Kin. 15:29, 30
Wars against
Asa .... 1 Kin. 15:16, 32
Restricts access to
Judah .... 1 Kin. 15:17
Contravened by Asa's league with
Ben-Hadad .... 1 Kin. 15:18-22
Evil reign .... 1 Kin. 15:33, 34

Babbler—*an inane talker*

The mumblings of
drunkards .... Prov. 23:29-35
Like a serpent ..... Eccl. 10:11
Paul called such ... Acts 17:18
Paul's warnings   (1 Tim. 6:20
against .... \2 Tim. 2:16

Babe, Baby—*an infant child*

A. *Natural:*
   Moses .... Ex. 2:6
   John Baptist ... Luke 1:41, 44
   Christ .... Luke 2:12, 16
   Offspring ...... Ps. 17:14
B. *Figurative of:*
   Unenlight-
   ened .... Rom. 2:20
   True   (Matt. 11:25
   believers ..... \Matt. 21:16
   New
   Christians .... 1 Pet. 2:2
   Carnal   (1 Cor. 3:1
   Christians .... \Heb. 5:13

Babel—*confusion*

A city built by Nimrod in the plain
of Shinar .... Gen. 10:8-10

Babel, Tower of

A huge brick structure intended to
magnify man and preserve the
unity of the
race .... Gen. 11:1-4
Objectives thwarted by
God .... Gen. 11:5-9

Babylon, city of

A. *History of:*
   Built by
   Nimrod .... Gen. 10:8-10
   Tower built
   there .... Gen. 11:1-9
   Amraphel's
   capital .... Gen. 14:1
   Occupied by Assyrians in
   Manasseh's
   time .... 2 Chr. 33:11
   Greatest power under
   Nebuchad-
   nezzar .... Dan. 4:30
   A magnificent (Is. 13:19
   city .... \Is. 14:4
   Wide
   walls of ...... Jer. 51:44
   Gates of ...... Is. 45:1, 2
   Bel, god of .... Is. 46:1
   Jews carried   (2 Kin. 25:1-21
   captive to .... \2 Chr. 36:5-21
B. *Inhabitants, described as:*
   Enslaved by
   magic .... Is. 47:1, 9-13
   Idolatrous ..... Jer. 50:35, 38
                   Dan. 3:18
   Sacrilegious ... Dan. 5:1-3
C. *Prophecies concerning:*
   Babylon,   (Jer. 25:9
   God's agent .. \Jer. 27:5-8
   God fights
   with .... Jer. 21:1-7
   Jews, 70 years (Jer. 25:12
   in .... \Jer. 29:10
   First of great (Dan. 2:31-38
   empires .... \Dan. 7:2-4
   Cyrus, God's
   agent .... Is. 45:1-4
   Perpetual
   desolation   (Is. 13:19-22
   of .... \Jer. 50:13, 39

Downfall of....Is. 13:1-22
Jer. 50:1-46

Babylon in the New Testament

A. *The city on the Euphrates*
Listed as a point of
reference......Matt. 1:11, 12,
17
As the place of Israel's
exile ....Acts 7:43
As the place of Peter's
residence......1 Pet. 5:13

B. *The prophetic city*
Fall
predicted......Rev. 14:8
Wrath taken
on ....Rev. 16:19
Called "the Mother of
Harlots"......Rev. 17:1-18
Fall
described......Rev. 18:1-24

Babylonians—*sons of Babel*

Inhabitants of
Babylonia ....Ezek. 23:15-23

Babylonian garment—*a valuable robe
worn in Babylon*

Coveted by
Achan...........Josh. 7:21

Baca—*weeping*

Figurative of
sorrow ....Ps. 84:6

Bachelor—*unmarried man*

Described
literally...........1 Cor. 7:26-33
Described   (Is. 56:3-5
figura-   {Matt. 19:12
tively...........(Rev. 14:1-5
Not for elders .....Titus 1:5, 6

Bachrites

Family of
Becher ....Num. 26:35

Backbiting—*reviling another in secret;
slander*

A fruit of sin.....Rom. 1:28-30
Expressed by the
mouth...........Ps. 50:20
An offspring of
anger............Prov. 25:23
Merits
punishment .....Ps. 101:5
Keeps from God..Ps. 15:1, 3

To be laid aside ...1 Pet. 2:1
Unworthy of
Christians ....2 Cor. 12:20

Backsliding—*to turn away from God
after conversion*

A. *Described as:*
Turning from
God...........1 Kin. 11:9
Turning to
evil ....Ps. 125:5
Turning to
Satan ....1 Tim. 5:15
Turning back to the
world ....2 Tim. 4:10
Tempting
Christ.........1 Cor. 10:9
Turning from first
love...........Rev. 2:4
Turning from   (Gal. 1:6, 7
the Gospel ...(Gal. 3:1-5

B. *Prompted by:*
Haughty
spirit...........Prov. 16:18
Spiritual   (2 Pet. 1:9
blindness.....(Rev. 3:17
Murmuring .....Ex. 17:3
Lusting after
evil ....Ps. 106:14
Material   (Mark 4:18, 19
things........(1 Tim. 6:10
Prosperity .....Deut. 8:11-14
Tribulation ....Matt. 13:20, 21

C. *Results:*
Displeases
God...........Ps. 78:56-59
Punishment....Num. 14:43-45
Jer. 8:5-13
Blessings
withheld ....Is. 59:2
Unworthi-
ness..........Luke 9:62

D. *Examples of Israel's:*
At Meribah ....Ex. 17:1-7
At Sinai ....Ex. 32:1-35
In wilderness ..Ps. 106:14-33
After Joshua's   (Judg. 2:8-23
death ....(Ps. 106:34-43
In Solomon's (1 Kin. 11:4-40
life...........(Neh. 13:26
During Asa's
reign..........2 Chr. 15:1-4
During Manasseh's
reign..........2 Chr. 33:1-10

E. *Examples of, among believers:*
Lot ....Gen. 19:1-22

David.........2 Sam. 11:1-5
Ps. 51:1-19
Peter ....Matt. 26:69-75
Luke 22:31, 32
Galatians .....Gal. 1:6
Gal. 4:9-11
Corinthians....1 Cor. 5:1-13
Churches of { 2 Tim. 1:15
Asia.........{ Rev. 2; 3

See Apostasy

Badger

1. *Probably a specie of dolphin or porpoise*
Skins of, used
in tabernacle { Ex. 26:14
coverings ....{ Ex. 35:7
Used for
sandals........Ezek. 16:10
2. *The Syrian rock hyrax*
Called "rock { Lev. 11:5
hyrax"........{ Deut. 14:7
Lives among
rocks ....Ps. 104:18
Likened to
people ....Prov. 30:26

Bag—*a purse or pouch*

A. *Used for:*
Money.........2 Kin. 12:10
Stones.........1 Sam. 17:40, 49
Food
("vessels") ....1 Sam. 9:7
Weights ....Deut. 25:13
Prov. 16:11

B. *Figurative of:*
Forgiveness....Job 14:17
True righteous-
ness.........Prov. 16:11
True riches....Luke 12:33
Insecure
riches.........Hag. 1:6

Bahurim—*young men*

A village near
Jerusalem ......2 Sam. 3:16
Where Shimei cursed
David ....2 Sam. 16:5
Where two men hid in a
well ....2 Sam. 17:17, 18

Bakbakkar—*investigator*

A Levite ....1 Chr. 9:15

Bakbuk—*a flask*

Head of postexilic
family ....Ezra 2:51
Neh. 7:53

Bakbukiah—*Yahweh has poured out*

1. A Levite of high
position ....Neh. 11:17
2. Levite porter...Neh. 12:25

Baker—*one who cooks food* (bread)

A. *Kinds of:*
Household .....Gen. 18:6
Public ....Jer. 37:21
Royal.........Gen. 40:1, 2

B. *Features of:*
Usually a woman's
job............Lev. 26:26
Considered
menial ....1 Sam. 8:13

Balaam—*destroyer of the people*

A. *Information concerning:*
A son of
Beor ....Num. 22:5
From Mesopo-
tamia ....Deut. 23:4
A soothsayer ..Josh. 13:22
A prophet .....2 Pet. 2:15
Killed because
of his sin....Num. 31:1-8

B. *Mission of:*
Balak sent to { Num. 22:5-7
curse Israel ..{ Josh. 24:9
Hindered by
speaking { Num. 22:22-35
ass............{ 2 Pet. 2:16
Curse
becomes a { Deut. 23:4, 5
blessing......{ Josh. 24:10

C. *Prophecies of:*
Under { Num. 22:18, 38
divine { Num. 23:16, 20,
control......{ 26
By the Spirit's
prompting....Num. 24:2
Blessed Israel three
times ....Num. 24:10
Spoke of the Messiah in final
message.......Num. 24:14-19

D. *Nature of:*
"Unrighteousness"—
greed ....2 Pet. 2:14, 15
"Error"—
rebellion .....Jude 11

Baladan—*(Marduk) has given a son*

Father of Merodach-Baladan (*also
spelled* Berodach-
Baladan) ....2 Kin. 20:12

Balak, Balac—*empty*

A Moabite king ...Num. 22:4
Hired Balaam to curse
Israel............Num. 22–24

Balances—*an instrument for weighing;
scales*

A. *Used for weighing:*
Things.........Lev. 19:36
Money.........Jer. 32:10

B. *Laws concerning:*
Must be just...Lev. 19:36
False, an abomi-
nation ....Prov. 11:1
Deceit,
condemned ...Amos 8:5

C. *Figurative of:*
God's justice...Job 31:6
Man's   ⎰Ps. 62:9
smallness .... ⎱Is. 40:12, 15
God's
judgment .....Dan. 5:27
Man's
tribulation ...Rev. 6:5

Baldness—*a head without hair*

A. *Natural:*
Not a sign of
leprosy.......Lev. 13:40, 41
Elijah mocked
for ....2 Kin. 2:23, 24

B. *Artificial:*
A sign of
mourning .....Is. 22:12
An idolatrous ⎰Lev. 21:5
practice......⎱Deut. 14:1
Inflicted upon
captives.......Deut. 21:12
Forbidden to
priests ....Ezek. 44:20
A part of Nazirite
vow...........Num. 6:2, 9, 18

C. *Figurative of judgment, upon:*
Israel...........Is. 3:24
                Amos 8:10
Moab...........Is. 15:2
Philistia.......Jer. 47:5
Tyre...........Ezek. 27:2, 31

Ball—*spherical object*

Prophetic ....Is. 22:18

Ballad singers

Rendered "those who speak in
proverbs" ....Num. 21:27

Balm—*an aromatic resin or gum*

A product of
Gilead...........Jer. 8:22
Sent to Joseph ...Gen. 43:11
Exported to
Tyre.............Ezek. 27:17
Healing   ⎰Jer. 46:11
qualities of .....⎱Jer. 51:8

Bamah—*high place*

A place of
idolatry.........Ezek. 20:29

Bamoth—*high places*

Encampment
site..............Num. 21:19, 20
Also called Bamoth
Baal..............Josh. 13:17

Bamoth Baal—*high places of Baal*

Assigned to
Reuben...........Josh. 13:17

Ban (see Excommunication)

Bandage

Used as disguise...1 Kin. 20:37-41
In prophecy against
Egypt...........Ezek. 30:20-22

Bani—*built*

1. Gadite
warrior ....2 Sam. 23:36
2. A Judahite...1 Chr. 9:4
3. A postexilic   ⎰Ezra 2:10
family ....⎱Neh. 10:14
4. A Merarite
Levite.........1 Chr. 6:46
5. A Levite; father of
Rehum.........Neh. 3:17
6. Signed
document.....Neh. 10:13
7. Head of Levitical
family.........Ezra 10:34
8. A postexilic
Levite.........Ezra 10:38
9. A descendant of
Asaph.........Neh. 11:22

Banishment—*forceful expulsion from
one's place*

A. *Political, of:*
Absalom by
David..........2 Sam. 14:13, 14

The Jews into
exile ....2 Chr. 36:20, 21
The Jews from
Rome ....Acts 18:2

B. *Moral and spiritual, of:*
Adam from
Eden..........Gen. 3:22-24
Cain from
others.........Gen. 4:12, 14
Lawbreaker....Ezra 7:26
John to
Patmos ....Rev. 1:9
Satan from
heaven........Rev. 12:7-9
The wicked to ⎰Rev. 20:15
lake of fire ...⎱Rev. 21:8

Bank—*A place for money:*

Exchange
charges.......John 2:15
Interest paid ⎰Matt. 25:27
on deposits ....⎱Luke 19:23

Bankruptcy—*inability to pay one's
debts*

A. *Literal:*
Condition of David's
men...........1 Sam. 22:1, 2
Unjust
steward ......Matt. 18:23-27

B. *Moral and spiritual:*
Israel's
condition .....Hos. 4:1-5
Mankind's ⎰Rom. 1:20-32
condition.....⎱Rom. 3:9-19
Individual's ⎰Phil. 3:4-8
condition.....⎱1 Tim. 1:13

Banner—*a flag or standard*

A. *Literal:*
Used by
armies ....Num. 2:2, 3
Signal for
assembling ....Is. 18:3
Hosts ....Num. 1:52
Enemy.........Ps. 74:4, 5

B. *Figurative of:*
Yahweh's name ("Yahweh is
my banner") ..Ex. 17:15
God's ⎰Ps. 20:5
salvation.....⎱Ps. 60:4
God's
protection.....Song 2:4
God's power...Song 6:4, 10
Enemy force...Is. 5:26
God's uplifted
hand..........Is. 31:9
Christ ....Is. 11:10, 12

Banquet—*a sumptuous feast*

A. *Reasons for:*
Birthday......Gen. 40:20
Marriage.......Gen. 29:22
Reunion ......Luke 15:22-25
State affairs ..⎰Esth. 1:3, 5
⎱Dan. 5:1

B. *Features of:*
Invitations ⎰Esth. 5:8, 9
sent..........⎱Luke 14:16, 17
Non-acceptance
censure......Luke 14:18-24
Courtesies to
guests.........Luke 7:34-46
Special ⎰Matt. 22:11
garment.......⎱Rev. 3:4, 5
A presiding
governor......John 2:8
Protocol of ⎰Gen. 43:33
seating.......⎱Prov. 25:6, 7
Anointing oil ..Ps. 45:7
Honor guest
noted ....1 Sam. 9:22-24

Baptism, Christian

A. *Commanded by:*
Christ ....Matt. 28:19, 20
Mark 16:15, 16
Peter ....Acts 10:46-48
Christian
ministers......Acts 22:12-16

B. *Administered by:*
The apostles ...Acts 2:1, 41
Ananias ....Acts 9:17, 18
Philip.........Acts 8:12
Acts 8:36-38
Peter ....Acts 10:44-48
Paul ....Acts 18:8
1 Cor. 1:14-17

C. *Places:*
Jordan........Matt. 3:13-16
Mark 1:5-10
Jerusalem.....Acts 2:5, 41
Samaria ......Acts 8:5, 12
A house ....Acts 10:44-48
A jail ....Acts 16:25-33

D. *Subjects of:*
Believing
Jews..........Acts 2:14, 41
Believing ⎰Acts 10:44-48
Gentiles......⎱Acts 18:8
Households ....Acts 16:14, 15,
27, 33
1 Cor. 1:16

E. *Characteristics of:*
By water ......Acts 10:47

Only one ...... Eph. 4:5
Necessary ..... Acts 2:38, 41
Source of
power........ Acts 1:5
Follows faith .. Acts 2:41
Acts 18:8

F. *Symbolism of:*
Forecast in ⎰ Joel 2:28, 29
prophecy..... ⎱ Acts 2:16-21
Prefigured in ⎰ 1 Cor. 10:2
types........ ⎱ 1 Pet. 3:20, 21
Visualized by
the Spirit's ⎰ John 1:32, 33
descent ...... ⎱ Acts 2:3, 4, 41
Expressive of
spiritual ⎰ 1 Cor. 12:13
unity........ ⎱ Gal. 3:27, 28
Figurative of
regen- ⎰ John 3:3, 5, 6
eration....... ⎱ Rom. 6:3, 4, 11
Illustrative of
cleansing..... Titus 3:5

Baptism, John's

Administrator—
John .... Matt. 3:4-7
Place—
at Jordan........ Matt. 3:6, 13, 16
in Aenon........ John 3:23
Persons—people ⎰ Mark 1:5, 9
and Jesus........ ⎱ Acts 13:24
Character—
repentance ...... Luke 3:3
Reception—rejected by
some .... Luke 7:29, 30
Nature—
of God— .... Matt. 21:25, 27
Insufficiency—
rebaptism .... Acts 19:1-7
Intent— ⎰ Matt. 3:11, 12
to ⎰ Acts 11:16
prepare.......... ⎱ Acts 19:4
Jesus' submission to—fulfilling all
righteousness..... Matt. 3:13-17

Barabbas—*son of Abba (father)*

A murderer
released
in place of ⎰ Matt. 27:16-26
Jesus............ ⎱ Acts 3:14, 15

Barachel—*God has blessed*

Father of Elihu.... Job 32:2, 6

Barak—*lightning*

Defeats Jabin ..... Judg. 4:1-24
A man of faith .... Heb. 11:32

Barbarian—*rude*

Primitive people... Rom. 1:14
Those included in the
Gospel .... Col. 3:11

Barber—*one who cuts hair*

Expressive of
divine ⎰ Is. 7:20
judgment........ ⎱ Ezek. 5:1

Bare—*uncovered; naked*

Figurative of:

Destitution........ Ezek. 16:22, 39
Uncleanness ...... Lev. 13:45
Undeveloped state,
immaturity .... Ezek. 16:7
Power revealed.... Is. 52:10
Destruction .... Joel 1:7
Mourning .... Is. 32:9-11

Barefoot—*bare feet*

Expression of great
distress........... 2 Sam. 15:30
Forewarning of
judgment........ Is. 20:2-4
Indicative of
reverence .... Ex. 3:5

Bargain—*an agreement between persons*

A disastrous....... Gen. 25:29-34
A blessed .... Gen. 28:20-22
Involving a wife... Gen. 29:15-20
Deception of ...... Prov. 20:14
Resulting in
death............. Matt. 14:7-10
History's most
notorious......... Matt. 26:14-16

Barhumite (another form of Baharumite)

One of David's mighty
men............. 2 Sam. 23:31

Bariah—*fugitive*

A descendant of
David .... 1 Chr. 3:22

Bar-Jesus (Elymas)

A Jewish
imposter.......... Acts 13:6-12

Bar-Jonah—*son of Jonah*

Surname of
Peter............. Matt. 16:17

Barkos—*parti-colored*

Postexilic family ..Ezra 2:53

Barley—*a bearded cereal grass*

Food for
animals...........1 Kin. 4:28
Used by the
poor..............Ruth 2:17
A product of   (Deut. 8:8
Palestine ....(Ruth 1:22
Used in trade .....2 Chr. 2:10
In a miracle.......John 6:9, 13

Barn—*a storehouse*

A. *Literal:*
   A place of   (Deut. 28:8
   storage.......(Joel 1:17
   Full, prayed
   for ....Ps. 144:13

B. *Spiritual, of:*
   God's   (Prov. 3:10
   blessings .....(Mal. 3:10
   Man's vanity..Luke 12:16-21
   Heaven itself ..Matt. 13:30, 43

Barnabas—*son of exhortation*

Gives property ....Acts 4:36, 37
Supports Paul.....Acts 9:27
Assists in
Antioch ....Acts 11:22-24
Brings Paul from
Tarsus............Acts 11:25, 26
Carries relief to
Jerusalem ....Acts 11:27-30
Travels with
Paul...............Acts 13:2
Called Zeus by the
multitudes........Acts 14:12
Speaks before Jerusalem
Council ....Acts 15:1, 2, 12
With Paul, takes decree to
churches ....Acts 15:22-31
Breaks with Paul over John
Mark..............Acts 15:36-39
Highly regarded   (1 Cor. 9:6
by Paul..........(Gal. 2:1, 9
Not always
steady............Gal. 2:13

Barren—*unable to reproduce*

A. *Physically, of:*
   Unproductive   (Ps. 107:34
   soil ....(Joel 2:20
   Trees ....Luke 13:6-9
   Females ....Prov. 30:16

B. *Significance of:*
   A reproach ....Gen. 16:2

A judgment....2 Sam. 6:23
Absence of
   God's   (Ex. 23:26
   blessing ......(Deut. 7:14
God's
   protection.....Ps. 113:9

C. *Spiritually:*
   Removal of,
   in new   (Is. 54:1
   Israel ....(Gal. 4:27
   Remedy
   against.......2 Pet. 1:5-8

D. *Examples of:*
   Sarah..........Gen. 21:2
   Rebekah......Gen. 25:21
   Rachel........Gen. 30:22
   Manoah's
   wife ....Judg. 13:2, 3, 24
   Hannah........1 Sam. 1:18-20
   The Shunammite
   woman.......2 Kin. 4:12-17
   Elizabeth ......Luke 1:7, 13, 57

Barsabas—*son of Saba*

1. Nominated to replace
   Judas ....Acts 1:23
2. Sent to
   Antioch.......Acts 15:22

Barter—*to exchange for something*

Between Joseph and the
Egyptians ....Gen. 47:15-17
Between Solomon and
Hiram............1 Kin. 5:10, 11

Bartholomew—*son of Talmai*

Called
Nathanael.......John 1:45, 46
One of Christ's
apostles ....Matt. 10:3
                    Acts 1:13

Bartimaeus—*son of Timaeus*

Blind beggar healed by
Jesus.............Mark 10:46-52

Baruch—*blessed*

1. Son of
   Neriah ......Jer. 32:12, 13
   Jeremiah's faithful friend and
   scribe........Jer. 36:4-32
   The Jewish remnant takes him
   to Egypt ......Jer. 43:1-7
2. Son of
   Zabbai ......Neh. 3:20
   Signs
   document.....Neh. 10:6

3. A Shilonite of
   Judah........Neh. 11:5

Barzillai—*of iron*

1. Helps David with
   food ....2 Sam. 17:27-29
   Age restrains him from
   following
   David........2 Sam. 19:31-39
2. Father of
   Adriel........2 Sam. 21:8
3. A postexilic
   priest ....Ezra 2:61

Basemath—*fragrance*

1. Wife of Esau...Gen. 26:34
   Called Adah ...Gen. 36:2
2. Wife of Esau...Gen. 36:3, 4, 13
   Called
   Mahalath .....Gen. 28:9
3. A daughter of
   Solomon .....1 Kin. 4:15

Bashan—*smooth soil*

A vast highland east of
the Sea of Chinnereth
(Galilee)..........Num. 21:33-35
Ruled by Og .....Deut. 29:7
Conquered by
Israel.............Neh. 9:22
Assigned to
Manasseh ......Deut. 3:13
Smitten by
Hazael ....2 Kin. 10:32, 33
Fine cattle ......Ezek. 39:18
Typical of ⎰Ps. 22:12
cruelty ......⎱Amos 4:1

Bashan Havoth Jair

A district named after
Jair ....Deut. 3:14

Basin—*cup or bowl for containing
liquids*

Moses used ......Ex. 24:6
Made for the ⎰Ex. 38:3
altar............⎱Ex. 27:3
Brought for
David ....2 Sam. 17:28, 29
Hiram made......1 Kin. 7:40

Baskets—*something made to hold
objects*

A. *Used for carrying:*
   Produce ....Deut. 26:2
   Food ....Matt. 14:20

Ceremonial
offerings ......Ex. 29:3, 23
Paul..............Acts 9:24, 25
Other objects
(heads)........2 Kin. 10:7

B. *Symbolic of:*
   Approaching
   death ....Gen. 40:16-19
   Israel's
   judgment .....Amos 8:1-3
   Judah's
   judgment .....Jer. 24:1-10
   Hiding good
   works........Matt. 5:15

Bastard—*an illegitimate child*

A. *Penalty attached
   to.............Deut. 23:2*

B. *Examples of:*
   Moab and
   Ammon.......Gen. 19:36-38
   Sons of Tamar by
   Judah........Gen. 38:12-30
   Jephthah ......Judg. 11:1

C. *Figurative of:*
   A mixed race ..Zech. 9:6
   The unregenerate
   state ....Heb. 12:8

Bat—*a flying mammal*

Listed among ⎰Lev. 11:19
unclean birds....⎱Deut. 14:18
Lives in dark
places ....Is. 2:19-21

Bath—*a liquid measure* (about 9
gallons)

A tenth of a
homer............Ezek. 45:10, 11
For measuring oil ⎰2 Chr. 2:10
and wine ....⎱Is. 5:10

Bathing

A. *For pleasure:*
   Pharaoh's
   daughter .....Ex. 2:5
   Bathsheba .....2 Sam. 11:2, 3

B. *For purification:*
   Cleansing the ⎰Gen. 24:32
   feet ....⎱John 13:10
   Ceremonial ⎰Lev. 14:8
   cleansing.....⎱2 Kin. 5:10-14
   Jewish
   rituals........Mark 7:2

Before performing priestly
duties........Ex. 30:19-21
Lev. 16:4, 24

Bath Rabbim—*daughter of multitudes*

Gate of
Heshbon ....Song 7:4

Bathsheba—*daughter of an oath*

Wife of Uriah .....2 Sam. 11:2, 3
Commits adultery with
David.........2 Sam. 11:4, 5
Husband's death contrived by
David.........2 Sam. 11:6-25
Mourns husband's
death.............2 Sam. 11:26
Becomes David's
wife...............2 Sam. 11:27
Her first child
dies...........2 Sam. 12:14-19
Solomon's
mother.........2 Sam. 12:24
Secures throne for
Solomon ....1 Kin. 1:15-31
Deceived by
Adonijah.........1 Kin. 2:13-25

Bathshua—*daughter of prosperity*

Same as
Bathsheba........1 Chr. 3:5

Batten—*a wooden or metal peg*

Used in a weaver's
loom ....Judg. 16:13, 14

See Nail

Battering ram (see Armor)

Used in
destroying { Ezek. 4:2
walls............ { Ezek. 21:22

Battle (See War)

Battle-ax—*an instrument of war*

Applied to Israel ..Jer. 51:19, 20

Bavai—*wisher*

Postexilic
worker...........Neh. 3:18

Bay—*inlet*

Dead Sea's cove at Jordan's
mouth............Josh. 15:5

Bazluth—*stripping*

Head of a family ..Ezra 2:52
Called
Bazlith in........Neh. 7:54

Bdellium—*an oily gum, or a white pearl*

A valuable mineral of
Havilah ....Gen. 2:12
Manna colored
like...............Num. 11:7

Beach—*coast; shore*

Place of:

Jesus' preaching ..Matt. 13:2
Fisherman's
task..............Matt. 13:48
Jesus' meal with
disciples.........John 21:8, 9
A prayer
meeting ....Acts 21:5
A notable
shipwreck ....Acts 27:39-44
A miracle ....Acts 28:1-6

Bealiah—*Yahweh is Lord*

A warrior ....1 Chr. 12:5

Bealoth—*mistresses*

Village of Judah...Josh. 15:24

Beam

A. *Physical:*
Wood undergirding
floors ....1 Kin. 7:2
Part of weaver's
frame ....1 Sam. 17:7

B. *Figurative of:*
The cry for
vengeance ....Hab. 2:11
God's power ...Ps. 104:3

Bean—*a food*

Brought to David
by friends ....2 Sam. 17:27, 28
Mixed with grain for
bread.............Ezek. 4:9

Bear—*a wild animal*

A. *Natural:*
Killed by
David.........1 Sam. 17:34, 35
Two tore up forty-two
lads ....2 Kin. 2:23, 24

B. *Figurative of:*
Fierce
revenge.......2 Sam. 17:8
Fool's folly.....Prov. 17:12
Wicked
rulers ....Prov. 28:15
World
empire ....Dan. 7:5

Final
antichrist .....Rev. 13:2
Messianic
times ....Is. 11:7
A constel-
lation ....Job 9:9

Bear—*to carry, yield*

A. *Used literally of:*
Giving birth ...Gen. 17:19
Carrying a   {Josh. 3:13
load .... {Jer. 17:21
Cross.........Matt. 27:32

B. *Used figuratively of:*
Excessive
punishment ...Gen. 4:13
Divine
deliverance....Ex. 19:4
Responsibility {Lev. 5:17
for sin ...... {Lev. 24:15
Burden of
leadership.....Deut. 1:9, 12
Personal
shame ....Ezek. 16:54
Evangelism ....Acts 9:15
Spiritual help ..Gal. 6:1, 2
Spiritual produc-
tivity........John 15:2, 4, 8

Beard—*hair grown on the face*

A. *Long, worn by:*
Aaron ....Ps. 133:2
David.........1 Sam. 21:12, 13

B. *In mourning:*
Plucked........Ezra 9:3
Clipped........Jer. 48:37, 38

C. *Features regarding:*
Leper's must be
shaven........Lev. 13:29-33
Half-shaven, an
indignity ......2 Sam. 10:4, 5
Marring of,
forbidden ....Lev. 19:27
Shaven, by
Egyptians .....Gen. 41:14
Spittle on, sign of
lunacy ....1 Sam. 21:12, 13
Holding to, a token of
respect........2 Sam. 20:9

Beasts—*four-footed animals; mammals*

A. *Characteristics of:*
God-created ...Gen. 1:21
Of their own
order..........1 Cor. 15:39
Named by
Adam ....Gen. 2:20

Suffer in man's
sin............Rom. 8:20-22
Perish at
death ....Ps. 49:12-15
Follow   {Is. 1:3
instincts ..... {Jude 10
Under God's
control........1 Sam. 6:7-14
Wild..........Mark 1:13
For man's   {Gen. 9:3
food .... {Acts 10:12, 13
Used in
sacrifices.....Lev. 27:26-29
Spiritual
lessons   {1 Kin. 4:30-33
from .... {Job 12:7
Eat people ....1 Sam. 17:46
                1 Cor. 15:32

B. *Treatment of:*
No sexual relation
with ....Lev. 20:15, 16
Proper care of, sign of a
righteous   {Gen. 33:13, 14
man.......... {Prov. 12:10
Abuse of,
rebuked.......Num. 22:28-32
Extra food
for, while   {Deut. 25:4
working...... {1 Tim. 5:18

C. *Typical of:*
Man's folly ....Ps. 73:22
Unregenerate
men...........Titus 1:12
False
prophets ......2 Pet. 2:12
Antichrist......Rev. 13:1-4

See Animals

Beaten silver—*silver shaped by hammering*

Overlaid idols .....Is. 30:22
                    Hab. 2:19
In trade..........Jer. 10:9

Beatings—*striking the body with blows; floggings*

A. *Inflicted on:*
The wicked ....Deut. 25:3
The guilty .....Lev. 19:20
Children .....Prov. 22:15
The disobe-   {Prov. 26:3
dient .... {Luke 12:47, 48

B. *Victims of unjust beatings:*
A servant......Luke 20:10, 11
Christ ....Is. 50:6
                Mark 15:19
The apostles ...Acts 5:40
Paul ....Acts 16:18-24

Beatitudes—*pronouncements of blessings*

Jesus begins His sermon with..... { Matt. 5:3-12 / Luke 6:20-22 }

Beautiful gate—*gate at east of Temple area*

Lame man healed there............Acts 3:1-10

Beauty, physical

A. *Temporal:*
  Seen in nature........ { Hos. 14:6 / Matt. 6:28, 29 }
  Consumed in dissipation....Is. 28:1
  Contest Abishag, winner of.....1 Kin. 1:1-4
  Esther, winner of.....Esth. 2:1-17
  Destroyed by sin.........Ps. 39:11
  Ends in grave.........Ps. 49:14

B. *In Women:*
  Vain...........Prov. 31:30
  Without discretion....Prov. 11:22
  Enticements of.........Prov. 6:25
  Source of temptation... { Gen. 6:2 / 2 Sam. 11:2-5 }
  Leads to marriage......Deut. 21:10-13
  A bride's.........Ps. 45:11
  Sarah's.........Gen. 12:11
  Rebekah's.....Gen. 24:15, 16
  Rachel's.....Gen. 29:17
  Daughters of Job.........Job 42:15
  Abigail's.......1 Sam. 25:3
  Bathsheba's..2 Sam. 11:2, 3
  Tamar's.....2 Sam. 13:1
  Abishag's.......1 Kin. 1:3, 4
  Vashti's.......Esth. 1:11
  Esther's.......Esth. 2:7

C. *In Men:*
  Of man........Is. 44:13
  Of the aged....Prov. 20:29
  Joseph's ......Gen. 39:6
  David's.........1 Sam. 16:12, 13
  Absalom's .....2 Sam. 14:25

Beauty, spiritual

The Messiah ......Ps. 110:3
                     Is. 52:7

The true Israel............ { Ps. 45:8-11 / Song 1:8 }
The meek.........Ps. 149:4
Spiritual worship ....2 Chr. 20:21
Christian ministers ....Rom. 10:15
Holy garments ...Is. 52:1
Christ's rejection by Israel............Zech. 11:7-14

Bebai—*fatherly*

1. Family head ...Ezra 2:11
2. One who signs document.....Neh. 10:15

Becher—*young camel*

1. Benjamin's son ......Gen. 46:21
2. Son of Ephraim ......Num. 26:35
   Called Bered...1 Chr. 7:20

Bechorath—*the first birth*

Ancestor of Saul ..1 Sam. 9:1

Bed

A. *Made of:*
  The ground....Gen. 28:11
  Iron, 13½ feet long ....Deut. 3:11
  Ivory ....Amos 6:4
  Gold and silver ....Esth. 1:6

B. *Used for:*
  Sleep ....Luke 11:7
  Rest ....2 Sam. 4:5-7
  Sickness.......Gen. 49:33
  Meals.........Amos 6:4
  Prostitution....Prov. 7:16, 17
  Evil............Ps. 36:4
  Marriage. { Song 3:1 / Heb. 13:4 }
  Singing ....Ps. 149:5

C. *Figurative of:*
  The grave .....Job 17:13-16
  Divine support ....Ps. 41:3
  Worldly security.......Is. 57:7

Bed—*a garden plot*

Used literally......Song 6:2
Used figuratively.......Song 5:13

Bedad—*separation*

Father of Hadad ..Gen. 36:35

Bedan—*son of judgment*

1. Judge of
    Israel ....1 Sam. 12:11
2. Descendant of
    Manasseh .....1 Chr. 7:17

Bedeiah—*servant of Yahweh*

Son of Bani ......Ezra 10:34, 35

Bedfellows

Provide mutual
  warmth ....Eccl. 4:11

Bedroom

A place of sleep ...2 Sam. 4:7
Elijah's special ...2 Kin. 4:8, 10
Secrets of ....2 Kin. 6:12
Joash hidden in ...2 Kin. 11:2

Bee—*insect*

Abundant in
  Canaan...........Judg. 14:8
Amorites
  compared to......Deut. 1:44
David's enemies
  compared to......Ps. 118:12
Assyria
  compared to....Is. 7:18

See Honey

Beef, boiled

Elisha gives
  people............1 Kin. 19:21

Beeliada—*the Lord knows*

Son of David......1 Chr. 14:7
Called Eliada......2 Sam. 5:14-16

Beelzebub

Prince of
  demons...........Matt. 12:24
Identified as
  Satan ....Matt. 12:26, 27
Jesus thus called ..Matt. 10:25

Beer—*a well*

1. Moab station ..Num. 21:16-18
2. Jotham's place of
    refuge........Judg. 9:21

Beera—*a well*

An Asherite.......1 Chr. 7:37

Beerah—*a well*

Reubenite
  prince............1 Chr. 5:6

Beer Elim

Well dug by leaders of
  Israel.............Is. 15:8

Beeri—*expounder*

1. Esau's father-in-
    law ....Gen. 26:34
2. Hosea's
    father.........Hos. 1:1

Beer Lahai Roi—*the well of The Living
One who sees me*

Angel met Hagar
  there ....Gen. 16:7-14
Isaac dwelt in.....Gen. 24:62

Beeroth—*wells*

Gibeonite city.....Josh. 9:17

Beerothite, Berothite

An inhabitant of { 2 Sam. 4:2
Beeroth ....   1 Chr. 11:39

Beersheba—*well of the oath*

A. *God appeared to:*
    Hagar ....Gen. 21:14,
                        17-19
    Isaac ....Gen. 26:19-24
    Jacob..........Gen. 46:1-5
    Elijah..........1 Kin. 19:3-7

B. *Other features of:*
    Named after { Gen. 21:31-33
    an oath...... { Gen. 26:26-33
    Isaac's residence
      at............Gen. 26:23-25
    Jacob's departure
      from ....Gen. 28:10
    Assigned to
      Judah.........Josh. 15:20, 28
    Later assigned to
      Simeon ....Josh. 19:1, 2, 9
    Judgeship of Samuel's
      sons ....1 Sam. 8:2
    Became seat { Amos 5:5
    of idolatry.... { Amos 8:14
    "From Dan to
      Beersheba"....2 Sam. 17:11

Be Eshterah—*temple of Ashterah*

A Levitical city....Josh. 21:27
Same as
Ashtaroth ....1 Chr. 6:71

Beggar—*needy*

A. *Statements concerning:*
Shame of ......Luke 16:3
Seed of righteous,
kept from .....Ps. 37:25
Punishment
of..............Ps. 109:10
Object of
prayer ....1 Sam. 2:1, 8

B. *Examples of:*
Bartimaeus ....Mark 10:46
Lazarus.......Luke 16:20-22
Blind man .....Luke 18:35
Lame man .....Acts 3:2-6

Beginning—*the starting point; origin of*

Creation ....Gen. 1:1
              John 1:1-3
Sin................Gen. 3:1-6
              Rom. 5:12-21
Death.............Gen. 3:3, 22-24
Salvation ....2 Thess. 2:13, 14
Satan.............John 8:44
The Gospel.......Gen. 3:15
              Gal. 3:8
The old
covenant ....Ex. 19:1-5
              Heb. 8:7-9
The   (Jer. 31:31-34
new   { Matt. 26:28
covenant ....(Heb. 9:14-28

Begotten—*from "beget" meaning to bring into being*

A. *Applied to Christ:*
Predicted ......Ps. 2:7
              Acts 13:33
Prefigured .....Heb. 11:17
Proclaimed ....John 1:14
Proffered ......John 3:16
Professed ......Heb. 1:5, 6

B. *Applied to Christians:*
By the
Gospel ....1 Cor. 4:15
In bonds.......Philem. 10
Unto hope .....1 Pet. 1:3
For
safekeeping ...1 John 5:18

Behavior—*one's conduct*

A. *Strange:*
Feigned
insanity.......1 Sam. 21:12, 13
Supposed drunken-
ness...........1 Sam. 1:12-16
Pretended
grief ....2 Sam. 14:1-8

Professed
loyalty ....Matt. 26:48-50
Insipid
hypocrisy .....Esth. 6:5-11
Counterfeit
religion ....2 Cor. 11:13-15

B. *True:*
Reverent ......Titus 2:7
Orderly ....2 Thess. 3:7
Good ....1 Tim. 3:2
Without
blame.........1 Thess. 2:10

Beheading—*a form of capital punishment*

Ishbosheth........2 Sam. 4:5-7
John the Baptist ..Matt. 14:10
James.............Acts 12:2
Martyrs...........Rev. 20:4

Behemoth—*a colossal beast*

Described ....Job 40:15-24

Bekah—*see Jewish measures*

Half a shekel......Ex. 38:26

Bel—*lord*

Patron god of   (Is. 46:1
Babylon ....{ Jer. 51:44
Merodach title ...(Jer. 50:2

Bela, Belah—*destruction*

1. King of
Edom ....Gen. 36:32
2. Reubenite
chief..........1 Chr. 5:8
3. Benjamin's
son ....Gen. 46:21
4. A city ....Gen. 14:2, 8

Belial

A. *Hebrew word translated:*
Corrupt.......Deut. 13:13
Perverted .....Judg. 19:22
Worthless .....1 Sam. 30:22
Scoundrels....1 Kin. 21:10, 13

B. *Applied to:*
Satan..........2 Cor. 6:15

Believers—*those who have received Christ; Christians*

Applied to   (Acts 5:14
converts.........(1 Tim. 4:12

Bellows—*an instrument used in forcing air at fire*

A figure of
affliction . . . . Jer. 6:29
Descriptive of God's
judgment. . . . . Jer. 6:27-30

Bells

On Aaron's $\left\{\begin{array}{l}\text{Ex. 28:33, 34}\\\text{Ex. 39:25, 26}\end{array}\right.$
garment . . . .
Attention-
getters . . . . Is. 3:16, 18
Symbols of
consecration. . . . . Zech. 14:20

Beloved—*a title of endearment*

A. *Applied naturally to:*
A husband . . . . . Song 6:1-3

B. *Applied spiritually to:*
Christ . . . . Matt. 3:17
Spiritual
Israel . . . . . . Rom. 9:25
Believers. . . . . . Col. 3:12
Christian
friends . . . . Rom. 16:8, 9
Saints' abode . . Rev. 20:9

Belshazzar—*Bel protect the king*

Son of Nebuchad-
nezzar. . . . . Dan. 5:2
Gives feast . . . . Dan. 5:1, 4
Disturbed by
handwriting . . . . . . Dan. 5:5-12
Seeks Daniel's
aid . . . . Dan. 5:13-16
Daniel interprets for
him . . . . Dan. 5:17-29
Last Chaldean
king. . . . . Dan. 5:30, 31

Belteshazzar—*Bel protect his life*

Daniel's Babylonian
name. . . . . Dan. 1:7

Ben—*son*

Levite
porter . . . . 1 Chr. 15:18

Benaiah—*Yahweh has built*

1. Jehoiada's
son . . . . 2 Sam. 23:20
A mighty
man . . . . 2 Sam. 23:20, 21
David's
bodyguard . . . . 2 Sam. 8:18
Faithful to $\left\{\begin{array}{l}\text{2 Sam. 15:18}\\\text{2 Sam. 20:23}\end{array}\right.$
David . . . .
Escorts Solomon to the
throne . . . . 1 Kin. 1:38-40

Executes
Adonijah, $\left\{\begin{array}{l}\text{1 Kin. 2:25,}\\\text{29-34}\end{array}\right.$
Joab and
Shimei . . . . 1 Kin. 2:46
Commander-in-
chief . . . . 1 Kin. 2:28-35
2. One of David's mighty
men . . . . 2 Sam. 23:30
Divisional
commander . . . 1 Chr. 27:14
3. Levite
musician . . . . . . 1 Chr. 15:18-20
4. Priestly $\left\{\begin{array}{l}\text{1 Chr. 15:24}\\\text{1 Chr. 16:6}\end{array}\right.$
trumpeter . . . . .
5. Levite of Asaph's
family . . . . 2 Chr. 20:14
6. Simeonite. . . . . . 1 Chr. 4:36
7. Levite
overseer . . . . . 2 Chr. 31:13
8. Father of leader
Pelatiah . . . . Ezek. 11:1, 13
9-12. Four postexilic Jews who
divorced their foreign
wives . . . . Ezra 10:25-43

Ben-Ammi—*son of my kinsman*

Son of Lot; father of the
Ammonites. . . . . . Gen. 19:38

Bene Berak—*sons of berak* (lightning)

A town of Dan . . . . Josh. 19:45

Ben-Deker—*piercing; mattock*

One of Solomon's
officers . . . . 1 Kin. 4:9

Benediction—*an act of blessing*

A. *Characteristics of:*
Instituted by
God. . . . . Gen. 1:22, 28
Divinely
approved. . . . . . Deut. 10:8
Aaronic form . . Num. 6:23-26
Apostolic
form . . . . 2 Cor. 13:14
Jesus' last
words . . . . Luke 24:50, 51

B. *Pronounced upon:*
Creation . . . . . . Gen. 1:22, 28
New world. . . . . Gen. 9:1, 2
Abraham . . . . . Gen. 14:19, 20
Marriage. . . . . . Gen. 24:60
Son
(Jacob). . . . . . Gen. 27:27-29

Monarch
(Pharaoh)....Gen. 47:7, 10
Sons
(Joseph's)....{ Gen. 48:15, 16, 20
Tribes
(Israel's)......Deut. 33:1-29
Foreigner......Ruth 1:8, 9
People.........2 Sam. 6:18
Jesus...........Luke 2:34
Song of
Zacharias.....Luke 1:68-79
Children's
blessing......Mark 10:16

Benefactor—*one who bestows benefits*

A. *Materially, God as:*
The poor ......Deut. 7:6-26
Unbeliever's...Acts 14:15-18
Christian's.....Phil. 4:19

B. *Spiritually:*
By God ....Eph. 1:3-6
Through
Christ.........Eph. 2:13-22
For
enrichment ...Eph. 1:16-19

C. *Attitudes toward:*
Murmuring .....Num. 11:1-10
Forgetful-
ness...........Ps. 106:7-14
Rejection ......Acts 13:44-47
Remem-
brance ....Luke 7:1-5
Gratefulness...Acts 13:48

Benefice—*an enriching act or gift*

Manifested by a
church ....Phil. 4:15-17
Encouraged in a
friend ....Philem. 17-22
Justified in
works ....James 2:14-17
Remembered in
heaven ....1 Tim. 6:17-19

Bene Jaakan—*sons of Jaakan*

A wilderness
station ....Num. 33:31

Benevolence—*generosity toward others*

A. *Exercised toward:*
The poor ......Gal. 2:10
The needy ....Eph. 4:28
Enemies ......Prov. 25:21
God's
servant ......Phil. 4:14-17

B. *Measured by:*
Ability.........Acts 11:29
Love...........1 Cor. 13:3
Sacrifice ......Mark 12:41-44
Bountiful-
ness..........2 Cor. 9:6-15

C. *Blessings of:*
Fulfills a
grace ....Rom. 12:6, 13
Performs a spiritual
sacrifice.......Heb. 13:16
Makes us "more
blessed".......Acts 20:35
Enriches the {Prov. 11:25
giver..........{Is. 58:10, 11
Reward........1 Tim. 6:17-19

Ben-Hadad—*son of the god Hadad*

1. Ben-Hadad I, king of Damascus.
Hired by Asa, king of Judah, to
attack Baasha, king of
Israel ....1 Kin. 15:18-21
2. Ben-Hadad II, king of
Damascus. Makes war on
Ahab, king of
Israel ....1 Kin. 20:1-21
Defeated by
Israel ....1 Kin. 20:26-34
Fails in siege
against {2 Kin. 6:24-33
Samaria......{2 Kin. 7:6-20
Killed by
Hazael........2 Kin. 8:7-15
3. Ben-Hadad III, king of
Damascus. Loses all Israelite
conquests made by Hazael, his
father.........2 Kin. 13:3-25

Ben-Hail—*son of strength*

A teacher ....2 Chr. 17:7

Ben-Hanan—*son of the gracious one*

A son of Shimon ..1 Chr. 4:20

Beninu—*our son*

A Levite document
signer ....Neh. 10:13

Benjamin—*son of the right hand*

Jacob's youngest
son...............Gen. 35:16-20
Jacob's favorite {Gen. 42:4
son...............{Gen. 43:1-14
Loved by Joseph ..Gen. 43:29-34
Judah intercedes
for ....Gen. 44:18-34

Joseph's
gifts to . . . . .Gen. 45:22
Father of five
sons. . . . . .1 Chr. 8:1, 2
Head of a tribe. . . .Num. 26:38-41
Jacob's prophecy
concerning . . . . . . .Gen. 49:27

Benjamin (others bearing this name)

1. A son of
   Bilhan . . . . .1 Chr. 7:10
2. Son of Harim . .Ezra 10:18, 31,
   32
   Same as in. . . . .Neh. 3:23

Benjamin, tribe of

A. *Background features of:*
   Descendants
   of Jacob's
   youngest ⎧Gen. 35:17, 18,
   son . . . .⎨24
   Family
   divisions of. . . .Num. 26:38-41
   Strength of . . . .Num. 1:36, 37
   Bounds of . . . . .Josh. 18:11-28
   Prophecies ⎧Gen. 49:27
   respecting. . . .⎨Deut. 33:12

B. *Memorable events of:*
   Almost destroyed for protecting
   men of
   Gibeah. . . . . . .Judg. 20:12-48
   Wives provided for, to preserve
   the tribe . . . . . .Judg. 21:1-23
   Furnished Israel her first
   king . . . . .1 Sam. 9:1-17
   Hailed David's
   return. . . . . . . .2 Sam. 19:16, 17

C. *Celebrities belonging to:*
   Ehud, a
   judge . . . . .Judg. 3:15
   Saul, Israel's first
   king . . . . .1 Sam. 9:1
   Abner, David's
   general. . . . . . .1 Sam. 17:55
   Mordecai . . . . . .Esth. 2:5
   The apostle
   Paul . . . . .Phil. 3:5

Beno—*his son*

A Merarite
Levite. . . . . .1 Chr. 24:26, 27

Ben-Oni—*son of my sorrow*

Rachel's name for
Benjamin. . . . . . . .Gen. 35:16-18

Ben-Zoheth—*son of Zoheth*

A man of Judah. . .1 Chr. 4:20

Beon—*house of On*

A locality east of
Jordan . . . . .Num. 32:3
Same as
Baal Meon. . . . . . .Num. 32:37, 38

Beor—*a burning*

1. Father of
   Bela. . . . . .Gen. 36:32
2. Father of ⎧Num. 22:5
   Balaam . . . . . .⎨2 Pet. 2:15

Bera—*excellent*

A king of
Sodom . . . . .Gen. 14:2

Berachah—*blessing*

1. David's
   warrior . . . . . .1 Chr. 12:3
2. A valley in Judah near
   Tekoa. . . . . . . .2 Chr. 20:26

Beraiah—*Yahweh has created*

A Benjamite
chief . . . . .1 Chr. 8:21

Berea—*watered*

A city of Macedonia visited by
Paul. . . . . .Acts 17:10-15

Bereavement—*the emotional state after
a loved one's death*

A. *General attitudes in:*
   Horror. . . . . . . .Ex. 12:29, 30
   Great
   emotion. . . . . .2 Sam. 18:33
   Complaint . . . . .Ruth 1:20, 21
   Genuine
   sorrow. . . . . . .Gen. 37:33-35
   Submission . . . .Job 1:18-21

B. *Christian attitudes in:*
   Unlike
   world's. . . . . . .1 Thess. 4:13-18
   Yet sorrow ⎧John 11:32-35
   allowed . . . . . .⎨Acts 9:39
   With hope of
   reunion . . . . . .John 11:20-27

C. *Unusual circumstances of,
   mourning:*
   Forbidden . . . . .Lev. 10:6
   Of great
   length. . . . . . . .Gen. 50:1-11
   Turned to
   joy. . . . . .John 11:41-44

Berachiah—*blessed by Yahweh*

1. Asaph's
   father........1 Chr. 6:39
2. Levite
   doorkeepers...1 Chr. 15:23, 24
3. Head man of
   Ephraim ......2 Chr. 28:12
4. Son of
   Zerubbabel....1 Chr. 3:20
5. Levite ....1 Chr. 9:16
6. Postexilic
   workman .....Neh. 3:4, 30
7. Father of   { Zech. 1:1, 7
   Zachariah.... { Matt. 23:35

Bered—*hail*

1. A place in the wilderness of
   Shur..........Gen. 16:7, 14
2. An
   Ephraimite....1 Chr. 7:20

Beri—*belonging to a well*

An Asherite.......1 Chr. 7:36

Beriah—*evil*

1. Son of Asher ..Gen. 46:17
2. Ephraim's
   son...........1 Chr. 7:22, 23
3. Chief of
   Benjamin .....1 Chr. 8:13, 16
4. Levite ....1 Chr. 23:10, 11

Berites

Descendants of
   Beriah ....Num. 26:44

Berites

A people in north { 2 Sam. 20:14,
   Palestine .... {   15

Berith—*covenant*

Shechem idol .....Judg. 9:46
Same as   { Judg. 8:33
Baal-Berith ...... { Judg. 9:4

Bernice—*victorious*

Sister of Herod
   Agrippa II......Acts 25:13, 23
Hears Paul's
   defense..........Acts 26:1-30

Berodach-Baladan

A king of
   Babylon ....2 Kin. 20:12-19
Also called Merodach-
   Baladan ....Is. 39:1

Berothah, Berothai—*wells*

City of Syria taken by
   David ....2 Sam. 8:8
Boundary in the ideal
   kingdom ....Ezek. 47:16

Beryl—*a precious stone*

In breastplate of { Ex. 28:15-21
   high priest....... { Ex. 39:8-14
Ornament of a
   king..............Ezek. 28:12, 13
Describes a
   lover ....Song 5:14
Applied to an
   angel.............Dan. 10:5, 6
Wheels like color
   of ....Ezek. 1:16
In New
   Jerusalem ....Rev. 21:20

Besai

A family head.....Ezra 2:49

Besodeiah—*in the counsel of Yahweh*

Father of
   Meshullam ....Neh. 3:6

Besor—*cold*

A brook south of { 1 Sam. 30:9, 10,
   Ziklag........... {   21

Bestial—*beast like*

Condemned ....Ex. 22:19
Punishment of ....Lev. 20:13

Best Seats—*seats or places of honor*

Sought by scribes { Matt. 23:1, 6
   and Pharisees.... { Mark 12:38, 39
Not to be
   sought ....Luke 14:7-11

Betah—*trust, confidence*

Cities of
   Hadadezer.......2 Sam. 8:8
Called Tibhath ....1 Chr. 18:8

Beten—*valley*

City of Asher .....Josh. 19:25

Beth—*house*

Second letter of the Hebrew
   alphabet..........Ps. 119:9-16

Bethabara—*house of passage*

A place beyond Jordan where John
   baptized..........John 1:28

Beth Acacia

A town of Judah..Judg. 7:22

Beth Anath—*house of Anath* (the goddess)

A town of
Naphtali.........Josh. 19:38, 39
Canaanites
remain in........Judg. 1:33

Beth Anoth—*house of Anoth* (the goddess)

A town of Judah..Josh. 15:59

Bethany—*house of poverty*

A town on Mt. of
Olives............Luke 19:29
Home of
Lazarus..........John 11:1
Home of Simon, the
leper.............Matt. 26:6
Jesus visits ⎧Mark 11:1, 11,
there............⎨   12
Scene,
Ascension.......Luke 24:50, 51

Beth Arabah—*house of desert*

A village of
Judah............Josh. 15:6, 61
Assigned to
Benjamin........Josh. 18:21, 22

Beth Arbel—*house of God's ambush*

A town destroyed by
Shalman.........Hos. 10:14

Beth Aven—*house of nothingness* (vanity)

A town of
Benjamin........Josh. 7:2
Israel defeated Philistines
there.............1 Sam. 13:5

Beth Baal Meon

City of Reuben....Josh. 13:17

Beth Barah—*house of the ford*

A passage over
Jordan...........Judg. 7:24

Beth Biri—*house of my creation*

A town of
Simeon...........1 Chr. 4:31
Probably same as Beth
Lebaoth..........Josh. 19:6

Beth Car—*house of a lamb*

Site of Philistines'
retreat...........1 Sam. 7:11

Beth Dagon—*house of Dagon*

1. Village of
Judah.........Josh. 15:41
2. Town of
Asher.........Josh. 19:27

Beth Diblathaim—*house of fig cakes*

A Moabite town...Jer. 48:21, 22

Bethel—*house of God*

1. A town of
Benjamin.....Judg. 21:19
Abraham settles
near..........Gen. 12:7, 8
Site of Abraham's
altar.........Gen. 13:3, 4
Scene of Jacob's
ladder........Gen. 28:10-19
Luz becomes
Bethel........Gen. 28:19
Jacob
returns to.....Gen. 35:1-15
On Ephraim's
border........Josh. 16:1-4
Samuel judged
there.........1 Sam. 7:15, 16
Site of worship and
sacrifice......1 Sam. 10:3
Center of
idolatry.......1 Kin. 12:28-33
School of
prophets......2 Kin. 2:1, 3
Youths from, mock
Elisha.........2 Kin. 2:23, 24
Josiah destroys
altars of.......2 Kin. 23:4,
              15-20
Denounced by a man of
God...........1 Kin. 13:1-10
Denounced by
Amos.........Amos 7:10-13
Denounced by
Jeremiah......Jer. 48:13
Denounced by
Hosea........Hos. 10:15
2. Simeonite
town..........1 Sam. 30:27
Called Bethul
and   ⎧Josh. 19:4
Bethuel......⎨1 Chr. 4:30

Beth Emek—*house of the valley*

A town of Asher..Josh. 19:27

Bether—*separation*

Designates
mountains........Song 2:17

Bethesda—*house of mercy*

Jerusalem pool....John 5:2-4

Beth Ezel—*a place near*

A town of Judah..Mic. 1:11

Beth Gader—*house of the wall*

A town of Judah..1 Chr. 2:51
Probably same as
Geder ....Josh. 12:13

Beth Gamul—*house of recompense*

A Moabite town...Jer. 48:23

Beth Haccherem—*house of the vineyard*

Town of Judah....Jer. 6:1

Beth Haram—*mountain house*

A town of Gad....Josh. 13:27
Same as
Beth Haran....Num. 32:36

Beth Hoglah—*house of the partridge*

A village of {Josh. 15:6
Benjamin.......{Josh. 18:19, 21

Beth Horon—*house of the hollow*

Twin towns of
Ephraim.........Josh. 16:3, 5
The nether, built by Sheerah, a
woman...........1 Chr. 7:24
Assigned to Kohathite
Levites.........Josh. 21:20, 22
Fortified by
Solomon.........2 Chr. 8:3-5
Prominent in {Josh. 10:10-14
battles.........{1 Sam. 13:18

Beth Jeshimoth, Beth Jesimoth—*house of the wastes*

A town near
Pisgah...........Josh. 12:3
Israel camps
near............Num. 33:49
Assigned to
Reubenites ......Josh. 13:20
Later a town of
Moab............Ezek. 25:9

Beth Lebaoth—*house of lionesses*

A town in south Judah; assigned to

Simeonites ....Josh. 19:6
Called Lebaoth...Josh. 15:32

Bethlehem (of Judah)—*house of bread*

A. *Significant features of:*
Built by
Salma..........1 Chr. 2:51
Originally called
Ephrath.......Gen. 35:16
Burial of
Rachel........Gen. 35:19
Two
wandering {Judg. 17:1-13
Levites of ....{Judg. 19:1-30
Naomi's
home ....Ruth 1:1, 19
Home of
Boaz..........Ruth 4:9-11
Home of
David.........1 Sam. 16:1-18
Stronghold of
Philistines.....2 Sam. 23:14, 15
Fortified by
Rehoboam ....2 Chr. 11:5, 6
Refuge of Gedaliah's
murderers.....Jer. 41:16, 17

B. *Messianic features of:*
Sought for the
tabernacle ....Ps. 132:5-7
Predicted place of the Messiah's
birth ....Mic. 5:2
Fulfillment
cited ....Matt. 2:1, 5, 6
Infants of,
slain by {Jer. 31:15
Herod........{Matt. 2:16-18

Bethlehem (of Zebulun)

Town assigned to
Zebulun..........Josh. 19:15, 16
Home of judge
Ibzan..........Judg. 12:8-11

Beth Maacah—*house of Maacah*

Tribe of Israel.....2 Sam. 20:14, 15

Beth Marcaboth—*house of the chariots*

Town of Simeon ..Josh. 19:5

Beth Meon—*house of habitation*

Moabite town .....Jer. 48:23

Beth Millo—*house of a terrace*

Stronghold at
Shechem ....Judg. 9:6, 20

Beth Nimrah—*house of the leopard*

Town of Gad......Num. 32:3, 36

Beth Pazzez—*house of dispersion*

Town of
Issachar..........Josh. 19:21

Beth Pelet—*house of escape*

Town of Judah....Josh. 15:27

Beth Peor—*house of Peor*

Town near
Pisgah............Deut. 3:29
Valley of Moses' burial
place ....Deut. 34:6
Assigned to
Reubenites ....Josh. 13:15, 20

Bethphage—*house of unripe figs*

Village near
Bethany..........Mark 11:1
Near Mt. of
Olives ....Matt. 21:1

Beth Rapha—*house of a giant*

A town or family of
Judah ....1 Chr. 4:12

Beth Rehob—*house of a street*

A town in north
Palestine ....Judg. 18:28
Inhabited by
Syrians...........2 Sam. 10:6

Bethsaida—*place of fishing*

A city of Galilee...Mark 6:45
Home of Andrew,
Peter and   {John 1:44
Philip............{John 12:21
Blind man
healed............Mark 8:22, 23
Near feeding of
5,000 ....Luke 9:10-17
Unbelief of,   {Matt. 11:21
denounced .....{Luke 10:13

Beth Shan, Beth Shean—*house of security*

A town in
Issachar..........Josh. 17:11
Assigned to
Manasseh ....1 Chr. 7:29
Tribute paid by....Josh. 17:12-16
Users of iron
chariots ....Josh. 17:16
Saul's corpse   {1 Sam. 31:10-13
hung up at ....{2 Sam. 21:12-14

Beth Shemesh—*house of the sun*

1. A border town between Judah
and Dan ......Josh. 15:10
Also called
Ir Shemesh ...Josh. 19:41
Assigned to
priests..........Josh. 21:16
Ark brought
to...........1 Sam. 6:12-19
Joash defeats
Amaziah at ...2 Kin. 14:11
Taken by
Philistines.....2 Chr. 28:18
2. A town of
Naphtali ......Josh. 19:38
3. A town of
Issachar ......Josh. 19:22
4. Egyptian city .Jer. 43:13

Beth Tappuah—*house of apples*

A town of Judah ..Josh. 15:53

Bethuel—*abode of God*

1. Father of
Laban and   {Gen. 22:20-23
Rebekah .....{Gen. 24:29
2. Simeonite
town..........1 Chr. 4:30
Called Bethul ..Josh. 19:4

Beth Zur—*house of a rock*

A town of Judah ..Josh. 15:58
Fortified by
Rehoboam........2 Chr. 11:7
Help to rebuild....Neh. 3:16

Betonim—*pistachio nuts*

A town of Gad ....Josh. 13:26

Betrayal—*a breach of trust*

A. *Of Christ:*
Predicted ......Ps. 41:9
Frequently   {Matt. 17:22
mentioned ...{John 13:21
Betrayer
identified......John 13:26
Sign of, a
kiss ....Matt. 26:48, 49
Guilt of.......Matt. 27:3, 4
Supper
before........1 Cor. 11:23
Jewish nation   {Matt. 27:9, 10
guilty of .....{Acts 7:51-53

B. *Examples of:*
Israelites by
Gibeonites ....Josh. 9:22
Samson by
Delilah........Judg. 16:18-20
The woman of En Dor by
Saul ....1 Sam. 28:9-12

Jesus by
Judas ....Matt. 26:14-16
Christians .....Matt. 10:21

Betrothed—*given in marriage*

Treatment of......Ex. 21:8, 9

Beulah—*married*

A symbol of true
Israel............Is. 62:4, 5

Beverage—*a drink*

A. *Literal:*
Milk...........Judg. 4:19
Judg. 5:25
Strong drink...Prov. 31:6
Water ....Matt. 10:42
Wine ....1 Tim. 5:23

B. *Figurative:*
Christ's
blood ....John 6:53
Cup of
suffering .....John 18:11
Living water...John 4:10
Water of life...Rev. 22:17

Beware—*be wary of; guard against*

A. *Of evil things:*
False
prophets ......Matt. 7:15
Evil men......Matt. 10:17
Covetous-
ness...........Luke 12:15
Dogs
(figurative)....Phil. 3:2

B. *Of possibilities:*
Disobeying
God...........Ex. 23:20, 21
Forgetting
God...........Deut. 6:12
Being led
away..........2 Pet. 3:17

Bewitch—*to charm, captivate, or astound*

Activity of
Simon............Acts 8:9-11
Descriptive of
legalism ....Gal. 3:1

Bezai—*shining, high*

Postexilic family ⎰Ezra 2:17
head ....⎱Neh. 7:23
Signs document...Neh. 10:18

Bezaleel—*in the shadow* (protection) *of God*

1. Hur's
grandson......1 Chr. 2:20
Tabernacle ⎰Ex. 31:1-11
builder ⎱Ex. 35:30-35
2. Divorced foreign
wife...........Ezra 10:18, 30

Bezek—*scattering*

1. Town near
Jerusalem .....Judg. 1:4, 5
2. Saul's army gathered
there..........1 Sam. 11:8

Bezer—*fortress*

1. An Asherite....1 Chr. 7:37
2. City of
Reuben ....Deut. 4:43
Place of
refuge........Josh. 20:8

Bible history, outlined

A. *Pre-patriarchal period, the:*
Creation.......Gen. 1:1-2:25
Fall of man ....Gen. 3:1-24
Development of
wickedness....Gen. 4:1-6:8
Flood..........Gen. 6:9-8:22
Establishment of
nations........Gen. 9:1-10:32
Confusion of
tongues ....Gen. 11:1-32

B. *Patriarchal period:*
Abraham ......Gen. 12:1-25:11
Isaac ....Gen. 21:1-28:9
Gen. 35:27-29
Jacob..........Gen. 25:19-37:36
Gen. 45:21-46:7
Gen. 49:1-33
Joseph.........Gen. 37:1-50:26

C. *Egypt and the Exodus:*
Preparation of
Moses.........Ex. 1:1-7:7
Plagues and
Passover......Ex. 7:8-12:36
From Egypt
to Sinai ....Ex. 12:37-18:27
The Law and
tabernacle ....Ex. 19:1-40:38

D. *Wilderness:*
Spies at
Kadesh ⎰Num. 13:1-
Barnea.......⎱14:38
Fiery
serpents.......Num. 21:4-9
Balak and ⎰Num. 22:1-
Balaam ......⎱24:25

Appointment of
Joshua........Num. 27:18-23
Death of
Moses........Deut. 34:1-8

E. *Conquest and settlement:*
Spies received by
Rahab........Josh. 2:1-21
Crossing
Jordan........Josh. 3:14-17
Fall of
Jericho........Josh. 6:1-27
Southern and central
mountains....Josh. 7:1-11
Victory at
Merom........Josh. 11:1-14
Division of the
land..........Josh. 14:1-21:45

F. *Period of the judges:*
Later
conquests.....Judg. 1:1-2:23
Othniel........Judg. 3:8-11
Ehud........Judg. 3:12-30
Shamgar......Judg. 3:31
Deborah and
Barak........Judg. 4:1-5:31
Gideon........Judg. 6:11-8:35
Abimelech....Judg. 9:1-57
Tola and Jair....Judg. 10:1-5
Jephthah......Judg. 11:1-12:7
Ibzan, Elon, and
Abdon........Judg. 12:8-15
Samson........Judg. 13:1-16:31
Tribal wars....Judg. 17:1-21:25

G. *From Samuel to David:*
Eli and
Samuel........1 Sam. 1:1-4:22
Samuel as
judge..........1 Sam. 5:1-8:22
The first
king..........1 Sam. 9:1-12:25
Battle of ⎰ 1 Sam.
Michmash....⎱ 13:1-14:52
Saul and the
Amalekites....1 Sam. 15:1-35
David chosen..1 Sam. 16:1-13
David and
Goliath........1 Sam. 17:1-58
David in ⎰ 1 Sam.
exile..........⎱ 18:5-31:13

H. *Kingdom united:*
David's reign
at Hebron.....2 Sam. 2:1-4:12
David's
reign at
Jerusalem.....2 Sam. 5:1-10:19
David's sin.....2 Sam. 11:1-25

Absalom's ⎰ 2 Sam.
rebellion......⎱ 15:1-18:33
David's
death..........1 Kin. 2:10-12
Accession of ⎰ 1 Kin. 1:32-53
Solomon ⎱ 1 Chr. 29:20-25
The Temple....1 Kin. 6:1-9:9
2 Chr. 2:1-7:22
Death of ⎰ 1 Kin. 11:41-43
Solomon ⎱ 2 Chr. 9:29-31

I. *Kingdom divided:*
Rebellion of
Israel..........2 Chr. 10:1-19
Rehoboam ⎰ 2 Chr. 10:1-
and Abijah...⎱ 13:22
Jeroboam ⎰ 1 Kin. 12:25-
and ⎱ 14:20
Nadab ⎱ 1 Kin. 15:25-31
Asa............1 Kin. 15:9-24
2 Chr. 14:1-16:14
Baasha, Elah, Zimri and
Omri..........1 Kin. 15:32-16:27

J. *Mutual alliance:*
Ahab and ⎰ 1 Kin.
Elijah........⎱ 16:28-18:19
Contest on Mt.
Carmel......1 Kin. 18:20-40
Ahab and Ben-
Hadad........1 Kin. 20:1-34
Murder of
Naboth........1 Kin. 21:1-29
Revival under
Jehosh- ⎰ 1 Kin. 22:41-50
aphat........⎱ 2 Chr. 17:1-19
Battle of
Ramoth ⎰ 1 Kin. 22:1-40
Gilead ⎱ 2 Chr. 18:1-34
Wars of
Jehosh- ⎰ 2 Chr.
aphat........⎱ 19:1-20:30
Translation of
Elijah..........2 Kin. 2:1-11
Jehoshaphat and
Jehoram......2 Kin. 3:1-27
Ministry of ⎰ 2 Kin. 4:1-6:23
Elisha ⎱ 2 Kin. 8:1-15
Siege of
Samaria.......2 Kin. 6:24-7:20
Death of
Elisha........2 Kin. 13:14-20

K. *Decline of both kingdoms:*
Accession of
Jehu..........2 Kin. 9:1-10:31
Athaliah and ⎰ 2 Kin. 11:1-
Joash........⎱ 12:21

Amaziah and
Jeroboam ....2 Kin. 14:1-29
Captivity of ⎰2 Kin. 15:29
Israel ....⎱2 Kin. 17:1-6
Reign ⎧2 Kin. 18:1–
of ⎪   20:21
Heze- ⎨2 Chr. 29:1–
kiah ....⎩   32:33
Reign of ⎰2 Kin. 21:1-18
Manasseh ....⎱2 Chr. 33:1-20
⎰2 Kin. 22:1–
⎱   23:30
Josiah's ⎰2 Chr. 34:1–
reforms ......⎱   35:27
Captivity ⎰2 Kin. 24:1–
of ⎨   25:30
Judah ....⎩2 Chr. 36:5-21

L. *Captivity:*
Daniel and Nebuchad-
nezzer ....Dan. 1:1-4:37
Belshazzar and
Darius ....Dan. 5:1-6:28
Rebuilding the
Temple ....Ezra 1:1-6:15
Rebuilding
Jerusalem .....Neh. 1:1-6:19
Esther and
Mordecai ......Esth. 2:1-10:3

M. *Ministry of Christ:*
Birth ....⎰Matt. 1:18-25
              ⎱Luke 2:1-20
Childhood .....Luke 2:40-52
Baptism ....⎰Matt. 3:13-17
              ⎱Luke 3:21, 22
Temptation ....⎰Matt. 4:1-11
              ⎱Luke 4:1-13
First miracle...John 2:1-11
With Nico-
demus ....John 3:1-21
The Samaritan
woman.........John 4:5-42
Healing........Luke 4:31-41
Controversy on the
Sabbath ....Luke 6:1-11
Apostles ⎰Mark 3:13-19
chosen.......⎱Luke 6:12-16
Sermon on ⎰Matt. 5:1-7:29
the Mount ...⎱Luke 6:20-49
Raises dead
son ....Luke 7:11-17
Anointed ......Luke 7:36-50
Accused of ⎰Matt. 12:22-37
blasphemy ...⎱Mark 3:19-30
Calms the ⎰Matt. 8:23-27
sea..........⎱Mark 4:35-41
Demoniac ⎰Matt. 8:28-34
healed ......⎱Mark 5:1-20

Daughter of
Jairus ⎰Matt. 9:18-26
healed ....⎱Luke 8:41-56
Feeds 5,000 ....⎰Matt. 14:13-21
              ⎱Mark 6:30-44
Feeds 4,000 ....Matt. 15:32-39
Peter confesses
Jesus is ⎰Matt. 16:5-16
Christ........⎱Mark 8:27-29
Foretells ⎰Matt. 16:21-26
death ....⎱Luke 9:22-25
Transfig- ⎰Matt. 17:1-13
uration.......⎱Luke 9:28-36
Forgiving of
adulteress.....John 7:53-8:11
Resurrection of
Lazarus.......John 11:1-44
Blesses the ⎰Matt. 19:13-15
children......⎱Mark 10:13-16
Bartimaeus ⎰Matt. 20:29-34
healed ....⎱Mark 10:46-52
Meets
Zacchaeus ....Luke 19:1-10
Triumphant ⎰Matt. 21:1-9
entry.........⎱Luke 19:29-44
Anointed ......⎰Matt. 26:6-13
              ⎱Mark 14:3-9
The Passover ..⎰Matt. 26:17-19
              ⎱Luke 22:7-13
The Lord's ⎰Matt. 26:26-29
Supper.......⎱Mark 14:22-25
Gethsemane ...Luke 22:39-46
Betrayal and ⎰Matt. 26:47-56
arrest ....⎱John 18:3-12
Before the ⎰Matt. 26:57-68
Sanhedrin....⎱Luke 22:54-65
Denied by
Peter.........John 18:15-27
Before Pilate...⎰Matt. 27:2-14
              ⎱Luke 23:1-7
Before Herod ..Luke 23:6-12
Returns to ⎰Matt. 27:15-26
Pilate ....⎱Luke 23:13-25
Crucifixion ....⎰Matt. 27:35-56
              ⎱Luke 23:33-49
Burial.........⎰Matt. 27:57-66
              ⎱Luke 23:50-56
Resurrection...⎰Matt. 28:1-15
              ⎱John 20:1-18
Appearance to ⎰Luke 24:36-43
disciples......⎱John 20:19-25
Appearance to
Thomas.......John 20:26-31
Great
commission ...Matt. 28:16-20
Ascension .....Luke 24:50-53

N. *The early church:*
Pentecost......Acts 2:1-42
In Jerusalem...Acts 2:3–6:7
Martyrdom of
Stephen.......Acts 6:8–7:60
In Judea and
Samaria.......Acts 8:1–12:25
Conversion of
Saul ....Acts 9:1-18
First
missionary
journey ....Acts 13:1–14:28
Jerusalem
conference ....Acts 15:1-35
Second missionary
journey ....Acts 15:36–18:22
Third
missionary
journey ....Acts 18:23–21:16
Captivity of
Paul ....Acts 21:27–28:31

Bichri—*firstborn*

Father of Sheba..2 Sam. 20:1

Bidkar—*servant of Kar*

Captain under
Jehu ....2 Kin. 9:25

Bigamist—*having more than one wife*

First, Lamech .....Gen. 4:19

Bigamy (see Marriage)

Bigotry—*excessive prejudice; blind fanaticism*

A. *Characteristics of:*
Name-calling ..John 8:48, 49
Spiritual
blindness......John 9:39-41
Hatred.........Acts 7:54-58
Self-righteous-
ness..........Phil. 3:4-6
Ignorance .....1 Tim. 1:13

B. *Examples of:*
Haman ....Esth. 3:8-10
The
Pharisees .....John 8:33-48
The Jews ......1 Thess. 2:14-16
Saul (Paul) ....Acts 9:1, 2
Peter ....Acts 10:14, 28

See Intolerance; Persecution

Bigtha—*gift of God*

An officer of
Ahasuerus........Esth. 1:10

Bigthan, Bigthana—*gift of God*

Conspired against {Esth. 2:21
Ahasuerus.......{Esth. 6:2

Bigvai—*happy*

1. Zerubbabel's {Ezra 2:2
companion...{Neh. 7:7, 19
2. One who signs
covenant......Neh. 10:16

Bildad—*Bel has loved*

One of Job's
friends ....Job 2:11
Makes {Job 8:1-22
three {Job 18:1-21
speeches ....{Job 25:1-6

Bileam—*greed*

A town of
Manasseh ....1 Chr. 6:70

Bilgah—*brightness, cheerfulness*

1. A descendant of
Aaron.........1 Chr. 24:1, 6, 14
2. A chief of the
priests ....Neh. 12:5, 7, 18
Same as Bilgai; signs
document .....Neh. 10:8

Bilhah—*foolish, simple*

1. Rachel's
maid.........Gen. 29:29
The mother of Dan and
Naphtali .....Gen. 30:1-8
Commits incest with
Reuben ....Gen. 35:22
2. Simeonite
town.........1 Chr. 4:29
Same as
Baalah ....Josh. 15:29

Bilhan—*foolish, simple*

1. A Horite
chief; son of {Gen. 36:27
Ezer ....{1 Chr. 1:42
2. A Benjamite family
head ....1 Chr. 7:10

Bilshan—*searcher*

A postexilic {Ezra 2:2
leader ....{Neh. 7:7

Bimhal—*with pruning*

An Asherite.......1 Chr. 7:33

Bin

For food storage ..1 Kin. 17:12-16

Binding—*a restraint; a tying together*

A. *Used literally of:*
Tying a man...Gen. 22:9
Imprison-   (2 Kin. 17:4
ment.   (Acts 22:4
Ocean's
shores ....Prov. 30:4

B. *Used figuratively of:*
A fixed
agreement ....Num. 30:2
God's Word....Prov. 3:3
The broken-
hearted ......Is. 61:1
Satan..........Luke 13:16
The wicked....Matt. 13:30
Ceremon-
ialism........Matt. 23:4
The keys ......Matt. 16:19
A determined
plan..........Acts 20:22
Marriage.......Rom. 7:2

Binea

A son of Moza ....1 Chr. 8:37

Binnui—*built*

1. Head of postexilic
family........Neh. 7:15
Called Bani ....Ezra 2:10
2. Son of Pahath-
Moab........Ezra 10:30
3. Son of Bani....Ezra 10:38
4. Postexilic
Levite........Neh. 12:8
Henadad's
son ....Neh. 10:9
Family of, builds
wall..........Neh. 3:24

Bird cage

Used
figuratively......Jer. 5:27

Birds—*vertebrates with feathers and wings*

A. *List of:*
Buzzard ......Lev. 11:13
Dove ....Gen. 8:8
Eagle ....Job 39:27
Falcon..........Deut. 14:13
Hawk ....Job 39:26
Hen ....Matt. 23:37
Heron ....Lev. 11:19
Hoopoe......Lev. 11:19
Jackal ......Job 30:29
Kite ....Deut. 14:13

Ostrich ......Job 30:29
Owls..........Lev. 11:16
Desert ....Ps. 102:6
Fisher ......Lev. 11:17
Screech ....Lev. 11:17
Little ....Lev. 11:17
Partridge ....1 Sam. 26:20
Pelican ......Ps. 102:6
Pigeon........Lev. 12:6
Quail ......Num. 11:31, 32
Raven ....Job 38:41
Rooster......Matt. 26:34, 74
Mark 14:30
Luke 22:61
John 18:27
Sparrow ......Matt. 10:29-31
Stork ....Ps. 104:17
Swallow ....Ps. 84:3
Swift ......Jer. 8:7
Turtledove.....Song 2:12
Vulture......Lev. 11:13

B. *Features regarding:*
Created by
God..........Gen. 1:20, 21
Named by
Adam........Gen. 2:19, 20
Clean,
unclean ......Gen. 8:20
Differ from
animals ......1 Cor. 15:39
Under man's
dominion ....Ps. 8:6-8
For food......Gen. 9:2, 3
Belong to
God..........Ps. 50:11
God provides (Ps. 104:10-12
for ....(Luke 12:23, 24
Can be
tamed........James 3:7
Differ in
singing ......Song 2:12
Some
migratory .....Jer. 8:7
Solomon
writes of ......1 Kin. 4:33
Clean,
used in   (Lev. 1:14
sacrifices.....(Luke 2:23, 24
Worshiped by
man ....Rom. 1:23

C. *Figurative of:*
Escape from
evil ....Ps. 124:7
A wanderer....Prov. 27:8
Snares of
death ....Eccl. 9:12
Cruel kings....Is. 46:11

Hostile nations	Jer. 12:9
Wicked rich	Jer. 17:11
Kingdom of heaven	Matt. 13:32
Maternal love	Matt. 23:37

Birsha—*with wickedness*

A king of
Gomorrah ....Gen. 14:2, 8, 10

Birth—*the act of coming into life*

A. *Kinds of:*

Natural	Eccl. 7:1
Figurative	Is. 37:3
Supernatural	Matt. 1:18-25
The new	John 3:5

See New birth

B. *Natural, features regarding:*

Pain of, results from sin	Gen. 3:16
Produces a sinful being	Ps. 51:5
Makes ceremonially unclean	Lev. 12:2, 5 / Luke 2:22
Affliction from	John 9:1
Twins of, differ	Gen. 25:21-23
Sometimes brings death	Gen. 35:16-20
Pain of, forgotten	John 16:21

Birthday—*date of one's birth*

Job and Jeremiah
curse theirs...... { Job 3:1-11 / Jer. 20:14, 15 }

Celebration:

| Pharaoh's | Gen. 40:20 |
| Herod's | Mark 6:21 |

Birthright—*legal rights inherited by birth*

A. *Blessings of:*

Seniority	Gen. 43:33
Double portion	Deut. 21:15-17
Royal succession	2 Chr. 21:3

B. *Loss of:*

Esau's— by sale	Gen. 25:29-34 / Heb. 12:16
Reuben's— as a punishment	Gen. 49:3, 4 / 1 Chr. 5:1, 2
Manasseh's— by Jacob's will	Gen. 48:15-20 / 1 Chr. 5:1, 2
David's brother—by divine will	1 Sam. 16:2-22
Adonijah's—by the Lord	1 Kin. 2:13, 15
Hosah's son's—by his father's will	1 Chr. 26:10

C. *Transferred to:*

Jacob	Gen. 27:6-46
Judah	Gen. 49:8-10
Solomon	1 Chr. 28:5-7

See Firstborn

Births, foretold

A. *Over a short period:*

Ishmael's	Gen. 16:11
Isaac's	Gen. 18:10
Samson's	Judg. 13:3, 24
Samuel's	1 Sam. 1:11, 20
Shunammite's son's	2 Kin. 4:16, 17
John the Baptist's	Luke 1:13

B. *Over a longer period:*

Josiah's	1 Kin. 13:2
Cyrus'	Is. 45:1-4
Christ's	Gen. 3:15 / Mic. 5:1-3

Birzaith—*olive well*

An Asherite......1 Chr. 7:31

Bishlam—*in peace*

A Persian officer ..Ezra 4:7

Bishop—*an overseer; elder*

A. *Qualifications of, given by:*

| Paul | 1 Tim. 3:1-7 |
| Peter, called "elder" | 1 Pet. 5:1-4 |

B. *Office of:*

Same as overseer or elder	Acts 20:17, 28
Several in a church	Acts 20:17, 28 / Phil. 1:1
Follows ordination	Titus 1:5, 7

Held by
Christ.........1 Pet. 2:25

C. *Duties of:*
Oversee the {Acts 20:17,
church....... 28-31
Feed God's
flock.........1 Pet. 5:2
Watch over men's
souls..........Heb. 13:17
Teach ....1 Tim. 5:17

Bit—*a part of a horse's bridle*

Figurative, of man's stubborn
nature............Ps. 32:9
James 3:3

Bithiah—*daughter of Yahweh*

Pharaoh's daughter; wife of
Mered............1 Chr. 4:18

Bithron—*ravine, gorge*

A district east of
Jordan ....2 Sam. 2:29

Bithynia—*a province of Asia Minor*

The Spirit keeps Paul
from ....Acts 16:7
Peter writes to
Christians of .....1 Pet. 1:1

Bitter herbs

Part of Passover {Ex. 12:8
meal ....{Num. 9:11

"Bitter is sweet"

Descriptive of man's
hunger ....Prov. 27:7

Bittern—*a nocturnal member of heron
family*

Sings in desolate
windows ....Zeph. 2:14

Bitter

A. *Used of:*
The soul ....Job 3:20
Words ....Ps. 64:3
Water ....Num. 5:24
Demanding
woman.......Eccl. 7:26
Sin ....Prov. 5:4
Death ....Jer. 31:15

B. *Avoidance of:*
Toward a
wife............Col. 3:19

As contrary to the
truth..........James 3:14

Bitterness—*extreme enmity; sour
temper*

A. *Kinds of:*
The heart......Prov. 14:10
Death ....1 Sam. 15:32

B. *Causes of:*
Childlessness ..1 Sam. 1:5, 10
A foolish son ..Prov. 17:25
Sickness.......Is. 38:17

C. *Avoidance of:*
Toward
others.........Eph. 4:31
As a source of
defilement ....Heb. 12:15

Bitter waters

Made sweet by a
tree ....Ex. 15:23-25
Swallowed by suspected
wife ....Num. 5:11-31

Bizjothjah—*contempt of Yahweh*

A town in south
Judah ....Josh. 15:28

Biztha—*eunuch*

An officer under
Ahasuerus.......Esth. 1:10

Blackness—*destitute of light*

A. *Literally of:*
Hair ....Song 5:11
Horse..........Zech. 6:2
Sky............1 Kin. 18:45
Mountain ......Heb. 12:18
Night..........Prov. 7:9

B. *Figuratively of:*
Hell ....Jude 13

C. *Specifically:*
Let blackness of the
day ....Job 3:5
Clothe heaven
with ....Is. 50:3

Blamelessness—*freedom from fault;
innocency*

A. *Used ritualistically of:*
Priests.........Matt. 12:5
Proper
observance....Luke 1:6
Works, righteous-
ness..........Phil. 3:6

B. *Desirable in:*

Bishops
(elders) ...... { 1 Tim. 3:2
{ Titus 1:6, 7
Deacons .... 1 Tim. 3:10
Widows........ 1 Tim. 5:7

C. *Attainment of:*

Desirable
now.......... Phil. 2:15
At
Christ's { 1 Cor. 1:8
{ 1 Thess. 5:23
return........ { 2 Pet. 3:14

Blasphemy—*cursing God*

A. *Arises out of:*

Pride .... Ps. 73:9, 11
Ezek. 35:12, 13
Hatred.......... Ps. 74:18
Affliction ...... Is. 8:21
Injustice ...... Is. 52:5
Defiance....... Is. 36:15-20
Scepticism..... Ezek. 9:8
Mal. 3:13, 14
Self-
deification.... { Dan. 11:36, 37
{ 2 Thess. 2:4
Unworthy { 2 Sam. 12:13, 14
conduct...... { Rom. 2:24

B. *Instances of:*

Job's wife...... Job 2:9
Shelomith's
son .... Lev. 24:11-16, 23
Sennacherib ... 2 Kin. 19:4, 10,
22
The beast...... { Dan. 7:25
{ Rev. 13:1, 5, 6
The Jews ...... Luke 22:65
Saul of
Tarsus .... 1 Tim. 1:13
Gentiles .... Rom. 1:28-32
Hymenaeus... 1 Tim. 1:20

C. *Those falsely accused of:*

Naboth .... 1 Kin. 21:12, 13
Jesus .... Matt. 9:3
Matt. 26:65
Stephen .... Acts 6:11, 13

D. *Guilt of:*

Punishable by
death .... Lev. 24:11, 16
Christ accused
of............. John 10:33, 36

See Revile

Blasphemy against the Holy Spirit

Attributing Christ's miracles to
Satan .... Matt. 12:22-32
Never forgivable .. Mark 3:28-30

Blasting—*injure severely*

Shows God's
power .... Ex. 15:8
Sent as
judgment........ Amos 4:9
Figurative of
death............ Job 4:9

Blastus—*sprout*

Herod's
chamberlain ...... Acts 12:20

Blemish—*any deformity or injury*

A. *Those without physical:*

Priests......... Lev. 21:17-24
Absalom....... 2 Sam. 14:25
Animals
used in { Lev. 22:19-25
sacrifices..... { Mal. 1:8

B. *Those without moral:*

Christ .... Heb. 9:14
The Church.... Eph. 5:27

C. *Those with:*

Apostates...... 2 Pet. 2:13

Bless—*to bestow blessings upon*

To give divine { Gen. 1:22
blessings .... { Gen. 9:1-7
To adore God for { Gen. 24:48
His blessings .... { Ps. 103:1
To invoke
blessings upon { Gen. 24:60
another .... { Gen. 27:4, 27

Blessed—*the objects of God's favors*

A. *Reasons for, they:*

Are chosen .... Eph. 1:3, 4
Believe .... Gal. 3:9
Are forgiven ... Ps. 32:1, 2
Are justified ... Rom. 4:6-9
Are
instructed..... Ps. 94:12
Keep God's
Word .... Rev. 1:3

B. *Time of:*

Eternal past ... Eph. 1:3, 4
Present .... Luke 6:22
Eternal
future.......... Matt. 25:34

Blessings—*the gift of God's grace*

A. *Physical and temporal:*

Prosperity ..... Mal. 3:10-12
Food, { Matt. 6:26,
clothing...... { 30-33

Sowing,
harvest ......Acts 14:17
Longevity ....Ex. 20:12
Children ......Ps. 127:3-5

B. *National and Israelitish:*
General......Gen. 12:1-3
Specific.......Rom. 9:4, 5
Fulfilled ......Rom. 11:1-36
Perverted ....Rom. 2:17-29
Rejected......Acts 13:46-52

C. *Spiritual and eternal:*
Salvation ......John 3:16
Election ......Eph. 1:3-5
Regen-
eration........2 Cor. 5:17
Forgiveness....Col. 1:14
Adoption ......Rom. 8:15-17
No condem-
nation ....Rom. 8:1
Holy Spirit....Acts 1:8
Justification ...Acts 13:38, 39
New
covenant......Heb. 8:6-13
Fatherly chastise-
ment........Heb. 12:5-11
Christ's
intercession ...Rom. 8:34
Sanctifi-
cation........Rom. 8:3-14
Perse-
verance ......John 10:27-29
Glorification ...Rom. 8:30

Blindfold—*a covering over the eyes*

A prelude to
execution ....Esth. 7:8
Put on Jesus ......Luke 22:63, 64

Blindness—*destitute of vision*

A. *Causes of:*
Old age........Gen. 27:1
Disobedi-
ence ....Deut. 28:28, 29
Miracle ....2 Kin. 6:18-20
Judgment......Gen. 19:1-11
Captivity ......Judg. 16:20, 21
Condition of
servitude ......1 Sam. 11:2
Defeat in
war ....2 Kin. 25:7
Unbelief ......Acts 9:8, 9
God's glory ....John 9:1-3

B. *Disabilities of:*
Keep from
priesthood ......Lev. 21:17, 18

Offerings
unaccept-⎰Lev. 22:22
able..........⎱Mal. 1:8
Make
protection.....Lev. 19:14
Helplessness ...Judg. 16:26
Occasional
derision ......2 Sam. 5:6-8

C. *Remedies for:*
Promised in
Christ..........Is. 42:7, 16
Proclaimed in ⎰Luke 4:18-21
the Gospel ...⎱Acts 26:18
Portrayed in a ⎰John 9:1-41
miracle.......⎱Acts 9:1-18
Perfected in ⎰John 11:37
faith ....⎱Eph. 1:15-19
Perverted by disobedi-
ence ....1 John 2:11

Blood

A. *Used to designate:*
Unity of
mankind ......Acts 17:26
Human
nature ....John 1:13
Human
depravity .....Ezek. 16:6, 22
The individual
soul..........Ezek. 33:8
The essence ⎰Gen. 9:4
of life ....⎱Lev. 17:11, 14
The sacredness of
life ....Gen. 9:5, 6
Means of
atonement ...Lev. 17:10-14
Regen-⎰Is. 4:4
eration......⎱Ezek. 16:9
New
covenant......Matt. 26:28
The new life ...John 6:53-56
Christ's
atonement ....Heb. 9:14
Redemption....Zech. 9:11

B. *Miracles connected with:*
Water turns
to.............Ex. 7:20, 21
Water appears
like ....2 Kin. 3:22, 23
The moon ⎰Acts 2:20
turns to......⎱Rev. 6:12
Flow of,
stops.......Mark 5:25, 29
Sea becomes...Rev. 11:6
Believers become
white in......Rev. 7:14

C. *Figurative of:*

Sin	Is. 59:3
Cruelty	Hab. 2:12
Abomi- nations	Is. 66:3
Inherited guilt	Matt. 23:35
Guilt	2 Sam. 1:16
	Matt. 27:25
Vengeance	Ezek. 35:6
Retribution	Is. 49:25, 26
Slaughter	Is. 34:6-8
Judgment	Rev. 16:6
Victory	Ps. 58:10

Blood of Christ

A. *Described as:*

Innocent	Matt. 27:4
Precious	1 Pet. 1:19
Necessary	Heb. 9:22, 23
Sufficient	Heb. 9:13, 14
Final	Heb. 9:24-28
Cleansing	1 John 1:7
Conquering	Rev. 12:11

B. *Basis of:*

Recon- ciliation	Eph. 2:13-16
Redemption	Rom. 3:24, 25
Justification	Rom. 5:9
Sanctifi- cation	Heb. 10:29
Communion	Matt. 26:26-29
Victory	Rev. 12:11
Eternal life	John 6:53-56

Bloodguiltiness—*guilt incurred by murder*

Incurred by willful murderer	Ex. 21:14
Not saved by altar	1 Kin. 2:29
Provision for innocent	Ex. 21:13
	1 Kin. 1:50-53
David's prayer concerning	Ps. 51:14
Judas' guilt in	Matt. 27:3, 4
The Jews' admission of	Matt. 27:23-25
Of Christ- rejectors	Acts 18:5, 6

Blood-money

Payment made to Judas	Matt. 26:14-16

Bloodthirsty—*Descriptive of:*

Saul's house	2 Sam. 21:1
David	2 Sam. 16:6, 7

Bloody—*Descriptive of:*

Cities	Ezek. 22:2
	Ezek. 24:6, 9

Bloody sweat—*(believed to be caused by agony or stress)*

Agony in Gethsemane	Luke 22:44

Blossom—*to open into blossoms; to flower*

Aaron's rod	Num. 17:5, 8
A fig tree	Hab. 3:17
A desert	Is. 35:1, 2
Israel	Is. 27:6

Blot—*to rub or wipe off*

One's name in God's Book	Ex. 32:32, 33
Legal ordinances	Col. 2:14
One's sins	Ps. 51:1, 9
	Acts 3:19
Amalek	Deut. 25:19
Israel as a nation	2 Kin. 14:27

Blue

Often used in tabernacle	Ex. 25:4
	Ex. 28:15
Used by royalty	Esth. 8:15
Imported	Ezek. 27:7

Blush—*to redden in the cheeks*

Sin makes impossible	Jer. 6:15
	Jer. 8:12

Boanerges—*sons of thunder*

Surname of James and John	Mark 3:17

Boar—*male wild hog*

Descriptive of Israel's enemies	Ps. 80:13

Boasting—*to speak of with pride; to brag*

A. *Excluded because of:*

Man's limited knowledge	Prov. 27:1, 2
Uncertain issues	1 Kin. 20:11
Evil incurred thereby	Luke 12:19-21
	James 3:5

Salvation by
grace ....Eph. 2:9
God's
sovereignty ...Rom. 11:17-21

B. *Examples of:*
Goliath ....1 Sam. 17:44
Ben-Hadad.....1 Kin. 20:10
Rabshakeh ....2 Kin. 18:27, 34
Satan..........Is. 14:12-15
                Ezek. 28:12-19

See Haughtiness; Pride

Boasting in God

Continual duty....Ps. 34:2
Always in the
Lord ....2 Cor. 10:13-18
Necessary to refute the
wayward ....2 Cor. 11:5-33
Of spiritual rather than
natural...........Phil. 3:3-14

Boats

In Christ's time ...Matt. 8:23-27
                    John 6:22, 23
Lifeboats.........Acts 27:30
Ferryboats.........2 Sam. 19:18
Used for fishing ...John 21:3-8

Boaz—*strength*

1. A wealthy Bethehem-
ite ....Ruth 2:1, 4-18
Husband of
Ruth..........Ruth 4:10-13
Ancestor of
Christ.........Matt. 1:5
2. Pillar of
Temple........1 Kin. 7:21

Bocheru—*firstborn*

A son of Azel .....1 Chr. 8:38

Bochim—*weepers*

A place near
Gilgal ....Judg. 2:1-5

Body of Christ

A. *Descriptive of His own body:*
Prepared by
God............Heb. 10:5
Conceived by the Holy
Spirit ......Luke 1:34, 35
Subject to   (Luke 2:40, 52
growth.......(Heb. 5:8, 9
Part of our
nature ....Heb. 2:14
Without sin ....2 Cor. 5:21

Subject to human
emotions......Heb. 5:7
Raised without
corruption ....Acts 2:31
Glorified by
resurrection...Phil. 3:21
Communion
with ....1 Cor. 11:27

B. *Descriptive of the true church:*
Identified ......Col. 1:24
Described ......Eph. 2:16
Christ, the
head of ....Eph. 1:22
Christ
dwells in ......Eph. 1:23

Body of man

A. *By creation:*
Made by God ..Gen. 2:7, 21, 22
Various
organs of .....1 Cor. 12:12-25
Bears God's   (Gen. 9:6
image........(Col. 3:10
Wonderfully
made ....Ps. 139:14

B. *By sin:*
Subject to
death ....Rom. 5:12
Destroyed .....Job 19:26
Instrument of
evil ....Rom. 1:24-32

C. *By salvation:*
A Temple of the Holy
Spirit ....1 Cor. 6:19
A living
sacrifice......Rom. 12:1
Dead to the
Law..........Rom. 7:4
Dead to sin ....Rom. 8:1-4
Control over...Rom. 6:12-23
Christ, the   (Rom. 6:8-11
center of .....(Phil. 1:20, 21
Sins against,
forbidden .....1 Cor. 6:13, 18
Needful
requirements (1 Cor. 7:4
of ....(Col. 2:23

D. *By resurrection, to be:*
Redeemed .....Rom. 8:23
Raised.........John 5:28, 29
Changed.......Phil. 3:21
Glorified......Rom. 8:29, 30
Judged ....2 Cor. 5:10-14
Perfected .....1 Thess. 5:23

E. *Figurative descriptions of:*
House ....2 Cor. 5:1

House of
clay..........Job 4:19
Earthen
vessel........2 Cor. 4:7
Tent...........2 Pet. 1:13
Temple of
God..........1 Cor. 3:16, 17
Members of
Christ........1 Cor. 6:15

Bohan—*thumb*

1. Reuben's son ..Josh. 15:6
2. Border mark...Josh. 18:17

Boil—*an inflamed ulcer*

Sixth Egyptian
plague...........Ex. 9:8-11
A symptom of
leprosy ....Lev. 13:18-20
Satan afflicts Job
with............Job 2:7
Hezekiah's life
endangered by....2 Kin. 20:7, 8

Boiling—*the state of bubbling*

A part of
cooking ....1 Kin. 19:21
Of a child, in
famine ....2 Kin. 6:29

Boldness—*courage; bravery; confidence*

A. *Comes from:*
Righteous-
ness...........Prov. 28:1
Prayer........Eph. 6:18, 19
Fearless
preaching .....Acts 9:26-29
Christ ....Eph. 3:11, 12
Phil. 1:20
Testimony ....Phil. 1:14
Communion with
God...........Heb. 4:16
Perfect love....1 John 4:17

B. *Examples of:*
Tribe of Levi..Ex. 32:26-28
David..........1 Sam. 17:45-49
Three Hebrew
men..........Dan. 3:8-18
Daniel ....Dan. 6:10-23
The apostles ...Acts 4:13-31
Paul ....Acts 9:26-29
Paul,
Barnabas.....Acts 13:46

See Courage; Fearlessness

Bondage, literal

Israel in Egypt ....Ex. 1:7-22

Gibeonites to
Israel...........Josh. 9:17-23
Judah in
Babylon ....2 Kin. 25:1-21
Israel in Assyria ..2 Kin. 17:6, 20,
23
Denied by Jews ...John 8:33

Bondage, spiritual

A. *Subjection to:*
The devil ......2 Tim. 2:26
Sin ....John 8:34
Fear of death ..Heb. 2:14, 15
Death ....Rom. 7:24
Corruption.....2 Pet. 2:19

B. *Deliverance from:*
Promised ......Is. 42:6, 7
Proclaimed ....Luke 4:18, 21
Through
Christ.........John 8:36
By obedience ..Rom. 6:17-19
By the truth ...John 8:32

Bones—*structural parts of the body*

A. *Descriptive of:*
Unity of male and
female ....Gen. 2:23
Physical
being ....Luke 24:39
Family unity...Gen. 29:14
Tribal unity...1 Chr. 11:1

B. *Prophecies concerning:*
The paschal
lamb's........{ Ex. 12:46
{ John 19:36
Jacob's ....Gen. 50:25
Heb. 11:22
Valley of dry...Ezek. 37:1-14

C. *Figurative of health, affected
by:*
Shameful
wife..........Prov. 12:4
Good report ...Prov. 15:30
Broken spirit...Prov. 17:22

Books—*written compositions*

A. *Features of:*
Old ....Job 19:23, 24
Made of papyrus
reeds.........Is. 19:7
Made of
parchment ..2 Tim. 4:13
Made in a
roll...........Jer. 36:2
Written with
ink............3 John 13
Dedicated......Luke 1:3

Sealed .... Rev. 5:1
Many .... Eccl. 12:12
Quotations
in .... Matt. 21:4, 5
Written by
secretary ..... Jer. 36:4, 18

B. *Contents of:*
Genealogies .... Gen. 5:1
Law of
Moses .... Deut. 31:9, 24,
              26
Geography ..... Josh. 18:9
Wars .... Num. 21:14
Records .... Ezra 4:15
Miracles ...... Josh. 10:13
Legislation ... 1 Sam. 10:25
Lamenta-
tions .... 2 Chr. 35:25
Proverbs ...... Prov. 25:1
Prophecies .... Jer. 51:60-64
Symbols ...... Rev. 1:1
The Messiah ... Luke 24:27, 44
              Heb. 10:7

C. *Mentioned but not preserved:*
Book of wars .. Num. 21:14
Book of
Jasher .... Josh. 10:13
Chronicles of
David .... 1 Chr. 27:24
Book of Gad ... 1 Chr. 29:29
Story of prophet
Iddo .... 2 Chr. 13:22
Book of
Nathan .... 1 Chr. 29:29
Book of Jehu .. 2 Chr. 20:34

Book of God's judgment

In visions of
Daniel and   {Dan. 7:10
John .... {Rev. 20:12

Book of the law

Called "the law of
Moses" .... Josh. 8:31, 32
Copied .... Deut. 17:18
Placed in the
ark .... Deut. 31:26
Foundation of Israel's
religion .... Deut. 28:58
Lost and found .... 2 Kin. 22:8
Produces
reformation ...... 2 Kin. 23:2-14
Produces revival .. Neh. 8:2, 8-18
Quoted .... 2 Kin. 14:6
To be   {Josh. 1:7, 8
remembered ..... {Mal. 4:4

Prophetic of
Christ .... Luke 24:27, 44

Book of life

A. *Contains:*
The names of the
saved .... Phil. 4:3
The deed of the
righteous ..... Mal. 3:16-18

B. *Excludes:*
Renegades ..... Ex. 32:33
              Ps. 69:28
Apostates ...... Rev. 13:8
              Rev. 17:8

C. *Affords, basis of:*
Joy .... Luke 10:20
Hope .... Heb. 12:23
Judgment ..... Dan. 7:10
              Rev. 20:12-15

Booths—*stalls made of branches*

Used for cattle .... Gen. 33:17
Required in feast   {Lev. 23:40-43
of tabernacle .... {Neh. 8:14-17

Booty—*spoils taken in war*

A. *Stipulations concerning:*
No
Canaanites .... Deut. 20:14-17
No accursed
thing .... Josh. 6:17-19
Destruction of
Amalek .... 1 Sam. 15:2, 3
Destruction of
Arad .... Num. 21:1-3
The Lord's
judgment ..... Jer. 49:30-32

B. *Division of:*
On percentage
basis .... Num. 31:26-47
Rear troops
share in .... 1 Sam. 30:22-25

Border—*boundary*

A. *Marked by:*
Natural
landmarks .... Josh. 18:16
Rivers .... Josh. 18:19
Neighbor's
landmark ..... Deut. 19:14

B. *Enlargement of:*
By God's
power .... Ex. 34:24
A blessing ..... 1 Chr. 4:10

Born again—*new birth, regeneration*

A. *Necessity of, because of:*
Inability . . . . . . John 3:3, 5
The flesh . . . . . . John 3:6
Deadness . . . . . . Eph. 2:1

B. *Produced by:*
The Holy ⎰ John 3:5, 8
Spirit . . . . . . ⎱ Titus 3:5
The Word of ⎰ James 1:18
God . . . . ⎱ 1 Pet. 1:23
Faith . . . . 1 John 5:1

C. *Results of:*
New
creature . . . . . . 2 Cor. 5:17
Changed life . . Rom. 6:4-11
Holy life . . . . . . 1 John 3:9
Righteous-
ness . . . . 1 John 2:29
Love . . . . 1 John 3:10
Victory . . . . 1 John 5:4

Borrow—*to get by loan*

A. *Regulations regarding:*
From other
nations, ⎰ Deut. 15:6
forbidden . . . . ⎱ Deut. 28:12
Obligation to
repay . . . . Ex. 22:14, 15
Non-payment,
wicked . . . . Ps. 37:21
Involves
servitude . . . . . . Prov. 22:7
Evils of,
corrected . . . . . Neh. 5:1-13
Christ's
words on . . . . . Matt. 5:42

B. *Examples of:*
Jewels . . . . Ex. 11:2
A widow's
vessels . . . . . . 2 Kin. 4:3
A woodsman's
ax . . . . 2 Kin. 6:5
Christ's transpor-
tation . . . . Matt. 21:2, 3

Bosom—*the breast as center of affections*

A. *Expressive of:*
Prostitution . . . . Prov. 6:26, 27
Anger . . . . Eccl. 7:9
Protection . . . . . Is. 40:11
Iniquity . . . . Job 31:33

B. *Symbolic of:*
Man's
impatience . . . . Ps. 74:11
Christ's deity . . John 1:18

Eternal
peace . . . . Luke 16:22, 23

Bottle—*a hollow thing* (vessel)

A. *Used for:*
Milk . . . . Judg. 4:19
Water . . . . Gen. 21:14
Wine . . . . Hab. 2:15

B. *Made of:*
Clay . . . . Jer. 19:1, 10, 11
Skins . . . . Matt. 9:17
Mark 2:22

C. *Figurative of:*
God's remem-
brance . . . . Ps. 56:8
God's
judgments . . . Jer. 13:12-14
Sorrow . . . . Ps. 119:83
Impatience . . . . Job 32:19
Clouds of
rain . . . . Job 38:37
Old and new
covenants . . . . . Matt. 9:17

Bottomless pit

Apollyon,
king of . . . . Rev. 9:11
Beast comes ⎰ Rev. 11:7
from . . . . ⎱ Rev. 17:8
Devil, cast into . . . . Rev. 20:1-3
A prison . . . . Rev. 20:7

Bough—*branch of a tree*

A. *Used:*
To make ceremonial
booths . . . . Lev. 23:39-43
In siege of
Shechem . . . . . . Judg. 9:45-49

B. *Figurative of:*
Joseph's
offspring . . . . . Gen. 49:22
Judgment . . . . . . Is. 17:1-11
Israel . . . . Ps. 80:8-11

Bow—*an instrument for shooting arrows*

A. *Uses of:*
For hunting . . . . Gen. 27:3
For war . . . . Is. 7:24
As a token of
friendship . . . . . 1 Sam. 18:4
As a commemorative
song . . . . 2 Sam. 1:18

B. *Illustrative of:*
Strength . . . . Job 29:20
The tongue . . . . Ps. 11:2

Defeat . . . . Hos. 1:5
Peace . . . . Hos. 2:18, 19

Bowing, Bowing the knee

A. *Wrong:*
Before idols . . . . Ex. 20:5
In mockery . . . . Matt. 27:29
Before an
angel . . . . Rev. 22:8, 9

B. *True, in:*
Prayer . . . . 1 Kin. 8:54
Homage . . . . . . 2 Kin. 1:13
Repentance . . . . Ezra 9:5, 6
Worship . . . . . . Ps. 95:6
Submission . . . . Eph. 3:14
Phil. 2:10

Bowl—*a vessel*

Full of incense . . . . Rev. 5:8
Filled with God's
wrath . . . . Rev. 16:1-17

Box tree—*an evergreen tree*

Descriptive of messianic
times . . . . Is. 41:19, 20

Boy—*male child*

Esau and Jacob . . . Gen. 25:27
Payment for a
harlot . . . . Joel 3:3
Play in streets . . . . . Zech. 8:5

See Children; Young men

Bozez—*shining*

Rock of
Michmash . . . . 1 Sam. 14:4, 5

Bozkath—*height*

A town in south
Judah . . . . Josh. 15:39
Home of
Jedidah . . . . 2 Kin. 22:1

Bozrah—*fortress; sheepfold*

1. City of Edom . . Gen. 36:33
Destruction of,
foretold . . . . . . Amos 1:12
Figurative, of Messiah's
victory . . . . Is. 63:1
2. City of Moab . . Jer. 48:24

Bracelet—*ornament*

Worn by both
sexes . . . . Ezek. 16:11
Given to
Rebekah . . . . Gen. 24:22

Worn by King
Saul . . . . 2 Sam. 1:10
A sign of
worldliness . . . . . . Is. 3:19

Braided hair

Contrasted to spiritual
adornment . . . . 1 Tim. 2:9, 10

Bramble—*a thorny bush*

Emblem of a
tyrant . . . . Judg. 9:8-15
Symbol of
destruction . . . . . . Is. 34:13

Branch—*a limb*

A. *Used naturally of:*
Limbs of tree . . Num. 13:23

B. *Used figuratively of:*
Israel . . . . Rom. 11:16, 21
The Messiah . . . Is. 11:1
Christians . . . . . John 15:5, 6
Adversity . . . . . . Job 15:32
Nebuchadnezzar's
kingdom . . . . . . Dan. 4:10-12

Brass—*an alloy of copper and zinc* (tin)

Used of:
Christ's glory . . Rev. 1:15

Bravery, moral

Condemning sin . . . 2 Sam. 12:1-14
Denouncing
hypocrisy . . . . Matt. 23:1-39
Opposing
enemies . . . . Phil. 1:28
Exposing
inconsistency . . . . . Gal. 2:11-15
Uncovering false
teachers . . . . 2 Pet. 2:1-22
Rebuking
Christians . . . . . . {1 Cor. 6:1-8
{James 4:1-11

Breach—*a break*

Used figuratively of:
Sin . . . . Is. 30:13

Bread—*food*

A. *God's provision for:*
Earned by
sweat . . . . Gen. 3:19
Object of
prayer . . . . Matt. 6:11
Without work,
condemned . . . 2 Thess. 3:8, 12
A gift . . . . Ruth 1:6
2 Cor. 9:10

B. *Uses of unleavened, for:*
Heavenly
visitors........Gen. 19:3
The Passover ..Ex. 12:8
Priests.........2 Kin. 23:9
Nazarites ......Num. 6:13, 15
Lord's
Supper........Luke 22:7-19

C. *Special uses of:*
Provided by
ravens ....1 Kin. 17:6
Strength........1 Kin. 19:6-8
Satan's ....Matt. 4:3
Miracle ....Matt. 14:19-21
Insight ....Luke 24:35

D. *Figurative of:*
Adversity......Is. 30:20
Christ ....John 6:33-35
Christ's
death ....1 Cor. 11:23-28
Communion ⎰Acts 2:46
with Christ...⎱1 Cor. 10:17
Extreme
poverty ....Ps. 37:25
Heavenly
food ....Ps. 78:24
Prodigality.....Ezek. 16:49
Wickedness....Prov. 4:17
Idleness ......Prov. 31:27

E. *Bread of life:*
Christ is ....John 6:32-35
Same as
manna........Ex. 16:4, 5
Fulfilled in Lord's
Supper........1 Cor. 11:23, 24

Breaking of bread—*a meal*

Prayer before .....Matt. 14:19
Insight through ...Luke 24:35
Fellowship
thereby..........Acts 2:42
Strength
gained by ....Acts 20:11

See Lord's Supper

Breastplate—*protection*

A. *Worn by:*
High priest ....Ex. 28:4, 15-20
"Locusts"......Rev. 9:7, 9

B. *Figurative of:*
Christ's righteous-
ness...........Is. 59:17
Faith's righteous-
ness..........Eph. 6:14

Breasts—*the female teats*

A. *Literally of:*
Married ⎰Prov. 5:19
love..........⎱Song 1:13
An infant's ⎰Job 3:12
life...........⎱Ps. 22:9
Posterity.......Gen. 49:25

B. *Figuratively, of:*
Mother
Jerusalem.....Is. 66:10, 11

Breath

Comes from
God ....Gen. 2:7
Necessary for all ..Eccl. 3:19
Held by God ....Dan. 5:23
Taken by God.....Ps. 104:29
Figurative, of new
life ....Ezek. 37:5-10

Breath of God

Cause of:
Life............Job 33:4
Destruction....2 Sam. 22:16
Is. 11:4
Death ....Job 4:9

Brevity of human life

A. *Compared to:*
Pilgrimage.....Gen. 47:9
A sigh ....Ps. 90:9
Sleep ....Ps. 90:5
Flower.........Job 14:2
Grass..........1 Pet. 1:24
Vapor ....James 4:14
Shadow........Eccl. 6:12
Moment.......2 Cor. 4:17
A weaver's
shuttle........Job 7:6

B. *Truths arising from:*
Prayer can
prolong ....Is. 38:2-5
Incentive to improve-
ment..........Ps. 90:12
Some kept from old
age ....1 Sam. 2:32, 33
Some know their
end ....2 Pet. 1:13, 14
Hope
regarding .....Phil. 1:21-25
Life's
completion....2 Tim. 4:6-8

Bribery—*gifts to pervert*

A. *The effects of:*

Makes
sinners........Ps. 26:10

Corrupts
conscience ....Ex. 23:8

Perverts
justice........Is. 1:23

Brings chaos...Amos 5:12

Merits
punishment ...Amos 2:6

B. *Examples of:*

Balak..........Num. 22:17, 18, 37

Delilah ....Judg. 16:4, 5

Samuel's
sons..........1 Sam. 8:3

Ben-Hadad.....1 Kin. 15:18, 19

Shemaiah......Neh. 6:10-13

Haman ....Esth. 3:8, 9

Judas and
priests.......Matt. 27:3-9

Soldiers........Matt. 28:12-15

Simon ....Acts 8:18

Felix..........Acts 24:25, 26

Brick—*baked clay*

Babel built of .....Gen. 11:3

Israel forced to
make..........Ex. 1:14

Altars made of ....Is. 65:3

Forts made of.....Is. 9:10

Bridal

Gift:

A burned city .....1 Kin. 9:16

Veil:

Rebekah wears
first ....Gen. 26:64-67

Bride—*newly wed woman*

Wears
adornments ......Is. 61:10

Receives
presents ....Gen. 24:53

Has damsels.......Gen. 24:59, 61

Adorned for
husband..........Rev. 19:7, 8

Husband
rejoices..........Is. 62:5

Stands near
husband..........Ps. 45:9

Receives
benediction.......Ruth 4:11, 12

Must forget father's
house ....Ruth 1:8-17

Must be chaste....2 Cor. 11:2

Figurative of
Israel............Ezek. 16:8-14

Figurative of
Church...........Rev. 21:2, 9

Bridegroom—*newly wed man*

Wears special
garments.........Is. 61:10

Attended by
friends..........John 3:29

Rejoices over
bride ....Is. 62:5

Returns with
bride ....Matt. 25:1-6

Exempted from military
service ....Deut. 24:5

Figurative of
God ....Ezek. 16:8-14

Figurative of
Christ............John 3:29

Bridle—*a harness*

A. *Used literally of:*
An ass...........Prov. 26:3

B. *Used figuratively of:*
God's control . .Is. 30:28
Self-control....James 1:26
Imposed
control........Ps. 32:9

Briers—*thorny shrub*

A. *Used literally of:*
Thorns ....Judg. 8:7, 16

B. *Used figuratively of:*
Sinful nature ..Mic. 7:4
Change of
nature ....Is. 55:13
Rejection ......Is. 5:6

Brimstone—*sulphur*

Falls upon
Sodom ....Gen. 19:24

Sent as
judgment........Deut. 29:23

State of wicked ...Ps. 11:6

Condition of hell . .Rev. 14:10

Broiled fish

Eaten by Jesus....Luke 24:42, 43

Broken-handed

Disqualifies for
priesthood.......Lev. 21:19

Brokenhearted—*grieving*

Christ's
mission to........Is. 61:1

Bronze—an alloy of copper and tin

A. *Used for:*
Tabernacle
vessels . . . . Ex. 38:2-31
Temple
vessels . . . . 1 Kin. 7:41-46
Armor . . . . 2 Chr. 12:10
Mirrors, etc. . . . Ex. 38:8
Is. 45:2

B. *Workers in:*
Tubal-Cain . . . . Gen. 4:22
Hiram . . . . 1 Kin. 7:14

C. *Figurative of:*
Grecian
Empire . . . . Dan. 2:39
Obstinate
sinners . . . . Is. 48:4
Endurance . . . . . Jer. 15:20
God's
decrees . . . . . . Zech. 6:1
Christ's glory . . Dan. 10:6

Bronze serpent

Occasion of ruin . . 2 Kin. 18:4

Brooks—streams

A. *Characteristics of:*
Numerous . . . . . Deut. 8:7
Produce
grass . . . . 1 Kin. 18:5
Abound in
fish . . . . Is. 19:8
Afford
protection . . . . . Is. 19:6

B. *Names of:*
Arnon . . . . . . Num. 21:14, 15
Besor . . . . 1 Sam. 30:9
Gaash . . . . 2 Sam. 23:30
Cherith . . . . . . 1 Kin. 17:3, 5
Kidron . . . . 2 Sam. 15:23
Kishon . . . . Ps. 83:9

C. *Figurative of:*
Wisdom . . . . . . Prov. 18:4
Prosperity . . . . Job 20:17
Deception . . . . Job 6:15
Refreshment . . . Ps. 110:7

Broth—thin, watery soup

Served by
Gideon . . . . Judg. 6:19, 20
Figurative of
evil . . . . Is. 65:4

Brother, brethren

A. *Used naturally of:*
Sons of same
parents . . . . Gen. 42:4
Common
ancestry . . . . . . Gen. 14:12-16
Same race . . . . . Deut. 23:7
Same
humanity . . . . . Gen. 9:5

B. *Used figuratively of:*
An ally . . . . Amos 1:9
Christian
disciples . . . . Matt. 23:8
A spiritual
companion . . . . 1 Cor. 1:1

C. *Characteristics of Christian
brothers:*
One Father . . . . Matt. 23:8, 9
Believe . . . . Luke 8:21
Some weak . . . . 1 Cor. 8:11-13
In need . . . . James 2:15
Of low
degree . . . . James 1:9
Disorderly . . . . 2 Thess. 3:6
Evil . . . . James 4:11
Falsely judge . . Rom. 14:10-21
Need admon-
ishment . . . . . . 2 Thess. 3:15

Brotherhood of man

A. *Based on common:*
Creation . . . . . . Gen. 1:27, 28
Blood . . . . Acts 17:26
Needs . . . . Prov. 22:2
Mal. 2:10

B. *Disrupted by:*
Sin . . . . 1 John 3:12
Satan . . . . John 8:44

Brotherly kindness (love)

A. *Toward Christians:*
Taught by
God . . . . 1 Thess. 4:9
Commanded . . . Rom. 12:10
Explained . . . . . . 1 John 4:7-21
Fulfills the
Law . . . . Rom. 13:8-10
Badge of new
birth . . . . John 13:34
A Christian
grace . . . . 2 Pet. 1:5-7
Must
continue . . . . . . Heb. 13:1

B. *Toward others:*
Neighbors . . . . . Matt. 22:39
Enemies . . . . . . Matt. 5:44

Brothers (brethren) of Christ

Four: James,
Joses, Simon, ⎰Matt. 13:55
Judas (Jude).....⎱Mark 6:3
Born after ⎰Matt. 1:25
Christ ....⎱Luke 2:7
Travel with
Mary...........Matt. 12:47-50
Disbelieve
Christ ....John 7:4, 5
Become
believers ....Acts 1:14
Work for Christ...1 Cor. 9:5
One (James) becomes
prominent........Acts 12:17
Wrote an epistle ..James 1:1
Another (Jude) wrote an
epistle.........Jude

Brothers, Twin

Figureheads on Paul's ship to
Rome, called Castor and
Pollux...........Acts 28:11

Brought up—reared

Ephraim's children—by
Joseph ....Gen. 50:23
Esther—by
Mordecai........Esth. 2:5-7, 20
Jesus—at
Nazareth ....Luke 4:16
Paul—at Gamaliel's
feet ....Acts 22:3

Brow

The forehead......Is. 48:4
Top of hill ....Luke 4:29

Bruised—injured

A. *Used literally of:*
Physical
injuries ......Luke 9:39

B. *Used figuratively of:*
Evils...........Is. 1:6
The Messiah's
pains..........Is. 53:5
Satan's ⎰Gen. 3:15
defeat ....⎱Rom. 16:20

Bucket—container for water

Figurative of
blessing ....Num. 24:7
Pictures God's
magnitude........Is. 40:15

Buffet—to strike

Descriptive of
Paul.............2 Cor. 12:7

Build—construct or erect

A. *Used literally, of:*
City ....Gen. 4:17
Altar ....Gen. 8:20
Tower ....Gen. 11:4
House ....Gen. 33:17
Sheepfolds.....Num. 32:16
Fortifica- ⎰Deut. 20:20
tions........⎱Ezek. 4:2
Temple ......⎰1 Kin. 6:1, 14
   ⎱Ezra 4:1
High place.....1 Kin. 11:7
Walls.........Neh. 4:6
Tombs........Matt. 23:29
   Luke 11:47
Synagogue.....Luke 7:2-5

B. *Used figuratively, of:*
Obeying
Christ........Matt. 7:24-27
Church........Matt. 16:18
Christ's res- ⎰Matt. 26:61
urrection.....⎱John 2:19-21
Return to
legalism.......Gal. 2:16-20
Christian
unity.........Eph. 2:19-22
   ⎰Acts 20:32
Spiritual ⎰Col. 2:7
growth.........⎱1 Pet. 2:5

See Edification

Bukki

1. Danite chief ...Num. 34:22
2. A descendant of
Aaron........1 Chr. 6:5, 51

Bukkiah—proved of Yahweh

A Levite
musician ....1 Chr. 25:4, 13

Bul—growth

Eighth Hebrew
month...........1 Kin. 6:38

Bull—male of any bovine animal

Used in
sacrifices ....Heb. 9:13
Blood of,
insufficient ....Heb. 10:4
Symbol of evil
men.............Ps. 22:12
Symbol of mighty
men.............Ps. 68:30
Restrictions on....Deut. 15:19, 20
Sacrifices of,
inadequate ....Ps. 69:30, 31
Blood of,
unacceptable .....Is. 1:11

Figurative of the Lord's
sacrifice . . . . Is. 34:6, 7
Figurative of
strength . . . . Deut. 33:17

Bullock—*young bull*

Used in
sacrifices . . . . Ex. 29:1, 10-14
Figurative of the Lord's
sacrifice . . . . Is. 34:6, 7

Bulrush—*a reed*

Used in Moses'
ark . . . . Ex. 2:3
Found in river
banks . . . . Job 8:11
Figurative of
judgment . . . . Is. 9:14

See Papyrus; Rush

Bulwark—*defensive wall*

Around
Jerusalem . . . . Ps. 48:13
Used in wars . . . . . . Eccl. 9:14

Bunah—*intelligence*

A descendant of
Judah . . . . 1 Chr. 2:25

Bunni—*erected*

1. A preexilic
Levite . . . . Neh. 11:15
2. A postexilic
Levite . . . . Neh. 9:4
3. Signer of
document . . . . . Neh. 10:15

Burden—*load*

A. *Used physically of:*
Load, cargo . . . . Neh. 4:17
B. *Used figuratively of:*
Care . . . . Ps. 55:22
Prophet's
message . . . . . . Hab. 1:1
Rules, rites . . . . Luke 11:46
Sin . . . . Ps. 38:4
Responsi-
bility . . . . Gal. 6:2, 5
Christ's law . . . . Matt. 11:30

Burden-bearer

Christ is the
believer's . . . . Ps. 55:22

Burial

A. *Features regarding:*
Body washed . . Acts 9:37

Ointment
used . . . . Matt. 26:12
Embalm
sometimes . . . . Gen. 50:26
Body
wrapped . . . . . . John 11:44
Placed in
coffin . . . . Gen. 50:26
Carried on a
bier . . . . Luke 7:14
Mourners
attend . . . . John 11:19
Graves
provided . . . . . Gen. 23:5-20
Tombs
erected . . . . Matt. 23:27-29

B. *Places of:*
Abraham and
Sarah . . . . Gen. 25:7-10
Deborah . . . . . . Gen. 35:8
Rachel . . . . Gen. 35:19, 20
Miriam . . . . Num. 20:1
Moses . . . . Deut. 34:5, 6
Gideon . . . . Judg. 8:32
Samson and
Manoah . . . . . . Judg. 16:30, 31
Saul and his
sons . . . . { 1 Sam. 31:12,
13
David . . . . 1 Kin. 2:10
Joab . . . . 1 Kin. 2:33, 34
Solomon . . . . . . 1 Kin. 11:43
Rehoboam . . . . 1 Kin. 14:31
Asa . . . . 1 Kin. 15:24
Manasseh . . . . . 2 Kin. 21:18
Amon . . . . 2 Kin. 21:23-26
Josiah . . . . 2 Chr. 35:23, 24
Jesus . . . . Luke 23:50-53
Lazarus . . . . John 11:14, 38

Buried alive

Two rebellious
families . . . . Num. 16:27-34
Desire of some . . . . Rev. 6:15, 16

Burning bush

God speaks
from . . . . Ex. 3:2

Business—*one's work*

A. *Attitudes toward:*
See God's
hand . . . . James 4:13
Be diligent . . . . . Prov. 22:29
Be
industrious . . . . Rom. 12:8, 11
Be honest . . . . . . 2 Cor. 8:20-22
Put God's
first . . . . Matt. 6:33, 34

Keep heaven in
mind.........Matt. 6:19-21
Give portion...Mal. 3:8-12
Avoid
anxiety......Luke 12:22-30
Remember the
fool..........Luke 12:15-21

B. *Those diligent in:*
Joseph.........Gen. 39:11
Moses.........Heb. 3:5
Workers in
Israel.........2 Chr. 34:11, 12
Daniel.........Dan. 6:4
Mordecai......Esth. 10:2, 3
Paul...........Acts 20:17-35

Busybodies—*meddlers*

Women
guilty of..........1 Tim. 5:13
Some ⎰ 2 Thess. 3:11,
Christians ⎱ 12
Admonitions
against..........1 Pet. 4:15

See Slander; Whisperer

Butler—*an officer*

Imprisonment of
Pharaoh's........Gen. 40:1-13
Same as
"cupbearer"......1 Kin. 10:5

Butter—*curdled milk*

Set before
visitors..........Gen. 18:8
Got by churning..Prov. 30:33
Figurative of smooth
words...........Ps. 55:21

See Curds

Buz—*contempt*

1. A Gadite.......1 Chr. 5:14
2. An Aramean tribe descending
from Nahor...Gen. 22:20, 21

Buzi—*descendant of Buz*

Father of
Ezekiel..........Ezek. 1:3

Buzite—*belonging to Buz*

Of the tribe of
Buz.............Job 32:2

Buzzard

Unclean bird......Lev. 11:13

Byway—*winding or secluded path*

Used by
travelers..........Judg. 5:6

Byword—*saying; remark*

Predicted as a
taunt............Deut. 28:37
Job describes
himself..........Job 17:6

C

Cabbon—*surround*

Village of Judah...Josh. 15:40

Cabul—*unproductive*

1. Town of
Asher........Josh. 19:27
2. A district of Galilee offered to
Hiram.........1 Kin. 9:12, 13
Solomon placed people
in.............2 Chr. 8:2

Caesar—*a title of Roman emperors*

A. *Used in reference to:*

1. Augustus Caesar (31 B.C.–A.D.
14) Decree of brings Joseph
and Mary to
Bethlehem....Luke 2:1
2. Tiberius Caesar (A.D. 14–37)
Christ's ministry dated
by ....Luke 3:1-23
Tribute paid
to............Matt. 22:17-21
Jews side
with.........John 19:12
3. Claudius Caesar (A.D. 41–54)
Famine in time
of............Acts 11:28
Banished Jews from
Rome........Acts 18:2
4. Nero Caesar (A.D. 54–68) Paul
appealed to ...Acts 25:8-12
Converts in household
of............Phil. 4:22
Paul before ....2 Tim. 4:16-18
Called
Augustus .....Acts 25:21

B. *Represented Roman authority*
Image ⎰ Matt. 22:19-21
on ⎱ Mark 12:15, 16
coins........ Luke 20:24
Received tax..Matt. 22:19, 21
Mark 12:14, 17
Luke 20:25
Jesus called ⎰ Luke 23:2
threat to .....⎱ John 19:12
Pilate's loyalty to
questioned ...John 19:12

Chosen over
Jesus.........John 19:12

Caesar's household—*the imperial staff*

Greeted the
Philippians ....Phil. 4:22

Caesarea—*pertaining to Caesar*

Home of Philip....Acts 8:40
                  Acts 21:8
Roman capital of { Acts 12:19
Palestine ....{ Acts 23:33
Home of
Cornelius.........Acts 10:1, 24, 25
Peter
preached at ......Acts 10:34-43
Paul
escorted to ......Acts 23:23, 33
Paul
imprisoned at.....Acts 25:4
Paul appealed to
Caesar at.........Acts 25:8-13
Paul preached here three
times..............Acts 9:26-30
                Acts 18:22
                Acts 21:8

Caesarea Philippi

A city in north Palestine; scene of
Peter's great
confession.......Matt. 16:13-20
Probable place of the
transfiguration ...Matt. 17:1-13

Cage—*an enclosure*

Judah
compared to.....Jer. 5:27
Figurative of
captivity ....Ezek. 19:9
Babylon called ....Rev. 18:2

Caiaphas—*depression*

Son-in-law of Annas; high
priest.............John 18:13
Makes prophecy ..John 11:49-52
Jesus before ......John 18:23, 24
Apostles before ...Acts 4:1-22

Cain—*smith, spear*

Adam's son ....Gen. 4:1
Offering   { Gen. 4:2-7
rejected ....{ Heb. 11:4
Was of the wicked
one...............1 John 3:12
Murders Abel .....Gen. 4:8
Becomes a
vagabond........Gen. 4:9-15

Builds city ....Gen. 4:16, 17
A type of evil .....Jude 11

Cainan—*fixed*

1. A son of
Arphaxad ....Luke 3:36
2. A son
of   { Gen. 5:9-14
         { 1 Chr. 1:1, 2
Enosh........{ Luke 3:37, 38

Cake—*a bread*

A. *Kinds of:*
Unleavened....Num. 6:19
Fig ....1 Sam. 30:12
Raisin ....1 Chr. 16:3
Barley ....Ezek. 4:12
Of fine flour ...Lev. 2:4
Baked with   { Ex. 29:23
oil ....{ Num. 11:8

B. *Used literally of:*
Food ....2 Sam. 13:6
Idolatry........Jer. 44:19
Food prepared for
Elijah ....1 Kin. 17:13

C. *Used figuratively of:*
Defeat.........Judg. 7:13
Weak
religion ....Hos. 7:8

Calah

A great city of Assyria built by
Nimrod..........Gen. 10:11, 12

Calamities—*disasters*

A. *Kinds of:*
Personal ......Job 6:2
Tribal.........Judg. 20:34-48
National ......Lam. 1:1-22
Punitive ......Num. 16:12-35
Judicial ....Deut. 32:35
Worldwide....Luke 21:25-28
Sudden ......Prov. 6:15
             1 Thess. 5:3

B. *Attitudes toward:*
Unrepen-
tance ....Prov. 1:24-26
Repentance....Jer. 18:8
Hardness of
heart..........Ex. 14:8, 17
Bitterness......Ruth 1:20, 21
Defeat........1 Sam. 4:15-18
Submission ...Job 2:9, 10
Prayer-
fulness........Ps. 141:5
Hopefulness ...Ps. 27:1-3

Calamus—*the sweet cane*

Figurative of
love .... Song 4:14
Rendered "sweet
cane" .... Jer. 6:20

Calcol, Chalcol

A son of Zerah .... 1 Chr. 2:6
Famous for
wisdom .... 1 Kin. 4:31

Caldron—*a large kettle*

A. *Used literally of:*
Temple
vessels .... 2 Chr. 35:13

B. *Used figuratively of:*
Safety .... Ezek. 11:3, 7, 11
Oppression .... Mic. 3:3

Caleb—*dog; also bold*

1. Son of
Jephunneh .... Josh. 15:13
Sent as spy .... Num. 13:2, 6
Gave good
report ..... Num. 13:27, 30
His life saved .. Num. 14:5-12
Told to divide
Canaan .... Num. 34:17, 19
Entered
Canaan .... Num. 14:24-38
Eighty-five at end of
conquest ...... Josh. 14:6-13
Given   ⎰ Josh. 14:14, 15
Hebron   ⎱ Josh. 15:13-16
Gave daughter to
Othniel ...... Judg. 1:12-15
Descendants
of .... 1 Chr. 4:15
2. Son of
Hezron .... 1 Chr. 2:18, 42

Caleb Ephratah

Hezron died at .... 1 Chr. 2:24

Calendar—*a system of dating*

Year divided ...... 1 Chr. 27:1-15
Determined by
moon .... Ps. 104:19

See Jewish calendar

Calf—*the young of a cow*

A. *Characteristics of:*
Playfulness
of .... Ps. 29:6
Used for
food .... Amos 6:4

A delicacy ..... Luke 15:23, 27
In sacrifice .... Lev. 9:2, 3
Redeemed, if
firstborn ..... Num. 18:17

B. *Figurative of:*
Saints
sanctified ..... Mal. 4:2
Nimbleness ... Ezek. 1:7

Calf, Calves of Gold

A. *Making of:*
Inspired by Moses'
delay .... Ex. 32:1-4
Repeated by
Jeroboam ..... 1 Kin. 12:25-28
To represent
God .... Ex. 32:4, 5
To replace Temple
worship .... 1 Kin. 12:26, 27
Priests appointed
for .... 1 Kin. 12:31
Sacrifices   ⎰ Ex. 32:6
offered to .... ⎱ 1 Kin. 12:32, 33

B. *Sin of:*
Immorality ... 1 Cor. 10:6-8
Great .... Ex. 32:21, 30, 31
An apostasy ... Ex. 32:8
Wrathful ...... Deut. 9:14-20
Brings
punishment ... Ex. 32:26-29, 35
Repeated by   ⎰ Hos. 1:1
Jeroboam .... ⎱ Hos. 8:5, 6

Call

To:

Name .... Gen. 1:5
Pray .... Gen. 4:26
Be in reality .... Luke 1:35
Set in office ...... Ex. 31:2
                    Is. 22:20
Give privileges .... Luke 14:16, 17
Offer salvation .... Matt. 9:13
Engage in work .. 1 Cor. 7:20

Calling—*one's vocation*

Faith and one's ... 1 Cor. 7:20-22

Calling, the Christian

A. *Manifested through:*
Christ .... Matt. 9:13
Holy Spirit ..... Rev. 22:17
Gospel .... 2 Thess. 2:14

B. *Described as:*
Heavenly ...... Heb. 3:1
Holy .... 2 Tim. 1:9
High .... Phil. 3:14

Irrevocable ....Rom. 11:29
By grace.......Gal. 1:15
                  2 Tim. 1:9
According to God's
  purpose.......2 Tim. 1:9

C. *Goals of:*
  Fellowship with
  Christ.........1 Cor. 1:9
  Holiness.......1 Thess. 4:7
  Liberty........Gal. 5:13
  Peace..........1 Cor. 7:15
  Glory and
  virtue.........2 Pet. 1:3
  Eternal glory ..2 Thess. 2:14
  Eternal life ...1 Tim. 6:12

D. *Attitudes toward:*
  Walk worthy
  of............Eph. 4:1
  Make it sure ...2 Pet. 1:10
  Of Gentiles ...Eph. 4:17-19

Calneh—*fort of Ana*

1. Nimrod's city ..Gen. 10:9, 10
2. A city linked with Hamath and
   Gath..........Amos 6:2
   Same as
   Calno.........Is. 10:9

Calvary—*from the Latin "calvaria"*
(skull)

Christ was crucified
  there.............Luke 23:33
Same as "Golgotha" in
  Hebrew.........John 19:17

Camel—*humpbacked animal*

A. *Used for:*
  Riding.........Gen. 24:61, 64
  Trade..........Gen. 37:25
  War............Judg. 7:12
  Hair of, for
  clothing.......Matt. 3:4
  Used for garment worn by John
  the Baptist ....Matt. 3:4
  Wealth.........Job 42:12

B. *Features of:*
  Docile.........Gen. 24:11
  Unclean........Lev. 11:4
  Adorned........Judg. 8:21, 26
  Prize for
  booty.........Job 1:17
  Treated well ...Gen. 24:31, 32
  Illustrative of the
  impossible.....Matt. 19:24

Camon—*elevation*

Jair was buried
  there.............Judg. 10:5

Camp—*to pitch a tent; take residence*

A. *The Lord's guidance of, by:*
  An angel ......Ex. 14:19
                  Ex. 32:34
  His presence...Ex. 33:14
  A cloud........Ps. 105:39

B. *Israel's:*
  On leaving
  Egypt.........Ex. 13:20
  At Sinai.......Ex. 18:5
  Orderly........Num. 2:2-34
  Tabernacle in
  center of......Num. 2:17
  Exclusion of:
  Unclean ......Deut. 23:10-12
  Lepers.........Lev. 13:46
  Dead..........Lev. 10:4, 5
  Executions
  outside........Lev. 24:23
  Log kept of ....Num. 33:1-49
  In battle......Josh. 10:5, 31, 34

C. *Spiritual significance of:*
  Christ's crucifixion
  outside........Heb. 13:12, 13
  God's people...Rev. 20:9

Cana of Galilee

A village of upper Galilee; home of
Nathanael.......John 21:2
Christ's first
  miracle at ......John 2:1-11
Healing at......John 4:46-54

Canaan—*low*

1. A son of
   Ham..........Gen. 10:6
   Cursed by
   Noah.........Gen. 9:20-25
2. Promised
   Land.........Gen. 12:5

Canaan, Land of

A. *Specifications regarding:*
  Boundaries ....Gen. 10:19
  Fertility.......Ex. 3:8, 17
  Seven
  nations........Deut. 7:1
  Language......Is. 19:18

B. *God's promises concerning,
  given to:*
  Abraham ......Gen. 12:1-3
  Isaac ....Gen. 26:2, 3

Jacob..........Gen. 28:10-13
Israel..........Ex. 3:8

C. *Conquest of:*
Announced....Gen. 15:7-21
Preceded by
spies..........Num. 13:1-33
Delayed by
unbelief........Num. 14:1-35
Accomplished by the
Lord..........Josh. 23:1-16
Done only in (Judg. 1:21,
part..........(27-36

Canaan, names of

Canaan ....Gen. 11:31
Land of
Hebrews..........Gen. 40:15
Palestina..........Ex. 15:14
Land of Israel.....1 Sam. 13:19
Immanuel's land ..Is. 8:8
Beulah ....Is. 62:4
Glorious ....Dan. 8:9
The Lord's land ..Hos. 9:3
Holy land ....Zech. 2:12
Land of the
Jews ....Acts 10:39
Land of promise...Heb. 11:9

Canaanites—*original inhabitants of Palestine*

A. *Described as:*
Descendants of
Ham..........Gen. 10:5, 6
Under a
curse..........Gen. 9:25, 26
Amorites ......Gen. 15:16
Seven
nations........Deut. 7:1
Fortified ....Num. 13:28
Idolatrous .....Deut. 29:17
Defiled ....Lev. 18:24-27

B. *Destruction of:*
Commanded by
God............Ex. 23:23, 28-33
Caused by
wickedness....Deut. 9:4
In God's
time ....Gen. 15:13-16
Done in
degrees ....Ex. 23:29, 30

C. *Commands prohibiting:*
Common league
with ....Deut. 7:1, 2
Intermarriage
with ....Deut. 7:1, 3
Idolatry of....Ex. 23:24
Customs of ...Lev. 18:24-27

Canaanites—*a Jewish sect*

1. "Simon the
Canaanite"....Matt. 10:4
Called the
Zealot ....Luke 6:15
2. Woman from that
region........Matt. 15:22

Candace—*dynastic title of Ethiopian queens*

Conversion of
eunuch of ....Acts 8:27-39

Cane—*a tall sedgy grass*

Used in (Is. 43:24
sacrifices ....(Jer. 6:20
Used in holy oil ..Ex. 30:23

Canneh

Trading city......Ezek. 27:23

Cannibalism—*using human flesh as food*

Predicted as a
judgment........Deut. 28:53-57
Fulfilled in a
siege ....2 Kin. 6:28, 29

Capacity—*ability to perform*

Hindered by sin ...Gal. 5:17
Fulfilled in
Christ ....Phil. 4:13

Capernaum—*village of Nahum*

A. *Scene of Christ's healing of:*
Centurion's
servant ....Matt. 8:5-13
Nobleman's
son ....John 4:46-54
Peter's mother-in-
law ....Matt. 8:14-17
The
demoniac .....Mark 1:21-28
The paralytic ..Matt. 9:1-8
Various
diseases.......Matt. 8:16, 17

B. *Other events connected with:*
Jesus' head-
quarters.......Matt. 4:13-17
Simon Peter's
home ....Mark 1:21, 29
Jesus' sermon on the Bread of
Life............John 6:24-71
Other important
messages......Mark 9:33-50
Judgment pronounced
upon..........Matt. 11:23, 24

Caph

Eleventh letter of Hebrew
alphabet.........Ps. 119:81-88

Caphtor—*cup*

The place (probably Crete) from
which the Philistines came to
Palestine ....Jer. 47:4

Caphtorim

Those of
Caphtor ....Deut. 2:23
Descendants of
Mizraim.........Gen. 10:13, 14
Conquerors of the
Avim.........Deut. 2:23

Capital punishment—*the death penalty*

A. *Institution of:*
By God ....Gen. 9:5, 6
　　　　　　　　Ex. 21:12-17

B. *Crimes punished by:*
Murder ....Gen. 9:5, 6
Adultery.........Lev. 20:10
Incest ....Lev. 20:11-14
Sodomy ....Lev. 20:13
Rape ....Deut. 22:25
Witchcraft.........Ex. 22:18
Disobedience to
parents ....Ex. 21:17
Blasphemy.........Lev. 24:11-16, 23
False
doctrines.........Deut. 13:1-10

Capitals—*tops of posts or columns*

Variegated decorations
of ....Ex. 36:38
Part of temple.........1 Kin. 7:16,
　　　　　　　　19, 20

Cappadocia—*a province of Asia Minor*

Natives of, at
Pentecost ....Acts 2:1, 9
Christians of, addressed by
Peter.........1 Pet. 1:1
Adnah ....2 Chr. 17:14

Capstone

Placed with shouts of
"Grace" ....Zech. 4:7

Captain—*a civil or military officer*

A. *Applied literally to:*
Arioch.........Dan. 2:15
Potiphar.........Gen. 37:36
David as
leader.........1 Sam. 22:2

Jehohanan.........2 Chr. 17:15
Temple police
head ....Luke 22:4

B. *Applied spiritually to:*
Angel of the
Lord ....Josh. 5:14

Captain, chief of the Temple—*priest who kept order*

Conspired with
Judas.........Luke 22:3, 4
Arrested Jesus ....Luke 22:52-54
Arrested
apostles ....Acts 5:24-26

Captive—*an enslaved person*

A. *Good treatment of:*
Compassion ....Ex. 6:4-8
Kindness ....2 Chr. 28:15
Mercy ....2 Kin. 6:21-23

B. *Bad treatment of:*
Forced labor.........2 Sam. 12:31
Blinded ....Judg. 16:21
Maimed.........Judg. 1:6, 7
Ravished ....Lam. 5:11-13
Enslaved ....2 Kin. 5:2
Killed.........1 Sam. 15:32, 33

C. *Applied figuratively to those:*
Under Satan.........2 Tim. 2:26
Under sin ....2 Tim. 3:6
Liberated by
Christ.........Luke 4:18

Captivity—*a state of bondage; enslavement*

A. *Foretold regarding:*
Hebrews in
Egypt.........Gen. 15:13, 14
Israelites ....Deut. 28:36-41
Ten tribes
(Israel).........Amos 7:11
Judah.........Is. 39:6

B. *Fulfilled:*
In Egypt.........Ex. 1:11-14
In many
captivities.........Judg. 2:14-23
In Assyria ....2 Kin. 17:6-24
In Babylon ....2 Kin. 24:11-16
Under Rome.........John 19:15

C. *Causes of:*
Disobedi-
ence ....Deut. 28:36-68
Idolatry.........Amos 5:26, 27

Caravan—*a group traveling together*

Ishmaelite
traders ....Gen. 37:25

Jacob's family....Gen. 46:5, 6
Jacob's funeral....Gen. 50:7-14
Queen of Sheba...1 Kin. 10:1, 2
Returnees from
exile..............Ezra 8:31

Carcas—*severe*

Eunuch under
Ahasuerus........Esth. 1:10

Carcass—*a dead body, corpse*

A. *Used literally of:*
Sacrificial
animals.......Gen. 15:9, 11
Unclean
beasts.........Lev. 5:2
Lion...........Judg. 14:8
Men...........Deut. 28:25, 26
Idols..........Jer. 16:18

B. *Used figuratively of:*
Those in hell...Is. 66:24
Idolatrous
kings.........Ezek. 43:7, 9
Attraction.....Matt. 24:28

C. *Laws regarding:*
Dwelling made unclean
by.............Num. 19:11-22
Contact with, makes
unclean.......Lev. 11:39
Food made
unclean.......Lev. 11:40

Carchemish

Eastern capital of Hittites on the
Euphrates..........2 Chr. 35:20
Conquered by
Sargon II.........Is. 10:9
Josiah wounded
here..............2 Chr. 35:20-24

Care, carefulness—*wise and provident concern*

A. *Natural concern for:*
Children.......Luke 2:44-49
Duties.........Luke 10:40
Mate..........1 Cor. 7:32-34
Health.........Is. 38:1-22
Life...........Mark 4:38
Possessions....Gen. 33:12-17

B. *Spiritual concern for:*
Duties.........Phil. 2:20
Office.........1 Tim. 3:1-8
A minister's
needs.........Phil. 4:10-12
The flock of {John 10:11
God..........{1 Pet. 5:2, 3
Christians.....1 Cor. 12:25

Spiritual
things.........Acts 18:12-17

Care, divine—*God's concern for His creatures*

For the world.....Ps. 104:1-10
For animals......Ps. 104:11-30
For pagans.......Jon. 4:11
For Christians....Matt. 6:25-34
Nineveh..........Zeph. 2:10-15

Careah—*made bold*

Father of
Johanan.........2 Kin. 25:23
Same as Kareah...Jer. 40:8

Cares, worldly—*overmuch concern for earthly things, anxiety*

A. *Evils of:*
Chokes the
Word.........Matt. 13:7, 22
Gluts the
soul..........Luke 21:34
Obstructs the
Gospel.......Luke 14:18-20
Hinders Christ's
work..........2 Tim. 2:4
Manifests
unbelief.......Matt. 6:25-32

B. *Antidotes for God's:*
Protection.....Ps. 37:5-11
Provision......Matt. 6:25-34
Promises......Phil. 4:6, 7

Carelessness—*lack of proper concern*

Babylon...........Is. 47:1, 8-11
Ethiopians.......Ezek. 30:9
Inhabitants of
coastlands......Ezek. 39:6
Nineveh..........Zeph. 2:15
Women of
Jerusalem.......Is. 32:9-11
Gallio............Acts 18:12-17

Carmel—*field, park, garden*

1. Rendered as:
"Fruitful
field"..........Is. 10:18
"Plentiful
field"..........Is. 16:10
"Bountiful
country".....Jer. 2:7
2. City of
Judah........Josh. 15:55
Site of Saul's
victory........1 Sam. 15:12

Home of David's
wife...........1 Sam. 27:3
3. A mountain of
Palestine......Josh. 19:26
Joshua defeated king
there.........Josh. 12:22
Scene of Elijah's
triumph.......1 Kin. 18:19-45
Elisha visits....2 Kin. 2:25
Place of
beauty ....Song 7:5
Figurative of
strength ......Jer. 46:18
Barrenness
foretold ......Amos 1:2

Carmelite, Carmelitess

Nabal.............1 Sam. 30:5
                 2 Sam. 2:2
Hezrai............2 Sam. 23:35
Abigail...........1 Sam. 27:3

Carmi—*vinedresser*

1. Son of
Reuben ....Gen. 46:9
2. Father of
Achan ....Josh. 7:1

Carnal—*fleshly, worldly*

Used literally of:

Sexual relations...Lev. 19:20
Paul calls
himself...........Rom. 7:14
Paul calls brethren at
Corinth ....1 Cor. 3:1, 3

Carob pod—*seedcase of the carob, or
locust tree*

Rendered "pod"; fed to
swine.............Luke 15:16

Carpenter—*a skilled woodworker*

David's house
built by ....2 Sam. 5:11
Temple
repaired by .....2 Chr. 24:12
Temple
restored by ......Ezra 3:7
Joseph
works as ....Matt. 13:55

Carpentry tools—*implements for the
carpentry trade*

Ax.................Deut. 19:5
Hammer ....Jer. 23:29
Line ....Zech. 2:1
Nail...............Jer. 10:4
Saw...............1 Kin. 7:9

Carpus—*fruit*

Paul's friend at
Troas............2 Tim. 4:13

Carriage

A vehicle ....Is. 46:1

Carrion vulture

Unclean bird......Lev. 11:18

Carshena—*plowman*

Prince of Persia ...Esth. 1:14

Cart—*a wagon*

Used in moving ...Gen. 45:19, 21
Made of wood.....1 Sam. 6:14
Sometimes
covered ....Num. 7:3
Drawn by cows ...1 Sam. 6:7
Used in
threshing.........Is. 28:28
Used for hauling ..Amos 2:13
Ark carried by ....2 Sam. 6:3
Figurative of sin ..Is. 5:18

Carving—*cutting figures in wood or
stone; grave*

Used in worship...Ex. 31:1-7
Found in homes...1 Kin. 6:18
Employed by
idolators..........Judg. 18:18
Used in the
Temple...........1 Kin. 6:35

Casiphia—*silvery*

Home of exiled
Levites ....Ezra 8:17

Casluhim

A tribe descended from
Mizraim ....Gen. 10:14
Descendant of
Ham ....1 Chr. 1:8, 12

Cassia—*amber*

An ingredient of holy
oil...............Ex. 30:24, 25
An article of
commerce........Ezek. 27:19
Noted for
fragrance.........Ps. 45:8

Castaway—*worthless; reprobated*

The   ⎰ Matt. 25:30
rejected ....⎱ 2 Pet. 2:4

Caste—*divisions of society*

Some leaders of
low...................Judg. 11:1-11
David aware of....1 Sam. 18:18, 23
Jews and Samaritans
observe............John 4:9
Abolished.........Acts 10:28-35

Castle—*fortress*

Used figuratively of:

Offended
brother...........Prov. 18:19

Castor and Pollux—*sons of Jupiter*

Gods in Greek and Roman
mythology; figureheads on Paul's
ship to Rome....Acts 28:11

Castration—*removal of male testicles*

Disqualified for
congregation.....Deut. 23:1
Rights restored in new
covenant.........Is. 56:3-5
Figurative of absolute
devotion.........Matt. 19:12

Caterpillar—*an insect living on
vegetation*

Works with
locust...........Is. 33:4

Cattle—*animals* (collectively)

Created by God...Gen. 1:24
Adam named......Gen. 2:20
Entered the ark...Gen. 7:13, 14
Taken as
plunder..........Josh. 8:2, 27
Belong to God....Ps. 50:10
Nebuchadnezzar eats
like..............Dan. 4:33
Pastureless.......Joel 1:18

Caulkers—*sealers*

Used on Tyrian
vessels..........Ezek. 27:9, 27

Caution—*provident care; alertness*

For safety.........Acts 23:10,
                    16-24
For defense.......Neh. 4:12-23
For attack........1 Sam. 20:1-17
A principle........Prov. 14:15, 16
Neglect of.........1 Sam. 26:4-16

Cave—*a cavern*

A. *Used for:*
Habitation......Gen. 19:30

Refuge........1 Kin. 18:4
Burial...........John 11:38
Conceal-
ment..........1 Sam. 22:1
Protection.....Is. 2:19
                Rev. 6:15

B. *Mentioned in Scripture:*
Machpelah....Gen. 23:9
Makkedah.....Josh. 10:16, 17
Adullam......1 Sam. 22:1
En Gedi.......1 Sam. 24:1, 3

Cedar—*an evergreen tree*

A. *Used in:*
Ceremonial
cleansing......Lev. 14:4-7
Building
Temple........1 Kin. 5:5, 6
Building
palaces........2 Sam. 5:11
Gifts............1 Chr. 22:4
Making idols...Is. 44:14, 17

B. *Figurative of:*
Israel's glory....Num. 24:6
Christ's glory..Ezek. 17:22, 23
Growth of
saints.........Ps. 92:12
Mighty
nations........Amos 2:9
Arrogant
rulers.........Is. 2:13

Ceiling—*upper surface of a room*

Temple's..........1 Kin. 6:15

Celebrate—*to commemorate; observe;
keep*

Feast of Weeks...Ex. 34:22
Feast of
Ingathering......Ex. 34:22
The Sabbath....Lev. 23:32, 41
Passover..........2 Kin. 23:21
Feast of Unleavened
Bread............2 Chr. 30:13
Feast of
Tabernacles......Zech. 14:16

Celestial—*heavenly*

Bodies called......1 Cor. 15:40

Celibacy—*the unmarried state*

Useful
sometimes........Matt. 19:10, 12
Not for bishops...1 Tim. 3:2
Requiring, a sign of
apostasy..........1 Tim. 4:1-3

Figurative of absolute
devotion..........Rev. 14:4

Cemetery—*a burial place*

Bought by
Abraham.........Gen. 23:15, 16
Pharisees
compared to....Matt. 23:27
Man dwelt in......Mark 5:2, 3
A resurrection
from ....Matt. 27:52

Cenchrea—*millet*

A harbor of
Corinth ....Acts 18:18
A church in ......Rom. 16:1

Censer—*firepan*

Used for $\left\{\begin{array}{l}\text{Num. 16:6, 7,}\\\text{39}\end{array}\right.$
incense..........
Made of bronze ...Num. 16:39
Used in idol
worship ....Ezek. 8:11
Typical of Christ's
intercession ......Rev. 8:3, 5

Censoriousness—*a critical spirit*

Rebuked by
Jesus.............Matt. 7:1-5
Diotrephes........3 John 9, 10
Apostates ....Jude 10-16

Census—*counting the population*

At Sinai...........Ex. 38:25, 26
Military ....Num. 1:2, 18, 20
In Moab ....Num. 26:1-64
By David.........2 Sam. 24:1-9
Provoked by
Satan ....1 Chr. 21:1
Completed by
Solomon ....2 Chr. 2:17
Of exiles ....Ezra 2:1-70
By Rome ....Luke 2:1, 2

Centurion—*a Roman officer*

Servant of,
healed............Matt. 8:5-13
Watches
crucifixion.......Matt. 27:54
Is converted ......Acts 10:1-48
Protects Paul.....Acts 22:25-28
Takes Paul to
Rome ....Acts 27:1

Cephas—*stone*

Name of Peter ....John 1:42

Ceremonialism—*adherence to forms and rites*

Jews guilty of.....Is. 1:11-15
Christ condemns ..Matt. 15:1-9
Apostles reject ....Acts 15:12-28
Sign of apostasy ..1 Tim. 4:1-3
Exhortations
against ....Col. 2:14-23

Certainties—*absolute truths*

Sin's exposure.....Num. 32:23
The Gospel........Luke 1:4
Jesus' claims .....Acts 1:3
Apostolic
testimony ....2 Pet. 1:16-21
Death's
approach.........Heb. 9:27
Ultimate
judgment.........Acts 17:31

Chaff—*the husk of threshed grain*

Describes the
ungodly ....Ps. 1:4
Emptiness.........Is. 33:11
False doctrine.....Jer. 23:28
God's judgment ...Is. 17:13
Punishment.......Matt. 3:12

Chain—*a series of connected links*

A. *A badge of office:*
On Joseph's
neck ....Gen. 41:42
Promised to
Daniel ....Dan. 5:7

B. *An ornament:*
Worn by
women........Is. 3:20

C. *A means of confinement of:*
Paul ....Eph. 6:20

D. *Used figuratively of:*
Oppression.....Lam. 3:7
Sin's
bondage .....Jer. 40:3, 4
Punishment....Jude 6
Satan's
defeat.........Rev. 20:1

Chalcedony—*from Chalcedon*

Variegated
stone.............Rev. 21:19

Chaldea

Originally, the south portion of
Babylonia ....Gen. 11:31
Applied later to all
Babylonia ....Dan. 3:8

Abraham came
from ....Gen. 11:28, 31
Ezekiel
prophesies in .....Ezek. 1:3

Chaldeans, Chaldees

Abraham, a
native ....Gen. 11:31
Ur, a city of.......Neh. 9:7
Babylon, "the
glory of" ....Is. 13:19
Attack Job........Job 1:17
Nebuchadnezzar,
king of ....2 Kin. 24:1
God's agent ....Hab. 1:6
Predicted captivity of Jews
among ....Jer. 25:1-26
Jerusalem
defeated by.......2 Kin. 25:1-21
Noted for
astrologers ......Dan. 2:2, 5, 10

Chalkstone—limestone

Used
figuratively.......Is. 27:9

Chamber—inner room; enclosed place

A. Used literally of:
Place of
idolatry ....2 Kin. 23:12

B. Used figuratively of:
Heavens ....Ps. 104:3, 13
Death ....Prov. 7:27

Chamberlain—a high official; a eunuch

Blastus, serving
Herod ....Acts 12:20

See Eunuch

Chameleon—a lizard-like reptile

Unclean..........Lev. 11:30

Champion—a mighty one; a winner

Goliath ....1 Sam. 17:23, 51
David ....1 Sam. 17:45-54

Chance, second

Not given to:

Angels ....2 Pet. 2:4
Noah's world.....2 Pet. 2:5
Esau ....Heb. 12:16, 17
Israelites.........Num. 14:26-45
Saul ....1 Sam. 16:1, 14
Judas ....John 13:26-30
Apostates ....Heb. 10:26-31
Those in hell .....Luke 16:19-31

Change of garments—gala, festal clothes

A gift ....Gen. 45:22
A wager ....Judg. 14:12-19
From a king ......2 Kin. 5:5

Character—one's total personality

A. Traits of:
Described propheti-
cally ....Gen. 49:1-28
Indicated before
birth ....Gen. 25:21-34
Seen in
childhood .....Prov. 20:11
Fixed in hell ....Rev. 22:11, 15

B. Manifested by:
Decisions
(Esau) ....Gen. 25:29-34
Destiny
(Judas).......John 6:70, 71
Desires
(Demas) ......2 Tim. 4:10
Deeds
(Saul).........1 Sam. 15:1-35

Character of God's people

A. Their dedication:
Hear Christ....John 10:3, 4
Follow
Christ.........John 10:4, 5, 27
Receive
Christ.........John 1:12

B. Their standing before God:
Blameless......Phil. 2:15
Faithful........Rev. 17:14
Godly..........2 Pet. 2:9
Holy...........Col. 3:12

C. Their graces:
Humble........1 Pet. 5:5
Loving.........1 Thess. 4:9
Humility.......Phil. 2:3, 4
Gentle.........Matt. 5:5
Merciful ....Matt. 5:7
Obedient ......Rom. 16:19
Pure...........Matt. 5:8
Sincere ....2 Cor. 1:12
Zealous ....Titus 2:14
Courteous .....1 Pet. 3:8
Unity of
mind..........Rom. 15:5-7
Hospitable ....1 Pet. 4:9
Generous .....2 Cor. 8:1-7
Peaceable......Heb. 12:14
Patient ....James 5:7, 8
Content ....Heb. 13:5
Steadfast ......1 Cor. 15:58

Character of the wicked

A. *Their attitude toward God:*
Hostile.........Rom. 8:7
Denial.........Ps. 14:1
Disobedi-
ence..........Titus 1:16

B. *Their spiritual state:*
Blindness......2 Cor. 4:4
Slavery to
sin............2 Pet. 2:14, 19
Deadness......Eph. 2:1
Inability......Rom. 8:8

C. *Their works:*
Boastful.......Ps. 10:3-6
Full of evil....Rom. 1:29-32
Haters of the
Gospel........John 3:19, 20
Sensual.......2 Pet. 2:12-22

Charashim—*craftsmen*

Called the "Valley of
Craftsmen".......Neh. 11:35

Charchemish (see Carchemish)

Chariot—*a vehicle*

A. *Used for:*
Travel.........Gen. 46:29
War...........1 Kin. 20:25

B. *Employed by:*
Kings.........1 Kin. 22:35
Persons of
distinction....Gen. 41:43
God...........2 Kin. 2:11, 12

C. *Illustrative of:*
Clouds........Ps. 104:3
God's
judgments....Is. 66:15
Angels........2 Kin. 6:16, 17

Chariot, war machine

A. *Used by:*
Egyptians......Ex. 14:7
Canaanites....Josh. 17:16
Philistines....1 Sam. 13:5
Syrians.......2 Sam. 10:18
Assyrians......2 Kin. 19:20, 23
Jews..........2 Kin. 8:21

B. *Numbers employed by:*
Pharaoh—
600...........Ex. 14:7
Jabin—
900...........Judg. 4:3
Philistines—
30,000........1 Sam. 13:5

Chariot cities

Many in Solomon's
time.............1 Kin. 9:19

Chariot horses

Hamstrung........1 Chr. 18:4

Chariot of fire

Used in Elijah's exit from
earth............2 Kin. 2:11

Chariots of the sun—*used in sun worship*

Destroyed.........2 Kin. 23:11

Charitableness—*a generous spirit toward others*

Bearing burdens..Gal. 6:2-4
Showing
forgiveness.......2 Cor. 2:1-10
Seeking concord..Phil. 4:1-3
Helping the
tempted.........Gal. 6:1
Encouraging the
weak...........Rom. 14:1-15
Not finding fault..Matt. 7:1-3
Descriptive of
Dorcas..........Acts 9:36

Charmers—*users of magic*

Falsified by God..Ps. 58:4, 5

Chastisement—*fatherly correction*

A. *Sign of:*
Sonship........Prov. 3:11, 12
God's love.....Deut. 8:5

B. *Design of, to:*
Correct........Jer. 24:5, 6
Prevent sin....2 Cor. 12:7-9
Bless..........Ps. 94:12, 13

C. *Response to:*
Penitence......2 Chr. 6:24-31
Submission....2 Cor. 12:7-10

Chastity—*sexual purity*

A. *Manifested in:*
Dress..........1 Pet. 3:1-6
Looks.........Matt. 5:28, 29
Speech........Eph. 5:4
Intentions.....Gen. 39:7-12

B. *Aids to:*
Shun the
unchaste......1 Cor. 5:11
Consider your
sainthood....Eph. 5:3, 4
Dangers of
unchastity....Prov. 6:24-35

Let marriage
suffice............1 Cor. 7:1-7
"Keep yourself
pure"..........1 Tim. 5:22

C. *Examples of:*
Job.............Job 31:1, 9-12
Joseph..........Gen. 39:7-20
Ruth............Ruth 3:10, 11
Boaz............Ruth 3:13, 14
Saints ....Rev. 14:4

Cheating—*defrauding by deceitful means; depriving*

The Lord..........Mal. 3:8, 9
One's soul........Matt. 16:26
The needy ....Amos 8:4, 5
Others ....1 Cor. 7:5

See Dishonesty

Chebar—*joining*

River in
Babylonia ....Ezek. 1:3
Site of Ezekiel's visions and Jewish
captives ....Ezek. 10:15, 20

Chedorlaomer—*servant of the god Lagamar*

A king of Elam; invaded
Canaan...........Gen. 14:1-16

Cheek—*side of face*

Micaiah struck
on................1 Kin. 22:24
Struck on.........Job 16:10
Messiah's
plucked ....Is. 50:6

Description of:

Beauty............Song 5:13
Patience ....Matt. 5:39
Victory ....Ps. 3:7
Attack ....Mic. 5:1

Cheerfulness—*serene joyfulness*

A. *Caused by:*
A merry
heart..........Prov. 15:13
The Lord's
goodness......Zech. 9:16, 17
The Lord's
presence ......Mark 6:54, 55
Victory ....John 16:33
Confidence ....Acts 24:10

B. *Manifested in:*
Giving..........2 Cor. 9:7
Christian
graces ....Rom. 12:8

Times of
danger ....Acts 27:22-36

Cheese—*a dairy product*

Used for food .....1 Sam. 17:18
Received by
David ....2 Sam. 17:29
Figurative of
trials ....Job 10:10

Chelal—*completeness; perfection*

A son of
Pahath-Moab.....Ezra 10:30

Cheluh—*robust*

A son of Bani .....Ezra 10:35

Chelub—*basket; bird's cage*

1. A brother of
Shuah ....1 Chr. 4:11
2. Father of
Ezri............1 Chr. 27:26

Chelubai

A son of Hezron ..1 Chr. 2:9

Chemosh—*fire, hearth*

The god of the
Moabites ....Num. 21:29
Children
sacrificed to ......2 Kin. 3:26, 27
Solomon builds
altars to ....1 Kin. 11:7
Josiah destroys
altars of..........2 Kin. 23:13

Chenaanah feminine form of *Canaan*

1. A Benjamite ...1 Chr. 7:10
2. Father of
Zedekiah......2 Chr. 18:10

Chenani contraction of *Chenaniah*

A reforming
Levite ....Neh. 9:4

Chenaniah—*Yahweh has established*

1. A chief Levite in David's
reign..........1 Chr. 15:22, 27
2. A reforming Levite; contracted
to Chenani....Neh. 9:4

Chephar Haammonai—*village of the Ammonite*

A village of
Benjamin.........Josh. 18:24

Chephirah—*village*

A city of the
Gibeonites.........Josh. 9:17
Assigned to
Benjamin.........Josh. 18:26
Residence of
exiles............Ezra 2:25

Cheran—*lyre*

A Horite, son of
Dishon.............1 Chr. 1:41

Cherethites—*Cretans in southwest Palestine*

Tribes in southwest
Canaan............1 Sam. 30:14
Identified with
Philistines........Ezek. 25:16
In David's
bodyguard........2 Sam. 8:18
Serve Solomon....1 Kin. 1:37, 38

Cherith—*cut; brook*

Elijah hid there ...1 Kin. 17:3-6

Cherub

A district in ⎰Ezra 2:59
Babylonia ......⎱Neh. 7:61

Cherubim (plural of cherub)

A. *Appearances of:*
Fully
described......Ezek. 1:5-14
B. *Functions of:*
Guard ....Gen. 3:22-24
Fulfill God's
purposes......Ezek. 10:9-16
Show God's
majesty ....2 Sam. 22:11
C. *Images of:*
On the mercy
seat......Ex. 25:18-22
On the veil ....Ex. 26:31
On curtains....Ex. 36:8
In the
Temple.......1 Kin. 8:6, 7

Chesalon—*trust*

A town of Judah ..Josh. 15:10

Chesed

Fourth son of
Nahor............Gen. 22:22

Chesil—*a fool*

A village of
Judah ....Josh. 15:30

Probably same as
Bethul and ⎰Josh. 19:4
Bethuel..........⎱1 Chr. 4:30

Chest—*case or box*

For offering ....2 Kin. 12:9, 10
For levy fixed by
Moses............2 Chr. 24:8, 9
Used to safeguard
valuables.........1 Sam. 6:8-15

Chestnut tree—*plane tree*

Used by Jacob ....Gen. 30:37
In Eden, God's
garden ....Ezek. 31:8, 9

Chesulloth—*loins or slopes*

A border town of
Issachar..........Josh. 19:18

Chezib—*deceitful*

Same as Azib; birthplace of
Shelah ....Gen. 38:5

Chicken—*domestic fowl*

Hen and brood ....Luke 13:34
Rooster ....Luke 22:34

Chicks—*the young of a hen*

Figurative of
Israel............Matt. 23:37

Chiding—*to reprove or rebuke*

A. *Between men:*
Jacob with
Laban.........Gen. 31:36
Israelites with
Moses.........Ex. 17:2
Ephraimites
with ⎰Judg. 7:24, 25
Gideon.......⎱Judg. 8:1
Paul with
Peter.........Gal. 2:11, 14
B. *By Christ, because of:*
Unbelief ......Matt. 11:20-24
Spiritual
dullness.......Matt. 16:8-12
Censo-
riousness......Mark 10:13-16
Sluggishness...Matt. 26:40

Chidon—*a javelin*

Where Uzza was struck
dead ....1 Chr. 13:9, 10
Called Nachon ....2 Sam. 6:6

Child-bearing

Agreeable to God's
command ....Gen. 1:28
Result of
marriage ....1 Tim. 5:14
Attended with
pain ....Gen. 3:16
Productive of
joy ....John 16:21
Productive of the
Messiah ....Luke 2:7
Means of
salvation ....1 Tim. 2:15
Expressed in
symbols ....Rev. 12:2, 5

Childhood, characteristics of

Dependence.......1 Thess. 2:7
Immaturity ....1 Cor. 13:11
Foolishness ......Prov. 22:15
Unstableness.....Eph. 4:14
Humility ....Matt. 18:1-5
Need for
instruction ......Prov. 22:6
Influence on
adults ....Is. 49:15

Childishness—an immature spirit

Manifested by
Saul...........1 Sam. 18:8, 9
Seen in Haman....Esth. 6:6-9

Childlikeness

Requirement of God's
kingdom ....Mark 10:15
An element in spiritual
growth............1 Pet. 2:2
A model to be
followed..........1 Cor. 14:20

Children, figurative

Disciples of a
teacher..........Mark 10:24
God's own ......Rom. 8:16, 17
Christians........Eph. 5:8
Devil's own ......1 John 3:10
Those who show such
trait ....Matt. 11:16-19

See Sonship of Believers

Children, illegitimate

No inheritance ....Gal. 4:30
No fatherly care..Heb. 12:8
Not in
congregation .....Deut. 23:2
Despised ....Judg. 11:2

Children, natural

A. *Right estimate of:*
God's gifts.....Gen. 33:5
God's
heritage......Ps. 127:3-5
Crown of old
men..........Prov. 17:6

B. *Characteristics of:*
Imitate
parents ....1 Kin. 15:11, 26
Diverse in
nature ....Gen. 25:27
Playful........Matt. 11:16-19

C. *Capacities of:*
Glorify God...Matt. 21:15, 16
Come to
Christ.........Mark 10:13-16
Understand
Scripture......2 Tim. 3:15
Receive the
promises ......Acts 2:39
Believe ......Matt. 18:6
Receive
training.......Eph. 6:4
Worship in God's
house.........1 Sam. 1:24, 28

D. *Parental obligations toward:*
Nourish-
ment..........1 Sam. 1:22
Discipline......Eph. 6:4
Instruction ....Gal. 4:1, 2
Employment ...1 Sam. 17:15
Inheritance ....Luke 12:13, 14

E. *Duties of:*
Obedience .....Eph. 6:1-3
Honor to
parents ....Heb. 12:9
Respect for
age ....1 Pet. 5:5
Care for
parents ....1 Tim. 5:4
Obedience to
God...........Deut. 30:2
Remembering
God...........Eccl. 12:1

F. *Description of ungrateful:*
Stubborn ......Deut. 21:18-21
Scorners.......Prov. 30:17
Robbers ....Prov. 28:24
Strikers........Ex. 21:15
Cursers........Lev. 20:9

G. *Examples of good:*
Isaac ....Gen. 22:6-10
Joseph.........Gen. 45:9, 10
Jephthah's
daughter......Judg. 11:34-36

Samuel ....1 Sam. 2:26
David.........1 Sam. 17:20
Josiah ....2 Chr. 34:1-3
Esther ....Esth. 2:20
Daniel........Dan. 1:1-6
John the
  Baptist.......Luke 1:80
Jesus ....Luke 2:51
In the
  Temple.......Matt. 21:15, 16
Timothy ......2 Tim. 3:15

H. *Examples of bad:*

Esau...........Gen. 26:34, 35
Job's haters....Job 19:18
Sons of Eli....1 Sam. 2:12, 17
Sons of
  Samuel ......1 Sam. 8:1-3
Absalom.......2 Sam. 15:10
Adonijah ......1 Kin. 1:5, 6
Elisha's
  mockers ......2 Kin. 2:22, 23
Adram-
  melech ....2 Kin. 19:37

I. *Acts performed upon:*

Naming.......Ruth 4:17
Blessing ......Luke 1:67, 76-79
Circum-
  cision ....Luke 2:21

J. *Murder of:*

By Pharaoh....Ex. 1:15, 16
By Herod the
  Great ....Matt. 2:16-18
In war ....Num. 31:12-17

Chileab—*restraint of father*

A son of David....2 Sam. 3:3
Also called
Daniel...........1 Chr. 3:1

Chilion—*wasting away*

Elimelech's son....Ruth 1:2
Orpah's deceased
  husband.......Ruth 1:4, 5
Boaz redeems his
  estate ....Ruth 4:9

Chilmad

A town or country trading with
Tyre..............Ezek. 27:23

Chimham—*pining*

A son of
  Barzillai ....2 Sam. 19:37-40
Inn bearing his
  name............Jer. 41:17

Chinnereth, Cinneroth—*lyre*

1. A city of
  Naphtali .....Deut. 3:17
2. The region of
  Chinneroth ...1 Kin. 15:20
  Same as plain of
  Gennesaret....Matt. 14:34
3. The Old Testament name for
  Sea of
  Galilee........Num. 34:11
  Also called Lake of Gennesaret
  and Sea of
  Galilee........Luke 5:1

Chios—*snow*

An island of the Aegean Sea; on
Paul's voyage ....Acts 20:15

Chislev

Ninth month of Hebrew
year...............Neh. 1:1

Chislon—*trust, hope*

Father of Elidad...Num. 34:21

Chisloth Tabor—*the flanks of Tabor*

A locality near Mt.
Tabor ....Josh. 19:12
Probably same as
Chesulloth ....Josh. 19:18

Chittim, Kittim

The island of Cyprus; inhabited by
descendants of Japheth (through
Javan)............Gen. 10:4
Ships of, in Balaam's
prophecy.........Num. 24:24

Chiun—*detestable thing*

Pagan deity worshiped by
Israel.............Amos 5:26

Chloe—*verdure*

Woman of
  Corinth ....1 Cor. 1:11

Choice, choose

A. *Of human things:*

Wives ....Gen. 6:2
Land ....Gen. 13:11
Soldiers........Ex. 17:9
King..........1 Sam. 8:18
Apostles ......Luke 6:13
Church
  officers........Acts 6:5
Missionaries ...Acts 15:40
Delegates......Acts 15:22, 25

B. *Of God's choice:*

Moses as
leader........Num. 16:28
Levites to
priesthood ....1 Sam. 2:28
Kings..........1 Sam. 10:24
Jerusalem......Deut. 12:5
Israel as His
people ....Deut. 7:6-8
Cyrus as
deliverer ......Is. 45:1-4
The Servant (the
Messiah)......Is. 42:1-7
The new Israel (the
Church).......1 Pet. 2:9
The weak as God's
own..........1 Cor. 1:27, 28
The elect ......Matt. 20:16

C. *Kind of:*

God and the
Devil.........Gen. 3:1-11
Life and
death ....Deut. 30:19, 20
God and
idols ....Josh. 24:15-28
Obedience and disobedi-
ence ....1 Sam. 15:1-35
God and
Baal ....1 Kin. 18:21-40
Wisdom and
folly ....Prov. 8:1-21
Obedience and
sin ....2 Pet. 2:4
Christ and
antichrist .....1 John 2:18, 19

D. *Factors determining choice,
man's:*

First choice....Rom. 5:12
Depraved
nature ....John 3:19-21
Spiritual
deadness......Eph. 4:17-19
Blindness ......John 9:39-41
Inability ......Rom. 8:7, 8

E. *Bad choice made by:*

Disobeying
God..........Num. 14:1-45
Putting the flesh
first..........Gen. 25:29-34
Following a false
prophet ....Matt. 24:11, 24
Letting the world
overcome ......Matt. 19:16-22
Rejecting God's
promises ......Acts 13:44-48

F. *Good choice made by:*

Using God's
Word ....Ps. 119:9-11
Believing
God...........Heb. 11:24-27
Obedience .....Acts 26:19-23
Prayer ....Eph. 1:16-19
Faith ....Heb. 11:8-10

Choir—*musicians trained to sing
together*

Appointed by
Nehemiah ....Neh. 12:31
In house of God...Neh. 12:40
Under instructor ..1 Chr. 15:22, 27

Chorazin

A city denounced for its
unbelief ....Matt. 11:21

Chozeba

Town of Judah....1 Chr. 4:22

Christ—*the Anointed One*

A. *Pre-existence of:*

Affirmed in Old
Testament ....Ps. 2:7
Confirmed by
Christ.........John 8:58
Proclaimed by
apostles.......Col. 1:15-19

B. *Birth of:*

Predicted ......Is. 7:14
Fulfilled ......Matt. 1:18-25
In the fullness of
time ....Gal. 4:4

C. *Deity of:*

Prophecy ......Is. 9:6
Acknowledged by
Christ.........John 20:28, 29
Acclaimed by
witnesses .....John 1:1, 14, 18
Affirmed by   (Rom. 9:5
apostles......(Heb. 1:8

D. *Attributes of:*

All-powerful ...Matt. 28:18
All-knowing ...Col. 2:3
Ever-present ...Matt. 18:20
Eternal ....John 1:1, 2, 15

E. *Humanity of:*

Foretold ....Gen. 3:15
             1 Cor. 15:45-47
Took man's   (John 1:14
nature ....(Heb. 2:9-18

Seed of
woman........Gal. 4:4
A son of
man ....Luke 3:38
Of David's
line ....Matt. 22:45
A man..........1 Tim. 2:5
Four
brothers......Mark 6:3

F. *Mission of:*
Do God's will ..John 6:38
Save sinners...Luke 19:10
Bring in everlasting right-
eousness ......Dan. 9:24
Destroy
Satan's ⎰Heb. 2:14
works........⎱1 John 3:8
Fulfill the Old
Testament ....Matt. 5:17
Give life ......John 10:10, 28
Abolish ceremo-
nialism........Dan. 9:27
Complete
revelation ....Heb. 1:1

G. *Worship of, by:*
Old Testament
saints........Josh. 5:13-15
Demons ....Mark 5:2, 6
Men ....John 9:38
Angels.........Heb. 1:6
Disciples......Luke 24:52
Saints in
glory..........Rev. 7:9, 10
All............Phil. 2:10, 11

H. *Character of:*
Holy...........Luke 1:35
Righteous .....Is. 53:11
Just ....Zech. 9:9
Guileless.......1 Pet. 2:22
Sinless........2 Cor. 5:21
Spotless ....1 Pet. 1:19
Innocent ......Matt. 27:4
Gentle........Matt. 11:29
Merciful ......Heb. 2:17
Humble........Phil. 2:8
Forgiving.....Luke 23:34

I. *Types of:*
Adam...........Rom. 5:14
Abel ....Heb. 12:24
Moses ....Deut. 18:15
Passover.......1 Cor. 5:7
Manna.........John 6:32
Bronze
serpent........John 3:14

J. *Other names for:*
Adam, the
second ....1 Cor. 15:45-47

Advocate .....1 John 2:1
Alpha and
Omega........Rev. 9:11
Amen..........Rev. 3:14
Ancient of
Days.........Dan. 7:9
Angel of his
presence ......Is. 63:9
Anointed above His
fellows........Ps. 45:7
Anointed of the
Lord ....Ps. 2:2
Apostle of our
confession ....Heb. 3:1
Arm of the
Lord ....Is. 51:9, 10
Author and finisher of
our faith .....Heb. 12:2
Author of eternal
salvation ......Heb. 5:9
Babe...........Luke 2:16
Banner to the
People ....Is. 11:10
Beginning and
end ....Rev. 21:6
Beloved........Eph. 1:6
Beloved of
God...........Matt. 12:18
Beloved Son ..Mark 1:11
Branch ....Zech. 3:8
Branch of
righteous-   ⎰Jer. 23:5
ness.........⎱Jer. 33:15
Bread.........John 6:41
Bread of Life..John 6:35
Bridegroom....John 3:29
Bright morning
star ....Rev. 22:16
Author of
salvation......Heb. 2:10
Carpenter......Mark 6:3
Carpenter's
son ....Matt. 13:55
Chief corner ⎰Ps. 118:22
stone.........⎱Mark 12:10
Chief
Shepherd .....1 Pet. 5:4
Child ....Is. 9:6
Child Jesus ...Luke 2:27
Chosen of
God...........1 Pet. 2:4
Christ, the.....John 1:41
Acts 9:22
Christ a King ..Luke 23:2
Christ, Jesus...Rom. 8:2
Christ Jesus our
Lord ....Rom. 8:39
Christ of God,
the............Luke 9:20

Christ of God, His Chosen One . . . . Luke 23:35
Christ the Lord . . . . Luke 2:11
Christ, the power of God . . . . 1 Cor. 1:24
Christ, the Son of the Blessed. . . . . . . Mark 14:61
Commander . . . Is. 55:4
Consolation of Israel . . . . Luke 2:25
Counselor . . . . . Is. 9:6
Covenant of the people . . . . Is. 42:6
Dayspring . . . . . Luke 1:78
Morning star . . 2 Pet. 1:19
Deity . . . . Col. 2:9
Deliverer . . . Rom. 11:26
Desire of all nations. . . . . Hag. 2:7
Diadem . . . . Is. 28:5
Door . . . . John 10:2
Door of the sheepfold . . . . . John 10:1
Eternal life . . . 1 John 5:20
Everlasting Father . . . . Is. 9:6
Faithful and True . . . . Rev. 19:11
Faithful witness . . . . . . Rev. 1:5
Firmly placed foundation . . . . Is. 28:16
Firstborn . . . . . . Heb. 1:6
Firstborn from the dead . . . . Col. 1:18
Firstborn of the dead . . . . Rev. 1:5
Firstborn of creation. . . . . . . Col. 1:15
Firstborn among many brethren . . . . . Rom. 8:29
First fruits. . . . . 1 Cor. 15:23
First and last . Rev. 22:13
Forerunner . . . Heb. 6:20
Foundation laid in Zion . . . . Is. 28:16
Friend of tax collectors and sinners. . . . . . . Luke 7:34
God . . . . John 20:28
God blessed forever. . . . . . . Rom. 9:5
God of Israel . Is. 45:15
God, our Savior . . . 1 Tim. 2:3
God with us . . . Matt. 1:23
Good Master. . Mark 10:17
Great God . . . . . Titus 2:13

Great High Priest . . . . Heb. 4:14
Great Shepherd . . . . . Heb. 13:20
Head, even Christ. . . . . Eph. 4:15
Head of all . . . . . Col. 2:10
Head of every man . . . . 1 Cor. 11:3
Head of the body, the church. . . . . . . Col. 1:18
Head over all things. . . . . Eph. 1:22
Heir of all things. . . . . Heb. 1:2
High Priest . . . . Heb. 4:14
His beloved Son . . . . Col. 1:13
Holy One . . . . . . 1 John 2:20
Holy and Just One . . . . Acts 3:14
Holy One of God. . . . . Luke 4:34
Holy One of Israel . . . . Is. 37:23
Holy Servant . . Acts 4:27
Hope of glory. . . . . Col. 1:27
Horn of salvation . . . . . . Luke 1:69
Husband. . . . . . 2 Cor. 11:2
I Am . . . . John 8:58
Image of God. . . . . 2 Cor. 4:4
Image of the Invisible God . . . . Col. 1:15
Immanuel . . . . . Is. 7:14
Jesus . . . . Luke 1:31
Jesus Christ . . . Rom. 1:4
Jesus Christ our Lord . . . . Rom. 6:23
Jesus Christ our Savior . . . . Titus 3:6
Jesus of Nazareth. . . . . . Luke 24:19
Jesus, the Son of God. . . . . Heb. 4:14
Jesus, the (supposed) son of Joseph . . . . Luke 3:23
Judge of Israel . . . . Mic. 5:1
Judge of the living and the dead . . . . Acts 10:42
Just man . . . . . Matt. 27:19
King. . . . . John 12:13
King eternal . . . 1 Tim. 1:17
King of glory . . Ps. 24:7
King of Israel . . . . John 12:13

King of
kings ....1 Tim. 6:15
King of the
Jews.........Matt. 27:37
King of Zion...Zech. 9:9
Lamb.........Rev. 13:8
Lamb of God ..John 1:36
Leader.........Is. 55:4
Life............John 14:6
Light ....John 1:9
Light of the
Gentiles........Acts 13:47
Light of the
World.........John 9:5
Lily of the
valleys ....Song 2:1
Lion of the tribe of
Judah.........Rev. 5:5
Living bread ..John 6:51
Living stone ...1 Pet. 2:4
Lord.........John 21:7
Lord Christ ...Col. 3:24
Lord God
Almighty......Rev. 4:8
Lord Jesus.....Acts 19:17
Lord Jesus
Christ.........2 Thess. 2:1
Lord and Savior Jesus
Christ.........2 Pet. 2:20
Lord both of dead and
living .....Rom. 14:9
Lord of all ..Acts 10:36
Rom. 10:12
Lord of glory ..1 Cor. 2:8
Lord of hosts ..Is. 54:5
Lord of lords...1 Tim. 6:15
Lord of
Sabbath.......Luke 6:5
Lord our righteous-
ness..........Jer. 23:6
Lord, your
redeemer......Is. 43:14
Majestic
Lord ....Is. 33:21
Man of
sorrows ......Is. 53:3
Mediator.......Heb. 12:24
Messenger of the
covenant......Mal. 3:1
Messiah ......John 4:25, 26
Mighty God...Is. 9:6
Mighty One....Ps. 45:3
Mighty One of
Jacob ....Is. 60:16
Minister of the
circumcision ..Rom. 15:8
Minister of the
sanctuary .....Heb. 8:1, 2

Morning star ..Rev. 22:16
Nazarene ......Matt. 2:23
Only begotten of the
Father.......John 1:14
Only begotten
Son...........John 1:18
Only wise
God...........1 Tim. 1:17
Our Passover ..1 Cor. 5:7
Our peace .....Eph. 2:14
Physician .....Luke 4:23
Power of
God...........1 Cor. 1:24
Precious
corner-   (Is. 28:16
stone.........(1 Pet. 2:6
Priest.........Heb. 5:6
Prince........Acts 5:31
Prince of life..Acts 3:15
Prince of
peace ....Is. 9:6
Prince of the kings of the
earth.........Rev. 1:5
Prophet.......Deut. 18:15, 18
Propitiation ..Rom. 3:25
Purifier and
refiner ......Mal. 3:3
Rabbi.........John 6:25
Rabboni ......John 20:16
Ransom ......1 Tim. 2:6
Redeemer......Is. 59:20
Resurrection and the
life...........John 11:25
Righteous
Judge ....2 Tim. 4:8
Righteous
Servant ......Is. 53:11
Rock ....1 Cor. 10:4
Rock of
offense........Rom. 9:33
Rod of the stem of
Jesse..........Is. 11:1
Root of
David ....Rev. 22:16
Root of Jesse ..Is. 11:10
Rose of
Sharon........Song 2:1
Ruler in   (Matt. 2:6
Israel ....(Mic. 5:2
Ruler over the kings
of the earth ...Rev. 1:5
Salvation .....Luke 2:30
Savior ....1 Tim. 4:10
Savior Jesus
Christ.........2 Pet. 2:20
Savior, God
our ....Titus 1:3

Savior of the
world . . . . 1 John 4:14
Scepter out of
Israel . . . . Num. 24:17
Second man . . . 1 Cor. 15:47
Seed of
David . . . . John 7:42
Seed of the
woman. . . . . . . Gen. 3:15
Shepherd . . . . . John 10:11
Shepherd and overseer of
souls . . . . 1 Pet. 2:25
Shoot of the stem of
Jesse. . . . . Is. 11:1
Son of the
Blessed. . . . . . . Mark 14:61
Son of David . . Matt. 9:27
Son of God . . . . Rom. 1:4
Son of Man. . . . Acts 7:56
Son of Mary . . . Mark 6:3
Son of the
Father . . . . 2 John 3
Son of the
Highest . . . . . . Luke 1:32
Sower . . . . Matt. 13:3, 37
Star out of
Jacob . . . . Num. 24:17
Stone. . . . . Dan. 2:45
Stone
rejected. . . . . . Luke 20:17
Stone of
stumbling . . . . . Rom. 9:32, 33
Sun of righteous-
ness. . . . . Mal. 4:2
Teacher from
God. . . . . John 3:2
Tried stone . . . Is. 28:16
True vine . . . . . John 15:1
Truth . . . . John 14:6
Unspeakable
gift . . . . 2 Cor. 9:15
Way . . . . John 14:6
Wonderful . . . . Is. 9:6
Word . . . . 1 John 1:1
Word of God . . Rev. 19:13
Word of Life . . 1 John 1:1

Christian attributes

A. *Manifested toward God:*
Belief . . . . Heb. 11:6
Holiness . . . . . . Heb. 12:10, 14
Godliness . . . . . Titus 2:12
Love . . . . Matt. 22:36, 37
Faith . . . . Mark 11:22
Joy . . . . Phil. 4:4

B. *Manifested toward Christ:*
Faith . . . . 2 Tim. 1:12
Worship . . . . . . Phil. 2:4-11

Obedience . . . . . 2 Thess. 1:8
Imitation . . . . . . 1 Cor. 11:1
Fellowship. . . . . 1 John 1:3

C. *Manifested toward the Holy
Spirit:*
Walking in . . . . Gal. 5:16
Filled with. . . . . Eph. 5:18
Guided by . . . . John 16:13
Praying in . . . . . Jude 20
Quench not. . . . 1 Thess. 5:19
Taught by . . . . . John 14:26
Living in. . . . . . Gal. 5:25
Grieve not . . . . . Eph. 4:30

D. *Manifested in the world:*
Chastity . . . . 1 Tim. 5:22
Content-
ment. . . . . Heb. 13:5
Diligence . . . . . . 1 Thess. 3:7, 8
Forbearance . . . Eph. 4:2
Honesty . . . . . . Eph. 4:25
Industry . . . . 1 Thess. 4:11, 12
Love toward
enemies . . . . . Matt. 5:44
Peacefulness. . . Rom. 14:17-19
Temperance . . . . 1 Cor. 9:25
Tolerance . . . . . Rom. 14:1-23
Zealous for good
deeds . . . . Titus 2:14

E. *Manifested toward other
Christians:*
Bearing
burdens . . . . . Gal. 6:2
Helping the
needy . . . . Acts 11:29, 30
Fellowship. . . . . Acts 2:42
Brotherly
kindness . . . . . . 1 Pet. 4:7-11
Mutual
edification . . . . 1 Thess. 5:11

F. *Manifested as signs of faith:*
Spiritual
growth. . . . . . . 2 Pet. 3:18
Fruitfulness. . . . John 15:1-6
Perse-
verance . . . . . . 1 Cor. 15:58
Persecution . . . 2 Tim. 3:9-12
Obedience . . . . Phil. 2:12
Good works . . . James 2:14-26

G. *Manifested as internal graces:*
Kindness . . . . . Col. 3:12, 13
Humility. . . . . . 1 Pet. 5:5, 6
Gentleness. . . . . James 3:17, 18
Love . . . . 1 Cor. 13:1-13
Self-control . . . Gal. 5:23
Peace. . . . . Phil. 4:7

Christianity, a way of life

Founded on
Christ . . . . 1 Cor. 3:10, 12
Based on
doctrines . . . . 1 Cor. 15:1-4
Designed for all . . . Matt. 28:18-20
Centers in
salvation . . . . Acts 4:12
Produces
change . . . . 1 Cor. 6:11

Christians—*Believers in Jesus Christ*

First applied at
Antioch . . . . Acts 11:26
Agrippa almost
becomes. . . . . Acts 26:28
Proof of, by
suffering . . . . 1 Pet. 4:16

Sometimes referred to as:

Believers . . . . Acts 5:14
Brethren . . . . Rom. 7:1
Brethren,
beloved. . . . . 1 Thess. 1:4
Brethren, holy . . . . Heb. 3:1
Children . . . . 2 Cor. 6:13
Children of God . . . Rom. 8:16
Children of
Light. . . . . Eph. 5:8
Dear children . . . . . Eph. 5:1
Disciples . . . . Acts 9:25
Elect, the . . . . Rom. 8:33
Friends . . . . John 15:14
Heirs of God and joint heirs
with. . . . . Rom. 8:17
Light in the
Lord . . . . Eph. 5:8
Light of the
world . . . . Matt. 5:14
Little children. . . . . 1 John 2:1
Members . . . . 1 Cor. 12:18, 25
Pilgrims. . . . . 1 Pet. 2:11
Priests . . . . Rev. 1:6
Saints. . . . . Rom. 8:27
Salt of the earth . . Matt. 5:13
Servants of God. . . Acts 16:17
Sheep. . . . . John 10:27
Soldier . . . . 2 Tim. 2:4
Sons of God . . . . . . Rom. 8:14
Vessels for
honor . . . . 2 Tim. 2:21
Witnesses . . . . Acts 1:8

Christlikeness

Model. . . . . 2 Cor. 3:18
Motivation . . . . 2 Cor. 5:14-17
Manifestation . . . . . Gal. 5:22, 23

Means . . . . Rom. 8:1-17
Mystery. . . . . 1 John 3:2

Chronicles—*two books of Old
Testament from Heb. meaning "the
words of the days"*

Chrysolite—*gold stone*

In New
Jerusalem . . . . Rev. 21:20

Chrysoprase—*golden-green stone*

In New
Jerusalem . . . . Rev. 21:20

Chub

Desolation of,
predicted . . . . Ezek. 30:5

Chun—*founding*

A town of Syria . . . 1 Chr. 18:8
Called Berothah . . Ezek. 47:16

Church—*the called out ones*

A. *Descriptive of:*
Local church . . Acts 8:1
Churches
generally . . . . . . Rom. 16:4
Believers
gathered . . . . . . Rom. 16:5
The body of
believers . . . . . . 1 Cor. 12:27, 28
Body of
Christ. . . . . Eph. 1:22, 23

B. *Title applied to:*
The Bride of
Christ. . . . . Eph. 5:22-32
The body . . . . . . Col. 1:18
One body . . . . . . 1 Cor. 12:18-24
Body of
Christ. . . . . Eph. 4:12
The Church. . . . Eph. 3:21
Church of the first-
born . . . . Heb. 12:23
Church of
God. . . . . 1 Cor. 1:2
Church of the Living
God. . . . . 1 Tim. 3:15
Churches of
Christ. . . . . Rom. 16:16
Church of the
Gentiles. . . . . . . Rom. 16:4
City of God . . . . Heb. 12:22
Flock. . . . . Acts 20:28
Flock of God . . 1 Pet. 5:2
God's
building. . . . . . . 1 Cor. 3:9

God's field . . . . . 1 Cor. 3:9
Habitation of
God . . . . Eph. 2:22
Household of
God . . . . Eph. 2:19
Israel of God . . Gal. 6:16
Jerusalem . . . . . . Gal. 4:24-26
Kingdom . . . . . . Heb. 12:28
Kingdom of the Son of His
love . . . . Col. 1:13
Lamb's wife . . . Rev. 19:7
Mt. Zion . . . . . . Heb. 12:22
People of
God . . . . 1 Pet. 2:10
Spiritual
house . . . . 1 Pet. 2:5
Temple of
God . . . . 1 Cor. 3:16

C. *Relation to Christ:*
Saved by . . . . . . Eph. 5:25-29
Purchased by . . Acts 20:28
Sanctified by . . Eph. 5:26, 27
Founded on . . . . Eph. 2:19, 20
Built by . . . . Matt. 16:18
Loved by . . . . . . Eph. 5:25
Subject to . . . . . Rom. 7:4

D. *Members of:*
Added by
faith . . . . Acts 2:41
Added by the
Lord . . . . Acts 2:47
Baptized by one
Spirit . . . . 1 Cor. 12:13
Edified by each
other . . . . Eph. 4:15, 16
Persecuted . . . . Acts 8:1-3
Disciplined . . . . . Matt. 18:15-17
Worship . . . . Acts 20:7
Fellowship
together . . . . . Acts 2:42-46
Urged to
attend . . . . Heb. 10:25
Subject to pastoral
oversight . . . . . . 1 Pet. 5:1-3
Unified in
Christ . . . . Gal. 3:28

E. *Organization of:*
Under
bishops . . . . 1 Tim. 3:1-7
Function of
deacons . . . . . . Acts 6:3-6
Place of
evangelists . . . . Eph. 4:11
Official
assemblies . . . . Acts 15:1-31
Function of the
presbytery . . . . 1 Tim. 4:14

F. *Mission of:*
Evangelize the
world . . . . Matt. 28:18-20
Guard the
truth . . . . 2 Tim. 2:1, 2
Edify the
saints . . . . Eph. 4:11-16
Discipline
unruly . . . . 2 Cor. 13:1-10

G. *Local, examples of:*
Antioch . . . . Acts 11:26
Asia . . . . 1 Cor. 16:19
                Rev. 1:11
Babylon . . . . 1 Pet. 5:13
Caesarea . . . . . . Acts 18:22
Cenchrea . . . . . . Rom. 16:1
Colosse . . . . Col. 1:2
Corinth . . . . 1 Cor. 1:2
Ephesus . . . . . . Acts 20:17
Galatia . . . . Gal. 1:2
Jerusalem . . . . . Acts 8:1
Judea . . . . Gal. 1:22
Laodicea . . . . . . Col. 4:15
Macedonia . . . . . 2 Cor. 8:1
Pergamos . . . . . Rev. 2:12
Philadelphia . . . Rev. 3:7
Philippi . . . . Phil. 1:1
Rome . . . . Rom. 1:7
Sardis . . . . Rev. 3:1
Smyrna . . . . Rev. 2:8
Thyatira . . . . . . Rev. 2:18
Thessalonica . . . 1 Thess. 1:1

Church sleeper

Falls from window during Paul's
sermon . . . . Acts 20:7-12

Chushan-Rishathaim—*extra wicked*

A Mesopotamian king; oppressed
Israel . . . . Judg. 3:8
Othniel delivers Israel
from . . . . Judg. 3:9, 10

Chuza

Herod's steward . . . Luke 8:3

Cilicia—*a province of Asia Minor*

Paul's country . . . . Acts 21:39
Students from, argued with
Stephen . . . . Acts 6:9
Paul labors in . . . . . Gal. 1:21

Cinnamon—*a laurel-like spicy plant*

Used in holy oil . . . Ex. 30:23
A perfume . . . . Prov. 7:17

In Babylon's trade..............Rev. 18:13
Figurative of a lover............Song 4:12, 14

Circle—*a curved line equally distant from a common center*

Used of the earth.............Is. 40:22

Circuit—*circle, regular course*

Judge's itinerary ..1 Sam. 7:16
Sun's orbit ....Ps. 19:6

Circumcision—*a cutting*

A. *The physical rite:*
Instituted by God.............Gen. 17:9-14
A seal of righteousness...........Rom. 2:25-29
Performed on the eighth day ....Luke 1:59
Child named when performed.....Luke 1:59, 60
Allowed right to Passover ......Ex. 12:48
Neglect of, punished......Ex. 4:24, 25
Neglected during wilderness ....Josh. 5:7
A sign of covenant relation ......Rom. 4:11

B. *Necessity of:*
Asserted in old dispensation........Gen. 17:9-14
Abolished by the Gospel ... {Gal. 5:1-4 / Eph. 2:11, 15
Avails nothing ...... {Gal. 5:6 / Col. 3:10, 11
Avowed by false teachers ....Acts 15:1
Acclaimed a yoke.........Acts 15:10
Abrogated by apostles......{Acts 15:5-29 / 1 Cor. 7:18, 19

C. *Spiritual significance of:*
Regeneration.........{Deut. 10:16 / Deut. 30:6 / Jer. 4:4
The true Jew (Christian) ....Rom. 2:29
The Christian.....{Phil. 3:3 / Col. 2:11

Circumstances

A. *Relationship to Christian:*
Work for good ....Rom. 8:28

Produce perseverance ....Rom. 5:3
Not cause for anxiety ....Phil. 4:6
Test and purify.........1 Pet. 1:5-7
To be met with thanksgiving.........{Eph. 5:20 / Phil. 4:6
Can be overcome .....Phil. 4:11-13

B. *Examples, victory over:*
Moses...........Ex. 14:10-31
Joshua.........Josh. 6:8-21
Shamgar.......Judg. 3:31
Gideon ....Judg. 7:19-23
Hannah........1 Sam. 1:9-20
David...........1 Sam. 17:40-51
Widow of Zarephath ...1 Kin. 17:8-16
Hezekiah ......2 Kin. 20:1-11
Peter ....Acts 12:5-17
Paul...........{Acts 14:19-20 / Acts 16:19-26

Cistern—*an underground reservoir for water*

A. *Literal uses of:*
Water ....2 Kin. 18:31
Imprisonment (when empty)........Jer. 38:6

B. *Figurative uses of:*
Wife...........Prov. 5:15
False religion ..Jer. 2:13

C. *Kinds of:*
Family cisterns ....Is. 36:16

Cities—*organized population centers*

A. *Features regarding:*
Walled.........{Lev. 25:29-31 / Deut. 3:5
Earliest.......Gen. 4:17
Often built on hills.........Matt. 5:14
Gates guarded.......Acts 9:24
Guard posted ....{2 Kin. 7:10 / Neh. 13:19
Difficult to attack.........Prov. 16:32
Business at gate.........{Gen. 23:10, 11 / Ruth 4:1-11

B. *Descriptions of:*
Sodom— wicked........Gen. 13:13

Jerusalem—
like Sodom....Is. 1:1, 10
Nineveh—
repentant.....Jon. 3:5-10
Capernaum—
arrogant......Matt. 11:23
Athens—
idolatrous.....Acts 17:16

Cities, Levitical

Forty-eight.......Num. 35:7
Six designed for
refuge............Deut. 19:1-13

Cities of refuge

Given to Levites..Num. 35:6
For the
manslayer.......Num. 35:11

Cities of the mountains

Avoided by
Israel............Deut. 2:37

Cities of the plain

Admah............Gen. 14:8
Bela..............Gen. 14:2
Gomorrah........Gen. 19:28
                        Jude 7
Sodom............Gen. 19:28-29
Zeboiim...........Gen. 14:8
Dibon, Bamoth Baal, Beth Baal
Meon.............Josh. 13:17

Cities of the lowland

Restored.........Jer. 32:44

Citizen, citizenship

A. *Kinds of:*
   Hebrew........Eph. 2:12
   Roman ....Acts 22:25-28
   Spiritual......Eph. 2:19, 20
             Phil. 3:20
   Christian (see below)
B. *Duties of Christian citizens:*
   Be subject to
   rulers.........Rom. 13:1-7
   Pray for
   rulers.........1 Tim. 2:1, 2
   Honor rulers...1 Pet. 2:17
   Seek peace ...Jer. 29:7
   Pay taxes......Matt. 22:21
   Obey God
   first...........Acts 5:27-29
   Love one's
   nation ....Neh. 2:3
   Live
   righteously...1 Pet. 3:8-17

City builder

Cain builds first ...Gen. 4:17
Woe to, who uses
bloodshed ....Hab. 2:12

City clerk—*a keeper of court records*

Appeases the
people............Acts 19:35

City, Holy

Applied to   { Dan. 9:24
Jerusalem ....{ Rev. 11:2
Prophecy
concerning ......Joel 3:17
Clothed with beautiful
garments.........Is. 52:1
New Jerusalem....Rev. 21:2

City of David

Applied to the stronghold of
Zion..............1 Chr. 11:5
Taken by David from
Jebusites.........1 Chr. 11:4-8
Ark brought to....1 Chr. 15:1-29
Bethlehem
called ....Luke 2:4

City of destruction

Prophecy concerning an Egyptian
city ....Is. 19:18

City of God

Prophetic description of
Zion.............Ps. 48:1-14
Dwelling place of
God ....Ps. 46:4, 5
Sought by the
saints ....Heb. 11:9, 10, 16
Descriptive of the heavenly
Jerusalem ....Rev. 21:2

City of Moab

Where Balak met
Balaam...........Num. 22:36

City of palm trees—*Jericho*

Seen by Moses ....Deut. 34:1-3
Occupied by
Kenites...........Judg. 1:16
Captured by
Eglon ....Judg. 3:12-14

City of Salt

Near the Dead
Sea..............Josh. 15:62

Civil

1. Righteousness
   Principle of .... Prov. 14:34
   Precepts of ... Zech. 8:16, 17
   Practice of.... Mic. 4:2
   Perversion of .. Mic. 7:1-4
2. Service
   A. *Characteristics of:*
      Loyalty .... Neh. 2:3
      Industry ...... Gen. 41:37-57
      Esteem .... Esth. 10:3

   B. *Examples of:*
      Joseph......... Gen. 39:1-6
      Daniel .... Dan. 1:17-21
      Mordecai ...... Esth. 8:1, 2, 9
      Nehemiah ..... Neh. 2:1-8

3. Authority:
   Obedience to
     com- ⎰ Eccl. 8:2-7
     manded ..... ⎱ Rom. 13:1-7
   Submit for Christ's
     sake .... 1 Pet. 2:13-15

Civility—*good breeding; courtesy*

Shown by
  Joseph .... Gen. 47:1-10
Taught by
  Christ .... Luke 14:8-10
Shown by
  Timothy......... Phil. 2:19-23
Shown by Gaius .. 3 John 1-6

Class distinction

Egyptians—against
  Hebrews.......... Gen. 43:32
Haman—against
  Hebrews........ Esth. 3:8, 9
Jews—against
  Samaritans ...... John 4:9
Jews—against
  Gentiles .... Acts 22:21, 22
Forbidden........ Ex. 12:48, 49

Clauda—*lamentable*

Small island southeast of
  Crete............ Acts 27:16

Claudia

Disciple at
  Rome .... 2 Tim. 4:21

Claudius Lysias

Roman commander who protected
  Paul.............. Acts 24:22-24, 26

Clay—*firm, plastic earth*

A. *Uses of:*
   Making
     bricks........ 2 Sam. 12:31
   Making
     pottery........ Is. 41:25
   Sealing .... Job 38:14
   Miracle .... John 9:6, 15

B. *Figurative of:*
   Man's
     weakness ..... Is. 64:8
   Unstable
     kingdom ..... Dan. 2:33-35, 42
   Trouble........ Ps. 40:2

Clean—*pure, innocent*

A. *Used physically:*
   Outward
     purity........ Matt. 23:26

B. *Used ceremonially of:*
   Clean
     animals ...... Gen. 7:2
   Freedom from
     defilement .... Luke 5:14, 15

C. *Used spiritually of:*
   Men's nature .. Job 9:30, 31
   Repentance.... Gen. 35:2
                   James 4:8
   Regener-
     ation.......... Ezek. 36:25
   Sanctifi-
     cation........ Ps. 24:4
   Glorification ... Rev. 19:8, 14

Cleanliness

Required of
  priests........... Is. 52:11
Acceptability of
  worship .... Heb. 10:22
Inner, better than
  outward......... Matt. 23:25-28

Cleansing, spiritual

Promise of .... Jer. 33:8
Need of .... Ps. 51:2
Extent of .... Ps. 19:12
Command
  regarding........ 2 Cor. 7:1
Means of......... 1 John 1:7, 9
Perfection of..... Eph. 5:25, 26

Cleanthes—*Stoic teacher not mentioned by name in the Bible*

Quoted by Paul ... Acts 17:28

Clement—*mild, merciful*

Paul's
companions ......Phil. 4:3

Cleopas—*of a renowned father*

Christ appeared
to ....Luke 24:18

Climate—*temperature and weather
conditions*

A. *Elements of:*
Cold...........Job 37:9
              Acts 28:2
Clouds........Job 35:5
Thirsty
  ground........Deut. 8:15
Heat...........Is. 49:10
Rain...........Ezra 10:13
Snow..........1 Chr. 11:22
Sunshine ......Ex. 16:21
Wind ....Matt. 14:24

B. *Order of:*
Promised ......Gen. 8:22
Controlled by
  God...........Job 37:5-13
Used in   (Jer. 50:38
  judgment ....\Hag. 1:9-11
Tool of
  correction.....Jon. 1:3, 4
Shows deity of
  Christ.........Mark 4:37-39

Cloak—*outer garment*

A. *Used literally of:*
Outer
  garment ......Matt. 5:40

B. *Used figuratively of:*
Covering for
  sin...........1 Thess. 2:5
Covering for
  vice...........1 Pet. 2:16

Clopas—*of a renowned father*

Husband of
  Mary...........John 19:25
Called Alphaeus...Matt. 10:3

Closet

A place of
prayer............Matt. 6:6

Clothing—*garments*

A. *Need of:*
Cover
  nakedness.....Gen. 3:10, 11

Maintain
  modesty ......1 Pet. 3:1-5
Keep warm ....2 Tim. 4:13
Remove
  anguish ....Esth. 4:3, 4

B. *Unusual features regarding:*
Lasted forty
  years.........Deut. 8:4
Torn into twelve
  pieces.........1 Kin. 11:29, 30
Obtained from
  enemies.......Ex. 12:35
Some
  stripped of ....Luke 10:30

C. *Regulations concerning:*
Wearing opposite sex's,
  forbidden .....Deut. 22:5
Gaudy,
  denounced ....Is. 3:16-24
Ostentatious,
  prohibited.....1 Tim. 2:9
Warnings
  concerning....Matt. 7:15
Judgments by,
  deceptive .....Luke 16:19-23
Proper sign of
  sanity.........Mark 5:15

Clothing, tearing of—*symbolic
expression of grief*

By Reuben........Gen. 37:29, 34
By Joshua........Josh. 7:6
By Tamar........2 Sam. 13:19
By Job...........Job 1:20
By Ezra..........Ezra 9:3
By high priest.....Mark 14:63
By Paul and
  Barnabas........Acts 14:14
Forbidden to
  Aaron..........Lev. 10:6

Cloud—*a visible mass of vapor*

A. *Miraculous uses of:*
Israel's
  guidance......Ex. 13:21, 22
Manifesting the divine
  glory.........Ex. 16:10
Manifesting the divine
  presence ......2 Chr. 5:13
Jesus' transfig-
  uration........Luke 9:34, 35
Jesus'
  ascension .....Acts 1:9-11
Jesus' return...Matt. 24:30

B. *Figurative of:*
God's unsearch-
  ableness.......Ps. 97:2

Sins . . . . Is. 44:22
Witnesses. . . . . . Heb. 12:1
False
  teachers . . . . . . 2 Pet. 2:17
Baptism . . . . 1 Cor. 10:1, 2
Boasting . . . . Prov. 25:14

Cloudburst—*a sudden downpour of rain*

Sent as a
  punishment . . . . . . Ezra 10:9-14

Cloud, pillar of

A. *Designed to:*
   Regulate Israel's
     movements . . . Ex. 40:36, 37
   Guide Israel . . Ex. 13:21
   Defend Israel . . Ex. 14:19, 20
   Cover the
     tabernacle . . . . Ex. 40:34

B. *Special manifestations of, at:*
   Time of
     murmuring . . Ex. 16:9, 10
   Giving of
     Law . . . . Ex. 19:9, 16
   Rebellion of Aaron and
     Miriam . . . . Num. 12:1-9
   Korah's
     rebellion . . . . . . Num. 16:19-21,
                            42

Clusters—*bunches*

Kinds of:
  Grapes . . . . Num. 13:23
  Henna
    blossoms . . . . Song 1:14
  Raisins . . . . 1 Sam. 25:18

Cnidus—*age*

City of Asia Minor on Paul's
  voyage . . . . Acts 27:7

Coal—*charcoal*

A. *Uses of:*
   Heating . . . . John 18:18
   Cooking . . . . John 21:9
   By smiths . . . . . . Is. 44:11, 12

B. *Figurative of:*
   Lust . . . . Prov. 6:25-28
   Purification . . . . Is. 6:6, 7
   Good deeds . . . Rom. 12:20
   Posterity . . . . 2 Sam. 14:7

Coat of mail

Worn by priests . . . Ex. 28:32
                       Ex. 39:23

Cobra—*venomous snake*

Figurative of evil
  deeds. . . . . Is. 11:8
Figurative of man's evil
  nature. . . . . Deut. 32:33

Coffin—*a box-like container for a corpse*

In Joseph's
  burial . . . . Gen. 50:26
Jesus touched . . . . . Luke 7:14

Coins—*metal mediums of exchange*

Bekah (½
  shekel) . . . . Ex. 38:26
Copper. . . . . Matt. 10:9
                          Matt. 10:29
Denarius. . . . . Matt. 20:2
Dram . . . . Ezra 2:69
Gerah. . . . . Ex. 30:13
Mina. . . . . Ezek. 45:12
Mite . . . . Mark 12:42
Shekels of gold. . . . 2 Kin. 5:5
Piece of money. . . . Matt. 17:27
Piece of silver. . . . . Matt. 26:15

Cold—*absence of heat*

A. *Used literally of:*
   Winter. . . . . Gen. 8:22
   Cold weather . . John 18:18

B. *Used figuratively of:*
   God's power . . Ps. 147:17
   Indolence. . . . . . Prov. 20:4
   Good news . . . Prov. 25:25
   Apostasy . . . . . Jer. 18:14
   Spiritual
     decay . . . . Matt. 24:12

Col-Hozeh—*all seeing*

A man of   {Neh. 3:15
Judah . . . . {Neh. 11:5

Collaborators

Delilah. . . . . Judg. 16:4-21
Doeg. . . . . 1 Sam. 21:7
                          1 Sam. 22:7-23
Judas . . . . Matt. 26:14-16

Collection box

For temple
  offerings. . . . . 2 Kin. 12:9

Collection of money

The temple tax . . 2 Chr. 24:6, 9
For saints . . . . Rom. 15:25, 26

Colony—*citizens transported to another land*

A. *Illustrated by:*
Israel in
Egypt . . . . Gen. 46:26-28
Israel in
Assyria . . . . 2 Kin. 17:6, 24
Judah in
Babylon . . . . . . 2 Kin. 25:8-12

B. *Applied to:*
Philippi as a Roman
colony . . . . Acts 16:12
Philippian
Christians . . . . . Phil. 3:20

Colors

A. *White, descriptive of:*
Glory and
majesty . . . . Dan. 7:9
Rev. 20:11
Purity, glory . . . Rev. 1:14
Victory . . . . Rev. 6:2
Completion . . . . John 4:35

B. *Black, descriptive of:*
Sorrow,
calamity . . . . . . Rev. 6–12
Hell . . . . Jude 13

C. *Green, descriptive of:*
Spiritual
privileges . . . . . Jer. 11:16
Spiritual life . . . Ps. 52:8
Ps. 92:12-15

D. *Red (crimson), descriptive of:*
Atonement . . . . Is. 63:2
Military
might . . . . Nah. 2:3
Persecution . . . . Rev. 12:3
Drunken-
ness . . . . Prov. 23:29
Sinfulness . . . . . Is. 1:18

E. *Purple, descriptive of:*
Royalty . . . . Judg. 8:26
Wealth . . . . Luke 16:19
Luxury . . . . Rev. 17:4

F. *Blue, descriptive of:*
Heavenly
character . . . . . Ex. 28:31

Colosse—*punishment*

A city in Asia
Minor . . . . Col. 1:2
Evangelized by
Epaphras . . . . Col. 1:7
Not visited by
Paul . . . . Col. 2:1

Paul writes against
errors of . . . . Col. 2:16-23

Colossians, the epistle to the

Written by Paul . . . Col. 1:1

Colt—*young beast of burden*

Descriptive of
Messiah . . . . Gen. 49:10, 11
Christ rides on . . . . Matt. 21:2, 5, 7
Of camel, as gift . . Gen. 32:13, 15

Come—*to approach; arrive*

Of invitation . . . . . . Is. 1:18
Of salvation . . . . Matt. 18:11
Of rest . . . . Matt. 11:28
Of promise . . . . John 14:3
Of prayer . . . . Heb. 4:16
The final . . . . Rev. 22:17, 20

Comfort—*to relieve distress; to console*

A. *Sources of:*
God . . . . 2 Cor. 1:3, 4
Christ . . . . Matt. 9:22
Holy Spirit . . . . Acts 9:29-31
The
Scriptures . . . . Rom. 15:4
Christian
friends . . . . 2 Cor. 7:6

B. *Those in need of:*
Afflicted . . . . . . Is. 40:1, 2
Sorrowful . . . . . 2 Cor. 2:6, 7
Weak . . . . 1 Thess. 5:14
Discouraged . . . 2 Cor. 2:6, 7
Troubled . . . . . . 2 Cor. 7:5-7
One another . . . 1 Thess. 4:18

Coming of Christ (see Second Coming
of Christ)

Commander—*a leading official*

Names of:
Phichol . . . . Gen. 21:32
Sisera . . . . Judg. 4:7
Saul . . . . 1 Sam. 9:15, 16
Abner . . . . 1 Sam. 17:55
Shobach . . . . 2 Sam. 10:16
Joab . . . . 2 Sam. 24:2
Amasa . . . . 1 Kin. 2:32
Zimri . . . . 1 Kin. 16:9
Omri . . . . 1 Kin. 16:16
Shophach . . . . . . 1 Chr. 19:16
Rehum . . . . Ezra 4:8
Lysias . . . . Acts 24:7

Commandment—*a rule imposed by authority*

A. *God's, described as:*
Faithful . . . . Ps. 119:86

Broad.........Ps. 119:96
A lamp ....Prov. 6:23
Holy..........Rom. 7:12
Not burden-
some.........1 John 5:3

B. *Christ's, described as:*
New..........John 13:34
Obligatory.....Matt. 5:19, 20
Promissory....John 15:10, 12
Eternal life ....John 12:49, 50

Commandments, divine

Sought by men....Phil. 3:6-15
Not material ......Rom. 14:1-23
Lives an
epistle of ....2 Cor. 3:1-3
Revealed at
judgment........Matt. 25:20, 21

Commandment, the new

Given by Christ ...John 13:34, 35
Based on old ......1 John 2:7-11
                            2 John 5
Fulfills the Law ...Matt. 22:34-40

Commandments, The Ten

Divine origin......Ex. 20:1
Written by God ...Ex. 32:16
Described ....Ex. 20:3-17
Christ sums up....Matt. 22:35-40
Spiritual nature ...Matt. 5:27, 28
Love fulfills ....Rom. 13:8-10

Commerce—*trade on a large scale*

A. *Engaged in:*
Locally ....Prov. 31:14-18
Nationally .....2 Chr. 9:21
Inter-
nationally....Rev. 18:10-24

B. *Abuses of:*
Sabbath
trading........Neh. 13:15-22
Temple
business......John 2:13-16
Ignoring the
Lord ....James 4:13-17
Pride ....Ezek. 28:2-18

Commission—*special assignment*

A. *Kinds of:*
Christ's—to
mankind....John 3:16-18
Israel's—to the
Gentiles.......Acts 13:45-47
The Church's—to the
world ....Matt. 28:19, 20

B. *Requirements of:*
Faithfulness ...2 Tim. 4:1-8
Diligence ......Rom. 15:15-32
Willingness ...1 Sam. 3:9, 10

Common—*public; general*

Normal, natural ...1 Cor. 10:13
Ceremonially
unclean ....Acts 10:14
Ordinary people...Jer. 26:23
Shared
togetherness......Acts 2:44
Things believed
alike ....Titus 1:4

Common people

Burial place of ....Jer. 26:23

Commonwealth—*a nation*

Descriptive of
Israel.............Eph. 2:12

Communion of the Lord's Supper (see Lord's Supper)

Communion of the Saints (see Fellowship)

Communion with Christ

A. *Based on:*
Redemption....Heb. 2:10-13
Regener-
ation...........1 Cor. 6:14-17
Resurrection
(spiritual) .....Col. 3:1-3

B. *Identifies Christians, in:*
Name..........1 Pet. 4:12-16
Character......John 14:23
Hope ....1 John 3:1-3

Communion with God

A. *Prerequisites of:*
Reconcili-
ation..........2 Cor. 5:18, 19
Acceptance of
Christ....John 14:6
Obedience .....John 14:23
Holiness ....2 Cor. 6:14-18

B. *Saints:*
Desire such....Heb. 11:10
Seek it through
prayer......Matt. 6:6-15
Realized fully in
eternity ....Rev. 7:13-17

Communism, Christian

A. *Supposedly found in:*
Early church...Acts 2:44, 45

B. *Differs from modern Communism:*

In being
voluntary .....Acts 5:4
Confined to
Christians.....Acts 4:32
Not under government
control.......Acts 4:34-37

Companion—*a fellow worker*

Wife ....Mal. 2:14
Companion in
tribulation........Rev. 1:9
Co-worker ....Ezra 4:7, 9, 11
Fellow fool.......Prov. 13:20
Fellow believer...Ps. 119:63
Fellow worker ...Phil. 2:23, 25

Companions, evil

A. *Cause:*

Rebellion ......Num. 16:1-50
Idolatry.......Ex. 32:1-8
Violence,
death ....Acts 23:12-22
Persecution....Acts 17:5-9

B. *Warnings against:*

Do not consent with
them.........Prov. 1:10-19
Avoid them....1 Cor. 5:9-11
Remember their
end ....Rev. 22:11, 14, 15

Comparison—*likeness; similarity*

A. *Worthy comparisons, between:*

God's holiness
and man's   {Is. 46:12, 13
sinfulness ....{Is. 55:6-9
Christ's glory and
humiliation ...Phil. 2:5-11
Israel's call and responsibility.......Rom. 2:17-29
Gentile faith and Jewish
unbelief.......Matt. 12:41, 42
Former and present
unbelief.......Matt. 11:20-24
Old and new
covenants.....2 Cor. 3:6-18
The believer's status now and
hereafter......1 John 3:1-3

B. *Unworthy comparisons, based on:*

Position ......Num. 16:3
Privileges......1 Cor. 3:1-9
Wealth ....James 2:1-9

Compassion—*suffering with another, mercy*

A. *God's, described as:*

Overabun-
dant ....Ps. 86:13, 15
New every
morning ......Lam. 3:22, 23
Great...........Is. 54:7
Kindled........Hos. 11:8

B. *God's, expressed:*

Fully ....Ps. 78:38
Sovereignly...Rom. 9:15
Unfailingly ....Lam. 3:22
Willingly.......Luke 15:18-20

C. *Christ's, expressed toward the:*

Weary ....Matt. 11:28-30
Tempted......Heb. 2:17, 18
Helpless ......Mark 9:20-22
Sorrowful......Luke 7:13, 14
Multitude......Matt. 15:32

D. *Examples of:*

David in
sorrow ....Ps. 51:1-12
God to Israel ..Hos. 11:8
Christ to
sinners........Matt. 9:12, 13

E. *Christian's:*

Commanded ...Zech. 7:9
                Col. 3:12
                Jude 22
Expressed......Heb. 10:34
                1 Pet. 3:8
Illustrated .....Luke 10:30, 33
Unified ....Phil. 2:1, 2

Complete—*to finish*

Used of:

Purification rites ..Esth. 2:12
Priestly ministry ..Luke 1:23
Time of
pregnancy.......Luke 2:6

Complicity—*partnership in wrongdoing*

In Adam's sin .....Rom. 5:12
In the sins of
others............Ps. 50:18
In national guilt...Matt. 27:24-26

Composure—*calmness; tranquility; self-possession*

Before enemies....Neh. 4:1-23
Under great
strain ....Acts 27:21-26
Facing death......Acts 7:59, 60
Lack of ....Dan. 6:18-20

Compromise—*agreement by concession*

A. *Forbidden with:*

Ungodly .... Ps. 1:1
Evil .... Rom. 12:9
Unbelievers .... 2 Cor. 6:14-18
False
teachers. { Gal. 1:8-10
         { 2 John 7-11
Spiritual
darkness ...... Eph. 5:11

B. *Examples:*

Lot .... Gen. 13:12, 13
              Gen. 19:1-29
Samson .... Judg. 16:1-21
Solomon .... 1 Kin. 11:1-14
Asa .... 2 Chr. 16:1-9
Jehoshaphat ... 2 Chr. 18:1-3
              2 Chr. 19:1, 2
              2 Chr. 20:35-37

Concealment—*keeping something secret*

Of sin,
impossible .... Is. 29:15
Of intrigue,
exposed .... Esth. 2:21-23
Of intentions,
revealed .... Acts 23:12-22

Conceit—*self-flattery*

Of persons:

Goliath .... 1 Sam. 17:42-44
Haman .... Esth. 6:6-9
The wicked ..... Prov. 6:12-17
Christians,
deplored .... Rom. 12:16

Characteristic of:

False teachers .... 1 Tim. 6:3, 4
New convert ...... 1 Tim. 3:6

Conceited—*a self-righteous spirit; haughty*

Christians warned
against .... Rom. 11:20
Rich tempted to ... 1 Tim. 6:17
To prevail in last
days .... 2 Tim. 3:1-5

Conception of children

In marriage .... Gen. 21:1-3
In adultery .... 2 Sam. 11:2-5
In virginity ...... Matt. 1:18-21

Conclude—*to finish*

The main issue .... Eccl. 12:13

Concubine—*a "wife" who is not legally a wife*

A. *Features regarding:*

Could be
divorced ...... Gen. 21:10-14
Has certain
rights .... Deut. 21:10-14
Children of,
legitimate ..... Gen. 22:24
Unfaithfulness
of .... Judg. 19:1, 2
Source of
trouble .... Gen. 21:9-14
Incompatible with
Christianity ... Matt. 19:5

B. *Men who had:*

Abraham ...... Gen. 25:6
Nahor .... Gen. 22:23, 24
Jacob .... Gen. 30:1, 4
Eliphaz .... Gen. 36:12
Gideon .... Judg. 8:30, 31
Saul .... 2 Sam. 3:7
David .... 2 Sam. 5:13
Solomon ...... 1 Kin. 11:1-3
Caleb .... 1 Chr. 2:46
Manasseh ..... 1 Chr. 7:14
Rehoboam ..... 2 Chr. 11:21
Belshazzar .... Dan. 5:2

Concupiscence—*sinful desire*

A. *Causes of:*

Learning evil .. Rom. 16:19
Making provision for
flesh .... Rom. 13:14
Not fearing { Prov. 8:13
God .... { Prov. 9:10
Not seeing
conse-   { Ex. 34:6, 7
quences of { Rom. 6:23
sin .... { Heb. 11:25

B. *Fruits of:*

Evil
inclinations ... Rom. 7:7, 8
Temptations ... James 1:14
Unchastity ..... 1 Thess. 4:5
Reprobation ... Rom. 1:21-32

C. *Remedy for:*

Repentance .... 2 Cor. 7:9, 10
              James 4:9, 10
Submitting to { Rom. 12:1, 2
God .... { James 4:7
Resisting the
devil .... James 4:7
Drawing near to
God .... James 4:8
Walking in the
Spirit .... Rom. 8:1-8

Condemnation—*the judicial act of declaring one guilty*

A. *Causes of:*
Adam's sin.....Rom. 5:12, 15-19
Actual sin.....Matt. 27:3
Our words.....Matt. 12:37
Self-
judgment ....{Rom. 2:1
{Titus 3:10, 11
Legal require-
ments.........2 Cor. 3:9
Rejection of
Christ.........John 3:18, 19

B. *Escape from:*
In Christ ......Rom. 8:1, 3
By faith........John 3:18, 19

C. *Described as:*
Having
degrees ....Matt. 23:14
Just ....Rom. 3:8
Self-inflicted ..1 Cor. 11:29
Merited........1 Tim. 5:11, 12

D. *Inflicted:*
Now...........Rom. 14:23
In eternity.....Matt. 23:33

Condescend—*to humble oneself to the level of others*

Christ's example ..John 13:3-5
The believer's
practice ....Rom. 12:16
The divine
model ....Phil. 2:3-11

Condolence—*an expression of sympathy*

A. *Received by:*
Job from
friends ....Job 2:11
Hanun from
David ....2 Sam. 10:2
Hezekiah from a
king ....2 Kin. 20:12
Mary from
Jesus.........John 11:23-35

B. *Helps in expressing, assurance of:*
Trust ....Ps. 23:1-6
Hope ....John 14:1-4
Resurrection...1 Thess. 4:13-18
Help...........Is. 40:10, 11

Confessing Christ

A. *Necessity of:*
For salvation...Rom. 10:9, 10
A test of
faith ....1 John 2:23

An evidence of spiritual
union ....1 John 4:15
His confessing
us............Matt. 10:32

B. *Content of:*
Christ's
incarnation ...1 John 4:2, 3
Christ's
Lordship ......Phil. 2:11

C. *Prompted by:*
Holy Spirit.....1 Cor. 12:3
Faith ....Rom. 10:9

D. *Hindrances to:*
Fear of men ...John 7:13
Persecution....Mark 8:34, 35
False
teachers ......2 John 7

Confession of sin

A. *Manifested by:*
Repentance....Ps. 51:1-19
Self-
abasement ....Jer. 3:25
Godly sorrow ..Ps. 38:18
Turning from
sin............Prov. 28:13
Restitution ....Num. 5:6, 7

B. *Results in:*
Forgiveness....1 John 1:9, 10
Pardon ....Ps. 32:1-5
Renewed
fellowship.....Ps. 51:12-19
Healing........James 5:16

C. *Instances of:*
Aaron ....Num. 12:11
Israelites ......1 Sam. 12:19
David.........2 Sam. 24:10
Ezra..........Ezra 9:6
Nehemiah .....Neh. 1:6, 7
Daniel ....Dan. 9:4
Peter ....Luke 5:8
Thief ....Luke 23:39-43

Confidence—*assurance*

A. *True, based upon:*
God's Word...:Acts 27:22-25
Assurance .....2 Tim. 1:12
Trust ....Hab. 3:17-19
Christ's
promise ....Phil. 1:6
Illustrated .....1 Sam. 17:45-50

B. *False, based upon:*
Unwarranted use of sacred
things.........1 Sam. 4:5-11
Presumption...Num. 14:40-45
Pride ....1 Sam. 17:43, 44

C. *The believer's:*

Source of......1 John 3:21, 22
In prayer ......1 John 5:14, 15
In testimony...Acts 28:31
In others ......2 Cor. 2:3
⠀⠀⠀⠀⠀⠀⠀⠀⠀⠀2 Cor. 7:16
Of God's will..Phil. 1:25, 26
Of faith's
⠀finality........Phil. 1:6
Of future
⠀things.........2 Cor. 5:6, 8
Must be held ..Heb. 10:35

Confirmation—*making something steadfast and sure; establishing*

Human things.....Ruth 4:7
⠀⠀⠀⠀⠀⠀⠀⠀⠀⠀⠀⠀Esth. 9:31, 32
A kingdom........2 Kin. 14:5
An oath...........Heb. 6:17
A covenant ....Gal. 3:17
Prophecy.........Dan. 9:12, 27
Promises..........Rom. 15:8
Defense of faith..Phil. 1:7
Establishing ⎰Acts 14:22
faith⠀⠀⠀⠀⠀⠀⎱Acts 15:32, 41
To the world,
⠀forbidden.........Rom. 12:2

Conform—*to make one thing like another*

Used of:

The world,
⠀forbidden.........Rom. 12:2
World's lust.......1 Pet. 1:14
Believer, to
⠀Christ ....Phil. 3:21

Confused—*disorderly; perplexed*

Concerning:

God's will........1 Sam. 23:1-12
The Messiah .....Matt. 11:2, 3
A great event....Acts 2:1-13

Confusion—*bewilderment, perplexity*

A. *Aspects of:*
⠀⠀God not author
⠀⠀⠀of..............1 Cor. 14:33
⠀⠀Typical of
⠀⠀⠀evil ....James 3:16
⠀⠀Prayer
⠀⠀⠀concerning....Ps. 70:2
⠀⠀Illustrations
⠀⠀⠀of.............Acts 19:29

B. *Examples of:*
⠀⠀Babel ....Gen. 11:9
⠀⠀Philistines .....1 Sam. 7:10

⠀⠀Egyptians......Ex. 14:24
⠀⠀City of Shu-
⠀⠀⠀shan ....Esth. 3:15
⠀⠀Jerusalem......Acts 21:31

Congratulate—*to express happiness to another*

Tou to David......1 Chr. 18:9, 10

Congregation—*an assembly of people*

A. *Used of:*
⠀⠀The political
⠀⠀⠀Israel ....Ex. 12:3, 19, 47
⠀⠀A religious
⠀⠀⠀assembly......Acts 13:42, 43

B. *Regulations concerning:*
⠀⠀Ruled by represen-
⠀⠀⠀tatives ....Num. 16:6
⠀⠀Summoned by
⠀⠀⠀trumpets......Num. 10:3, 4, 7
⠀⠀Bound by decisions of represen-
⠀⠀⠀tatives ....Josh. 9:15-21
⠀⠀Atonement of
⠀⠀⠀sin of ....Lev. 4:13-21
⠀⠀Exclusion of certain ones
⠀⠀⠀from ....Deut. 23:1-8

Coniah—*Yahweh is creating*

King of Judah.....Jer. 22:24, 28
Same as
Jehoiachin........2 Kin. 24:8

Connivance at wrong—*tacit approval of evil*

Involves guilt .....Ps. 50:18-22
Aaron's, at Sinai ..Ex. 32:1, 2, 22
Pilate's, at Jesus'
⠀trial ....Matt. 27:17-26
Saul's (Paul's) at
Stephen's⠀⠀⠀⠀⎰Acts 7:57-60
death.⠀⠀⠀⠀⠀⠀⎱Acts 8:1

Cononiah, Conaniah—*Yahweh has established*

1. A Levite ......2 Chr. 31:11, 12, 13
2. A Levite
⠀⠀official ....2 Chr. 35:9

Conscience—*the inner judge of moral issues*

A. *Described as:*
⠀⠀Good ....Acts 23:1
⠀⠀Pure..........1 Tim. 3:9
⠀⠀Evil..........Heb. 10:22
⠀⠀Defiled........1 Cor. 8:7
⠀⠀Seared........1 Tim. 4:2

B. *Functions of:*

A witness......Rom. 2:14, 15
An accuser ....John 8:9
An upholder ...1 Tim. 1:19
Server of
good..........Rom. 13:4, 5
Source of joy ..2 Cor. 1:12
Dead ....Prov. 30:20

C. *Limitations of:*

Needs
cleansing......Heb. 9:14
Subject to
others'........1 Cor. 10:28, 29
Differs.........1 Cor. 8:7-13
Fallible ....Prov. 16:25

Conscience, clear—*freedom from guilt feelings*

A. *Necessary for:*

Freedom from dead
works.........Heb. 9:13, 14
Access to
God...........Heb. 10:21, 22
Liberty in
witnessing ....1 Pet. 3:15, 16
Christian
love...........1 Tim. 1:5
Confidence in
prayer ....1 John 3:21, 22
Proud
confidence ....2 Cor. 1:12

B. *Requirements for:*

Doctrinal
purity......... { 1 Tim. 1:3-5, 18-2:1 / 1 Tim. 4:1, 2 }
Proper
conduct....... { Acts 24:10-13, 16 / Rom. 13:4-6 }
Faith in Christ's
blood ....Heb. 9:14
             Heb. 10:19-22
Knowledge ....1 Cor. 8:7
Belief..........Titus 1:15
Submissive
spirit..........1 Pet. 2:18, 19
Faith in God's
greatness .....1 John 3:20
Consideration of
others.........1 Cor. 10:28, 29
Seeking
forgiveness... { Prov. 28:13 / Matt. 5:23, 24 }

Conscription—*to enroll for compulsory service*

Employed by { 1 Kin. 7:13, 14
Solomon .... 1 Kin. 9:20, 21 }
To build Temple...1 Kin. 5:2, 3, 13

To restore cities...1 Kin. 9:15-17
Led to revolt .....1 Kin. 12:3-16

See Levy

Consecration—*dedication to God's service*

A. *Applied to:*

Israel..........Ex. 19:6
Priests.........Lev. 8:1-13
Levites ....Num. 8:5, 6, 14
Individuals ....1 Sam. 1:11
Firstborn ......Ex. 13:2, 12
Possessions ....Lev. 27:28, 29
Christ ....Heb. 2:10

B. *The Christian's:*

By Christ .....John 17:23
Complete and
entire ....Rom. 12:1, 2
Separation from
world ....2 Cor. 6:14-18
Devotion to
Christ.........Rev. 14:1-7
Sacred
anointing .....1 John 2:20, 27
New
priesthood ....1 Pet. 2:5, 9

Conservation—*preserving worthwhile things*

Material things...John 6:12, 13
Spiritual things...Rev. 3:2, 3
Good ....Acts 26:22, 23
Unwise ....Luke 5:36, 37

Consolation—*comfort fortified with encouragement*

God, source of ....Rom. 15:5
Simeon waits
for ....Luke 2:25
Source of joy .....Acts 15:30, 31
To be shared......2 Cor. 1:4-11

Conspiracy—*a plot to overthrow lawful authority*

Against:

Joseph ....Gen. 37:18-20
Moses...........Num. 16:1-35
Samson ....Judg. 16:4-21
Daniel ....Dan. 6:4-17
Jesus...........Matt. 12:14
Paul ....Acts 23:12-15

Constancy—*firmness of purpose*

Ruth's, to
Naomi...........Ruth 1:16

Jonathan's, to
David . . . . 1 Sam. 20:12-17
Virgins, to
Christ . . . . Rev. 14:4, 5

Constellation—*a group of stars*

The Great Bear	Job 9:9
	Job 38:32
The Serpent	Job 26:13
Orion	Job 38:31
	Amos 5:8
Pleiades (seven stars)	{Job 9:9
	{Job 38:31
Castor and Pollux	Acts 28:11
Judgment on	Is. 13:10, 11
Incense burned to	2 Kin. 23:5

Consultation—*seeking advice from others*

Demonical	1 Sam. 28:7-25
Divided	1 Kin. 12:6, 8
Determined	Dan. 6:7
Devilish	John 12:10, 11
	Matt. 26:3, 4

Contempt—*scorn compounded with disrespect*

A. *Forbidden toward:*

Parents	Prov. 23:22
Weak Christians	{Matt. 18:10
	{Rom. 14:3
Believing masters	1 Tim. 6:2
The poor	James 2:1-3

B. *Objects of:*

The righteous	Ps. 80:6
Spiritual things	Matt. 22:2-6
Christ	John 9:28, 29

C. *Examples of:*

Nabal	1 Sam. 25:10, 11
Michal	2 Sam. 6:16
Sanballat	Neh. 2:19
Jews	Matt. 26:67, 68
False teachers	2 Cor. 10:10
The wicked	Prov. 18:3

Contention—*a quarrelsome spirit*

A. *Caused by:*

Pride	Prov. 13:10
Disagreement	Acts 15:36-41
Divisions	1 Cor. 1:11-13

A quarrelsome
spirit . . . . Gal. 5:15

B. *Antidotes:*

Avoid the contentious	Prov. 21:19
Avoid controversies	Titus 3:9
Abandon the quarrel	Prov. 17:14
Follow peace	Rom. 12:18-21

Contentious woman

Gets Samson's secret	Judg. 16:13-17
Called brawling	Prov. 21:9, 19
Undesirable	Prov. 25:24
	Prov. 27:15

Contentment—*an uncomplaining acceptance of one's share*

A. *Opposed to:*

Worry	Matt. 6:25, 34
Murmuring	1 Cor. 10:10
Greed	Heb. 13:5
Envy	James 3:16

B. *Shown by our recognition of:*

Our unworthiness	Gen. 32:9, 10
Our trust	Hab. 3:17-19
God's care	Ps. 145:7-21
God's provisions	1 Tim. 6:6-8
God's promises	Heb. 13:5

Contracts—*covenants legally binding*

A. *Ratified by:*

Giving presents	Gen. 21:25-30
Public witness	Ruth 4:1-11
Oaths	Josh. 9:15, 20
Joining hands	Prov. 17:18
Pierced ear	Ex. 21:2-6

B. *Examples of:*

Abraham and Abimelech	Gen. 21:25-32
Solomon and Hiram	1 Kin. 5:8-12

Contrition—*a profound sense of one's sinfulness*

Of the heart	Ps. 51:17
The tax collector	Luke 18:13
Peter's example	Matt. 26:75

Controversy—*dispute between people*

Between men	Deut. 25:1
A public	Acts 15:1-35
A private	Gal. 2:11-15

Conversion—*turning to God from sin*

A. *Produced by:*

God	Acts 21:19
Christ	Acts 3:26
Holy Spirit	1 Cor. 2:13
The Scriptures	Ps. 19:7
Preaching	Rom. 10:14

B. *Of Gentiles:*

Foretold	Is. 60:1-5
Explained	Rom. 15:8-18
	Acts 15:3
Illustrated	Acts 10:1-48
	Acts 16:25-34
Confirmed	Acts 15:1-31
Defended	Gal. 3:1-29

C. *Results in:*

Repentance	Acts 26:20
New creation	2 Cor. 5:17
Transformation	1 Thess. 1:9, 10

D. *Fruits of:*

Faithfulness	Matt. 24:45-47
Gentleness	1 Thess. 2:7
Patience	Col. 1:10-12
Love	1 John 3:14
Obedience	Rom. 15:18
Peacefulness	James 3:17, 18
Self-control	2 Pet. 1:6
Self-denial	John 12:25

Conviction—*making one conscious of his guilt*

A. *Produced by:*

Holy Spirit	John 16:7-11
The Gospel	Acts 2:37
Conscience	John 8:9
	Rom. 2:15
The Law	James 2:9

B. *Instances of:*

Adam	Gen. 3:8-10
Joseph's brothers	Gen. 42:21, 22
Israel	Ex. 33:2-4
David	Ps. 51:1-17
Isaiah	Is. 6:1-5
Men of Nineveh	Matt. 12:41
Peter	Luke 5:8
Saul of Tarsus	Acts 9:4-18

Philippian jailer	Acts 16:27-30

Convocation—*a gathering for worship*

A. *Applied to:*

Sabbaths	Lev. 23:2, 3
Passover	Ex. 12:16
Pentecost	Lev. 23:16-21
Feast of Trumpets	Num. 29:1
Feast of Weeks	Num. 28:26
Feast of Tabernacles	Lev. 23:34-36
Day of Atonement	Lev. 23:27

B. *Designed to:*

Gather the people	Josh. 23:1-16
Worship God	2 Kin. 23:21, 22

Cooking—*making food palatable*

Done by women	Gen. 18:2-6
Carefully performed	Gen. 27:3-10
Savory dish	Gen. 27:4
Vegetables	Gen. 25:29
Forbidden on the Sabbath	Ex. 35:3
Fish	Luke 24:42

Cooperation—*working together*

A. *Kinds of:*

Man with man	Ex. 17:12
God with man	Phil. 2:12, 13

B. *Needed to:*

Complete job	Neh. 4:16, 17
Secure results	Matt. 18:19
Win converts	John 1:40-51
Maintain peace	Mark 9:50

C. *Basis:*

Obedience to God	Ps. 119:63
Faith	Rom. 14:1-4

Cos

An island between Rhodes and Miletus	Acts 21:1

Copper

A. *Used for:*

Money	Matt. 10:9

B. *Workers in:*
Alexander .....2 Tim. 4:14

Coral—*a rocklike substance formed from skeletons of sea creatures*

Wisdom more valuable
than..............Job 28:18
Bought by
traders ....Ezek. 27:16

Corban—*an offering*

Money
dedicated.........Mark 7:11

Cordiality—*sincere affection and kindness*

Abraham's ....Gen. 18:1-8
Seen in
Jonathan.........1 Sam. 20:11-23
Lacking in
Nabal ....1 Sam. 25:9-13

Coriander

A plant whose seed is compared to
manna ....Ex. 16:31

Corinth—*a city of Greece*

Paul labors at .....Acts 18:1-18
Site of church.....1 Cor. 1:2
Visited by
Apollos...........Acts 19:1
Abode of
Erastus...........2 Tim. 4:20

Corinthians, epistles to the—*two books of the New Testament*

Written by Paul...1 Cor. 1:1
2 Cor. 1:1

Cornelius—*a horn*

A religious
Gentile ....Acts 10:1-48

Cornerstone—*a stone placed to bind two walls together*

Laid in Zion.......Is. 28:16
Rejected ....Ps. 118:22
Christ is ....1 Pet. 2:6, 8
Christ fulfills .....Acts 4:11
1 Pet. 2:7

Correction—*punishment designed to restore*

A. *Means of:*
God's
judgments ....Jer. 46:28
The rod........Prov. 22:15
Wickedness....Jer. 2:19

Prayer.........Jer. 10:24
Scriptures .....2 Tim. 3:16

B. *Benefits of:*
Needed for
children.......Prov. 23:13
Sign of
sonship ....Prov. 3:12
Brings rest.....Prov. 29:17
Makes happy ..Job 5:17

Corrosion (see Rust)

Corruption—*rottenness; depravity*

A. *Descriptive of:*
Physical
blemishes .....Mal. 1:14
Physical
decay ....Matt. 6:19, 20
Moral decay ...Gen. 6:12
Eternal ruin ...Gal. 6:8

B. *Characteristics of:*
Unregenerate
men..........Luke 6:43-45
Apostates......2 Cor. 2:6, 7
2 Pet. 2:12, 19

C. *Deliverance from:*
By Christ ......Acts 2:27, 31
Promised ......Rom. 8:21
Through
conversion ...1 Pet. 1:18, 23
Perfected in
heaven........1 Cor. 15:42, 50

Corruption, mount of

Site of pagan
altars.............1 Kin. 11:7
Altars of,
destroyed.........2 Kin. 23:13

Corruption of body

Results from Adam's
sin ....Rom. 8:21
Begins in this
life ....2 Cor. 5:4
Consummated by
death.............John 11:39
Freedom from,
promised ....Rom. 8:21
Freedom from,
accomplished.....1 Cor. 15:42

Cosam—*a diviner*

Father of Addi ....Luke 3:28

Cosmetics

Used by Jezebel...2 Kin. 9:30
Futility of.........Jer. 4:30

Cosmic conflagration—*to destroy by fire*

Day of
judgment.........2 Pet. 3:7-10

Council—*Jewish Sanhedrin*

A judicial court ... Matt. 5:22
Christ's trial ..... Matt. 26:57-59
Powers of,
limited .... John 18:31
Apostles before .. Acts 4:5-30
Stephen before .. Acts 6:12-15
Paul before ...... Acts 23:1-5

Counsel, God's

A. *Called:*
Immutable....Heb. 6:17
Faithful........Is. 25:1
Wonderful.....Is. 28:29
Great........Jer. 32:19
Sovereign.....Dan. 4:35
Eternal ......Eph. 3:11

B. *Events determined by:*
History ....Is. 46:10, 11
Christ's
death ......Acts 2:23
Salvation .....Rom. 8:28-30
Union in
Christ........Eph. 1:9, 10

C. *Attitudes toward:*
Christians
declare.......Acts 20:27
Proper
reserve.......Acts 1:7
Wicked
despise........Is. 5:19
They reject ....Luke 7:30

Counsel, man's

Jethro's,
accepted ....Ex. 18:13-27
Hushai's
followed..........2 Sam. 17:14
Of a woman, brings
peace............2 Sam. 20:16-20
David's dying .....1 Kin. 2:1-10
Of old men,
rejected ....1 Kin. 12:8, 13
Of friends,   { Esth. 5:14
avenged ....{ Esth. 7:10

Counselor—*an advisor*

Christ is ....Is. 9:6
Your testimonies
are ....Ps. 119:24
Safety in many....Prov. 11:14

Brings security....Prov. 15:22
Jonathan, a ....1 Chr. 27:32
Gamaliel ....Acts 5:33-40

Count—*to number*

Things counted:

Stars..............Gen. 15:5
Days...............Lev. 15:13
Years ....Lev. 25:8
Plunder ....Num. 31:26
Weeks ....Deut. 16:9
Money ....2 Kin. 22:4
People ....1 Chr. 21:17
Bones.............Ps. 22:17
Towers............Ps. 48:12
Houses............Is. 22:10

Countenance—*facial expression, visage*

A. *Kinds of:*
Unfriendly ....Gen. 31:1, 2
Fierce ....Deut. 28:50
Awesome.....Judg. 13:6
Sad............Neh. 2:2, 3
Handsome ....1 Sam. 16:12
Cheerful ......Prov. 15:13
Angry ....Prov. 25:23

B. *Transfigured:*
Moses'........2 Cor. 3:7
Christ's........Matt. 17:1, 2
The
believer's......2 Cor. 3:18

Counterfeit—*a spurious imitation of the real thing*

A. *Applied to persons:*
Christ ....Matt. 24:4, 5, 24
Apostles .....2 Cor. 11:13
Ministers .....2 Cor. 11:14, 15
Christians ....Gal. 2:3, 4
Teachers .....2 Pet. 2:1
Prophets.......1 John 4:1
The
antichrist .....Rev. 19:20

B. *Applied to things:*
Worship ......Matt. 15:8, 9
Gospel........Gal. 1:6-12
Miracles ......2 Thess. 2:7-12
Knowledge ...1 Tim. 6:20
Command-
ments........Titus 1:13, 14
Doctrines .....Heb. 13:9
Religion ......James 1:26
Prayers.......James 4:3

Country—*the land of a nation*

Commanded to
leave . . . . Gen. 12:1-4
Love of native . . . . Gen. 30:25
Exiled from . . . . Ps. 137:1-6
A prophet in his
own . . . . Luke 4:24
A heavenly . . . . Heb. 11:16

Courage—*fearlessness in the face of danger*

A. *Manifested:*
Among
enemies . . . . Ezra 5:1-17
In battle . . . . 1 Sam. 17:46
Against great
foes . . . . Judg. 7:7-23
Against great
odds . . . . 1 Sam. 17:32, 50
When
threatened . . . . Dan. 3:16-18
When
intimidated . . . . Dan. 6:7-13
When facing
death . . . . Judg. 16:28-30
In youth . . . . 1 Sam. 14:6-45
In old age . . . . . Josh. 14:10-12
Before a king . . Esth. 4:8, 16
In moral
crises . . . . Neh. 13:1-31
In preaching
Christ . . . . Acts 3:12-26
In rebuking . . . . Gal. 2:11-15

B. *Men encouraged to:*
Leaders . . . . Deut. 31:7
Joshua . . . . Josh. 1:5-7
Gideon . . . . Judg. 7:7-11
Philistines . . . . . 1 Sam. 4:9
Zerubbabel . . . . Hag. 2:4
Solomon . . . . . . 1 Chr. 28:20

Course—*onward movement; advance*

A ship's
direction . . . . Acts 16:11
A prescribed
path . . . . Judg. 5:20
The age . . . . Eph. 2:2
The cycle of life . . . James 3:6

Courtesy—*visible signs of respect*

A. *Shown in:*
Manner of
address . . . . Gen. 18:3
Gestures of
bowing . . . . Gen. 19:1
Rising before
superiors . . . . . . Lev. 19:32

Well-wishing
remarks . . . . . . Gen. 43:29
Expressions of
blessing . . . . . . Ruth 2:4

B. *Among Christians:*
Taught . . . . Rom. 12:9-21
Illustrated . . . . . 3 John 1-6, 12

Courts—*institution designed for justice*

A. *Kinds of:*
Circuit . . . . 1 Sam. 7:15-17
Superior and
inferior . . . . Ex. 18:21-26
Ecclesias-
tical . . . . Matt. 18:15-18

B. *Places held:*
At the
tabernacle . . . . Num. 27:1-5
Outside the
camp . . . . Lev. 24:13, 14
At the city's
gates . . . . Ruth 4:1, 2
Under a tree . . . Judg. 4:4, 5

C. *Features of:*
Witness
examined . . . . . Deut. 19:15-21
Accused
speaks . . . . Mark 15:1-5
Sentence of,
final . . . . Deut. 17:8-13
Contempt of,
forbidden . . . . . Acts 23:1-5
Corruption of,
deplored . . . . . . Matt. 26:59-62

Courtship—*the period leading to marriage*

Isaac and
Rebekah . . . . Gen. 24:1-67
Jacob and
Rachel . . . . Gen. 29:9-30
Samson . . . . Judg. 14:1-7
Boaz and Ruth . . . . Ruth 3:4-14
Ahasuerus and
Esther . . . . Esth. 2:17

Courtyard, Court—*an enclosed area*

Tabernacle . . . . Ex. 27:9
Temple . . . . 1 Kin. 6:36
Prison . . . . Jer. 32:2
House . . . . 2 Sam. 17:18
Garden place . . . . . . Esth. 1:5

Covenant—*agreement between men*

A. *Designed for:*
Mutual
protection.....Gen. 31:50-52
Securing
peace ....Josh. 9:15, 21
Friendship.....1 Sam. 18:3
Promoting
commerce.....1 Kin. 5:6-11

B. *Requirements of:*
Witnessed .....Gen. 23:16-18
Confirmed by an
oath ....Gen. 21:23, 31
Specified.......1 Sam. 11:1, 2
Written and
sealed.........Neh. 9:38

C. *Examples of:*
Abraham and
Abimelech ....Gen. 21:27-32
Laban and
Jacob ....Gen. 31:43-55
David and
elders.........2 Sam. 5:1-3
Ahab and Ben-
Hadad ....1 Kin. 20:34
New
covenant......Matt. 26:28
New Testament dispen-
sation..........2 Cor. 3:6
Superiority of the
new...........Heb. 8:6-13
Descriptive of a person's
will ....Heb. 9:15-17

Covenant—*spiritual agreement*

A. *Between a leader and people:*
Joshua's ....Josh. 24:1-28
Jehoiada's .....2 Kin. 11:17
Hezekiah's.....2 Chr. 29:1, 10
Josiah's........2 Kin. 23:3
Ezra's ....Ezra 10:3

B. *Between God and man:*
Adam..........Gen. 2:16, 17
Noah ....Gen. 9:1-17
Abraham ......Gen. 15:18
Isaac ....Gen. 26:1-5
Jacob..........Gen. 28:13-22
Israel..........Ex. 19:5
Levi ....Mal. 2:4-10
Phinehas ......Num. 25:11-13
David ....Ps. 89:3, 28, 34

C. *The old* (Sinaitic):
Instituted at
Sinai..........Ex. 19:5

Ratified by ⎰Ex. 24:6-8
sacrifice....⎱Heb. 9:16
Does not annul the
Abrahamic....Gal. 3:16-18
Designed to lead to
Christ.........Gal. 3:17-25
Consists of outward
rites ....Heb. 9:1-13
Sealed by circum-
cision ....Gen. 17:9-14
Prefigures the
Gospel ....Heb. 9:8-28

D. *The new* (evangelical):
Promised in
Eden..........Gen. 3:15
Proclaimed to
Abraham......Gen. 12:3
Dated in
prophecy......Dan. 9:24-27
Fulfilled in
Christ.........Luke 1:68-79
Ratified by His
blood ....Heb. 9:11-23
Remembered in the Lord's
Supper........1 Cor. 11:25
Called
everlasting ....Heb. 13:20

Covenant-breakers

Under God's
judgment.........Is. 24:5
By abominations ..Ezek. 44:7

Covenant-keepers

God's blessing
upon ....Ex. 19:5

Covenant of salt—*of perpetual purity*

Descriptive of
Priests...........Num. 18:19
Descriptive of
David ....2 Chr. 13:5
Used
figuratively.......Mark 9:50

Covered carts

Used as
offerings.........Num. 7:3

Coverings

Symbolic of:
Immorality......Prov. 7:16

Covert—*hiding place*

Used by Abigail ...1 Sam. 25:20
Figurative of
protection ....Is. 32:2

Covetousness—*an insatiable desire for worldly gain; greed*

A. *Described as:*
Idolatry........Col. 3:5
Root of evil....1 Tim. 6:9-11
Never
satisfied.......Hab. 2:9
Vanity..........Ps. 39:6

B. *Productive of:*
Theft ....Josh. 7:20, 21
Lying ....2 Kin. 5:20-27
Murder ....Prov. 1:18, 19
Falsehood .....Acts 5:1-10
Harmful
lusts ....1 Tim. 6:9
Apostasy ....1 Tim. 6:10

C. *Excludes from:*
God's
kingdom ....{1 Cor. 6:10
              {Eph. 5:5
Sacred
offices.........1 Tim. 3:3
Heaven.........Eph. 5:5

D. *Examples of:*
Achan ....Josh. 7:21
Saul ....1 Sam. 15:9, 19
Judas..........Matt. 26:14, 15
Ananias ....Acts 5:1-11

See Avarice

Cowardice, spiritual

A. *Causes of:*
Fear of life.....Gen. 12:11-13
Fear of
others.........Ex. 32:22-24
Unbelief ....Num. 13:28-33
Fear of
rulers ....John 9:22

B. *Results in:*
Defeat..........Num. 14:40-45
Escape.........2 Sam. 15:13-17
Compromise...John 19:12-16
Denial ....Matt. 26:69-74

C. *Guilty conscience makes:*
Joseph's
brothers.......Gen. 42:21-28
David..........2 Sam. 12:1-14
Pharisees ......John 8:1-11

Cows

Jacob's
possessions......Gen. 32:15
Found in Egypt ...Gen. 41:2
Use of milk ....2 Sam. 17:29
Used in rituals ....Lev. 3:1

Cozbi—*false*

Slain by
Phinehas ....Num. 25:6-18

Craft

A trade ....Rev. 18:22

Craftiness—*cunning deception*

Applied to
David ....1 Sam. 23:19-22
Man's thwarted by
God..............Job 5:13
A harlot's heart ...Prov. 7:10
Man's, known by
God..............1 Cor. 3:19
Enemies', perceived by
Christ............Luke 20:23
Use of, rejected ...2 Cor. 4:2
Warning against ..Eph. 4:14

Craftsmen—*men who work at a trade*

Makers of idols....Deut. 27:15
Destroyed in
Babylon ....Rev. 18:21, 22

Crane—*a migratory bird*

Chatters ....Is. 38:14

Creation—*causing what did not exist to exist*

A. *Author of:*
God ....Heb. 11:3
Jesus Christ ...Col. 1:16, 17
Holy Spirit.....Ps. 104:30

B. *Objects of:*
Heaven,
earth..........Gen. 1:1-10
Vegetation.....Gen. 1:11, 12
Animals ......Gen. 1:21-25
Man ....Gen. 1:26-28
Stars ....Is. 40:26

C. *Expressive of God's:*
Deity ....Rom. 1:20
Power ....Is. 40:26, 28
Glory..........Ps. 19:1
Goodness......Ps. 33:5, 6
Wisdom ....Ps. 104:24
Sovereignty....Rev. 4:11

D. *Illustrative of:*
The new
birth ....2 Cor. 5:17
Renewal of
believers ......Ps. 51:10
The eternal
world ....{Is. 65:17
              {2 Pet. 3:11, 13

E. *The first:*
Subject to
vanity..........Rom. 8:19, 20
Will be
delivered......Rom. 8:21

Creator—*the Supreme Being*

A title of God.....Is. 40:28
Man's disrespect
of................Rom. 1:25
To be
remembered......Eccl. 12:1

Creditor—*one to whom a debt is payable*

Interest,
forbidden.........Ex. 22:25
Debts remitted....Neh. 5:10-12
Some very cruel...Matt. 18:28-30
Christian
principle..........Rom. 13:8

Cremation—*burning a body*

Two hundred fifty were
consumed.......Num. 16:35
Zimri's end........1 Kin. 16:15-19

Crescens—*growing*

Paul's assistant....2 Tim. 4:10

Crete—*an island in the Mediterranean Sea*

Some from, at
Pentecost.......Acts 2:11
Paul visits........Acts 27:7-21
Titus
dispatched to.....Titus 1:5
Inhabitants of, evil and
lazy..............Titus 1:12

Crib

Animals feed
from.............Is. 1:3

Criminal—*a lawbreaker*

Paul
considered a......Acts 25:16, 27
Christ
accused of........John 18:28-30
Christ crucified
between..........Luke 23:32, 33
One unrepentant; one
repentant........Luke 23:39-43

Cripple—*one physically impaired*

Mephibosheth, by a
fall...............2 Sam. 4:4

Paul's
healing of........Acts 14:8-10
Jesus heals........Matt. 15:30, 31

Crisis—*the crest of human endurance*

Bad advice in.....Job 2:9, 10
God's advice in....Luke 21:25-28

Crispus—*curled*

Chief ruler of synagogue at
Corinth..........Acts 18:8
Baptized by Paul..1 Cor. 1:14

Crop—*the craw of a bird*

Removed by
priest.............Lev. 1:16

Cross—*a method of execution*

A. *Used literally of:*
Christ's
death.........Matt. 27:32

B. *Used figuratively of:*
Duty..........Matt. 10:38
Christ's
sufferings.....1 Cor. 1:17
The Christian
faith.........1 Cor. 1:18
Reconcili-
ation..........Eph. 2:16

Crown—*an emblem of glory*

A. *Worn by:*
High priest....Lev. 8:9
Kings..........2 Sam. 12:30
Queens........Esth. 2:17
Ministers of
state.........Esth. 8:15

B. *Applied figuratively to:*
A good wife...Prov. 12:4
Old age........Prov. 16:31
Grand-
children.......Prov. 17:6
Honor.........Prov. 27:24
Material
blessings......Ps. 65:11

C. *Applied spiritually to:*
Christ.........Ps. 132:18
Christ at His
return........Rev. 19:12
Christ
glorified.......Heb. 2:7-9
The church...Is. 62:3
The Christian's
reward.......2 Tim. 2:5
The minister's
reward.......Phil. 4:1
Soul winners...1 Thess. 2:19

The Christian's incorruptible
prize . . . . 1 Cor. 9:25

Crown—*the top of the head*

Figurative of
retribution . . . . Ps. 7:16

Crown of thorns

Placed on   { Matt. 27:29
Christ . . . . { John 19:2

Crowns of Christians

Joy . . . . 1 Thess. 2:19
Righteousness. . . . . 2 Tim. 4:8
Life . . . . James 1:12
Glory . . . . 1 Pet. 5:4
Imperishable . . . . . 1 Cor. 9:25

Crucifixion—*death on a cross*

A. *Jesus' death by:*
    Predicted . . . . . . Matt. 20:19
    Demanded. . . . . Mark 15:13, 14
    Gentiles . . . . Matt. 20:19
    Jews. . . . . Acts 2:22, 23, 36
    Between
    thieves. . . . . Matt. 27:38
    Nature of, unrecog-
    nized. . . . . 1 Cor. 2:7, 8

B. *Figurative of:*
    Utter
    rejection . . . . Heb. 6:6
    Apostasy . . . . . . Rev. 11:8
    Union with
    Christ. . . . . Gal. 2:20
    Separation . . . . . Gal. 6:14
    Sanctifi-
    cation. . . . . Rom. 6:6
    Dedication. . . . . 1 Cor. 2:2

Cruelty—*violence*

Descriptive of the
wicked . . . . Ps. 74:20
To animals,
forbidden. . . . . Num. 22:27-35

Crumbs—*fragments of bread*

Dogs eat of . . . . Matt. 15:27
Lazarus begs for . . Luke 16:20, 21

Crying—*an emotional upheaval*

Accusation. . . . . Gen. 4:10
Remorse . . . . Heb. 12:17
Pretense . . . . Judg. 14:15-18
Sorrow. . . . . 2 Sam. 18:33
Others' sins . . . . . . Ps. 119:136

Pain . . . . Heb. 5:7, 8
None in heaven . . . Rev. 21:4

Crystal—*rock crystal*

Wisdom
surpasses. . . . . Job 28:17-20
Gates of Zion . . . . Is. 54:12
Descriptive of
heaven . . . . Rev. 4:6

Cubs—*offspring of beasts*

Figurative of:

Babylonians. . . . . . . Jer. 51:38
Assyrians . . . . Nah. 2:11, 12
Princes of Israel. . . Ezek. 19:2-9

Cucumber—*an edible fruit grown on a vine*

Lusted after. . . . . . . Num. 11:5
Grown in
gardens . . . . Is. 1:8

Cud—*partly digested food*

Animals chew
again. . . . . Lev. 11:3-8

Cummin—*an annual of the parsley family*

Seeds threshed by a
rod. . . . . Is. 28:25, 27
A trifle of
tithing. . . . . Matt. 23:23

Cup

A. *Literal use of:*
    For drinking . . . 2 Sam. 12:3

B. *Figurative uses of:*
    One's portion . . Ps. 11:6
    Blessings . . . . . . Ps. 23:5
    Suffering . . . . . . Matt. 20:23
    New
    covenant. . . . . . 1 Cor. 10:16
    Hypocrisy . . . . . Matt. 23:25, 26
                  Luke 11:39

Cupbearer—*a high court official*

Many under
Solomon . . . . 1 Kin. 10:5
Nehemiah, a
faithful. . . . . Neh. 1:11

Curds

Article of diet . . . . . 2 Sam. 17:29
Fed to infants . . . . Is. 7:15, 22
Illustrative of
prosperity . . . . Deut. 32:14

See Butter

Cure—*to restore to health*

Of the body ...... Matt. 17:16
Of the mind ...... Mark 5:15
Of the
  demonized ...... Matt. 12:22
With means ...... Is. 38:21
By faith ...... Num. 21:8, 9
By prayer ...... James 5:14, 15
By God's mercy ... Phil. 2:27
Hindered ...... 2 Kin. 8:7-15

Curiosity—*seeking to know things forbidden or private*

Into God's secrets,
  forbidden ...... John 21:21, 22
Leads 50,070 to
  death ...... 1 Sam. 6:19

Curiosity seekers

Eve ...... Gen. 3:6
Israelites ...... Ex. 19:21, 24
Babylonians ...... 2 Kin. 20:12, 13
Herod ...... Matt. 2:3-8
Zacchaeus ...... Luke 19:1-6
Certain Greeks ... John 12:20, 21
Lazarus' visitors.. John 12:9
Peter ...... Matt. 26:58
At the
  crucifixion ...... Matt. 27:46-49
Athenians ...... Acts 17:21

Curse, cursing—*a violent expression of evil upon others*

A. *Pronounced upon:*
  The earth ...... Gen. 3:17, 18
  Cain ...... Gen. 4:9-11
  Canaan ...... Gen. 9:25
  Two sons ...... Gen. 49:5-7
  Disobedient .... Deut. 28:15-45
  Meroz ...... Judg. 5:23
  Jericho's
    rebuilders ...... Josh. 6:26

B. *Forbidden upon:*
  Parents ...... Ex. 21:17
  Ruler ...... Ex. 22:28
  Deaf ...... Lev. 19:14
  Enemies ...... Luke 6:28
  God ...... Job 2:9
  God's people ... Gen. 12:3

C. *Instances of:*
  Goliath's ...... 1 Sam. 17:43
  Balaam's
    attempted ..... Num. 22:1-12
  The fig tree .... Mark 11:21
  Peter's ...... Matt. 26:69-74
  The crucified .. Gal. 3:10, 13

D. *Manifested by:*
  Rebellious ..... 2 Sam. 16:5-8

Curtains—*an awning-like screen*

Ten, in
  tabernacle ...... Ex. 26:1-13
Figurative of the
  heavens ...... Ps. 104:2

Cush—*black*

1. Ham's oldest
   son ...... 1 Chr. 1:8-10
2. Means
   Ethiopia ...... Is. 18:1
3. A Benjamite ... Ps. 7 (Title)

Cushan—*blackness*

Probably same as
  Cush ...... Hab. 3:7

Cushan-Rishathaim—*extra wicked*

A. *Mesopotamian King*
  Oppressed
    Israel ...... Judg. 3:8
  Othniel delivers Israel
    from ...... Judg. 3:9, 10

Cushi—*an Ethiopian*

1. Ancestor of
   Jehudi ...... Jer. 36:14
2. Father of
   Zephaniah .... Zeph. 1:1

Cushite—*an Ethiopian*

David's servant ... 2 Sam. 18:21-32

Custom—*tax; usage*

A. *As a tax:*
  Levites excluded
    from ...... Ezra 7:24
  Imposed by
    Jews ...... Ezra 4:20
  Imposed upon
    Jews ...... Ezra 4:13
  Kings require .. Matt. 17:25

B. *As a common practice:*
  Abominable.... Lev. 18:30
  Vain ...... Jer. 10:3
  Worthy ...... Luke 4:16
  Traditional.... Acts 21:21

Cuth, Cuthah—*burning*

People from, brought to
  Samaria ...... 2 Kin. 17:24, 30

Cymbal—*hollow of a vessel*

A musical   { 1 Chr. 13:8
  instrument ...... { 1 Chr. 15:28

Figurative of
pretense..........1 Cor. 13:1

Cypress—*a hardwood tree*

Used by idol-
makers...........Is. 44:14-17

Cyprus—*fairness*

Ships of, in Balaam's
prophecy.........Num. 24:24
A haven for Tyre's
ships..............Is. 23:1-12
Mentioned in the
prophets..........Jer. 2:10
A large Mediterranean island;
home of
Barnabas.........Acts 4:36
Christians reach...Acts 11:19, 20
Paul visits.........Acts 13:4-13
Barnabas visits....Acts 15:39
Paul twice sails
past..............Acts 21:3

Cyrene—*wall*

A Greek colonial city in north
Africa; home of
Simon............Matt. 27:32
People from, at
Pentecost........Acts 2:10
Synagogue of.....Acts 6:9
Some from, become
missionaries......Acts 11:20

Cyrus—*sun; throne*

A. *Prophecies concerning, God's:*
"Anointed".....Is. 45:1
Liberator.......Is. 45:1
Rebuilder.......Is. 44:28

D

Dabbasheth—*hump*

Town of
Zebulun..........Josh. 19:10, 11

Daberath—*pasture*

Correct rendering of
Dabareh..........Josh. 21:28
Assigned to
Gershomites......1 Chr. 6:71, 72

Dagon—*fish*

The national god of the
Philistines........Judg. 16:23
Falls before ark...1 Sam. 5:1-5

Daleth

The fourth letter in the Hebrew
alphabet..........Ps. 119:25-32

Dalmanutha

A place near the Sea of
Galilee..........Mark 8:10

Dalmatia—*deceitful*

A region east of the
Adriatic Sea; Titus
departs to........2 Tim. 4:10

Dalphon—*crafty*

A son of Haman..Esth. 9:7-10

Damages and Remuneration

A. *In law for:*
Personal
injury..........Ex. 21:18, 19
Causing
miscarriage...Ex. 21:22
Injuries by
animals.......Ex. 21:28-32
Injuries to
animals.......Ex. 21:33-35
Losses.........Ex. 22:1-15
Stealing.......Lev. 6:1-7
Defaming a
wife...........Deut. 22:13-19
Rape..........Deut. 22:28, 29

B. *In practice:*
Jacob's........Gen. 31:38-42
Samson's......Judg. 16:28-30
Tamar's.......2 Sam. 13:22-32
Zacchaeus'....Luke 19:8
Paul's.........Acts 16:35-39
Philemon's.....Philem. 10-18

Damaris—*gentle*

An Athenian woman converted by
Paul..............Acts 17:33, 34

Damascus—*chief city of Aram*

A. *In the Old Testament:*
Abram passed
through........Gen. 14:14, 15
Abram heir
from..........Gen. 15:2
Captured by
David.........2 Sam. 8:5, 6
Rezon,
king of........1 Kin. 11:23, 24
Ben-Hadad,
king of........1 Kin. 15:18

Rivers of,
mentioned ....2 Kin. 5:12
Elisha's
prophecy in ...2 Kin. 8:7-15
Taken by
Assyrians .....2 Kin. 16:9
Prophecies
concerning....Is. 8:3, 4

B. *In the New Testament, Paul:*
Journeys to....Acts 9:1-9
Is converted
near ....Acts 9:3-19
First
preaches at ...Acts 9:20-22
Escapes from ..2 Cor. 11:32, 33
Revisits........Gal. 1:17

Dan—*judge*

1. Jacob's son by
   Bilhah ....Gen. 30:5, 6
   Prophecy
   concerning....Gen. 49:16, 17
2. *Tribe of:*
   Census of......Num. 1:38, 39
   Position of....Num. 2:25, 31
   Blessing of....Deut. 33:22
   Inheritance
   of.............Josh. 19:40-47
   Conquest by ...Josh. 19:47
   Failure of.....Judg. 1:34, 35
   Idolatry of....Judg. 18:1-31
3. *Town of:*
   Called
   Leshem ....Josh. 19:47
   Captured by
   Danites ....Josh. 19:47
   Northern boundary of
   Israel ....Judg. 20:1
   Center of
   idolatry ......1 Kin. 12:28-30
   Destroyed by Ben-
   Hadad ....1 Kin. 15:20
   Later references
   to.............Jer. 4:15-17

Dance—*an emotional movement of the body*

A. *Kinds of:*
   Joyful ....Ps. 30:11
   Evil...........Ex. 32:19

B. *Designed to:*
   Express joy in
   victory........1 Sam. 18:6, 7
   Greet a returning
   son ....Luke 15:21-25
   Rejoice in the
   Lord ....2 Sam. 6:14-16
   Inflame lust ...Matt. 14:6

C. *Performed by:*
   Children ......Matt. 11:16, 17
   Women.........Judg. 11:34
   David..........2 Sam. 6:14, 16
   Worshipers ....Ps. 149:3

Dancing

David only ....2 Sam. 6:14-16
Greeting a   (Luke 15:20,
prodigal ....(23-25
Lustful
exhibition ....Mark 6:22
Religious
exercise ....1 Chr. 15:25-29
Time of
rejoicing ....1 Sam. 18:6, 7
Time to dance.....Eccl. 3:4
Young women
alone..............Judg. 21:20, 21

Danger—*risk; peril*

Physical...........Acts 27:9-44
Spiritual ....Heb. 2:1-3
Comfort in........Acts 27:22-25
Jesus sought in ...Luke 8:22-24
Of many kinds ....2 Cor. 11:23-33
Paul's escape
from ....Acts 9:22-25

Daniel—*God is my judge*

1. Son of David ..1 Chr. 3:1
   Called
   Chileab ....2 Sam. 3:2, 3
2. Postexilic
   priest ....Ezra 8:1, 2
   Signs
   covenant......Neh. 10:6
3. Taken to
   Babylon.......Dan. 1:1-7
   Refuses king's choice
   foods ....Dan. 1:8
   Interprets
   dreams........Dan. 2:1-45
   Honored by Nebuchad-
   nezzar ....Dan. 2:46-49
   Interprets
   handwriting...Dan. 5:10-29
   Made a high
   official ......Dan. 6:1-3
   Conspired
   against........Dan. 6:4-15
   Cast into lion's
   den ....Dan. 6:16-22
   Honored by
   Belshazzar ....Dan. 5:29
   Vision of
   beasts........Dan. 7:1-28
   Vision of ram and
   goat ....Dan. 8:1-27

Great confession
of..............Dan. 9:1-19
Vision of the seventy
weeks........Dan. 9:20-27
Vision by the great
river..........Dan. 10:1-21
Vision of the
kings..........Dan. 11:1-45
Vision of the two
men..........Dan. 12:1-13

Daniel—*book of Bible*

History in
Babylon..........Dan. 1-6
Prophecy of
nations..........Dan. 2:4-45
Visions..........Dan. 7, 8
Kingdom..........Dan. 9-12

Danites

Descendants of
Dan..............Judg. 13:2

Dan Jaan

Town near
Zidon.............2 Sam. 24:6

Dannah—*low ground*

A city of Judah...Josh. 15:49

Darda—*pearl of wisdom*

Famed for
wisdom...........1 Kin. 4:31
Also called Dara..1 Chr. 2:6

Darius—*possessing the good*

1. *Darius the Mede:*
Son of
Ahasuerus....Dan. 9:1
Succeeds
Belshazzar....Dan. 5:30, 31
Co-ruler with
Cyrus..........Dan. 6:28
Made king of the
Chaldeans.....Dan. 9:1

2. *Darius Hystaspis* (521–486 B.C.)
King of all
Persia.........Ezra 4:5
Confirms Cyrus' royal
edict...........Ezra 6:1-14
Temple work dated by his
reign...........Ezra 4:24
Prophets during his
reign...........Hag. 1:1

3. *Darius the Persian*
(424–404 B.C.)

Priestly records made during his
reign..........Neh. 12:22

Dark sayings

Speaks openly.....Num. 12:8
Utter of old.......Ps. 78:2

Darkness—*absence of light*

A. *Kinds of:*
Pre-
creational.....Gen. 1:2-4
Natural.......Gen. 15:17
Miraculous....Ex. 10:21, 22
Super-
natural.......Matt. 27:45
Spiritual....Acts 13:8-11
Eternal.......Matt. 8:12

B. *Illustrative of:*
God's unsearch-
ableness.......Ps. 97:2
The way of
sin............Eph. 5:11
Afflictions.....Ps. 112:4
Moral
depravity.....Rom. 13:12
Ignorance.....1 John 2:8-11
Death..........Job 10:21, 22
Hell...........Matt. 22:13

Darkon—*scatterer*

Founder of a
family............Neh. 7:58

Dart—*a pointed weapon*

Figurative of Satan's
weapons..........Eph. 6:16

Dathan—*fount*

A Reubenite......Num. 26:7-11
Joins Korah's
rebellion..........Num. 16:1-35
Swallowed up by the
earth..........Ps. 106:17

Daughter—*a female descendant*

A. *Applied to:*
Female child...Gen. 20:12
Female inhabitants of a
city............Judg. 21:1
Female worshipers of
God...........Is. 43:6
Citizens of a
town..........Ps. 9:14

B. *Described as:*
Licentious.....Gen. 19:30-38

Dutiful ....Judg. 11:36-39
Ideal...........Prov. 31:29
Beautiful .....Ps. 45:9-13
Complacent...Is. 32:9-11
Prophesy .....Joel 2:28

C. *Daughter-in-law:*
Bride, son's wife
Ruth, a loyal...Ruth 1:11-18
Strife against ..Matt. 10:35

Daughter of Zion—*a name referring to Jerusalem and the inhabitants therein*

Show praise to ....Ps. 9:14
Gaze on
Solomon ....Song 3:11
Left desolate ......Is. 1:8
The King
comes to ....Matt. 21:5

David—*well-beloved*

A. *Early life of:*
Born at Beth-
lehem.........1 Sam. 17:12
Son of Jesse ..Ruth 4:17, 22
Genealogy of ..1 Chr. 2:3-15
Of tribe of
Judah..........1 Chr. 28:4
Youngest
son ....1 Sam. 16:10-13
Handsome ....1 Sam. 17:42
A shepherd ....1 Sam. 16:11
Strong.........1 Sam. 17:34-36
Chosen by
God...........1 Sam. 16:1, 13

B. *His life under King Saul:*
Royal harpist ..1 Sam. 16:14-23
Armor-
bearer.........1 Sam. 16:21
Kills Goliath ...1 Sam. 17:4-49
Subdues
Philistines.....1 Sam. 17:32-54
Loved by
Jonathan......1 Sam. 18:1-4
Wise
behavior of....1 Sam. 18:5-30
Writes a
Psalm..........Ps. 59 (Title)

C. *The fugitive hero:*
Flees from
Saul ....1 Sam. 19:1-18
Takes refuge with
Samuel ....1 Sam. 19:20-24
Makes covenant with
Jonathan......1 Sam. 20:1-42
Eats show-
bread ....Matt. 12:3, 4

Feigns insanity in
Gath..........1 Sam. 21:10-15
Dwells in
cave ....1 Sam. 22:1-8
Saves Keilah...1 Sam. 23:1-13
God   ⎰1 Sam. 23:14,
delivers ⎱   15
Second covenant with
Jonathan......1 Sam. 23:16-18
Betrayed but
saved ....1 Sam. 23:19-29
Writes a
Psalm.........Ps. 54 (Title)
Spares Saul's
life............1 Sam. 24:1-22
Scorned by
Nabal.........1 Sam. 25:1-38
Marries Nabal's
widow ....1 Sam. 25:39-42
Again spares Saul's
life............1 Sam. 26:1-25
Dwells in
Ziklag ....1 Sam. 27:5-7
Rejected by
Philistines.....1 Sam. 29:1-11
Smites the
Amalekites....1 Sam. 30:1-31
Kills Saul's
murderer......2 Sam. 1:1-16
Laments Saul's
death ....2 Sam. 1:17-27

D. *King over Judah:*
Anointed at
Hebron ......2 Sam. 2:1-4, 11
List of
supporters ....1 Chr. 12:23-40
Long war with Saul's
house.........2 Sam. 3:1
Abner, rebuffed, makes
covenant with
David.........2 Sam. 3:6-21
Mourns Abner's
death ....2 Sam. 3:28-39
Punishes Ishbosheth's
murderers.....2 Sam. 4:1-12

E. *King over all Israel:*
Recognized as
king ....2 Sam. 5:1-5
Takes Zion from
Jebusites......2 Sam. 5:6-10
Builds a
house.........2 Sam. 5:11
Strengthens
kingdom ......2 Sam. 5:11-16
Strikes down the
Philistines....2 Sam. 5:17-25

Escorts ark to
Jerusalem.....2 Sam. 6:1-16
Organizes
worship.......1 Chr. 15:1-29
Organizes
musicians.....1 Chr. 25:1-31
Blesses the
people ....2 Sam. 6:17-19
Upbraided by
Michal........2 Sam. 6:20-23
Receives eternal
covenant.......2 Sam. 7:1-29
Subdues
many   ⎰2 Sam. 8:1-18
nations......⎱2 Sam. 10:1-19
Commits
adultery.......2 Sam. 11:1-27
Rebuked by
Nathan ....2 Sam. 12:1-14
Afflictions
follow..........2 Sam. 12:15-23
Repents ....Ps. 32:1-11
            Ps. 51:1-19
Family strife...2 Sam. 13:1-39
Absalom's
rebellion ......2 Sam. 15:1-31
Flees from
Jerusalem.....2 Sam. 15:13-37
Mourns Absalom's
death ....2 Sam. 19:1-10
Returns to
Jerusalem.....2 Sam. 19:15-43
Sheba's
conspiracy ....2 Sam. 20:1-26
Atones for Saul's
crime ....2 Sam. 21:1-14
Further
conflicts ......2 Sam. 21:15-22
Song of
deliverance....2 Sam. 22:1-51
Last
words of ......2 Sam. 23:1-7
His mighty
men...........2 Sam. 23:8-39
Sins by numbering
people ....2 Sam. 24:1-17
Buys Araunah's threshing
floor ....2 Sam. 24:18-25
Secures Solomon's
succession ....1 Kin. 1:5-53
Gives dying charge to
Solomon ......1 Kin. 2:1-11
Reign of forty
years..........1 Kin. 2:11

F. *Spiritual significance of:*
Prophet........Acts 2:29, 30
Musician ......2 Sam. 23:1

Inspired man ..Matt. 22:43
Type of
Christ.........Jer. 23:5, 6
Name designates
Christ.........Ezek. 34:23, 24
Christ,
son of,........Matt. 1:1
"Kingdom
of"............Mark 11:10
"Throne of" ...Luke 1:32
"Tabernacle
of"............Acts 15:16
"Key of".......Is. 22:22
Faith ....Heb. 11:32, 33
Covenant
with ....2 Sam. 7:4-17

David, Root of—*a title of Christ*

Opens sealed
book ....Rev. 5:5
Jesus describes Himself
as.................Rev. 22:16

David, Tower of—*fortress built by
David, location now unknown*

Symbolic of
strength..........Song 4:4

Dawn, Dawning

Not even one
remained........2 Sam. 17:22
Worked from .....Neh. 4:21
"The dawning of the
day" ....Job 3:9
Continually tossing
until..............Job 7:4
Murderer
"rises with the
light".............Job 24:14
Mary came to the⎰Matt. 28:1
grave at ....⎱Luke 24:1

Day—*a division of time*

A. *Natural uses of:*
The daylight...Gen. 1:5, 16
Twelve hours ..John 11:9
Opposite of
night.........Mark 5:5
The civil day (24
hours) ....Luke 13:14
Divisions of...Neh. 9:3
Security of...Gen. 8:22

B. *Extended uses of:*
Noah's time....Matt. 24:37
Gospel age.....John 9:4
Long period....2 Pet. 3:8

C. *Descriptive of:*

Believers.......	1 Thess. 5:5, 8
Christ's return.........	1 Thess. 5:2
Prophetic period........	Dan. 12:11 / Rev. 2:10
Eternity.....	Dan. 7:9, 13
Present age....	Heb. 1:2

Day of the Lord

A. *In Old Testament:*

Punishment of faithless...	Is. 13:6-13 / Amos 5:18-20
Day of wrath..	Is. 2:6-22
Restoration of remnant.....	Is. 10:20-22 / Hos. 2:16-20

B. *In New Testament:*

The last times........	Matt. 24:29 / 2 Pet. 3:10
The great day..........	Rev. 16:14

Day, Joshua's long

Described........Josh. 10:12-14

Day's Journey

Described as:

A distance.......	Gen. 30:36 / Gen. 31:23
Traveled to make a sacrifice.......	Ex. 3:18 / Ex. 5:3 / Ex. 8:27

Deaconess—*a female attendant*

Phoebe thus called ("a servant").........Rom. 16:1

Deacons—*church officers*

Ordained by the apostles..........	Acts 6:1-6
Stephen, the first martyr of........	Acts 6:5-15
Named with bishops..........	Phil. 1:1
Qualifications of..	1 Tim. 3:8-13

Dead—*lacking life*

A. *Used literally of:*

Lost physical functions......	Rom. 4:19
Those in the other world........	Rev. 20:12

B. *Used figuratively of:*

Unregenerate..........	Eph. 2:1
Unreal faith...	James 2:17, 19
Decadent church........	Rev. 3:1
Legal requirements.........	Heb. 9:14
Freedom from sin's power.........	Rom. 6:2, 8, 11
Freedom from the Law...........	Rom. 7:4

Dead Sea

Called the:

Salt Sea...........	Gen. 14:3
Sea of the Arabah...........	Deut. 3:17

Deaf—*unable to hear*

Protection afforded..........	Lev. 19:14
Healing of........	Matt. 11:5
Figurative of spiritual inability..........	Is. 42:18, 19
Figurative of patience..........	Ps. 38:13

Death, eternal

A. *Described as:*

Everlasting punishment...	Matt. 25:46
Resurrection of condemnation.......	John 5:29
God's wrath...	1 Thess. 1:10
Destruction..........	2 Thess. 1:9 / 2 Pet. 2:12
Second death..	Rev. 20:14

B. *Truths regarding:*

A consequence of man's sin............	Gen. 3:17-19
The punishment of the wicked........	Matt. 25:41, 46
Separates from God..........	2 Thess. 1:9
Christ saves from..........	John 3:16
Saints shall escape from.......	1 Cor. 15:54-58 / Rev. 2:11
Vividly described..........	Luke 16:22-26

Death, natural

A. *Features regarding:*

Consequence of sin..........	Rom. 5:12
Lot of all......	Heb. 9:27
Ends earthly life............	Eccl. 9:10
Christ delivers from fear of........	Heb. 2:14, 15

Some escaped
from . . . . Gen. 5:24
Some will
escape . . . . 1 Cor. 15:51, 52
All to be raised
from . . . . Acts 24:15
Illustrates regenera-
tion . . . . Rom. 6:2

B. *Described as:*
Return to
dust. . . . . Gen. 3:19
Removal of {Gen. 25:8
breath {Acts 5:10
Removal from
tent. . . . . 2 Cor. 5:1
Naked . . . . 2 Cor. 5:3, 4
Sleep . . . . John 11:11-14
Departure . . . . . Phil. 1:23

C. *Recognition after:*
Departed saints recognized by
the living . . . . . Matt. 17:1-8
Greater knowledge in future
world . . . . 1 Cor. 13:12
The truth
illustrated . . . . . Luke 16:19-24

Death of saints

A. *Described as:*
Sleep in
Jesus. . . . . 1 Thess. 4:14
Blessed . . . . Rev. 14:13
A gain . . . . Phil. 1:21
Peace. . . . . Is. 57:1, 2
Crown of righteous-
ness. . . . . 2 Tim. 4:8

B. *Exemplified in:*
Abraham . . . . . . Gen. 25:8
Isaac . . . . Gen. 35:28, 29
Jacob. . . . . Gen. 49:33
Elisha . . . . 2 Kin. 13:14, 20
The criminal . . . Luke 23:39-43

Death of wicked

Result of sin . . . . . . Rom. 5:12
Often {Ex. 23:25-29
punishment {Is. 65:11, 12
Unpleasant for
God . . . . Ezek. 33:11
Without hope . . . . . 1 Thess. 4:13
Rev. 20:10, 14,
15

Death penalty—*legal execution*

By stoning . . . . Deut. 13:6-10
Deut. 17:5

Debate—*discussion, contention*

With a neighbor . . . Prov. 25:9
Wicked, full of . . . . Rom. 1:29
Saints must
avoid . . . . 2 Cor. 12:20

Debir—*oracle*

1. King of
Eglon . . . . Josh. 10:3-26
2. City of
Judah . . . . Josh. 15:15
Also called Kirjath
Sepher . . . . Josh. 15:15
Captured by
Joshua . . . . Josh. 10:38, 39
Recaptured by {Josh. 15:15-17
Othniel. . . . . . . {Judg. 1:11-13
Assigned to
priests . . . . Josh. 21:13, 15
3. A place east of the
Jordan . . . . Josh. 13:26
4. Town of
Judah . . . . Josh. 15:7

Deborah—*a bee*

1. Rebekah's
nurse . . . . Gen. 35:8
2. A prophetess and
judge . . . . Judg. 4:4-14
Composed song of
triumph . . . . . . Judg. 5:1-31

Debt, debtor

A. *Safeguards regarding:*
No oppression
allowed . . . . . . Deut. 23:19, 20
Collateral
protected . . . . . Ex. 22:25-27
Time limitation
of . . . . Deut. 15:1-18
Non-payment
forbidden . . . . . Neh. 5:4, 5
Debts to be
honored. . . . . . . Rom. 13:6
Interest (usury)
forbidden . . . . . Ezek. 18:8-17
Love, the
unpayable. . . . . Rom. 13:8
Parable
concerning . . . . Matt. 18:23-35

B. *Evils of:*
Causes
complaint . . . . . 2 Kin. 4:1-7
Produces
strife. . . . . Jer. 15:10
Makes
outlaws . . . . 1 Sam. 22:2

Endangers
property ......Prov. 6:1-5
Brings
slavery........Lev. 25:39, 47,
48

C. *Figurative of:*
Sins ....Matt. 6:12
Works..........Rom. 4:4
Moral
obligation .....Rom. 1:4
God's mercy ...Ps. 37:26

Decalogue (see Ten Commandments)

Decapolis—*league of ten cities*

Multitudes from, follow
Jesus...........Matt. 4:25
Healed demon-possessed, preaches
in ....Mark 5:20

Deceit, deceivers, deception

A. *The wicked:*
Devise..........Ps. 35:20
Speaks.........Jer. 9:8
Are full of .....Rom. 1:29
Increase in ....2 Tim. 3:13

B. *Agents of:*
Satan...........2 Cor. 11:13, 14
Sin ....Rom. 7:11
Self.............1 Cor. 3:18
                James 1:22
Others..........2 Thess. 2:3
                2 Tim. 3:13

C. *Warnings against:*
Among religious
workers........2 Cor. 11:3-15
As a sign of
apostasy ......2 Thess. 2:9, 10
Sign of latter
days...........1 Tim. 4:1
As a sign of the
antichrist .....1 John 4:1-6

D. *Examples of:*
Eve.............1 Tim. 2:14
Abram..........Gen. 12:11-13
Isaac...........Gen. 26:6, 7
Jacob...........Gen. 27:18-27
Joseph's
brothers......Gen. 37:28-32
Pharaoh ....Ex. 8:29
David...........1 Sam. 21:12, 13
Amnon ....2 Sam. 13:6-14
Gehazi.........2 Kin. 5:20-27
Elisha..........2 Kin. 6:18-23
Herod ....Matt. 2:7, 8
Pharisees ......Matt. 22:15, 16
Peter ....Mark 14:70, 71

Ananias ....Acts 5:1-11
The earth......Rev. 13:11-14

Deceive—*to delude or mislead*

A. *In Old Testament:*
Eve, by
Satan ....Gen. 3:13
Israel, by the
Midianites....Num. 25:17, 18
Joshua, by the
Gibeonites ....Josh. 9:22

B. *Of Christians:*
By flattering
words........Rom. 16:18
By false
report........2 Thess. 2:3
By false
reasoning .....Col. 2:4
By evil
spirits.........1 Tim. 4:1
By false   ⎰Mark 13:22
prophets .....⎱2 Tim. 3:13

Decision—*determination to follow a
course of action*

A. *Sources of:*
Loyalty........Ruth 1:16
Prayer.........1 Sam. 23:1-13
The Lord ......1 Kin. 12:15
Satan ....1 Chr. 21:1
The world .....Luke 14:16-24
Human need....Acts 11:27-30
Disagree-
ment..........Acts 15:36-41
Faith ....Heb. 11:24-28

B. *Wrong, leading to:*
Spiritual
decline........Gen. 13:7-11
Repentance....Heb. 12:16, 17
Defeat.........Num. 14:40-45
Rejection ......1 Sam. 15:6-26
Apostasy ......1 Kin. 11:1-13
Division ....1 Kin. 12:12-20
Death ....Acts 1:16-20

C. *Good, manifested in:*
Siding with the
Lord ....Ex. 32:26
Following   ⎰Num. 14:24
God...........⎱Josh. 14:8
Loving God....Deut. 6:5
Seeking God ...2 Chr. 15:12
Obeying God ..Neh. 10:28-30

Decision, valley of—*location unknown*

Called "Valley of
Jehoshaphat".....Joel 3:2, 12

Refers to final
judgment........Joel 3:1-21

Decisiveness—*showing firmness of decision*

In serving God....Josh. 24:15, 16
                    Heb. 11:24, 25
Toward family ....Ruth 1:15-18
Toward a leader...2 Kin. 2:1-6
To complete a
task..............Neh. 4:14-23
In morality.......Gen. 39:10-12
                    Dan. 1:8
In prayer ....Dan. 6:1-16

Decree—*a course of action authoritatively determined*

A. *As a human edict:*
   Issued by
   kings ....Dan. 6:7-14
   Considered
   inflexible......Dan. 6:15-17
   Published
   widely ....Esth. 3:13-15
   Providentially
   nullified.......Esth. 8:3-17
   Sometimes
   beneficial .....Dan. 4:25-28

B. *As a divine edict, to:*
   Govern
   nature ....Jer. 5:22

Dedan—*low*

1. Raamah's
   son ....Gen. 10:7
2. Jokshan's
   son ....Gen. 25:3
3. Descendants of Raamah; a
   commercial ⎰Ezek. 27:15, 20
   people ....⎱Ezek. 38:13

Dedication—*setting apart for a sacred use*

A. *Of things:*
   Tabernacle....Ex. 40:34-38
   Solomon's
   Temple........1 Kin. 8:12-66
   Second
   temple ....Ezra 6:1-22

B. *Offerings in, must be:*
   Voluntary .....Lev. 22:18-25
   Without
   blemish ....Lev. 1:3
   Unre-
   deemable .....Lev. 27:28, 29

C. *Examples of:*
   Samuel ....1 Sam. 1:11, 22
   The believer ...Rom. 12:1, 2

Dedication, Feast of

Jesus attended ....John 10:22, 23

Deeds—*things done*

A. *Descriptive of one's:*
   Past record ....Luke 11:48
   Present achieve-
   ments.........Acts 7:22
   Future
   action.........2 Cor. 10:11

B. *Expressive of one's:*
   Evil nature ....2 Pet. 2:7, 8
   Parentage ....John 8:41
   Record ....Luke 24:19
   Profession ....3 John 10
   Love..........1 John 3:18
   Judgment......Rom. 2:5, 6

C. *Toward God:*
   Weighed.......1 Sam. 2:3
   Wrong
   punished......Luke 23:41

D. *Lord's are:*
   Righteous ....Judg. 5:11
                   1 Sam. 12:7
   Mighty ....Ps. 106:2
   Beyond
   description....Ps. 106:2

E. *Considered positively:*
   Example of ....Titus 2:7
   Zealous for ...Titus 2:14
   Careful to
   engage in .....Titus 3:8, 14
   Stimulate to ...Heb. 10:24
   In heaven .....Rev. 14:13

Deeds, the unbeliever's

A. *Described as:*
   Evil...........Col. 1:21
   Done in dark
   place..........Is. 29:15
   Abominable....Ps. 14:1
   Unfruitful .....Eph. 5:11

B. *God's attitude toward, will:*
   Never forget...Amos 8:7
   Render according
   to.............Prov. 24:12
   Bring to
   judgment .....Rev. 20:12, 13

C. *Believer's relation to:*
   Lay aside ......Rom. 13:12
   Not partici-
   pate in ....Eph. 5:11

Be delivered
from ....2 Tim. 4:18

Deer

A. *Literally:*
Listed as
clean.........Deut. 14:5
Hurt by
drought......Jer. 14:5

B. *Figurative of:*
Spiritual
vivacity......2 Sam. 22:34
Buoyancy of
faith ....Hab. 3:19
Good wife .....Prov. 5:19

Defense—*protection during attack*

Of a city ....2 Kin. 19:34
Of Israel ....Judg. 10:1
Of a plot ....2 Sam. 23:11, 12
Of the upright ....Ps. 7:10
Of one accused....Acts 22:1
Of the Gospel .....Phil. 1:7, 16

Deference—*respectful yielding to another*

To a woman's
entreaty......Ruth 1:15-18
To an old man's
wish.............2 Sam. 19:31-40
Results in
exaltation ....Matt. 23:12
Commanded .....Heb. 13:17

Defilement—*making the pure impure*

A. *Ceremonial causes of:*
Childbirth .....Lev. 12:2-8
Leprosy........Lev. 13:3, 44-46
Bodily
discharge .....Lev. 15:1-15
Copulation.....Lev. 15:17
Menstrua-
tion...........Lev. 15:19-33
Touching the
dead ....Lev. 21:1-4, 11

B. *Spiritual manifestations of:*
Abomina-
tions..........Jer. 32:34

C. *Objects of:*
Conscience ....1 Cor. 8:7
Fellowship.....Heb. 12:15
Flesh ....Jude 8
Hands ....Mark 7:2

Defrauding—*depriving others through deceit*

Forbidden........Mark 10:19

To be accepted....1 Cor. 6:5-8
Paul, not
guilty of.........2 Cor. 7:2
Product of sexual
immorality ......1 Thess. 4:3-6

Degrees—*ascents; steps*

The sun dial ......2 Kin. 20:9-11
Rank in society ...Luke 1:52
Advancement in
service ....1 Tim. 3:13

Dehavites—*people who settled in Samaria during the exile*

Opposed rebuilding of
Jerusalem ....Ezra 4:9-16

Deity of Christ (see Christ)

Delaiah—*Yahweh has delivered*

1. Descendant of
Aaron.........1 Chr. 24:18
2. Son of Shemaiah; urges
Jehoiakim not to burn
Jeremiah's
roll............Jer. 36:12, 25
3. Founder of a
family.........Ezra 2:60
4. A son of
Elioenai.......1 Chr. 3:24

Delegation—*an official commission*

Coming to seek
peace.............Luke 14:32

Deliberation—*careful consideration of elements involved in a decision*

Necessary in life ..Luke 14:28-32
Illustrated in
Jacob ....Gen. 32:1-23

Delicacies—*savory food*

Used as a
warning..........Prov. 23:3-6
Unrighteous
fellowship........Ps. 141:4

Delight—*great pleasure in something*

A. *Wrong kind of:*
Showy
display........Esth. 6:6-11
Physical
strength ......Ps. 147:10
Abomi-
nations........Is. 66:3
Sacrifices .....Ps. 51:16
Is. 1:11

B. *Right kind of:*
   God's will......Ps. 40:8
   God's command-
   ments.........Ps. 112:1
   God's
   goodness......Neh. 9:25
   Lord Himself...Is. 58:14

Delilah—*lustful*

Deceives
Samson ....Judg. 16:4-22

Deliver—*to rescue or save from evil*

A. *By Christ, from:*
   Trials..........2 Tim. 3:11
   Evil............2 Tim. 4:18
                  2 Pet. 2:9
   Death ....2 Cor. 1:10
   Power of
   darkness......Col. 1:13
   God's wrath ...1 Thess. 1:10

B. *Examples of, by God:*
   Noah..........Gen. 8:1-22
   Lot............Gen. 19:29, 30
   Jacob.........Gen. 33:1-16
   Israel........Ex. 12:29-51
   David.........1 Sam. 23:1-29
   Jews..........Esth. 9:1-19
   Daniel ....Dan. 6:13-27
   Jesus ....Matt. 2:13-23
   Apostles .....Acts 5:17-26
   Paul ....2 Cor. 1:9, 10

Deluge, the—*the Flood*

A. *Warnings of:*
   Believed by
   Noah ....Heb. 11:7
   Disbelieved by the
   world ....2 Pet. 2:5

B. *Coming of:*
   Announced ...Gen. 6:5-7
   Dated.........Gen. 7:11
   Sudden ....Matt. 24:38, 39

C. *Purpose of:*
   Punish sin .....Gen. 6:1-7
   Destroy the
   world ....2 Pet. 3:5, 6

D. *Its non-repetition based on
   God's:*
   Promise.......Gen. 8:21, 22
   Covenant.....Gen. 9:9-11
   Token (the
   rainbow)......Gen. 9:12-17
   Pledge........Is. 54:9, 10

E. *Type of:*
   Baptism ....1 Pet. 3:20, 21
   Christ's
   coming........Matt. 24:36-39
   Destruction....Is. 28:2, 18
   The end ....2 Pet. 3:5-15

Delusions, common—*self-deception*

Rejecting God's
existence .....Ps. 14:1
Supposing God does
not see ....Ps. 10:1-11
Trusting in one's
heritage ....Matt. 3:9
Living for time
alone..........Luke 12:17-19
Presuming on
time...........Luke 13:23-30
Believing
antichrist........2 Thess. 2:1-12
Denying facts .....2 Pet. 3:5, 16, 17

Demagogue—*one who becomes a leader
by mass prejudice*

Absalom ....2 Sam. 15:2-12
Haman...........Esth. 3:1-11
Judas of Galilee ...Acts 5:37

Demas—*popular*

Follows Paul .....Col. 4:14
Forsakes Paul.....2 Tim. 4:10

Demetrius

1. A silversmith at
   Ephesus.......Acts 19:24-31
2. A good
   Christian......3 John 12

Demon—*an evil spirit*

A. *Nature of:*
   Evil............Luke 10:17, 18
   Powerful......Luke 8:29
   Numerous .....Mark 5:8, 9
   Unclean ......Matt. 10:1
   Under Satan...Matt. 12:24-30

B. *Ability of:*
   Recognize
   Christ........Mark 1:23, 24
   Possess human
   beings ....Matt. 8:28, 29
   Overcome
   men...........Acts 19:13-16
   Know their
   destiny........Matt. 8:29-33
   Receive
   sacrifice......1 Cor. 10:20

Instigate
deceit.........1 Tim. 4:1

Demon possession

A. *Recognized as:*
Not insanity ...Matt. 4:24
Not disease ....Mark 1:32
Productive
harm.........Mark 5:1-5

B. *Instances of:*
Man in the
synagogue ....Mark 1:23-26
Blind and mute
man ....Matt. 12:22, 23
Two men of the
Gergesenes....Matt. 8:28-34
Mute man .....Matt. 9:32, 33
Canaanite woman's
daughter......Matt. 15:22-28
Epileptic
child.........Matt. 17:14-21
Mary
Magdalene ....Mark 16:9

Denarius, Denarii

Debt of 100 ....Matt. 18:28
Day laborer's
pay...............Matt. 20:2-13
Roman coin.......Matt. 22:19-21
Two, the cost of
lodging.........Luke 10:35
Ointment, worth
300.............John 12:5
Famine prices.....Rev. 6:6

See Jewish measures

Den of lions

Daniel placed in...Dan. 6:16-24

Denial of Christ

A. *The realm of:*
Doctrine.......Mark 8:38
                2 Tim. 1:8
Practice ....Titus 1:16

B. *The agents of:*
Individuals ....Matt. 26:69-75
Jews...........John 18:40
False
teachers ......2 Pet. 2:1
Antichrist......1 John 2:22, 23

C. *The consequences of:*
Christ denies
them...........Matt. 10:33
They merit
destruction....2 Pet. 2:1

Deportation—*exile from a nation*

Captives carried
into ....2 Kin. 15:29
To Babylon ......2 Kin. 24:8-17

Deposit—*a pledge of full payment*

The Holy Spirit in the
heart.............2 Cor. 1:22
Given by God.....2 Cor. 5:5
Guarantee of future
redemption.......Eph. 1:13, 14

Depravity of man

A. *Extent of:*
Universal......Gen. 6:5
In the heart ...Jer. 17:9
Man's whole
being ....Rom. 3:9-19
From birth.....Ps. 51:5

B. *Effects of:*
Impenitence ...Rom. 2:5
Inability to   (Jer. 17:23
listen.........\2 Pet. 2:14, 19
Lovers of
evil ....John 3:19
Defilement of
conscience ....Titus 1:15, 16

Deputy—*a person empowered to act for another*

King..............1 Kin. 22:47

Derbe—*a city of Lycaonia*

Paul visits........Acts 14:6, 20
Paul meets Timothy
here..............Acts 16:1
Gaius, native of ...Acts 20:4

Derision—*contempt manifested by laughter*

Heaped on God's
people............Jer. 20:7, 8

Descend

As a   (Matt. 3:16
dove ....\John 1:32
The angels of
God ....John 1:51

Desert—*a wilderness place*

Israel journeys
through ....Is. 48:21
Place of great
temptation ....Ps. 106:14

Rejoicing of,
predicted . . . . Is. 35:1
A highway in . . . . . Is. 40:3
John's home in . . . . . Luke 1:80
Israel received
manna in . . . . John 6:31

Desertion—*forsaking a person or thing*

Jesus, by His
disciples . . . . Matt. 26:56
Jesus, by God . . . . . Matt. 27:46
Paul, by others . . . . 2 Tim. 4:16
Christ, by professed
disciples . . . . 2 Pet. 2:15

Desire, spiritual

Renewed
fellowship . . . . 1 Thess. 2:17
Church office . . . . . 1 Tim. 3:1
Spiritual
knowledge . . . . 1 Pet. 2:2
Spiritual gifts . . . . . 1 Cor. 14:1

Desire of all nations

A title descriptive of the
Messiah . . . . Hag. 2:6, 7

Despair—*a hopeless state*

A. *Results from:*
Heavy
burdens . . . . Num. 11:10-15
Disobedi-
ence . . . . 1 Sam. 28:16-25
Disap-
pointment . . . . . 2 Sam. 17:23
Impending
death . . . . Esth. 7:1-10
Futility of human
things . . . . Eccl. 6:1-12
Rejection . . . . . . Matt. 27:3-5
Rebellion against
God . . . . Rev. 9:4-6
Hopeless-
ness . . . . Luke 16:23-31

B. *Remedies against:*
Hope in God . . . Ps. 42:5, 11
God's
faithfulness . . . 1 Cor. 10:13
Accept God's
chastening . . . . Heb. 12:5-11
Cast your care upon the
Lord . . . . 1 Pet. 5:7

Despondency—*depression of spirits*

A. *Causes of:*
Mourning . . . . . . Gen. 37:34, 35
Sickness . . . . Is. 38:9-12

Sorrow . . . . 2 Sam. 18:32, 33
                     2 Cor. 2:7
Adversity . . . . . . Job 9:16-35
Fears . . . . 2 Cor. 7:5, 6

B. *Examples of:*
Moses . . . . Ex. 14:15
Joshua . . . . Josh. 7:7-9
Elijah . . . . 1 Kin. 19:2, 4
David . . . . Ps. 42:6
Jonah . . . . Jon. 4:3, 8
Two disciples . . Luke 24:13-17

Destitute—*a state of extreme need*

The soul . . . . Ps. 102:17
The body . . . . James 2:14-17
Spiritual
realities . . . . Prov. 15:21

Destruction—*a state of ruin*

A. *Past:*
Cities . . . . Gen. 19:29
People . . . . 1 Cor. 10:9, 10
Nations . . . . Jer. 48:42

B. *Present:*
Satan's power
of . . . . 1 Cor. 5:5
Power of
lusts . . . . 1 Tim. 6:9
Wicked on way
to . . . . Rom. 3:16

C. *Future:*
Men
appointed   (Prov. 31:8
to . . . . {2 Pet. 2:12
Men fitted
for . . . . Rom. 9:22
End of the enemies of
Christ . . . . Phil. 3:18, 19
Sudden . . . . 1 Thess. 5:3
Swift . . . . 2 Pet. 2:1
Everlasting . . . . 2 Thess. 1:9

Determinate counsel

God's fixed
purpose . . . . Acts 2:22, 23

Determination—*resolute persistence*

Against popular   (Num. 13:26-31
opposition . . . . . . {Num. 14:1-9
Against great
numbers . . . . 1 Sam. 14:1-5
Beyond human
advice . . . . 2 Kin. 2:1-6
In perilous
situation . . . . Esth. 4:10-16
In spite of
persecution . . . . . . Acts 6:8-7:60

Deuel—*invocation of God*

Father of
Eliasaph..........Num. 1:14

Deuteronomy—*book of the Old
Testament containing the farewell
speeches of Moses*

Written and spoken by
Moses.............Deut. 31:9, 22,
24

Devil—*the chief opponent of God*

A. *Titles of:*
Abaddon.......Rev. 9:11
Accuser ....Rev. 12:10
Adversary .....1 Pet. 5:8
Angel of the bottomless
pit ....Rev. 9:11
Apollyon.......Rev. 9:11
Beelzebub .....Matt. 12:24
Belial ....2 Cor. 6:15
God of this
age ....2 Cor. 4:4
Murderer ......John 8:44
Prince of
demons ....Matt. 12:24
Prince of the power
of the air......Eph. 2:2
Ruler of
darkness......Eph. 6:12
Ruler of this
world ....John 14:30
Satan..........Luke 10:18
Serpent.........Gen. 3:4
Serpent of
old............Rev. 20:2
Wicked one....Matt. 13:19

B. *Origin of:*
Heart lifted up in
pride..........Is. 14:12-20
Perfect until sin
came..........Ezek. 28:14-19
Greatest of fallen
angels.........Rev. 12:7-9
Tempts man to
sin............Gen. 3:1-7
Father of lies ..John 8:44

C. *Character of:*
Cunning.......Gen. 3:1
2 Cor. 11:3
Slanderous.....Job 1:9
Fierce ....Luke 8:29
Deceitful ......2 Cor. 11:14
Powerful.......Eph. 2:2
Proud..........1 Tim. 3:6
Cowardly......James 4:7
Wicked........1 John 2:13

D. *Power of, over the wicked:*
They are his ⎧Acts 13:10
children......⎨1 John 3:10
They do his
will ....John 8:44
He possesses...Luke 22:3
He blinds .....2 Cor. 4:4
He deceives....Rev. 20:7, 8
He ensnares ...1 Tim. 3:7
They are punished with
him ....Matt. 25:41

E. *Power of, over God's people:*
Tempt ....1 Chr. 21:1
Afflict ....Job 2:7
Oppose ....Zech. 3:1
Sift ....Luke 22:31
Deceive........2 Cor. 11:3
Disguise ......2 Cor. 11:14, 15

F. *The believer's power over:*
Watch
against........2 Cor. 2:10, 11
Fight against ..Eph. 6:11-16
Resist..........James 4:7
1 Pet. 5:9
Overcome .....1 John 2:13
Rev. 12:10, 11

G. *Christ's triumph over:*
Predicted ......Gen. 3:15
Portrayed......Matt. 4:1-11
Proclaimed ....Luke 10:18
Perfected ....Mark 3:22-28

Devotion to God

A. *How?*
With our ⎧Prov. 3:9
whole ⎨Rom. 12:1
selves........⎩1 Cor. 6:20

B. *Why? Because of:*
God's ⎧1 Sam. 12:24
goodness.....⎨1 Thess. 2:12
Christ's
death ....2 Cor. 5:15
Our
redemption....1 Cor. 6:19, 20

Devotion to the ministry of saints

Household of
Stephanas........1 Cor. 16:15

Devotions, morning

Jacob's..........Gen. 28:16-18
Samuel's
parents' ....1 Sam. 1:17-19
Hezekiah's ....2 Chr. 29:20-31
Job's.............Job 1:5
Jesus' ....Mark 1:35

Devout—*pious, religious, sincere*

Simeon	Luke 2:25
Cornelius	Acts 10:1, 2, 7
Ananias	Acts 22:12
Those who buried Stephen	Acts 8:2
Converts	Acts 13:43
Women of Antioch	Acts 13:50
Greeks in Thessalonica	Acts 17:4
Gentiles	Acts 17:17
Men	Is. 57:1

Dew—*moisture condensed on the earth*

A. *Used literally of:*

Natural dew	Ex. 16:13, 14
A miraculous test	Judg. 6:37-40
A curse	1 Kin. 17:1
	Hag. 1:10

B. *Used figuratively of:*

God's blessings	Gen. 27:28
God's truth	Deut. 32:2
The Messiah	Is. 26:19
Man's fickleness	Hos. 6:4
Peace and harmony	Ps. 133:3

Dexterity—*skill in using one's hands or body*

Of 700 men	Judg. 20:16
David's	1 Sam. 17:40-50

Diadem—*a crown*

Reserved for God's people	Is. 28:5
Restored by grace	Is. 62:3

Dial—*an instrument for telling time*

Miraculous movement of	Is. 38:8

Diamond—*crystallized carbon*

Sacred	Ex. 28:18
Precious	Ezek. 28:13

Diblah—*rounded cake*

An unidentified place	Ezek. 6:14

Diblaim—*twin fig cakes*

Hosea's father-in-law	Hos. 1:3

Dibon—*a wasting away*

1. Amorite

town	Num. 21:30
Taken by Israel	Num. 32:2-5
Rebuilt by Gadites	Num. 32:34
Called Dibon Gad	Num. 33:45, 46
Later given to Reubenites	Josh. 13:9, 15, 17
Destruction of foretold	Jer. 48:18, 22

2. A village of

Judah	Neh. 11:25

Dibri—*loquacious; wordy*

A Danite	Lev. 24:11-14

Dictator—*ruler with absolute authority*

A. *Powers of, to:*

Take life	1 Kin. 2:45, 46
Judge	1 Kin. 10:9
Tax	2 Kin. 15:19, 20
Levy labor	1 Kin. 5:13-15
Make war	1 Kin. 20:1
Form alliances	1 Kin. 15:18, 19

B. *Examples, evil:*

Pharaoh	Ex. 1:8-22
Ahab	1 Kin. 16:28-33
Herod	Matt. 2:16

C. *Examples, benevolent:*

Solomon	1 Kin. 8:12-21
	1 Kin. 10:23-24
Cyrus	Ezra 1:1-4

Didymus—*twin*

Surname of Thomas	John 11:16

Diet

Of the Hebrews	Lev. 11:1-47

Differing weights

Prohibited	Deut. 25:13, 14

Difficulties—*problems hard to solve*

A. *Kinds of:*

Mental	Ps. 139:6, 14
Moral	Ps. 38:1-22
Theological	John 6:48-60

B. *Examples of:*
Birth of a child in old
age .... Gen. 18:9-15
Testing of
Abraham ...... Gen. 22:1-14
Slaughter of
Canaanites .... Ex. 23:27-33
God's
providence .... Ps. 44:1-26
Prosperity of
wicked .... Ps. 73:1-28
Israel's
unbelief ...... John 12:39-41

C. *Negative attitudes toward:*
Rebellion
against .... Num. 21:4, 5
Unbelief
under .... Heb. 3:12-19

D. *Positive attitudes toward:*
Submission
under .... Num. 14:7-9
Prayer
concerning .... Mark 11:23, 24
Admission of .. 2 Pet. 3:15, 16

Diklah—*palm tree*

Son of Joktan ..... Gen. 10:27

Dilean—*cucumber*

Town of Judah .... Josh. 15:38

Dilemma—*unpleasant alternatives*

Given to David .... 1 Chr. 21:9-17
Presented to
Jews .... Matt. 21:23-27

Diligence—*faithful applications to one's work*

A. *Manifested in:*
A child's
education ..... Deut. 6:6, 7
Dedicated
service .... Rom. 12:11
A minister's
task .... 2 Tim. 4:1-5

B. *Special objects of:*
The soul ...... Deut. 4:9
God's command-
ments .... Deut. 6:17
The heart ..... Prov. 4:23
Christian
qualities ...... 2 Pet. 1:5-9
One's calling .. 2 Pet. 1:10

C. *Rewards of:*
Prosperity ..... Prov. 10:4
Ruling hand ... Prov. 12:24

Persever-
ance .... 2 Pet. 1:10

Dimnah—*dung heap*

City of Zebulun ... Josh. 21:35
Same as
Rimmon .... 1 Chr. 6:77

Dimon—*river bed*

Place in Moab ..... Is. 15:9

Dimonah

Town in Judah .... Josh. 15:22
Same as Dibon .... Neh. 11:25

Dinah—*judgment*

Daughter of
Leah .... Gen. 30:20, 21
Defiled by
Shechem .... Gen. 34:1-24
Avenged by
brothers .... Gen. 34:25-31
Guilt concerning .. Gen. 49:5-7

Dinaites

Foreigners who settled in
Samaria .... Ezra 4:9

Dinhabah—*give judgment*

City of Edom ..... Gen. 36:32

Dionysius—*of the (god) Dionysos*

Prominent Athenian; converted by
Paul .... Acts 17:34

Diotrephes—*nurtured by Zeus*

Unruly church
member .... 3 John 9, 10

Diplomacy—*the art of managing affairs of state*

Joseph, an
example in .... Gen. 41:33-46
Mordecai's advancement
in .... Esth. 10:1-3
Daniel's
ability in .... Dan. 2:48, 49
Paul's resort to ... Acts 21:20-25

Disappointment—*the non-fulfillment of one's hopes*

A. *Concerning one's:*
Sons .... 1 Sam. 2:12-17
Mate .... 1 Sam. 25:23-31
Failure .... 2 Sam. 17:23
Wisdom .... Eccl. 1:12-18
Acceptance .... Jer. 20:7-9

Mission . . . . .Jon. 4:1-9
Hopes . . . . .Luke 24:17-24

B. *Antidotes against:*
Let trust
prevail . . . . . . .Hab. 3:17-19
Put God first . . .Hag. 1:2-14
Accept God's
plan . . . . .Rom. 8:28
Remember God's
promises . . . . . .Heb. 6:10-12

Disarmament—*abolishing weapons of war*

Imposed upon
Israel . . . . .1 Sam. 13:19-22
Figurative of
peace . . . . .Is. 2:4

Discernment, spiritual

Requested by
Solomon . . . . .1 Kin. 3:9-14
Prayed for by the
psalmist . . . . .Ps. 119:18
Sought by
Daniel . . . . .Dan. 7:15, 16
Denied to the
unregenerate . . . . .1 Cor. 2:14
Necessity of . . . . . .1 John 4:1-6

Disciples—*followers of a teacher*

John the
Baptist's . . . . .John 1:35
Jesus' . . . . .John 2:2
Moses' . . . . .John 9:28
False teachers' . . . .Acts 20:30

Discipleship—*adherence to a teacher's faith*

A. *Tests of:*
Obedience . . . . .John 14:15
Faithfulness . . .John 15:8
Persever-
ance . . . . .John 8:31
Love . . . . .John 13:35
Humility . . . . . .Matt. 10:24, 25
Surrender
of all . . . . .Luke 14:26, 33
Bearing the
cross . . . . .Matt. 16:25

B. *Rewards of:*
Acknowledged by
Christ . . . . .Matt. 12:49, 50
Enlightened by
Christ . . . . .John 8:12
Guided by the
Spirit . . . . .John 16:13

Honored by the
Father . . . . . . .John 12:26

Discipline of the church

A. *Needed to:*
Maintain sound
faith . . . . .Titus 1:13
Correct
disorder . . . . . .2 Thess. 3:6-15
Remove the
wicked . . . . . . .1 Cor. 5:3-5, 13

B. *How performed:*
In gentleness . .Gal. 6:1
In love . . . . . . .2 Cor. 2:6-8
In
submission . . . .Heb. 13:17
For
edification . . . .2 Cor. 10:8

Discipline, parental

A. *Needed to:*
Produce under-
standing . . . . . .Prov. 10:13
Drive out
foolishness . . . .Prov. 22:15
Deliver from hell
(Sheol) . . . . . . .Prov. 23:13, 14
Produce
obedience . . . . .Prov. 19:18
Develop
reverence . . . . .Heb. 12:8-10

B. *How performed:*
Without
anger . . . . .Eph. 6:4
In love . . . . . . .Heb. 12:5-7

Disclosure—*an unfolding of the unknown*

A person's
identity . . . . .Gen. 45:1-5
Desirable
information . . . .1 Sam. 23:10-12
God's plan . . . . . . .Rom. 16:25-27

Discontentment—*unhappy at the condition of things*

Between Jacob and
Laban . . . . .Gen. 31:1-16
Between Moses and
Miriam . . . . .Num. 12:1-16
Among soldiers . . .Luke 3:14

Discord—*lack of love; disagreement*

Caused by
contention . . . . . . .Prov. 26:20, 21

Envy.............1 Cor. 3:3
Caused by lies ....Prov. 6:16-19
Among Jews ......John 6:41-43

Discouragement—*depression of one's spirits*

A. *Causes of:*
Heavy
burden........Num. 11:10-15
Defeat........Josh. 7:7-9
Apparent
failure........1 Kin. 19:2-4
Sickness........Is. 38:9-20

B. *Remedies against:*
"What are you doing
here?" ....1 Kin. 19:9-18
"Cast your burden on the
Lord" ....Ps. 55:22
"Come aside by
yourselves" ...Mark 6:31
"Lift up your
heads" ....Luke 21:28

Discourtesy—*rudeness in manners*

Nabal's............1 Sam. 25:3, 14
Hanun's ....2 Sam. 10:1-5
Simon's ....Luke 7:44

Discretion—*action based upon caution*

Joseph chosen
for ....Gen. 41:33, 39
The value of .....Prov. 2:11
A woman
without ....Prov. 11:22
Women to have...Titus 2:5
God teaches.......Is. 28:26
Trait of a good
man ....Ps. 112:5

Discrimination—*making distinctions*

A. *Forbidden, on basis of:*
Wealth ....James 2:1-9
Personal righteous-
ness..........Rom. 3:10, 23

B. *Between truth and error:*
Test the
spirits.........1 John 4:1-6
Spirit of
truth..........John 14:16, 17
Word is ⎰Ps. 119:160
truth..........⎱John 17:17
Satan, father of
lies.............John 8:44

C. *Between God's Word and man's:*
Paul
preached......1 Thess. 2:13

God's Word
inspired.......2 Tim. 3:16
By Spirit.......1 Cor. 2:10-16

Diseases—*physical impairments of health*

A. *Kinds of:*
Atrophy ....Job 16:8
Blindness .....Matt. 9:27
Boil.............2 Kin. 20:7
Boils...........Ex. 9:10
Consump-
tion...........Deut. 28:22
Deafness......Mark 7:32
Dropsy ....Luke 14:2
Dumbness ....Matt. 9:32
Dysentery ....2 Chr. 21:12-19
Epilepsy ......Matt. 4:24
Fever..........Matt. 8:14, 15
Flow of
blood ....Matt. 9:20
Inflamma-
tion...........Deut. 28:22
Insanity ......Dan. 4:33
Itch ....Deut. 28:27
Leprosy.......2 Kin. 5:1
Paralysis......Matt. 4:24
Plague........2 Sam. 24:15-25
Scab..........Deut. 28:27
Sores ....Luke 16:20
Tumors........1 Sam. 5:6, 12
Weakness ....Ps. 102:23

B. *Causes of:*
Man's original
sin............Gen. 3:16-19
Man's actual ⎰2 Kin. 5:25-27
sin............⎱2 Chr. 21:12-19
Satan's ⎰Job 2:7
afflictions ....⎱Luke 13:16
God's
sovereign ⎰John 9:1-3
will ....⎱2 Cor. 12:7-10

C. *Cures of:*
From ⎰2 Chr. 16:12
God..........⎱Ps. 103:2, 3
By Jesus......Matt. 4:23, 24
By prayer.....Acts 28:8, 9
James 5:14, 15
By the use of ⎰Is. 38:21
means ....⎱Luke 10:34

See Sickness

Disfigured face

Disqualifies for
service ....Lev. 21:18

Disgrace—*shame produced by evil conduct*

Treachery..........2 Sam. 10:1-5
Private............2 Sam. 13:6-20
Public............Esth. 6:6-13
Posthumous........Jer. 8:1-3
Permanent........Matt. 27:21-25
Paramount........Matt. 27:26-44

Disgraceful—*comtemptuous reproach or shame*

Immorality........Gen. 34:7
Transgression....Josh. 7:15
Rape.............2 Sam. 13:12

Dish

Tabernacle
 implement........Ex. 25:29
Figurative of annihilating
 Jerusalem ....2 Kin. 21:13

Dishan—*antelope*

Son of Seir........Gen. 36:21, 28

Dishes—*platters used for food*

In the
 tabernacle........Ex. 25:29
A common.........Matt. 26:23
Man washing .....2 Kin. 21:13

Dishon—*antelope*

1. Son of Seir ....Gen. 36:21-30
2. Grandson of
   Seir ....Gen. 36:25

Dishonesty—*untruthfulness*

A. *Manifested in:*
 Half-truths.....Gen. 12:11-20
 Trickery ....Gen. 27:6-29
 Falsifying one's
  word..........Gen. 34:1-31
 Wicked
  devices........Prov. 1:10-19
 Theft ....John 12:4-6
 Unpaid
  wages.........James 5:4

B. *Consequences of:*
 Uncovered by
  God...........1 Kin. 21:17-26
 Uncovered by
  men...........Josh. 9:3-22
 Condemned by
  conscience ....Matt. 27:3-5

Disobedience—*rebellion against recognized authority*

A. *Sources of:*
 Satan's
  temptations ...Gen. 3:1-13
 Lust ....James 1:13-15
 Rebellion ......Num. 20:10-24
                 1 Sam. 15:16-23

B. *Consequences of:*
 Death ....Rom. 5:12-19
 The flood ......1 Pet. 3:18-20
 Exclusion from the promised
  land..........Num. 14:26-39
 Defeat.........Judg. 2:2, 11-15
 Doom ....1 Pet. 2:7, 8

Disorderly—*unruly and irregular*

Paul not guilty ....1 Thess. 5:14
Some guilty.......2 Thess. 3:6-11

Dispensation—*a stewardship or administration*

Of divine
 working..........Eph. 1:10
Paul's special privilege
 in ....Eph. 3:2

Dispersion—*a scattering abroad*

Of Noah's
 generation........Gen. 11:8
Of Israelites......2 Kin. 17:5, 6
Because of
 disobedience......Hos. 9:1-12
Of the early
 Christians ....1 Pet. 1:1

Display—*an unusual exhibition*

A. *Of God's:*
 Power ....Ex. 14:23-31
 Glory ....Ex. 33:18-23
 Wrath ....Num. 16:23-35
 Universe.......Job 38:1-41
 Holiness ......Is. 6:1-10

B. *Of man's:*
 Kingdom ......Esth. 1:2-7
 Pride ....Esth. 5:10, 11
 Wealth ....Is. 39:1, 2
 Hypocrisy .....Luke 20:46, 47

Displeasure—*disapproval; anger*

God's, at man .....1 Chr. 21:7
Man's, at God....Jon. 4:1
Man's, at men.....Mark 10:41

Disposition—*natural temperament*

Ambitious
Absalom.........2 Sam. 15:1-6
Boastful Nebuchad-
nezzar.............Dan. 4:30
Cowardly Peter ...Matt. 26:57, 58
Devilish Judas ...John 13:20-30
Envious Saul ....1 Sam. 18:6-12
Foolish Nabal .....1 Sam. 25:10-25
Gullible Haman ...Esth. 6:6-11
Humble Job.......Job 1:20-22

Distress, distressed

Used of:

Lust ....2 Sam. 13:2
God's
punishment ......Ps. 2:5

Ditch—*a trench*

Miraculously
filled ....2 Kin. 3:16-20
Wicked fall into...Ps. 7:15
Blind leaders fall
into ....Luke 6:39

Diversity—*variety*

Among hearers....Mark 13:3-8
Of God's gifts .....1 Cor. 12:4-11
Of God's times ....Heb. 1:1

Divination—*attempt to foretell the unknown by occult means*

A. *Considered as:*
System of
fraud..........Ezek. 13:6, 7
Lucrative employ-
ment..........Acts 16:16
Abomination..Deut. 18:11, 12
Punishable by
death ....Lev. 20:6, 27

B. *Practiced by:*
Astrologers ....Is. 47:13
Diviners ....Deut. 18:14
False
prophets .....Jer. 14:14
Magicians .....Gen. 41:8
Medium ....Deut. 18:11
Necro-
mancer ....Deut. 18:11
Soothsayers ...Is. 2:6
Sorcerers .....Acts 13:6, 8
Sorceress .....Ex. 22:18
Spiritist........Deut. 18:11

Division—*diversity; discord*

A. *Causes of:*
Real faith......Luke 12:51-53
Carnal spirit ...1 Cor. 3:3

B. *Opposed to:*
Prayer of
Christ.........John 17:21-23
Unity of
Christ.........1 Cor. 1:13
Unity of the   (John 10:16
church ....(1 Cor. 12:13-25

Division of Priests—*assignments for service*

Outlined by
David ....1 Chr. 24:1-19
Determined by
casting lots......1 Chr. 24:5, 7
Of Zacharias .....Luke 1:5

Divorce—*breaking of the marriage tie*

A. *The Old Testament teaching:*
Permitted......Deut. 24:1-3
Divorced may not
return to first
husband .....Deut. 24:4
Denied to those making false
claims........Deut. 22:13-19
Denied to those seducing a
virgin ....Deut. 22:28, 29
Unjust,
reproved .....Mal. 2:14-16
Required, foreign wives put
away.........Ezra 10:1-16
Disobedience, a cause among
heathen.......Esth. 1:10-22
A prophet's concern
with ....Hos. 2:1-22

B. *In the New Testament:*
Marriage
binding
as long as   (Mark 10:2-9
life...........(Rom. 7:2, 3
Divorce allowed because of
adultery......Matt. 5:27-32
Marriage of the divorced
constitutes
adultery......Luke 16:18
Reconciliation
encouraged ...1 Cor. 7:10-17

Dizahab—*abounding in gold*

Location of Moses' farewell
addresses.........Deut. 1:1

Doctrine—*teaching*

A. *Statements of:*
Founda-
tional ....Heb. 6:1, 2
Traditional.....1 Cor. 15:1-4
Creedal........2 Tim. 3:16

B. *Essentials of:*
The Bible's
inspiration ....2 Tim. 3:16
Christ's deity ..1 Cor. 12:3
Christ's
incarnation ...1 John 4:1-6
Christ's
resurrection...1 Cor. 15:12-20
Christ's
return.........2 Pet. 3:3-13
Salvation by
faith ....Acts 2:38

C. *Attitudes toward:*
Obey ....Rom. 6:17
Receive........1 Cor. 15:1-4
Hold fast ......2 Tim. 1:13
Adorn ....Titus 2:10

Doctrine, false

A. *What constitutes:*
Perverting the ⎰Gal. 1:6, 7
Gospel ....⎱1 John 4:1-6
Satanic
deception ....2 Cor. 11:13-15

B. *Teachers of:*
Deceive
many ....Matt. 24:5, 24
Attract many ..2 Pet. 2:2
Speak perverse
things.........Acts 20:30
Are savage ....Acts 20:29
Deceitful ......2 Cor. 11:13
Ungodly ......Jude 4, 8
Proud.........1 Tim. 6:3, 4
Corrupt.......2 Tim. 3:8
Love error .....2 Tim. 4:3, 4

C. *Christian attitude toward:*
Avoid.........Rom. 16:17, 18
Test ....1 John 4:1
Detest ....Jude 23

Dodai

An Ahohite ....1 Chr. 27:4

Dodanim

Descendants of
Javan ....Gen. 10:4

Dodavah—*beloved of Yahweh*

Eliezer's father....2 Chr. 20:37

Dodo—*loving*

1. A descendant of
Issachar ......Judg. 10:1
2. A mighty man of
David's ......2 Sam. 23:9
Called Dodai...1 Chr. 27:4
3. Father of
Elhanan.......2 Sam. 23:24

Doe—*female deer*

Figurative of peaceful
quietude..........Song 2:7

Doeg—*fearful*

An Edomite; chief of Saul's
herdsmen ....1 Sam. 21:7
Betrays David.....1 Sam. 22:9, 10
Kills 85 priests ....1 Sam. 22:18, 19

Dogs—*a domesticated animal*

A. *Described as:*
Carnivorous ...1 Kin. 14:11
Blood-eating...1 Kin. 21:19
Dangerous....Ps. 22:16
Domesti-
cated ....Matt. 15:26, 27
Unclean ......Is. 66:3

B. *Figurative of:*
Promiscuity....Deut. 23:18
Contempt....1 Sam. 17:43
Worthless-
ness..........2 Sam. 9:8
Satan.........Ps. 22:20
Hypocrite......Matt. 7:6
Gentiles ......Matt. 15:26
False
teachers ......2 Pet. 2:22
The unsaved...Rev. 22:15

Dominion—*supreme authority to govern*

A. *Man's:*
Delegated by
God...........Gen. 1:26-28
Under God's
control........Jer. 25:12-33
Misused ....Dan. 5:18-23

B. *Satan's:*
Secured by
rebellion ......Is. 14:12-16
Offered to
Christ.........Luke 4:6
Destroyed by
Christ.........1 John 3:8
Abolished at Christ's
return.........2 Thess. 2:8, 9

C. *Christ's:*
Predicted ......Is. 11:1-10
Announced ....Luke 1:32, 33
Secured by
His resurrec- ⎰Acts 2:24-36
tion...........⎱Rev. 1:18
Perfected at His
return........1 Cor. 15:24-28

Donkey

A. *Used for:*
Riding ....Gen. 22:3
Carrying
burdens......Gen. 42:26
Food ....2 Kin. 6:25
Royalty.......Judg. 5:10

B. *Regulations concerning:*
Not to be yoked with an
ox ....Deut. 22:10
To be rested ⎰Ex. 23:12
on Sabbath...⎱Luke 13:15
To be redeemed with a
lamb ....Ex. 34:20

C. *Special features regarding:*
Spoke to
Balaam ......Num. 22:28-31
Knowing his
owner........Is. 1:3
Jawbone kills
many ....Judg. 15:15-17
Jesus rides ⎰Zech. 9:9
upon one.....⎱Matt. 21:2, 5
All cared for by
God..........Ps. 104:1, 10, 11

D. *Figurative of:*
Wildness (in Hebrew, "wild
donkey")......Gen. 16:12
Stubborn-
ness...........Hos. 8:9
Promiscuity....Jer. 2:24

Door—*an entrance*

A. *Used literally of:*
City gates .....Neh. 3:1-6
Prison gates ...Acts 5:19

B. *Used figuratively of:*
Christ ....John 10:7, 9
Christ's
return........Matt. 24:33
Day of
salvation.....Matt. 25:10
Inclusion of
Gentiles......Acts 14:27
Opportunity ...2 Cor. 2:12

Doorkeeper

Descriptive of:

Maaseiah ....Jer. 35:4
Watchman.......Mark 13:34
Good shepherd....John 10:3
One who was spoken to by a
disciple..........John 18:16

Doorpost

Private homes.....Ex. 12:7
Servant's ears
pierced at ....Ex. 21:6
Tabernacle........1 Sam. 1:9
Command to
strike.............Amos 9:1

Dophkah—*cattle driving*

A desert
encampment .....Num. 33:12, 13

Dor—*habitation*

Jabin's ally........Josh. 11:1, 2
Taken by
Joshua........Josh. 12:23
Assigned to
Manasseh .....Josh. 17:11
Inhabitants
unexpelled ......Judg. 1:27

Dorcas—*gazelle*

Good woman .....Acts 9:36
Raised to life.....Acts 9:37-42
Called Tabitha ...Acts 9:36, 40

Dothan—*wells*

Ancient town .....Gen. 37:14-25
Joseph sold
there............Gen. 37:17-28
Elisha strikes
Syrians at ....2 Kin. 6:8-23

Double-mindedness—*inability to hold a fixed belief*

Makes one
unstable.........James 1:8

Double-tongued—*two-faced, hypocritical*

Condemned in
deacons ....1 Tim. 3:8

Doubt—*uncertainty of mind*

A. *Objects of, Christ's:*
Miracles ....Matt. 12:24-30

Resurrection...John 20:24-29
Messiahship ...Luke 7:19-23
Return.........2 Pet. 3:4

B. *Causes of:*
Satan..........Gen. 3:4
Unbelief......Luke 1:18-20
Worldly
  wisdom......1 Cor. 1:18-25
Spiritual
  instability....James 1:6, 7

C. *Removal of, by:*
Putting God (Judg. 6:36-40
  to the test....{John 7:16-18
Searching the
  Scriptures.....Acts 17:11, 12
Believing God's
  Word.........Luke 16:27-31

Dove—*pigeon*

A. *Features regarding:*
Sent from
  ark..........Gen. 8:8, 10, 12
Sold in
  Temple.......Matt. 21:12

B. *Figurative of:*
Loveliness.....Song 2:14
Desperate
  mourning.....Is. 38:14
Foolish
  insecurity.....Hos. 7:11
Israel's
  restoration....Hos. 11:11
Holy Spirit.....Matt. 3:16
Harmless-
  ness..........Matt. 10:16

Dove's dropping

Sold in Samaria...2 Kin. 6:25

Dowry—*gifts given to bride's father for the bride*

A. *Regulations regarding:*
Sanctioned in the
  Law..........Ex. 22:16, 17
Amount of,
  specified......Deut. 22:28, 29
Sometimes given by bride's
  father.........Josh. 15:16-19

B. *Instances of:*
Abraham (Isaac) for
  Rebekah......Gen. 24:22-53
Jacob for
  Rachel.......Gen. 29:15-20
Shechem for
  Dinah.........Gen. 34:11-14

David for
  Michal.......1 Sam. 18:20-25

Dragon

Applied to:
Satan.............Rev. 12:9
Antichrist........Rev. 12:3

Drawers of water—*a lowly servant classification*

Women..........Gen. 24:13
                1 Sam. 9:11
Defeated
  enemies.........Josh. 9:21
Young men......Ruth 2:9
Included in
  covenant........Deut. 29:10-13

Dreams—*thoughts visualized in sleep*

A. *Purposes of:*
Restrain from
  evil...........Gen. 20:3
Reveal God's
  will...........Gen. 28:11-22
Encourage.....Judg. 7:13-15
Reveal
  future.........Gen. 37:5-10
Instruct.......Matt. 1:20

B. *The interpretation of:*
Sought
  anxiously.....Dan. 2:1-3
Belong to
  God...........Gen. 40:8
Revealed by
  God...........Gen. 40:8
Sought for God's
  will...........Num. 12:6
Sometimes
  delusive.......Is. 29:7, 8
False, by false
  prophets......Deut. 13:1-5

C. *Notable examples of:*
Abimelech.....Gen. 20:3
Jacob..........Gen. 28:10, 12
Laban..........Gen. 31:24
Joseph.........Gen. 37:5
Pharaoh.......Gen. 41:1-13
Unnamed
  person.......Judg. 7:13, 14
Solomon.......1 Kin. 3:5-10
Job............Job 7:14
Nebuchad-
  nezzar.......Dan. 2:1-13
Joseph.........Matt. 1:19, 20
Pilate's wife...Matt. 27:13, 19

Dregs—*the sediments of liquids; grounds*

Wicked shall drink
down.............Ps. 75:8
Contains God's
fury.............Is. 51:17, 22
Figurative of negligence and
ease............Jer. 48:11

Drink—*to swallow liquids*

A. *Used literally of:*
    Water ....Gen. 24:14
    Wine ....Gen. 9:21

B. *Used figuratively of:*
    Famine ....2 Kin. 18:27
    Misery.........Is. 51:22, 23
    Married
    pleasure.......Prov. 5:15-19
    Unholy
    alliances ......Jer. 2:18
    God's
    blessings ......Zech. 9:15-17
    Spiritual
    communion ...John 6:53, 54
    Holy Spirit.....John 7:37-39

Drink offerings

Of wine...........Hos. 9:4
Of water..........1 Sam. 7:6

Dromedary—*a specie of camel*

Noted for speed...Jer. 2:23
Figurative of Gospel
blessings ....Is. 60:6

Dropsy—*an unnatural accumulation of fluid in parts of the body*

Healing of.........Luke 14:2-4

Dross—*impurities separated from metals*

Result of
refinement ....Prov. 25:4
Figurative of
Israel.............Is. 1:22, 25

Drought—*an extended dry season*

Unbearable
in the day ....Gen. 31:40
Seen in the
wilderness........Deut. 8:15
Comes in
summer ....Ps. 32:4
Sent as a
judgment.........Hag. 1:11
Only God can
stop ....Jer. 14:22
Descriptive of spiritual
barrenness ....Jer. 14:1-7
The wicked
dwell in ....Jer. 17:5, 6
The righteous
endure ....Jer. 17:8
Longest ....1 Kin. 18:1
                Luke 4:25

Drown

Of the
Egyptians ....Ex. 14:27-30
Jonah saved
from ....Jon. 1:15-17
Of severe
judgment.........Matt. 18:6
The woman saved
from ....Rev. 12:15, 16
Figurative of
lusts.............1 Tim. 6:9

Drowsiness—*the mental state preceding sleep*

Prelude to
poverty...........Prov. 23:21
Disciples
guilty of.........Matt. 26:36-43

Drunkenness—*state of intoxication*

A. *Evils of:*
    Debases ....Gen. 9:21, 22
    Provokes
    brawling ......Prov. 20:1
    Poverty........Prov. 23:21
    Perverts
    justice ....Is. 5:22, 23
    Confuses the
    mind..........Is. 28:7
    Licentious-
    ness..........Rom. 13:13
    Disorderli-
    ness..........Matt. 24:48-51
    Hinders watchful-
    ness...........1 Thess. 5:6, 7

B. *Actual instances of the evil of:*
    Defeat in
    battle ....1 Kin. 20:16-21
    Degradation ...Esth. 1:10, 11
    Debauchery....Dan. 5:1-4
    Weakness .....Amos 4:1
    Disorder.......1 Cor. 11:21, 22

C. *Penalties of:*
    Death ....Deut. 21:20, 21
    Exclusion from
    fellowship.....1 Cor. 5:11

Exclusion from
heaven........1 Cor. 6:9, 10

D. *Figurative of:*
Destruction......Is. 49:26
Roaring
waves.........Ps. 107:25-27
Giddiness......Is. 19:14
Error ....Is. 28:7
Spiritual
blindness......Is. 29:9-11
International
chaos ....Jer. 25:15-29
Persecution....Rev. 17:6

Drusilla—*feminine of "Drusus"*

Wife of Felix; hears
Paul.............Acts 24:24, 25

Dumah—*silence*

1. Descendants (a tribe) of
   Ishmael......Gen. 25:14
2. Town in
   Judah........Josh. 15:52

Dumb—*inability to speak*

A. *Used literally of dumbness:*
Imposed ......Ezek. 3:26, 27
Demonized ....Mark 9:17, 25

B. *Used figuratively of:*
Inefficient
leaders........Is. 56:10
Helplessness ...1 Cor. 12:2

See Mute

Dung—*excrement; refuse*

A. *Used for:*
Fuel ....Ezek. 4:12, 15
Food in
famine........2 Kin. 6:25

B. *Figurative of:*
Something
worthless ....2 Kin. 9:37

Dungeon—*an underground prison*

Joseph in .....Gen. 40:8, 15
Jeremiah in ......Jer. 37:16

Dunghills—*heaps of manure*

Pile of manure ....Luke 14:34, 35

Dura—*circuit, wall*

Site of Nebuchadnezzar's golden
image ....Dan. 3:1

Dust—*powdery earth*

A. *Used literally of:*
Man's body ....Gen. 2:7
Dust of
Egypt.........Ex. 8:16, 17
Particles of
soil ....Num. 5:17

B. *Used figuratively of:*
Man's
mortality......Gen. 3:19
Descendants...Gen. 13:16
Judgment......Deut. 28:24
Act of
cursing........2 Sam. 16:13
Dejection......Job 2:12
Subjection.....Is. 49:23
The grave .....Is. 26:19
Rejection......Matt. 10:14

Duty—*an obligation*

A. *Toward men:*
Husband to
wife...........Eph. 5:25-33
Wife to
husband .....Eph. 5:22-24
Parents to
children.......Eph. 6:4
Children to
parents ....Eph. 6:1-3
Subjects to
rulers ....1 Pet. 2:12-20
Rulers to
subjects......Rom. 13:1-7
Men to men ...1 Pet. 3:8-16
The weak......1 Cor. 8:1-13

B. *Toward God:*
Love..........Deut. 11:1
Obey ....Matt. 12:50
Serve ....1 Thess. 1:9
Worship ......John 4:23

Dwarf—*a diminutive person*

Excluded from
priesthood.......Lev. 21:20

Dwelling, God

In the
tabernacle.......Ex. 29:43-46
In the temple ....1 Kin. 6:11-13
                 2 Chr. 7:1-3
In Zion ....Is. 8:18
In Christ..........Col. 2:9
Among men......John 1:14
In our hearts......1 John 4:12-16
In the Holy
Spirit...........1 Cor. 3:16
In the New
Jerusalem ....Rev. 7:15

Dyeing—*coloring*

Leather . . . . Ex. 25:5

Dysentery

Cured by Paul . . . . . Acts 28:8

E

Eagle—*a bird of prey of the falcon species*

A. *Described as:*
Unclean . . . . Lev. 11:13
A bird of
prey . . . . Job 9:26
Large . . . . Ezek. 17:3, 7
Swift . . . . 2 Sam. 1:23
Keen in
vision . . . . Job 39:27-29
Nesting high . . Jer. 49:16

B. *Figurative of:*
God's care . . . . . Ex. 19:4
Swift armies . . . Jer. 4:13
Spiritual
renewal . . . . . . Is. 40:31
Flight of
riches . . . . Prov. 23:5
False
security . . . . . . Jer. 49:16

Ear—*the organ of hearing*

A. *Ceremonies respecting:*
Priest's,
anointed . . . . . Ex. 29:20
Leper's,
anointed . . . . . Lev. 14:2, 14, 25
Servant's
bored . . . . Ex. 21:5, 6

B. *The hearing of the
unregenerate:*
Deafened . . . . . Deut. 29:4
Stopped . . . . . . Ps. 58:4
Dulled . . . . Matt. 13:15
Disobedient . . . . Jer. 7:23, 24
Uncir-
cumcised . . . . . Acts 7:51
Itching . . . . 2 Tim. 4:3, 4

C. *Promises concerning, in:*
Prophecy . . . . . Is. 64:4
Fulfillment . . . . . Matt. 13:16, 17
A miracle . . . . . Mark 7:35
A foretaste . . . . 2 Cor. 12:4
Final
realization . . . . 1 Cor. 2:9

Early, arose

A. *For spiritual purposes:*
Abraham—looked on Sodom
and
Gomorrah . . . . . Gen. 19:27, 28
Abraham—to offer a burnt
offering . . . . . . Gen. 22:2, 3
Jacob—to worship the
Lord . . . . Gen. 28:18-22
Moses—to meet God on
Sinai . . . . Ex. 34:4, 5
Elkanah and Hannah—to
worship God . . 1 Sam. 1:19-28
Hezekiah—to worship
God . . . . 2 Chr. 29:20-24
Job—to offer
sacrifices . . . . . . Job 1:5
Jesus—to
pray . . . . Mark 1:35
Jesus—to prepare to
teach . . . . John 8:2
The people—to hear
Jesus . . . . Luke 21:38

B. *For military reasons:*
Joshua—to lead Israel over
Jordan . . . . Josh. 3:1-17
Joshua—to capture
Jericho . . . . Josh. 6:12-27
Joshua—to
capture Ai . . . . Josh. 8:10
People of Jerusalem—to see
dead men . . . . . 2 Kin. 19:35

C. *For personal reasons:*
Gideon—to examine the
fleece . . . . Judg. 6:36-38
Samuel—to meet
Saul . . . . 1 Sam. 15:12
David—to obey his
father . . . . 1 Sam. 17:20
The ideal woman—to do her
work . . . . Prov. 31:15
Drunkards—to pursue strong
drink . . . . Is. 5:11
Certain women—to visit
Christ's
grave . . . . Mark 16:1, 2

Early rising

Hezekiah to worship
God . . . . 2 Chr. 29:20-24

Earnest—*a pledge of full payment*

The Holy Spirit in the
heart . . . . 2 Cor. 1:22
Given by God . . . . . 2 Cor. 5:5

Guarantee of future
redemption........Eph. 1:13, 14

Earnestness—*a serious and intense spirit*

Warning
men.............$\begin{cases} \text{Gen. 19:15-17} \\ \text{Ezek. 18:1-32} \end{cases}$
Accepting
promises.........Gen. 28:12-22
Admonishing a
son..............1 Chr. 28:9, 10
Public prayer......2 Chr. 6:12-42
Asking
forgiveness.......Ps. 51:1-19
Calling to
repentance.......Acts 2:38-40
Seeking
salvation.........Acts 16:30-34
Preaching the
Gospel..........Acts 20:18-38
Contend for the
faith.............Jude 3-5

Earrings—*ornaments worn on the ear*

Sign of
worldliness.......Gen. 35:2-4
Made into a golden
calf..............Ex. 32:2-4
Spoils of war......Judg. 8:24-26
Used
figuratively.......Ezek. 16:12

Earth—*our planet*

A. *Described as:*
Inhabitable....Is. 45:18
God's
footstool......Is. 66:1
A circle........Is. 40:22
Full of
minerals......Deut. 8:9

B. *Glory of God's:*
Goodness......Ps. 33:5
Glory.........Is. 6:3
Riches.........Ps. 104:24
Mercy.........Ps. 119:64

C. *History of:*
Created by
God...........Gen. 1:1
Given to
man...........Gen. 1:27-31
Affected by
sin............Rom. 8:20-23
Destroyed.....Gen. 7:6-24
Final
destruction....2 Pet. 3:7-12
To be
renewed......Is. 65:17

D. *Unusual events of:*
Swallows several
families......Num. 16:23-35
Reversed in
motion........2 Kin. 20:8-11
Shaking.......Heb. 12:26
Striking.......Mal. 4:6
Earthquake....Matt. 27:51-54

E. *Man's relation to:*
Made of.......1 Cor. 15:47, 48
Given dominion
over..........Gen. 1:26
Brings
curse on......Gen. 3:17
Returns to
dust...........Gen. 3:19

F. *Promises respecting:*
Continuance of
seasons.......Gen. 8:21, 22
No more
flood..........Gen. 9:11-17
God's knowledge to
fill............Is. 11:9
The gentle shall
inherit........Matt. 5:5
Long life
upon..........Eph. 6:2, 3
To be
renewed......Is. 65:17

Earthquake—*a trembling of the earth*

A. *Expressive of God's:*
Power.........Heb. 12:25-29
Presence......Ps. 68:7, 8
Anger.........Ps. 18:7
Judgments.....Is. 24:18-21
Overthrowing
of
kingdoms....$\begin{cases} \text{Hag. 2:6, 7} \\ \text{Rev. 16:18-21} \end{cases}$

B. *Mentioned in the Scriptures:*
Mt. Sinai......Ex. 19:18
The
wilderness....Num. 16:31, 32
Saul's time.....1 Sam. 14:15, 16
Ahab's reign...1 Kin. 19:11, 12
Uzziah's
reign..........Amos 1:1
Christ's
death.........Matt. 27:50, 51
Christ's
resurrection...Matt. 28:2
Philippi........Acts 16:26
This age......Matt. 24:7

Ease—*contentment of body and mind*

Israel's............Amos 6:1
Pagan nations'....Zech. 1:15

East country—*southeastern Palestine; Arabia*

Abraham sent family
there .... Gen. 25:6

East gate—*a gate of Jerusalem*

In Temple area.... Ezek. 10:19
Ezek. 11:1

East wind—*a scorching desert wind; the sirocco*

Destroys
vegetation....... { Gen. 41:6
Ezek. 17:10
Destroys
ships .... { Ps. 48:7
Ezek. 27:25, 26
Brings judgment .. Is. 27:8
Dries springs and
fountains......... Hos. 13:15
Afflicts Jonah ..... Jon. 4:8
Called
Euroclydon....... Acts 27:14

Eat, eating

A. *Restrictions on:*
Forbidden
tree .... Gen. 2:16, 17
Blood .... Acts 15:19, 20
Unclean
things....... { Lev. 11:1-47
Deut. 14:1-29
Excess, con-
demned ...... { Eccl. 10:16, 17
Phil. 3:19
Anxiety concerning,
prohibited..... Matt. 6:24-34

B. *Spiritual significance of:*
Covenant...... Ex. 24:11
Adoption...... Jer. 52:33, 34
Fellowship..... Luke 22:15-20

C. *Christian attitude toward:*
Tradition
rejected....... Mark 7:1-23
Disorderliness
condemned ... 1 Cor. 11:20-22
Regard for weaker
brother ...... Rom. 14:1-23
No work, no
eating......... 2 Thess. 3:7-10

Ebal—*to be bare, stony*

1. Son of
Shobal .... Gen. 36:23
Same as
Obal .... Gen. 10:28
2. Mountain in
Samaria....... Deut. 27:12, 13
Law to be written
upon.......... Deut. 27:1-8

Fulfilled by
Joshua........ Josh. 8:30-35

Ebed—*slave*

1. Gaal's father... Judg. 9:28, 30
2. Son of
Jonathan...... Ezra 8:6

Ebed-Melech—*slave of the king*

Ethiopian eunuch; rescues
Jeremiah .... Jer. 38:7-13
Promised divine
protection .... Jer. 39:15-18

Ebenezer—*stone of help*

Site of Israel's
defeat .... 1 Sam. 4:1-10
Ark transferred
from .... 1 Sam. 5:1
Site of memorial
stone............ 1 Sam. 7:10, 12

Eber—*the region beyond*

1. Great-
grandson { Gen. 10:21-24
of Shem...... 1 Chr. 1:25
Progenitor of the:
Hebrews ...... Gen. 11:16-26
Arabians and
Arameans..... Gen. 10:25-30
Ancestor of
Christ........ Luke 3:35
2. Son of Elpaal .. 1 Chr. 8:12
3. Son of
Shashak ...... 1 Chr. 8:22, 25
4. Postexilic
priest .... Neh. 12:20

Ebiasaph—*gatherer*

Forefather of
Samuel........... 1 Chr. 6:23
Same as
Abiasaph ...... Ex. 6:16, 18, 24

Ebony

Black, heavy hardwood; article
of trade .... Ezek. 27:15

Ebron—*alliance*

Town of Asher.... Josh. 19:28

See Hebron

Ecclesiastes, Book of—*from Gr. word "assembly" and Heb. word "one who assembles"*

Vanity of earthly
things .... Eccl. 1:2
Material goods .... Eccl. 5:10-12

Eclipse of the sun

Foretold .... Amos 8:9

Economy—*living thriftily*

The law of .... Prov. 11:24
The wrong kind ... Hag. 1:6, 9-11
Exemplified by
Jesus .... John 6:11, 12

Eczema

Makes an animal
unacceptable ..... Lev. 22:22

Eden—*delight; pleasantness*

1. First home ..... Gen. 2:8-15
   Zion becomes
   like .... Is. 51:3
   Called the "garden of
   God" .... Ezek. 28:13
   Terrible
   contrast ...... Joel 2:3
2. Region in Mesopo-
   tamia .... Is. 37:12
3. Gershonite
   Levite .... 2 Chr. 29:12

Eder—*a flock*

1. Tower .... Gen. 35:21
2. Town in
   Judah .... Josh. 15:21
3. Benjamite ..... 1 Chr. 8:15
4. Levite .... 1 Chr. 23:23

Edification—*building up one's faith*

A. *Objects of:*
   The church .... 1 Cor. 14:4-12
   The body of
   Christ .... Eph. 4:12
   One another ... Rom. 14:19

B. *Accomplished by:*
   The ministry ... 2 Cor. 12:19
   Christian
   gifts .... 1 Cor. 14:3-12
   Word of God .. Acts 20:32
   Love .... 1 Cor. 8:1
   Spiritual
   things .... Rom. 14:19
   Seeking another's
   goods .... Rom. 15:2

God's
authority ...... 2 Cor. 10:8

C. *Hindrances of:*
   Carnal spirit ... 1 Cor. 3:1-4
   Disputes ...... 1 Tim. 1:3, 4
   Spiritual luke-
   warmness ..... Rev. 3:14-22
   Worldly
   spirit .... James 4:1-6

Edom—*red*

1. Name given to
   Esau .... Gen. 25:30
2. Edomites ...... Num. 20:18-21
3. Land of Esau; called
   Seir .... Gen. 32:3
   Called Edom and
   Idumea ...... Mark 3:8
   Mountainous
   land .... Jer. 49:16, 17
   People of,
   cursed .... Is. 34:5, 6

Edomites—*descendants of Esau*

A. *Character of:*
   Warlike .... Gen. 27:40
   Idolatrous ..... 2 Chr. 25:14, 20
   Super-
   stitious .... Jer. 27:3, 9
   Proud .... Jer. 49:16
   Strong .... Jer. 49:19
   Vindictive ..... Ezek. 25:12

B. *Relations with Israel:*
   Descendants of
   Esau .... Gen. 36:9
   Refused
   passage to .... Num. 20:18-20
   Enemies of ... Ezek. 35:5-7
   Wars against .. 1 Sam. 14:47
   Joined
   enemies of .... 2 Chr. 20:10
   Aided Babylon
   against .... Ps. 137:7

C. *Prophecies concerning:*
   Subjection to
   Israel .... Gen. 27:37
   Punishment for persecuting
   Israel .... Is. 34:5-8
   Utter desolation
   of .... Is. 34:9-17
   Figurative of
   Gentiles ...... Amos 9:11, 12

Edrei—*mighty*

1. Capital of
   Bashan .... Deut. 3:10

Site of Og's
defeat.........Num. 21:33-35
2. City of
Naphtali ......Josh. 19:37

Education—*instruction in knowledge*

A. *Performed by:*
Parents........Eph. 6:4
Guardians .....Gal. 4:1-3
Teachers......2 Chr. 17:7-9
Learned men ..Acts 22:3

B. *Method of:*
Sharing........Gal. 6:6
Recalling God's
works.........Ps. 78:1-8
Learning from
nature ....Prov. 6:6-11
Step by step ...Is. 28:10
Asking
questions .....Luke 2:46

C. *Examples of:*
Moses ....Acts 7:22
Daniel.........Dan. 1:17
Paul ....Acts 22:3
Timothy ....2 Tim. 3:15, 16

Effeminate—*a man with female traits*

Curse on Egypt ...Is. 19:16
The weakness of
Nineveh.......Nah. 3:13
Rebuked by
Paul.............1 Cor. 16:13
Shall not inherit the kingdom of
God ....1 Cor. 6:9

Effort—*using energy to get something
done*

Organized.........Neh. 4:15-23
Diligence in ......Neh. 6:1-4
Inspired to ....Hag. 1:12-14
Ill-considered ....Luke 14:28-30
The highest ....Phil. 3:11-14

Egg

Prohibition concerning that of
birds ....Deut. 22:6
Article of food ....Luke 11:12
White of, without
taste ....Job 6:6

Eglah—*heifer*

Wife of David.....2 Sam. 3:2, 5

Eglaim—*two ponds*

Moabite town .....Is. 15:8

Eglon—*heifer-like*

1. Moabite king ..Judg. 3:12-15
2. City of
Judah........Josh. 15:39

Egotism—*a sinful exultation of one's
self*

Satan ....Is. 14:13-15
Luke 4:5, 6
Goliath ....1 Sam. 17:4-11
Haman............Esth. 6:6-12
Simon.............Acts 8:9-11
Herod.............Acts 12:20-23
Diotrephes ....3 John 9, 10
Sign of
antichrist........2 Thess. 2:3, 4
Sign of the last
days.............2 Tim. 3:1-5

Egypt—*black*

A. *Israel's contact with:*
Abram visits ...Gen. 12:10
Joseph sold
into.........Gen. 37:28, 36
Joseph becomes
leader in ......Gen. 39:1-4
Hebrews
move to......Gen. 46:5-7
Persecution
by ....Ex. 1:15-22
Israel leaves ...Ex. 12:31-33
Army of,
perishes......Ex. 14:26-28

B. *Characteristics of:*
Super-
stitious.......Is. 19:3
Unprofitable ...Is. 30:1-7
Treacherous ...Is. 36:6
Ambitious .....Jer. 46:8, 9

C. *Prophecies concerning:*
Israel's
sojourn in.....Gen. 15:13
Destruction
of............Ezek. 30:24, 25
Ever a lowly
kingdom ......Ezek. 29:14, 15
Conversion
of............Is. 19:18-25
Christ, called
out of........Matt. 2:15

Egyptian, the—*an unknown
insurrectionist*

Paul
mistaken for......Acts 21:37, 38

Ehi—*brotherly*

Benjamin's son....Gen. 46:21
Same as Ahiram ..Num. 26:38

Ehud—*union*

1. Great-grandson of
   Benjamin .....1 Chr. 7:10
2. Son of Gera ...Judg. 3:15
   Slays Eglon ..Judg. 3:16-26

Eker—*offshoot*

Descendant of
  Judah ....1 Chr. 2:27

Ekron—*extermination*

Philistine city .....Josh. 13:3
Captured by
  Judah ....Judg. 1:18
Assigned to Dan ..Josh. 19:40, 43
Ark sent to ....1 Sam. 5:10
Denounced by the
  prophets.........Jer. 25:9, 20

El—*ancient word for God, often used as prefix to Hebrew names*

El Bethel..........Gen. 35:6, 7

Eladah—*God has adorned*

A descendant of
  Ephraim..........1 Chr. 7:20

Elah—*an oak*

1. Duke of
   Edom ....Gen. 36:41
2. Son of Caleb...1 Chr. 4:15
3. King of   (1 Kin. 16:6,
   Israel   ⎰   8-10
4. Benjamite .....1 Chr. 9:8
5. Father of
   Hoshea ....2 Kin. 15:30
6. Valley of.......1 Sam. 17:2, 19
7. Father of
   Shimei ....1 Kin. 4:18

Elam—*hidden*

1. Son of Shem...Gen. 10:22
2. Benjamite .....1 Chr. 8:24
3. Korahite
   Levite.........1 Chr. 26:1, 3
4. Head of postexilic
   families ....Ezra 2:7
5. Another family
   head ....Ezra 2:31
6. One who signs
   covenant......Neh. 10:1, 14
7. Priest..........Neh. 12:42

Elamites—*descendants of Elam*

A Semite (Shem)
  people...........Gen. 10:22
An ancient
  nation...........Gen. 14:1
Connected with
  Media ....Is. 21:2
Destruction of ....Jer. 49:34-39
In Persian
  empire ....Ezra 4:9
Jews from, at
  Pentecost ....Acts 2:9

Elasah—*God has made*

1. Shaphan's
   son ....Jer. 29:3
2. Son of
   Pashur........Ezra 10:22

Elath—*a grove*

Seaport on Red
  Sea..............1 Kin. 9:26
Built by Azariah ..2 Kin. 14:21, 22
Captured by
  Syrians...........2 Kin. 16:6
Same as Ezion
  Geber ....2 Chr. 8:17

El Bethel—*God of Bethel*

Site of Jacob's
  altar..............Gen. 35:6, 7

Eldaah—*God has called*

Son of Midian.....Gen. 25:4

Eldad—*God has loved*

Elder of Moses ....Num. 11:26-29

Elderly

A. *Contributions of:*
   Counsel ....1 Kin. 12:6-16
                 Job 12:12

   Spiritual
     service.......Luke 2:36-38
   Fruitfulness....Ps. 92:13, 14
   Leadership.....Josh. 24:2, 14,
                 15, 29

B. *Attitude toward:*
   Minister to
     needs ....1 Kin. 1:15
   Respect........Ps. 71:18, 19
   As cared for by
     God............Is. 46:4
   Honor ....Lev. 19:32
                 Prov. 16:31

Elders of Israel

A. *Functions of, in Mosaic period:*
Rule the
people . . . . Judg. 2:7
Represent the
nation . . . . Ex. 3:16, 18
Share in national
guilt . . . . Josh. 7:6
Assist in
government . . . Num. 11:16-25
Perform religious
acts . . . . Ex. 12:21, 22

B. *Functions of, in later periods:*
Choose a
king . . . . 2 Sam. 3:17-21
Ratify a
covenant . . . . 2 Sam. 5:3
Assist at a
dedication . . . . . 1 Kin. 8:1-3
Counsel   { 1 Kin. 12:6-8,
kings . . . . {   13
Legislate
reforms . . . . Ezra 10:7-14
Try civil
cases . . . . Matt. 26:3-68

Elders in the church

A. *Qualifications of, stated by:*
Paul . . . . Titus 1:5-14
Peter . . . . 1 Pet. 5:1-4

B. *Duties of:*
Administer
relief . . . . Acts 11:29, 30
Correct error . . Acts 15:4, 6, 23
Hold fast the faithful
Word . . . . Titus 1:5, 9
Rule well . . . . . . 1 Tim. 5:17
Minister to the
sick . . . . James 5:14, 15

C. *Honors bestowed on:*
Ordination . . . . . Acts 14:21, 23
Obedience . . . . Heb. 13:7, 17
Due respect . . . . 1 Tim. 5:1, 19

See Bishop

Elead—*God has testified*

Ephraimite . . . . 1 Chr. 7:21

Elealeh—*God has ascended*

Moabite town . . . . . Is. 15:1, 4
Rebuilt by
Reubenites . . . . Num. 32:37

Eleasah—*God has made*

1. Descendant of
Judah . . . . 1 Chr. 2:2-39

2. Descendant of
Saul . . . . 1 Chr. 8:33-37

Eleazar—*God has helped*

1. Son of Aaron . . Ex. 6:23
Father of
Phinehas . . . . . . Ex. 6:25
Consecrated a
priest . . . . Ex. 28:1
Ministers in priest's
position . . . . Lev. 10:6, 7
Made chief
Levite . . . . Num. 3:32
Succeeds
Aaron . . . . Num. 20:25-28
Aids Joshua . . . Josh. 14:1
Buried at
Ephraim . . . . . . Josh. 24:33
2. Merarite
Levite . . . . 1 Chr. 23:21, 22
3. Son of Abinadab; custodian of
the ark . . . . 1 Sam. 7:1
4. One of David's mighty
men . . . . 2 Sam. 23:9
5. Priest . . . . Ezra 8:33
6. Son of
Parosh . . . . Ezra 10:25
7. Musician
priest . . . . Neh. 12:27-42
8. Ancestor of
Jesus . . . . Matt. 1:15

Elect, Election—*chosen*

A. *Descriptive of:*
The Messiah . . . Is. 42:1
Israel . . . . Is. 45:4
Good angels . . . 1 Tim. 5:21
Christians . . . . . Matt. 24:22, 31
Christian
ministers . . . . . . Acts 9:15
Lady or
church . . . . 2 John 1, 13

B. *Characteristics of:*
Eternal . . . . Eph. 1:4
Personal . . . . . . Acts 9:15
Sovereign . . . . . . Rom. 9:11-16
Unmerited . . . . . Rom. 9:11
God's fore-
knowledge . . . . 2 Pet. 1:3, 4
Of grace . . . . . . Rom. 11:5, 6
Through
faith . . . . 2 Thess. 2:13
Recorded in
heaven . . . . Luke 10:20
Knowable . . . . . 1 Thess. 1:4
Of high
esteem . . . . 2 Tim. 2:4

C. *Results in:*
Adoption ....Eph. 1:5
Salvation ......2 Thess. 2:13
Conformity to
Christ.........Rom. 8:29
Good works ...Eph. 2:10
Eternal glory ..Rom. 9:23
Inheritance ....1 Pet. 1:2, 4, 5

D. *Proof of:*
Faith ....2 Pet. 1:10
Holiness ....Eph. 1:4, 5
Divine
protection.....Mark 13:20
Manifest it in
life............Col. 3:12

El Elohe Israel—*God, the God of Israel*

Name of Jacob's
altar..............Gen. 33:20

Elements—*basic parts of anything*

A. *Used literally of:*
Basic forces of
nature ....2 Pet. 3:10, 12

B. *Used figuratively of:*
"Basic principles" of
religion ....Gal. 4:3, 9
"Rudiments" of
tradition ......Col. 2:8, 20
"First principles" of
religion ....Heb. 5:12

Eleph—*ox*

Town of
Benjamin.........Josh. 18:28

Eleven, the—*the disciples without Judas*

Were told of
resurrection....Luke 24:9, 33, 34
Met Jesus.........Matt. 28:16
At Pentecost .....Acts 2:1, 14

Elhanan—*God has been gracious*

1. Son of Dodo ...2 Sam. 23:24
Brave man.....1 Chr. 11:26
2. Son of Jair....1 Chr. 20:5
Slays a giant..2 Sam. 21:19

Eli—*my God*

Jesus' cry on the
cross...........Matt. 27:46
Same as "Eloi"....Mark 15:34

Eli—*high (that is, God is high)*

Officiates in
Shiloh............1 Sam. 1:3

Blesses Hannah ...1 Sam. 1:12-19
Becomes Samuel's
guardian.....1 Sam. 1:20-28
Samuel ministers
before ....1 Sam. 2:11
Sons of ....1 Sam. 2:12-17
Rebukes sons .....1 Sam. 2:22-25
Rebuked by a man of
God ....1 Sam. 2:27-36
Instructs
Samuel...........1 Sam. 3:1-18
Death of ....1 Sam. 4:15-18

Eliab—*God is father*

1. Son of Helon ..Num. 1:9
Leader of
Zebulun.......Num. 7:24, 29
2. Father of Dathan and
Abiram ......Num. 16:1, 12
3. Ancestor of
Samuel ....1 Chr. 6:27, 28
4. Brother of
David ....1 Sam. 16:5-13
Fights in Saul's
army..........1 Sam. 17:13
Discounts
David's   ⎧ 1 Sam. 17:28,
worth........ ⎨   29
5. Gadite
warrior ....1 Chr. 12:1-9
6. Levite
musician ......1 Chr. 15:12-20

Eliada, Eliadah—*God has known*

1. Son of David ..2 Sam. 5:16
Also called
Beeliada.......1 Chr. 14:7
2. Father of
Rezon.........1 Kin. 11:23
3. Benjamite
warrior ....2 Chr. 17:17

Eliah—*my God is Yahweh*

Divorced foreign
wife.............Ezra 10:18, 26

Eliahba—*God conceals*

One of David's
mighty men ......2 Sam. 23:32

Eliakim—*God will establish*

1. Son of
Hilkiah........2 Kin. 18:18
Confers with
Rabshakeh....Is. 36:3, 11-22
Sent to
Isaiah.........Is. 37:2-5

Becomes type of the
Messiah........Is. 22:20-25
2. Son of King
   Josiah.........2 Kin. 23:34
   Name changed to
   Jehoiakim.....2 Chr. 36:4
3. Postexilic
   priest ....Neh. 12:41
4. Ancestor of   { Matt. 1:13
   Christ........   { Luke 3:30

Eliam—*God of the people*

1. Father of
   Bathsheba ....2 Sam. 11:3
   Called
   Ammiel.......1 Chr. 3:5
2. Son of
   Ahithophel....2 Sam. 23:34

Eliasaph—*God has added*

1. Gadite prince ..Num. 1:4, 14
   Presents
   offering.......Num. 7:41, 42
2. Levite ....Num. 3:24

Eliashib—*God will restore*

1. Davidic
   priest ....1 Chr. 24:1, 12
2. Divorced
   foreign   { Ezra 10:24
   wife.......   { Ezra 10:27
3. High priest ...Neh. 12:10
   Rebuilds Sheep
   Gate ....Neh. 3:1, 20, 21
   Allies with
   foreigners.....Neh. 13:4, 5, 28
4. Descendant of
   Zerubbabel....1 Chr. 3:19-24

Eliathah—*God has come*

Son of Heman ....1 Chr. 25:1-27

Elidad—*God has loved*

Benjamite leader ..Num. 34:17, 21

Eliel—*God is God*

1. Ancestor of
   Samuel ....1 Chr. 6:33, 34
2. One of David's mighty
   men...........1 Chr. 11:26, 46
3. Another of David's mighty
   men...........1 Chr. 11:47
4. Gadite
   warrior ....1 Chr. 12:1-11
5. Levite ....1 Chr. 15:9, 11
6. Benjamite .....1 Chr. 8:1-21
7. Benjamite, son of
   Shashak ......1 Chr. 8:22, 25

8. Manassite
   chief..........1 Chr. 5:23, 24
9. Overseer of
   tithes ....2 Chr. 31:12, 13

Elienal—*toward God are my eyes*

Benjamite chief ...1 Chr. 8:1, 20

Eliezer—*God of help*

1. Abraham's
   servant ....Gen. 15:2
2. Son of Moses ..Ex. 18:2-4
3. Son of Zichri ..1 Chr. 27:16
4. Son of
   Becher........1 Chr. 7:8
5. Priest of
   David.........1 Chr. 15:24
6. Prophet........2 Chr. 20:37
7. Ezra's
   delegate.......Ezra 8:16
8, 9, 10. Three men who divorced
   their foreign
   wives.........Ezra 10:18-31
11. An ancestor of
   Christ.........Luke 3:29

Elihoenai—*toward God are my eyes*

Son of Zerahiah...Ezra 8:4

Elihoreph—*God of autumn*

One of Solomon's
scribes ....1 Kin. 4:3

Elihu—*He is my God*

1. Ancestor of
   Samuel ....1 Sam. 1:1
   Also called Eliab and
   Eliel ....1 Chr. 6:27, 34
2. David's
   brother ....1 Chr. 27:18
   Called Eliab...1 Sam. 16:6
3. Manassite
   captain........1 Chr. 12:20
4. Temple
   servant ....1 Chr. 26:1, 7
5. One who reproved Job and his
   friends ....Job 32:2, 4-6

Elijah—*Yahweh is God*

A. Life of the prophet:
   Denounces
   Ahab..........1 Kin. 17:1
   Hides by the brook
   Cherith ....1 Kin. 17:3
   Fed by
   ravens ....1 Kin. 17:4-7
   Fed by
   widow ....1 Kin. 17:8-16

Restores widow's
son . . . . 1 Kin. 17:17-24
Sends message to
Ahab. . . . . 1 Kin. 18:1-16
Overthrows Baal
prophets . . . . . . 1 Kin. 18:17-46
Flees from
Jezebel. . . . . 1 Kin. 19:1-3
Fed by
angels. . . . . 1 Kin. 19:4-8
Hears God . . . . . 1 Kin. 19:9-14
Sent on a
mission . . . . 1 Kin. 19:15-21
Condemns
Ahab. . . . . 1 Kin. 21:15-29
Condemns
Ahaziah. . . . . . . 2 Kin. 1:1-16
Taken up to
heaven. . . . . 2 Kin. 2:1-15

B. *Miracles of:*
Widow's oil . . . 1 Kin. 17:14-16
Dead child
raised . . . . 1 Kin. 17:17-24
Causes rain . . . . 1 Kin. 18:41-45
Causes fire to consume
sacrifices . . . . . . 1 Kin. 18:24-38
Causes fire to consume
soldiers . . . . . . 2 Kin. 1:10-12

C. *Prophecies of:*
Drought . . . . 1 Kin. 17:1
Ahab's
destruction. . . . 1 Kin. 21:17-29
Ahaziah's
death . . . . 2 Kin. 1:2-17
Plague. . . . . 2 Chr. 21:12-15

D. *Significance of:*
Prophecy of his
coming. . . . . Mal. 4:5, 6
Appears with
Christ. . . . . Matt. 17:1-4
Type of John the
Baptist. . . . . . . Luke 1:17

Elijah—*Yahweh is God*

1. Priest who divorced his foreign
wife. . . . . Ezra 10:21
2. Son of
Jehoram . . . . . . 1 Chr. 8:27

Elika—*God has spewed out*

David's warrior . . . 2 Sam. 23:25

Elim—*large trees*

Israel's
encampment . . . . Ex. 15:27
Place of palm
trees . . . . Num. 33:9, 10

Elimelech—*God is king*

Man of Judah . . . . . Ruth 1:1, 2
Dies in Moab. . . . . . Ruth 1:3
Kinsman of
Boaz . . . . Ruth 2:1, 3
Boaz buys his
land. . . . . Ruth 4:3-9

Elioenai—*toward God are my eyes*

1. Descendant of
Benjamin . . . . . 1 Chr. 7:8
2. Simeonite
head . . . . 1 Chr. 4:36
3. Son of
Neariah . . . . 1 Chr. 3:23, 24
4. Postexilic
priest . . . . Neh. 12:41
Divorced his foreign
wife. . . . . Ezra 10:19, 22
5. Son of Zattu; divorced his
foreign wife. . . Ezra 10:27

Eliphal—*God has judged*

David's warrior . . . 1 Chr. 11:26, 35
Called Eliphelet . . 2 Sam. 23:34

Eliphaz—*God is fine gold*

1. Son of Esau . . . Gen. 36:2, 4
2. One of Job's
friends . . . . Job 2:11
Rebukes Job . . . Job 4:1, 5
Is forgiven. . . . . Job 42:7-9

Elipheleh—*whom God makes
distinguished*

Levite singer . . . . . . 1 Chr. 15:18, 21

Eliphelet—*God is deliverance*

1. Son of David . . 1 Chr. 3:5, 6
2. Another son of
David . . . . 2 Sam. 5:16
3. Descendant of
Jonathan. . . . . . 1 Chr. 8:33, 39
4. David's
warrior . . . . 2 Sam. 23:34
5. Returnee from
Babylon . . . . . . Ezra 8:13
6. Son of Hashum; divorced his
foreign wife. . . Ezra 10:33

Elisha—*God is salvation*

A. *Life of:*
Succeeds
Elijah . . . . 1 Kin. 19:16
Follows
Elijah . . . . 1 Kin. 19:19-21

Sees Elijah
translated.....2 Kin. 2:1-12
Is recognized as a
prophet ......2 Kin. 2:13-22
Mocked........2 Kin. 2:23-25
Deals with
kings ....2 Kin. 3:11-20
Helps two
women........2 Kin. 4:1-17

B. *Miracles of:*
Divides
Jordan ....2 Kin. 2:14
Purifies
water ....2 Kin. 2:19-22
Increases widow's
oil ....2 Kin. 4:1-7
Raises Shunammite's
son ....2 Kin. 4:18-37
Neutralizes
poison ....2 Kin. 4:38-41
Multiplies
bread ....2 Kin. 4:42-44
Heals Naaman the
leper ....2 Kin. 5:1-19
Inflicts Gehazi with
leprosy.......2 Kin. 5:26, 27
Causes iron to
float ....2 Kin. 6:6
Reveals secret
counsels ......2 Kin. 6:8-12
Opens servant's
eyes ....2 Kin. 6:13-17
Strikes Syrian army with
blindness......2 Kin. 6:18-23

C. *Prophecies of:*
Birth of a
child ....2 Kin. 4:16
Abundance ....2 Kin. 7:1
Official's
death ....2 Kin. 7:2
Great famine ..2 Kin. 8:1-3
Hazael's
cruelty........2 Kin. 8:7-15
Joash's
victories ......2 Kin. 13:14-19

Elishah—*God is salvation*

Son of Javan......Gen. 10:4

Elishama—*God has heard*

1. Son of
   Ammihud.....Num. 1:10
   Ancestor of
   Joshua........1 Chr. 7:26
2. Man of
   Judah.........1 Chr. 2:41
3. Son of David ..1 Chr. 3:1, 5, 6

Also called
Elishama........2 Sam. 5:15
4. Another son of
   David.........2 Sam. 5:16
5. Teaching
   priest ....2 Chr. 17:7, 8
6. Scribe ....Jer. 36:12, 20, 21

Elishaphat—*God has judged*

Captain ....2 Chr. 23:1

Elisheba—*God is an oath*

Wife of Aaron.....Ex. 6:23

Elishua—*God is salvation*

Son of David......2 Sam. 5:15
Called Elishama ..1 Chr. 3:6

Eliud—*God is mighty*

Father of
Eleazar...........Matt. 1:14, 15

Elizabeth—*God is an oath*

Wife of
Zacharias ....Luke 1:5
Barren ....Luke 1:7, 13
Conceives son...Luke 1:24, 25
Relative of Mary ..Luke 1:36
Salutation to
Mary...........Luke 1:39-45
Mother of John the
Baptist ....Luke 1:57-60

Elizaphan—*God has concealed*

1. Chief of
   Kohathites....Num. 3:30
   Heads family ..1 Chr. 15:5, 8
   Family
   consecrated...2 Chr. 29:12-16
2. Son of
   Parnach.......Num. 34:25

Elizur—*God is a rock*

Reubenite
warrior...........Num. 1:5

Eljehoenai—*toward God are my eyes*

Korahite
gatekeeper ....1 Chr. 26:1-3

Elkanah—*God has possessed*

1. Father of
   Samuel ....1 Sam. 1:1-23
2. Son of Korah ..Ex. 6:24
   Escapes
   judgment .....Num. 26:11
3. Levite ....1 Chr. 6:23-36

4. Descendant of
   Korah..........1 Chr. 6:22, 23
5. Levite ....1 Chr. 9:16
6. Korahite
   warrior ....1 Chr. 12:1, 6
7. Officer under
   Ahaz..........2 Chr. 28:7
8. Doorkeeper of
   the ark........1 Chr. 15:23

Elkoshite—*an inhabitant of Elkosh*

Descriptive of
Nahum...........Nah. 1:1

Ellasar

Place in Babylon ..Gen. 14:1, 9

Elmodam

Ancestor of
Christ ....Luke 3:28

Elnaam—*God is pleasantness*

Father of two
warriors........1 Chr. 11:26, 46

Elnathan—*God has given*

1. Father of
   Nehushta .....2 Kin. 24:8
   Goes to
   Egypt.........Jer. 26:22
   Entreats with
   king..........Jer. 36:25
2, 3, 4. Three
   Levites........Ezra 8:16

Eloi (same as Eli)

Jesus' cry ....Mark 15:34

Elon—*oak*

1. Hittite ....Gen. 26:34
2. Son of
   Zebulun......Gen. 46:14
3. Judge in
   Israel ....Judg. 12:11, 12
4. Town of Dan ..Josh. 19:43

Elon Beth Hanan—*oak of house of grace*

Town of Dan......1 Kin. 4:9

Elonites—*belonging to Elon*

Descendants of
Elon.............Num. 26:26

Eloquent—*fluent and persuasive in speech*

Moses is not ......Ex. 4:10
Paul rejects.......1 Cor. 2:1, 4, 5

Apollos is ....Acts 18:24
False prophets
boast of ....2 Pet. 2:18

Elpaal—*God has wrought*

Benjamite.........1 Chr. 8:11-18

El Paran—*oak of Paran*

Place in Canaan...Gen. 14:6

Elpelet—*God of deliverance*

Son of David......1 Chr. 14:3, 5
Same as
Eliphelet ....1 Chr. 3:6

Eltekeh—*God is dread*

City of Dan ....Josh. 19:44
Assigned to
Levites ....Josh. 21:23

Eltekon—*founded by God*

Village in Judah...Josh. 15:59

Eltolad—*kindred of God*

Town in Judah....Josh. 15:21, 30
Assigned to
Simeonites ......Josh. 19:4
Called Tolad .....1 Chr. 4:29

Elul—*vine*

Sixth month of Hebrew
year..............Neh. 6:15

Eluzai—*God is my defense*

Ambidextrous warrior of
David ....1 Chr. 12:1, 5

Elymas—*a wise man*

Arabic name of Bar-Jesus, a false
prophet ....Acts 13:6-12

Elzabad—*God has bestowed*

1. Gadite
   warrior ....1 Chr. 12:8, 12
2. Korahite
   Levite.........1 Chr. 26:7, 8

Elzaphan contraction of *Elizaphan*

Son of Uzziel .....Ex. 6:22
Given instructions by
Moses............Lev. 10:4

Emancipation—*a setting free from slavery*

Of Hebrew
nation............Ex. 12:29-42
Of Hebrew
slaves ....Ex. 21:2

In the year of
jubilee............Lev. 25:8-41
Proclaimed by
Zedekiah........Jer. 34:8-11
By Cyrus.........2 Chr. 36:23
Ezra 1:1-4

Emasculation—*castration*

Penalty of.........Deut. 23:1

Embalming—*preserving a corpse from decay*

Unknown to
Abraham.........Gen. 23:1-4
Practiced in
Egypt ....Gen. 50:2, 3, 26
Manner of, among
Jews ....2 Chr. 16:14
Limitation of.....John 11:39, 44

Embroider—*to decorate by needlework*

In tabernacle
curtains.........Ex. 26:1, 36
Bezaleel and Aholiab
inspired in.......Ex. 35:30-35
On Sisera's
garments.........Judg. 5:30

Emek Keziz—*cut off*

City of
Benjamin.........Josh. 18:21

Emerald—*a precious stone of the beryl variety*

In high priests'
garments.........Ex. 28:17
In Tyre's trade....Ezek. 27:16
Used for
ornamentation ...Ezek. 28:13
Foundation
stone............Rev. 21:19

Emim—*terrors*

Giant race of Anakim east of the
Dead Sea.........Gen. 14:5

Emmaus—*hot spring*

Town near
Jerusalem ....Luke 24:13-18

Emotion—*a person's response to living situations*

A. *Objects of:*
Self............Job 3:1-26
Nation..........Ps. 137:1-6
Family..........Gen. 49:1-28
Mate ....1 Sam. 25:24, 25
Foreigners.....Ruth 1:16-18

B. *Kinds of:*
Conviction.....Acts 2:37
Contempt......1 Sam. 17:42-44
Despond-
ency ....1 Kin. 19:4-10
Disap-
pointment.....Luke 18:23
Disgust ....Neh. 4:1-3
Envy ....1 Sam. 17:28
Fear ....1 Kin. 19:1-3
Flattery........1 Sam. 25:23-31
Hate...........Acts 7:54, 57
Joy ....Luke 15:22-24
Love...........Ex. 32:26-29
Loyalty........2 Sam. 18:32, 33
Regret.........Luke 16:27-31
Revenge........Gen. 27:41-45
Sorrow ....2 Sam. 12:13-19

C. *Control of:*
Unsup-
pressed ....1 Sam. 20:30-33
Suppressed ....Is. 36:21
Uncon-
trollable.......Mark 5:4, 5
Controlled .....Mark 5:18, 19

Employees—*those who work for others*

A. *Types of:*
Diligent.........Gen. 30:27-31
Discon-
tented.........Matt. 20:1-15
Unworthy .....Matt. 21:33-41

B. *Duties of:*
Content-
ment..........Luke 3:14
Fulfilling
terms ....Matt. 20:1-15
Respect........1 Tim. 6:1
Diligence ......Prov. 22:29

C. *Rights of:*
Equal wage....Matt. 10:10
Prompt
payment ......Lev. 19:13
Good
treatment .....Ruth 2:4

D. *Oppression of, by:*
Arbitrary
changes.......Gen. 31:38-42
Unscrupulous
landowners ...James 5:4-6

Employers—*those who hire others to work for them*

Must not
oppress...........Deut. 24:14
Must be
considerate.......Job 31:31

Must be just and
fair..............Col. 4:1

Employment—*the state of one who has regular work*

A. *Usefulness of:*
Manifest
graces ....Prov. 31:10-31
Provided
food ....2 Thess. 3:7-12

B. *Examples of:*
Adam..........Gen. 2:15
Workmen after the
exile ....Neh. 4:15-23
Paul ....1 Thess. 2:9-11

Enam—*two springs*

Village of Judah...Josh. 15:20, 34

Enan—*having fountains*

Father of Ahira ...Num. 1:15

Encampment—*a resting place on a march or journey*

Israel's, on leaving
Egypt ....Ex. 13:20
At Sinai.........Ex. 18:5
List of ....Num. 33:10-49
In battle ....Josh. 10:5, 31, 34

Enchantment—*the practice of magical arts*

A. *Practiced in:*
Egypt..........Ex. 7:11
Judah.........2 Kin. 17:16, 17
Babylon ....Ezek. 21:21
Chaldea ....Dan. 5:11
Greece.........Acts 16:16
Asia Minor ....Acts 19:13, 19

B. *Futility of:*
Vanity of ......Is. 47:9-15
Inability of ....Ex. 7:11, 12
Abomination
of.............Deut. 18:9-12

C. *Examples of:*
Simon ....Acts 8:9
Bar-Jesus ......Acts 13:6-12
Slave-girl ......Acts 16:16
Itinerant
Jews..........Acts 19:13
Jannes and
Jambres.......2 Tim. 3:8

Encouragement—*inspiration to hope and service*

A. *Needed by:*
Prophets........1 Kin. 19:1-19
People..........Neh. 4:17-23

Servants.......2 Kin. 6:15-17
Kings..........2 Kin. 11:10-21
Heathen ....Dan. 6:18-23

B. *Agents of:*
Angels of:
Angels.......Gen. 32:1, 2
A dream......Gen. 28:11-22
God's
promises .....Josh. 1:1-9
A friend ......1 Sam. 23:16-18
A relative.....Esth. 4:13-16
Paul..........Acts 27:21-26

C. *Reasons for, Christ is:*
Risen ....1 Cor. 15:11-58
Present ....Matt. 28:19, 20
Coming........Luke 21:25-28

Encumbrance—*that which hinders freedom of action*

Universal ....Gen. 3:16-19
Imposed ....Gen. 32:31, 32
Perpetual ....Matt. 27:25
Moral............Titus 1:12, 13
Spiritual ....Heb. 12:1

End of the world

A. *Events connected with:*
Day of salvation
ended.........Matt. 24:3, 14
Harvest of
souls..........Matt. 13:36-43
Defeat of man of
sin............2 Thess. 2:1-12
Judgment......Matt. 25:31-46
Destruction of
world ....2 Thess. 1:6-10

B. *Coming of:*
Denied by
scoffers ....2 Pet. 3:3-5
Preceded by
lawlessness....Matt. 24:12
Preceded by
apostasy ......Luke 18:8
Without
warning.......Matt. 24:37-42
With fire......2 Thess. 1:7-10

C. *Attitude toward:*
Watchful-
ness..........Matt. 25:1-13
Industry ......Matt. 25:14-30
Hopefulness ..Luke 21:25-28
Holy   {Rom. 13:12-14
living .... {2 Pet. 3:11, 14
Seeking the
lost ....2 Pet. 3:9, 15
Waiting for   {2 Pet. 3:13
eternity ...... {Rev. 21:1

En Dor—*fountain of habitation*

Town of
Manasseh . . . . Josh. 17:11
Site of memorable
defeat . . . . Ps. 83:9, 10
Home of notorious
witch. . . . . 1 Sam. 28:1-10

Endurance, blessedness of

Commanded . . . . . . Matt. 10:22
2 Tim. 2:3
Exemplified . . . . . . 2 Tim. 2:10
Heb. 10:32, 33
Rewarded. . . . . 2 Tim. 3:11
James 1:12

Enduring things

God's
faithfulness. . . . . . Ps. 89:33
God's mercies . . . . . Ps. 103:17
God's Word . . . . . . Matt. 24:35
Spiritual
nourishment. . . . . . John 6:27
Spiritual
rewards . . . . 1 Cor. 3:14
Graces. . . . . 1 Cor. 13:13
The real things . . . 2 Cor. 4:18
God's kingdom . . . . Heb. 12:27, 28

En Eglaim—*fountain of calf*

Place near the Dead
Sea. . . . . Ezek. 47:10

Enemies—*foes; adversaries; opponents*

A. *Applied to:*
Foreign
nations. . . . . . . Gen. 14:20
Israel . . . . Mic. 2:8
Gentiles . . . . . . Col. 1:21
Unregenerate
men. . . . . Rom. 5:10
The world . . . . . Matt. 22:44
Satan. . . . . Matt. 13:39
Death . . . . 1 Cor. 15:26

B. *Characteristics of, hate for:*
God . . . . Rom. 1:30
The Gospel . . . . 1 Thess. 2:14-18
The light . . . . . . John 3:19-21

C. *Examples of:*
Amalek against
Israel . . . . Ex. 17:8-16
Saul against
David . . . . 1 Sam. 18:29
Jezebel against
Elijah . . . . 1 Kin. 19:1, 2
Ahab against
Elijah . . . . 1 Kin. 21:20

Haman against the
Jews . . . . Esth. 3:10
Jews against   ⎰Acts 7:54-60
Christians. . . . . ⎱Acts 22:13, 21,
22

D. *Christian attitude toward:*
Overcome by
kindness . . . . . . 1 Sam. 26:18-21
Do not curse. . . Job 31:29, 30
Feed. . . . . Rom. 12:20
Love. . . . . Luke 6:27, 35
Forgive . . . . Matt. 6:12-15
Pray for . . . . . . Luke 23:34

Energy—*effective force to perform work*

A. *God's, in nature:*
Creative . . . . . . Job 38:4-11
Beyond natural
law . . . . Job 26:12
Maintains
matter . . . . Heb. 1:3

B. *God's, in man:*
To be
witnesses . . . . . Acts 1:8
For abundant
living . . . . Rom. 15:13
For
edification . . . . Rom. 15:14
To raise   ⎰1 Cor. 6:14
dead . . . . ⎱2 Cor. 13:4

En Gannim—*fountains of gardens*

1. Village of
Judah . . . . Josh. 15:34
2. Border town of
Issachar . . . . . . Josh. 19:21
Assigned to
Levites. . . . . . . Josh. 21:29

En Gedi—*fountain of a kid*

May have been originally called
Hazazon Tamar . 2 Chr. 20:2
Occupied by the
Amorites . . . . . . Gen. 14:7
Assigned to
Judah . . . . Josh. 15:62, 63
David's hiding
place . . . . 1 Sam. 23:29
Noted for
vineyards. . . . . . Song 1:14

Engraving—*cutting or carving on some hard substance*

Stone set in priest's
breastplate . . . . . . Ex. 28:9-11, 21

Bezaleel,
inspired in .... Ex. 35:30-33
Of a signet .... Ex. 28:21
                    Ex. 39:6
Of cherubim ..... 1 Kin. 6:29

En Haddah—*swift fountain*

Frontier village of
Issachar .... Josh. 19:17, 21

En Hakkore—*fountain of him who called*

Miraculous
spring .... Judg. 15:14-19

En Hazor—*fountain of a village*

City of Naphtali .. Josh. 19:32, 37

Enjoyment—*satisfaction in something*

A. *Of material things:*
   Depends upon
   obedience ..... Deut. 7:9-15
   Withheld for disobe-
   dience .... Hag. 1:3-11
   Must not
   trust in ...... Luke 12:16-21
   Cannot fully
   satisfy .... Eccl. 2:1-11

B. *Of spiritual things:*
   Abundant ...... 1 Tim. 6:17
   Never-ending .. Is. 58:11
   Satisfying ..... Is. 55:1, 2
   Internal ...... John 7:37-39
   For God's people
   only .... Is. 65:22-24
   Complete in
   heaven .... Ps. 16:11

Enlargement—*extension in quantity or quality*

Japheth's
territory .... Gen. 9:27
Israel's
prosperity .... Ex. 34:24
Solomon's
kingdom .... 1 Kin. 4:20-25
Solomon's
wisdom .... 1 Kin. 4:29-34
Pharisaical
hypocrisy .... Matt. 23:5
Spiritual:
Relationship .... 2 Cor. 6:11, 13
Knowledge ...... Eph. 1:15-19
Opportunity ..... Is. 54:1-3

Enlightenment, spiritual

A. *Source of:*
   From God ..... Ps. 18:28
   Through God's
   Word .... Ps. 19:8
   By prayer ...... Eph. 1:18
   By God's
   ministers ..... Acts 26:17, 18

B. *Degrees of:*
   Partial now .... 1 Cor. 13:9-12
   Hindered by
   sin .... 1 Cor. 2:14
   Complete in
   heaven .... Is. 60:19

Enoch—*dedicated*

1. Son of Cain .... Gen. 4:17
2. City built by
   Cain .... Gen. 4:17
3. Father of Methu-
   selah .... Gen. 5:21
   Walks with
   God .... Gen. 5:22
   Taken up to
   heaven .... Gen. 5:24
   Prophecy of,
   cited .... Jude 14, 15

Enos, Enosh—*mortal*

Grandson of
Adam .... Gen. 4:25, 26
Son of Seth ...... Gen. 5:6-11
Ancestor of
Christ .... Luke 3:38
Genealogy of .... 1 Chr. 1:1

En Rimmon—*fount of pomegranates*

Reinhabited after the
exile .... Neh. 11:29
Same as
Rimmon .... Zech. 14:10

En Rogel—*the fuller's fountain*

Fountain outside
Jerusalem .... 2 Sam. 17:17
On Benjamin's
boundary .... Josh. 18:11, 16
Seat of Adonijah's
plot .... 1 Kin. 1:5-9

En Shemesh—*fountain of the sun*

Spring and town near
Jericho .... Josh. 15:7

En Tappuah—*fountain of the apple tree*

Town of
Ephraim.........Josh. 17:7, 8

Entertainment—*affording an enjoyable occasion*

A. *Occasions of:*
Child's
weaning ......Gen. 21:8
Ratifying
covenants.....Gen. 31:54
King's
coronation ....1 Kin. 1:9, 18, 19
National
deliverance....Esth. 9:17-19
Marriage......Matt. 22:2
Return of loved
ones ....Luke 15:23-25

B. *Features of:*
Invitations
sent..........Luke 14:16
Preparations
made ....Matt. 22:4
Helped by
servants.......John 2:5
Under a
leader........John 2:8, 9
Often with
music........Luke 15:25
Sometimes out of
control........1 Sam. 25:36
Unusual ......Heb. 13:2

Enthusiasm—*a spirit of intense zeal*

Caleb's.........Num. 13:30-33
Phinehas' ....Num. 25:7-13
David's ....2 Sam. 6:12-22
Saul's (Paul's)....Acts 9:1, 2
Paul's..........Phil. 3:7-14

Enticers—*those who allure to evil*

A. *Means of:*
Man ....Ex. 22:16
Spirit ....2 Chr. 18:20
Sinners ....Prov. 1:10
Lusts ....James 1:14
Human
wisdom ....1 Cor. 2:4

B. *Reasons proposed:*
Turn from
God...........Deut. 13:6-8
Obtain
secrets........Judg. 16:4, 5
Defeat a
king ....2 Chr. 18:4-34
Commit a sin ..James 1:14

Entrails—*bowels, intestines*

Used literally:

Amasa's poured
out...............2 Sam. 20:10
Jehoram's came
out...............2 Chr. 21:14-19
Judas's gushed
out...............Acts 1:16-18

Envy—*resentment against another's success, jealousy*

A. *Characterized as:*
Powerful.......Prov. 27:4
Dominant in unregenerate
nature ....Rom. 1:29
Of the flesh....Gal. 5:19-21
Source of
evil ....1 Tim. 6:4

B. *The evil of, among Christians:*
Hinders
growth........1 Pet. 2:1, 2

C. *Examples of:*
Philistines .....Gen. 26:14
Joseph's
brothers.......Gen. 37:5, 11
Aaron and
Miriam.......Num. 12:1, 2
Korah ....Num. 16:1-3
Asaph ....Ps. 73:3, 17-20
Haman ....Esth. 5:13
Chief priests ...Mark 15:10
The Jews ......Acts 13:45

Epaenetus

Addressed by
Paul..............Rom. 16:5

Epaphras

Leader of the Colossian
church ....Col. 1:7, 8
Suffers as a prisoner in
Rome ....Philem. 23

Epaphroditus—*lovely, charming*

Messenger from
Philippi.........Phil. 2:25-27
Brings a gift to
Paul............Phil. 4:18

Ephah (I)—*dark one*

1. Son of
Midian ....Gen. 25:4
2. Concubine of
Caleb ....1 Chr. 2:46
3. Son of
Jahdai ....1 Chr. 2:47

Ephah (II)—*a measure*

Dry measure ..... Ex. 16:36
Used for measuring
barley .... Ruth 2:17

Ephai—*bird-like*

Netophathite ..... Jer. 40:8

Epher—*young deer*

1. Son of
   Midian .... Gen. 25:4
2. Man of
   Judah .... 1 Chr. 4:17
3. Chief in
   Manasseh ..... 1 Chr. 5:23, 24

Ephes Dammim—*end of bloods*

Philistine
encampment ..... 1 Sam. 17:1
Called Pas-
dammim .... 1 Chr. 11:13

Ephesians, the Epistle to the—*a book of the New Testament*

Written by Paul .. Eph. 1:1
Election .... Eph. 1:4-6
Salvation by { Eph. 1:7, 8
grace .... { Eph. 2:8
Headship of
Christ .... Eph. 4:15, 16

Ephesus—*a city of Asia Minor*

Site of Jewish
synagogue .... Acts 18:19
Paul visits .... Acts 18:18-21
Miracles done
here .... Acts 19:11-21
Demetrius stirs
up riot in .... Acts 19:24-29
Elders of, addressed by Paul at
Miletus .... Acts 20:17-38
Letter sent to ..... Eph. 1:1
Paul sends
Tychicus .... Eph. 6:21
Paul leaves
Timothy .... 1 Tim. 1:3
One of seven
churches .... Rev. 1:11

Ephlal—*judgment*

A descendant of
Judah .... 1 Chr. 2:37

Ephod—*a vest*

1. Worn by:
   The high
   priest .... Ex. 28:4-35

Samuel .... 1 Sam. 2:18
David .... 2 Sam. 6:14
Used in asking counsel of
God .... 1 Sam. 23:9-12
Used in
idolatry .... Judg. 8:27
2. Father of
   Hanniel .... Num. 34:23

Ephphatha—*be opened*

Christ's
command .... Mark 7:34

Ephraim—*doubly fruitful*

1. Joseph's younger
   son .... Gen. 41:52
   Obtains Jacob's
   blessing .... Gen. 48:8-20
2. Tribe of
   Ephraim ...... Josh. 16:4, 10
   Predictions
   concerning .... Gen. 48:20
   Large
   number of .... Num. 1:33
   Joshua, an
   Ephraimite .... Josh. 19:49, 50
   Territory
   assigned to .... Josh. 16:1-10
   Make Canaanites
   slaves .... Judg. 1:28, 29
   Assist
   Deborah ...... Judg. 5:14, 15
   Assist
   Gideon .... Judg. 7:24, 25
   Quarrel with
   Gideon .... Judg. 8:1-3
   Quarrel with
   Jephthah ...... Judg. 12:1-4
   Attend David's
   coronation .... 1 Chr. 12:30
   Leading tribe of kingdom of
   Israel .... Is. 7:2-17
   Provoke God
   by sin .... Hos. 12:7-14
   Many of, join
   Judah .... 2 Chr. 15:8, 9
   Bethel, idolatrous
   city of .... 1 Kin. 12:29
   Captivity of,
   predicted ...... Hos. 9:3-17
   Mercy
   promised to ... Jer. 31:9, 20
   Messiah
   promised to ... Zech. 9:9-13
3. Hill country in
   Palestine ...... 1 Sam. 1:1
4. Forest where Absalom was
   killed .... 2 Sam. 18:6-18

5. Gate in
   Jerusalem.....2 Kin. 14:13
6. Town to which Jesus
   withdrew .....John 11:54
7. Ten tribes considered as a
   unit...........Hos. 4:16, 17

Ephrathah—*fruitfulness*

1. Ancient name of Beth-
   lehem.........Ruth 4:11
   Prophecy
   concerning....Mic. 5:2
2. Land of
   Palestine......Ps. 132:6
3. Wife of
   Caleb ....1 Chr. 2:19, 50

Ephrathite

1. Inhabitant of Bethlehem
   (Ephrath) .....Ruth 1:2
2. David was the
   son of.........1 Sam. 17:12
   Also called
   Ephraimites...Judg. 12:5, 6

Ephron—*fawn-like*

1. Hittite who sold Machpelah to
   Abraham......Gen. 23:8-20
2. Landmarks of
   Judah........Josh. 15:9

Epicureans—*followers of Epicurus*

Sect of pleasure-loving
philosophers......Acts 17:18

Equality of man

A. *Seen in same:*
   Creation.......Acts 17:26
   Guilt ....Rom. 5:12-21
   Sinfulness .....Rom. 3:10-19
   Salvation .....John 3:16
   Judgment......2 Cor. 5:10

B. *Consistent with:*
   God's plan .....Rom. 9:6-33
   Different
   talents ....Matt. 25:14-30
   Different
   gifts ....1 Cor. 12:4-31
   Different
   functions {Eph. 5:22-33
   {Eph. 6:1-9
   Rule...........Ps. 9:8

Equity—*justice*

Yahweh judges
with.............Ps. 98:9

Er—*watching*

1. Son of {Gen. 38:1-7
   Judah........{Gen. 46:12
2. Descendant of
   Judah........1 Chr. 4:21
3. Ancestor of
   Christ........Luke 3:28

Eran—*watchful*

Founder of the
Eranites..........Num. 26:36

Erastus—*beloved*

1. Paul's friend {Acts 19:21, 22
   at Ephesus...{2 Tim. 4:20
2. Treasurer of
   Corinth ......Rom. 16:23
   May be same person as 1.

Erech—*size*

City of Shinar.....Gen. 10:10

Eri—*watching*

Son of Gad.......Gen. 46:16
Founder of the
Erites ....Num. 26:16

Error—*a departure from the truth*

Deceptive ....2 Tim. 3:13
False.............Matt. 24:4, 11
Produces misunder-
standing........Matt. 22:29
Against Christ ....1 John 4:1-6
Sign of the end....1 Tim. 4:1

Esarhaddon—*Ashur has given a brother*

Son of Sennacherib; king of
Assyria (681–669
B.C.).............2 Kin. 19:36, 37

Esau—*hairy*

Son of Isaac ......Rom. 9:11-13
Hairy ....Gen. 25:25
Hunter...........Gen. 25:27
Isaac's favorite
son. .....Gen. 25:28
Sells his
birthright........Gen. 25:29-34
Unable to
repent...........Heb. 12:16, 17
Marries two
women...........Gen. 26:34
Deprived of
blessing ....Gen. 27:1-40
Hates his brother
Jacob ....Gen. 27:41-45

Reconciled to
Jacob ....Gen. 33:1-17
With Jacob, buries his
father ....Gen. 35:29
Descendants of....Gen. 36:1-43
Ancestor of
Edomites ....Jer. 49:7, 8
Prophecy
concerning ......Obad. 18

Escape—to flee from

A. Physical things:
Flood..........Gen. 7:7, 8
City of
destruction....Gen. 19:15-30
Mob ....Luke 4:28-30
Insane king....1 Sam. 19:9-18
Wicked
queen.........2 Kin. 11:1-3
Assassi-
nation ....Esth. 2:21-23
Hanging ......Esth. 5:14
Esth. 7:9
Prison ....Acts 5:18-20
Sinking ship...Acts 27:30-44

B. Spiritual things:
Sin ....Gen. 39:10-12
Destruction.....Luke 21:36
Corruption.....2 Pet. 1:4
God's wrath ...1 Thess. 1:9, 10
The great
tribulation ....Rev. 7:13-17

Eschatology—teaching dealing with final destiny

A. In Old Testament:
Judgment......Is. 2:12-22
Messianic   { Jer. 23:4-18
kingdom ......{ Jer. 33:14-17

B. In New Testament:
Coming of   { Matt. 24
Christ........{ Luke 21:5-36
Resurrection   { 1 Cor. 15:51-58
of dead......{ 1 Thess. 4:13-18
Destruction of
earth..........2 Pet. 3:10-13
Reign of
Christ.........Rev. 20:4, 6

Esek—strife

A well in Gerar ...Gen. 26:20

Esh-Baal—man of Baal

Son of Saul ....1 Chr. 8:33

Eshban—wise man

Son of Dishon.....Gen. 36:26

Eshcol—cluster of grapes

1. Brother of Aner and
Mamre........Gen. 14:13, 24
2. Valley near   { Num. 13:22-27
Hebron   { Deut. 1:24

Eshean—support

City of Judah .....Josh. 15:52

Eshek—oppression

Descendant of
Saul..............1 Chr. 8:39

Eshtaol—a way

Town of Judah....Josh. 15:20, 33
Assigned to
Danites...........Josh. 19:40, 41
Near Samson's home and burial
site..............Judg. 16:31

Eshtaolites

Inhabitants of
Eshtaol...........1 Chr. 2:53

Eshtemoa, Eshtemoh—obedience

Town of Judah....Josh. 15:20, 50
Assigned to
Levites ....Josh. 21:14
David sends   { 1 Sam. 30:26,
spoils to.........{ 28

Eshton—restful

Man of Judah .....1 Chr. 4:1-12

Esli—reserved

Ancestor of
Christ ....Luke 3:25

Establish—a permanent condition

A. Of earthly things:
Kingdom ......2 Chr. 17:5
Festival.......Esth. 9:21

B. Of spiritual things:
Messiah's
kingdom ......2 Sam. 7:13
God's Word....Ps. 119:38
Our:
Hearts........1 Thess. 3:13
Faith ....Col. 2:7
Works........2 Thess. 2:17
Lives ....1 Pet. 5:10

C. Accomplished by:
God ....2 Cor. 1:21, 22

Esther—*star*

Daughter of
Abihail . . . . .Esth. 2:15
Mordecai's
cousin . . . . .Esth. 2:7, 15
Selected for
harem . . . . .Esth. 2:7-16
Chosen queen . . . .Esth. 2:17, 18
Seeks to help
Mordecai . . . . .Esth. 4:4-6
Told of Haman's
plot . . . . .Esth. 4:7-9
Sends message to
Mordecai . . . . .Esth. 4:10-12
Told to act . . . . .Esth. 4:13, 14
Seeks Mordecai's
aid . . . . .Esth. 4:15-17
Appears before
Ahasuerus . . . . .Esth. 5:1-5
Invites Ahasuerus to
banquet . . . . .Esth. 5:4-8
Reveals Haman's
plot . . . . .Esth. 7:1-7
Given Haman's
house . . . . .Esth. 8:1, 2
Secures change of
edict . . . . .Esth. 8:3-6
Makes further
request . . . . .Esth. 9:12, 13
With Mordecai, institutes
Purim . . . . .Esth. 9:29-32

Estrangement from God

Caused by:

Adam's sin . . . . .Gen. 3:8-11, 24
Personal sin . . . . . . .Ps. 51:9-12
National sin . . . . . . .Jer. 2:14-17

Etam—*Wild beasts' lair*

1. Village of
   Simeon . . . . . . .1 Chr. 4:32
2. Rock where Samson took
   refuge . . . . .Judg. 15:8-19
3. Town of
   Judah . . . . .2 Chr. 11:6

Eternal, everlasting—*without end*

A. *Applied to Trinity:*
   God . . . . .Ps. 90:2
   Christ . . . . .Prov. 8:23
   Holy Spirit . . . . .Heb. 9:14

B. *Applied to God's attributes:*
   Home . . . . .Eccl. 12:5
   Power . . . . .Rom. 1:20
   Covenant . . . . . . .Is. 55:3
   Gospel . . . . .Rev. 14:6
   Counsels . . . . . . .Eph. 3:10, 11

Righteous-
ness . . . . .Ps. 119:142, 144
Kingdom . . . . . .Ps. 145:13
Truth . . . . .Ps. 100:5
Love . . . . .Jer. 31:3
Father . . . . .Is. 9:6

C. *Applied to the believer:*
   Comfort . . . . . . .2 Thess. 2:16
   Life . . . . .John 3:15
   Redemption . . . .Heb. 9:12
   Salvation . . . . . .Heb. 5:9
   Inheritance . . . .Heb. 9:15
   Glory . . . . .1 Pet. 5:10
   Kingdom . . . . . .2 Pet. 1:11
   Reward . . . . .John 4:36
   Name . . . . .Is. 56:5
   Glory . . . . .2 Tim. 2:10
   Light . . . . .Is. 60:19, 20
   Joy . . . . .Is. 51:11
   Dwellings . . . . . .Luke 16:9
   Purpose . . . . . . .Eph. 3:11

D. *Applied to the wicked:*
   Condem-
   nation . . . . . . .Mark 3:29
   Judgment . . . . .Heb. 6:2
   Punishment . . . .Matt. 25:46
   Destruction . . . .2 Thess. 1:9
   Contempt . . . . .Dan. 12:2
   Bonds . . . . .Jude 6
   Fire . . . . .Matt. 25:41
   Sin . . . . .Mark 3:29

Eternity—*time without end mentioned once*

God's habitation . .Is. 57:15

Etham—*sea bound*

Israel's
encampment . . . . .Ex. 13:20

Ethan—*perpetuity*

1. One noted for
   wisdom . . . . . . .1 Kin. 4:31
2. Levite . . . . .1 Chr. 6:44
3. Ancestor of
   Asaph . . . . .1 Chr. 6:42, 43

Ethanim—*incessant rains*

Seventh month in the Hebrew
year . . . . .1 Kin. 8:2

Ethbaal—*with Baal*

Father of
Jezebel . . . . .1 Kin. 16:31

Ether—*plenty*

Town of Judah . . . .Josh. 15:42

Ethics—*a system setting forth standards of right conduct*

Perversion of......Rom. 1:19-32
Law of............Rom. 2:14-16
Summary of
Christian.........Rom. 12:1-21

Ethiopia (Cush)—*burnt face*

Country south of
Egypt.............Ezek. 29:10
Home of the Sons of
Ham ....Gen. 10:6
Famous for
minerals..........Job 28:19
Merchandise of....Is. 45:14
Wealth of ....Is. 43:3
Militarily strong...2 Chr. 12:2, 3
Anguished
people............Ezek. 30:4-9
Defeated by Asa ..2 Chr. 14:9-15
Subdued ....Dan. 11:43
Prophecies
against...........Is. 20:1-6
Hopeful promise ..Ps. 68:31

Ethiopians—*descendants of Cush*

Skin of,
unchangeable ....Jer. 13:23
Moses'
marriage to......Num. 12:1
Ebed-Melech saves
Jeremiah ....Jer. 38:7
Eunuch
converted ....Acts 8:26-40

Eth Kazin—*time of a judge*

On border of
Zebulun..........Josh. 19:13, 16

Ethnan—*hire*

Judahite ....1 Chr. 4:5-7

Ethni—*liberal*

Levite.............1 Chr. 6:41

Eubulus—*prudent*

Christian at
Rome ....2 Tim. 4:21

Eucharist (see Lord's Supper)

Eunice—*blessed with victory*

Mother of
Timothy..........2 Tim. 1:5

Eunuch—*an officer or official, emasculated*

A. *Rules concerning:*
Excluded from congre-
gation.........Deut. 23:1
Given
promise.......Is. 56:3-5

B. *Duties of:*
Keeper of
harem.........Esth. 2:3, 14
Attendant .....Dan. 1:3, 7, 10,
11
Treasurer.....Acts 8:27
Seven, serving
Ahasuerus ....Esth. 1:10, 15

Euodias—*good journey*

Christian woman at
Philippi..........Phil. 4:2

Euphrates—*that which makes fruitful*

River of Eden .....Gen. 2:14
Assyria bounded
by................2 Kin. 23:29
Babylon on.......Jer. 51:13, 36
Boundary of   {Gen. 15:18
God's promise ...{1 Kin. 4:21, 24
Scene of battle ...Jer. 46:2, 6, 10
Exiled Jews weep
there............Ps. 137:1
Angels bound
there............Rev. 9:14

Euroclydon—*east wind*

Violent wind......Acts 27:14

Eutychus—*fortunate*

Sleeps during Paul's
sermon..........Acts 20:9
Restored to life....Acts 20:12

Evangelism—*declaring Gospel to the unregenerate*

A. *Scope:*
To all   {Matt. 28:19, 20
nations.......{Mark 16:15
House to
house.........Acts 5:42
Always ....1 Pet. 3:15
As ambas-
sadors.........2 Cor. 5:18-20

B. *Source:*
Jesus Christ ...Gal. 1:6-12
The Father ....John 6:44, 65
The Spirit......Acts 1:8

Evangelist—*one who proclaims good news*

Distinct ministry . . Eph. 4:11
Applied to Philip . . Acts 21:8
Timothy
works as . . . . 2 Tim. 4:5

Eve—*life*

Made from
 Adam's rib . . . . . . Gen. 2:18-22
Named by Adam . . Gen. 3:20
Deceived by
 Satan . . . . Gen. 3:1-24
Leads Adam
to sin . . . . 1 Tim. 2:13, 14

Evening—*last hours of sunlight*

Labor ceases . . . . . Judg. 19:16
 Ruth 2:17
Workers paid . . . . Deut. 24:15
Ritual impurity ⎰Lev. 11:24-28
ends . . . . ⎱Num. 19:19
Meditation . . . . . . Gen. 24:63
Prayer . . . . Matt. 14:15, 23
Eating . . . . Luke 24:29, 30
Sacrifice . . . . Ex. 29:38-42
 Num. 28:3-8

Evening sacrifice—*part of Israelite worship*

Ritual described . . . Ex. 29:38-42
Part of continual
offering . . . . Num. 28:3-8

Events, Biblical, classified

A. *Originating, originating other events:*
 Creation . . . . Gen. 1
 Fall of man . . . . Rom. 5:12

B. *Epochal, introducing new period:*
 Flood . . . . Gen. 6-8
 The death of ⎰Matt. 27:50, 51
 Christ . . . . ⎱Heb. 9

C. *Typical, foreshadowing some New Testament event:*
 The
 Passover— ⎰Ex. 12
 Christ as ⎰John 1:35-37
 Lamb . . . . ⎱1 Cor. 5:7, 8
 Jonah and great fish—
 Christ's death and
 resurrec- ⎰Jon. 1, 2
 tion . . . . ⎱Matt. 12:38-41

D. *Prophetic, prophesying future events:*
 Return from ⎰2 Chr. 36:22, 23
 exile . . . . ⎱Jer. 29:10
 Destruction of ⎰Luke 19:41-44
 Jerusalem . . . . ⎱Luke 21:20-24

E. *Redemptive, connected with man's salvation:*
 Advent of ⎰Luke 2:11
 Christ . . . . ⎱Gal. 4:4, 5
 Death ⎰Matt. 20:28
 of ⎰Luke 24:44-47
 Christ . . . . . . ⎱1 Tim. 1:15

F. *Unique, those without parallel:*
 Creation . . . . . . Gen. 1
 Virgin birth . . . . Matt. 1:18-25
 Luke 1:30-37

G. *Miraculous, those produced by supernatural means:*
 Plagues on
 Egypt . . . . Ex. 7-12
 Crossing Red
 Sea . . . . Ex. 14-15
 Fall of
 Jericho . . . . Josh. 6
 Sun's standing
 still . . . . Josh. 10:12-14

H. *Judgmental, those judging people for sins:*
 Flood . . . . 2 Pet. 2:5
 Sodom and ⎰Gen. 19
 Gomorrah . . . . ⎱2 Pet. 2:6
 Killing of ⎰Ex. 32:25-35
 Israelites . . . . . ⎱Num. 25:1-9

I. *Transforming, those producing a change:*
 Christ's trans-
 formation . . . . . Matt. 17:1-8
 Conversion of ⎰Acts 9
 Paul . . . . ⎱1 Tim. 1:12-14
 Believer's
 regenera- ⎰John 3:1-8
 tion . . . . ⎱2 Cor. 5:17

J. *Providential, those manifesting God's providence:*
 Baby's cry . . . . . Ex. 2:5-10
 Joseph's being
 sold into ⎰Gen. 37:26-28
 Egypt . . . . ⎱Gen. 45:1-9
 King's sleepless
 night . . . . Esth. 6:1-10

K. *Confirmatory, those confirming some promise:*
 Worship at
 Sinai . . . . Ex. 3:12

Aaron's rod....Num. 17:1-11
Thunder and
rain..........1 Sam. 12:16-18
Sun's shadow
moved   {2 Kin. 20:8-11
backward ....{Is. 38:1-8

L. *Promissory, those fulfilling
some promise:*
Pentecost......{Joel 2:28-32
                {Acts 2
               {Luke 24:49
Spirit's   {Acts 1:4, 5, 8
coming.......{Acts 2:1-4
Possession   {Gen. 15:18-21
of   {Josh. 24:3,
land..........{11-19

M. *Eschatological, those connected
with Christ's return:*
Doom of
antichrist .....2 Thess. 2:1-12
Resurrection   {1 Cor. 15:35-38,
and   {42
translation ..{1 Thess. 4:13-18
Resurrection   {Matt. 25:31-46
and   {Acts 17:31
judgment ....{Rev. 20:11-15
Destruction of the
world ....2 Pet. 3:7-15

Evi—*desirous*

King of Midian....Num. 31:8
Land of, assigned to
Reuben..........Josh. 13:15, 21

Evidence—*ground for belief*

A. *Based upon:*
Testimony of
witnesses .....Matt. 18:16
Personal
testimony .....Acts 26:1-27
Fulfilled
prophecy......Matt. 1:22, 23
Supernatural
testimony .....Matt. 3:17
New life ....1 John 3:14

B. *Kinds of:*
Circum-
stantial ......Gen. 39:7-19
False ....Matt. 26:59-61
Fabricated.....Gen. 37:29-33
Confirmed.....Heb. 2:3, 4
Satanic ....2 Thess. 2:9, 10
Indisputable ...1 Cor. 15:1-19

C. *Need of:*
Confirm weak
faith ....Luke 7:19, 22

Remove
doubt ....John 20:24-29
Refute
mockers ......2 Pet. 3:3-7
Attest a messenger of
God...........Ex. 8:18, 19
Produce faith ..John 20:30, 31

Evil—*that which is morally injurious*

A. *Origin of:*
Begins with
Satan ..,.....Is. 14:12-14
Enters world...Rom. 5:12
Comes from
man ....Matt. 15:18, 19
Inflamed by
lust ....James 1:14

B. *Applied to:*
Men ....Matt. 12:35
Heart..........Jer. 17:9
Imaginations ..Gen. 6:5
Generation ....Matt. 12:39
Age...........Gal. 1:4
Our days ......Eph. 5:16
Conscience ....Heb. 10:22
Spirits ....Matt. 12:45

C. *Satan as "the evil one":*
Lord safeguards
against........John 17:15

D. *The Christian should guard
against, evil:*
Heart of
unbelief.......Heb. 3:12
Thoughts ......James 2:4
Boastings ......James 4:16
Things.........Rom. 12:9
Deeds ....2 John 9
Appearance....1 Thess. 5:22

Evil—*that which is physically harmful:
floods, earthquakes, etc.*

Part of man's
curse...........Gen. 3:17-19
Men cry out
against ....Rev. 9:18-21
Can be
misinterpreted....Luke 13:1-3
Foreseen by
prudent ....Prov. 22:3
Will continue to
the end...........Matt. 24:6-8, 14
Believers
share in ....2 Cor. 12:7-10
To be borne   {Job 2:7-10
patiently ....{James 5:11

Prospects of relief
from ....Rom. 8:18-39
Relieved now by
faith............Heb. 3:17-19
None in heaven ...Rev. 7:14-17

Evil companions (see Association)

Evildoers—*workers of evil*

Christians wrongly
called ....1 Pet. 2:12
Christians should
not be............1 Pet. 4:15
Christians cry
against........Ps. 119:115
Punished by
magistrates.......Rom. 13:1-4
End of, certain ....Ps. 34:16

Evil eye

Descriptive of a man's inner
being............Mark 7:21, 22
Shown in
attitudes ....Matt. 20:15

Evil-Merodach—*man of Marduk*

Babylonian king (562–560 B.C.);
follows Nebuchad-
nezzar............2 Kin. 25:27-30

Evil speaking

A. *The evil of:*
Sign of unregen-
eracy ....Ps. 10:7
Aimed at
righteous .....Ps. 64:2-5
Defiles the whole
body ....James 3:5-10
Disrupts
fellowship.....3 John 9-11
Severely
condemned ...James 4:11
Punished ......1 Cor. 6:9, 10

B. *Not to be confused with:*
Denunciation of
vice...........Titus 1:12, 13
Description of
sinners........Acts 13:9, 10
Defense of the
faith.........Jude 4, 8-16

Evil spirits—*demons*

Sent upon King
Saul.............1 Sam. 16:14
Ahab prompted to evil
by...............1 Kin. 22:1-23

Cast out by
Jesus............Luke 7:21
Cast out by Paul ..Acts 19:11, 12

Evolution—*development of life from
lower to higher forms*

A. *Conflicts with:*
God's   {Gen. 1:26, 27
description... {Gen. 2:21-25
Moses'   {Ex. 20:11
record........ {Deut. 4:32

B. *Not accepted by:*
Jesus ....Matt. 19:4-6
                Rom. 5:12-19
Paul ....1 Cor. 15:22, 45
                1 Tim. 2:13, 14

Exaltation—*the state of being raised up*

A. *Of evil man:*
Originates in
Satan ....Luke 4:5, 6
Defies God .....2 Kin. 18:28-35
Perverts
religion ....Dan. 11:36, 37
Brings   {Esth. 6:6-14
downfall ..... {Esth. 7:9
Merits
punishment ...1 Kin. 16:1-4
Displayed by
Herod.........Acts 12:21-23
Seen in
antichrist .....2 Thess. 2:4, 9

B. *Of good men:*
Principle of ....Matt. 23:12
Follows
humility ......1 Pet. 5:6
Restrictions
upon.........2 Cor. 10:5
Brings glory ...James 1:9
False, brings
sorrow........1 Cor. 4:6-14
Final, in
heaven........Rev. 22:5

C. *Of Christ:*
Promised ......Ps. 2:8, 9
Predicted by
Christ........Matt. 26:64
The
ascension .....Acts 2:33, 34
Seen by
Stephen.......Acts 7:55, 56
Taught by the
apostles.......Eph. 1:20-22
Set forth as a
reward........Phil. 2:9-11
Introduces priestly
intercession ...Heb. 1:3

Examination of others

Of Jesus .... Luke 23:13, 14
Of Peter .... Acts 4:8, 9
Of Paul .... Acts 22:24, 25

Examination of self

Sought by David .. Ps. 26:2
Must precede Lord's
  Supper .... 1 Cor. 11:28
Necessary for real
  faith............. 2 Cor. 13:5

Example—*a pattern to follow*

A. *Purposes of:*
   Set forth sin's
     punishment ... 2 Pet. 2:6
   Show unbelief's con-
     sequences..... Heb. 4:11
   Restrain from
     evil .... 1 Cor. 10:6-11
   Illustrate   {John 13:14, 15
     humility...... {1 Pet. 3:5
   Exemplify   {James 5:10, 11
     patience..... {1 Pet. 2:20-22
   Portray Christian
     conduct....... Phil. 3:17

B. *Of evil men:*
   Covetousness—
     Achan .... Josh. 7:20, 21
   Immorality—
     Eli's sons...... 1 Sam. 2:22-25
   Rebellion—
     Saul .... 1 Sam. 15:17-23
   Folly—Nabal.. 1 Sam. 25:25-37
   Idolatry—
     Jeroboam ..... 1 Kin. 12:26-33

C. *Of good men:*
   Holy zeal—
     Phinehas..... Num. 25:7-13
   Faith—Caleb .. Josh. 14:6-15
   Fidelity—
     Joshua....... Josh. 24:15-25
   Courage—
     David .... 1 Sam. 17:32-37
   Holy life—
     Daniel .... Ezek. 14:14, 20
   Perseverance—
     Job .... James 5:10, 11
   Christian living—
     Paul .... Phil. 3:17

Example of Christ, the

A. *Virtues illustrated by:*
   Gentleness..... Matt. 11:29
   Self-denial ..... Matt. 16:24
   Love.......... John 13:34

Obedience ..... John 15:10
Benevolence... 2 Cor. 8:7, 9
Humility....... Phil. 2:5-8
Forgiveness.... Col. 3:13
Suffering
  wrongfully .... 1 Pet. 2:21-23
Purity .... 1 John 3:3

B. *The Christian approach to:*
   Progressive .... 2 Cor. 3:18
   Instructive.... Eph. 4:20-24
   Imitative ...... 1 Pet. 2:21-23
   Perfective...... Rom. 8:29

Excitement—*something that stirs us
  emotionally*

A. *Causes of:*
   Great sin ...... Ex. 32:17-20
   Great victory ... 1 Sam. 17:52
   God's power ... 1 Kin. 18:22-41
   King's
     coronation .... 2 Kin. 11:12-16
   Human
     destruction.... Esth. 9:1-19
   Handwriting on the
     wall.......... Dan. 5:5-9
   Miracle .... Acts 19:13-20

B. *Time of:*
   The giving of the
     Law.......... Heb. 12:18-21
   Christ's
     death .... Matt. 27:51-54
   Pentecost...... Acts 2:1-47
   Christ's
     return........ Luke 21:25-28

Exclusiveness—*setting boundaries
  against others*

A. *Christianity's, only one:*
   Door .... John 10:1, 7, 9
   Way........... John 14:6
   Salvation ...... Acts 4:12

B. *The Bible's, only book:*
   Inspired .... 1 Tim. 3:16
   Revealing
     God.......... Heb. 1:1
   Written to save
     men.......... John 20:30, 31
   Containing true
     prophecies .... John 5:45-47

Excommunication—*expulsion from
  membership in a body*

A. *Separation from.*
   Kingship....... 1 Sam. 16:1
   Foreigners ..... Neh. 13:1-3
   Priesthood..... Neh. 13:27, 28

B. *Practice of:*
To intimidate
people........John 9:19-23
Against true
Christians.....John 16:1, 2
Against false
teachers ......2 John 10, 11

C. *Method of:*
Described.......Matt. 18:15-17
Illustrated .....1 Cor. 5:1-13
Perverted......3 John 9, 10

Excuse—*an invalid reason for neglect of duty*

A. *Nature of, blaming:*
Wife...........Gen. 3:12
The people.....1 Sam. 15:20, 21
God's mercy ...Jon. 4:1-4
God's
providence ...Num. 14:1-23

B. *Invalidity of:*
Shown to
Moses........Ex. 3:10-12
Proved to
Gideon.......Judg. 6:36-40
Made plain to
Esther ....Esth. 4:13-17
Illustrated by
Christ........Luke 14:16-24
Relayed to Hades'
inhabitants....Luke 16:27-31
Made evident to
Thomas......John 20:24-28

Exhortation—*encouraging others to commendable conduct*

A. *Objects of:*
Call to
repentance....Luke 3:17, 18
Continue in the
faith ....Acts 14:22
Convict
gainsayers ....Titus 1:9
Warn the
unruly ....1 Thess. 5:14
Encourage
soberness .....Titus 3:1
Strengthen
godliness......1 Thess. 4:1-6
Stir up
liberality ......2 Cor. 9:5-7

B. *Office of:*
Commended ...Rom. 12:8
Part of the
ministry.......Titus 2:15
Needed in
times ....2 Tim. 4:2-5

C. *Nature of:*
Daily duty .....Heb. 3:13
For holiness ...1 Thess. 2:3, 4
Worthy of
reception......Heb. 13:22
Belongs
to all..........Heb. 10:25
Special
need of ......Jude 3, 4

Exile—*banished from one's native land; captive*

David............1 Sam. 21:10-15
Jeroboam.......1 Kin. 11:40
Jeremiah........Jer. 43:4-7
Christ...........Matt. 2:13-15
John ....Rev. 1:9
Jehoiachin .....2 Kin. 24:15
Judah...........2 Kin. 25:21
Jeconiah ....Jer. 27:20
Nebuchad-
nezzar.......Jer. 29:1
Chemosh.........Jer. 48:7
Syrians.........Amos 1:5

See Captivity

Exodus—*a departure*

Israel's, from
Egypt ....Ex. 12:41

Exodus, Book of—*a book of the Old Testament*

Escape from
Egypt ....Ex. 12:31-42
The Law ....Ex. 20:1-17
The tabernacle and
priesthood.......Ex. 24:12-31:18

Exorcists—*those who use oaths to dispel evil spirits*

Paul encounters...Acts 19:13, 19

Expanse—*firmament; vault*

Created by God ...Gen. 1:8
Stars placed in ....Gen. 1:14, 17
Compared to a tent
curtain ....Ps. 104:2
Expressive of God's
glory ....Ps. 19:1
Saints
compared to......Dan. 12:3

Expectation—*looking forward*

Conquest ....Num. 14:1-24
Victory ....Josh. 7:4-13
Relief ....1 Kin. 12:4-15
Impending
doom.............2 Kin. 23:25-27

Elevation . . . . .Esth. 6:6-14
The wicked . . . . . . .Prov. 10:28
Righteous. . . . . .Ps. 62:5
Death. . . . . .Acts 28:3-6

Expediency—*a method of justifying an act*

To fulfill God's
plan . . . . .John 11:50
To avoid offense . .1 Cor. 8:8-13
To save men . . . . . .1 Cor. 9:19-23
To accomplish a
task . . . . .2 Cor. 8:10-12
Illustrations . . . . . . .Acts 16:3

Expense—*the cost involved*

Royalty, foretold . .1 Sam. 8:11-18
Royalty, realized . .1 Kin. 4:22, 23

Experiment—*a test designed to prove something*

Jacob . . . . .Gen. 30:37-43
Aaron's sons . . . . . .Lev. 10:1-3
Philistines. . . . . .1 Sam. 6:1-18
Daniel . . . . .Dan. 1:11-16
God's goodness . . .Mal. 3:10-12

Expiation—*atonement*

Under ⎰Lev. 14:11-20
Law. . . . . ⎱Lev. 16:11-28
Prophecy of
Isaiah . . . . .Is. 53:1-12
Fulfilled in ⎰Acts 8:27-39
Christ . . . . ⎱1 Pet. 2:21-25

Explanation—*making simple and plain*

Of a condition. . . . .Luke 16:25-31
Of a
phenomenon . . . . .Acts 2:1-21
Of a decision. . . . . .Acts 15:15-31

Expulsion—*driving out by force from*

Eden. . . . . .Gen. 3:22-24
The priesthood. . . .Neh. 13:27-29
A city. . . . . .Luke 4:16-29
By persecution . . . .Acts 13:50, 51

Extortion—*money obtained by force or threat*

Innocency from,
pretended . . . . . . .Matt. 23:25
Fellowship with,
forbidden. . . . . .1 Cor. 5:10, 11
Sin of,
proscribed. . . . . . . .Luke 3:13, 14
Examples of. . . . . . .Gen. 47:13-26

Extremity—*the greatest degree of something*

Human faith . . . . . .Gen. 22:1-3
Grief. . . . . .2 Sam. 18:33
Pride. . . . . .Is. 14:13, 14
Pain . . . . .Matt. 27:46-50
Degradation. . . . . . .Luke 15:13-16
Torments . . . . .Luke 16:23, 24
Human
endurance. . . . . . . .2 Cor. 1:8-10

Eye—*the organ of sight*

A. *Affected by:*
Age. . . . . .Gen. 27:1
Wine . . . . .Gen. 49:12
Sorrow . . . . .Job 17:7
Disease . . . . .Lev. 26:16
Grief . . . . .Ps. 6:7
Light . . . . .Acts 22:11

B. *Of God, figurative of:*
Omniscience. . .2 Chr. 16:9
Holiness . . . . . . .Hab. 1:13
Guidance . . . . . .Ps. 32:8
Protection . . . . .Ps. 33:18

C. *Of man, figurative of:*
Revealed
knowledge . . . .Num. 24:3
Lawlessness . . .Judg. 17:6
Jealousy . . . . . .1 Sam. 18:9
Under-
standing . . . . .Ps. 19:8
Agreement. . . . .Is. 52:8
Great sorrow . .Jer. 9:1
Retaliation . . . .Matt. 5:38
The essential
nature . . . . . . .Matt. 6:22, 23
Moral state . . . .Matt. 7:3-5
Spiritual
inability. . . . . . .Matt. 13:15
Spiritual
dullness. . . . . .Mark 8:17, 18
Future glory . .1 Cor. 2:9
Illumination . . .Eph. 1:18
Unworthy
service. . . . . . .Eph. 6:6
Worldliness. . . .1 John 2:16
Evil desires . . .2 Pet. 2:14

D. *Prophecies concerning:*
Shall see the
Redeemer . . . . .Job 19:25-27
Gentiles
shall see . . . . . .Is. 42:6, 7
Blind
shall see . . . . . .Is. 29:18
Will see the
King . . . . .Is. 33:17

Will see
Jesus.........Rev. 1:7
Tears of, shall be wiped
away.........Rev. 7:17

Eyebrows—*the arch of hair over the eyes*

Of lepers,
shaved off.......Lev. 14:2, 9

Eye salve—*an ointment*

Christ mentions...Rev. 3:18

Eyeservice—*service performed only when watched by another*

Highly
obnoxious........Eph. 6:6

Eyewitness—*a firsthand observer*

Consulted by
Luke.........Luke 1:1, 2
Of Christ's
majesty ....2 Pet. 1:16

Ezbai—*shining*

Naarai's father ....1 Chr. 11:37

Ezbon—*bright*

1. Son of Gad ....Gen. 46:16
2. Benjamite .....1 Chr. 7:7

Ezekiel—*God strengthens*

A. *Life of:*
  Hebrew prophet; son of
  Buzi ....Ezek. 1:3
  Carried captive to
  Babylon.......Ezek. 1:1-3
  Lived among
  exiles ....Ezek. 3:15-17
  His wife died..Ezek. 24:18
  Persecuted.....Ezek. 3:25
  Often
  consulted ....Ezek. 8:1
  Prophetic
  minister.......Ezek. 3:17-21

B. *Visions of:*
  God's glory ....Ezek. 1:4-28
  Abomina-
  tions..........Ezek. 8:5-18
  Valley of dry
  bones ....Ezek. 37:1-14
  Messianic
  times ....Ezek. 40—48
  River of life....Ezek. 47:1-5

C. *Methods employed by:*
  Threatens
  dumbness.....Ezek. 3:26
  Symbolizes siege of
  Jerusalem .....Ezek. 4:1-3
  Shaves
  himself.......Ezek. 5:1-4
  Removes
  belongings ....Ezek. 12:3-16
  Uses
  boiling pot ....Ezek. 24:1-14
  Does not mourn for
  wife..........Ezek. 24:16-27
  Uses
  parables......Ezek. 17:2-10

Ezekiel, Book of—*a Book of the Old Testament*

Prophecies against
Israel.............Ezek. 1:1-24:27
Prophecies against the
nations...........Ezek. 25:1-32:32
Prophecies of
restoration ......Ezek. 33:1-39:29
The messianic
kingdom ....Ezek. 40:1-48:35

Ezel—*departure*

David's hiding
place ....1 Sam. 20:19

Ezem—*bone*

Village of Judah...Josh. 15:29
Assigned to
Simeon...........Josh. 19:3

Ezer—*help*

1. Horite tribe....1 Chr. 1:38
  Son of Seir ....Gen. 36:21
2. Ephraimite.....1 Chr. 7:21
3. Judahite.......1 Chr. 4:1, 4
4. Gadite
  warrior ....1 Chr. 12:9
5. Son of
  Jeshua........Neh. 3:19
6. Postexilic
  priest ....Neh. 12:42

Ezion Geber—*backbone of a giant*

Town on the Red
Sea...............1 Kin. 9:26
Israelite
encampment .....Num. 33:35
Seaport of Israel's
navy ....1 Kin. 22:48
See Elath

Eznite—*spear; to be sharp*

Warrior of
David ....2 Sam. 23:8
Called
Tachmonite ......2 Sam. 23:8
Called
Hachmonite ......1 Chr. 11:11

Ezra—*help*

1. Postexilic
  priest ....Neh. 12:1, 7
  Called
  Azariah ....Neh. 10:2
2. Scribe, priest and reformer
  of postexilic
  times ....Ezra 7:1-6
  Commissioned by
  Artaxerxes....Ezra 7:6-28
  Takes exiles
  with him......Ezra 8:1-20
  Proclaims a
  fast ....Ezra 8:21-23
  Commits treasures to the
  priests ....Ezra 8:24-30
  Comes to
  Jerusalem.....Ezra 8:31, 32
  Institutes
  reforms ....Ezra 9:1-15
  Reads the
  Law...........Neh. 8:1-18
  Helps in
  dedication.....Neh. 12:27-43

Ezra, Book of—*a book of the Old
Testament*

Return from
exile.............Ezra 1:1—2:70
Rebuilding the
Temple..........Ezra 3:1—6:22
Reformation .....Ezra 9:1—10:44

Ezrahite—*belonging to Ezrach*

Family name of Ethan and
Heman ....1 Kin. 4:31

Ezri—*my help*

David's farm
overseer..........1 Chr. 27:26

F

Fable—*a fictitious story*

A. *Form of allegory:*
  The trees ......Judg. 9:7-15
  The thistle ....2 Kin. 14:9

B. *Form of fiction, contrary to:*
  Edification.....1 Tim. 1:4
  Godliness......1 Tim. 4:6, 7
  Truth..........2 Tim. 4:4
  Facts ....2 Pet. 1:16

Face—*front part of head*

A. *Acts performed on:*
  Spitting on ....Deut. 25:9
  Disfiguring
  of............Matt. 6:16
  Painting of ....2 Kin. 9:30
  Hitting ....2 Cor. 11:20

B. *Acts indicated by:*
  Falling on—
  worship.......Gen. 17:3
  Covering of—
  mourning......2 Sam. 19:4
  Hiding of—
  disapproval ...Deut. 31:17, 18
  Turning away of—
  rejection ......2 Chr. 30:9
  Setting of—deter-
  mination......2 Kin. 12:17

Face of the Lord

A. *Toward the righteous:*
  Shine on.......Num. 6:25
  Do not hide....Ps. 102:2
  Hide from our
  sins ....Ps. 51:9
  Shall see ......Rev. 22:4

B. *Toward the wicked:*
  Is against......Ps. 34:16
  Set against ....Jer. 21:10
  They hide
  from ....Rev. 6:16

Failure

A. *Causes of:*
  Contrary to God's
  will ....Gen. 11:3-8
  Disobe-
  dience........Num. 14:40-45
  Sin ....Josh. 7:3-12
  Lack of   { Matt. 17:15-20
  prayer ......{ Mark 9:24-29
  Not counting the
  cost...........Luke 14:28-32
  Unbelief ......Heb. 4:6

B. *Examples of:*
  Esau...........Gen. 25:29-34
  Eli's sons ......1 Sam. 2:12-17
  King Saul......1 Sam. 16:1
  Absalom ....2 Sam. 18:6-17
  Hananiah......Jer. 28:1-17
  Haman ....Esth. 7:1-10

Fainting, faintheartedness—*a loss of vital powers; weary*

A. *Causes of:*
Physical
fatigue........Gen. 25:29, 30
Famine........Gen. 47:13
Unbelief........Gen. 45:26
Fear...........Josh. 2:24
Sin............Lev. 26:31
Sickness.......Job 4:5
Human
weakness.....Is. 40:29-31
Ecstasy of
visions........Dan. 8:27
Disappoint-
ment..........Jon. 4:8

B. *Antidotes against:*
Removal of the
fearful........Deut. 20:8

Fair—English rendering of numerous Hebrew and Greek words

Beautiful..........Song 1:15, 16
Good.............Matt. 16:2

Fair Havens

Harbor of Crete...Acts 27:8

Faith—*confidence in the testimony of another*

A. *Nature of:*
Fruit of the
Spirit.........Gal. 5:22, 23
Work of God...John 6:29
God's gift......Eph. 2:8
Comes from the
heart...........Rom. 10:9, 10
Substance of unseen
things..........Heb. 11:1

B. *Results from:*
Scriptures.....John 20:30, 31
Preaching......John 17:20
Gospel........Acts 15:7

C. *Objects of:*
God...........John 14:1
Christ.........John 20:31
Moses'
writings.......John 5:46
Writings of the
prophets......Acts 26:27
Gospel........Mark 1:15
God's
promises......Rom. 4:21

D. *Kinds of:*
Saving.........Rom. 10:9, 10

Temporary....Luke 8:13
Intellectual...James 2:19
Dead.........James 2:17, 20

E. *Described as:*
Boundless.....John 11:21-27
Common......Titus 1:4
Great.........Matt. 8:10
Holy..........Jude 20
Humble.......Luke 7:6, 7
Little.........Matt. 8:26
Mutual.......Rom. 1:12
Perfect.......James 2:22
Precious.....2 Pet. 1:1
Rootless......Luke 8:13
Small.........Matt. 17:20
Unfeigned....1 Tim. 1:5
United........Mark 2:5
Vain.........1 Cor. 15:14, 17
Venturing.....Matt. 14:28, 29

F. *The fruits of:*
Remission of
sins...........Acts 10:43
Justification...Acts 13:39
Freedom from condem-
nation.......John 3:18
Salvation......Mark 16:16
Sanctifi-
cation.........Acts 15:9
Freedom from spiritual
death.........John 11:25, 26
Spiritual
light.........John 12:36, 46
Spiritual life...John 20:31
Eternal life....John 3:15, 16
Adoption......John 1:12
Access to
God...........Eph. 3:12
Edification.....1 Tim. 1:4
Preservation...John 10:26-29
Inheritance....Acts 26:18
Peace and
rest..........Rom. 5:1

G. *Place of, in Christian life:*
Live by......Rom. 1:17
Walk by......Rom. 4:12
Pray by.......Matt. 21:22
Resist
evil by........Eph. 6:16
Overcome
world by.....1 John 2:13-17
Die in........Heb. 11:13

H. *Growth of, in Christian life:*
Stand
fast in........1 Cor. 16:13
Continue in....Acts 14:22
Be strong in...Rom. 4:20-24

Abound in .....2 Cor. 8:7
Be grounded
 in ....Col. 1:23
Hold fast ....1 Tim. 1:19
Pray for
 increase of ....Luke 17:5
Have assurance
 of ....2 Tim. 1:12

I. *Examples of, in Old Testament:*
   Abel ....Heb. 11:4
   Enoch ....Heb. 11:5
   Noah ....Heb. 11:7
   Abraham ......Rom. 4:16-20
   Sarah..........Heb. 11:11
   Jacob..........Heb. 11:21
   Joseph.........Heb. 11:22
   Moses ....Heb. 11:23-29
   Caleb..........Josh. 14:6, 12
   Rahab ....Heb. 11:31
   Jonathan ......1 Sam. 14:6
   David..........1 Sam. 17:37
   Jehoshaphat ...2 Chr. 20:5, 12
   Three Hebrew
    captives.......Dan. 3:16, 17
   Job ....Job 19:25
   Others.........Heb. 11:32-39

J. *Examples of, in New
   Testament:*
   Centurion .....Matt. 8:5-10
   Jairus.........Mark 5:22, 23
   Sick woman ...Mark 5:25-34
   Syro-Phoenician
    woman.......Mark 7:24-30
   Bartimaeus ....Mark 10:46-52
   Sinful
    woman.......Luke 7:36-50
   Ten lepers ....Luke 17:11-19
   Certain
    nobleman ....John 4:46-54
   Mary and
    Martha.......John 11:1-32
   Thomas........John 20:24-29
   Multitudes ....Acts 5:14
   Stephen ....Acts 6:8
   Samaritans ...Acts 8:5-12
   Ethiopian
    eunuch ......Acts 8:26-39
   Barnabas ......Acts 11:22-24
   Lydia ....Acts 16:14, 15
   Philippian
    jailer.........Acts 16:25-34
   Paul ....Acts 27:23-25

Faith as a body of belief

Priests
 obedient to ....Acts 6:7
Churches
 established in.....Acts 16:5

Stand fast in ......1 Cor. 16:13
Paul preaches .....Gal. 1:23
Now revealed .....Gal. 3:23
Household of......Gal. 6:10
Contending for....Phil. 1:27
Hold purely ....1 Tim. 3:9
Denial of ....1 Tim. 5:8
Some erred from ..1 Tim. 6:10, 21
Reprobate ....2 Tim. 3:8
Paul keeps ....2 Tim. 4:7
Chosen of God ....Titus 1:1
Common among
 redeemed........Titus 1:4
To be
 sound in........Titus 1:13

Faithfulness—*making faith a living
 reality in one's life*

A. *Manifested in:*
   God's service ..Matt. 24:45
   Declaring God's
    Word ....Jer. 23:38
   Bearing
    witness ......Prov. 14:5
   Keeping
    secrets ....Prov. 11:13
   Helping
    others.........3 John 5
   Doing work....2 Chr. 34:12
   Positions of
    trust ....Neh. 13:13
   Reproving
    others.........Prov. 27:6
   Conveying
    messages......Prov. 25:13
   Smallest
    things........Luke 16:10-12

B. *Illustrated in lives of:*
   Abraham .....Gal. 3:9
   Abraham's
    servant .....Gen. 24:32, 33
   Joseph.........Gen. 39:22, 23
   Moses ....Num. 12:7
   David.........2 Sam. 22:22-25
   Elijah..........1 Kin. 19:10, 14
   Josiah.........2 Kin. 22:1, 2
   Abijah.........2 Chr. 13:4-12
   Micaiah........2 Chr. 18:12, 13
   Jehoshaphat ...2 Chr. 20:1-30
   Azariah........2 Chr. 26:16-20
   Hanani and
    Hananiah ....Neh. 7:1, 2
   Isaiah ....Is. 39:1-8
   Jeremiah ......Jer. 26:1-15
   Daniel ....Dan. 6:10
   John the
    Baptist ....Luke 3:7-19
   Jesus ....Heb. 3:1, 2

Peter .... Acts 4:8-12
Paul .... Acts 17:16, 17

Faithfulness of God

A. *Described as:*
Everlasting .... Ps. 119:90
Established .... Ps. 89:2
Unfailing .... Ps. 89:33
Infinite .... Ps. 36:5
Great .... Lam. 3:23
Incompar-
able........... Ps. 89:8

B. *Manifested in:*
Counsels... Is. 25:1
Covenant-
keeping .... Deut. 7:9
Forgiving
sins .... 1 John 1:9
Testimonies... Ps. 119:138
Judgments... Jer. 51:29
Promises....... 1 Kin. 8:20

Falcon

Unclean bird ..... Deut. 14:12, 13

Fall of man

A. *Occasion of:*
Satan's
temptation .... Gen. 3:1-5
Eve's
yielding .... 2 Cor. 11:3
Adam's dis-
obedience ..... Rom. 5:12-19

B. *Temporal consequences of:*
Driven from
Paradise ..... Gen. 3:24
Condemned to hard
labor.......... Gen. 3:16, 19
Condemned
to die .... 1 Cor. 15:22

C. *Spiritual consequences of:*
Separated from
God........... Eph. 4:18
Born in sin.... John 3:6
Evil in heart .. Matt. 15:19
Corrupt and
perverse ...... Rom. 3:12-16
In bondage
to sin .... Rom. 6:19
In bondage to
Satan .... Heb. 2:14, 15
Dead in sin .... Col. 2:13
Spiritually
blind.......... Eph. 4:18
Utterly
depraved ..... Titus 1:15

Change from, not in
man .... Jer. 2:22
Only God can
change........ John 3:16

Fallow ground—*a field plowed and left for seeding*

Used   (Jer. 4:3
figuratively.. (Hos. 10:12

False accusations

A. *Against men:*
Joseph........ Gen. 39:7-20
Moses .... Num. 16:1-3, 13
Ahimelech ... 1 Sam. 22:10-16
David......... Ps. 41:5-9
Elijah......... 1 Kin. 18:17, 18
Naboth .... 1 Kin. 21:1-14
Jeremiah ..... Jer. 26:8-11
Amos.......... Amos 7:10, 11
Stephen ...... Acts 6:11, 13
Paul .... Acts 21:27-29

B. *Against Christ:*
Gluttony...... Matt. 11:19
Blasphemy.... Matt. 26:64, 65
Insanity ...... Mark 3:21
Demon
possession .... John 7:20
Sabbath
desecration ... John 9:16
Treason....... John 19:12

False apostles

Opposed Paul ..... 2 Cor. 11:1-15

False Christs

Christ foretells their
coming........... Matt. 24:24
Christ warns
against .... Mark 13:21-23

See Antichrist

False confidence

A. *Characteristics of:*
Self-
righteous ..... Rom. 2:3
Spiritually
blind.......... Is. 28:15, 19
Sensualist ..... Gal. 6:7, 8
Worldly
secure .... 1 Thess. 5:3

B. *Causes of trusting in:*
Riches......... 1 Tim. 6:17
Worldly
success .... Luke 12:19, 20

Men . . . . .Is. 30:1-5
Oneself . . . . .Matt. 26:33-35
Ignoring God's
providence . . . .James 4:13-15

C. *Warnings against:*
Curse on . . . . . .Jer. 17:5
Do not glory in
men . . . . .1 Cor. 3:21
Man's
limitation . . . . .2 Cor. 1:9
Mighty will
fail . . . . .Ps. 33:16, 17
Boasting . . . . . . .1 Kin. 20:11

D. *Instances of:*
Babel's men . . .Gen. 11:4
Sennacherib . . .2 Kin. 19:20-37
Asa . . . . .2 Chr. 16:7-12
Peter . . . . .Luke 22:33, 34

Falsehood—*turning truth into a lie*

A. *Manifested by false:*
Witnesses . . . . . .Ps. 27:12
Balances . . . . . . .Prov. 11:1
Tongue . . . . .Ps. 120:3
Report . . . . .Ex. 23:1
Prophets . . . . . .Jer. 5:2, 31
Knowledge . . . .1 Tim. 6:20

B. *God's people:*
Must avoid . . . .Ex. 23:7
Must hate . . . . .Ps. 119:104, 128
Must endure . . .Acts 6:13
Are falsely
charged   {Jer. 37:14
with . . . .{Matt. 5:11

False professions

A. *Pretending to be:*
Harmless . . . . . .Josh. 9:3-16
Innocent . . . . . .Matt. 27:24
Divine . . . . .Acts 12:21-23
Sincere . . . . . . .Matt. 26:47-49
True
prophets . . . . . .1 Kin. 22:6-12

B. *Exposed by:*
Prophets . . . . . .Jer. 28:1-17
Christ . . . . .John 13:21-30
Apostles . . . . . . .Acts 5:1-11

False prophets

A. *Tests of:*
Doctrine . . . . . . .Is. 8:20
Prophecies . . . . .1 Kin. 13:1-32
Lives . . . . .Matt. 7:15, 16

B. *Characteristics of:*
Prophesy
peace . . . . .Jer. 23:17
Teach a lie . . . . .Jer. 28:15
Pretend to be
true . . . . .Matt. 7:22, 23
Teach
corruption . . . .2 Pet. 2:10-22

C. *Examples of:*
Zedekiah . . . . . .1 Kin. 22:11, 12
Hananiah . . . . . .Jer. 28:1-17
In the last
days . . . . .Matt. 24:3, 11

False teachers

A. *Characteristics of:*
Grace-
perverters . . . . .Gal. 1:6-8
Money-lovers . .Luke 16:14
Christ-
deniers . . . . .2 Pet. 2:1
Truth-
resisters . . . . . . .2 Tim. 3:8
Fable-lovers . . .2 Tim. 4:3, 4
Destitute of the
truth . . . . .1 Tim. 6:3-5
Bound by
traditions . . . . .Matt. 15:9
Unstable . . . . . . .1 Tim. 1:6, 7
Deceitful . . . . . .Eph. 4:14
Lustful . . . . .2 Pet. 2:12-19

B. *Prevalence of:*
In Paul's
time . . . . .2 Tim. 1:14, 15
During this
age . . . . .1 Tim. 4:1-3
At Christ's
return . . . . .2 Tim. 4:3, 4

C. *Examples of:*
Balaam . . . . .Rev. 2:14
Bar-Jesus . . . . . .Acts 13:6
Ephesian   {Acts 20:30
elders . . . .{Rev. 2:2
Epicureans . . . . .Acts 17:18
False   {2 Cor. 11:5, 13
apostles . . . . . .{2 Cor. 12:11
Freedmen . . . . . .Acts 6:9
Herodians . . . . .Mark 3:6
                     Mark 12:13
Hymenaeus . . . .2 Tim. 2:17
Nicolaitanes . . .Rev. 2:15
Pharisees . . . . . .Matt. 23:26
Philetus . . . . . . .2 Tim. 2:17
Sadducees . . . . .Matt. 16:12
Scribes . . . . .Matt. 12:38, 39

Serpent
(Satan) ....Gen. 3:4
Stoic philo-
sophers ....Acts 17:18

False weights

Prohibited.........Deut. 25:13, 14

False witnesses

A. *Defined as:*
Deceptive......Prov. 12:17
Cruel..........Prov. 25:18
Utters lies ....Prov. 6:19
Shall perish ....Prov. 21:28
Hated by
God..........Zech. 8:17
Forbidden .....Ex. 20:16

B. *Sin of:*
Comes from corrupt
heart..........Matt. 15:19
Causes
suffering ......Ps. 27:12
Merits
punishment ...Prov. 19:5, 9

C. *Punishment of:*
Specified......Lev. 6:1-5
Described......Deut. 19:16-20
Visualized ....Zech. 5:3, 4

D. *Examples of, against:*
Ahimelech ....1 Sam. 22:8-18
Naboth ....1 Kin. 21:13
Jeremiah ......Jer. 37:12-14
Jesus ....Matt. 26:59-61
Stephen ....Acts 6:8-13
Paul ....Acts 16:19-21

Fame—report; renown; news

A. *As report or news of:*
Joseph's
brothers.......Gen. 45:16
Israel's
departure .....Num. 14:15
Jesus'
ministry.......Matt. 4:24

B. *As reputation or renown of:*
Nation.........Ezek. 16:14, 15
Joshua's
exploits ....Josh. 6:27
God's works ....Josh. 9:9
Solomon's
wisdom ....1 Kin. 4:30, 31
David's
power.........1 Chr. 14:17
The Temple's
greatness .....1 Chr. 22:5

God's glory ....Is. 66:19
Mordecai's
fame..........Esth. 9:4
Jesus' works ...Matt. 9:31

Familiar spirits

A. *Described as:*
Source of
defilement ....Lev. 19:31
Abominable....Deut. 18:10-12
Vain...........Is. 8:19

B. *The practicers of, to be:*
Cut off ....Lev. 20:6
Put to death ...Lev. 20:27

C. *Consulted by:*
Saul ....1 Sam. 28:3-25
Manasseh......2 Kin. 21:6

Family

A. *Founded on:*
Divine
creation.......Gen. 1:27, 28
Marriage.......Matt. 19:6
Monogamy ....Ex. 20:14
Unity of
parents ....Ex. 20:12
Headship of
husband ......1 Cor. 11:3-7
Subordination of
children.......Eph. 6:1-4
Common
concern.......Luke 16:27, 28

B. *Disturbed by:*
Polygamy......Gen. 4:19-24
Jealousy.......Gen. 37:3, 4,
18-27
Hatred.........Gen. 4:5, 8
Deceit.........Gen. 37:31-35
Ambition ......2 Sam. 15:1-16
Wayward-
ness...........Luke 15:11-18
Insubor-
dination.......Gen. 34:6-31
Unbelief ......John 7:3-10
Lust ....Gen. 34:1-31

C. *Unity of:*
Husband and
wife...........1 Cor. 7:3
Parents and
children.......Jer. 35:1-19
Worship ....1 Cor. 16:19
Faith ....2 Tim. 1:5
Baptism ....Acts 16:14, 15

D. *Worship in:*
Led by the
father..........Gen. 18:19

Instructed in the
Scriptures.....Eph. 6:4
Observing
religious
rites......... { Acts 10:2, 47,
                48
Common conse-
cration........Josh. 24:15

Famine—*deficiency of food*

A. *Kinds of:*
Physical ....Gen. 12:10
Prophetic......Matt. 24:7
                Rev. 6:5-8
Spiritual ......2 Chr. 15:3
                Amos 8:11

B. *Causes of:*
Hail storms ....Ex. 9:23
Insects ....Joel 1:4
Enemies ......Deut. 28:49-51
Siege ....2 Kin. 6:24, 25
Sin ....Ezek. 14:12, 13
Punishment....2 Kin. 8:1

C. *Characteristics of:*
Often long.....Gen. 41:27
Often severe...Deut. 28:49-53
Suffering
intense........Jer. 14:1, 5, 6
Destructive ....Jer. 14:12, 15

D. *Instances of, in:*
Abram's time .Gen. 12:10
Isaac's time....Gen. 26:1
Joseph's
time .... { Gen. 41:53-56
                Acts 7:11-13
Time of
judges ....Ruth 1:1
David's reign ..2 Sam. 21:1
Elisha's time...2 Kin. 4:38
Samaria's
siege..........2 Kin. 6:24, 25
Reign of Claudius
Caesar ....Acts 11:28
Jeremiah's
time ....Jer. 14:1-6
Ahab's reign ...1 Kin. 17:1

Fan—*to toss about*

A. *Used literally of:*
Fork for winnowing
grain..........Is. 30:24

B. *Used figuratively of judgments:*
God's...........Is. 30:24
Christ's........Matt. 3:12

Fanaticism—*unbridled obsession*

A. *Kinds of:*
Personal ......Acts 9:1, 2
Group ....1 Kin. 18:22-29
Civic ....Acts 19:24-41
National ......John 19:15

B. *Characteristics of:*
Intolerance ....Acts 7:57
Persecution....1 Thess. 2:14-16
Inhumanity....Rev. 11:7-10
Insanity ....1 Sam. 18:9-12

Fangs

Used figuratively of:

Power over   { Job 29:17
the wicked ......{ Prov. 30:14

Farewell message

Joshua's ....Josh. 24:1-28
David's ....1 Kin. 2:1-9
Christ's ....Matt. 28:18-20
Paul's ....2 Tim. 4:1-8

Farewells—*expressions at departing*

Naomi's, to
Orpah............Ruth 1:11-14
Paul's, to
Ephesians ....Acts 18:18-21
Paul's, to elders ...Acts 20:17-38
Paul's, to
Tyrians...........Acts 21:3-6
Paul's, to Jews ....Acts 28:23-29

Farm—*a cultivated field*

Preferred more than a
wedding.........Matt. 22:1-5

Farmer—*one who farms*

Cain, the first .....Gen. 4:2
Noah ....Gen. 9:20
Elisha ....1 Kin. 19:19, 20
Remain in land....2 Kin. 25:12
Uzziah............2 Chr. 26:9, 10
Diligence
required in ....Prov. 24:30-34
Reward of.........2 Cor. 9:6-11
Unwise ....Luke 12:16-21
Takes share of
crops.............2 Tim. 2:6

Farming—*the art of agriculture*

Rechabites forbidden to
engage in ....Jer. 35:5-10

Fasting—*abstaining from physical
nourishment*

A. Occasions of:
Public
disasters ...... 1 Sam. 31:11-13
Private
emotions...... 1 Sam. 1:7
Grief .... 2 Sam. 12:16
Anxiety...... Dan. 6:18-20
Approaching
danger....... Esth. 4:16
National
repentance.... 1 Sam. 7:5, 6
Sad news...... Neh. 1:4
Sacred
ordination..... Acts 13:3

B. Accompaniments of:
Prayer .... Luke 2:37
Confession..... Neh. 9:1, 2
Mourning..... Joel 2:12
Humiliation..... Neh. 9:1

C. Safeguards concerning:
Avoid display .. Matt. 6:16-18
Remember
God........... Zech. 7:5-7
Chasten the
soul........... Ps. 69:10
Humble the
soul........... Ps. 35:13
Consider the true
meaning of.... Is. 58:1-14

D. Results of:
Divine
guidance...... Judg. 20:26-28
Victory over
temptation.... Matt. 4:1-11

E. Instances of:
Moses .... Ex. 34:27, 28
Israelites ...... Judg. 20:26
Samuel .... 1 Sam. 7:5, 6
David.......... 2 Sam. 12:16
Elijah......... 1 Kin. 19:2, 8
Ninevites ...... Jon. 3:5-8
Nehemiah ..... Neh. 1:4
Darius......... Dan. 6:9, 18
Daniel .... Dan. 9:3
Anna .... Luke 2:36, 37
Jesus .... Matt. 4:1, 2
John's disciples and the
Pharisees ..... Mark 2:18
Early
Christians..... Acts 13:2
Apostles ...... 2 Cor. 6:4, 5
Paul .... 2 Cor. 11:27

Fat

Figurative of
best .... Gen. 45:18

Of sacrifices,   {Ex. 29:13
burned .... {Lev. 4:26
Figurative of
pride .... Ps. 119:69, 70
Sacrificed by
Abel.............. Gen. 4:4
Offered to God .... Ex. 23:18
Lev. 3:14-16

Father—male parent

A. Kinds of:
Natural........ Gen. 28:13
Ancestors...... Jer. 35:6
Natural
leaders........ Rom. 9:5
Head of
households.... Ex. 6:14

B. Figurative of:
Source......... Job 38:28
Original
inventor ...... Gen. 4:20
Creator........ James 1:17
Spiritual
likeness ...... John 8:44
Counselor ..... Gen. 45:8
Superior ...... 2 Kin. 2:12
Praise-
seeking ...... Matt. 23:9

C. Powers of in Old Testament times:
Arrange son's
marriage...... Gen. 24:1-9
Sell children .. Ex. 21:7

D. Duties of, toward his children:
Love.......... Gen. 37:4
Command ..... Gen. 50:16
Instruct .... Prov. 1:8
Guide and
warn.......... 1 Thess. 2:11
Train .... Hos. 11:1-3
Rebuke....... Gen. 34:30
Restrain ...... 1 Sam. 3:12, 13
Punish........ Deut. 21:18-21
Chasten ...... Heb. 12:7
Nourish....... Is. 1:2
Supply needs . Matt. 7:8-11
Do not
provoke....... Eph. 6:4

E. Examples of devout:
Abraham ...... Gen. 18:18, 19
Isaac .... Gen. 26:12, 13
Joshua........ Josh. 24:15
Job .... Job 1:5

F. Christ's command about:
"Do not call anyone on earth
your father" .. Matt. 23:9

Fatherhood of God

Of all men .... Mal. 2:10
Of Israel .... Jer. 31:9
Of Gentiles .... Rom. 3:29
Of Christians ...... John 1:12, 13

Fatherless—orphans

A. *Proper attitude toward:*
   Share blessings
   with .... Deut. 14:28, 29
   Leave gleanings
   for .... Deut. 24:19-22
   Do not
   defraud .... Prov. 23:10
   Defend .... Ps. 82:3
   Visit .... James 1:27
   Oppress not .... Zech. 7:10
   Do no violence
   to .... Jer. 22:3

B. *God's help toward:*
   Father of ...... Ps. 68:5
   Helper of ...... Ps. 10:14
   Hears cry of ... Ex. 22:22, 23
   Executes judgment
   of .... Deut. 10:18

Father's house

The family   ⎰ Gen. 12:1
home.   ⎱ 1 Sam. 18:2
A household ...... Ex. 12:3
Tribal divisions .... Num. 3:15, 20
                    Num. 17:2, 3
Temple .... John 2:14-16
Heaven .... John 14:2

Fathom—a sea measure; about six feet

Mentioned in Paul's
shipwreck .... Acts 27:28

Fatigue—physical or mental exhaustion

From:

Marching .... 1 Sam. 30:9, 10
Fighting .... 2 Sam. 23:10, 15
Much study .... Eccl. 12:12
Fasting .... Acts 27:21

In:

Sleeping .... Matt. 26:45

Fault—an imperfection

A. *Examples of:*
   A promise
   forgotten ...... Gen. 41:9
   Unworthy
   conduct .... 1 Sam. 29:3

   Guilt .... John 18:38
   Deficient
   behavior ...... Matt. 18:15

B. *Absence of:*
   Flawless
   devotion ...... Rev. 14:5
   Ultimate
   sinlessness .... Jude 24

Faultfinders—carping critics

A. *Motives behind:*
   Supposed
   injustice ...... Matt. 20:9-12
   Supposed
   defilement .... Luke 5:29, 30
   Greed and
   avarice .... John 12:3-6

B. *Against God's:*
   Choice .... Num. 12:1, 2
   Leading .... Num. 14:1-4
   Mercy .... Jon. 4:1-11
   Government ... Rom. 9:19-23

C. *Guilt of:*
   Punishable ..... Num. 12:2, 8-13
   Productive of
   evil .... 3 John 10

Faultless—without blame

David .... 1 Sam. 29:3, 6
Daniel .... Dan. 6:4
Christ .... Luke 23:4, 14

Favoritism—being unfairly partial

A. *Forbidden to:*
   Parents .... Deut. 21:15-17
   Judges .... Deut. 25:1-3
   Ministers ...... 1 Tim. 5:21

B. *Results in:*
   Family
   friction .... Gen. 27:6-46
   Jealousy ...... Gen. 37:3-35

Fear—anxiety caused by approaching danger

A. *Causes of:*
   Diso-
   bedience ...... Gen. 3:10
   Impending
   judgment ..... Heb. 11:7
   Persecution .... John 20:19
   Events of
   nature .... Acts 27:17, 29
   Suspicion ...... Acts 9:26
   Uncertainty .... 2 Cor. 11:3

Final events ...Luke 21:26
Death ....Heb. 2:15

B. *Effects of:*
Demorali-
zation.........1 Sam. 13:5-8
Paralysis.......Matt. 28:4
Silent
testimony.....John 9:22

C. *Instances of:*
Abraham ......Gen. 20:11
Jacob..........Gen. 32:9-11
Soldiers.......Matt. 27:54

Fear, godly

A. *Defined as:*
Hating evil....Prov. 8:13
Life-giving ....Prov. 14:27
Sanctifying ...Ps. 19:9
Beginning of
wisdom .....Prov. 1:7

B. *Motives to, God's:*
Majesty.......Jer. 10:7
Holiness ......Rev. 15:4
Forgiveness....Ps. 130:4
Power ....Josh. 4:23, 24
Goodness......1 Sam. 12:24
Judgment......Rev. 14:7

C. *Examples of:*
Noah ....Heb. 11:7
Abraham ......Gen. 22:12
Jacob..........Gen. 28:16, 17
Joseph.........Gen. 42:18
David..........Ps. 5:7
Obadiah ....1 Kin. 18:7, 12
Job ....Job 1:8
Nehemiah .....Neh. 5:15
Early
Christians.....Acts 9:31

Fearlessness—*without fear*

A. *Source of:*
Believing God's
promises ......Num. 13:30
Challenge of
duty ....Ex. 32:26-29
Regard for God's
holiness ......Num. 25:1-9
Believing
God...........Acts 27:22-26

B. *Exemplified by:*
Abram..........Gen. 14:14-16
Jonathan ......1 Sam. 14:6-14
David..........1 Sam. 17:34-37
Nehemiah .....Neh. 4:1-23
Hebrew men...Dan. 3:16-30

Peter and
John ....Acts 4:13
Paul ....Acts 21:10-14

Feasts, Hebrew

A. *Three annual:*
Passover.......Lev. 23:5-8
Weeks
(Pentecost)...Ex. 23:16
Tabernacle.....Lev. 23:34-44

B. *Purposes of:*
Unify the
nation ....Deut. 12:5-14
Worship God ..Ex. 5:1
Illustrate spiritual
truths........John 7:37-39
Foretell the
Messiah.......1 Cor. 11:23-26

C. *Brief history of:*
Pre-Sinaitic
observance....Ex. 12:1-27
Three instituted at
Sinai..........Ex. 23:14-17
Celebrated in the
wilderness ....Num. 9:3-5
Again at beginning of
conquest......Josh. 5:10, 11
At dedication of
Temple........1 Kin. 8:2, 65
"Dedication" introduced by
Solomon ......2 Chr. 7:9-11
Idolatrous
counterfeits
introduced by
Jeroboam .....1 Kin. 12:27-33
Observed in Hezekiah's
reign..........2 Chr. 30:1
Perversion of, by
Jews..........Is. 1:13, 14
Restored in Josiah's
reformation ...2 Kin. 23:22, 23
Failure in, cause of
exile ....2 Chr. 36:20, 21
Restored after the
exile ....Ezra 3:4
Purim instituted by
Mordecai......Esth. 9:17-32
Christ   { John 2:23
attends......{ John 13:1
Christ fulfills the
Passover ......1 Cor. 5:7, 8
Christianity begins with
Pentecost ....Acts 2:1-41
All fulfilled in
Christ.........2 Cor. 3:3-18

Feasts, social

A. *Worldly, occasions of:*
Idolatry........Ex. 32:6

Drunken-
ness...........1 Sam. 25:36
Proud
display.......Esth. 1:1-8
Profane
carousals......Dan. 5:1-16
Licen-
tiousness......Mark 6:21, 22

B. *Proper, occasions of:*
Refreshment...Gen. 19:1-3
Recon-
ciliation.......Gen. 31:54, 55
Reunion.......Gen. 43:16-34
Restoration....Luke 15:22-24

See Entertainment

Feeble—*powerless*

Moab.............Is. 16:14

Feed—*to supply food to*

A. *Used naturally of:*
Food for
men...........2 Sam. 19:33
Food for
animals.......Gen. 30:36
God's
provision......Matt. 6:26

B. *Used figuratively of:*
Messiah.......Ezek. 34:23
Good deeds....Matt. 25:37
Supernatural
supply........Rev. 12:6
Elemental
teaching......1 Cor. 3:2
Change of
nature........Is. 11:7
Corruption.....Ps. 49:14
Vanity........Hos. 12:1

Feet—*the lower parts of the body*

A. *Acts performed by or on, indicating:*
Subjection....Josh. 10:24
Conquest......2 Sam. 22:39
Humiliation....Judg. 5:27
Submission
and   { 1 Sam. 25:24,
entreaty......{ 41
Great love....Luke 7:38, 44-46
Worship.......Rev. 19:10
Learner's
position......Luke 10:39
Humility......John 13:5-14
Changed
nature........Luke 8:35
Rejection......Matt. 10:14

B. *Figurative of:*
God's
holiness......Ex. 3:5
God's nature...Ex. 24:10
Clouds........Nah. 1:3
God's
messengers...Rom. 10:15
Final
conquest......Rom. 16:20

C. *Unusual features concerning:*
No swelling....Neh. 9:21
Lameness......2 Sam. 9:3, 13
Neglected.....2 Sam. 19:24
Impotent......Acts 14:8-10
Binding........Acts 21:11

See Foot

Feet washing

Performed on
guests...........Gen. 18:4
Proffered by   { 1 Sam. 25:40,
Abigail.........{ 41
On Jesus, with
tears............Luke 7:44
Performed by
Jesus...........John 13:5
Duty of saints.....1 Tim. 5:10

Felix—*happy*

Governor of
Judea............Acts 23:24, 26
Letter
addressed to......Acts 23:25-30
Paul's defense
before...........Acts 24:1-21
Convicted, but
unchanged......Acts 24:22-25
Subject to
bribery..........Acts 24:26, 27

Fellow citizens

With the saints...Eph. 2:19

Fellow countryman

Shall not hate.....Lev. 19:17
Becomes poor.....Lev. 25:25
Judge
righteously......Deut. 1:16
Lord gives rest......Deut. 3:20
Save some........Rom. 11:14

Fellow servant

Who owed a hundred
denarii.......Matt. 18:28-33
Evil slave beats...Matt. 24:48, 49
Were to be
killed.............Rev. 6:11

Who hold fast the testimony of
Jesus............Rev. 19:10
Who heed the
words ....Rev. 22:9

Fellowship—*sharing together*

A. *Based upon common:*
Purpose..........Ps. 133:1-3
Belief..........Acts 2:42
Conviction.....1 Pet. 3:8
Work..........Neh. 4:1-23
Hope ....Heb. 11:39, 40
Faith ....1 Sam. 20:30-42
Suffering ......Dan. 3:16-30
Need ....2 Cor. 8:1-15

B. *Persons sharing together:*
Father, the Son, and
Christians.....1 John 1:3
Christ and
Christians.....1 Cor. 1:9
Holy Spirit and
Christians.....Phil. 2:1
Apostles ....Acts 2:42
Believers ....1 John 1:7

C. *Things shared together:*
Material
things..........2 Cor. 8:4
Suffering ......Phil. 3:10
The Gospel
ministry.......Gal. 2:9
Gospel
privileges .....Phil. 1:5
Gospel
mystery.......Eph. 3:9

Fellow workers

In the truth.......3 John 8
In the kingdom ...Col. 4:11
Prisca and Aquila
described as ....Rom. 16:3
Urbanus..........Rom. 16:9
Timothy ....Rom. 16:21
Paul ....1 Cor. 3:1-9
Titus.............2 Cor. 8:23
Epaphroditus....Phil. 2:25
Philemon ....Philem. 1
Marcus, Aristarchus, Demas,
Lucas ....Philem. 24

Ferryboats

David's use of.....2 Sam. 19:16-18

Festus—*feastful, joyful*

Governor of
Judaea ....Acts 24:27
Paul's defense made
to ....Acts 25:1-22

Fetters—*shackle for binding the feet*

A. *Used literally of:*
Imprison-
ment..........Ps. 105:18

B. *Used figuratively of:*
Trouble........Job 36:8
Subjection.....Ps. 149:8

Fetus—*unborn child*

Protected by
law..............Ex. 21:22, 23
Possesses sin
nature...........Ps. 51:5
Fashioned by
God ....Ps. 139:13-16
Called by God.....Is. 49:1
                 Jer. 1:5
Active ....Luke 1:41

Fever—*abnormal body temperature*

Sent as a
judgment.........Deut. 28:22
Rebuked by
Christ ....Luke 4:38, 39
Healed by Paul....Acts 28:8

Few—*the opposite of many*

Days..............Gen. 47:9
Do not determine God's
power ....1 Sam. 14:6
Words in prayer...Eccl. 5:2
The saved........Matt. 7:14
Gospel
messengers......Matt. 9:37
The chosen ......Matt. 22:14

Fidelity—*faithfulness in the
performance of duty*

In finances........2 Kin. 12:15
In industry........2 Chr. 34:11, 12
Seen in Joseph ...Gen. 39:6
Seen in Daniel ....Dan. 6:1-3, 28

Field—*open or cleared land*

A. *Used literally of:*
Cultivated
land...........Gen. 47:20
A city ....Ps. 78:12, 43

B. *Laws regarding:*
Fires............Ex. 22:6
Mixed seed ....Lev. 19:19
Coveting
others'........Deut. 5:21
Destruction of
trees of.......Deut. 20:19, 20
Total harvest
of.............Deut. 24:19-22

Sabbath rest...Lev. 25:3-12
Redemption
of............Lev. 27:16-24
Title of ......Ruth 4:5-11

C. *Figurative of:*
World ....Matt. 13:38
Harvest of
souls..........John 4:35

Field of Blood

A field, predicted in the Old
Testament, bought as a cemetery
for Judas' {Zech. 11:12, 13
burial ....{Matt. 27:1-10

Fiery serpents

Attack Israelites ..Num. 21:6, 8

Fig—*pear-shaped fruit of fig tree*

Destruction
foretold ....Hos. 2:12

Fig lumps

Prescribed for
boils..............Is. 38:21

Fig tree

A. *The leaves of, used for:*
Covering
nakedness......Gen. 3:7
Shade ....John 1:48, 50

B. *Fruit of:*
Used for
food ....1 Sam. 30:12
Sent as
present.......1 Sam. 25:18
Sold in
markets.......Neh. 13:15
Used for
healing........Is. 38:21
Sometimes
fails..........Hab. 3:17

C. *Figurative of:*
Prosperity and
peace ....1 Kin. 4:25
Righteous and the
wicked.......Jer. 24:1-10
Fathers of
Israel ....Hos. 9:10
Barren
religion ....Matt. 21:19
Jewish
nation ....Luke 13:6-9
Christ's
return.........Matt. 24:32, 33
Final
judgment ....Rev. 6:13

Fight—*a conflict*

A. *Used literally of:*
War ....Ex. 17:8, 10
Individual {1 Sam. 17:10,
combat ......{ 32

B. *Used figuratively of:*
Determined
resolve........1 Cor. 9:26
Opposition of evil
men..........1 Cor. 15:32
Christian life...1 Tim. 6:12
Dissension.....James 4:1, 2
Spiritual
conflict ....Rev. 12:7

Fighting against God

A. *Manifested by:*
Pharaoh ....Ex. 5:1, 2
Rabshakeh.....2 Kin. 18:28-36
Jeroboam......2 Chr. 13:8-19

B. *Futility of:*
Seen by
Gamaliel .....Acts 5:34, 39
Admitted by
Pharisees .....Acts 23:9
Experienced by
Satan ....Rev. 12:7-17
Blasphemy of unregen-
erate..........Rev. 16:9-21

Figurehead—*symbol on ship's prow*

Twin Brothers.....Acts 28:11

Figures of speech

Allegory ....Gal. 4:24
Fable ....Judg. 9:8-15
                    1 Tim. 4:7
Hyperbole.........1 Sam. 13:5
                    John 21:25
Interrogation .....1 Cor. 12:29, 30
Irony ....Luke 15:7-10
Metaphor ....Luke 13:32
Parable ....Matt. 13:10
Parallelism........Gen. 4:23, 24
Personification ....Is. 55:12
Proverb ....1 Kin. 4:32
Sarcasm ....Matt. 27:29
Simile.............Is. 1:8, 9
Similitude.........Ps. 90:4-6

Filial devotion

A. *Duty of:*
Commanded...Ex. 20:12
Corrupted .....Matt. 15:4-6
Confirmed.....Eph. 6:1-3

B. *Examples of:*
Joseph.........Gen. 47:12
David.........1 Sam. 22:3
Solomon......1 Kin. 2:19
Elisha ....1 Kin. 19:19, 20
Young man....Matt. 19:16-20

C. *Obedience:*
Continual......Prov. 6:20-22
Total ....Col. 3:20
Lack of, severely
punished......Deut. 21:18-21
Lack of,
cursed ....Prov. 20:20

Filth—*uncleanness, defilement, corruption*

Men ....Job 15:16
                Ps. 14:2, 3
Garments
and   ⎰Is. 4:1-4
furniture ......⎱Is. 28:8; James 2:2
Ceremonial
uncleanness.....Ezek. 22:15
Unrigh-   ⎰Is. 64:6
teousness......⎱Ezek. 16:6

Fine—*penalty payment*

Paid by guilty.....Ex. 21:23-30
                   Deut. 22:19
Restitution.......Ex. 22:5-15
                 Num. 5:6, 7

Finger

A. *Used literally of:*
Man's fingers ..John 20:25, 27
Deformity ......2 Sam. 21:20
Measure-
ment..........Jer. 52:21
Mysterious
hand..........Dan. 5:5

B. *Used figuratively of:*
God's power ...Ex. 8:19
Inspiration.....Ex. 31:18
Sugges-
tiveness.......Prov. 6:13
Contrast of
burdens........1 Kin. 12:10
Lord's
authority......Luke 11:20

Finish

Used of:

The Messiah's
advent ....Dan. 9:24-27
Final events.......Dan. 12:7

Fins

Signs of a clean
fish...............Lev. 11:9

Fir—*a tree of the pine family*

Used in ships......Ezek. 27:5
Used for musical
instruments ......2 Sam. 6:5

Fire

A. *Physical uses of:*
Warmth ....John 18:18
Cooking ....Ex. 16:23
Signs ....Judg. 20:38, 40
Sacrifices ......Gen. 8:20, 21
Refining ....Ps. 12:6
Torture ....Dan. 3:6
Sacrifice of
children........2 Kin. 16:3

B. *Supernatural uses of:*
Manifest God ..Ex. 3:2
Indicate God's
power..........Ex. 9:24
Express God's
approval ....Lev. 9:24
Vindicate God's
wrath ....2 Kin. 1:9-12
Guide Israel ...Ex. 13:21, 22
Transport a saint to
heaven........2 Kin. 2:11

C. *Used figuratively of:*
God's
protection.....Zech. 2:5
God's
vengeance ....Heb. 12:29
God's Word....Jer. 5:14
Christ ....Mal. 3:2
Holy Spirit.....Acts 2:3
Angels.........Heb. 1:7
Tongue........James 3:6
Persecution...Luke 12:49-53
Affliction......Is. 43:2
Purification....Is. 6:5-7
Love...........Song 8:6
Lust ....Prov. 6:27, 28

D. *Final uses of:*
Destroy
world ....2 Pet. 3:10-12
Punish
wicked........Matt. 25:41

Fire, Lake of—*place of eternal punishment*

The beast ....Rev. 19:20
The false
prophet ....Rev. 19:20

The devil.........Rev. 20:10

Death and
Hades..........Rev. 20:14

Sinners ....Rev. 21:8

Firebrand—*torch*

Figurative of
enemies ....Is. 7:4

Thrown by a
madman.........Prov. 26:18

Have no fear of..Is. 7:4

All who encircle...Is. 50:11

Snatched from a
blaze ....Amos 4:11

Firepan—*a shovel used for carrying fire*

Part of the altar...Ex. 27:3

Firmament—*expanse*

Created by God...Gen. 1:8

Stars placed in ....Gen. 1:14, 17

Compared to a
tent ....Ps. 104:2

Expressive of God's
glory...............Ps. 19:1

Saints compared
to ....Dan. 12:3

First

Came out red .....Gen. 25:25

This came out.....Gen. 38:28

These should set
forth ....Num. 2:9

Amalek, of
nations...........Num. 24:20

Hands of witness
shall be...........Deut. 17:7

Altar Saul built ....1 Sam. 14:35

Case pleaded.....Prov. 18:17

Seek ....Matt. 6:33

Cast out   { Matt. 7:5
plank...........   { Luke 6:42

Last state worse
than...............Luke 11:26

The blade, then the
head ....Mark 4:28

Let the children...Mark 7:27

Desire to be......Mark 9:35

Commandment...Mark 12:28

Gospel must, be
preached ....Mark 13:10

Appeared to Mary
Magdalene ......Mark 16:9

Not sit down......Luke 14:28

Stepped in, made
whole ....John 5:4

Gave themselves ..2 Cor. 8:5

Trusted in
Christ ....Eph. 1:12

A falling away ....2 Thess. 2:3

Let these also .....1 Tim. 3:10

Dwelt.............2 Tim. 1:5

He takes away ....Heb. 10:9

First (things mentioned)

Altar.............Gen. 8:20

Archer...........Gen. 21:20

Bigamist ....Gen. 4:19

Birthday
celebration .....Gen. 40:20

Book.............Gen. 5:1

Bridal veil........Gen. 24:64-67

Cave dwellers.....Gen. 19:30

Christian martyr ..Acts 22:19, 20

City builder......Gen. 4:17

Coffin............Gen. 50:26

Command.........Gen. 1:3

Commanded by
Christ ....Matt. 6:33

Craftsman.......Gen. 4:22

Cremation ....1 Sam. 31:12

Curse............Gen. 3:14

Death............Gen. 4:8

Doubt.............Gen. 3:1

Dream ....Gen. 20:3

Drunkenness.....Gen. 9:20, 21

Emancipator ......Ex. 3:7-22

Embalming........Gen. 50:2, 3

European
convert..........Acts 16:14, 15

Execution.........Gen. 40:20-22

Family ....Gen. 4:1, 2

Famine ....Gen. 12:10

Farewell address ..Josh. 23:1-16

Farmer...........Gen. 4:2

Female
government .....Judg. 4:4, 5

Ferry boat ....2 Sam. 19:18

Food control .....Gen. 41:25-36

Frying pan........Lev. 2:7

Gardener.........Gen. 2:15

Gold.............Gen. 2:11

Harp.............Gen. 4:21

Hebrew (Jew)....Gen. 14:13

High priest.......Ex. 28:1

Hunter...........Gen. 10:8, 9

Idolatry..........Josh. 24:2

"In-law" trouble ..Gen. 26:34, 35

Iron bedstead ....Deut. 3:11

Kiss.............Gen. 27:26, 27

Left-handed
man.............Judg. 3:15

Letter...........2 Sam. 11:14

Liar.............Gen. 3:1-5

Magistrates ....Dan. 3:2

Man to hang
himself ....2 Sam. 17:23
Man to shave .....Gen. 41:14
Man to wear a
ring.............Gen. 41:42
Miracles of
Christ ....John 2:1-11
Mother of twins...Gen. 25:21-28
Murderer ....Gen. 4:8
Musician..........Gen. 4:21
Navy.............1 Kin. 9:26
Oath ....Gen. 21:24
Orchestra ....2 Sam. 6:5
Pilgrim............Gen. 12:1-8
Prayer ....Gen. 4:26
Prison............Gen. 39:20
Prophecy ....Gen. 3:15
Prophetess ....Ex. 15:20
Proposal of
adultery..........Gen. 39:7-12
Pulpit............Neh. 8:4
Purchase of land . .Gen. 23:3-20
Question ....Gen. 3:1
Rainbow ....Gen. 9:13, 14
Rape.............Gen. 34:1-5
Riddle............Judg. 14:12-18
Sabbath...........Gen. 2:2, 3
Sacrifice ....Gen. 8:20
Saddle ....Gen. 22:3
Scribe............Ex. 24:4
Selective Service . .Num. 31:3-6
Shepherd ....Gen. 4:2
Shepherdess ......Gen. 29:9
Shipbuilder.......Gen. 6:14
Sin...............Gen. 3:1-24
Singing school ... .1 Chr. 25:5-7
Sunstroke ....2 Kin. 4:18-20
Surveying of
land..............Josh. 18:8, 9
Temptation ......Gen. 3:1-6
Theater ....Acts 19:29-31
To be named before
birth ....Gen. 16:11
To confess
Christ ....John 1:49
Tombstone.......Gen. 35:20
Tower ....Gen. 11:4, 5
Vagabond.........Gen. 4:9-12
Voluntary
fasting...........Judg. 20:26
Wage contract ....Gen. 29:15-20
War..............Gen. 14:2-12
Warships.........Num. 24:24
Well ....Gen. 16:14
Whirlwind ....2 Kin. 2:1
Wife ....Gen. 3:20
Woman thief......Gen. 31:19
Woman to curse . .Judg. 17:1, 2

Woman to use
cosmetics ....2 Kin. 9:30
Words spoken to
man..............Gen. 1:28
Worship ....Gen. 4:3-5

Firstborn

Said to the   ⌠Gen. 19:31
younger..........⌡Gen. 19:34
Bore a son ....Gen. 19:37
Give younger
before............Gen. 29:26
According to
birthright.........Gen. 43:33
Israel is My ......Ex. 4:22
Will slay your.....Ex. 4:23
All in the land of
Egypt ....Ex. 11:5
Killed all the .....Ex. 13:15
                   Ps. 105:36
Will smite all......Ex. 12:12
Sanctify to
Me all ....Ex. 13:2
Of Israel are
Mine ....Num. 3:13
Lay
foundation with . .Josh. 6:26
Of death shall.....Job 18:13
Gave birth ....Luke 2:7
Of all creation....Col. 1:15
So that he who
destroyed.........Heb. 11:28

A. *Privileges of:*
First in
family..........Gen. 48:13, 14
Delegated
authority of . . .Gen. 27:1-29
Received father's special
blessing.......Gen. 27:4, 35
Bears father's
title............2 Chr. 21:1, 3
Given double portion of
inheritance....Deut. 21:17
Object of special
love...........Jer. 31:9, 20
Precious and
valuable.......Mic. 6:7

B. *Laws concerning:*
Dedicated to
God...........Ex. 22:29-31
To be
redeemed .....Ex. 34:20
Redemption
price of ....Num. 3:46-51
Tribe of Levi substituted
for............Num. 3:11, 45

Death of, next brother
substituted......Matt. 22:24-28
Change of,
forbidden.....Deut. 21:15-17
Forfeited by evil
deeds........Gen. 49:3, 4, 8
Forfeited by
sale...........Heb. 12:16, 17
Changed
sovereignty...1 Sam. 16:6-12
Christ
subject to.....Luke 2:22-24

C. *Figurative of, Christ in:*
Authority......Ps. 89:27
Honor.........Heb. 1:6
Resurrection...Col. 1:18
Church.......Rom. 8:29
Glory.......Heb. 12:22, 23

First day of the week—*Sunday*

Day of Christ's ⎰Mark 16:9
resurrection.....⎱John 20:1, 19
Day after the ⎰Matt. 28:1
Sabbath.........⎱Mark 16:1, 2
Day of ⎰Acts 20:7
worship.........⎱1 Cor. 16:1, 2
Called "the Lord's
day".............Rev. 1:10

Firstfruits

A. *Regulations concerning:*
Law specified..Lev. 23:9-14
Brought to God's
house.........Ex. 34:26
Ritual of,
described......Deut. 26:3-10
Considered
holy..........Ezek. 20:40
God honored
by.............Prov. 3:9

B. *Figurative of:*
Israel's
position.......Rom. 11:16
Christ's place in
resurrection...1 Cor. 15:20, 23
Christians.....James 1:18
First
converts......Rom. 16:5

Firstlings

Abel brought......Gen. 4:4
Set apart ⎰Ex. 13:12
every...........⎱Ex. 34:19
Of a donkey you ⎰Ex. 13:13
shall redeem.....⎱Ex. 34:20
Lords, no man shall
sanctify.........Lev. 27:26

Of unclean
beasts............Num. 18:15
You shall bring, of your
herd..........Deut. 12:6
Males sanctify....Deut. 15:19
Glory is like......Deut. 33:17

Fish

A. *Features regarding:*
Created by
God..........Gen. 1:20, 21
Worship of
forbidden.....Deut. 4:15-18
Caught by
net...........Matt. 4:18
Some disciples called as
fishermen.....Matt. 4:18-21

B. *Miracles concerning:*
Jonah's
life in.........Jon. 1:17
Multiplied by
Christ.........Matt. 14:17-21
Bearing a
coin..........Matt. 17:27

C. *Figurative of:*
Men in the sea of
life...........Ezek. 47:9, 10
Ministers as
fishermen.....Matt. 4:19
Ignorant
men..........Eccl. 9:12

Fish Gate—*a gate of Jerusalem*

Manasseh built wall
there..........2 Chr. 33:13, 14
Built by sons of
Hassenaah.....Neh. 3:3
Two choirs took their
stand.............Neh. 12:38-40
A cry there
prophesied.......Zeph. 1:10

Fish hook—*hook for catching fish*

Cannot catch
Leviathan........Job 41:1
Fishing in the
brooks...........Is. 19:8

Fist fighting

Punishment of....Ex. 21:18, 19

Flask—*a small vessel*

Used for
anointing.........1 Sam. 10:1

Flattery—*unjustified praise*

A. *Used by:*
False
prophets ......Rom. 16:18
Hypocrites.....Ps. 78:36
Wicked........Ps. 36:1-4
Seductresses...Prov. 2:16

B. *Attitude of saints toward:*
Should avoid
users of ....Prov. 20:19
Pray against ...Ps. 5:8, 9
Should not
use ....1 Thess. 2:5

C. *Dangers of:*
Leads to ruin ..Prov. 26:28
Brings
deception .....Prov. 29:5
Corrupts.......Dan. 11:21, 25,
27
Brings death ...Acts 12:21-23

Flax—*the flax plant*

Grown in Egypt and
Palestine ....Ex. 9:31

Used for:
Cords ....Judg. 15:14
Weaving ....Is. 19:9
Garments
("linen") ....Deut. 22:11

Flea—*a parasitic, blood-sucking insect*

Figurative of
insignificance.....1 Sam. 24:14

Fleece—*freshly sheared wool*

Given to priests ...Deut. 18:3, 4
Sign to Gideon ....Judg. 6:36-40
Warm.............Job 31:20

Flesh

A. *Used to designate:*
All created   { Gen. 6:13, 17,
life.............{ 19
Kinsmen (of same
nature) ....Rom. 9:3, 5, 8
The body ......Job 33:25
Marriage.......Matt. 19:5
Human
nature ....John 1:14
Christ's mys-   { John 6:51,
tical nature .. { 53-63
Human
weakness .....Matt. 16:17
Outward
appearance....2 Cor. 5:16
The evil principle in
man ....Rom. 7:18

B. *In a bad sense, described as:*
Having
passions.......Gal. 5:24
Producing evil
works.........Gal. 5:19-21
Dominating the
mind..........Eph. 2:3
Absorbing the
affections .....Rom. 13:14
Seeking outward
display........Gal. 6:12, 13
Antagonizing the
Spirit ....Gal. 5:17
Fighting against God's
Law...........Rom. 8:5-9
Reaping
corruption ....Gal. 6:8
Producing
death ....Rom. 7:5

C. *Christian's attitude toward:*
Still
confronts .....Rom. 7:18-23
Source of
opposition.....Gal. 5:17
Make no provision
for............Rom
13:14
Do not love....1 John 2:15-17
Do not
walk in ....Rom. 8:1, 4
Do not
live in.........Rom. 8:12, 13
Crucified ......Gal. 5:24

Fleshhook—*fork*

In tabernacle......Ex. 27:3
Num. 4:14
By priests ....1 Sam. 2:12-14
In Temple.........1 Chr. 28:11, 17
2 Chr. 4:16

Flies—*small winged insects*

Cause of evil
odor.............Eccl. 10:1
Figurative of
Egypt ....Is. 7:18
Plague upon the { Ex. 8:21-31
Egyptians ....{ Ps. 78:45

Flint—*a very hard stone*

Water from ....Deut. 8:15
Oil from..........Deut. 32:13
Turning into fountain of
water ....Ps. 114:8
Hoofs shall seem
like..............Is. 5:28
Figurative of a   { Is. 50:7
fixed course .... { Ezek. 3:9

Flock—*a group of domesticated animals*

Sheep and goats . . Gen. 27:9
Nations . . . . Jer. 51:23
National leaders . . . Jer. 25:34, 35
Jewish people . . . . . Jer. 13:17, 20
True church . . . . . . Is. 40:11
Acts 20:28

Flood—*overflowing of water*

A. *Used literally of:*
Earth's flood . . . Gen. 6:17

B. *Used figuratively of:*
Great trouble . . . Ps. 32:6
Hostile world
powers . . . . Ps. 93:3
An invading
army . . . . Jer. 46:7, 8
Great
destruction . . . . Dan. 9:26
Testing . . . . Matt. 7:25, 27
Persecution . . . . Rev. 12:15, 16

Floor

For threshing ⎰ Judg. 6:37
wheat . . . . ⎱ 1 Kin. 22:10
Of a building . . . . . . 1 Kin. 6:15

Flour—*finely ground wheat*

Offered in
sacrifices . . . . Lev. 5:11, 13

Flowers

A. *Described as:*
Wild . . . . Ps. 103:15, 16
Beautiful . . . . . . Matt. 6:28, 29
Sweet . . . . Song 5:13
Fading . . . . Is. 40:7, 8

B. *Figurative of:*
Shortness of
life . . . . Job 14:2
Israel . . . . Is. 28:1
Man's glory . . . . James 1:10, 11

Flute—*a hollow musical instrument*

A. *Used in:*
Babylon . . . . Dan. 3:5
Prophecy . . . . . . 1 Sam. 10:5
Worship . . . . Ps. 150:4

B. *Figurative of:*
Joyful
deliverance . . . . Is. 30:29
Mournful
lamentation . . . Jer. 48:36
Inconsistent
reactions . . . . . Matt. 11:17

**Spiritual
discernment** . . . 1 Cor. 14:7

Foal—*a colt, young donkey*

Given to Esau . . . . . Gen. 32:13-15
Ridden by ⎰ Zech. 9:9
Christ . . . . ⎱ Matt. 21:5

Fodder—*food for domestic animals*

Given to oxen
and wild ⎰ Job 6:5
ass . . . . ⎱ Is. 30:24

Following

A. *In Old Testament:*
Commanded . . . Deut. 8:6
Brought
reward . . . . Deut. 19:9
Covenant . . . . . . 2 Kin. 23:3

B. *In New Testament:*
Multitudes . . . . . Matt. 4:25
Matt. 12:15
Disciples . . . . . . Matt. 8:19
Luke 5:11, 27, 28
Left all . . . . Matt. 4:18-22
In light . . . . John 8:12
After
Christ's ⎰ John 13:15
example . . . . . . ⎱ 1 John 2:6
⎧ Phil. 3:17
Example of ⎨ Heb. 6:12
Godly men . . . ⎩ James 5:10

Folly—*contemptuous disregard of holy things*

A. *Associated with:*
Deception . . . . . Prov. 14:8
Hasty spirit . . . . Prov. 14:29
Gullibility . . . . . . Prov. 13:16
Fero-
ciousness . . . . Prov. 17:12
Disgust . . . . Prov. 26:11

B. *Warnings against:*
Saints not to
return to . . . . . Ps. 85:8
Prophets
guilty of . . . . . . Jer. 23:13
Apostles
subject to . . . . . 2 Cor. 11:1

Food

A. *Features regarding:*
Given by
God . . . . Ps. 104:21, 27
Necessary for
man . . . . Gen. 1:29, 30

Gives physical
strength ......Acts 9:19
Revives the
spirit.........1 Sam. 30:12
Object of daily
prayer ....Matt. 6:11
Object of thanks-
giving.........1 Sam. 9:13
Sanctified by
prayer ....1 Tim. 4:4, 5
Scruples
recognized ....Rom. 14:2-23

B. *Lack of:*
Testing of
faith ....Hab. 3:17

C. *Provided by:*
God ....Ps. 145:15
Christ ....John 21:5, 6

D. *Prohibitions concerning:*
Dead animals ..Ex. 22:31
Eating blood...Deut. 12:16
Clean and
unclean ....Deut. 14:4-20
Wine ....Prov. 23:29-35
Strangled
animals ....Acts 21:25
Not in itself commend-
able ....1 Cor. 8:8
Not to be a stumbling
block ....1 Cor. 8:13
Life more important
than ....Matt. 6:25

E. *Miracles connected with:*
Destruction
of.............Ps. 105:29-35
Provision for...Ps. 105:40, 41
Supply of......1 Kin. 17:4-6
Multiplication
of.............John 6:5-13
Refused........Matt. 4:1-4

F. *Figurative of:*
God's will......John 4:32, 34
Christ ....John 6:27, 55
Strong
doctrines......1 Cor. 3:2

Food control

First ....Gen. 41:25-36
Final.............Rev. 13:11-17

Food, spiritual

A. *Elements of:*
The Word .....Ps. 19:9, 10
Christ ....John 6:48-51

B. *Need of, by:*
The naive......Prov. 9:1-5

The
immature .....1 Cor. 3:1, 2
The mature....Heb. 5:14
All............Matt. 22:4

C. *Characteristics of:*
Abundant......Is. 55:1-3
Satisfying......Ps. 22:26
Enduring......John 6:48-51
Life-giving.....John 6:53-63

Foods of Bible times

A. *Obtaining; storing; use:*
Shall be for ....Gen. 6:21
Let them
gather ....Gen. 41:35
But to buy.....Gen. 42:10
Go again,
buy ....Gen. 43:2
Buy............Gen. 43:4
Much..........Prov. 13:23
Of the
offering ....Lev. 3:11
Of Holy
things.........Lev. 22:7
In giving
him ....Deut. 10:18
Seeking in
wilderness ....Job 24:5
Man did eat that of
angels'........Ps. 78:25
Bring forth ....Ps. 104:14

B. *Specific kinds:*
Almonds.......Gen. 43:11
Barley.........Judg. 7:13
Beans..........Ezek. 4:9
Beef ....1 Kin. 4:22, 23
Beef stew......1 Kin. 19:21
Bread..........1 Sam. 17:17
Broth..........Judg. 6:19
Cakes ....2 Sam. 13:8
Cheese ....Job 10:10
Cucumbers ....Num. 11:5
Curds of
cows..........Deut. 32:14
Eggs...........Deut. 22:6
Figs ....Num. 13:23
Fish ....Matt. 7:10
Fowl...........1 Kin. 4:23
Fruit..........2 Sam. 16:2
Garlic ....Num. 11:5
Goat's milk ....Prov. 27:27
Grain..........Ruth 2:14
Grapes.........Deut. 23:24
Grass-
hoppers.......Lev. 11:22
Herbs..........Ex. 12:8
Honey ....Is. 7:15

Leeks.........Num. 11:5
Lentils.......Gen. 25:34
Locusts.......Matt. 3:4
Meal.........Matt. 13:33
Melons.......Num. 11:5
Milk.........Gen. 18:7, 8
Nuts.........Gen. 43:11
Oil...........Prov. 21:17
Olives........Deut. 28:40
Onions.......Num. 11:5
Pome-
  granates.....Num. 13:23
Quail........Num. 11:32, 33
Raisins......2 Sam. 16:1
Salt.........Job 6:6
Sheep........Deut. 14:4
Spices.......Gen. 43:11
Stew.........Gen. 25:30
Vinegar......Num. 6:3
Venison......Gen. 25:28
Wild honey...Matt. 3:4
Wine.........John 2:3, 10

Foolish—*those who misuse wisdom*

A. *Those described as:*
Clamorous
  woman........Prov. 9:13
Builder on
  sand.........Matt. 7:26
Five virgins....Matt. 25:1-13
Galatians......Gal. 3:1, 3
Gentiles.......Titus 3:3

B. *Things described as:*
The Heart.....Rom. 1:21
Things........1 Cor. 1:27
Lusts.........1 Tim. 6:9
Disputes......2 Tim. 2:23

C. *Characteristics of:*
Destructive....Prov. 10:14
Despicable....Prov. 15:20
Disap-
  pointing......Prov. 19:13

Foolishness—*a disregard of final issues*

A. *Characteristics of:*
Form of sin....Prov. 24:9
Originates in the
  heart..........Mark 7:21-23
Sign of
  wickedness....Eccl. 7:25
Known by
  God...........Ps. 69:5

B. *Consequences of:*
Brings
  sorrow........Ps. 38:4-10

Perverts man's
  way...........Prov. 19:3
Spiritual
  blindness......1 Cor. 1:18

Fools—*those who misuse true wisdom*

A. *Described as:*
Atheistic.......Ps. 14:1
Blasphe-
  mous.........Ps. 74:18
Contentious...Prov. 18:6
Hypocritical...Luke 11:39, 40
Idle............Eccl. 4:5
Vexation......Prov. 12:16
Materialistic...Luke 12:16-21
Quarrelsome...Prov. 20:3
Mischievous...Prov. 10:23
Mocking.......Prov. 14:9
Raging........Prov. 14:16
Self-
  confident......Prov. 28:26
Self-
  righteous.....Prov. 12:15
Self-
  sufficient......Rom. 1:22
Slandering....Prov. 10:18
Wasteful......Prov. 21:20
Wordy........Eccl. 10:12-14

B. *Further characteristics of:*
Hate
  knowledge....Prov. 1:22
Come to
  shame........Prov. 3:35
Mock at sin....Prov. 14:9
Cannot attain to
  wisdom.......Prov. 24:7
Trust in their
  hearts.........Prov. 28:26
Walk in
  darkness......Eccl. 2:14

C. *Examples of:*
Nabal.........1 Sam. 25:3, 25
Rehoboam.....1 Kin. 12:6-13
Pharisees....Matt. 23:17, 19
The rich man..Luke 12:16-21

Foot

A. *To sit at, figurative of:*
Teach-
  ableness......Luke 10:39

B. *To be under, figurative of:*
Man's
  sovereignty...Ps. 8:6
Christ's
  victory........Ps. 110:1
Conquest......Josh. 10:24

C. *Examples, figurative of:*
Prosperity	Deut. 33:24
Possession	Josh. 1:3
Reverence	Josh. 5:15
Whole person	Prov. 1:15

See Feet

Footstool

A. *Used literally of:*
In the Temple	2 Chr. 9:18
Prominent seat	James 2:3

B. *Used figuratively of:*
Earth	Matt. 5:35
Ark	1 Chr. 28:2
Temple worship	Ps. 99:5
Subjection	Acts 2:35

Forbearance of God

A. *God's withholding of judgment upon:*
The Amorites	Gen. 15:16
Sodom	Gen. 18:23-32
Israel	Neh. 9:30, 31
Nineveh	Jon. 4:10, 11
The world	Rom. 3:25

B. *Attitudes toward:*
Not to be despised	Rom. 2:4
To be remembered	2 Pet. 3:8-10
Means of preparation	Mal. 3:1-6

Forbearance toward others

Expression of love	1 Cor. 13:7
Christian grace	Eph. 4:2

Forced labor—*conscripted workers or slaves*

Prisoners of war	Deut. 20:10, 11
As slaves	Ex. 13:3
By Solomon	1 Kin. 9:20, 21

Forces—*military power*

Assembling great	Dan. 11:10, 38
Weakness of	Zech. 4:6
Destruction of great	Rev. 20:7-10

Forceful—*powerful*

Power of right words	Job 6:25

Ford—*a shallow crossing of a body of water*

Of the Jabbok	Gen. 32:22
Of the Jordan	Judg. 3:28

Forehead—*the upper part of the face*

A. *Used literally of:*
Aaron's	Ex. 28:38
Philistines'	1 Sam. 17:49
Uzziah's	2 Chr. 26:19, 20

B. *Used figuratively of:*
Shamelessness	Rev. 17:5
Stronger power	Ezek. 3:8, 9
Devotion to God	Ezek. 9:4
Christ's true servants	Rev. 7:3

Foreign affairs—*dealings with other countries*

War	Gen. 14:1-16
	Josh. 8:1-29
Treaties	Josh. 9:1-27
Trade agreement	1 Kin. 5:1-18
Alliances	1 Kin. 15:16-22
	1 Kin. 22:1-6
Conquest	2 Kin. 25:1-11

Foreigners—*sojourners in Israel*

Kept from feast	Ex. 12:43-45
Taxable	Deut. 15:2, 3
Figurative of Gentiles	Eph. 2:19

See Strangers

Foreign missionaries

Jonah as	Jon. 1:1, 2
Came from Antioch church	Acts 13:1-3
Report of	Acts 15:7-12

Foreknowledge of Christ

Concerning:
Men's nature	John 1:47, 48
Men's acts	John 6:64
His death and resurrection	Matt. 20:18, 19
	John 13:1
Jerusalem's destruction	Luke 19:41-44
Prophetic events	Matt. 24:1-51

Foreknowledge of God

A. *Manifested in:*
Naming a
person ....1 Kin. 13:2, 3
Naming a
place...........Matt. 2:5, 6
Setting a
time ....Mark 1:15
Determining the boundaries of
nations........Acts 17:26
Indicating successive
nations....... Dan. 2:26-47
Announcing Israel's
captivity ......Jer. 25:11, 12
Foretelling Christ's
death ....Acts 2:23

B. *Based upon God's:*
Infinite
knowledge ....Is. 41:22, 23
Eternal being .. Is. 43:9-13
Foredetermination of
events ....Rom. 8:29

C. *Plan of Salvation:*
Planned in
eternity ....Eph. 1:3-12
Announces from
beginning .....Gen. 3:15
Expanded to include
Gentiles.......Gal. 3:8
Elaborated in
details ....Is. 53:1-12
Visualized in
prophecy......Zech. 3:1-10
Consummated in Christ's
death ....John 19:30

Foresee—*to see something before it
takes place*

Approaching
evil...............Prov. 22:3
Resurrection of
Christ ....Acts 2:31
Salvation of
Gentiles ....Gal. 3:8

Foreskin (see Circumcision)

A. *Used literally of:*
Circum-
cision ....Gen. 17:9-17
Death ....1 Sam. 18:25

B. *Figuratively of:*
Regen-
eration.......Jer. 4:4

Forest

A. *Descriptive of wooded areas in:*
Hareth.........1 Sam. 22:5
Lebanon.......1 Kin. 7:2
Bethel ....2 Kin. 2:23, 24
Arabia.........Is. 21:13

B. *Used figuratively of:*
Army...........Is. 10:18, 19
Kingdom ......Jer. 21:14
Unfruit-   {Jer. 26:18
fulness........{Hos. 2:12

Forethought—*thinking ahead*

In meeting a
danger ....Gen. 32:3-23
In anticipating
evil................Prov. 22:3
Concerning physical
needs..............Phil. 4:10-19
Neglect of,
dangerous........Matt. 25:8-13
Examples of
ant, in............Prov. 6:6-8
For eternal
riches ....Luke 12:23-34

Foretold—*made known beforehand*

Destruction of
Jerusalem ....Mark 13:1, 2
Gospel blessings...Acts 3:24
Paul's trip to
Corinth ....2 Cor. 13:2

Forewarn—*to warn beforehand*

God's judgment...Luke 12:5
God's vengeance ..1 Thess. 4:6

Forfeit—*loss incurred by one's failure*

Leadership ....1 Sam. 15:16-28
Possessions ....Ezra 10:8
Salvation ....Matt. 16:26

Forfeiting spiritual rights

Birthright ....Gen. 25:34
Headship..........Gen. 49:3, 4
Apostleship ....Matt. 26:14-16
Spiritual
heritage..........Acts 13:45-48

Forger—*a counterfeiter*

Applied to David's
enemies ....Ps. 119:69

Forget—*be unable to remember*

God does not......Is. 49:15
Our sinful past ....Phil. 3:13

Forgetful—*unable to remember*

Concerning our
hearing...........James 1:25

Forgetting of God

A. *Seen in forgetting God's:*
Covenant......Deut. 4:23
Works.........Ps. 78:7, 11
Blessings......Ps. 103:2
Law...........Ps. 119:153, 176
Word..........James 1:25

B. *Characteristics of:*
Wicked........Is. 65:11
Form of
backsliding....Jer. 3:21, 22
Instigated by false
teachers......Jer. 23:26, 27

Forgiveness—*an act of pardon*

A. *Synonyms of:*
"Blots out".....Is. 43:25
"Remission"...Matt. 26:28
"Pardon".......Is. 55:7
"Remember no
more"........Jer. 31:34
"Healed".......2 Chr. 30:18-20

B. *Basis of:*
God's nature...Ps. 86:5
God's grace....Luke 7:42
Shedding of
blood.........Heb. 9:22
Christ's
death.........Col. 1:14
Son's power...Luke 5:21-24
Man's
repentance....Acts 2:38
Our
forgiveness....Matt. 6:12-14
Faith in
Christ.........Acts 10:43

C. *Significance of:*
Shows God's righteous-
ness.........Rom. 3:25, 26
Makes salvation
real..........Luke 1:77
Must be
preached......Luke 24:47

Forgiving one another

A. *The measure of:*
Seventy times
seven........Matt. 18:21, 22
Unlimited......Luke 17:3, 4
As God forgave
us...........Eph. 4:32

B. *Benefits of:*
Means of our
forgiveness....Mark 11:25, 26
Restored Christian
fellowship.....2 Cor. 2:7-10

Spiritual
cleansing......James 5:15, 16

C. *Examples of:*
Esau and
Jacob........Gen. 33:4-15
Joseph........Gen. 45:8-15
Moses.........Num. 12:1-13
David.........2 Sam. 19:18-23
Solomon.......1 Kin. 1:52, 53
Jesus.........Luke 23:34
Stephen.......Acts 7:59, 60
Paul..........2 Tim. 4:16

Fork

In tabernacle......Ex. 27:3
Num. 2:12-14
In temple.........1 Chr. 28:11, 17
2 Chr. 4:16

Form—*the outward appearance*

A. *Of physical things:*
Earth
without.......Gen. 1:2
Man in the
womb........Is. 44:24
Sexes.........1 Tim. 2:13
Idols.........Is. 44:10

B. *Of spiritual realities:*
Incarnate   {Is. 53:2
Christ.......{Rom. 9:20
Molder........Rom. 9:20
Christian
truth.........Rom. 6:17
New birth.....Gal. 4:19
World passing
away.........1 Cor. 7:31

Formalism—*forms performed mechanically*

A. *Characterized by:*
Outward forms of
religion......Is. 1:10-15
Lifelessness....Is. 58:1-14
Lukewarm-
ness.........Rev. 3:14-18

B. *Sign of:*
Hypocrisy.....Luke 18:10-14
Deadness......Phil. 3:4-8
Last days......2 Tim. 3:1, 5

Formula—*a prescribed method*

Success...........Prov. 22:29
Prosperity.........Matt. 6:32, 33
Peace.............Is. 26:3
Making friends....Prov. 18:24

Fornication—*sex relations among the unmarried*

Evil of:

Comes from evil
heart..............Matt. 15:19
Sins against the
body ....1 Cor. 6:18
Excludes from God's
kingdom ....1 Cor. 6:9
Disrupts Christian
fellowship........1 Cor. 5:9-11
Spiritual fornication symbolized in
final apostasy ....Rev. 17:1-5

Forsaken—*left deserted*

God's house.......Neh. 13:11
God's children ....Ps. 37:25
Messiah...........Is. 53:3
God's Son........Matt. 27:46

Forsaking Christ

Disciples left ......Matt. 26:56
Cause of
separation........John 6:66-70

Forsaking God

A. *Manifested in:*
Going after
idols ....1 Kin. 11:33
Going
backward .....Jer. 15:6
Following human
forms ....Jer. 2:13

B. *Evil of:*
Manifests
ingratitude....Jer. 2:5-12
Brings
confusion .....Jer. 17:13
Merits God's
wrath ....Ezra 8:22

C. *Examples of:*
Israel...........2 Kin. 17:7-18
Judah...........2 Chr. 12:1, 5

Fortifications—*walls or towers for protection*

Cities ....1 Kin. 9:15
                      2 Chr. 11:5-11
City of David .....2 Sam. 5:7-9

Fortified cities

Means of
protection........2 Sam. 20:6
Mighty and
strong............Deut. 9:1

Conquerable ......Deut. 3:4, 5
Utterly
destroyed........2 Kin. 3:19, 25
No substitute for
God ....Hos. 8:14

Fortress—*center of military strength*

Nation's
security ....2 Chr. 26:9
Illustrative of God's
protection ....Ps. 18:2
Typical of Christ ..Is. 33:16, 17
Applied to God's
prophet ....Jer. 6:27

Fortunatus—*fortunate*

Christian at
Corinth ....1 Cor. 16:17

Forty days

Length of flood ...Gen. 7:17
Israel's
embalming.....Gen. 50:2, 3
Moses on Mt.
Sinai ....Ex. 24:18
Spies in Canaan...Num. 13:25
Moses' prayer.....Deut. 9:25-29
The Philistine's
arrogance ......1 Sam. 17:16
Elijah's fast ....1 Kin. 19:2, 8
Nineveh's
probation........Jon. 3:4
Christ's
temptation ......Luke 4:1, 2
Christ's ministry after His
resurrection ......Acts 1:3

Forty stripes

Limit for
scourging ....Deut. 25:3
Paul's, one less ...2 Cor. 11:24

Forty years

Isaac's age at
marriage ....Gen. 25:20
Israel's diet ....Ex. 16:35
Israel's
wanderings.....Num. 32:13
Same sandals
for ....Deut. 29:5
Period of rest .....Judg. 3:11
Egypt's
desolation ......Ezek. 29:11-13
Saul's reign ....Acts 13:21
David's reign......1 Kin. 2:11
Solomon's reign...1 Kin. 11:42

Forwardness—*haste; overboldness*

Peter's faltering . . . Matt. 14:28, 29
Matt. 26:31-35

Foundation

A. *Used literally of:*
Cities . . . . Josh. 6:26
Walls . . . . Ezra 4:12
Houses . . . . Luke 6:48
Prison house . . Acts 16:26
House of the
Lord . . . . 1 Kin. 6:37
Towers . . . . . . Luke 14:28, 29

B. *Used figuratively of:*
Christian
truth . . . . Eph. 2:20
Christ . . . . Is. 28:16
Matt. 16:18
God decrees . . . 2 Tim. 2:19
Security of
parents . . . . . . 1 Tim. 6:19
Eternal city . . . Heb. 11:10

C. *Importance of:*
Must be on a ⎰ Matt. 7:24
rock . . . . ⎱ Matt. 16:18
Must be firm . . . Luke 6:48
Must be
Christ . . . . 1 Cor. 3:11
Without,
hopeless . . . . . . Ps. 11:3

Foundation, Gate of the—*a gate of Jerusalem*

Levites stationed
there . . . . 2 Chr. 23:2-5
Possibly the ⎰ 2 Kin. 11:16
Horse Gate ⎱ 2 Chr. 23:15

Fountain—*a flow of water from the earth*

Figurative of:

Rich blessings . . . . . Jer. 2:13

Fountain Gate—*a gate of Jerusalem*

Viewed by
Nehemiah . . . . Neh. 2:13, 14
Repaired . . . . Neh. 3:15

Foursquare

Altar . . . . Ex. 27:1
Breastplate . . . . Ex. 39:8, 9
City of God . . . . . . Rev. 21:16

Fowler—*one who catches birds*

Law restricting . . . . Deut. 22:6, 7

Figurative of false
prophets . . . . Hos. 9:8
Figurative of ⎰ Ps. 91:3
trials . . . . ⎱ Ps. 124:7

Fox—*a dog-like animal*

A. *Described as:*
Plentiful . . . . Judg. 15:4
Destructive . . . . Neh. 4:3
Crafty . . . . Luke 13:32
Living in
holes . . . . Matt. 8:20
Loves grapes . . Song 2:15

B. *Figurative of:*
False
prophets . . . . . . Ezek. 13:4
Enemies . . . . Song 2:15
Deceivers . . . . . Luke 13:32

Fragment—*a part of a larger whole*

Of food . . . . Mark 6:43

Fragrance—*a sweet odor*

Of perfume . . . . John 12:3
Figurative of
restoration . . . . . . Hos. 14:6

Frankincense—*a fragrant gum of a tree*

Used in holy oil . . . Ex. 30:34-38
Used in meal
offerings . . . . Lev. 2:1, 2, 15
Excluded from certain
offerings . . . . Lev. 5:11
Used in the
showbread . . . . . . Lev. 24:7
Presented to
Jesus . . . . Matt. 2:11

Fratricide—*murder of a brother*

Abel, by Cain . . . . . Gen. 4:8
70, by
Abimelech . . . . Judg. 9:1, 5
Amnon, by
Absalom . . . . 2 Sam. 13:28, 29
Adonijah, by
Solomon . . . . 1 Kin. 2:23-25
Six, by Jehoram . . 2 Chr. 21:4
Predicted . . . . Matt. 10:21

Fraud—*something designed to deceive*

A. *Examples of:*
Rebekah's, on
Isaac . . . . Gen. 27:5-36
Laban's, on
Jacob . . . . Gen. 29:21-25
Gibeonites', on
Israelites . . . . . . Josh. 9:3-9

Jonathan's, on
Saul .... 1 Sam. 20:11-17

B. *Discovery of, by:*
A miracle ...... Ex. 7:9-12
Events .... Matt. 28:11-15
Character ..... Matt. 26:47-50

Free moral agency of man—*ability to choose*

Resulted in sin .... Gen. 2:16, 17
Recognized by   { Gen. 4:6-10
God   { John 7:17
Appealed to ...... Is. 1:18-20
Jer. 36:3, 7

Freedmen

Jews opposing
Stephen .... Acts 6:9

Freedom—*unrestricted action*

A. *Of the unregenerate, limited by:*
Sin .... John 8:34
Inability .... John 8:43
Satan .... John 8:41, 44
Bondage ...... Rom. 6:20
Deadness ..... Eph. 2:1

B. *Of the regenerate:*
Made free by
Christ .... John 8:36
Freed from
bondage ..... Rom. 6:18, 22
Not of
license .... 1 Pet. 2:16
Not of bondage
again .... Gal. 5:1
Not of the
flesh .... Gal. 5:13

Freewill offerings

Obligatory .... Deut. 12:6
Must be perfect ... Lev. 22:17-25
Eaten in tabernacle by the
priests .... Lev. 7:16, 17
Firstfruits .... Prov. 3:9
According to one's
ability .... Deut. 16:17
Willing mind ...... 2 Cor. 8:10-12
Cheerful heart .... 2 Cor. 9:6, 7

Fretting—*a peevish state of mind*

Of the saints,
forbidden .... Ps. 37:1, 7, 8

Friend

A. *Nature of, common:*
Interest .... 1 Sam. 18:1

Love .... 1 Sam. 20:17
Sympathy ..... Job 2:11
Sacrifice .... John 15:13

B. *Value of:*
Constructive
criticism ...... Prov. 27:6
Helpful
advice .... Prov. 27:7
Valuable in time of
need .... Prov. 27:10
Always
faithful .... Prov. 17:17

C. *Dangers of:*
May entice to
sin .... Deut. 13:6-8
Some are
necessary ..... Prov. 14:20
Some are untrust-
worthy .... Ps. 41:9

D. *Examples of:*
God and
Abraham ...... Is. 41:8
David and
Jonathan ...... 1 Sam. 18:1
David and
Hushai .... 2 Sam. 15:37
Elijah and
Elisha .... 2 Kin. 2:1-14
Christ and His
disciples ...... John 15:13-15
Paul and
Timothy ...... 2 Tim. 1:2

Friendless—*lacking friends*

David's plight ..... Ps. 142:4
Prodigal son ...... Luke 15:15, 16

Friendship

A. *Kinds of:*
True .... 1 Sam. 18:1-3
Close .... Prov. 18:24
Ardent .... 2 Cor. 2:12, 13
Treacherous ... Matt. 26:48-50
Dangerous .... Deut. 13:6-9
Unfaithful ..... Job 19:14-19
False .... 2 Sam. 16:16-23
Worldly .... James 4:4

B. *Tests of:*
Continued
loyalty .... 2 Sam. 1:23
Willingness to
sacrifice ...... John 15:13
Obedient
spirit .... John 15:14, 15
Likeminded-
ness .... Phil. 2:19-23

Frog—*a small, leaping creature*

Plague on Egypt . . Ps. 78:45
Of unclean
spirits . . . . Rev. 16:13

Frontlets—*ornaments worn on the
forehead*

Of God's Word . . . . Deut. 6:6-9

Frost

Figurative of God's creative
ability . . . . Job 38:29

Frugality—*thrift*

Manifested by
Jesus . . . . John 6:11-13
Wrong kind . . . . Prov. 11:24, 25

Fruit—*product of life*

A. *Used literally of:*
Produce of
trees . . . . Gen. 1:29
Produce of the
earth. . . . . Gen. 4:3

B. *Factors destructive of:*
Blight. . . . . Joel 1:12
Locusts . . . . Joel 1:4
Enemies . . . . . . Ezek. 25:4
Drought . . . . . . Hag. 1:10, 11
God's anger . . . Jer. 7:20

C. *Used figuratively of:*
Repentance . . . . Matt. 3:8
Industry . . . . Prov. 31:16, 31
Christian
graces . . . . . . Gal. 5:22, 23
Holy life . . . . . . Prov. 11:30
Christ . . . . Ps. 132:11
Sinful life . . . . . Matt. 7:15, 16
Reward of righ-
teousness . . . . . Phil. 1:11

Fruit-bearing—*productiveness of*

Old age . . . . Ps. 92:14
Good hearers . . . . . Matt. 13:23
Christian
converts. . . . . Col. 1:6, 10
Abiding . . . . John 15:2-8

Fruitfulness

A. *Literally, dependent upon:*
Right soil . . . . . . Matt. 13:8
Rain . . . . James 5:18
Sunshine . . . . . . Deut. 33:14
Seasons. . . . . . . Matt. 21:34
Cultivation . . . . Luke 13:8

God's
blessing . . . . Acts 14:17

B. *Spiritually, dependent upon:*
Death . . . . John 12:24
New life . . . . . . Rom. 7:4
Abiding in
Christ . . . . John 15:2-8
Yielding to
God . . . . Rom. 6:13-23
Christian
effort . . . . 2 Pet. 1:5-11
Absence of,
reprobated . . . . Matt. 21:19

Fruitless discussion—*self-conceited talk
against God*

Characteristic of false
teachers. . . . . 1 Tim. 1:6, 7

Fruit trees

Protected by
Law. . . . . Lev. 19:23-25

Frying pan

Mentioned in . . . . . . Lev. 2:7

Fulfill—*to bring to its designed end*

A. *Spoken of God's:*
Word . . . . Ps. 148:8
Prophecy . . . . . 1 Kin. 2:27
Threat. . . . . 2 Chr. 36:20, 21
Promise. . . . . . . Acts 13:32, 33
Righteous-
ness. . . . . Matt. 3:15
Good
pleasure. . . . . . 2 Thess. 1:11

B. *Spoken of the believer's:*
Love. . . . . Rom. 13:8
Right-
teousness . . . . . Rom. 8:4
Burden-
bearing . . . . . . Gal. 6:2
Mission . . . . Col. 1:25
Ministry . . . . . . Col. 4:17

Full—*complete*

A. *Of natural things:*
Years. . . . . Gen. 25:8
Pails. . . . . Job 21:24
Children . . . . . . Ps. 127:5
Cart . . . . Amos 2:13
Leprosy. . . . . . . Luke 5:12

B. *Of miraculous things:*
Guidance . . . . . Judg. 6:38
Supply. . . . . 2 Kin. 4:4, 6
Protection . . . . . 2 Kin. 6:17

C. *Of evil emotions:*

Evil............Eccl. 9:3
Fury............Dan. 3:19
Wrath ....Acts 19:28
Envy ....Rom. 1:29
Cursing.........Rom. 3:14
Deadly
poison ....James 3:8
Adultery....2 Pet. 2:14

D. *Of good things:*

Power ....Mic. 3:8
Grace, truth ...John 1:14
Joy.............John 15:11
Faith ....Acts 6:5, 8
Good works ...Acts 9:36
Holy Spirit.....Acts 11:24

Fuller—*one who treats or dyes cloth*

Outside city......2 Kin. 18:17
                   Is. 7:3
God is like ....Mal. 3:2

Fullness—*completion*

A. *Of time:*
Christ's
advent ....Gal. 4:4
Gentile age ....Rom. 11:25
Age of grace...Eph. 1:10

B. *Of Christ:*
Eternal
Christ.........Col. 2:9
Incarnate
Christ.........John 1:16
Glorified
Christ.........Eph. 1:22, 23

Funeral—*burial rites*

Sad ....1 Kin. 13:29, 30
Joyful............Luke 7:11-17

Furnace—*fire made very hot*

A. *Used literally of:*
Smelting
ovens ....Gen. 19:28
Baker's oven...Hos. 7:4

B. *Used figuratively of:*
Egyptian
bondage ......Deut. 4:20
Spiritual
refinement ...Ps. 12:6
Lust ....Hos. 7:4
Hell ....Matt. 13:42, 50
Punishment....Ezek. 22:18-22

Furnace, fiery

Deliverance
from ....Dan. 3:8-26

Furniture

Tabernacle ....Ex. 31:7
Room............2 Kin. 4:8-10

Futile, futility—*vain; useless*

Used of:

Thoughts ....Ps. 94:11
Worship ....Jer. 51:17, 18
Customs ....Jer. 10:3
Sacrifice ....Is. 1:13
Obedience.........Deut. 32:46, 47
Visions...........Ezek. 13:7
Faith.............1 Cor. 15:17
Imaginations....Rom. 1:21
Mind.............Eph. 4:17

Future—*that which is beyond the present*

Only God knows ..Is. 41:21-23
Revealed by:

Christ............John 13:19
The Spirit.........John 16:13
Man's
ignorance of.....Luke 19:41-44
No provision for,
dangerous.......Luke 12:16-21
Proper provision
for ....Matt. 6:19-34

G

Gaal—*loathing*

Son of Ebed; vilifies
Abimelech........Judg. 9:26-41

Gaash—*quaking*

Hill of Ephraim ...Judg. 2:9
Joshua's burial
near.............Josh. 24:30

Gaba—*a hill*

City of
Benjamin.........Josh. 18:21, 24

Gabbai—*tax gatherer*

Postexilic
Benjamite ....Neh. 11:8

Gabbatha—*pavement*

Place of Pilate's
court.............John 19:13

Gabriel—*man of God*

Interprets Daniel's
vision ....Dan. 8:16-27

Reveals the prophecy of 70
weeks............Dan. 9:21-27
Announces John's
birth.............Luke 1:11-22
Announces Christ's
birth.............Luke 1:26-38
Stands in God's
presence........Luke 1:19

Gad—*good fortune*

1. Son of Jacob by
   Zilpah.......Gen. 30:10, 11
   Father of seven sons who
   founded tribal
   families......Gen. 46:16
2. Descendants of the tribe of
   Gad...........Deut. 27:13
   Census of.....Num. 1:24, 25
   Territory of...Num. 32:20-36
   Captivity of....1 Chr. 5:26
   Later references
   to.............Rev. 7:5
3. Seer of
   David........1 Sam. 22:5
   Message of, to
   David.........2 Sam. 24:10-16

Gadarenes, Gergesenes

People east of the Sea of
Galilee...........Mark 5:1
Healing of demon-possessed
here............Matt. 8:28-34

Gaddi—*fortunate*

Manassite spy.....Num. 13:11

Gaddiel—*Gad (fortune) is God*

Zebulunite spy....Num. 13:10

Gadi—*a Gadite*

Father of King
Menahem........2 Kin. 15:14

Gaham—*burning*

Son of Nahor.....Gen. 22:23, 24

Gahar—*hiding place*

Head of a family of Temple
servants..........Ezra 2:47

Gain through loss

A. *Elements of:*
   Death first.....John 12:24
   Servant
   status.........Mark 9:35
   Discount all temporal
   gains.........Matt. 19:29
   Loss of "life"..Mark 8:35

B. *Examples of:*
   Abraham......Heb. 11:8-19
   Moses.........Heb. 11:24-27
   Ruth..........Ruth 1:16-18
   Abigail........1 Sam. 25:18-42
   Esther.........Esth. 2:1-17
   Christ.........Phil. 2:5-11

Gains unjustly gotten

By:

Deceit.............Josh. 7:15-26
Violence..........Prov. 1:19
Oppression........Prov. 22:16
Divination........Acts 16:16, 19
Unjust wages.....James 5:4

Gaius—*commended*

1. Companion of
   Paul..........Acts 19:29
2. Convert at
   Derbe.........Acts 20:4
3. Paul's host at
   Corinth.......Rom. 16:23
   Corinthian
   convert.......1 Cor. 1:14
4. One addressed by
   John..........3 John 1-5

Galal—*a rolling*

1. Levite.........1 Chr. 9:15
2. Another
   Levite.........1 Chr. 9:16

Galatia—*a province of Asia Minor*

Paul's first
visit to...........Acts 16:6
Paul's second
visit to...........Acts 18:23
Churches of.....1 Cor. 16:1
Peter writes to
Christians in.....1 Pet. 1:1

Galatians—*people of Galatia*

Paul's:

Rebuke of their
instability........Gal. 1:6, 7
Defense of the Gospel among
them.............Gal. 1:8-24
Concern for
them.............Gal. 4:9-31
Confidence in
them.............Gal. 5:7-13

Galatians, the Epistle to—*a book of the
New Testament*

True gospel . . . . Gal. 1:6-12
Freedom from the
Law . . . . Gal. 2:15—4:31
Fruits of the Holy
Spirit . . . . Gal. 5:22, 23

Galbanum—*a yellowish-brown aromatic resin*

Used in the holy
oil . . . . Ex. 30:34

Galeed—*heap of witness*

Memorial site . . . . . Gen. 31:48

Galilean—*an inhabitant of Galilee*

Speech of . . . . Mark 14:70
Slaughter of . . . . . . Luke 13:1
Faith of . . . . John 4:45
Pilate's cruelty
toward . . . . Luke 13:1, 2

Galilee—*circle, circuit*

A. *History of:*
Moses' prophecy
concerning . . . . . . Deut. 33:18-23
Conquered by
Syrians . . . . 1 Kin. 15:18, 20
Conquered by
Assyrians . . . . . 2 Kin. 15:29
Dialect of,
distinctive . . . . . Matt. 26:73
Herod's jurisdiction
over . . . . Luke 3:1
Christian
churches in . . . Acts 9:31

B. *Christ's contacts with:*
Resided in . . . . . Matt. 2:22
Chooses disciples
from . . . . Matt. 4:18, 21
Fulfills prophecy
concerning . . . . . Matt. 4:14, 15
Performs many
miracles in . . . . Matt. 4:23
People of, receive
Him . . . . Matt. 4:25
Seeks
refuge in . . . . . . John 4:1, 3
Women of, minister to
Him . . . . Matt. 27:55
Seen in, after His
resurrection . . . Matt. 26:32

Galilee, Sea of

Scene of many events in
Christ's life . . . . . . Mark 7:31
Called
Chinnereth . . . . Num. 34:11

Later called
Gennesaret . . . . Luke 5:1

Gall—*bile*

Used literally of:

Liver secretion . . . . Job 16:13
Poisonous herb . . . . Amos 6:12
Matt. 27:34

Gallantry—*a chivalrous act of bravery*

Example of . . . . Ex. 2:16-21

Gallim—*heaps*

Village north of
Jerusalem . . . . Is. 10:29, 30
Home of Palti . . . . . 1 Sam. 25:44

Gallio—*who lives on milk*

Roman proconsul of Achaia;
dismisses charges against
Paul . . . . Acts 18:12-17

Gallows—*a structure used for hanging*

Haman had
made . . . . Esth. 5:14
Haman
hanged on . . . . Esth. 7:9, 10
Haman's sons
hanged on . . . . Esth. 9:13, 25

Gamaliel—*God has rewarded*

1. Leader of
Manasseh . . . . . Num. 2:20
2. Famous Jewish
teacher . . . . Acts 22:3
Respected by
people . . . . Acts 5:34-39

Game—*the flesh of wild animals*

Isaac's favorite
dish . . . . Gen. 27:1-33

Games—*various kinds of contests*

Figurative examples of, (as of a race):

Requiring
discipline . . . . 1 Cor. 9:25-27
Requiring obedience to
rules . . . . 2 Tim. 2:5
Testing the
course . . . . Gal. 2:2
Press on to the
goal . . . . Phil. 3:13, 14

Gammad—*warrior*

Manned Tyre's
towers . . . . Ezek. 27:11

Gamul—*rewarded*

Descendant of
Aaron . . . . 1 Chr. 24:17

Garden—*a protected and cultivated place*

A. *Notable examples of:*
In Eden . . . . Gen. 2:15
In Egypt . . . . . . Deut. 11:10
In Shushan . . . . Esth. 1:5
In Geth-
semane . . . . . . Mark 14:32
A royal . . . . 2 Kin. 25:4

B. *Used for:*
Festivities . . . . . Esth. 1:5
Idolatry . . . . Is. 65:3
Meditations . . . . Matt. 26:36
Burial . . . . John 19:41

C. *Figurative of:*
Desolation . . . . . Amos 4:9
Fruitfulness . . . . Is. 51:3
Prosperity . . . . . Is. 58:11
Righ-
teousness . . . . . Is. 61:11

Gardener—*one whose work is gardening*

Adam, the first . . . . Gen. 2:15
Christ,
mistaken for . . . . . John 20:15, 16

Gareb—*scab*

1. One of David's
warriors . . . . . . 2 Sam. 23:38
2. Hill near
Jerusalem . . . . . Jer. 31:39

Garland—*ceremonial headdress or wreath*

Brought by priests of
Jupiter . . . . Acts 14:13

Garlic—*an onion-like plant*

Egyptian food . . . . . Num. 11:5

Garments (see Clothing)

Garmite—*bony*

Gentile name applied to
Keilah . . . . 1 Chr. 4:19

Garrison—*a military post*

Smitten by
Jonathan . . . . 1 Sam. 13:3, 4
Attacked by
Jonathan . . . . 1 Sam. 14:1-15

Gatam—*puny*

Esau's grandson; chief of Edomite
clan . . . . Gen. 36:11-16

Gate—*an entrance*

A. *Made of:*
Wood . . . . Neh. 2:3, 17
Iron . . . . Acts 12:10
Bronze . . . . Ps. 107:16
Stones . . . . Rev. 21:12

B. *Opening for:*
Cities . . . . Judg. 16:3
Citadel . . . . Neh. 2:8
Sanctuary . . . . . Ezek. 44:1, 2
Tombs . . . . Matt. 27:60
Prisons . . . . Acts 12:5, 10

C. *Used for:*
Business trans-
actions . . . . 1 Kin. 22:10
Legal
business . . . . . . Ruth 4:1-11
Criminal
cases . . . . Deut. 25:7-9
Procla-
mations . . . . . . Jer. 17:19, 20
Festivities . . . . . Ps. 24:7
Protection . . . . . 2 Sam. 18:24, 33

D. *Figurative of:*
Satanic
power . . . . Matt. 16:18
Death . . . . Is. 38:10
Righteous-
ness . . . . Ps. 118:19, 20
Salvation . . . . . Matt. 7:13
Heaven . . . . Rev. 21:25

Gatekeeper

Duty of:

Zechariah	1 Chr. 9:21
Shallum	1 Chr. 9:17
Akkub	1 Chr. 9:17
Talmon	1 Chr. 9:17
Ahiman	1 Chr. 9:17
Ben	1 Chr. 15:18
Jaaziel	1 Chr. 15:18
Shemiramoth	1 Chr. 15:18
Jehiel	1 Chr. 15:18
Unni	1 Chr. 15:18
Eliab	1 Chr. 15:18
Benaiah	1 Chr. 15:18
Maaseiah	1 Chr. 15:18
Mattithiah	1 Chr. 15:18
Elipheleh	1 Chr. 15:18
Mikneiah	1 Chr. 15:18
Obed-Edom	1 Chr. 15:18
Jehiel	1 Chr. 15:18

Jeiel	1 Chr. 15:18
Heman	1 Chr. 15:17
Asaph	1 Chr. 15:17
Ethan	1 Chr. 15:17
Berechiah	1 Chr. 15:23
Elkanah	1 Chr. 15:23
Jehiah	1 Chr. 15:24
Jeduthun	1 Chr. 16:38
Hosah	1 Chr. 16:38

Gates of Jerusalem

1. Corner Gate ... 2 Chr. 26:9
2. Refuse Gate .. Neh. 12:31
3. Of Ephraim .... Neh. 8:16
4. Fish Gate ...... Zeph. 1:10
5. Fountain
   Gate .... Neh. 12:37
6. Horse Gate ... Jer. 31:40
7. Benjamin's
   Gate .... Zech. 14:10
8. "Gate of the
   Prison" .... Neh. 12:39
9. Sheep Gate .. Neh. 3:1
10. Upper Benjamin
    Gate .... Jer. 20:2
11. Valley Gate.... Neh. 2:13
12. Water Gate .. Neh. 8:16

Gath—*winepress*

1. Philistine
   city .... 1 Sam. 6:17
   Last of Anakim
   here .... Josh. 11:22
   Ark carried
   to.............. 1 Sam. 5:8
   Home of
   Goliath .... 1 Sam. 17:4
   David takes
   refuge in ..... 1 Sam. 21:10-15
   David's second
   flight to..... 1 Sam. 27:3-12
   Captured by
   David .... 1 Chr. 18:1
   Captured by
   Hazael ...... 2 Kin. 12:17
   Rebuilt by
   Rehoboam .... 2 Chr. 11:5, 8
   Uzziah broke down
   walls of ...... 2 Chr. 26:6
   Destruction of,
   prophetic .... Amos 6:1-3
   Name becomes
   proverbial..... Mic. 1:10

2. Musical instrument or
   tune .... Ps. 8; 81; 84
   (titles)

Gath Hepher—*winepress of the pit*

Birthplace of
Jonah .... 2 Kin. 14:25
Boundary of
Zebulun .... Josh. 19:13

Gath Rimmon—*pomegranate press*

1. City of Dan ... Josh. 19:40-45
   Assigned to
   Levites........ Josh. 21:24
2. Town in
   Manasseh ..... Josh. 21:25

Gaza—*strong place*

Philistine city ..... Josh. 13:3
Conquered by
Joshua .... Josh. 10:41
Refuge of
Anakim .... Josh. 11:22
Assigned to
Judah .... Josh. 15:47
Gates of, removed by
Samson .... Judg. 16:1-3
Samson deceived by Delilah
here........... Judg. 16:1-20
Samson blinded
here........... Judg. 16:21
Ruled by
Solomon .... 1 Kin. 4:22, 24
Sin of,
condemned...... Amos 1:6, 7
Judgment pronounced
upon .... Jer. 25:20
Philip
journeys to..... Acts 8:26

Gazelle—*medium-sized antelope; translated "roe"; "roebuck"*

A. *Described as:*
   Fit for food .... Deut. 12:15, 22
   Swift .... 1 Chr. 12:8
   Wild........... 2 Sam. 2:18
   Hunted by
   men........... Prov. 6:5
   In Solomon's
   provisions..... 1 Kin. 4:23

B. *Figurative of:*
   Timidity .... Is. 13:14
   Swiftness ..... 2 Sam. 2:18
   Church .... Song 4:5
   Christ .... Song 2:9, 17

Gazez—*shearer*

1. Son of Caleb... 1 Chr. 2:46
2. Grandson of
   Caleb .... 1 Chr. 2:46

Gazingstock—*an object of contempt*

Ignominy of......Nah. 3:6
Lot of
Christians........Heb. 10:33

Gazites

Inhabitants of
Gaza.............Judg. 16:2

Gazzam—*consuming*

Head of family of Temple
servants.........Ezra 2:48

Geba, Gaba—*a hill*

City of
Benjamin.........Josh. 18:24
Assigned to
Levites...........Josh. 21:17
Rebuilt by Asa....1 Kin. 15:22
Idolatrous........2 Kin. 23:8
Repossessed after the
exile..............Neh. 11:31

Gebal—*mountain*

1. Phoenician maritime
   town.........Ezek. 27:9
   Inhabitants
   called   (Josh. 13:5
   Gebalites.....(1 Kin. 5:18
2. Mountainous region in
   Edom.........Ps. 83:7

Geber—*strong one; hero*

Solomon's
purveyors........1 Kin. 4:19

Gebim—*ditches*

Place north of
Jerusalem........Is. 10:31

Gedaliah—*Yahweh has made great*

1. Jeduthun's
   son...........1 Chr. 25:3, 9
2. Pashur's son...Jer. 38:1
3. Grandfather of
   Zephaniah....Zeph. 1:1
4. Ahikam's
   son...........Jer. 39:14
   Made governor of
   Judea.........2 Kin. 25:22-26
   Befriends
   Jeremiah......Jer. 40:5, 6
   Murdered by
   Ishmael......Jer. 41:2, 18
   Postexilic
   priest......Ezra 10:18

Geder—*wall*

Town of Judah....Josh. 12:13

Gederah—*sheepfold*

Town in Judah....Josh. 15:36

Gederathite

Native of
Gederah.........1 Chr. 12:4

Gederite

Native of Geder...1 Chr. 27:28

Gederoth—*sheepfolds*

Town of Judah....Josh. 15:41
Captured by
Philistines.......2 Chr. 28:18

Gederothaim—*two sheepfolds*

Town of Judah....Josh. 15:36

Gedor—*wall*

1. Town of
   Judah.........Josh. 15:58
2. Simeonite
   town..........1 Chr. 4:39
3. Town of
   Benjamin.....1 Chr. 12:7
4. Family in
   Judah.........1 Chr. 4:4
5. A son of
   Jeiel and
   brother of   (1 Chr. 8:30, 31
   Ner...........(1 Chr. 9:35-37
6. The son of
   Jered.........1 Chr. 4:18

Ge Harashim

A craftsman.......1 Chr. 4:14

Gehazi—*valley of vision*

Elisha's servant...2 Kin. 5:25
Seeks reward from
Naaman..........2 Kin. 5:20-24
Afflicted with
leprosy..........2 Kin. 5:25-27
Relates Elisha's deeds to
Jehoram.........2 Kin. 8:4-6

Gehenna (see Hell)

Geliloth—*circles*

Probably Gilgal, in the land of
Benjamin.........Josh. 18:17

Gemalli—*camel driver*

Father of
Ammiel..........Num. 13:12

Gemariah—*Yahweh has perfected*

1. Hilkiah's son...Jer. 29:3
2. Shaphan's
   son ....Jer. 36:10-25

Gems—*precious stones*

On breastplate ....Ex. 28:15-21
Figurative of value ....{Prov. 3:15 / Prov. 31:10}
In commerce......Ezek. 27:16
In New
Jerusalem......Rev. 21:19-21

Genealogies—*ancestral lineage*

A. *Importance:*
   Chronology....Matt. 1:17
   Priesthood
   claims........{Ezra 2:61, 62 / Neh. 7:63, 64}
   Messiahship ...Matt. 1:1-17

B. *Lists of:*
   Patriarchs' ....Gen. 5:1-32
   Noah's.........Gen. 10:1-32
   Shem's ....Gen. 10:21-32
   Abraham's.....1 Chr. 1:28-34
   Jacob's ....Gen. 46:8-27
   Esau's ....Gen. 36:1-43
   Israel's ....1 Chr. 9:1
   David's ....1 Chr. 3:1-16
   Levites'........1 Chr. 6:1-81

Genealogy of Jesus

Seed of
Abraham.........Gal. 3:16
Through Joseph...Matt. 1:2-17
Through Mary ....Luke 3:23-38

General—*chief military authority*

Commander......1 Chr. 27:34
               Rev. 6:15
Also rendered
"princes".........Gen. 12:15

Generation

Descriptive of:

Period of time.....Gen. 9:12
Living people or
race..............Matt. 24:34

Genesis, Book of—*first book of the Old Testament*

Creation ....Gen. 1:1–2:25
The fall ....Gen. 3:1-24
The flood ....Gen. 6:8–7:24
Abraham.........Gen. 12:1–25:18
Isaac.............Gen. 25:19–26:35
Jacob ....Gen. 27:1–36:43
Joseph ....Gen. 37:1–50:26

Genius—*unusual mental ability*

Applicable to
Solomon ....1 Kin. 4:29-34

Gentiles—*non-Jews*

A. *Described as:*
   Supersti-
   tious..........Deut. 18:14
   Knowing
   God...........Rom. 1:21
   Without the
   Law..........Rom. 2:14
   Wicked ......Rom. 1:23-32
   Idolatrous .....1 Cor. 12:2
   Uncircum-
   cised..........Eph. 2:11
   Without
   Christ.........Eph. 2:12
   Dead in sins ...Eph. 2:1

B. *Blessings promised to:*
   Given to
   Christ ....Ps. 2:8
   Included in God's
   covenant........{Gen. 12:3 / Gal. 3:8}
   Conversion
   predicted.......{Is. 11:10 / Rom. 15:9-16}
   Christ their
   light ....Is. 49:6
   Included in "all
   flesh".........Joel 2:28-32
   Called "other
   sheep".........John 10:16

C. *Conversion of:*
   Predicted ......Is. 60:1-14
   Proclaimed ....Matt. 4:12-17
   Anticipated ....John 10:16
   Questioned ....Acts 10:9-29
   Realized ....Acts 10:34-48
   Explained......Acts 11:1-18
   Hindered ......Acts 13:45-51
   Debated ....Acts 15:1-22
   Confirmed .....Acts 15:23-31
   Vindicated.....Acts 28:25-29

D. *Present position:*
   Barrier
   removed ......Eph. 2:11-22
   Brought near ..Eph. 2:13
   Fellow
   citizens ....Eph. 2:19
   Fellow heirs ...Eph. 3:6
   In body........Eph. 3:6

Gentleness—*mildness combined with tenderness*

A. *Examples of:*
   God's ....2 Sam. 22:36

Christ's........Matt. 11:29
Paul's..........1 Thess. 2:7
Holy Spirit.....Gal. 5:22, 23

B. *A Christian essential in:*
Living in the
world ....Titus 3:1, 2
Instruction ...2 Tim. 2:24, 25
Restoring a
brother ......Gal. 6:1
Calling ....Eph. 4:1, 2
Marriage.......1 Pet. 3:1-4

C. *Commandments concerning:*
Follow after ...1 Tim. 6:11

Genubath—*theft*

Edomite..........1 Kin. 11:20

Geology—*study of the earth*

Allusions to.......Gen. 1:9, 10

Gera—*grain*

1. Son of Bela ....Gen. 46:21
2. A descendant of
Bela...........1 Chr. 8:3-8
3. Father of
Ehud...........Judg. 3:15
4. Father of
Shimei.........2 Sam. 16:5

Gerah—*smallest coin and weight
among the Jews*

Twentieth part {Ex. 30:13
of a shekel ......{Lev. 27:25

Gerar—*region*

Town of
Philistia ....Gen. 10:19
Visited by
Abraham.........Gen. 20:1-18
Visited by Isaac...Gen. 26:1-17
Abimelech,
king of ....Gen. 26:1, 26

Gerizim—*cutters*

Mountain of blessing in
Ephraim.........Deut. 11:29
Jotham's
parable...........Judg. 9:7
Samaritans' sacred
mountain........John 4:20, 21

Gershom, Gershon—*exile*

1. Son of Levi ....Ex. 6:16
1 Chr. 6:16-20
Father of Libni and
Shimei ....Ex. 6:17

Founder of
Gershonites ...Num. 3:17-26
2. Son of Moses ..Ex. 2:21, 22
Circumcised ...Ex. 4:25
Founder of Levite
family.........1 Chr. 23:14-16
3. Descendant of
Phinehas......Ezra 8:2
4. Father of
Jonathan......Judg. 18:30

Gershonites

Descendants of
Gershon.........Num. 3:21, 22
Tabernacle
servants.........Num. 3:25, 26
Achievements of ..1 Chr. 15:7-19

Geshan—*firm*

Descendant of
Caleb.............1 Chr. 2:47

Geshem—*shower*

Opposes
Nehemiah ....Neh. 6:6

Geshur—*bridge*

Not expelled .....Josh. 13:13
Talmai, king of....2 Sam. 3:3
Absalom
flees to ....2 Sam. 13:37, 38

Geshurites

1. People of
Geshur........Deut. 3:14
2. People living south of
Philistia.......1 Sam. 27:8

Gether—*fear*

Son of Aram ......Gen. 10:23

Gethsemane—*oil press*

Garden near
Jerusalem ......Matt. 26:30, 36
Scene of Christ's
agony and {Matt. 26:36-56
betrayal ....{John 18:1-12
Often visited by
Christ ....Luke 22:39

Geuel—*majesty of God*

Gadite spy ....Num. 13:15, 16

Gezer—*portion*

Canaanite city ....Josh. 10:33
Not expelled .....Josh. 16:10

Assigned to
Kohathites ....Josh. 21:21
Scene of
warfare..........1 Chr. 14:16
Burned by Egyptian
king..............1 Kin. 9:16
Rebuilt by
Solomon ....1 Kin. 9:17

Ghost

Christ thought to { Matt. 14:26
be................ { Mark 6:49

Giah—*waterfall*

Place near
Ammah ....2 Sam. 2:24

Giants—*men of unusual size*

A. *Names of:*
Rephaim.......Gen. 14:5
Anakim........Num. 13:28-33
                    Josh. 11:21
Emim..........Gen. 14:5
Zamzummim ..Deut. 2:20
Goliath ....1 Sam. 17:4-7
Og.............Deut. 3:11, 13
Others.........2 Sam. 21:16-22

B. *Destroyed by:*
Moses ....Deut. 3:3-11
Joshua........Josh. 11:21
David..........1 Sam. 17:48-51
David and his
men...........2 Sam. 21:16-22

Gibbar—*huge*

Family head.......Ezra 2:20

Gibbethon—*mound*

Town of Dan......Josh. 19:44
Assigned to
Levites ....Josh. 21:20-23
Nadab's assassination
at ....1 Kin. 15:27, 28
Besieged by
Omri ....1 Kin. 16:17

Gibea—*hill*

Caleb's
grandson ....1 Chr. 2:49

Gibeah—*hill*

1. Village of
Judah.........Josh. 15:57
2. Town of
Benjamin .....Judg. 19:14-16
Known for
wickedness....Judg. 19:12-30

Destruction....Judg. 20:1-48
Saul's
birthplace.....1 Sam. 10:26
Saul's political
capital ....1 Sam. 15:34
Saul's sons
executed......2 Sam. 21:6-10
Wickedness of, long remembered ....Hos. 9:9

Gibeathites

Inhabitants of
Gibeah ....1 Chr. 12:3

Gibeon—*hill town*

Hivite town ....Josh. 9:3, 7
Mighty, royal
city ....Josh. 10:2
Sun stands still
at ....Josh. 10:12
Assigned to
Benjamin......Josh. 18:25
Given to Levites ..Josh. 21:17
Location of
tabernacle......1 Chr. 16:39
Joab struck
Amasa ....2 Sam. 20:8-10
Joab killed here ...1 Kin. 2:28-34
Site of Solomon's sacrifice
and dream......1 Kin. 3:5-15
Natives of, return from
exile.............Neh. 3:7

Gibeonites—*inhabitants of Gibeon*

Deceive Joshua ...Josh. 9:3-15
Deception
discovered......Josh. 9:16-20
Made
woodcutters.....Josh. 9:21-27
Rescued by
Joshua.........Josh. 10:1-43
Massacred by
Saul.............2 Sam. 21:1
Avenged by
David ....2 Sam. 21:2-9

Giddalti—*I have made great*

Son of Heman ....1 Chr. 25:4

Giddel—*very great*

1. Head of family of Temple
servants.......Ezra 2:47
2. Children of
Solomon's   { Ezra 2:56
servants......{ Neh. 7:58

Gideon—*cutter of trees*

Son of Joash .....Judg. 6:11
Called by an
angel............Judg. 6:11-24
Destroys Baal's
altar...........Judg. 6:25-32
Fleece confirms call from
God...........Judg. 6:36-40
His army
reduced ....Judg. 7:2-8
Encouraged by a
dream............Judg. 7:9-15
Employs successful
strategy ....Judg. 7:16-25
Soothes angry
Ephraimites .....Judg. 8:1-3
Takes revenge on Succoth and
Penuel ....Judg. 8:4-22
Refuses kingship ...Judg. 8:22, 23
Unwisely makes an
ephod ....Judg. 8:24-27
Judgeship of forty
years..........Judg. 8:28, 29
Father of 71
sons..............Judg. 8:30, 31
His death brings
apostasy ....Judg. 8:32-35
Called Jerubbaal . Judg. 8:35
Man of faith ......Heb. 11:32

Gideoni—*a cutting down*

Benjamite.........Num. 1:11
Father of
Abidan ....Num. 1:11
Brought offering for the tribe of
Benjamin.........Num. 7:60-65
Over tribal army of
Benjamin.........Num. 10:24

Gidom—*a cutting off*

Village of
Benjamin.........Judg. 20:45

Gifts

A. *Of God:*

1. *Material:*
Food ....Matt. 6:25, 26
Rain............Matt. 5:45
Health.........Phil. 2:25-30
Sleep ....Prov. 3:23-25
Rest ....Deut. 12:10
All things......1 Tim. 6:17
All needs .....Phil. 4:19
2. *Spiritual:*
Christ ....John 3:16
Holy Spirit.....Luke 11:13
Grace..........James 4:6

Wisdom ....James 1:5
Repentance ....Acts 11:18
Faith ....Eph. 2:8
New spirit ....Ezek. 11:19
Peace..........Phil. 4:7
Rest ....Heb. 4:1, 9
Glory ....1 Pet. 5:10
Eternal life ...John 10:28

B. *Of man:*

1. *Purposes of:*
Confirm
covenants.....Gen. 21:27-32
Appease
anger ....1 Sam. 25:27-35
Show respect ..Judg. 6:18-21
Manifest
friendship.....1 Sam. 30:26-31
Reward........2 Sam. 18:11, 12
Memorialize an
event ....Esth. 9:20-22
Render
worship......Matt. 2:11
Give help.....Phil. 4:10-18
Seal
friendship.....1 Sam. 18:3, 4
2. *Times given:*
Betrothals ....Gen. 24:50-53
Weddings.....Ps. 45:12
Departures ....Gen. 45:21-24
Returns
home ....Luke 15:22, 23
Times of
recovery .....Job 42:10, 11
Trials,
forbidden .....Ex. 23:8

C. *Spiritual:*
Listed and   { Rom. 12:6-8
explained ....   { 1 Cor. 12:4-30
Came from
God...........James 1:17
Assigned
sovereignty ...1 Cor. 12:11, 28
Cannot be
bought........Acts 8:18-20
Always for
edification ....Rom. 1:11
Counterfeited by
Satan ....2 Cor. 11:13-15
Spiritually
discerned ....1 Cor. 12:2, 3
Love, the
supreme ....1 Cor. 13:1-13

Gihon—*bursting forth*

1. River of
Eden..........Gen. 2:13

2. Spring outside
Jerusalem.....1 Kin. 1:33-45
3. Source of water
supply ....2 Chr. 32:30

Gilalai—*weighty*

Levite musician ...Neh. 12:36

Gilboa—*bubbling fountain*

Range of limestone hills in
Issachar ......1 Sam. 28:4
Scene of Saul's
death............1 Sam. 31:1-7
Philistines desecrate Saul's
body ....1 Sam. 31:8, 9
Under David's
curse............2 Sam. 1:17, 21

Gilead—*rocky or strong*

1. Grandson of
Manasseh .....Num. 26:29, 30
2. Father of
Jephthah......Judg. 11:1
3. Gadite ....1 Chr. 5:14
4. Condemned
city ....Hos. 6:8
5. Mountain......Judg. 7:3
6. Tableland east of the Jordan
between the Arnon and Jab-
bok rivers.....Judg. 20:1
Possessed by
Israel ....Num. 21:21-31
Assigned to Reuben, Gad, and
Manasseh .....Deut. 3:12-17
Rebuked by
Deborah ......Judg. 5:17
Hebrews
flee to.........1 Sam. 13:7
Ishbosheth's rule
over ....2 Sam. 2:8, 9
David { 2 Sam. 17:26,
takes { 27
refuge in ..{ 2 Sam. 19:31
In David's
census ....2 Sam. 24:1, 6
Elijah's
birthplace.....1 Kin. 17:1
Smitten by
Hazael ....2 Kin. 10:32, 33
Mentioned by
Amos ....Amos 1:3, 13

Gilead, Balm of—*an aromatic gum for
medicinal purposes*

Figurative of:

National { Jer. 8:22
healing ....{ Jer. 51:8

Gilgal—*a circle, a wheel*

1. Memorial site between Jordan
and Jericho ...Josh. 4:19-24
Israel
circumcised ...Josh. 5:2-9
Passover
observed ......Josh. 5:10
Site of Gibeonite
covenant......Josh. 9:3-15
On Samuel's
circuit ....1 Sam. 7:15, 16
Saul made
king ....1 Sam. 11:15
Saul rejected ..1 Sam. 13:4-15
Denounced for
idolatry ......Hos. 9:15
2. Town near
Bethel.........2 Kin. 2:1
Home of
Elisha.........2 Kin. 4:38

Giloh—*exile*

Town of Judah....Josh. 15:51

Gilonite—*Giloh native*

Ahithophel
called ....2 Sam. 15:12

Gimel

Third letter in Hebrew
alphabet.........Ps. 119:17-24

Gimzo—*producing sycamores*

Village of Judah..2 Chr. 28:18

Ginath—*protection*

Father of Tibni ...1 Kin. 16:21, 22

Ginnethoi—*gardener*

Postexilic priest ...Neh. 12:4

Ginnethon—*gardener*

Family head and signer of
document ......Neh. 10:6
Probably same as Ginnethoi

Gird—*to put on, as a belt*

A. *Purposes of:*
Strength-
ening ....Prov. 31:17

B. *Figurative of:*
Gladness.......Ps. 30:11
Truth..........Eph. 6:14
Readiness......1 Pet. 1:13

C. *Those girding:*
Priests........Ex. 28:4, 39
Warriors.......1 Sam. 18:4
Jesus ....John 13:3, 4

Girgashites—*an original tribe of Canaan*

Descendants of
Canaan.............Gen. 10:15, 16
Land of, given to Abraham's
descendants.........Gen. 15:18, 21
Delivered to
Israel.............Josh. 24:11

Girl—*a female child; young woman*

Sold for wine .....Joel 3:3
Prophecy
concerning ....Zech. 8:4, 5
Raised by Jesus ..Mark 5:39-42
Demands John's
head ....Matt. 14:10, 11
Questions Peter ...John 18:17
Is disbelieved .....Acts 12:13-17
Healed by Paul....Acts 16:16-18

Girzites—*inhabitants of Gezer*

Raided by David ..1 Sam. 27:8

Gishpa—*fondle*

Overseer ....Neh. 11:21

Gittaim—*two winepresses*

Village of
Benjamin.........Neh. 11:31, 33
Refuge of the
Beerothites.......2 Sam. 4:2, 3

Gittites—*natives of Gath*

600 follow David ..2 Sam. 15:18-23

Giving to God

A. *Manner of:*
Without
show..........Matt. 6:1-4
According to
ability.........1 Cor. 16:1, 2
Willingly.......1 Chr. 29:3-9
Liberally.......2 Cor. 9:6-15
Cheerfully .....2 Cor. 9:7
Propor-
tionately ......Mal. 3:10

B. *Examples of:*
Israelites ......Ex. 35:21-29
Leaders of
Israel ....Num. 7:2-28
Poor widow....Luke 21:1-4
Macedonian
churches......2 Cor. 8:1-5

Gizonite

Hashem thus
described.........1 Chr. 11:34

Gladness—*cheerfulness*

A. *Causes of:*
Salvation ......Is. 51:3, 11
John 8:56
Forgiveness....Ps. 51:8
Recovery of a
son ....Luke 15:32
Restoration of
hope..........John 20:20
Temporal
blessings......Acts 14:17
Christ's
coming........1 Pet. 4:13

B. *Wrong kinds of:*
At an enemy's
downfall ......Prov. 24:17
At
wickedness....Hos. 7:3

Glass

A. *Used literally of:*
Crystal ....Job 28:17, 18

B. *Used figuratively of:*
God's nature...Rev. 4:6
New
Jerusalem.....Rev. 21:18, 21

Gleaning—*gathering grain left by
reapers*

Laws providing
for ....Lev. 19:9, 10
Illustrated by
Ruth ....Ruth 2:2-23
Gideon's
reference to ......Judg. 8:2

Glorification of Christ

A. *Nature of:*
Predicted ......Is. 55:5
Prayed for .....John 12:28
Not of
Himself ....Heb. 5:5
Prede-
termined......John 17:1

B. *Accomplished by:*
Father.........John 13:31, 32
Holy Spirit.....John 16:13, 14
Miracles ....John 11:4
His
resurrection...Acts 3:13
Believers......Acts 21:20

Glorifying God

A. *By means of:*
Praise ....Ps. 50:23
Fruitfulness....John 15:8

Service ....1 Pet. 4:11
Suffering ......1 Pet. 4:14, 16

B. *Reason for:*
Deliverance....Ps. 50:15
Mercy shown..Rom. 15:9
Subjection.....2 Cor. 9:13

C. *Extent of:*
Universal......Ps. 86:9
In body and
soul...........1 Cor. 6:20

Glory—*honor; renown*

A. *Of temporal things:*
Granted by
God...........Dan. 2:37
Used to
entrap ....Matt. 4:8
Not to be
sought ....1 Thess. 2:6
Quickly
passes........1 Pet. 1:24

B. *Of believers:*
Given by
God...........John 17:22
Transformed by the
Spirit ....2 Cor. 3:18
Through Christ's
death ....Heb. 2:9, 10
Follows
salvation .....2 Tim. 2:10
In suffering...Rom. 5:3
In the cross....Gal. 6:14
Greater than present
suffering .....Rom. 8:18
Hope of.......Col. 1:27
At Christ's
advent .....Col. 3:4

Glory of Christ

A. *Aspects of:*
Manifested to
men..........John 2:11
Not selfish.....John 8:50
Given by
God..........John 17:22
Crowned
with ....Heb. 2:9
Ascribed to
forever.......Heb. 13:21

B. *Stages of:*
Before
creation.......John 17:5
Revealed in Old
Testament ....John 12:41
In His
incarnation ...John 1:14

In His trans-
figuration .....Luke 9:28-36
In His
resurrection...Luke 24:26
In His
exaltation .....1 Tim. 3:16
At His return..Matt. 25:31
In heaven .....Rev. 5:12

Glory of God

A. *Manifested to:*
Moses ....Ex. 24:9-17
Stephen ....Acts 7:55

B. *Reflected in:*
Christ ....John 1:14
Man ....1 Cor. 11:7

C. *Appearances of:*
The
tabernacle ....Ex. 40:34
The temple ....1 Kin. 8:11
At Jesus'
birth ....Luke 2:8-11

D. *The believer's relation to:*
Does all for....1 Cor. 10:31
Illuminated
by ....2 Cor. 4:6
Will stand in
presence of ...Jude 24

E. *Man's relation to:*
Corrupts.......Rom. 1:23
Falls short of ..Rom. 3:23
Refuse to give to
God...........Acts 12:23

Glory of man

Prefigured in
creation ....Heb. 2:6-8
Lost by sin.......Rom. 3:23
Soon passes
away.............1 Pet. 1:24
Removed by
death............Ps. 49:17
Restored by
Christ ....2 Cor. 5:17

Gluttony—*excessive appetite*

Sternly
forbidden........Prov. 23:1-3
Characteristic of the
wicked ....Phil. 3:19
Leads to poverty ..Prov. 23:21
Christ
accused of.......Matt. 11:19

Gnat—*small insect*

Used as
illustration ....Matt. 23:24

Gnosticism—*early heresy based on knowledge instead of faith*

Warned against ...Col. 2:8, 18
Arrogant..........1 Cor. 8:1
False.............1 Tim. 6:20
Surpassed by
Christ ....Eph. 3:19

Goad—*a pointed rod*

Used as a
weapon ....Judg. 3:31
Figurative of pointed
morals ....Eccl. 12:11
Figurative of
conscience ....Acts 26:14
Sharpened by
files ....1 Sam. 13:21

Goals, spiritual

Provide
motivation ....Phil. 3:12-14
Promise reward ...1 Cor. 9:24, 25

Goat—*a domesticated animal*

A. *Literal uses of:*
Clothing.......Num. 31:20
Heb. 11:37
Milk of, food...Prov. 27:27
Curtains.......Ex. 26:7
Wineskins .....Josh. 9:4
Sacrifices .....Ex. 12:5

B. *Figurative uses of:*
Kingdom of
Greece ....Dan. 8:5, 21
Wicked ....Matt. 25:32, 33

Goath—*constance*

Place near
Jerusalem ....Jer. 31:39

Gob—*a pit*

Plain where Hebrews and
Philistines
fought............2 Sam. 21:18, 19
Also called
Gezer ....1 Chr. 20:4

Goblet—*a bowl or basin*

Used as a
comparison......Song 7:2
Same word
translated
"basins" and   {Ex. 24:6
"cups" ....   {Is. 22:24

God—*the Supreme Being*

A. *Names of:*
God ....Gen. 1:1
LORD God .....Gen. 2:4
Most high
God..........Gen. 14:18-22
Lord God .....Gen. 15:2, 8
Almighty
God..........Gen. 17:1, 2
Everlasting
God..........Gen. 21:33
God
Almighty.....Gen. 28:3
I Am ....Ex. 3:14
Jealous ....Ex. 34:14
Eternal God ...Deut. 33:27
Living God ...Josh. 3:10
God of hosts...Ps. 80:7
Lord of hosts ..Is. 1:24
Holy One of
Israel ....Is. 43:3, 14, 15
Mighty God...Jer. 32:18
God of
heaven........Jon. 1:9
Heavenly
Father ....Matt. 6:26
King eternal ...1 Tim. 1:17
Only
Potentate .....1 Tim. 6:15
Father of
lights ....James 1:17

B. *Manifestations of:*
Face of ....Gen. 32:30
Voice of ....Deut. 5:22-26
Glory of ....Ex. 40:34, 35
Angel of ....Gen. 16:7-13
Name of.......Ex. 34:5-7
Form of ....Num. 12:6-8
Comes from
Teman........Hab. 3:3

C. *Nature of:*
Spirit ....John 4:24
One ....Deut. 6:4
Personal......John 17:1-3
Trinitarian....2 Cor. 13:14
Omnipotent....Rev. 19:6

D. *Natural attributes of:*
Incom-
parable........2 Sam. 7:22
Invisible ......John 1:18
Inscrutable ...Is. 40:28
Unchange-
able..........Num. 23:19
Unequaled ...Is. 40:13-25
Unsearch-
able...........Rom. 11:33, 34
Infinite ....1 Kin. 8:27
Eternal ....Is. 57:15

Omnip-
otence . . . . Jer. 32:17, 27
(All-powerful)
Omni-
presence . . . . . . Ps. 139:7-12
(Ever-present)
Omniscience . . . 1 John 3:20
(All-knowing)
Fore-
knowledge . . . . Is. 48:3, 5
Wise. . . . . Acts 15:18

E. *Moral attributes of:*
Goodness (see Goodness of
God)
Hatred. . . . . Ps. 5:5, 6
Holiness . . . . Rev. 4:8
Impartiality . . . . 1 Pet. 1:17
Justice. . . . . Ps. 89:14
Long-
suffering . . . . . Ex. 34:6, 7
Love. . . . . 1 John 4:8, 16
Mercy . . . . Lam. 3:22, 23
Truth. . . . . Ps. 117:2
Vengeance. . . . Deut. 32:34-41
Wrath . . . . Deut. 32:22

F. *Human expressions applied to:*
Fear . . . . Deut. 32:26, 27
Grief . . . . Gen. 6:6
Repentance . . . Gen. 6:7
Jealousy . . . . . . Ex. 34:14
Swearing . . . . . Jer. 44:26
Laughing . . . . . Ps. 2:4
Sleeping . . . . . . Ps. 78:65
Human parts . Ex. 33:21-23

G. *Titles given to:*
Creator . . . . Is. 40:12, 22, 26
Judge. . . . . Ps. 96:10, 13
King. . . . . Ps. 47:2, 7, 8
Defender . . . . . . Ps. 59:1
Preserver . . . . . Ps. 121:3-8
Shepherd . . . . . Gen. 49:24

H. *Works of, described as:*
Awesome . . . . . Ps. 66:3
Incompar-
able. . . . . Ps. 86:8
Great. . . . . Ps. 92:5
Manifold. . . . . . Ps. 104:24
Marvelous . . . . Ps. 139:14

I. *Ways of, described as:*
Perfect . . . . Ps. 18:30
Knowl-
edgeable . . . . . Ps. 86:11
Made known . Ps. 103:7
Righteous . . . . . Ps. 145:17

Not like
man's . . . . Is. 55:8, 9
Everlasting . . . . Hab. 3:6
Inscrutable . . . . Rom. 11:33
Just and true . . Rev. 15:3

See Goodness of God; Love of God;
Power of God

Godhead—*the Deity*

Revealed to
mankind . . . . Rom. 1:20
Corrupted by
mankind . . . . Acts 17:29
Incarnated in Jesus
Christ . . . . Col. 2:9

Godliness—*holy living*

Profitable . . . . 1 Tim. 4:7, 8
Perverted . . . . 1 Tim. 6:5
Pursuit . . . . 1 Tim. 6:11
Duty . . . . Titus 2:12

See Holiness of Christians

Gods, false

A. *Names of:*
Adrammelech
(Syria) . . . . 2 Kin. 17:31
Anammelech
(Babylon) . . . . . 2 Kin. 17:31
Artemis
(Greek) . . . . Acts 19:34
Ashtoreth
(Canaan). . . . . . 1 Kin. 11:5, 33
Baal
(Canaan). . . . . . 1 Kin. 18:19
Baal of Peor
(Moab). . . . . Num. 25:1-9
Beelzebub
(Philistine) . . . . Luke 11:19-23
Bel
(Babylon) . . . . . Jer. 51:44
Calf worship
(Egypt) . . . . Ex. 32:1-6
Chemosh
(Moab). . . . . 1 Kin. 11:7
Dagon
(Philistine) . . . 1 Sam. 5:1-7
Hermes
(Greek) . . . . Acts 14:12, 13
Milcom
(Ammon) . . . . . 1 Kin. 11:5
Molech
(Ammon) . . . . . 1 Kin. 11:7
Nebo
(Babylon) . . . . . Is. 46:1
Nisroch
(Assyria) . . . . . . 2 Kin. 19:37

Rimmon
(Syria) .... 2 Kin. 5:18
Tammuz
(Babylon) .... Ezek. 8:14
Zeus (Greek) .. Acts 14:12, 13

B. *Evils connected with:*
Immorality .... Num. 25:1-9
Prostitution .... 2 Kin. 23:7
Divination ..... Lev. 20:1-6
Sacrilege ...... Dan. 5:4
Pride .... 2 Kin. 18:28-35
Persecution .... 1 Kin. 19:1-3
Child
sacrifice .... Jer. 7:29-34

Gog—*mountain*

1. Reubenite ..... 1 Chr. 5:4
2. Prince of Rosh, Meshech,
   and Tubal ..... Ezek. 38:2, 3
3. Leader of the final
   battle .... Rev. 20:8-15

Golan—*circuit*

City of Bashan .... Deut. 4:43
Assigned to
Levites .... Josh. 21:27
City of refuge .... Josh. 20:8

Gold

A. *Found in:*
Havilah .... Gen. 2:11, 12
Ophir .... 1 Kin. 9:28
Sheba .... 1 Kin. 10:2, 10
Arabia .... 2 Chr. 9:14

B. *Used for:*
Money .... Matt. 10:9
Offerings ...... Ex. 35:22
Presents ...... Matt. 2:11
Holy
adornment .... Ex. 28:4-6
Jewelry .... Gen. 24:22
Physical
adornment .... Ex. 36:34, 38
Idols .... Ex. 32:31

C. *Figurative of:*
Saints
refined .... Job 23:10
Babylonian
empire .... Dan. 2:38
Redeemed ..... 2 Tim. 2:20
Faith
purified ...... 1 Pet. 1:7
Christ's
doctrine ...... Rev. 3:18

Golden apples

Appropriate
word .... Prov. 25:11

Golden city

Babylon called .... Is. 14:4

Golden rule

For Christian conduct .... {Matt. 7:12 / Luke 6:31

Golden wedge

Figurative term ... Is. 13:12

Goldsmiths

In the
tabernacle .... Ex. 31:1-4
Refiners .... Mal. 3:3
Shapers of
objects .... Ex. 25:11, 18
Makers of idols .... Num. 33:52
Guilds .... Neh. 3:8, 32

Golgotha—*place of a skull*

Where Jesus
died .... Matt. 27:33-35

Goliath—*exile*

1. Giant of
   Gath .... 1 Sam. 17:4
   Killed by
   David .... 1 Sam. 17:50
2. Brother of above; killed by
   Elhanan .... 2 Sam. 21:19

See Giant

Gomer—*completion*

1. Son of Japheth {Gen. 10:2, 3 / 1 Chr. 1:5, 6
   Northern
   nation .... Ezek. 38:6
2. Wife of
   Hosea .... Hos. 1:2, 3

Gomorrah—*submersion*

In a fruitful
valley .... Gen. 13:10
Defeated by
Chedorlaomer .... Gen. 14:8-11
Destroyed by
God .... Gen. 19:23-29
Symbol of evil .... Is. 1:10
Symbol of
destruction .... Amos 4:11
Punishment of .... Matt. 10:15

Good for evil

Illustrated by
Joseph .... Gen. 45:5-15
Christian duty .... Luke 6:27, 35

Goodness of God

A. *Described as:*
Abundant......Ex. 34:6
Great.........Ps. 31:19
Enduring......Ps. 52:1
Satisfying.....Ps. 65:4
Universal.....Ps. 145:9

B. *Manifested in:*
Material
blessings ..... {Matt. 5:45 / Acts 14:17}
Spiritual
blessings ..... Ps. 31:19
Forgiving sin .. Ps. 86:5

C. *Saints' attitude toward:*
Rejoice in .....Ex. 18:9
Remember.....Ps. 145:7
Be satisfied
with ....Jer. 31:14

Gopher wood

Used in Noah's
ark..............Gen. 6:14

Gore—*to push or thrust*

By an ox.........Ex. 21:28-32
Rendered
"push" {Deut. 33:17 / Ezek. 34:21}

Goshen

1. District of Egypt where Israel
   lived ....Gen. 45:10
   Land of
   pastures......Gen. 47:1-6
   Called the land of
   Rameses .....Gen. 47:6-11
2. Region in south
   Judah.........Josh. 10:41
3. City of
   Judah.........Josh. 15:51

Gospel—*good news*

A. *Described as, of:*
God ....Rom. 1:1
Christ ....2 Cor. 2:12
The kingdom ..Matt. 24:14
Grace of God ..Acts 20:24
Peace.........Eph. 6:15
Salvation .....Eph. 1:13
Glory of
Christ.........2 Cor. 4:4

B. *Defined as:*
Of supernatural
origin ....Gal. 1:10-12
God's power ...Rom. 1:16
Mystery ....Eph. 6:19

Revelation .....Eph. 3:1-6
Deposit of
truth.........1 Cor. 15:1-4

C. *Source of:*
Hope ....Col. 1:23
Salvation .....2 Thess. 2:13, 14
Faith ....Acts 15:7
Life..........1 Cor. 4:15
Immortality...2 Tim. 1:10
Afflictions ....Phil. 1:16
Peace.........Eph. 6:15

D. *Proclaimed by or in:*
Old
Testament ....Gal. 3:8
Prophets.......Rom. 1:1, 2
John..........Mark 1:1-4
Jesus Christ ..Mark 1:14, 15
Chosen men ..1 Pet. 1:12

E. *Should be proclaimed:*
To all people..Mark 16:15, 16
Everywhere....Rom. 15:19, 20
At all times....Rev. 14:6
With great
urgency.......1 Cor. 9:16
With
boldness .....Eph. 6:19
As a
testimony .....Matt. 24:14

F. *Proclaimers of, are:*
Separated......Rom. 1:1
Called ....Acts 16:10
Entrusted
with it ....1 Thess. 3:2
Set apart for its
defense ......Phil. 1:7, 16, 27
Under divine
orders.........1 Cor. 9:16

G. *Negative reactions to, some:*
Disobey......2 Thess. 1:8
Are blinded
to.............2 Cor. 4:3, 4
Hinder........1 Cor. 9:12
Pervert ....Gal. 1:7

H. *Believer's reaction to:*
Believing .....Eph. 1:13
Submitting
to.............2 Cor. 9:13
Being established
by ....Rom. 16:25
Living by.....Phil. 1:27
Defending ....Phil. 1:7, 16, 27

Gossip—*idle talk or rumors about others; talebearer*

Forbidden.........Lev. 19:16
Cause of friction ..Prov. 16:28

Destructive ....1 Tim. 5:13
Warns against associating
with.............Prov. 20:19
Called
"talebearer" ....{Prov. 11:13
Called "talkers"...{Prov. 20:19
Ezek. 36:3
Called
"whisperers" .....Rom. 1:29
Called
"whisperings" ....2 Cor. 12:20

Gourd—*a running plant with large leaves*

Poison variety.....2 Kin. 4:39-41

Government—*recognized rulership*

A. *Types of:*
Patriarchal, in
families ....Gen. 27:29-39
Theocratic, under
God...........Ex. 18:13-26
Monarchial, under
kings ....1 Sam. 8:5-22
Antichristian, under
antichrist .....2 Thess. 2:3-12
Absolute and final, under
Christ..........Is. 9:6, 7

B. *Characteristics of:*
Ruled by
God..........Is. 45:1-13
Successions of, determined by
God..........Dan. 2:28-45
Ignorant of spiritual
things..........1 Cor. 2:8
Providentially
used ....Acts 26:32

C. *Christian attitude toward:*
Occupy
positions in ...Gen. 42:6
Pay taxes to ...Matt. 22:18-21
Pray for ....1 Tim. 2:1-3
Obey
rules of ....Rom. 13:1-7
But obey God
first...........Acts 5:29

Governor—*a ruler*

Title used of
Zerubbabel ......Ezra 2:63
Applied to
Nehemiah ....Neh. 8:9
Prime minister ....Gen. 42:6
Provincial ruler ...Acts 23:24, 26

Gozan—*quarry*

Town and district in
Mesopotamia.....2 Kin. 17:6

Israelites
deported to.......2 Kin. 18:11

Grace—*unmerited favor*

A. *Descriptive of:*
God's favor ....Gen. 6:8
God's forgiving
mercy.........Rom. 11:6
Gospel.........John 1:17
Gifts (miracles,
etc.) ....1 Pet. 4:10
Eternal life ....1 Pet. 1:13

B. *Is the source of:*
Salvation ......Acts 15:11
Call of God ....Gal. 1:15
Faith ....Acts 18:27
Justification ...Rom. 3:24
Forgiveness....Eph. 1:7
Consolation ...2 Thess. 2:16

C. *Described as:*
All-abundant ..Rom. 5:15-20
All-sufficient ..2 Cor. 12:9
Glorious ......Eph. 1:6
Great.........Acts 4:33
Manifold......1 Pet. 4:10
Rich..........Eph. 2:4, 5
Undeserved ...1 Tim. 1:12-16

D. *Believers:*
Are under .....Rom. 6:14
Receive......John 1:16
Stand in ......Rom. 5:2
Abound in.....2 Cor. 9:8
Be strong in ..2 Tim. 2:1
Grow in ....2 Pet. 3:18
Speak with ...Eph. 4:29
Inherit........1 Pet. 3:7

E. *Dangers of, can:*
Be abused .....Jude 4
Be frustrated ..Gal. 2:21
Be turned
from ....Gal. 5:3, 4

Graces, Christian

Growth in,
commanded ......2 Pet. 1:5-8

Grafting—*uniting a portion of one plant to another*

Gentiles, on Israel's
stock.............Rom. 11:17, 24

Grain—*the generic term for cereal grasses*

A. *Features regarding:*
Grown in
Palestine......2 Kin. 18:32

Article of
food .... Gen. 42:1, 2, 19
Offered mixed with
oil .... Lev. 2:14, 15
Roasted .... Ruth 2:14

B. *Figurative of:*
Blessings ...... Ezek. 36:29
Christ .... John 12:24
Life's
maturity ...... Job 5:26

Grandchildren

Lot becomes father of, through
incest .... Gen. 19:30-38
Abdon's .... Judg. 12:13, 14
Widow's .... 1 Tim. 5:4
Iniquity visited
on .... Ex. 34:7
Served idols .... 2 Kin. 17:41
Crown of old
men .... Prov. 17:6
Practice piety toward
family .... 1 Tim. 5:4

Grandmother

Lois thus called ... 2 Tim. 1:5

Grapes

Grown in
Palestine .... Num. 13:23
Used for wine .... Num. 6:3
"Sour grapes" .... Ezek. 18:2
Figurative of
judgment .... Rev. 14:18

See Vine, vineyard

Grass

A. *Features:*
Created by
God .... Gen. 1:11, 12
Produced by
rain .... Deut. 32:2
Adorns earth .. Matt. 6:30
Failure of, a
calamity ..... Jer. 14:5, 6
Nebuchadnezzar
eats .... Dan. 4:1, 33
Disappears ..... Prov. 27:25
Withered
away .... Is. 15:6

B. *Figurative of:*
Life's
shortness ..... Ps. 90:5, 6
Prosperous
wicked .... Ps. 92:7
God's grace .... Ps. 72:6

Grasshopper—*locust*

Used as food ..... Lev. 11:22
Inferiority .... Num. 13:33
Insignificance ..... Is. 40:22
Burden .... Eccl. 12:5

See Locust

Gratitude (see Thankfulness)

Gratitude to man

A. *Reasons for:*
Deliverance from an
enemy .... Judg. 8:22, 23
Deliverance from
death .... 1 Sam. 26:21-25
Interpretation of a
dream ..... Dan. 2:46-48
Rescue from
murderers ..... Esth. 6:1-6

B. *Examples of:*
Ruth to Boaz .. Ruth 2:8-17
Israelites to
Jonathan ...... 1 Sam. 14:45
Abigail to
David .... 1 Sam. 25:40-42
David to
Jonathan ...... 2 Sam. 9:1
David to
Hanun .... 2 Sam. 10:1, 2
Pagans to
Paul .... Acts 28:1-10

Grave—*a place of burial*

A. *Features regarding:*
Dug in
ground .... Gen. 50:5
Some in
caves .... Gen. 23:9
Marker
set on .... Gen. 35:20
Touching of, makes
unclean .... Num. 19:16, 18

B. *Resurrection from:*
Symbolized .... Ezek. 37:1-14

Graveclothes—*clothes for the dead*

Lazarus attired
in .... John 11:43, 44
Jesus lays His
aside .... Luke 24:12

Gravel—*small pebbles*

Figurative of:
Distress .... Prov. 20:17

Numerous offspring; rendered
"grains".........Is. 48:19
Suffering.........Lam. 3:16

Graven image—*an idol*

Of Canaanites, to ⎰Deut. 7:1-5, 25
be destroyed.....⎱Deut. 12:2, 3
Cause of God's   ⎰Ps. 78:58
anger...........⎱Jer. 8:19

See Idols, idolatry

Great

A. *Descriptive of:*
  Sun and
  moon.........Gen. 1:16
  Euphrates.....Gen. 15:18
  Mediter-
  ranean......Josh. 1:4
  Nineveh......Jon. 3:2, 3
  Babylon......Rev. 14:8

B. *Applied to God's:*
  Nature.......Deut. 10:17
  Works........Judg. 2:7
  Victory......2 Sam. 23:10, 12
  Mercy........2 Chr. 1:8
  Wrath........2 Chr. 34:21
  Glory........Ps. 21:5

C. *Descriptive of Christ as:*
  God..........Titus 2:13
  Prophet......Luke 7:16
  Priest.......Heb. 4:14
  King.........Luke 1:32, 33
               Rev. 11:17
  Shepherd.....Heb. 13:20

D. *Applied to the believer's:*
  Reward.......Matt. 5:12
  Faith........Matt. 15:28
  Joy..........Acts 8:8
  Zeal.........Col. 4:13
  Affliction...2 Cor. 8:2
  Boldness.....1 Tim. 3:13
  Promises.....2 Pet. 1:4

E. *Applied to final things:*
  Gulf fixed.....Luke 16:26
  Wrath........Rev. 6:17
  Tribulation....Rev. 7:14
  White throne
  judgment.....Rev. 20:11

Great fish
  Swallows   ⎰Jon. 1:17
  Jonah.........⎱Matt. 12:40

Greatness, true

Hinges on:

God's gentleness..Ps. 18:35

Great work.......Neh. 6:3
Unselfishness....Jer. 45:5
Servanthood.....Matt. 23:11
God's estimate...Matt. 5:19

Greece—*the southern extremity of the
Balkan peninsula*

Prophecy
concerning.....Dan. 8:21
Paul preaches in..Acts 17:16-31
Called Javan.....Is. 66:19
Vision of in Daniel's
visions..........Dan. 8:21
Conflict with....Zech. 9:13

Greed—*excessive desire for things*

A. *Productive of:*
  Defeat.......Josh. 7:11-26
  Murder.......1 Kin. 21:1-16
  Betrayal.....Luke 22:1-6

B. *Examples of:*
  Samuel's
  sons.........1 Sam. 8:1, 3
  False
  prophets.....Is. 56:10, 11
  False
  teachers.....2 Pet. 2:14, 15

See Avarice; Covetousness

Greek

1. Native of   ⎰Joel 3:6
   Greece.......⎱Acts 16:1
   Spiritual
   state of.....Rom. 10:12
   Some believe..Acts 14:1
2. Foreigners speaking
   Greek........John 12:20
3. Language of
   Greece.......Acts 21:37

Greeting

A. *Normal:*
  Between:
    Brothers......1 Sam. 17:22
    Social ranks..Gen. 47:7
    Strangers.....1 Sam. 10:3, 4
    Christians....1 Pet. 5:14
    On visits.....Rom. 16:21-23

B. *Examples of forms used in:*
  "God be
  gracious".....Gen. 43:29
  "Peace be with
  you"..........Judg. 19:20
  "The LORD be with
  you"..........Ruth 2:4
  "The LORD bless
  you"..........Ruth 2:4

"Blessed are
you" .... Ruth 3:10
"Hail" .... Luke 1:28
"Joy to you" .... Matt. 28:9

See Benediction

Greyhound—*a tall, slender hound*

Poetically
described .... Prov. 30:29, 31

Grief

A. *Causes of:*
Son's
marriage ..... Gen. 26:34, 35
Barrenness ..... 1 Sam. 1:11, 16
Death .... 2 Sam. 19:1, 2
Disease .... Job 2:11-13
Sinners .... Ps. 119:158
Foolish son ... Prov. 17:25

B. *Descriptive of:*
Messiah ...... Is. 53:3, 4, 10
God .... Ps. 95:10
Holy Spirit ..... Eph. 4:30
Is. 63:10

See Sorrow

Grow—*to increase*

A. *Of material things:*
Power .... 2 Sam. 3:1

B. *Of immaterial things:*
Spirituality .... Luke 2:40
Old covenant .. Heb. 8:13
God's
kingdom ...... Luke 13:18, 19

Growth, spiritual

A. *Expressed by words indicating:*
Fruitfulness .... John 15:2, 5
Increase ...... 2 Cor. 9:10
Addition ...... 2 Pet. 1:5-10
Growth .... 1 Pet. 2:2
Building up .... Jude 20

B. *Hindrances to:*
Lack of
knowledge .... Acts 18:24-28
Carnality ...... 1 Cor. 3:1-3
Instability ..... Eph. 4:14, 15
Dullness .... Heb. 5:11-14

Grudge—*to harbor resentment*

Forbidden .... Lev. 19:18

Guard

A. *Aspects of:*
Called
mighty .... 2 Sam. 23:8-23

Often
foreigners ..... 2 Sam. 20:7
Respected ..... Jer. 40:1-5

B. *Duties of:*
Run before
chariots .... 2 Sam. 15:1
Form a military
guard .... 1 Sam. 22:17
Keep watch .... 2 Kin. 11:5, 6
Carry out command-
ments .... Jer. 39:11-14
Execute
criminals ..... Dan. 2:14

Guardians, stewards—*custodians*

Christ, of our
souls .... 2 Tim. 1:12
Referred to by
Paul .... Gal. 4:2

Guardian angels

Helpers .... Gen. 24:7
Heb. 1:1-14
Protectors .... Ps. 91:11
Matt. 18:10
Aided apostles .... Acts 5:17-19
Acts 8:26

Gudgodah—*cutting; cleft*

Israelite
encampment ..... Deut. 10:7
Also called
Hor Hagidgad .... Num. 33:32

Guest

Kinds of:

Terrified .... 1 Kin. 1:41, 49
Dead .... Prov. 9:18
Unwelcomed ..... Prov. 25:17
Unprepared ...... Matt. 22:11
Criticized .... Luke 7:39-50
Congenial .... Acts 18:1-3
Courteous .... 1 Cor. 10:27
Angelic .... Heb. 13:2

Guidance, divine

To meek .... Ps. 25:9
To wise .... Prov. 23:19
To good man ...... Ps. 112:5
In God's
strength .... Ex. 15:13
On every side .... 2 Chr. 32:22
With God's eye ... Ps. 32:8
With counsel ..... Ps. 73:24
Like a flock ...... Ps. 78:52
By skillfulness ... Ps. 78:72
Continually ...... Is. 58:11

Guide—*a leader*

A. *Kinds of:*
Human . . . . Num. 10:29-32
Super-
natural. . . . . . . Ex. 13:20-22
Blind . . . . Matt. 23:16, 24

B. *Goals of:*
Peace. . . . . Luke 1:79
Truth. . . . . John 16:13
God's word . . . . Acts 8:30, 31

Guilt, universality of

Described as:

Filthy rags . . . . . . Is. 64:6
Fall short . . . . . . Rom. 3:23
All declared . . . . Rom. 5:12-14
Gal. 3:22

Guni—*colored*

1. One of Naphtali's
sons . . . . Gen. 46:24
1 Chr. 7:13
Descendants called
Gunites . . . . . Num. 26:48

2. Gadite. . . . . 1 Chr. 5:15

Gur—*lion's cub*

Site of Ahaziah's
death. . . . . 2 Kin. 9:27

Gur Baal—*sojourn of Baal*

Place in Arabia. . . . 2 Chr. 26:7

H

Haahashtari—*runner*

Son of Ashur. . . . . . 1 Chr. 4:5, 6

Habaiah—*Yahweh has hidden*
Father of
excommunicated {Ezra 2:61, 62
Jewish priests . . .{Neh. 7:63, 64

Habakkuk—*embrace*

A. *Complaints of:*
God's silence . . Hab. 1:2-4
God's
response . . . . . . Hab. 1:5-11
Chaldean
cruelty. . . . . . . Hab. 1:12-17
God's
response . . . . . Hab. 2:1-20

B. *Prayer of:*
Praise of
God. . . . . Hab. 3:1-19

Habakkuk, the Book of—*a book of the Old Testament*

Author. . . . . Hab. 1:1
Setting. . . . . Hab. 1:2-4
Historical
reference . . . . Hab. 1:6
The life of the
just . . . . Hab. 2:4

Habazziniah

Grandfather of
Jaazaniah . . . . Jer. 35:3

Habit—*a custom*

Kinds of:

Doing evil. . . . . Jer. 13:23
Doing good . . . . . . Acts 10:38
Of animals,
instinctive. . . . . . . 2 Pet. 2:22

Habitation—*a place of residence*

A. *Used literally of:*
Canaan . . . . Num. 15:2
A tree . . . . Dan. 4:20, 21
Nation. . . . . Acts 17:26

B. *Used figuratively of:*
Eternity . . . . . . Is. 57:15
God's throne. . Is. 63:15
Sky. . . . . Hab. 3:11
Heaven . . . . Luke 16:9
New
Jerusalem . . . . . Is. 33:20

Habor—*joined together*

The river of
Gozan. . . . . 2 Kin. 17:6

Hachaliah—*darkness of Yahweh*

Father of
Nehemiah . . . . . . Neh. 1:1

Hachilah—*dark; gloomy*

Hill in the wilderness of Ziph
where David
hid . . . . 1 Sam. 23:19-26

Hachmoni

Father of a tutor to David's
son. . . . . 1 Chr. 27:32

Hadad—*fierceness*

1. Ishmael's
   son ....1 Chr. 1:30
2. King of
   Edom ....Gen. 36:35, 36
3. Another king of
   Edom ....1 Chr. 1:50
   Called Hadar ..Gen. 36:39
4. Edomite
   leader........1 Kin. 11:14-25

Hadadezer—*Hadad is a help*

King of Zobah ..2 Sam. 8:3-13
Defeated by
David ....2 Sam. 10:6-19

Hadad and Rimmon

Name of the two Aramean deities;
a place in
Jezreel ....Zech. 12:11

Hadashah—*new*

Village of Judah...Josh. 15:37

Hadassah—*myrtle*

Esther's Jewish
name.............Esth. 2:7

Hadattah—*new*

Town in south Judah; possibly
should be read as Hazor-
Hadattah ....Josh. 15:25

Hadid—*sharp*

Town of
Benjamin.........Neh. 11:31, 34

Hadlai—*restful*

Ephraimite........2 Chr. 28:12

Hadoram—*Hadar is exalted*

1. Son of
   Joktan........Gen. 10:26, 27
2. Son of Tou ....1 Chr. 18:9, 10
3. Rehoboam's tribute
   officer.........2 Chr. 10:18
   Called
   Adoram......1 Kin. 12:18
   Probably same as
   Adoniram .....1 Kin. 4:6

Hadrach—*periodical return*

Place in Syria .....Zech. 9:1

Hagab—*locust*

Head of a family of Temple
servants..........Ezra 2:46

Hagabah—*locust*

Head of a family
of Temple   {Neh. 7:46, 48
servants........   {Ezra 2:43, 45

Hagar—*flight*

Sarah's Egyptian
handmaid ....Gen. 16:1
Flees from
Sarah ....Gen. 16:5-8
Returns; becomes mother of
Ishmael ....Gen. 16:3-16
Abraham sends her
away.............Gen. 21:14
Paul's
allegory of.......Gal. 4:22-26

Hagerite—*a descendant of Hagar*

Jaziz, keeper of David's
flocks ....1 Chr. 27:31

Haggai—*festive*

Postexilic
prophet ....Ezra 5:1, 2
Contemporary of
Zechariah ....Ezra 6:14
Prophecies of, dated in reign of
Darius
Hystaspes   {Hag. 1:1, 15
(520 B.C.)....... {Hag. 2:1, 10, 20

Haggai, the Book of—*a book of the Old Testament*

Purpose.........Hag. 1:1-15
The coming
glory ....Hag. 2:4-9
On Levitical
cleanliness ......Hag. 2:10-14

Hagri—*a Hagerite*

Father of one of David's
warriors..........1 Chr. 11:38
Called "Bani the
Gadite" in........2 Sam. 23:36

Haggi—*festal*

Son of Gad.......Gen. 46:16
Head of tribal
family ....Num. 26:15

Haggiah—*festival of Yahweh*

Merarite Levite ...1 Chr. 6:30

Haggith—*festal*

One of David's
wives.............2 Sam. 3:4
Mother of
Adonijah ....1 Kin. 1:5

Hagrites

Nomad people east of
Gilead............1 Chr. 5:10-22
Called Hagarites ..Ps. 83:6

Hail—*frozen rain*

Illustrative of God's:

Wonders..........Job 38:22
Glory.............Ps. 18:12
Chastening........Is. 28:2, 17
Wrath ....Rev. 8:7
Power.............Ps. 147:17

Hail—*a salutation*

Gabriel to Mary...Luke 1:26-28
Soldiers to
Christ ....Matt. 27:27-29

Hair

A. *Of women:*
  Covering ......1 Cor. 11:15
  Uses of ....Luke 7:38
  Prohibitions (1 Tim. 2:9
  concerning...(1 Pet. 3:3
B. *Of men:*
  Not to be worn
  long ....1 Cor. 11:14
  Rules for
  cutting........Lev. 19:27
  Long, during Nazirite
  vow...........Num. 6:5
  Gray, sign
  of age.........1 Sam. 12:2
  Absalom's
  beautiful......2 Sam. 14:25, 26
  Numbered .....Matt. 10:30
C. *Figurative of:*
  Minuteness ....Judg. 20:16
  Complete
  safety.........1 Sam. 14:45
  Fear...........Job 4:14, 15
  Great
  numbers ......Ps. 40:12
  Grief..........Ezra 9:3
  Respect........Prov. 16:31
  Attrac-
  tiveness......Song 5:2, 11
  Affliction ......Is. 3:17, 24
  Entire
  destruction....Is. 7:20
  Decline and
  fall...........Hos. 7:9

Hakkatan—*the smallest*

Johanan's father ..Ezra 8:12

Hakkoz—*the thorn*

Descendant of
Aaron............1 Chr. 24:1, 10
Called Koz.......Ezra 2:61, 62
Descendants of, kept from
priesthood.......Neh. 7:63, 64

Hakupha—*crooked*

Ancestor of certain Temple
servants.........Ezra 2:42, 43, 51

Halah—*a district of Assyria*

Israelite captives
carried to........2 Kin. 17:6

Halak—*smooth*

Mountain near
Seir ....Josh. 11:17

Half-shekel tax—*a temple tax*

Commanded ......Ex. 30:13, 14
Christ paid.......Matt. 17:24-27

Half-tribe of Manasseh—*the part of Manasseh east of the Jordan*

Clans of:

Machir............Josh. 17:1

Halhul—*contorted*

A city in Judah ...Josh. 15:20,
                  21, 58

Hali—*necklace*

Town of Asher....Josh. 19:25

Hallohesh—*enchanter*

Repairs walls and signs
covenant.........Neh. 3:12
                  Neh. 10:24

Ham—*hot*

1. Noah's youngest
   son ....Gen. 5:32
   Enters ark .....Gen. 7:7
   His immoral behavior merits
   Noah's curse ...Gen. 9:22-25
   Father of descendants of
   repopulated
   earth..........Gen. 10:6-20
2. Poetical name of
   Egypt ....Ps. 105:23, 27
3. Hamites at
   Gedor.........1 Chr. 4:39, 40
4. Place where Chedorlaomer
   defeated the
   Zuzim ....Gen. 14:5

Haman

Plots to destroy
Jews ....Esth. 3:3-15
Invited to Esther's
banquet ....Esth. 5:1-14
Forced to honor
Mordecai.........Esth. 6:5-14
Hanged on his own
gallows...........Esth. 7:1-10

Hamath—*fortification*

Hittite city north of
Damascus ....Josh. 13:5
Spies visit........Num. 13:21
Israel's northern
limit...............Num. 34:8
Solomon's
boundary.........1 Kin. 8:65
Storage cities
built...............2 Chr. 8:3, 4
Captured by the
Assyrians.........2 Kin. 18:30, 34
People of, deported to
Samaria ....2 Kin. 17:24, 30
Israelites exiled ...Is. 11:11
Mentioned by
Jeremiah ....Jer. 49:23
Limit of Ezekiel's
prophecy.........Ezek. 47:16-20

Hamathites

People of
Hamath ....Gen. 10:18

Hamath Zobah—*fortress of Zobah*

Captured by
Solomon ....2 Chr. 8:3

Hammath—*hot springs*

1. City of
   Naphtali ......Josh. 19:35
   Probably the same as Hammon
   and Hammoth
   Dor ....1 Chr. 6:76
2. Founder of the
   Rechabites ....1 Chr. 2:55

Hammedatha—*given by Ham*

Father of
Haman ....Esth. 3:1

Hammer—*a workman's tool*

A. *Literal uses of:*
   Drive tent
   pegs ....Judg. 4:21
   Not used in
   Temple........1 Kin. 6:7

Straighten
metal ....Is. 41:7

B. *Figurative uses of:*
   God's Word....Jer. 23:29
   Babylon ......Jer. 50:23

Hammered gold—*gold shaped by forceful blows*

Ornamental
shields.
{ 1 Kin. 10:16, 17
{ 2 Chr. 9, 15, 16

Hammoleketh—*the queen*

Sister of Gilead ...1 Chr. 7:17, 18

Hammon—*glowing*

1. Village of
   Asher ....Josh. 19:28
2. Town of
   Naphtali ......1 Chr. 6:76

See Hammath 1

Hammoth Dor—*hot springs of Dor*

City of refuge.....Josh. 21:32

See Hammath 1

Hamonah—*multitude*

Site of Gog's
defeat ....Ezek. 39:11-16

Hamon Gog—*multitude of Gog*

Memorial name of Gog's
burial ....Ezek. 39:11

Hamor—*ass*

Sells land to
Jacob.
{ Gen. 33:18-20
{ Acts 7:16
Killed by Jacob's
sons..............Gen. 34:1-31

Hamran

Descendant of
Seir ....1 Chr. 1:41

See Hemdan

Hamstring—*to cut the tendons of the leg*

To render
captured animals
useless
{ Josh. 11:6, 9
{ 2 Sam. 8:4

Hamuel—*anger of God*

Son of Mishma....1 Chr. 4:26

Hamul—*spared*

Son of Pharez.....Gen. 46:12
Founder of tribal
family............Num. 26:21

Hamutal—*kinsman of dew*

Wife of King
Josiah . . . . 2 Kin. 23:30, 31
Mother of Jehoahaz and
Zedekiah . . . . 2 Kin. 24:18
Daughter of Jeremiah of
Libnah . . . . Jer. 52:1

Hanameel—*God has pitied*

Cousin of Jeremiah the
prophet . . . . Jer. 32:7

Hanan—*merciful*

1. One of David's mighty
   men. . . . . 1 Chr. 11:26, 43
2. Benjamite . . . . . 1 Chr. 8:23, 25
3. Descendant of
   Jonathan. . . . . . . 1 Chr. 8:38
4. Prophet. . . . . Jer. 35:4
5. Head of Temple
   servants. . . . . . . Ezra 2:46
6. Explained
   Law. . . . . Neh. 8:7
7. Nehemiah's assistant
   treasurer. . . . . . . Neh. 13:13
8, 9. Signers of the
   covenant. . . . . . Neh. 10:22, 26

Hananeel—*God has been gracious*

Tower at
Jerusalem . . . . Jer. 31:38

Hanani—*gracious*

1. Father of Jehu the
   prophet . . . . 1 Kin. 16:1, 7
   Rebukes Asa; confined to
   prison. . . . . 2 Chr. 16:7-10
2. Son of Heman; head of Levitical
   course . . . . 1 Chr. 25:4, 25
3. Priest who divorced his foreign
   wife. . . . . Ezra 10:20
4. Nehemiah's brother; brings
   news concerning the
   Jews . . . . Neh. 1:2
   Becomes a governor of
   Jerusalem . . . . . Neh. 7:2
5. Levite
   musician . . . . . . Neh. 12:35, 36

Hananiah—*Yahweh has been gracious*

1. Benjamite
   chief. . . . . 1 Chr. 8:24, 25
2. Son of Heman; head of Levitical
   division . . . . . . 1 Chr. 25:4, 23
3. One of King Uzziah's
   captains. . . . . . . 2 Chr. 26:11

4. Father of
   Zedekiah. . . . . . Jer. 36:12
5. False prophet who contradicts
   Jeremiah. . . . . . Jer. 28:1-17
6. Ancestor of
   Irijah . . . . Jer. 37:13-15
7. Hebrew name of
   Shadrach . . . . . Dan. 1:6, 7, 11
8. Son of
   Zerubbabel. . . . 1 Chr. 3:19-21
   Perhaps the same as
   Joannas. . . . . . . Luke 3:27
9. Son of Bebai; divorced his
   foreign wife. . . Ezra 10:28
10. Postexilic
    workman . . . . . Neh. 3:8, 30
11. Postexilic
    priest . . . . Neh. 12:41
12. Postexilic chief; signs
    document . . . . . Neh. 10:23
13. Postexilic
    ruler . . . . Neh. 7:2
14. Priest of Joiakim's
    time . . . . Neh. 12:12

Hand

Mysterious. . . . . . . Dan. 5:1-6
Healing
withered . . . . Mark 3:1-3
Offending, to be cut
off. . . . . Matt. 18:8

Handbreadth—*a linear measurement*

Border of . . . . Ex. 37:12
Figurative of human
life . . . . Ps. 39:5

Handful

Of fine flour. . . . . Lev. 2:2–5:12
Of grain offering . . Num. 5:26
Of barley. . . . . Ezek. 13:19

Handkerchief

Touch of, brings
healing . . . . Acts 19:12
Placed on the
dead . . . . John 20:7

Handle—*to manage with the hands*

Hold . . . . 2 Chr. 25:5
Touch. . . . . Luke 24:39
Feel. . . . . Ps. 115:7

Handmaid—*female servant*

Examples of:

Hagar. . . . . Gen. 16:1

Zilpah ....Gen. 29:24
Bilhah ....Gen. 30:4

Hand of God

Expressive of:

Judgment ....Ex. 9:3
Chastening ....Job 19:21
Security ....John 10:29
Miracles ....Ex. 3:20
Providence ....Ps. 31:15
Provision ....Ps. 145:16
Protection ....Ps. 139:10
Punishment ......Ps. 75:8
Pleading ....Is. 65:2

Hands

Clapping—
in joy ....2 Kin. 11:12
Washing—
in innocency .....Matt. 27:24
Joining—
in agreement .....2 Kin. 10:15
Striking—
in suretyship .....Prov. 17:16-18
Striking—
in anger ....Num. 24:10
Under thigh—
in oaths ....Gen. 47:29, 31

Right hand, expressive of:

Honor ....Ps. 45:9
Power ....Ps. 110:1
Love ....Song 2:6
Oath ....Is. 62:8
Opposition ....Zech. 3:1
Self-denial ......Matt. 5:30
Fellowship ....Gal. 2:9

Hands, laying on of

A. *In the Old Testament:*
   Blessing a
   person ....Gen. 48:14, 20
   Transferring one's
   guilt ....Lev. 4:14, 15
   Setting apart for
   service ....Num. 8:10, 11
   Inaugurating a
   successor .....Num. 27:18-23

B. *In the New Testament:*
   Blessing ....Matt. 19:13-15
   Healing ....Matt. 9:18
   Ordaining
   deacons ....Acts 6:6
   Sending out mission-
   aries ....Acts 13:2, 3

Ordaining
officers ....1 Tim. 4:14
In bestowing the Holy
Spirit ....Acts 8:17, 18

Handwriting

Of a king,
changeable ......Dan. 6:8-27
Of God,
unchangeable ....Dan. 5:5-31

Hanes—*mercury*

Probably an Egyptian
city ....Is. 30:4

Hanging—*a form of punishment*

Absalom ....2 Sam. 18:9-17
Ahithophel ....2 Sam. 17:23
Judas ....Matt. 27:5
Chief baker ......Gen. 40:19, 22
King of Ai ....Josh. 8:29
Five Canaanite
kings ....Josh. 10:26, 27
Ishbosheth's
murderers ....2 Sam. 4:12
Bodies of Saul and
Jonathan ....2 Sam. 21:5-12
Law of ....Ezra 6:11
Haman ....Esth. 7:10
Haman's sons .....Esth. 9:14
Curse of ....Gal. 3:13
Saul's
descendants ......2 Sam. 21:8, 9
Jesus Christ ......John 19:17, 18, 31

Haniel—*God has been gracious*

Descendant of
Asher ....1 Chr. 7:30, 39

Hannah—*graciousness*

Favored wife of
Elkanah ....1 Sam. 1:5
Childless ....1 Sam. 1:5, 6
Provoked by
Peninnah ....1 Sam. 1:2, 6, 7
Wrongly accused by
Eli ....1 Sam. 1:14
Prayerful ....1 Sam. 1:10
Attentive to her
child ....1 Sam. 1:22
Fulfills her vows .1 Sam. 1:11-28
Magnifies God ....1 Sam. 2:1-10
Recognizes the Messiah ("his
anointed") ....1 Sam. 2:10
Model of Mary's
song ....Luke 1:46-54

Hannathon—*regarded with favor*

Town of
Zebulun..........Josh. 19:14

Hanniel—*God has been gracious*

Manassite
prince............Num. 34:23

Hanoch—*dedicated*

1. Descendant of ⎰Gen. 25:4
   Abraham.....⎱1 Chr. 1:33
2. Son of
   Reuben.......Gen. 46:9
3. Head of tribal
   family........Num. 26:5

Hanun—*favored*

1. King of
   Ammon.......2 Sam. 10:1
   Disgraces David's ambas-
   sadors........2 Sam. 10:2-5
   Is defeated by
   David.........2 Sam. 10:6-14
2, 3. Postexilic
   workmen.....Neh. 3:13, 30

Haphraim—*double pit*

Town of
Issachar.........Josh. 19:19

Happiness of the saints

A. *Is derived from:*
   Fear of God....Ps. 128:1, 2
   Trust in God...Prov. 16:20
   Obedience to
   God...........John 13:15, 17
   Wisdom's
   ways..........Prov. 3:13-18

B. *Examples of:*
   Israel..........Deut. 33:29
   Mary..........Luke 1:46-55
   Paul...........Acts 26:2

C. *In spite of:*
   Discipline......Job 5:17
   Suffering......1 Pet. 4:12-14
   Persecution....Matt. 5:10-12
   Lack...........Phil. 4:6, 7
   Trouble........2 Cor. 4:7-18

D. *Described as:*
   Blessed.......Matt. 5:3-12
   Filled.........Ps. 36:8
   In God alone..Ps. 73:25, 26

See Gladness; Joy

Happiness of the wicked

A. *Described as:*
   Short.........Job 20:5
   Uncertain......Luke 12:20
   Vain..........Eccl. 2:1, 2
   Limited to this
   life...........Luke 16:24, 25
   Under God's ⎰Job 15:20, 21
   judgment....⎱Ps. 73:12, 18-20

B. *Derived from:*
   Prominence....Job 21:7
        Ps. 37:35
   Prosperity.....Ps. 17:14
        Ps. 37:7
   Sensuality.....Is. 22:13

C. *Saints:*
   Sometimes
   stumble at....Ps. 73:2, 3
   Should not
   envy..........Ps. 37:1, 7
   Will see end...Ps. 73:17-20

Happizzez

Chief of a priestly
course............1 Chr. 24:15

Hara—*hill*

Place in Assyria where captive
Israelites
settled............1 Chr. 5:26

Haradah—*fear*

Israelite
encampment.....Num. 33:24

Haran—*mountainous*

1. Abraham's younger
   brother........Gen. 11:26-31
2. Gershonite
   Levite.........1 Chr. 23:9
3. Son of Caleb...1 Chr. 2:46
4. City of Mesopo-
   tamia.........Gen. 11:31
   Abraham
   lives in.......Acts 7:2, 4
   Abraham
   leaves........Gen. 12:4, 5
   Jacob
   flees to.......Gen. 27:43
   Jacob
   dwells at......Gen. 29:4-35
   Center of ⎰Gen. 35:2
   idolatry......⎱2 Kin. 19:12

Hararite—*mountaineer*

Applied to
David's mighty ⎰2 Sam. 23:11,
men............. ⎱33
⎱1 Chr. 11:34, 35

Harass, harassed

Used of:

Temptations ......Num. 25:18
King ....Acts 12:1
Enemies ....Judg. 10:8

Harbona—*bald man*

Chamberlain of
Ahasuerus........Esth. 1:10
Same as
Harbonah ....Esth. 7:9

Harbor—*a sheltered bay*

Unacceptable .....Acts 27:12

Hard labor

A. *Spiritual:*
Subduing
flesh ....1 Cor. 9:24-27
Striving against
sin.............Heb. 12:4
Reaching
goal............Phil. 3:11-14

B. *Physical:*
Jacob..........Gen. 31:40-42
Israelites ......Ex. 1:11-14
Gibeonites ....Josh. 9:3-27
Samson........Judg. 16:20, 21

Hardness of heart

A. *Causes of:*
God ....Rom. 9:18
Man...........Job 9:4
Unbelief ......John 12:40
Sin ....Heb. 3:13

B. *Examples of:*
Pharaoh ....Ex. 4:21
Zedekiah ......2 Chr. 36:11-13
Israel.........Ezek. 3:7
Nebuchad-
nezzar........Dan. 5:20
Jews..........Mark 3:5
Believers......Mark 6:52

C. *Warnings against:*
Recognized by
Egyptians .....1 Sam. 6:6
Unheeded by
Israel ....Jer. 5:3
Lamented by the
prophets ......Is. 63:17

Addressed to ⎰Heb. 3:8-15
Christians....⎱Heb. 4:7

Harem—*group of females associated
with one man*

Esther a member of King
Ahasuerus' ....Esth. 2:8-14

Hareph—*plucking*

Son of Caleb .....1 Chr. 2:50, 51

Harhaiah—*Yahweh is protecting*

Father of Uzziel...Neh. 3:8

Harhas—*splendor*

Grandfather of
Shallum ....2 Kin. 22:14

Harhur—*fever*

Ancestor of returning Temple
servants..........Ezra 2:43, 51

Harim—*consecrated to God*

1. Descendant of
Aaron.........1 Chr. 24:1, 6, 8
2. Postexilic
leader.........Ezra 2:32, 39
3. Father of
Malchijah.....Neh. 3:11
4. Signer of the
covenant......Neh. 10:1, 5
5. Signer of the
covenant......Neh. 10:1, 27
6. Family house of
priests ....Neh. 12:12, 15
7. Descendants of, divorced
foreign
wives ....Ezra 10:19, 21

Hariph—*autumn rain*

Family of
returnees........Neh. 7:24
Signers of
covenant........Neh. 10:19
Same as Jorah ....Ezra 2:18

Harlot—*a prostitute*

A. *Characteristics of:*
Shameless .....Jer. 3:3
Painted ......Ezek. 23:30, 40
Enticing ......Prov. 9:14-18
Roaming
streets ......Prov. 7:12
Expensive .....Prov. 29:3

B. *Evils of:*
Profanes God's
name ....Amos 2:7

Connected with
idolatry . . . . Ex. 34:15, 16
Brings spiritual
error . . . . Hos. 4:10-19
Cause of
divorce . . . . Jer. 3:8, 14

C. *Prohibitions concerning:*
Forbidden in
Israel . . . . Lev. 19:29
Priests not to
marry . . . . Lev. 21:1, 7, 14
To be
shamed . . . . . . Prov. 5:3-20
Punishment . . . . Lev. 21:9

D. *Examples of:*
Tamar . . . . Gen. 38:13-20
Rahab . . . . Josh. 2:1-21
Jephthah's
mother . . . . Judg. 11:1
Samson's . . . . . Judg. 16:1
Hosea's wife . . . Hos. 1:2
The great . . . . . Rev. 17:1-18

E. *Figurative of:*
Tyre . . . . Is. 23:15, 17
Israel . . . . Is. 1:21
Spiritual ⎧ Is. 57:7-9
adultery . . . . ⎨ Rev. 17:1-18

See Adultery

Harmony—*agreement, co-operation*

Husband ⎧ 1 Cor. 7:3-6
and ⎨ Eph. 5:22-23
wife . . . . ⎩ Col. 3:18, 19
Christians . . . . . . John 13:34, 35
Rom. 15:5-7
Christians and ⎧ Rom. 12:16-18
unbelievers . . . . . ⎨ Heb. 12:14

Harnepher

Asherite . . . . 1 Chr. 7:36

Harness—*to equip*

Horses . . . . Jer. 46:4

Harod—*fountain of trembling*

Well near Gideon's
camp . . . . Judg. 7:1

Harodite

Inhabitant of
Harod . . . . 2 Sam. 23:25
Same as
Harorite . . . . 1 Chr. 11:27

Haroeh—*the seer*

Judahite . . . . 1 Chr. 2:50, 52
Called Reaiah . . . . 1 Chr. 4:2

Harosheth Hagoyim—*carving of the nations*

Residence of
Sisera . . . . Judg. 4:2, 13, 16

Harp—*a stringed musical instrument*

Used by:

The wicked . . . . . Is. 5:11, 12
David . . . . 1 Sam. 16:16, 23
Prophets . . . . 1 Sam. 10:5
Temple
orchestra . . . . 1 Chr. 16:5
Temple
worshipers . . . . . . Ps. 33:2
Celebrators . . . . . . 2 Chr. 20:27, 28
Jewish captives . . Ps. 137:2
Worshipers in
heaven . . . . Rev. 5:8

Harpoon—*a barbed spear for hunting large fish*

Used against
Leviathan . . . . Job 41:7

Harsha—*enchanter*

Head of Temple ⎧ Ezra 2:43, 52
servants . . . . ⎨ Neh. 7:46, 54

Harum—*exalted*

Judahite . . . . 1 Chr. 4:8

Harumaph—*flat-nosed*

Father of
Jedaiah . . . . Neh. 3:10

Haruphite

Designation of
Shephatiah . . . . . . 1 Chr. 12:5
Member of Hariph's
family . . . . Neh. 7:24

Haruz—*active*

Father-in-law of King
Manasseh . . . . 2 Kin. 21:19

Harvest—*the time when the crops are ripe*

A. *Occasion of:*
Great joy . . . . . . Is. 9:3
Bringing the first
fruits . . . . Lev. 23:10
Remembering the
poor . . . . Lev. 19:9, 10

B. *Figuratively of:*
Seasons of
grace . . . . Jer. 8:20

Judgment......Jer. 51:33
God's wrath ...Rev. 14:15
Gospel opportunities ....Matt. 9:37, 38
World's end....Matt. 13:30, 39
Measure of fruitfulness....2 Cor. 9:6

C. *Promises concerning:*
To continue ...Gen. 8:22
Rain.........Jer. 5:24
Patience......James 5:7

D. *Failure caused by:*
Drought.......Amos 4:7
Locusts........Joel 1:4
Sin ....Is. 17:4-12

Hasadiah—*Yahweh has been gracious*

Son of
Zerubbabel.......1 Chr. 3:20

Hashabiah—*Yahweh has imputed*

1. Merarite
   Levite.........1 Chr. 6:44, 45
   Perhaps the same
   as in ....1 Chr. 9:14
2. Levite
   musician......1 Chr. 25:3, 19
3. Kohathite
   Levite.........1 Chr. 26:30
4. Levite ruler....1 Chr. 27:17
5. Chief Levite during Josiah's
   reign.........2 Chr. 35:9
6. Postexilic
   Levite.........Ezra 8:19, 24
   Probably the
   same in ....Neh. 10:11
7. Postexilic
   ruler ....Neh. 3:17
8. Descendant of
   Asaph.........Neh. 11:22
9. Priest in the time of
   Joiakim ....Neh. 12:21

Hashabnah—*covenant sealer*

Signed covenant ..Neh. 10:25

Hashabniah—*Yahweh has regarded me*

1. Father of
   Hattush ......Neh. 3:10
2. Postexilic
   Levite.........Neh. 9:5

Probably the same as Hashabiah 6.

Hashbadana—*thoughtful judge*

Assistant to
Ezra..............Neh. 8:4

Hashem—*shining*

Father of David's
warriors..........1 Chr. 11:34
Also called
Jashen ....2 Sam. 23:32

Hashmonah—*fertility*

Israelite
encampment .....Num. 33:29

Hashub, Hasshub—*thoughtful*

1. Postexilic
   workman .....Neh. 3:11
2. Signer of the
   covenant......Neh. 10:23
3. Levite chief....Neh. 11:15

Hashubah—*esteemed*

Son of
Zerubbabel.......1 Chr. 3:19, 20

Hashum—*opulent*

Founder of postexilic
family...........Ezra 2:19
Assists Ezra and signs
document ....Neh. 8:4
Neh. 10:18

Hasrah—*want*

Grandfather of
Shallum ....2 Chr. 34:22
Called Harhas.....2 Kin. 22:14

Hassenaah—*thorny*

Father of postexilic
workmen........Neh. 3:3
Same as ⎧Ezra 2:35
Senaah ....⎩Neh. 7:38

Hassenuah—*thorny*

Benjamite
family...........1 Chr. 9:7
Called Senuah ....Neh. 11:7-9

Haste—*to do something quickly*

Prompted by ⎧2 Chr. 35:21
good ....⎩Luke 19:5, 6
Prompted by ⎧Prov. 14:29
evil.............⎩Prov. 28:20

Hasupha—*naked*

Head of Temple ⎧Ezra 2:43
servants........⎩Neh. 7:46

Hate—*to dislike something with strong feeling*

A. *Meanings of:*
React as God
does .... Rev. 2:6
Twist moral
judgments .... Prov. 8:36
Esteem of less
value .... John 12:25
Make a vital
distinction .... Luke 14:26
Despise .... Is. 1:14

B. *Causes of:*
Parental
favoritism..... Gen. 37:4, 5
Rape .... 2 Sam. 13:14, 15,
22
Failure to
please......... 1 Kin. 22:8
God's
purpose ...... Ps. 105:25
Belonging to
Christ........ Matt. 24:9, 10
Evil nature .... John 3:20

C. *Objects of:*
God's people... Gen. 26:27
God .... Ex. 20:5
Christ .... John 15:25
Light .... John 3:20
Evil men...... Ps. 26:5
Wickedness.... Ps. 45:7

D. *Toward Christians, sign of their:*
Discipleship... Matt. 24:9
Election ...... John 15:19
Regen-
eration........ 1 John 3:13-15

Hathach—*chamberlain*

Esther's
attendant........ Esth. 4:5-10

Hathath—*terror*

Son of Othniel .... 1 Chr. 4:13

Hatipha—*captive*

Head of Temple
servants.......... Ezra 2:43, 54

Hatita—*dug up*

Father of ⎰Ezra 2:42
porters ....⎱Neh. 7:45

Hattil—*vacillating*

Ancestor of
Solomon's ⎰Ezra 2:55, 57
servants..........⎱Neh. 7:57-59

Hattush—*assembled*

1. Descendant of
David .... Ezra 8:2

2. Man of
Judah......... 1 Chr. 3:22
Probably the same as 1
3. Priest returning with
Zerubbabel.... Neh. 12:1, 2
4. Postexilic
workman ..... Neh. 3:10
5. Priest who signs
covenant...... Neh. 10:1, 4

Haughtiness—*an arrogant spirit*

Precedes a fall .... Prov. 16:18
To be brought
low............... Is. 2:11, 17
Guilt of ⎰Ezek. 16:50
Jerusalem for....⎱Zeph. 3:11

Hauran—*hollow land*

District southeast of Mt.
Hermon........ Ezek. 47:16

Haven—*a sheltered area*

Zebulun's assets.. Gen. 49:13
Desired .... Ps. 107:30
Near Lasea........ Acts 27:8

Havilah—*circle*

1. Son of Cush .. Gen. 10:7
2. Son of
Joktan........ Gen. 10:29
3. District of
Arabia .... Gen. 2:11
Limit of Ishmaelite
territory ...... Gen. 25:18
Saul defeated
Amalekites.... 1 Sam. 15:7

Havoth Jair—*tent villages of Jair*

Villages of Jordan in
Gilead........... Num. 32:40, 41
Or in Bashan.... Deut. 3:13, 14
Taken by Jair ..... Num. 32:41

Hawk—*a plundering bird*

Ceremonially
unclean .... Lev. 11:16
Migratory........ Job 39:26

Hay—*food for cattle*

Build with........ 1 Cor. 3:12
Rendered
"leeks"........... Num. 11:5

Hazael—*God has seen*

King over Syria .. 1 Kin. 19:15-17
Defeats Joram of
Israel............ 2 Kin. 8:25-29
Defeats Jehu ...... 2 Kin. 10:31, 32

Oppresses Israel...2 Kin. 13:3-7, 22
His son defeated ..2 Kin. 13:24, 25

Hazaiah—*Yahweh has seen*

Man of Judah .....Neh. 11:5

Hazar Addar—*village of Addar*

Place in Canaan...Num. 34:4

Hazar Enan—*village of springs*

Village of north
Palestine ....Num. 34:9, 10

Hazar Gaddah—*village of good fortune*

Town on the border of
Judah ....Josh. 15:21, 27

Hazar Hatticon—*the middle village*

Town on the border of
Hauran..........Ezek. 47:16

Hazarmaveth—*village of death*

Descendants of
Joktan ....Gen. 10:26

Hazar Shual—*fox village*

Town in south
Judah ....Josh. 15:21, 28
Assigned to
Simeon..........Josh. 19:1, 3
Reoccupied after
exile.............Neh. 11:27

Hazar Susah—*village of a mare*

Simeonite
village...........Josh. 19:5

Hazelelponi—*give shade, thou who
turnest toward me*

Female descendant of
Judah ....1 Chr. 4:3

Hazeroth—*courts*

Israelite camp.....Num. 33:17
Scene of sedition of Miriam and
Aaron............Num. 12:1-16

Hazezon Tamar—*pruning of the palm*

Dwelling of
Amorites ....Gen. 14:7
Also called En
Gedi.............2 Chr. 20:2

Haziel—*God sees*

Gershonite
Levite ....1 Chr. 23:9

Hazo—*seer*

Son of Nahor .....Gen. 22:22, 23

Hazor—*enclosure*

1. Royal Canaanite city destroyed
   by Joshua.....Josh. 11:1-13
   Rebuilt and assigned to
   Naphtali ......Josh. 19:32, 36
   Army of, defeated by Deborah
   and Barak.....Judg. 4:1-24
   Fortified by
   Solomon ......1 Kin. 9:15
   Captured by Tiglath-
   Pileser ....2 Kin. 15:29
2. Town in south
   Judah.........Josh. 15:21, 25
3. Town of south
   Judah.........Josh. 15:21, 23
4. Town of
   Benjamin .....Neh. 11:31, 33
5. Region in the Arabian
   desert........Jer. 49:28-33

He

Fifth letter of Hebrew
alphabet..........Ps. 119:33-40

Head

A. *Attitudes expressed by:*
   Covered, in
   grief ....2 Sam. 15:30
   Covered, in
   subjection.....1 Cor. 11:5
   Hand upon, in
   sorrow ....2 Sam. 13:19
   Dust upon, in
   dismay........Josh. 7:6
   Uncovered, in
   leprosy........Lev. 13:45
   Wagging, in
   derision ....Matt. 27:39
   Anointed, in
   dedication.....Matt. 6:17

See Hands, laying on of

B. *Figurative of:*
   God ....1 Cor. 11:3
   Christ ....Eph. 1:22
   Husband.......1 Cor. 11:3, 7
   Protection .....Ps. 140:7
   Judgment......Is. 15:2
   Confidence ....Luke 21:28
   Pride ....Ps. 83:2
   Exaltation .....Ps. 27:6
   Joy and
   prosperity ....Ps. 23:5

Headdresses

Part of feminine
attire.............Is. 3:20

Head of the Church—*position of preeminence in the Church*

Christ.............Eph. 1:22
Eph. 5:23
Col. 1:18
Prophesied.......Dan. 7:13, 14

Headship—*office of authority,
responsibility*

A. *Of Christ:*
Over all
things.........Eph. 4:15
Over man.....1 Cor. 11:3
Of Church....Eph. 5:23
Col. 1:18
Of the Corner {Acts 4:11
Stone {1 Pet. 2:7, 8

B. *Of the Father:*
Over Christ...1 Cor. 11:3
Gives {John 5:26, 27
authority.....{1 Cor. 15:25-28

C. *Of Man:*
Of human
race...........Rom. 5:12, 18, 21
Over woman..1 Cor. 11:3
Eph. 5:23

Heads of Grain

Seen in Pharaoh's
dream.............Gen. 41:5-7
Regulations
concerning.......Lev. 2:14
Ruth gleans.......Ruth 2:2
Christ's disciples
pluck.............Matt. 12:1

Healing—*restoration of health*

A. *Resulting from:*
Intercession.....Num. 12:10-15
Repentance....1 Kin. 13:1-6
Prayer.........James 5:14, 15
Faith.........Matt. 9:20-22
John 4:46-53
God's Word....Ps. 107:20

B. *Power of:*
Belongs to
God..........Gen. 20:17, 18
Possessed by {Matt. 4:24
Jesus.........{Matt. 8:16
Given to
apostles......Matt. 10:1-8
Given as a
gift ....1 Cor. 12:9

Eternal in
heaven........Rev. 22:2

See Diseases; Sickness

Healing, spiritual

A. *Source of:*
Only in God ...Jer. 17:14
Through
Christ.........Is. 53:5
Through the
Gospel ....Ezek. 47:8-11

B. *Provided for:*
Heartbroken...Ps. 147:3
Repentant .....2 Chr. 7:14
Egyptians......Is. 19:22-25
Faithful........Mal. 4:2

C. *Necessary because of man's:*
Sin ....Ps. 41:4
Backsliding ....Jer. 3:22
Spiritual
sickness.......Is. 6:10

Health—*the body freed from disease*

A. *Factors conducive to:*
Exercise ......1 Tim. 4:8
Food ....Acts 27:34
Temperance ...Jer. 35:5-8
Obedience ....Prov. 4:20-22
Cheerfulness..Prov. 17:22
God's will.....John 9:1-3

B. *Factors destructive of:*
Moral
looseness......Prov. 7:22-27
Wickedness...Ps. 55:23
Disease ....1 Sam. 5:6-12
Injury ....Luke 10:30
Debauchery....Titus 1:12

Heap of stones—*a monument of stones*

Symbolic of:
Shameful acts..Josh. 7:20-26
Covenant ......Gen. 31:46-52

Hearers—*those who hear*

A. *Element necessary in:*
Atten-
tiveness.......Neh. 8:1-3
Belief..........Rom. 10:14
Conviction.....Acts 2:37
Discrim-
ination ....Luke 8:18

B. *Reactions of:*
Responsive-
ness...........2 Sam. 7:17-29
Repentance....2 Sam. 12:12, 13
Rebellion .....Ezek. 33:30-33

Retreat . . . . John 6:60-66
Resistance . . . . . Acts 7:51-54
Rejoicing . . . . . . Acts 13:48
Rejection . . . . . . Acts 28:23-29
Research . . . . . . Acts 17:11

Heart

A. *Seat of:*
Adultery . . . . . . Matt. 5:28
Concern . . . . . . Jer. 31:20
Desire . . . . Rom. 10:1
Doubt . . . . Mark 11:23
Evil . . . . Ps. 28:3
Fear . . . . Is. 35:4
Hatred . . . . Lev. 19:17
Love . . . . Mark 12:30, 33
Lust . . . . Rom. 1:24
Meditation . . . . . Ps. 19:14
Obedience . . . . . Rom. 6:17
Pride . . . . Prov. 16:5
Purpose . . . . . . 2 Cor. 9:7
Reason . . . . Mark 2:8
Rebellion . . . . . . Jer. 5:23
Rejoicing . . . . . . Acts 2:26
Sorrow . . . . John 14:1
Suffering . . . . . . Ps. 22:14
Thought . . . . . . Matt. 9:4

B. *Of the wicked, described as:*
Blind . . . . Eph. 4:18
Darkened . . . . . . Rom. 1:21
Covetous . . . . . . 2 Pet. 2:14
Full of evil . . . . . Gen. 6:5
Unrepentant . . . . Rom. 2:5
Lustful . . . . Prov. 6:25
Proud . . . . Jer. 49:16
Rebellious . . . . . Jer. 5:23
Uncir-
cumcised . . . . . Acts 7:51

C. *God's action upon:*
Knows . . . . Ps. 44:21
Searches . . . . . . 1 Chr. 28:9
Enlightens . . . . . 2 Cor. 4:6
Opens . . . . Acts 16:14
Recreates . . . . . Ezek. 11:19
Tests . . . . Jer. 12:3
Strengthens . . . . Ps. 27:14
Establishes . . . . 1 Thess. 3:13

D. *Regenerate's, described as:*
Circumcised . . . Rom. 2:29
Contrite . . . . . . Ps. 51:17
Enlarged . . . . . . Ps. 119:32
Enlightened . . . . 2 Cor. 4:6
Joyful in
God . . . . 1 Sam. 2:1
Meditative . . . . . Ps. 4:4
Perfect . . . . Ps. 101:2
Pure . . . . Ps. 73:1
                     Matt. 5:8

Prayerful . . . . . . 1 Sam. 1:12, 13
Glad and
sincere . . . . Acts 2:46
Steadfast . . . . . Ps. 57:7
Tender . . . . 2 Kin. 22:19
Treasury of
good . . . . Matt. 12:35
Wise . . . . Prov. 10:8

E. *Regenerate's, responses of:*
Believe with . . . . Rom. 10:10
Keep with
diligence . . . . . Prov. 4:23
Love God
with all . . . . . . Matt. 22:37
Sanctify God
in . . . . 1 Pet. 3:15
Serve God
with all . . . . . . Deut. 26:16
Walk before God
with all . . . . . . 1 Kin. 2:4
Trust the Lord
with all . . . . . . Prov. 3:5
Regard not iniquity
in . . . . Ps. 66:18
Do God's will
from . . . . Eph. 6:6

Hearth—*a place for fire*

Bed of live   ⎰ Is. 30:14
coals . . . . ⎱ Ps. 102:3

Heartlessness—*without moral feeling;
cruelty*

A. *Among unbelievers:*
Philistines, toward
Samson . . . . . . Judg. 16:21
Saul, toward
David . . . . 1 Sam. 18:25
Nabal, toward
David . . . . 1 Sam. 25:4-12
Haman, toward
Jews . . . . Esth. 8-10
Levite, toward a certain
man . . . . Luke 10:30-32

B. *Among professing believers:*
Laban, toward
Jacob . . . . Gen. 31:7, 36-42
Jacob's sons, toward
Joseph . . . . . . Gen. 37:18-35
David, toward
Uriah . . . . 2 Sam. 11:9-27

Heat, hot

Figurative of:

God's wrath . . . . . . Deut. 9:19
Man's anger . . . . . . Deut. 19:6
Determination . . . . Gen. 31:36

Zeal . . . . .Ps. 39:3
Persecution . . . . . . .Matt. 13:6, 21
Heavy toil. . . . . . . .Matt. 20:12
Real faith . . . . .Rev. 3:15

Heathen (see Gentiles)

Heave offering

A. *Consisted of:*
Firstfruits. . . . . . .Num. 15:18-21
Tenth of all
tithes . . . . .Num. 18:21-28

B. *Part of:*
All gifts. . . . . . .Num. 18:29
Spoils. . . . . .Num. 31:26-47
Offerings . . . . . . .Ex. 29:27
Lev. 7:14, 32

C. *Requirements concerning:*
To be the
best. . . . . .Num. 18:29
Brought to God's
house . . . . .Deut. 12:5, 6
Given to
priests . . . . . . .Ex. 29:27, 28
Sanctified the whole
offering . . . . . .Num. 18:27-32
Eaten in a clean
place. . . . . .Lev. 10:12-15

Heaven—*the place of everlasting bliss*

A. *Inhabitants of:*
God . . . . .1 Kin. 8:30
Christ . . . . .Heb. 9:12, 24
Holy Spirit. . . . .Ps. 139:7, 8
Angels. . . . . .Matt. 18:10
Just men . . . . . .Heb. 12:22, 23

B. *Things lacking in:*
Marriage. . . . . . .Matt. 22:30
Death . . . . .Luke 20:36
Flesh and
blood . . . . .1 Cor. 15:50
Imper-
ishable. . . . . . .1 Cor. 15:42, 50
Sorrow . . . . .Rev. 7:17
Pain . . . . .Rev. 21:4
Curse. . . . . .Rev. 22:3
Night. . . . . .Rev. 22:5
Wicked
people . . . . . . .Rev. 22:15
End. . . . . .Matt. 25:46
Rev. 22:5

C. *Positive characteristics of:*
Joy . . . . .Luke 15:7, 10
Rest . . . . .Rev. 14:13
Peace. . . . . .Luke 16:19-25
Righ-
teousness . . . . .2 Pet. 3:13

Service . . . . .Rev. 7:15
Reward. . . . . .Matt. 5:11, 12
Inheritance . . . .1 Pet. 1:4
Glory. . . . . .Rom. 8:17, 18

D. *Entrance into, for:*
Righteous . . . . .Matt. 5:20
Changed. . . . . . .1 Cor. 15:51
Saved. . . . . .John 3:5, 18, 21
Called . . . . .2 Pet. 1:10, 11
Overcomers. . . .Rev. 2:7, 10, 11
Those
recorded . . . . .Luke 10:20
Obedient. . . . . .Rev. 22:14
Holy. . . . . .Rev. 19:8

E. *Believer's present attitude
toward:*
Given
foretaste of . . .Acts 7:55, 56
Earnestly
desires . . . . . . .2 Cor. 5:2, 8
Looks for . . . . . .2 Pet. 3:12
Considers "far better" than
now. . . . . .Phil. 1:23
Puts treasure
there. . . . . .Luke 12:33

F. *Described as:*
House . . . . .John 14:2
Kingdom . . . . . .Matt. 25:34
Abraham's
bosom . . . . . . .Luke 16:22, 23
Paradise . . . . . .2 Cor. 12:2, 4
Better
country . . . . . .Heb. 11:10, 16
Holy city . . . . .Rev. 21:2, 10-27
Rev. 22:1-5

Heavens, natural

A. *Facts regarding:*
Created by
God. . . . . .Gen. 1:1
Stretched   {Is. 42:5
out. . . . .{Jer. 10:12
Will be   {Heb. 1:10-12
destroyed . . . .{2 Pet. 3:10
New heavens   {Is. 65:17
to follow . . . . .{2 Pet. 3:13

B. *Purposes of:*
To declare God's
glory. . . . . .Ps. 19:1
To declare God's righ-
teousness . . . . .Ps. 50:6
To manifest God's
wisdom . . . . . .Prov. 8:27

Heaviness—*a spirit of grief or anxiety*

Unrelieved by
mirth. . . . . .Prov. 14:13

God's children
experience........Phil. 2:26
Needed
exchange........James 4:9
Experienced by
Christ............Ps. 69:20, 21
Remedy for.......Prov. 12:25

Heavy—*oppressive*

A. *Used literally of:*
Eli's weight....1 Sam. 4:18
Absalom's
hair...........2 Sam. 14:26
Stone..........Prov. 27:3

B. *Used figuratively of:*
Fatigue........Matt. 26:43
Burdens........2 Chr. 10:11, 14
Sins...........Is. 24:20
God's
judgments....1 Sam. 5:6, 11

Heber, Eber—*associate*

1. Son of
Beriah........Gen. 46:17
Descendants called
Heberites.....Num. 26:45
2. Husband of Jael, the slayer of
Sisera........Judg. 4:11-24
3. Descendant of
Ezra..........1 Chr. 4:17, 18
4. Gadite chief...1 Chr. 5:11, 13
5. Benjamite.....1 Chr. 8:17

Hebrew—*one from the other side*

Applied to:

Abram...........Gen. 14:13
Israelites..........1 Sam. 4:6, 9
Jews..............Acts 6:1
Paul, a sincere....Phil. 3:5

Hebrew language

Spoken by
Rabshakeh.......2 Kin. 18:26, 28
Alphabet of, in
divisions........Ps. 119
Language of {John 19:13, 20
Christ's time....{Acts 21:40

See Aramaic

Hebrews, Epistle of the—*a book of the New Testament*

Christ greater than the
angels...........Heb. 1:3, 4
Christ of the order of
Melchizedek......Heb. 4:14–5:10

The new
covenant.........Heb. 8:1–10:18
The life of faith...Heb. 10:19–13:17

Hebron—*alliance*

1. Ancient town in
Judah.........Num. 13:22
Originally called Kirjath
Arba..........Gen. 23:2
Abram dwells
here..........Gen. 13:18
Abraham buys cave
here..........Gen. 23:2-20
Isaac and Jacob sojourn
here..........Gen. 35:27
Visited by
spies.........Num. 13:21, 22
Defeated by
Joshua........Josh. 10:1-37
Caleb expels Anakim
from..........Josh. 14:12-15
Assigned to
Levites.......Josh. 21:10-13
City of
refuge........Josh. 20:5-7
David's original
capital.......2 Sam. 2:1-3, 11
Birthplace of David's
sons..........2 Sam. 3:2
Abner's death
here..........2 Sam. 4:1
Absalom's rebellion
here..........2 Sam. 15:7-10
Fortified by
Rehoboam.....2 Chr. 11:10
2. Son of
Kohath........Ex. 6:18
Descendants called
Hebronites....Num. 3:19, 27
3. Descendant of
Caleb.........1 Chr. 2:42, 43

Hebronites (see Hebron 3)

Hedge—*a fence or barrier*

Illustrative of:

God's protection..Job 1:10
Afflictions.........Job 19:8
Slothfulness.......Prov. 15:19
Removal of
protection.......Ps. 80:12

Heedfulness—*giving proper attention to something important*

A. *Objects of:*
God's command-
ments.........Josh. 22:5

Our ways......Ps. 39:1
False
  teachers ......Matt. 16:6
God's Word....2 Pet. 1:19

B. *Admonitions to Christians,*
  concerning:
Deception .....Matt. 24:4
Outward
  display........Matt. 6:1
Worldliness....Luke 21:34
Duty ....Acts 20:28-31
Foundation ....1 Cor. 3:10
Liberty ....1 Cor. 8:9
Security ....1 Cor. 10:12
Effec-
  tiveness.......Gal. 5:15
Ministry.......Col. 4:17
Fables ....1 Tim. 1:4
Unbelief ....Heb. 3:12

See Caution

Heel—*the back part of the human foot*

Used literally of:

Esau's.............Gen. 25:26

Used figuratively of:

Seed of the
  woman...........Gen. 3:15
Enemy of Dan ....Gen. 49:17
The wicked ....Job 18:5, 9
Friend of David ...Ps. 41:9

Hegai—*the sprinkler*

Eunuch under King
Ahasuerus........Esth. 2:3, 8, 15

Heifer—*a young cow*

A. *Ceremonial uses of:*
In a
  covenant......Gen. 15:9
In
  purification ...Num. 19:1-22

B. *Red heifer, ceremony*
  concerning:
Without spot ..Num. 19:2
Never yoked...Num. 19:2
Slaughtered and burned outside
  the camp....Num. 19:3-8
Ashes kept ....Num. 19:9, 10
Ashes, with water, used to
  purify........Num. 19:11-22
Significance
  of.............Heb. 9:13, 14

C. *Figurative of:*
Improper
  advantage.....Judg. 14:18

Content-
  ment..........Jer. 50:11

Heirs, natural

A. *Persons and property involved:*
Firstborn ......Deut. 21:15-17
Sons of
  concubines....Gen. 21:10
Daughters .....Num. 27:1-11
Widows........Ruth 3:12, 13
Order of
  succession ....Num. 27:8-11

B. *Exceptions:*
Father could make concubines'
  sons heirs....Gen. 49:1, 12-27
Daughters receive marriage
  portion....Gen. 29:24, 29
Daughters sometimes share
  with sons .....Job 42:15
Daughters receive, if no
  sons ....Num. 27:8

C. *Examples of heirship changes*
  by divine election:
Ishmael to
  Isaac.........Gen. 21:10, 11
Esau to   {Gen. 27:35-37
  Jacob .... {Rom. 9:13
Reuben to
  Joseph ....Gen. 49:22-26
Adonijah to
  Solomon ......1 Kin. 1:11-14

See Birthright; Inheritance, earthly

Heirs, spiritual

A. *Of Christ:*
Recognized ....Matt. 21:38
Appointed .....Heb. 1:2

B. *Of Christians, means of:*
By promise ....Gal. 3:29
Through
  Christ........Gal. 4:7
Through
  faith ....Rom. 4:13, 14
By grace.......Gal. 4:21-31

C. *Of Christians, receiving:*
Grace..........1 Pet. 3:7
Promise........Heb. 11:9
Kingdom ......James 2:5
Salvation ......Heb. 1:14
Righ-
  teousness .....Heb. 11:7
Eternal life ....Titus 3:7

See Inheritance, spiritual

Helah—*ornament*

One of Asher's
wives............1 Chr. 4:5, 7

Helam—*fortress*

Place between Damascus and
Hamath where David defeated
Syrians..........2 Sam. 10:16-19

Helbah—*fertility*

City of Asher .....Judg. 1:31

Helbon—*fertile*

City north of
Damascus........Ezek. 27:18

Heldai—*worldly*

1. One of David's
captains........1 Chr. 27:15
Probably same as Heled and
Heleb..........1 Chr. 11:30
2. Exile from Babylon bearing
gifts ....Zech. 6:10, 11
Called Helem ..Zech. 6:14

Helek—*portion*

Son of Gilead .....Num. 26:30
Founder of a
family............Josh. 17:2

Helem—*strength*

1. Asherite ....1 Chr. 7:34, 35
2. Same as
Heldai ....Zech. 6:10, 11
Called
Hotham.......1 Chr. 7:32

Heleph—*strong*

Frontier town of
Naphtali.........Josh. 19:32, 33

Helez—*strong*

1. One of David's
captains.......2 Sam. 23:26
2. Judahite ......1 Chr. 2:39

Heli—*climbing*

Father of Joseph, husband of
Mary.............Luke 3:23

Helkai—*portion*

Postexilic priest ...Neh. 12:15

Helkath—*portion, field*

Frontier town of
Asher ....Josh. 19:24, 25

Assigned to
Levites...........Josh. 21:31
Same as Hukok ...1 Chr. 6:75

Hell—*the place of eternal torment*

A. *Described as:*
Everlasting
fire............Matt. 25:41
Everlasting
punishment ...Matt. 25:46
Outer
darkness......Matt. 8:12
Everlasting
destruction...2 Thess. 1:9
Lake of fire....Rev. 19:20

B. *Prepared for:*
Devil and his
angels.........Matt. 25:41
Wicked........Rev. 21:8
Disobedient....Rom. 2:8, 9
Fallen angels ..2 Pet. 2:4
Beast and the false
prophet ....Rev. 19:20
Worshipers of the
beast..........Rev. 14:11
Rejectors of the
Gospel ....Matt. 10:15

C. *Punishment of, described as:*
Bodily ....Matt. 5:29, 30
In the soul.....Matt. 10:28
With degrees ..Matt. 23:14

Hellenists

Greek-speaking
Jews ....Acts 6:1
Hostile to Paul ....Acts 9:29
Gospel preached
to ....Acts 11:20

Helmet—*armor for the head*

Used figuratively of salvation:

Prepared ....Is. 59:17
Provided..........Eph. 6:17
Promised..........1 Thess. 5:8

Helon—*strong*

Father of Eliab ....Num. 1:9

Helper—*one who assists another*

A. *Used of:*
God ....Heb. 13:6
Christ ....Heb. 4:15, 16
Holy Spirit.....Rom. 8:26
Angels.........Dan. 10:13
Woman........Gen. 2:18, 20
Christians .....Acts 16:9

B. *As the Holy Spirit:*

Abides with
believers ......John 14:16
Teaches ......John 14:26
Testifies of
Christ.........John 15:26
Convicts.......John 16:7-11
Guides into
truth..........John 16:13
Glorifies
Christ.........John 16:14, 15

Helps—*the acts of bearing another's burden*

A gift to the
Church...........1 Cor. 12:28
Christians
admonished to....1 Thess. 5:14
Elders
admonished to....Acts 20:28, 35

Hemam—*raging*

Son of Lotan......Gen. 36:22
Same as Homam ..1 Chr. 1:39

Heman—*faithful*

1. Famous wise
   man ....1 Kin. 4:31
   Judahite.......1 Chr. 2:6
   Composer of a
   Psalm.........Ps. 88 (Title)
2. Musician under David;
   grandson of
   Samuel ....1 Chr. 6:33
   Appointed as chief
   singer.........1 Chr. 15:16, 17
   Man of spiritual
   insight ....1 Chr. 25:5

Hemdan—*pleasant*

Descendant of
Seir ....Gen. 36:26
Same as
Hamran ....1 Chr. 1:41

Hemorrhage—*a flow of blood*

Healed...........Luke 8:43, 44
Woman suffered
from, for 12 {Matt. 9:20
years............{Mark 5:25

Hen—*favor*

1. Son of
   Zephaniah ....Zech. 6:14
2. Domestic
   fowl ....Matt. 23:37

Hena—*low land*

City captured by the
Assyrians.........2 Kin. 18:34

Henadad—*favor of Hadad*

Postexilic Levite ..Ezra 3:9
Sons of, help
Nehemiah ....Neh. 3:18, 24

Henna—*a fragrant shrub*

Illustrative of
beauty ....Song 1:14

Henoch

1. Same as
   Enoch.........1 Chr. 1:3
2. Same as
   Hanoch 1 .....1 Chr. 1:33

Hepher—*pit, well*

1. Town west of the
   Jordan ....Josh. 12:17
   Name applied to a
   district........1 Kin. 4:10
2. Founder of
   Hepherites ....Num. 26:30, 32
3. Son of Ashur ..1 Chr. 4:5, 6
4. One of David's
   guards ....1 Chr. 11:26, 36

Hephzibah—*my delight is in her*

Mother of King
Manasseh ....2 Kin. 21:1

Herald

Of Nebuchad-
nezzar............Dan. 3:3-6
Of Pharaoh ......Gen. 41:42, 43
Zion ....Is. 40:9

Herbs—*grass or leafy vegetables*

Bitter, used at
Passover........Ex. 12:8
Poisonous,
not fit ....2 Kin. 4:39, 40

Herdsman—*one who tends cattle*

Conflict among ...Gen. 13:7, 8

Heredity—*transmission of physical and mental traits*

A. *Factors involved:*
Likeness of
nature ....Gen. 5:3
Common trans-
gression.......Rom. 5:12
Sinful nature ..John 3:6, 7

Family and national
traits.........Titus 1:12
God's purpose of
plan.........Gen. 9:22-27

B. *Consistent with:*
Individual respon-
sibility......Jer. 31:29, 30
God's sovereign
plan..........Rom. 9:6-16
Need of a new
nature ....John 3:1-12
Family
differences ....1 John 3:11, 12
Child different from his
parents ....1 Sam. 8:1-5

Heres—*sun*

1. Mountain in
Dan..........Judg. 1:35, 36
Probably connected with Beth
Shemesh or   (1 Kin. 4:9
Ir Shemesh ..(Josh. 19:40, 41
2. Egyptian city; probably is
the "city of destruction"
referred to ....Is. 19:18

Heresh—*silent*

Levite.............1 Chr. 9:15

Heresy—*a teaching contrary to the
truth*

A. *Characteristics of:*
Damnable .....2 Pet. 2:1
Contagious ....2 Pet. 2:2
Subversive.....Gal. 1:7

B. *Attitude toward:*
Recognize
purpose ....1 John 2:18, 19
Withdraw......1 Tim. 6:4, 5, 11
Do not
receive........2 John 9-11

Hereth

Forest in Judah ...1 Sam. 22:5

Heritage, earthly

A. *Of believers:*
Children.......Ps. 127:3
Long life.......Ps. 91:16

B. *Of Israel:*
Promised
Land..........Ex. 6:8
Forsaken of
God...........Jer. 12:7-9
Discontinue....Jer. 17:4
Return to......Jer. 12:15

Heritage, spiritual

A. *Described as:*
Laid up........Ps. 31:19
Col. 1:5
Reserved ......1 Pet. 1:4
Prepared.......1 Cor. 2:9

B. *Consists of:*
Protection .....Is. 54:17
Provision ......Is. 58:14
Unseen
things........Matt. 25:34
Kingdom ......1 Cor. 2:9-12
All things......Rom. 8:32

Hermas

Christian at
Rome ....Rom. 16:14

Hermes

1. Paul acclaimed
as.............Acts 14:12
2. Christian at
Rome.........Rom. 16:14

Hermogenes—*sprung from Hermes*

Turns from Paul ..2 Tim. 1:15

Hermon—*sacred mountain*

Highest mountain (9,166 ft.) in
Syria; also called Sirion,
Shenir............Deut. 3:8, 9
Northern limit of
conquest ....Josh. 11:3, 17
Joined with Tabor, Zion, and
Lebanon in Hebrew
poetry............Ps. 89:12

Hero—*a person acclaimed for unusual
deeds*

Caleb, a rejected ..Num. 13:30-33
Phinehas, a
rewarded........Num. 25:7-13
Deborah, a
militant.........Judg. 4:4-16
Jonathan, a   (1 Sam. 14:6-17,
rescued..........(38-45
David, a popular ..1 Sam. 18:5-8
Esther, a
hesitant ....Esth. 4:10-17

Herod—*family name of Idumaean rulers
of Palestine*

1. Herod the Great,
procurator of Judea
(37–4 B.C.).....Luke 1:5
Inquires of Jesus'
birth ....Matt. 2:3-8

Slays Bethlehem
infants.......Matt. 2:12-18
2. Archelaüs (4 B.C.–A.D. 6)
succeeds Herod the
Great.........Matt. 2:22
3. Herod Antipas, the tetrarch,
ruler of Galilee and Perea (4
B.C.–A.D. 39)...Luke 3:1
Imprisons John the
Baptist.......Luke 3:18-21
Has John the Baptist
beheaded.....Matt. 14:1-12
Disturbed about
Jesus.........Luke 9:7-9
Jesus sent to
him..........Luke 23:7-11
Becomes Pilate's
friend.........Luke 23:12
Opposes
Jesus.........Acts 4:27
4. Philip, tetrarch of Iturea and
Trachonitis
(4 B.C.–A.D.   {Luke 3:1
34)..........{Acts 13:1
5. Herod Philip, disinherited
son of Herod
the Great.....Matt. 14:3
6. Herod Agrippa I
(A.D. 37–44)...Acts 12:1, 19
Kills James....Acts 12:1, 2
Imprisons
Peter.........Acts 12:3-11, 19
Slain by an
angel.........Acts 12:20-23
7. Herod Agrippa II (A.D. 53–70)
Called Agrippa
and King
Agrippa......Acts 25:22, 23
              Acts 25:24, 26
Festus tells him about
Paul.........Acts 25:13-27
Paul makes a defense
before.........Acts 26:1-23
Rejects the
Gospel.......Acts 26:24-30
Recognizes Paul's
innocency.....Acts 26:31, 32
8. Aristobulus; identified by some
as son of Herod the
Great.........Rom. 16:10

Herodians—*an influential Jewish party*

Join Pharisees against
Jesus............Mark 3:6
Seek to trap
Jesus...........Matt. 22:15-22
Jesus warns
against..........Mark 8:15

Herodias—*feminine form of Herod*

Granddaughter of Herod the Great;
plots John's
death............Matt. 14:3-12
Married her
uncle............Mark 6:17, 18

Herodion

Christian at
Rome...........Rom. 16:11

Heron
Unclean bird.....{Lev. 11:19
               {Deut. 14:18

Hesed—*mercy*

Father of one of Solomon's
officers...........1 Kin. 4:7, 10

Heshbon—*intelligence*

Ancient Moabite city; taken by
Sihon, king of the
Amorites.........Num. 21:25-34
Taken by Moses...Num. 21:23-26
Assigned to
Reubenites.......Num. 32:1-37
Built by Reuben...Num. 32:37
On Gad's southern
boundary.........Josh. 13:26
Levitical city.....Josh. 21:39
Later held by
Moabites.........Is. 15:1-4
Judgment of,
announced.......Is. 16:8-14
Fall of, predicted..Jer. 48:2, 34, 35
Pools in..........Song 7:4

Heshmon—*fatness*

Town of Judah....Josh. 15:21, 27

Hesitation—*delay prompted by
indecision*

Causes of:

Uncertain about God's
will...............1 Sam. 23:1-13
Fear of man......John 9:18-23
Selfish
unconcern........2 Cor. 8:10-14
Unbelief.........John 20:24-28

Heth

Eighth letter in Hebrew
alphabet..........Ps. 119:57-64

Heth—*terror*

Son of Canaan ....Gen. 10:15
Ancestor of the
  Hittites..........Gen. 23:10
Abraham buys field from
  sons of ....Gen. 23:3-20
Esau marries
  daughters of......Gen. 27:46

See Hittites

Hethlon—*hiding place*

Place indicating Israel's ideal
  northern
  boundary.........Ezek. 47:15

Hizki—*my strength*

Benjamite.........1 Chr. 8:17

Hezekiah—*Yahweh strengthens*

1. King of
     Judah.........2 Chr. 29:1-3
   Reforms Temple
     services ....2 Chr. 29:3-36
   Restores pure
     worship ....2 Chr. 31:1-19
   Military
     exploits of ....2 Kin. 18:7-12
   Defeated by Senna-
     cherib.........2 Kin. 18:13
   Sends messengers to
     Isaiah.........2 Kin. 19:1-5
   Rabshakeh's further
     taunts.........2 Kin. 19:8-13
   Prays
     earnestly......2 Kin. 19:14-19
   Encouraged by
     Isaiah.........2 Kin. 19:20-37
   Healed; his life prolonged 15
     years.........2 Kin. 20:1-11
   His thanks.....Is. 38:9-22
   Rebuked for his
     pride.........2 Kin. 20:12-19
   Death of.......2 Kin. 20:20, 21
   Ancestor of
     Christ.........Matt. 1:9
2. Ancestor of returning
     exiles ....Ezra 2:1, 16
3. Ancestor of
     Zephaniah ....Zeph. 1:1
4. Postexilic workman who
     returned with
     Zerubbabel....Ezra 2:16
5. Son of
     Neariah ....1 Chr. 3:23
6. Ancestor of returning
     exiles ....Neh. 10:17

Hezion—*vision*

Grandfather of
  Ben-Hadad ....1 Kin. 15:18

Hezir—*swine*

1. Descendant of
     Aaron.........1 Chr. 24:1, 15
2. One who signs
     document.....Neh. 10:1, 20

Hezro—*having a fixed habitation*

One of David's mighty
  men.............1 Chr. 11:37

Hezron—*enclosure*

1. Place in south
     Judah.........Josh. 15:1, 3
2. Son of
     Reuben ....Gen. 46:9
   Founder of the
     Hezronites ....Num. 26:6
3. Son of Perez...Gen. 46:12
   Head of tribal
     family.........Num. 26:21
   Ancestor of
     David.........Ruth 4:18-22
   Ancestor of
     Christ.........Matt. 1:3

Hiddai—*joyful*

One of David's
  warriors..........2 Sam. 23:30
Same as Hurai ....1 Chr. 11:32

Hiddekel—*rapid*

Hebrew name of ⎰Gen. 2:14
the river Tigris .⎱Dan. 10:4

Hide—*to conceal*

A. *Used literally of:*
   Man in Eden...Gen. 3:10
   Baby Moses...Ex. 2:2, 3
   Spies ....Josh. 6:17, 25

B. *Used figuratively of:*
   God's face .....Deut. 31:17, 18
   Protection .....Is. 49:2
   Darkness .....Ps. 139:12
   Believer's life ..Col. 3:3

Hiel—*God lives*

Native of Bethel; rebuilds
  Jericho...........1 Kin. 16:34
Fulfills Joshua's
  curse.............Josh. 6:26

Hierapolis—*sacred city*

City of Asia Minor; center of
Christian
activity..........Col. 4:13

High—*exalted, lofty*

Descriptive of:

Rich ....Ps. 49:2
Eminent people ...1 Chr. 17:17
God's mercy ......Ps. 103:11

High places—*places of idolatrous
worship*

A. *Evils of:*
Contrary to one
sanctuary .....Deut. 12:1-14
Source of
idolatry ....2 Kin. 12:3
Place of child
sacrifices......Jer. 7:31
Cause of
God's {1 Kin. 14:22, 23
wrath........{Ps. 78:58
Denounced by
the {Ezek. 6:1-6
prophets ....{Hos. 4:11-14
Cause of
exile ....Lev. 26:29-34

B. *Built by:*
Solomon......1 Kin. 11:7-11
Jeroboam.....1 Kin. 12:26-31
Jehoram ......2 Chr. 21:9, 11
Ahaz ....2 Chr. 28:24, 25
Manasseh....2 Kin. 21:1, 3
People of
Judah.........1 Kin. 14:22, 23
People of
Israel ....2 Kin. 17:9
Sepharvites....2 Kin. 17:32

C. *Destroyed by:*
Asa............2 Chr. 14:3, 5
Jehoshaphat ...2 Chr. 17:6
Hezekiah ......2 Kin. 18:4, 22
Josiah ....2 Kin. 23:5, 8, 13

High priest

A. *Duties of:*
Offer gifts and
sacrifices......Heb. 5:1
Make
atonement ....Lev. 16:1-34
Inquire of
God...........1 Sam. 23:9-12
Consecrate
Levites........Num. 8:11-21
Anoint kings...1 Kin. 1:34

Bless the
people ....Num. 6:22-27
Preside over {Matt. 26:3,
courts........{ 57-62

B. *Typical of Christ's priesthood:*
Called of
God...........Heb. 5:4, 5
Making
atonement ....Lev. 16:32, 33
Subject to
temptation....Heb. 2:18
Exercise of
compassion ...Heb. 4:15, 16
Holiness of
position ......Lev. 21:14, 15
Marrying a
virgin ....2 Cor. 11:2
Alone entering Holy of
Holies.........Heb. 9:7, 12, 24
Ministry of
inter- {Num. 16:43-48
cession........{Heb. 7:25
Blessing
people ....Acts 3:26

Highway—*a thoroughfare, road*

A. *Characteristics of:*
Roads for public
use ....Num. 20:19
Straight and
broad ....Is. 40:3
Made to cities of
refuge.........Deut. 19:2, 3
Robbers use ...Luke 10:30-33
Animals
infest ....Is. 35:8, 9
Beggars sit
by ....Matt. 20:30
Byways sometimes
better.........Judg. 5:6

B. *Figurative of:*
Holy way ......Prov. 16:17
Israel's
restoration....Is. 11:16
Gospel's call ...Is. 40:3
Way of
salvation ......Is. 35:8-10
Two
destinies ......Matt. 7:13, 14
Christ ....John 14:6

Hilen—*strong place*

Town of Judah....1 Chr. 6:57, 58
Also called
Holon ....Josh. 15:51

Hilkiah—*Yahweh is my portion*

1. Levite, son of
   Amzi..........1 Chr. 6:45, 46
2. Levite, son of
   Hosah..........1 Chr. 26:11
3. Father of
   Eliakim.......Is. 22:20
4. Priest, father of
   Jeremiah......Jer. 1:1
5. Father of
   Gemariah.....Jer. 29:3
6. Shallum's
   son..........1 Chr. 6:13
   High priest in Josiah's
   reign.......2 Chr. 34:9-22
   Oversees Temple
   work.........2 Kin. 22:4-7
   Finds the book of the
   Law..........2 Kin. 22:8-14
   Aids in
   reformation...2 Kin. 23:4
7. Chief of postexilic
   priest.........Neh. 12:1, 7
   Later descendants
   of.............Neh. 12:12, 21
8. One of Ezra's
   assistants.....Neh. 8:4

Hill, hill country—*an elevation of the earth's surface*

Rendered
"Gibeah".........1 Sam. 11:4
Sinners plead for their
covering.........Luke 23:30

Hillel—*he has praised*

Father of Abdon the
judge.............Judg. 12:13, 15

Hindrances—*things which obstruct one's way*

A. *Physical:*
   Heavy armor..1 Sam. 17:38, 39
   Ship's cargo...Acts 27:18-38

B. *Spiritual:*
   Satanic
   temptations...Matt. 4:8-10
   Riches.........Matt. 19:24
   Unbelief.......Matt. 11:21-24
   Ceremo-
   nialism.......Matt. 15:1-9
   Love of
   world.........2 Tim. 4:10
   Sin............Heb. 12:1

C. *Removal of, by:*
   Faith..........Matt. 17:20, 21
   God's armor...Eph. 6:11-18

Walking in the
Spirit.........Gal. 5:16, 17
Self-control....1 Cor. 9:25-27

Hinge—*a pivot of a door*

Of gold...........1 Kin. 7:50

Hinnom, Valley of (Ben-Hinnom)

A. *Location of:*
   Near
   Jerusalem.....Jer. 19:2
   Boundary
   line...........Josh. 15:8
   Tophet........Jer. 19:6, 11-14

B. *Uses of:*
   For idol
   worship.......1 Kin. 11:7
   For sacrificing
   children.......2 Chr. 28:3
   Defiled by
   Josiah........2 Kin. 23:10-14
   Jeremiah addresses people
   here..........Jer. 19:1-5
   Will become "Valley of
   Slaughter"...Jer. 7:31, 32
   Make holy.....Jer. 31:40

Hirah—*nobility*

Adullamite, a friend of
Judah............Gen. 38:1, 12

Hiram—*highborn*

1. King of Tyre...2 Sam. 5:11
   Provides men and material
   for David's
   palace.........1 Chr. 14:1
   David's
   friend.........1 Kin. 5:1
   Provides men and material
   for Solomon's
   Temple........1 Kin. 5:1-12
   Refuses gifts of cities from
   Solomon......1 Kin. 9:10-13
   Helps Solomon⎰1 Kin. 9:14,
   with money ⎱   26-28
   and seamen..⎰1 Kin. 10:11
2. Craftsman; a son of a Tyrian
   and a widow of
   Naphtali.....1 Kin. 7:13, 14
   Sent by King Solomon
   to work on ⎰1 Kin. 7:14-40,
   Temple........⎱   45
   Writes to
   Solomon.....2 Chr. 2:11

Hire—*wages*

A. *Used literally of payments to:*
   Prostitute......Deut. 23:18

Priests.........Judg. 18:4
Mercenary
soldiers.......2 Sam. 10:6
Mercenary
prophets......Deut. 23:4

B. *Used figuratively of:*
Spiritual
adultery.......Ezek. 16:33
Sexual
relations......Gen. 30:16

See Wages, hire

Hireling—*a common laborer*

Anxious for the day to
close.............Job 7:1, 2
Figurative of man's
life................Job 14:6
Guilty of neglect..John 10:12, 13

History, Biblical

A. *Characteristics of:*
Dated with
human   (Hag. 1:1, 15
events.......(Luke 3:1
Inspired.......2 Tim. 3:16
Free of
fables.........2 Pet. 1:16

B. *Valuable for:*
Outline of ancient
history........Acts 7:1-53
Spiritual
lessons........1 Cor. 10:1-11
Prophecy and
fulfillment.....Acts 4:24-28

Hittites—*an ancient nation*

A. *Facts concerning:*
Descendants of
Canaan.......Gen. 10:15
One of seven Canaanite
nations.......Deut. 7:1
Original inhabitants of
Palestine.....Ezek. 16:3, 45
Ruled by
kings.........1 Kin. 10:29
Great nation...2 Kin. 7:6
Their land promised to
Israel.........Gen. 15:18, 20
Destruction of, com-
manded.......Deut. 7:1, 2, 24
Destruction of,
incomplete....Judg. 3:5

B. *Intermarriage with:*
By Esau.......Gen. 36:2
By Israelites after the
conquest.....Judg. 3:5, 6

By Solomon...1 Kin. 11:1
By Israelites after the
exile..........Ezra 9:1, 2

C. *Notable persons of:*
Ephron·........Gen. 49:30
Ahimelech.....1 Sam. 26:6
Uriah..........2 Sam. 11:6, 21

Hivites

Descendants of
Canaan..........Gen. 10:15, 17
One of seven Canaanite
nations...........Deut. 7:1
Esau intermarries
with..............Gen. 36:2
Gibeonites
belong to.........Josh. 9:3, 7
Land of,
promised to   (Ex. 3:8
Israel............(Ex. 23:23
Destruction of:
Commanded.....Deut. 7:1, 2, 24
Incomplete.......Judg. 3:3

Hobah—*hiding place*

Town north of
Damascus........Gen. 14:15

Hod—*majesty*

Asherite.........1 Chr. 7:30, 37

Hodaviah—*praise ye Yahweh*

1. Son of
Elioenai.......1 Chr. 3:24
2. Chief of
Manasseh.....1 Chr. 5:23, 24
3. Benjamite....1 Chr. 9:7
4. Levite, founder of a
family........Ezra 2:40
Called Judah..Ezra 3:9

Hodesh—*new moon*

Wife of
Shaharaim.......1 Chr. 8:8, 9

Hodiah, Hodijah—*splendor of Yahweh*

1. Judahite.......1 Chr. 4:1, 19
2. Levite
interpreter....Neh. 8:7
Leads in
prayer........Neh. 9:5
Probably the same as one of the
signers of the
covenant......Neh. 10:10, 13
3. Signer of the
covenant......Neh. 10:18

Hoglah—*partridge*

Daughter of
Zelophehad.......Num. 26:33

Hoham—*Yahweh protests*

Amorite king defeated by
Joshua ....Josh. 10:3-27

Hold fast

Good thing.......1 Thess. 5:21
Faithful word .....Titus 1:9
Our confidence....Heb. 3:6
Our confession....Heb. 4:14
What we have ....Rev. 2:25
　　　　　　　　Rev. 3:11

Holiness of Christ

A. *Announced in:*
Psalms.........Ps. 16:10
Prophets.......Is. 11:4, 5

B. *Proclaimed by:*
Gabriel ....Luke 1:35
Demons ....Mark 1:24
Centurion ....Luke 23:47
Peter ....Acts 4:27, 30
Paul ....2 Cor. 5:21
John..........1 John 2:1, 29

C. *Manifested negatively in
freedom from:*
Sin ....1 John 3:5
Guilt ....John 8:46
Defilement.....Heb. 7:26, 27

D. *Manifested as "the Holy One"
applied by:*
Demons ......Mark 1:24
Peter ....Acts 2:27
Paul ....Acts 13:35
John..........1 John 2:20
Christ
Himself ......Rev. 3:7

Holiness of Christians

A. *In their calling:*
Elected to .....Rom. 8:29
Called to.......1 Thess. 4:7
Created in ....Eph. 4:24
Possessed by...1 Cor. 3:16, 17

B. *In their lives:*
Bodies ....Rom. 6:13, 19
Manner of
life.............1 Pet. 1:15
Fruitfulness....John 15:8

C. *Reasons for:*
God's
holiness.......1 Pet. 1:15, 16
God's
mercies ....Rom. 12:1, 2

Christ's love ...2 Cor. 5:14, 15
World's end....2 Pet. 3:11
Inheritance in
kingdom ......Eph. 5:5

D. *God's means of:*
Word.........John 17:17
Chastise-
ment.........Heb. 12:10
Grace.........Titus 2:3, 11, 12

See Godliness; Sanctification

Holiness to the Lord

Breastplate
insignia ....Ex. 28:36

Holon—*strong place*

1. City of
Judah.........Josh. 15:51
2. City of Moab ..Jer. 48:21

Holy Day—*any of the Jewish religious
holidays*

Sabbath...........Ex. 35:2
"Festival".........Col. 2:16
Rendered
"Feast"..........Luke 2:41

Holy Land (see Canaan, Land of)

Holy of Holies

A. *Described as:*
Sanctuary .....Lev. 4:6
Holy
Sanctuary....Lev. 16:33
Holy place....Ex. 28:29
Most Holy ....Ex. 26:33
Holiest of All ..Heb. 9:3
Inner
sanctuary.....1 Kin. 6:5-20

B. *Contents of:*
Ark of the
testimony .....Ex. 26:33
Mercy seat.....Ex. 26:34
Cherubim......Ex. 25:18-22
Altar of
incense ....Heb. 9:4
Pot of
manna........Ex. 16:33
Aaron's rod....Num. 17:10
Written copy ⎰Deut. 31:26
of the Law... ⎱2 Kin. 22:8

C. *Entrance to, by the high priest:*
Not at all
times ....Lev. 16:2
Alone, once a
year ....Heb. 9:7
With blood ....Lev. 16:14, 15

To make   { Lev. 16:15-17,
atonement . . . {   33, 34

D. *Significance of:*
Abolished by Christ's
death . . . . Matt. 27:51
Typical of
heaven. . . . . . . Ps. 102:19
Believers now enter
boldly. . . . . Heb. 10:19

See Tabernacle

Holy Spirit

A. *Titles applied to:*
Spirit of:
  God . . . . Gen. 1:2
  The Lord
   God. . . . . Is. 61:1
  Your Father . . Matt. 10:20
  Grace. . . . . Zech. 12:10
  Truth. . . . . John 14:17
  Holiness . . . . . . Rom. 1:4
  Life. . . . . Rom. 8:2
  Christ . . . . Rom. 8:9
  Adoption . . . . . Rom. 8:15
  His Son. . . . . . Gal. 4:6
  Glory . . . . 1 Pet. 4:14
  Prophecy . . . . . Rev. 19:10
  My Spirit . . . . . Gen. 6:3
  Holy Spirit . . . . Ps. 51:11
  The Helper . . . John 14:16, 26
  Eternal Spirit . . Heb. 9:14

B. *Deity of:*
Called God . . . . Acts 5:3, 4
Joined with the Father and
Son . . . . Matt. 28:19
            2 Cor. 13:14
Eternal . . . . Heb. 9:14
Omnipotent. . . Luke 1:35
Omniscient . . . . 1 Cor. 2:10, 11
Omnipresent . . Ps. 139:7-13
Creator . . . . Gen. 1:2
Sovereign. . . . . . 1 Cor. 12:6, 11
New creation . . John 3:3, 8
Sin against,
  eternal . . . . . . Matt. 12:31, 32

C. *Personality of:*
Speaks. . . . . Acts 28:25
Teaches . . . . . . John 14:26
Strives with
  sinners. . . . . . . Gen. 6:3
Comforts . . . . . . Acts 9:31
Helps our
  weaknesses . . . Rom. 8:26
Is grieved. . . . . . Eph. 4:30
Is resisted . . . . . Acts 7:51

D. *Work in the world:*
Creates . . . . Job 33:4
Renews. . . . . Is. 32:15
Convicts
  men. . . . . John 16:8-11

E. *Work of, in Christ's ministry:*
Christ conceived
  by . . . . Luke 1:35
Miracles performed
  by . . . . Matt. 12:28
Anointed by . . . Matt. 3:16
Supported by . . Luke 4:1, 17, 18
Filled by . . . . . . Luke 4:1
Offered to
  God by. . . . . . . Heb. 9:14
Raised by . . . . . Rom. 1:4
Justified by . . . . 1 Tim. 3:16

F. *Work of, in the Scriptures:*
Speaks in:
  Prophets. . . . . Acts 28:25
  Psalms. . . . . . . Acts 1:16, 17
  All
   Scripture. . . . 2 Tim. 3:16
His sword. . . . . . Eph. 6:17

G. *Ministry of, among believers:*
Regenerates . . . John 3:3, 5
Indwells . . . . . . Rom. 8:11
Anoints . . . . 1 John 2:20, 27
Baptizes . . . . . . Acts 2:17-41
Guides. . . . . John 16:13
Empowers . . . . . Mic. 3:8
Sanctifies. . . . . . Rom. 15:16
             2 Thess. 2:13
Bears   { Rom. 8:16
witness . . { Heb. 10:15
Helps. . . . . John 14:16-26
Gives joy . . . . . Rom. 14:17
Gives discern- { 1 Cor. 2:10-16
ment . . . . . . { 1 John 4:1-6
Bears fruit . . . . . Gal. 5:22, 23
Gives gifts. . . . . 1 Cor. 12:3-11

H. *Ministry of, in the Church:*
Fills . . . . Acts 2:4
Baptizes . . . . . . 1 Cor. 12:13
Appoints
  officers. . . . . . . Acts 20:17, 28
Sends out mission-
  aries . . . . Acts 13:2, 4
Directs mission-
  aries . . . . Acts 8:29
Comforts the
  Church . . . . . . Acts 9:31
Sanctifies the
  Church . . . . . . Rom. 15:16

I. *Reception of:*
Promised . . . . . . Joel 2:28-32

Awaits Christ's
glorification . . . John 7:38, 39
Realized at
Pentecost . . . . . Acts 2:1-21
Realized by
Gentiles . . . . Acts 10:45
Can be sinned
against . . . . Matt. 12:31, 32
Contingent . . . . Acts 2:38
Acts 5:32

J. *Filling of:*
Bezaleel . . . . Ex. 31:2
Jesus . . . . Luke 4:1
John the
Baptist . . . . Luke 1:15, 60
Elizabeth . . . . . Luke 1:41
Zacharias . . . . . Luke 1:67
Pentecost
Christians . . . . Acts 2:1-4
Peter . . . . Acts 4:8
Seven men . . . . Acts 6:3-5
Stephen . . . . . . Acts 7:55
Barnabas . . . . . Acts 11:22, 24
Paul . . . . Acts 13:9
Certain
disciples . . . . . Acts 13:52

K. *As teacher:*
Illuminates   {1 Cor. 2:12, 13
the mind . . . . . {Eph. 1:16, 17
Reveals things   {Is. 40:13, 14
of God . . . .   {1 Cor. 2:10, 13

Home—*center of family life*

Things associated with:

Eating . . . . 1 Cor. 11:34
Homemaking . . . . Titus 2:5
Religious
training . . . . 1 Tim. 5:4
Entertainment . . . Luke 15:6
Domestic:
Counsel . . . . 1 Cor. 14:35
Discord . . . . 2 Sam. 14:13-24
Ruth 4:3
Land . . . . Ruth 4:3
Friends . . . . Mark 5:19
Present life . . . . . . 2 Cor. 5:6

See House

Homeless

Christ's
condition . . . . Luke 9:58
True of apostles
also . . . . 1 Cor. 4:11

Homer—*a heap*

Measure; equal to about 11
bushels . . . . Ezek. 45:11, 14

Homesickness

Jacob . . . . Gen. 30:25
Edomite Hadad . . . 1 Kin. 11:21, 22
Exiles . . . . Ps. 137:1-6
Prodigal son . . . . . Luke 15:11-19
Epaphroditus . . . . . Phil. 2:25, 26

Homestead—*the family dwelling*

Redeemable . . . . Lev. 25:25-30

Homicide

Provisions provided:

Distinction
between guilty   {Ex. 21:12-14
and innocent . . . . {Num. 35:16-23
Determination of
guilt . . . . Num. 35:24, 30
Detention in   {Num. 35:11, 15,
cities of refuge . . { 25-29
Defilement of land by slack
justice . . . . Num. 35:31-34

See Murder

Homosexuality

Forbidden . . . . Lev. 18:22
Considered an
abomination . . . . . . 1 Kin. 14:24
Punishment . . . . . . Lev. 20:13
Unclean . . . . Rom. 1:24, 26, 27

Honest, honesty—*uprightness*

A. *Necessity of:*
Means of
testimony . . . . . 1 Pet. 2:12
Obligatory upon
Christians . . . . . 2 Cor. 13:7
Signs of a righteous
man . . . . Ps. 1:1-3
Luke 8:15

B. *Blessings of:*
Brings advance-
ment . . . . Is. 33:15-17
Makes acceptable with
God . . . . Ps. 15:1, 2

C. *Examples of:*
Samuel . . . . 1 Sam. 12:1-5
David . . . . 1 Sam. 25:7, 15
Workmen . . . . . . 2 Kin. 12:15
Zacchaeus . . . . . Luke 19:8
Paul . . . . 2 Cor. 8:20, 21

Honey—*a sweet substance*

A. *Characteristics of:*
Product of
bees . . . . Judg. 14:8, 9

Not acceptable in
offerings ......Lev. 2:11
Offered as part of first
fruits..........2 Chr. 31:5

B. *Figurative of:*
God's Word....Ps. 19:10
God's
blessings ......Ex. 3:8, 17
Wisdom ......Prov. 24:13, 14
Prostitute's
enticements...Prov. 5:3
Immanuel's
diet ....Is. 7:14, 15

Honor—*to esteem or regard highly*

A. *Those worthy of:*
God ....1 Tim. 1:17
Christ ....John 5:23
Parents........Eph. 6:2
Aged ....1 Tim. 5:1, 3
Church
officers.......Phil. 2:25, 29

B. *Obtainable by:*
Wisdom ......Prov. 3:16
Gracious-
ness..........Prov. 11:16
Discipline......Prov. 13:18
Humility......Prov. 15:33
Peaceable-
ness..........Prov. 20:3
Righteousness and
mercy......Prov. 21:21
Honoring
God..........1 Sam. 2:30
Serving
Christ........John 12:26

C. *Those advanced to:*
Joseph.........Gen. 41:41-43
Phinehas ......Num. 25:7-13
Joshua........Num. 27:18-20
Solomon ......1 Kin. 3:13
Abishai ....1 Chr. 11:20, 21
Daniel ....Dan. 2:48
Mordecai ......Esth. 8:15
Apostles ......Matt. 19:27-29

Hoof—*the horny covering of the
extremities of certain animals*

Test of clean
animals...........Lev. 11:3-8
All must leave with
Israel.............Ex. 10:26
Like flint..........Is. 5:28
Cause noise ......Jer. 47:3

Hook

Used:

For curtains.......Ex. 26:32, 37
In fishing ....Job 41:1, 2
For pruning.......Is. 2:4
Expressive of God's
sovereignty......2 Kin. 19:28

Hoopoe—*a bird of the plover family*

Unclean bird......Lev. 11:19

Hope—*the expectation of future good*

A. *Kinds of:*
Natural
expectation ...Acts 27:20
Sinful
expectation ...Acts 24:26
Impossible.....Rom. 4:18
Spiritual
assurance .....2 Cor. 1:7

B. *Described as:*
Living ....1 Pet. 1:3
Blessed ....Titus 2:13
Good ....2 Thess. 2:16
Better ....Heb. 7:19
Sure and
steadfast......Heb. 6:19
One of the great
virtues ....1 Cor. 13:13

C. *Productive of:*
Purity ....1 John 3:3
Patience ....Rom. 8:25
Courage ......Rom. 5:4, 5
Joy ....Rom. 12:12
Salvation ......Rom. 8:23
Assurance .....Heb. 6:18, 19
Stability ....Col. 1:23

D. *Grounds of:*
God's Word....Ps. 119:42-81
Rom. 15:4
God's {Acts 26:6, 7
promises .....{Titus 1:2

E. *Objects of:*
God ....Ps. 39:7
Christ ....1 Cor. 15:19
Salvation ......Rom. 5:1-5
Resurrection ...Acts 23:6
Eternal life ....Titus 1:2
Glory ....Rom. 5:2
Christ's
return.........Rom. 8:22-25

Hopelessness—*without hope*

Condition of the
wicked ....Eph. 2:12

Their unchangeable
condition . . . . Luke 16:23-31

Hophni—*fighter*

Son of Eli; brother of
Phinehas . . . . 1 Sam. 1:3
Called
"reprobates" . . . . . . 1 Sam. 2:12
Guilty of unlawful
practices . . . . 1 Sam. 2:13-17
Immoral . . . . 1 Sam. 2:22
Eli's warning
rejected by . . . . 1 Sam. 2:23-25
Cursed by a man of
God . . . . 1 Sam. 2:27-36
Warned by
Samuel . . . . 1 Sam. 3:11-18
Ark taken to
battle by . . . . 1 Sam. 4:1-8
Slain in battle . . . . 1 Sam. 4:11
News of, causes Eli's
death . . . . 1 Sam. 4:12-18

Hor—*mountain*

1. Mountain of
   Edom . . . . Num. 20:23
   Scene of
   Aaron's { Num. 20:22-29
   death . . . . . . { Num. 33:37-39
2. Prominent peak of the Lebanon
   range . . . . Num. 34:7, 8

Horam—*elevated*

King of Gezer . . . . . Josh. 10:33

Horeb—*desert*

God appears to
Moses . . . . Ex. 3:1-22
Water flows
from . . . . Ex. 17:6
Law given here . . . Mal. 4:4
Site of Israel's { Deut. 9:8, 9
great sin . . . . . . { Ps. 106:19
Covenant made . . . Deut. 29:1
Elijah lodged here 40
days . . . . 1 Kin. 19:8, 9

See Sinai

Horem—*consecrated*

City of Naphtali . . . Josh. 19:32, 38

Hor Hagidgad—*cavern of Gidgah*

Israelite
encampment . . . . Num. 33:32

See Gudgodah

Hori—*cave dweller*

1. Son of { Gen. 36:22
   Lotan . . . . { 1 Chr. 1:39
2. Horites . . . . Gen. 36:21-30
3. Father of Shaphat
   the spy . . . . Num. 13:5

Horites—*cave dwellers*

Inhabitants of
Mt. Seir . . . . Gen. 36:20
Defeated by
Chedorlaomer . . . Gen. 14:5, 6
Ruled by
chieftains . . . . Gen. 36:29, 30
Driven out by
Esau's { Gen. 36:20-29
descendants . . . . { Deut. 2:12, 22

Hormah—*devoted to destruction*

Originally called
Zephath . . . . Judg. 1:17
Scene of Israel's
defeat . . . . Num. 14:45
Destroyed by
Israel . . . . Num. 21:1-3
Assigned to
Judah . . . . Josh. 15:30
Transferred to
Simeon . . . . Josh. 19:4
David sends
spoils to . . . . 1 Sam. 30:26, 30

Horn—*bone-like protrusion from an animal's head*

A. *Descriptive of:*
   Ram's . . . . Gen. 22:13
   Ox's . . . . Ex. 21:29
   Wild Ox . . . . . . Ps. 92:10
   Goat's . . . . Dan. 8:5
   Altar's . . . . 1 Kin. 1:50

B. *Uses of:*
   For trumpets . . Josh. 6:4, 13
   For vessels . . . . 1 Sam. 16:1-13

C. *Figurative of:*
   Christ's
   power . . . . Rev. 5:6
   Power of the
   wicked . . . . Ps. 22:21
   Power of earthly
   kingdoms . . . . . Dan. 7:7, 8, 24
   Power of the
   antichrist . . . . . Rev. 13:1
   Arrogance . . . . 1 Kin. 22:11
   Conquests . . . . Deut. 33:17
   Exaltation . . . . 1 Sam. 2:1, 10
   Destruction . . . . Jer. 48:25
   Salvation . . . . . Luke 1:69

D. *As musical instrument:*

Used on
occasions ..... 1 Chr. 15:28
A part of
worship .... 2 Chr. 15:14
Used in
Babylon .... Dan. 3:7, 10

Hornets—*a large, strong wasp*

God's agents ...... Ex. 23:28
Deut. 7:20
Kings driven
out by .... Josh. 24:12

Horns of the altar—*the protruding
points at the four corners of an altar*

Description .... Ex. 27:2
Provides
sanctuary .... 1 Kin. 1:50

Horonaim—*two caverns*

Moabite city ...... Is. 15:5

Horonite

Native of
Horonaim .... Neh. 2:10, 19

Horoscope—*fortune-telling by astrology*

Forbidden .... Jer. 10:2
Unprofitable ...... Deut. 17:2-5
Punishment .... Is. 47:13, 14

Horse

A. *Used for:*

Travel .... Deut. 17:16
War .... Ex. 14:9
Bearing
burdens ...... Neh. 7:68
Sending
messages ..... Esth. 8:10
Idolatry ...... 2 Kin. 23:11

B. *Figurative of:*

Human trust ... Hos. 14:3
Obstinacy ...... Ps. 32:9
James 3:3
Impetuosity in
sin ...... Jer. 8:6
God's
protection .... 2 Kin. 2:11

Horse traders

Tyre famous for ... Ezek. 27:2, 14

Horse Gate—*a gate of Jerusalem*

Restored by
Nehemiah .... Neh. 3:28

Hosah—*seeking refuge*

1. Village of
Asher .... Josh. 19:29
2. Temple
porter .... 1 Chr. 16:38

Hosanna—*save, now, we beseech thee*

Triumphal ⎰ Matt. 21:9, 15
acclaim .... ⎱ Mark 11:9

Hosea—*salvation*

Son of Beeri, prophet
of the northern
kingdom .... Hos. 1:1
Reproved
idolatry .... Hos. 1-2
Threatens God's judgment; calls to
repentance ...... Hos. 3-6
Foretells impending
judgment .... Hos. 7-10
Calls an ungrateful people to
repentance; promises God's
blessings .... Hos. 11-14

Hoshaiah—*Yahweh has saved*

1. Father of Jezaniah and
Azariah .... Jer. 42:1
2. Participant in a
dedication ...... Neh. 12:31, 32

Hoshama—*Yahweh has heard*

Son of King
Jeconiah .... 1 Chr. 3:17, 18

Hoshea—*save*

1. Original name
of Joshua,
the son of ⎰ Deut. 32:44
Nun.......... ⎱ Num. 13:8, 16
See Joshua, Jehoshua
2. Ephraimite
chieftain ..... 1 Chr. 27:20
3. One who signs
covenant ...... Neh. 10:1, 23
4. Israel's last king; usurps
throne .... 2 Kin. 15:30
5. Reigns wickedly; Israel taken to
Assyria during
reign.......... 2 Kin. 17:1-23

Hospitality—*reception and
entertainment of strangers*

A. *Kinds of:*

Treacherous ... Judg. 4:17-21
Rewarded ...... Josh. 6:17-25
Unwise .... 2 Kin. 20:12-19
Critical .... Luke 7:36-50

Unwel-
comed ....Luke 9:51-53
Joyful ....Luke 19:5, 6
Turbulent......Acts 17:5-9
Forbidden .....3 John 1, 9, 10

B. *Act of:*
Commanded...Rom. 12:13
Required of church
leaders........1 Tim. 3:2
Discipleship....Matt. 25:35

C. *Courtesies of:*
Protection
provided ......Gen. 19:6-8
Food ....Luke 11:5-8
Washing of
feet ....Luke 7:44
Kissing ....Luke 7:45
Denied with ⎰Judg. 19:15-28
indignities....⎱Luke 10:10-16

D. *Examples of:*
Abraham to
angels.........Gen. 18:1-8
Lot to an
angel ....Gen. 19:1-11
Laban to Abraham's
servant ....Gen. 24:31-33
Joseph to his
brothers.......Gen. 43:31-34
Pharaoh to
Jacob ....Gen. 45:16-20
Rahab to the
spies ....Josh. 2:1-16
David to Mephibo-
sheth ....2 Sam. 9:6-13
Martha to
Jesus.........Luke 10:38-42
Lydia to Paul and
Silas ....Acts 16:14, 15
Barbarians to
Paul ....Acts 28:2, 7

Host—*one who entertains*

One who entertains
hospitably ....Rom. 16:23

Hostage—*a person held as security*

Captive for ⎰2 Kin. 14:14
pledge...........⎱2 Chr. 25:24

Host of Heaven

A. *Used of stars as objects of
worship:*
Objects of
idolatry ....Deut. 4:19

Practiced in
Israel ....2 Kin. 17:16
Introduced by
Manasseh .....2 Kin. 21:5
Abolished by
Josiah.........2 Kin. 23:4-12
Worship of, on
roofs..........Jer. 19:13

B. *Used of stars as created things:*
Created by
God...........Is. 45:12
Cannot be
numbered ......Jer. 33:22
Named by
God...........Is. 40:26
To be
dissolved......Is. 34:4

C. *Used of angels:*
Created by
God...........Neh. 9:6
Around the
throne ....1 Kin. 22:19

Hosts, Lord of—*a title of God*

Commander of:
Israel's armies.....1 Sam. 17:45
Is. 31:4
Armies ⎰Gen. 28:12, 13
(angels) of ⎰Ps. 89:6-8
heaven ....⎱Hos. 12:4, 5
Same as
Sabaoth ....Rom. 9:29

Hotham—*determination*

1. Asherite ....1 Chr. 7:30, 32
2. Father of two of David's valiant
men..........1 Chr. 11:26, 44

Hothir—*abundance*

Son of Heman; a
musician ....1 Chr. 25:4, 28

Hour—*a division of time*

A. *Used literally of:*
One-twelfth of
daylight.......Matt. 20:1-12
One-twelfth of
night.........Luke 12:39

B. *Jewish reckoning (from 6 P.M.
and from 6 A.M.):*
Third
(9 A.M.) ....Matt. 20:3
Sixth and ninth (12 noon; 3
P.M.) ....Matt. 20:5

Ninth
(3 P.M.).......Acts 3:1
Eleventh
(5 P.M.).......Matt. 20:6, 9, 12
Third
(9 P.M.).......Acts 23:23

C. *Used literally and descriptively of Christ's:*
Death ....Mark 14:35
.................John 13:1
Betrayal ......Matt. 26:45
Set time.......John 7:30
Predestined
time ....John 12:27

D. *Used prophetically of:*
Gospel age.....John 4:21
Great
tribulation ....Rev. 3:10
God's
judgment ....Rev. 14:7, 15
Christt's
return, ... {Matt. 24:42, 44, 50}

Hours of prayer

A. *Characteristics of:*
Jewish
custom.......Luke 1:10
Directed toward
Jerusalem.....1 Kin. 8:48

B. *Times of:*
Three times
daily ....Dan. 6:10
First, at third hour
(9 A.M.) ....Acts 2:15
Second, at sixth hour
(12 noon) .....Acts 10:9
Third, at ninth hour
(3 P.M.).......Acts 3:1

House

A. *Descriptive of:*
Family
dwelling ..... {Judg. 11:34 / Acts 16:34 / Gen. 14:14}
Descendants...Luke 2:4
Racial or religious
group.........Is. 7:13
.................Jer. 31:31
Tabernacle or {Ex. 34:26
Temple........1 Kin. 6:1}

B. *Figurative of:*
Grave ....Job 30:23
Body ....2 Cor. 5:1
True Church...Heb. 10:21
Earthly life ...Ps. 119:54
Heaven.......John 14:2

Security and
insecurity .....Matt. 7:24-27
Division ....Mark 3:25

See Home

Household idols

Laban's stolen by
Rachel ....Gen. 31:19-35

Housekeeper

Sarah ....Gen. 18:6
Rebekah ....Gen. 27:6-9
Abigail............1 Sam. 25:41, 42
Happy ....Ps. 113:9
Ideal woman......Prov. 31:10-31
Martha...........Luke 10:40, 41

House of God

Tabernacle
called ....Luke 6:4
Temple
described........Ezra 5:2, 8
Church named ...1 Tim. 3:15
Center of God's
worship ....Ps. 42:4

House of prayer

Corrupted into a {Matt. 21:13
den of thieves ...Mark 11:17}

Houses—*dwellings made for habitations*

Rechabites refuse to
dwell in ....Jer. 35:5-10

Hukkok—*decreed*

Border town of
Naphtali.........Josh. 19:32, 34

Hukok

Land given as place of
refuge............1 Chr. 6:75

Hul—*circle*

Aram's second
son..............Gen. 10:23

Huldah—*weasel, mole*

Wife of Shallum...2 Kin. 22:14
Foretells
Jerusalem's {2 Kin. 22:15-17
ruin ....{2 Chr. 34:22-25}
Exempts Josiah from
trouble ....2 Kin. 22:18-20

Human dignity

Based on:

God's image.......Gen. 1:26

Elevated by God . .Ps. 8:3-8
Loved. . . . . .John 3:16
Chosen . . . . .John 15:16

Humaneness—*a kind spirit*

Toward animals . . .Ex. 23:5
Not shown by
Balaam. . . . . .Num. 22:27-30

Humanitarianism—*promoting the welfare of humanity*

Illustrated by
Jesus. . . . . .Luke 10:30-37
Enjoined on
Christians . . . . .1 Thess. 5:15

Human nature of Christ

A. *Predicted as seed of:*
Woman. . . . . . . .Gen. 3:15
Abraham . . . . . .Gal. 3:8, 16
David. . . . . .Luke 1:31, 32

B. *Proved by:*
Virgin's
conception . . . .Matt. 1:18
Birth . . . . .Matt. 1:16, 25
Incarnation. . . .John 1:14
Circum-
cision . . . . . . .Luke 2:21
Growth . . . . . . .Luke 2:52
Genealogy . . . . .Matt. 1:1-17

C. *Manifested in:*
Hunger . . . . . . .Matt. 4:2
Thirst. . . . . .John 19:28
Weariness . . . . .John 4:6
Sleep . . . . .Matt. 8:24
Suffering . . . . . .Luke 22:44
Death . . . . .John 19:30
Burial. . . . . .Matt. 27:59, 60
Resurrection. . . .Luke 24:39
Touch . . . . .1 John 1:1, 2

D. *Importance of, necessary for:*
Sinlessness . . . .John 8:46
His death . . . . . .Heb. 2:14, 17
His
resurrection. . .2 Tim. 2:8
His
exaltation. . . . .Phil. 2:9-11
His priestly
intercession . .Heb. 7:26, 28
His return . . . . .Heb. 9:24-28
Faith . . . . .2 John 7-11

See Incarnation of Christ

Human sacrifice

A. *Practiced by:*
Canaanites . . . .Deut. 12:31
Ammonites . . . .Lev. 20:2, 3

Moabites . . . . . .2 Kin. 3:26, 27
Phoenicians. . . .Jer. 19:5
Israel. . . . . .2 Kin. 16:3, 4
Judah. . . . . .2 Chr. 28:3

B. *Sin of:*
Condemned. . . .Lev. 18:21
Source of
defilement . . . .Ezek. 20:31
Source of
demonism. . . . .Ps. 106:37, 38
Cause of
captivity . . . . . .2 Kin. 17:17, 18

Humiliation—*state of deflated pride*

A. *Causes of:*
Pride . . . . .Esth. 6:6-13
Arrogance . . . . .Dan. 4:29-33
Boastfulness . . .1 Sam. 17:42-50
National sins . . .Dan. 9:1-21
Self-will . . . . . . .Luke 15:11-19

B. *Remedies against:*
Be humble. . . . .Luke 14:8-11
Avoid
sinners. . . . . . .Judg. 16:16-21
Obey God. . . . . .Josh. 7:11-16
Avoid self-
sufficiency . . . .Luke 22:31-34
Rely upon God's
grace . . . . .2 Cor. 12:6-10

Humiliation of Christ—*the state that He took while on earth*

A. *Exhibited in His:*
Taking our
nature . . . . . . .Phil. 2:7
Birth . . . . .Matt. 1:18-25
Obedience . . . . .Luke 2:51
Submission to
ordinances . . . .Matt. 3:13-15
Becoming a
servant . . . . . .Matt. 20:28
Menial acts . . . .John 13:4-15
Suffering . . . . . .Matt. 26:67, 68
Death . . . . .John 10:15-18

B. *Rewards of:*
Exalted by
God. . . . . .Acts 2:22-36
Crowned
king . . . . .Heb. 1:1, 2
Perfected
forever. . . . . . . .Heb. 2:10
Acceptable high
priest . . . . .Heb. 2:17

Humility

A. *Factors involved in sense of:*
One's
sinfulness . . . . .Luke 18:13, 14

One's unworthi-
ness...........Luke 15:17-21
One's
limitations ....1 Kin. 3:6-14
God's
holiness.......Is. 6:1-8
God's righ-
teousness .....Phil. 3:4-9

B. *Factors producing:*
Affliction ......Deut. 8:3
Impending
doom ....2 Chr. 12:5-12
Submis-
siveness.......Luke 10:39
Christ's
example.......Matt. 11:29

C. *Rewards of:*
Road to
honor..........1 Kin. 3:11-14
Leads to
riches..........Prov. 22:4
Brings
blessings......2 Chr. 7:14, 15
Guarantees
exaltation .....James 4:10
Insures God's
presence ......Is. 57:15
Makes truly
great..........Matt. 18:4
Unlocks more ⌠Prov. 3:34
grace ⌡James 4:6

D. *Christians exhorted to:*
Put on.........Col. 3:12
Be clothed
with ....1 Pet. 5:5
Walk with .....Eph. 4:1, 2
Avoid false ....Col. 2:18-23

E. *Examples of:*
Abraham ......Gen. 18:27, 32
Jacob..........Gen. 32:10
Moses ....Ex. 3:11
Joshua.........Josh. 7:6
David..........1 Sam. 18:18-23
Job ....Job 42:2-6
Jeremiah ......Jer. 1:6
Daniel ....Dan. 2:30
Elizabeth ......Luke 1:43
John the
Baptist.......John 3:29, 30
Jesus ....Matt. 11:29
Paul...........Acts 20:19

Humtah—*a place of lizards*

Town of Judah....Josh. 15:54

Hunchback

Barred from
priesthood........Lev. 21:20, 21

Hunger, physical

A. *Causes of:*
Fasting ....Matt. 4:1-3
Fatigue........Gen. 25:29, 30
Famine ....Luke 15:14-17
God's
judgment .....Is. 9:19-21

B. *Some results of:*
Selling
birthright .....Gen. 25:30-34
Murmuring ...Ex. 16:2, 3
Breaking God's
Law...........1 Sam. 14:31-34
Cannibalism ...2 Kin. 6:28, 29
Cursing God...Is. 8:21

C. *Satisfaction of:*
Supplied:
By friends ....2 Sam. 17:27-29
Super-
naturally....Ex. 16:4-21
Sent as a
judgment .....Ps. 106:14, 15
Provided by
God...........Matt. 6:11
Christian
duty ....1 Sam. 30:11, 12
Complete in
heaven........Rev. 7:14-17

D. *Examples of:*
David..........1 Sam. 21:3-6
Elijah..........1 Kin. 17:11-13
Jeremiah ......Jer. 38:9
Peter ....Acts 10:10
Paul...........1 Cor. 4:11

E. *Strike:*
By forty men ..Acts 23:11-16

Hunger, spiritual

More important than
physical ....Deut. 8:3
Sent as a
judgment........Amos 4:11-13
Will be satisfied ..Is. 55:1, 2
Blessing of ....Matt. 5:6
Satisfied by
Christ..........John 6:33-35

Hunter, hunting

A. *Purposes of:*
Kill harmful
beasts.........1 Sam. 17:34-36

B. *Methods of:*
Noose ....Job 18:10
Snare..........Amos 3:5
Pits...........2 Sam. 23:20

Bows and
quiver........Gen. 27:3
Sword, etc. ....Job 41:26-30

C. *Examples of:*
Nimrod........Gen. 10:8, 9
Ishmael........Gen. 21:20
Esau........Gen. 27:3, 5, 30

Hupham—*protected*

Son of Benjamin; founder of
Huphamites ......Num. 26:39
Called Huppim ....Gen. 46:21

Huppah—*covering*

Descendant of
Aaron ....1 Chr. 24:1, 13

Huppim—*protection*

1. Son of
Benjamin .....Gen. 46:21
2. Son of Ir ......1 Chr. 7:12

See Hupham

Hur—*splendor*

1. Man of Judah; of Caleb's
house ......1 Chr. 2:18-20
Grandfather of
Bezaleel ......Ex. 31:1, 2
Supports Moses'
hands........Ex. 17:10-12
Aids Aaron ....Ex. 24:14
2. Prince of
Midian ....Josh. 13:21
3. Father of
Rephaiah .....Neh. 3:9

Hurai—*free, noble*

One of David's mighty
men..............1 Chr. 11:32

Huram—*noble, free*

Son of Bela ....1 Chr. 8:5

Huri—*linen worker*

Gadite ....1 Chr. 5:14

Husband—*married man*

A. *Regulations concerning:*
One flesh ......Matt. 19:5, 6
Until death ....Rom. 7:2, 3
Rights of ......1 Cor. 7:1-5
Sanctified by
wife...........1 Cor. 7:14-16

B. *Duties of, toward wife:*
Love...........Eph. 5:25-33

Live with for
life............Matt. 19:3-9
Be faithful to ..Mal. 2:14, 15
Be satisfied
with ....Prov. 5:18, 19
Instruct ....1 Cor. 14:34, 35
Honor ....1 Pet. 3:7
Confer with....Gen. 31:4-16
Provide for ....1 Tim. 5:8
Rule over......Gen. 3:16

C. *Kinds of:*
Adam,
blaming.......Gen. 3:9-12
Isaac, loving...Gen. 24:67
Elkanah, sympa-
thetic ....1 Sam. 1:8-23
Nabal, evil .....1 Sam. 25:3
Ahab, weak....1 Kin. 21:5-16
David,
ridiculed .....2 Sam. 6:20
Job, strong ....Job 2:7-10

Hushah—*haste*

Judahite ....1 Chr. 4:4

Hushai—*hasty*

Archite; David's
friend ....2 Sam. 15:32-37
Feigns sympathy with
Absalom..........2 Sam. 16:16-19
Defeats Ahithophel's
advice............2 Sam. 17:5-23

Husham—*hastily*

Temanite king of
Edom ....Gen. 36:34, 35

Hushathite

Inhabitant of
Hushah ....2 Sam. 21:18

Hushim—*hasters*

1. Head of a Danite
family........Gen. 46:23
Called
Shuham......Num. 26:42
2. Sons of Aher ..1 Chr. 7:12
3. Wife of
Shaharaim ....1 Chr. 8:8, 11

Huz

Son of Nahor .....Gen. 22:20, 21

Huzzab—*uncertain meaning*

May refer to Assyrian queen or to
Nineveh; or may be rendered "it is
decreed" ....Nah. 2:7

Hymenaeus—*belonging to Hymen*

False teacher excommunicated
by Paul...........1 Tim. 1:19, 20
Teaches error .....2 Tim. 2:17, 18

Hymn—*a spiritual song*

A. *Occasions producing:*
Great
deliverance....Ex. 15:1-19
Great victory ..Judg. 5:1-31
Prayer
answered .....1 Sam. 2:1-10
Mary's "Magnifi-
cat".........Luke 1:46-55
Father's
ecstasy ....Luke 1:68-79
Angel's
delight ....Luke 2:14
Old man's
faith ....Luke 2:29-32
Heaven's eternal
praise ....Rev. 5:9-14

B. *Purposes of:*
Worship God ..2 Chr. 23:18
Express joy ....Matt. 26:30
Edify ....1 Cor. 14:15
Testify to
others.........Acts 16:25

Hypocrisy, hypocrite—*showy, empty
display of religion*

A. *Kinds of:*
Worldly........Matt. 23:5-7
Legalistic ......Rom. 10:3
Evangelical ....2 Pet. 2:10-22
Satanic ....2 Cor. 11:13-15

B. *Described as:*
Self-
righteous .....Luke 18:11, 12
"Holier than
you"..........Is. 65:5
Blind ....Matt. 23:17-26
Covetous ......2 Pet. 2:3
Showy.........Matt. 6:2, 5, 16
Highly
critical........Matt. 7:3-5
Indignant......Luke 13:14-16
Bound by
traditions .....Matt. 15:1-9
Neglectful of major
duties.........Matt. 23:23, 24
Pretended but
unpracticed ..Ezek. 33:31, 32
Interested in the
externals......Luke 20:46, 47
Fond of titles ..Matt. 23:6, 7
Inwardly unregen-
erate..........Luke 11:39

C. *Examples of:*
Jacob..........Gen. 27:6-35
Jacob's sons ...Gen. 37:29-35
Delilah........Judg. 16:4-20
Ishmael........Jer. 41:6, 7
Herod ....Matt. 2:7, 8
Pharisees ......John 8:4-9
Judas..........Matt. 26:25-49
Ananias ....Acts 5:1-10
Peter ....Gal. 2:11-14

Hyssop—*a small plant*

Grows from
walls ....1 Kin. 4:33
Used in sprinkling
blood.............Ex. 12:22
Used to offer Jesus
vinegar...........John 19:28, 29
Typical of spiritual
cleansing ....Ps. 51:7

I

I AM—*a title indicating self-existence*

Revealed to
Moses...........Ex. 3:14
Said by Christ.....John 8:57, 58

Christ expressing, refers to:

Bread of   ⎰John 6:35, 41
life ....⎱   48, 51
Light of the   ⎰John 8:12
world ....⎱John 9:5
Door of the
sheep...........John 10:7, 9
Good shepherd....John 10:11, 14
Resurrection and the
life ....John 11:25
True and living
way ....John 14:6
True vine ....John 15:1, 5

Ibleam—*he destroys the people*

City assigned to
Manasseh ......Josh. 17:11, 12
Canaanites
remain in........Judg. 1:27
Called Bileam .....1 Chr. 6:70
Ahaziah slain
near.............2 Kin. 9:27

Ibneiah—*Yahweh builds up*

Head of a Benjamite
family............1 Chr. 9:8

Ibnijah—*Yahweh builds up*

Father of Reuel ...1 Chr. 9:8

Ibri—*a Hebrew*

Son of Jaaziah ....1 Chr. 24:27

Ibzan—*active*

Judge of Israel ....Judg. 12:8
Father of 60
children ....Judg. 12:8, 9

Ice

Figurative of:

By reason of .....Job 6:16

Ichabod—*inglorious*

Son of Phinehas...1 Sam. 4:19-22

Iconium—*image-like*

City of Asia Minor; visited by
Paul...............Acts 13:51
Many converts
in ....Acts 14:1-6
Paul visits again ..Acts 14:21
Timothy's
ministry..........Acts 16:1, 2
Paul persecuted ...2 Tim. 3:11

Iconoclast—*a breaker of images*

Moses, an angry ..Ex. 32:19, 20
Gideon, an
inspired ....Judg. 6:25-32
Jehu, a subtle .....2 Kin. 10:18-31
Josiah, a
reforming ....2 Kin. 23:12-25

Idalah—*memorial of God*

Border town of
Zebulun..........Josh. 19:15

Idbash—*honey-sweet*

Man of Judah .....1 Chr. 4:3

Iddo—*festal*

1. Chief officer under
   David........1 Chr. 27:21
2. Father of
   Ahinadab .....1 Kin. 4:14
3. Leader of Jews at
   Casiphia ......Ezra 8:17-20
4. Gershonite
   Levite.........1 Chr. 6:20, 21
   Called
   Adaiah........1 Chr. 6:41
5. Seer whose writings are
   cited ....2 Chr. 9:29

6. Grandfather of Zechariah the
   prophet ....Zech. 1:1, 7
7. Postexilic
   priest ....Neh. 12:4, 16

Identification—*proving something or
somebody to be what it or he really is*

A. *Among men:*
   At birth........Gen. 25:22-26
   By the life .....Luke 6:43-45
   By speech .....Judg. 12:6
   By a search ....2 Kin. 10:23
   By a kiss ......Matt. 26:48, 49

B. *Of Christ the Messiah, by:*
   A divine sign ..John 1:31-34
   A divine
   voice..........Matt. 17:5
   Divine works ..Matt. 11:2-6
   Human
   testimony .....John 3:26-36
   Scriptures .....John 5:39-47

C. *Of spiritual things:*
   New birth .....2 Cor. 5:17
   Apostates......Matt. 7:22, 23
   Antichrist......2 Thess. 2:1-12
   Believers and
   unbelievers ...Matt. 25:31-46

Identifying with Christ

A. *Proper time, when tempted:*
   To harm.......Prov. 1:10-19
   To violate
   convictions ...Dan. 1:8
   To conform to
   world ....Rom. 12:2
   To rebellion....Rom. 13:1-5
   With improper
   associations ...2 Cor. 6:14-17
   To learn evil...Rom. 16:19
                   Prov. 19:27

B. *Results:*
   Hatred........John 17:14
   Separation.....Luke 6:22, 23
   Suffering .....1 Pet. 2:20, 21
   Witness........1 Pet. 3:15
   Good
   conscience ....1 Pet. 3:16

C. *Basis:*
   Future glory...Rom. 8:18
   Life of Christ ..Gal. 2:20
   Reward........2 Tim. 2:12

Idleness—*inactivity; slothfulness*

A. *Consequences of:*
   Poverty........Prov. 20:13
   Begging ......Prov. 20:4

Hunger . . . . .Prov. 19:15
Bondage . . . . .Prov. 12:24
Ruin. . . . . .Prov. 24:30-34

B. *Admonitions against, consider:*
Ant. . . . . .Prov. 6:6-11
Ideal woman. . . . .Prov. 31:10-31
Lord . . . . .John 9:4
Apostles . . . . . . .2 Thess. 3:7-9
Judgment. . . . . . .1 Cor. 3:8-15

See Laziness; slothfulness

Idol makers

Maachah. . . . . .1 Kin. 15:13
Foreign peoples . . .Is. 45:16
Men of Judah . . . . .Is. 2:1, 20
People of
Jerusalem . . . . . .Ezek. 22:3

Idol making

Described by
Isaiah . . . . .Is. 44:9-18

Idols, idolatry—*worship of idols*

A. *Described as:*
Irrational . . . . . .Acts 17:29
Degrading . . . . . .Rom. 1:22, 23
Demonical . . . . . .1 Cor. 10:20, 21
Defiling. . . . . . . .2 Cor. 6:15-18
Enslaving. . . . . . .Gal. 4:8, 9
Abominable. . . .1 Pet. 4:3

B. *Brief history of:*
Begins in man's
apostasy . . . . . .Rom. 1:21-25
Prevails in
Ur . . . . .Josh. 24:2, 14
In Laban's
household. . . . .Gen. 31:19-35
Judgments on
Egyptian . . . . . .Num. 33:4
Brought from Egypt by
Israel . . . . .Josh. 24:14
Forbidden in Law at
Sinai. . . . . .Ex. 20:1-5
Warnings against, at
Sinai. . . . . .Ex. 34:13-16
Israel yields to, at
Sinai. . . . . .Ex. 32:1-8
Moabites entice
Israel to. . . . . . .Num. 25:1-18
Early zeal
against. . . . . . . .Josh. 22:10-34
Gideon
destroys. . . . . . .Judg. 6:25-32
Gideon becomes an
occasion of. . . .Judg. 8:24-27
Enticements to
Baalism . . . . . . .Judg. 10:6-16

Levite corrupted
by . . . . .Judg. 17:1-13
Danites establish, at
Shiloh. . . . . . . .Judg. 18:30, 31
Overthrow of
Philistines. . . . .1 Sam. 5:1-12
Revival against, under
Samuel . . . . . . .1 Sam. 7:3-6
Solomon
yields to . . . . . .1 Kin. 11:1-8
Jeroboam establishes
in   (1 Kin. 12:26-33
Jerusalem . . . . .(2 Chr. 11:14, 15
Rehoboam tolerates in
Judah. . . . . .1 Kin. 14:22-24
Conflict—Elijah and
Ahab. . . . . .1 Kin. 18:1-46
Wicked kings (1 Kin. 21:25, 26
of Israel. . . . .(2 Kin. 16:2, 3
Prophet denounces in
Israel . . . . .Hos. 4:12-19
Cause of Israel's
exile . . . . .2 Kin. 17:5-23
Judah follows Israel's
example. . . . . . .2 Chr. 28:1-4
Manasseh climaxes
Judah's   (2 Kin. 21:1-18
apostasy in. (2 Chr. 33:1-11
Reformation against, under
Asa . . . . .2 Chr. 14:3-5
Under
Hezekiah. . . . . .2 Chr. 29:15-19
Under Josiah . .2 Kin. 23:1-20
Prophets denounce in
Judah. . . . . .Jer. 16:11-21
Cause of Judah's
exile . . . . .2 Kin. 23:26, 27

C. *Christians warned against:*
No company
with . . . . .1 Cor. 5:11
Flee from. . . . . .1 Cor. 10:14
No fellowship
with . . . . .1 Cor. 10:19, 20
Keep from . . . . .1 John 5:21
Testify
against. . . . . . . .Acts 14:15
Turn from . . . . .1 Thess. 1:9

D. *Enticements to, due to:*
Heathen
back-   (Josh. 24:2
ground. . . . . . (Ezek. 16:44, 45
Contact with
idolaters . . . . . .Num. 25:1-6
Inter-
marriage . . . . . .1 Kin. 11:1-13

Imagined
good.........Jer. 44:15-19
Corrupt
heart.........Rom. 1:21-23

E. *Removed through:*
Punishment....Deut. 17:2-5
Display of
power-
lessness......$\begin{cases} \text{1 Sam. 5:1-5} \\ \text{1 Kin. 18:25-29} \end{cases}$
Logic..........Is. 44:6-20
Display of God's
power.........2 Kin. 19:10-37
Denuncia-
tion..........Mic. 1:5-7
Exile..........Hos. 8:5-14
Zeph. 1:4-6
New
birth.........$\begin{cases} \text{Hos. 14:1-9} \\ \text{Amos 5:26, 27} \end{cases}$

Idumea—*pertaining to Edom*

Name used by Greek and Romans
to designate
Edom ....Mark 3:8

See Edom

Igal—*He (God) redeems*

1. Issachar's
spy ....Num. 13:2, 7
2. One of David's mighty
men............2 Sam. 23:36
3. Shemaiah's
son ....1 Chr. 3:22

Igdaliah—*great is Yahweh*

Father of Hanan the
prophet ....Jer. 35:4

Ignorance—*lack of knowledge*

A. *Kinds of:*
Pardonable....Luke 23:34
Pretended .....Luke 22:57-60
Innocent ......Acts 19:2-5
Excusable ....Acts 17:30
Judicial........Rom. 1:28
Guilty ....Rom. 1:19-25
Partial ....1 Cor. 13:12
Confident......Heb. 11:8

B. *Causes of:*
Unregen-
eracy ....Eph. 4:18
Unbelief ....1 Tim. 1:13
Spiritual:
Darkness .....1 John 2:11
Immaturity ...1 Cor. 8:7-13

C. *Productive of:*
Unbelief ....John 8:19-43
Error ....Matt. 22:29

D. *Objects of:*
God ....John 8:55
Scriptures .....Matt. 22:29
Christ's
return........$\begin{cases} \text{1 Thess. 4:13,} \\ \text{14} \end{cases}$

Iim—*ruins*

Town of Judah....Josh. 15:29

Ije Abarim—*ruins of the Abarim*
(regions beyond)

Wilderness
camp.............Num. 21:11
Same as Ijim......Num. 33:44, 45

Ijon—*heap*

Town of Naphtali; captured by
Ben-Hadad ....1 Kin. 15:20
Captured by Tiglath-
Pileser...........2 Kin. 15:29

Ikkesh—*crooked*

Father of Ira .....2 Sam. 23:26
Commander of
24,000 ....1 Chr. 27:9

Ilai—*supreme*

One of David's mighty
men.............1 Chr. 11:26, 29
Called Zalmon ....2 Sam. 23:28

Illumination—*enlightenment,
understanding*

Of Daniel ....Dan. 5:11, 14

Illumination, spiritual

By Christ ....John 1:9
At conversion.....Heb. 6:4
In Christian
truth.............Eph. 1:18
By Holy Spirit.....John 16:13-16
By God ....1 Cor. 4:5

Illustration—*something used to explain
something else*

From:

Ancient history ...1 Cor. 10:1-14
Current history ...Mark 12:1-11
Nature ....Prov. 6:6-11

Illyricum—*a province of Europe*

Paul preaches .....Rom. 15:19

Image (see Idols; idolatry)

Image of God

A. *In man:*

Created in .....Gen. 1:26, 27
Reason for sanctity of
life.........Gen. 9:6
Reason for man's
headship ......1 Cor. 11:7
Restored by
grace ....Col. 3:10
Transformed
of............2 Cor. 3:18

B. *In Christ:*

In essential
nature ....Col. 1:15
Manifested on
earth.........John 1:14, 18
Believers
conformed ....Rom. 8:29

Imagination—*creating mental picture of*

A. *Described as:*

Willful.......Jer. 18:12
Deceitful ......Prov. 12:20

B. *Cleansing of:*

Promised .....Jer. 3:17

See Thought

Imitation—*attempting to duplicate*

Of the good:

God.............Eph. 5:1
Paul's conduct ....2 Thess. 3:7, 9
Apostles .....1 Thess. 1:6
Heroes of the
faith.............Heb. 6:12
Good.............3 John 11
Other churches ...1 Thess. 2:14

See Example of Christ, the

Imla, Imlah—*fullness*

Father of
Micaiah   {2 Chr. 18:7, 8
the prophet......{1 Kin. 22:8, 9

Immanuel—*God (is) with us*

Name given to
the child born of {Is. 7:14
the virgin ....{Matt. 1:23
Emmanuel in.....Matt. 1:23

Immer—*eloquent*

1. Descendant of
Aaron.........1 Chr. 24:1-14
2. Father of
Pashur......Jer. 20:1
3. Founder of a postexilic
family.........Ezra 2:37

The same as the father of
Meshille-
mith ....1 Chr. 9:12
Also the ancestor of priests
marrying
foreigners.....Ezra 10:19, 20
4. Person or place in
Babylonia .....Neh. 7:61
5. Zadok's
father.........Neh. 3:29

Immorality—*state of a wrongful act or
relationship; fornication*

Attitude toward:

Consider sanctity of the
body ....1 Cor. 6:13-20
Flee from it ....1 Cor. 6:18
Get married ....1 Cor. 7:2
Abstain from it...1 Thess. 4:3
Mention it not ....Eph. 5:3
Corrupts the
earth.............Rev. 19:2

Immortality—*eternal existence*

A. *Proof of, based upon:*

God's image in
man ....Gen. 1:26, 27
Translation of
Enoch and   {Gen. 5:24
Elijah.........{2 Kin. 2:11, 12
Promises of   {John 11:25, 26
Christ.........{John 14:2, 3
Appearance of Moses and
Elijah ....Matt. 17:2-9
Eternal
rewards and
punish-   {Matt. 25:31-46
ments.........{Luke 16:19-31
Resurrection   {Rom. 8:11
of Christ .....{1 Cor. 15:12-58
Resurrection   {Dan. 12:2, 3
of men.......{John 5:28, 29

B. *Expression indicative of:*

"I am".........Matt. 22:32
"Today" ....Luke 23:43
"Shall never
die"..........John 11:25, 26
"The redemption of our
body".........Rom. 8:22, 23
"Neither
death".........Rom. 8:38, 39
"We know".....2 Cor. 5:1-10
"A living
hope"..........1 Pet. 1:3-8
"We shall be like
Him"..........1 John 3:2

See Eternal, everlasting; Life, eternal

Immunity—*exemption from something*

From:

Egyptian
plagues..........Ex. 8:22, 23
Disease ....Deut. 7:15
Corruption.......Ps. 16:10, 11
Harm ....Luke 10:19
Second death .....Rev. 20:6

Immutability—*unchangeableness*

A. *Of God, expressed by:*
"I AM".........Ex. 3:14
"You are the
same"...........Ps. 102:25-27
"I do not
change".......Mal. 3:6
"Are
irrevocable"..Rom. 11:29
"Who cannot
lie".............Titus 1:2
"The immut-
ability".........Heb. 6:17, 18
"No
variation".....James 1:17

B. *Of Christ, expressed by:*
"I AM".........John 8:58
"You are the
same".........Heb. 1:12
"Unchange-
able"..........Heb. 7:22-24
"The same"...Heb. 13:8
"I am Alpha and
Omega".......Rev. 1:8-18

C. *Of God, characteristics of:*
Unique ....Is. 43:10
Purposive......Ps. 138:8
Active ....Phil. 1:6

Imna—*he keeps back*

Asherite chief.....1 Chr. 7:35

Imnah—*prosperity*

1. Eldest son of
Asher.........1 Chr. 7:30
Called Jimna {Num. 26:44
and Jimnah .. {Gen. 46:17
2. Levite in Hezekiah's
reign..........2 Chr. 31:14

Impartiality—*that which is equitable,
just, and fair*

In God's:
Material
blessings ....Matt. 5:45

Spiritual
blessings ....Acts 10:34, 35
Judgments ....Rom. 2:3-12

Impatience—*inability to control one's
desire for action*

A. *Causes of:*
Lust ....Gen. 19:4-9
Revenge ....Gen. 34:25-27
Irritability .....Num. 20:10

B. *Consequences of:*
Kept from promised
land...........Num. 20:10-12
Great sin ......Ex. 32:1, 21, 30
Foolish
statements....Job 2:7-9
Loss of
birthright ....Gen. 25:29-34
Shipwreck .....Acts 27:29-34

Impeccability (see Holiness of Christ)

Impediment—*something that hinders
one's activity*

In speech, cured ..Mark 7:32-35
Avoided by
obedience ....Prov. 4:10, 12

Impenitence—*without a change of mind*

A. *Expressed by:*
Willful disobedi-
ence ....Jer. 44:15-19
Hardness of
heart..........John 12:37-40
Refusing to
hear ....Luke 16:31
Rebellion against the
truth..........1 Thess. 2:15, 16

B. *Consequences of:*
Spiritual
bondage ......John 8:33-44
Judicial
blindness......John 9:39-41
Eternal
destruction....2 Thess. 1:8, 9

Imperfection of man

A. *Manifested in:*
Falling short of God's
glory..........Rom. 3:23
Total
corruption ....Is. 1:5, 6

B. *Remedy for:*
New
creature.......2 Cor. 5:17
Conformity to
Christ..........1 John 3:2, 3

Impertinence—*an action or remark inappropriate for the occasion*

Christ rebukes
Peter's .... Mark 8:31-33

Impetuousness—*acting suddenly with little thought*

Characterized by:

Ill-considered
judgment......... Esth. 1:10-22
Enraged
disposition........ Gen. 34:25-31
Hasty action ...... Josh. 22:10-34

Import—*to receive from other countries*

Things imported:

Horses .... 1 Kin. 10:28
Chariots .... 2 Chr. 1:17
Fish............. Neh. 13:16

Importunity in prayer

Need involved..... Luke 11:5-13
Christ's example .. Luke 22:44
Great
intensity of...... Acts 12:5
Results of .... Mark 7:24-30

See Prayer

Impossibilities—*powerless, weak*

A. *Natural:*
   Change one's
   color.......... Jer. 13:23
   Hide from
   God........... Ps. 139:7-12
   Change one's
   size .... Matt. 6:27
   Control the
   tongue....... James 3:7, 8
B. *Spiritual:*
   God to sin ..... Hab. 1:13
   God to fail His
   promises ...... Titus 1:2
   Believers to
   perish........ John 10:27-29

Imposter—*a pretender*

A. *Characteristics of:*
   Not
   believed as .... Jer. 40:14-16
   Speaks
   falsely .... Josh. 9:3-14
   Poses as real .. 2 Cor. 11:13-15
   Much like the
   real.......... Matt. 7:21-23
   Deception of, revealed to
   prophets ...... Acts 13:8-12

B. *Examples of:*
   Jannes and
   Jambres....... 2 Tim. 3:8
   Judas.......... John 13:18-30
   Antichrist...... 2 Thess. 2:1-4

Imprecation—*pronouncing a curse*

God's enemies..... Ps. 55:5-15
One's enemies..... Ps. 35:4-8, 26
Heretics........... Gal. 1:9
Persecutors .... Jer. 11:18-20
Forbidden........ Luke 9:54-56

See Curse, cursing

Imprisonment—*physical confinement in jail*

A. *Of Old Testament persons:*
   Joseph......... Gen. 39:20
   Simeon .... Gen. 42:19, 24
   Samson........ Judg. 16:21, 25
   Jehoiachin..... 2 Kin. 25:27-29
   Micaiah........ 2 Chr. 18:25, 26
   Jeremiah....... Jer. 32:2, 8, 12
B. *Of New Testament persons:*
   John the
   Baptist........ Mark 6:17-27
   Apostles........ Acts 5:18
   Peter .... Acts 12:4
   Paul and
   Silas.......... Acts 16:24
   Paul .... Acts 23:10, 18
   John........... Rev. 1:9

See Prisoners

Improvement—*a betterment*

Expressed by:

Growth .... 1 Pet. 2:2
Addition .... 2 Pet. 1:5-11
Press on .... Phil. 3:13-15

Improvidence—*wasting present possession*

Material things.... Luke 15:11-13
Spiritual things.... Luke 12:16-23
Eternal things.... Luke 16:19-31

Impurity (see Unclean)

Imputation—*counting or crediting something to another*

A. *Described as charging:*
   Evil to an innocent
   person .... Philem. 18
   Evil to an evil
   person .... Lev. 17:4
   Good to a good
   person .... Ps. 106:30, 31

B. Of Adam's sin to the race:
Based on the
fall............Gen. 3:1-19
Explained
fully ....Rom. 5:12-21
The wider implications
of............Rom. 8:20-23

C. Of the believer's sin to Christ:
Our iniquity laid on
Him............Is. 53:5, 6
Made to be sin
for us.........2 Cor. 5:21
Became a curse
for us.........Gal. 3:13
Takes away ... (John 1:29
our sins ...... (Heb. 9:28

D. Of Christ's righteousness to the
believer:
Negatively
stated.........Rom. 4:6-8
Positively
affirmed.......Rom. 10:4-10
Explained
graphically....Luke 15:22-24
God justifies the
ungodly.........Rom. 5:18, 19
Christ becomes our righteousness............1 Cor. 1:30
We become the righteousness
of God in
Him............2 Cor. 5:21
Illustrated by Abraham's
faith............Rom. 4:3

See Justification

Imrah—*He* (God) *resists*

Son of Zophah ....1 Chr. 7:36

Imri—*eloquent*

1. Son of Bani....1 Chr. 9:4
2. Father of
Zaccur........Neh. 3:2

Inability (see Impossibilities)

Incarnation of Christ

A. Foreshadowed by:
Angel..........Josh. 5:13-15
Prophecies.....Is. 7:14

B. Described as:
Becoming
flesh ....John 1:14
Born of
woman........Gal. 4:4

Coming in
flesh ....1 John 4:2
Appearing in
flesh ....1 Tim. 3:16
Our likeness ...Rom. 8:3
Heb. 2:14
Body ....Heb. 10:5, 10
1 John 1:1-3
Dying in ..... (1 Pet. 3:18
flesh ....(1 Pet. 4:1

C. Purposes of:
Reveal the
Father ....John 14:8-11
Do God's will ..Heb. 10:5-9
Fulfill
prophecy......Luke 4:17-21
Die for our
sins ....1 Pet. 3:18
Fulfill all righteous-
ness............Matt. 3:15
Reconcile the
world ....2 Cor. 5:18-21
Become our high
priest ....Heb. 7:24-28
Become our
example.......1 Pet. 2:21-23

D. Importance of:
Evidence Christ's
deity ....Rom. 9:3-5
Confirm Christ's
resurrection...Acts 2:24-32
Mark of
believers ......1 John 4:1-6

See Human nature of Christ

Incense—*sweet perfume; frankincense*

A. Offered:
By priests......Lev. 16:12, 13
On the altar ...Ex. 30:1-8
On day of
atonement ....Lev. 16:12, 13
According to strict
formula......Ex. 30:34-36

B. Illegal offering of:
Forbidden .....Ex. 30:37, 38
Excluded from certain
offerings ......Lev. 5:11
Punished ..... (Lev. 10:1, 2
severely......(2 Chr. 26:16-21
Among
idolaters ......Is. 65:3

C. Typical of:
Worship ....Ps. 141:2
Prayer.........Rev. 5:8
Rev. 8:3, 4

Praise ....Mal. 1:11
Approved
service........Eph. 5:2

D. *Purposes of:*
Used in holy
oil ....Ex. 30:34-38
Used in meal
offerings ......Lev. 2:1, 2, 15
Excluded from certain
offerings ......Lev. 5:11
Used in the
showbread ....Lev. 24:7
Product of
Arabia ....Is. 60:6
Presented to
Jesus.........Matt. 2:11
Figurative of
worship.......Ps. 141:2

Incentives to good works

Reap kindness ....Hos. 10:12
Remain ....John 15:16
Reap.............Gal. 6:7-10

Incest—*sexual relations between persons related*

A. *Relations prohibited:*
Same family ...Lev. 18:6-12
Grand-
children......Lev. 18:10
Aunts and
uncles........Lev. 18:12-14
In-laws........Lev. 18:15, 16
Near kin.......Lev. 18:17, 18

B. *Punishment for:*
Death ....Lev. 20:11-17
Child-
lessness......Lev. 20:19-21
A curse........Deut. 27:20-23

C. *Examples of:*
Lot—with his
daughters.....Gen. 19:30-38
Reuben—with his father's
concubine.....Gen. 35:22

Inconsistency—*the non-agreement of two things*

Between:

Criticism of ourselves and
others............Matt. 7:3
Legalism and human
mercy............John 7:23
Profession and
reality...........Luke 22:31-62
Preaching and
practice ....Rom. 2:21-23

Private and public
convictions......Gal. 2:11-14
Faith and works ..James 2:14-26
Profession and
works ....Titus 1:16

Inconstancy—*inability to stand firm in crisis*

A. *Causes of:*
Little faith.....Matt. 13:19-22
Satan..........Luke 22:31-34
False
teachers ......Gal. 1:6-10
Doubt ....James 1:6-8
Immaturity ....2 Pet. 1:5-10

B. *Remedies against:*
Firm
foundation ....Matt. 7:24-27
Strong faith ...Hab. 3:16-19
Full armor.....Eph. 6:10-20

Incontinency—*uncontrolled indulgence of the passions*

A. *Expressed in:*
Unbridled sexual
morals........Ex. 32:6, 18, 25
Abnormal sexual
desires........2 Sam. 13:1-15
Unnatural
sexual   (Gen. 19:5-9
appetites.....(Rom. 1:26, 27

B. *Sources of:*
Lust ....1 Pet. 4:2, 3
Satan...........1 Cor. 7:5
Apostasy ......2 Tim. 3:3

Incorruptible—*enduring; lasting forever*

Resurrected   (1 Cor. 15:42, 52,
body ....(53
Christian's
inheritance.......1 Pet. 1:4
Seed of Christian
life ....1 Pet. 1:23

Increase—*to become more abundant*

A. *Used literally of:*
Knowledge ....Dan. 12:4

B. *Used spiritually of:*
Messiah's
kingdom ......Is. 9:7
Wisdom ....Luke 2:52
Faith ....Luke 17:5
Esteem ....John 3:30
Knowledge of
God...........Col. 1:10
Love...........1 Thess. 4:9, 10
Ungodliness ...2 Tim. 2:16

Incredulity—*an unwillingness to believe*

Characterized by:

Exaggerated demand for
evidence ....John 20:24, 25
Desire for more
signs ....Judg. 6:37-40
Attempts to nullify plain
evidence ....John 9:13-41
Blindness of
mind ....Acts 28:22-29

Indecency

Noah guilty of ....Gen. 9:21-23
Forbidden, to
priests ....Ex. 20:26
Michal rebukes David
for ....2 Sam. 6:20-23
Men committing ...Rom. 1:27

Indecision—*inability to decide between vital issues*

A. *Manifested in, mixing:*
Truth and
idolatry ....1 Kin. 18:21
Duty and compro-
mise ....John 19:12-16
Holiness and
sin ....Gal. 5:1-7
Faith and
works..........Gal. 3:1-5

B. *Results in:*
Spiritual
unfitness......Luke 9:59-62
Instability ....James 1:6-8
Sinful compro-
mise ....2 Cor. 6:14-18
Spiritual
defeat.........Rom. 6:16-22
Spiritual
deadness......Rev. 3:15-17

C. *Examples of:*
Israel at
Kadesh ....Num. 13:26-33
Joshua at Ai ...Josh. 7:6-10
David at
Keilah ....1 Sam. 23:1-5
Pilate ....Matt. 27:11-24
Felix..........Acts 24:25, 26

See Inconstancy

Independence—*control of one's affairs apart from outside influences*

A. *Virtues of:*
Freedom of
action.........Gen. 14:22-24

Respon-
sibility ....John 9:21, 23

B. *Evils of:*
Arbitrary use of
authority......1 Sam. 14:24-45
Selfishness.....1 Sam. 25:1-11
Mismanage-
ment..........Luke 15:12-16
Arrogance .....3 John 9, 10

India

Eastern limit of Persian
Empire ....Esth. 1:1

Indictment—*formal accusation for a crime*

A. *For real crimes:*
Korah's
company......Num. 16:1-50
Achan ....Josh. 7:1-26
Baal
worshipers ....1 Kin. 18:19-42
David..........2 Sam. 12:1-14
Ananias ....Acts 5:1-10

B. *For supposed crimes:*
Certain
tribes ....Josh. 22:10-34
Naboth ....1 Kin. 21:1-16
Three Hebrew
men..........Dan. 3:1-28
Jews..........Ezra 5:3-17
Esth. 3:8, 9
Christ ....Matt. 26:61-65
Stephen ....Acts 6:11, 13
Paul..........Acts 16:20, 21
Acts 17:7

Indifference—*not concerned for or against something*

A. *Characteristic of:*
Unbelievers....Luke 17:26-30
Backsliders ....Rev. 3:15, 16

B. *As a good feature concerning, worldly:*
Comforts ......Phil. 4:11-13
Applause ......Gal. 1:10
Traditions .....Col. 2:16-23

C. *As a bad feature:*
Inhumani-
tarianism.....Luke 10:30-32
In the use of one's
talents ....Luke 19:20-26
Moral
callousness....Matt. 27:3, 4

Religious
unconcern ....Acts 18:12-16

Indignation—*boiling wrath against something sinful*

A. *God's:*
Irresistible .....Nah. 1:6
Victorious .....Hab. 3:12
Poured out ....Zeph. 3:8
Toward His
enemies......Is. 66:14
On Israel ......Deut. 29:28
Against Edom
forever.. ....Mal. 1:4
Angels, instruments
of............Ps. 78:49
On believers ...Job 10:17
Will hide His own
from ....Is. 26:20
Entreated, on the
wicked........Ps. 69:24
As
punishment ...Rom. 2:8

B. *Man's against:*
Others........Esth. 5:9
Jews..........Neh. 4:1
Christ ....Luke 13:14
Christians .....Acts 5:17

Indignities suffered by Christ

A. *Against His body:*
Spit on ....Matt. 26:67
Struck.........John 18:22, 23
Crowned with
thorns ....Matt. 27:29
Crucified .....Matt. 27:31-35

B. *Against His person:*
Called guilty without a
trial............John 18:30, 31
Mocked and {Matt. 27:29, 31,
derided.....{ 39-44
Rejected in favor of a
murderer......Matt. 27:16-21
Crucified between two
men...........John 19:18

Indiscrimination—*showing lack of distinction in*

Devastation........Is. 24:1-4
Judgment........Ezek. 18:1-32
God's
providences ......Matt. 5:45

Indulge—*to yield to desires*

Fleshly desires ....Eph. 2:3
Corrupt desires....2 Pet. 2:10

Gross
immorality ....Jude 7

Indulgence—*a kindness often misused*

Parental ....1 Sam. 3:11-14
Kingly ....2 Sam. 13:21-39
Priestly ....Judg. 17:1-13

Industry—*diligence in one's work*

A. *Characteristics of:*
Established ....Gen. 2:15
Commanded...1 Thess. 4:11
Commend-
able..........Prov. 27:23-27
Done
willingly ......Prov. 31:13
Mark of
wisdom ......Prov. 10:5
Suspended on
Sabbath......Ex. 20:10
Neglect of,
rebuked.......2 Thess. 3:10-12

B. *Necessity of:*
Our needs .....1 Thess. 2:9
Needs of
others.........Acts 20:35
Faithful
witness ....1 Tim. 5:8

C. *Blessings of:*
Wealth ....Prov. 10:4, 5
Praise ....Prov. 31:28, 31
Food
sufficient......Prov. 12:11
Will rule......Prov. 12:24

Indwelling, of believers

A. *By Christ:*
Through
faith ....Eph. 3:14-19
Mystery ....Col. 1:27

B. *Spirit:*
Every
believer......Rom. 8:9-11
Body, a temple of
God..........1 Cor. 3:16

Infant salvation

Suggested by {Matt. 18:3-5, 10
scripture ....{Matt. 19:14

Infants

A. *Acts performed upon:*
Naming.......Ruth 4:17
Blessing ......Luke 1:67, 76-79
Circumcision ..Luke 2:21

B. *Capacity to:*
Believe ....Matt. 18:6
Know the
Scriptures.....2 Tim. 3:15
Receive
training.......Eph. 6:4
Worship in God's
house ....1 Sam. 1:24, 28

C. *Murder of:*
By Pharaoh....Ex. 1:16
By Herod the
Great ....Matt. 2:16-18
In war........Num. 31:17

Infidelity—*unbelief in God's revelation*

A. *Causes of:*
Unregenerate
heart..........Rom. 2:5
Hatred of the
light ....John 3:19-21
Spiritual
blindness......1 Cor. 2:8, 14
Self-trust .....Is. 47:10, 11
Unbelief ......Acts 6:10-15
Inveterate
prejudice......Acts 7:54, 57
Worldly
wisdom ....1 Cor. 1:18-22

B. *Manifested in:*
Rejecting God's
Word ....2 Pet. 3:3-5
Scoffing at God's
servants.......2 Chr. 30:6, 10
Hiding under
lies...........Is. 28:15
Living without
God...........Job 22:13-17
Using derisive
words.........Matt. 12:24
Doubting God's righteous-
ness...........Ps. 10:11, 13
Calling religion
worthless .....Mal. 3:14

C. *Punishment of:*
Eternal separation from
God...........2 Thess. 1:8, 9
God's wrath ...1 Thess. 2:14-16
Hell ....Luke 16:23-31
Severe
punishment ...Heb. 10:28, 29

D. *Remedies against:*
Remember the
end ....Ps. 73:16-28
Trust when you can't
explain........Job 2:9, 10
Stand upon the
Word ....Matt. 4:3-11

Use God's
armor.........Eph. 6:10-19
Grow
spiritually .....2 Pet. 1:4-11

Infinite—*extending immeasurably*

God's
understanding ....Ps. 147:5

Infirmities—*weaknesses of our human
nature*

A. *Kinds of:*
Sickness or
disease........Matt. 8:17
Imperfections of the
body ....2 Cor. 11:30

B. *Our duties with reference to:*
Rejoice in .....2 Cor. 12:10
Help those afflicted
with ....Gal. 6:1
Not to despise in
others.........Gal. 4:13, 14

Influence—*that invisible force in one's
personality that causes others to act*

Christians, should be:

As salt ....Matt. 5:13
As light ....Matt. 5:14-16
Phil. 2:15
As examples ......1 Thess. 1:7, 8
Beneficial to   {1 Cor. 7:14, 16
spouse............{1 Pet. 3:1, 2
Above criticism ...1 Cor. 8:10-13
Honorable........1 Tim. 6:1
Permanent ....Heb. 11:4
Beneficial to
others............1 Pet. 2:11, 12
Without
reproach ....Phil. 2:15, 16

Ingenuity—*skill shown in unusual
contrivances*

Of God...........Job 38:4-41
Ps. 139:13-16
Gen. 27:7-29
Of man ....Ex. 2:1-9
Ex. 35:30-33

Ingratitude—*unthankfulness for
blessings received*

A. *Characteristics of:*
Inconsider-
ate.............Deut. 32:6, 7
Unreason-
able...........Jer. 2:5-7

Unnatural .....Is. 1:2, 3
Ungrateful....Jer. 5:7-9, 24

B. *Causes of:*
Prosperity .....Deut. 6:10-12
Self-
sufficiency ....Deut. 8:12-18
Forgetful-
ness.........Luke 17:12-18
Fear...........1 Sam. 23:5, 12
Greed..........1 Sam. 25:4-11
Pride ....Dan. 5:18-20

C. *Attitudes toward:*
Acknowl-
edged........1 Sam. 24:17-19
Abused ....2 Chr. 24:22
Revealed .....1 Sam. 23:5-12
Forgiven by
kindness ......1 Sam. 25:14-35
Long remem-
bered........Deut. 25:17-19
Overcome by
faithfulness ...Gen. 31:38-44

D. *Examples of:*
Moses by
Israel........Ex. 17:1-3
Gideon by
Israel ....Judg. 8:33-35
God by Saul ...1 Sam. 15:16-23
God by
David ....2 Sam. 12:7-14
Jeremiah by
Judah........Jer. 18:19, 20
God by the
world ....Rom. 1:21

Inheritance, earthly

A. *Among Israelites:*
God the
owner.........Lev. 25:23, 28
Possessed by
families ....Num. 27:4, 7
Law of trans-
mission ....Num. 27:8-11
If sold, restored in year of
jubilee ....Lev. 25:25-34
Must remain in
tribe ....Num. 36:6-10
Repossessed by
kinsman ......Ruth 4:3-5, 10

B. *General characteristics of:*
From fathers...Prov. 19:14
Uncertain
use ....Eccl. 2:18, 19
Object of ⎰ 1 Kin. 21:3, 4
seizure.....⎱ Matt. 21:38
Squandered....Luke 15:11-13

Foolish not
blessed........Prov. 11:29
Descendants
blessed........Ps. 25:12, 13

See Heirs, natural

Inheritance of Israel

A. *Basic features of:*
Lord, Israel's...Deut. 9:26, 29
Land promised to Abraham's
seed ....Gen. 15:7-18
Limits
defined........Gen. 15:18-21
Limits
fulfilled ....1 Kin. 4:21, 24
Possession of, based on
obedience .....2 Kin. 21:12-15
Blessed by the
Lord ....Deut. 15:4
Tribes destroyed
from ....Deut. 20:16-18
Possessed by
degrees ....Ex. 23:29-31
Apportioned ...Josh. 13:7-33
Tribes encouraged to
possess........Josh. 18:1-10
Levites excluded
from ....Num. 18:20-24
Lost by sin ....Ps. 79:1
Restored after the
captivity ......Neh. 11:20

B. *Figurative of:*
Messianic
blessings ......Ps. 2:8
Call of the
Gentiles.......Is. 54:3
Elect
remnant ......Is. 65:8, 9
Eternal
possessions....Is. 60:21

Inheritance, spiritual

A. *Objects of:*
Kingdom ......Matt. 25:34
Eternal life ....Matt. 19:29
Promises.......Heb. 6:12
Blessing ......1 Pet. 3:9
All things......Rev. 21:7
Glory ....Prov. 3:35

B. *Nature of:*
Sealed by the
Spirit ....Eph. 1:13, 14
Received from the
Lord ....Col. 3:24
Results from Christ's
death ....Heb. 9:15

Depends on
belief ....Gal. 3:18, 22
Incorruptible ..1 Pet. 1:4
Final, in
heaven........1 Pet. 1:4

C. *Restrictions upon, only:*
For the
righteous .....1 Cor. 6:9, 10
For the
sanctified .....Acts 20:32
In Christ ......Eph. 1:11, 12
For the trans-
formed .....1 Cor. 15:50-53

See Heirs, spiritual

Inhospitality—*unwillingness to
entertain strangers*

Edomites.........Num. 20:17-21
Sihon ....Num. 21:22, 23
Gibeah...........Judg. 19:15
Nabal ....1 Sam. 25:10-17
Samaritans.......Luke 9:53
Diotrephes.......3 John 10
Penalty for.......Deut. 23:3, 4
                       Luke 10:10-16

Iniquity—*the depth of sin; lawlessness*

A. *Sources of:*
Heart ....Ps. 41:6
                       Matt. 23:28

B. *Effects upon man:*
Insatiable appetite
for ....Ezek. 7:16, 19
Perversion .....Ezek. 9:9

C. *God's attitude toward:*
Cannot look
on ....Hab. 1:13
Does not do ...Zeph. 3:5
Remembers and
punishes ......Jer. 14:10
Visits on
children........Ex. 34:7
Pardons and
subdues.......Mic. 7:18, 19
Takes away from
us..............Zech. 3:4
Lays upon the
Messiah.......Is. 53:5, 6, 11
Remembers no
more..........Heb. 8:12

D. *Christ's relation to:*
Bears our ......Is. 53:5, 6, 11
Makes reconciliation
for ....Dan. 9:24
Redeems us....Titus 2:14

E. *Believer's relation to:*
Will
declare it.......Ps. 38:18
Confesses .....Neh. 9:2
Prays for
pardon of .....Ps. 25:11
Forgiven of ....Ps. 32:5
Must depart
from ....2 Tim. 2:19
Protection
from ....Ps. 125:3
Separation from
God...........Is. 59:2
Prays for freedom
from ....Ps. 119:133
Hindrance to
prayer ....Ps. 66:18

F. *Punishment for:*
Wanderings....Num. 14:34
Loss of
strength ......Ps. 31:10
Destruction....Gen. 19:15
Captivity .....Ezra 9:7
Death ....Ezek. 18:24, 26
Less than
deserved .....Ezra 9:13
Remembered
forever.......1 Sam. 3:13, 14
In hell........Ezek. 32:27

Injustice—*that which violates another's
rights*

A. *Examples of, among men:*
Laban's treatment of
Jacob ....Gen. 31:36-42
Saul's treatment of:
Priests ....1 Sam. 22:15-23
David.........1 Sam. 24:8-22
                       1 Sam. 26:14-25
David's treatment of
Uriah ....2 Sam. 12:1-12
Irijah's treatment of
Jeremiah......Jer. 37:11-21

B. *Charges made against God for
His:*
Choice.........Num. 16:1-14
Inequality .....Ezek. 18:25
Partiality ......Rom. 9:14
Delay..........Rev. 6:10

C. *Punishment on executed:*
Severely .....1 Sam. 15:32, 33
Swiftly ....Esth. 7:9, 10
According to
prophecy......1 Kin. 22:34-38

See Just, justice

Ink—*a writing fluid*

Used for writing a
book . . . . Jer. 36:18
Used in letter {2 John 12
writing {3 John 13

Inkhorn—*a case for pens and ink*

Writer's tool . . . . . . Ezek. 9:2, 3

Inn—*a shelter providing lodging for travelers*

Lodging place . . . . . Jer. 9:2
Place for rest . . . . . . Luke 2:7

Inner group

At girl's bedside . . . Mark 5:35-40
At Christ's
transfiguration . . . Mark 9:2
In Gethsemane . . . . . Matt. 26:36, 37

Inner man—*man's genuine identity*

Often hidden . . . . . . Matt. 23:27, 28
Seen by God . . . . . . 1 Sam. 16:7
Strengthened . . . . . Eph. 3:16

Inner natures, conflict of

A. *Sin nature:*
Called flesh . . . . Rom. 8:5
Called old
self . . . . Col. 3:9
Corrupt and
deceitful . . . . . . Eph. 4:22
Works of . . . . . . Gal. 5:19-21
Cannot please
God . . . . Rom. 8:8
To be
mortified . . . . . . Col. 3:5

B. *New nature:*
By Spirit's
indwelling . . . . . 1 Cor. 3:16
Strengthened by
Spirit . . . . Eph. 3:16
Called inward
man . . . . 2 Cor. 4:16
Called new
man . . . . Col. 3:10
Fruits of . . . . . . Gal. 5:22, 23

C. *Conflict:*
Called {Rom. 7:19-23
warfare . . . . . . {Gal. 5:17

D. *Victory:*
Recognize
source . . . . James 1:14-16
Realize former
condition . . . . . Eph. 2:1-7
Put off former
conduct . . . . . . Eph. 4:22

Make no
provision . . . . . . Rom. 13:14
Complete surrender to
God . . . . Rom. 12:1, 2
Spiritual
food . . . . 1 Pet. 2:1, 2

Innocence—*freedom from guilt or sin*

A. *Loss of, by:*
Disobedi-
ence . . . . Rom. 5:12
Idolatry . . . . Ps. 106:34-39

B. *Kinds of:*
Absolute . . . . 2 Cor. 5:21
Legal . . . . Luke 23:4
Moral . . . . Josh. 22:10-34
Spiritual . . . . 2 Pet. 3:14

C. *Of Christ:*
In prophecy . . . Is. 53:7-9
In type . . . . 1 Pet. 1:19
In reality . . . . . 1 Pet. 3:18
By exami-
nation . . . . Luke 23:13-22
By testimony . . Acts 13:28

Innocents, massacre of

Mourning
foretold . . . . Jer. 31:15
After Jesus'
birth . . . . Matt. 2:16-18

Inns, Three

Place about 30 miles south of
Rome . . . . Acts 28:15

Innumerable—*uncounted multitude*

Evils . . . . Ps. 40:12
Animal life . . . . Ps. 104:25
Descendants . . . . . Heb. 11:12
People . . . . Luke 12:1
Angels . . . . Heb. 12:22

Inquiry—*a consulting or seeking for counsel*

By Israel . . . . Ex. 18:15
With ephod . . . . 1 Sam. 23:9, 11
Unlawful
method . . . . 1 Sam. 28:6, 7
Through prayer . . . 2 Cor. 12:7-9
James 1:5

Insanity—*mental derangement*

A. *Characteristics of:*
Abnormal
behavior . . . . . . Dan. 4:32-34
Self-
destruction . . . . Matt. 17:14-18

Distinct from demon
possession ....Matt. 4:24

B. *Figurative of:*
The result of
moral $\left\{\begin{array}{l}\text{Jer. 25:15-17}\\\text{Jer. 51:7}\end{array}\right.$
instability
God's
judgment .....Zech. 12:4

Inscription—*a statement written or engraved*

On Christ's $\left\{\begin{array}{l}\text{Luke 23:38}\\\text{John 19:19-22}\end{array}\right.$
cross
On an altar ......Acts 17:23
Roman coin .....Mark 12:16

Insects of the Bible

A. *Characteristics of:*
Created by
God.............Gen. 1:24, 25
Some clean ....Lev. 11:21, 22
Some
unclean ......Lev. 11:23, 24

B. *List of:*
Ant.............Prov. 6:6
Bee............Judg. 14:8
Cricket ....Lev. 11:22
Caterpillar....Ps. 78:46
Flea ....1 Sam. 24:14
Fly ....Eccl. 10:1
Gnat...........Matt. 23:24
Grasshopper ...Lev. 11:22
Hornet.........Deut. 7:20
Leech...........Prov. 30:15
Locust.........Ex. 10:4
Moth ....Is. 50:9
Spider ....Prov. 30:28
Worms ....Ex. 16:20

C. *Illustrative of:*
Design in
nature ....Prov. 30:24-28
Troubles.....Ps. 118:12
Insignifi-
cance ....1 Sam. 24:14
Desolation....Joel 1:4
Appetite ......Prov. 30:15
Transitori- $\left\{\begin{array}{l}\text{Is. 51:8}\\\text{Matt. 6:20}\end{array}\right.$
ness...........
Vast
numbers .....Judg. 6:5

Insecurity—*a state of anxiety about earthly needs*

A. *Descriptive of:*
Wicked........Ps. 37:1, 2, 10
Riches..........1 Tim. 6:17
Those trusting in
themselves....Luke 12:16-21

B. *Cure of:*
Steadfast of
mind..........Is. 26:3
Rely upon God's
promises ......Ps. 37:1-26
Remember God's
provision......Phil. 4:9-19
Put God first...Matt. 6:25-34

Insensibility—*deadness of spiritual life*

A. *Kinds of:*
Physical ....Judg. 19:26-29
Spiritual.......Jer. 5:3, 21
Judicial.......Acts 28:25-28

B. *Causes of:*
Seared
conscience ....1 Tim. 4:2
Spiritual
ignorance .....Eph. 4:18, 19
Wanton
pleasure.......1 Tim. 5:6

Insincerity—*hypocritical deceitfulness*

A. *Manifested in:*
Mock
ceremonies....Is. 58:3-6
Unwilling
preaching ....Jon. 4:1-11
Trumped up
questions .....Matt. 22:15-22
Boastful
pretentions....Luke 22:33

B. *Those guilty of:*
Hypocrites.....Luke 11:42-47
False
teachers ......Gal. 6:12, 13
Immature
Christians.....1 Cor. 4:17-21

See Hypocrisy

Insomnia—*inability to sleep*

A. *Causes of:*
Excessive
work..........Gen. 31:40
Worry........Esth. 6:1
Dreams........Dan. 2:1
Conscience ....Dan. 6:9-18

B. *Cure of:*
Trust ....Ps. 3:5, 6
Peacefulness...Ps. 4:8
Confidence ....Ps. 127:1, 2
Obedience .....Prov. 6:20-22

Inspiration of the Scriptures

A. *Expressed by:*
"Thus the Lord said to
me"...........Jer. 13:1

"The word of the Lord
came"........1 Kin. 16:1
"It is
written" ......Rom. 10:15
"As the Holy Spirit
says" ....Heb. 3:7
"According to the
Scripture"....James 2:8
"My words in your
mouth" ......Jer. 1:9, 10

B. *Described as:*
Inspired by
God...........2 Tim. 3:16
Moved by the Holy
Spirit ....2 Pet. 1:21
Christ-   {Luke 24:27
centered .....{2 Cor. 13:3

C. *Modes of:*
Different.......Heb. 1:1
Inner   {Judg. 13:25
impulse .....{Jer. 20:9
A voice ....Rev. 1:10
Dreams........Dan. 7:1
Visions ....Ezek. 11:24, 25

D. *Proofs of:*
Fulfilled   {Jer. 28:15-17
prophecy ....{Luke 24:27, 44,
                    45
Miracles   {Ex. 4:1-9
attesting .....{2 Kin. 1:10-14
Teachings   {Deut. 4:8
supporting ...{Ps. 19:7-11

E. *Design of:*
Reveal God's   {Amos 3:7
mysteries ....{1 Cor. 2:10
Reveal the   {Acts 1:16
future.........{1 Pet. 1:10-12
Instruct and   {Mic. 3:8
edify ....{Acts 1:8
Counteract   {2 Cor. 13:1-3
distortion ....{Gal. 1:6-11

F. *Results of Scriptures:*
Unbreakable...John 10:34-36
Eternal ....Matt. 24:35
Authori-
tative ....Matt. 4:4, 7, 10
Trustworthy ...Ps. 119:160
                {Matt. 22:32,
Verbally   {   43-46
accurate .....{Gal. 3:16
Sanctifying ...2 Tim. 3:16, 17
Effective.......Jer. 23:29
                    2 Tim. 3:15

See Word of God

Instability—*lack of firmness of
convictions*

A. *Causes of:*
Deception .....Gal. 3:1
                    Col. 2:4-8
Immaturity ...1 Tim. 3:6
False   {2 Cor. 11:3, 4
teaching .....{Gal. 1:6-11
Lack of
depth ....Heb. 5:11-14
Unsettled   {Eph. 4:14
mind.........{James 1:6-8

B. *Examples of:*
Pharaoh ....Ex. 10:8-20
Israel..........Judg. 2:17
Solomon ......1 Kin. 11:1-8
Disciples......John 6:66
John Mark.....Acts 15:37, 38
Galatians ......Gal. 1:6

Instinct—*inbred characteristic of*

Animals...........Is. 1:3
Birds..............Jer. 8:7

Instruction—*imparting knowledge to
others*

A. *Given by:*
Parents........Deut. 6:6-25
Priests.........Deut. 24:8
God ....Jer. 32:33
Pastors ....Eph. 4:11
Pedagogues...Neh. 8:7, 8
Paraclete (the Holy
Spirit)........John 14:26

B. *Means of:*
Nature.........Prov. 6:6-11
Human
nature ....Prov. 24:30-34
Law ....Rom. 2:18
Proverbs......Prov. 1:1-30
Songs.........Deut. 32:1-44
History ....1 Cor. 10:1-11
God's Word....2 Tim. 3:15, 16

See Education; Teaching, teachers

Instrument—*a tool or implement*

For threshing .....2 Sam. 24:22
For sacrifices......Ezek. 40:42
Of iron ....2 Sam. 12:31
Body members,
used as..........Rom. 6:13

Insult—*to treat insolently*

Ignored by King
Saul...............1 Sam. 10:26, 27
Job treated with ..Job 30:1, 9, 10
Children punished
because of........2 Kin. 2:23, 24

Pharisees treat Jesus
with.............Matt. 12:24, 25
Paul's
reaction to......Acts 23:1-5
Forbidden.........1 Pet. 3:8, 9

Insurrection—*rebellion against constituted authority*

In Jerusalem......Ezra 4:19
Absalom's
miserable.........2 Sam. 18:32, 33
Attempted by
Jews ....Mark 15:7

Integrity—*moral uprightness*

A. *Manifested in:*
Moral
uprightness ...Gen. 20:3-10
Unselfish
service........Num. 16:15
Performing
vows..........Jer. 35:12-19
Rejecting
bribes.........Acts 8:18-23
Honest
behavior ......2 Cor. 7:2

B. *Illustrated in:*
Job's life.......Job 2:3, 9, 10
David's
kingship ......Ps. 7:8
Nehemiah's
service........Neh. 5:14-19
Daniel's rule ...Dan. 6:1-4
Paul's
ministry.......2 Cor. 4:2

Intemperance—*not restraining the appetites*

A. *Manifested in:*
Drunken-
ness...........Prov. 23:19-35
Gluttony.......Titus 1:12
Immorality ....Rom. 1:26, 27

B. *Evils of:*
Puts the flesh
first..........Phil. 3:19
Brings about
death ....1 Sam. 25:36-38

See Drunkenness

Intention—*a fixed determination to do a specified thing*

A. *Good:*
Commended but not
allowed ......1 Kin. 8:17-19

Planned but
delayed ....Rom. 15:24-28

B. *Evil:*
Restrained by
God...........Gen. 31:22-31
Turned to good by
God...........Gen. 45:4-8
Overruled by God's
providence ....Esth. 9:23-25

C. *Of Christ:*
Predicted .....Ps. 40:6-8
Announced ....Matt. 20:18-28
Misunder-
stood ....Matt. 16:21-23
Fulfilled ......John 19:28-30
Explained......Luke 24:25-47

Interbreeding—*crossbreed*

Forbidden:

In animals, vegetables,
cloth ....Lev. 19:19

Intercession—*prayer offered in behalf of others*

A. *Purposes of:*
Secure
healing........James 5:14-16
Avert
judgment .....Num. 14:11-21
Insure
deliverance....1 Sam. 7:5-9
Give
blessings ......Num. 6:23-27
Obtain
restoration ....Job 42:8-10
Encourage
repentance....Rom. 10:1-4

B. *Characteristics of:*
Pleading......Gen. 18:23-33
Specific.......Gen. 24:12-15
Victorious.....Ex. 17:9-12
Very intense...Ex. 32:31, 32
Quickly
answered ...Num. 27:15-23
Confessing.....2 Sam. 24:17
Personal.......1 Chr. 29:19
Covenant
pleading ......Neh. 1:4-11
Unselfish ......Acts 7:60

C. *Examples of:*
Moses ....Ex. 32:11-13
Joshua.........Josh. 7:6-9
Jehoshaphat ...2 Chr. 20:5-13
Isaiah ....2 Chr. 32:20
Daniel.........Dan. 9:3-19

Christ ....John 17:1-26
Paul ....Col. 1:9-12

Intercourse—*copulation*

Kinds of, forbidden:

With neighbor's
wife... ....Lev. 18:20
With animal .....Lev. 18:23

Interest—*money charged on borrowed money; usury*

From a poor man,
forbidden.........Ex. 22:25
From a stranger,
permitted.........Deut. 23:19, 20
Exaction of,
unprofitable .....Prov. 28:8
Condemned as a
sin ....Ezek. 18:8-17
Exaction of,
rebuked ....Neh. 5:1-13
Reward for non-exaction
of ....Ps. 15:5
Used to
illustrate ....Luke 19:23

Intermediate state—*the state of the believer between death and the resurrection*

A. *Described as:*
Like sleep .....John 11:11-14
"Far better" ...Phil. 1:21, 23
"Present with the
Lord" ....2 Cor. 5:6, 8

B. *Characteristics of:*
Persons
identifiable....Matt. 17:3
Conscious and (Ps. 17:15
enjoyable ....｛Luke 16:25
Unchange-
able..........Luke 16:26
Without the ｛2 Cor. 5:1-4
body ....｛Rev. 6:9
Awaiting the ｛Phil. 3:20, 21
resur-
rection......｛1 Thess. 4:13-18

See Immortality

Interpretation—*making the unknown known*

A. *Things in need of:*
Dreams.......Gen. 41:15-36
Languages.....Gen. 42:23
Writings......Dan. 5:7-31
Scripture .....Acts 8:30-35
Tongues ......1 Cor. 12:10

B. *Agents of:*
Jesus Christ ...Luke 24:25-47
Holy Spirit.....1 Cor. 2:11-16
Angels........Luke 1:26-37
Prophets and
apostles.......Eph. 3:2-11

Intestines (see Entrails)

Intimidation—*suggesting possible harm if one acts contrary to another's wishes*

Attitudes toward:

Discovers its
deceit ....Neh. 6:5-13
Do not yield ......Jer. 26:8-16
Go steadfastly
on.................Dan. 6:6-10
Answer boldly ....Amos 7:12-17

Intolerance—*active opposition to the views of others*

A. *Of the state against:*
Jews...........Esth. 3:12, 13
Rival
religions ......Dan. 3:13-15
Christian
faith ....Rev. 13:1-18

B. *Of the Jews against:*
Their
prophets ......Matt. 23:31-35
Christ ....Luke 4:28-30
Christians ....Acts 5:40, 41
Christianity ..Acts 17:1-8

C. *Of the Church against:*
Evil............2 Cor. 6:14-18
False
teaching ......2 John 10, 11
False
religions ......Gal. 1:6-9

D. *Manifestations of:*
Prejudice ......Acts 21:27-32
Persecution ....Acts 13:50
Passion ....Acts 9:1, 2, 21

Intrigue—*using hidden methods to cause another's downfall*

A. *Characteristics of:*
Deceit ....Gen. 27:6-23
Plausible
arguments ....Judg. 9:1-6
Subtle
maneuvers ....2 Sam. 15:1-13
False front ....2 Kin. 10:18-28
Political
trickery ....Esth. 3:5-10

B. *Against Christ by:*
Herod .... Matt. 2:8, 12-16
Satan.......... Matt. 4:3-11
Jews........... Luke 11:53, 54

Investigation—*close examination*

A. *Characteristics of:*
Involves
research ..... Ezra 6:1-13
Causes sought
out .... Eccl. 1:13, 17
Claims
checked...... Num. 13:1-25
Suspicions followed
through...... Josh. 22:10-30
Historic parallels
cited ..... Jer. 26:17-24

B. *Lack of:*
Cause of later
trouble........ Josh. 9:3-23
Productive of
evil .... Dan. 5:22, 23

Investments, spiritual

In heavenly
riches .... Matt. 6:20
Dividends later
paid............ 1 Tim. 6:19

Invisible—*the unseeable*

God is .... 1 Tim. 1:17
Faith sees........ Heb. 11:27

Invitations of the Bible

Come:

And reason ..... Is. 1:18
My people .... Is. 26:20
Buy wine and
milk......... Is. 55:1
"To Me" ...... Is. 55:3
And see.......... John 1:46
And rest ...... Matt. 11:28
After Me........ Mark 1:17
Take up the
cross .... Mark 10:21
To the marriage... Matt. 22:4
Everything is
ready........... Luke 14:17
The blessed ...... Matt. 25:34
Threefold .... Rev. 22:17

Iphdeiah—*the Lord redeems*

A descendant of
Benjamin........ 1 Chr. 8:1, 25

Ira—*watchful*

1. Priest to
David .... 2 Sam. 20:26

2. One of David's
mighty ⎰ 2 Sam. 23:26
men......... ⎱ 1 Chr. 11:28

3. Ithrite .... 2 Sam. 23:38
1 Chr. 11:40

Irad—*fugitive*

Son of Enoch; grandson of
Cain.............. Gen. 4:18

Iram—*aroused*

Edomite chief ..... Gen. 36:43
1 Chr. 1:54

Iri—*urbane*

Benjamite......... 1 Chr. 7:7

Irijah—*Yahweh sees*

Accuses Jeremiah of
desertion .... Jer. 37:13, 14

Ir-Nahash—*serpent city*

City of Judah ..... 1 Chr. 4:1, 12

Iron—*a useful metal*

A. *Features concerning:*
Used very
early.......... Gen. 4:22
Used in
weapons ...... Job 20:24

B. *Items made of:*
Armor .... 2 Sam. 23:7
Axe............ 2 Kin. 6:5
Bedstead....... Deut. 3:11
Chariot....... Josh. 17:16, 18
Gate........... Acts 12:10
Gods .... Dan. 5:4, 23
Iron pen ...... Job 19:24
Tools .... 1 Kin. 6:7
2 Sam. 12:31
Vessels .... Josh. 6:24
Weapons ...... Job 20:24
Yokes .... Deut. 28:48
Implements.... Gen. 4:22

C. *Figurative of:*
Affliction ...... Deut. 4:20
Barrenness.... Deut. 28:23
Authority...... Ps. 2:9
Stubborn-
ness........... Is. 48:4
Slavery .... Jer. 28:13, 14
Strength....... Dan. 2:33-41
Insensibility ... 1 Tim. 4:2

Iron—*conspicuous*

City of Naphtali... Josh. 19:38

Irony—*a pretense of ignorance*

Show contempt ...2 Sam. 6:20
Mockery ....1 Kin. 18:27
Rebuke distrust ...1 Kin. 22:13-17
Multiply
transgression.....Amos 4:4
Mocked honor .....Matt. 27:29
Deflate the wise..2 Cor. 11:19, 20

Irpeel—*God heals*

Town of
Benjamin.........Josh. 18:21, 27

Irreconcilable—*violators of agreements;
opposing compromise*

Characteristic of the last
days..............2 Tim. 3:1, 3

Irrigation—*supply with water*

Not usually
needed ....Deut. 11:11, 14
Source of ....Eccl. 2:5, 6
Figurative of {Is. 43:19, 20
spiritual life .....{Is. 58:11

Irritability—*the quality of easily being
provoked to anger*

A. *Characteristics of:*
  Quick
  temper........1 Sam. 20:30-33
  Morose {1 Sam. 25:3,
  disposition ...{ 36-39
  Hotheaded.....Gen. 49:6
  Complaining ...Ex. 14:10-14

B. *Cure by God's:*
  Love...........1 Cor. 13:4-7
  Peace..........Phil. 4:7, 8
  Spirit.........Gal. 5:22-26

Ir Shemesh—*city of the sun*

Danite city........Josh. 19:41
Same as Beth
Shemesh ....1 Kin. 4:9

Iru—*watchful*

Son of Caleb ......1 Chr. 4:15

Isaac—*laughter*

A. *Life of:*
  Son of Abraham and
  Sarah ....Gen. 21:1-3
  His birth
  promised......Gen. 17:16-18
  Heir of the
  covenant......Gen. 17:19, 21

Born and
circumcised ...Gen. 21:1-8
Offered up as a
sacrifice.....Gen. 22:1-19
Secures Rebekah as
wife..........Gen. 24:1-67
Buries his
father.........Gen. 25:8, 9
Father of Esau and
Jacob ....Gen. 25:19-26
Prefers Esau ...Gen. 25:27, 28
Lives in
Gerar ....Gen. 26:1, 6
Covenant reaffirmed
with ....Gen. 26:2-5
Calls Rebekah his
sister.........Gen. 26:7-11
Becomes
prosperous ....Gen. 26:12-14
Trouble over
wells.........Gen. 26:14-22
Covenant with
Abimelech ....Gen. 26:23-33
Grieves over
Esau ....Gen. 26:34, 35
Deceived by
Jacob ....Gen. 27:1-25
Blesses his
sons ....Gen. 27:26-40
Dies in his old
age ....Gen. 35:28, 29

B. *Character of:*
  Obedient.......Gen. 22:9
  Peaceable.....Gen. 26:14-22
  Thoughtful ....Gen. 24:63
  Prayerful .....Gen. 25:21
              Gen. 26:25

C. *Significance of:*
  Child of
  promise ....Gal. 4:22, 23
  Man of faith ...Heb. 11:9, 20
  Type of
  believers ......Gal. 4:28-31
  Ancestor of
  Christ.........Luke 3:34
  Patriarch of
  Israel ....Ex. 32:13

Isaiah—*Yahweh is salvation*

A. *Life of:*
  Son of Amoz ..Is. 1:1
  Prophesies during reigns of
  Uzziah, Jotham, Ahaz and
  Hezekiah......Is. 1:1
  Contemporary of Amos and
  Hosea.........Hos. 1:1
              Amos 1:1

Responds to prophetic
call . . . . .Is. 6:1-13
Protests against policy of
Ahaz. . . . . .Is. 7:1-25
                      Is. 8:1-22
Gives symbolic names to his
sons . . . . .Is. 8:1-4, 18
Walks naked and
barefoot. . . . . . .Is. 20:2, 3
Encourages
Hezekiah. . . . . .2 Kin. 19:1-34
Warns Hezekiah of
death . . . . .2 Kin. 20:1
Instructs Hezekiah
concerning his
recovery . . . . . .2 Kin. 20:4-11
Upbraids Hezekiah for his
acts. . . . . .2 Kin. 20:12-19
Writes Uzziah's
biography . . . . .2 Chr. 26:22
Writes Hezekiah's
biography . . . . .2 Chr. 32:32

B. *Messianic prophecies of:*
Christ's birth . .Is. 7:14
                      Is. 11:1-9
                      Matt. 1:22, 23
John's   ⎰Is. 40:3
coming. . . . . . .⎱Matt. 3:3
Christ's   ⎰Is. 61:1, 2
mission . . . . . .⎱Luke 4:17-19
                      ⎰Is. 53:1-12
Christ's   ⎱Matt. 8:17
death . . . . 1 Pet. 2:21-25
Christ as   ⎰Is. 42:1-4
Servant . . . . . .⎱Matt. 12:17-21
Gospel   ⎰Is. 55:1-13
invitation . . . .⎱Acts 13:34
Conversion of   ⎰Is. 11:10
Gentiles. . . . . .⎱Rom. 15:8-12

C. *Other prophecies of:*
Assyrian
invasion. . . . . .Is. 8:1-4
Babylon's fall . .Is. 13:1-22
Devastation of
Moab . . . . .Is. 16:1-14
Tyre and Sidon
condemned . . .Is. 23:1-18
Destruction of Sennach-
erib . . . . .Is. 37:14-38
Babylonian
captivity . . . . .Is. 39:3-7

D. *Other features concerning:*
Calls Christ
Immanuel. . . . .Is. 7:14
Names Cyrus . .Is. 45:1-3

Eunuch reads ⎰Acts 8:27, 28,
from . . . .⎱ 30
                      ⎰Rom. 9:27, 29
Quoted   ⎱Rom. 10:16, 20,
in New   21
Testament . . .⎰Rom. 11:26, 27

Isaiah, the Book of—*a book of the Old
Testament*

Call of Isaiah . . . . .Is. 6
Promise of
Immanuel. . . . . . .Is. 7:10-25
Prophecies against
nations. . . . . .Is. 13-23
Historical
section . . . . .Is. 36-39
Songs of the
servant. . . . . .Is. 42, 49-53
Future hope of
Zion. . . . . .Is. 66

Iscah—*watchful*

Daughter of
Haran . . . . .Gen. 11:29

Iscariot, Judas—*man of Kerioth*

A. *Life of:*
Listed among the
Twelve. . . . . . .Mark 3:14, 19
Called Iscariot and a
traitor . . . . . . .Luke 6:16
Criticizes
Mary. . . . . .John 12:3-5
Treasurer . . . . . .John 13:29
Identified as
betrayer. . . . . .John 13:21-26
Sells out
Christ. . . . . . . .Matt. 26:14-16
Betrays Christ ⎰Mark 14:10, 11,
with a kiss . . .⎱ 43-45
Returns betrayal
money . . . . . . .Matt. 27:3-10
Commits
suicide . . . . . . .Matt. 27:5
Goes to his own
place. . . . . .Acts 1:16-20, 25
Better not to have been
born . . . . .Matt. 26:24

B. *Described as:*
Thief . . . . .John 12:6
Callous . . . . . . .John 12:4-6
Deceitful . . . . . .Matt. 26:14-16
Possessed by
Satan . . . . .John 13:27
Son of
perdition . . . . . .John 17:12
Devil . . . . .John 6:70, 71

Ishbah

Ishbah—*he praises*

Man of Judah . . . . . 1 Chr. 4:17

Ishbak—*leaving*

Son of Abraham and
Keturah . . . . Gen. 25:2

Ishbi-Benob—*my dwelling is at Nob*

Philistine giant . . . . 2 Sam. 21:16, 17

Ishbosheth—*man of shame*

One of Saul's
sons . . . . 2 Sam. 2:8
Made king . . . . 2 Sam. 2:8-10
Offends Abner . . . . 2 Sam. 3:7-11
Slain; but assassins
executed . . . . 2 Sam. 4:1-12

Ishhod—*man of majesty*

Manassite . . . . 1 Chr. 7:18

Ishi—*salutary*

1. Son of
   Appaim . . . . 1 Chr. 2:31
2. Descendant of
   Judah . . . . 1 Chr. 4:20
3. Simeonite whose sons destroyed
   Amalekites . . . . 1 Chr. 4:42
4. Manassite
   leader . . . . 1 Chr. 5:23, 24

Ishiah—*Yahweh will lend*

Son of Izrahiah . . . 1 Chr. 7:3
See Isshiah

Ishijah—*Yahweh will lend*

Son of Harim . . . . . Ezra 10:31

Ishma—*desolate*

Man of Judah . . . . . 1 Chr. 4:1, 3

Ishmael—*God hears*

1. Abram's son by
   Hagar . . . . Gen. 16:3, 4, 15
   Angel foretells his name and
   character . . . . . Gen. 16:11-16
   Circumcised at
   13 . . . . Gen. 17:25
   Mocks at Isaac's
   feast . . . . Gen. 21:8, 9
   Evidence of fleshly
   origin . . . . Gal. 4:22-31
   Becomes an
   archer . . . . Gen. 21:20
   Dwells in
   wilderness . . . . Gen. 21:21

Marries an
Egyptian . . . . . . Gen. 21:21
Buries his
father . . . . Gen. 25:9
Dies at age
137 . . . . Gen. 25:17
His
generations . . . Gen. 25:12-19
His descen-
dants . . . . 1 Chr. 1:29-31
2. Descendant of
   Jonathan . . . . . . 1 Chr. 8:38
3. Father of
   Zebadiah . . . . . . 2 Chr. 19:11
4. Military officer under
   Joash . . . . 2 Chr. 23:1-3, 11
5. Son of Nethaniah; instigates
   murder of
   Gedaliah . . . . . . 2 Kin. 25:22-25
6. Priest who divorced his foreign
   wife . . . . Ezra 10:22

Ishmaelites—*descendants of Ishmael*

Settle at Havilah . Gen. 25:17, 18
Joseph sold to . . . . . Gen. 37:25-28
Sell Joseph to
Potiphar . . . . Gen. 39:1
Wear golden
earrings . . . . Judg. 8:22, 24
Become known as
Arabians . . . . 2 Chr. 17:11

Ishmaiah—*Yahweh hears*

1. Gibeonite . . . . . . 1 Chr. 12:4
2. Tribal chief in
   Zebulun . . . . 1 Chr. 27:19

Ishmerai—*Yahweh keeps*

Benjamite . . . . 1 Chr. 8:18

Ishpan—*he will hide*

Son of Shashak . . . 1 Chr. 8:22, 25

Ish-Tob—*man of Tob*

Small kingdom of
Aram . . . . 2 Sam. 10:6, 8
Jephthah seeks asylum
in . . . . Judg. 11:3, 5

Ishuah—*he is equal*

Son of Asher . . . . . . Gen. 46:17
Called Ishvah . . . . . 1 Chr. 7:30

Ishvi—*man of Yahweh*

Son of Asher and
chief . . . . 1 Chr. 7:30

Island—*surrounded by water*

List of:

Caphtor (Crete?) . . Jer. 47:4
Clauda . . . . Acts 27:16
Chios . . . . Acts 20:15
Cos . . . . Acts 21:1
Crete . . . . Acts 27:12
Cyprus. . . . . Acts 11:19
Elishah. . . . . Ezek. 27:7
Malta . . . . Acts 28:1, 7, 9
Patmos . . . . Rev. 1:9
Rhodes. . . . . Acts 21:1
Samos . . . . Acts 20:15
Samothrace . . . . Acts 16:11
Syracuse . . . . Acts 28:12
Tyre . . . . Is. 23:1, 2

Ismachiah—*Yahweh will sustain*

Temple overseer . . 2 Chr. 31:13

Ispah—*to lay bear*

Benjamite . . . . 1 Chr. 8:16

Israel—*God strives*

A. *Used literally of:*
　Jacob . . . . Gen. 32:28
　Descendants of
　　Jacob . . . . Gen. 49:16, 28
　Ten northern tribes (in contrast
　　to Judah) . . . . . 1 Sam. 11:8
　Restored nation after
　　exile . . . . Ezra 9:1

B. *Used spiritually of:*
　Messiah . . . . Is. 49:3
　God's redeemed
　　ones . . . . Rom. 9:6-13
　True church . . . Gal. 6:16

Israelites—*descendants of Israel* (Jacob)

A. *Brief history of:*
　Begin as a nation in
　　Egypt . . . . Ex. 1:12, 20
　Afflicted in
　　Egypt . . . . Ex. 1:12-22
　Moses becomes their
　　leader . . . . Ex. 3:1-22
　Saved from
　　plagues . . . . Ex. 9:4, 6, 26
　Expelled from
　　Egypt . . . . Ex. 12:29-36
　Pass through Red
　　Sea . . . . Ex. 14:1-31
　Receive Law at
　　Sinai . . . . Ex. 19:1-25
　Sin at Sinai . . . . Ex. 32:1-35

Rebel at
　Kadesh . . . . Num. 13:1-33
Wander 40
　years. . . . . Num. 14:26-39
Cross Jordan . . Josh. 4:1-24
Conquer
　Canaan . . . . Josh. 12:1-24
Ruled by
　judges . . . . Judg. 2:1-23
Samuel becomes
　leader. . . . . 1 Sam. 7:1-17
Seek to have a
　king . . . . 1 Sam. 8:1-22
Saul chosen
　king . . . . 1 Sam. 10:18-27
David becomes
　king . . . . 2 Sam. 2:1-4
Solomon becomes
　king . . . . 1 Kin. 1:28-40
Kingdom
　divided. . . . . 1 Kin. 12:1-33
Israel (northern kingdom)
　carried
　captive. . . . . 2 Kin. 17:5-23
Judah (southern kingdom)
　carried
　captive. . . . . 2 Kin. 24:1-20
70 years in
　exile . . . . 2 Chr. 36:20, 21
Return after
　exile . . . . Ezra 1:1-5
Nation rejects
　Christ. . . . . Matt. 27:20-27
Nation　　　　{ Luke 21:20-24
　destroyed . . . . { 1 Thess. 2:14-16

B. *Blessed with:*
　Great leaders . . Heb. 11:8-40
　Inspired
　　prophets . . . . . . 1 Pet. 1:10-12
　God's oracles . . Rom. 3:2
　Priesthood . . . . . Rom. 9:3-5
　The Law. . . . . . . Gal. 3:16-25
　Messianic
　　promises . . . . . . Acts 3:18-26
　Tabernacle. . . . . Heb. 9:1-10
　Messiah . . . . Dan. 9:24-27
　God's
　　covenant. . . . . . Jer. 31:31-33
　Regathering . . Is. 27:12
　　　　　　　　　　Jer. 16:15, 16

C. *Sins of:*
　Idolatry. . . . . . . Hos. 13:1-4
　Hypocrisy . . . . . Is. 1:11-14
　Disobedi-
　　ence . . . . Jer. 7:22-28
　Externalism. . . . Matt. 23:1-33
　Unbelief . . . . Rom. 11:1-31

Works—righ-
teousness ..... Phil. 3:4-9

D. *Punishments upon:*
Defeat........Lev. 26:36-38
Curses upon ...Deut. 28:15-46
Captivity .....Judg. 2:13-23
Destruction....Luke 19:42-44
Dispersion .....Deut. 4:26-28
Blindness ......Rom. 11:25
Forfeiture of
blessings ......Acts 13:42-49
Replaced by
Gentiles.......Rom. 11:11-20

See Jews

Israel, the religion of

A. *History of:*
Call of
Abraham......Gen. 12:1-3
Canaan
promised......Gen. 15:18-21
Covenant at
Sinai..........Ex. 20
Covenant at
Shechem......Josh. 24:1-28
Ark brought to
Jerusalem .....2 Sam. 6
Dedication of the
Temple........1 Kin. 8:1-66
Reform move- ⌠2 Kin. 23:4-14
ments........⌡2 Chr. 29:3-36
Destruction of
Jerusalem .....Jer. 6
Restoration of the
Law...........Neh. 8, 9

B. *Beliefs about God:*
Creator ....Gen. 1:1
Ps. 104:24
Sustainer of
creation.......Ps. 104:27-30
Active in human
affairs.........Deut. 26:5-15
Omniscient ....Ps. 139:1-6
Omnipresent ..Jer. 23:23, 24
Everlasting ....Ps. 90:2
Moral..........Ex. 34:6, 7

Issachar—*man of hire*

1. Jacob's fifth
son ....Gen. 30:17, 18
2. Tribe of, descendants of Jacob's
fifth son ......Num. 26:23, 24
Prophecy
concerning....Gen. 49:14, 15
Census at
Sinai..........Num. 1:28, 29

On Gerizim ....Deut. 27:12
Inheritance
of...............Josh. 19:17-23
Assists
Deborah ....Judg. 5:15
At David's
coronation ...1 Chr. 12:32
Census in David's
time ....1 Chr. 7:1-5
Attended Hezekiah's
Passover ......2 Chr. 30:18
Prominent person
of.............Judg. 10:1
3. Doorkeeper....1 Chr. 26:1, 5

Isshiah, Jisshiah, Jesshiah—*Yahweh exists*

1. Mighty man of
David.........1 Chr. 12:1, 6
2. Kohathite   ⌠1 Chr. 23:20
Levite........⌡1 Chr. 24:25
3. Levite and family
head ....1 Chr. 24:21

Isui (see Ishvi)

Italy—*a peninsula of southern Europe*

Soldiers of, in
Caesarea ....Acts 10:1
Jews expelled
from ....Acts 18:2
Paul sails for......Acts 27:1, 6
Christians in .....Acts 28:14

Itching ears—*descriptive of desire for something exciting*

Characteristic of the last
days..............2 Tim. 4:2, 3

Ithai—*with me* (is Yahweh)

Son of Ribai ......1 Chr. 11:31
Also called Ittai ...2 Sam. 23:29

Ithamar—*island of palms*

Youngest son of
Aaron............Ex. 6:23
Consecrated as
priest.............Ex. 28:1
Duty
entrusted to......Ex. 38:21
Jurisdiction over Gershonites and
Merarites.......Num. 4:21-33
Founder of Levitical
family............1 Chr. 24:4-6

Ithiel—*God is with me*

1. Man addressed by
Agur...........Prov. 30:1
2. Benjamite .....Neh. 11:7

Ithmah—*bereavement*

Moabite of David's mighty
men...............1 Chr. 11:46

Ithnan—*perennial*

Town in south
Judah ....Josh. 15:23

Ithran, Jithran—*excellent*

1. Son of
   Dishon........Gen. 36:26
2. Son of
   Zophah ....1 Chr. 7:37
   Same as
   Jether.........1 Chr. 7:38

Ithream—*residue of the people*

Son of David.....2 Sam. 3:2-5

Ithrite—*pre-eminence*

Family dwelling at Kirjath
Jearim............1 Chr. 2:53
One of David's
guard ....2 Sam. 23:38

Itinerary, Israelites in Wilderness

Leave Egypt ......Ex. 12:29-36
Cross Red Sea ....Ex. 14:1-31
Bitter water
sweetened........Ex. 15:22-26
Manna in
wilderness........Ex. 16:1-36
Water from a
rock..............Ex. 17:1-7
Defeat of
Amalek ....Ex. 17:8-16
At Sinai...........Ex. 19:1-25
Depart Sinai .....Num. 10:33, 34
Lord sends
quails ....Num. 11:1-35
Twelve spies .....Num. 13:1-33
Rebellion at
Kadesh...........Num. 14:1-45
Korah's
rebellion..........Num. 16:1-34
Aaron's rod ....Num. 17:1-13
Moses' sin........Num. 20:2-13
Fiery serpents.....Num. 21:4-9
Balak and   { Num. 22:1-
Balaam...........   24:25
Midianites
conquered........Num. 31:1-24
Death of Moses ...Deut. 34:1-8
Accession of
Joshua ....Deut. 34:9

Ittai—*with me* (is Yahweh)

1. One of David's
   guard ....2 Sam. 23:23-29

2. Native of Gath; one of
   David's com-
   manders ......2 Sam. 15:18-22

Iturea—*pertaining to Jetur*

Ruled by Philip....Luke 3:1

Ivah—*sky*

City conquered by the
Assyrians.........Is. 37:13

Ivory—*the tusks of certain mammals*

Imported from
Tharshish ....1 Kin. 10:22
Imported from
Chittim...........Ezek. 27:6, 15
Ahab's palace
made of ....1 Kin. 22:39
Thrones
made of ....1 Kin. 10:18
Beds made of .....Amos 6:4
Sign of luxury.....Amos 3:15
Figuratively
used.............Song 5:14
Descriptive of
wealth ....Ps. 45:8
Among Babylon's
trade.............Rev. 18:12

Izhar, Izehar—*shining*

Son of Kohath ....Ex. 6:18, 21
                    Num. 3:19
Ancestor of the   { Num. 3:27
Izharites .... { 1 Chr. 6:38

Izrahiah—*Yahweh will shine*

Chief of
Issachar.........1 Chr. 7:1, 3

Izrahite—*descendant of Zerah*

Applied to
Shamhuth........1 Chr. 27:8

J

Jaakan, Jakan, Akan

Son of Ezer ....1 Chr. 1:42
Also called
Akan.............Gen. 36:27
Of Horite origin...Gen. 36:20-27
Tribe of, at
Beeroth ....Deut. 10:6
Dispossessed by
Edomites ....Deut. 2:12

Same as Bene
Jaakan........Num. 33:31, 32

Jaakobah—*heel catcher*

Simeonite........1 Chr. 4:36

Jaala, Jaalah—*wild she-goat*

Family head of exile
returnees........Ezra 2:56
Descendants of Solomon's
servants..........Neh. 7:57, 58

Jaalam

Son of Esau......Gen. 36:5, 18

Jaanai—*answerer*

Gadite chief.......1 Chr. 5:12

Jaare-Oregim—*forests of weavers*

Father of
Elhanan..........2 Sam. 21:19
Also called Jair....1 Chr. 20:5

Jaareshiah—*Yahweh nourishes*

Benjamite head ...1 Chr. 8:27

Jaasai—*Yahweh makes*

Sons of Bani; divorced foreign
wife..............Ezra 10:37

Jaasiel—*God makes*

1. One of David's mighty
   men...........1 Chr. 11:47
2. Son of Abner ..1 Chr. 27:21

Jaazaniah—*Yahweh hearkens*

1. Military commander supporting
   Gedaliah ......2 Kin. 25:23
2. Rechabite
   leader..........Jer. 35:3
3. Idolatrous Israelite
   elder ....Ezek. 8:11
4. Son of Azur; seen in Ezekiel's
   vision ....Ezek. 11:1

Jaaziah—*Yahweh strengthens*

Merarite Levite ...1 Chr. 24:26, 27

Jaaziel—*God strengthens*

Levite musician ...1 Chr. 15:18, 20

Jabal—*moving*

Son of Lamech; father of
herdsmen ....Gen. 4:20

Jabbok—*luxuriant river*

River entering the Jordan
about 20 miles north of the

Dead Sea........Num. 21:24
Scene of Jacob's
conflict..........Gen. 32:22-32
Boundary
marker..........Deut. 3:16

Jabesh—*dry*

1. Father of { 2 Kin. 15:10, 13,
   Shallum....{ 14
2. Abbreviated name of Jabesh
   Gilead ....1 Sam. 11:1-10

Jabesh Gilead—*Jabesh of Gilead*

Consigned to
destruction ......Judg. 21:8-15
Saul struck the Ammonites
here..............1 Sam. 11:1-11
Citizens of, rescue
Saul's body.......1 Sam. 31:11-13
David thanks
citizens of ....2 Sam. 2:4-7

Jabez—*he makes sorrowful*

1. City of
   Judah.........1 Chr. 2:55
2. Man of Judah noted for his
   prayer ....1 Chr. 4:9, 10

Jabin—*He (God) perceives*

1. Canaanite king of Hazor; leads
   confederacy against
   Joshua ....Josh. 11:1-14
2. Another king of Hazor;
   oppresses
   Israelites......Judg. 4:2
   Defeated by Deborah and
   Barak......Judg. 4:3-24
   Immortalized in
   poetry ....Judg. 5:1-31

Jabneel—*built of God*

1. Town in north
   Judah........Josh. 15:11
   Probably same as
   Jabneh......2 Chr. 26:6
2. Town of
   Naphtali ......Josh. 19:33

Jachan—*troubled*

Gadite chief.......1 Chr. 5:13

Jachin—*He (God) establishes*

1. Son of
   Simeon....Gen. 46:10
   Family head ...Num. 26:12
   Called Jarib....1 Chr. 4:24
2. Descendant of
   Aaron.........1 Chr. 24:1, 17

Representatives
of..............Neh. 11:10
3. One of two pillars in front of
Solomon's
Temple.......1 Kin. 7:21, 22

Jacinth—*a sapphire stone*

In high priest's
breastplate ....Ex. 28:19
Foundation
stone.............Rev. 21:20

Jacob—*supplanter*

Son of Isaac and ⎰Gen. 25:20-26
Rebekah.........⎱Hos. 12:2, 3
Born in answer to
prayer.............Gen. 25:21
Rebekah's
favorite ....Gen. 25:27, 28
Obtains Esau's ⎰Gen. 25:29-34
birthright.......⎱Heb. 12:16
Obtains Isaac's
blessing ....Gen. 27:1-40
Hated by Esau ...Gen. 27:41-46
Departs for
Haran ....Gen. 28:1-5
Sees heavenly
ladder............Gen. 28:10-19
Makes a vow......Gen. 28:20-22
Meets Rachel and
Laban.............Gen. 29:1-14
Serves for Laban's
daughters ....Gen. 29:15-30
His children......Gen. 29:31-35
Requests departure from
Laban ....Gen. 30:25-43
Flees from
Laban ....Gen. 31:1-21
Overtaken by
Laban ....Gen. 31:22-43
Covenant with
Laban............Gen. 31:44-55
Meets angels......Gen. 32:1, 2
Sends message to
Esau ....Gen. 32:3-8
Prays earnestly....Gen. 32:9-12
Sends gifts to
Esau ....Gen. 32:13-21
Wrestles with an ⎰Gen. 32:22-32
angel............⎱Hos. 12:3, 4
Name becomes
Israel............Gen. 32:28
Reconciled to
Esau ....Gen. 33:1-16
Erects altar at
Shechem.........Gen. 33:17-20
Trouble over
Dinah ....Gen. 34:1-31
Renewal at
Bethel............Gen. 35:1-15

Buries Rachel .....Gen. 35:16-20
List of 12 sons ....Gen. 35:22-26
Buries Isaac.......Gen. 35:27-29
His favoritism toward
Joseph ....Gen. 37:1-31
Mourns over
Joseph ....Gen. 37:32-35
Sends sons to Egypt for
food.............Gen. 42:1-5
Allows Benjamin
to go ....Gen. 43:1-15
Revived by good
news ....Gen. 45:25-28
Goes with family to
Egypt ....Gen. 46:1-27
Meets Joseph .....Gen. 46:28-34
Meets Pharaoh....Gen. 47:7-12
Makes Joseph
swear ....Gen. 47:28-31
Blesses Joseph's
sons.............Gen. 48:1-22
Blesses his own
sons.............Gen. 49:1-28
Dies in Egypt .....Gen. 49:29-33
Burial in
Canaan...........Gen. 50:1-14

Jacob

Father of Joseph, Mary's
husband.........Matt. 1:15, 16

Jacob's oracles—*blessings and curses
on twelve tribes*

Recorded ....Gen. 49:1-27

Jacob's well

Christ teaches a Samaritan
woman..........John 4:5-26

Jada—*knowing*

Grandson of ⎰1 Chr. 2:26, 28,
Jerahmeel ......⎱ 32

Jaddai—*praised*

Son of Nebo ......Ezra 10:43

Jaddua—*known*

1. Chief layman who signs the
document.....Neh. 10:21
2. Levite who returns with
Zerubbabel....Neh. 12:8, 11

Jadon—*he judges*

Meronothite
worker ....Neh. 3:7

Jael—*mountain goat*

Wife of Heber the
Kenite.............Judg. 4:17
Slays Sisera.......Judg. 4:17-22
Praised by
Deborah..........Judg. 5:24-27

Jagur—*lodging place*

Town in south
Judah ....Josh. 15:21

Jahath—*comfort, revival*

1. Grandson of
Judah.........1 Chr. 4:2
2. Great-grandson of
Levi...........1 Chr. 6:20, 43
3. Son of
Shimei........1 Chr. 23:10
4. Son of
Shelomoth ....1 Chr. 24:22
5. Merarite
Levite.........2 Chr. 34:12

Jahaz, Jahaza—*a place trodden under
foot*

Town in Moab at which Sihon was
defeated...........Num. 21:23
Assigned to
Reubenites ....Josh. 13:18
Levitical city .....Josh. 21:36
Regained by
Moabites ....Is. 15:4
Same as Jahzah ...1 Chr. 6:78

Jahaziah—*Yahweh sees*

Postexilic
returnee..........Ezra 10:15

Jahaziel—*God sees*

1. Kohathite
Levite.........1 Chr. 23:19
2. Benjamite
warrior ....1 Chr. 12:4
3. Priest...........1 Chr. 16:6
4. Inspired
Levite.........2 Chr. 20:14

Jahdai—*Yahweh leads*

Judahite ....1 Chr. 2:47

Jahdiel—*God makes glad*

Manassite chief ...1 Chr. 5:24

Jahdo—*union*

Gadite ....1 Chr. 5:14

Jahleel—*wait for God*

Son of Zebulun ...Gen. 46:14
Family head.......Num. 26:26

Jahleelites

Descendants of
Jahleel ....Num. 26:26

Jahmai—*may God protect*

Descendant of
Issachar..........1 Chr. 7:1, 2

Jahzeel—*God divides*

Son of Naphtali ...Gen. 46:24
Same as Jahziel ...1 Chr. 7:13

Jahzeelites

Descendants of
Jahzeel...........Num. 26:48

Jahzerah—*prudent*

Priest ....1 Chr. 9:12
Called Ahzai .....Neh. 11:13

Jahziel—*God divides*

Son of Naphtali ...1 Chr. 7:13

Jailer—*one who guards a prison*

At Philippi, converted by
Paul..............Acts 16:19-34

Jair—*he enlightens*

1. Manassite   {Num. 32:41
warrior.......{Deut. 3:14
Conquers towns in
Gilead ....Num. 32:41
2. Eighth judge of
Israel ....Judg. 10:3-5
3. Father of Mordecai, Esther's
uncle ....Esth. 2:5
4. Father of
Elhanan......1 Chr. 20:5
Called Jaare-
Oregim.......2 Sam. 21:19

Jairite

Descendant of Jair, the
Manassite ....2 Sam. 20:26

Jairus—*Greek form of Jair*

Ruler of the synagogue;
Jesus raises his   {Mark 5:22-24,
daughter ....{ 35-43

Jakeh—*pious*

Father of Agur....Prov. 30:1

Jakim—*He* (God) *raises up*

1. Descendant of
   Aaron......1 Chr. 24:1, 12
2. Benjamite.....1 Chr. 8:19

Jalon—*passing the night*

Calebite, son of
Ezra..........1 Chr. 4:17

Jambres—*opposer*

Egyptian
magician.........2 Tim. 3:8

See Jannes and Jambres

James—*a form of Jacob*

1. Son of
   Zebedee......Matt. 4:21
   Fisherman......Matt. 4:21
   One of the
   Twelve........Matt. 10:2
   In business with
   Peter..........Luke 5:10
   Called
   Boanerges.....Mark 3:17
   Of fiery
   disposition....Luke 9:52-55
   Makes a
   contention....Mark 10:35-45
   One of inner
   circle.........Matt. 17:1
   Sees the risen
   Lord..........John 21:1, 2
   Awaits the Holy
   Spirit.........Acts 1:13
   Slain by Herod
   Agrippa.......Acts 12:2
2. Son of Alphaeus; one of the
   Twelve........Matt. 10:3, 4
   Identified usually as "the
   Less".........Mark 15:40
   Brother of
   Joses.........Matt. 27:56
3. Son of Joseph and
   Mary..........Matt. 13:55, 56
   Lord's
   brother.......Gal. 1:19
   Rejects Christ's
   claim.........Mark 3:21
   Becomes a
   believer......Acts 1:13, 14
   Sees the risen
   Lord..........1 Cor. 15:7
   Becomes moderator of
   Jerusalem
   Council......Acts 15:13-23
   Paul confers with
   him..........Gal. 2:9, 12

Wrote an
epistle........James 1:1
Brother of
Jude..........Jude 1

James, the Epistle of—*a book of the New Testament*

Trials............James 1:2-8
Temptation......James 1:12-18
Doing the word..James 1:19-25
Faith and works..James 2:14-26
Patience.........James 5:7-11
Converting the
sinner...........James 5:19, 20

Jamin—*the right hand*

1. Son of
   Simeon.......Gen. 46:10
   Family head...Ex. 6:14, 15
2. Man of
   Judah.........1 Chr. 2:27
3. Postexilic Levite; interprets the
   law...........Neh. 8:7, 8

Jaminites

Descendants of
Jamin.............Num. 26:12

Jamlech—*whom He* (God) *makes king*

Simeonite chief...1 Chr. 4:34

Janna—*a form of John*

Ancestor of
Christ...........Luke 3:23, 24

Jannes and Jambres

Two Egyptian magicians; oppose
Moses............2 Tim. 3:8
Compare
account..........Ex. 7:11-22

Janoah—*rest; quiet*

Town of
Naphtali.........2 Kin. 15:29

Janohah—*Border town of*

Border town of
Ephraim..........Josh. 16:6,7

Janum—*sleep*

Town near
Hebron...........Josh. 15:53

Japheth—*widespreading*

One of Noah's three
sons.............Gen. 5:32

Saved in the ark ..1 Pet. 3:20
Receives messianic
blessing ....Gen. 9:20-27
His descendants occupy Asia Minor
and Europe......Gen. 10:2-5

Japhia—*may He (God) cause to shine forth*

1. King of Lachish; slain by
   Joshua........Josh. 10:3-27
2. One of David's
   sons ....2 Sam. 5:13-15
3. Border town of
   Zebulun.......Josh. 19:10, 12

Japhlet—*He (God) will deliver*

Asherite family....1 Chr. 7:32, 33

Japhletites

Unidentified tribe on Joseph's
boundary........Josh. 16:1, 3

Jarah—*honeycomb*

Descendant of King
Saul..............1 Chr. 9:42
Called
Jehoaddah......1 Chr. 8:36

Jareb—*he will contend*

Figurative description of Assyrian
king..............Hos. 5:13

Jared—*descent*

Father of Enoch...Gen. 5:15-20
Ancestor of
Noah..............1 Chr. 1:2
Ancestor of
Christ ....Luke 3:37

Jarha

Egyptian slave; marries master's
daughter ....1 Chr. 2:34-41

Jarib—*he contends*

1. Head of a Simeonite
   family........1 Chr. 4:24
   Called Jachin ..Gen. 46:10
2. Man sent to search for
   Levites....Ezra 8:16, 17
3. Priest who divorced his foreign
   wife..........Ezra 10:18

Jarmuth—*height*

1. Royal city of
   Canaan ....Josh. 10:3
   King of, slain by
   Joshua........Josh. 10:3-27

Assigned to
Judah........Josh. 15:20, 35
Inhabited after
exile ....Neh. 11:29
2. Town in Issachar assigned to
   the Levites....Josh. 21:28, 29
   Called
   Ramoth.......1 Chr. 6:73
   Called
   Remeth ......Josh. 19:21

Jaroah—*new moon*

Gadite chief......1 Chr. 5:14

Jashen—*sleeping*

Sons of, in David's
bodyguard........2 Sam. 23:32
Called Hashem....1 Chr. 11:34

Jasher—*upright*

Book of, quoted...Josh. 10:13

Jashobeam—*let the people return*

1. Chief of David's mighty
   men..........1 Chr. 11:11
   Becomes military
   captain.......1 Chr. 27:2, 3
2. Benjamite
   warrior......1 Chr. 12:1, 2, 6

Jashub—*he returns*

1. Issachar's
   son ....1 Chr. 7:1
   Head of
   family........Num. 26:24
   Called Job .....Gen. 46:13
2. Son of Bani; divorced his
   foreign wife...Ezra 10:29

Jashubi-Lehem—*bread returns*

A man of Judah...1 Chr. 4:22

Jashubites

Descendants of
Jashub ....Num. 26:24

Jason—*Greek equivalent for Joshua or Jesus*

Welcomes Paul at
Thessalonica .....Acts 17:5-9
Described as Paul's
kinsman..........Rom. 16:21

Jasper—*a precious stone (quartz)*

Set in high priest's
breastplate ....Ex. 28:20
Descriptive of:

Tyre's
adornments ......Ezek. 28:12, 13
Heavenly vision...Rev. 4:3

Jathniel—*God bestows*

Korahite
porters ....1 Chr. 26:1, 2

Jattir—*preeminence*

Town of Judah....Josh. 15:48
Assigned to Aaron's
children ....Josh. 21:13, 14
David sends
spoil to...........1 Sam. 30:26, 27

Javan—*Greece* (Ionia)

Son of Japheth....Gen. 10:2, 4
Descendants of, to receive
good news........Is. 66:19, 20
Trade with Tyre...Ezek. 27:13, 19
King of, in Daniel's
visions ....Dan. 8:21
Conflict with......Zech. 9:13

Javelin—*a light, short spear*

Used by Saul......1 Sam. 18:10

Jaw—*jawbone*

Used figuratively of:
God's
sovereignty.......Is. 30:28

Jawbone—*cheekbone*

Weapon used by
Samson ....Judg. 15:15-19

Jazer—*helpful*

Town east of Jordan near
Gilead............2 Sam. 24:5
Amorites driven
from ....Num. 21:32
Assigned to Gad ..Josh. 13:24, 25
Becomes Levitical
city ....Josh. 21:34, 39
Taken by
Moabites ....Is. 16:8, 9
Desired by sons of Reuben and
Gad ....Num. 32:1-5

Jaziz—*shining*

Shepherd over David's
flocks ....1 Chr. 27:31

Jealous, jealousy

A. *Kinds of:*
   Divine ....Ex. 20:5
   Marital ....Num. 5:12-31
   Motherly ......Gen. 30:1
   Brotherly ......Gen. 37:4-28
   Sectional ......2 Sam. 19:41-43
   National.......Judg. 8:1-3

B. *Good causes of:*
   Zeal for the
   Lord ....Num. 25:11
   Concern over
   Christians.....2 Cor. 11:2

C. *Evil causes of:*
   Favoritism.....Gen. 37:3-11
   Regard for
   names ....1 Cor. 3:3-5
   Carnality ......Amos 3:12-15
                 2 Cor. 12:20

D. *Described as:*
   Implacable.....Prov. 6:34, 35
   Cruel..........Song 8:6
   Burning ....Deut. 29:20
   Godly..........2 Cor. 11:2

Jearim—*forests*

Mountain 10 miles west of
Jerusalem ....Josh. 15:10

Jeatherai—*steadfast*

Descendant of
Levi..............1 Chr. 6:21
Also called
Ethni.............1 Chr. 6:41

Jeberechiah—*Yahweh blesses*

Father of Zechariah (not the
prophet)..........Is. 8:2

Jebus—*trodden under foot*

Same as
Jerusalem ....1 Chr. 11:4
Entry denied to
David ....1 Chr. 11:5
Levite came
near..............Judg. 19:1, 11

See Zion; Sion

Jebusites

Descendants of
Canaan...........Gen. 10:15, 16
Mountain tribe ...Num. 13:29
Land of, promised to
Israel.............Gen. 15:18-21
Adoni-Zedek, their king, raises
confederacy .....Josh. 10:1-5
Their king killed by
Joshua ....Josh. 10:23-26
Join fight against
Joshua ....Josh. 11:1-5

Assigned to
Benjamin.........Josh. 18:28
Royal city not
taken ....Judg. 1:21
Taken by David...2 Sam. 5:6-8
Old inhabitants
remain ....2 Sam. 24:16-25
Become slaves ....1 Kin. 9:20, 21

Jecamiah (see Jekamiah)

Jecholiah—*Yahweh is able*

Mother of King {2 Kin. 15:2
Azariah ....{2 Chr. 26:3

Jeconiah—*Yahweh establishes*

Variant form of
Jehoiachin........1 Chr. 3:16, 17
Abbreviated to
Coniah ....Jer. 22:24, 28
Son of Josiah ....Matt. 1:11

See Jehoiachin

Jedaiah—*Yahweh has been kind*

1. Priestly
   family.........1 Chr. 24:7
2. Head of the
   priests ....Neh. 12:6
3. Another head
   priest ....Neh. 12:7, 21
4. Simeonite......1 Chr. 4:37
5. Postexilic
   worker........Neh. 3:10
6. One who brings gifts for the
   Temple........Zech. 6:10, 14

Jediael—*known of God*

1. Son of Benjamin and family
   head ....1 Chr. 7:6, 10, 11
2. Manassite; joins
   David ....1 Chr. 12:20
3. One of David's mighty
   men..........1 Chr. 11:45
4. Korahite
   porter.........1 Chr. 26:1, 2

Jedidah—*beloved*

Mother of King
Josiah ....2 Kin. 22:1

Jedidiah—*beloved of Yahweh*

Name given to Solomon by
Nathan...........2 Sam. 12:24, 25

Jeduthun—*praising*

1. Levite musician appointed by
   David ....1 Chr. 16:41, 42

Heads a family of
musicians .....2 Chr. 5:12
Name appears in Psalm
titles.........Ps. 39; 62; 77
Family officiates after
Exile.........Neh. 11:17
Possibly same as
Ethan ....1 Chr. 15:17, 19
2. Father of
   Obed-Edom ...1 Chr. 16:38

Jegar Sahadutha—*heap of testimony*

Name given by Laban to memorial
stones...........Gen. 31:46, 47

Jehaleleel, Jehalelel—*God will flash
light*

1. Man of Judah and family
   head.........1 Chr. 4:16
2. Merarite
   Levite.........2 Chr. 29:12

Jehdeiah—*Yahweh will make glad*

1. Kohathite
   Levite.........1 Chr. 24:20
2. Meronothite in charge of
   David's
   asses.........1 Chr. 27:30

Jehezekel—*God will strengthen*

Descendant of
Aaron ....1 Chr. 24:1, 16

Jehiah—*Yahweh lives*

Doorkeeper ....1 Chr. 15:24

Jehiel—*God lives*

1. Levite
   musician......1 Chr. 15:18, 20
2. Gershonite and family
   head ....1 Chr. 23:8
3. Son of
   Hachmoni.....1 Chr. 27:32
4. Son of King Jehosh-
   aphat ....2 Chr. 21:2, 4
5. Hemanite
   Levite........2 Chr. 29:14
6. Overseer in Hezekiah's
   reign.........2 Chr. 31:13
7. Official of the
   Temple........2 Chr. 35:8
8. Father of Obadiah, a returned
   exile ....Ezra 8:9
9. Father of
   Shechaniah ...Ezra 10:2
10. Postexilic
    priest ....Ezra 10:21

11. Postexilic
     priest ....Ezra 10:26

Jehieli

A Levite family ...1 Chr. 26:21, 22

Jehizkiah—*Yahweh strengthens*

Ephraimite chief ..2 Chr. 28:12

Jehoaddah—*whom Yahweh adorns*

Descendant of
Saul............1 Chr. 8:36
Also called
Jarah.............1 Chr. 9:42

Jehoaddan—*Yahweh delights*

Mother of
Amaziah ....2 Kin. 14:2

Jehoahaz—*Yahweh has taken hold of*

1. Son and successor of Jehu, king
   of Israel.......2 Kin. 10:35
   Seeks the Lord in
   defeat.........2 Kin. 13:2-9
2. Son and successor of Josiah,
   king of
   Judah ....2 Kin. 23:30-34
   Called
   Shallum.......1 Chr. 3:15
3. Another form of Ahaziah,
   youngest son of King
   Joram.........2 Chr. 21:17

Jehoash (see Joash)

Jehohanan—*Yahweh is gracious*

1. Korahite
   Levite.........1 Chr. 26:3
2. Captain under Jehosh-
   aphat ....2 Chr. 17:10, 15
3. Father of Ishmael, Jehoiada's
   supporter .....2 Chr. 23:1
4. Priestly family
   head ....Neh. 12:13
5. Priest who divorced his
   wife...........Ezra 10:28
6. Son of Tobiah the
   Ammonite ....Neh. 6:17, 18
7. Postexilic
   singer.........Neh. 12:42

See Johanan

Jehoiachin—*Yahweh establishes*

Son of Jehoiakim; next to the last
king of Judah ....2 Kin. 24:8
Deported to
Babylon ....2 Kin. 24:8-16

Liberated by Evil-
Merodach ....Jer. 52:31-34

See Jeconiah

Jehoiada—*Yahweh knows*

1. Aaronite supporter of
   David.........1 Chr. 12:27
2. Father of Benaiah, one of
   David's
   officers........2 Sam. 8:18
3. Son of Benaiah; one of David's
   counselors ....1 Chr. 27:34
4. High priest ....2 Kin. 11:9
   Proclaims Joash
   king..........2 Kin. 11:4-16
   Institutes a
   covenant......2 Kin. 11:17-21
   Instructs
   Joash ....2 Kin. 12:2
   Commanded to repair the
   Temple........2 Kin. 12:3-16
   Receives honorable
   burial ....2 Chr. 24:15, 16
5. Deposed
   priest ....Jer. 29:26
6. Postexilic
   returnee ......Neh. 3:6

See Joiada

Jehoiakim—*Yahweh raises up*

Son of King
Josiah ....2 Kin. 23:34, 35
Made Pharaoh's
official...........2 Kin. 23:34,36
Wicked king ......2 Chr. 36:5, 8
Burns Jeremiah's
roll..............Jer. 36:1-32
Becomes Nebuchadnezzar's
servant...........2 Kin. 24:1
Punished by the
Lord ....2 Kin. 24:2-4
Taken by Nebuchad-
nezzar............2 Chr. 36:5, 6
Returns to
idolatry ....2 Chr. 36:5, 8
Treats Jeremiah with
contempt.........Jer. 36:21-28
Kills a true
prophet ....Jer. 26:20-23
Bound in fetters...2 Chr. 36:6
Buried as a
donkey...........Jer. 22:18, 19
Curse on ....Jer. 36:30, 31

Jehoiarib—*Yahweh contends*

Descendant of
Aaron ....1 Chr. 24:1, 6, 7

Founder of an order of
priests............1 Chr. 9:10, 13

Jehonadab—*Yahweh is liberal*

A Rechabite.......2 Kin. 10:15

See Jonadab

Jehonathan—*Yahweh has given*

1. Levite
teacher ....2 Chr. 17:8
2. Postexilic
priest ....Neh. 12:1, 18
3. Uncle of King
David.........1 Chr. 27:32

See Jonathan

Jehoram—*Yahweh is high*

1. King of Judah; son and
successor of Jehosh-
aphat ....1 Kin. 22:50
Called Joram ..2 Kin. 8:21, 23,
24
Marries Athaliah, who leads
him astray ....2 Kin. 8:18, 19
Reigns eight
years..........2 Kin. 8:16, 17
Killed his
brothers.......2 Chr. 21:2, 4, 13
Edom revolts
from.........2 Kin. 8:20-22
Elijah predicts his terrible
end ....2 Chr. 21:12-15
Nations fight
against........2 Chr. 21:16, 17
Smitten by the Lord; dies in
disgrace.......2 Chr. 21:18-20
2. King of Israel; son of
Ahab..........2 Kin. 1:17
Reigns 12
years..........2 Kin. 3:1
Puts away
Baal ....2 Kin. 3:2
Called Joram ..2 Kin. 8:16, 25,
28
Joins Jehoshaphat against
Moabites......2 Kin. 3:1-27
Naaman sent to, for
cure ....2 Kin. 5:1-27
Informed by Elijah of Syria's
plans..........2 Kin. 6:8-23
Wounded in war with
Syria.........2 Kin. 8:28, 29
3. Levite
teacher ....2 Chr. 17:8

See Joram

Jehoshabeath—*Yahweh is an oath*

Safeguards Joash from
Athaliah.........2 Chr. 22:11

Jehoshaphat—*Yahweh has judged*

1. King of Judah; son and
successor of
Asa ....1 Kin. 15:24
Reigns 25
years..........1 Kin. 22:42
Fortifies his
kingdom ......2 Chr. 17:2
Institutes
reforms ....2 Chr. 17:3
Inaugurates public
instruction ....2 Chr. 17:7-9
Honored and
respected ....2 Chr. 17:10-19
Joins Ahab against Ramoth
Gilead ....1 Kin. 22:1-36
Rebuked by a
prophet ....2 Chr. 19:2, 3
Develops legal
system........2 Chr. 19:4-11
By faith defeats invading
forces.........2 Chr. 20:1-30
Navy of,
destroyed ....2 Chr. 20:35-37
Provision for his
children ....2 Chr. 21:2, 3
Death of......2 Chr. 21:1
Ancestor of
Christ........Matt. 1:8
2. Son of
Ahilud ....2 Sam. 8:16
Recorder under David and
Solomon ....2 Sam. 20:24
3. Father of King
Jehu ....2 Kin. 9:2

Jehoshaphat, Valley of

Described as a place of
judgment........Joel 3:2, 12

Jehosheba—*Yahweh is an oath*

King Joram's
daughter ....2 Kin. 11:2

Jehozabad—*Yahweh has bestowed*

1. Son of Obed-
Edom ....1 Chr. 26:4
2. Son of a Moabitess; assassinates
Joash ....2 Kin. 12:20, 21
Put to death ...2 Chr. 25:3
3. Military captain under King
Jehosh-
aphat ....2 Chr. 17:18

Jehozadak—*Yahweh has justified*

Son of Seraiah, the high
priest.............1 Chr. 6:14
His father killed...2 Kin. 25:18-21
Carried captive to
Babylon..........1 Chr. 6:15
Father of Joshua the high
priest.............Hag. 1:1, 12, 14

Jehu—*Yahweh is He*

1. Benjamite
   warrior ....1 Chr. 12:3
2. Prophet and son of
   Hanani........1 Kin. 16:1
   Denounces
   Baasha........1 Kin. 16:2-4, 7
   Rebukes Jehosh-
   aphat ....2 Chr. 19:2, 3
   Writes Jehoshaphat's
   biography.....2 Chr. 20:34
3. Descendant of
   Judah..........1 Chr. 2:38
4. Simeonite......1 Chr. 4:35
5. Grandson of
   Nimshi........2 Kin. 9:2
   Commander under
   Ahab..........2 Kin. 9:25
   Divinely commissioned to
   destroy Ahab's
   house.........1 Kin. 19:16, 17
   Carries out orders with
   zeal..........2 Kin. 9:11-37
   Killed Ahab's
   sons ....2 Kin. 10:1-17
   Destroys worshipers of
   Baal ....2 Kin. 10:18-28
   Serves the Lord
   outwardly.....2 Kin. 10:29-31

Jehubbah—*he hides*

Asherite ....1 Chr. 7:34

Jehucal—*Yahweh is able*

Son of Shelemiah; sent by
Zedekiah to
Jeremiah.........Jer. 37:3
Also called Jucal ..Jer. 38:1

Jehud—*praise*

Town of Dan......Josh. 19:40, 45

Jehudi—*a man of Judah; a Jew*

Reads Jere-   { Jer. 36:14, 21,
miah's roll.......{ 23

Jehudijah—*a Jewess*

One of Mered's two wives; should
be rendered "the
Jewess" ....1 Chr. 4:18

Jeiel—*God snatches away*

1. Ancestor of
   Saul...........1 Chr. 9:35-39
2. One of David's mighty
   men...........1 Chr. 11:44
   Reubenite
   prince........1 Chr. 5:6, 7
3. Levite
   musician......1 Chr. 16:5
4. Porter ....1 Chr. 15:18, 21
   May be the same
   as 3...........1 Chr. 16:5
   Called Jehiah ..1 Chr. 15:24
5. Inspired
   Levite.........2 Chr. 20:14
6. Levite chief....2 Chr. 35:9
7. Scribe ....2 Chr. 26:11
8. Temple
   Levite.........2 Chr. 29:13
9. One who divorced his foreign
   wife..........Ezra 10:19, 43

Jekabzeel—*God will gather*

Town in Judah....Neh. 11:25
Called Kabzeel ..Josh. 15:21
Home of Benaiah, David's
friend ....2 Sam. 23:20

Jekameam—*people will rise*

Kohathite Levite ..1 Chr. 23:19

Jekamiah, Jecamiah—*Yahweh will rise*

1. Son of
   Shallum.......1 Chr. 2:41
2. Son of
   Jeconiah ......1 Chr. 3:17, 18

Jekuthiel—*God will support*

Man of Judah .....1 Chr. 4:18

Jemimah—*dove*

Job's daughter ....Job 42:14

Jemuel—*day of God*

Son of Simeon ....Gen. 46:10
Called Nemuel ....Num. 26:12

Jephthah—*he will open*

Gilead's son by a
harlot ....Judg. 11:1

Flees to Tob; becomes a
leader..............Judg. 11:2-11
Cites historical precedents against
invading
Ammonites.......Judg. 11:12-27
Makes a vow before
battle............Judg. 11:28-31
Defeats
Ammonites.......Judg. 11:32, 33
Fulfills vow.........Judg. 11:34-40
Defeats quarrelsome
Ephraimites .....Judg. 12:1-7
Cited by Samuel ..1 Sam. 12:11
In faith's
chapter...........Heb. 11:32

Jephunneh—*it will be prepared*

1. Caleb's
   father........Num. 13:6
2. Asherite ......1 Chr. 7:38

Jerah—*moon*

Son of Joktan; probably an
Arabian tribe.....Gen. 10:26
1 Chr. 1:20

Jerahmeel—*may God have compassion*

1. Great-grandson of
   Judah..........1 Chr. 2:9, 25-41
2. Son of Kish, not Saul's
   father...........1 Chr. 24:29
3. King Jehoiakim's
   officer..........Jer. 36:26

Jerahmeelites

Raided by David ..1 Sam. 27:10

Jered—*descent*

A descendant of
Judah ....1 Chr. 4:18

See Jared

Jeremai—*high*

One who divorced his foreign
wife..............Ezra 10:19, 33

Jeremiah (I)—*Yahweh establishes*

A. *Life of:*
Son of Hilkiah; a
Benjamite.....Jer. 1:1
Native of
Anathoth .....Jer. 1:1
Called before
birth..........Jer. 1:4-10
Prophet under kings Josiah,
Jehoiakim, and
Zedekiah.....Jer. 1:2, 3

Imprisoned by
Pashur........Jer. 20:1-6
Writes his prophecy; Jehoiakim
burns it ....Jer. 36:1-26
Prophecy
rewritten......Jer. 36:27-32
Accused of
defection......Jer. 37:1-16
Released by
Zedekiah......Jer. 37:17-21
Cast into a
dungeon ......Jer. 38:1-6
Saved by an
Ethiopian .....Jer. 38:7-28
Set free by Nebuchad-
nezzar ....Jer. 39:11-14
Given liberty of choice by
Nebuzar-
adan ....Jer. 40:1-6
Forced to flee to
Egypt.........Jer. 43:5-7
Last prophecies at Tahpanhes,
Egypt........Jer. 43:8-13

B. *Characteristics of:*
Forbidden to
marry.........Jer. 16:1-13
Has internal
conflicts ......Jer. 20:7-18
Has incurable
pain...........Jer. 15:18
Motives misunder-
stood ....Jer. 37:12-14
Tells captives to build in
Babylon.......Jer. 29:4-9
Denounces false prophets in
Babylon.......Jer. 29:20-32
Rebukes
idolatry ......Jer. 7:9-21

C. *Prophecies of, foretell:*
Egypt's fall ....Jer. 43:8-13
70 years of
captivity ......2 Chr. 36:21
Restoration to
land...........Jer. 16:14-18
New
covenant......Jer. 31:31-34
Herod's
massacre......Jer. 31:15

D. *Teachings of:*
God's
sovereignty ...Jer. 18:5-10
God's
knowledge ....Jer. 17:5-10
Shame of
idolatry ......Jer. 10:14, 15
Spirituality of worship,
etc. ....Jer. 3:16, 17

Need of regeneration........Jer. 9:26
Man's sinful nature ....Jer. 2:22
Gospel salvation......Jer. 23:5, 6
Call of the Gentiles.......Jer. 3:17-19

Jeremiah (II)

1. Benjamite warrior ....1 Chr. 12:4
2. Gadite warrior ....1 Chr. 12:10
3. Another Gadite warrior ....1 Chr. 12:13
4. Manassite head..........1 Chr. 5:23, 24
5. Father of Hamutal, a wife of Josiah.........2 Kin. 23:31
6. Father of Jaazaniah.....Jer. 35:3
7. Postexilic priest ....Neh. 12:1, 7
   Head of a priestly line ....Neh. 12:12
8. Priest who signs the covenant......Neh. 10:2

Jeremiah, the Book of—*a book of the Old Testament*

Jeremiah's call ....Jer. 1:1-19
Jeremiah's life.....Jer. 26:1-45:5
Israel's sin against God..............Jer. 2:1-10:25
Against false prophets..........Jer. 23:9-40
Against foreign nations.........Jer. 46:1-51:64
The messianic king..............Jer. 23:1-8

Jeremoth—*elevation*

1. Benjamite .....1 Chr. 8:14
2. Merarite Levite.........1 Chr. 23:23
3. Musician of David.........1 Chr. 25:22
4. One who divorced his foreign wife...Ezra 10:26
5. Another who divorced his foreign wife...Ezra 10:27
6. Spelled Jerimoth......1 Chr. 24:30

See Jerimoth

Jeriah, Jerijah—*Yahweh sees*

Kohathite Levite ..1 Chr. 23:19, 23
Hebronite chief ...1 Chr. 26:31

Jeribai—*Yahweh contends*

One of David's warriors.........1 Chr. 11:46

Jericho—*place of fragrance*

City near the Jordan ....Num. 22:1
Viewed by Moses............Deut. 34:1-3
Called the city of palm trees ....Deut. 34:3
Viewed by spies....Josh. 2:1
Home of Rahab the harlot ....Heb. 11:31
Scene of Joshua's vision ....Josh. 5:13-15
Destroyed by Joshua ....Heb. 11:30, 31
Curse of rebuilding of .....Josh. 6:26
Assigned to Benjamin......Josh. 16:1, 7
Moabites retake...Judg. 3:12, 13
David's envoys stay here ....2 Sam. 10:4, 5
Rebuilt by Hiel....1 Kin. 16:34
Visited by Elijah and Elisha ....2 Kin. 2:4-22
Zedekiah captured here ....2 Kin. 25:5
Reinhabited after exile.............Ezra 2:34
People of, help rebuild Jerusalem ......Neh. 3:2
Blind men of, healed by Jesus...........Matt. 20:29-34
Home of Zacchaeus.......Luke 19:1-10

Jeriel—*God sees*

Son of Tola ....1 Chr. 7:2

Jerimoth

1. Son of Bela ....1 Chr. 7:7
2. Warrior of David.........1 Chr. 12:5
3. Musician of David.........1 Chr. 25:4
4. Son of David ..2 Chr. 11:18
5. Levite overseer ......2 Chr. 31:13
6. Son of Becher........1 Chr. 7:8

7. Ruler of
   Naphtali ......1 Chr. 27:19
8. Spelled
   Jeremoth......1 Chr. 23:23

See Jeremoth

Jerioth—*tent curtains*

One of Caleb's
wives.............1 Chr. 2:18

Jeroboam—*may the people increase*

1. Son of Nebat ..1 Kin. 11:26
   Rebels against
   Solomon ......1 Kin. 11:26-28
   Ahijah's prophecy
   concerning....1 Kin. 11:29-39
   Flees to
   Egypt.........1 Kin. 11:40
   Recalled,   { 1 Kin. 12:1-3, 12,
   made king ... { 20
   Perverts the true
   religion ....1 Kin. 12:25-33
   Casts Levites
   out ....2 Chr. 11:14
   Rebuked by a man of
   God..........1 Kin. 13:1-10
   Leads people
   astray......1 Kin. 13:33, 34
   His wife consults
   Ahijah ....1 Kin. 14:1-18
   War with
   Abijam........1 Kin. 15:7
   Reigns 22
   years..........1 Kin. 14:20
   Struck by the
   Lord ....2 Chr. 13:20
2. Jeroboam II; king of
   Israel ....2 Kin. 13:13
   Successor of Joash
   (Jehoash) .....2 Kin. 14:16, 23
   Conquers Hamath and
   Damascus ...2 Kin. 14:25-28
   Reigns wickedly 41
   years..........2 Kin. 14:23, 24
   Denounced by
   Amos ....Amos 7:7-13
   Death of.......2 Kin. 14:29

Jeroham—*he is pitied*

1. Grandfather of
   Samuel ....1 Sam. 1:1
2. Benjamite .....1 Chr. 9:8
3. Father of Benjamite chief
   men............1 Chr. 8:27
4. Benjamite of
   Gedor.........1 Chr. 12:7

5. Father of
   Adaiah........1 Chr. 9:12
6. Danite chief's
   father.........1 Chr. 27:22
7. Military
   captain........2 Chr. 23:1

Jerubbaal—*Baal contends*

Name given to Gideon for
destroying Baal's
altar..............Judg. 6:32

Jerubbesheth—*let shame contend*

Father of
Abimelech.......2 Sam. 11:21

Jeruel—*founded by God*

Wilderness west of the Dead
Sea................2 Chr. 20:16

Jerusalem—*possession of peace*

A. *Names applied to:*
   City of God....Ps. 46:4
   City of David ..2 Sam. 5:6, 7
   City of
   Judah.........2 Chr. 25:28
   Zion...........Ps. 48:12
   Jebus..........Josh. 18:28
   Holy city .....Matt. 4:5
   Faithful city ..Is. 1:21, 26
   City of righteous-
   ness...........Is. 1:26
   City of Truth ..Zech. 8:3
   City of the great
   King..........Ps. 48:2
   Salem ....Gen. 14:18

B. *History of:*
   Originally
   Salem.........Gen. 14:18
   Occupied by
   Jebusite.......Josh. 15:8
   King of, defeated by
   Joshua........Josh. 10:5-23
   Assigned to
   Benjamin .....Josh. 18:28
   Attacked by
   Judah.........Judg. 1:8
   Jebusites
   remain in .....Judg. 1:21
   David brings Goliath's
   head to ....1 Sam. 17:54
   Conquered by
   David.........2 Sam. 5:6-8
   Name
   changed .....2 Sam. 5:7-9
   Ark
   brought to ....2 Sam. 6:12-17

Saved from
destruction....2 Sam. 24:16
Solomon builds temple
here ....1 Kin. 5:5-8
Suffers in
war.......1 Kin. 14:25-27
Plundered by
Israel......2 Kin. 14:13, 14
Besieged by
Syrians ....Is. 7:1
Earthquake
damages ......Amos 1:1
Miraculously
saved ....2 Kin. 19:31-36
Ruled by
Egypt......2 Kin. 23:33-35
Besieged by
Babylon.......2 Kin. 24:10, 11
Captured by
Babylon......Jer. 39:1-8
Desolate 70
years.........Jer. 25:11, 12
Temple
rebuilt in......Ezra 1:1-4
Exiles
return to......Ezra 2:1-70
Work on,
hindered ......Ezra 5:1-17
Walls of,
dedicated .....Neh. 12:27-47
Christ:
Enters
as king.......Matt. 21:9, 10
Laments for ...Matt. 23:37
Crucified at....Luke 9:31
Weeps over....Luke 19:41, 42
Predicts destruc-
tion...........Luke 19:43, 44
Gospel
preached at ...Luke 24:47
Many miracles performed
in ....John 4:45
Church begins
here ....Acts 2:1-47
Christians of,
persecuted ....Acts 4:1-30
Stephen
martyred at ...Acts 7:1-60
First Christian council held
here ....Acts 15:1-29
Paul:
Visits.........Acts 20:16
Arrested in ...Acts 21:30-36
Taken from...Acts 23:12-33

C. *Prophecies concerning:*
Destruction by
Babylon.......Jer. 20:5
Utter ruin .....Jer. 26:18

Rebuilding by
Cyrus.........Is. 44:26-28
Christ's entry
into...........Zech. 9:9
Gospel proclaimed
from ....Is. 2:3
Perilous
times ....Matt. 24:1-22
Being under
Gentiles......Luke 21:24

D. *Described:*
Physically— ⎧ Ps. 48:12, 13
strong........⎩ Ps. 125:2
Morally— ⎧ Is. 1:1-16
corrupt ......⎩ Jer. 5:1-5
Spiritually—the
redeemed ....Gal. 4:26-30
Prophetically—New
Jerusalem.....Rev. 21:1-27

See Zion; Sion

Jerusha—*possessed* (married)

Wife of King
Uzziah ....2 Kin. 15:33
Called Jerushah ...2 Chr. 27:1

Jeshaiah—*Yahweh saves*

1. Musician of
David.........1 Chr. 25:3
2. Grandson of
Zerubbabel....1 Chr. 3:21
3. Levite in David's
reign........1 Chr. 26:25
4. Son of Athaliah; returns from
Babylon......Ezra 8:7
5. Levite who returns with
Ezra ....Ezra 8:19
6. Benjamite .....Neh. 11:7

Jeshanah—*old*

City of Ephraim taken by
Abijah...........2 Chr. 13:19

Jesharelah—*upright toward God*

Levite musician ...1 Chr. 25:14
Called
Asharelah ....1 Chr. 25:2

Jeshebeab—*may the father tarry* (live)

Descendant of
Aaron.............1 Chr. 24:13

Jesher—*uprightness*

Caleb's son........1 Chr. 2:18

Jeshimon—*waste*

Wilderness west of the
Dead Sea.........1 Sam. 23:19, 24

Jeshishai—*aged*

Gadite ....1 Chr. 5:14

Jeshohaiah—*humbled by Yahweh*

Leader in
Simeon...........1 Chr. 4:36

Jeshua—*Yahweh is salvation*

1. Descendant of
   Aaron.........Ezra 2:36
2. Levite
   treasurer......2 Chr. 31:14, 15
3. Postexilic high
   priest ....Zech. 3:8
   Returns with
   Zerubbabel....Ezra 2:2
   Aids in Temple
   rebuilding.....Ezra 3:2-8
   Withstands
   opponents.....Ezra 4:1-3
   Figurative act performed
   on ....Zech. 3:1-10
4. Called
   Jeshua........Hag. 1:1
   See Joshua (3)
5. Levite
   assistant .....Ezra 2:40
   Explains the
   Law..........Neh. 8:7
   Leads in
   worship.......Neh. 9:4, 5
   Seals the
   covenant......Neh. 10:1, 9
6. Repairer of the
   wall..........Neh. 3:19
7. Man of the house of Pahath-
   Moab........Ezra 2:6
8. Village in south
   Judah.........Neh. 11:26

Jeshurun—*upright one*

Poetic name of endearment for
Israel............Deut. 32:15

Jesimiel—*God sets up*

Simeonite leader ..1 Chr. 4:36

Jesse—*Yahweh exists*

Grandson of Ruth and
Boaz ....Ruth 4:17-22
Father of:
David ....1 Sam. 16:18, 19

Eight sons ....1 Sam. 16:10, 11
Two daughters...1 Chr. 2:15, 16
Citizen of Beth-
lehem ....1 Sam. 16:1, 18
Protected by
David ....1 Sam. 22:1-4
Of humble
origin ....1 Sam. 18:18, 23
Mentioned in
prophecy.........Is. 11:1, 10
Ancestor of
Christ ....Matt. 1:5, 6

Jesshiah (see Isshiah)

Jesting—*mocking; joking*

Condemned.......Eph. 5:4
Lot appeared
to be ....Gen. 19:14
Of godless men....Ps. 35:16

Jesus (see Christ)

Jether—*abundance*

1. Gideon's oldest
   son ....Judg. 8:20, 21
2. Descendant of
   Judah.........1 Chr. 2:32
3. Son of Ezra....1 Chr. 4:17
4. Asherite; probably same as
   Ithran ....1 Chr. 7:30-38
5. Amasa's
   father.........1 Kin. 2:5, 32

Jetheth—*subjection*

Chief of Edom ....Gen. 36:40

Jethlah—*an overhanging place*

Danite town ......Josh. 19:42

Jethro—*excellent*

Priest of Midian; Moses'
father-in-law .....Num. 10:29
Also called
Reuel ....Num. 10:29
Moses marries his daughter
Zipporah ....Ex. 2:16-22
Moses departs
from ....Ex. 4:18-26
Visits and counsels
Moses ....Ex. 18:1-27

Jetur

Son of Ishmael....Gen. 25:15
Conflict with
Israel.............1 Chr. 5:18, 19
Tribal descendants of; the
Itureans..........Luke 3:1

Jeuel—*snatching away*

Son of Zerah......1 Chr. 9:6

Jeush—*may he aid*

1. Son of Esau and Edomite
   chief..........Gen. 36:5, 18
2. Benjamite
   head..........1 Chr. 7:10
3. Gershonite
   Levite..........1 Chr. 23:10, 11
4. Descendant of
   Jonathan..........1 Chr. 8:39
5. Rehoboam's
   son ....2 Chr. 11:19

Jeuz—*counseling*

Benjamite..........1 Chr. 8:8, 10

Jewels—*ornaments used on the body*

A. *Used for:*
   Ornaments.....Is. 3:18-24
   Evil offering ...Ex. 32:1-5
   Good
   offering ......Ex. 35:22
   Spoils of war ..2 Chr. 20:25
   Farewell
   gifts ....Ex. 11:2

B. *Significance of:*
   Betrothal
   present........Gen. 24:22, 53
   Sign of
   wealth ....James 2:2
   Standard of
   value ....Prov. 3:15
   Tokens of
   repentance....Gen. 35:4
   Tokens of
   love..........Ezek. 16:11-13
   Indications of
   worldliness....1 Tim. 2:9
   Figurative of God's
   own..........Matt. 13:45, 46

Jewess—*a female Jew*

Woman of the Hebrew
race..............Acts 24:24

Jewish alphabet

Given topically....Ps. 119

Jewish calendar

A. *List of months of:*
   Abib, or Nisan
   (March—
   April) ....Ex. 13:4

Ziv or Iyyar
(April—
May).........1 Kin. 6:1, 37
Sivan (May—
June) ....Esth. 8:9
Tammuz (June—
July)..........Jer. 39:2
Ab (July—
August)......Num. 33:38
Elul (August—
September) ..Neh. 6:15
Ethanim or Tishri
(September—
October) .....1 Kin. 8:2
Bul or Heshvan
(October—
November)...1 Kin. 6:38
Chislev
(November—
December)...Neh. 1:1
Tebeth (December—
January)......Esth. 2:16
Shebat or Sebat
(January—
February)....Zech. 1:7
Adar (February—
March).......Esth. 3:7

B. *Feasts of:*
   Abib (14)—
   Passover......Ex. 12:18
   Abib (15-21)—
   Unleavened
   Bread ....Lev. 23:5, 6
   Abib (16)—
   Firstfruits.....Lev. 23:10, 11
   Ziv (14)—Later
   Passover.....Num. 9:10, 11
   Sivan (6)—
   Pentecost, Feast of Weeks,
   Harvest ......Lev. 23:15-21
   Ethanim (1)—
   Trumpets....Lev. 23:24
   Ethanim (10)—
   Day of
   Atonement...Lev. 16:29-34
   Ethanim (15-21)—
   Tabernacles..Lev. 23:34, 35
   Ethanim (22)—
   Holy Convo-
   cation........Lev. 23:36
   Chislev (25)—
   Dedication....John 10:22

Jewish measures (Metrology)

A. *Long Measures:*
   Finger
   (¾ inch) ......Jer. 52:21

Handbreadth
(3 to 4
inches)......Ex. 25:25
Span (about 9
inches)......Ex. 28:16
Cubit of man (about 18
inches)........Gen. 6:15
Pace (about 3
feet).........2 Sam. 6:13
Fathom (about 6
feet) ....Acts 27:28
Rod (about 11
feet) ....Ezek. 40:5
Line ....Ezek. 40:3

B. *Land measures:*
Cubit of God
(1¾ feet)......Josh. 3:4
Mile
(1,760 yds.) ...Matt. 5:41
Sabbath day's journey
(3/5 mile).....Acts 1:12
Day's journey (24
miles).........Gen. 30:36

C. *Weights and dry measures:*
Kab (about 2
quarts)........2 Kin. 6:25
Omer (about 7
pints) ....Ex. 16:16-18, 36
Ephah (about 4½
pecks) ....Ex. 16:36
Homer (about ⎰ Num. 11:32
11 bushels)...⎱ Hos. 3:2
Talent (about 93
pounds)......Ex. 25:39

D. *Liquid measures:*
Log (about 1
pint) ....Lev. 14:10, 15
Hin (about 1½
gallons) ......Num. 15:4-10
Bath (about 9
gallons) ......Is. 5:10
Homer or Kor
(c. 85
gallons) ......Ezek. 45:11, 14

Jews—*the Hebrew people*

A. *Descriptive of:*
Hebrew race...Esth. 3:6, 13
Postexilic Hebrew
nation ....Ezra 5:1, 5
Believers.......Rom. 2:28, 29

B. *Kinds of:*
Hypocritical ...Matt. 23:1-31
Persecuting....1 Thess. 2:14, 15
Prejudiced .....John 4:9
Penitent ....John 12:10, 11

C. *Their sins:*
Self-righteous-
ness..........Rom. 10:1-3
Hypocrisy .....Rom. 2:17-25
Persecution....1 Thess. 2:14, 15
Rejection of
Christ........Matt. 27:21-25
Rejection of the
Gospel......Acts 13:42-46
Embitter
Gentiles......Acts 14:2-6
Spiritual
blindness......John 3:1-4
Ignorance ....Luke 19:41, 42

D. *Their punishment:*
Blinded........Rom. 11:25
Cast out ....Matt. 8:11, 12
Desolation as a
nation ....Luke 21:20-24
Scattered .....Deut. 28:48-64

Jezaniah—*Yahweh answers*

Judahite military
officer ....Jer. 40:7, 8
Seeks advice from
Jeremiah ....Jer. 42:1-3
Called Jaazaniah ..2 Kin. 25:23

Jezebel—*unmarried, chaste*

1. Daughter of Ethbaal;
Ahab's wife ...1 Kin. 16:31
Follows her
idolatry ....1 Kin. 16:32, 33
Destroyed Jehovah's
prophets.....1 Kin. 18:4-13
Plans Elijah's
death.......1 Kin. 19:1, 2
Secures Naboth's
death ....1 Kin. 21:1-15
Sentence:
Pronounced
upon.......1 Kin. 21:23
Fulfilled by
Jehu ....2 Kin. 9:7, 30-37
2. Type of paganism in the
church........Rev. 2:20

Jezer—*form, purpose*

Son of Naphtali ...Gen. 46:24
Family head of the
Jezerites..........Num. 26:49

Jeziah—*Yahweh sprinkles*

One who divorced his foreign
wife..............Ezra 10:25

Jeziel—*God sprinkles*

Benjamite
warrior..........1 Chr. 12:2, 3

Jezrahiah—*Yahweh shines*

Leads singing at dedication
service ....Neh. 12:42

Jezreel—*God sows*

1. Fortified city of
Issachar ......Josh. 19:17, 18
Gideon fights Midianites in
valley of ......Judg. 6:33
Israelites camp
here ....1 Sam. 29:1, 11
Center of Ishbosheth's
rule..........2 Sam. 2:8, 9
Capital city ....1 Kin. 18:45
Home of
Naboth ......1 Kin. 21:1, 13
Site of Jezebel's
tragic end.....1 Kin. 21:23
Heads of Ahab's sons piled
here ....2 Kin. 10:1-10
City of
bloodshed.....Hos. 1:4
Judgment in
valley of ......Hos. 1:5
2. Town of
Judah ....Josh. 15:56
David's wife
from ....1 Sam. 25:43
3. Judahite......1 Chr. 4:3
4. Symbolic name of
Hosea's son ...Hos. 1:4
5. Symbolic name of the
new Israel ....Hos. 2:22, 23

Jezreelite—*a person from Jezreel*

Naboth ....1 Kin. 21:1

Jezreelitess—*a female from Jezreel*

Ahinoam..........1 Sam. 30:5

Jibsam—*fragrant*

Descendant of
Issachar..........1 Chr. 7:2

Jimnah—*prosperity*

Son of Asher......Gen. 46:17

Jidlaph—*he weeps*

Son of Nahor .....Gen. 22:22

Jiphthah El—*God will open*

Valley between Asher and
Naphtali..........Josh. 19:10-27

Jiphtah—*he will open*

City of Judah .....Josh. 15:43

Jishui

Son of Saul ....1 Sam. 14:49

Jithra—*excellence*

Israelite (or Ishmaelite); father of
Amasa ....2 Sam. 17:25
Called Jether....1 Kin. 2:5, 32

Jizliah—*Yahweh delivers*

Son of Elpaal .....1 Chr. 8:18

Jizri—*fashioner*

Leader of Levitical
Choir............1 Chr. 25:11
Also called Zeri ...1 Chr. 25:3

Joab—*Yahweh is father*

1. Son of Zeruiah, David's half-
sister..........2 Sam. 8:16
Leads David's army to
victory over
Ishbosheth....2 Sam. 2:10-32
Assassinates Abner
deceptively....2 Sam. 3:26, 27
David rebukes
him ....2 Sam. 3:28-39
Commands David's army
against
Edomites......1 Kin. 11:14-17
Defeats Syrians and
Ammonites ...2 Sam. 10:1-14
Obeys David's orders
concerning
Uriah ....2 Sam. 11:6-27
Allows David to besiege
Rabbah ....2 Sam. 11:1
Makes David favorable toward
Absalom ......2 Sam. 14:1-33
Remains loyal to
David.........2 Sam. 18:1-5
Killed
Absalom ......2 Sam. 18:9-17
Rebukes David's
grief ....2 Sam. 19:1-8
Demoted by
David.........2 Sam. 19:13
Puts down Sheba's
revolt ....2 Sam. 20:1-22
Killed Amasa ..2 Sam. 20:8-10
Regains
command .....2 Sam. 20:23
Opposes David's
numbering of the
people ....2 Sam. 24:1-9
                    1 Chr. 21:1-6

Supports
Adonijah......1 Kin. 1:7
David's dying words
against.........1 Kin. 2:1-6
His crimes punished by
Solomon ......1 Kin. 2:28-34
2. Son of
Seraiah ....1 Chr. 4:13, 14
3. Family head of
exiles ....Ezra 2:6

Joah—*Yahweh is brother*

1. Son of Obed-
Edom ....1 Chr. 26:4
2. Gershonite
Levite.........1 Chr. 6:21
Hezekiah's
assistant ......2 Chr. 29:12
3. Son of Asaph; a recorder under
Hezekiah......Is. 36:3, 11, 22
4. Son of
Joahaz........2 Chr. 34:8

Joahaz—*Yahweh has laid hold of*

Father of Joah, a
recorder.......2 Chr. 34:8

Joanna—*Yahweh has been gracious*

Wife of Chuza, Herod's
steward ....Luke 8:1-3
With others, heralds Christ's
resurrection ......Luke 23:55, 56

Joannas—*Yahweh has been gracious*

Ancestor of
Christ ....Luke 3:27

Joash, Jehoash (I)—*Yahweh has given*

1. Father of
Gideon........Judg. 6:11-32
2. Judahite ....1 Chr. 4:21, 22
3. Benjamite
warrior ....1 Chr. 12:3
4. Son of Ahab ...1 Kin. 22:26
5. Son and successor of Ahaziah,
king of
Judah.........2 Kin. 11:1-21
Rescued and hid by
Jehosheba.....2 Kin. 11:1-3
Proclaimed king by
Jehoiada ......2 Kin. 11:4-12
Instructed by
Jehoiada ......2 Kin. 12:1, 2
Repairs the
Temple........2 Kin. 12:4-16
Turns to idols after Jehoiada's
death ....2 Chr. 24:17-19

Murdered Zechariah,
Berechiah's
son ....Matt. 23:35
Killed, not buried with
kings ....2 Chr. 25:23-28
6. Son and successor of Jehoahaz,
king of
Israel ....2 Kin. 13:10-13
Follows
idolatry ....2 Kin. 13:11
Laments Elijah's
sickness......2 Kin. 13:14-19
Defeats:
Syria ....2 Kin. 13:24, 25
Amaziah......2 Kin. 13:12

Joash (II)—*Yahweh has come to help*

1. Benjamite .....1 Chr. 7:8
2. Officer of
David.........1 Chr. 27:28

Job—*returning*

A. *Life of:*
Lives in Uz ....Job 1:1
Afflicted by
Satan ....Job 1:6-19
Debate between Job and his
three friends ..Job 3–33
Elihu
intervenes.....Job 34–37
Lord answers
Job ....Job 38–41
His final
reply..........Job 42:1-6
The Lord rebukes Job's three
friends ....Job 42:7-9
Restored to
prosperity.....Job 42:10-15
Dies "old and full of
days".........Job 42:16, 17

B. *Strength of his:*
Faith ....Job 19:23-27
Perseverance ..James 5:11
Integrity.......Job 31:1-40

C. *Sufferings of:*
Lost
property ......Job 1:13-17
Lost children ..Job 1:18, 19
Lost health ...Job 2:4-8
Misunder-   ⎰Job 4:1-8
stood by   ⎱Job 8:1-6
friends ....⎰Job 11:1-20

D. *Restoration of:*
After
repentance....Job 42:1-6
After prayer ..Job 42:8-10

To greater
prosperity.....Job 42:11-17

Job, the Book of—*a book of the Old
Testament*

Wisdom
described........Job 1:1-5
Wisdom tested....Job 1:6—2:10
Wisdom sought...Job 3—37
God challenges
Job..............Job 38—41
Wisdom in
humility.........Job 42:1-6

Jobab—*to call shrilly*

1. Son of
   Joktan........Gen. 10:29
   Tribal head...1 Chr. 1:23
2. King of
   Edom.........Gen. 36:31, 33
3. Canaanite king defeated by
   Joshua........Josh. 11:1, 7-12
4. Benjamite.....1 Chr. 8:9
5. Another
   Benjamite.....1 Chr. 8:18

Jochebed—*Yahweh is glory*

Daughter of Levi; mother of
Miriam, Aaron, and
Moses............Ex. 6:20

Joed—*Yahweh is witness*

Benjamite.........Neh. 11:7

Joel—*Yahweh is God*

1. Son of
   Samuel......{ 1 Sam. 8:1, 2
              { 1 Chr. 6:28, 33
   Father of Heman the
   singer.........1 Chr. 15:17
2. Kohathite
   Levite.........1 Chr. 6:36
3. Leader of
   Simeon.......1 Chr. 4:35
4. Reubenite
   chief..........1 Chr. 5:4, 8, 9
5. Gadite chief...1 Chr. 5:12
6. Chief man of
   Issachar......1 Chr. 7:3
7. One of David's mighty
   men...........1 Chr. 11:38
8. Gershonite   { 1 Chr. 15:7, 11,
   Levite.......{   17
   Probably the
   same as in ....1 Chr. 23:8
9. Manassite chief
   officer.........1 Chr. 27:20

10. Kohathite Levite during
    Hezekiah's
    reign.........2 Chr. 29:12
11. Son of Nebo; divorced his
    foreign wife...Ezra 10:43
12. Benjamite overseer under
    Nehemiah.....Neh. 11:9
13. Prophet........Joel 1:1

Joel, Book of

Prophecies of:

Predict
Pentecost ....Joel 2:28-32
Proclaim salvation in
Christ...........Joel 2:32
Portray the universal
judgment.......Joel 3:1-16
Picture the eternal
age..............Joel 3:17-21

Joelah—*let him help*

David's recruit at
Ziklag............1 Chr. 12:7

Joezer—*Yahweh is help*

One of David's supporters at
Ziklag............1 Chr. 12:6

Jogbehah—*lofty*

Town in Gilead ...Judg. 8:11

Jogli—*exiled*

Father of Bukki, a Danite
prince............Num. 34:22

Joha—*Yahweh is living*

1. Benjamite .....1 Chr. 8:16
2. One of David's mighty
   men...........1 Chr. 11:45

Johanan—*Yahweh is gracious*

1. One of David's mighty
   men...........1 Chr. 12:2, 4
2. Gadite captain of
   David.........1 Chr. 12:12, 14
3. Father of Azariah the
   priest ....1 Chr. 6:10
4. Ephraimite
   leader.........2 Chr. 28:12
5. Son of King
   Josiah.........1 Chr. 3:15
6. Son of
   Careah........2 Kin. 25:22, 23
   Supports
   Gedaliah .....Jer. 40:8, 9
   Warns Gedaliah of assassination
   plot...........Jer. 40:13, 14

Avenges Gedaliah's
murder........Jer. 41:11-15
Removes Jewish remnant to
Egypt against Jeremiah's
warning.......Jer. 41:16-18
7. Elioenai's
son ....1 Chr. 3:24
8. Returned
exile ....Ezra 8:12
9. Postexilic high
priest ....Neh. 12:22

See Jehohanan

John—*Yahweh has been gracious*

1. Jewish
official ....Acts 4:6
2. Also called
Mark ....Acts 12:12, 25
3. John the
Baptist........Matt. 3:1
4. John the
Apostle......Matt. 4:21

John the Apostle

A. *Life of:*
Son of
Zebedee.......Matt. 4:21
Fisherman .....Luke 5:1-11
Leaves his business for
Christ........Matt. 4:21, 22
Called to be an
apostle........Matt. 10:2
Rebuked by   {Mark 13:3
Christ.......   {Luke 9:54, 55
Sent to prepare
Passover .....Luke 22:8-13
Close to Jesus at Last
Supper......John 13:23-25
Christ commits His mother
to.............John 19:26, 27
Witnesses Christ's
ascension .....Acts 1:9-13
With Peter, heals a
man ....Acts 3:1-11
Imprisoned with
Peter.........Acts 4:1-21
With Peter, becomes a
missionary ....Acts 8:14-25
Encourages
Paul ....Gal. 2:9
Exiled on
Patmos ......Rev. 1:9
Wrote a
Gospel ......John 21:23-25
Wrote   {1 John
three   {2 John
epistles.......{3 John
Wrote the
Revelation ....Rev. 1:1, 4, 9

B. *Described as:*
Uneducated....Acts 4:13
Intolerant .....Mark 9:38
Ambitious ....Mark 10:35-37
Trustworthy ...John 19:26, 27
Humble.......Rev. 19:10
Beloved by
Jesus.........John 21:20

John the Baptist

A. *Life of:*
Prophecies:
Concerning ...Is. 40:3-5
Fulfilled by ...Matt. 3:3
Angel anounces
birth of ....Luke 1:11-20
Set apart as   {Num. 6:2, 3
Nazirite ...... {Luke 1:15
Lives in
deserts........Luke 1:63, 80
Ministry of,
dated ....Luke 3:1-3
Public
confusion .....Luke 3:15
Identifies Jesus as the
Messiah......John 1:29-36
Bears witness to
Christ........John 5:33
Exalts Christ...John 3:25-36
Baptizes
Christ........Matt. 3:13-16
Doubts ....Matt. 11:2-6
Identified with
Elijah ....Matt. 11:13, 14
Public
reaction to....Matt. 11:16-18
Christ's testimony
concerning....Matt. 11:9-13
Reproves Herod for
adultery.......Mark 6:17, 18
Imprisoned by
Herod.........Matt. 4:12
Beheaded by
Herod.........Matt. 14:3-12

B. *Described as:*
Fearless ....Matt. 14:3, 4
Holy...........Mark 6:20
Humble........John 3:25-31
Faithful........Acts 13:24, 25
Resourceful....Matt. 3:4
Baptism of,   {Acts 18:24-26
insufficient... {Acts 19:1-5
Preaching a baptism of
repentance....Luke 3:2-18

John, the Epistles of—*books of the New Testament*

A. *1 John:*
God is light....1 John 1:5-7
True
knowledge....1 John 2:3, 4
Love one
another......1 John 3:11-24
God is love....1 John 4:7-21
Eternal life....1 John 5:13-21

B. *2 John:*
Commandment to
love...........2 John 4-6
Warning against
deceit.........2 John 7-11

C. *3 John:*
Walking in
truth.........3 John 3, 4
Service to the
brethren.....3 John 5-8
Rebuke to
Diotrephes...3 John 9, 10
Do good.......3 John 11, 12

John, the Gospel of—*a book of the New Testament*

Deity of Christ....John 1:1-18
Testimony of the
Baptist.........John 1:19-34
Wedding at
Cana.............John 2:1-11
Samarian
mission...........John 4:1-42
Feast of
Tabernacles.....John 7:1-53
The good
shepherd........John 10:1-42
Lazarus raised....John 11:1-57
Priestly prayer....John 17:1-26
Sufferings and ⎰ John 18:1–
glory...........⎱ 20:31
Purpose of.......John 20:30, 31

Joiada—*Yahweh knows*

Postexilic high ⎰Neh. 12:10,
priest...........⎱ 11, 22
Son banished from
priesthood.......Neh. 13:28

See Jehoiada

Joiakim—*Yahweh establishes*

Postexilic high priest; son of
Jeshua ....Neh. 12:10-26

Joiarib—*Yahweh contends*

1. Teacher sent by
Ezra..........Ezra 8:16, 17
2. Postexilic Judahite
chief..........Neh. 11:5
3. Founder of an order of
priests........Neh. 11:10
4. Postexilic
priest.........Neh. 12:6
Father of
Joiakim.......Neh. 12:19

Jokdeam—*anger of the people*

City of Judah.....Josh. 15:56

Jokim—*Yahweh raises up*

Judahite..........1 Chr. 4:22

Jokmeam—*let the people arise*

Town of
Ephraim..........1 Chr. 6:68
Home of Kohathite
Levites...........1 Chr. 6:66, 68
Same as
Kibzaim in.......Josh. 21:22
Called Jokneam...1 Kin. 4:12

Jokneam—*let the people inquire*

1. Town near Mt.
Carmel.......Josh. 12:22
In tribe of
Zebulun.......Josh. 19:11
Assigned to
Levites.......Josh. 21:34
2. Town of
Ephraim......1 Kin. 4:12

See Jokmeam

Jokshan—*fowler*

Son of Abraham and
Keturah..........Gen. 25:1, 2

Joktan—*he will be made small*

A descendant of
Shem.............Gen. 10:21, 25

Joktheel—*God's reward of victory*

1. Village of
Judah..........Josh. 15:20, 38
2. Name given by King Amaziah
to Selah.......2 Kin. 14:7

Jonadab—*Yahweh is bounteous*

1. Son of Shimeah; David's
nephew.......2 Sam. 13:3

Very subtle man.......... { 2 Sam. 13:3-6, 32-36

2. Son of
Rechab.....Jer. 35:6
Makes Rechabites
primitive and
temperate.....Jer. 35:5-17
Blessing
upon.........Jer. 35:18, 19
Opposes { 2 Kin. 10:15, 16,
idolatry.....{ 23
Called
Jehonadab...2 Kin. 10:15, 23

Jonah—*dove*

1. Son of
Amittai.......Jon. 1:1
Ordered to go to
Nineveh.......Jon. 1:2
Flees to
Tarshish.....Jon. 1:3
Cause of storm; cast into
sea...........Jon. 1:4-16
Swallowed by a great
fish...........Jon. 1:17
Prays in fish's
belly.........Jon. 2:1-9
Vomited upon
land...........Jon. 2:10
Obeys second order to go to
Nineveh.......Jon. 3:1-10
Grieved at Nineveh's
repentance.....Jon. 4:1-3
Taught God's
mercy.........Jon. 4:4-11
Type of Christ's
resurrection...Matt. 12:39, 40

2. Father of Simon
Peter..........John 1:42
Peter called Bar-
Jonah.........Matt. 16:17

Jonan—*Yahweh has been gracious*

Ancestor of
Christ...........Luke 3:30

Jonathan—*Yahweh has given*

1. Levite; becomes Micah's
priest.........Judg. 17:1-13
Follows Danites to idolatrous
Dan...........Judg. 18:3-31
Grandson of Moses
(Manasseh)...Judg. 18:30

2. King Saul's eldest
son...........1 Sam. 14:49
Smites Philistine
garrison.......1 Sam. 13:2, 3

Attacks
Michmash.....1 Sam. 14:1-14
Saved from his father's
vow...........1 Sam. 14:24-45
Makes covenant with
David.........1 Sam. 18:1-4
Pleads for David's
life.............1 Sam. 19:1-7
Warns David of Saul's
wrath.........1 Sam. 20:1-42
Makes second covenant with
David.........1 Sam. 23:15-18
Killed by
Philistines.....1 Sam. 31:2, 8
Mourned by
David.........2 Sam. 1:17-27
David provides for his
son...........2 Sam. 9:1-8

3. Son of the high priest
Abiathar.....2 Sam. 15:27
Remains faithful to
David.........2 Sam. 15:26-36
Brings David Absalom's
plans.........2 Sam. 17:15-22
Informs Adonijah of David's
choice.......1 Kin. 1:41-49

4. Son of
Shimeah.....2 Sam. 21:21, 22

5. One of David's mighty
men...........2 Sam. 23:32

6. Judahite.......1 Chr. 2:32, 33

7. Son of
Kareah........Jer. 40:8, 9

8. Scribe.........Jer. 37:15, 20

9. Opponents of Ezra's
reforms.......Ezra 10:15

10. Descendant of
Adin...........Ezra 8:6

11. Levite of Asaph's
line...........Neh. 12:35

12. Head of a priestly
house.........Neh. 12:14

13. Postexilic high
priest.........Neh. 12:11

Joppa—*beauty*

Allotted to Dan...Josh. 19:40, 46
Seaport city......2 Chr. 2:16
Center of
commerce.......Ezra 3:7
Scene of Peter's
vision...........Acts 10:5-23, 32

Jorah—*rain*

Family of
returnees.........Ezra 2:18
Called Hariph.....Neh. 7:24

Jorai—*rainy*

Gadite chief.......1 Chr. 5:13

Joram, Jehoram—*Yahweh is exalted*

1. Son of Toi, king of
   Hamath.......2 Sam. 8:10
   Called
   Hadoram.......1 Chr. 18:10
2. Levite.......1 Chr. 26:25
3. Son of Ahab, king of
   Israel ....2 Kin. 3:1
   Institutes some
   reforms ....2 Kin. 3:2, 3
   Joins Judah against
   Moab.......2 Kin. 3:1-27
   Slain by
   Jehu.........2 Kin. 9:14-26
   Called
   Jehoram ....2 Kin. 1:17
4. Priest sent to teach the
   people ....2 Chr. 17:8
5. Son and successor of
   Jehoshaphat, king of
   Judah.......2 Kin. 8:16
   Murders his
   brothers.......2 Chr. 21:1-4
   His wife, Ahab's daughter, leads
   him astray ....2 Kin. 8:17, 18
   Edomites revolt
   against.......2 Chr. 21:8-10
   Unable to withstand
   invaders ....2 Chr. 21:16, 17
   Elijah's prophecy
   against.......2 Chr. 21:12-15
   Dies horribly without
   mourners .....2 Chr. 21:18-20
   Called
   Jehoram ....2 Chr. 21:1, 5

See Jehoram

Jordan—*the descender; a river in
   Palestine*

Canaan's eastern
   boundary.......Num. 34:12
Despised by
   foreigners ....2 Kin. 5:10, 12
Lot dwells near ...Gen. 13:8-13
Jacob crosses .....Gen. 32:10
Moses forbidden to
   cross ....Deut. 3:27
Israel crosses
   miraculously .....Josh. 3:1-17
Stones commemorate
   crossing of ....Josh. 4:1-24
David crosses in
   flight.............2 Sam. 17:22, 24

Divided by
   Elijah ....2 Kin. 2:5-8
Divided by
   Elisha.........2 Kin. 2:13, 14
Naaman
   healed in ....2 Kin. 5:10, 14
John's
   baptism in........Matt. 3:6
Christ
   baptized in .....Matt. 3:13-17

Jorim—*Yahweh is exalted*

Ancestor of
   Christ............Luke 3:29

Jorkoam

Judahite family
   name.............1 Chr. 2:44
May be same as Jokdeam
   in ....Josh. 15:56

Jose

Ancestor of
   Christ............Luke 3:29

Joseph—*may He (Yahweh) add*

1. Son of Jacob by
   Rachel.........Gen. 30:22-24
2. Father of one of the
   spies ....Num. 13:7
3. Son of Asaph ..1 Chr. 25:2, 9
4. One who divorced his foreign
   wife...........Ezra 10:32, 42
5. Preexilic ancestor of
   Christ.........Luke 3:30
6. Priest in the days of
   Joiakim ....Neh. 12:14
7. Postexilic ancestor of
   Christ.........Luke 3:26
8. Son of Mattathiah, in Christ's
   ancestry...Luke 3:24, 25
9. Husband of Mary, Jesus'
   mother.......Matt. 1:16
   Of Davidic
   lineage........Matt. 1:20
   Angel explains Mary's condition
   to............Matt. 1:19-25
   With Mary at Jesus'
   birth ....Luke 2:16
   Obeys Old Testament
   ordinances ....Luke 2:21-24
   Takes Jesus and Mary to
   Egypt.........Matt. 2:13-15
   Returns to Nazareth with
   family.........Matt. 2:19-23
   Jesus subject
   to.............Luke 2:51

10. Man of
   Arimathea ....John 19:38
   Devout man ...Luke 23:50, 51
   Secret
   disciple ......John 19:38
   Obtains Christ's body; prepares
   it ....Mark 15:43, 46
   Receives Nicodemus's
   help........John 19:39, 40
   Puts Christ's body in his new
   tomb.........Luke 23:53
11. Called Barsabas; one of two
   chosen to occupy Judas's
   place.........Acts 1:22-26

Joseph—*increaser*

A. *Life of:*
   Jacob's son by
   Rachel........Gen. 30:22-25
   Jacob's
   favorite ......Gen. 37:3
   Aroused his brothers'
   hatred ......Gen. 37:4
   Sold into
   Egypt.........Gen. 37:25-30
   Wins esteem in
   Egypt.........Gen. 39:1-23
   Interprets Pharaoh's
   dream.........Gen. 41:1-37
   Made Pharaoh's Prime
   Minister......Gen. 41:38-46
   Recognizes his
   brothers......Gen. 42:1-8
   Reveals his
   identity ......Gen. 45:1-16
   Invites Jacob to
   Egypt.........Gen. 45:17-28
   Enslaves
   Egypt.........Gen. 47:13-26
   Put under oath by
   Jacob ....Gen. 47:28-31
   His sons blessed by
   Jacob ....Gen. 48:1-22
   Blessed by
   Jacob ....Gen. 49:22-26
   Mourns his father's
   death ....Gen. 50:1-14
   Deals kindly with his
   brothers......Gen. 50:15-21
   His death at
   110............Gen. 50:22-26
   Descendants
   of............Num. 26:28-37

B. *Character of:*
   Spiritually
   sensitive ......Gen. 37:2
   Wise and
   prudent ......Gen. 41:38-49
   Of strong
   emotions......Gen. 43:29-31
   Sees God's hand in human
   events ....Gen. 45:7, 8
   Forgiving......Gen. 50:19-21
   Man of faith ...Heb. 11:22

Joses—*increaser*

1. One of Christ's
   brothers.......Matt. 13:55
2. The name of
   Barnabas......Acts 4:36

Josah—*Yahweh's gift*

Simeonite leader ..1 Chr. 4:34, 38

Joshaphat—*Yahweh has judged*

1. Mighty man of
   David.........1 Chr. 11:43
2. Priestly
   trumpeter.....1 Chr. 15:24

Joshaviah—*Yahweh is equality*

One of David's mighty
men..............1 Chr. 11:46

Joshbekashah—*he returns a hard fate*

Head of musical
order.............1 Chr. 25:4, 24

Josheb-Basshebeth—*one who sat on the seat*

Chief of David's mighty
men..............2 Sam. 23:8
Called
Jashobeam ....1 Chr. 11:11

Joshibiah—*Yahweh causes to dwell* (in peace)

Simeonite.........1 Chr. 4:35

Joshua, Jeshua—*Yahweh is salvation*

1. Native of Beth
   Shemesh ....1 Sam. 6:14, 18
2. Governor of Jerusalem during
   Josiah's
   reign..........2 Kin. 23:8
3. High priest during Zerubbabel's
   time ....Hag. 1:1, 12, 14
   Called Jeshua in Ezra and
   Nehemiah.....Ezra 2:2
   Type of
   Christ.........Zech. 6:11-13
4. Son of Nun ....Num. 13:8, 16

See Jeshua (4)

Joshua—*Yahweh saves*

A. *Life of:*
Defeats
Amalek . . . . Ex. 17:8-16
Minister under
Moses. . . . . Ex. 24:13
One of the ⎧ Num. 13:1-3,
spies . . . . ⎩ 8, 16
Reports
favorably . . . . . Num. 14:6-10
Moses'
successor . . . . . Num. 27:18-23
Inspired by
God. . . . . Num. 27:18
Unifies the
people . . . . Josh. 1:10-18
Sends spies
out . . . . Josh. 2:1-24
Crosses
Jordan . . . . Josh. 3:1-17
Destroys
Jericho. . . . . . . Josh. 6:1-27
Conquers
Canaan . . . . . . Josh. 10-12
Divides the
land. . . . . Josh. 13-19
Orders Israel's
leaders . . . . Josh. 23:1-16
Final address to the
nation . . . . . . Josh. 24:1-28
Dies at 110. . . . . Josh. 24:29, 30
Called
Hoshea . . . . . . Num. 13:8, 16

B. *Character of:*
Courageous. . . . Num. 14:6-10
Emotional . . . . . Josh. 7:6-10
Wise military
man . . . . Josh. 8:3-29
Easily
beguiled. . . . . . Josh. 9:3-27
Prophetic . . . . . Josh. 6:26, 27
Strong religious
leader . . . . Judg. 2:7

Joshua, the Book of—*a book of the Old Testament*

Entering Promised
Land . . . . Josh. 1:1-5:12
The divine
captain . . . . Josh. 5:13-6:5
Capture of
Jericho . . . . Josh. 6:6-27
Capture of Ai . . . . . Josh. 8:1-29
Apportionment of the
land . . . . Josh. 13:1-22:34
Covenant at
Shechem . . . . Josh. 24:1-28
Death of Joshua . . Josh. 24:29-33

Josiah—*Yahweh heals*

1. Son and successor of Amon,
king of
Judah. . . . . 2 Kin. 21:25, 26
Crowned at 8; reigns
righteously 31
years. . . . . 2 Kin. 22:1
Named before
birth . . . . 1 Kin. 13:1, 2
Repairs the
Temple. . . . . . . 2 Kin. 22:3-9
Receives the Book of
Law. . . . . 2 Kin. 22:10-17
Saved from predicted
doom . . . . 2 Kin. 22:18-20
Reads the
Law. . . . . 2 Kin. 23:1, 2
Makes a
covenant. . . . . . 2 Kin. 23:3
Destroys ⎧ 2 Kin. 23:4, 20,
idolatry ⎩ 24
Observes the
Passover . . . . . . 2 Kin. 23:21-23
Exceptional
king . . . . 2 Kin. 23:25
Slain in
battle . . . . 2 Chr. 35:20-24
Lamented by
Jeremiah. . . . . . 2 Chr. 35:25-27
Commended by
Jeremiah. . . . . . Jer. 22:15-18
Ancestor of
Christ. . . . . Matt. 1:10, 11
2. Son of
Zephaniah . . . . Zech. 6:10

Josiphiah—*Yahweh will increase*

Father of a postexilic
Jew . . . . Ezra 8:10

Jot—*Greek iota* (i); *Hebrew yodh* (y)

Figurative of the smallest
detail. . . . . Matt. 5:18

Jotbah—*pleasantness*

City of Haruz, the father of
Meshullemeth . . . . 2 Kin. 21:19

Jotbathah—*pleasantness*

Israelite ⎧ Num. 33:33
encampment . . . . ⎩ Deut. 10:7

Jotham—*Yahweh is perfect*

1. Gideon's youngest
son . . . . Judg. 9:5
Escapes Abimelech's
massacre. . . . . . Judg. 9:5, 21

Utters a prophetic
parable.........Judg. 9:7-21
Sees his prophecy
fulfilled ....Judg. 9:22-57
2. Son and successor of Azariah
(Uzziah), king of
Judah.........2 Kin. 15:5, 7
Reign of, partly
good ....2 Kin. 15:32-38
Conquers
Ammonites ...2 Chr. 27:5-9
Contemporary of Isaiah and
Hosea.........Is. 1:1
Ancestor of
Christ.........Matt. 1:9
3. Son of
Jahdai ....1 Chr. 2:47

Journey—*an extended trip*

Preparation for, by:

Prayer ....Rom. 1:10
God's providence
acknowledged ....James 4:13-17

Joy—*gladness of heart*

A. *Kinds of:*
Foolish.......Prov. 15:21
Temporary.....Matt. 13:20
Motherly ......Ps. 113:9
Figurative .....Is. 52:9
Future.........Matt. 25:21, 23

B. *Described as:*
Everlasting ....Is. 51:11
Great..........Acts 8:8
Full...........1 John 1:4
Abundant......2 Cor. 8:2
Unspeakable...1 Pet. 1:8

C. *Causes of:*
Victory.......1 Sam. 18:6
Christ's birth ..Luke 2:10, 11
Christ's
resurrection...Matt. 28:7, 8
Sinner's
repentance....Luke 15:5, 10
Miracles among the
Gentiles......Acts 8:7, 8
Forgiveness...Ps. 51:8, 12
God's Word....Jer. 15:16
Spiritual
discovery .....Matt. 13:44
Names written in
heaven......Luke 10:17, 20
True faith .....1 Pet. 1:8

D. *Place of, in:*
Prayer.........Is. 56:7

Christian:
Fellowship....Phil. 1:25
Tribulation ...2 Cor. 7:4-7
Giving........2 Cor. 8:2

E. *Contrasted with:*
Weeping.......Ezra 3:12, 13
Ps. 30:5
Tears ....Ps. 126:5
Sorrow ....Is. 35:10
Mourning.....Jer. 31:13
Pain ....John 16:20, 21
Loss...........Heb. 10:34
Heb. 13:17
Adversity......Eccl. 7:14
Discipline.....Ps. 51:8
Heb. 12:11
Persecution....Luke 6:22, 23

F. *Of angels:*
At creation ....Job 38:4, 7
At Christ's
birth.........Luke 2:10, 13, 14
At sinner's
conversion....Luke 15:10

G. *Expressed by:*
Songs.........Gen. 31:27
Musical
instruments...1 Sam. 18:6
Sounds ....1 Chr. 15:16
Praises........2 Chr. 29:30
Shouting .....Ezra 3:12, 13
Heart.........1 Kin. 21:7

See Gladness; Happiness of the Saints

Jozabad—*Yahweh has bestowed*

1, 2, 3. Three of David's mighty
men...........1 Chr. 12:4, 20
4. Levite overseer in Hezekiah's
reign..........2 Chr. 31:13
5. Chief Levite in Josiah's
reign..........2 Chr. 35:9
6. Levite, son of
Jeshua ....Ezra 8:33
Probably the
same as in ....Ezra 10:23
7. Expounder of the
Law...........Neh. 8:7
8. Levitical
chief.........Neh. 11:16
Some consider 6, 7, 8 the same
person
9. Priest who divorced his foreign
wife..........Ezra 10:22

Jozachar—*Yahweh has remembered*

Assassin of
Joash...........2 Kin. 12:19-21
Called Zabad......2 Chr. 24:26

Jozadak—*Yahweh is righteous*

Postexilic priest ...Ezra 3:2

Jubal—*playing*

Son of Lamech....Gen. 4:21

Jubilee, Year of:

A. *Regulations concerning:*
Introduced by
trumpet.......Lev. 25:9
After 49
years.........Lev. 25:8
Rules for
fixing   {Lev. 25:15, 16,
prices........{ 25-28

B. *Purposes of:*
Restore liberty (to the
enslaved) .....Lev. 25:38-43
Restore property (to the
original
owner).......Lev. 25:23-28
Remit debt (to the
indebted) .....Lev. 25:47-55
Restore rest
(to the   {Lev. 25:11, 12,
land).........{ 18-22

C. *Figurative of:*
Christ's
mission ....Is. 61:1-3
Earth's
jubilee ....Rom. 8:19-24

Judah—*let Him (God) be praised*

1. Son of Jacob and
Leah..........Gen. 29:15-35
Intercedes for
Joseph ....Gen. 37:26, 27
Marries a
Canaanite.....Gen. 38:1-10
Fathers Perez and Zerah by
Tamar ....Gen. 38:11-30
Through Tamar, an ancestor of
David........Ruth 4:18-22
Ancestor of
Christ.........Matt. 1:3, 16
Offers himself as Benjamin's
ransom....Gen. 44:33, 34
Leads Jacob to
Goshen ....Gen. 46:28
Jacob bestows birthright
on ....Gen. 49:3-10
Messiah promised
through.......Gen. 49:10

2. Judah, Tribe of
See separate article

3. Postexilic
Levite........Ezra 3:9
4. Levite returning with
Zerubbabel...Neh. 12:8
5. Levite divorced his foreign
wife..........Ezra 10:23
6. Postexilic
overseer ......Neh. 11:9
7. Priest and
musician......Neh. 12:36
Probably same as 4 and 5
8. Postexilic
prince.........Neh. 12:32-34

Judah, Tribe of

Descendants of
Judah ....Gen. 29:35
Prophecy
concerning ......Gen. 49:8-12
Five families of....Num. 26:19-22
Leads in wilderness
journey ....Num. 2:3, 9
Numbering of, at
Sinai ....Num. 1:26, 27
Numbering of, in
Moab............Num. 26:22
Leads in conquest of
Canaan.........Judg. 1:1-19
Territory assigned
to ....Josh. 15:1-63
Fights against
Gibeah ....Judg. 20:18
Makes David
king............2 Sam. 2:1-11
Elders of, upbraided by
David ....2 Sam. 19:11, 15
Conflict with other
tribes.............2 Sam. 19:41-43
Loyal to David during Sheba's
rebellion.........2 Sam. 20:1, 2
Loyal to Davidic house at
Jeroboam's
rebellion..........1 Kin. 12:20
Becomes leader of southern
kingdom
(Judah)...........1 Kin. 14:21, 22
Taken to
Babylon ....2 Kin. 24:1-16
Returns after
exile..............2 Chr. 36:20-23
Christ comes of ...Luke 3:23-33

Judas—*Greek form of Judah*

See Judah 1

1. Judas Lebbaeus, surnamed
Thaddaeus ....Matt. 10:3
One of Christ's
apostles.......Luke 6:13, 16

Offers a
question ......John 14:22
2. Betrayer of Christ (see
Iscariot) ......Luke 6:13, 16
3. Brother of Christ (see Brethren
of Christ) .....Matt. 13:55
4. Leader of an
insurrection...Acts 5:37
See Jude
5. Jew of
Damascus.....Acts 9:11
6. Judas Barsabas, a chief
deputy ....Acts 15:22-32
Probably related to the disciple
Joseph ....Acts 1:23

Jude, Judas

Brother of
Christ ....Matt. 13:55
Does not believe in
Christ ....John 7:5
Becomes Christ's
disciple............Acts 1:14
Writes an
Epistle ....Jude 1

See Judas 5

Jude, the Epistle of—*a book of the New Testament*

Author............Jude 1
Against false
teachers ....Jude 3-5
Against the
ungodly ....Jude 6-16
Exhortation ....Jude 17-23

Judea—*a district in southern Palestine*

District under a
governor ....Luke 3:1
All Palestine ......Luke 23:5
All the land of the
Jews ....Acts 10:37
Rural people outside
Jerusalem ....Matt. 4:25
Wilderness country near Dead
Sea...............Matt. 3:1
Christ born in.....Matt. 2:1, 5, 6
Hostile toward
Christ ....John 7:1
Gospel
preached in.......Acts 8:1, 4
Churches
established in.....Acts 9:31

Judge—*an official authorized to hear and decide cases of law*

A. *History of, in scripture:*
Family head ...Gen. 38:24

Established by { Ex. 18:13-26
Moses........ { Deut. 1:9-17
Rules for ......Deut. 16:18-20
                Deut. 17:2-13
Circuit..........1 Sam. 7:6,
                15-17
King acts as ...2 Sam. 15:2
                1 Kin. 3:9, 28
Jehoshaphat established
court..........2 Chr. 19:5-11
Levites
assigned ......1 Chr. 23:1-4
Restored after
exile ....Ezra 7:25

B. *Procedure before:*
Public trial......Ex. 18:13
Case   { Deut. 1:16
presented .... { Deut. 25:1
Position of
parties ....Zech. 3:1
Accused
heard ....John 7:51
Witness........Deut. 19:15-19
Priests.........Deut. 17:8-13
Oath...........Ex. 22:11
                Heb. 6:16
Casting of lots sometimes
used ....Prov. 18:18
Divine will
sought ....Lev. 24:12-14

C. *Office of:*
Divinely
instituted .....2 Sam. 7:11
Limits to human
affairs.........1 Sam. 2:25
Restricted by righteous-
ness..........Deut. 16:18-20
Needful of great
wisdom ....1 Kin. 3:9
Easily
corrupted .....Mic. 7:3
Unjustly   { Acts 23:3
used .... { Acts 25:9-11
Fulfilled
perfectly in { Is. 2:4
the   { Is. 11:3, 4
Messiah...... { Acts 17:31

Judge, God as

Manner of:

According to
righteousness.....1 Pet. 2:23
According to one's
works ....1 Pet. 1:17
Openly...........Rom. 2:16
By Christ ....John 5:22, 30
In a final way.....Joel 3:12-14

Judges of Israel

A. *Characteristics of era:*
No central authority..... Judg. 17:6
Judg. 21:25
Spiritual decline....... Judg. 2:16-18
Judg. 18:1-31

B. *List of:*
Othniel .... Judg. 3:9-11
Ehud .... Judg. 3:15-30
Shamgar....... Judg. 3:31
Deborah and Barak .... Judg. 4:4-9
Gideon .... Judg. 6:11-40
Abimelech ..... Judg. 9:1-54
Tola .... Judg. 10:1, 2
Jair .... Judg. 10:3-5
Jephthah ..... Judg. 12:1-7
Ibzan .... Judg. 12:8-10
Elon .... Judg. 12:11, 12
Abdon .... Judg. 12:13-15
Samson .... Judg. 15:20
Eli............. 1 Sam. 4:15, 18
Samuel .... 1 Sam. 7:15
Samuel's sons .... 1 Sam. 8:1-3

Judges, the Book of—*a book of the Old Testament*

The death of Joshua .... Judg. 2:6-10
Deborah and Barak .... Judg. 4:1–5:31
Gideon .... Judg. 6:1–8:32
Jephthah......... Judg. 10:6–11:40
Samson .... Judg. 13:1–16:31
Micah and the Danites.......... Judg. 18
The war against Benjamin...... Judg. 19:1–21:25

Judgment, divine

A. *Design of:*
Punish evil .... Ex. 20:5
Chasten .... 2 Sam. 7:14, 15
Manifest God's righteous-ness.......... Ex. 9:14-16
Correct .... Hab. 1:12
Warn others ... Luke 13:3, 5

B. *Causes of:*
Disobedi-ence .... 2 Chr. 7:19-22
Rejecting God's warnings...... 2 Chr. 36:16, 17
Idolatry....... Jer. 7:30-34
Sins of rulers .. 2 Chr. 21:1-17
Loving evil .... Rom. 1:18-32

C. *Kinds of:*
Physical destruction.... Deut. 28:15-68
Material loss... Mal. 3:11
Spiritual blindness...... Is. 6:9, 10
Eternal destruction... Luke 12:16-21
Luke 16:19-31

D. *Avoidance of, by:*
Turning to God.......... Deut. 30:1-3
Turning from sin .... Jer. 7:3-7
Humiliation.... Jon. 1:1-17
Prayer......... 2 Kin. 19:14-36
2 Chr. 20:5-30

Judgment Hall

Of Solomon .... 1 Kin. 7:1, 7

Judgment, human

A. *Weaknesses of:*
Often circum-stantial .... Josh. 22:10-34
Sometimes wrong .... Gen. 39:10-20
Hasty and revengeful .... 1 Sam. 25:20-35
Full of conceit........ Esth. 5:11-14
Prejudicial..... Luke 7:38-50

B. *Rules regarding:*
Begin with self-judgment ..... Matt. 7:1-5
Become spiritually minded........ 1 Cor. 2:12-15
Abound in love.......... Phil. 1:9, 10
Await the final judgment ..... Rom. 14:10

C. *Basis of:*
Circum-stance .... Gen. 39:10-20
Opinion........ Acts 28:22
Moral law ..... Rom. 2:14-16
Conscience ... 1 Cor. 10:27-29
Nature......... 1 Cor. 11:13, 14
Apostolic authority...... 1 Cor. 5:3, 4
Law of Christ......... Gal. 6:2-4
Divine illumination ... Josh. 7:10-15

Judgment, the last

A. *Described as:*
Day of wrath .. Rom. 2:5

Day of
judgment .....2 Pet. 3:7
Judgment seat of
Christ.......Matt. 25:31

B. *Time of:*
After death ....Heb. 9:27
At Christ's
return........Matt. 25:31
Appointed
day ....Acts 17:31
After the world's
destruction....2 Pet. 3:7-15

C. *Grounds of:*
One's works ...1 Cor. 3:11-15
One's faith.....Matt. 7:22, 23
Conscience ...Rom. 2:12,
14-16
Law ....Rom. 2:12
Gospel.......James 2:12
Christ's
Word ....John 12:48
Book of Life ...Rev. 20:12, 15

D. *Results of:*
Separation of righteous from
the wicked....Matt. 13:36-43
Retribution for disobe-
dience ......2 Thess. 1:6-10
Crown of righteous-
ness..........2 Tim. 4:8

E. *Attitudes toward:*
Be prepared
for............1 Thess. 5:1-9
Beware of
deception .....Matt. 7:21-27
Warn the wicked
concerning ...2 Cor. 5:10, 11

Judith—*Jewess*

Hittite wife of
Esau ....Gen. 26:34
Called
Aholibamah ......Gen. 36:2

Julia—*feminine form of Julius*

Christian woman at
Rome ....Rom. 16:15

Julius—*the family name of the Caesars*

Roman centurion assigned to guard
Paul...........Acts 27:1, 3
Disregards Paul's
warning........Acts 27:11
Accepts Paul's
warning........Acts 27:31
Saves Paul's life...Acts 27:42-44

Junia—*a kinsman of Paul*

Jewish Christian at
Rome ....Rom. 16:7

Juniper—*a shrub of the broom family*

Symbolic of
devastation.......Jer. 48:6

Jushab-Hesed—*kindness returned*

Son of
Zerubbabel.......1 Chr. 3:20

Just, justice—*integrity of character*

A. *Descriptive of:*
Righteous
man ....Gen. 6:9
Upright
Gentile........Acts 10:22
God's nature...Deut. 32:4
Promised
Messiah.......Zech. 9:9
Christ ....Acts 3:14
Saved.........Heb. 12:23

B. *Produced by:*
True wisdom ..Prov. 8:15
Parental
instruction ....Gen. 18:19
True faith .....Heb. 10:38

See Injustice

Justification—*accounting the guilty just
before God*

A. *Negatively considered, not by:*
The Law.......Rom. 3:20, 28
Men's righteous-
ness...........Rom. 10:1-5
Human
works.........Rom. 4:1-5
Faith mixed {Acts 15:1-29
with works. {Gal. 2:16
A dead faith ...James 2:14-26

B. *Positively considered, by:*
Grace.........Rom. 5:17-21
Christ:
Blood........Rom. 5:9
Resur-
rection......Rom. 4:25
Righteous-
ness.........Rom. 10:4
Faith ....Rom. 3:26, 27

C. *Fruits of:*
Forgiveness of
sins..........Acts 13:38, 39
Peace.........Rom. 5:1

Holiness .... Rom. 6:22
Imputed righteous-
ness.......... 2 Cor. 5:21
Outward righteous-
ness........... Rom. 8:4
Eternal life .... Titus 3:7

D. *Evidence of:*
Works (by
faith) .... James 2:18
Wisdom ...... James 3:17
Patience ...... James 5:7, 8
Suffering ..... James 5:10, 11

See Imputation

Justus—*righteous*

1. Surname of
   Joseph .... Acts 1:23
2. Man of Corinth; befriends
   Paul .... Acts 18:7
3. Converted
   Jew .... Col. 4:11

Juttah—*extended*

Town of Judah.... Josh. 15:55
Assigned to the
priests........... Josh. 21:13, 16

Juvenile delinquents

A. *Examples of:*
Eli's sons ...... 1 Sam. 2:12-17
Samuel's
sons .... 1 Sam. 8:1-5
Elisha's
mockers ..... 2 Kin. 2:22-24

B. *Safeguards against:*
Praying
mother........ 1 Sam. 1:9-28
Strict
discipline...... Prov. 13:24
Early
training ...... Prov. 22:6

K

Kab—*a hollow vessel*

Jewish measure; about 2
quarts............ 2 Kin. 6:25

Kabzeel—*God's gathering*

Town in south
Judah .... Josh. 15:21
Benaiah's home
town .... 2 Sam. 23:20
Called Jekabzeel .. Neh. 11:25

Kadesh—*holy*

Location of .... Num. 27:14
Captured by
Chedorlaomer .... Gen. 14:5-7
Hagar flees near.. Gen. 16:7, 14
Abraham dwells
here.............. Gen. 20:1
Spies sent from .. Num. 13:3, 26
Miriam buried
here.............. Num. 20:1
Moses strikes rock
here.............. Num. 20:1-13
Request passage through Edom
here.............. Num. 20:14-22
Figurative of God's
power .... Ps. 29:8
Boundary in the new
Israel........... Ezek. 47:19

Kadesh Barnea—*another name for Kadesh*

Boundary of promised
land.............. Num. 34:1-4
Extent of Joshua's military
campaign......... Josh. 10:41

Kadmiel—*God is the Ancient One*

1. Levite family head; returns
   from
   Babylon....... Ezra 2:40
2. Takes part in
   rebuilding..... Ezra 3:9
   Participates in national
   repentance... Neh. 9:4, 5

Kadmonites—*easterners*

Tribe whose land Abraham is to
inherit............ Gen. 15:18, 19

Kallai—*smith*

Postexilic priest ... Neh. 12:1, 20

Kanah—*place of reeds*

1. Brook between Ephraim and
   Manasseh ..... Josh. 16:8
2. Border town of
   Asher .... Josh. 19:28

Karkaa—*floor, ground*

Place in south
Judah .... Josh. 15:3

Karkor—*even ground*

Place in east
Jordan .... Judg. 8:10

Karnaim—*two peaks*

Conquered .... Amos 6:13

Kartah—*city*

Levitical town in
Zebulun..........Josh. 21:34

Kartan—*town*

Town in Naphtali assigned to
Levites............Josh. 21:32
Called
Kirjathaim ....1 Chr. 6:76

Kattath—*little*

Town of
Zebulun..........Josh. 19:15, 16
Same as Kitron ....Judg. 1:30

Kedar—*dark*

Son of Ishmael....Gen. 25:12, 13
Skilled archers ....Is. 21:17
Prophecy
against ....Jer. 49:28, 29
Inhabit villages ...Is. 42:11
Famous for
flocks ....Is. 60:7
Tents of, called
dark...............Song 1:5
Type of barbarous
people............Ps. 120:5

Kedemah—*toward the east*

Ishmaelite tribe ...Gen. 25:15

Kedemoth—*ancient places*

City east of the Jordan assigned to
the tribe of
Reuben............Josh. 13:15, 18
Assigned to Merarite
Levites ....Josh. 21:34, 37
Messengers sent
from ....Deut. 2:26

Kedesh—*sacred place*

1. Town in south
   Judah.........Josh. 15:23
2. City of Issachar assigned to
   Gershonite
   Levites.........1 Chr. 6:72
   Called
   Kishion ....Josh. 19:20
3. Canaanite town taken by
   Joshua and assigned to
   Naphtali ......Josh. 12:22
   Called Kedesh in
   Galilee........Josh. 20:7
   Called Kedesh in
   Naphtali ......Judg. 4:6
   City of
   refuge.........Josh. 21:27, 32

Home of
Barak.........Judg. 4:6
People of, carried
captive........2 Kin. 15:29

Keeper—*one who watches over, or guards*

Guardian of:

Sheep.............Gen. 4:2
Brother ....Gen. 4:9
Wardrobe ....2 Kin. 22:14
Gate ....Neh. 3:29
Door..............1 Chr. 9:21
Women ....Esth. 2:3, 8
Prison.............Acts 16:27

Keeping—*holding or observing something firmly*

A. *Christian objects of:*
   Christ's command-
   ments........John 14:15-23
   God's com-
   mandments ...1 John 5:2
   God's Word....Rev. 22:7, 9
   Unity of the
   Spirit ....Eph. 4:3
   Faith ....2 Tim. 4:7
   Purity ....1 Tim. 5:22
   Oneself ....1 John 5:18
   In God's love ..Jude 21

B. *Manner of, by God's:*
   Power ....John 10:28, 29
   Name..........John 17:11, 12

C. *Promises respecting:*
   Provision ......Ps 121:3-8
   Preservation ...John 17:11, 12
   Power ....Rev. 2:26
   Purity ....Rev. 16:15

See Heart

Kehelathah—*assembly*

Israelite camp....Num. 33:22, 23

Keilah—*enclosed*

Town of Judah....Josh. 15:21, 44
Rescued from Philistines by
David ....1 Sam. 23:1-5
Betrays David.....1 Sam. 23:6-12
David escapes
from ....1 Sam. 23:13
Reoccupied after the
exile..............Neh. 3:17

Kelaiah—*Yahweh is light*

Levite who divorced foreign wife .... { Ezra 10:18, 19, 23

See Kelita

Kelita—*dwarf*

Levite who divorced foreign
wife .... Ezra 10:23
Explains the
Law .... Neh. 8:7
Called Kelaiah .... Ezra 10:23

Kemuel—*congregation of God*

1. Son of Nahor; father of six
   sons .... Gen. 22:20, 21
2. Ephraimite
   prince .... Num. 34:24
3. Levite in David's
   time .... 1 Chr. 27:17

Kenath—*possession*

City of Gilead near Bozrah taken
by Nobah .... Num. 32:40, 42
Reconquered by Geshur and
Aram .... 1 Chr. 2:23

Kenaz—*side, flank*

1. Descendant of
   Esau .... Gen. 36:10, 11
2. Edomite
   duke .... Gen. 36:42
3. Caleb's brother; father of
   Othniel ...... Josh. 15:17
   Family called
   Kenezzites .... Num. 32:12
4. Grandson of
   Caleb .... 1 Chr. 4:15

Kenezzite

1. Canaanite tribe whose land is
   promised to Abraham's
   seed .... Gen. 15:19
2. Title applied to
   Caleb .... Num. 32:12
   Probably related to Kenaz, the
   Edomite ...... Gen. 36:11-42
   Edomite ...... Gen. 36:11-42

Kenites—*pertaining to coppersmiths*

Canaanite tribe whose land is
promised to Abraham's
seed .... Gen. 15:19
Subjects of Balaam's
prophecy .... Num. 24:20-22

Mix with
Midianites .... Num. 10:29
Member of, becomes Israel's
guide .... Num. 10:29-32
Settle with
Judahites .... Judg. 1:16
Heber separates from
Kenites .... Judg. 4:11
Heber's wife (Jael) slays
Sisera .... Judg. 4:17-22
Spared by Saul in war with
Amalekites .... 1 Sam. 15:6
David shows
friendship to ...... 1 Sam. 30:29
Recorded among Judahites;
ancestors of
Rechabites .... 1 Chr. 2:55

Keren-Happuch—*horn of eye paint*

Daughter of Job... Job 42:14

Kerioth—*cities*

1. Town in south
   Judah .... Josh. 15:25
2. City of Moab .. Amos 2:2

Keros—*bent*

Head of a Nethinim family
returning
from exile .... Ezra 2:44

Kettle—*pot*

Large cooking
vessel .... 1 Sam. 2:14
Same word rendered
"baskets" .... Ps. 81:6

Keturah—*incense*

Abraham's second
wife .... Gen. 25:1
Sons of:
Listed .... Gen. 25:1, 2
Given gifts and sent
away .... Gen. 25:6

Key—*a small instrument for unlocking doors*

Used literally for:

Doors .... Judg. 3:25

Used figuratively of:

Prophetic authority of
Christ .... Is. 22:22
Present authority of
Christ .... Rev. 1:18
Plenary authority of Christ's
apostles .... Matt. 16:19
Teachers .... Luke 11:52

Keziah—*cassia*

Daughter of Job...Job 42:14

Kibroth Hattaavah—*graves of lust*

Burial site of Israelites slain by God..............Num. 11:33-35

Kibzaim—*double heap*

Ephraimite city assigned to Kohathite Levites..........Josh. 21:22
Called Jokmeam ..1 Chr. 6:68

See Jokmeam

Kid—*a young goat*

A. *Used for:*
   Food ....Gen. 27:9
   Payment......Gen. 38:17-23
   Sacrifices ......Lev. 4:23
   Offerings ......Judg. 13:15, 19
   Festive occasions .....Luke 15:29

B. *Figurative of:*
   Weakness .....Judg. 14:6
   Peacefulness...Is. 11:6

See Goat

Kidnappers—*those who seize others by unlawful force*

Condemned by law...............1 Tim. 1:10

Kidnapping

A. *Punishment for:*
   Death ....Ex. 21:16
   Condemned ...1 Tim. 1:10

B. *Examples of:*
   Joseph.........Gen. 37:23-28
   Daughters of Shiloh.......Judg. 21:20-23
   Joash..........2 Kin. 11:1-12
   Jeremiah ......Jer. 43:1-8

Kidneys

Select internal organs of an animal ....Ex. 29:13, 22
Translated "wheat".........Deut. 32:14

Kidron—*dark, turbid*

Valley (dry except for winter torrents) near Jerusalem.........John 18:1
East boundary of Jerusalem ....Jer. 31:40
Crossed by David and Christ............John 18:1
Site of dumping of idols.............2 Chr. 29:16

Killing—*causing life to cease*

A. *Reasons for:*
   Take another's wife.........Gen. 12:12
   Take another's property ......1 Kin. 21:19
   Take revenge......Gen. 27:42
   Satisfy anger ..Num. 22:29
   Hate...........John 5:18
   Execute God's wrath ....{Num. 31:2, 16-19
   Destroy people ....Ex. 1:16
   Seize a throne ....2 Kin. 15:25
   Put down rebellion ......1 Kin. 12:27
   Fulfill prophecy......1 Kin. 16:1-11
   Fear of punishment ...Acts 16:27
   Get rid of an unwanted person ....Matt. 21:38

B. *Reasons against:*
   God's Law.....Ex. 20:13
   Regard for:
   Life............Gen. 37:21
   One's position ......{1 Sam. 11, 1 Sam. 24:10

C. *Of Christians:*
   In God's hand..........Luke 12:4, 5
   Result of persecution ...Matt. 24:9
   Time will come.........John 16:2
   Under antichrist ....{Rev. 11:7, Rev. 13:15

Kinah—*lamentation*

Village in south Judah ....Josh. 15:22

Kindness—*a friendly attitude toward others*

A. *Kinds of:*
   Extra-ordinary ......Acts 28:2
   Acquired ......Col. 3:12
   Developed .....Prov. 31:26

Commended...2 Cor. 6:6
Divine..........Neh. 9:17

B. *Of God, described as:*
Great..........Neh. 9:17
Everlasting ....Is. 54:8
Shall not
depart ....Is. 54:10
Manifested.....Ps. 31:21
Through
Christ.........Eph. 2:7
Cause of man's
salvation......Titus 3:4-7

C. *Manifestation of:*
Rewarded......1 Sam. 15:6
Recalled.......2 Sam. 2:5, 6
Rebuffed.......2 Sam. 3:8
Remem-
bered ....2 Sam. 9:1-7
Refused........2 Sam. 10:1-6

Kindred—*one's family connections*

Manifestation of:

Felt with great
emotion ....Esth. 8:6
Through faith.....Josh. 6:23
By gospel ....Acts 3:25
                   Rev. 14:6

Kine—*archaic for cow, ox, steer*

Used for:

Ox................Deut. 7:13
Cattle............Deut. 32:14
Cow...............Gen. 32:15
                  1 Sam. 6:7

King, Christ as

A. *In Old Testament prophecy:*
Judah's tribe...Gen. 49:10
With a
scepter........Num. 24:15-17
David's
lineage........2 Sam. 7:1-29
Divine origin ..Is. 9:6, 7
In righ-
teousness .....Is. 11:1-5
At God's appointed
time ....Ezek. 21:27
Will endure
forever........Dan. 2:44
Born in Beth-
lehem.........Mic. 5:2, 3
As Priest-
king ....Zech. 6:9-15
Having
salvation......Zech. 9:9
He is coming ..Mal. 3:1-5

B. *Christ's right to rule,
determined by:*
Divine
decree ....Ps. 2:6, 7
Prophecy ......Ps. 45:6, 7
Birth ....Is. 9:6, 7
Being seated ⎧Ps. 16:8-11
at God's right ⎨Ps. 110:1, 2
hand..........⎩Acts 2:34-36
Crowning......Zech. 6:11-15

C. *Described as:*
Eternal ....Rev. 11:15
Spiritual ......John 18:36, 37
Not for immoral or impure
person ....Eph. 5:5
The Son of His
love...........Col. 1:13

Kingdom of God

A. *Described as, of:*
God ....Mark 1:15
Heaven........Matt. 3:2
Christ and
God..........Eph. 5:5
Their Father...Matt. 13:43
My Father's ...Matt. 26:29
His dear Son...Col. 1:13

B. *Special features of:*
Gospel of .....Matt. 24:14
Word of ....Matt. 13:19
Mysteries of ..Mark 4:10-13
Key of David ..Rev. 3:7

C. *Entrance into, by:*
New birth .....John 3:1-8
Granted ....Luke 22:29
Divine call.....1 Thess. 2:12
Repentance....Matt. 3:2

D. *Members of:*
Seek it first ....Matt. 6:33
Suffer
tribulation ....Acts 14:22
Preach it ......Acts 8:12
Pray for it ....Matt. 6:10
Work in ....Col. 4:11

E. *Nature of:*
Spiritual.......Rom. 14:17
Eternal ....2 Pet. 1:11

Kings, earthly

A. *Some characteristics of:*
Arose over
Egypt.........Ex. 1:8
Desired by
people ....1 Sam. 8:5, 6

Under God's
control.......Dan. 4:25, 37
Rule by God's
permission....Dan. 2:20, 21
Subject to
tempta-   ⎰2 Sam. 11:1-5
tions.........⎱Prov. 31:5
Good..........2 Kin. 22:1, 2
Evil...........2 Kin. 21:1-9

B. *Position of before God, by God:*
Chosen.......1 Chr. 28:4-6
Anointed.....1 Sam. 16:12
Removed and
established....Dan. 2:21
Rejected.......1 Sam. 15:10-26

C. *Duties of:*
Make
covenants.....Gen. 21:22-32
Read
Scriptures.....Deut. 17:19
Make war.....1 Sam. 11:5-11
Pardon........2 Sam. 14:1-11
              2 Sam. 19:18-23
Judge.........2 Sam. 15:2
Govern
righteously....2 Sam. 23:3, 4
Keep Law.....1 Kin. 2:3
Make
decrees.......Dan. 3:1-6, 29

King's Garden—*a garden of Jerusalem*

Near a gate.........2 Kin. 25:4
By the Pool of
Shelah..........Neh. 3:15

King's Highway—*an important
passageway connecting Damascus
and Egypt*

Use of,
requested........Num. 20:17

Kings of ancient Israel

A. *Over the United Kingdom:*
Saul...........1 Sam.
              11:15-31:13
David.........2 Sam. 2:4-
              1 Kin. 2:11
Solomon......1 Kin. 1:39-11:43

B. *Over Israel* (the northern
kingdom):
Jeroboam   ⎰1 Kin.
(22 yrs.)......⎱ 12:20-14:20
Nadab   ⎰1 Kin. 15:25-27,
(2 yrs.)......⎱ 31
Baasha   1 Kin. 15:28-34
(24 yrs.)......1 Kin. 16:1-7
Elah (2 yrs.)...1 Kin. 16:8-14

Zimri
(7 days).......1 Kin. 16:15
Omri
(12 yrs.)......1 Kin. 16:23-28
Ahab   ⎰1 Kin.
(22 yrs.)......⎱ 16:29-22:40
Ahaziah
(2 yrs.)........1 Kin. 22:51-53
Jehoram (Joram)
(12 yrs.)......2 Kin. 3:1-9:26
Jehu   ⎰2 Kin. 9:2-
(28 yrs.)......⎱ 10:36
Jehoahaz
(17 yrs.)......2 Kin. 13:1-9
Jehoash (Joash)
(16 yrs.)......2 Kin. 13:10-25
Jeroboam II
(41 yrs.)......2 Kin. 14:23-29
Zechariah
(6 mos.).......2 Kin. 15:8-12
Shallum
(1 mo.)........2 Kin. 15:13-15
Menahem
(10 yrs.)......2 Kin. 15:16-22
Pekahiah
(2 yrs.)........2 Kin. 15:23-26
Pekah
(20 yrs.)......2 Kin. 15:27-31
Hoshea
(9 yrs.)........2 Kin. 17:1-6

C. *Over Judah* (the southern
kingdom):
Rehoboam
(17 yrs.).......1 Kin. 12:21-24
Abijam (Abijah)
(3 yrs.)........1 Kin. 15:1-8
Asa (41 yrs.)...1 Kin. 15:9-24
Jehoshaphat
(25 yrs.)......1 Kin. 22:41-50
Jehoram (Joram)
(8 yrs.)........2 Kin. 8:16-24
Ahaziah
(1 yr.).........2 Kin. 8:25-29
Athaliah (Queen) (usurper)
(6 yrs.)........2 Kin. 11:1-3
Joash (Jehoash)
(40 yrs.)......2 Kin. 12:1, 21
Amaziah
(29 yrs.)......2 Kin. 14:1-20
Azariah (Uzziah)
(52 yrs.)......2 Kin. 15:1, 2
Jotham
(16 yrs.)......2 Kin. 15:32-38
Ahaz
(16 yrs.)......2 Kin. 16:1-20
Hezekiah
(29 yrs.)......2 Kin. 18:1-20:21
Manasseh
(55 yrs.)......2 Kin. 21:1-18

Amon
(2 yrs.)........2 Kin. 21:19-26
Josiah
(31 yrs.)......2 Kin. 22:1-23:30
Jehoahaz (Shallum)
(3 mos.)......2 Kin. 23:31-33
Jehoiakim
(11 yrs.)......2 Kin. 23:34-24:6
Jehoiachin (Jeconiah)
(3 mos.)......2 Kin. 24:8-16
Zedekiah (Mattaniah)
(11 yrs.)......2 Kin. 24:17-25:7

Kings, the Books of—*books of the Old Testament*

A. 1 Kings
Solomon ascends to the
throne ....1 Kin. 1:1-2:46
The kingdom ⎰1 Kin. 3:1-
of Solomon ⎱　　10:29
The fall of
Solomon ......1 Kin. 11:1-40
Rehoboam against
Jeroboam .....1 Kin. 12:1-33
Ahab and
Jezebel........1 Kin. 16:29-34
Ministry of ⎰1 Kin. 17:1-
Elijah ....⎱　　19:21
Syria against
Samaria.......1 Kin. 20:1-34
Ahab and
Naboth ....1 Kin. 21:1-29

B. 2 Kings
Ministry of Elijah and
Elisha.........2 Kin. 1:1-9:11
Reign of ⎰2 Kin. 9:11-
Jehu ....⎱　　10:36
Fall of Israel...2 Kin. 17:1-41
Reign of ⎰2 Kin. 18:1-
Hezekiah... ⎱　　20:21
Reform of ⎰2 Kin. 22:1-
Judah........⎱　　23:30
Fall of
Jerusalem.....2 Kin. 25:1-21

Kingship of God—*the position of God as sovereign ruler of the universe*

Over Jerusalem ...Matt. 5:35
Over all ....Ps. 103:19
Of all kingdoms ...2 Kin. 19:15

Kir—*wall*

1. Place mentioned by Amos to
which Syrians were
taken ....Amos 1:5
Tiglath-Pileser carries
people of Damascus
here ....2 Kin. 16:9
Inhabitants of, against
Judah.........Is. 22:6

2. Fortified city of
Moab ....Is. 15:1
Same as Kir ⎰Is. 16:7
Hareseth .....⎱2 Kin. 3:25

Kirjath—*city*

Town of
Benjamin........Josh. 18:21, 28

Kirjathaim—*twin cities*

1. Assigned to
Reuben ....Num. 32:37
Repossessed by
Moabites......Jer. 48:1-23
2. Town in
Naphtali ......1 Chr. 6:76
Same as
Kartan........Josh. 21:32

Kirjath Arba—*city of Arba, or fourfold city*

Ancient name of
Hebron........Gen. 23:2
Named after Arba the
Anakite ....Josh. 15:54
City of refuge ......Josh. 20:7
Possessed by
Judah ....Judg. 1:10

Kirjath Jearim—*city of forests*

Gibeonite town ...Josh. 9:17
Assigned to
Judah ....Josh. 15:60
Reassigned to
Benjamin........Josh. 18:28
Ark taken from ...1 Chr. 13:5
Home of Urijah ...Jer. 26:20
Called:
Baalah ....Josh. 15:9, 10
Kirjath..........Josh. 18:28
Kirjath Baal......Josh. 15:60
Baale of Judah ...2 Sam. 6:2
Shortened to Kirjath
Arim ....Ezra 2:25

Kirjath Sannah—*city of destruction*

City of Judah; also called
Debir.............Josh. 15:49

Kirjath Sepher—*city of books*

Same as Debir ....Judg. 1:11-13
Taken by
Othniel ....Josh. 15:15-17

Kish—*bow*

1. Benjamite of Gibeah;
father of ⎰1 Sam. 9:1-3
King Saul ....⎱Acts 13:21

2. Benjamite of
   Jerusalem.....1 Chr. 8:30
3. Merarite Levite in David's
   time..........1 Chr. 23:21, 22
4. Another Merarite Levite in
   Hezekiah's
   time..........2 Chr. 29:12
5. Benjamite and great-
   grandfather of
   Mordecai......Esth. 2:5

Kishi—*snarer*

One of David's
singers...........1 Chr. 6:31, 44
Called Kushaiah ..1 Chr. 15:17

Kishion—*hardness*

Border town of
Issachar.........Josh. 19:17, 20
Called Kishon.....Josh. 21:28

See Kedesh 2

Kishon—*bending*

River of north Palestine; Sisera's
army swept away
by...............Judg. 4:7, 13
Elijah slew Baal
prophets here ....1 Kin. 18:40

Kiss—*a physical sign of affection*

A. *Times employed, at:*
   Departure .....Gen. 31:28, 55
   Separation.....Acts 20:37
   Reunions ......Luke 15:20
   Great joy......Luke 7:38, 45
   Blessing ......Gen. 48:10-16
   Anointings.....1 Sam. 10:1
   Reconcilia-
   tion...........Gen. 33:4
   Death ....Gen. 50:1

B. *Figurative of:*
   Complete:
   Submission to
   evil ....Hos. 13:2
   Submission to
   God...........Ps. 2:12
   Recon-
   ciliation......Ps. 85:10
   Utmost
   affection ......Song 1:2

C. *Kinds of:*
   Deceitful .....2 Sam. 20:9, 10
                  Luke 22:48
   Insincere .....2 Sam. 15:5
   Fatherly ......Gen. 27:26, 27
   Friendship ....Ex. 18:7
                  1 Sam. 20:41

Esteem ....2 Sam. 19:32, 39
Sexual love ....Gen. 29:11
                Song 1:2
Illicit love .....Prov. 7:13
False   (1 Kin. 19:18
religion ...... { Hos. 13:2
Holy love......Rom. 16:16
                1 Cor. 16:20

Kite—*a bird of the falcon family*

Ceremonially
unclean ....Lev. 11:12-14

Kithlish—*a man's wall*

Town of Judah....Josh. 15:1, 40

Kitron—*shortened, little*

Town in
Zebulun..........Judg. 1:30

Kittim

Sons of
Javan ....Gen. 10:4

Kneading—*mixing elements together*

Part of food
process...........Gen. 18:6
Done by women ..Jer. 7:18

Kneading bowl—*used for kneading
dough*

Overcome by
frogs ....Ex. 8:3
Carried out of
Egypt ....Ex. 12:33-34

Knee

A. *Place of weakness, due to:*
   Terror ....Dan. 5:6
   Fasting ....Ps. 109:24
   Disease........Deut. 28:35
   Lack of faith...Is. 35:3

B. *Lying upon:*
   Sign of true parentage or
   adoption ......Gen. 30:3
   Place of
   fondling.......Is. 66:12
   Place of
   sleep..........Judg. 16:19

C. *Bowing of:*
   Act of:
   Respect........2 Kin. 1:13
   False
   worship.......1 Kin. 19:18
   True worship ..Rom. 14:11

D. *Bowing of, in prayer:*
   Solomon.......2 Chr. 6:13, 14

Daniel . . . . Dan. 6:10
Christ . . . . Luke 22:41
Stephen . . . . Acts 7:59, 60
Peter . . . . Acts 9:40
Paul . . . . Acts 20:36
Christians . . . . . Acts 21:5

Knife—*a sharp instrument for cutting*

A. *Used for:*
Slaying
animals . . . . . . Gen. 22:6-10
Circum-
cision . . . . Josh. 5:2, 3
Dismembering a
body . . . . Judg. 19:29
Sharpening
pens . . . . Jer. 36:23

B. *Figurative of:*
Inordinate
appetite . . . . . . Prov. 23:2
Cruel
oppressors . . . . Prov. 30:14

Knob—*an ornament*

Round protrusions on
lampstand . . . . Ex. 25:31-36

Knock—*to rap on a door*

Rewarded . . . . . . Luke 11:9, 10
Expectant . . . . Luke 12:36
Disappointed . . . . . Luke 13:25-27
Unexpected . . . . . . Acts 12:13, 16
Invitation . . . . Rev. 3:20

Knowledge

A. *Kinds of:*
Natural . . . . Matt. 24:32
Deceptive . . . . . . Gen. 3:5
Sinful . . . . Gen. 3:7
Personal . . . . . . Josh. 24:31
Practical . . . . . . Ex. 36:1
Experi-
mental . . . . . . Ex. 14:4, 18
Friendly . . . . . . Ex. 1:8
Intuitive . . . . . . 1 Sam. 22:22
Intellectual . . . . John 7:15, 28
Saving . . . . John 17:3
Spiritual . . . . . . 1 Cor. 2:14
Revealed . . . . . . Luke 10:22

B. *Sources of:*
God . . . . Ps. 94:10
Nature . . . . Ps. 19:1, 2
Scriptures . . . . . 2 Tim. 3:15
Doing God's
will . . . . John 7:17

C. *Believer's attitude toward:*
Not to be puffed
up . . . . 1 Cor. 8:1
Should grow
in . . . . 2 Pet. 3:18
Should add
to . . . . 2 Pet. 1:5
Not to be forgetful
of . . . . 2 Pet. 3:17
Accept our limitations
of . . . . 1 Cor. 13:8-12
Be filled with . . Phil. 1:9

D. *Christ's, of:*
God . . . . Luke 10:22
Man's nature . . John 2:24, 25
Man's
thoughts . . . . . . Matt. 9:4
Believers . . . . John 10:14, 27
Things
future . . . . 2 Pet. 1:14
All things . . . . . . Col. 2:3

E. *Attitude of sinful men toward:*
Turn from . . . . . Rom. 1:21
Ignorant of . . . . 1 Cor. 1:21
Raised up
against . . . . 2 Cor. 10:5
Did not acknowledge
God . . . . Rom. 1:28
Never able to come
to . . . . 2 Tim. 3:7

F. *Value of:*
Superior to
gold . . . . Prov. 8:10
Increases
strength . . . . . . Prov. 24:5
Keeps from
destruction . . . . Is. 5:13
Insures
stability . . . . Is. 33:6

Koa

People described as enemies of
Jerusalem . . . . Ezek. 23:23

Kohath—*assembly*

Second son of
Levi . . . . Gen. 46:8, 11
Goes with Levi to
Egypt . . . . Gen. 46:11
Brother of Jochebed,
mother of Aaron
and Moses . . . . Ex. 6:16-20
Dies at age 133 . . . . Ex. 6:18

Kohathites—*descendants of Kohath*

A. *History of:*
Originate in Levi's son
(Kohath)......Gen. 46:11
Divided into 4 groups (Amram,
Izhar, Hebron,
Uzziel).......Num. 3:19, 27
Numbering
of.............Num. 3:27, 28
Duties assigned
to.............Num. 4:15-20
Cities assigned
to.............Josh. 21:4-11

B. *Privileges of:*
Aaron and
Moses.........Ex. 6:20
Special charge of sacred
instruments...Num. 4:15-20
Temple music by Heman the
Kohathite.....1 Chr. 6:31-38
Under Jehoshaphat, lead in
praise.........2 Chr. 20:19
Under Hezekiah,
help to cleanse
Temple........2 Chr. 29:12, 15

C. *Sins of:*
Korah (of
Izhar) leads ⎰Num. 16:1-35
rebellion .....⎱Jude 11

Kolaiah—*voice of Yahweh*

1. Father of the false prophet
Ahab.........Jer. 29:21-23
2. Postexilic Benjamite
family.........Neh. 11:7

Koph

Letter of the Hebrew
alphabet.........Ps. 119:145-152

Korah—*baldness*

1. Son of Esau ...Gen. 36:5, 14, 18
2. Son of Eliphaz and grandson of
Esau ....Gen. 36:16
3. Calebite ....1 Chr. 2:42, 43
4. Son of Izhar the
Kohathite.....Ex. 6:21, 24
Leads a rebellion against Moses
and Aaron ....Num. 16:1-3
Warned by
Moses.........Num. 16:4-27
Supernaturally
destroyed .....Num. 16:28-35
Sons of, not
destroyed ....Num. 26:9-11
Sons of,
porters........1 Chr. 26:19

Korahites

Descendants of
Korah............Ex. 6:24
Some become:
David's
warriors.........1 Chr. 12:6
Servants ....1 Chr. 9:19-31
Musicians.........1 Chr. 6:22-32
A contemplation
of ....Ps. 42 (Title)

Kore—*a partridge*

1. Korahite
Levite.........1 Chr. 9:19
2. Porter of the eastern
gate...........2 Chr. 31:14

Koz—*thorn*

Father of Anub ...1 Chr. 4:8

See Hakkoz

Kushaiah—*bow of Yahweh (that is,
rainbow)*

Merarite Levite
musician ....1 Chr. 15:17
Called Kishi.......1 Chr. 6:44

L

Laadah—*festival*

Judahite ....1 Chr. 4:21

Laadan

1. Son of Gershon, the son of
Levi...........1 Chr. 23:7-9
Called Libni ...1 Chr. 6:17
2. Ephraimite.....1 Chr. 7:26

Laban—*white*

1. Son of
Bethuel ....Gen. 24:24, 29
Brother of
Rebekah ......Gen. 24:15, 29
Father of Leah and
Rachel ....Gen. 29:16
Chooses Rebekah for
Isaac..........Gen. 24:29-60
Entertains
Jacob ....Gen. 29:1-14
Deceives Jacob in
marriage arrange-
ment..........Gen. 29:15-30
Agrees to Jacob's
business arrange-
ment..........Gen. 30:25-43

Changes attitude toward
Jacob . . . . Gen. 31:1-9
Pursues after fleeing
Jacob . . . . Gen. 31:21-25
Rebukes
Jacob . . . . Gen. 31:26-30
Rebuked by
Jacob . . . . Gen. 31:31-42
Makes covenant with
Jacob . . . . Gen. 31:43-55
2. City in the
wilderness . . . . Deut. 1:1

Labor—*physical or mental effort*

A. *Physical:*

Nature of:
As old as
creation . . . . . . Gen. 2:5, 15
Ordained by
God . . . . Gen. 3:17-19
One of the command-
ments . . . . Ex. 20:9
From morning until
night . . . . Ps. 104:23
With the
hands . . . . 1 Thess. 4:11
To life's end . . Ps. 90:10
Without God,
vanity . . . . Eccl. 2:11
Shrinking from,
denounced . . . 2 Thess. 3:10

Benefits of:
Profit . . . . Prov. 14:23
Happiness . . . . . Ps. 128:2
Proclaim
gospel . . . . 1 Thess. 2:9
Supply of
other's   {Acts 20:35
needs . . . . {Eph. 4:28
Restful sleep . . . Eccl. 5:12
Double
honor . . . . 1 Tim. 5:17
Eternal life . . . . John 6:27
Not in vain . . . . 1 Cor. 15:58
Phil. 2:16

B. *Spiritual:*

Characteristics of:
Commissioned by
Christ . . . . John 4:38
Accepted by
few . . . . Matt. 9:37, 38
Working with
God . . . . 1 Cor. 3:9
By God's
grace . . . . 1 Cor. 15:10
Result of
faith . . . . 1 Tim. 4:10

Characterized by
love . . . . 1 Thess. 1:3
Done in
prayer . . . . Col. 4:12
Subject to
discourage-   {Is. 49:4
ment . . . . {Gal. 4:11
Interrupted by
Satan . . . . 1 Thess. 3:5

See Work, the Christian's

C. *Problems:*
Inspired by
opposition . . . . Ezra 4:1-6
Complaint over
wages . . . . Matt. 20:1-16
Mistreatment of
employees . . . . . Matt. 21:33-35
Characteristics of last
days . . . . James 5:1-6

Labor, (childbirth)

A. *Of a woman's, described as:*
Fearful . . . . Ps. 48:6
Painful . . . . Is. 13:8
Hazardous . . . . . Gen. 35:16-19
Joyful
afterwards . . . . John 16:21

B. *Figurative of:*
New Israel . . . . Is. 66:7, 8
Messiah's
birth . . . . Mic. 4:9, 10
Redemption . . . Mic. 5:3
New birth . . . . . Gal. 4:19
Creation's
rebirth . . . . Rom. 8:22

Lachish

Town in south
Judah . . . . Josh. 15:1, 39
Joins coalition against
Gibeonites . . . . Josh. 10:3-5
Defeated by
Joshua . . . . Josh. 10:6-33
Fortified by
Rehoboam . . . . . . 2 Chr. 11:5, 9
City of sin . . . . Mic. 1:13
Amaziah   {2 Kin. 14:19
murdered here . . . {2 Chr. 25:27
Taken by
Sennacherib . . . . . 2 Kin. 18:13-17
Military   {Is. 36:1, 2
headquarters . . . . {Is. 37:8
Fights against Nebuchad-
nezzar . . . . Jer. 34:1, 7
Reoccupied after
exile . . . . Neh. 11:30

Lack—*something still needed*

A. *How to avoid:*
Remember God's
promises ...... Deut. 2:7
Work
diligently..... { 1 Thess. 4:11,
12
Live chastely .. Prov. 6:32
Share in
common ...... Acts 4:34
Obey .... Amos 4:6

B. *Things subject to:*
Food .... 2 Sam. 3:29
Physical
needs .... { 2 Chr. 8:14
2 Cor. 11:9
Possessions .... 1 Sam. 30:19
Service to
others........ Phil. 2:30
Entire commit-
ment....... Luke 18:22
Wisdom ...... James 1:5
Graces......... 2 Pet. 1:9

See Want

Lad—*a young boy*

Heard by God..... Gen. 21:17-20
Saved by God..... Gen. 22:12
Loved by his
father .... Gen. 44:22-34
Slain with
Samson .... Judg. 16:26-30
Unsuspecting ..... 1 Sam. 20:21-41
Tattling.......... 2 Sam. 17:18
Providing .... John 6:9

Ladder

Jacob's........... Gen. 28:10-12

Lady

Applied to females of high
rank.............. Judg. 5:29
Among royalty.... Esth. 1:18
Elect.............. 2 John 1, 5
Figurative of
Babylon .... Is. 47:5-7

Lael—*belonging to God*

Gershonite
Levite .... Num. 3:24

Lahad—*oppression*

Judahite .... 1 Chr. 4:2

Lahai Roi—*of the Living One who sees me*

Name of a well.... Gen. 24:62
Same as Beer Lahai
Roi............... Gen. 6:7, 14

Lahmam—*place of light*

City of Judah ..... Josh. 15:1, 40

Lahmi—*Bethlehemite*

Brother of Goliath slain by
Elhanan .... 1 Chr. 20:5

Laish—*lion*

1. Benjamite ..... 1 Sam. 25:44
2. City in north Palestine at the
head of the
Jordan .... Judg. 18:7, 14
Called
Leshem .... Josh. 19:47
3. Village in Benjamin between
Anathoth and
Gallim .... Is. 10:30

Lake

Sea of Galilee is { Luke 5:1, 2
called .... { Luke 8:22-33
Bottomless pit
described as ...... Rev. 19:20

Lake of fire—*the place of final punishment*

A. *Those consigned to:*
The beast and false
prophet .... Rev. 19:20
The devil ...... Rev. 20:10
Death and
hell .... Rev. 20:14
Those whose names are not in
book of life ... Rev. 20:15

B. *Described as:*
Burning
brimstone..... Rev. 19:20
Second death .. Rev. 20:14

Lakkum—*obstruction*

Town of
Naphtali......... Josh. 19:32, 33

Lama—*the Aramaic for why*

Spoken by Christ on the
cross .... Matt. 27:46

Lamb—*a young sheep*

A. *Used for:*
Food .... 2 Sam. 12:4
Clothing....... Prov. 27:26
Trade.......... Ezra 7:17
Tribute .... 2 Kin. 3:4
Covenants..... Gen. 21:28-32
Sacrifices ...... Ex. 12:5

B. *Figurative of:*
God's people...Is. 5:17
Weak
 believers ......Is. 40:11
God's
 ministers......Luke 10:3
Messiah's
 reign..........Is. 11:6

Lamb of God, the (Christ)

A. *Descriptive of Christ as:*
Predicted ......Is. 53:7
Presented to
 Israel ....John 1:29
Preached to
 world ....Acts 8:32-35
Praised throughout
 eternity ......Rev. 5:6, 13

B. *Descriptive of Christ as:*
Sacrifice ....1 Pet. 1:19
              Rev. 7:13, 14
Redeemer......Rev. 5:9
King..........Rev. 15:3

Lame, lameness—*inability to walk properly*

A. *Healing of, by:*
Christ ....Matt. 11:5
Peter ....Acts 3:2-7
Philip.........Acts 8:5-7

B. *Figurative of:*
Extreme
 weakness .....2 Sam. 5:6, 8
Incon-
 sistency......Prov. 26:7
Weak
 believers ......Jer. 31:8
Healed........Is. 35:6

C. *Causes of:*
Birth defect....Acts 3:2
Accident.......2 Sam. 4:4

D. *Renders unfit for:*
Priesthood.....Lev. 21:17, 18
Sacrifice.......Deut. 15:21
Active life .....2 Sam. 9:13
              2 Sam. 19:24-26

Lamech—*wild man*

1. Son of Methusael, of Cain's
 race..........Gen. 4:17, 18
Had two
 wives ....Gen. 4:19
2. Son of Methuselah; father of
 Noah ....Gen. 5:25-31

Man of faith ...Gen. 5:29
In Christ's
 ancestry ......Luke 3:36

Lamed

Letter of the Hebrew
 alphabet.........Ps. 119:89-96

Lamentation—*mournful speeches; elegies; dirges*

A. *Historical of:*
Jeremiah over
 Josiah.........2 Chr. 35:25
David over
 Saul.........2 Sam. 1:17-27
David over
 Abner.........2 Sam. 3:33, 34
Jeremiah over
 Jerusalem.....Lam. 1:1

B. *Prophetic of:*
Isaiah over
 Babylon.......Is. 14:1-32
Jeremiah over
 Jerusalem.....Jer. 7:28-34
Ezekiel over
 Tyre ....Ezek. 27:2-36
Christ over
 Jerusalem.....Luke 19:41-44
Kings over
 Babylon.......Rev. 18:1-24

Lamentations, the Book of—*a book of the Old Testament*

The suffering of
 Zion..............Lam. 1:1-2:22
Individual
 prayer............Lam. 3:1-66
Collective
 prayer............Lam. 5:1-22

Lamp

A. *Used in:*
Tabernacle.....Ex. 37:23
Temple ....1 Chr. 28:15
Processions....Matt. 25:1-8

B. *Figurative of:*
God ....2 Sam. 22:29
God's   ⎰Ps. 119:105
 Word ....⎱Prov. 6:23
God's justice...Zeph. 1:12
Conscience ....Prov. 20:27
Prosperity .....Job 29:3
Industry ......Prov. 31:18
Death ....Job 18:6
Churches ......Rev. 1:20
Christ ....Rev. 1:14

Lampstand, The Golden

A. *Specifications regarding:*
Made of gold . . Ex. 25:31
After a divine
model. . . . . Ex. 25:31-40
Set in holy
place. . . . . Heb. 9:2
Continual burning
of . . . . Ex. 27:20, 21
Carried by
Kohathites . . . . Num. 4:4, 15
Temple's ten branches
of . . . . 1 Kin. 7:48-50
Taken to
Babylon. . . . . . . Jer. 52:19

B. *Used figuratively of:*
Christ . . . . Zech. 4:2, 11
The church . . . . Rev. 1:13, 20

Lance—*a spear*

Used in war . . . . . . Jer. 50:42
Used by Baal's
priests. . . . . 1 Kin. 18:28

Landmark—*a boundary marker*

Removal of,
forbidden . . . . Deut. 19:14

Land of promise (Canaan)

A. *Described as:*
The land of
promise . . . . Heb. 11:9
The land of
Canaan . . . . . . Ezek. 16:3, 29
The land of the
Jews. . . . . Acts 10:39
The Holy
Land. . . . . Zech. 2:12
"Beulah" . . . . . Is. 62:4

B. *Conquest of, by:*
Divine
command . . . . Ex. 23:24
God's angel. . . Ex. 23:20, 23
Hornets. . . . . . . Ex. 23:28
Degrees. . . . . . . Ex. 23:29, 30

C. *Inheritance of:*
Promised to Abraham's
seed . . . . Gen. 12:1-7
Awaits God's
time . . . . Gen. 15:7-16
Boundaries of,
specified . . . . . Gen. 15:18-21
Some kept
from . . . . Deut. 1:34-40
For the
obedient . . . . . Deut. 5:16

Sin separates
from . . . . Deut. 28:49-68

D. *Laws concerning:*
Land allotted to 12
tribes . . . . Num. 26:52-55
None for
priests . . . . Num. 18:20, 24
Sale and redemption
of . . . . Lev. 25:15-33
Transfer of
title. . . . . Ruth 4:3-8
Witness of
sale . . . . Ruth 4:9-11
Relieved of debt
on . . . . Neh. 5:3-13
Leased to
others. . . . . Matt. 21:33-41
Widow's right
in . . . . Ruth 4:3-9
Rights of unmarried women
in . . . . Num. 27:1-11
Rest of, on the seventh
years. . . . . Ex. 23:11

E. *Original inhabitants of:*
Seven gentile   (Deut. 7:1
  nations. . . . . . \Josh. 24:11
Mighty . . . . Deut. 4:38
Tall. . . . . Deut. 9:1, 2
Mingled with
Israel . . . . Ps. 106:34-38
Idolatrous . . . . . Ex. 23:23, 24
                      Deut. 12:29-31
Corrupt. . . . . . . Lev. 18:1-30
                      Ezek. 16:47

Language—*man's means of
communication*

A. *Kinds of:*
Hebrew . . . . . . 2 Kin. 18:28
Chaldean . . . . . Dan. 1:4
Aramaic . . . . . . 2 Kin. 18:26
Egyptian . . . . . Ps. 114:1
Arabic. . . . . Acts 2:11
Greek . . . . Acts 21:37
Latin . . . . John 19:19, 20
Lycaonian . . . . Acts 14:11
Medes and
Persians. . . . . Esth. 3:12

B. *Varieties of:*
Result of confusion
(Babel). . . . . . . Gen. 11:1-9
Result of division
of Noah's three
sons . . . . Gen. 10:5, 20, 31
Seen in one   (Esth. 1:22
empire . . . . \Dan. 3:4, 7, 29

Seen in Christ's
inscription ....John 19:19, 20
Witnessed at
Pentecost .....Acts 2:6-12
Evident in
heaven........Rev. 5:9

See Tongue

Lantern—*an enclosed lamp*

Used by soldiers arresting
Jesus..........John 18:3

Laodicea—*a chief city of Asia Minor*

Church of, sharply
rebuked ....Rev. 1:11
Epaphras labors
here...............Col. 4:12, 13
Paul writes letter
to...................Col. 4:16
Not visited by   (Col. 2:1
Paul.............. (Col. 4:15

Lap

A. *As a loose skirt of a garment:*
   For carrying
   objects........2 Kin. 4:39
   Lots cast
   into...........Prov. 16:33

B. *As an act of dogs:*
   For selecting Gideon's
   army.........Judg. 7:5, 6, 7

Lapidoth—*torches*

Husband of Deborah the
prophetess.......Judg. 4:4

Lasea

Seaport of Crete ..Acts 27:8

Lash—*a punishment imposed with a
whip or scourge*

Rendered
"blows" ....Deut. 25:3
Imposed on Paul (rendered
"stripes").......2 Cor. 11:24

Lasha—*bursting forth*

Boundary town of southeast
Palestine ....Gen. 10:19

Lasharon—*to Sharon*

Town possessed by
Joshua ....Josh. 12:1, 18

Last—*the terminal point*

A. *Senses of:*
   Final conse-
   quence.......Prov. 23:32
   God ....Is. 44:6

B. *Of events, last:*
   Day (resur-
   rection) ......John 6:39, 40
   Day
   (judgment)....John 12:48
   Days (present
   age)..........Acts 2:17
   Hour (present
   age)..........1 John 2:18
   Times (present
   age)..........1 Pet. 1:20
   Days (time before
   Christ's   (2 Tim. 3:1
   return).......(2 Pet. 3:3
   Enemy
   (death)........1 Cor. 15:26
   Time (Christ's
   return)........1 Pet. 1:5
   Trumpet (Christ's
   return)........1 Cor. 15:52

Last Supper

At Feast of
Unleavened   (Matt. 26:17
Bread ....(Mark 14:12
Fulfills Passover..Luke 22:15-18

Latin—*the Roman language*

Used in writing Christ's
inscription.......John 19:19, 20

Lattice—*a framework of crossed wood
or metal strips*

Window of Sisera's
mother............Judg. 5:28
Ahaziah fell
through ....2 Kin. 1:2
Looked through...Prov. 7:6

Laughter—*an emotion expressive of
joy, mirth or ridicule*

A. *Kinds of:*
   Divine ....Ps. 59:8
   Natural........Job 8:21
   Derisive ......Neh. 2:19
   Fake...........Prov. 14:13
   Scornful ......2 Chr. 30:10
   Confident......Job 5:22
   Joyful ....Ps. 126:2

B. *Causes of:*
   Man's folly ....Ps. 2:4

Something
unusual.......Gen. 18:12-15
Something
untrue.......Matt. 9:24
Ridicule.......2 Chr. 30:10
Highly contra-
dictory.......Ps. 22:7, 8

Laver—a basin for washing

Made for the
tabernacle.......Ex. 30:18

Law—an authoritative rule of conduct

Law of man.......Luke 20:22
Natural law written upon
the heart.......Rom. 2:14, 15
Law of Moses.....Gal. 3:17-21
Entire Old
Testament.......John 10:34
Expression of God's
will..............Rom. 7:2-9
Operating
principle..........Rom. 3:27

Law of Moses

A. *History of:*
Given at
Sinai..........Ex. 20:1-26
Called a
covenant......Deut. 4:13, 23
Dedicated with
blood.......Heb. 9:18-22
Called the Law of
Moses........Josh. 8:30-35
Restated in Deuter-
onomy.....Deut. 4:44-46
Written on
stone........Deut. 4:13
Plaster coated
stone.......Deut. 27:3-8
Placed with the
ark.......Deut. 31:9, 26
Given to
Joshua.......Josh. 1:1-9
Repeated by
Joshua.......Josh. 23:6-16
Disobeyed by:
Israel.........Judg. 2:10-20
Israel's
kings........2 Kin. 10:31
The Jews.....Is. 1:10-18
Finding of book
of.......2 Chr. 34:14-33
Disobedience to, cause of
exile..........2 Kin. 17:3-41
Read to postexilic
assembly.....Neh. 8:1-18

Recalled at close of Old
Testament....Mal. 4:4
Meaning of, fulfilled by
Christ.......Matt. 5:17-48
Pharisees insist on observance
of.......Acts 15:1-29

B. *Purposes of:*
Knowledge of
sin............Rom. 3:20
Manifest God's righ-
teousness.....Rom. 7:12
Lead to
Christ........Gal. 3:24, 25

C. *Christ's relation to:*
Born under....Gal. 4:4
Explains
proper ⎧ Matt. 5:17-48
meaning to... ⎩ Matt. 12:1-14
Redeems sinners from
curse of......Gal. 3:13
Shows fulfillment of, in
Himself.......Luke 24:27, 44

D. *Christian's relation to:*
Freed from....Acts 15:1-29
Spirit of, fulfilled in
love.......Rom. 13:8-10
Now written on the
heart..........2 Cor. 3:3-11

E. *Inadequacies of, cannot:*
Make worshiper
perfect........Heb. 9:9-15
Justify.........Acts 13:38, 39

Lawgiver—a lawmaker

Only one..........James 4:12
The LORD is.......Is. 33:22

Lawlessness—living outside or contrary to law

A. *Described as:*
Wickedness....Acts 2:23
Iniquity.......Matt. 13:41
Unrighteous-
ness...........2 Cor. 6:14

B. *Features concerning:*
Called sin.....1 John 3:4
Incompatible with righ-
teousness.....2 Cor. 6:14
Torments the ⎧ Matt. 24:12
righteous.....⎩ 2 Pet. 2:8
Led to
crucifixion....Acts 2:22, 23
Descriptive of
antichrist.....2 Thess. 2:7, 8
Scribes and Pharisees
full of........Matt. 23:27, 28

Basis for condem-
nation ....Matt. 7:23
Law made
for ....1 Tim. 1:9
Forgiven......Rom. 4:7
            Titus 2:14
Forgotten.....Heb. 8:12
            Heb. 10:17

Lawsuits—*suing another for damages*

Between
Christians,   { Matt. 5:25, 40
forbidden........{ 1 Cor. 6:1-8

Lawyers—*interpreters of the law*

Test Jesus........Matt. 22:34-40
Jesus answers
one.............Luke 10:25-37
Condemned by
Jesus.............Luke 11:45-52
Zenas, a
Christian ....Titus 3:13

Lazarus—*God has helped*

1. Beggar described in a
parable.......Luke 16:20-25
2. Brother of Mary and Martha;
raised from the
dead ....John 11:1-44
Attends a
supper ....John 12:1, 2
Jews seek to
kill.........John 12:9-11

Laziness

A. *Leads to:*
Poverty........Prov. 6:9-11
Waste ....Prov. 18:9
Loss of all .....Matt. 25:26-30

B. *Admonitions against:*
Make the most of
time ....Eph. 5:16
Have a great
work..........Neh. 6:3
Work day and
night..........1 Thess. 2:9
Consider the
ant...........Prov. 6:6-8
No work, no
eat...........2 Thess. 3:10-12

Lead—*a heavy metal*

Purified by fire ....Num. 31:22, 23
Engraved with ....Job 19:23, 24
Very heavy ....Ex. 15:10
Object of trade...Ezek. 27:12

Leader—*a guide*

A. *Kinds of:*
False ....Is. 3:12
Blind ....Luke 6:39
Young..........Is. 11:6
Safe ....Ps. 78:53
Gentle ....Is. 40:11
Faithful........Deut. 8:2, 15

B. *Used of:*
The LORD......Ex. 13:21
Christ ....John 10:3
The Lamb ....Rev. 7:17
The Spirit......Luke 4:1
            Gal. 5:18
Hananiah......Neh. 7:2
Tribal heads ...Num. 2:3, 5

C. *Course of, in:*
God's truth ....Ps. 25:5
Righ-
teousness .....Ps. 5:8
Way you should
go ....Is. 48:17
Unknown
ways..........Is. 42:16
Smooth path...Ps. 27:11
Everlasting
way..........Ps. 139:24

Leaf, leaves

Trees ....Matt. 21:19

League—*an agreement between two or
more parties*

Fraudulent........Josh. 9:3-6
Forbidden........Judg. 2:2
Secret.............1 Sam. 22:8
Conditional ....2 Sam. 3:12, 13
Acceptable........2 Sam. 3:21
Unifying ....2 Sam. 5:1-3
International......1 Kin. 5:12
Purchased........1 Kin. 15:18-21
Deceitful.........Dan. 11:23

Leah—*a wild cow*

Laban's eldest
daughter ....Gen. 29:16, 17
By Laban's deceit, becomes Jacob's
wife............Gen. 29:19-27
Unloved by
Jacob ....Gen. 29:30-33
Mother of seven
children ....Gen. 30:19-21
Buried in Machpelah's
cave............Gen. 49:30, 31
Builder of house of
Israel.............Ruth 4:11

Leaping—*to spring or bound forward suddenly*

A. *Used physically of:*
Insects ....Joel 2:5
Men ....1 Kin. 18:26
Unborn child ..Luke 1:41, 44
Lame man .....Acts 3:8

B. *Expressive of:*
Great joy ......2 Sam. 6:16
Renewed life...Is. 35:6
Victory in
persecution ...Luke 6:22, 23

Learning—*knowledge acquired through experience or instructions*

A. *Aspects of:*
God's
statutes ....Ps. 119:71, 73
Righteous-
ness...........Is. 26:9, 10
Good works ...Titus 3:14
Obedience .....Heb. 5:8

B. *Objects of:*
Abominable
things........Deut. 18:9
Heathen ⎰Deut. 18:9
ways..........⎱Ps. 106:35
Fear ⎧Deut. 14:23
of the ⎨Deut. 17:19
LORD........⎩Deut. 31:13

C. *Sources of:*
Experience.....Gen. 30:27
Worldly
knowledge ....John 7:15
Christian
experience ....Phil. 4:11
Scriptures .....Rom. 15:4

Leather—*an animal's dried skin*

Worn by John the
Baptist ....Matt. 3:4

Leaven—*dough in a state of fermentation*

A. *Forbidden in:*
Passover.......Ex. 12:8-20
Grain
offerings ......Lev. 2:11

B. *Permitted in:*
Peace
offerings .....Lev. 7:13
Firstfruits of ⎰Lev. 23:17
grain.........⎱Num. 15:20, 21

C. *Figurative of:*
Kingdom of
heaven........Matt. 13:33

Corrupt
teaching .....Matt. 16:6, 12
Infectious
sin ....1 Cor. 5:5-7
False
doctrine......Gal. 5:1-9

Lebanah—*white*

Founder of a family
of returning ⎰Ezra 2:43, 45
exiles............⎱Neh. 7:48
Called Lebana.....Neh. 7:48

Lebanon—*mountain range (10,000 ft.) in north Canaan*

A. *Source of:*
Wood for Solomon's
Temple........1 Kin. 5:5, 6
Stones for Solomon's
Temple.......1 Kin. 5:14, 18
Wood for the second
Temple.......Ezra 3:7

B. *Significant as:*
A sight desired by
Moses.........Deut. 3:25
Israel's northern
boundary .....Deut. 1:7
Captured by ⎰Josh. 11:16, 17
Joshua ......⎱Josh. 12:7
Assigned to
Israelites......Josh. 13:5-7
Not completely
conquered ....Judg. 3:1-3
Possessed by
Assyria ....Is. 37:24

C. *Figurative of:*
Great
kingdoms .....Is. 10:24, 34
Spiritual transfor-
mation........Is. 29:17
Jerusalem and the
Temple.......Ezek. 17:3
Spiritual
growth........Hos. 14:5-7
Messiah's
glory..........Is. 35:2

D. *Noted for:*
Blossoms .....Nah. 1:4
Wine ....Hos. 14:6, 7
Wild beast.....2 Kin. 14:9
Snow..........Jer. 18:14
Cedars........Song 5:15
Is. 14:8

Lebaoth—*lionesses*

Town of south
Judah ....Josh. 15:32

Also called Beth
Lebaoth .... Josh. 19:6

Lebbaeus (see Judas 3)

Surname of Judas
(Jude) .... Matt. 10:3

Lebonah—*incense*

Town north of
Shiloh .... Judg. 21:19

Lecah—*journey*

Descendant of
Judah .... 1 Chr. 4:21

Ledge—*a protrusion around an altar*

Part of altars rendered
rim .... Ex. 27:5

Leech

Figurative of insatiable
appetite .... Prov. 30:15, 16

Leek—*an onion-like plant*

Desired by
Israelites .... Num. 11:5

Left—*opposite of right*

A. *Of direction:*
  Making a
  choice .... Gen. 13:9
  Position .... Matt. 20:21-23

B. *Of the hand:*
  Unusual capacity of 700
  men .... Judg. 20:15, 16
  Lesser importance
  of .... Gen. 48:13-20

C. *Figurative of:*
  Weakness ..... Eccl. 10:2
  Shame......... Matt. 25:33, 41
  Bride's
  choice .... Song 2:6
  Singleness of
  purpose ...... Matt. 6:3
  Riches......... Prov. 3:16
  Ministry of
  God .... 2 Cor. 6:7

Left—*that which remains over*

A. *Descriptive of:*
  Aloneness ..... Gen. 32:24
  Entire
  destruction.... Josh. 11:11, 12
  Entire
  separation..... Ex. 10:26
  Survival .... Num. 26:65

Remnant ...... Is. 11:11, 16
Heir .... 2 Sam. 14:7

B. *Blessings upon:*
  Equal booty ... 1 Sam. 30:9-25
  Greater
  heritage....... Is. 49:21-23
  Holiness ...... Is. 4:3
  Lord's
  protection..... Rom. 11:3-5
  Not wasted .... Matt. 15:37

Legacy—*that which is bequeathed to heirs*

Left by:

Abraham......... Gen. 25:5, 6
David .... 1 Kin. 2:1-7
Christ............. John 14:15-27

Legal—*lawful*

Kingship, determined by
David .... 1 Kin. 1:5-48
Priests' rights, divinely
enforced......... 2 Chr. 26:16-21
Priesthood,
rejected .... Neh. 7:63-65
Right to rebuild,
confirmed .... Ezra 5:3-17
Mixed marriages,
condemned...... Ezra 10:1-44
David's act,
justified .... Matt. 12:3-8
Christ's trial,
exposed .... Matt. 27:4-31
Paul's right of appeal,
recognized ...... Acts 26:31, 32

Legion—*a great number or multitude*

Demons........... Mark 5:9, 15
Christ's angels .... Matt. 26:53

Legs—*lower parts of human or animal body*

A. *Used literally of:*
  Animal's....... Ex. 12:9
  Man's.......... 1 Sam. 17:6
  Christ's........ John 19:31, 33

B. *Used figuratively of:*
  Fool .... Prov. 26:7
  Man's
  weakness ..... Ps. 147:10
  Children of
  Israel .... Amos 3:12
  Strength....... Dan. 2:33, 40
  Christ's
  appearance.... Song 5:15

Lehabim—*flaming*

Nation (probably the Libyans)
related to the
Egyptians ....Gen. 10:13

Lehi—*cheek, jawbone*

Place in Judah; Samson kills
Philistines ....Judg. 15:9-19

Leisure—*spare time*

None found ......Mark 6:31

Lemuel—*devoted to God*

King taught by his
mother ....Prov. 31:1-31

Lending—*to give to another for
temporary use*

A. *As a gift to:*
   Expecting no
   return.........Luke 6:34, 35
   To the LORD ...1 Sam. 1:28
                  1 Sam. 2:20

B. *As a blessing:*
   Recognized by
   God...........Deut. 28:12, 44
   Remembered by
   God...........Ps. 112:5, 6
   Rewarded by
   God...........Ps. 37:25, 26

See Borrow

Length of life

A. *Factors prolonging:*
   Keeping command-
   ments.........1 Kin. 3:14
   Wisdom........Prov. 3:13, 16
   Prayer........2 Kin. 20:1-11
   Honor to
   parents ....Eph. 6:3
   Fear of the
   LORD..........Prov. 10:27

B. *Factors decreasing:*
   Killing.........2 Sam. 3:27
   God's
   judgment ....Job 22:15, 16
   Suicide ....Matt. 27:5

Lentil—*plant of the legume family*

Prepared as Esau's
pottage..........Gen. 25:29-34
Bread made of ....Ezek. 4:9

Leopard—*a wild, spotted animal*

A. *Characteristics of:*
   Swift ....Hab. 1:8
   Watches ....Jer. 5:6
   Lies in wait ....Hos. 13:7
   Lives in
   mountains ....Song 4:8

B. *Figurative of:*
   Man's inability to
   change........Jer. 13:23
   Transfor-
   mation........Is. 11:6
   Greek
   empire ....Dan. 7:6
   Antichrist......Rev. 13:2

Leprosy—*scourge; a cancer-like disease*

A. *Characteristics of:*
   Many diseased
   with ....Luke 4:27
   Unclean ....Lev. 13:44, 45
   Outcast.........2 Kin. 15:5
   Considered
   incurable......2 Kin. 5:7
   Often
   hereditary.....2 Sam. 3:29
   Excluded from the
   priesthood ....Lev. 22:2-4

B. *Kinds of, in:*
   Man ....Luke 17:12
   House ....Lev. 14:33-57
   Clothing.......Lev. 13:47-59

C. *Treatment of:*
   Symptoms
   described......Lev. 13:1-46
   Cleansing
   prescribed....Lev. 14:1-32
   Healing by a
   miracle....... Ex. 4:6, 7

D. *Used as a sign:*
   Miriam ....Num. 12:1-10
   Gehazi.........2 Kin. 5:25, 27
   Uzziah.........2 Chr. 26:16-21
   Moses ....Ex. 4:6, 7

Letters—*written communications;
epistles*

A. *Kinds of:*
   Forged.........1 Kin. 21:7, 8
   Rebellious .....Jer. 29:24-32
   Authori-
   tative ....Acts 22:5
   Instructive....Acts 15:23-29
   Weighty ....2 Cor. 10:10
   Causing
   sorrow ....2 Cor. 7:8

B. *Descriptive of:*
One's writing . . Gal. 6:11
Learning . . . . . . John 7:15
External . . . . . . Rom. 2:27, 29
Legalism . . . . . . Rom. 7:6
Christians . . . . 2 Cor. 3:1, 2

"Let us"

"Arise, go from
here" . . . . John 14:31
"Cast off the works of
darkness" . . . . Rom. 13:12
"Walk properly" . . Rom. 13:13
"Be sober" . . . . 1 Thess. 5:8
"Fear" . . . . Heb. 4:1
"Be diligent to enter that
rest" . . . . Heb. 4:11
"Come boldly" . . . . Heb. 4:16
"Go on to
perfection" . . . . Heb. 6:1
"Draw near" . . . . . . Heb. 10:22
"Hold fast" . . . . . . Heb. 10:23
"Consider one
another" . . . . Heb. 10:24
"Run with
endurance" . . . . Heb. 12:1
"Go forth" . . . . Heb. 13:13
"Offer sacrifice" . . . Heb. 13:15

Letushim—*sharpened*

Tribe descending from
Dedan . . . . Gen. 25:3

Leummim—*peoples*

Tribe descending from
Dedan . . . . Gen. 25:3

Levi—*joined*

1. Third son of Jacob and
Leah . . . . Gen. 29:34
Participates in
revenge . . . . Gen. 34:25-31
Father of Gershon, Kohath,
Merari . . . . Gen. 46:11
Descendants of, to be
scattered . . . . . Gen. 49:5-7
Dies in Egypt at age
137 . . . . Ex. 6:16
2. Ancestor of
Christ . . . . Luke 3:24
3. Another ancestor of
Christ . . . . Luke 3:29
4. Apostle called
Matthew . . . . . Luke 5:27, 29
5. Tribe descending from
Levi . . . . Ex. 32:26, 28

Leviathan—*twisted, coiled*

Great beast created by
God . . . . Ps. 104:26
Habit of, graphically
described . . . . Job 41:1-34
God's power
over . . . . Ps. 74:14

Levites—*descendants of Levi*

A. *History of:*
Descendants of Levi, Jacob's
son . . . . Gen. 29:34
Jacob's prophecy
concerning . . . . Gen. 49:5-7
Divided into three
families . . . . . . Ex. 6:16-24
Aaron, great-grandson of Levi,
chosen for
priesthood . . . . Ex. 28:1
Tribe of Levi rewarded for
dedication . . . . . Ex. 32:26-29
Chosen by God for holy
service . . . . Deut. 10:8
Not numbered among
Israel . . . . Num. 1:47-49
Substituted for Israel's first-
born . . . . Num. 3:12-45
Given as gifts to Aaron's
sons . . . . Num. 8:6-21
Rebellion among, led by
Korah . . . . Num. 16:1-50
Choice of, confirmed by the
Lord . . . . Num. 17:1-13
Bear ark of the covenant across
the Jordan . . . . Josh. 3:2-17
Hear Law
read . . . . Josh. 8:31-35
Cities (48)   ⌠Num. 35:2-8
assigned to . . . ⌡Josh. 14:3, 4
One of, becomes Micah's
idolatrous   ⌠Judg. 17:5-13
priest . . . . ⌡Judg. 18:18-31
Perform priestly
functions . . . . . . 1 Sam. 6:15
Appointed over service of
song . . . . 1 Chr. 6:31-48
Service of heads of
households . . . . 1 Chr. 9:26-34
Excluded by
Jeroboam . . . . . 2 Chr. 11:13-17
Help repair the
Temple . . . . 1 Chr. 23:2-4
Carried to
Babylon . . . . 2 Chr. 36:19, 20
Return from
exile . . . . Ezra 2:40-63
Tithes withheld
from . . . . Neh. 13:10-13

Intermarry with
foreigners.....Ezra 10:2-24
Seal the
covenant......Neh. 10:1, 9-28
Present defiled
offerings will ⎰Mal. 1:6-14
be purified ...⎱Mal. 3:1-4

B. *Duties of:*
Serve the
LORD..........Deut. 10:8
Serve the
priesthood ....Num. 3:5-9
Attend to sanctuary
duties........Num. 18:3
Distribute the
tithe ....2 Chr. 31:11-19
Prepare sacrifices for
priests ....2 Chr. 35:10-14
Teach the
people ....2 Chr. 17:8-11
Declare verdicts of
Law..........Deut. 17:9-11
Protect the
king ....2 Chr. 23:2-10
Perform
music.........1 Chr. 25:1-7
Precede the ⎰2 Chr. 20:19-21,
army.........⎱ 28

C. *Spiritual truths illustrated by:*
Representation—Duties of the
congre-
gation.........Num. 3:6-9
Substitution—
place of the ⎰Num. 3:12, 13,
firstborn .....⎱ 41, 45
Subordination—service to the
Temple........Num. 3:5-10
Consecration—separated
for God's
work..........Num. 8:9-14
Holiness—
cleansed ......Num. 8:6, 7, 21
Election—God's
choice ....Num. 17:7-13
Inheritance—in the
Lord ....Num. 18:20

See Priest

Leviticus, the Book of—*a book of the
Old Testament*

Laws of sacrifice ..Lev. 1:1-7:38
Laws of ⎰Lev. 11:1-
purity ....⎱ 15:33
Day of
atonement........Lev. 16:1-34
Laws of ⎰Lev. 17:1-
holiness ....⎱ 25:55

Blessings and
curses...........Lev. 26:1-46

Levy—*forced labor imposed upon a
people*

Israelites..........1 Kin. 5:13-15
Canaanites........1 Kin. 9:15, 21

Lewd, lewdness—*wickedness*

A. *Characteristics of:*
Shameful .....Ezek. 16:27
Sexual........Ezek. 22:11
Youthful......Ezek. 23:21
Adulterous....Jer. 13:27
Filthiness....Ezek. 24:13
Outrage ......Judg. 20:6

B. *Committed by:*
Men of
Gibeah........Judg. 20:5
Israel..........Hos. 2:10
Jerusalem.....Ezek. 16:27, 43

Liars, lies, lying—*manifestation of
untruth*

A. *Defined as:*
Nature of the
devil........John 8:44
Denial that Jesus is
Christ........1 John 2:22
Not keeping Christ's command-
ments........1 John 2:4
Hating one's
brother ......1 John 4:20
All that is not of the
truth.........1 John 2:21, 27

B. *Those who speak:*
Wicked........Ps. 58:3
False
witnesses ....Prov. 14:5, 25
Astrologers ....Dan. 2:9
Israel..........Hos. 7:3, 13
Judah..........Jer. 9:1-5

C. *Attitude of the wicked toward:*
Are always ....Titus 1:12
Forge against the
righteous .....Ps. 119:69
Change God's truth
for............Rom. 1:25

D. *Attitude of the righteous
toward:*
Keep far
from ....Prov. 30:8
Shall not
speak ....Zeph. 3:13

Pray for deliverance
from . . . . Ps. 120:2
"Put away" . . . . . . Eph. 4:25

E. *Attitude of God toward:*
Will not . . . . . Num. 23:19
Is an abomina-
tion . . . . Prov. 6:16-19
Will discover
man's . . . . Is. 28:15, 17
Is against . . . . . Ezek. 13:8

F. *Punishment of, shall:*
Not escape . . . . . Prov. 19:5
Be stopped . . . . . Ps. 63:11
Be silenced . . . . Ps. 31:18
Be short
lived . . . . Prov. 12:19
End in lake of
fire . . . . Rev. 21:8, 27

G. *The evils of:*
Produces
error . . . . Amos 2:4
Increases
wickedness . . . . Prov. 29:12
Destruction . . . . Hos. 10:13-15
Death . . . . Prov. 21:6
Zech. 13:3

Liberality—*a generous spirit in helping the needy*

A. *Object of:*
Poor . . . . Deut. 15:11
Strangers . . . . . . Lev. 25:35
Afflicted . . . . . . Luke 10:30-35
Servants
(slaves) . . . . . Deut. 15:12-18
All men . . . . Gal. 6:10
God's
children . . . . . 2 Cor. 8:1-9, 12

B. *Reasons for:*
Make our faith
real . . . . James 2:14-16
Secure true { Luke 12:33
riches . . . . . . { 1 Tim. 6:17-19
Follow Christ's
example . . . . . 2 Cor. 8:9
Help God's
kingdom . . . . . Phil. 4:14-18
Relieve
distress . . . . . . 2 Cor. 9:12

C. *Blessings of:*
God
remembers . . . . Prov. 3:9, 10
Will return
abundantly . . . . Prov. 11:24-27
Brings deliverance in time of
need . . . . Is. 58:10, 11

Insures
sufficiency . . . . Ps. 37:25, 26
Brings
reward . . . . Ps. 112:5-9
Matt. 25:40
Provokes others
to . . . . 2 Cor. 9:2

Liberty, civil

Obtained by:
Purchase . . . . Acts 22:28
Birth . . . . Acts 22:28
Release . . . . Deut. 15:12-15
Victory . . . . Ex. 14:30, 31

Liberty, spiritual

A. *Described as:*
Predicted . . . . . . Is. 61:1
Where the
spirit is . . . . 2 Cor. 3:17

B. *Relation of Christians toward, they:*
Are called to . . . Gal. 5:13
Abide by . . . . . . James 1:25
Should
walk at . . . . Ps. 119:45
Have in Jesus
Christ . . . . Gal. 2:4, 5

See Freedom

Libnah—*whiteness*

1. Israelite
camp . . . . Num. 33:20, 21
2. Canaanite city near
Lachish . . . . . . Josh. 10:29-32
Captured by
Joshua . . . . Josh. 10:30, 39
In Judah's
territory . . . . . . Josh. 15:42
Given to Aaron's descen-
dants . . . . Josh. 21:13
Fought against by
Assyria . . . . 2 Kin. 19:8, 9
Home of
Hamutal . . . . . . 2 Kin. 23:31

Libni—*white, pure*

1. Son of
Gershon . . . . . . Num. 3:18, 21
Family of, called
Libnites . . . . . . Num. 3:21
Called
Laadan . . . . 1 Chr. 23:7
2. Descendant of
Merari . . . . 1 Chr. 6:29

Libya, Libyans—*the land and people west of Egypt*

Called Lubim......Nah. 3:9
Will fall by the
sword ....Ezek. 30:5
Will be
controlled ....Dan. 11:43
Some from, at
Pentecost ....Acts 2:1-10

Lice—*some small, harmful insects*

Third plague upon Egypt, produced
from dust ....Ex. 8:16-18

License—*authority to do something*

Granted to Paul...Acts 21:40

Licentiousness—*unbridled lust*

Flows from the
heart.............Mark 7:20-23
Seen in the flesh ..Gal. 5:19
Characterizes the old
life ....1 Pet. 4:3
Found among
Gentiles ....Eph. 4:19, 20
Sign of apostasy ..Jude 4
Among Christians,
lamentable ....2 Cor. 12:21
Not to walk in ....Rom. 13:13

Life, eternal

A. *Defined as:*
Knowing the true
God..............John 17:3
God's command-
ment...........John 12:50
Jesus Christ ...1 John 1:2
He gives.......John 10:28, 29
God's gift.....Rom. 6:23

B. *Christ's relation to:*
It is in Him ....2 Tim. 1:1
Manifested through
Him...........2 Tim. 1:10
He has the
words of .....John 6:68
It comes through
Him...........Rom. 5:21

C. *Means of securing, by:*
God's gift......Rom. 6:22, 23
Having the
Son ....1 John 5:11, 12
Knowing the true
God...........John 17:3
Knowing the
Scriptures.....John 20:31
Believing the
Son ....John 3:15-36

Drinking the water of
life............John 4:14
Eating the bread of
life............John 6:50-58
Reaping ....John 4:36
Fight the good fight of
faith ....1 Tim. 6:12, 19

D. *Present aspect of, for Christians, they:*
Believe in the
Son ....John 3:36
Have assurance
of.............John 5:24
Have promise
of.............Titus 1:2
Have hope of ..Titus 3:7
Take hold of...1 Tim. 6:12, 19
Hates his life in this
world ....John 12:25

E. *Future aspect of, for Christians, they shall:*
Inherit.........Matt. 19:29
In the world to
come.........Luke 18:30
In them you think you
have ....John 5:39
Reap ....Gal. 6:8

Life, natural

A. *Origin of, by:*
God's
creation......Acts 17:28, 29
Natural birth ..Gen. 4:1, 2
Supernatural
conception ....Luke 1:31-35

B. *Shortness of, described as:*
Dream.........Job 20:8
Shadow........1 Chr. 29:15
Cloud..........Job 7:9
Flower.........Job 14:1, 2
Vapor ....James 4:14
Sleep ....Ps. 90:5
Sigh ....Ps. 90:9
Pilgrimage.....Gen. 47:9
Grass..........1 Pet. 1:24

C. *God's concern for, its:*
Preservation ...Gen. 7:1-3
Protection .....Ps. 34:7, 17, 19
Perpetuity (contin-
uance) ....Gen. 1:28
Provisions .....Ps. 104:27, 28
Punishment....Gen. 3:14-19
Perfection in
glory..........Col. 3:4

D. *Believer's attitude toward:*
Seeks to preserve
it ....Acts 27:10-31
Attends to needs
of ....Acts 27:34
Accepts suffering
of............Job 2:4-10
Makes God's kingdom first
in............Matt. 6:25-33
Gives it up for
Christ........Matt. 10:39
Lays it down for
others........Acts 15:26
Prizes it not too
highly........Acts 20:24
Puts Jesus first
in............2 Cor. 4:10-12
Regards God's will
in............James 4:13-15
Puts away the evil
of............Col. 3:5-9
Does not run
with ....1 Pet. 4:1-4
Praises God all the days
of............Ps. 63:3, 4
Doesn't fear enemies
of............Luke 12:4

E. *Cares of:*
Stunt spiritual
growth........Luke 8:14
Divide
loyalty........Luke 16:13
Delay pre-
paredness ....{Luke 17:26-30
{Luke 21:34
Hinder
service........2 Tim. 2:4

Life, spiritual

A. *Source of:*
God ....Ps. 36:9
Christ............John 14:6
Holy Spirit.....Ezek. 37:14
God's Word....James 1:18

B. *Described as:*
New birth .....John 3:3-8
Resurrection...John 5:24
Translation ....Acts 26:18
New creation ..2 Cor. 5:17
Seed ....1 John 3:9
Crucifixion ....Gal. 2:20

C. *Evidences of:*
Growth........1 Pet. 2:2
Love............1 John 3:14
Obedience .....Rom. 6:16-22
Victory ....Rom. 6:1-15
Spiritual-
mindedness ...Rom. 8:6

Possession of the
Spirit ....Rom. 8:9-13
Spirit's
testimony.....Rom. 8:15-17
Walking in the
Spirit ....Gal. 5:16, 25
Bearing the fruit of the
Spirit ....Gal. 5:22
Name in the
Book of {Phil. 4:3
Life ....{Rev. 17:8

D. *Growth of:*
Begins in
birth ....John 3:3-8
Feeds on milk in
infancy ....1 Pet. 2:2
Must not remain in
infancy ....Heb. 5:11-14
Comes to
adulthood.....1 John 2:13, 14
Arrives at
maturity ......Eph. 4:14-16

E. *Characteristics of:*
Imperish-
able...........John 11:25, 26
Trans-
forming ......Rom. 12:1, 2
Invisible ....Col. 3:3, 4
Abides
forever........1 John 2:17

F. *Enemies of:*
Devil ....Eph. 6:11-17
World ....1 John 2:15-17
Flesh ....Gal. 5:16-21

Life, triumphant Christian

A. *Over:*
Sorrow ....John 16:22-24
1 Thess. 4:13-18
The world .....John 16:33
1 John 5:4, 5
{Rom. 6:6-7,
{11-18
Transgres-   {Rom. 8:1-4
sions..........{Eph. 2:5, 6
{1 John 5:4, 5
Circum-   Rom. 8:37
stances........Phil. 4:11-13
Death ....Rom. 6:6-9
1 Cor. 15:54-57

B. *Through:*
Prayer.........John 16:22-24
Christ's
death ....Rom. 6:6, 7
Doctrine.......Rom. 6:17
Holy Spirit.....Rom. 8:1, 2
Christ ....Phil. 4:13

Grace.........Rom. 6:14
Eph. 2:7
Exaltation with
Christ........Eph. 2:5, 6
God's will.....Phil. 2:13
Hope of
resurrection...1 Thess. 4:16-18
Return of
Christ........1 Thess. 4:16, 17
Faith.........1 John 5:4, 5

C. *When?*:
Forever.......1 Cor. 15:54
Always.......2 Cor. 2:14

D. *By whom? Those who*:
Are in Christ ..Rom. 8:1
Were dead in transgres-
sions.......Eph. 2:5
Are born of
God..........1 John 5:4
Believe ....1 John 5:5

E. *Goal*:
To demonstrate God's
grace ....Eph. 3:7-10
To glorify   ⎰Rom. 8:16-18
Christ........⎱1 Pet. 4:11

Light—*the absence of darkness*

A. *Kinds of*:
Cosmic.......Gen. 1:3-5
Natural......Judg. 19:26
Miraculous ...Acts 12:7
Artificial......Acts 16:29

B. *Descriptive of God's*:
Nature.......1 John 1:5
Word........Ps. 119:105
Wisdom......Dan. 2:21, 22
Guidance.....Ps. 78:14
Ps. 89:15
Favor.........Ps. 4:6

C. *Descriptive of Christ's*:
Preincar-
nation ....John 1:4-9
Person........2 Cor. 4:6
Prediction .....Is. 42:6
Presentation to the
world ....Luke 2:32
Proclama-
tion..........John 8:12
Perfection in
glory.........Rev. 21:23, 24

D. *Descriptive of Christians as*:
Forerunners ...John 5:35
Examples......Matt. 5:14, 16
Missionaries ...Matt. 10:27
Transformed
people ....Eph. 5:8-14

Heirs of
glory.........Rev. 21:23

Lightning—*electrical discharges between the clouds and the earth*

A. *Used literally of God's*:
Visitation at
Sinai........Ex. 19:16
A power in
storms ....Job 38:35

B. *Descriptive of*:
Swiftness ......Nah. 2:4
Brightness .....Matt. 28:3
God's
judgments ....Rev. 11:19
Christ's
coming.......Luke 17:24
Satan's fall ....Luke 10:18

Likeness—*similarity of features*

Between:

Spiritual and the
moral ....2 Cor. 3:6
Spiritual and the
physical ....Jer. 23:29
Two events ....2 Chr. 35:18
God and idols .....Is. 46:5, 6, 9
Believers and
unbelievers ......Ps. 73:5
Now and the
future ....1 John 3:2

Likhi—*Yahweh is doctrine*

Manassite........1 Chr. 7:19

Lilith—*an evil female demon in Babylonian mythology*

Rendered "night creatures,"
suggesting
desolation ....Is. 34:14

Lily—*a bulbous plant*

Descriptive of:

Beauty............Song 5:13
Spiritual growth...Hos. 14:4, 5
Christ............Song 2:1
Shape of, used in Solomon's
Temple ....1 Kin. 7:19, 22

Lime—*containing limestone*

Descriptive of:

Cruel treatment...Amos 2:1
Devastating
judgment.........Is. 33:12

Line

A. *Literal uses of:*
As a measure-
ment..........Jer. 31:39
Rahab's cord...Josh. 2:18, 21

B. *Figurative uses of:*
God's
providences ...Ps. 16:6
God's
judgments ....Is. 28:17

Linen—*cloth made from flax*

A. *Used for:*
Priestly
garments......Ex. 28:1, 39
Tabernacle
curtains.......Ex. 26:1
Sacred veil.....Ex. 26:31, 36
Garments for
royalty........Esth. 8:15
Levitical
singers........2 Chr. 5:12
Gifts to a
woman........Ezek. 16:10, 13
Clothing of the
rich..........Luke 16:19
Embalming ....Matt. 27:59

B. *Figurative of:*
Righ-
teousness .....Rev. 19:8
Purity ....Rev. 19:14
Babylon's
pride..........Rev. 18:2, 16

Lintel—*a beam of wood overhanging the door*

Sprinkled with
blood.............Ex. 12:22, 23

Linus

Christian at
Rome ....2 Tim. 4:21

Lions

A. *Described as:*
Strongest among
beasts.........Prov. 30:30
Destructive ....Amos 3:12
Strong.........Judg. 14:18
Fierce ....Job 10:16
Stealthy ....Ps. 10:9
Majestic ....Prov. 30:29, 30
Provoking
fear............Amos 3:8

B. *God's use of:*
Slay the
disobedient....1 Kin. 13:24, 26
Punish
idolaters ......2 Kin. 17:25, 26
Show His power
over ....Dan. 6:16-24

C. *Figurative of:*
Tribe of
Judah..........Gen. 49:9
Christ ....Rev. 5:5
Devil ....1 Pet. 5:8
Transfor-
mation........Is. 11:6-8
Victory ....Ps. 91:13
Boldness ......Prov. 28:1
Persecutors....Ps. 22:13
World
empire ....Dan. 7:1-4
Antichrist......Rev. 13:2

Lips

A. *Described as:*
Uncir-
cumcised......Ex. 6:12, 30
Unclean ....Is. 6:5, 7
Stammering ...Is. 28:11
Flattering .....Ps. 12:2, 3
Perverse.......Prov. 4:24
Righteous .....Prov. 16:13
False ....Prov. 17:4
Burning ....Prov. 26:23

B. *Of the righteous, used for:*
Knowledge ....Job 33:3
Prayer.........Ps. 17:1
Silent prayer...1 Sam. 1:13
Righ-
teousness .....Ps. 40:9
Grace..........Ps. 45:2
Praise ....Ps. 51:15
Vows..........Ps. 66:13, 14
Singing ....Ps. 71:23
God's
judgments ....Ps. 119:13
Feeding
many ....Prov. 10:21
Spiritual fruit-{Hos. 14:2
fulness.......{Heb. 13:15

C. *Of the wicked, used for:*
Flattery........Prov. 7:21
Mocking ....Ps. 22:7
Defiance.......Ps. 12:4
Lying ....Is. 59:3
Poison..........Ps. 140:3, 9
Trouble-
making ....Prov. 24:2

Evil............Prov. 16:27, 30
Deception .....Prov. 24:28

D. *Warnings:*
Put away
perverse ....Prov. 4:24
Refrain from (Prov. 17:28
using........(1 Pet. 3:10
Of an adulteress,
avoid ....Prov. 5:3-13
Hypocrites.....Mark 7:6

Litigation—*a lawsuit*

Christ's warning
concerning ....Matt. 5:25, 40
Paul's warning
concerning ....1 Cor. 6:1, 2

Litter—*a covered framework for carrying a single passenger*

Of nations ....Is. 66:20

Liver—*body organ that secretes bile*

A. *Used literally of:*
Animals:
In sacrifice ...Ex. 29:13, 22
For
divination....Ezek. 21:21
B. *Used figuratively of:*
Extreme pain or
death ....Prov. 7:23

Livestock

Struck by God ....Ex. 12:29
Firstborn of, belong to
God ....Ex. 34:19
Can be unclean ...Lev. 5:2
East of Jordan good
for ....Num. 32:1, 4
Given as ransom ..Num. 3:45
See Cattle

Living, Christian

Source—Christ....John 14:19
Length—forever..John 11:25, 26
Means—faith in
Christ ....Rom. 1:17
Kind—
resurrected.......2 Cor. 5:15
End—to God......Rom. 14:7, 8
Purpose—for
Christ ....1 Thess. 5:10
Motivation—
Christ...........Gal. 2:20
Atmosphere—in the
Spirit.............Gal. 5:25
Manner—
righteously ....Titus 2:12

Enemies—flesh
and sin...........Rom. 8:12, 13
Price—
persecution.......2 Tim. 3:12

Living creatures—*a phrase referring to animals or living beings*

Aquatic animals..Gen. 1:21
Land animals ....Gen. 1:24
Angelic beings ....Ezek. 1:5

Lizard—*a small, swift reptile with legs*

Ceremonially
unclean ....Lev. 11:29, 30

Lo-Ammi—*not my people*

Symbolic name of Hosea's
son...............Hos. 1:8, 9

Loan (see Borrow; Lending)

Lock

Doors............Judg. 3:23, 24
Hair ....Judg. 16:13, 19
City gates........Neh. 3:6, 13, 14

Locust—*devastating, migratory insects*

A. *Types, or stages, of:*
Eating ....Joel 1:4
Devastating....Lev. 11:22
B. *Used literally of insects:*
Miraculously brought
forth..........Ex. 10:12-19
Sent as a (Deut. 28:38
judgment ....(1 Kin. 8:37
Used for
food ....Matt. 3:4
C. *Used figuratively of:*
Weakness .....Ps. 109:23, 24
Running
men...........Is. 33:4
Nineveh's departing
glory..........Nah. 3:15, 17
Final plagues ..Rev. 9:3, 7

See Grasshopper

Lod

Benjamite town ...1 Chr. 8:1, 12
Mentioned in postexilic
books ....Ezra 2:33
Aeneas healed here, called
Lydda ....Acts 9:32-35

Lo Debar

City in Manasseh
(in Gilead) ......2 Sam. 9:4, 5

Machir a native
of .... 2 Sam. 17:27

Lodge—*to pass the night*

Travelers—in a
house .... Judg. 19:4-20
Spies—in a
house .... Josh. 2:1
Animals—in
ruins .... Zeph. 2:14
Righteousness—in a
city .... Is. 1:21
Thoughts—in
Jerusalem .... Jer. 4:14

Loft—*a room upstairs*

Dead child taken
to .... 1 Kin. 17:19-24
Young man falls
from .... Acts 20:9

Loins

Used figuratively of source of
hope .... 1 Pet. 1:13

Lois

Timothy's
grandmother ..... 2 Tim. 1:5

Loneliness

Jacob—in
prayer.......... Gen. 32:23-30
Joseph—in
weeping.......... Gen. 43:30, 31
Elijah—in discourage-
ment .... 1 Kin. 19:3-14
Jeremiah—in
witnessing........ Jer. 15:17
Nehemiah—in a night
vigil............ Neh. 2:12-16
Christ—in
agony........... Matt. 26:36-45
Paul—in prison.... 2 Tim. 4:16

Longevity—*a great span of life*

Allotted years,
70................ Ps. 90:10

See Length of life

Long-suffering—*forbearance*

A. *Manifested in God's:*
Description of His
nature .... Ex. 34:6
Delay in executing
wrath .... Rom. 9:22

Dealing with sinful
men.......... Rom. 2:4
Desire for man's
salvation...... 2 Pet. 3:9, 15

B. *As a Christian grace:*
Exemplified by the prophets
("patience")... James 5:10
Manifested by Old Testament
saints
("patience")... Heb. 6:12
Produced by the
Spirit .... Gal. 5:22
Witnessed in
Paul's life ..... 2 Cor. 6:6
Taught as a
virtue......... Eph. 4:1
Given power
for............ Col. 1:11
Set for
imitation...... 2 Tim. 3:10
Needed by
preachers ..... 2 Tim. 4:2

Look—*focusing the eyes toward
something*

Promise........... Gen. 15:5
Warning against looking
back .... Gen. 19:17, 26
Astonishment ..... Ex. 3:2-6
Disdain .... 1 Sam. 17:42
Encouragement ... Ps. 34:5
Salvation .... Is. 45:22
Glory .... Acts 7:55

Lord—*title of majesty and kingship;
master*

A. *Applied to:*
God .... Gen. 3:1-23
Christ .... Luke 6:46
Masters........ Gen. 24:14, 27
Men ("sir") .... Matt. 21:30
Husbands...... Gen. 18:12
1 Pet. 3:6

B. *As applied to Christ, "kyrios"
indicates:*
Identity with
Jehovah....... Joel 2:32
Confession of Christ's Lordship
("Jesus as
Lord") .... Rom. 10:9
Absolute
Lordship ...... Phil. 2:11

Lord's Day (see First day of week)

Lord's Prayer

Taught by Jesus to His
disciples .... Matt. 6:9-13

Lord's Supper

A. *Described as:*
   Sharing of
   communion ... 1 Cor. 10:16
   Breaking of
   bread .... Acts 2:42, 46
   Lord's supper .. 1 Cor. 11:20
   Eucharist "Giving of
   thanks" ...... Luke 22:17, 19

B. *Features concerning:*
   Instituted by
   Christ .... Matt. 26:26-29
   Commemorative of Christ's
   death .... Luke 22:19, 20
   Introductory to the new
   covenant ..... Matt. 26:28
   Means of Christian
   fellowship ..... Acts 2:42, 46
   Memorial
   feast .... 1 Cor. 11:23-26
   Inconsistent with demon
   fellowship ..... 1 Cor. 10:19-22
   Preparation for,
   required .... 1 Cor. 11:27-34
   Spiritually
   explained ..... John 6:26-58

Lordship—*supreme authority*

Human kings ..... Mark 10:42
Divine King ...... Phil. 2:9-11

Lo-Ruhamah—*not pitied*

Symbolic name of Hosea's
daughter .... Hos. 1:6

Loss, spiritual

A. *Kinds of:*
   One's self ...... Luke 9:24, 25
   Reward ...... 1 Cor. 3:13-15
   Heaven .... Luke 16:19-31

B. *Causes of:*
   Love of this
   life .... Luke 17:33
   Sin .... Ps. 107:17, 34

Lost—*not found*

Descriptive of men as:

Separated from
God .... Luke 15:24, 32

Unregenerated .... Matt. 15:24
Objects of Christ's
mission .... Luke 15:4-6
Blinded by
Satan .... 2 Cor. 4:3, 4
Defiled .... Titus 1:15, 16

Lot—*covering*

A. *Life of:*
   Abraham's
   nephew .... Gen. 11:27-31
   Goes with Abraham to
   Canaan ...... Gen. 12:5
   Accompanies Abraham to
   Egypt .... Gen. 13:1
   Settles in
   Sodom .... Gen. 13:5-13
   Rescued by
   Abraham .... Gen. 14:12-16
   Befriends
   angels .... Gen. 19:1-14
   Saved from Sodom's
   destruction.... Gen. 19:15, 22
   His wife, disobedient, becomes
   pillar of salt ... Gen. 19:15, 17,
                                     26
   His daughters commit incest
   with .... Gen. 19:30-38
   Unwilling father of
   Moabites and
   Ammonites ... Gen. 19:37, 38

B. *Character of:*
   Makes selfish
   choice .... Gen. 13:5-13
   Lacks moral
   stability .... Gen. 19:6-10
   Loses moral
   influence...... Gen. 19:14, 20
   Still "oppressed" by
   Sodomites..... 2 Pet. 2:7, 8

Lotan—*a covering*

Tribe of Horites ⎰ Gen. 36:20, 29
in Mt. Seir....... ⎱ 1 Chr. 1:38, 39

Lot(s)—*a means of deciding doubtful matters*

A. *Characteristic of:*
   Preceded by
   prayer .... Acts 1:23-26
   With divine
   sanction ...... Num. 26:55
   Considered
   final .... Num. 26:56
   Used also by the
   ungodly....... Matt. 27:35

B. *Used for:*
Selection of
scapegoat.....Lev. 16:8
Detection of a
criminal.......Josh. 7:14-18
Selection of
warriors.......Judg. 20:9, 10
Choice of a
king ....1 Sam. 10:19-21
Deciding priestly
rotation.......Luke 1:9

Lot's wife

Disobedient, becomes pillar of
salt...............Gen. 19:26
Event to be
remembered......Luke 17:32

Love, Christian

A. *Toward God:*
First command-
ment.........Matt. 22:37, 38
With all the
heart..........Matt. 22:37
More important than
ritual ....Mark 12:31-33
Gives
boldness ......1 John 4:17-19

B. *Toward Christ:*
Sign of true
faith ....John 8:42
Manifested in (John 14:15, 21,
obedience..... 23
Leads to
service........2 Cor. 5:14

C. *Toward others:*
Second
command .....Matt. 22:37-39
Commanded by
Christ........John 13:34
Described in
detail ....1 Cor. 13:1-13

Love of Christ, the

A. *Objects of:*
Father.........John 14:31
Believers.......Gal. 2:20
Church ....Eph. 5:2, 25

B. *Described as:*
Knowing........Eph. 3:19
Personal.......Gal. 2:20
Conquering....Rom. 8:37
Unbreakable....Rom. 8:35
Intimate.......John 14:21
Imitative ......1 John 3:16

Like the
Father's.......John 15:9
Sacrificial......Gal. 2:20

C. *Expressions of:*
In taking our
nature ....Heb. 2:16-18
In dying for
us.............John 15:13

Love of God, the

A. *Objects of:*
Christ ....John 3:35
Christians ....2 Thess. 2:16
Mankind.......Titus 3:4
Cheerful
giver..........2 Cor. 9:7

B. *Described as:*
Great..........Eph. 2:4
Everlasting ....Jer. 31:3
Sacrificial......Rom. 5:8

C. *As seen in believers':*
Hearts.........Rom. 5:5
Regen-
eration........Eph. 2:4, 5
Love...........1 John 4:7-12
Faith ....1 John 4:16
Security ....2 Thess. 3:5
Daily life ......1 John 2:15-17
Obedience .....1 John 2:5
Without fear...1 John 4:17-19
Glorification ...1 John 3:1, 2

Love, physical

Isaac and
Rebekah ....Gen. 24:67
Jacob and
Rachel ....Gen. 29:11-30
Samson and
Delilah ....Judg. 16:4, 15

Lovingkindness—*gentle and steadfast
mercy*

Attitude of believers, to:

Expect............Ps. 17:7
                 Ps. 36:10
Rejoice in........Ps. 63:3
                 Ps. 69:16

Loyalty—*fidelity to a person or cause*

A. *Kinds of:*
People ....Acts 25:7-11
Relatives ......Esth. 2:21-23
King...........1 Sam. 24:6-10
Cause ....2 Sam. 11:9-11
Oath...........2 Sam. 21:7

B. *Signs of:*
General
obedience . . . . . Rom. 13:1, 2
Prayer for
rulers . . . . Ezra 6:10
Hatred of
disloyalty . . . . . Josh. 22:9-20

Lucifer—*light-bearer*

Name applied to
Satan . . . . Is. 14:12
Allusion to
elsewhere . . . . Luke 10:18

Lucius—*of light*

1. Prophet and teacher at
Antioch . . . . . . Acts 13:1
2. Paul's companion in
Corinth . . . . . . Rom. 16:21

Lud, Ludim (plural)

1. Lud, a people descending from
Shem . . . . 1 Chr. 1:17
2. Ludim, a people descending
from Mizraim
(Egypt) . . . . . . Gen. 10:13

Luhith—*of tablets or planks*

Moabite town . . . . . Is. 15:5

Luke—*another name for Lucius*

"The beloved
physician" . . . . Col. 4:14
Paul's last
companion . . . . 2 Tim. 4:11

Luke, the Gospel of—*a book of the
New Testament*

The
annunciation . . . . . Luke 1:26-56
John the Baptist . . Luke 3:1-22
The temptation . . . Luke 4:1-13
Public ministry
begins . . . . Luke 4:15
The disciples
chosen . . . . Luke 6:12-19
The disciple's { Luke
instructions . . . . . { 10:25–13:21
The Jerusalem { Luke
ministry . . . . { 19:28–21:38
The Last Supper . . Luke 22:1-38
The { Luke
Crucifixion . . . . . . { 22:39–23:56
The
Resurrection . . . . . Luke 24:1-53

Lukewarm—*neither hot nor cold*

Descriptive of
Laodicea . . . . Rev. 3:14-16

Lunatic—*an insane person*

David acts as . . . . . 1 Sam. 21:13-15
Nebuchadnezzar
inflicted as . . . . . . Dan. 4:31-36
Christ declared . . . John 10:20
Paul called . . . . Acts 26:24

See Madness

Lust—*evil desire*

A. *Origin of, in:*
Satan . . . . . . 1 John 3:8-12
Heart . . . . Matt. 15:19
Flesh . . . . James 1:14, 15
World . . . . 2 Pet. 1:4

B. *Described as:*
Deceitful . . . . . Eph. 4:22
Enticing . . . . . . James 1:14, 15
Harmful . . . . . . 1 Tim. 6:9
Numerous . . . . 2 Tim. 3:6

C. *Among the unregenerate, they:*
Live and walk
in . . . . Eph. 2:3
Are punished
with . . . . Rom. 1:24-32

D. *Among false teachers, they:*
Walk after . . . . 2 Pet. 2:10-22
Will prevail in the last
days . . . . 2 Pet. 3:3
Are received because
of . . . . 2 Tim. 4:3, 4

E. *Among Christians:*
Once lived in . . Eph. 2:3
Consider it
dead . . . . Col. 3:5
Deny . . . . Titus 2:12
Flee from . . . . . 2 Tim. 2:22
Not carry
out . . . . Gal. 5:16

Lute—*musical instrument*

Used in worship . . . Ps. 150:3

Luxuries

A. *Characteristic of:*
Egypt . . . . Heb. 11:24-27
Tyre . . . . Ezek. 27:1-27
Ancient
Babylon . . . . . . Dan. 4:30
Israel . . . . Amos 6:1-7
Persia . . . . Esth. 1:3-11
Harlot
Babylon . . . . . . Rev. 18:10-13

B. *Productive of:*
Temptation . . . . Josh. 7:20, 21
Physical
weakness . . . . . Dan. 1:8, 10-16

Moral decay . . . Nah. 3:1-19
Spiritual
decay . . . . Rev. 3:14-17

Luz—*almond tree*

1. Ancient Canaanite
   town . . . . Gen. 28:19
   Called
   Bethel . . . . Gen. 35:6
2. Hittite town . . . Judg. 1:23-26

Lycaonia—*a rugged, inland district of Asia Minor*

Paul preaches in three of its
cities . . . . Acts 14:6, 11

Lycia—*a province of Asia Minor*

Paul:

Visits Patara, a city
of . . . . Acts 21:1, 2
Lands at Myra, a city
of . . . . Acts 27:5, 6

Lydia—*from Lud*

1. Woman of Thyatira;
   Paul's first
   European   { Acts 16:14, 15,
   convert . . . . . . {   40
2. District of Asia Minor
   containing Ephesus, Smyrna,
   Thyatira, and
   Sardis . . . . Rev. 1:11

Lye

Used for
cleansing . . . . Jer. 2:22

Lying (see Liars)

Lyre—*a musical instrument*

Used in Babylon . . Dan. 3:7, 10

Lysanias—*ending sadness*

Tetrarch of
Abilene . . . . Luke 3:1

Lysias, Claudius

Roman captain who rescues
Paul . . . . Acts 23:10
Listens to Paul's
nephew . . . . Acts 23:16-22
Sends Paul to
Felix . . . . Acts 23:23-31
Felix awaits arrival
of . . . . Acts 24:22

Lystra—*a city of Lycaonia*

Visited by Paul . . . . Acts 14:6, 21
Lame man healed
here . . . . Acts 14:8-10
People of, attempt to worship Paul
and Barnabas . . . . . Acts 14:11-18
Paul stoned here . . 2 Tim. 3:11
Home of
Timothy . . . . Acts 16:1, 2

M

Maacah, Maachah—*oppression*

1. Daughter of
   Nahor . . . . Gen. 22:24
2. Small Syrian kingdom near Mt.
   Hermon . . . . Deut. 3:14
   Not possessed by
   Israel . . . . Josh. 13:13
   Called Syria-
   maachah . . . . . . 1 Chr. 19:6, 7
3. Machir's wife . . 1 Chr. 7:15, 16
4. One of Caleb's
   concubines . . . . 1 Chr. 2:48
5. Father of
   Shephatiah . . . . 1 Chr. 27:16
6. Ancestress of   { 1 Chr. 8:29
   King Saul . . . . { 1 Chr. 9:35
7. One of David's
   warriors . . . . 1 Chr. 11:43
8. Father of Achish, king of
   Gath . . . . 1 Kin. 2:39
9. David's wife and mother of
   Absalom . . . . . . 2 Sam. 3:3
10. Wife of Rehoboam; mother of
    King Abijah . . 2 Chr. 11:18-21
    Makes idol, is deposed as
    queen-
    mother . . . . 1 Kin. 15:13

Maachathites, Maacathites—*inhabitants of Maachah*

Not conquered by
Israel . . . . Josh. 13:13
Among Israel's
warriors . . . . 2 Sam. 23:34

See Maacah, Maacath 2

Maadai—*ornament of Yahweh*

Postexilic Jew; divorced his foreign
wife . . . . Ezra 10:34

Maadiah

Priest who returns from Babylon
with
Zerubbabel . . . . . . Neh. 12:5, 7

Same as Moadiah
in .... Neh. 12:17

Maai—*compassionate*

Postexilic
trumpeter .... Neh. 12:35, 36

Maarath—*barren place*

Town of Judah.... Josh. 15:1, 59

Maaseiah—*work of Yahweh*

1. Levite musician during David's
   reign......... 1 Chr. 15:16, 18
2. Levite captain under
   Jehoiada ...... 2 Chr. 23:1
3. Official during King Uzziah's
   reign......... 2 Chr. 26:11
4. Son of Ahaz, slain by
   Zichri........ 2 Chr. 28:7
5. Governor of Jerusalem during
   King Josiah's
   reign......... 2 Chr. 34:1, 8
6. Father of the false prophet
   Zedekiah...... Jer. 29:21
7. Father of Zephaniah the
   priest .... Jer. 21:1
8. Temple
   doorkeeper.... Jer. 35:4
9. Judahite postexilic
   Jew........... Neh. 11:5
10. Benjamin ancestor of a
    postexilic
    Jew........... Neh. 11:7
11, 12, 13. Three priests who
    divorced
    their foreign ⎰ Ezra 10:18, 21,
    wives ⎱   22
14. Layman who divorced his
    foreign wife.. Ezra 10:30
15. Representative who signs the
    covenant...... Neh. 10:1, 25
16. One who stood by
    Ezra .... Neh. 8:4
17. Levite who explains the
    Law........... Neh. 8:7
18. Priest who takes part in
    dedication
    services....... Neh. 12:41
19. Another participating
    priest .... Neh. 12:42
20. Father or ancestor of
    Azariah ...... Neh. 3:23

Maasai—*work of Yahweh*

Priest of Immer's
family............ 1 Chr. 9:12

Maath—*to be small*

Ancestor of
Christ........... Luke 3:26

Maaz—*anger*

Judahite .... 1 Chr. 2:27

Maaziah—*Yahweh is a refuge*

1. Descendant of Aaron; heads a
   course of
   priests .... 1 Chr. 24:1-18
2. One who signs the
   covenant...... Neh. 10:1, 8

Macedonia—*Greece* (northern)

A. *In Old Testament prophecy:*
   Called the kingdom of
   Greece........ Dan. 11:2
   Bronze part of
   Nebuchadnezzar's
   image......... Dan. 2:32, 39
   Described as a leopard with
   four heads .... Dan. 7:6, 17
   Described as a ⎰ Dan. 8:5, 21
   male goat .... ⎱ Dan. 11:4

B. *In New Testament missions:*
   Man of, appeals
   to............. Acts 16:9, 10
   Paul preaches in,
   at Philippi, ⎰ Acts 16:10-
   etc. .... ⎱ 17:14
   Paul's troubles
   in............. 2 Cor. 7:5
   Churches of,
   very ⎰ Rom. 15:26
   generous..... ⎱ 2 Cor. 8:1-5

Machbanai—*clad with a cloak*

One of David's mighty
men.............. 1 Chr. 12:13

Machbenah—*lump*

Son of Sheva...... 1 Chr. 2:49

Machi

Father of the Gadite
spy............. Num. 13:15

Machir—*sold*

1. Manasseh's only
   son .... Gen. 50:23
   Founder of the family of
   Machirites .... Num. 26:29
   Conqueror of
   Gilead........ Num. 32:39, 40
   Name used of Manasseh
   tribe .... Judg. 5:14

2. Son of
Ammiel . . . . . . 2 Sam. 9:4, 5
Provides food for
David . . . . 2 Sam. 17:27-29

Machnadebai—*gift of the noble one*

Son of Bani; divorced foreign
wife . . . . Ezra 10:34, 40

Machpelah—*double*

Field containing a cave; bought by
Abraham . . . . Gen. 23:9-18
Sarah and Abraham buried
here . . . . Gen. 23:19; 25:9,
10
Isaac, Rebekah, Leah, and Jacob
buried here . . . . Gen. 49:29-31

Madai—*middle*

Third son of Japheth; ancestor of
the Medes . . . . Gen. 10:2

Made—*something brought into being*

A. *Why Christ was made for us:*
Sin . . . . 2 Cor. 5:21
In our
likeness . . . . Phil. 2:7
High priest . . . . Heb. 6:20

B. *What Christians are made by
Him:*
Righteous . . . . . 2 Cor. 5:21
Heirs . . . . Titus 3:7

Madmannah—*dunghill*

Town in south
Judah . . . . Josh. 15:20, 31
Son of Shaaph . . . . 1 Chr. 2:49

Madmen—*dunghill*

Moabite town . . . . . Jer. 48:2

Madmenah—*dunghill, or dungheap*

Town near
Jerusalem . . . . Is. 10:31

Madness—*emotional or mental
derangement*

A. *Kinds of:*
Extreme
jealousy . . . . 1 Sam. 18:8-11
Extreme rage . . Luke 6:11

B. *Causes of:*
Disobedience to God's
Laws . . . . Deut. 28:28

Judgment
sent by   ⎧Dan. 4:31-34
God . . . . ⎨Zech. 12:4

C. *Manifestations of:*
Irrational
behavior . . . . . . 1 Sam. 21:12-15
Uncontrollable
emotions . . . . . . Mark 5:1-5
Moral decay . . . Jer. 50:38

See Insanity; Lunatic

Madon—*contention*

Canaanite town . . Josh. 12:19
Joins confederacy against
Joshua . . . . Josh. 11:1-12

Magbish—*strong*

Town of Judah . . . . Ezra 2:30

Magdala—*tower*

City of Galilee . . . . Matt. 15:39

Magdalene—*of Magdala*

Descriptive of one of the
Marys . . . . Matt. 27:56

See Mary 3

Magdiel—*God is glory*

Edomite duke . . . . . Gen. 36:43

Magi—*a priestly sect in Persia*

Brings gifts to the infant
Jesus . . . . Matt. 2:1, 2

Magic, magician—*the art of doing
superhuman things by
"supernatural" means*

A. *Special manifestations of:*
At the
exodus . . . . Ex. 7:11
During apostolic
Christianity . . . Acts 8:9, 18-24

B. *Modified power of:*
Acknowledged in
history . . . . Ex. 7:11, 22
Recognized in
prophecy . . . . . . 2 Thess. 2:9-12
Fulfilled in
antichrist . . . . . Rev. 13:13-18

C. *Failure of, to:*
Perform
miracles . . . . Ex. 8:18, 19
Overcome
demons . . . . Acts 19:13-19

D. *Condemnation of, by:*
Explicit Law . . . Lev. 20:27
Their
inability . . . . Ex. 8:18
Final
judgment . . . . . Rev. 21:8

See Divination

Magistrates—*civil rulers*

A. *Descriptive of:*
Ruler . . . . Judg. 18:7
Authorities . . . . Luke 12:11

B. *Office of:*
Ordained by
God . . . . Rom. 13:1, 2
Due proper
respect . . . . Acts 23:5

C. *Duties of:*
To judge:
Impartially . . . Deut. 1:17
Righteously . . . Deut. 25:1

D. *Christian's attitude toward:*
Pray for . . . . 1 Tim. 2:1, 2
Honor . . . . Ex. 22:28
Submit to . . . . . . 1 Pet. 2:13, 14

Magnanimity—*loftiness*

A. *Expressions of, toward men:*
Abram's offer to
Lot . . . . Gen. 13:7-12
Jacob's offer to
Esau . . . . Gen. 33:8-11

B. *Expression of, toward God:*
Moses' plea for
Israel . . . . Ex. 32:31-33
Paul's prayer for
Israel . . . . Rom. 9:1-3

Magnificat—*he magnifies*

Poem of the Virgin
Mary . . . . Luke 1:46-55

Magnify—*to make or declare great*

A. *Concerning God's:*
Name . . . . 2 Sam. 7:26
Word . . . . Ps. 138:2
Law . . . . Is. 42:21
Christ's
name . . . . Acts 19:17

B. *Duty of, toward God:*
With others . . . . Ps. 34:3
With thanks-
giving . . . . Ps. 69:30
In the body . . . . Phil. 1:20

Magog—*region of Gog*

People among Japheth's
descendants . . . . . . Gen. 10:2
Associated with
Gog . . . . Ezek. 38:2
Representatives of final
enemies . . . . Rev. 20:8

Magor-Missabib—*terror on every side*

Name indicating Pashur's
end . . . . Jer. 20:3

Magpiash—*collector of a cluster of stars*

Signer of the
covenant . . . . Neh. 10:20

Mahalaleel—*praise of God*

1. Descendant of
Seth . . . . Gen. 5:12
Ancestor of
Christ . . . . Luke 3:37
2. Postexilic
Judahite . . . . . . Neh. 11:4

Mahalath—*sickness*

1. One of Esau's
wives . . . . Gen. 28:9
Called
Basemath . . . . . Gen. 36:3, 4, 13
2. One of Rehoboam's
wives . . . . 2 Chr. 11:18
3. Musical term . . Ps. 53 (Title)

Mahanaim—*two camps*

Name given by Jacob to a sacred
site . . . . Gen. 32:2
On boundary between Gad and
Manasseh . . . . . . Josh. 13:26, 30
Assigned to Merarite
Levites . . . . Josh. 21:38
Becomes Ishbosheth's
capital . . . 2 Sam. 2:8-29
David flees to, during Absalom's
rebellion . . . . 2 Sam. 17:24, 27
Solomon places Ahinadab
over . . . . 1 Kin. 4:14

Mahaneh Dan—*camp of Dan*

Place between Zorah and
Eshtaol . . . . Judg. 13:25

Maharai—*swift, hasty*

One of David's mighty
men . . . . 2 Sam. 23:28
Becomes an army
captain . . . . 1 Chr. 27:13

Mahath—*grasping*

1. Kohathite
Levite........1 Chr. 6:35
2. Levite in Hezekiah's
reign..........2 Chr. 29:12
Appointed an overseer of
tithes ....2 Chr. 31:13

Mahavite

Applied to Eliel....1 Chr. 11:46

Mahazioth—*visions*

Levite musician ...1 Chr. 25:4, 30

Maher-Shalal-Hash-Baz—*spoil speeds, prey hastes*

Symbolic name of Isaiah's second son; prophetic of the fall of Damascus and Samaria ....Is. 8:1-4

Mahlah—*disease*

1. Zelophehad's
daughter......Num. 26:33
2. Child of Ham-
moleketh......1 Chr. 7:18

Mahli—*weak, silly*

1. Eldest son of
Merari ....Num. 3:20
Father of three
sons ....1 Chr. 6:29
Father of tribal
family........Num. 3:33
Called
Mahali ....Ex. 6:19
2. Another Merarite
Levite; {1 Chr. 6:47
nephew {1 Chr. 23:23
of 1 {1 Chr. 24:30

Mahlon—*sickly*

Husband of Ruth; without
child ....Ruth 1:2-5

Mahol—*dance*

Father of certain wise
men..............1 Kin. 4:31

Mahseiah

Ancestor of
Baruch ....Jer. 32:12

Maid—*a young woman*

A. *Characteristics of:*
Obedient.......Ps. 123:2

B. *Provision for:*
Physical needs
of............Prov. 27:27
Accepted as
wives ....Gen. 30:3

Maidservant

Expressive of humility:

Ruth.............Ruth 2:13
Woman of {1 Sam. 28:7, 21,
Endor ....{ 22
Mary.............Luke 1:38

Mail

Letters were
sent ....Esth. 3:13

Mainsail—*the lowest sail on the foremast, providing directional control*

Hoisted ....Acts 27:40

Maintenance—*provision for support*

Household
supply............Prov. 27:27
King's service.....Ezra 4:14
Solomon's
supply............1 Kin. 4:22, 23

Majesty—*the dignity and power of a ruler*

A. *Of God:*
Splendor of ....Is. 2:2, 19, 21
Voice of ....Ps. 29:4
Clothed with...Ps. 93:1
B. *Of Christ:*
Promised to....Mic. 5:2-4
Laid upon .....Ps. 21:5
Eyewitness ....2 Pet. 1:16
C. *Of kings:*
Solomon.......1 Chr. 29:25
Nebuchad- {Dan. 4:28, 30, 36
nezzar ......{Dan. 5:18-21

Makaz—*end, boundary*

Town in Judah...1 Kin. 4:9

Makheloth—*assemblies*

Israelite camp.....Num. 33:25, 26

Makkedah—*place of shepherds*

Canaanite town assigned to
Judah ....Josh. 15:20, 41

Maktesh—*mortar*

Valley in
Jerusalem ....Zeph. 1:11

Malachi—*my messenger*

Prophet and
writer ....Mal. 1:1

Malachi, the Book of—*a book of the Old Testament*

God's love for
Jacob ....Mal. 1:1-5
The priesthood
rebuked ....Mal. 1:6–2:17
The messenger of the
LORD ....Mal. 3:1-5
The Day of the
LORD ....Mal. 4:1-6

Malcam—*their king*

Benjamite leader ..1 Chr. 8:9

Malchiah (see Malchijah)

Malchiel—*God is king*

Grandson of Asher; founder of
Malchielites ......Gen. 46:17

Malchijah, Malchiah—*Yahweh is king*

1. Gershonite
Levite.........1 Chr. 6:40
2. The father of ⎰1 Chr. 9:12
Pashur ......⎱Jer. 21:1
Called
Melchiah......Jer. 21:1
3. Head of a priestly
division ....1 Chr. 24:1, 6, 9
4. Royal prince...Jer. 38:1, 6
5, 6. Two sons of Parosh; divorced
their foreign
wives ....Ezra 10:25
7. Son of Harim; divorced his
foreign wife..Ezra 10:31
Helps rebuild
walls.........Neh. 3:11
8. Son of Rechab; repairs
gates..........Neh. 3:14
9. Postexilic
goldsmith .....Neh. 3:31
10. Ezra's
assistant ......Neh. 8:4
11. Signer of the
covenant......Neh. 10:1, 3
12. Choir
member.......Neh. 12:42

Malchiram—*the king is exalted*

Son of King
Jeconiah ....1 Chr. 3:17, 18

Malchishua—*the king is salvation*

Son of King
Saul..............1 Sam. 14:49
Killed at Gilboa ...1 Sam. 31:2

Malchus—*king*

Servant of the high
priest............John 18:10

Malformation—*irregular features*

Of a giant........2 Sam. 21:20

Malice—*active intent to harm others*

A. *Causes of:*
Unregenerate ⎰Prov. 6:14-16, 18,
heart........⎱ 19
Satanic
hatred ....1 John 3:12
Jealousy.......1 Sam. 18:8-29
Racial
prejudice......Esth. 3:5-15

B. *Christian's attitude toward:*
Pray for those guilty
of............Matt. 5:44
Clean out .....1 Cor. 5:7, 8
Put away......Eph. 4:31
Put off........Col. 3:8
Laying aside ...1 Pet. 2:1
Avoid manifes-
tations........1 Pet. 2:16

C. *Characteristics:*
Unregen- ⎰Rom. 1:29
erate......⎱Titus 3:3
God's wrath ...Rom. 1:18, 29
Brings own
punishment ...Ps. 7:15, 16

Malignity

Full of envy......Rom. 1:29

Mallothi—*I have talked*

Son of Heman ....1 Chr. 25:4, 26

Mallows—*saltiness*

Perennial shrub that grows in salty
marshes..........Job 30:4

Malluch—*reigning*

1. Merarite
Levite.........1 Chr. 6:44
2. Chief of postexilic
priests ....Neh. 12:2, 7
3. Son of Bani; divorced his
foreign wife...Ezra 10:29
4. Son of Harim; divorced his
foreign wife...Ezra 10:32

5, 6. Two who sign the
covenant......Neh. 10:4, 27

Malta—*an island in the Mediterranean*

Paul's shipwreck..Acts 28:1-8

Mammon—*wealth*

Served as a master other than
God..............Matt. 6:24

Mamre—*firmness*

1. Town or district near
Hebron.......Gen. 23:19
West of
Machpelah....Gen. 23:17, 19
Abraham dwelt by the oaks
of............Gen. 13:18
2. Amorite, brother of
Eschol........Gen. 14:13

Man—*human being, male or female*

A. *Original state of:*
Created for God's
pleasure and $\{$ Is. 43:7
glory........$\{$ Rev. 4:11
Created by
God...........Gen. 1:26, 27
Made in God's
image.........Gen. 9:6
Formed of
dust..........Gen. 2:7
Made upright ..Eccl. 7:29
Endowed with $\{$ Gen. 2:19, 20
intelligence ..$\{$ Col. 3:10
Wonderfully
made.........Ps. 139:14-16
Given wide
dominion.....Gen. 1:28
From one......Acts 17:26-28
Male and
female.......Gen. 1:27
Superior to
animals.......Matt. 10:31
Living
being.........Gen. 2:7

B. *Sinful state of:*
Result of Adam's
disobe- $\{$ Gen. 2:16, 17
dience- $\{$ Gen. 3:1-6
Makes all
sinners........Rom. 5:12
Brings $\{$ Gen. 2:16, 17,
physical $\{$ 19
death $\{$ Rom. 5:12-14
Makes spiritually
dead..........Eph. 2:1

C. *Redeemed state of:*
Originates in God's
love...........John 3:16
Provides salvation
for............Titus 2:11
Accomplished by Christ's
death.........1 Pet. 1:18-21
Fulfills the new
covenant......Heb. 8:8-13
Entered by new
birth.........John 3:1-12

D. *Final state of:*
Continues
eternally......Matt. 25:46
Cannot be
changed......Luke 16:26
Determined
by faith or by $\{$ John 3:36
unbelief......$\{$ 2 Thess. 1:6-10

E. *Christ's relation to:*
Gives light
to...........John 1:9
Knows nature
of............John 2:25
Took nature
of............Heb. 2:14-16
In the
likeness......Rom. 8:3
Only Mediator
for............1 Tim. 2:5
Died for......Heb. 9:26,28
1 Pet. 1:18-21

F. *Certain aspects of:*
First—Adam...1 Cor. 15:45, 47
Last—Christ...1 Cor. 15:45
Natural—unregen-
erate..........1 Cor. 2:14
Outward—
physical.......2 Cor. 4:16
Inner—
spiritual......Rom. 7:22
New—
regenerate....Eph. 2:15

Man of sin (see Antichrist)

Manaen—*comforter*

Prophet and teacher in church at
Antioch..........Acts 13:1

Manahath—*resting place*

1. Son of
Shobal........Gen. 36:23
2. City of exile for sons of
Ehud.........1 Chr. 8:6
Citizens of, called Manaheth-
ites...........1 Chr. 2:54

Manasseh—*making to forget*

1. Joseph's firstborn
   son ....Gen. 41:50, 51
   Adopted by
   Jacob ....Gen. 48:5, 6
   Loses his birthright to
   Ephraim ......Gen. 48:13-20
   Ancestor of a
   tribe ....Num. 1:34, 35
2. Sons of ....Num. 26:28-34
   Census of.....Num. 1:34, 35
   One half of, desire region in
   east Jordan ...Num. 32:33-42
   Help Joshua against
   Canaanites ...Josh. 1:12-18
   Division of, into eastern and
   western ....Josh. 22:7
   Region assigned to eastern
   half ....Deut. 3:12-15
   Land assigned to western
   half ....Josh. 17:1-13
   Zelophehad's daughters
   included in....Josh. 17:3, 4
   Question concerning
   altar ....Josh. 22:9-34
   Joshua's challenge
   to.............Josh. 17:14-18
   City (Golan) of refuge
   in.............Josh. 20:8
   Did not drive out
   Canaanites....Judg. 1:27, 28
   Gideon, a member
   of.............Judg. 6:15
   Some of, help
   David.........1 Chr. 12:19-31
   Many support
   Asa ....2 Chr. 15:9
   Attend
   Passovers .....2 Chr. 30:1-18
   Idols destroyed
   in.............2 Chr. 31:1
3. Intentional change of Moses'
   name to.......Judg. 18:30
4. Son and successor of
   Hezekiah, king of
   Judah.........2 Kin. 21:1
   Reigns wickedly;
   restores   {2 Kin. 21:1-16
   idolatry .....{2 Chr. 33:1-9
   Captured and taken to
   Babylon.......2 Chr. 33:10, 11
   Repents and is
   restored......2 Chr. 33:12, 13
   Removes idols and
   altars ....2 Chr. 33:14-20
5, 6. Two men who divorce their
   foreign
   wives ....Ezra 10:30, 33

Mandrake—*a rhubarb-like herb, having narcotic qualities*

Supposed to
induce human   {Gen. 30:14-16
fertility ......{Song 7:13

Manger—*a feeding place for cattle*

Place of Jesus'
birth ....Luke 2:7, 12
Called "crib".......Is. 1:3
Same as "stall"
in ....Luke 13:15

Manifest—*to make something clear or evident*

A. *Applied to God's:*
   Nature.........Rom. 1:19
   Revelation.....Col. 1:26
   Knowledge ....2 Cor. 2:14
   Love...........1 John 4:9

B. *Applied to Christ's:*
   Nature.........1 Tim. 3:16
   Presence.......John 1:31
   Life............1 John 1:2

C. *Applied to evil:*
   Works of the
   flesh ....Gal. 5:19
   Man's:
   Deeds ....John 3:21
   Folly ....2 Tim. 3:9

Manliness—*masculine characteristics at their best*

A. *Qualities of:*
   Self-control....1 Cor. 9:25-27
   Mature under-
   standing ......1 Cor. 14:20
   Courage in
   danger........2 Sam. 10:11, 12
   Endure
   hardship ......2 Tim. 2:3-5

B. *Examples of:*
   Caleb..........Num. 13:30
   Joshua.........Josh. 1:1-11
   Jonathan ......1 Sam. 14:1,
                           6-14
   Daniel ....Dan. 6:1-28

Manna—*what is it?*

A. *Features regarding:*
   Description
   of.............Num. 11:7-9
   Bread given   {Ex. 16:4, 15
   by God.......{John 6:30-32
   Previously
   unknown .....Deut. 8:3, 16

Fell at
evening......Num. 11:9
Despised by
people......Num. 11:4-6
Ceased at
conquest......Josh. 5:12

B. *Illustrative of:*
God's glory....Ex. 16:7
Christ as the true
bread........John 6:32-35

Manners—*a way of life*

A. *Evil kinds:*
Sexual
immorality....Gen. 19:31-36
Customs of other
nations.......Lev. 20:23
Careless
living.........Judg. 18:7

B. *Good kinds:*
Prayer.........Matt. 6:9
Faithfulness ...Acts 20:18

Manoah—*rest, quiet*

Danite; father of
Samson ....Judg. 13:1-25

Mantle—*a garment*

Female garment...Is. 3:22
Outer   {1 Kin. 19:13, 19
garment (robe) ..{2 Kin. 2:8, 13, 14

Maoch—*oppression*

Father of Achish, king of
Gath ....1 Sam. 27:2

Maon—*abode*

1. Village in
Judah........Josh. 15:55
David stayed
at............1 Sam. 23:24, 25
House of
Nabal.........1 Sam. 25:2
2. Shammai's
son ....1 Chr. 2:45
3. People called Maonites among
Israel's
oppressors ....Judg. 10:12
Called
Meunites......2 Chr. 26:7
Listed among {Ezra 2:50
returnees.....{Neh. 7:52

Mara—*bitter*

Name chosen by
Naomi...........Ruth 1:20

Marah—*bitterness*

First Israelite camp after passing
through the Red
Sea..............Num. 33:8, 9

Maralah—*downward slope*

Village in
Zebulun..........Josh. 19:11

Marble—*crystalline limestone*

In columns.......Esth. 1:6
In Babylon's
trade.............Rev. 18:12

Mareshah—*summit*

1. Father of
Hebron ....1 Chr. 2:42
2. Judahite.....1 Chr. 4:21
3. Town of
Judah.........Josh. 15:44
City built for defense by
Rehoboam ....2 Chr. 11:5, 8
Great battle here between Asa
and Zerah.....2 Chr. 14:9-12

Mariners—*sailors; seamen*

Skilled ....1 Kin. 9:27
Fearful............Jon. 1:5
Weeping ....Ezek. 27:8-36
Storm-tossed.....Acts 27:27-31

Mark

As object, thing:

Sign for preserva-
tion.............Ezek. 9:4-6
Sign of those   {Rev. 13:16, 17
following   {Rev. 14:9, 11
antichrist........{Rev. 20:4

Mark (John)—*a large hammer*

Son of Mary, a
believer ....Acts 12:12
Cousin of
Barnabas.........Col. 4:10
Returns with Barnabas to
Antioch ....Acts 12:25
Leaves Paul and Barnabas at
Perga ....Acts 13:13
Paul refuses to take him
again..............Acts 15:37-39
Paul's approval
of.................2 Tim. 4:11
Peter's
companion ....1 Pet. 5:13
The author of the second
Gospel ....Mark 1:1 (Title)

Mark, the Gospel of—*a book of the New Testament*

John the Baptist .. Mark 1:1-11
Choosing of the
disciples.......... Mark 3:13-19
Parables .... Mark 4:1-34
Galilean ⎰Mark 1:21-45
tours ....⎱Mark 6:1-44
Peter's
confession........ Mark 8:27-30
The
transfiguration ... Mark 9:1-13
Foretelling of Jesus'
death............. Mark 10:32-34
Entry into
Jerusalem .... Mark 11:1-11
Controversy with ⎰Mark
Jews ....⎱ 11:27-12:40
Events of the ⎰Mark
crucifixion........⎱ 14:43-15:47
The resurrection .. Mark 16:1-20

Marketplace

Place of:

Greetings .... Matt. 23:7
Public trial .... Acts 16:19, 20
Evangelism .... Acts 17:17

Maroth—*bitter fountains*

Town of Judah.... Mic. 1:12

Marred face

Disqualifies for
service .... Lev. 21:18

Marriage

A. *Described as:*

Instituted by
God.......... Gen. 2:18-24
Honorable among
all .... Heb. 13:4
Permanent
bond.......... Matt. 19:6
Intimate
bond.......... Matt. 19:5
Blessed of God for having
children....... Gen. 1:27, 28
Dissolved by
death.......... Rom. 7:2, 3
Means of sexual
love.......... Prov. 5:15-19
Centered in love and
obedience ..... Eph. 5:21-33
Worthy of Jesus'
presence ...... John 2:1-11

B. *Prohibitions concerning:*

Near of kin .... Lev. 18:6-18

Fornication excludes
remarriage .... Matt. 5:32
Polygamy
forbidden ..... Lev. 18:18
Idol
worshipers .... Ex. 34:16

C. *Arrangements for* (among Hebrews):

Arranged by
parents .... Gen. 21:21
Parties
consenting .... Gen. 24:8
Parental concern
in............. Gen. 26:34, 35
Romance involved
in............. Gen. 29:10, 11
Commitment considered
binding ...... Gen. 24:58, 60
Unfaithfulness in, brings God's
judgment ..... Heb. 13:4

D. *Ceremonies of* (among Hebrews):

Time of joy .... Jer. 7:34
Bride richly
attired .... Ps. 45:13-15
Bride veiled... Gen. 24:65
Bridegroom decks
himself........ Is. 61:10
Wedding feast in bridegroom's
house........ Matt. 22:1-10
Distinctive clothing of
guests........ Matt. 22:11, 12
Christ
attends........ John 2:1-11
Festivities
following...... John 2:8-10
Gifts bestowed
at............. Ps. 45:12
Parental blessing
on .... Gen. 24:60
Change of
name .... Ps. 45:10, 16
Consummation
of............. Gen. 29:23
Proof of
virginity ...... Deut. 22:13-21

E. *Purposes of:*

Man's
happiness ..... Gen. 2:18
Continuance of the
race.......... Gen. 1:28
Godly
offspring ..... Mal. 2:14, 15
Prevention of
fornication.... 1 Cor. 7:2, 9
Complete
satisfac- ⎰Prov. 5:19
tion.......... ⎱1 Tim. 5:14

F. *Denial of:*
As a prophetic
sign .... Jer. 16:2
For a specific
purpose ...... Matt. 19:10-12
As a sign of
apostasy ..... 1 Tim. 4:1-3
To those in
heaven .... Matt. 22:30

G. *Figurative of:*
God's union with
Israel .... Is. 54:5
Christ's union with His
Church ...... Eph. 5:23-32

Marrow—*the vascular tissue which occupies the cavities of bones*

A. *Used literally of:*
Healthy man...Job 21:23, 24
Inner being....Heb. 4:12

B. *Used figuratively of:*
Spiritual
sustenance....Ps. 63:5

Marsena—*forgetful man*

Persian prince.....Esth. 1:14

Mars Hill (see Areopagus)

Marsh—*an area of grassy, soft, wet land*

Spelled "marish" ..Ezek. 47:11

Mart—*market*

Tyre, to all
nations...........Is. 23:1-4

Martha—*lady, mistress*

Sister of Mary and
Lazarus ....John 11:1, 2
Welcomes Jesus into her
home.............Luke 10:38
Rebuked by
Christ ....Luke 10:38-42
Affirms her faith ..John 11:21-32
Serves supper .....John 12:1-3

Martyrdom—*death for the sake of one's faith*

A. *Causes of:*
Evil deeds ....1 John 3:12
Antichrist's
persecution ...Rev. 13:15
Harlot Babylon's
hatred ....Rev. 17:5, 6
Our Christian
faith ....Rev. 6:9

B. *Believer's attitude toward:*
Remember Christ's
warning........Matt. 10:21, 22
Do not fear....Matt. 10:28
Be prepared....Matt. 16:24, 25
Be ready to, if
necessary .....Acts 21:13

C. *Examples of:*
Prophets and
apostles.......Luke 11:50, 51
John the
Baptist........Mark 6:18-29
Stephen ....Acts 7:58-60
Early disciples of the
Lord..........Acts 9:1, 2

Marvel—*to express astonishment*

A. *Expressed by Christ because of:*
Centurion's
faith ....Matt. 8:10

B. *Expressed by men because of Christ's:*
Power ....Matt. 8:27
Knowledge ....John 7:15

Mary—*same as Miriam*

1. Jesus'
mother........Matt. 1:16
Prophecies
concerning....Is. 7:14
Engaged to
Joseph ....Luke 1:26, 27
Told of virginal
conception ....Luke 1:28-38
Visits
Elizabeth......Luke 1:39-41
Offers praise ...Luke 1:46-55
Gives birth to
Jesus.........Luke 2:6-20
Flees with Joseph to
Egypt.........Matt. 2:13-18
Mother of other
children........Mark 6:3
Visits Jerusalem with
Jesus.........Luke 2:41-52
Intrusted to John's
care..........John 19:25-27
2. Wife of
Clopas ....John 19:25
Mother of James and
Joses.........Matt. 27:56
Looking on the crucified
Savior ....Matt. 27:55, 56
Follows Jesus' body to the
tomb.........Matt. 27:61
Sees the risen
Lord ....Matt. 28:1, 9, 10

Tells His disciples
of resur-
rection . . . . Matt. 28:7-9 / Luke 24:9-11

3. Mary
Magdalene . . . . Matt. 27:56, 61
Delivered from seven
demons . . . . Luke 8:2
Contributes to support of
Christ . . . . Luke 8:2, 3
Looks on the crucified
Savior . . . . Matt. 27:55, 56
Follows Jesus' body to the
tomb . . . . Matt. 27:61
Visits Jesus' tomb with Mary,
mother of
James . . . . Mark 16:1-8
Tells the
disciples . . . . . John 20:2
First to see
the risen / Mark 16:9
Lord . . . . . \ John 20:11-18

4. Mary, the sister of Martha and
Lazarus . . . . . . John 11:1, 2
Commended by
Jesus . . . . Luke 10:38-42
Grieves for / John 11:19, 20,
Lazarus . . . . \ 28-33
Anoints
Jesus . . . . John 12:1-3, 7
Commended again by
Jesus . . . . Matt. 26:7-13

5. Mark's
mother . . . . Acts 12:12-17

6. Christian disciple at
Rome . . . . Rom. 16:6

Mash

Division of the
Arameans . . . . . . Gen. 10:23
Called Meshech . . 1 Chr. 1:17

Mashal

Refuge city given to the
Levites . . . . 1 Chr. 6:74
Called / Josh. 19:26
Mishal . . . . \ Josh. 21:30

Mason—one who lays stones or bricks

Sent by Hiram to help:
David . . . . 2 Sam. 5:11
Solomon . . . . 1 Kin. 5:18
Used in Temple:
Repairs . . . . 2 Chr. 24:12
Rebuilding . . . . . Ezra 3:7

Masrekah—vineyard

City of Edom . . . . Gen. 36:36

Massa—burden

Son of Ishmael . . . . Gen. 25:12, 14

Massah and Meribah—testing and strife

Named together . . . Ex. 17:7
Named
separately . . . . Deut. 33:8
First, at Rephidim, Israel just out
of Egypt . . . . Ex. 17:1-7
Levites proved . . . . Deut. 33:8
Second, at Kadesh-Barnea, 40 years
later . . . . Num. 20:1-13
Moses and Aaron rebel
here . . . . Num. 20:24
Tragic events recalled by
Moses . . . . Deut. 6:16
Events later
recalled . . . . Ps. 81:7
Used as a boundary of the
land . . . . Ezek. 47:17, 19
Used for spiritual
lesson . . . . Heb. 3:7-12

Mast—a vertical support for sails and rigging on a sailing ship

A. *Used literally of:*
Cedars of
Lebanon . . . . . . Ezek. 27:5

B. *Used figuratively of:*
Strength of
enemies . . . . . . Is. 33:23

Master

A. *Descriptive of:*
Owner of
slaves . . . . Ex. 21:4-6
King . . . . 1 Chr. 12:19
Prophet . . . . 2 Kin. 2:3, 5

B. *Kinds of:*
Unmerciful . . . 1 Sam. 30:13-15
Angry . . . . Luke 14:21
Good . . . . Gen. 24:9-35
Believing . . . . . 1 Tim. 6:2
Heavenly . . . . . Col. 4:1

Master builder

Paul describes himself
as . . . . 1 Cor. 3:10

Master workmen—craftsmen

Bezaleel . . . . Ex. 31:1-5
Hiram of Tyre . . . . 1 Kin. 7:13-50
Aquila and
Priscilla . . . . Acts 18:2, 3
Demetrius . . . . Acts 19:24

Mate—the male or female of a pair

God provides for . . Is. 34:15, 16

Materialistic—*concerned for worldly goods only*

Christ condemns . . Luke 12:16-21
Sadducees
described . . . . Acts 23:8
Christians forbidden to live
as . . . . 1 Cor. 15:30-34

Mathematics, spiritual

A. *General:*

Addition:
God's Word . . . . Deut. 4:2
Knowledge will
increase . . . . Dan. 12:4
Increased
riches . . . . Ps. 62:10

Subtraction:
God's command-
ments . . . . Deut. 12:32

Multiplication:
Human
family . . . . Gen. 1:28

B. *Unrighteous:*

Addition:
Wealth . . . . Ps. 73:12
Guilt . . . . 2 Chr. 28:13
Sin . . . . Is. 30:1

Subtraction:
Wealth obtained by
fraud . . . . Prov. 13:11
Life $\begin{cases}$ Ps. 55:23
shortened . . . . $\end{cases}$ Prov. 10:27

Multiplication:
Sorrow by
idolatry . . . . Ps. 16:4
Trans-
gression . . . . Prov. 29:16

C. *Righteous:*

Addition:
Years . . . . Prov. 3:1, 2
Prov. 4:10
Blessing without
sorrow . . . . Prov. 10:22
By putting God
first . . . . Matt. 6:33
Graces . . . . 2 Pet. 1:5-7
In latter
years . . . . Job 42:12

Subtraction:
Disease . . . . Ex. 15:26
Taken from
evil . . . . Is. 57:1

Multiplication:
Prosperity . . . . . Deut. 8:1, 11-13
Length of $\begin{cases}$ Deut. 11:18-21
days . . . . $\end{cases}$ Prov. 9:11
Mercy, peace,
love . . . . Jude 2
Church . . . . Acts 9:31

Matred—*expulsion*

Mother-in-law of Hadar (Hadad),
an Edomite
king . . . . Gen. 36:39

Matri—*rainy*

Saul's Benjamite
family . . . . 1 Sam. 10:21

Mattan—*gift*

1. Priest of Baal . . 2 Kin. 11:18
Killed by the
people . . . . 2 Chr. 23:16, 17
2. Father of
Shephatiah . . . . Jer. 38:1

Mattanah—*gift*

Israelite camp . . . . . Num. 21:18, 19

Mattaniah—*gift of Yahweh*

1. King Zedekiah's original
name . . . . 2 Kin. 24:17
2. Son of Mica, a Levite and
Asaphite . . . . . . 1 Chr. 9:15
3. Musician, son of
Heman . . . . 1 Chr. 25:4, 16
4. Spirit of the LORD came
upon . . . . 2 Chr. 20:14
5. Levite under King
Hezekiah . . . . . . 2 Chr. 29:13
6. Postexilic Levite and
singer . . . . Neh. 11:17
7. Levite
gatekeeper . . . . Neh. 12:25
8. Postexilic
Levite . . . . Neh. 12:35
9. Levite in charge of
treasuries . . . . . Neh. 13:13
10, 11, 12, 13. Four postexilic Jews
who divorced foreign
wives . . . . Ezra 10:26-37

Mattathah—*gift* (of God)

Son of Nathan; ancestor of
Christ . . . . Luke 3:31

Mattathias—*Greek form of Mattathiah*

1. Postexilic ancestor of
Christ . . . . Luke 3:25

2. Another postexilic ancestor of
Christ........Luke 3:26

Mattattah—*gift of Yahweh*

Jew who put away his foreign
wife.............Ezra 10:33

Mattenai—*gift of Yahweh*

1. Priest in the time of
Joiakim.......Neh. 12:19
2, 3. Two postexilic Jews who put
away their foreign
wives.........Ezra 10:33, 37

Matter—*something*

A. *Descriptive of:*
Lawsuit.......1 Cor. 6:1
Sum of
something....Eccl. 12:13
Love affair.....Ruth 3:18
News.........Mark 1:45

B. *Kinds of:*
Evil.............Ps. 64:5
Unknown......Dan. 2:5, 10

Matthan—*gift*

Ancestor of
Joseph..........Matt. 1:15, 16

Matthat—*gift*

1. Ancestor of
Christ........Luke 3:24
2. Another ancestor of
Christ.........Luke 3:29

Matthew—*gift of Yahweh*

Tax gatherer......Matt. 9:9
Becomes Christ's
follower..........Matt. 9:9
Appointed an
apostle..........Matt. 10:2, 3
Called Levi, the son of
Alphaeus........Mark 2:14
Entertains Jesus with a great
feast..........Mark 2:14, 15
In the upper
room..........Acts 1:13
Author of the first
Gospel..........Matt. 1:1 (Title)

Matthew, the Gospel of—*a book of the New Testament*

Events of Jesus'　⎰Matt. 1:18–
birth.............⎱　2:23
John the Baptist..Matt. 3:1-17
The temptation...Matt. 4:1-11
Jesus begins His
ministry..........Matt. 4:12-17

The Great
Sermon..........Matt. 5:1-7:29
Christ, about John the
Baptist..........Matt. 11:1-19
Conflict with the Pharisees and
Sadducees.......Matt. 15:39–16:6
Peter's
confession.......Matt. 16:13-20
Prophecy of death and
resurrection.....Matt. 20:17-19
Jerusalem entry...Matt. 21:1-11
Authority of　　⎰Matt.
Jesus............⎱　21:23–22:14
Woes to the
Pharisees........Matt. 23:1-36
Garden of
Gethsemane......Matt. 26:36-56
Crucifixion and
burial............Matt. 27:27-66
Resurrection of
Christ............Matt. 28:1-20

Matthias—*gift of Yahweh*

Chosen by lot to replace
Judas.............Acts 1:15-26

Mattithiah—*gift of Yahweh*

1. Korahite
Levite.........1 Chr. 9:31
2. Levite, son of Jeduthun, and
Temple
musician......1 Chr. 15:18, 21
3. Jew who put away his foreign
wife...........Ezra 10:43
4. Levite attendant to
Ezra..........Neh. 8:4

Mattock—*an agricultural instrument for digging and hoeing*

Sharpened for
battle............1 Sam. 13:20-22

Maturity, spiritual

Do away with childish
things............1 Cor. 13:11
Be mature in your
thinking..........1 Cor. 14:20
Solid food is for...Heb. 5:11-14
Overcoming the evil
one...............1 John 2:14

Mazzaroth—*the signs of the Zodiac or a constellation*

Descriptive of God's
power............Job 38:32

Meah, tower of the

Restored by
Eliashib..........Neh. 3:1

Meal—*ground grain used for food*

One-tenth of an ephah
of ....Num. 5:15
Used in
offerings..........1 Kin. 4:22
"Then bring".....2 Kin. 4:41
Millstones and
grind.............Is. 47:2
Three measures
of ....Matt. 13:33

Meals—*times of eating*

A. *Times of:*
Early
morning ......John 21:4-12
At noon (for
laborers) ......Ruth 2:14
In the
evening ....Gen. 19:1-3

B. *Extraordinary and festive:*
Guests
invited........Matt. 22:3, 4
Received with a
kiss ....Luke 7:45
Feet washed...Luke 7:44
Anointed with
ointment......Luke 7:38
Proper dress ...Matt. 22:11, 12
Seated according to
rank ....Matt. 23:6
Special guest
honored.....1 Sam. 9:22-24
Entertainment
provided ......Luke 15:25
Temperate habits
taught ....Prov. 23:1-3
Intemperance
condemned ...Amos 6:4-6

See Entertainment; Feasts

Means of grace

A. *Agents of:*
Holy Spirit.....Gal. 5:16-26
God's Word....1 Thess. 2:13
Prayer.........Rom. 8:15-27
Christian
fellowship.....Mal. 3:16-18
Public
worship.......1 Thess. 5:6
Christian
witnessing ....Acts 8:4

B. *Words expressive of:*
Stir up the
gift ....2 Tim. 1:6
Neglect not the spiritual
gift ....1 Tim. 4:14

Take heed to the
ministry.......Col. 4:17
Grow in
grace ....2 Pet. 3:18

C. *Use of, brings:*
Assurance .....2 Pet. 1:5-12
Stability ....Eph. 4:11-16

D. *Enemies of:*
Devil ....1 Thess. 3:5
World ....1 John 2:15-17
Coldness.......Rev. 3:14-18

Mearah—*cave*

Unconquered by
Joshua ....Josh. 13:1, 4

Measure—*a standard of size, quantity
or values*

A. *Objectionable:*
Differing
(different).....Deut. 25:14, 15
Short ....Mic. 6:10
Using themselves as a
gauge.........2 Cor. 10:12

B. *As indicative of:*
Earth's
weight ....Is. 40:12
Punishment
inflicted.......Matt. 7:2

C. *Figurative of:*
Great size .....Hos. 1:10
Sin's ripeness ..Matt. 23:32
The Spirit's
infilling ......John 3:34
Man's ability...2 Cor. 10:13
Perfection of
faith ....Eph. 4:13, 16

Measuring line—*a cord of specified
length for measuring*

Signifies hope .....Jer. 31:38-40
                 Zech. 2:1

Mebunnai—*built*

One of David's mighty
men..............2 Sam. 23:27
Called Sibbechai ..1 Chr. 11:29

Mecherathite—*a dweller in Mecharah*

Descriptive of Hepher, one of
David's mighty
men..............1 Chr. 11:36

Meconah—*foundation*

Town of Judah....Neh. 11:25, 28

Medad—*beloved*

One of the seventy elders receiving
the Spirit........Num. 11:26-29

Medan—*judgment*

Son of Abraham by
Keturah........Gen. 25:1, 2

Meddling—*interfering with the affairs
of others*

Brings a king's
death............2 Chr. 35:21-24
Christians........1 Pet. 4:15
Such called
"busybodies"......2 Thess. 3:11

Medeba—*full waters*

Old Moabite
town.............Num. 21:29, 30
Assigned to
Reuben...........Josh. 13:9, 16
Syrians defeated
here.............1 Chr. 19:6, 7
Reverts to Moab..Is. 15:2

Medes, Media—*the people and country
of the Medes*

A. *Characteristics of:*
Part of Medo-Persian
empire........Esth. 1:19
Inflexible laws
of..............Dan. 6:8, 12, 15
Among those at
Pentecost......Acts 2:9

B. *Kings of, mentioned in the
Bible:*
Cyrus...........Ezra 1:1
Ahasuerus......Ezra 4:6
Artaxerxes I...Ezra 4:7
Darius.........Ezra 6:1
Xerxes.........Dan. 11:2
Artaxerxes.....Ezra 6:14

C. *Place of, in Bible history:*
Israel deported
to..............2 Kin. 17:6
Babylon falls
to..............Dan. 5:30, 31
"Darius the Mede," new ruler of
Babylon........Dan. 5:31
Daniel rises high in the
kingdom of ...Dan. 6:1-28
Cyrus, king of Persia, allows
Jews to
return.........2 Chr. 36:22, 23
Esther and Mordecai live under
Ahasuerus, king
of..............Esth. 1:3, 19

D. *Prophecies concerning:*
Agents in Babylon's
fall............Is. 13:17-19
Cyrus, king of, God's
servant ....Is. 44:28
"Inferior"
kingdom ......Dan. 2:39
Compared to a
bear ....Dan. 7:5
Kings of ......Dan. 11:2
War with
Greece........Dan. 11:2

Mediation—*a friendly intervention
designed to render assistance*

A. *Purposes of:*
Save a life .....Gen. 37:21, 22
Save a
people ....Ex. 32:11-13
Obtain a wife ..1 Kin. 2:13-25
Obtain
justice ....Job 9:33

B. *Motives prompting:*
People's fear ..Deut. 5:5
Regard for human
life............Jer. 38:7-13
Sympathy for (2 Kin. 5:6-8
a sick man ...(Matt. 17:15

C. *Methods used:*
Intense
prayer ....Deut. 9:20-29
Flattery........1 Sam. 25:23-35
Appeal to self-preserva-
tion...........Esth. 4:12-17

Mediator, Christ our

A. *His qualifications:*
Bears God's
image, man's (Phil. 2:6-8
likeness......(Heb. 2:14-17
Is both sinless
and sin-   (Is. 53:6-10
bearer........(Eph. 2:13-18
Endures God's wrath,
brings God's righ-
teousness .....Rom. 5:6-19
Is sacrifice
and the   (Heb. 7:27
priest ....(Heb. 10:5-22

B. *How He performs the function,
by:*
Took our
nature ....1 John 1:1-3
Died as our
substitute.....1 Pet. 1:18, 19
Reconciled us to
God...........Eph. 2:16

Medicine—*something prescribed to cure an illness*

A. *General prescriptions:*
Merry heart ...Prov. 15:13
Rest ....Ps. 37:7-11
Sleep ....John 11:12, 13
Quarantine ....Lev. 12:1-4
Sanitation .....Deut. 23:10-14

B. *Specific prescriptions:*
Figs ....Is. 38:21
Leaves.........Ezek. 47:12
Wine ....1 Tim. 5:23

C. *Used figuratively of:*
Salvation ......Jer. 8:22
Incurable-
ness.........Jer. 46:11
Spiritual stubborn-
ness..........Jer. 51:8, 9

See Diseases

Meditation—*quiet contemplation of spiritual truths*

A. *Objects of, God's:*
Word..........Ps. 119:148
Law ....Josh. 1:8
Instruction ....1 Tim. 4:15

B. *Value of, for:*
Under-
standing ......Ps. 49:3
Spiritual
satisfaction ...Ps. 63:5, 6
Superior
knowledge ....Ps. 119:99

C. *Extent of:*
All the day ....Ps. 119:97
At evening.....Gen. 24:63
In night
watches.......Ps. 119:148

Mediterranean Sea

Described as:

Sea ....Gen. 49:13
Great ⎰Josh. 1:4
Sea..............⎱Josh. 9:1
Sea of the
Philistines........Ex. 23:31
Western Sea .....Deut. 11:24
                  Joel 2:20
                  Zech. 14:8

Mediums

A. *Described as:*
Source of
defilement ....Lev. 19:31

Abomination...Deut. 18:10-12
Whisperers ....Is. 8:19

B. *The practicers, to be:*
Cut off ....Lev. 20:6
Put to death ...Lev. 20:27

C. *Consulted by:*
Saul ....1 Sam. 28:3-25
Manasseh......2 Kin. 21:6

D. *Condemned by:*
Josiah ....2 Kin. 23:24

Meek

Receiving the
Word.............James 1:21
Stating our
assurance ....James 3:13

Megiddo—*place of troops*

City conquered by
Joshua ....Josh. 12:21
Assigned to
Manasseh ....Josh. 17:11
Inhabitants of, made
slaves ....Judg. 1:27, 28
Canaanites defeated
here...............Judg. 5:19-21
Site of Baana's
headquarters .....1 Kin. 4:12
Fortified by
Solomon ....1 Kin. 9:15-19
King Ahaziah dies
here...............2 Kin. 9:27
King Josiah killed
here...............2 Kin. 23:29, 30
Mentioned in
prophecy.........Zech. 12:11
Site of
Armageddon .....Rev. 16:16

Mehetabeel—*God benefits*

1. King Hadar's
wife...........Gen. 36:39
2. Father of
Delaiah ....Neh. 6:10

Mehida—*renowned*

Ancestor of a family of returning
Temple
servants..........Ezra 2:52

Mehir—*price*

Judahite ....1 Chr. 4:11

Meholathite—*a native of Meholah*

Descriptive of
Adriel............1 Sam. 18:19

Mehujael—*smitten of God*

Cainite; father of
Methusael.......Gen. 4:18

Mehuman—*faithful*

Eunuch under King
Ahasuerus.......Esth. 1:10

Me Jarkon—*waters of yellow color*

Territory of Dan near
Joppa ....Josh. 19:40, 46

Melatiah—*Yahweh has set free*

Postexilic
workman.........Neh. 3:7

Melchi—*my king*

Two ancestors of
Jesus.............Luke 3:24, 28

Melchizedek—*king of righteousness*

A. *Described as:*
King of
Salem.........Gen. 14:18
Priest of God ..Gen. 14:18
Receiver of a tenth of Abram's
goods ....Gen. 14:18-20
King of righ-
teousness .....Heb. 7:2
Without
parentage.....Heb. 7:3
Great man.....Heb. 7:4

B. *Typical of Christ's:*
Eternity ....Heb. 7:3
Priesthood.....Ps. 110:4
Kingship.......Heb. 8:1

Melea

Ancestor of
Jesus.............Luke 3:31

Melech—*king*

Son of Micah, grandson of
Jonathan.........1 Chr. 8:35

Melichu—*reigning*

Head of a
household ....Neh. 12:14

Melon—*the watermelon*

Desired by Israelites in
wilderness........Num. 11:5

Melting—*making a solid a liquid*

Used figuratively of:

Complete
destruction.......Ex. 15:15

Discourage-
ment.............Josh. 7:5
Defeatism........Josh. 5:1
National discourage-
ment ....Is. 19:1
Destruction of the
wicked ....Ps. 68:2
God's presence....Mic. 1:4
Testings.........Jer. 9:7
Troubled sea ......Ps. 107:26
Christ's pain on the
cross ....Ps. 22:14

Mem

Letter of the Hebrew
alphabet.........Ps. 119:97-104

Member—*a part of a larger whole*

A. *Descriptive of:*
Parts of the
body ....Matt. 5:29, 30
Union with
Christ.........1 Cor. 6:15
True Church...1 Cor. 12:27

B. *Of the body:*
Effect of sin
in.............Rom. 7:5
Struggle in ....Rom. 7:23

C. *Illustrative of:*
Variety of Christian
gifts ....Rom. 12:4, 5
God's design
in.............1 Cor. 12:18, 24

Memorials—*things established to commemorate an event or a truth*

A. *Established by men:*
Jacob's stone ..Gen. 28:18-22
Altar at
Jordan ....Josh. 22:9-16
Feast of
Purim.........Esth. 9:28

B. *Established by God:*
Passover.......Ex. 12:14
Pot of
manna ....Ex. 16:32-34
Lord's
Supper........Luke 22:19

Memories—*the ability to revive past experiences*

A. *Uses of, to recall:*
Past
blessings ......Ezra 9:5-15
Past sins.......Josh. 22:12-20
God's
blessings ......Neh. 9:1-38

God's
promises......Neh. 1:8-11
Christian
truths........2 Pet. 1:15-21
Prophecies.....John 2:19-22
Lost opportun-
ities..........Ps. 137:1-3

B. *Aids to:*
Reminder......2 Sam. 12:1-13
Prick of
conscience....Gen. 41:9
Holy Spirit.....John 14:26

Memphis—*haven of good*

Ancient capital of
Egypt ....Hos. 9:6
Prophesied against by
Isaiah ....Is. 19:13
Jews flee to ......Jer. 44:1
Called Noph ......Jer. 46:19
Denounced by the
prophets..........Jer. 46:19

Memucan

Persian prince.....Esth. 1:14-21

Menahem—*comforter*

Cruel king of
Israel............2 Kin. 15:14-18

Menan

Ancestor of
Jesus.............Luke 3:31

Mending—*restoring something*

Of nets...........Matt. 4:21
Used
figuratively......Luke 5:36

Mene—*numbered*

Sentence of
doom.............Dan. 5:25, 26

Mene, Tekel, Upharsin

Written by God ...Dan. 5:5, 25
Interpreted by
Daniel............Dan. 5:24-29

Menstruation—*a woman's monthly flow*

Intercourse during,
prohibited........Lev. 18:19
End of, in old
age................Gen. 18:11

Called:

"Sickness" ....Lev. 20:18
"The manner of
women".........Gen. 31:35

Meonenim—*augurs*

Tree or place where soothsayers
performed........Judg. 9:37

Meonothai—*my habitations*

Judahite ....1 Chr. 4:14

Mephaath—*splendor*

Reubenite town ...Josh. 13:18
Assigned to Merarite
Levites ....Josh. 21:34, 37
Repossessed by
Moabites ....Jer. 48:21

Mephibosheth—*one who destroys shame*

1. Son of King
Saul ....2 Sam. 21:8
2. Grandson of King Saul; crippled
son of
Jonathan......2 Sam. 4:4-6
Reared by
Machir........2 Sam. 9:4-6
Sought out and honored by
David.........2 Sam. 9:1-13
Accused by
Ziba ....2 Sam. 16:1-4
Later explains his side to
David.........2 Sam. 19:24-30
Spared by
David.........2 Sam. 21:7
Father of
Micha.........2 Sam. 9:12
Called Merib-
Baal ....1 Chr. 8:34

Merab—*increase*

King Saul's eldest
daughter ....1 Sam. 14:49
Saul promises her to David, but
gives her to
Adriel ....1 Sam. 18:17-19

Meraiah—*rebellious*

Postexilic priest ...Neh. 12:12

Meraioth—*rebellious*

1. Levite ....1 Chr. 6:6, 7
2. Son of Ahitub and father of
Zadok ....1 Chr. 9:11
3. Priestly household in Joiakim's
time ....Neh. 12:15
Called
Meremoth.....Neh. 12:3

Merari—*bitter*

1. Third son of Levi; brother of
   Gershon and
   Kohath ...... Gen. 46:11
   Goes with Jacob to
   Egypt .... Gen. 46:8, 11
2. Descendants of Merari; called
   Merarites .... Num. 26:57
   Divided into two
   groups .... Ex. 6:19
   Duties assigned
   to .... Num. 3:35-37
   Follow Judah in
   march .... Num. 10:14, 17
   Twelve cities assigned
   to .... Josh. 21:7, 34-40
   Superintend Temple
   music .... 1 Chr. 6:31-47
   Help David bring up the
   ark .... 1 Chr. 15:1-6
   Divided into
   courses .... 1 Chr. 23:6-23
   Their duties
   described ..... 1 Chr. 26:10-19
   Participate in cleansing the
   house of the
   LORD .... 2 Chr. 29:12-19
   After exile, help
   Ezra .... Ezra 8:18, 19

Merarites (see Merari 2)

Merathaim—*double rebellion*

Name applied to
Babylon .... Jer. 50:21

Merchandise—*things for sale in trade*

A. *Characteristics of:*
   Countries employed
   in .... Is. 45:14
   Men occupied
   with .... Matt. 22:5
   Not mixed with spiritual
   things .... John 2:16
   To be
   abolished ..... Rev. 18:11, 12

B. *Figurative of:*
   Wisdom's
   profit .... Prov. 3:13, 14
   Gospel trans-
   formation ..... Is. 23:18

Merchants—*traders*

Characteristics of:

Crossed the sea ... Is. 23:2
Lamentation
over .... Ezek. 27:2-36

Some do not observe the
Sabbath .... Neh. 13:19-21
Burden people with
debts .... Neh. 5:1-13
Peddle goods ...... Neh. 13:16
Trade with
farmers .... Prov. 31:24
Form guilds .... Neh. 3:8-32
Destroyed with
Babylon .... Rev. 18:3-19
Sailors, in Solomon's
service .... 1 Kin. 9:27, 28
Bring gold to
Solomon .... 2 Chr. 9:14
Bring horses to
Solomon .... 2 Chr. 9:28

Mercy

A. *Described as:*
   Great .... Is. 54:7
   Sure .... Is. 55:3
   Abundant ..... 1 Pet. 1:3
   Tender .... Ps. 25:6
   New every
   morning ..... Lam. 3:22, 23

B. *Of God, seen in:*
   Regener-
   ation .... 1 Pet. 1:3
   Salvation ..... Titus 3:5
   Christ's
   mission ...... Luke 1:72, 78
   Forgiveness ... Ps. 51:1

C. *In the Christian life:*
   Received in
   salvation ..... 1 Cor. 7:25
   Taught as a principle of
   life .... Matt. 5:7
   Practiced as a
   gift .... Rom. 12:8
   Evidenced in God's
   provinces ..... Phil. 2:27
   Obtained in
   prayer .... Heb. 4:16
   Reason of conse-
   cration .... Rom. 12:1
   Reason for
   hope .... Jude 21

D. *Special injunctions concerning:*
   Put on .... Col. 3:12

E. *Examples of:*
   David to
   Saul .... 1 Sam. 24:10-17
   Christ to
   sinners .... Matt. 9:13

F. *Attitude of believers, to:*
Cast themselves
on ....2 Sam. 24:14
Look for ......Jude 21

Mercy seat—*the covering of the ark*

Made of pure
gold.............Ex. 25:17
Blood sprinkled
upon..........Lev. 16:14, 15
God manifested
over............Lev. 16:2
Figurative of
Christ ....Heb. 9:5-12

Mered—*rebellion*

Judahite ....1 Chr. 4:17
Had two wives....1 Chr. 4:17, 18

Meremoth—*elevations*

1. Signer of the
   covenant......Neh. 10:5
   Called
   Meraioth......Neh. 12:15
2. One who divorced his foreign
   wife..........Ezra 10:34, 36
3. Priest, son of Uriah; weighs
   silver and
   gold.........Ezra 8:33
   Repairs wall of
   Jerusalem.....Neh. 3:4, 21

Meres—*the forgetful one*

Persian prince..'...Esth. 1:13, 14

Merib-Baal—*Baal contends*

Another name for
Mephibosheth ....1 Chr. 8:34

Merit—*reward given for something
done additionally*

A. *Of man, impossible because:*
None is good ..Rom. 3:12
None is
righteous .....Rom. 3:10
We are all
sinful ....Is. 6:5
Our good comes from
God..........1 Cor. 15:9, 10
Our righteousness:
Is unavail-
ing...........Matt. 5:20
Is Christ's ....2 Cor. 5:21
Cannot save ..Rom. 10:1-4

B. *Of Christ:*
Secured by
obedience.....Rom. 5:17-21

Secured by His
death ....Is. 53:10-12
Obtained by
faith ....Phil. 3:8, 9

Merodach—*bold*

Supreme deity of the
Babylonians .....Jer. 50:2
Otherwise called
Bel...............Is. 46:1

Merodach-Baladan—*Merodach has
given a son*

Sends ambassadors to
Hezekiah.........Is. 39:1-8
Also called Berodach-
Baladan.......2 Kin. 20:12

Merom—*high place*

Lake on Jordan north of the Sea of
Galilee ....Josh. 11:5, 7

Meronothite

Citizen of
Meronoth ....1 Chr. 27:30

Meroz—*refuge*

Town cursed for failing to help the
Lord ....Judg. 5:23

Merry—*a spirit of gaiety; cheerful*

A. *Good, comes from:*
Heart..........Prov. 15:13, 15
Restoration....Jer. 30:18, 19
Christian joy ..James 5:13

B. *Evil, results from:*
Careless
unconcern ....Judg. 9:27
Drunkenness ..1 Sam. 25:36
False
optimism......1 Kin. 21:7
Sinful glee.....Rev. 11:10

Mesha—*retreat*

1. Border of Joktan's descendants ....Gen. 10:30
2. Benjamite .....1 Chr. 8:8, 9
3. Son of Caleb...1 Chr. 2:42
4. King of
   Moab ....2 Kin. 3:4

Meshach—*the shadow of the prince*

Name given to
Mishael ....Dan. 1:7
Advanced to high
position ....Dan. 2:49
Remains faithful in
testing ....Dan. 3:13-30

Meshech—*tall*

1. Son of
   Japheth ....Gen. 10:2
   Called
   Mesech ....Ps. 120:5
   Famous
   traders........Ezek. 27:13
   Confederates with
   Gog..........Ezek. 38:2, 3
   Inhabitants of the nether
   world ....Ezek. 32:18, 26
2. Son of Shem...1 Chr. 1:17
   Same as
   Mash ....Gen. 10:23

Meshelemiah—*Yahweh repays*

Father of
Zechariah ....1 Chr. 9:21
Porter in the
Temple............1 Chr. 26:1
Called
Shelemiah........1 Chr. 26:14

Meshezabeel—*God delivers*

1. Postexilic wall
   repairer ....Neh. 3:4
2. One who signs
   covenant......Neh. 10:21
3. Judahite ....Neh. 11:24

Meshillemith—*recompense*

Postexilic priest ...1 Chr. 9:10-12
Called
Meshillemoth.....Neh. 11:13

Meshillemoth—*acts of recompense*

Ephraimite
leader ....2 Chr. 28:12

Meshobab—*restored*

Descendant of
Simeon...........1 Chr. 4:34-38

Meshullam—*recompensed; rewarded*

1. Benjamite .....1 Chr. 8:17
2. Gadite leader ..1 Chr. 5:11, 13
3. Shaphan's
   grandfather ...2 Kin. 22:3
4. Hilkiah's
   father.........1 Chr. 9:11
5. Son of
   Zerubbabel...1 Chr. 3:19
6. A priest........1 Chr. 9:10-12
7. Kohathite
   overseer ......2 Chr. 34:12
8. A second
   Benjamite.....1 Chr. 9:7

9. Another
   Benjamite.....1 Chr. 9:8
10. Man commissioned to secure
    Levites........Ezra 8:16
11. Levite who supports Ezra's
    reforms ....Ezra 10:15
12. One who divorced his foreign
    wife..........Ezra 10:29
13. Postexilic
    workman .....Neh. 3:4, 30
    His daughter married Tobiah's
    son ....Neh. 6:18
14. Postexilic
    workman .....Neh. 3:6
15. One of Ezra's
    attendants ....Neh. 8:4
16, 17. Two priests who sign
    covenant......Neh. 10:7, 20
18, 19. Two priests in Joiakim's
    time ....Neh. 12:13, 16
20. Porter ....Neh. 12:25
21. Participant in dedication
    services ......Neh. 12:33

Meshullemeth—*feminine form of Meshullam*

Wife of King
Manasseh ....2 Kin. 21:18, 19

Mesopotamia—*the country between two rivers*

Abraham's native
home.............Acts 7:2
Place of Laban's
household ....Gen. 24:4, 10, 29
Called:
Padan Aram .....Gen. 25:20
Syria...........Gen. 31:20, 24
Balaam came
from ....Deut. 23:4
Israel enslaved
to................Judg. 3:8, 10
Chariots and horsemen hired
from ....1 Chr. 19:6
Called Haran; conquered by
Sennacherib....2 Kin. 19:12, 16
People from, at
Pentecost ....Acts 2:9

Messenger—*one sent on a mission*

A. *Mission of, to:*
Appease
wrath........Gen. 32:3-6
Ask for
favors.......Num. 20:14-17
Spy out........Josh. 6:17, 25
Assemble a
nation ....Judg. 6:35

Secure
  provisions.....1 Sam. 25:4-14
Relay news ....1 Sam. 11:3-9
Stir up war ....Judg. 11:12-28
Sue for
  peace ....2 Sam. 3:12, 13
Offer
  sympathy .....1 Chr. 19:2
Call for help ...2 Kin. 17:4
Issue an
  ultimatum ....1 Kin. 20:2-9
Deliver the LORD's
  message.......Hag. 1:13

B. *Reception of:*
Rejected.......Deut. 2:26-30
Humiliated.....1 Chr. 19:2-4
Rebuked.......2 Kin. 1:2-5, 16

C. *Significant examples of:*
John the
  Baptist.......Mal. 3:1
Paul's thorn ...2 Cor. 12:7
Gospel   (2 Cor. 8:23
  workers......(Phil. 2:25

Messiah, the

A. *Described as:*
Seed of
  woman........Gen. 3:15
Promised   (Gen. 12:1-3
  seed..........(Gal. 3:16
Star out of   (Num. 24:17
  Jacob ....(Luke 3:34
Of Judah's   (Gen. 49:10
  tribe ....(Heb. 7:14
Son of David ..Is. 11:1-10
              Matt. 1:1
Prophet.......Deut. 18:15-19
              Acts 3:22, 23
Priest after Melchi-
  zedek's   (Ps. 110:4
  order........(Heb. 6:20
King of   (Jer. 23:5
  David's line (Luke 1:32, 33
Son of God ....Ps. 2:7, 8
              Acts 13:33
Son of Man....Dan. 7:13
              Mark 8:38
Immanuel .....Is. 7:14
              Matt. 1:22, 23
Branch ....Jer. 23:5
              Zech. 3:8
Headstone.....Ps. 118:22
              1 Pet. 2:4, 7
Servant........Is. 42:1-4
              Matt. 12:18, 21

B. *Mission of, to:*
Introduce the
  new   (Jer. 31:31-34
  covenant....(Matt. 26:26-30
Preach the   (Is. 61:1-3
  Gospel ......(Luke 4:17-19
Bring peace...Is. 9:6, 7
              Heb. 2:14-16
Die for man's (Is. 53:4-6
  sin...........(1 Pet. 1:18-20
Unite God's   (Is. 19:23-25
  people ....(Eph. 2:11-22
Call the   (Is. 11:10
  Gentiles......(Rom. 15:9-12
Rule from
  David's   (Ps. 45:5-7
  throne.......(Acts 2:30-36
Be a priest....Zech. 6:12, 13
              Heb. 1:3
              Heb. 8:1
Destroy   (Rom. 16:20
  Satan ....(1 John 3:8
Bring in
  everlasting (Dan. 9:24
  righteous-   (Matt. 3:15
  ness.........(2 Cor. 5:21

C. *Christ the true Messiah, proved
   by:*
Birth at   (Mic. 5:2
  Bethlehem ...(Luke 2:4-7
Born of a   (Is. 7:14
  virgin ....(Matt. 1:18-25
Appearing in
  the second   (Hag. 2:7, 9
  Temple.......(John 18:20
Working   (Is. 35:5, 6
  miracles......(Matt. 11:4, 5
Rejection by the
  Jews ....John 1:11
Vicarious   (Is. 53:1-12
  death ....(1 Pet. 3:18
Coming at the
  appointed   (Dan. 9:24-27
  time ....(Mark 1:15

D. *Other prophecies concerning:*
Worship ....Ps. 72:10-15
              Matt. 2:1-11
Flight to   (Hos. 11:1
  Egypt........(Matt. 2:13-15
Forerunner ....Mal. 3:1
              Mark 1:1-8
Zeal ....Ps. 69:9
              John 2:17
Triumphal   (Zech. 9:9, 10
  entry........(Matt. 21:1-11
Betrayal ......Ps. 41:9
              Mark 14:10

Being sold . . . . Zech. 11:12
Matt. 26:15
Silent defense ⎰ Is. 53:7
⎱ Matt. 26:62, 63
Being spit on . Is. 50:6
Mark 14:65
Being crucified with sinners ⎰ Is. 53:12
⎱ Matt. 27:38
Piercing of hands and feet ⎰ Ps 22:16
⎱ John 19:36, 37
Being mocked . . . . . ⎰ Ps. 22:6-8
⎱ Matt. 27:39-44
Dying drink . . . Ps. 69:21
John 19:29
Side pierced . . Zech. 12:10
John 19:34
Prayer for the enemies . . . . . . ⎰ Ps. 109:4
⎱ Luke 23:34
Garments gambled for . . . . ⎰ Ps. 22:18
⎱ Mark 15:24
Death without broken bones . . . . ⎰ Ps. 34:20
⎱ John 19:33
Separation from God . . . . ⎰ Ps. 22:1
⎱ Matt. 27:46
Burial with the rich . . . . . ⎰ Is. 53:9
⎱ Matt. 27:57-60
Preservation from decay . . . ⎰ Ps. 16:8-10
⎱ Acts 2:31
Ascension . . . . . Ps. 68:18
Eph. 4:8-10
Exaltation . . . . . Ps. 2:6-12
Phil. 2:9, 10

See Christ

Metallurgy—*mining and processing of metal*

Mining and refining . . . . Job 28:1, 2
Heat needed . . . . . . Jer. 6:29

Metaphors—*graphic comparisons*

A. *Concerning God, as:*
Rock . . . . Deut. 32:4
Sun and shield . . . . Ps. 84:11
Consuming fire . . . . Heb. 12:29
Husbandman . . John 15:1

B. *Concerning Christ, as:*
Bread of life . . John 6:35
Light of the world . . . . John 8:12
Door . . . . John 10:9

Good Shepherd . . . . . John 10:14
Way, Truth, Life . . . . John 14:6
True vine . . . . . . John 15:1

C. *Concerning Christians, as:*
Light . . . . Matt. 5:14
Salt . . . . Matt. 5:13
Epistles . . . . 2 Cor. 3:3
Living stones . . 1 Pet. 2:5

D. *Concerning the Bible, as:*
Fire . . . . Jer. 5:14
Light; lamp . . . Ps. 119:105
Sword . . . . Eph. 6:17

Metheg Ammah—*power of the metropolis*

Probably a figurative name for Gath . . . . 2 Sam. 8:1

Methuselah—*man of a javelin*

Son of Enoch . . . . . Gen. 5:21
Oldest man on record . . . . Gen. 5:27
Ancestor of Christ . . . . Luke 3:37

Methusael—*man of God*

Cainite, father of Lamech . . . . Gen. 4:18

See Maon

Meunites

Arabian tribe near Mount Seir . . . . 2 Chr. 26:7
Smitten by Simeonites . . . . 1 Chr. 4:39-42
Descendants of, serve as Nethinim . . . . Ezra 2:50

Mezahab—*waters of gold*

Grandfather of Mehetabel, wife of King Hadar . . . . . . Gen. 36:39

Mezobaite—*found of Yahweh*

Title given Jasiel . . 1 Chr. 11:47

Mibhar—*choice*

One of David's mighty men . . . . 1 Chr. 11:38

Mibsam—*sweet odor*

1. Son of Ishmael . . . . Gen. 25:13
2. Simeonite . . . . . . 1 Chr. 4:25

Mibzar—*stronghold*

Edomite duke.....Gen. 36:42

Micah, Micha, Micah—*who is like Yahweh?*

1. Ephraimite who hires a traveling Levite.........Judg. 17:1-13
2. Reubenite .....1 Chr. 5:1, 5
3. Son of Mephibosheth ....2 Sam. 9:12
4. Descendant of Asaph.........1 Chr. 9:15
   Called Michaiah......Neh. 12:35
5. Kohathite Levite.........1 Chr. 23:20
6. Father of Abdon .....2 Chr. 34:20
7. Prophet, contemporary of Isaiah........ {Is. 1:1 {Mic. 1:1
8. One who signs the covenant......Neh. 10:11

Micah, the Book of—*a book of the Old Testament*

Judgment of Israel and Judah ....Mic. 1:2-16
Promise to the remnant.........Mic. 2:12, 13
Judgment on those in authority.........Mic. 3:1-12
The coming peace.............Mic. 4:1-8
The Redeemer from Bethlehem.......Mic. 5:1-4
Hope in God ......Mic. 7:8-20

Micaiah, Michaiah—*who is like Yahweh?*

1. Wife of King Rehoboam ....2 Chr. 13:2
2. Prophet who predicts Ahab's death ....1 Kin. 22:8-28
3. Teaching official ....2 Chr. 17:7
4. Father of Achbor........2 Kin. 22:12
   Called Micah ..2 Chr. 34:20
5. Contemporary of Jeremiah......Jer. 36:11-13
6. Descendant of Asaph.........Neh. 12:35
7. Priest in dedication service ....Neh. 12:41

Michael—*who is like God?*

1. Father of an Asherite spy ....Num. 13:13
2, 3. Two Gadites ....1 Chr. 5:13, 14
4. Levite ancestor of Asaph.........1 Chr. 6:40
5. Issacharian chief..........1 Chr. 7:3
6. Benjamite .....1 Chr. 8:16
7. Manassite chief under David........1 Chr. 12:20
8. Father of Omri..........1 Chr. 27:18
9. Son of King Jehoshaphat ......2 Chr. 21:2
10. Father of Zebadiah......Ezra 8:8
11. Chief prince ...Dan. 10:13, 21
    Stands against forces.........Dan. 10:21
    Disputes with Satan ....Jude 9
    Fights the dragon ....Rev. 12:7-9

Michal—*who is like God?*

Daughter of King Saul........1 Sam. 14:49
Loves and marries David ....1 Sam. 18:20-28
Saves David from Saul.............1 Sam. 19:9-17
Given to Palti.....1 Sam. 25:44
David demands her from Abner............2 Sam. 3:13-16
Ridicules David; becomes barren........2 Sam. 6:16-23

Michmash, Michmas—*hidden place*

Town occupied by Saul's army ....1 Sam. 13:2
Site of battle with Philistines....... {1 Sam. 13:5, 11, 16, 23
Scene of Jonathan's victory .....1 Sam. 14:1-18
Mentioned in prophecy.........Is. 10:28
Exiles return ......Ezra 2:1, 27

Michmethah—*lurking place*

Place on the border of Ephraim and Manasseh ....Josh. 16:5, 6

Michri—*purchase price*

Benjamite.........1 Chr. 9:8

Michtam

Word of unknown meaning used in
titles of...........Ps. 16; 56 to 60

Middin—*extensions*

In the
wilderness.......Josh. 15:61

Midian—*place of judgment*

1. Son of Abraham by
Keturah......Gen. 25:1-4
2. Region in the Arabian desert
occupied by
the   (Gen. 25:6
Midianites....(Ex. 2:15

Midianites—*descendants of Midian*

A. *Characteristics of:*
Descendants of Abraham by
Keturah......Gen. 25:1, 2
Moses fled to..Ex. 2:15
Retain worship of
Yahweh.......Ex. 2:16
Ruled by
kings ....Num. 31:8
Immoral
people ....Num. 25:18

B. *Contacts with Israel:*
Joining Moab in
cursing.......Num. 22:4-7
Seduction of...Num. 25:1-18
Defeat because
of.............Num. 31:1-18
Being sent as
punishment...Judg. 6:1-10

Midnight

A. *Significant happenings at:*
Death in
Egypt.........Ex. 11:4
Prayer
meeting.......Acts 16:25
Possible time of Christ's
return.......Matt. 25:6

B. *Other happenings at:*
Quick
departure .....Judg. 16:2, 3
Friend's need ..Luke 11:5
Great fear .....Job 34:20

Midwife—*one who assists at childbirth*

Helps in the birth of a
child ....Gen. 35:17

Migdal El—*tower of God*

City of Naphtali...Josh. 19:38

Migdal Gad—*a tower of Gad* (fortune)

Town of Judah....Josh. 15:37

Migdol—*tower*

1. Israelite encamp-
ment..........Ex. 14:2
2. Place in Egypt to which Jews
flee ....Jer. 44:1

Might—*effective power*

A. *God's:*
Irresistible.....2 Chr. 20:6
God's hand
is ....1 Chr. 29:12
Unutterable....Ps. 106:2

B. *Man's physical:*
Boasted in, brings
destruction....Dan. 4:30-33
Not to be gloried
in.............Deut. 8:17
Will fail.......Jer. 51:30
Exhortation
concerning....Eccl. 9:10

C. *Man's intellectual and moral:*
Invites self-
glory..........Jer. 9:23
Makes salvation
difficult ......1 Cor. 1:26

D. *Man's spiritual, comes from:*
God ....Eph. 1:19
Christ........Col. 1:28, 29
The Spirit......Mic. 3:8

Mighty

Literally of:

Hunter............Gen. 10:9
Nation .....'.....Gen. 18:18
Prince.............Gen. 23:6
Waters............Ex. 15:10
Hand ....Ex. 32:11
Acts ....Deut. 3:24
Men of valor......1 Chr. 7:9-11
Warrior ....2 Chr. 32:21
Kings ....Ezra 4:20
Strength ....Job 9:4
Fear ....Job 41:25

Mighty man—*a powerful man; a valiant warrior*

Men of renown....Gen. 6:4
Gideon............Judg. 6:11, 12
Warriors of
David ....2 Sam. 10:7

Migron—*precipitous* (very steep)

1. Place where Saul
stayed ....1 Sam. 14:2

2. Village north of
Michmash.....Is. 10:28

Mijamin—*from the right side*

1. Descendant of
Aaron........1 Chr. 24:1, 6, 9
2. Chief priest; returns with
Zerubbabel....Neh. 12:5, 7
Probably same as 1
3. Divorced his foreign
wife..........Ezra 10:25
4. Priest who signs the
covenant......Neh. 10:7
Same as Minjamin
in............Neh. 12:17, 41

Mikloth—*rods*

1. Ruler under
David........1 Chr. 27:4
2. Benjamite .....1 Chr. 8:32

Mikneiah—*possession of Yahweh*

Porter and musician in David's
time.............1 Chr. 15:18, 21

Milalai—*eloquent*

Levite musician in dedication
service ....Neh. 12:36

Milcah—*counsel*

1. Wife of
Nahor........Gen. 11:29
Mother of eight
children....Gen. 22:20-22
Grandmother of
Rebekah.....Gen. 22:23
2. Daughter of
Zelophehad ...Num. 26:33

Milcom—*an Ammonite god*

Solomon went
after ....1 Kin. 11:5
Altar destroyed by
Josiah..........2 Kin. 23:12, 13

Mildew—*a disease of grain due to dampness*

Threatened as a
punishment ......Deut. 28:22
Sent upon Israel ..Amos 4:9
Removed by
repentance ....1 Kin. 8:37-39

Mile—*a thousand paces* (about 12/13 of an English mile)

Used
illustratively......Matt. 5:41

See Jewish measures

Miletus—*a city of Asia Minor*

Paul meets Ephesian elders
here.............Acts 20:15-38
Paul leaves Trophimus
here.............2 Tim. 4:20

Milk—*a white liquid secreted by mammary glands*

A. *Produced by:*
Goats.........Prov. 27:27
Sheep........Deut. 32:14
Camels ....Gen. 32:15
Cows..........1 Sam. 6:7, 10
Humans ......Is. 28:9

B. *Figurative of:*
Abundance ....Deut. 32:14
Egypt's supposed
blessings .....Num. 16:13
Elementary
teaching ......1 Cor. 3:2
Pure
doctrine.......1 Pet. 2:2

Mill, millstone

A. *Uses of:*
Grinding
grain..........Num. 11:8
Weapon ....Judg. 9:53
Pledge,
forbidden ....Deut. 24:6
Weight ....Matt. 18:6

B. *Operated by:*
Women........Matt. 24:41
Maidservant ...Ex. 11:5
Prisoners.....Judg. 16:21

C. *Figurative of:*
Courage ....Job 41:24
Old age........Eccl. 12:4
Desolation ....Jer. 25:10

Millennium—*thousand years*

Latin for a thousand
years.............Rev. 20:1-10

Millet—*a cereal*

Ezekiel makes bread
of ....Ezek. 4:9

Millo—*terrace, elevation*

Fort at
Jerusalem ....2 Sam. 5:9
Prepared by
Solomon ....1 Kin. 9:15
Strengthened by
Hezekiah.........2 Chr. 32:5
Scene of Joash's
death............2 Kin. 12:20, 21

Mina—*Greek money*

Used in parable ...Luke 19:12-27

Mincing—*affected elegance in walking*

Denounced........Is. 3:16

Mind—*the reasoning faculty*

A. *Faculties of:*
Perception.....Luke 9:47
Remem-
  brance........Titus 3:1
Reasoning.......Rom. 7:23, 25
Feelings ....2 Sam. 17:8
Desire ....Neh. 4:6
Intent ....Gen. 6:5
Purpose........2 Cor. 1:15, 17

B. *Of the unregenerate, described as:*
Alienated......Ezek. 23:17-22
              Col. 1:21
Spiteful........Ezek. 36:5
Debased ....Rom. 1:28
Hardened ......2 Cor. 3:14
Defiled ....Titus 1:15

C. *Of the regenerate, described as:*
Willing ....1 Chr. 28:9
In peace ......Rom. 8:6
Right ....Luke 8:35
Renewed ......Rom. 12:2
Having
  Christ's ....1 Cor. 2:16
Obedient......Heb. 8:10

D. *Dangers of, to the Christian:*
Worry ....Luke 12:29
Doubt ....Rom. 14:5
Disunity ......Rom. 12:16
              Phil. 4:2
Grow weary ...Heb. 12:3
Mental
  disturbance ...2 Thess. 2:2
Spiritual
  disturbance ...Rom. 7:23, 25

E. *Exhortations concerning, to Christians:*
Love God with
  all ....Matt. 22:37

Minerals of the Bible

A. *Features concerning:*
Mined ....Job 28:1-11
Plentiful in
  Canaan ....Deut. 8:9
Refined by
  fire...........Ezek. 22:18, 20
Trade in ....Ezek. 27:12

B. *List of:*
Asphalt
  (bitumen).....Gen. 11:3
Brimstone
  (sulphur).....Deut. 29:23
Bronze.........Num. 21:9
Chalk..........Is. 27:9
Clay...........Is. 41:25
Copper ....Deut. 8:9
Coral ....Job 28:18
Flint...........Deut. 32:13
Gold...........Gen. 2:11, 12
Iron ....Gen. 4:22
Lead...........Job 19:24
Lime...........Amos 2:1
Pitch
  (asphalt) .....Gen. 6:14
Salt...........Gen. 14:3
Sand...........Prov. 27:3
Silver.........Gen. 44:2
Tin ....Num. 31:22

Mingle, mix—*to put different elements together*

A. *Instances of:*
Offerings .....Lev. 2:4, 5
Garment.......Lev. 19:19
Judgments.....Rev. 8:7
Human
  sacrifice......Luke 13:1
Inter-
  marriage ......Ezra 9:2

B. *Figurative of:*
Sorrow ....Ps. 102:9
Wisdom ....Prov. 9:2, 5
Instability .....Is. 19:14
Severity ....Ps. 75:8
Impurity......Is. 1:22
Intoxication ...Is. 5:22
Worldliness....Hos. 7:8

Miniamin, Minjamin—*fortunate*

1. Levite
   assistant ......2 Chr. 31:14, 15
2. Postexilic
   priest ....Neh. 12:17
3. Priestly participant in
   dedication.....Neh. 12:41

Minister—*one who serves*

A. *Descriptive of:*
Court
  attendants ....1 Kin. 10:5
Angels.........Ps. 103:20
Priests and
  Levites........Joel 1:9, 13
Servant........Matt. 20:22-27

Ruler ....Rom. 13:3-5
Christ.........Rom. 15:8
Christ's
messengers ...1 Cor. 3:5
False
teachers ......2 Cor. 11:15

B. *Christian, qualifications of:*
Able to teach ..1 Tim. 3:2
Diligent........1 Cor. 15:10
Faithful........Rom. 15:17-19
Impartial ......1 Tim. 5:21
Industrious ....2 Cor. 10:12-16
Meek ....2 Tim. 2:25
Obedient.......Acts 16:9, 10
Persevering ....2 Cor. 11:23-33
Prayerful ......Acts 6:4
Quick
temper........Acts 20:22-24
Sincere ....2 Cor. 4:1, 2
Spirit-filled.....Acts 1:8
Studious.......1 Tim. 4:13, 15
Sympathetic ...Heb. 5:2
Temperate.....1 Cor. 9:25-27
Willing ....1 Pet. 5:2
Worthy of
imitation......1 Tim. 4:12

C. *Sins to avoid:*
Arrogance .....1 Pet. 5:3
Conten-
tiousness......Titus 1:7
Discourage-
ment..........2 Cor. 4:8, 9
Insincerity.....Phil. 1:15, 16
Perverting the
truth..........2 Cor. 11:3-15
Unfaith-
fulness........Matt. 24:48-51

D. *Duties of:*
Preach:
Gospel........1 Cor. 1:17
Christ
crucified .....1 Cor. 1:23
Christ's
riches........Eph. 3:8-12
Feed the
Church ....John 21:15-17
Edify the
Church ....Eph. 4:12
Pray for
people ....Col. 1:9
Teach ....2 Tim. 2:2
Exhort........Titus 1:9
Rebuke........Titus 2:15
Warn of
apostasy .....2 Tim. 4:2-5
Comfort ......2 Cor. 1:4-6
Win souls.....1 Cor. 9:19-23

E. *Attitude of believers toward:*
Pray for ....Eph. 6:18-20
Follow the example
of.............1 Cor. 11:1
Obey ....Heb. 13:17
Esteem
highly.........1 Thess. 5:12, 13
Provide for ....1 Cor. 9:6-18

Minni—*a people* (Manneans) *of Armenia*

Summoned to destroy
Babylon ....Jer. 51:27

Minnith—*distribution*

Wheat-growing Ammonite
town ....Ezek. 27:17

Minority—*the lesser number*

On God's side .....Num. 14:1-10
To be preferred ...Ex. 23:2
Saved are ....Matt. 7:13-23

Mint—*a fragrant herb*

Tithed by
Pharisees.........Matt. 23:23

Miphkad—*appointed place*

Gate of Jerusalem rebuilt by
Nehemiah ....Neh. 3:31

Miracle

A. *Described:*
Signs ....Acts 4:30
Wonders.......Acts 6:8
Works.........John 10:25-38

B. *Kinds of, over:*
Nature.........Josh. 10:12-14
Animals ....Num. 22:28
Human
beings ....Gen. 19:26
Nations........Ex. 10:1, 2
Sickness and
disease........2 Kin. 5:10-14
Natural laws...2 Kin. 6:5-7
Future
events ....2 Kin. 6:8-13
Death ....John 11:41-44

C. *Produced by:*
God's power ...Acts 15:12
Christ's
power.........Matt. 10:1
Spirit's
power.........Matt. 12:28

D. *Design of:*
  Manifest:
    God's glory ...John 11:40-42
    Christ's
      glory.........John 2:11
    God's
      presence .....Judg. 6:11-24
    Proof of God's messen-
      gers..........Ex. 4:2-9
    Produce
      obedience ....Ex. 16:4
    Vindicate
      God..........Ex. 17:4-7
    Produce
      faith ....John 20:30, 31
    Proof of Jesus as the
      Messiah......Matt. 11:2-5
    Signs of a true
      apostle.......2 Cor. 12:12
    Authenticate the
      Gospel ......Rom. 15:18, 19
    Fulfill
      prophecy....John 12:37-41

E. *Effect of, upon people:*
  Forced
    acknowledg-   ⎰John 11:47
      ment.........⎱Acts 4:16
  Amazement....Mark 6:49-51
  Faith ....John 2:23
                 John 11:42
  God glorified..Matt. 9:1-8

F. *False:*
  Not to be
    followed ......Deut. 13:1-3
  Sign of   ⎰2 Thess. 2:3, 9
    antichrist ....⎱Rev. 13:13
  Predicted by
    Christ........Matt. 24:24

G. *Evidence of:*
  Logic..........John 9:16
  Sufficient to   ⎰John 3:2
    convince .....⎱John 6:14
  Insufficient to ⎰Luke 16:31
    convince .....⎱John 12:37
  Sought by
    Jews..........John 2:18
  Demanded unrea-
    sonably ....Matt. 27:42, 43
  Incurs guilt....Matt. 11:20-24
                   John 15:24

Miracles of the Bible—*Old Testament*

Creation ....Gen. 1:1-31
Enoch's
  translation ......Gen. 5:24
The Flood.........Gen. 7:17-24

Confusion of tongues at
  Babel............Gen. 11:3-9
Sodom and Gomorrah
  destroyed........Gen. 19:24
Lot's wife turned to a pillar of
  salt.............Gen. 19:26
Ass speaking .....Num. 22:21-35

*Those associated with Moses and
Aaron:*

Burning bush .....Ex. 3:3
Moses' rod changed into a
  serpent..........Ex. 4:3, 4, 30
Moses' hand made
  leprous..........Ex. 4:6, 7, 30
Aaron's rod changed into a
  serpent..........Ex. 7:8-10

Ten plagues:
  River turned to
    blood...........Ex. 7:20-25
  Frogs ....Ex. 8:1-15
  Lice..............Ex. 8:16-19
  Flies.............Ex. 8:20-24
  Pestilence........Ex. 9:1-7
  Boils.............Ex. 9:8-12
  Hail..............Ex. 9:18-24
  Locusts ....Ex. 10:1-20
  Darkness..........Ex. 10:21-23
  Firstborn
    destroyed.......Ex. 12:29, 30
Pillar of cloud   ⎰Ex. 13:21, 22
  and fire..........⎱Ex. 14:19, 20
Crossing the sea ..Ex. 14:21, 23
Bitter waters
  sweetened........Ex. 15:25
Manna sent ....Ex. 16:13-36
Water from the rock at
  Rephidim.........Ex. 17:5-8
Amalek defeated ..Ex. 17:9-13
Fire on Aaron's
  sacrifice ....Lev. 9:24
Nadab and Abihu
  devoured.........Lev. 10:1, 2
Israel's judgment by
  fire..............Num. 11:1-3
Miriam's leprosy ..Num. 12:10-15
Destruction of
  Korah............Num. 16:31-35
Aaron's rod
  blossoms ....Num. 17:8
Water from the rock in
  Kadesh...........Num. 20:8-11
Bronze serpent....Num. 21:9

Those associated with Joshua:

Jordan divided ....Josh. 3:14-17
Fall of Jericho ....Josh. 6:6-20
Sun and moon stand
  still..............Josh. 10:12-14

Those associated with Samson:

Lion killed ....Judg. 14:5, 6
Thirty Philistines
killed............Judg. 14:19
Water from the hollow place in
Lehi..............Judg. 15:19
Gates of the city carried
away............Judg. 16:3
Dagon's house pulled
down............Judg. 16:29, 30

Those associated with Elijah:

Drought ....1 Kin. 17:1
 James 5:17
Fed by ravens.....1 Kin. 17:4-6
Widow's oil and meal
increased.........1 Kin. 17:12-16
Widow's son raised from
dead ....1 Kin. 17:17-23
Sacrifice consumed by
fire................1 Kin. 18:38
Rain in answer to
prayer............1 Kin. 18:41
Captains consumed by
fire...............2 Kin. 1:9-12
Jordan divided ....2 Kin. 2:8
Translated to heaven in a chariot
of fire ....2 Kin. 2:11

Those associated with Elisha:

Jordan divided ....2 Kin. 2:14
Waters of Jericho
healed............2 Kin. 2:20-22
Mocking young men destroyed by
bears.............2 Kin. 2:24
Water supplied for
Jehoshaphat......2 Kin. 3:16-20
Widow's oil
multiplied ....2 Kin. 4:1-7
Shunammite's child raised from
dead ....2 Kin. 4:19-37
Poisoned pottage made
harmless ....2 Kin. 4:38-41
Hundred fed with twenty
loaves ....2 Kin. 4:42-44
Naaman cured of
leprosy...........2 Kin. 5:10-14
Gehazi struck with
leprosy ....2 Kin. 5:27
Axe head caused to
float..............2 Kin. 6:5-7
Ben-Hadad's plans
revealed..........2 Kin. 6:8-13
Syrian army
defeated..........2 Kin. 6:18-20
Revival of a man by touch with
Elisha's bones ....2 Kin. 13:21

Those associated with Isaiah:

Hezekiah healed ..2 Kin. 20:7
Shadow turns backward on sun
dial...............2 Kin. 20:11

*Other miracles of the Old
Testament:*

Dew on Gideon's
fleece ....Judg. 6:37-40
Dagon's fall before the
ark...............1 Sam. 5:1-12
Men of Beth Shemesh
destroyed........1 Sam. 6:19, 20
Thunder and rain in
harvest..........1 Sam. 12:18
Uzzah's death.....2 Sam. 6:6, 7
Jeroboam's hand withered and
restored..........1 Kin. 13:4-6
Rending of the
altar..............1 Kin. 13:5
Sennacherib's army
destroyed........2 Kin. 19:35
Uzziah afflicted with
leprosy ....2 Chr. 26:16-21
Three men protected from the fiery
furnace..........Dan. 3:19-27
Daniel delivered from the lion's
den...............Dan. 6:16-23
Preservation of Jonah in stomach
of fish three
days..............Jon. 2:1-10

Miracles of the Bible—*New Testament*

Of Christ (listed chronologically):

Water made wine
(Cana) ....John 2:1-11
Son of nobleman healed
(Cana) ....John 4:46-54
Passed unseen through crowd
(Nazareth) ......Luke 4:28-30
Man with unclean spirit in
synagogue cured ⎧ Mark 1:23-26
(Capernaum) ....⎩ Luke 4:33-35
Peter's mother- ⎧ Matt. 8:14-17
in-law healed ⎨ Mark 1:29-31
(Capernaum) ....⎩ Luke 4:38, 39
Net full of fishes (Lower
Galilee)..........Luke 5:1-11
Leper ⎧ Matt. 8:1-4
cleansed ⎨ Mark 1:40-45
(Capernaum) ....⎩ Luke 5:12-15
Paralytic ⎧ Matt. 9:1-8
cured ⎨ Mark 2:3-12
(Capernaum) ....⎩ Luke 5:18-26
Man healed
(Jerusalem).......John 5:1-9
Withered hand ⎧ Matt. 12:10-13
restored ⎨ Mark 3:1-5
(Galilee).........⎩ Luke 6:6-11

Centurion's servant
cured of palsy {Matt. 8:5-13
(Capernaum) .... Luke 7:1-10
Widow's son raised from dead
(Nain) .... Luke 7:11-17
Demon-possessed man
healed {Matt. 12:22, 23
(Galilee) .... Luke 11:14
Windstorm stilled {Matt. 8:23-27
Mark 4:37-41
(Lower
Galilee) .... Luke 8:22-25
Two demon-
possessed men {Matt. 8:28-34
Mark 5:1-20
cured (Gadara) .. Luke 8:26-39
Raised Jairus' {Matt. 9:24-26
daughter Mark 5:23
(Capernaum) .... Luke 8:41
Woman with
flow of blood {Matt. 9:20-22
healed Mark 5:25-34
(Capernaum) .... Luke 8:43-48
Blind men cured
(Capernaum) ..... Matt. 9:27-31
Mute spirit cast out
(Capernaum) ..... Matt. 9:32, 33
Five {Matt. 14:15-21
thousand Mark 6:35-44
fed (Lower Luke 9:10-17
Galilee) .... John 6:1-14
Walking on the {Matt. 14:25-33
sea (Lower Mark 6:48-52
Galilee) .... John 6:15-21
Canaanite's or Syro-Phoenician's
daughter healed
(District of {Matt. 15:21-28
Tyre) .... Mark 7:24-30
Four thousand
fed (Lower {Matt. 15:32-39
Galilee) .... Mark 8:1-9
Deaf and dumb man cured
(Lower Galilee) ... Mark 7:31-37
Blind man healed
(Bethsaida) ...... Mark 8:22-26
Demon cast out {Matt. 17:14-18
of boy (near Mark 9:14-29
Caesarea) .... Luke 9:37-43
Tribute money provided
(Capernaum) ..... Matt. 17:24-27
Passed unseen through crowd (in
Temple) .... John 8:59
Ten lepers cleansed
(Samaria) .... Luke 17:11-19
Man born blind, healed
(Jerusalem) ...... John 9:1-7
Lazarus raised from dead
(Bethany) .... John 11:38-44
Woman with sickness cured
(Peraea) .... Luke 13:11-17

Man with dropsy cured
(Peraea) .... Luke 14:1-6
Two blind {Matt. 20:29-34
men cured Mark 10:46-52
(Jericho) .... Luke 18:35-43
Fig tree withered {Matt. 21:18-22
(Mt. Olivet) ...... Mark 11:12-14
Malchus' ear healed
(Gethsemane) .... Luke 22:50, 51
Second net full of fishes
(Lower Galilee) ... John 21:1-14
Resurrection of {Luke 24:6
Christ .... John 10:18

*Appearances of Christ after His
resurrection, to:*

Mary Magdalene
(Jerusalem) ...... Mark 16:9
Other women
(Jerusalem) ...... Matt. 28:9
Two disciples
(Emmaus) .... Luke 24:15-31
Peter
(Jerusalem) ...... 1 Cor. 15:5
Ten apostles, Thomas absent
(Jerusalem) ...... John 20:19, 24
Eleven apostles, Thomas present
(Jerusalem) ...... John 20:26-28
Seven disciples fishing
(Lower Galilee) ... John 21:1-24
Eleven apostles
(Galilee) .... Matt. 28:16, 17
Five hundred
brethren .... 1 Cor. 15:6
James .... 1 Cor. 15:7
Eleven apostles on day of His
ascension
(Bethany) .... Acts 1:2-9
Paul at his {Acts 9:1-5
conversion 1 Cor. 15:8

Those associated with Peter:

Lame man cured .. Acts 3:6
Death of Ananias and
Sapphira .... Acts 5:5, 10
Sick healed .... Acts 5:15
Aeneas healed of
palsy .... Acts 9:34
Dorcas restored to
life .... Acts 9:40
His release from
prison .... Acts 12:7-11

Those associated with Paul:

His sight {Acts 9:17-18
restored .... Acts 22:12-13
Elymas blinded .... Acts 13:11
Lame man cured .. Acts 14:10

Girl freed of evil spirits .... { Acts 16:18 / Acts 19:11, 12

Earthquake at Philippi.......... Acts 16:25, 26

Evil spirits overcame Sceva's seven sons. .... Acts 19:13-16

Eutychus restored to life .... Acts 20:10

Unharmed by viper's bite .... Acts 28:5

Publius' father healed.......... Acts 28:8

Other miracles of the New Testament:

Outpouring of the Holy Spirit.......... Acts 2:1-21

Gift of tongues.... { Acts 2:3, 4, 11 / Acts 10:46 / Acts 19:6

Apostles freed from prison...... { Acts 5:19 / Acts 12:7-11

Agabus' prophesies...... { Acts 11:28 / Acts 21:11

Visions: { Matt. 17:1, 2 / Luke 9:32

Of Christ, by dying:

Stephen........... { Acts 7:55, 56

Ananias' .... Acts 9:10

Peter's.......... { Acts 10:1-48 / Acts 11:1-30

Cornelius'.......... { Acts 10:3, 4, 30-32

Paul's.......... { Acts 16:9 / 2 Cor. 12:1-5

John's on Patmos.......... { Rev. 1:10 / Rev. 4-22

Miracles by the seventy.......... Luke 10:17

Stephen performed great miracles.......... Acts 6:8

Philip cast out unclean spirits .... Acts 8:6-13

Miracles pretended, or false

Egyptian magicians .... { Ex. 7:11-22 / Ex. 8:18, 19

In support of false religions.......... Deut. 13:1-3

Witch of Endor ... 1 Sam. 28:9-12

False prophets .... { Matt. 7:22, 23 / Matt. 24:24

False christs ...... Matt. 24:24

Deceive the ungodly .... { Rev. 13:13 / Rev. 19:20

Sign of apostasy.......... { 2 Thess. 2:3, 9 / Rev. 13:13

Mire—*deep mud*

A. *Places of:*
Dungeon ...... Jer. 38:22
Streets.......... Is. 10:6

B. *Figurative of:*
Affliction ...... Job 30:19
Insecurity ..... Is. 57:20
Plentifulness... Zech. 9:3

Miriam—*obstinacy* (stubbornness)

1. Sister of Aaron and Moses........ Num. 26:59
Chosen by God; called a prophetess .... Ex. 15:20
Leads in victory song .... Ex. 15:20, 21
Punished for rebellion ...... Num. 12:1-16
Buried at Kadesh ...... Num. 20:1

2. Judahite .... 1 Chr. 4:17

Mirma, Mirmah—*deceit*

Benjamite.......... 1 Chr. 8:10

Mirror

In the tabernacle........ Ex. 38:8
Of cast metal ..... Job 37:18
Used figura- tively.......... { 1 Cor. 13:12 / 2 Cor. 3:18 / James 1:23, 25

Mirth—*a spirit of gaiety*

Occasions of .... { Gen. 31:27 / Neh. 8:10-12

Absence of .... { Jer. 25:10, 11 / Hos. 2:11

Inadequacy of .... { Prov. 14:13 / Eccl. 2:1, 2

Miscarriage—*premature ejection of a fetus from the mother's womb, resulting in the death of the fetus*

Against the wicked .... Ps. 58:8
Wished for........ Job 3:16
Eccl. 6:3

Miscegenation—*intermarriage of different races*

A. Restrictions in Law of Moses...... Ex. 34:12-16

B. *Notable examples:*
Moses .... Num. 12:1-10
Ruth .... Matt. 1:5

C. *Unity of all races:*
Descended
from Adam... (Gen. 3:20 \ Rom. 5:12
From one......Acts 17:26

D. *Christian marriage:*
Spiritual
basis..........Matt. 19:6
In the Lord....1 Cor. 7:39
2 Cor. 6:14

Miser—*a covetous man*

A. *Characteristics of:*
Selfish.........Eccl. 4:8
Covetous......Luke 12:15
Divided
loyalty........Matt. 6:24

B. *Punishment of:*
Dissatis-
faction........Eccl. 5:10
Loss...........Matt. 6:19
Sorrows.......1 Tim. 6:10
Destruction....Ps. 52:5, 7

C. *Examples of:*
Rich fool......Luke 12:16-21
Rich ruler.....Luke 18:18-23
Ananias and
Sapphira......Acts 5:1-11

Miserable—*the wretched*

A. *State of:*
Wicked.........Rom. 3:12-16
Trapped.......Rom. 7:24
Lost...........Luke 13:25-28

B. *Caused by:*
Forgetfulness of
God...........Is. 22:12-14
Ignorance.....Luke 19:42-44

Misfortune—*an unexpected adversity*

Explained by the
nations..........Deut. 29:24-28
Misunderstood by
Gideon...........Judg. 6:13
Understood by
David...........2 Sam. 16:5-13
Caused by sin....Is. 59:1, 2

Mishael—*who is like God?*

1. Kohathite
Levite.........Ex. 6:22
Removes dead
bodies.........Lev. 10:4, 5
2. Hebrew name of
Meshach......Dan. 1:6-19
3. One of Ezra's
assistants.....Neh. 8:4

Mishal

Town in Asher....Josh. 19:24, 26
Assigned to
Levites..........Josh. 21:30
Called Mashal.....1 Chr. 6:74

Misham—*swift*

Son of Elpaal.....1 Chr. 8:12

Mishma—*hearing*

1. Son of (Gen. 25:13, 14
Ishmael...\1 Chr. 1:30
2. Descendant of
Simeon.......1 Chr. 4:25

Mishmannah—*fatness*

One of David's Gadite
warriors..........1 Chr. 12:10

Mishraites

Family living in Kirjath
Jearim............1 Chr. 2:53

Mispar—*writing*

Exile returnee.....Ezra 2:2
Called
Mispereth........Neh. 7:7

Misrephoth—*burning of waters*

Haven of fleeing
Canaanites......Josh. 11:8
Near the
Sidonians........Josh. 13:6

Missionaries—*those sent out to spread the Gospel*

Jonah.............Jon. 3:2, 3
The early
church..........Acts 8:4
Philip............Acts 8:5
Some from Cyrene become
missionaries......Acts 11:20
Paul and
Barnabas........Acts 13:1-4
Peter..............Acts 15:7
Apollos...........Acts 18:24
Noah.............2 Pet. 2:5

Mission of Christ

Do God's will.....John 6:38
Save sinners......Luke 19:10
Bring in everlasting
righteousness.....Dan. 9:24
Destroy Satan's (Heb. 2:14
works...........\1 John 3:8

Fulfill the Old
Testament........Matt. 5:17
Give life ....John 10:10, 28
Stop sacrifices.....Dan. 9:27
Complete
revelation ....Heb. 1:1-3

Missions

A. *Commands concerning:*
"Will be" ......Matt. 24:14
"Go" ....Matt. 28:18-20
"Tarry"........Luke 24:49
"Come"........Acts 16:9

B. *Motives prompting:*
God's love .....John 3:16
Christ's love ...2 Cor. 5:14, 15
Mankind's
need ....Rom. 3:9-31

C. *Equipment for:*
Word..........Rom. 10:14, 15
Spirit ....Acts 1:8
Prayer........Acts 13:1-4

Mist—*a vapor (physical and spiritual)*

Physical (vapor)..Gen. 2:6
Spiritual
(blindness) ....Acts 13:11
Eternal
(darkness)........2 Pet. 2:17

Mistake—*an error arising from human weakness*

Causes of:

Motives
misunderstood....Josh. 22:9-29
Appearance
misjudged........1 Sam. 1:13-15
Trust misplaced...Josh. 9:3-27

Mistress—*a married woman*

Over a maid......Gen. 16:4, 8, 9
Figurative of
Nineveh..........Nah. 3:4

Misunderstandings—*disagreements among*

Israelites..........Josh. 22:9-29
Christ's disciples ..Matt. 20:20-27
Apostles ....Gal. 2:11-15
Christians.........Acts 6:1

Misused—*putting to a wrong use*

Guilt of, brings
wrath ....2 Chr. 36:16

Mite—*Jews' smallest coin*

Widow's ....Mark 12:42

Mithkah—*sweetness*

Israelite
encampment .....Num. 33:28, 29

Mithnite

Descriptive of Joshaphat, David's
officer ....1 Chr. 11:43

Mithredath—*consecrated to Mithra*

1. Treasurer of
Cyrus..........Ezra 1:8
2. Persian
official ....Ezra 4:7

Mitylene—*a city on the island of Lesbos*

Visited by Paul....Acts 20:13-15

Mix (see Mingle; Miscegenation)

Mizar—*small*

Hill east of
Jordan ....Ps. 42:6

Mizpah—*watchtower*

1. Site of covenant between Jacob
and Laban ....Gen. 31:44-53
2. Town in Gilead; probably same
as 1...........Judg. 10:17
Jephthah's   (Judg. 11:11, 29,
home ....   (34
Probably same as Ramath
Mizpah ....Josh. 13:26
3. Region near Mt.
Hermon.......Josh. 11:3, 8
4. Town in
Judah.........Josh. 15:1, 38
5. Place in Moab; David brings his
parents to.....1 Sam. 22:3, 4
6. Town of
Benjamin ....Josh. 18:21, 26
Outraged Israelites gather
here ....Judg. 20:1, 3
Samuel
gathers   (1 Sam. 7:5-16
Israel .... (1 Sam. 10:17-25
Built by Asa ...1 Kin. 15:22
Residence of
Gedaliah ......2 Kin. 25:23, 25
Home of exile
returnees .....Neh. 3:7, 15, 19

Mizraim—*Egypt*

1. Son of Ham; ancestor of Ludim,
Anamim,
etc. ....1 Chr. 1:8, 11
2. Hebrew name for
Egypt.........Gen. 50:11
Called the land of
Ham ....Ps. 105:23, 27

Mizzah—*fear*

Grandson of Esau; a duke of
Edom ....Gen. 36:13, 17

Mnason

Christian of Cyprus and Paul's
host..............Acts 21:16

Moab—*seed*

1. Son of Lot.....Gen. 19:33-37
2. Country of the
   Moabites......Deut. 1:5

Moabites—*inhabitants of Moab*

A. *History of:*
   Descendants of
   Lot ....Gen. 19:36, 37
   Became a great
   nation ....Num. 21:28, 30
   Governed by ⎰Num. 23:7
   kings.........⎱Josh. 24:9
   Driven out of their territory by
   Amorites......Num. 21:26
   Refused to let Israel
   pass.........Judg. 11:17, 18
   Joined Midian to curse
   Israel ....Num. 22:4
   Excluded from
   Israel ....Deut. 23:3-6
   Friendly relation with
   Israel .....Ruth 1:1, 4, 16
   Defeated by
   Saul ....1 Sam. 14:47
   Refuge for David's
   parents ......1 Sam. 22:3, 4
   Defeated by
   David ....2 Sam. 8:2, 12
   Solomon married
   women of.....1 Kin. 11:1, 3
   Paid tribute to
   Israel ....2 Kin. 3:4
   Fought Israel and
   Judah ....2 Kin. 3:5-7
   Conquered by Israel and
   Judah........2 Kin. 3:8-27
   Intermarried ⎰Ezra 9:1, 2
   with Jews....⎱Neh. 13:23

B. *Characteristics of:*
   Idolatrous ....1 Kin. 11:7
   Wealthy ......Jer. 48:1, 7
   Super-
   stitious.......Jer. 27:3, 9
   Satisfied .....Jer. 48:11
   Proud.........Jer. 48:29

C. *Prophecies concerning their:*
   Desolation .....Is. 15:1-9

Ruin and
destruction....Jer. 27:3, 8
Punishment....Amos 2:1-3
Subjection.....Is. 11:14

Mob—*a lawless crowd*

Caused Pilate to pervert
justice............Matt. 27:20-25
Made unjust
charges.........Acts 17:5-9
Paul saved from...Acts 21:27-40

Mocking—*imitating in fun or derision*

A. *Evil agents of:*
   Children ....2 Kin. 2:23
   Men of Israel ..2 Chr. 30:10
   Men of
   Judah..........2 Chr. 36:16
   Fools ....Prov. 14:9
   Wine ....Prov. 20:1
   Jews...........Matt. 20:19
   Roman
   soldiers ....Luke 23:36
   False
   teachers ......Jude 18

B. *Good agents of:*
   Donkey.......Num. 22:29
   Samson........Judg. 16:10-15
   Elijah..........1 Kin. 18:27
   Wisdom
   (God) ....Prov. 1:20, 26
   The Lord ....Ps. 2:4

C. *Reasons for, to:*
   Show
   unbelief......2 Chr. 36:16
   Portray
   scorn ....2 Chr. 30:10
   Ridicule ....Acts 2:13
   Insult..........Gen. 39:14, 17

D. *Objects of:*
   Christ ....Luke 23:11, 36
   Believers......Heb. 11:36

Modesty in dress

A. *Of women:*
   Instructed ....1 Tim. 2:9
   Illustrated in
   Israel ....1 Pet. 3:3-5
   Lack of, an
   enticement....2 Sam. 11:2-5

B. *Of men:*
   Lack of,
   condemned ...Gen. 9:21-27
   Illustrated ...John 21:7
   Manifested in
   conversion ....Mark 5:15

Moladah—*birth, origin*

Town of Judah....Josh. 15:1, 26
Inheritance of
Simeon..........Josh. 19:1, 2
Returning Levites
inhabit ....Neh. 11:26

Molded, molten—*made of melted metal*

A. *Applied to:*
Great basin in the
Temple........1 Kin. 7:16-33
Mirror..........Job 37:18
Images ....Ex. 32:4, 8

B. *Of images:*
Making of
forbidden .....Ex. 34:17
Made by
Israel ....2 Kin. 17:16
Worshiped by
Israel ....Ps. 106:19
Destroyed by
Josiah.........2 Chr. 34:3, 4
Folly of........Is. 42:17
Vanity.........Is. 41:29

See Gods, false

Molding—*a decorative ledge of gold*

Around:

Ark ....Ex. 25:11
Incense altar.....Ex. 30:3, 4

Moldy—*musty or stale*

Applied to bread ..Josh. 9:5, 12

Mole—*a small, burrowing mammal*

Among unclean
animals...........Is. 2:20

Molech—*king*

A. *Worship of:*
By Ammon-
ites ....1 Kin. 11:7
By human
sacrifice.......2 Kin. 23:10
Strongly
condemned ...Lev. 18:21
Introduced by
Solomon ....1 Kin. 11:7

B. *Prevalence of, among Jews:*
Favored by
Solomon ......1 Kin. 11:7

See Human sacrifice

Molid—*begetter*

Judahite ....1 Chr. 2:29

Moment—*a small unit of time*

A. *Descriptive of:*
Man's life......Job 34:20
Lying
tongues.......Prov. 12:19
Satan's
temptation....Luke 4:5

B. *Descriptive of God's:*
Anger ....Num. 16:21, 45
Punishment....Is. 47:9
Destruction....Jer. 4:20

C. *Descriptive of the believer's:*
Problems ......Job 7:18
Protection .....Is. 26:20, 21
Perfection in
glory..........1 Cor. 15:52

Monarchy—*the rule of one man (king)*

Described by
Samuel...........1 Sam. 8:11-18

Money—*an authorized medium of
exchange*

A. *Wrong uses of:*
Misuse.........Gen. 31:15
Forced
tribute ....2 Kin. 15:20
Make interest
on ....Ps. 15:5
Bribe ....Ps. 15:5
Miser ....Matt. 25:18
Buy spiritual
gifts ....Acts 8:18, 20

B. *Good uses of:*
Buy property ..Gen. 23:9, 13
Buy food ......Deut. 2:6, 28
Give as an
offering ......Deut. 14:22-26
Repair God's
house ....2 Kin. 12:4-15
Pay   (Matt. 17:27
taxes.......(Matt. 22:19-21
Use for the
Lord ....Matt. 25:27

C. *Evils connected with:*
Greed..........2 Kin. 5:20-27
Debts..........Neh. 5:2-11

Moneychangers—*dealers in changing
money*

Christ drives them
out...............Matt. 21:12

Monkeys

Imported by Solomon from
Tarshish..........1 Kin. 10:22
Trade item ....2 Chr. 9:21

Monogamy—*marriage to one spouse*

Commanded ......Matt. 19:3-9
1 Cor. 7:1-16
Example of Christ and the
Church...........Eph. 5:25-33
Demanded of
bishop............1 Tim. 3:2

Monotheism—*a belief in one god*

Statements of:

The great
commandment ...Deut. 6:4, 5
Song of Moses ....Deut. 32:36-39
About eternal
life ....John 17:3, 22

Moon—*earth's satellite*

A. *Miraculous use of:*
Standing still ..Hab. 3:11
Darkened......Is. 13:10
Turned to
blood ....Acts 2:20

B. *Worship of:*
Among Jews...Jer. 7:18
Forbidden .....Deut. 4:19
Punishable.....Jer. 8:1-3

C. *Illustrative of:*
Eternity ....Ps. 72:5, 7
Universal
praise........Is. 66:23
God's
faithfulness ...Jer. 31:35-37
Greater light of Gospel
age ....Is. 30:26

D. *Purpose of:*
Rule the
night.........Gen. 1:16
Marking
time ....Gen. 1:14
Designating
seasons ....Ps. 104:19
Signaling
prophetic   ⎰Matt. 24:29
events ....⎱Luke 21:25

Morality—*principles of right conduct*

A. *Of the unregenerate:*
Based upon
conscience ....Rom. 2:14, 15
Commanded by
law ....John 8:3-5

Limited to outward
appearance....Is. 1:14, 15
Object of
boasting ......Mark 10:17-20

B. *Of the regenerated:*
Based upon the new
birth ....2 Cor. 5:17
Prompted by the
Spirit ....Gal. 5:22, 23
Comes from the
heart..........Heb. 8:10
No boasting
except in   ⎰1 Cor. 15:10
Christ........⎱Phil. 3:7-10

Morasthite—*a native of Moresheth*

Descriptive of
Micah ....Jer. 26:18

Mordecai—*dedicated to Mars*

1. Jew exiled in
Persia..........Esth. 2:5, 6
Brings up
Esther ....Esth. 2:7
Directs Esther's
movements ...Esth. 2:10-20
Reveals plot to kill the
king ....Esth. 2:22, 23
Refuses homage to
Haman.........Esth. 3:1-6
Gallows made
for............Esth. 5:14
Honored by the
king ....Esth. 6:1-12
Is highly
exalted........Esth. 8:7, 15
Becomes
famous........Esth. 9:4
Writes to Jews about Feast of
Purim.........Esth. 9:20-31
2. Postexilic
returnee ......Ezra 2:2

More—*something in addition*

A. *"More than" promises:*
Repentance....Matt. 18:13
Love...........John 21:15

B. *"Much more" promises:*
Grace..........Rom. 5:9-17
Witnessing ....Phil. 1:14
Obedience .....Phil. 2:12

C. *"No more" promises:*
Christ's
death ....Rom. 6:9
Remember
sin............Heb. 8:12

Moreh—*teacher, soothsayer*

1. Place (oak tree or grove) near
   Shechem......Gen. 12:6
   Probably place of:
   Idol-burying . Gen. 35:4
   Covenant-
   stone ....Josh. 24:26
2. Hill in the valley of
   Jezreel.......Judg. 7:1

Moresheth Gath—*possession of Gath*

Birthplace of Micah the
prophet ....Mic. 1:14

Moriah

God commands Abraham to
sacrifice Isaac
here.............Gen. 22:1-13
Site of Solomon's
temple ....2 Chr. 3:1

Morning—*the first part of the day*

A. *Early risers in:*
   Do the LORD's
   will ....Gen. 22:3
   Worship ....Ex. 24:4
   Do the LORD's
   work..........Josh. 6:12
   Fight the LORD's
   battles ....Josh. 8:10
   Depart on a
   journey ....Judg. 19:5, 8
   Correct an
   evil ....Dan. 6:19
   Pray..........Mark 1:35
   Visit the
   tomb.........Mark 16:2
   Preach........Acts 5:21

B. *For the righteous, a time for:*
   Joy ....Ps. 30:5
   God's loving-
   kindness ......Ps. 92:2
   God's
   mercies ....Lam. 3:22, 23

C. *For the unrighteous, a time of:*
   Dread ....Deut. 28:67
   Destruction....Is. 17:14

D. *Figurative of:*
   Man's unrigh-
   teousness .....Hos. 6:4
   Judgment......Zeph. 3:5
   God's light.....Amos 5:8
   Christ's
   return........Rev. 2:28

Morning sacrifice—*part of Israelite
worship*

Ritual described...Ex. 29:38-42
Part of continual
offering ....Num. 28:3-8
Under Ahaz.......2 Kin. 16:15

Morning Star

Figurative of Christ:

To church at
Thyatira.........Rev. 2:24, 28
Christ, of
Himself..........Rev. 22:16
Applied to
Christ ....2 Pet. 1:19

Morsel—*a small piece of food*

Offered to
angels............Gen. 18:5
Rejected by a doomed
man..............1 Sam. 28:22
Asked of a dying
woman..........1 Kin. 17:11, 12
Better than
strife ....Prov. 17:1
Exchanged for a
birthright........Heb. 12:16

Mortar (I)—*a vessel*

Vessel used for beating
grains ....Num. 11:8
Used
figuratively......Prov. 27:22

Mortar (II)—*a building material*

Made of:

Clay ....Is. 41:25
Asphalt ....Gen. 11:3
Plaster ....Lev. 14:42, 45

Mortgage—*something given in security
for debt*

Postexilic Jews burdened
with..............Neh. 5:3

Mortification—*a putting to death*

A. *Objects of:*
   Law ....Rom. 7:4
   Sin ....Rom. 6:6, 11
   Flesh ....Rom. 13:14
   Members of earthly
   body..........Col. 3:5

B. *Agents of:*
   Holy Spirit.....Rom. 8:13
   Our
   obedience .....Rom. 6:17-19

Moserah (sing.), **Moseroth** (pl.)—*bond*

Place of Aaron's death and
burial .... Deut. 10:6
Israelite
encampment ..... Num. 33:30, 31

Moses—*drawn out*

A. *Early life of* (first 40 years):
Descendant of
Levi. .... Ex. 2:1
Son of Amram and
Jochebed. ..... Ex. 6:16-20
Brother of Aaron and
Miriam. .... Ex. 15:20
Born under
slavery. .... Ex. 2:1-10
Hid by
mother. .... Ex. 2:2, 3
Educated in Egyptian
wisdom ...... Acts 7:22
Refused Egyptian
sonship ...... Heb. 11:23-27
Defended his
people .... Ex. 2:11-14
Rejected, flees to
Midian .... Ex. 2:15

B. *In Midian* (second 40 years):
Married
Zipporah ...... Ex. 2:16-21
Father of two { Ex. 2:22
sons .... { Acts 7:29
Became Jethro's
shepherd. ..... Ex. 3:1

C. *Leader of Israel* (last 40 years;
to the end of his life):
Heard God's
voice. .... Ex. 3:2-6
God's plan revealed to
him .... Ex. 3:7-10
Argued with
God. .... Ex. 4:1-17
Met Aaron. ..... Ex. 4:14-28
Assembled elders of
Israelites ..... Ex. 4:29-31
Rejected by Pharaoh and
Israel .... Ex. 5:1-23
Conflict with Pharaoh; ten
plagues sent .. Ex. 7-12
Commanded to
institute the { Ex. 12:1-29
Passover ..... { Heb. 11:28

D. *From Egypt to Sinai:*
Led people from
Egypt. .... Ex. 12:30-38
Observed the
Passover ...... Ex. 12:39-51

Healed bitter
waters .... Ex. 15:22-27
People hunger; flesh
and manna { Ex. 16:1-36
supplied. ..... { John 6:31, 32
Came to
Sinai. .... Ex. 19:1, 2

E. *At Sinai:*
Called to God's
presence ...... Acts 7:38
Prepared Israel for the
Law. .... Ex. 19:7-25
Received the
Law. .... Ex. 20-23
Confirmed the covenant with
Israel .... Ex. 24:1-11
Stayed 40 days on
Sinai. .... Ex. 24:12-16
Shown the pattern of the
tabernacle .... Ex. 25-31
Israel sins; Moses
interceded .... Ex. 32:1-35
Recommissioned and
encouraged ... Ex. 33:1-23
Instructions received;
tabernacle
erected. .... Ex. 36-40
Consecrated
Aaron. .... Lev. 8:1-36
Numbered the
men. .... Num. 1:1-54
Observed the
Passover ...... Num. 9:1-5

F. *From Sinai to Kadesh Barnea:*
Resumed journey to
Canaan ...... Num. 10:11-36
Complained; 70 elders
appointed .... Num. 11:1-35
Spoke against by Miriam and
Aaron. .... Num. 12:1-6

G. *At Kadesh Barnea:*
Sent spies to
Canaan ...... Num. 13:1-33
Pleaded with rebellious
Israel .... Num. 14:1-19
Announced God's
judgment ..... Num. 14:20-45

H. *Wanderings:*
Instructions
received. ...... Num. 15:1-41
Sinned in
anger .... Num. 20:1-13
Sent messengers to
Edom .... Num. 20:14-21
Made a
bronze { Num. 21:4-9
serpent. ...... { John 3:14

Traveled toward
Canaan ......Num. 21:10-20
Ordered
destruction....Num. 25:1-18
Numbered the
people ....Num. 26:1-65
Gave instruction concerning
inheritance....Num. 27:1-11
Commissioned Joshua as his
successor .....Num. 27:12-23
Received further
laws ....Num. 28-30
Conquered
Midianites....Num. 31:1-54
Final instruction and
records.......Num. 32-36
Enough.......Deut. 3:24-27
Reinterpreted the
Law..........Deut. 1-31
Gave farewell
messages......Deut. 32-33
Committed written Law to the
priests ....Deut. 31:9, 26
Saw the promised
land.........Deut. 34:1-4
Died, in full strength, at
120..........Deut. 34:5-7
Israel wept
over ....Deut. 34:8

I. *Character of:*
Believer.......Heb. 11:23-28
Faithful.......Num. 12:7
                      Heb. 3:2-5
Humble.......Num. 12:3
Respected .....Ex. 33:8-10
Logical ....Num. 14:12-20
Impatient......Ex. 5:22, 23
Given to
anger ....Ex. 32:19

Moses, oracles of—*blessings on tribes of
Israel*

Pronounced......Deut. 33:6-25
Song introduces...Deut. 33:2-5
Song concludes...Deut. 33:26-29

Most assuredly—*a strong affirmation*

A. *Concerning Christ's:*
Glory..........John 1:51
Eternity ......John 8:58
Uniqueness....John 10:1, 7
Mission.......John 6:32
Betrayal ......John 13:21
Death ....John 12:24

B. *Concerning man's:*
Spiritual
bondage .....John 8:34

Spiritual
darkness ......John 6:26
Need of
regeneration ..John 3:3, 5
Need of
salvation......John 5:24, 25
Means of
salvation......John 6:47, 53
Life eternal ....John 8:51

C. *Concerning the believer's:*
Fickleness .....John 13:38
Work..........John 14:12
Mission.......John 13:16, 20
Prayer........John 16:23
Life............John 21:18

Most High—*a name of God*

Melchizedek,
priest of.........Heb. 7:1
Applied to Jesus by
demons..........Mark 5:7, 8
Paul and Silas called servants
of ....Acts 16:17

Moth—*a garment-destroying insect*

Used figuratively of:

Inner corruption ..Is. 50:9
God's judgments ..Hos. 5:12
Man's insecurity ..Job 4:19
Man's fading
glory ....Job 13:28

Mother

A. *Described as:*
Loving.........Ex. 2:1-25
Appreciative ...2 Kin. 4:19-37
Weeping.......Luke 7:12-15
Remem-
bering.......Luke 2:51

B. *Kinds of:*
Idolatrous .....Judg. 17:1-4
Troubled.......1 Kin. 17:17-24
Cruel ....2 Kin. 11:1, 2
Joyful ....Ps. 113:9
Good ....Prov. 31:1
Scheming ......Matt. 20:20-23
Prayerful ......Acts 12:12

C. *Duties toward:*
Honor ....Eph. 6:2
Obedience .....Deut. 21:18, 19
Protection .....Gen. 32:11
Provision ......John 19:25-27

D. *Figurative of:*
Israel..........Hos. 2:2, 5
Judah..........Ezek. 19:2, 10

Heavenly
Jerusalem . . . . . Gal. 4:26

E. *Duties performed by:*
Selecting son's
wife. . . . . Gen. 21:21
Hospitality . . . . . Gen. 24:55
Nourish-
ment. . . . . Ex. 2:8, 9
Provision . . . . . . 1 Kin. 1:11-21
Comfort . . . . Is. 66:12, 13

F. *Dishonor of, punished by:*
Death . . . . Lev. 20:9
Shame. . . . . Prov. 19:26
Darkness . . . . . . Prov. 20:20
Destruction. . . . Prov. 28:24

Motherhood

A. *Described as:*
Painful . . . . Gen. 3:16
Sometimes
dangerous. . . . . Gen. 35:16-20
Yet joyful . . . . . John 16:21
Object of
prayer . . . . Gen. 25:21

B. *Blessings of:*
Fulfills divine
Law. . . . . Gen. 1:28
Makes joyful . . . Ps. 113:9
Woman will be saved
in . . . . 1 Tim. 2:15

Mother-in-law

Judith's—grief . . . . Gen. 26:34, 35
Ruth's—loved . . . . . Ruth 1:14-17
Peter's—healed by
Christ . . . . Matt. 8:14, 15

Motive—*inner impulse producing outward action*

A. *Good:*
Questioned . . . . 2 Kin. 5:5-8
Misapplied. . . . . Esth. 6:6-11
Misrep-
resented . . . . . . Job 1:9-11
Misunder-
stood . . . . Acts 21:26-31

B. *Evil:*
Prompted by
Satan . . . . Matt. 16:22, 23
Designed to
deceive . . . . Acts 5:1-10

Mount Baalah—*mistress*

Part of the territory of
Judah . . . . Josh. 15:11

Mount Baal Hermon—*possessor of Hermon*

Lived on by nations that tested
Israel. . . . . Judg. 3:3, 4

Mount Carmel—*fruitful*

Prophets gathered together
here . . . . 1 Kin. 18:19, 20
Elisha journeyed
to . . . . 2 Kin. 2:25
Shunammite woman comes to
Elisha . . . . 2 Kin. 4:25

Mount Ebal—*bald*

Cursed by God . . . . Deut. 11:29
Joshua built an altar
here . . . . Josh. 8:30

Mount Gaash—*quaking*

Place of Joshua's
burial . . . . Josh. 24:30

Mount Gerizim—*rocky*

Place the blessed
stood. . . . . Deut. 27:12
Jotham spoke to people of
Shechem here . . . . Judg. 9:7

Mount Gilboa—*bubbling spring*

Men of Israel
slain. . . . . 1 Sam. 31:1
Saul and his sons slain
here . . . . 1 Sam. 31:8

Mount Gilead—*heap of witness*

Gideon divides the people for
battle . . . . Judg. 7:3

Mount Hor—*mountain*

LORD spoke to Moses and
Aaron . . . . Num. 20:23
Aaron died
there . . . . Num. 20:25-28

Mount Horeb—*desolate*

Sons of Israel stripped of
ornaments. . . . . . . Ex. 33:6
The same as
Sinai . . . . Ex. 3:1

Mount of Olives

Prophecy
concerning . . . . . . Zech. 14:4
Jesus sent
disciples for {Matt. 21:1, 2
donkey . . . . {Mark 11:1, 2

Jesus speaks of
the signs of His {Matt. 24:3
coming ....{Mark 13:3, 4
After the Lord's
supper went out {Matt. 26:30
to ....{Mark 14:26
Called Mount {Luke 19:29
Olivet ....{Luke 21:37

Mount Seir—*rugged*

Horites defeated by
Chedorlaomer ....Gen. 14:5, 6

Mount Shepher—*beauty*

Israelites camped
at ....Num. 33:23, 24

Mount Sinai

Lord descended upon, in
fire..............Ex. 19:18
Lord called Moses to the
top..............Ex. 19:20
The glory of the LORD rested on,
for six days......Ex. 24:16

Mount Tabor—*broken*

Deborah sent Barak there to defeat
Canaanites ......Judg. 4:6-14

Mount Zion

Survivors shall go out
from ....2 Kin. 19:31

Mountain—*a high elevation of earth*

A. *Mentioned in the Bible:*
Abarim ......Num. 33:47, 48
Ararat ....Gen. 8:4
Bashan ....Ps. 68:15
Carmel ....1 Kin. 18:19
Ebal ....Deut. 27:13
Gaash ....Judg. 2:9
Gerizim.......Deut. 11:29
Gilboa ....2 Sam. 1:6, 21
Hachilah.......1 Sam. 23:19
Hermon ......Josh. 13:11
Hor..........Num. 34:7, 8
Horeb (same as
Sinai)........Ex. 3:1
Lebanon......Deut. 3:25
Moreh ....Judg. 7:1
Moriah ......Gen. 22:2
Nebo ....Deut. 34:1
Olives or
Olivet........Matt. 24:3
Pisgah........Num. 21:20
Sinai.........Ex. 19:2-20
Sion or Zion ...2 Sam. 5:7
Tabor.........Judg. 4:6-14

B. *In Christ's life, place of:*
Temptation ....Matt. 4:8
Sermon........Matt. 5:1
Prayer........Matt. 14:23
Transfigura-
tion...........Matt. 17:1, 2
Prophecy .....Matt. 24:3
Agony ....Matt. 26:30, 31
Ascension .....Luke 24:50

C. *Uses of:*
Boundaries ....Num. 34:7, 8
Distant
vision ....Deut. 3:27
Hunting ......1 Sam. 26:20
Warfare ......1 Sam. 17:3
Protection .....Amos 6:1
Refuge ....Matt. 24:16
Idolatrous
worship........Is. 65:7
Assembly
sites ....Josh. 8:30-33

D. *Significant Old Testament
events on:*
Ark rested upon
(Ararat).......Gen. 8:4
Abraham's testing
(Moriah) ......Gen. 22:1-19
Giving of the Law
(Sinai) ....Ex. 19:2-25
Moses' view of Canaan
(Pisgah)........Deut. 34:1
Combat with Baalism
(Carmel) ......1 Kin. 18:19-42
David's city
(Zion)..........2 Sam. 5:7

E. *Figurative of:*
God's:
Protection ....Is. 31:4
Dwelling......Is. 8:18
Judgments...Jer. 13:16
Gospel age.....Is. 27:13
Messiah's
advent ....Is. 40:9
Great joy .....Is. 44:23
Great
difficulties.....Matt. 21:21
Pride of man...Luke 3:5
Supposed
faith ....1 Cor. 13:2

Mourning—*expression of sorrow*

A. *Caused by:*
Death ....Gen. 50:10
Defection......1 Sam. 15:35
Diso-
bedience ......Ezra 9:4-7

Desolation.....Joel 1:9, 10
Defeat........Rev. 18:11
Discourage-
ment..........Ps. 42:9
Disease.......Job 2:5-8

B. *Transformed into:*
Gladness.......Is. 51:11
Hope..........John 11:23-28
Everlasting
joy............Is. 35:10

C. *Signs of:*
Tearing of
clothing.......2 Sam. 3:31, 32
Ashes on
head..........2 Sam. 13:19
Sackcloth......Gen. 37:34
Neglect of
appearance...2 Sam. 19:24
Presence of
mourners.....John 11:19, 31
Apparel........2 Sam. 14:2
Shave head....Jer. 16:6, 7

Mouse, mice—*a small quadruped*

Accounted
unclean..........Lev. 11:29
Eaten by idolatrous
Israelites.........Is. 66:17

Mouth

A. *Descriptive of:*
Top of a well..Gen. 29:2, 3, 8
Opening of a
sack..........Gen. 42:27, 28
Man's.........Job 3:1

B. *Exhortations concerning:*
Make all
acceptable....Ps. 19:14
Keep with a
muzzle........Ps. 39:1
Set a guard
before........Ps. 141:3
Keep the corrupt
from..........Eph. 4:29
Keep filthy language
from..........Col. 3:8

C. *Of unregenerate, source of:*
Lying........1 Kin. 22:13, 22, 23
Idolatry.......1 Kin. 19:18
Unfaith-
fulness........Ps. 5:9
Cursing........Ps. 10:7
Pride..........Ps. 17:10
Evil............Ps. 50:19
Lies...........Ps. 63:11

Vanity.........Ps. 144:8, 11
Foolishness....Prov. 15:2, 14

D. *Of regenerate, used for:*
Prayer........1 Sam. 1:12
God's Law.....Josh. 1:8
Praise.........Ps. 34:1
Wisdom.......Ps. 37:30
Testimony.....Eph. 6:9
Confession.....Rom. 10:8-10
Righ-
teousness.....Ps. 71:15

Move—*to change the position*

A. *Of God's Spirit in:*
Creation.......Gen. 1:2
Man...........Judg. 13:25
Prophets.......2 Pet. 1:21

B. *Of things immovable:*
City of God...Ps. 46:4, 5
Eternal
kingdom.....Ps. 96:10

Mowing—*to cut grass*

First growth for
taxes...........Amos 7:1
Left on the
ground..........Ps. 72:6

Moza—*a going forth*

1. Descendant of
Judah.........1 Chr. 2:46
2. Descendant of
Saul..........1 Chr. 8:36, 37

Mozah—*drained*

A Benjamite
town.............Josh. 18:21, 26

Mulberry tree

Referred to by
Jesus.............Luke 17:6

Mule—*a hybrid between a horse and a donkey*

Breeding of,
forbidden.........Lev. 19:19
Sign of kingship..1 Kin. 1:33
Used in trade.....Ezek. 27:14
Considered
stubborn.........Ps. 32:9

Multiply—*to increase in quantity or quality*

A. *Of good things:*
Holy seed.....Jer. 30:19
Churches.....Acts 9:31

Word of God ..Acts 12:24
God's
wonders ......Ex. 7:3
Loaves and ⎰ Matt. 15:32-39
fish ....⎱ John 6:1-15

B. *Secret of:*
God's:
Promise.......Gen. 16:10
Oath..........Gen. 26:3, 4
Man's
obedience .....Deut. 7:12, 13

Multitude—*a large number of people*

A. *Dangers of:*
Mixed, source of
evil ....Ex. 12:38
Follow after in doing
evil ....Ex. 23:2
Sacrifices,
vain..........Is. 1:11

B. *Christ's compassion upon:*
Teaching ......Matt. 5:1
Healing........Matt. 12:15
Teaching parables
to.............Matt. 13:1-3, 34
Feeding........Matt. 14:15-21

C. *Their attitude toward Christ:*
Reaction to....Matt. 9:8, 33
Recognition ⎰ Matt. 14:5
of ....⎱ Matt. 21:46
Reception of...Matt. 21:8-11
Running
after ....John 6:2
Rejection of ...Matt. 27:20

Munificence—*generous in giving*

Measure of, on:
God's part ....Mal. 3:10
Israel's part.....Ex. 36:3-7
Judah's part......1 Chr. 29:3-9
Christian's part ..2 Cor. 8:1-5

Muppim—*obscurities*

Son of Benjamin ..Gen. 46:21
Called Shupham ..Num. 26:39
Shuppim and ⎰ 1 Chr. 7:12, 15
Shephuphan.....⎱ 1 Chr. 8:5

Murder

A. *Defined as:*
Coming out of the
heart.........Matt. 15:19
Result from
anger ....Matt. 5:21, 22
Work of the
flesh ....Gal. 5:19-21

Excluding from eternal
life............1 John 3:15

B. *Guilt of:*
Determined by
witnesses .....Num. 35:30
Not
redeemable....Num. 35:30
Not forgiven by flight to the
altar ....Ex. 21:14

C. *Penalty of:*
Ordained by
God...........Gen. 9:6
Executed by avenger of
blood ....Deut. 19:6

See Homicide

Murmuring—*sullen dissatisfaction with things*

A. *Caused by:*
Thirst ....Ex. 15:24
Hunger ......Ex. 16:2, 3, 8
Fear...........Num. 14:1-4

B. *Against Christ, because of His:*
Practices ......Luke 15:1, 2
Pronounce-
ments........John 6:41-61

C. *Of Christians:*
Provoked......Acts 6:1
Forbidden ....John 6:43
Excluded .....Phil. 2:14

Mushi—*drawn out*

Son of Merari .....Ex. 6:19
Descendants of,
called ⎰ Num. 3:33
Mushites ....⎱ Num. 26:58

Music

A. *Used in:*
Farewells ......Gen. 31:27
Entertain-
ments.........Is. 5:12
Weddings ....Jer. 7:34
Funerals......Matt. 9:18, 23
Sacred
processions ...1 Chr. 13:6-8
Victory
celebrations...Ex. 15:20, 21
Coronation
services ....2 Chr. 23:11, 13
Dedication
services ....2 Chr. 5:11-13

B. *Influence of, upon:*
Mental ⎰ 1 Sam. 16:14-17,
disorders.....⎱ 23
Sorrowful.....Ps. 137:1-4

C. *List of instruments of:*
Cymbal........1 Cor. 13:1
Flute ....Ps. 150:4
Is. 30:29
Harp...........1 Sam. 16:16, 23
Psaltery ....1 Sam. 10:5
Dan. 3:5, 10
Tambourine ...Is. 5:12
Horn ....Dan. 3:5, 7
Lyre...........Dan. 3:5, 7
Sistrums......2 Sam. 6:5
Timbrel........Gen. 31:27
Ex. 15:20
Trumpet.......Josh. 6:4
Complete
orchestra .....2 Sam. 6:5

Music in Christian worship

From heart........Eph. 5:19
Means of
teaching..........Col. 3:16

Must—*something that is imperative*

A. *Concerning Christ's:*
Preaching.....Luke 4:43
Suffering ......Matt. 16:21
Death ....John 3:14
Fulfillment of
Scripture.....Matt. 26:54
Resurrection...John 20:9
Ascension .....Acts 3:21
Reign..........1 Cor. 15:25

B. *Concerning the believer's:*
Belief.........Heb. 11:6
Regener-
ation..........John 3:7
Salvation .....Acts 4:12
Worship ....John 4:24
Duty ....Acts 9:6
Suffering .....Acts 9:16
Mission ....Acts 19:21
Moral life.....Titus 1:7
Inner life .....2 Tim. 2:24
Judgment......2 Cor. 5:10

C. *Concerning prophecy:*
Gospel's procla-
mation........Mark 13:10
Gentiles'
inclusion......John 10:16
Earth's
tribulations ...Matt. 24:6
Resurrection...1 Cor. 15:53

Mustard seed—*very small seed*

Kingdom compared
to ....Matt. 13:31

Faith compared
to ....Matt. 17:20

Mutability—*capable of change*

A. *Asserted of:*
Physical
world ....Matt. 5:18
Earthly
world ....1 John 2:15-17
Old covenant ..Heb. 8:8-13
Present order ..2 Cor. 4:18

B. *Denied of:*
God ....Mal. 3:6
Christ ....Heb. 1:10, 11
Heb. 13:8

See Immutability; Move

Mute—*inability to speak*

A. *Used literally of dumbness:*
Natural........Ex. 4:11
Penalized .....Luke 1:20

B. *Used figuratively of:*
External
calamity ......Ps. 38:13
Submissive-
ness...........Is. 53:7
Lamb before shearer
is ....Acts 8:32
With silence ...Ps. 39:2

Mutilation—*to maim, to damage, to
disfigure*

A. *Object of, forbidden:*
On the body ...Lev. 19:28
For:
Priesthood....Lev. 21:18
Sacrifice......Lev. 22:22
Mourning.....Jer. 41:5-7

B. *Practiced by:*
Jews...........Judg. 19:29, 30
Philistines ....Judg. 16:21
Canaanites ...Judg. 1:6, 7
Baal
prophets ......1 Kin. 18:28

C. *Used of:*
Legalistic
circumcision ..Phil. 3:2

Mutiny—*revolt against authority*

By Israelites ......Num. 14:1-4

Mutual—*a common interest*

Spoken of faith ...Rom. 1:12

Muzzling

Applied:

To oxen..........Deut. 25:4
Figuratively, to
Christians.......1 Cor. 9:9-11

Myra—*a city of Lycia*

Paul changes ships
here..............Acts 27:5, 6

Myrrh

A. *Dried gum (Heb., mor) of a
balsam tree, used:*
In anointing
oil ....Ex. 30:23
As a perfume . Ps. 45:8
For beauty
treatment.....Esth. 2:12
Brought as
gifts ....Matt. 2:11
Given as a
sedative.......Mark 15:23
Used for
embalming....John 19:38, 39

B. *Fragrant resin (Heb., lot) used:*
In commerce . Gen. 37:25
As presents....Gen. 43:11

Myrtle—*a shrub*

Found in mountains; booths
made of..........Neh. 8:15
Figurative of the
Gospel ....Is. 41:19
Used
symbolically.....Zech. 1:10, 11

Mysia—*a province of Asia Minor*

Paul and Silas pass
through.........Acts 16:7, 8

Mystery—*something unknown except
by divine revelation*

A. *Concerning God's:*
Secrets ....Deut. 29:29
Providence ....Rom. 11:33-36
Sovereignty...Rom. 9:11-23
Prophecies.....1 Pet. 1:10-12
Predesti-
nation ....Rom. 8:29, 30

B. *Concerning Christianity:*
Christ's
incarnation ...1 Tim. 3:16
Christ's
nature ....Col. 2:2
Kingdom of
God...........Luke 8:10

Christian
faith ....1 Tim. 3:9
Indwelling
Christ.........Col. 1:26, 27
Union of all
believers ......Eph. 3:4-9
Israel's
blindness......Rom. 11:25
Lawlessness ...2 Thess. 2:7
Harlot
Babylon.......Rev. 17:5, 7
Resurrection of
saints ....1 Cor. 15:51
God's completed
purpose.......Rev. 10:7

Mythology, referred to

Zeus..............Acts 14:12, 13
Hermes...........Acts 14:12
Pantheon ....Acts 17:16-23
Diana..........Acts 19:24-41
Castor and Pollox (Twin
Brothers)........Acts 28:11

Myths—*speculative and philosophical
fable or allegory*

Condemned ......1 Tim. 1:4
Fables ....1 Tim. 4:7
False.............2 Tim. 4:4

N

Naam—*pleasantness*

Son of Caleb .....1 Chr. 4:15

Naamah—*sweet, pleasant*

1. Daughter of
Lamech.......Gen. 4:19-22
2. Ammonite wife of Solomon;
mother of King
Rehoboam ....1 Kin. 14:21, 31
3. Town of
Judah.........Josh. 15:1, 41

Naaman—*pleasant*

1. Son of
Benjamin .....Gen. 46:21
2. Captain in the Syrian
army..........2 Kin. 5:1-11
Healed of his
leprosy........2 Kin. 5:14-17
Referred to by
Christ........Luke 4:27

Naamathite—*an inhabitant of Naamah*

Applied to Zophar, Job's
friend ....Job 2:11

Naamites

Descendants of
Naaman.........Num. 26:40

Naarah—*girl*

1. Wife of
   Ashur.........1 Chr. 4:5, 6
2. Town of
   Ephraim ......Josh. 16:7
   Same as
   Naaran.......1 Chr. 7:28

Naarai—*pleasantness of Yahweh*

One of David's mighty
men..............1 Chr. 11:37

Naashon (see Nahshon)

Nabal—*fool*

Wealthy sheep
owner............1 Sam. 25:2, 3
Refuses David's
request............1 Sam. 25:4-12
Abigail, wife of, appeases David's
wrath against ....1 Sam. 25:13-35
Drunk, dies of a
stroke............1 Sam. 25:36-39
Widow of, becomes David's
wife..............1 Sam. 25:39-42

Naboth—*sprout*

Owner of vineyard coveted by King
Ahab..............1 Kin. 21:1-4
Accused falsely of blasphemy and
disloyalty.........1 Kin. 21:5-16
Murder of,
avenged..........1 Kin. 21:17-25

Nachon—*prepared*

Threshingfloor, site of Uzzah's
death..............2 Sam. 6:6, 7

Called:
Perez Uzzah
("breach")........2 Sam. 6:8
Chidon...........1 Chr. 13:9

Nadab—*willing, liberal*

1. Eldest of Aaron's four
   sons ....Ex. 6:23
   Takes part in affirming
   covenant......Ex. 24:1, 9-12
   Becomes
   priest ....Ex. 28:1
   Consumed by
   fire............Lev. 10:1-7
   Dies childless ..Num. 3:4

2. Judahite.......1 Chr. 2:28, 30
3. Benjamite .....1 Chr. 8:30
4. King of
   Israel ....1 Kin. 14:20
   Killed by
   Baasha........1 Kin. 15:25-31

Naggai

Ancestor of
Christ ....Luke 3:25

Nahalal, Nahallal, Nahalol—*drinking place for flocks*

Village of
Zebulun..........Josh. 19:10, 15
Assigned to Merarite
Levites ....Josh. 21:35
Canaanites not driven
from ....Judg. 1:30

Nahaliel—*valley of God*

Israelite camp.....Num. 21:19

Naham—*consolation*

Father of Keilah ..1 Chr. 4:19

Nahamani—*compassionate*

Returned after the
exile..............Neh. 7:7

Naharai—*snorting*

Armor-bearer of {2 Sam. 23:37
Joab.   {1 Chr. 11:39

Nahash—*serpent*

1. King of Ammon; makes
   impossible
   demands......1 Sam. 11:1-15
2. King of Ammon who treats
   David kindly ..2 Sam. 10:2
   Son of, helps
   David........2 Sam. 17:27-29
3. Father of Abigail and Zeruiah,
   David's half
   sisters.........2 Sam. 17:25

Nahath—*descent*

1. Edomite
   chief..........Gen. 36:13
2. Kohathite
   Levite.........1 Chr. 6:26
   Called Tohu ...1 Sam. 1:1
3. Levite in Hezekiah's
   reign..........2 Chr. 31:13

Nahbi—*concealed*

Spy of Naphtali ...Num. 13:14

Nahor, Nachor—*snorting*

1. Grandfather of
   Abraham......Gen. 11:24-26
2. Son of Terah, brother of
   Abraham......Gen. 11:27
   Marries Milcah, fathers eight
   sons by her and four by
   concubine.....Gen. 11:29
   City of
   Haran........Gen. 24:10
   God of........Gen. 31:53

Nahshon, Naashon

Judahite leader....Num. 1:4, 7
Aaron's brother-in-
law..............Ex. 6:23
Ancestor of
David ....Ruth 4:20-22
Ancestor of
Christ ....Matt. 1:4

Nahum—*full of comfort*

Inspired prophet to Judah
concerning
Nineveh..........Nah. 1:1

Nahum, the Book of—*a book of the Old
Testament*

The awesomeness of
God ....Nah. 1:1-15
The destruction of
Nineveh..........Nah. 2-3

Nail

A. *Significant uses of:*
Killing a
man ....Judg. 4:21
Fastening Christ to
cross.........John 20:25

B. *Figurative uses of:*
Words fixed in the
memory......Eccl. 12:11
Atonement for man's
sin ....Col. 2:14

Nain—*pleasant*

Village south of Nazareth; Jesus
raises widow's son
here..............Luke 7:11-17

Naioth—*habitations*

Prophets' school {1 Sam. 19:18, 19,
in Ramah........{ 22, 23

Naked, nakedness—*nude, nudity*

A. *Used of man's:*
Original state ..Gen. 2:25

Sinful state ....Gen. 3:7, 10, 11
State of
grace ....Rom. 8:35
Disembodied
state ....2 Cor. 5:3

B. *Evil of:*
Strictly
forbidden .....Lev. 18:6-20
Brings a
curse.........Gen. 9:21-25
Judged by
God..........Ezek. 22:10

C. *Instances of:*
Noah guilty
of............Gen. 9:21-23
Forbidden, to
priests ....Ex. 20:26
Michal rebukes David
for...........2 Sam. 6:20-23

D. *Putting clothing on:*
Indicates a changed
life...........Mark 5:15
Promises a
reward.......Matt. 25:34-40
Takes away
shame ....Rev. 3:18
Sign of true
faith ....James 2:15-17

E. *Figurative of:*
Separation from
God..........Is. 20:3
Israel's unworthi-
ness..........Ezek. 16:7-22
Judah's spiritual
adultery......Ezek. 16:36-38
God's
judgment .....Ezek. 16:39
Spiritual
need ....Hos. 2:9
Wickedness....Nah. 3:4, 5
Needy ....Matt. 25:36, 38
God's
knowledge ....Heb. 4:13
Unprepared-
ness..........Rev. 16:15

Name—*a word used to identify a
person, animal, or thing*

A. *Determined by:*
Events of the
time ....Gen. 30:8
Prophetic
position ......Gen. 25:26
Fondness of
hope ....Gen. 29:32-35

Change of
  character .....John 1:42
Innate
  character .....1 Sam. 25:25
Coming
  events ....Is. 8:1-4
Divine
  mission ....Matt. 1:21

B. Of God, described as:
Great ....Josh. 7:9
Secret ....Judg. 13:18
Glorious ......Is. 63:14
Everlasting ....Ps. 135:13
Exalted ....Ps. 148:13
Holy...........Is. 57:15

C. Of God, evil acts against:
Taken in
  vain..........Ex. 20:7
Sworn falsely ..Lev. 19:12
Lies spoken
  in ....Zech. 13:3
Despised ......Mal. 1:6

D. Of God, proper attitude toward:
Exalt ....Ps. 34:3
Praise ....Ps. 54:6
Love...........Ps. 69:36

E. Of Christ:
Given before
  birth ....Matt. 1:21, 23
Hated by the
  world ....Matt. 10:22
Believers baptized
  in ....Acts 2:38
Miracles performed
  by ....Acts 3:16
Believers suffer
  for ....Acts 5:41
Speaking in....Acts 9:27, 29
Gentiles called
  by ....Acts 15:14, 17
Final subjection
  to............Phil. 2:9, 10

F. Of believers:
Called
  everlasting ....Is. 56:5
Written in
  heaven........Luke 10:20
Called evil by
  world ....Luke 6:22
Known by
  Christ.........John 10:3
Confessed by
  Christ.........Rev. 3:5
"Called by"....Is. 62:2
  Rev. 3:12

Names of Christ (see Christ, names of)

Naomi—my delight

Widow of
  Elimelech ....Ruth 1:1-3
Returns to Bethlehem with
  Ruth ....Ruth 1:14-19
Arranges Ruth's marriage to
  Boaz ....Ruth 3–4
Considers Ruth's child (Obed)
  her own..........Ruth 4:16, 17

Naphish—numerous

Ishmael's eleventh
  son..............Gen. 25:15

Naphtali—my wrestling

1. Son of Jacob by
  Bilhah ....Gen. 30:1; 8
  Sons of, form
    tribe ....Gen. 46:24
  Receives Jacob's
    blessing ......Gen. 49:21, 28
2. Tribe of.......Num. 1:42
  Stationed
    last ....Num. 2:29-31
  Territory assigned
    by ....Josh. 19:32-39
  Canaanites not driven out
    by ....Judg. 1:33
  Barak becomes
    famous.......Judg. 4:6, 14-16
  Bravery of,
    praised.......Judg. 5:18
  Warriors of, under
    Gideon.......Judg. 7:23
  Warriors of, help
    David.........1 Chr. 12:34
  Conquered by
    wars ....1 Kin. 15:20
  Taken
    captive........2 Kin. 15:29
  Prophecy of a great light
    in.............Is. 9:1-7
  Fulfilled in Christ's ministry
    in.............Matt. 4:12-16

Naphtuhim

Fourth son of Mizraim; probably
district around ...Gen. 10:13

Narcissus

Christian in
  Rome ....Rom. 16:11

Nathan—gift

1. Son of David ..2 Sam. 5:14
  Mary's lineage traced
    through.......Zech. 12:12
2. Judahite ....1 Chr. 2:36

3. Prophet under David and
   Solomon ......1 Chr. 29:29
   Reveals God's plan to
   David.........2 Sam. 7:2-29
   Rebukes David's
   sin..........2 Sam. 12:1-15
   Renames
   Solomon
   as Jedidiah....2 Sam. 12:24, 25
   Reveals Adonijah's
   plot.......1 Kin. 1:10-46
   Sons of, in official
   positions ......1 Kin. 4:1, 2, 5
4. Father of
   Igal...........2 Sam. 23:36
5. A chief among
   returnees .....Ezra 8:16
6. One who divorced his foreign
   wife..........Ezra 10:34, 39

Nathanael—*God has given*

One of Christ's
disciples.........John 1:45-51

Nathan-Melech—*the king has given*

An official in Josiah's
reign ....2 Kin. 23:11

National duties (see Citizen, citizenship)

Nations—*people under a sovereign
government*

A. *Of the world:*
   Descendants of Noah's
   sons ....Gen. 10:32
   Originate in a
   person ....Gen. 19:37, 38
   Made from one
   blood ....Acts 17:26
   Separated by
   God............Deut. 32:8
   Inherit separate character-
   istics..........Gen. 25:23
   Laden with
   iniquity ......Is. 1:4
   Destroyed by
   corruption ....Lev. 18:26-28
   Exalted by righ-
   teousness .....Prov. 14:34
   Father of many
   nations........Gen. 17:4
   LORD will set you high
   above all......Deut. 28:1
   Subject to
   repentance....Jer. 18:7-10
   Judged by
   God............Gen. 15:14

   Under God's
   control........Jer. 25:8-14
   Future of,
   revealed.......Dan. 2:27-45
   Gospel to be preached
   to all.........Matt. 24:14
   Sarah shall be mother of
   many ....Gen. 17:16

B. *Of Israel:*
   Descendants
   of   ⎰Gen. 12:2
   Abraham.....⎱John 8:33, 37
   Designated ....Ex. 19:6
   Given   ⎰Deut. 4:7, 8
   blessings......⎱Rom. 9:4, 5
   Punished by
   God............Jer. 25:1-11
   Scattered
   among   ⎰Neh. 1:8
   nations........⎱Luke 21:24
   Christ died
   for ....John 11:51

C. *Of the true people of God:*
   Described as
   righteous .....Is. 26:2
   Born in a
   day ....Is. 66:8
   Accounted
   fruitful........Matt. 21:43
   Believers are...1 Pet. 2:9

Nations, table of

Record...........Gen. 10:1-32

Natural—*that which is innate and real;
not artificial or man-made*

A. *Described as:*
   Physical
   origin ....James 1:23
   Normal ....Rom. 1:26
   Unre-
   generate .....1 Cor. 2:14
   Unnatural ....2 Pet. 2:12
   Temporal ....1 Cor. 15:46

B. *Contrasted with:*
   Acquired ......Rom. 11:21, 24
   Perverted......Rom. 1:26, 27
   Spiritual
   (life)..........1 Cor. 2:14
   Spiritual
   (body) ....1 Cor. 15:44-46

Naturalization—*becoming a citizen of
an adopted country*

Natural level,
rights of.........Acts 22:25-28

Spiritual level,
blessings of......Eph. 2:12-19

Natural man

Does not accept things of
God..............1 Cor. 2:14
Contrasted with
spiritual..........1 Cor. 15:44-46

Natural religion

A. *Contents of, God's:*
Glory........Ps. 19:1-3
Nature........Rom. 1:19, 20
Sovereignty....Acts 17:23-31
Goodness......Acts 14:15-17

B. *Characteristics of:*
Original........Rom. 1:19, 20
Universal......Rom. 10:18
Inadequate....Rom. 2:12-15
Corrupted.....Rom. 1:21-32
Valuable......Dan. 5:18-23

Nature—*the essential elements resident
in something*

A. *Descriptive of:*
Right order of
things........Rom. 1:26
Natural sense of
right..........Rom. 2:14
Non-
existence......Gal. 4:8
Man's natural
depravity.....Eph. 2:3
Divine........2 Pet. 1:4

B. *Of man's unregenerate,
described as:*
Under wrath...Eph. 2:3
Source of:
Iniquity......James 3:6
Corruption....2 Pet. 2:12

Nature, beauties of

Reveal God's
glory.........Ps. 19:1-6
Greater than outward
appearance......Matt. 6:28-30
Descriptive of spiritual
blessings......Is. 35:1, 2

Navel—*the point at which the umbilical
cord is attached*

A. *Used literally of:*
Lover's
appeal.......Song 7:2

B. *Used figuratively of:*
Israel's wretched
condition.....Ezek. 16:4

Navy—*ships owned by a country*

Solomon's.........1 Kin. 9:26
Jehoshaphat's.....1 Kin. 22:48

Nazarene—*a native of Nazareth*

Jesus to be
called...........Matt. 2:23
Descriptive of Jesus'
followers.........Acts 24:5

Nazareth

A. *Town in Galilee:*
Considered
obscure.......John 1:46
City of Jesus'
parents.......Matt. 2:23
Early home of
Jesus.........Luke 2:39-51
Jesus departs
from..........Mark 1:9
Jesus rejected
by............Luke 4:16-30

B. *As a title of honor descriptive
of Jesus:*
Anointed by the
Spirit.........Acts 10:38
Risen Lord......Acts 22:8

Nazirite—*one especially consecrated to
God*

A. *Methods of becoming, by:*
Birth.........Judg. 13:5, 7
Vow...........Num. 6:2

B. *Requirements of:*
Separation....Num. 6:4
No:
Wine.........Num. 6:3, 4
Shaving......Num. 6:5
Defilement...Num. 6:6, 7
Corruption....Amos 2:11, 12
Holiness......Num. 6:8

C. *Examples of:*
Samson........Judg. 16:14-17
Samuel........1 Sam. 1:11-28
John the
Baptist.......Luke 1:13, 15
Christians.....2 Cor. 6:17

Neah—*the settlement*

Town in
Zebulun..........Josh. 19:13

Neapolis—*new city*

Seaport of
Philippi..........Acts 16:11

Near—*close at hand* (in place or time)

A. *Of dangers, from:*
   Prostitute......Prov. 7:8
   Destruction....Prov. 10:14
   God's
   judgment .....Joel 3:14

B. *Of the messianic salvation, as:*
   Promised .....Is. 50:8
   Available .....Is. 51:5

C. *Of Christ's return, described by:*
   Christ ....Matt. 24:33
   Paul ....Rom. 13:11

Neariah—*Yahweh drives away*

1. Descendant of
   David.........1 Chr. 3:22, 23
2. Simeonite
   captain........1 Chr. 4:42

Nearness of God

A. *Old Testament:*
   In sense of   ⎰Is. 46:13
   time ....⎱Zeph. 1:14
   In prayer .....Is. 55:6

B. *New Testament:*
   In sense of   ⎰Rev. 1:1-3
   time ....⎱Rev. 22:10
   In prayer .....Phil. 4:5-9

Nebai—*projecting*

Leader who signs the sealed
covenant.........Neh. 10:19

Nebaioth, Nebajoth

Descendants of, from Arabian
tribe..............Is. 60:7
Eldest son of
Ishmael ....Gen. 25:13

Neballat—*hard, firm*

Postexilic town of
Benjamin.....Neh. 11:31, 34

Nebat—*look*

Father of
Jeroboam ....1 Kin. 11:26

Nebo—*height*

1. Babylonian god of literature
   and science ...Is. 46:1
2. Mountain peak near
   Jericho........Num. 33:47

Name of Pisgah's
summit ......Deut. 34:1
3. Moabite town near Mt.
   Nebo.......Num. 32:3
   Restored by
   Reubenites....Num. 32:37, 38
   Mentioned in the
   prophecy......Is. 15:2
4. Town in
   Judah.........Ezra 2:29

Nebuchadnezzar—*Nebo, defend the
boundary*

A. *Life of:*
   Monarch of the Neo-Babylonian
   Empire (605–562 B.C.);
   defeats Pharaoh
   Necho at
   Car-   ⎰2 Chr. 35:20
   chemish......⎱Jer. 46:2
   Besieges Jerusalem; carries
   captives to
   Babylon.......Dan. 1:1-3
   Crushes Jehoiachin's revolt
   (597 B.C.)......2 Kin. 24:10-17
   Carries sacred vessels to
   Babylon.......2 Kin. 24:11-13
   Destroys Jerusalem;
   captures Zedekiah
   (587 B.C.)......Jer. 39:5, 6
   Leads attack on
   Tyre ....Ezek. 26:7

B. *Features concerning:*
   Builder of
   Babylon.......Dan. 4:30
   First of four great
   empires ......Dan. 2:26-48
   Instrument of God's
   judgment .....Jer. 27:8
   Called God's
   servant ......Jer. 25:9
   Afflicted with
   insanity......Dan. 4:28-37

C. *Prophecies concerning his:*
   Conquest of Judah and
   Jerusalem ....Jer. 21:7, 10
   Destruction of
   Jerusalem....Jer. 32:28-36
   Conquest of other
   nations.......Jer. 27:7-9
   Conquest of
   Egypt.........Jer. 43:10-13
   Destruction of
   Tyre ....Ezek. 26:7-12
   Utter
   destruction....Is. 14:4-27

Nebushasban—*Nebo delivers me*

Babylonian
officer . . . . Jer. 39:13

Nebuzaradan—*Nebo has given seed*

Nebuchadnezzar's captain at siege
of Jerusalem . . . . . . 2 Kin. 25:8-20
Carries out Nebuchadnezzar's
commands . . . . 2 Kin. 25:8-20
Protects
Jeremiah . . . . Jer. 39:11-14

Necessary, necessity—*something
imperative*

A. *As applied to God's plan:*
Preaching to the Jews
first . . . . Acts 13:46
Change of the
Law . . . . Heb. 7:12
Of Christ's
sacrifice . . . . Heb. 8:3

B. *In the Christian's life:*
Wise
decisions . . . . . . 2 Cor. 9:5
Personal
needs . . . . Acts 20:34

See Must

Neck

A. *Uses of:*
Ornaments . . . . . Ezek. 16:11
Beauty . . . . Song 4:4
Authority . . . . . . Gen. 41:42

B. *Significant acts performed by:*
Emotional
salutation . . . . . Gen. 45:14
Subjection of
enemies . . . . Josh. 10:24

C. *Figurative of:*
Servitude . . . . . . Gen. 27:40
Severe punish-
ment . . . . Is. 8:8
Rescue . . . . Is. 52:2

See Yoke

Necklace—*an ornament worn about the
neck*

Signifying rank . . . Gen. 41:41, 42
Worn by
animals . . . . Judg. 8:26

Nedabiah—*Yahweh has been gracious*

Son of King
Jeconiah . . . . 1 Chr. 3:18

Need(s)—*an inner or outward lack; a
compulsion to something*

A. *Physical necessity, arising from
lack of:*
Food . . . . Deut. 15:8
Provisions . . . . . 2 Chr. 2:16

B. *Moral necessity, arising from:*
Spiritual
immaturity . . . . Heb. 5:12
Order of
things . . . . Matt. 3:14
Spiritual
need . . . . Luke 10:42

C. *Promises concerning supply of:*
Promised . . . . . . Matt. 6:8, 32
Provided . . . . . . Acts 2:45
Fulfilled . . . . Rev. 21:23

D. *Caused by:*
Riotous
living . . . . Luke 15:14

E. *Provision against, by:*
Help of
others . . . . 2 Cor. 9:12

F. *Reaction to, shown in:*
Humble submission to God's
will . . . . Phil. 4:11, 12

See Must; Necessary, necessity

Needle—*a sharp instrument used in
sewing or embroidering*

Figurative of something
impossible . . . . Matt. 19:24

Needy—*the poor*

A. *Evil treatment of:*
Oppression . . . . . Amos 4:1
Injustice
toward . . . . Is. 10:2

B. *Promise toward:*
God's:
Remembrance
of . . . . Ps. 9:18
Deliverance . . . Ps. 35:10
Salvation of . . . Ps. 72:4-13
Exaltation of . . . Ps. 113:7
Strength of . . . . Is. 25:4

C. *Right treatment of:*
Recom-
mended . . . . . . Deut. 24:14, 15
Remem-
bered . . . . Jer. 22:16
Rewarded . . . . . . Matt. 25:34-40

See Poor, poverty

Neglect—*to fail to respond to duties*

A. *Of material things:*
One's
appearance....2 Sam. 19:24
Needs of the
body..........Col. 2:23

B. *Of spiritual things:*
Gospel.........Matt. 22:2-5
Salvation ......Heb. 2:1-3

C. *Consequences of:*
Kept out.......Matt. 25:1-13
Sent to hell....Matt. 25:24-30
Reward lost....1 Cor. 3:10-15

Nehelamite

Term applied to Shemaiah, a false
prophet ....Jer. 29:24-32

Nehemiah (I)—*Yahweh has comforted*

1. Leader in the postexilic
community....Ezra 2:2
2. Postexilic
workman .....Neh. 3:16

Nehemiah (II)—*Yahweh has comforted*

A. *Life of:*
Son of
Hachaliah.....Neh. 1:1
Cupbearer to the Persian King
Artaxerxes I (465–424
B.C.) ....Neh. 1:11
Grieves over Jerusalem's
desolation.....Neh. 1:4-11
Appointed
governor......Neh. 5:14
Sent to rebuild
Jerusalem.....Neh. 2:1-8
Unwelcome by non-
Jews ....Neh. 2:9, 10
Views walls at
night..........Neh. 2:11-20
Gives list of
builders ....Neh. 3:1-32
Continues work in spite of
opposition.....Neh. 4:1-23
Makes reforms among
Jews ....Neh. 5:1-19
Opposition continues, but work
completed.....Neh. 6:1-19
Introduces law and
order..........Neh. 7:1-73
Participates with Ezra in
restored
worship.......Neh. 8–10
Registers
inhabitants....Neh. 11:1-36

Registers priests and
Levites........Neh. 12:1-26
Returns to Artaxerxes; revisits
Jerusalem.....Neh. 13:6, 7
Institutes
reforms ....Neh. 13:1-31

B. *Character of:*
Patriotic.......Neh. 1:1-4
Prayerful .....Neh. 1:5-11
Perceptive ....Neh. 2:17-20
Persistent......Neh. 4:1-23
Persuasive ....Neh. 5:1-13
Pure in
motives ....Neh. 5:14-19
Persevering ...Neh. 6:1-19

See the next article

Nehemiah, the Book of—*a book of the Old Testament*

Nehemiah's
prayer...........Neh. 1:4-11
Inspection of the
wall ....Neh. 2:11-16
Rebuilding the
wall ....Neh. 3:1-32
The enemies'
plot ....Neh. 6:1-14
The reading of the
Law ....Neh. 8:1-18
Confession of the
priests............Neh. 9:4-38
Nehemiah's
reform ....Neh. 13:7-31

Nehum—*consolation*

Postexilic
returnee..........Neh. 7:7
Called Rehum.....Ezra 2:2

Nehushta—*of bronze*

Wife of King
Jehoiakim ....2 Kin. 24:8

Nehushtan—*piece of brass*

Applied to brazen
serpent...........2 Kin. 18:4

Neiel—*dwelling of God*

Town in Asher ....Josh. 19:24, 27

Neigh—*to cry lustfully*

Used of:
Horses ....Jer. 8:16
Lustful desires ....Jer. 5:8
Rendered
"bellow"..........Jer 50:11

Neighbor

A. *Sins against, forbidden:*
False witness . . Ex. 20:16
Coveting . . . . . Ex. 20:17
Lying . . . . Lev. 6:2-5
Hating . . . . Deut. 19:11-13
Despising . . . . . Prov. 14:21
Enticing . . . . . . Prov. 16:29
Deception . . . . . Prov. 26:19
Flattery . . . . Prov. 29:5
Failure to
pay . . . . Jer. 22:13
Adultery . . . . . . Jer. 29:23

B. *Duties toward, encouraged:*
Love . . . . Rom. 13:9, 10
Speak truth
to . . . . Eph. 4:25
Teach . . . . Jer. 31:34
Show mercy
to . . . . Luke 10:29, 37

Nekoda—*dotted*

Founder of a family of temple
servants . . . . Ezra 2:48
Genealogy of,
rejected . . . . . . Ezra 2:59, 60

Nemuel—*God is spreading*

1. Brother of Dathan and
Abiram . . . . . . Num. 26:9
2. Eldest son of
Simeon . . . . 1 Chr. 4:24
Head of
Nemuelites . . . . Num. 26:12
Called
Jemuel . . . . Gen. 46:10

Nepheg—*sprout*

1. Izhar's son; Korah's
brother . . . . . . Ex. 6:21
2. David's son born in
Jerusalem . . . . 2 Sam. 5:13-15

Nephtoah—*opening*

Border town between Judah and
Benjamin . . . . Josh. 15:9

Nepotism—*putting relatives in public offices*

Joseph's . . . . Gen. 47:11, 12
Saul's . . . . 1 Sam. 14:50
David's . . . . 2 Sam. 8:16-18
Nehemiah's . . . . Neh. 7:2

Ner—*lamp*

Father of Abner;
grandfather of { 1 Sam. 14:50,
Saul . . . . { 51

Nereus—*the name of a sea god*

Christian at
Rome . . . . Rom. 16:15

Nergal—*a Babylonian god of war*

Worshiped by men of
Cuth . . . . 2 Kin. 17:30

Nergal-Sharezer—*Nergal preserve the king*

Babylonian prince during capture
of Jerusalem . . . . . . Jer. 39:3, 13

Neri

Ancestor of
Christ . . . . Luke 3:27

Neriah—*Yahweh is a lamp*

Father of
Baruch . . . . Jer. 32:12

Nest

A. *Kinds of:*
Eagle's . . . . Job 39:27
Swallow's . . . . . Ps. 84:3
Snake's . . . . Is. 34:15
Dove's . . . . Jer. 48:28

B. *Figurative of:*
False
security . . . . . . Num. 24:21, 22
Lord's resting
place . . . . Matt. 8:20
Full maturity . . Job 29:18
Something out of
place . . . . Prov. 27:8
Helplessness . . . Is. 10:14

Net

A. *Kinds of:*
Design in a
structure . . . . . Ex. 27:4, 5
Trapping a bird or
animal . . . . . . Prov. 1:17
Catching fish . . John 21:6-11

B. *Figurative of:*
Plots of evil
men . . . . Ps. 9:15
Predatory
men . . . . Ps. 31:4
God's chastise-
ments . . . . Job 19:6
Flattery . . . . Prov. 29:5
God's
sovereign { Ezek. 12:13
plan . . . . { Ezek. 17:20

Nethaneel, Nethaneal, Nethanel—*God has given*

1. Leader of Issachar ......Num. 1:8
2. Jesse's fourth son ....1 Chr. 2:13, 14
3. Levite trumpeter.....1 Chr. 15:24
4. Levite scribe...1 Chr. 24:6
5. Obed-Edom's fifth son ....1 Chr. 26:4
6. Prince sent to teach Judah ....2 Chr. 17:7
7. Levite chief....2 Chr. 35:9
8. Priest who married a foreign wife..Ezra 10:18-22
9. Priest in Joiakim's time ....Neh. 12:21
10. Levite musician in dedication service ....Neh. 12:36

Nethaniah—*Yahweh has given*

1. Son of Asaph ..1 Chr. 25:2, 12
2. Levite teacher in Jehoshaphat's reign..........2 Chr. 17:8
3. Father of Jehudi ....Jer. 36:14
4. Father of Ishmael, struck down Gedaliah ......2 Kin. 25:23, 25

Nethinim—*given*

A. *Described as:*
   Servants of the Levites.......Ezra 8:20

B. *Probable origin of:*
   Midianites .....Num. 31:2, 41
   Gibeonites .....Josh. 9:23, 27
   Solomon's slaves ....1 Kin. 9:20, 21

C. *Characteristics of:*
   Governed by captains.......Neh. 11:21
   Assigned certain cities..........1 Chr. 9:2
   Exempt from taxes..........Ezra 7:24
   Zealous for Israel's covenant......Neh. 10:28, 29
   Assigned important jobs..........Ezra 8:17
   Returned from exile in large numbers ......Ezra 2:43-54

Netophathite—*an inhabitant of Netophah*

Town of Judah near Jerusalem ....1 Chr. 2:54

Occupied by returning Levites ....1 Chr. 9:16
Applied to two of David's mighty men..............2 Sam. 23:28, 29
Loyalty of, demonstrated.....2 Kin. 25:23, 24

Nettles—*thorn bushes*

Sign of:
   Indolence ....Prov. 24:31
   Desolation ....Is. 34:13
Retreat for cowards..........Job 30:7

Network—*artistic handwork in*

Tabernacle........Ex. 27:4
Temple............2 Kin. 7:18-41

Neutrality

Impossibility of, taught...........{ Matt. 6:24 / Matt. 12:30 }
Invitation to, rejected ......Josh. 24:15, 16

Never—*not ever*

A. *Concerning God's spiritual promises:*
   Satisfaction....John 4:14
   Stability ......Ps. 55:22
   Security ......John 10:28

B. *Concerning God's threats:*
   Chastisement..........2 Sam. 12:10
   Desolation ....Is. 13:20
   Forgiveness....Mark 3:29

New—*something recent or fresh*

Commandment....John 13:34
Covenant ....Jer. 31:31
Creature ......2 Cor. 5:17
Fruit.............Ezek. 47:12
Earth ....Is. 65:17
Spirit ....Ezek. 11:19
Heaven ....Is. 66:22
Jerusalem ....Rev. 21:2
Name ....Is. 62:2
Man ....Eph. 2:15
Song.............Is. 42:10
New thing (Christ's birth)..............Jer. 31:22
All things new ....Rev. 21:5

New birth—*regeneration*

A. *Described as:*
   One heart......Ezek. 11:19
   Resurrection...Rom. 6:4-10
   New creature.......2 Cor. 5:17

Circum-
cision . . . . Deut. 30:6
Holy seed . . . . . . 1 John 3:9
Begotten . . . . . . 1 Pet. 1:3
Name written in
heaven . . . . Luke 10:20

B. *Productive of:*
Growth . . . . 1 Pet. 2:1, 2
Knowledge . . . . 1 Cor. 2:12-16
Change . . . . 2 Cor. 3:18
Fruitfulness . . . . John 15:1-8
Victory . . . . 1 John 5:4
Discipline . . . . . . Heb. 12:3-11

See Born again

New covenant

A. *Described as:*
Everlasting . . . . Is. 55:3
Of peace . . . . . . Ezek. 34:25
Of life . . . . Mal. 2:5

B. *Elements of:*
Author—God . . Eph. 2:4
Cause—God's
love . . . . John 3:16
Mediator—
Christ . . . . 1 Tim. 2:5
Time originated—in
eternity . . . . Rom. 8:29, 30
Time instituted—at man's
sin . . . . Gen. 3:15
Time realized—at Christ's
death . . . . Eph. 2:13-22
Time consummated—in
eternity . . . . . . Eph. 2:7
Duties—faith and
repentance . . . . Mark 1:15

C. *Ratification of, by:*
God's
promise . . . . . . Gen. 3:15
God's oath . . . . . Is. 54:9, 10
Christ's
blood . . . . Heb. 9:12-26
Spirit's
sealing . . . . 2 Cor. 1:22

D. *Superiority of, to the old:*
Hope . . . . Heb. 7:19
Priesthood . . . . . Heb. 7:20-28
Covenant . . . . . . Heb. 8:6
Sacrifice . . . . . . Heb. 9:23

New Gate—*a temple gate*

Princes meet at . . . Jer. 26:10

New Jerusalem

Vision, seen by
Abraham . . . . Heb. 11:10, 16

Reality of, experienced by
believers . . . . Gal. 4:26, 31
Consummation of, awaits
eternity . . . . Heb. 13:14

New man (see New birth)

New moon

A festival
day . . . . {Ps. 81:3
{Col. 2:16
A point of
reference . . . . Is. 66:23

News

A. *Kinds of:*
Distressing . . . . . Gen. 32:6-8
Disturbing . . . . . Josh. 22:11-20
Alarming . . . . . 1 Sam. 4:13-22
Agonizing . . . . . 2 Sam. 18:31-33
Sorrowful . . . . . . Neh. 1:2-11
Joyful . . . . Luke 2:8-18
Fatal . . . . 1 Sam. 4:14-19

B. *Of salvation:*
Bringer of
peace . . . . Is. 52:7
By Christ . . . . . . Is. 61:1-3

See Tidings

New Year

Erection of the tabernacle
on . . . . Ex. 40:17, 18

Neziah—*preeminent*

Head of a Nethinim
family . . . . Ezra 2:43, 54

Nezib—*garrison*

Town of Judah . . . . Josh. 15:1, 43

Nibhaz

Idol of Avites . . . . . 2 Kin. 17:31

Nibshan—*the furnace*

Town of Judah . . . . Josh. 15:1, 62

Nicanor—*victorious*

One of the seven men chosen as
deacons . . . . Acts 6:1-5

Nicodemus—*conqueror of the people*

Pharisee; converses with
Jesus . . . . John 3:1-12
Protests unfairness of Christ's
trial . . . . John 7:50-52
Brings gifts to anoint Christ's
body . . . . John 19:39, 40

Nicolaitanes—*early Christian sect*

Group teaching moral
looseness...........Rev. 2:6-15

Nicolas—*victor over the people*

Non-Jewish proselyte
deacon...........Acts 6:5

Nicopolis—*city of victory*

Town in Epirus (near
Actium)...........Titus 3:12

Niger—*black*

Latin surname of Simeon, a
teacher in
Antioch...........Acts 13:1

Night—*the time of darkness*

A. *Important facts concerning:*
Made by God..Ps. 104:20
Named at
creation.......Gen. 1:5
Begins at
sunset.........Gen. 28:11
Established by God's
covenant......Gen. 8:22
Displays God's
glory..........Ps. 19:2
Designed for
rest...........Ps. 104:23
Wild beasts creep
in.............Ps. 104:20-22
None in
heaven........Zech. 14:7
Divided into "watches" and
hours..........Mark 13:35

B. *Special events in:*
Jacob's
wrestling......Gen. 32:22-31
Egypt's greatest
plague.........Ex. 12:12-31
Ordinance of the
Passover.......Ex. 12:42
King's sleepless-
ness...........Esth. 6:1
Nehemiah's
vigil..........Neh. 2:11-16
Belshazzar
slain..........Dan. 5:30
Angelic
revelation.....Luke 2:8-15
Nicodemus'
talk...........John 3:2
Release from
prison.........Acts 5:19
Paul's escape..Acts 9:24, 25
Wonderful
conversion....Acts 16:25-33

Lord's return..Mark 13:35

C. *Good acts in:*
Toil...........Luke 5:5
Prayer.........1 Sam. 15:11
               Luke 6:12
Song...........Job 35:10
               Ps. 42:8
Flight from   {1 Sam. 19:10
evil...........{Matt. 2:14
Dreams.........Matt. 2:12, 13, 19

D. *Evil acts in:*
Drunken-
ness...........Is. 5:11
Thievery.......Obad. 5
               Matt. 27:64
Debauchery....1 Thess. 5:2-7
Betrayal.......Matt. 26:31, 34,
               46-50
Death..........Luke 12:20

E. *Figurative of:*
Present age....Rom. 13:11, 12
Death..........John 9:4
Unregenerate
state..........1 Thess. 5:5, 7
Judgment......Mic. 3:6

Night creature—*a nocturnal creature*

Dwells in ruins....Is. 34:14

Nighthawk

Unclean bird......Lev. 11:16

Nile—*Egypt's main river*

A. *Called:*
Shihor.........Is. 23:3
Brook of
Egypt.........Is. 27:12
Sea............Nah. 3:8

B. *Characteristics of:*
Has seven
streams.......Is. 11:15
Overflows
annually......Jer. 46:8
Source of Egyptian
wealth........Is. 19:5-8

C. *Events connected with:*
Drowning of male
children.......Ex. 1:22
Moses placed
in.............Ex. 2:3
Water of, turned to
blood.........Ex. 7:15, 20

D. *Figurative of:*
Judgment......Ezek. 30:12
               Amos 9:5
Army..........Jer. 46:7-9

Nimrah—*an abbreviation of Beth Nimrah*

Town in Gilead ...Num. 32:3, 36

Nimrim—*wholesome waters*

Place in south
Moab.............Is. 15:6

Nimrod—*strong*

Ham's grandson...Gen. 10:6-8
Becomes a mighty
hunter ....Gen. 10:8, 9
Establishes cities ..Gen. 10:10-12
Land of Assyria, thus
described........Mic. 5:6

Nimshi—*Yahweh reveals*

Grandfather of King
Jehu ....2 Kin. 9:2, 14
Called Jehu's
father ....2 Kin. 9:20

Nineveh—*the capital of ancient Assyria*

A. *History of:*
Built by
Nimrod ......Gen. 10:8-12
Capital of
Assyria ......2 Kin. 19:36
Jonah preaches
to..............Jon. 1:1, 2
Citizens of:
Repent ....Jon. 3:5-9
At the judgment
seat..........Matt. 12:41

B. *Prophecies concerning its:*
Destruction by
Babylon.......Nah. 2:1-4
Internal
weakness .....Nah. 3:11-17
Utter
desolation ....Nah. 3:18, 19

C. *Described as:*
Great city .....Jon. 3:2, 3
Wealthy ....Nah. 2:9
Fortified ....Nah. 3:8, 12
Wicked.......Jon. 1:2
Idolatrous ....Nah. 1:14
Careless ....Zeph. 2:15
Full of lies ....Nah. 3:1

Ninth hour—*that is, 3 P.M.*

Time of Christ's
death.............Matt. 27:46
Customary hour of
prayer.........Acts 3:1
Time of Cornelius'
vision ....Acts 10:1, 3

Nisan—*beginning*

Name of Abib (first month of
Jewish year) after the
exile.............Neh. 2:1

See Jewish calendar

Nisroch—*eagle, hawk*

Sennacherib's
god..............2 Kin. 19:37

No Amon—*the Egyptian city Thebes*

Nineveh compared
to ....Nah. 3:8

Noadiah—*Yahweh has met by appointment*

1. Levite in Ezra's
time ....Ezra 8:33
2. Prophetess who tries
to frighten
Nehemiah.....Neh. 6:14

Noah (I)—*rest*

A. *Life of:*
Son of
Lamech.......Gen. 5:28, 29
Father of Shem, Ham, and
Japheth ......Gen. 5:32
Finds favor with
God..........Gen. 6:8
Lives in the midst of
corruption ....Gen. 6:1-13
Instructed to build the
ark ....Gen. 6:13-22
Preacher of righ-
teousness ....2 Pet. 2:5
Enters ark with family and
animals ....Gen. 7:1-24
Preserved during
flood..........Gen. 8:1-17
Builds an
altar ....Gen. 8:18-22
Covenant established
with ....Gen. 9:1-19
Plants a vineyard; becomes
drunk.......Gen. 9:20, 21
Pronounces curse and
blessings......Gen. 9:22-27
Dies at 950....Gen. 9:28, 29

B. *Character of:*
Righteous .....Gen. 6:9
Obedient.......Heb. 11:7
In fellowship with
God..........Gen. 6:9
Notable in
history........Ezek. 14:14, 20

Noah (II)—*trembling*

Daughter of
Zelophehad.......Num. 26:33

Nob—*height*

City of priests; David
flees to...........1 Sam. 21:1-9
Priests of, killed by
Saul.............1 Sam. 22:9-23
Near Jerusalem ...Is. 10:32
Reinhabited after the
exile..............Neh. 11:32

Nobah—*barking*

1. Manassite
   leader.........Num. 32:42
2. Town in Gad ..Judg. 8:11

Nobleman—*one who belongs to the
   upper class*

Jesus:

Heals son of......John 4:46-54
Cites in parable ...Luke 19:12-27

Nod—*wandering exile*

Place (east of Eden) of Cain's
abode ....Gen. 4:16, 17

Nodab—*nobility*

Arabian tribe......1 Chr. 5:19

Nogah—*brilliance*

One of David's
sons..............1 Chr. 3:1, 7

Nohah—*rest*

Benjamin's fourth
son...............1 Chr. 8:1, 2

Noise—*a sound of something*

A. *Kinds of:*
   Sea............Ps. 65:7
   Sound of
   Songs.........Ezek. 26:13
                  Amos 5:23
   Battle.........Is. 13:4
                  Jer. 47:3
   Mourners......Matt. 9:23
   Outcry........1 Sam. 4:13, 14
   Revelry......Ex. 32:17, 18
   Growl of
   Dog..........Ps. 59:6
   God's glory ....Ezek. 43:2

B. *Figurative of:*
   Strong
   opposition.....Is. 31:4
   Worthless-
   ness..........Jer. 46:17

Nomad—*wanderer*

Life style of   {Gen. 12:1-9
patriarchs .... {Gen. 13:1-18
Israel's history ....Deut. 26:5

Noon—*midday*

A. *Time of:*
   Eating ....Gen. 43:16, 25
   Resting ....2 Sam. 4:5
   Praying ....Ps. 55:17
   Crying aloud...Ps. 55:17
   Drunken-
   ness...........1 Kin. 20:16
   Destruction....Ps. 91:6
   Death ....2 Kin. 4:20

B. *Figurative of:*
   Blindness ......Deut. 28:29
   Cleansing......Job 11:17

Nophah—*windy place*

Moabite town .....Num. 21:29, 30

North

Refers to:

A geographical   {Gen. 28:14
direction .... {Ps. 107:3
Invading forces ...Is. 14:31
                   Jer. 6:1

Nose, nostrils—*the organ of breathing*

A. *Used literally for:*
   Breathing......Gen. 2:7
   Smelling.......Amos 4:10
   Ornamen-
   tation.........Is. 3:21
   Bondage.......Is. 37:29
   Blood
   (forced)......Prov. 30:33
   Behemoth .....Job 40:15-24
   Idols..........Ps. 115:6
   Nosebleeding produced by
   wringing......Prov. 30:33

B. *Used figuratively of:*
   Man's life......Job 27:3
   God's:
   Power ....Ex. 15:8
   Sovereign
   control........2 Kin. 19:28
   Over-
   indulgence ....Num. 11:20

National hope
(Zedekiah)....Lam. 4:20
Something very
offensive......Is. 65:5

Nose jewels

Worn by women ..Is. 3:21
Put in swine's
snout...........Prov. 11:22

Not my people, Not loved—*symbolic names of Hosea's children*

Lo-Ammi ....Hos. 1:9
Lo-Ruhamah......Hos. 1:6

Nothing—*not a thing*

A. *Descriptive of:*
Something:
  Without
  payment .....Gen. 29:15
Service without:
  Christ ....John 15:5
  Love.........1 Cor. 13:3
Circumcision ..1 Cor. 7:19
Flesh ....John 6:63

B. *Time of:*
Past ....Neh. 4:15
Future.........Ps. 33:10

C. *Things that will come to:*
Wicked ....Job 8:22
Wicked
  counsel ......Is. 8:10
Babylon ....Rev. 18:17

Nourish—*provide means of growth to*

A. *Descriptive of the growth or care of:*
Children.......Acts 7:20, 21
Animals ....2 Sam. 12:3
Plants ....Is. 44:14
Family.........Gen. 45:11
Country ....Acts 12:20

B. *Figurative of:*
Protection .....Is. 1:2
Provision ......Ruth 4:15
Pampering.....James 5:5
Preparedness ..1 Tim. 4:6

Novice—*one who is inexperienced. A recent Christian convert*

Bishops, not to
be................1 Tim. 3:1, 6

Now—*the present time*

A. *As contrasted with:*
Old
  Testament ....John 4:23
Past ....John 9:25

Future........John 13:7, 19
Two
  conditions.....Luke 16:25

B. *In Christ's life, descriptive of His:*
Atonement ....Rom. 5:11
Humiliation....Heb. 2:8
Resurrection ..1 Cor. 15:20
Glorification ...John 13:31
Intercession ...Heb. 9:24
Return.........1 John 2:28

C. *In the Christian's life, descriptive of:*
Salvation ......Rom. 13:11
Regener-
  ation.........John 5:25
Reconcili-
  ation..........Col. 1:21, 22
Justification ...Rom. 5:9
Victory ....Gal. 2:20
Worship ....John 4:23
Suffering ......1 Pet. 1:6-8
Hope ....Rev. 12:10
Glorification ...Rom. 8:21, 22
                1 John 3:2

D. *Descriptive of the present age as:*
Time of:
  Oppor-
    tunity........2 Cor. 6:2
  Evil..........1 Thess. 2:6
God's:
  Greater
    revelation....Eph. 3:5
  Completed redemp-
    tion..........Col. 1:26, 27
  Final dealing with
    mankind .....Heb. 12:26

Nuisance—*something very irritating*

Descriptive of:

Widow...........Luke 18:2-5

Numbers

Symbolic of:

One—unity ....Deut. 6:4
                Matt. 19:6
Two—unity ......Gen. 1:27
Two—division.....1 Kin. 18:21
                Matt. 7:13, 14
Three—the   ⎧ Matt. 28:19
  Trinity ....⎨ 2 Cor. 13:14
                ⎩ (Hos. 6:1, 2
Three—   ⎧ Matt. 12:40
  resurrection ....⎨ Luke 13:32
Three—
  completion ......1 Cor. 13:13

Three—testing . . . . Judg. 7:16

Four—comple-
tion { Matt. 13:4–8
John 4:35

Five—
incompletion { Matt. 25:2
Matt. 25:15–20

Six—man's
testing { Gen. 1:27, 31
Rev. 13:18

Seven—
completion . . . . . Ex. 20:10

Seven—
fulfillment . . . . . . Josh. 6:4

Seven—
perfection . . . . . . Rev. 1:4

Eighth—new
beginning { Ezek. 43:27
1 Pet. 3:20

Ten—
completion . . . . . Dan. 7:7

Tenth—God's
part { Gen. 14:20
Mal. 3:10

Twelve—God's
purpose { John 11:9
Rev. 21:12–17

Forty—
testing { Jon. 3:4
Matt. 4:2

Forty—
judgment . . . . . . { Num. 14:33
Ps. 95:10

Seventy—God's
completed
purpose { Jer. 25:11
Dan. 9:24

Numbers, the Book of—*a book of the
Old Testament*

The census . . . . Num. 1:1–4:49
Cleansing of
Levites . . . . Num. 8:5–22
The cloud and the
tabernacle . . . . . . Num. 9:15–23
The provision of
manna . . . . Num. 11:4–9
The spies . . . . Num. 13:1–14:45
The rebellion of
Korah . . . . Num. 16:1–35
The sin of
Moses . . . . Num. 20:1–13
Aaron's death . . . . . Num. 20:22–29
Balaam and
Balak . . . . { Num. 22:2–
24:25
Offerings and
feasts . . . . { Num. 28:1–
29:40
Settlements in
Gilead . . . . Num. 32:1–42
Preparation for
Canaan . . . . { Num.
33:50–35:34

Nun—*fish*

1. Father of
Joshua,
Israel's
military
leader . . . . { Josh. 1:1
1 Chr. 7:27

2. Letter in the Hebrew
alphabet . . . . . . Ps. 119:105–112

Nurse—*nourishment and protection to
the young*

A. *Duties of:*
Provide nourish-
ment . . . . Gen. 21:7
Protect . . . . 2 Kin. 11:2
Rear "the
sons" . . . . 2 Kin. 10:1, 5

B. *Figurative of:*
Judgment . . . . . Lam. 4:3, 4
Provision . . . . . . Num. 11:12
Gentleness . . . . . 1 Thess. 2:7

Nuts

Provided as gifts . . Gen. 43:11
Grown in
gardens . . . . Song 6:11

Nymphas—*sacred to the nymphs*

Christian of
Laodicea . . . . Col. 4:15

O

Oak—*a large and strong tree*

A. *Uses of:*
Place of rest . . . 1 Kin. 13:14
Place of
idolatry . . . . . . Is. 44:14
For oars . . . . . . Ezek. 27:6

B. *Figurative of:*
Strength . . . . Amos 2:9
Haughtiness . . . Is. 2:11, 13

Oars—*wooden blades used for rowing*

Made of oak . . . . . Ezek. 27:6, 29
Used on galleys . . Is. 33:21

Oaths—*solemn promises*

A. *Expressions descriptive of:*
"As the LORD
lives" . . . . 1 Sam. 19:6
"God is
witness" . . . . . . Gen. 31:50
"The LORD . . . be
witness" . . . . . . Jer. 42:5
"God judge between
us" . . . . Gen. 31:53
"The LORD make you
like" . . . . Jer. 29:22

" 'I adjure
You".........Matt. 26:63
"I call God as
witness" ......2 Cor. 1:23

B. *Purposes of:*
Confirm
covenant......Gen. 26:28
Insure
protection.....Gen. 31:44-53
Establish
truth..........Ex. 22:11
Confirm
fidelity ....Num. 5:19-22
Guarantee
duties.........Gen. 24:3, 4
Sign a
covenant......2 Chr. 15:12-15
Fulfill
promises .....Neh. 5:12, 13

C. *Sacredness of:*
Obligatory .....Num. 30:2-16
Maintained even in
deception .....Josh. 9:20
Upheld by
Christ.........Matt. 26:63, 64
Rewarded......2 Chr. 15:12-15
Maintained in
fear...........1 Sam. 14:24, 26

D. *Prohibitions concerning, not:*
In idol's
name ....Josh. 23:7
In creature's
name ....Matt. 5:34-36
Falsely.........Lev. 19:12
Among
Christians.....Matt. 5:34

Oaths of God

A. *Made in Old Testament
concerning:*
Promise to
Abraham......Gen. 50:24
Davidic
covenant......2 Sam. 7:10-16
Messianic
priesthood ....Ps. 110:4, 5

B. *Fulfilled in New Testament in
Christ's:*
Birth ....Luke 1:68-73
Kingship on David's
throne ....Luke 1:32, 33
Priesthood.....Heb. 7:20-28

See Swearing

Obadiah—*servant of Yahweh*

1. King Ahab's
steward.......1 Kin. 18:3-16

2. Descendant of
David........1 Chr. 3:21
3. Chief of
Issachar......1 Chr. 7:3
4. Descendant of
Saul ....1 Chr. 8:38
5. Gadite
captain........1 Chr. 12:8, 9
6. Man of
Zebulun.......1 Chr. 27:19
7. Prince sent by Jehoshaphat to
teach ....2 Chr. 17:7
8. Levite
overseer ......2 Chr. 34:12
9. Leader in the postexilic
community....Ezra 8:9
10. Priest who signs the
covenant......Neh. 10:5
11. Levite ....1 Chr. 9:16
Called Abda ...Neh. 11:17
12. Postexilic
porter.........Neh. 12:25
13. Prophet of
Judah.........Obad. 1

Obadiah, the Book of—*a book of the Old Testament*

Against Edom.....Obad. 1-9
Edom against
Judah ....Obad. 10-14
The day of the
LORD ....Obad. 15, 16
Zion's victory .....Obad. 17-21

Obal—*to be bare*

Descendants of
Joktan ....Gen. 10:28

Obduracy—*resistance to pleadings of mercy*

Expressed by:

"Stiff-necked".....Ex. 33:3, 5
"Uncircum-
cised"..........Lev. 26:41
"Impenitent"......Rom. 2:5
"Harden your
hearts"...........1 Sam. 6:6
"Nor will I let"....Ex. 5:1, 2
"I will not hear" ..Jer. 22:21
"Do not seek" ....John 5:44
"Increasingly
unfaithful" ....2 Chr. 28:22-25
"Being past
feeling" ....Eph. 4:18, 19
"God gave them
up"...............Rom. 1:24-28

"Therefore they could not
believe" ....John 12:39
"That cannot cease from
sin" ....2 Pet. 2:14
"They were
appointed" ....1 Pet. 2:8
"Let him be unjust
still" ....Rev. 22:11

See Hardness of heart; Impenitence

Obed—*servant*

1. Son of Ephlal ..1 Chr. 2:37, 38
2. Son of Boaz and
   Ruth.........Ruth 4:17-22
3. One of David's mighty
   men..........1 Chr. 11:47
4. Korahite
   porter.........1 Chr. 26:7
5. Father of
   Azariah ....2 Chr. 23:1

Obed-Edom—*servant of Edom*

1. Philistine from Gath;
   ark of the Lord
   left in his   {2 Sam. 6:10-12
   house........ {1 Chr. 13:13, 14
2. Overseer
   of the
   storehouse ....1 Chr. 26:4-8, 15
3. Levitical
   musician ......1 Chr. 16:5
4. Guardian of the sacred
   vessels ....2 Chr. 25:24

Obedience—*submission to authority*

A. *Relationship involved:*
   God—man .....Acts 5:29
   Parent—   {Gen. 28:7
   child......... {Eph. 6:1
   Husband—
   wife............1 Cor. 14:34, 35
   Master—
   servant ....Eph. 6:5
   Ruler—   {Titus 1:1
   subject....... {1 Pet. 2:13, 14
   Leader—
   follower.......Acts 5:36, 37
   Pastor—
   people ....Heb. 13:17
   Man—nature ..James 3:3
   God—nature...Matt. 8:27
   God—
   demons......Mark 1:27

B. *Spiritual objects of:*
   God ....Acts 5:29
   Christ ....Heb. 5:9

Truth.........Gal. 5:7
Faith ....Acts 6:7

C. *In the Christian's life:*
   Comes from the
   heart.......Rom. 6:17
   Needs testing ..2 Cor. 2:4
   Aided by the
   Spirit ....1 Pet. 1:22
   Manifested in
   Gentiles.......Rom. 15:18
   In pastoral
   relations .....2 Cor. 7:15

D. *Lack of, brings:*
   Rejection ......1 Sam. 15:20-26
   Captivity .....2 Kin. 18:11, 12
   Death ....1 Kin. 20:36
   Retribution ....2 Thess. 1:8

E. *Examples of:*
   Noah ....Gen. 6:22
   Abram ....Gen. 12:1-4
   Israelites ......Ex. 12:28
   Caleb and
   Joshua........Num. 32:12
   David..........Ps. 119:106
   Asa...........1 Kin. 15:11, 14
   Elijah..........1 Kin. 17:5
   Hezekiah ......2 Kin. 18:6
   Josiah ....2 Kin. 22:2
   Zerubbabel ....Hag. 1:12
   Christ ....Rom. 5:19
   Paul ....Acts 26:19
   Christians .....Phil. 2:12

Obedience of Christ, our example

To death ....Phil. 2:5-11
Learned..........Heb. 5:7-10
Submissive........Matt. 26:39, 42

Obedience to civil government

Meet obligation ...Mark 12:13-17
Of God............Rom. 13:1-7
Duty ....Titus 3:1
For Lord's sake ...1 Pet. 2:13-17

Obeisance—*bending or bowing*

As an act of:
Respect ....Ex. 18:7
Reverence ......Matt. 2:11
Flaunting
fidelity ....2 Sam. 1:2-16
Fawning favor ....2 Sam. 14:2-4
Feigned flattery ...2 Sam. 15:5, 6

Obil—*camel driver*

Ishmaelite in charge of
camels ....1 Chr. 27:30

Obituary—*an account of a person's life; a death notice*

Written of
Moses............Deut. 34:1-12

Objectors—*those who oppose something*

A. *Argue against God's:*
Power ....Ex. 14:10-15
Provision ......Ex. 16:2-17
Promises ......Num. 14:1-10

B. *Overcome by:*
Prophecies
cited ....Jer. 26:8-19
Promises
claimed ......Acts 4:23-31

Oblivion—*the state of being forgotten*

God's punishment on the
wicked ....Ps. 34:16

Oboth—*water skins*

Israelite camp.....Num. 21:10, 11
Num. 33:43, 44

Observe—*to keep; to remember*

A. *Descriptive of:*
Laws ....Ex. 31:16
Obedience .....Matt. 28:20
Watch-
fulness.......Jer. 8:7
False rituals ...Gal. 4:10

B. *Blessings of proper:*
Material
prosperity.....Deut. 6:3
Righteous-
ness..........Deut. 6:25
Elevation .....Deut. 28:1, 13
Loving-
kindness ......Ps. 107:43

C. *Manner of proper:*
Carefully .....Deut. 12:28
Without
change.......Deut. 12:32
Diligently .....Deut. 24:8
Forever........2 Kin. 17:37
Without
preference ....1 Tim. 5:21

Obstacles—*obstructions*

Eliminated by:

God's help ......Is. 45:2
Christ's help ....Is. 49:9-11
Spirit's help .....Zech. 4:6, 7

Obstacles to faith

Men's honor ......John 5:44
Highminded-
ness.............Rom. 11:20

Obstinacy—*stubbornness*

Continuing in
sin ....2 Chr. 28:22, 23
Rejecting
counsel.........1 Kin. 12:12-15
Refusing to
change ....Jer. 44:15-27

Obstruct—*to hamper progress*

Attempted ....Ezra 4:1-5
Condemned.......3 John 9, 10

Obtain—*to bring into one's possession*

A. *Of material things:*
Advance-
ment.........Esth. 2:9-17

B. *Of spiritual things:*
Favor..........Prov. 8:35
Joy and
gladness ......Is. 35:10
Divine help ....Acts 26:22
Salvation ......Rom. 11:7
Better
resurrection...Heb. 11:35
Faith ....2 Pet. 1:1

Occultism—*pertaining to supernatural, especially evil, influences*

A. *Forms of:*
Astrology......Is. 47:13
Charming......Deut. 18:11
Spiritism......Deut. 18:11
Divination .....Deut. 18:14
Magic ....Gen. 41:8
Necromancy...Deut. 18:11
Soothsaying ...Is. 2:6
Sorcery........Ex. 7:11
Ex. 22:18
Witchcraft .....Deut. 18:10
Wizardry ......Deut. 18:11

B. *Attitude toward:*
Forbidden .....Deut. 18:10, 11
Jer. 27:9
Punished by (Ex. 22:18
death ....(Lev. 20:6, 27
Forsaken ......Acts 19:18-20

Ocran—*troubled*

Man of (Num. 1:13
Asher ....(Num. 2:27

Oded

1. Father of Azariah the
prophet ....2 Chr. 15:1

2. Prophet of
   Samaria.......2 Chr. 28:9-15

Odors, sweet

A. *Used literally of:*
   Sacrificial
   incense ....Lev. 26:31
   Ointment
   fragrance .....John 12:3

B. *Used figuratively of:*
   New life ......Hos. 14:7
   Prayers........Rev. 5:8
   Christian
   service........Phil. 4:18

Offend, offense

A. *Causes of:*
   Christ ....Matt. 11:6
   Persecution....Matt. 24:10
   The cross......1 Cor. 1:23

B. *Causes of, in Christ's:*
   Lowly
   position ......Matt. 13:54-57
   Being the
   Rock..........Is. 8:14
   Being the
   Bread.........John 6:58-66
   Being the righteousness of
   God...........Rom. 9:31-33

C. *Christians forbidden to give:*
   In anything....2 Cor. 6:3
   At any time....Phil. 1:10

See Stumble

Offering of Christ

Of Himself:

Predicted ....Ps. 40:6-8
Prepared........Heb. 5:1-10
Proclaimed......Heb. 10:5-9
Purified........Heb. 9:14
Personalized .....Heb. 7:27
Perfected ....Heb. 10:11-14
Praised..........Eph. 5:2

Offerings

A. *Characteristics of:*
   Made to God
   alone ....Ex. 22:20
   Limitation of ..Heb. 9:9
   Prescribed under the
   Law...........Mark 1:44

B. *Thing offered must be:*
   Perfect ....Lev. 22:21
   Ceremonially
   clean..........Lev. 27:11, 27
   Best ....Mal. 1:14

C. *Offerer must:*
   Not delay......Ex. 22:29, 30
   Offer in righ-
   teousness ....Mal. 3:3
   Offer with thanks-
   giving.........Ps. 27:6

D. *Classification of:*
   Private and
   public.........Lev. 4:1-12
   Physical and
   spiritual.......Lev. 5:1-13
   Voluntary and
   required.......Lev. 1:3
   Accepted and
   rejected........Judg. 6:17-24
   Purified and
   perverted .....Mal. 3:3, 4
   Passing and
   permanent ....Jer. 7:21-23
   Typical and
   fulfilled ....Gen. 22:2, 13

Offerings of the leaders—*by heads, of
twelve tribes*

1. Six wagons and twelve oxen to
   transport
   tabernacle ....Num. 7:1-89
2. Dedication
   gift ....Num. 7:1-89

Office—*a position of trust*

Holders of:

Butler............Gen. 40:13
Judge ....Deut. 17:9
Priest............Deut. 26:3
Ministers of
song ....1 Chr. 6:32
Gatekeeper ......1 Chr. 9:22
Tax collector.....Matt. 9:9
Bishop ....1 Tim. 3:1

Officers—*men appointed to rule over
others*

A. *Descriptive of:*
   Magistrate.....Luke 12:58
   Principal
   officer.........1 Kin. 4:5, 7

B. *Functions of:*
   Administer
   justice ....Num. 11:16

Offices of Christ

As Prophet........Deut. 18:18, 19
                   Is. 61:1-3
As Priest..........Ps. 110:4
                   Is. 53:1-12

As King..........2 Sam. 7:12-17
Luke 1:32, 33

Offscouring—*something vile or worthless*

Jews thus
described........Lam. 3:45

Offspring—*issue* (physical or spiritual)

A. *Used literally of:*
Set apart firstlings { Ex. 13:12
{ Ex. 34:19
Of a donkey you shall redeem... { Ex. 13:13
{ Ex. 34:20
Man's issue (children) .....Job 5:25
Man as created by God..........Acts 17:28, 29
Christ as a descendant of David......Rev. 22:16

B. *Used figuratively of:*
True believer ..Is. 22:24
New Israel.....Is. 44:3-5
Gentile church........Is. 61:9
True Church...Is. 65:23

Og—*giant*

Amorite king of Bashan...........Deut. 3:1, 8
Extent of rule.....Deut. 3:8, 10
Residences at Ashtaroth and Edrei............Josh. 12:4
Man of great size ....Deut. 3:11
Defeated and killed by Israel............Num. 21:32-35
Territory of, assigned to Manasseh ....Deut. 3:13
Memory of, long remembered......Ps. 135:11

Ohad—*powerful*

Son of Simeon ....Gen. 46:10

Ohel—*family*

Son of Zerubbabel......1 Chr. 3:19, 20

Oholah—*tent woman*

Symbolic name of Samaria..........Ezek. 23:4, 5, 36

Oil—*a liquid extracted from olives*

A. *Features concerning:*
Given by God..........Ps. 104:14, 15
Subject to tithing ....Deut. 12:17

B. *Uses of:*
Food ....Num. 11:8
Anointing......1 Sam. 10:1
Beautifi- cation........Ruth 3:3
Perfumer's ointment......Eccl. 10:1
Illumination ....Ex. 25:6
Ex. 30:26-32
Matt. 25:3-8

C. *Types of oil:*
Anointing......Ex. 25:6
Pure..........Ex. 27:20
Baking........Ex. 29:23
Pressed.......Ex. 29:40
Olive ....Ex. 30:24
Precious ointment......2 Kin. 20:13
Golden ......Zech. 4:12

D. *Figurative of:*
Prosperity .....Deut. 32:13
Joy and gladness ......Is. 61:3
Waste- fulness........Prov. 21:17
Brotherly love..........Ps. 133:2
Real grace....Matt. 25:4
Holy Spirit.....1 John 2:20, 27

Oil tree

Signifies restoration ....Is. 41:17-20

Ointment—*a salve made of olive oil and spices*

A. By special prescription for tabernacle .....Ex. 30:23-25
Misuse of, forbidden .....Ex. 30:37, 38
Ingredients stirred together ......Job 41:31

B. *Features concerning:*
Considered very valuable.......2 Kin. 20:13
Carried or stored in containers ....Matt. 26:7
Can be polluted.......Eccl. 10:1

C. *Uses of:*
Cosmetic ......Eccl. 9:8
Sign of
hospitality ....Luke 7:46
Embalming
agent ....Luke 23:55, 56
Sexual
attraction .....Is. 57:9

Old—*mature; ancient*

A. *Descriptive of:*
Age............Gen. 25:8
Elders ....1 Kin. 12:6-13
Experienced ...Ezek. 23:43
Ancient
times ....Mal. 3:4
Old Testament
age ....Matt. 5:21-33
Old
Testament ....2 Cor. 3:14
Unregenerate
nature ....Rom. 6:6

B. *Of man's age, infirmities of:*
Waning sexual
desire ....Luke 1:18
Physical
handicaps.....1 Kin. 1:1, 15
Failing
strength ......Ps. 71:9

C. *Of man's age, dangers of:*
Spiritual
decline........1 Kin. 11:4
Not receiving
instruction ....Eccl. 4:13
Disrespect
toward........Deut. 28:50

D. *Of man's age, blessing of:*
God's care .....Is. 46:4
Continued
fruitfulness...Ps. 92:14
Security of
faith ....Prov. 22:6
Fulfillment of life's
goals..........Is. 65:20
Honor ....Lev. 19:32
Grand-
children.......Prov. 17:6
Men dream
dreams........Acts 2:17

See Length of life

Old Testament

A. *Characteristics of:*
Inspired ....2 Tim. 3:16

Authorita-
tive ....John 10:34, 35
Written by the Holy
Spirit ....Heb. 3:7
Uses many figurative
expressions ...Is. 55:1, 12, 13
Written for our
admonition....1 Cor. 10:1-11
Israel now blinded
to.............2 Cor. 3:14-16
Foreshadows the
New ....Heb. 9:1-28

B. *With the New Testament,
unified in:*
Authorship ....Heb. 1:1
Plan of
salvation......1 Pet. 1:9-12
Presenting Christ (see Messiah,
the)..........Luke 24:25-44

Olive groves

Freely given ......Josh. 24:13
Taken in greed....2 Kin. 5:20, 26

Olive tree

A. *Used for:*
Oil of, many uses
(see Oil).......Ex. 27:20
Temple
furniture......1 Kin. 6:23
Temple construc-
tion...........1 Kin. 6:31-33
Booths.........Neh. 8:15

B. *Cultivation of:*
By grafting ....Rom. 11:24
Hindered by
disease........Deut. 28:40
Failure of, a great
calamity ......Hab. 3:17, 18
Poor provided
for...........Deut. 24:20
Palestine suitable
for ....Deut. 6:11

C. *Figuratively of:*
Peace.........Gen. 8:11
Kingship......Judg. 9:8, 9
Israel.........Jer. 11:16
The
righteous .....Ps. 52:8
Faithful
remnant ......Is. 17:6
Gentile
believers ......Rom. 11:17, 24
True Church...Rom. 11:17, 24
Prophetic
symbols.......Zech. 4:3, 11, 12

Olives, Mount of

A. *Described as:*
"The Mount of
  Olives".......Zech. 14:4
"The hill that is east of
  Jerusalem"....1 Kin. 11:7
"The Mount of
  Corruption"...2 Kin. 23:13
"The
  mountain" ....Neh. 8:15

B. *Scene of:*
David's flight ..2 Sam. 15:30
Solomon's
  idolatry ....2 Kin. 23:13
Ezekiel's
  vision.........Ezek. 11:23
Postexilic
  festivities .....Neh. 8:15
Zechariah's
  prophecy......Zech. 14:4
Triumphal
  entry..........Matt. 21:1
Weeping.......Luke 19:37, 41
Great prophetic
  discourse......Matt. 24:3
Ascension .....Acts 1:12

Olympas

Christian in
  Rome ....Rom. 16:15

Omar—*eloquent*

Grandson of   {Gen. 36:11, 15
  Esau ....{1 Chr. 1:36

Omega—*the last letter in the Greek alphabet*

Descriptive of   {Rev. 1:8, 11
Christ's   {Rev. 21:6
  infinity ....{Rev. 22:13

Omen—*a portent; a sign*

Forbidden.........Deut. 18:10
The LORD causes to
  fail ....Is. 44:25

Omission, sins of

A. *Concerning ordinances:*
Moses' neglect of circum-
  cision ....Ex. 4:24-26
Israel's neglect of the
  tithe ....Mal. 3:7-12
Christians neglecting to
  assemble .....Heb. 10:25

B. *Concerning moral duties:*
Witnessing ....Ezek. 33:1-6

Warning.......Jer. 42:1-22
Watch-   {Matt. 24:42-51
  fulness........{Matt. 26:36-46

Omnipotence—*infinite power*

A. *Of God, expressed by His:*
Names ("Almighty,"
  etc.) ....Gen. 17:1, 2
Creative
  word...........Gen. 1:3
Control of:
  Nature........Amos 4:13
  Nations.......Amos 1:1–2:3
  All things.....Ps. 115:3
Power ....Rom. 4:17-24
Unweariness ..Is. 40:28

B. *Of Christ, expressed by His power over:*
Disease ....Matt. 8:3
Unclean
  spirit..........Mark 1:23-27
Devil ....Matt. 4:1-11
Death ....John 10:17, 18
Destiny........Matt. 25:31-33

C. *Of the Holy Spirit, expressed by:*
Christ's
  anointing .....Is. 11:2
Confirmation of the
  Gospel ....Rom. 15:19

Omnipresence—*universal presence of*

God................Jer. 23:23, 24
Christ.............Matt. 18:20
Holy Spirit ....Ps. 139:7-12

Omniscience—*infinite knowledge of*

God................Is. 40:14
Christ.............Col. 2:2, 3
Holy Spirit ....1 Cor. 2:10-13

Omri—*Yahweh apportions*

1. Descendant of
   Benjamin ....1 Chr. 7:8
2. Judahite ....1 Chr. 9:4
3. Chief officer of
   Issachar .....1 Chr. 27:18
4. King of Israel; made king
   by Israel's
   army..........1 Kin. 16:15, 16
   Prevails over Zimri and
   Tibni.........1 Kin. 16:17-23
   Builds
   Samaria.......1 Kin. 16:24
   Reigns
   wickedly......1 Kin. 16:25-28

On—*stone*

1. Reubenite leader; joins Korah's rebellion . . . . . . Num. 16:1
2. City of Lower Egypt; center of sun-worship. . . Gen. 41:45, 50
   Called Beth Shemesh . . . . . . Jer. 43:13

See Heres

Onam—*vigorous*

1. Horite chief . . . . Gen. 36:23
2. Man of Judah . . . . 1 Chr. 2:26, 28

Onan—*strong*

Second son of Judah; slain for failure to consummate union . . . . Gen. 38:8-10

Oneness—*unity*

A. *Of Christ, with:*
   The Father . . . . John 10:30
   Christians . . . . . Heb. 2:11

B. *Among Christians of:*
   Baptized . . . . . . 1 Cor. 12:13
   Union . . . . Ezek. 37:16-24
   Headship . . . . . Ezek. 34:23
   Faith . . . . Eph. 4:4-6
   Mind . . . . Phil. 2:2
   Heart . . . . Acts 4:32

See Unity of believers

Onesimus—*useful*

Slave of Philemon converted by Paul in Rome . . . . . Philem. 10-17
With Tychicus, carries Paul's letters to Colosse and to Philemon . . . . Col. 4:7-9

Onesiphorus—*profit-bearing*

Ephesian Christian commended for his service . . . . 2 Tim. 1:16-18

Onion—*a bulbous plant used for food*

Lusted after by Israelites . . . . Num. 11:5

Only begotten

Of Christ's:

Incarnation . . . . . . John 1:14
Godhead . . . . . . John 1:18
Mission . . . . John 3:16, 18
                  1 John 4:9

Ono—*strong*

Town of Benjamin rebuilt by Shamed . . . . 1 Chr. 8:12
Reinhabited by returnees . . . . . Ezra 2:1, 33

Onycha—*nail; claw; husk*

Ingredient of holy incense . . . . Ex. 30:34

Onyx—*fingernail* (Greek)

Translation of a Hebrew word indicating a   { Job 28:16
precious stone . . . { Ezek. 28:13
Found in Havilah . . . . Gen. 2:11, 12
Placed in high priest's ephod . . . . . . Ex. 28:9-20
Gathered by David . . . . 1 Chr. 29:2

Open—*to unfasten; to unlock; to expose*

A. *Descriptive of miracles on:*
   Earth . . . . . Num. 16:30, 32
   Eyes . . . . John 9:10-32
   Ears . . . . Mark 7:34, 35
   Mouth . . . . Luke 1:64
   Prison doors . . . Acts 5:19, 23
   Death . . . . 2 Kin. 4:35
   Graves . . . . . . Matt. 27:52

B. *Descriptive of spiritual things:*
   God's provision . . . . . . Ps. 104:28
   God's bounty . . Mal. 3:10
   Christ's blood . . . . Zech. 13:1
   Man's corruption . . . . Rom. 3:13
   Spiritual eyesight . . . . . Luke 24:31, 32
   Door of faith . . Acts 14:27
   Opportunity . . . 1 Cor. 16:9

Ophel—*bulge, hill*

South extremity of Jerusalem's eastern hill . . . . . . Neh. 3:15-27
Fortified by Jotham and Manasseh . . . . 2 Chr. 27:3
Residence of Nethinim . . . . Neh. 3:26

Ophir—*rich*

1. Son of Joktan . . . . Gen. 10:26, 29
2. Land, probably in southeast Arabia, inhabited by descendants of 1 . . . . Gen. 10:29, 30

Famous for its
gold..........1 Chr. 29:4

Ophni—*the high place*

Village of
Benjamin........Josh. 18:24

Ophrah—*hind*

1. Judahite.......1 Chr. 4:14
2. Town in Benjamin near
   Michmash.....Josh. 18:21, 23
3. Town in Manasseh; home of
   Gideon.......Judg. 6:11, 15
   Site of Gideon's
   burial.........Judg. 8:32

Opportunity—*the best time for
something*

A. *Kinds of:*
   Rejected.......Matt. 23:37
   Spurned.......Luke 14:16-24
   Prepared.......Acts 8:35-39
   Providential ...1 Cor. 16:9
   Good ....Gal. 6:10

B. *Loss of, due to:*
   Unbelief.......Num. 14:40-43
   Neglect.......Jer. 8:20
   Unprepared-
   ness..........Matt. 24:50, 51
   Blindness......Luke 19:41, 42

Oppression—*subjection to unjust
hardships*

A. *Kinds of:*
   Personal......Is. 38:14
   National......Ex. 3:9
   Economic......Mic. 2:1, 2
   Messianic.....Is. 53:7
   Spiritual......Acts 10:38

B. *Those subject to:*
   Widows........Zech. 7:10
   Hired
   servant ......Deut. 24:14
   Poor...........Ps. 12:5
   People.........Is. 3:5
   Soul ....Ps. 54:3

C. *Evils of, bring:*
   Guilt ....Is. 59:12, 13
   Reproach ......Prov. 14:31
   Poverty........Prov. 22:16
   Judgment......Ezek. 18:12, 13

D. *Punishment of:*
   God's
   judgment .....Is. 49:26
   Captivity ......Is. 14:2, 4
   Destruction
   of............Ps. 72:4

E. *Protection against:*
   Sought in
   prayer ....Deut. 26:7
   Given by the
   LORD..........Ps. 103:6
   Secured in
   refuge.........Ps. 9:9

F. *Agents of:*
   Nations........Judg. 10:12
   Enemy.........Ps. 42:9
                Ps. 106:42
   Wicked........Ps. 55:3
   Man ....Ps. 119:134
   Leaders........Prov. 28:16
   Sword ....Jer. 46:16
                Jer. 50:16
   Devil ....Acts 10:38
   Rich ....James 2:6

Oracle—*a revelation; a wise saying*

A. *Descriptive of the high priest's
   ephod:*
   Source of
   truth..........1 Sam. 23:9-12

B. *Descriptive of God's Word:*
   Received by
   Israel ....Acts 7:38
   Test of truth...1 Pet. 4:11

Oration, orator

Character of:
   Egotistical ....Acts 12:21-23
   Prejudiced ......Acts 24:1-9
   Inspired..........Acts 26:1-29

Orchard—*a cultivated garden or park*

Source of fruits ...Song 4:13
Source of nuts ...Song 6:11

Orchestra—*group of musicians playing
together*

Instituted by
David ....2 Sam. 6:5

Ordain, ordained—*to establish, appoint,
set, decree*

A. *As appointment to office:*
   Prophet........Jer. 1:5

B. *As appointment of temporal
   things:*
   World order ...Ps. 8:3
   Institution of:
   Offering ....Num. 28:6

C. *As appointment of eternal
   things:*
   Hidden
   wisdom ......1 Cor. 2:7

See Appoint

Order—*harmony; symmetry; in proper places*

A. *As an arrangement in rows:*
Wood for
sacrifices......Gen. 22:9
Battle
formation.....1 Chr. 12:38
Words logically
developed.....Job 33:5
Consecutive
narrative......Luke 1:3
Absence of ....Job 10:22

B. *As a classification according to work:*
Priestly
service........2 Kin. 23:4
Christ's
priesthood ....Ps. 110:4
Church
services.......1 Cor. 11:34
Church
officers........Titus 1:5

C. *Of something prescribed:*
Ritual
regulations....1 Chr. 15:13
Church
regulations....1 Cor. 14:40
Subjection to ..1 Chr. 25:2, 6

D. *Of preparation for death:*
Ahithophel's...2 Sam. 17:23
Hezekiah's.....2 Kin. 20:1

E. *Figurative of:*
God's
covenant......2 Sam. 23:5
Believer's life ..Ps. 37:23
Man's sins .....Ps. 50:21

Ordinances—*regulations established for proper procedure*

A. *Descriptive of:*
Ritual
observance....Heb. 9:1, 10
God's laws....Is. 24:5
God's laws in
nature ....Jer. 31:35
Man's
regulations....Neh. 10:32
Man's laws ....1 Pet. 2:13
Apostolic
messages......1 Cor. 11:2
Jewish
legalism......Eph. 2:15

B. *Of the Gospel:*
Baptism ....Matt. 28:19

Lord's
Supper........1 Cor. 11:23-29
Preaching the
Word ....Rom. 10:15

Oreb—*a raven*

1. Midianite prince slain by
Gideon........Judg. 7:25
2. Rock on which Oreb was
slain ....Judg. 7:25

Oren—*a fir or cedar tree*

Judahite ....1 Chr. 2:25

Orion—*strong*

Brilliant
constellation .....Job 9:9

Ornaments—*outward adornments of the body*

Figurative of:

Wisdom's
instruction ......Prov. 1:9
Reproof
received..........Prov. 25:12
God's provisions ..Ezek. 16:7-14
Apostasy from
God ....Jer. 4:30

See Clothing; Jewels

Orpah—*neck*

Ruth's sister-in-
law..............Ruth 1:4, 14

Orphans—*children deprived of parents*

Description of.....Lam. 5:3
Provision for......Deut. 24:17, 21
Job helps.........Job 29:12
Visitation of,
commended .....James 1:27
Christians not left
"orphans".......John 14:18

Osnapper—*probably the Aramaean name for Ashurbanipal, an Assyrian king*

Called "the great and
noble"...........Ezra 4:10

Ostentatious—*vain, ambitious*

Manifested in:

Boastfulness ......Luke 18:10-14
Hypocrisy.........Matt. 6:1-7, 16
Conceit ....2 Sam. 15:1-6
Egotism..........Acts 12:20-23

Ostracism—*exclusion of a person from society*

Accepted.........Luke 6:22

See Excommunication

Ostrich—*a two-toed, swift and flightless bird*

Figurative of
cruelty ....Lam. 4:3

Othni—*abbreviation of Othniel*

Son of
Shemaiah ....1 Chr. 26:7

Othniel—*God is force*

Son of Kenaz, Caleb's youngest
brother...........Judg. 1:13
Captures Kirjath Sepher; receives
Caleb's daughter as
wife..............Josh. 15:15-17
First judge of
Israel............Judg. 3:9-11

Ought—*something morally imperative*

A. *Of duties not properly done:*
Use of
talents ....Matt. 25:27
Accusation ....Acts 24:19
Growth........Heb. 5:12

B. *Of acts wrongly done:*
Worship ......John 4:20, 21
Death ....John 19:7
Wrong
behavior ....2 Cor. 2:3
Inconsistent
speaking .....James 3:10

C. *Of moral duties among Christians:*
Witnessing ....Luke 12:12
Prayer........Luke 18:1
Service ....John 13:14
Obedience .....1 Thess. 4:1
Helping the
weak.........Rom. 15:1
Love toward
wife.........Eph. 5:28
Proper
behavior .....2 Thess. 3:7
Holy conduct ..2 Pet. 3:11
Willingness to
sacrifice .....1 John 3:16
Love of one
another ......1 John 4:11

See Must; Necessary, necessity

Outcasts—*dispossessed people*

Israel among the
nations...........Ps. 147:2
Israel as objects of
mercy............Is. 16:3, 4
New Israel ....Jer. 30:17-22

Oven—*a place for baking or cooking*

A. *Characteristics of:*
Used for
cooking......Ex. 8:3
Fuel for,
grass.......Matt. 6:30
Made on
ground.......Gen. 18:6

B. *Figurative of:*
Scarcity in
famine ....Lev. 26:26
Lust ....Hos. 7:4, 6, 7
God's
judgments ....Ps. 21:9
Effects of
famine ....Lam. 5:10

Overcome—*to conquer*

A. *Means of, by:*
Wine ....Jer. 23:9
Fleshly
desire ....2 Pet. 2:19, 20
God ....Rom. 8:37

B. *Objects of:*
World ....John 16:33
Evil...........Rom. 12:21
Satan..........1 John 2:13, 14
Evil spirits.....1 John 4:4
Two
witnesses .....Rev. 11:7
Evil powers ....Rev. 17:13, 14

C. *Promises concerning, for Christians:*
Eating of the tree of
life..........Rev. 2:7
Exemption from the second
death ....Rev. 2:11
Power over the
nations........Rev. 2:26
Clothed in white
garments......Rev. 3:5
Made a pillar in God's
Temple.......Rev. 3:12
Rulership with
Christ.........Rev. 3:21

Overlay—*to spread or place over*

Materials used:

Gold ....Ex. 26:32

Bronze............Ex. 38:2
Silver ....Ex. 38:17

Objects overlaid:

Pillar—with gold . . Ex. 26:32
Board—with
gold...............Ex. 36:34
Altar—with
cedar............1 Kin. 6:20
Sanctuary—with
gold...............1 Kin. 6:21
Cherubim—with
gold...............1 Kin. 6:28
Earthen vessel—with
silver dross ....Prov. 26:23
Images—with
silver..............Is. 30:22

Overseer—*a leader or supervisor*

Kinds of:

Prime minister ....Gen. 39:4, 5
Managers ....Gen. 41:34
Elders.............Acts 20:17, 28

Overthrow—*to throw down; destroy*

Agents of:

God................Prov. 21:12
Evil.................Ps. 140:11
Wickedness ....Prov. 11:11
Evil ruler..........Dan. 11:41
Christ..............John 2:15

Overwork—*too much work*

Complaint of
Israelites ....Ex. 5:6-21
Solution of, for
Moses..........Ex. 18:14-26

Owe—*an obligation of*

Financial debt.....Matt. 18:24, 28
Moral debt ....Philem. 18, 19
Spiritual debt .....Rom. 13:8

Owl—*a large-eyed bird of prey*

Varieties of, all
unclean ....Lev. 11:13-17
Solitary in habit...Ps. 102:6

Ownership—*title of possession*

A. *By men, acquired by:*
Purchase ......Gen. 23:16-18
Inheritance ....Luke 15:12
Covenant......Gen. 26:25-33

B. *By God, of:*
World ....Ps. 24:1
Souls of men . . Ezek. 18:4
Redeemed .....1 Cor. 6:19, 20

Ox

A. *Uses of:*
Pulling covered
carts ....Num. 7:3
Plowing ....1 Kin. 19:19
Food ....Deut. 14:4
Sacrifice ......Ex. 20:24
Means of
existence......Job 24:3
Designs in
Temple........1 Kin. 7:25

B. *Laws concerning:*
To rest on
Sabbath.......Ex. 23:12
Not to be:
Yoked with an
ass...........Deut. 22:10
Muzzled while
treading......Deut. 25:4
To be
restored......Ex. 22:4, 9-13

C. *Figurative of:*
Easy victory ...Num. 22:4
Youthful
rashness ......Prov. 7:22
Preach the
Gospel ....Is. 32:20
Minister's
support ....1 Cor. 9:9, 10

D. *Descriptive of:*
Of great
strength ......Num. 23:22
Very wild and
ferocious......Job 39:9-12
Frisky in
youth ....Ps. 29:6

Ox goad—*spike used to drive oxen*

As a weapon ......Judg. 3:31

Ozem—*anger*

1. Son of Jesse ...1 Chr. 2:13, 15
2. Descendant of
Judah.........1 Chr. 2:25

Ozni—*gives ear*

Son of Gad and head of a
family............Num. 26:15, 16
Called Ezbon......Gen. 46:16

P

Paarai—*devotee of Peor*

One of David's mighty
men..............2 Sam. 23:35
Called Naarai .....1 Chr. 11:37

Pacification—*causing anger to rest*

A. *Means of:*
Gift............Prov. 21:14
Wise man......Prov. 16:14
Yielding.......Eccl. 10:4

B. *Examples of:*
Esau, by
Jacob.........Gen. 32:11-19
Lord, toward His
people.........Ezek. 16:63
Ahasuerus, by Haman's
death.........Esth. 7:10

Pack animals

Used by
Israelites.........1 Chr. 12:40

Padan Aram—*the plain of Aram* (Mesopotamia)

Home of Isaac's
wife.............Gen. 25:20
Jacob flees to.....Gen. 28:2-7
Jacob returns
from.............Gen. 31:17, 18
Same as
Mesopotamia.....Gen. 24:10
People of, called
Syrians...........Gen. 31:24
Language of, called
Aramaic..........2 Kin. 18:26

See Aramaic

Padon—*ransom*

Head of Nethinim {Ezra 2:44
family {Neh. 7:47

Pagan gods

A. *Mentioned:*
Molech.......Lev. 18:21
Chemosh......Judg. 11:24
Dagon........Judg. 16:23
Baal..........2 Kin. 17:16
Nergal........2 Kin. 17:30
Succoth
Benoth........2 Kin. 17:30
Ashima........2 Kin. 17:30
Nibhaz........2 Kin. 17:31
Tartak........2 Kin. 17:31
Adram-
melech........2 Kin. 17:31
Anam-
melech........2 Kin. 17:31
Nisroch.......Is. 37:38
Zeus..........Acts 14:12
Hermes........Acts 14:12
Greek
Pantheon.....Acts 17:16-23
Diana.........Acts 19:23-37

B. *Worship of condemned:*
By apostolic
command.....1 Cor. 10:14
By Law........Ex. 20:3, 4
Deut. 5:7

Pagiel—*God meets*

Son of Ocran, chief of Asher's
tribe..............Num. 1:13

Pahath Moab—*governor of Moab*

Family of postexilic
returnees.........Ezra 2:6
Members of, divorced foreign
wives..............Ezra 10:19, 30
One of, signs
covenant.......Neh. 10:1, 14
Hashub, one of, helps
Nehemiah........Neh. 3:11

Pain—*physical or mental suffering*

A. *Kinds of:*
Childbirth.....Rev. 12:2
Physical
fatigue.........2 Cor. 11:27
Physical
afflictions.....Job 33:19
Mental
disturbance...Ps. 55:4

B. *Characteristics of:*
Affects face....Joel 2:6
Means of
chastening....Job 15:20
Affects the whole
person.........Jer. 4:19
Common to all
men...........Rom. 8:22

C. *Remedies for:*
Balm..........Jer. 51:8
Prayer.........Ps. 25:17, 18
God's
deliverance....Acts 2:24
Heaven........Rev. 21:4

D. *Figurative of:*
Mental
anguish.......Ps. 48:6
Impending
trouble.........Jer. 22:23
Distressing
news..........Is. 21:2, 3
Israel's
captivity......Is. 26:17, 18

Paint—*to apply liquid colors*

Applied to a wide
house............Jer. 22:14
Used by women...2 Kin. 9:30

Used especially | Jer. 4:30
by prostitutes ... | Ezek. 23:40

Paintings

Of Chaldeans .....Ezek. 23:14
Of animals and idols (on a
secret wall).......Ezek. 8:7-12

Pair—*two*

Sandals ....Amos 2:6
Turtledoves ......Luke 2:24
Balances ....Rev. 6:5

Palace—*a royal building*

A. *Descriptive of:*
King's house...2 Chr. 9:11
Foreign city ...Is. 25:2
Dwellings in
Zion ....Ps. 48:3
Heathen king's
residence......Ezra 6:2

B. *Characteristics of:*
Place of
luxury ....Luke 7:25
Subject to
destruction....Is. 13:22

C. *Figurative of:*
Messiah's
temple ....Ps. 45:8, 15
Divine workman-
ship...........Ps. 144:12
Eternal city ....Jer. 30:18

Palal—*judge*

Postexilic
laborer ....Neh. 3:25

Pale—*deficient in color*

Figurative of:
Shame ....Is. 29:22

Palestine (see Canaan, Land of)

Palliation of sin—*excusing sin*

A. *Manifested by:*
Calling bad men
good..........Mal. 2:17
Describing sin as
good..........Is. 5:20
Justifying the
wicked.........Is. 5:23
Encouraging the
wicked........Ezek. 13:22
Calling the proud
blessed........Mal. 3:13-15
Envying the
wicked........Ps. 73:3-15

Supposing God cannot
see sin ....Ps. 10:11-13
Ignoring
reproof........Job 34:5-36
Sinning
defiantly .....Is. 5:18, 19
Considering God indifferent
to evil........Zeph. 1:12
Misjudging
people ....Matt. 11:18, 19
Questioning God's
Word ....Ezek. 20:49

B. *Caused by:*
Moral
darkness .....Matt. 6:23
Man-made
concepts .....Matt. 16:3-6
Hypocrisy .....Matt. 23:15-23
Evil heart......Luke 16:15
False
teaching ......2 Pet. 2:1-19

Pallu—*distinguished*

Son of Reuben; | Gen. 46:9
head of tribal | Ex. 6:14
family ....| Num. 26:5, 8

Palm of the hand

Used literally of:

Priest's hand .....Lev. 14:15, 26
Idol's hand........1 Sam. 5:4
Daniel's hand .....Dan. 10:10
Soldier's hand....Matt. 26:67

Palm tree

A. *Uses of:*
Fruit of, for
food ....Joel 1:12
Figures of, carved on
Temple........1 Kin. 6:29-35
Branches of, for
booths ....Lev. 23:40-42
Places of, at Elim and
Jericho.......Ex. 15:27
Site of, for
judgeship .....Judg. 4:5

B. *Figurative of:*
Righteous .....Ps. 92:12
Beauty........Song 7:7
Victory........John 12:13

Palms, city of

Moabites
conquer ....Judg. 3:12, 13

Palti—*abbreviation of Pelatiah*

1. Benjamite
spy ....Num. 13:9

2. Man to whom Saul gives
   Michal, David's wife-to-be, in
   marriage ...... 1 Sam. 25:44

Paltiel—*God has delivered*

1. Prince of
   Issachar ...... Num. 34:26
2. Same as
   Palti 2 ...... 2 Sam. 3:15

Paltite, the

Native of Beth
Pelet .... Josh. 15:27
Home of one of David's mighty
men.............. 2 Sam. 23:26
Same referred to as the
Pelonite..... 1 Chr. 11:27

Pamphylia—*coastal region in South
Asia Minor*

People from, at
Pentecost .... Acts 2:10
Paul visits......... Acts 13:13
John Mark
returns home   ⎰Acts 13:13
from .... ⎱Acts 15:38
Paul preaches in
cities of .... Acts 14:24, 25
Paul sails past..... Acts 27:5

Pan—*thin plate*

Offering in .... Lev. 2:5
Cooking .... Lev. 6:21
Pouring .... 2 Sam. 13:9

Panic—*fright*

A. *Among Israelites:*
At the Red
Sea .... Ex. 14:10-12
Before the
Philistines..... 1 Sam. 4:10
Of Judah before
Israel .... 2 Kin. 14:12

B. *Among nations:*
Egyptians ..... Ex. 14:27
Philistines ..... 1 Sam. 14:22
Syrians .... 2 Kin. 7:6, 7
Ammonites and
Moabites...... 2 Chr. 20:22-25

Paper—*sheet*

Writing material .. 2 John 12

See Papyrus

Paphos—*capital of Cyprus*

Paul blinds
Elymas........... Acts 13:6-13

Papyrus—*a tall marsh plant growing in
the Nile river region*

Referred to as
bulrush in .... Ex. 2:3
Cannot grow without
marsh .... Job 8:11

See Paper

Parables—*an earthly story with a
heavenly meaning*

A. *Descriptive of:*
Prophecy ...... Num. 23:7-24
Discourse...... Job 27:1-23
Wise saying.... Prov. 26:7, 9
Prophetic
message....... Ezek. 17:1-10
Illustration (especially true of
Christ's) ...... Matt. 13:18

B. *Of Christ, characteristics of:*
Numerous ..... Mark 4:33, 34
Illustrative..... Luke 12:16-21

Meaning of:
Self-evident.... Mark 12:1-12
Unknown...... Matt. 13:36
Explained...... Luke 8:9-15
Prophetic...... Luke 21:29-36

C. *Design of:*
Bring under
conviction .... 2 Sam. 12:1-6
Teach a spiritual
truth.......... Is. 5:1-6
Illustrate a
point.......... Luke 10:25-37
Fulfill
prophecy...... Matt. 13:34, 35
Conceal truth from the
unbelieving ... Matt. 13:10-16

D. *Of Christ, classification of:*
Concerning God's love in Christ:
Lost sheep..... Luke 15:4-7
Lost money.... Luke 15:8-10
Prodigal son .. Luke 15:11-32
Hidden
treasure...... Matt. 13:44
Pearl of great
price.......... Matt. 13:45, 46

Concerning Israel:
Barren fig
tree........... Luke 13:6-9
Two sons...... Matt. 21:28-32
Wicked husband-
man .... Matt. 21:33-46

*Concerning Christianity (the
Gospel) in this age:*
New cloth ..... Matt. 9:16
New wine ..... Matt. 9:17

Sower ....Matt. 13:3-8
Tares ....Matt. 13:24-30
Mustard seed ..Matt. 13:31, 32
Leaven ....Matt. 13:33
Net...........Matt. 13:47-50
Great supper...Luke 14:16-24
Seed growing
secretly ....Mark 4:26-29

Concerning salvation:
House built on the
rock ....Matt. 7:24-27
Pharisee and
publican .....Luke 18:9-14
Two debtors ..Luke 7:36-50
Marriage of the king's
Son ....Matt. 22:1-14

Concerning Christian life:
Lamp under a
basket ....Matt. 5:15, 16
Unmerciful
servant ......Matt. 18:23-35
Friend at
midnight.....Luke 11:5-13
Importunate
widow ....Luke 18:1-8
Tower ....Luke 14:28-35
Good
Samaritan.....Luke 10:25-37
Unjust
steward ......Luke 16:1-13
Laborers in the
vineyard .....Matt. 20:1-16

*Concerning rewards and
punishments:*
Ten virgins ...Matt. 25:1-13
Talents ....Matt. 25:14-30
Minas ....Luke 19:12-27
Sheep and
goats ....Matt. 25:31-46
Master and
servant ......Luke 17:7-10
Servants ⎰Mark 13:33-37
watching.....⎱Luke 12:36-40
Rich fool .....Luke 12:16-21
Rich man and
Lazarus......Luke 16:19-31

Paraclete—*called to one's side*

Greek word
translated ⎰John 14:16-18
"Helper" and ⎰John 15:26
"Advocate".....⎱1 John 2:1

Paradise—*an enclosed park similar to
the Garden of Eden*

Applied in the ⎰Luke 23:43
New Testament ⎰2 Cor. 12:4
to heaven ......⎱Rev. 2:7

Paradox—*a statement appearing to be
untrue or contradictory*

Getting rich by
poverty..........Prov. 13:7
Dead burying the
dead ....Matt. 8:22
Finding life by
losing it ....Matt. 10:39
Not peace, but a
sword ....Matt. 10:34-38
Wise as serpents; harmless
as doves.........Matt. 10:16
Hating and
loving ....Luke 14:26
Becoming great by
serving ....Mark 10:43
Dying in order to
live...............John 12:24, 25
Becoming a fool to be
wise..............1 Cor. 3:18

Parah—*young cow*

City in
Benjamin........Josh. 18:23

Paralytic—*one affected with
incapacitation*

Brought to ⎰Matt. 9:2
Jesus...........⎱Mark 2:3
Healed by Jesus...Matt. 4:24
Luke 5:24
Healed by Jesus, through
Peter.............Acts 9:33
Healed by
Christians ....Acts 8:7

Paramours—*illegal lovers*

Applied to the male
lover ....Ezek. 23:20

Paran—*a wilderness region in the
Sinaitic Peninsula*

Mountainous
country ....Hab. 3:3
Residence of exiled
Ishmael ....Gen. 21:21
Israelites camp
in ....Num. 10:12
Headquarters of
spies ....Num. 13:3, 26
Site of David's
refuge............1 Sam. 25:1

Parapet—*a low wall to protect the edge
of a roof*

For safety........Deut. 22:8

Parbar—suburb

Precinct or colonnade west of the
Temple . . . . 1 Chr. 26:18
Same word translated
"court" in . . . . 2 Kin. 23:11

Parched—roasted, dry

Grain . . . . Josh. 5:11
2 Sam. 17:28

Parchments—writing material made
from animal skin

Paul sends
request . . . . 2 Tim. 4:13

Pardon—to forgive

A. Objects of our:
Transgres-
sions . . . . Ex. 23:21
Iniquities . . . . . . Ex. 34:9
Backslidings . . . Jer. 5:6, 7

B. God's, described as:
Not granted . . 2 Kin. 24:4
Requested . . . . . Num. 14:19, 20
Abundant . . . . . . Is. 55:7
Covering all
sins . . . . Jer. 33:8
Belonging to the faithful
remnant . . . . . . Is. 40:2

C. Basis of:
LORD's name . . Ps. 25:11
Repentance . . . Is. 55:7
Seeking the
faith . . . . Jer. 5:1

See Forgiveness

Parents—fathers and mothers

A. Kinds of:
Faithful
(Abraham) . . . . Gen. 18:18, 19
Neglectful
(Moses) . . . . . . Ex. 4:24-26
Presumptuous
(Jephthah) . . . Judg. 11:30-39
Holy
(Hannah) . . . . 1 Sam. 1:11
Indulgent
(Eli) . . . . 1 Sam. 2:22-29
Distressed
(David) . . . . . . 2 Sam. 18:32, 33
Honored
(Jonadab) . . . Jer. 35:5-10
Arrogant
(Haman) . . . . . Esth. 3:1-10
Forgiving (prodigal son's
father) . . . . . . Luke 15:17-24

B. Duties toward:
Obedience . . . . Eph. 6:1
Honor . . . . Ex. 20:12
Reverence . . . . Lev. 19:3

C. Duties of, toward children:
Protection . . . . Heb. 11:23
Training . . . . . . Deut. 6:6, 7
Education . . . . Gen. 18:19
Deut. 4:9
Correction . . . . Deut. 21:18-21
Provision . . . . . . 2 Cor. 12:14

D. Sins of:
Favoritism . . . . . Gen. 25:28
Not restraining
children . . . . . . 1 Sam. 2:27-36
Bad example . . 1 Kin. 15:26
Anger . . . . Eph. 6:4

E. Sins against, by children:
Disobedi-
ence . . . . Rom. 1:30
Cursing . . . . Ex. 21:17
Mocking . . . . . . Prov. 30:17
Disrespect . . . . Gen. 9:21-27

Parmashta—the very first

Haman's son . . . . . Esth. 9:9

Parmenas

One of the seven
deacons . . . . Acts 6:5

Parnach

Zebulunite . . . . Num. 34:25

Parosh—flea

1. Head of a
postexilic   (Ezra 2:3
family . . . . (Ezra 8:3
Members of, divorced foreign
wives . . . . Ezra 10:25
One of, Pedaiah, helps
rebuild . . . . Neh. 3:25
2. Chief who seals the
covenant . . . . . . Neh. 10:1, 14

Parricide—murder of one's father and/
or mother

Sennacherib's sons guilty
of . . . . 2 Kin. 19:36, 37

Parshandatha—inquisitive

Haman's son . . . . . Esth. 9:7

Parsimony—stinginess; living like a
miser

A. Characteristics of:
Choosing
selfishly . . . . . . Gen. 13:5-11

Living
luxuriantly....Amos 6:4-6
Showing
greediness.....John 12:5, 6
Withholding God's
tithe...........Mal. 3:8
Unmerciful toward the
needy..........Zech. 7:10-12

B. *Punishment of:*

Brings:

Poverty........Prov. 11:24, 25
A curse........Prov. 11:26
Revenge........Prov. 21:13
The closing of God's
kingdom......Luke 18:22-25

Part—*a portion of the whole*

Mary chooses the
good..............Luke 10:42
Israel's
blindness..........Rom. 11:25
Our knowledge....1 Cor. 13:9-12

Partake—*to share in*

A. *Of physical things:*
Sacrifices......1 Cor. 10:18
Suffering......2 Cor. 1:7
Benefit.........1 Tim. 6:2
Human
nature.........Heb. 2:14
Discipline.....Heb. 12:8
Bread..........1 Cor. 10:17

B. *Of evil things:*
Evil............Eph. 5:3-7
Demonism.....1 Cor. 10:21

C. *Of spiritual things:*
Divine
nature........2 Pet. 1:4
Christ.........Heb. 3:14
Holy Spirit.....Heb. 6:4
Heavenly
calling........Heb. 3:1
Grace..........Phil. 1:7
Gospel.........1 Cor. 9:23
Spiritual
blessings......Rom. 11:17
Future glory...1 Pet. 5:1
Promise of
salvation......Eph. 3:6
Holiness.......Heb. 12:10
Inheritance....Col. 1:12

Partakers

A. *Of physical things:*
Sacrifices......1 Cor. 10:18
Suffering......2 Cor. 1:7

B. *Of spiritual things:*
Holiness........Heb. 12:10
Communion...1 Cor. 10:16, 17
Spiritual
things.........Rom. 15:27
Inheritance....Col. 1:12

Parthians—*inhabitants of Parthia*

Some present at
Pentecost.......Acts 2:1, 9

Partiality—*favoritism*

A. *Manifested:*
In marriages...Gen. 29:30
Among
brothers.......Gen. 43:30, 34
Between parents and
children.......Gen. 25:28
In social life...James 2:1-4

B. *Inconsistent with:*
Household
harmony......Gen. 37:4-35
Justice in
law...........Lev. 19:15

Favoritism in:
Ministry........1 Tim. 5:21
Restriction of
salvation......Acts 10:28-35

C. *Consistent with:*
Choice of
workers.......Acts 15:36-40
Estimate of
friends........Phil. 2:19-22
God's predes-
tination.......Rom. 9:6-24

See Favoritism

Partition—*a dividing wall*

In the sanctuary...1 Kin. 6:21
Between people...Eph. 2:11-14

Partner—*an associate in*

Crime............Prov. 29:24
Business.........Luke 5:7, 10
Christian work....2 Cor. 8:23
Philem. 17

Partridge—*a wild bird meaning "the
caller" (in Heb.)*

Hunted in
mountains........1 Sam. 26:20
Figurative of ill-gotten
riches............Jer. 17:11

Paruah—*sprouting*

Father of Jehoshaphat, an officer of
Solomon.........1 Kin. 4:17

Parvaim

Unidentified place providing gold
for Solomon's
Temple . . . . 2 Chr. 3:6

Parzites

Descendants of
Perez . . . . Num. 26:20

Pasach—*divider*

Asherite . . . . 1 Chr. 7:33

Pasdammim—*boundary of bloodshed*

Philistines gathered
here . . . . 1 Chr. 11:13

Paseah—*lame*

1. Judahite . . . . 1 Chr. 4:12
2. Head of a family of
   Nethinim . . . . . . Ezra 2:43, 49
   One of, repairs
   walls . . . . Neh. 3:6
3. A family of temple
   servants . . . . . . Neh. 7:46, 51

Pashur, Pashhur—*free*

1. Official
   opposing ⎰Jer. 21:1
   Jeremiah . . . . . ⎱Jer. 38:1-13
   Descendants of,
   returnees . . . . . . Neh. 11:12
2. Priest who put Jeremiah in
   jail . . . . Jer. 20:1-6
3. Father of Gedaliah, Jeremiah's
   opponent . . . . . Jer. 38:1
4. Priestly family of
   returnees . . . . . Ezra 2:38
   Members of, divorced foreign
   wives . . . . Ezra 10:22
5. Priest who signs the
   covenant . . . . . . Neh. 10:3

Passing away—*ceasing to exist*

A. *Things subject to:*
   Our days . . . . . Ps. 90:9
   Old things . . . . 2 Cor. 5:17
   World's
   fashion . . . . 1 Cor. 7:31
   World's lust . . . 1 John 2:17
   Heaven and
   earth . . . . 2 Pet. 3:10

B. *Things not subject to:*
   Christ's
   words . . . . Luke 21:33
   Christ's
   dominion . . . . Dan. 7:14

Passion—*suffering*

A. *Descriptive of:*
   Christ's
   sufferings . . . . . Acts 1:3
   Lusts . . . . Rom. 1:26

B. *As applied* (theologically) *to
   Christ's sufferings:*
   Predicted . . . . . . Is. 53:1-12
   Portrayed
   visibly . . . . Mark 14:3-8
   Preached . . . . . Acts 3:12-18
   1 Pet. 1:10-12

Passover—*a Jewish festival commemorative of the exodus from Egypt*

A. *Features concerning:*
   Commemorative of the tenth
   plague . . . . Ex. 12:3-28
   Necessity of blood
   applied . . . . Ex. 12:7
   To be repeated
   annually . . . . . . Ex. 12:24-27

B. *Observances of:*
   At Sinai . . . . Num. 9:1-14
   At the
   conquest . . . . . Josh. 5:10-12
   By Christ . . . . . Matt. 26:18, 19

C. *Typical of the Lord's death* (the
   Lord's Supper):
   Lamb without
   blemish . . . . . . 1 Pet. 1:19
   One of their ⎰Ex. 12:5
   own . . . . ⎱Heb. 2:14, 17
   Lamb chosen . . Ex. 12:3
   1 Pet. 2:4
   Slain at God's
   appointed ⎰Ex. 12:6
   time . . . . ⎱Acts 2:23
   Christ is . . . . . . 1 Cor. 5:7

See Lamb of God, the

Password—*a secret word used to identify friends*

Used by
Gileadites . . . . Judg. 12:5, 6

Pastor—*shepherd*

To perfect the
saints . . . . Eph. 4:11, 12
Appointed by
God . . . . Jer. 3:15
Unfaithful ones are
punished . . . . . . Jer. 22:22

See Shepherd

Pasture—*a place for grazing animals*

A. *Used literally of places for:*
Cattle to
feed............Gen. 47:4
Wild animals to
feed...........Is. 32:14
God's material
blessings......Ps. 65:11-13

B. *Used figuratively of:*
Restoration and
peace.........Ezek. 34:13-15
True Israel....Ps. 95:7
Kingdom of
God............Is. 49:9, 10
Kingdom of
Israel.........Jer. 25:36
Gospel.........Is. 30:23
Abundant provision for
salvation......Ezek. 45:15

C. *Of the true Israel (the Church),
described as:*
God's people...Ps. 100:3
Provided for...John 10:9
Purchased.....Ps. 74:1, 2
Thankful......Ps. 79:13
Scattered by false
shepherds....Jer. 23:1

See Shepherd

Patara—*a port of Lycia in Asia Minor*

Paul changes ships
here.............Acts 21:1, 2

Path—*a walk; manner of life*

A. *Of the wicked:*
Brought to
nothing.......Job 6:18
Becomes
dark.........Job 24:13
Is crooked.....Is. 59:8
Leads to
death.........Prov. 2:18
Filled with
wickedness....Prov. 1:15, 16
Is
destructive....Is. 59:7
Followed by wicked
rulers.........Is. 3:12
Made difficult by
God...........Hos. 2:6

B. *Of believers:*
Beset with
difficulties.....Job 19:8
Under God's
control........Job 13:27

Hindered by the
wicked........Job 30:13
Enriched by the
LORD..........Ps. 23:3
Upheld by
God...........Ps. 17:5
Provided with
light..........Ps. 119:105
Known by
God...........Ps. 139:3
Like a shining
light..........Prov. 4:18
Directed by
God...........Is. 26:7
To be
pondered......Prov. 4:26
No death at the
end...........Prov. 12:28
Sometimes
unknown.....Is. 42:16
Sometimes seems
crooked......Lam. 3:9
To be made
straight.......Heb. 12:13

C. *Of righteousness:*
Taught by
father.........Prov. 4:1, 11
Kept...........Prov. 2:20
Shown to   ⎰ Ps. 16:11
Messiah......⎱ Acts 2:28
Taught to
believers.....Ps. 25:4, 5
Sought by   ⎰ Ps. 119:35
believers.....⎱ Is. 2:3
Rejected by
unbe-   ⎰ Jer. 6:16
lieving.......⎱ Jer. 18:15

D. *Of the Lord:*
True............Ps. 25:10
Smooth........Ps. 27:11
Rich...........Ps. 65:11
Guarded......Prov. 2:8
Upright........Prov. 2:13
Living.........Prov. 2:19
Peaceful......Prov. 3:17

Pathros—*the Southland*

Name applied to south (Upper)
Egypt............Ezek. 29:10-14
Described as a lowly
kingdom.........Ezek. 29:14-16
Refuge for dispersed
Jews.............Jer. 44:1-15
Jews to be regathered
from.............Is. 11:11

Pathrusim—*the inhabitants of Pathros*

Hamitic people descending from
Mizraim and living in
Pathros..........Gen. 10:14

Patience—*the ability to bear trials
without grumbling; perseverance*

A. *Of the Trinity:*
God, the author
of.............Rom. 15:5
Christ, the example
of.............2 Thess. 3:5
Spirit, the source
of.............Gal. 5:22

B. *Described as:*
Rewarded......Rom. 2:7
Endured with
joy............Col. 1:11

C. *Is a product of:*
Good heart ....Luke 8:15
Tribulation ....Rom. 5:3, 4
Testing of
faith ....James 1:3
Hope ....Rom. 8:25
Scriptures .....Rom. 15:4

D. *Necessary grace, in:*
Times of
crises ....Luke 21:15-19
Dealing with a
church........2 Cor. 12:12
Opposing
evil ....Rev. 2:2
Soundness of
faith ....Titus 2:2
Waiting for Christ's
return........James 5:7, 8

Patmos—*an Aegan island off the
southwestern coast of Asia Minor*

John, banished here, receives the
Revelation.......Rev. 1:9

Patriarchal age—*the time of Abraham,
Isaac, Jacob (between 1900 and 1600
B.C.)*

A. *Rulers of:*
Kings and
princes........Gen. 12:15-20
Family heads
(fathers) ......Gen. 18:18, 19

B. *Business of:*
Cattle, etc.....Gen. 12:16
Caravans .....Gen. 37:28-36

Selling, etc.....Gen. 23:1-20
Contracts......Gen. 21:27-30
Business
agreements ...Gen. 30:28-34

C. *Customs of:*
Prevalence of
polygamy .....Gen. 16:4
Existence of
slavery........Gen. 12:16
Son's wife, selected by his
father........Gen. 24:1-4
Children given significant
names ....Gen. 29:31-35

D. *Religion of:*
Existence of
idolatry ......Gen. 35:1, 2
Worship of God
Almighty......Gen. 14:19-22
God's covenant
recognized ....Gen. 12:1-3
Circumcision
observed .....Gen. 17:10-14
Headship of
father........Gen. 35:2
Obedience
primary ......Gen. 18:18, 19
Prayers and sacrifices
offered.......Gen. 12:8
Blessings and curses
pronounced by
father........Gen. 27:27-40
True faith ⎰ Matt. 15:28
believed......⎱ Heb. 11:8-22

Patriarchs—*ancient family, or tribal
heads*

Applied, in New Testament, to
Abraham, to Jacob's sons, and to
David ....Heb. 7:4

Patriotism—*love of one's country*

Manifested in:

Willingness to fight for one's
country ....1 Sam. 17:26-51
Concern for national
survival ....Esth. 4:13-17
Desire for national
revival ....Neh. 1:2-11
Loyalty to national
leader ....2 Sam. 2:10
Respect for national
leaders ....2 Sam. 1:18-27

Patrobas

Christian at
Rome ....Rom. 16:14

Pattern—*a copy; an example*

A. *Of physical things:*
Tabernacle.....Heb. 8:5
Temple ....1 Chr. 28:11-19

B. *Of spiritual things:*
Good works ...Titus 2:7
Heavenly
originals ......Heb. 9:23

See Example; Example of Christ, the

Pau, Pai—*groaning, bleating*

Edomite town, residence
of King Hadar   ⎰ Gen. 36:39
(Hadad) ....⎱ 1 Chr. 1:50

Paul—*little*

A. *Life of:*

From birth to conversion:
Born at Tarsus in
Cilicia.........Acts 22:3
Born a Roman
citizen ....Acts 22:25-28
Called Saul until
changed to   ⎰ Acts 9:11
Paul ....⎱ Acts 13:9
Benjamite
Jew ....Phil. 3:5
Citizen of
Tarsus ....Acts 21:39
By trade a
tentmaker....Acts 18:1, 3
Zealot for   ⎰ Gal. 1:14
Judaism......⎱ Phil. 3:5
Very strict   ⎰ Acts 23:6
Pharisee .....⎱ Phil. 3:5, 6
Educated under
Gamaliel ......Acts 22:3
His sister in
Jerusalem .....Acts 23:16
Apparently unmarried or a
widower ......1 Cor. 9:5
Member of Jewish
council........Acts 26:10
Zealous for the Mosaic
Law...........Acts 26:4, 5
Consented to   ⎧ Acts 7:58
Stephen's   ⎨ Acts 8:1
death ....⎩ Acts 22:20
Intensified   ⎧ Acts 9:1, 2
persecution   ⎨ Acts 22:3-5
of   ⎨ Acts 26:10, 11
Christians....⎩ Gal. 1:13
Conscientious ⎰ Acts 26:9
persecutor ...⎱ 1 Tim. 1:13

His conversion:
On road to
Damascus.....Acts 9:1-19
At noon ....Acts 26:13
Blinded by
supernatural   ⎰ Acts 9:3, 8
vision........⎱ 2 Cor. 12:1-7
Responded willingly to Jesus'
entreaty ......Acts 9:4-9
Given a divine
commis-   ⎰ Acts 9:6, 10-18
sion..........⎱ Eph. 3:1-8
Instructed and baptized by
Ananias.......Acts 9:6, 10-18
Repeated his
conversion   ⎰ Acts 22:1-16
story..........⎱ Acts 26:1-20
Referred   ⎧ 1 Cor. 9:1, 16
to it   ⎨ 1 Cor. 15:8-10
often..........⎩ Gal. 1:12-16
Considered himself
unworthy .....Eph. 3:1-8
Cites details of his
change........Phil. 3:4-10
Regretted former
life.............1 Tim. 1:12-16
Not ashamed   ⎰ Rom. 1:16
of Christ .....⎱ 2 Tim. 1:8-12
Preached Jesus as God's Son
and as the Christ (that is, the
Messiah) ......Acts 9:19-22
Persecuted by ⎧ Acts 9:23-25
Jews; went to ⎨ 2 Cor. 11:32, 33
Arabia ....⎩ Gal. 1:17
Returned to
Damascus .....Gal. 1:17
Visited
Jerusalem   ⎰ Acts 9:26-29
briefly........⎱ Gal. 1:18, 19
Received vision of his ministry
to Gentiles ....Acts 22:17-21
Sent by
disciples to   ⎰ Acts 9:29, 30
Tarsus ....⎱ Gal. 1:21
Brought to Antioch (in Syria)
by Barnabas...Acts 11:22-26
Sent to Jerusalem with
relief..........Acts 11:27-30
Returned to
Antioch ....Acts 12:25

First Missionary Journey:
Divinely chosen
and commis-   ⎰ Acts 13:1-4
sioned........⎱ Acts 26:19, 20
Accompanied by Barnabas and
John Mark ....Acts 13:1, 5

Preached in
Cyprus........Acts 13:4-12
Sailed to Perga; Mark left
him............Acts 13:13
Preached in Antioch
(in Pisidia);
rejected by {Acts 13:14-51
Jews.........{2 Tim. 3:11
Rejected in {Acts 13:51, 52
Iconium......{Acts 14:1-5
Stoned at {Acts 14:6-20
Lystra........{2 Tim. 3:11
Went to
Derbe........Acts 14:20, 21
Returned to Antioch (in
Syria)........Acts 14:21-26
Told Christians about his
work..........Acts 14:27, 28
Participated in
Jerusalem {Acts 15:2-22
Council ......{Gal. 2:1-10
Rebuked Peter in Antioch for
inconsist-
ency ....Gal. 2:11-21

Second Missionary Journey:
Rejected John Mark as
companion; took
Silas ....Acts 15:36-40
Strengthened churches in Syria
and Cilicia ....Acts 15:41
Revisited Derbe and
Lystra ....Acts 16:1
Took Timothy as
worker........Acts 16:1-5
Directed by the Spirit where to
preach ....Acts 16:6, 7
Responded to Macedonian
vision ....Acts 16:8, 9
Joined by Luke
("we") ....Acts 16:10
Entered
Macedonia ....Acts 16:10, 11
Converted Lydia at
Philippi ......Acts 16:12-15
Cast into prison; jailer
converted.....Acts 16:16-34
Used Roman
citizenship ....Acts 16:35-39
Preached {Acts 17:1-9
at Thessa- {1 Thess. 1:7
lonica........{1 Thess. 2:2-18
Received by the
Bereans.......Acts 17:10-13
Left Silas and Timothy; went to
Athens........Acts 17:14-17

Preached on Mars' Hill (the
Areopagus) ...Acts 17:18-34
Arrived in Corinth; stayed with
Aquila and
Priscilla ......Acts 18:1-5
Reunited with
Silas and {Acts 18:5
Timothy .....{1 Thess. 3:6
Wrote letters
to Thessa- {1 Thess. 3:1-6
lonians.......{2 Thess. 2:2
Established a church at
Corinth ......Acts 18:5-18
Stopped briefly at
Ephesus........Acts 18:19-21
Saluted Jerusalem church;
returned to Antioch (in
Syria)........Acts 18:22

Third Missionary Journey:
Strengthened churches of
Galatia and
Phrygia ......Acts 18:23
Gave direction for relief
collection .....1 Cor. 16:1
Ministered three
years in {Acts 19:1-12
Ephesus.......{Acts 20:31
Saved from angry
mob ....Acts 19:13-41
Probably wrote *Galatians*
here ....Gal. 1:1
Wrote *First Corinthians*
here ....1 Cor. 5:9
Went to Troas; failed to meet
Titus..........2 Cor. 2:12, 13
Reunited with
Titus in {Acts 20:1
Macedonia...{2 Cor. 7:5-16
Wrote *Second Corinthians*; sent
Titus to Corinth with this
letter..........2 Cor. 8:6-18
Traveled {Acts 20:2
extensively...{Rom. 15:19
Visited Greece and
Macedonia ....Acts 20:2, 3
Wrote *Romans* in
Corinth ......Rom. 1:1
Returned through
Macedonia....Acts 20:3
Preached long sermon in
Troas ....Acts 20:5-12
Gave farewell talk to Ephesian
elders at
Miletus ......Acts 20:14-38

Arrived in
Caesarea......Acts 21:1-8
Warned by
Agabus.......Acts 21:9-14

In Jerusalem and Caesarea:
Arrived in Jerusalem; welcomed
by church.....Acts 21:15-19
Falsely charged; riot
follows.......Acts 21:20-40
Defended his action; removed
by Roman
police.........Acts 22:1-30
Defended his action before
Jewish
council.......Acts 23:1-10
Saved from Jewish plot; taken
to Caesarea...Acts 23:11-35
Defended himself before
Felix.........Acts 24:1-23
Preached to Felix and
Drusilla.....Acts 24:24-26
Imprisoned for two
years.........Acts 24:27
Accused before Festus by
Jews.........Acts 25:1-9
Appealed to
Caesar.......Acts 25:10-12
Defended himself
before ⎧ Acts 25:13-27
Agrippa......⎨ Acts 26:1-32

Voyage to Rome:
Sailed from Caesarea to
Crete........Acts 27:1-13
Ship tossed by
storm........Acts 27:14-20
Assured by the
Lord.........Acts 27:21-25
Ship wrecked; all
saved........Acts 27:26-44
On island of
Malta........Acts 28:1-10
Continued journey to
Rome.........Acts 28:11-16
Rejected by Jews in
Rome.........Acts 28:17-29
Dwelt in Rome two
years.........Acts 28:30, 31
Wrote
Ephesians, ⎧ Eph. 3:1
Colossians, ⎪ Eph. 6:20
Philippians, ⎨ Phil. 1:7, 13
and Philemon ⎪ Col. 4:7-18
here.........⎩ Philem. 10, 22

Final ministry and death:
Released from
first Roman ⎧ Phil. 1:25
imprison- ⎨ Phil. 2:17, 24
ment.........⎩ 2 Tim. 4:16, 17
Wrote First
Timothy and ⎧ 1 Tim. 1:1-3
Titus.........⎨ Titus 1:1-5
Visited Macedonia and other
places.........2 Tim. 4:20
Wrote Second Timothy from
Roman ⎧ 2 Tim. 1:8
prison........⎨ 2 Tim. 4:6-8
Sent final news and
greetings......2 Tim. 4:9-22

B. **Missionary methods of:**
Pay his ⎧ Acts 18:3
own ⎨ Acts 20:33-35
way..........⎩ 2 Cor. 11:7, 9
Preach to the ⎧ Acts 13:46
Jews first ....⎨ Acts 17:1-5
Establish churches
in large ⎧ Acts 19:1-10
cities.........⎨ Rom. 1:7-15
Travel ⎧ Acts 15:40
with com- ⎨ Acts 20:4
panions ......⎩ Col. 4:14
Report work to
sending ⎧ Acts 14:26-28
church........⎨ Acts 21:17-20
Use his Roman
citizenship ⎧ Acts 16:36-39
when ⎨ Acts 22:24-29
necessary ....⎩ Acts 25:10-12
Seek to
evangelize ⎧ Col. 1:23-29
the world ....⎨ 2 Tim. 4:17

C. **Writings of:**
Inspired ⎧ 2 Cor. 13:3
by ⎨ 1 Thess. 2:13
God..........⎩ 2 Tim. 3:15, 16
Contain difficult
things.........2 Pet. 3:15, 16
Written by ⎧ Gal. 6:11
himself........⎨ 2 Thess. 3:17
Sometimes dictated to a
scribe.........Rom. 16:22
Considered weighty by
some...........2 Cor. 10:10
His name sometimes
forged.........2 Thess. 2:2
Reveal personal
infor- ⎧ 2 Cor. 11:1-33
mation........⎨ 2 Cor. 12:1-11
Convey personal
messages......Phil. 2:19-30
Contain salutation and
closing ⎧ 2 Cor. 1:2, 3
doxology.....⎨ 2 Cor. 13:14

Disclose personal plans ⎰ Phil. 2:19-24
⎱ Philem. 22

Some complimentary .... Phil. 4:10-19

Some filled with rebuke ⎰ Gal. 1:6-8
⎱ Gal. 5:1-10

D. *Characteristics of:*

Consecrated ... 1 Cor. 4:1-15
Phil. 3:7-14

Cheerful .... Acts 16:25
2 Cor. 4:8-10

Courageous .... Acts 9:29
Acts 20:22-24

Considerate of others ⎰ Phil. 2:25-30
⎱ Philem. 7-24

Conscientious ⎰ 2 Cor. 1:12-17
⎱ 2 Cor. 6:3, 4

Christ-centered ⎰ 2 Cor. 4:10, 11
⎱ Phil. 1:20-23

Conciliatory .. 2 Cor. 2:1-11
Gal. 2:1-15

Composed ..... 2 Cor. 12:8-10
2 Tim. 4:7, 8

Pauline theology

Given by revelation .... Gal. 1:11, 12
Salvation by grace .... Eph. 2:1-10
To Gentiles ...... Eph. 3:1-12

Paulus, Sergius

Roman proconsul of Cyprus .... Acts 13:4, 7

Pavement—*a terrace made of bricks or stones*

God's, made of sapphire .... Ex. 24:10
Shushan's, made of precious stones .... Esth. 1:5, 6
Of stone .... 2 Kin. 16:17
Ezekiel's temple, surrounded by .... Ezek. 40:17, 18
Judgment place of Pilate .... John 19:13

See Gabbatha

Pavilion—*a covered place, tent, booth*

Place of refuge .... Ps. 27:5
Canopy of God's abode .... Job 36:29
Protective covering ("tabernacle") .... Is. 4:6

Paws—*the feet of animals having claws*

Descriptive of certain animals .... Lev. 11:27
Of bears and lions .... 1 Sam. 17:37

Pay—*to give something for something*

Lord's blessing .... Prov. 19:17
Punishment .... Matt. 5:26
Servitude and forgiveness ...... Matt. 18:23-35
Sign of righteousness ..... Ps. 37:21

See Vow

Pe

Letter in the Hebrew alphabet .... Ps. 119:129-136

Peace

A. *Kinds of:*

International .. 1 Sam. 7:14
National .... 1 Kin. 4:24
Civil .... Rom. 14:19
Domestic ..... 1 Cor. 7:15
Individual .... Luke 8:48
False .... 1 Thess. 5:3
Hypocritical .. James 2:16
Spiritual ...... Rom. 5:1

B. *Source of:*

God .... Phil. 4:7
Christ .... John 14:27
Holy Spirit ..... Gal. 5:22

C. *Of Christ:*

Predicted ...... Is. 9:6, 7
Promised ..... Hag. 2:9
Announced ... Is. 52:7

D. *Lord's relation to, He:*

Reveals .... Jer. 33:6
Gives .... Ps. 29:11
Establishes ..... Is. 26:12

E. *Among the wicked:*

Not known by .... Is. 59:8
None for .... Is. 48:22

F. *Among believers, truths concerning:*

Comes through Christ's atonement ... Is. 53:5
Results from reconciliation ...... Col. 1:20
Product of justification ... Rom. 5:1
Obtained by faith .... Is. 26:3

G. *Among believers, exhortations regarding:*

Should live
in.............2 Cor. 13:11
Should
pursue........2 Tim. 2:22

Peacemakers—*those who work for peace*

Christ the great...2 Cor. 5:18-21
Christians
become.........(Matt. 5:9
(Rom. 14:19
Rules regarding...1 Pet. 3:8-13

Pearl—*a precious gem found in oyster shells*

A. *Used literally of:*
Valuable
gems..........Rev. 18:12, 16
Woman's
attire ....1 Tim. 2:9

B. *Used figuratively of:*
Spiritual
truths.........Matt. 7:6
Kingdom ......Matt. 13:45, 46
Worldly
adornment....Rev. 17:4
Wonders of heaven's
glories ....Rev. 21:21

Pedahel—*God saves*

Prince of
Naphtali..........Num. 34:28

Pedahzur—*the Rock (God) has redeemed*

Father of
Gamaliel ....Num. 1:10

Pedaiah—*Yahweh redeems*

1. Father of Joel, ruler in David's
reign...........1 Chr. 27:20
2. Grandfather of
Jehoiakim.....2 Kin. 23:36
3. Son of
Jeconiah ......1 Chr. 3:18, 19
4. Postexilic
workman .....Neh. 3:25
5. Ezra's Levite
attendant .....Neh. 8:4
6. Man appointed as
treasurer......Neh. 13:13
7. Postexilic
Benjamite.....Neh. 11:7

Peg

Used to hold idols in
place.............Is. 41:7

Figurative uses of:

Revived nation....Ezra 9:8
Messiah's
kingdom ...Is. 22:23, 24
Messiah's death ...Is. 22:25

Pekah—*opening (of the eye)*

Son of Remaliah; usurps Israel's
throne............2 Kin. 15:25-28
Forms alliance with Rezin of Syria
against Ahaz .....Is. 7:1-9
Alliance defeated; captives
returned..........2 Kin. 16:5-9
Territory of, overrun by Tiglath-
Pileser............2 Kin. 15:29
Assassinated by
Hoshea...........2 Kin. 15:30

Pekahiah—*Yahweh hath opened (the eyes)*

Son of Menahem; king of
Israel.............2 Kin. 15:22-26
Assassinated by
Pekah ....2 Kin. 15:23-25

Pekod—*visitation*

Aramean tribe during
Nebuchadnezzar's
reign ....Jer. 50:21

Pelaiah—*Yahweh is wonderful*

1. Judahite........1 Chr. 3:24
2. Ezra's Levite attendant; reads
covenant......Neh. 8:7

Pelaliah—*Yahweh has judged*

Postexilic priest ...Neh. 11:12

Pelatiah—*Yahweh has freed*

1. Simeonite captain in war with
Amalekites....1 Chr. 4:42, 43
2. Prince dying while Ezekiel
prophesies ....Ezek. 11:1-13
3. Descendant of
Solomon ......1 Chr. 3:21
4. One who signs the
covenant......Neh. 10:1, 22

Peleg—*division*

Brother of
Joktan ....Gen. 10:25
Son of Eber.......Luke 3:35

Pelet—*(God) has freed*

1. Judahite.......1 Chr. 2:47
2. Benjamite warrior under
David.........1 Chr. 12:3

Peleth—*swiftness*

1. Reubenite, father of
   On............Num. 16:1
2. Judahite.......1 Chr. 2:33

Pelethites—*perhaps a contraction of Philistines*

David's faithful soliders during
Absalom's and Sheba's
rebellions.........2 Sam. 15:18-22

See Cherethites

Pelican—*the vomiter*

Dwells in
wilderness........Ps. 102:6
Lives in ruins .....Is. 34:11
                   Zeph. 2:14

Pelonite

Descriptive of two of David's
mighty men ......1 Chr. 11:27, 36

Pen

Figurative of
tongue ....Ps. 45:1
False.............Jer. 8:8
Not preferred .....3 John 1:13

Penalties—*punishment inflicted for wrongdoing*

A. *For sexual sins:*
   Adultery—
     death ....Lev. 20:10
   Incest—
     death ....Lev. 20:11-14
   Sodomy—   (Gen. 19:13, 17,
     destruction...{ 24

B. *For bodily sins:*
   Drunken-
     ness—   (1 Cor. 5:11
     exclusion—   { 1 Cor. 6:9, 10
   Murder—
     death ....Ex. 21:12-15
   Persecution—God's
     judgment .....Matt. 23:34-36

C. *For following heathen ways:*
   Human sacrifice—
     death ....Lev. 20:2-5
   Witchcraft—
     death ....Ex. 22:18
   Idolatry—
     death ....Ex. 22:20

D. *For internal sins:*
   Ingratitude—
     punished ......Prov. 17:13

Pride—abomi-
  nation ....Prov. 16:5
Unbelief—
  exclusion .....Num. 20:12
Lying—   (Jer. 23:10
  curse.........{ Zech. 5:3
Blasphemy—   (Lev. 24:14-16,
  death ....{ 23

Peninnah—*coral, pearl*

Elkanah's second
wife..............1 Sam. 1:2, 4

Penitence—*state of being sorry for one's sins*

A. *Results of:*
   Forgiveness....Ps. 32:5, 6
   Restoration....Job 22:23-29
   Renewed
     fellowship.....Ps. 51:12, 13

B. *Examples of:*
   Job ....Job 42:1-6
   David..........Ps. 51:1-19
   Josiah ....2 Kin. 22:1, 19
   Tax collector ..Luke 18:13
   Thief on the
     cross.........Luke 23:39-42

C. *Elements:*
   Acknowledg-   (Job 33:27, 28
     ment of sin...{ Luke 15:18, 21
   Plea for
     mercy.......Luke 18:13
   Broken heart ..Ps. 34:18
                  Ps. 51:17
   Confession.....1 John 1:9

See Repentance

Pentecost—*fiftieth* (day)

A. *In the Old Testament:*
   Called "the Feast of
     Weeks".......Ex. 34:22, 23
   Marks completion of barley
     harvest ......Lev. 23:15, 16
   Called "Feast of
     Harvest"......Ex. 23:16
   Work during,
     prohibited.....Lev. 23:21
   Two loaves
     presented .....Lev. 23:17, 20
   Other sacrifices
     prescribed.....Lev. 23:18
   Offerings given by
     Levites........Deut. 16:10-14
   Time of conse-
     cration........Deut. 16:12, 13

Observed during Solomon's
time ....2 Chr. 8:12, 13

See Feasts, Hebrew

B. *In the New Testament:*
Day of the Spirit's coming; the
formation of the Christian
Church ......Acts 2:1-47
Paul desires to
attend ......Acts 20:16
Paul plans to stay in Ephesus
until ....1 Cor. 16:8

Penuel—*the face of God*

1. Place east of Jordan; site of
Jacob's wrestling with
angel ....Gen. 32:24-31
Inhabitants of, slain by
Gideon.......Judg. 8:8, 9, 17
Later refortified by
Jeroboam .....1 Kin. 12:25
2. Judahite.......1 Chr. 4:4
3. Benjamite .....1 Chr. 8:25

Penury—*extreme poverty; destitution*

Widow's gift in,
commended ......Luke 21:1-4

People

Found among
Israel.............Deut. 7:6
Not limited to
Israel.............Rom. 2:28, 29
Called the
remnant..........Is. 11:10, 11, 16
Gentiles included { Is. 19:25
in .... { Is. 65:1
{ Rom. 15:10, 11
Became such by
covenant........Jer. 31:31-34
Secured through the
Messiah ....Ezek. 34:22-31
Accomplished by { Matt. 1:21
Christ's death ... { Luke 1:68, 77
Separated from { 2 Cor. 6:16-18
others............ { Rev. 18:4
God's true
Church.........1 Pet. 2:9, 10
All nations { Rev. 5:9
included in ...... { Rev. 7:9
God's eternal
people...........Rev. 21:3

People of the land—*the conservative
element of the population consisting
mainly of landholders*

The influence of...2 Kin. 11:13-15
Taxed.............2 Kin. 23:35

Peor—*opening*

1. Mountain of Moab opposite
Jericho........Num. 23:28
Israel's camp seen
from ....Num. 24:2
2. Moabite god
called Baal of { Num. 25:3, 5,
Peor .... { 18
Israelites punished for worship
of.............Num. 31:16

Perceive, perception—*knowledge
derived through one of the senses*

Outward { 2 Sam. 12:19
circumstances ... { Acts 27:10
Outward
intentions ....John 6:15
Intuition ....1 Sam. 3:8
John 4:19
Unusual manifes- { 1 Sam. 12:17, 18
tations .... { Acts 10:34
Spiritual { Neh. 6:12
insight .... { Acts 14:9
God's blessings....Neh. 6:16
Bitter { Eccl. 1:17
experience...... { Eccl. 3:22
Obvious { Matt. 21:45
implication ...... { Luke 20:19
God's { Gal. 2:9
revelation ...... { 1 John 3:16
Internal { Luke 8:46
consciousness ... { Acts 8:23

Perdition—*the state of the damned;
destruction*

Judas Iscariot .....John 17:12
Lost ....Phil. 1:28
Antichrist........2 Thess. 2:3
Rev. 17:8, 11

Peres—*to split into pieces*

Sentence of
doom.............Dan. 5:28

Peresh—*dung*

Man of
Manasseh ....1 Chr. 7:16

Perez—*a breach*

One of Judah's twin sons by
Tamar............Gen. 38:24-30
Numbered among Judah's
sons..............Gen. 46:12
Founder of a tribal
family...........Num. 26:20, 21
Descendants of, notable in later
times............1 Chr. 27:3

Ancestor of David and
Christ .... Ruth 4:12-18

Perezites

Descendants of
Perez............ Num. 26:20

Perfection—*the extreme degree of
excellence; pure; complete; mature*

A. *Applied to natural things:*
Day .... Prov. 4:18
Gold........... 2 Chr. 4:21
Weights .... Deut. 25:15
Beauty........ Ezek. 28:12
Offering ...... Lev. 22:21

B. *Applied to spiritual graces:*
Patience ...... James 1:4
Love........... Col. 3:14
Holiness ...... 2 Cor. 7:1
Praise .... Matt. 21:16
Faith .... 1 Thess. 3:10
Good works ... Heb. 13:21
Unity......... John 17:23
Strength....... 2 Cor. 12:9

C. *Means of:*
God .... 1 Pet. 5:10
Christ .... Heb. 10:14
Holy Spirit..... Gal. 3:3
God's Word ... 2 Tim. 3:16, 17
Ministry ...... Eph. 4:11, 12
Sufferings .... Heb. 2:10

D. *Stages of:*
Eternally accom-
plished........ Heb. 10:14
Objective
goal........... Matt. 5:48
Subjective
process ...... 2 Cor. 7:1
Daily activity .. 2 Cor. 13:9
Present
possession .... 1 Cor. 2:6
Experience not yet
reached....... Phil. 3:12
Descriptive of the completed
Church ...... Heb. 11:40
Heaven's eternal
standard ...... 1 Cor. 13:10-12

Perfume—*a substance producing
pleasant scents*

A. *Made by:*
Apothecary .... Ex. 30:25, 35

Combining:
Various
ingredients.... Job 41:31

Olive oil with imported
aromatics ..... 1 Kin. 10:10

B. *Uses of:*
Incense and ointment for
tabernacle .... Ex. 30:22-28
Personal
adornment .... Prov. 27:9
Seduction...... Prov. 7:17

C. *Figurative of:*

Christ's:
Glories .... Ps. 45:8
Righteousness and
intercession ... Song 3:6
Spiritual
prostitution ... Is. 57:9

Perfumer—*to mix, compound*

Great art........ Ex. 30:25, 35
                   Eccl. 10:1
Used in
tabernacle....... Ex. 30:25, 35
Used in
embalming ...... 2 Chr. 16:14
A maker of
ointment .... Eccl. 10:1
Among
returnees........ Neh. 3:8

Perga—*the capital of Pamphylia*

Visited by Paul.... Acts 13:13, 14
                    Acts 14:25

Pergamos—*a leading city in Mysia in
Asia Minor*

One of the seven churches
here............. Rev. 1:11
Antipas martyred
here.............. Rev. 2:12, 13
Special message
to .... Rev. 2:12-17

Perida (see Peruda)

Perils—*physical or spiritual dangers*

Escape from, by:

Prayer .... Gen. 32:6-12
Pacifying gifts..... Gen. 32:13-20
Quick action ...... 1 Sam. 18:10, 11
Flight............. Matt. 2:12-15
Love of Christ .... Rom. 8:35
God............... 2 Cor. 1:10

Perish—*to be destroyed violently*

A. *Applied to:*
Universe........ Heb. 1:11

Old world......2 Pet. 3:6
Animals ......Ps. 49:12, 20
Vegetation.....Jon. 4:10
Food ....John 6:27
Gold..........1 Pet. 1:7
Human body...2 Cor. 4:16
Soul ....Matt. 10:28

B. *Safeguards against:*
  God's:
    Power ....John 10:28
    Will ....Matt. 18:14
    Providence ...Luke 21:18
  Christ's
    resurrection...1 Cor. 15:18, 19
  Repentance....Luke 13:3, 5

See Lost

Perizzites—*dwellers in the open country*

One of seven Canaanite
  nations...........Deut. 7:1
Possessed Palestine in Abraham's
  time..............Gen. 13:7
Land of, promised to Abraham's
  seed............Gen. 15:18, 20
Jacob's fear of ....Gen. 34:30
Israel commanded to utterly
  destroy.........Deut. 20:17
Israel forbidden to intermingle
  with..............Ex. 23:23-25
Defeated by
  Joshua.........Josh. 3:10
Many of, slain by
  Judah ....Judg. 1:4, 5
Israel intermarries
  with...............Judg. 3:5-7
Made slaves by
  Solomon ......1 Kin. 9:20, 21

See Canaanites

Perjury—*swearing falsely*

Condemned by the
  Law..............Lev. 19:12
Hated by God.....Zech. 8:17
Requires
  atonement........Lev. 6:2-7
Brings
  punishment .....{ Zech. 5:3, 4
                   { Mal. 3:5

See False Witnesses

Perpetual—*lasting forever*

Statute............Ex. 27:21
Incense ....Ex. 30:8
Covenant ....Ex. 31:16
Priesthood ....Ex. 40:15
Possession ....Lev. 25:34
Desolations ....Ps. 74:3
Pain ....Jer. 15:18

Hissing............Jer. 18:16
Sleep.............Jer. 51:39
Hills ....Hab. 3:6

Perplexity—*a state wherein no way out
is seen*

Predicted by
  Christ ....Luke 21:25

Persecution—*to afflict, oppress, torment*

A. *Caused by:*
  Man's sinful
    nature ....Gal. 4:29
  Hatred of
    God...........John 15:20-23
  Ignorance of
    God...........John 16:1-3
  Hatred of   { 1 Thess. 2:15
    Christ........ { Rev. 12:13
  Preaching the   { Gal. 5:11
    cross......... { Gal. 6:12
  Godly living ...Matt. 13:21
                   2 Tim. 3:12
  Mistaken   { Acts 13:50
    zeal.......... { Acts 26:9-11

B. *Christian's attitude under:*
  Flee from .....Matt. 10:23
  Rejoice in .....Matt. 5:12
  Be patient
    under ....1 Cor. 4:12
  Glorify God
    in ....1 Pet. 4:16
  Pray during....Matt. 5:44

Persecution psalm

Of David.........Ps. 69

Perseverance—*steadfastness;
persistence*

Elements involved in:

Spiritual growth...Eph. 4:15
Fruitfulness......John 15:4-8
God's armor......Eph. 6:11-18
Chastening.......Heb. 12:5-13
Assurance ...... 2 Tim. 1:12
Salvation ....Matt. 10:22
Reward ....Gal. 6:9

Persis—*Persian*

Christian woman in
  Rome ....Rom. 16:12

Personal devotions

A. *Prayer:*
  In morning ....Ps. 5:3
                   Ps. 119:147
  Three times   { Ps. 55:17
    daily .... { Dan. 6:10

Continually....1 Thess. 3:10
1 Tim. 5:5

B. *Study:*
Daily ....Deut. 17:19
For learning ...Acts 17:11
Rom. 15:4

Personal work—*seeking to win persons
to Christ*

Need of ....John 4:35-38
Model of ......John 4:4-30
Means of.........1 Thess. 1:5, 6
Power of......John 16:7-11
Methods of.......1 Cor. 9:19-22

Persuasion—*inclining another's will
toward something*

A. *Good, to:*
Worship ......Acts 18:13
Steadfast-
ness.........Acts 13:43
Belief ......Acts 18:4
Acts 19:8

Turn from
idolatry ......Acts 19:26
Trust Jesus ....Acts 28:23

B. *Evil, to:*
Unbelief ......2 Chr. 32:10-19
Unholy
alliance ......2 Chr. 18:2
Fatal conflict ..1 Kin. 22:20-22
Turmoil.......Acts 14:19
Error ....Gal. 5:8

C. *Objects of:*
Hereafter ......Luke 16:31
One's faith in
God..........Rom. 4:21
Personal
assurance ....Rom. 8:38
Personal
liberty ....2 Tim. 1:12
Another's
faith ....2 Tim. 1:5

Peruda, Perida—*separated*

One of Solomon's servants whose
descendants
return from ⎰Ezra 2:55
exile............⎱Neh. 7:57

Perverse, Perverseness—*willfully
continuing in sinful ways*

Heart ....Prov. 12:8
Generation.......Phil. 2:15
False doctrine.....Acts 20:30
Comes from the
heart............Prov. 6:14

Issues from the
mouth..........Prov. 2:12
Causes strife .....Prov. 16:28
Abomination to
God.............Prov. 11:20
Hard way ....Prov. 22:5
Shall be cut off....Prov. 10:31

Pervert—*to change something from its
right use*

A. *Evil of, in dealing with:*
Man's
judgment .....Deut. 24:17
God's:
Judgment.....Job 8:3
Word........Jer. 23:36
Ways.........Acts 13:10
Gospel.......Gal. 1:7

B. *Caused by:*
Drink..........Prov. 31:5
Worldly
wisdom ....Is. 47:10
Spiritual
blindness.....Luke 23:2, 14

Pestilence

Fifth Egyptian
plague............Ex. 9:1-16
Used for man's
corrections ......Ezek. 38:22
Precedes the Lord's
coming...........Hab. 3:5

Pestle—*instrument used for pulverizing
material*

Figurative of severe
discipline........Prov. 27:22

Peter

A. *Life of:*
Before his call:
Simon ⎰Matt. 16:17
Bar-Jonah....⎱John 21:15
Brother of
Andrew......Matt. 4:18
Married ⎰Mark 1:30
man..........⎱1 Cor. 9:5
Not highly
educated.....Acts 4:13
Fisherman....Matt. 4:18

From his call to Pentecost:
Brought to Jesus by
Andrew......John 1:40-42
Named Cephas by
Christ........John 1:42
Called to discipleship by
Christ........Matt. 4:18-22

Mother-in-law
healed ....Matt. 8:14, 15
Called as
apostle.......Matt. 10:2-4
Walks on
water ....Matt. 14:28-33
Confessed Christ's
deity..........Matt. 16:13-19
Rebuked by
Jesus..........Matt. 16:21-23
Witnesses
transfigura-   {Matt. 17:1-8
tion...........   {2 Pet. 1:16-18
Asked important
questions ....Matt. 18:21
Refuses Christ's menial
service ....John 13:6-10
Cuts off high priest's slave's
ear...........John 18:10, 11
Denies Christ three
times ....Matt. 26:69-75
Weeps
bitterly.......Matt. 26:75
Runs to Christ's
tomb..........John 20:1-8
Returns to
fishing ....John 21:1-14
Witnesses Christ's
ascension ....Matt. 28:16-20
Returns to
Jerusalem.....Acts 1:12-14
Leads
disciples.......Acts 1:15-26

From Pentecost onward:
Explains Spirit's coming at
Pentecost .....Acts 2:1-41
Heals lame
man ....Acts 3:1-11
Pronounces
judgment .....Acts 5:1-11
Heals.........Acts 5:14-16
Meets Paul ....Acts 9:26
                 Gal. 1:17, 18
Raises
Dorcas........Acts 9:36-43
Called to
Gentiles.......Acts 10:1-23
Preaches the Gospel to
Gentiles.......Acts 10:24-46
Explains his action to
apostles.......Acts 11:1-18
Imprisoned—
delivered......Acts 12:3-19
Attends Jerusalem
Council ....Acts 15:7-14
Rebuked by Paul for inconsis-
tency ....Gal. 2:14

Commends Paul's
writings.......2 Pet. 3:15, 16

B. *His life contrasted before and
after Pentecost, once:*
Coward; now   {Matt. 26:58,
courageous... {   69-74
Impulsive; now
humble ....John 18:10
Ignorant; now
enlightened ...Matt. 16:21, 22
Deeply inquisitive; now
submissive ....John 21:21, 22
Boastful of self; now boastful of
Christ........Matt. 26:33, 34
Timid and afraid; now
fearless ......Matt. 14:28-31

C. *Significance of:*
Often the representative for the
others.........Matt. 17:24-27
Only disciple personally
restored by the
Lord ....John 21:15-19
Leader in the early
church........Acts 3:12-26

Peter, the Epistles of—*books of the
New Testament*

A. *1 Peter*
God's
salvation......1 Pet. 1:3-12
Obedience and
holiness.......1 Pet. 1:13-23
Christ the corner-
stone ....1 Pet. 2:4-6
A royal
priesthood ....1 Pet. 2:9
Christ's
example.......1 Pet. 2:18-25
Husbands and
wives ....1 Pet. 3:1-7
Partakers of His
suffering ......1 Pet. 4:12-19
Be humble before
God...........1 Pet. 5:6-10

B. *2 Peter*
Things pertaining to
life............2 Pet. 1:1-4
Diligent
growth........2 Pet. 1:5-11
False
teachers ......2 Pet. 2:1-22
The hope of the
day ....2 Pet. 3:9, 10

Pethahiah—*Yahweh opens* (the womb)

1. Priest of David's
time ....1 Chr. 24:16

2. Judahite serving as a Persian official ....Neh. 11:24
3. Levite who divorced his foreign wife....Ezra 10:19, 23
   Prays with the other Levites........Neh. 9:4, 5

Pethor—*a town in North Mesopotamia*

Balaam's home....Num. 22:5, 7

Pethuel—*God delivers*

Father of Joel the prophet ....Joel 1:1

Petitions—*entreaties for favors*

A. *Offered to men:*
Treacherous ...Dan. 6:7

B. *Offered to God:*
Favored ....1 Sam. 1:17
Granted ....1 Sam. 1:27

Peulthai—*reward of Yahweh*

Levite doorkeeper ....1 Chr. 26:5

Phanuel—*face of God*

Father of Anna ...Luke 2:36

Pharaoh—*great house*

A. *Unnamed ones, contemporary of:*
Abraham ,.....Gen. 12:15-20
Joseph........Gen. 37:36
Moses (the oppression) ...Ex. 1:8-11
Moses (the exodus) ....Ex. 5-14
Solomon.......1 Kin. 3:1
1 Kin. 11:17-20
Hezekiah ......2 Kin. 18:21

B. *Named ones:*
Shishak........1 Kin. 14:25, 26
So............2 Kin. 17:4
Tirhakah ......2 Kin. 19:9
Nechoh........2 Kin. 23:29
Hophra........Jer. 44:30
Probably also referred to in ....Jer. 37:5, 7, 11

Pharisees—*separated ones*

A. *Characteristics of:*
Jewish sect ....Acts 15:5
Upholders of traditions ....{ Mark 7:3, 5-8
Gal. 1:14
Sticklers for Mosaic Law.........{ Acts 26:5
Phil. 3:5

Very careful in outward details ....{ Matt. 23:23
Luke 18:11
Rigid in fasting ....{ Luke 5:33
Luke 18:12
Zealous for Judaism......Matt. 23:15
Lovers of display.......Matt. 23:5-7
Covetous ......Luke 16:14
Cruel perse- cutors........{ Acts 9:1, 2
Phil. 3:5, 6

B. *Chief errors of, their:*
Outward righteous- ness..........Luke 7:36-50
Blindness to spiritual things........John 3:1-10
Emphasis on the ceremonial Law...........Matt. 15:1-9
Perversion of Scripture......Matt. 15:1, 9
Self-justification before men..........Luke 16:14, 15
Hindering potential believers ......John 9:16, 22
Refusal to accept Christ.........Matt. 12:24-34

C. *Christ's description of:*
Vipers ......Matt. 12:24, 34
Blind ....Matt. 15:12-14
Hypocrites....Matt. 23:13-19
Serpents......Matt. 23:33
Children of the devil ....John 8:13, 44

D. *Attitude of, toward Christ, sought to:*
Destroy Him...Matt. 12:14
Test Him ......Matt. 16:1
Matt. 19:3
Entangle Him..........Matt. 22:15
Accuse Him ...Luke 11:53, 54

Pharpar—*haste*

One of the two rivers of Damascus........2 Kin. 5:12

Phichol

Captain of King Abimelech's army ....Gen. 21:22, 32

Philadelphia—*brotherly love*

City of Lydia in Asia Minor; church established here.............Rev. 1:11

Philanthropy

A. *Manifested by:*
Ethiopian......Jer. 38:6-13
Samaritan .....Luke 10:30, 33
Roman
centurion .....Luke 7:2-5
Pagans ....Acts 28:2, 7, 10
Christians .....Acts 4:34-37

B. *Precepts concerning:*
"Do good to
all" ....Gal. 6:10
"Love your
enemies"......Matt. 5:43-48
"Pursue what is
good".........1 Thess. 5:15

Philemon—*loving*

Christian at Colosse to whom Paul
writes............Philem. 1
Paul appeals to him to receive
Onesimus ....Philem. 9-21

Philemon, the Epistle to—*a book of the New Testament*

Thanksgiving .....Philem. 4-7
Plea for
Onesimus ....Philem. 10-21
Hope through
prayer..........Philem. 22

Philetus—*worthy of love*

False teacher......2 Tim. 2:17, 18

Philip—*lover of horses*

1. Son of Herod the
Great ....Matt. 14:3
2. One of the twelve
apostles.......Matt. 10:3
Brought Nathanael to
Christ.........John 1:43-48
Tested by
Christ.........John 6:5-7
Introduced Greeks to
Christ.........John 12:20-22
Gently rebuked by
Christ.........John 14:8-12
In the upper
room..........Acts 1:13
3. One of the seven
deacons.......Acts 6:5
Called an
evangelist.....Acts 21:8
Father of four prophet-
esses..........Acts 21:8, 9
Preached in
Samaria......Acts 8:5-13
Led the Ethiopian eunuch to
Christ.........Acts 8:26-40

Visited by
Paul ....Acts 21:8

Philippi—*pertaining to Philip*

City of Macedonia (named after
Philip of Macedon); visited by
Paul..............Acts 16:12
Acts 20:6
Paul wrote letter to church
of ....Phil. 1:1

Philippians, the Epistle to the—*a book of the New Testament*

Thanksgiving .....Phil. 1:3-10
Christ is
preached ....Phil. 1:12-18
To live is Christ...Phil. 1:21
The humility of
Christ ....Phil. 2:5-11
Lights in the
world ....Phil. 2:12-16
Perseverance......Phil. 3
Rejoicing in the
Lord ....Phil. 4:1-13

Philistia—*the country of the Philistines*

"The land of the
Philistines".......Gen. 21:32, 34
"The territory of the
Philistines".......Josh. 13:2
Philistia...........Ps. 60:8

Philistines—*the people of Philistia*

A. *History of:*
Descendants of
Mizraim.......Gen. 10:13, 14
Originally on the island of
Caphtor.......Jer. 47:4
Israel commanded to
avoid ....Ex. 13:17
Not attacked by
Joshua........Josh. 13:1-3
Left to test
Israel ....Judg. 3:1-4
Israel sold
into...........Judg. 10:6, 7
Delivered from, by
Samson ......Judg. 13–16
Defeat Israel...1 Sam. 4:1-11
Take ark to house of
Dagon ....1 Sam. 4–5
Defeated at
Mizpah ....1 Sam. 7:7-14
Champion, Goliath,
killed ....1 Sam. 17:1-52
David seeks asylum
among ....1 Sam. 27:1-7

Gather at
Aphek; Saul
and sons { 1 Sam. 29:1
slain by ......{ 1 Sam. 31:1-13
Often defeated by
David.........2 Sam. 5:17-25
Besieged by
Nadab ....1 Kin. 15:27
War against
Jehoram ......2 Chr. 21:16, 17
Defeated by
Uzziah........2 Chr. 26:6, 7
Defeated by
Hezekiah......2 Kin. 18:8

B. *Prophecies concerning:*
Union against
Israel ....Is. 9:11, 12
Punishment
pronounced ...Jer. 25:15, 20
Hatred against Israel
revenged......Ezek. 25:15-17
Destruction by
Pharaoh ......Jer. 47:1-7
Ultimate
decay ....Zeph. 2:4-6

Philologus—*lover of words*

Christian at
Rome ....Rom. 16:15

Philosophy

Divisions of ......Acts 17:18
Deception of ......Col. 2:8

Phinehas—*oracle*

1. Eleazar's son; Aaron's
   grandson......Ex. 6:25
   Slays an Israelite and a
   Midianite
   woman........Num. 25:1-18
   Wonderfully
   rewarded......Ps. 106:30, 31
   Fights against
   Midianites.....Num. 31:6-12
   Settles dispute over memorial
   altar.......Josh. 22:11-32
   Prays for
   Israel.........Judg. 20:28
2. Younger son of
   Eli ....1 Sam. 1:3
   Worthless
   man ....1 Sam. 2:12-25
   Slain by
   Philistines.....1 Sam. 4:11, 17
   Wife of, dies in
   childbirth .....1 Sam. 4:19-22
3. Father of a postexilic
   priest ....Ezra 8:33

Phlegon—*scorching*

Christian at
Rome ....Rom. 16:14

Phoebe—*pure, bright*

Deaconess of the church at
Cenchrea........Rom. 16:1, 2

Phoenicia—*purple*

Mediterranean coastal region
including the cities of Ptolemais,
Tyre, Zarephath and Sidon;
evangelized by early
Christians ....Acts 11:19
Jesus preaches
here.............Matt. 15:21

Phoenix—*harbor in southern Crete*

Paul was to winter
there.............Acts 27:12

Phrygia—*a large province of Asia Minor*

Jews from, at
Pentecost ....Acts 2:1, 10
Visited twice by
Paul.......Acts 16:6

Phurah—*branch*

Gideon's servant ..Judg. 7:10, 11

Put—*foreign bowman*

1. Third son of
   Ham ....Gen. 10:6
2. Warriors (Libyans) allied with
   Egypt.........Ezek. 27:10
   Same as Libyans
   in.............Jer. 46:9

Phygellus—*fugitive*

Becomes an
apostate.........2 Tim. 1:15

Phylactery—*charm*

Scripture verses placed on the
forehead; based upon a literal
interpretation
of ....Ex. 13:9-16
Condemned by
Christ ....Matt. 23:5

Physicians—*trained healers*

God the only
true ....Deut. 32:39
Practiced
embalming ....Gen. 50:2, 26

Job's friends of no
value............Job 13:4
Consulted by
Asa ....2 Chr. 16:12
For the sick
only............Matt. 9:12
Proverb concerning,
quoted ....Luke 4:23
Payment for services
of ....Mark 5:26
Luke, "the
beloved" ....Col. 4:14

Pi Beseth—*the house of the goddess
Bast*

City of Lower Egypt 40 miles north
of Memphis ......Ezek. 30:17

Pictures—*drawn or carved
representations of life scenes*

Descriptive of idolatrous
images ....Num. 33:52

Piece—*part of a larger whole*

Silver ....1 Sam. 2:36
Fig cake ....1 Sam. 30:12
Money............Gen. 33:19
                    Job 42:11
Fish..............Luke 24:42

Pierce—*to push a pointed instrument
through something*

A. *Used literally of:*
Nail in Sisera ..Judg. 5:26
Messiah's predicted
death ....Ps. 22:16
Christ's
death ....John 19:34, 37

B. *Used figuratively of:*
God's
destruction....Num. 24:8
Egypt's
weakness .....2 Kin. 18:21
Harsh words...Prov. 12:18
Great conflict of
soul........Job 30:16, 17
God's Word....Heb. 4:12
Coveted
riches.........1 Tim. 6:10

Piety—*holy living*

A. *Aided by:*
God's Word ...2 Tim. 3:14-17
Godly
parents ....1 Sam. 1:11
Prayer.........James 5:16-18
Good works ...1 Tim. 5:10

Hope of Christ's
return........Titus 2:11-14

B. *Hindered by:*
World ....James 4:4
Flesh ....Rom. 8:1-13
Satan.........Luke 22:31
Envying and
strife.........1 Cor. 3:1-7

C. *Value of:*
Profitable now and
later ....1 Tim. 4:8
Safeguard in
temptation ....Gen. 39:7-9
Rewarded in
heaven.......Rev. 14:13

See Holiness of Christians;
Sanctification

Pigeon

As a sin offering ..Lev. 12:6
As a burnt
offering ....Lev. 1:14
Offered by Mary ..Luke 2:22, 24

See Dove

Pi Hahiroth—*the place of meadows*

Israelite camp
before crossing   (Ex. 14:2, 9
the Red Sea .....(Num. 33:7, 8

Pilate, Pontius

Governor of Judea
(A.D. 26–36)......Luke 3:1
Destroyed
Galileans ....Luke 13:1
Jesus brought
before...........Matt. 27:2
Washed hands in mock
innocency ......Matt. 27:24
Notorious in   (Acts 3:13
history ....(Acts 4:27, 28

Pildash—*steely*

Son of Nahor and
Milcah ....Gen. 22:20-22

Pilfering—*stealing*

Forbidden.........Titus 2:10

Pilgrims—*God's people as*

A. *Elements involved in:*
Forsaking all   (Luke 14:26, 27,
for Christ ....(33
Traveling by
faith...........Heb. 11:9
Faces set toward
Zion ....Jer. 50:5

Encouraged by God's
promises ......Heb. 11:13
Sustained by
God..........Is. 35:1-10

B. *Their journey in this world as:*
Pilgrims and
strangers......1 Pet. 2:11, 12
Lights ....Phil. 2:15
Salt.........Matt. 5:13
God's own .....1 Pet. 2:9, 10
Chosen out of ⌠John 17:6
the world ....⌡1 Pet. 1:1, 2

See Strangers

Pilha—*plowman*

Signer of the
covenant ....Neh. 10:24

Pillar—*a column or support*

A. *Descriptive of:*
Memorial
sites ....Gen. 28:18, 22
Woman turned to
salt ....Gen. 19:26
Altars of
idolatry ......Deut. 12:3
Supports for a ⌠Judg. 16:25, 26,
building ......⌡   29
Covenant
site ....Ex. 24:4-8
Miracles ......Joel 2:30

B. *Figurative of:*
God's
presence ......Ex. 33:9, 10
Earth's
supports ......Job 9:6
God's sovereignty over
nations........Is. 19:19
Man's legs.....Song 5:15
Important
persons ......Gal. 2:9
Church ....1 Tim. 3:15
True
believers ......Rev. 3:12
Angel's feet....Rev. 10:1

Pillar of cloud and fire

A. *As means of:*
Guiding
Israel ....Ex. 13:21, 22
Protecting
Israel ....Ex. 14:19, 24
Regulating Israel's
journeys .....Num. 9:15-23
Manifesting His glory to
Israel ....Ex. 24:16-18

Manifesting His
presence ......Ex. 34:5-8
Communicating with
Israel ....Ex. 33:9, 10

B. *Effect of:*
Cause of fear ..Ex. 19:9, 16
Repeated in the
Temple........1 Kin. 8:10, 11
Long remem-
bered ....Ps. 99:7
Recalled with
gratitude......Neh. 9:12, 19
Repeated in Christ's transfigur-
ation..........Matt. 17:5

C. *Figurative of God's:*
Wonders.......Joel 2:30
Departure from
Jerusalem .....Ezek. 9:3
Presence among
believers ......Matt. 18:20

Pillow—*a cushion*

Stone used as .....Gen. 28:11, 18
Made of goat's
hair ....1 Sam. 19:13, 16
Used on a ship ....Mark 4:38

Pilot—*one who guides*

Of Tyre's ships....Ezek. 27:8-29
Shipmaster........Jon. 1:6
Used
figuratively.......James 3:4

Piltai—*Yahweh delivers*

Priest of Joiakim's
time..............Neh. 12:12, 17

Pine away—*to waste away*

Jerusalem.........Lam. 4:9

Pine trees—*evergreen trees*

Product of
Lebanon..........Is. 60:13
Used
figuratively.......Is. 41:19

Pinnacle—*a summit; highest ledge*

Of the Temple ....Matt. 4:5

Pinon—*darkness*

Edomite chief .....Gen. 36:41
1 Chr. 1:52

Pipe, piper—*a flute*

A. *Descriptive of:*
Hollow tube ...Zech. 4:2, 12

Spiritual
discernment...1 Chr. 14:7

B. *Figurative of:*
Joyful
deliverance....Is. 30:29
Mournful
lamentation...Jer. 48:36
Inconsistent
reactions......Matt. 11:17
Spiritual discern-
ment..........1 Cor. 14:7

Piram—*indomitable*

Amorite king of
Jarmuth..........Josh. 10:3

Pirathon—*height*

Town in
Ephraim..........Judg. 12:15

Pirathonite—*inhabitant of Pirathon*

Descriptive of:

Abdon............Judg. 12:13-15
Benaiah...........2 Sam. 23:30

Pisgah—*a mountain peak in the Abarim range in Moab*

Balaam offers sacrifice
upon ....Num. 23:14
Moses views promised land
from ....Deut. 3:27
Site of Moses'
death............Deut. 34:1-7
Summit of, called
Nebo.............Deut. 32:49-52

See Nebo

Pishon—*freely flowing*

One of Eden's four
rivers.............Gen. 2:10, 11

Pisidia—*a mountainous district in Asia Minor*

Twice visited by { Acts 13:13, 14
Paul.............. { Acts 14:24

Pispah—*dispersion*

Asherite..........1 Chr. 7:38

Pit—*a hole*

Figurative of:

Grave............Ps. 30:9
Snare ....Ps. 35:7
Harlot ....Prov. 23:27
Mouth of strange
woman...........Prov. 22:14

Destruction ......Ps. 55:23
Self-destruction ...Prov. 28:10
Hell..............Ps. 28:1
Devil's abode......Rev. 9:1, 2, 11

See Abyss

Pitch

Ark covered
with.............Gen. 6:14

See Asphalt

Pitcher—*an earthenware vessel with handles*

A. *Used for:*
Water ....Gen. 24:16
Protection of a
torch..........Judg. 7:16, 19

B. *Figurative of:*
Heart..........Eccl. 12:6

Pithom—*mansion of the god Atum*

Egyptian city built by Hebrew
slaves.........Ex. 1:11

Pithon—*harmless*

Son of Micah .....1 Chr. 8:35

Pitilessness—*showing no mercy*

Examples of:

Rich man ....2 Sam. 12:1-6
Nebuchad-
nezzar............2 Kin. 25:6-21
Medes ....Is. 13:18
Edom ....Amos 1:11
Heartless
creditor ....Matt. 18:29, 30
Strict
religionists ....Luke 10:30-32
Merciless
murderers ....Acts 7:54-58

Pity—*to show compassion*

A. *Of God, upon:*
Heathen ....Jon. 4:10, 11
Israel..........Is. 63:9
Faithful
remnant .....Is. 54:8-10
Believer.......James 5:11

B. *Of men:*
Pleaded........Job 19:21
Upon the
poor ....Prov. 19:17
Upon
children.......Ps. 103:13
Encouraged....1 Pet. 3:8

See Compassion; Mercy

Plague—*a severe epidemic*

A. *Descriptive of:*
Divine
  judgment .....Ex. 9:14
Leprosy.........Lev. 13:1-59
Threatened by
  God...........Deut. 28:21
Final
  judgment .....Rev. 9:20

B. *Instances of:*
In Egypt.........Ex. 11:1
At Kibroth Hat-
  taavah ....Num. 11:33, 34
At Kadesh .....Num. 14:37
At Peor........Josh. 22:17
Among:
  Philistines ....1 Sam. 5:7
  Israelites .....2 Sam. 24:15
  Sennacherib's
    soldiers ......Is. 37:36

C. *Sent by God:*
Because of
  sin ....Gen. 12:17
As final
  judgments ....Rev. 15:1, 8

D. *Remedy against, by:*
Intervention ...Ps. 106:29, 30
Prayer and
  confession ....1 Kin. 8:37, 38
Separation.....Rev. 18:4
Promise........Ps. 91:10
Obedience .....Rev. 22:18

Plain—*a geographically flat area
(usually refers to specific regional
areas)*

Dry region ....Num. 22:1
                  Deut. 3:17
                  Deut. 34:3

Plans—*methods of action*

Acknowledging God
  in ....Prov. 3:6
Considering all
  possibilites ...Luke 14:31-33
Leaving God out ..Luke 12:16-21
Not trusting
  God ....Ps. 52:7

Plants

Created by God ...Gen. 1:11, 12
Given as food .....Gen. 1:28, 29

Plants of the Bible

Anise ....Matt. 23:23
Bean.............Ezek. 4:9

Bramble..........Judg. 9:14, 15
Brier.............Judg. 8:7, 16
Broom
  ("juniper") ......Ps. 120:4
Calamus.........Song 4:14
Cummin ....Is. 28:25, 27
Fitch.............Ezek. 4:9
Garlic............Num. 11:5
Gourd............2 Kin. 4:39
Grass............Ps. 103:15
Henna ....Song 1:14
Hyssop..........Ex. 12:22
Lily..............Song 5:13
Mallows..........Job 30:4
Mandrakes.......Gen. 30:14-16
Mint.............Matt. 23:23
Mustard..........Matt. 13:31
Myrtle...........Is. 55:13
Rose ....Is. 35:1
Rue..............Luke 11:42
Saffron...........Song 4:14
Spikenard........Song 4:13, 14
Thorn............Judg. 8:7
Vine of Sodom ....Deut. 32:32
Wormwood.......Deut. 29:18

Plaster—*building material used on*

Infested walls .....Lev. 14:42, 48
Mt. Ebal.........Deut. 27:2, 4
Babylon's walls....Dan. 5:5

See Lime; Mortar

Platform

Ezra reads law
  from ....Neh. 8:4-8

Platter

Deep dish or
  basin.............Matt. 14:8, 11
In tribal
  offerings.........Num. 7:13
Used for a dead man's
  head ....Matt. 14:8, 11

Play

Music.............1 Sam. 16:16-23
Immoral acts......Ex. 32:6
Dancing ....2 Sam. 6:5, 21
Fish.............Ps. 104:26
Children ....Is. 11:8

Plead—*to entreat intensely*

A. *Asking for judgment against:*
Idolatry.........Judg. 6:31, 32
Evil king.......1 Sam. 24:15

B. *Asking for protection of:*
Poor...........Prov. 22:23

Widows........Is. 1:17
Repentant .....Mic. 7:9

Please—*to satisfy*

A. *Applied to God's:*
Sovereignty....Ps. 115:3
Election ....1 Sam. 12:22
Method........1 Cor. 1:21
Reactions to
man ....1 Kin. 3:10
Purpose........Col. 1:19
Creative acts ..1 Cor. 12:18
Will ....Matt. 3:17

B. *Applied to the unregenerate's:*
Behavior......Rom. 8:8
Passions......Matt. 14:6
Ways..........1 Thess. 2:15
Prejudices .....Acts 12:3

C. *Applied to the regenerate's:*
Faith ....Heb. 11:5, 6
Calling ....2 Tim. 2:4
Concern for
others.........Rom. 15:26, 27
Example,
Christ.........John 8:29

Pleasure—*satisfying the sensations*

A. *Kinds of:*
Physical ......Eccl. 2:1-10
Sexual.......Gen. 18:12
Worldly.......Luke 8:14
Immoral.......Titus 3:3
Spiritual ......Ps. 36:8
Heavenly .....Ps. 16:11

B. *God's, described as:*
Sovereign......Eph. 1:5, 9
Creative ......Rev. 4:11
In righteous-
ness...........1 Chr. 29:17
Purpose........Luke 12:32
Not in evil.....Ps. 5:4
Not in the   { Ezek. 18:23, 32
wicked........{ Ezek. 33:11

C. *Christian's described as:*
Subject to God's
will ....2 Cor. 12:10
Inspired by
God...........Phil. 2:13
Fulfilled by
God...........2 Thess. 1:11

D. *The unbeliever's, described as:*
Unsatisfying ...Eccl. 2:1
Enslaving .....Titus 3:3
Deadening .....1 Tim. 5:6
Judged ....2 Thess. 2:12

Pledge—*something given for security of a debt*

A. *Of material things:*
Garments......Ex. 22:26
Regulations
concerning....Deut. 24:10-17
Evil of.........Job 22:6
Restoration of, sign of
righteous-
ness...........Ezek. 18:7, 16
Unlawfully held
back ....Ezek. 18:12

B. *Of spiritual things:*
The Holy Spirit in the
heart..........2 Cor. 1:22
Given by
God...........2 Cor. 5:5
Guarantee of future
redemption....Eph. 1:13, 14

See Borrow; Debt; Lending; Surety

Pleiades—*cluster of many stars*

Part of God's   { Job 9:9
creation ....{ Amos 5:8

Plentiful, plenty

A. *Of physical things:*
Food ....Gen. 41:29-47
Prosperity .....Deut. 28:11
Productivity ...Jer. 2:7
Rain...........Ps. 68:9
Water ....Lev. 11:36

B. *Of spiritual things:*
Souls in need ..Matt. 9:37

C. *How to obtain, by:*
Industry.......Prov. 28:19
Putting God
first...........Prov. 3:9, 10

See Abundance

Plottings

A. *Against:*
Poor...........Ps. 10:7-11
Prophets.......Jer. 18:18
Persecuted.....Matt. 5:11, 12

B. *Inspired by:*
Contempt......Neh. 4:1-8
Hatred.........Gen. 37:8-20
Devil ....John 13:27
Envy ....Matt. 27:18

C. *Examples of:*
Esau against
Jacob ....Gen. 27:41-45
Satan against
Job ....Job 1:8-22

Ahab against
Naboth ....1 Kin. 21:1-16
Jews against
Jeremiah......Jer. 26:8-15
Haman against the
Jews.........Esth. 7:3-6
Chaldeans against
Daniel ....Dan. 6:1-8
Jews against   {Matt. 26:1-5
Christ.........{John 11:47-53
Jews against
Paul ....Acts 23:12-22

Plow, plowing—*to dig up the earth for sowing seed*

A. *Used literally of:*
Elisha ....1 Kin. 19:19
Forbidden with mixed
animals ......Deut. 22:10
Job's
servants......Job 1:14, 15

B. *Used figuratively of:*
Proper
learning.......Is. 28:24, 26
Wrongdoing....Hos. 10:13
Punishment....Hos. 10:11
Affliction......Ps. 129:3
Destruction....Jer. 26:18
Persistent sin ..Job 4:8
Christian
labor..........1 Cor. 9:10
Information from a
wife..........Judg. 14:18
Constancy in
decision.......Luke 9:62
Perverse
action........Amos 6:12

Plowman—*a farmer*

Used literally of:

Farming ....Is. 28:24

Used figuratively of:

Prosperity........Amos 9:13
Christian
ministry..........1 Cor. 9:10

Plowshares—*the hard part of a plow*

Made into
swords ....Joel 3:10
Swords made
into ....Is. 2:4

Plumb Line—*a cord with a weight (plummet)*

Figurative of:

Destruction ....2 Kin. 21:13
God's judgment...Amos 7:7, 8
God's building ....Zech. 4:10

Plunder—*spoil*

Clothing ....Ex. 3:22
Sheep.............Num. 31:32
House.............Mark 3:27
Camp.............1 Sam. 17:53

See Spoil

Pochereth—*binder*

Descendants of, among Solomon's
servants.........Ezra 2:57
Neh. 7:59

Pods—*husks of the carob or locust tree*

Fed to swine .....Luke 15:15, 16

Poetry, Hebrew

A. *Classified according to form:*
Synonymous—repetition of
same
thoughts......Ps. 19:2
Progressive—advance of
thought in second
line ....Job 3:17
Synthetic—second line adds
something
new...........Ps. 104:19
Climactic—the thought climbs
to a climax....Ps. 121:3, 4
Antithetic—the second line
contrasted with
first ....Prov. 14:1
Comparative—the "as"
compared with the
"so" ....Prov. 10:26
Acrostic—
alphabetic.....Ps. 119:1-176

B. *Classified according to function:*
Didactic   {Deut. 32:1-43
(teaching)....{Book of Job
Lyrics ....Ex. 15:1-19
Judg. 5:1-31
Elegies.........2 Sam. 1:17-27
Psalms........Book of Psalms

Poison

Reptiles...........Deut. 32:24
Serpents ....Deut. 32:33
Gourd...........2 Kin. 4:39, 40
Hemlock..........Hos. 10:4
Waters...........Jer. 8:14

Asps . . . . .Ps. 140:3
                        Rom. 3:13
Cobras . . . . .Job 20:16

Politeness—*refined manners*

A. *Manifested by:*
   Kings. . . . . .Gen. 47:2-11
   Hebrews. . . . . . .Gen. 43:26-29
   Romans . . . . . . .Acts 27:3
   Pagans . . . . . . .Acts 28:1, 2
   Christians . . . . .Philem. 8-21

B. *Counterfeited by:*
   Trickery . . . . . .2 Sam. 20:9, 10
   Deceit . . . . .2 Sam. 15:1-6
   Hypocrisy . . . . .Matt. 22:7, 8
   Pride . . . . .Luke 14:8-10
   Snobbery . . . . .James 2:1-4
   Selfishness . . . .3 John 9, 10

See Courtesy

Politicians—*governmental officials*

A. *Evils manifested by:*
   Ambition . . . . . .2 Sam. 15:1-6
   Flattery. . . . . . .Dan. 6:4-15
   Indifference. . . .Acts 18:12-16
   Avarice. . . . . . .Acts 24:26

B. *Good manifested by:*
   Provision . . . . .Gen. 41:33-49
   Protection . . . . .Neh. 2:7-11
   Piety . . . . .2 Chr. 34:1-33
   Prayer. . . . . . . .2 Chr. 20:6-12
   Praise . . . . . . .2 Chr. 20:27-29

Pollute—*to defile*

A. *Described as something
   unclean:*
   Morally. . . . . . .Num. 35:33, 34
   Spiritually . . . .Acts 15:20

B. *Means of:*
   Blood. . . . . .Ps. 106:38
   Idolatry. . . . . . .Ezek. 20:30, 31
   Abomina-
   tions. . . . . . . .Jer. 7:30
   Unregenerate
   service. . . . . .Ezek. 44:7
   Wickedness . . . .Jer. 3:1, 2
   Contempt of the
   Lord . . . . .Mal. 1:7, 12

See Unclean

Polygamy—*having more than one wife*

A. *Caused by:*
   Barrenness of first
   wife. . . . . .Gen. 16:1-6
   Desire for large
   family. . . . . . .Judg. 8:30

Political ties with other
   countries. . . . . .1 Kin. 3:1
Sexual desire . .2 Chr. 11:23
Slavery . . . . .Gen. 16:1, 3

B. *Contrary to:*
   God's original
   Law. . . . . .Gen. 2:24
   Ideal picture of
   marriage . . . . . .Ps. 128:1-6
   God's command-
   ment. . . . . .Ex. 20:14
   God's equal distribution
   of the   { Gen. 1:27
   sexes. . . . .{ 1 Cor. 7:2
   Relationship between Christ
   and the
   Church . . . . . . .Eph. 5:22-33

C. *Productive of:*
   Dissension . . . . .Gen. 16:1-6
   Discord. . . . . . .1 Sam. 1:6
   Degeneracy. . . .1 Kin. 11:1-4

See Adultery; Family; Fornication;
Marriage

Pomegranate—*a small tree bearing an
apple-shaped fruit*

Grown in
Canaan. . . . . .Num. 13:23

Ornaments of:

Worn by priests. . .Ex. 28:33
In temple . . . . .1 Kin. 7:18
Sign of
fruitfulness. . . . . .Hag. 2:19
Used
figuratively. . . . . .Song 4:3

Pond, pool—*a reservoir of water*

A. *Used for:*
   Washing. . . . . .1 Kin. 22:38
   Water supply . .2 Kin. 20:20
   Irrigation. . . . . .Eccl. 2:6
   Healing. . . . . . .John 5:2-7

B. *Famous ones:*
   Gibeon . . . . . . .2 Sam. 2:13
   Hebron. . . . . . .2 Sam. 4:12
   Samaria . . . . . .1 Kin. 22:38
   Bethesda . . . . .John 5:2
   Siloam. . . . . . .John 9:7
   The upper . . . .Is. 7:3
   The lower . . . . .Is. 22:9, 11
   The King's. . . . .Neh. 2:14

Pontus—*a coastal strip of north Asia Minor*

Jews from, at
Pentecost ....Acts 2:5, 9
Home of Aquila ...Acts 18:2
Christians of, addressed by
Peter.............1 Pet. 1:1

Poor, poverty

A. *Descriptive of:*
Needy ....Luke 21:2
Lower
classes ....2 Kin. 24:14
Rebellious .....Jer. 5:3, 4

B. *Causes of:*
God's
sovereignty ...1 Sam. 2:7
Sloth ....Prov. 6:10, 11
Lack of
industry.......Prov. 24:30-34
Love of
pleasure.......Prov. 21:17
Stubborn-
ness...........Prov. 13:18
Empty
pursuits.......Prov. 28:19
Drunkenness ..Prov. 23:21

C. *Wrong treatment of:*
Reproaches
God...........Prov. 14:31
Brings
punishment ...Prov. 21:13
Brings
poverty ....Prov. 22:16
Regarded by
God..........Eccl. 5:8
Judged by
God..........Is. 3:13-15

D. *Legislation designed for
protection of:*
Daily payment of
wages........Lev. 19:13
Sharing of tithes
with ....Deut. 14:28, 29
Loans to, without
interest ......Lev. 25:35, 37
Right to
glean ....Lev. 19:9, 10
Land of, restored in jubilee
year ....Lev. 25:25-30
Equal participation in
feasts........Lev. 16:11, 14
Permanent bondage of,
forbidden ....Deut. 15:12-15

See Needy; Poverty, spiritual

Poor in spirit—*humble, self-effacing*

Promised
blessing ....Matt. 5:3

Poplar tree

Used in deception of
Laban ....Gen. 30:37
Pagan rites
among ....Hos. 4:13
Probably same as
"willows" in ......Lev. 23:40

Popularity—*one's esteem in the world*

Obtained by:

Heroic exploits....Judg. 8:21, 22
Unusual wisdom ..1 Kin. 4:29-34
Trickery ....2 Sam. 15:1-6
Outward display ..Matt. 6:2, 5, 16

Popularity of Jesus

A. *Factors producing His:*
Teaching ......Mark 1:22, 27
Healing........Mark 5:20
Miracles ......John 12:9-19
Feeding the
people ....John 6:15-27

B. *Factors causing decline of His:*
High ethical
standards .....Mark 8:34-38
Foretells His
death ....Matt. 16:21-28

Population—*the total inhabitants of a place*

Israel's, increased in
Egypt ....Ex. 1:7, 8
Nineveh's, great...Jon. 4:11
Heaven's, vast ...Rev. 7:9

Poratha

One of Haman's
sons..............Esth. 9:8

Porch

Portico for
pedestrians.......John 5:2
Roofed
colonnade.......John 10:23

Porcius Festus—*successor to Felix*

Paul stands trial
before............Acts 25:1-22

Porcupine

Symbolic of
devastation.......Is. 14:23

Pork—*swine's flesh*

Classified as
unclean ....Lev. 11:7, 8

Port—*a harbor*

At Joppa.........Jon. 1:3
Fair Havens.......Acts 27:8
Phoenix..........Acts 27:12
Syracuse.........Acts 28:12
Rhegium.........Acts 28:13
Puteoli..........Acts 28:13

Portion—*a stipulated part*

A. *Of things material:*
Inheritance ....Gen. 48:22
B. *Of good things:*
Spirit ....2 Kin. 2:9
Lord ....Ps. 119:57
Spiritual
riches.........Is. 61:7
C. *Of evil things:*
Things of the
world ....Ps. 17:14
D. *Of things eternal:*
Punishment of the
wicked........Ps. 11:6

See Inheritance

Position—*place of influence*

Sought after by
Pharisees.........Matt. 23:5-7
James and John
request...........Mark 10:37
Seeking after,
denounced ......Luke 14:7-11
Diotrephes, a seeker
after ....3 John 9

Possess—*to acquire*

A. *Objects of:*
Promised
land...........Deut. 4:1, 5
Country ....Is. 14:21
Spiritual
riches.........Is. 57:13
Christ ....Prov. 8:22
One's:
Soul ....Luke 21:19
Body of
wife..........1 Thess. 4:4
B. *Of Canaan:*
Promised ......Gen. 17:8
Under oath ....Neh. 9:15
Israel challenged
to............Num. 13:30

Possible—*that which can exist*

A. *Things possible:*
All, with God ..Matt. 19:26
All, to the
believer ......Mark 9:23
Peaceful
living ....Gal. 4:15
B. *Things impossible:*
Deception of the
saints ....Matt. 24:24
Removal of the
Cross ....Matt. 26:39
Christ's remaining in the
grave ....Acts 2:24
Removal of sins by animal
sacrifice......Heb. 10:4

Posthumous—*after death*

Mary of
Bethany.........Matt. 26:13
Abel ....Heb. 11:4
All believers......Rev. 14:13

Pot—*a rounded, open-mouthed vessel*

A. *Use of:*
Cooking ......Zech. 14:21
Refining ....Prov. 17:3
B. *Figurative of:*
Sudden
destruction....Ps. 58:9
Impending national
destruction....Jer. 1:13
Merciless
punishment ...Mic. 3:2, 3
Complete sanctifi-
cation.........Zech. 14:20, 21

Potentate—*a mighty one*

Christ the only
absolute..........1 Tim. 6:15

Potiphar—*whom Re (the sun god) has
given*

High Egyptian
officer ....Gen. 39:1
Puts Joseph in
jail ....Gen. 39:20

Poti Pherah

Egyptian priest of On
(Heliopolis)......Gen. 41:45-50
Father of Asenath, Joseph's
wife ....Gen. 46:20

Potsherd—*a fragment of broken pottery*

Figurative of:

Weakness........Ps. 22:15

Leviathan's
underparts ...... Job 41:30

Uses of:

Scraping .... Job 2:8
Scooping water ... Is. 30:14

Potsherd gate—*a gate of Jerusalem*

By valley of the Son of
Hinnom .... Jer. 19:2

Potter—*one who makes earthenware vessels*

A. *Art of, involves:*
Reducing clay to
paste........... Is. 41:25
Shaping by revolving
wheel.......... Jer. 18:1-4
Molding by
hands.......... Jer. 18:6

B. *Figurative of:*
Complete
destruction.... Is. 30:14
God's sovereignty over
men........... Is. 64:8
Israel's lack of under-
standing ...... Is. 29:16

Potter's Field—*burial place for poor people*

Judas' money used for
purchase of...... Matt. 27:7, 8

Poultice—*medicinal material*

Figs applied to Hezekiah's
boil.............. Is. 38:21

Pour—*to flow freely from something*

A. *Applied to:*
Rain from
clouds .... Amos 9:6
Oil from
vessels........ Gen. 35:14
Blood from
animals ...... Lev. 8:15
Water from
barrels .... 1 Kin. 18:33

B. *Used figuratively of:*
Christ's
death .... Ps. 22:14
Spirit's
coming....... Joel 2:28, 29
Holy Spirit..... Ezek. 39:29

God's:
Wrath .... 2 Chr. 34:21, 25
Blessings ..... Mal. 3:10
Sover-
eignty........ Job 10:9, 10
Prayer and
repentance.... Lam. 2:19
Extreme
emotions...... 1 Sam. 1:15

Poverty, spiritual

A. *In a bad sense, of spiritual:*
Decay .... Rev. 2:9
Immaturity .... 1 Cor. 3:1-3

B. *Used in a good sense, of:*
The contrite ... Is. 66:2
God's people... Is. 14:32

C. *Caused by:*
Hastiness ...... Prov. 21:5
Greed.......... Prov. 22:16
Laziness ...... Prov. 24:30-34

Power of Christ

A. *Described as:*
Given by
God........... John 17:2
Derived from the
Spirit .... Luke 4:14
Delegated to
others......... Luke 9:1
Determined by
Himself .... John 10:18

B. *Manifested as power in:*
Creation ...... John 1:3, 10
Upholds all
things........ Heb. 1:3
Miracles ...... Luke 4:36
Regen-
eration....... John 5:21-26
Salvation ..... Heb. 7:25
Resurrecting
believers ..... John 5:28, 29
His return .... Matt. 24:30

C. *Manifested as authority to:*
Forgive sins .. Matt. 9:6, 8
Teach .... Luke 4:32
Lay down His
life........... John 10:18
Authority..... Matt. 28:18

D. *Benefits from, to believers:*
Life........... John 17:2
Strength...... Phil. 4:13
Effective   { 1 Tim. 1:12
service....... { 2 Tim. 4:17
Perfected in
weakness ..... 2 Cor. 12:9

Conquest over
temptation....Heb. 2:18
Glorification ...Phil. 3:20, 21

Power of God

A. *Manifested in:*
Creation.......Jer. 51:15
Keeps watch on the
nations........Ps. 66:7
Christ's:
Birth ....Luke 1:35
Miracles ......Luke 11:20
Resurrec-
tion..........2 Cor. 13:4
Exaltation ....Eph. 1:19, 20
Regen-
eration........Eph. 1:19
Sanctifica-
tion..........Phil. 2:13
Believer's
resurrection...1 Cor. 6:14

B. *Believer's attitude toward:*
Renders praise
for...........Ps. 21:13
Sings of ....Ps. 59:16
Talks of ....Ps. 145:11

Power of the Holy Spirit

A. *Manifested in Christ's:*
Conception ....Luke 1:35
Ministry ......Luke 4:14
Miracles ......Luke 11:20
Resurrection..Rom. 1:4

B. *Manifested in the believer's:*
Regen-
eration........Ezek. 37:11-14
Effective
ministry......Luke 24:49

Power, spiritual

Sources of:

Holy Spirit ......1 Cor. 2:4, 5
Christ............1 Cor. 1:24
Gospel..........Rom. 1:16
God's kingdom ..Mark 9:1
God's Word ......Heb. 4:12
New life..........Eph. 1:19

Powerlessness—*ineffective testimony*

Produced by:

Worldliness......Gen. 19:14
Unbelief ....Matt. 17:16-20

Practice—*customary habit*

Wicked works.....Ps. 141:4
Ungodliness......Is. 32:6
Work evil.........Mic. 2:1

Praetorium—*the governor's official residence*

1. Pilate's,   ⎧ Mark 15:16
   in   ⎨ John 18:28
   Jerusalem....⎩ Matt. 27:27
2. Herod's palace at
   Caesarea......Acts 23:35

Praise of God

A. *Objects of:*
God Himself ...Ps. 139:14
God's:
Name.........1 Chr. 29:13
Ps. 99:3
Power ....Ps. 21:13
Wonders......Ps. 89:5
Loving-
kindness .....Ps. 138:2
Works........Ps. 145:4

B. *Times of:*
Daily ....Ps. 72:15
Continually....Ps. 71:6
Seven times
daily ....Ps. 119:164
All the day ....Ps. 35:28
At midnight ...Ps. 119:62
Acts 16:25
While I live....Ps. 146:2

Praise of men

A. *Worthy:*
From
another ......Prov. 27:2
For:
Faithful-
ness........Prov. 31:28
Obedience ....Rom. 13:3
Works........Prov. 31:31

B. *Unworthy for:*
Wicked ....Prov. 28:4
Disorder ......1 Cor. 11:17, 22
Self-seeking ...John 12:43

Prating—*foolish babbling*

Descriptive of:

Fool ....Prov. 10:8, 10
Diotrephes........3 John 10

Prayer—*a request to God*

A. *Kinds of:*
Secret ....Matt. 6:6
Family.........Acts 10:2, 30
Group ....Matt. 18:20
Public ....1 Cor. 14:14-17

B. *Parts of:*
Adoration .....Dan. 4:34, 35
Confession.....1 John 1:9
Supplication ...1 Tim. 2:1-3
Intercession ...James 5:14, 15
Thanks-
giving.........Phil. 4:6

C. *Personal requirements of:*
Purity of
heart.........Ps. 66:18, 19
Believing ......Matt. 21:22
In Christ's
name ....John 14:13
According to God's
will ....1 John 5:14

D. *General requirements of:*
Forgiving
spirit.........Matt. 6:14
Simplicity.......Matt. 6:5, 6
Humility and
repentance....Luke 18:10-14
Unity of
believers ......Matt. 18:19, 20
Tenacity.......Luke 18:1-8
Importunity ...Luke 11:5-8
Intensity.......Matt. 7:7-11
Confident
expectation ...Mark 11:24
Without many
words.........Matt. 6:7
Unceasingly ...1 Thess. 5:17

E. *Answers refused, because of:*
Sin ....Ps. 66:18
Selfishness.....James 4:3
Doubt ....James 1:5-7
Disobedi-
ence ....Prov. 28:9
Inhumanity....Prov. 21:13
Pride ....Luke 18:11, 12,
                14

F. *Posture for:*
Standing.......Neh. 9:5
Kneeling.......Ezra 9:5
Sitting.........1 Chr. 17:16-27
Bowing........Ex. 34:8
Hands
uplifted ....1 Tim. 2:8

Prayer meetings

In the upper
room.............Acts 1:13, 14
In a house ....Acts 12:5-17
By a river........Acts 16:13
On a beach ......Acts 21:5

Prayers of Christ

A. *Their nature:*
Adoration .....Matt. 11:25-27
Intercession ...John 17:1-26
Thanks-
giving.........John 11:41, 42

B. *Their great occasions:*
At His
baptism.......Luke 3:21, 22
Before selecting the
apostles.......Luke 6:12-16
At His transfig-
uration.......Luke 9:28, 29
In Geth-
semane ....Matt. 26:36-42

C. *Their times and places:*
Early in
morning .....Mark 1:35
In secret......Luke 5:16
                Luke 9:18
With others...Luke 11:1
On mountain ..Matt. 14:23

Preach, preaching—*proclaiming the Gospel*

A. *Of the Gospel:*
Necessity of ...1 Cor. 9:16
Without
charge ....1 Cor. 9:18
Extent of, to
all ....Col. 1:25
Only one ......Gal. 1:8, 9
Centers in the
Cross ....1 Cor. 1:23
Preacher's importance
in..............Rom. 10:14, 15

B. *Attitudes toward:*
Accepted ......Luke 11:32
Rejected.......2 Pet. 2:4, 5
Not perfected
by ....Heb. 4:2
Perverted......Gal. 1:6-9
Contentious
about ....Phil. 1:15-18
Counted
foolishness....1 Cor. 1:18-21
Ridiculed ......Acts 17:16-18
Not ashamed
of.............Rom. 1:15, 16

Preacher—*one who proclaims publically*

Author of
Ecclesiastes ......Eccl. 1:1, 2
Causes to hear ....Rom. 10:14
Paul, speaking of {1 Tim. 2:7
himself.........{2 Tim. 1:11

Noah, of
righteousness.....2 Pet. 2:5

Precepts—*specific charges;
commandments*

God's:

Commanded .....Heb. 9:19
Corrupted........Matt. 15:9
Kept..............Ps. 119:56-69
Sought.........Ps. 119:40-94
Not forgotten .....Ps. 119:93, 141
Loved...........Ps. 119:159
Source of
understanding....Ps. 119:100, 104

See Traditions

Precious—*something extremely
valuable*

A. *Applied to spiritual things:*
Wisdom ......Prov. 3:13, 15
One's life .....1 Sam. 26:21
                2 Kin. 1:13, 14
Redemption of a
soul...........Ps. 49:8
God's thoughts
to us..........Ps. 139:17
Death of God's
people ....Ps. 72:14
Christ ....Is. 28:16
Christ's
blood ....1 Pet. 1:19
Faith ....2 Pet. 1:1
Promises.......2 Pet. 1:4
Trial of faith ..1 Pet. 1:7

B. *Applied figuratively to:*
Knowledge ....Prov. 20:15
Sons of Zion...Lam. 4:2
Rewards.......1 Cor. 3:12-14
Final harvest ..James 5:7
Worldly
pomp ....Rev. 17:4
Heaven's
glory..........Rev. 21:11, 19

Precious promises

A. *To the troubled by:*
Doubts ....Ps. 73:1-28
Afflictions .....Ps. 34:1-22
Persecution....Matt. 5:11, 12
Anxiety.......Phil. 4:6
Temptation ....1 Cor. 10:13
Infirmities ....2 Cor. 12:7-10
Discipline......Heb. 12:3-13

B. *To the sorrowful over:*
Death ....1 Thess. 4:13-18
Sickness......James 5:13-16

Their sins......Ps. 32:1-11
Disappoint-
ment..........Rom. 8:28

C. *To those troubled by:*
World ....1 John 2:15-17
Flesh ....Gal. 5:16-18
Satan ....Luke 22:31, 32
Worry ....Matt. 6:31-34
Sin ....James 1:12-15
Pride ....1 Pet. 5:5-7

D. *To the active Christian in his:*
Giving.........Mal. 3:10
Zeal ....Phil. 4:13
Soul winning ..James 5:20
Fruitfulness....John 7:38, 39
Graces.........2 Pet. 1:5-11
Prayers ....James 5:16
Perse-
verance ......Gal. 6:9
Watchful-
ness..........Eph. 6:10-20
Assurance .....Rom. 8:32-39
Ministry ....Ps. 138:8

Predestination—*God's eternal plan*

A. *Described as:*
"Purpose" .....Rom. 8:28
"Prepared
beforehand"...Rom. 9:23
"Foreknowl-
edge" ....Acts 2:23
"Foreknew" ...Rom. 8:29
"Ordained" ...Acts 13:48
"Appointed" ...Acts 22:10
"Deter-
mined".......Luke 22:22
"Fore-
seeing".......Gal. 3:8
"Before time
began".......2 Tim. 1:9

B. *Determined by God's:*
Counsel ....Acts 2:23
Foreknowl-
edge ....Acts 2:23
Good   ⎧ Luke 12:32
pleasure......⎨ 1 Cor. 1:21
Will ....Eph. 1:5, 9, 11
Purpose........Eph. 3:11
Power ....Is. 40:10-17
                Rom. 9:15-24

C. *Expressed toward the believer
in:*
Election ......Eph. 1:4
Salvation .....2 Thess. 2:13,
                14
Justification ...Rom. 8:30

Sanctifi-
cation........2 Thess. 2:12, 13
Glorification ...Rom. 8:30
Eternal
destiny........Matt. 25:34

See Foreknowledge of God; Elect

Predict—*to foretell*

Astrologers ....Is. 47:13

Preeminence—*being supreme above all*

A. *Of creatures:*
   Sought by the
   devil ....Is. 14:12-15
   Sought by
   man ....Gen. 3:5, 6
   Illustrated by
   Diotrephes ....3 John 9, 10

B. *Of Christ:*
   Predicted ......Ps. 45:6, 7
   Proclaimed ....Luke 1:31-33
   Visualized ....Matt. 17:4, 5
   Realized ......Col. 1:19
   Acknowl-
   edged ....Phil. 2:9, 10

Pregnancy

Safeguards
provided.........Ex. 21:22-25
Evidences of ......Luke 1:44
God's call
during..........{Jer. 1:4, 5
               {Gal. 1:15

Prejudice—*a biased opinion*

A. *Toward men, based on:*
   Race..........Acts 19:34
   Social
   position ......James 2:1-4
   Jealousy ......Gen. 37:3-11

B. *Toward Christ, based on His:*
   Lowly origin ...Mark 6:3
   Residence in
   Galilee ......John 1:46
   Race..........John 4:9
   Teaching ......John 9:16-41

See Bigotry

Premeditation—*deliberate plan to perform an act*

With:

Evil intent ......Gen. 27:41-45
Good intent......Luke 14:28-33
Heavenly
sanctions.......James 4:13-17

Preparation Day

Evening..........Matt. 27:57, 62
Day before   {Mark 15:42
Sabbath ....{Luke 23:54

Prepare—*to make ready*

A. *Of spiritual things:*
   To build an
   altar ....Josh. 22:26
   God ....Amos 4:12
   God's throne..Ps. 9:7
   Heart.........Ezra 7:10
   Passover......Luke 22:8, 9
   Spiritual
   provision.....Ps. 23:5
   Service ....2 Tim. 2:21
   Redeemed
   people ....Rom. 9:23, 24

B. *Of eternal things:*
   Reward......Matt. 20:23
   Kingdom .....Matt. 25:34
   Heaven.......John 14:2, 3
   Heavenly
   city ....Heb. 11:16
   Everlasting
   fire..........Matt. 25:41

Presbytery—*the Christian eldership acting as a body*

Ordination ascribed
to ....1 Tim. 4:14

See Elders in the Church

Presence, divine

Described as:

Majesty..........1 Chr. 16:27
Joyful...........Ps. 16:11
Protective........Ps. 31:20
Everywhere......Ps. 139:7
Guide............Ex. 33:14, 15

Present, Present to—*to offer*

A. *As an introduction of:*
   Joseph's
   brothers......Gen. 47:2
   Joseph to his
   father.........Gen. 46:29
   Dorcas to her
   friends ....Acts 9:41
   Paul to a
   governor......Acts 23:33

B. *Descriptive of the Christian's life as:*
   Living and holy
   sacrifice....Rom. 12:1
   Chaste virgin ..2 Cor. 11:2

Holy..........Col. 1:22
Perfect ....Col. 1:28
Without
blemish ......Eph. 5:27
Resurrected...2 Cor. 4:14

Presents—gifts

A. Offered to:
Brother.......Gen. 32:13-20
King...........Is. 39:1
Foreign
nation ....Hos. 10:6

B. Purposes of:
Secure a
message......2 Kin. 8:7-10
Show
friendship ...2 Kin. 20:12, 13
Show
obedience.....Ps. 72:10

See Gifts of man

Preservation, God's

A. As manifested over:
World ....Neh. 9:6
King..........2 Sam. 8:6, 14
Animals ......Ps. 36:6
Nation........Gen. 45:5, 7
Messiah ......Is. 49:8
Apostle.......2 Tim. 4:18
Believers.....1 Thess. 5:23
Faithful.......Ps. 31:23

B. Special objects of:
Those who trust
Him..........Ps. 16:1
Holy..........Ps. 86:2
Souls of
saints ....Ps. 97:10
Simple........Ps. 116:6
Those who love
Him..........Ps. 145:20

C. Spiritual means of:
Integrity......Ps. 25:21
Loving-
kindness .....Ps. 40:11
Mercy and
truth.........Ps. 61:7
Wisdom ......Prov. 4:5, 6
Losing one's
life...........Luke 17:33
Prophet.......Hos. 12:13

Press—a machine for extracting the juice from grapes

Used literally......Neh. 13:15
Figurative of appointed
time.............Joel 3:13

Pressure—force exerted

A. As evil:
Perversion.....Gen. 19:9
Enticement ....Judg. 16:16

B. As a good, to:
Hear God's
Word ....Luke 5:1
Get into the
kingdom .....Luke 16:16
Attain a goal ..Phil. 3:14

Presumption—to speak or act without warrant

A. Manifested in:
Speaking without divine
warrant ......Deut. 18:20-22
Acting without God's
presence ......Num. 14:44, 45
Living without
God...........Luke 12:19-21
Performing functions without
authority......Num. 16:3-11
Supposing God will not judge
sin ....Ps. 73:8-12
Aspiring to divine
titles..........Is. 14:12-15
Posing as
righteous .....Luke 18:11, 12
Making plans without
God...........James 4:13, 14

B. Judgment upon:
Defeat.........Is. 37:23-36
Loss of
power.........Judg. 16:20
Quick
punishment ...2 Sam. 6:6, 7
Rejection......1 Sam. 15:3,
          9-23
Destruction....Lev. 10:1, 2

Pretense—a false or counterfeit profession

Pharisees condemned
for ....Matt. 23:14

Prevail—to get the mastery over

A. Of physical force:
Waters ....Gen. 7:18-24
Combat........1 Sam. 17:50

B. Of supernatural force in:
Battle.........Ex. 17:11
Combat........1 Sam. 17:9, 50
Accomplish
much ....1 Sam. 26:25
Conquest ......Jer. 20:7
Victory ....Rev. 5:5

Prevarication—*evasion of truth*

Ananias and Sapphira killed
for ....Acts 5:1-10
Solemn warning
against ....Col. 3:9

Prey—*that which is taken by attack*

Used figuratively of:

Enemies ....Gen. 49:9
Innocent
victims ....Ezek. 22:27

Pride—*a conceited sense of one's
superiority*

A. *Origin of, in:*
   Devil ....Is. 14:13-15
   Ambition ......Dan. 5:20-23
   Evil heart.....Mark 7:21, 22
   World ....1 John 2:16
   Self-righteous-
   ness..........Luke 18:11, 12
   Worldly
   power.........Ezek. 16:49, 56

B. *Evils of:*
   Hardens the
   mind..........Dan. 5:20
   Produces spiritual
   decay ....Hos. 7:9, 10
   Keeps from real
   progress ......Prov. 26:12
   Hinders coming to
   God..........Ps. 10:4
   Issues in self-
   deception .....Jer. 49:16
   Makes men reject God's
   Word ....Jer. 43:2
   Leads to ruin ..Prov. 16:18

C. *Characteristic of:*
   Wicked ....Ps. 73:6
   World rulers...Hab. 2:4, 5
   Last days ......2 Tim. 3:2

Priest

A. *Requirements of:*
   Must be a son of
   Aaron.........Ex. 29:9
   Sanctified to
   office..........Ex. 29:44
   Statute
   perpetual .....Ex. 27:21
   No physical
   blemish ....Lev. 21:17-23
   Genealogy of,
   necessary .....Ezra 2:62

B. *Duties of:*
   Keeping the
   sanctuary.....Num. 3:38
   Keep lamp burning
   continually....Ex. 27:20, 21
   Continuing the sacred
   fire...........Lev. 6:12, 13
   Covering furniture when
   moved ....Num. 4:5-15
   Burning
   incense ....Ex. 30:7, 8
   Offering
   sacrifices.....Lev. 1:1-17
   Blessing the
   people ....Num. 6:23-27
   Purifying the
   unclean ....Lev. 15:15-31
   Diagnosing
   leprosy........Lev. 13:2-59
   Blowing the
   trumpets......Num. 10:1-10
   Carrying the ark of the
   covenant......Josh. 3:6-17
   Teaching the
   Law..........Lev. 10:11

C. *Names of:*
   Aaron.........Ex. 31:10
   Abiathar......1 Sam. 23:9
   Ahimelech....1 Sam. 22:11
   Amariah......2 Chr. 19:11
   Ananias ......Acts 23:2
   Caiaphas .....Matt. 26:3
   Christ ....Heb. 3:1
   Eleazar ......Num. 16:39
   Eli............1 Sam. 1:9
   Eliashib.......Neh. 3:1
   Ezekiel ......Ezek. 1:3
   Ezra ....Ezra 7:11, 12
   Hilkiah ....2 Kin. 22:4
   Jehoiada......Num. 11:9
   Jehozadak ....Hag. 1:1
   Joshua........Zech. 3:1
   Maaseiah .....Jer. 37:3
   Mattan (of
   Baal).........2 Kin. 11:18
   Melchizedek ...Heb. 7:1
   Pashhur ......Jer. 20:1
   Phinehas .....Josh. 22:30
   Sceva.........Acts 19:14
   Seraiah ....2 Kin. 25:18
   Shelemiah ....Neh. 13:13
   Urijah ....2 Kin. 16:10
   Zabud ....1 Kin. 4:5
   Zacharias.....Luke 1:5
   Zadok ....2 Sam. 15:27
   Zephaniah ....2 Kin. 25:18

See Levites

Priesthood of believers

Typical of Israel...1 Pet. 2:9
Predicted in
prophecy.........Is. 61:6
Including all
believers ....Rev. 1:5, 6
Having access to
God..............Eph. 2:18
Body as a living
sacrifice ....Rom. 12:1
Spiritual
sacrifices ....1 Pet. 2:5
Praise and good
works ....Heb. 13:15, 16
Deeds of
kindness ....Phil. 4:18

Priesthood of Christ

A. *Superior to Aaron as:*
Man; Christ the Son of
God..........Heb. 7:28
Sinner; Christ,
sinless ....Heb. 7:26, 27
Typical; Christ's the
fulfillment.....Heb. 8:1-6
Subject to change; Christ's un-
changeable....Heb. 7:23, 24
Imperfect; Christ's
perfect........Heb. 7:11, 25

B. *Christ as priest:*
Satisfies God's
justice ....Rom. 3:24-28
Pacifies God's
wrath.........Rom. 5:9
Justifies the
sinner.........Rom. 5:1
Sanctifies the
believer ......1 Cor. 1:30

See High priest

Prince—*a ruler*

A. *Descriptive of:*
Ruler ....Judg. 5:15
Head or
captain........Ex. 2:14
Noble or
volunteer .....Ps. 47:9

B. *Of the Messiah:*
Of David's
line ....Ezek. 34:23, 24
Reign of,
forever........Ezek. 37:24, 25
Time of,
determined....Dan. 9:25, 26
Reign of,
peaceful.......Is. 9:6

Author of
life...........Acts 3:15
Exalted to be
Savior ....Acts 5:31

Principalities

Created by
Christ ....Col. 1:16
Subject to
Christ ....Eph. 1:20, 21
Beholders of God's
redemption......Eph. 3:10
Overcome by
Christ ....Col. 2:15
Fighting against
Christians ....Eph. 6:12
Powerless against
Christians ....Rom. 8:38

Principles—*elementary Christian truths*

To be
maintained ....1 Tim. 5:21
Christians must go
beyond...........Heb. 5:12

Print—*a recognizable sign*

On the hands,
desired ....John 20:25

Priscilla, Prisca

Wife of Aquila ....Acts 18:1-3
An instructed
Christian ....Acts 18:26
One of Paul's
helpers ....Rom. 16:3
Greetings sent
from ....1 Cor. 16:19
Timothy commanded to
greet ....2 Tim. 4:19

Prison—*place of confinement*

A. *Place of:*
Hard labor.....Judg. 16:21, 25
Confinement...Jer. 52:11
Guards ....Acts 12:3-6
Stocks ....Acts 16:23, 24
Torture........Acts 22:24, 25
Execution .....Matt. 14:10

B. *Notable occupants of:*
Joseph.........Gen. 40:2, 3
Micaiah........1 Kin. 22:26-28
Jeremiah ......Jer. 32:2, 8, 12
Hanani ....2 Chr. 16:7-10
Zedekiah ......Jer. 52:11
John the
Baptist........Luke 3:20
Apostles ....Acts 5:18, 19

Peter .... Acts 12:1-4
Paul .... Acts 16:24

See Imprisonment

Prisoners—*those confined to jails*

A. *Used literally of:*
Criminals ...... Matt. 27:15, 16
Christians ..... Eph. 4:1
                 Col. 4:10

B. *Used figuratively of:*
Gentiles .... Is. 42:6, 7
Those in
spiritual $\begin{cases} \text{Is. 49:9} \\ \text{Zech. 9:11, 12} \end{cases}$
darkness
Righteous $\begin{cases} \text{Ps. 69:33} \\ \text{Ps. 79:11} \\ \text{Ps. 146:7, 8} \end{cases}$
in their
need

Privileges of believers

Access to God .... Rom. 5:2
Christ's
intercession ...... Heb. 7:25, 26
Eternal life .... John 17:2, 3
Growth assured ... 1 Pet. 2:2
Intercession of the
Spirit .... Rom. 8:16, 17
Kinship with
Christ .... Heb. 2:10-14
Membership in God's
kingdom .... 1 Cor. 6:9-11
Names written in book of
life .... Rev. 20:15
Partakers of the divine
nature .... 2 Pet. 1:4
Reconciled to
God .... Rom. 5:10
Suffering with
Christ .... Acts 5:41
Trials overcome .. 1 Pet. 1:6-8
Victorious living .. Rom. 8:37-39

Privileges of Israel

A. *Consisted of:*
Chosen by
God .... Deut. 7:6-8
Entrusted with God's
revelation ..... Rom. 3:1, 2
Blessings bestowed
upon .... Rom. 9:4, 5
Messiah
(Christ) .... Acts 2:22-39
Gospel first
preached to ... Acts 3:18-26

B. *Lost because of:*
Unbelief .... Matt. 8:10-12
Spiritual
hardness ...... John 12:37-40

Spiritual
blindness ..... John 9:39-41

C. *Now given to:*
Gentiles .... Matt. 21:43
Faithful
remnant ...... Rom. 11:1-7
Church .... 1 Pet. 2:5-10

Prize—*a reward for faithful
accomplishment*

A. *Described as crown of:*
Righteous-
ness .... 2 Tim. 4:8
Glory .... 1 Pet. 5:4
Life .... James 1:12

B. *Factors involved in obtaining:*
Self-control ... 1 Cor. 9:24-27
Following the
rules .... 2 Tim. 2:5
Pressing
toward .... Phil. 3:14
Enduring
temptation .... James 1:12
Looking to
Jesus .... Heb. 12:1, 2
Loving His
appearing .... 2 Tim. 4:8

Probation—*a period of testing*

A. *Factors determining:*
God's
promises ..... Matt. 21:33-43
Specific time ... Dan. 9:24-27
Faith or $\begin{cases} \text{Acts 13:32-48} \\ \text{Rom. 10:1-21} \end{cases}$
unbelief

B. *None after death:*
No change
permitted ..... Luke 16:26
Judgment
final .... Rev. 20:11-15
Destinies eternally
fixed .... Matt. 25:46

Prochorus—*leader in advance*

One of the seven
deacons .... Acts 6:5

Proclaim—*to officially announce*

A. *Physical objects of:*
Idolatrous
feast .... Ex. 32:4, 5
Holy
convocation ... Lev. 23:2, 4, 21
Year of
jubilee .... Lev. 25:10
Fast .... 2 Chr. 20:3
Release .... Jer. 34:17

Peace..........Is. 52:7
Doom ....Jer. 4:15, 16

B. *Spiritual objects of:*
God's name....Ex. 33:19
God's Word....Jer. 3:12
Salvation ......Is. 62:11

Procrastination—*putting off something*

A. *Manifested in:*
Delaying a
decision.......Matt. 19:16-22
Putting other things
first............Luke 9:59-62
Presuming on
tomorrow.....Prov. 27:1
Postponing
service........2 Cor. 8:10-14
Rejecting
reproof........Prov. 29:1

B. *Evils of, missing:*
Salvation ......2 Cor. 6:1
Life's
importance....Eccl. 12:1
God's
opportunity ...Jer. 13:16

Prodigal son

Parable
concerning ......Luke 15:11-32

Profane—*to act or speak irreverently of
holy things; defile*

A. *Manifested in:*
Breaking God's
Law............Amos 2:7
Defiling God's
house..........Mal. 1:12, 13
Not observing the
Sabbath.......Neh. 13:17, 18
Committing abomi-
nations........Mal. 2:10, 11
Idolatry........Lev. 18:21
Swearing
falsely ....Lev. 19:12
Illegal
marriages.....Lev. 21:14, 15
Blemished
service........Lev. 21:21-23

B. *Punishment of:*
Excommuni-
cation.........Lev. 19:8
Death ....Lev. 21:9
Destruction....Ezek. 28:16

Profession—*to declare one's faith
publicly*

Harmful..........1 Tim. 6:20, 21

Inconsistent......Titus 1:16
Degrading........Rom. 1:22
Tragic ....Matt. 7:23

Profit—*gain*

A. *Things empty of:*
Wickedness....Prov. 10:2
Riches.........Prov. 11:4
Labor without
God...........Eccl. 2:11
Lying words ...Jer. 7:8
World ....Matt. 16:26
Flesh ....John 6:63
Word without
faith..........Heb. 4:2
Mere
profession.....James 2:14, 16

B. *Things full of:*
Spiritual gifts ..1 Cor. 12:7
Godliness......1 Tim. 4:8
Inspired
Word ....2 Tim. 3:16
Good works ...Titus 3:8

Prognosticators—*those who profess to
know the future*

Help from, vain ...Is. 47:13-15

Prohibition—*restraint placed against
evil tendencies*

A. *Against:*
Idolatry........1 John 5:21
Drunken-
ness..........Luke 21:34
Uncleanness ...Eph. 4:18, 19
Worldliness ...1 John 2:15-17

B. *Based upon:*
Sanctity of the
body..........1 Cor. 6:13-20
New life in
Christ.........Col. 3:1-10
God's
holiness.......1 Pet. 1:14-16

Promises of God

A. *Described as:*
Never
failing........{Josh. 23:5-15
{1 Kin. 8:56
Backed by God's
oath ....Heb. 6:12-20
Fulfilled on
schedule .....{Acts 7:6, 17
{Gal. 4:4
Given to
Israel ....Rom. 9:4
Confirmed by
Christ.........Rom. 15:8
Kept by faith ..Rom. 4:20, 21
Heb. 11:13-40

Centered in {2 Cor. 1:20
Christ........ {2 Tim. 1:1
Exceedingly
great.........2 Pet. 1:4
Not slow......2 Pet. 3:4-13

B. *Objects of, for Israel:*
Land of {Acts 7:5
Palestine..... {Heb. 11:9
Davidic
kingship ......2 Chr. 6:10-16
Messiah ....Acts 13:23-33
Gospel ....Acts 10:43
New heart ....Jer. 31:33

C. *Objects of, for Christians:*
Holy Spirit....Luke 24:49
Salvation .....Acts 2:39
Kingdom ......James 2:5
Life eternal ..Titus 1:2
Crown of life ..James 1:12
New earth ....2 Pet. 3:13

See Messiah, the

Promises to believers (see Privileges of
believers)

Promotion—*advancement in status*

Deserved.........Gen. 41:38-42
Desirable.........Prov. 4:8
Divine ....Ps. 75:6, 7
Despicable.......Num. 22:17, 37

Pronunciation—*giving the right sound
to words*

Peter's detected ...Matt. 26:73
Correct, required in
church ....1 Cor. 14:7-16

Property—*material possessions*

Acquired by:

Industry ....Gen. 31:36-42
Inheritance ....Eccl. 2:21
Purchase.........Gen. 23:7-20
Deception.........1 Kin. 21:1-16
Coveting.........Josh. 7:21

See Ownership

Prophecy—*inspired foretelling of events*

A. *Characteristics of:*
Given by
God...........Is. 41:22, 23
Centered in {Luke 24:26, 27,
Christ........ { 44
Inspired by the
Spirit ....2 Pet. 1:21
Not of one's own interpre-
tation ....2 Pet. 1:20

Always
relevant.......Rev. 22:10
Must not be changed by
man ....Rev. 22:18, 19

B. *True, based on:*
Inspiration.....Mic. 3:8
Foreknowl-
edge ....Is. 42:9

C. *False, evidenced by:*
Nonfulfill-
ment.........Jer. 28:1-17
Peaceful
message......Jer. 23:17-22
Apostasy from
God..........Deut. 13:1-5
Lying ....Jer. 23:25-34

D. *Fulfillment of:*
Uncondi-
tional ....Ezek. 12:25-28
Sometimes:
Conditional ...Jon. 3:1-10
Dated.........Dan. 9:24-27
Nonliteral ....Matt. 17:10-12
Unrecognized by
Jews..........Acts 13:27-29
Interpretation of,
needed........Luke 24:25-44
Often referred {Matt. 1:22, 23
to............ {Matt. 2:14-23

Prophetess—*a female prophet*

A. *Good:*
Miriam ....Ex. 15:20, 21
Deborah.......Judg. 4:4, 5
Huldah ....2 Kin. 22:12-20
Isaiah's wife ...Is. 8:1-3
Anna ....Luke 2:36
Daughters of
Philip ....Acts 21:8, 9
Prophecy
concerning....Joel 2:28

B. *False:*
Women of
Judah ....Ezek. 13:17
Noadiah ....Neh. 6:14
Jezebel ....Rev. 2:20

Prophets—*inspired messengers*

A. *Described as:*
God's
servants.......Zech. 1:6
God's
messengers ...2 Chr. 36:15
Holy
prophets ......Luke 1:70
Holy men......2 Pet. 1:21

Watchmen.....Ezek. 3:17
Prophets of
God.....Ezra 5:2

B. *Message of:*
Centered in
Christ.........Luke 10:24
Interpreted by
Christ.........Luke 24:27, 44
United in
testimony.....Acts 3:21, 24
Contains grace and
salvation.....1 Pet. 1:9-12
Abiding
revelation.....Matt. 5:17, 18

Prophets, names of

Enoch.............Gen. 5:21, 24
Noah..............Gen. 9:25-27
Abraham..........Gen. 20:1, 7
Jacob.............Gen. 49:1
Aaron.............Ex. 7:1
Moses.............Deut. 18:18
Joshua.............1 Kin. 16:34
One sent to
Israel.............Judg. 6:8-10
One sent to Eli....1 Sam. 2:27-36
Samuel............1 Sam. 3:20
David.............Acts 2:25, 30
Nathan............2 Sam. 7:2
Zadok.............2 Sam. 15:27
Gad...............2 Sam. 24:11-14
Ahijah............1 Kin. 11:29
One of Judah......1 Kin. 13:1
Iddo..............2 Chr. 9:29;
                      12:15
Shemaiah.........2 Chr. 12:5, 7, 15
Azariah...........2 Chr. 15:1-8
Hanani............2 Chr. 16:7-10
Jehu..............1 Kin. 16:1, 7, 12
Elijah.............1 Kin. 17:1
Elisha............1 Kin. 19:16
Micaiah...........1 Kin. 22:7, 8
Jonah.............2 Kin. 14:25
Isaiah............2 Kin. 19:2
Hosea.............Hos. 1:1
Amos.............Amos 1:1
Micah.............Mic. 1:1
Oded..............2 Chr. 28:9
Nahum............Nah. 1:1
Joel...............Joel 1:1
Zephaniah........Zeph. 1:1
Jeduthun.........2 Chr. 35:15
Jeremiah..........2 Chr. 36:12, 21
Habakkuk.........Hab. 1:1
Obadiah...........Obad. 1:1
Ezekiel............Ezek. 1:3
Daniel............Matt. 24:15
Haggai............Ezra 5:1

Zechariah.........Ezra 5:1
                      Zech. 1:1
Malachi...........Mal. 1:1
Zacharias
(same as
Zechariah) ......Luke 1:67
John the Baptist..Luke 7:26-28
Agabus...........Acts 11:28
Paul.............1 Tim. 4:1
Peter.............2 Pet. 2:1, 2
John.............Rev. 1:1

Prophets in the New Testament

A. *Office of, based upon:*
Christ's prophetic
office.........Deut. 18:15, 18
Old
Testament   {Joel 2:28
prediction....{Acts 2:18
Holy Spirit's
coming.......John 16:7, 13
Divine
institution.....1 Cor. 12:28

B. *Functions of:*
Strengthen.....Acts 15:32
Define God's
will..........Acts 13:1-3
Predict the
future.........Acts 21:10, 11

Propitiation—*appeasing or conciliating*

Elements in Christ's:

Dying for man's
sins.............1 Pet. 1:18, 19
Satisfying God's
justice..........Rom. 3:25, 26
Reconciling God and
man.............2 Cor. 5:18, 19
Offering believing sinner perfect
righteousness.....2 Cor. 5:20, 21

Proselyte—*convert to Judaism*

A. *Regulations imposed upon:*
Circum-
cision.........Gen. 17:13
Observance of the
Law..........Ex. 12:48, 49
Obedience to the
covenant......Deut. 29:10-13
Association with
Israel.........Ruth 1:16
Separation from
heathenism...Ezra 6:21
Participation   {John 12:20-22
in feasts......{Acts 8:27

B. *Special significance of:*
Typical of gentile
converts ......Is. 56:3-8
Concerned about
Christ........John 12:20
Among early
converts ......Acts 6:5
Source of gentile
church ....Acts 13:42-46

Prosperity—*a state of material or spiritual bountifulness*

A. *Kinds of:*
Material ....1 Cor. 16:2
National ......Ezek. 16:13, 14
Personal ......Dan. 6:28
Deceitful ......1 Kin. 22:12, 15
Evil...........Ps. 73:12
Spiritual ......3 John 2
Divine ....Is. 53:10

B. *Of the righteous:*
Promised ......Ps. 1:3
Prayed for .....Neh. 1:11
Perplexed......Jer. 12:1-3

C. *Of the wicked:*
Lack of understanding
over ....Ps. 73:3-12
Righteous must not fret
over ....Ps. 37:7
Terrible end
of............Jer. 20:11

D. *Hindrances to:*
Trans-
gression.......2 Chr. 24:20
Hiding one's
sins...........Prov. 28:13
Distrust of the
Lord ....Jer. 2:36, 37

E. *True secrets of:*
Lord's
blessings ......Ps. 35:27
Keeping God's
Law...........Josh. 1:7, 8
God's
guidance ......Gen. 24:40-56
Trust in God...Neh. 2:20
Dedication to
God...........2 Chr. 31:20, 21
Listening to God's
prophets ......Ezra 6:14
Belief in God's
Word ....2 Chr. 20:20

F. *Perils of:*
Forgetting   ⎰Deut. 8:10-12
God...........⎱Prov. 30:7-9
Rebellion ......Jer. 22:21

Prostitute—*one engaged in promiscuous sexual activity*

Forbidden.........Lev. 19:29

Prostitution (see Harlot)

Protection, divine

A. *Characteristics of:*
Continuous ....Ps. 121:3-8
Unfailing ......Josh. 1:5
Assuring.......Is. 41:10
Persevering ...John 10:28-30
Satisfying.....2 Cor. 12:9, 10
Necessary .....Ps. 124:1-5

B. *Provided against:*
Evil............2 Thess. 3:3
Temptation ....1 Cor. 10:13
Persecution ...Rev. 3:10
Enemies ....Ps. 56:9
Falling........Jude 24
Dangers ....Ps. 91:3-7
Calamities ....Ps. 57:1

Protector, divine

God as............Ps. 18:2
Christ as.........2 Tim. 4:17, 18

Proud—*the defiant and haughty*

A. *Descriptive of:*
Moabites ......Jer. 48:29
Babylonians ...Jer. 50:29-32
Wicked........Ps. 17:9, 10
Scoffers.......Prov. 21:24

B. *God's attitude toward:*
Does not
respect........Ps. 40:4
Rebukes ....Ps. 119:21
Resists........James 4:6

See Pride

Prove—*to show something to be true*

Objects of, among Christians:
Love ....2 Cor. 8:8
Sacrifice ....Rom. 12:2
Faith.............2 Cor. 13:5
Works ....Gal. 6:4
Abilities...........1 Tim. 3:10

Proverb—*a wise saying*

A. *Descriptive of:*
Wise saying....1 Sam. 24:13
Something generally
accepted ......Ezek. 12:22, 23
Object of
taunt ....Deut. 28:37

Figurative
language......John 16:25, 29

Remember ⎰ Ps. 37:1-40
God's hand...⎱ Ps. 139:10

B. *Characteristics of:*
Brief...........1 Sam. 10:12
Striking
statement.....Luke 4:23
Authorita-
tive.........Prov. 1:1-6
Emphasis by
repetition.....Prov. 3:17

Proverbs, the Book of—*a book of the Old Testament*

Tribute to
wisdom...........Prov. 1-2
Against
immorality.......Prov. 5:1-23
Parental counsel..Prov. 6-7
Miscellaneous
proverbs..........Prov. 10-24
Proverbs of Agur
and Lemuel......Prov. 30:1-31:9
The worthy
woman..........Prov. 31:10-31

Providence—*divine guidance of men and things*

A. *Described as:*
Universal......Ps. 103:19
Purposive......Gen. 45:5-8
Righteous.....Ps. 145:17
Something
mysterious....Job 11:7-9
Irresistible.....Dan. 4:35

B. *Manifested, in the world, in God's:*
Preserving the
world.........Neh. 9:6
Providing for His
possesions....Ps. 104:27, 28
Guiding world
events........Acts 17:26, 27
Ruling over the
elements......Is. 50:2, 3
Preserving
nature........Gen. 8:22
Ordering man's
life..........Ps. 75:6, 7
Controlling minute
details........Matt. 10:29, 30

C. *Attitude of believers toward:*
Acknowledge
in ⎰ 1 Chr. 29:11, 12
prosperity....⎱ Prov. 3:6
Humble himself
before in ⎰ Job 1:21
adversity.....⎱ Ps. 119:75

Province—*a governmental district*

A. *Ruled by:*
Governors.....Esth. 3:12
Proconsuls.....Acts 13:4, 7

B. *Characteristics of:*
Numerous.....Esth. 1:1
Ruled by one
man..........Dan. 2:48, 49
Justice perverted
in............Eccl. 5:8
People, citizens
of............Acts 23:34
News spreads
to............Esth. 9:4

C. *Of the Roman Empire:*
Achaia........Acts 18:12
Asia..........Acts 19:10
Bithynia......Acts 16:7
Cappadocia....Acts 2:9
Cyprus........Acts 13:4
Egypt.........Matt. 2:13
Galatia.......Acts 16:6
Macedonia.....Acts 16:12
Pamphylia.....Acts 13:13
Lycia.........Acts 27:5
Syria.........Matt. 4:24

Provision

Provide for own
house............1 Tim. 5:8
Provide for poor...Is. 58:7

Provoke—*to agitate another's soul*

A. *Between people:*
Two women...1 Sam. 1:7
Peoples
(nations)......Rom. 10:19
Father and
children.......Eph. 6:4

B. *Causes of, between God and man:*
Evil...........Deut. 4:25
Sins..........1 Kin. 16:2
Whoredoms...Ezek. 16:26

Prudence—*wisdom applied to practical matters*

A. *Characteristics of:*
Dwells with
wisdom.......Prov. 8:12
Observant.....Prov. 14:15
Foresees evil...Prov. 22:3

Regards
reproof........Prov. 15:5
Conceals
knowledge....Prov. 12:23
Crowned with
knowledge....Prov. 14:18
Keeps silent....Amos 5:13

B. *Descriptive of:*
David.........1 Sam. 16:18
Solomon.......2 Chr. 2:12
Messiah ....Is. 52:13
Wife.......Prov. 19:14
Believers......Hos. 14:9
Worldly wise ...Matt. 11:25

C. *Examples of:*
Jacob.........Gen. 32:3-23
Joseph.........Gen. 41:39-49
Gideon ....Judg. 8:1-3

Prune—*to cut back plants for the purpose of producing more growth*

Vineyards........Lev. 25:3, 4
Figurative of ⎰Is. 5:6
God's care......⎱John 15:2

Instruments used to:

Hooks ....Is. 2:4
Is. 18:5

Psalm—*a spiritual song*

Some written by
David ....2 Sam. 23:1
Prophetic of
Christ........Luke 24:44
Used in worship..Ps. 95:2
Used in church....1 Cor. 14:26

Psalms, the Book of—*a book of the Old Testament*

Book I—The Genesis Book
Concerning
Man..............Ps. 1-41
Blessed are the
righteous.........Ps. 1
The holy hill ......Ps. 15
The creation of
God ....Ps. 19
Messianic Psalm ..Ps. 22
Prayer for God's
help..............Ps. 28
Book II—The Exodus Book
Concerning Israel as a
Nation ....Ps. 42-72
Psalm of longing ..Ps. 42
Prayer for
cleansing.........Ps. 51

Prayer for
deliverance.......Ps. 70
Book III—The Leviticus Book
Concerning the
Sanctuary ....Ps. 73-89
Prayer for
restoration ....Ps. 80
Book IV—The Numbers Book
Concerning Israel and the
Nation ....Ps. 90-106
The Lord reigns...Ps. 93
God's wondrous
works ....Ps. 105
Book V—The Deuteronomy Book
Concerning God and His
word ....Ps. 107-150
On God's command-
ments ....Ps. 119
Psalm of
faithfulness.......Ps. 128
God is gracious ...Ps. 145
Psalms of ⎰Ps. 149
praise ....⎱Ps. 150

Psaltery—*a musical instrument*

Used in:

Government
proclamations ....Dan. 3:5, 10

Ptolemais—*a seaport city south of Tyre*

Paul lands at ....Acts 21:7
Same as Acco. ....Judg. 1:31

Public opinion

Rescues
Jonathan.........1 Sam. 14:45
Delays John's
death.............Matt. 14:1-5
Protects the
apostles ....Acts 5:26
Makes Saul sin....1 Sam. 15:24
Increases Pilate's
guilt.............Matt. 27:21-26
Incites
persecution.......Acts 12:1-3

Publish—*to proclaim publicly*

Descriptive of:

Message of
doom.............Jon. 3:7

Publius—*common*

Roman official; entertains
Paul.............Acts 28:7, 8

Pudens—*modest*

Believer at
Rome ....2 Tim. 4:21

Pul—*strong*

1. King of Assyria; same as
   Tiglath-
   Pileser ....2 Kin. 15:19
2. Country and people in
   Africa.........Is. 66:19

Punishment, everlasting (see Hell;
Eternal, everlasting)

Punishments—*penalties inflicted on
criminals*

A. *Agents of:*
   State ....Rom. 13:1-4
   Nation.........Josh. 7:25
   Prophet.......1 Sam. 15:33
   Witnesses.....John 8:3-7
   Soldiers.......Matt. 27:27-35

B. *Kinds of* (non-capital):
   Imprison-
   ment..........Matt. 5:25
   Fine ....Ex. 21:22
   Restitution ....Ex. 22:3-6
   Retaliation.....Deut. 19:21
   Scourging ....Acts 22:25
   Bondage.......Matt. 18:25
   Banishment...Rev. 1:9
   Torture.......Heb. 11:35
   Mutilation....Judg. 1:5-7

C. *Kinds of* (capital):
   Burning ......Gen. 38:24
   Hanging.......Esth. 7:9, 10
   Crucifying.....Matt. 27:35
   Beheading ....Mark 6:16, 27
   Stoning.......Lev. 24:14
   Cutting in
   pieces.........Dan. 2:5
   Exposing to
   lions ....Dan. 6:16, 24
   Killing with the
   sword........Acts 12:2

See Capital punishment

Punites

Descendants of
Pua ....Num. 26:23

Punon

Israelite camp.....Num. 33:42, 43

Pur—*a lot*

Cast for Jews'
slaughter.........Esth. 3:7
Origin of Purim ...Esth. 9:24-26

Purah—*branch*

Gideon's servant ..Judg. 7:10, 11

Purchase—*to buy*

A. *Used literally of:*
   Cave ....Gen. 49:32
   Field..........Jer. 32:9-16
   Wife..........Ruth 4:10

B. *Used figuratively of:*
   Israel's
   redemption....Ex. 15:16
   God's gifts.....Acts 8:20
   Church ....Acts 20:28

Pure, purity—*uncontaminated with
dross or evil*

A. *Descriptive of:*
   Chastity.......1 Tim. 5:2
   Innocent ......Acts 20:26
   Regenerated ...Titus 1:15

B. *Applied figuratively to God's:*
   Law ....Ps. 19:8
   Word ....Ps. 119:140
   Wisdom ....James 3:17

C. *Applied figuratively to the
   believer's:*
   Heart..........Ps. 24:4
   Mind ....2 Pet. 3:1
   Conscience ....1 Tim. 3:9
   Language .....Zeph. 3:9
   Body ....Heb. 10:22

D. *Applied to the Christian's life:*
   Source.........Titus 1:15
   Command ....1 Tim. 4:12
   Means ....Phil. 4:8
   Outward manifes-
   tation ....James 1:27
   Inward
   evidence ....1 Tim. 1:5
   Goal...........1 John 3:3
   Reward.......Matt. 5:8
   False ....Prov. 20:9

E. *Applied symbolically to:*
   New
   Jerusalem.....Rev. 21:18, 21

Purge—*to cleanse thoroughly*

A. *Used, in the Old Testament,
   ceremonially of:*
   Cleansing......Ezek. 20:38
   Separation from
   idolatry ....2 Chr. 34:3, 8

B. *Used, in the Old Testament,
   figuratively of:*
   Reformation ...Ezek. 24:13
   Regen-
   eration........Is. 4:4

Sanctifica-
tion..........Is. 1:25
Forgiveness....Ps. 51:7
Consecration ..Is. 6:7
Atonement ....Mal. 3:3, 4

Purification—*ceremonial or spiritual cleansing*

A. *Objects of:*
Israelites at
Sinai..........Ex. 19:10
Priests at
ordination.....Ex. 29:4
Levites at
ordination.....Num. 8:6, 7
Offerings ......2 Chr. 4:6
High priest ....Lev. 16:4, 24
People
unclean.......Lev. 15:2-13
Nazirite after
vow...........Acts 21:24, 26

B. *Accomplished by:*
Sprinkling .....Num. 19:13-18
Washing parts of the
body..........Ex. 30:18, 19
Washing the whole
body..........Lev. 8:6
Running
water.........Lev. 15:13

C. *Figurative of:*
Christ's
atonement ....Mal. 3:3
Regen-
eration........Acts 15:9
Sanctifica-
tion...........James 4:8
Obedience .....1 Pet. 1:22

Purim—*lots*

Jewish festival celebrating being
rescued from Haman's
plot ....Esth. 9:26-28

Purple

Used in the
tabernacle........Ex. 25:4
Sign of riches .....Luke 16:19
Worn by royalty ..Judg. 8:26
Lydia, seller of ....Acts 16:14

Purposes of God

Characteristics of:

Centered in
Christ ....Eph. 3:11
Irresistible ....Is. 14:26, 27

Unknown to the
wise...........Is. 19:11, 12
Made known......Jer. 50:45
Irreversible ......Jer. 4:28
Planned..........Is. 23:9
Fulfilled..........Rom. 9:11
Victorious........2 Chr. 32:2-22

Purposes of man

A. *Good:*
Hindered by evil
men...........Ezra 4:5
Known by
others.........2 Tim. 3:10
Permitted......Dan. 1:8-16
Accom-
plished........1 Kin. 5:5
Determine .....Ps. 17:3
Delayed ....Acts 19:21
Not
vacillating.....2 Cor. 1:17

B. *Evil:*
Known by
God...........Jer. 49:30
Designed against the
righteous .....Ps. 140:4
Hindered ......Dan. 6:17-23

Purse—*a bag*

One, forbidden ....Prov. 1:14

Pursue—*To go after*

"Enemy said, I
will" ....Ex. 15:9
"Will flee when no
one" ....Lev. 26:17
"I will arise
and" ....2 Sam. 17:1
"Seek peace,
and" ....Ps. 34:14
"Blood shall"......Ezek. 35:6

Puteoli—*little wells*

Seaport of Italy ...Acts 28:13

Puthites

Descendants of
Caleb.............1 Chr. 2:50, 53

Putiel—*God enlightens*

Father-in-law of
Eleazar...........Ex. 6:25

Puvah, Pua, Puah—*utterance*

1. Issachar's second
son ....Gen. 46:13

Descendants of
Punites ....Num. 26:23
2. Father of Tola, Israel's
judge ....Judg. 10:1

Q

Quail—*a small bird*

Sent to satisfy
hunger ....Ex. 16:12, 13
Sent as a
judgment........Num. 11:31-34

Quarantine—*restricted in public contacts*

Required of
lepers ....Lev. 13:45, 46
Miriam
consigned ....Num. 12:14-16
Imposed under King
Azariah ....2 Kin. 15:1-5

Quarrel—*a dispute*

A. *Caused by:*
Flesh ....James 4:1, 2
Hatred.........Mark 6:18, 19

B. *Productive of:*
Friction........Matt. 20:20-24
Separation.....Acts 15:37-40

C. *Cured by:*
Gentleness.....2 Tim. 2:24-26
Forgiveness....Col. 3:13
Unity of
mind..........Phil. 2:3, 4

See Contention; Strife

Quartus—*fourth*

Christian at
Corinth ....Rom. 16:23

Queen—*a king's wife*

A. *Applied to:*
Queen regent ..1 Kin. 10:1-13
Queen
mother.........1 Kin. 15:13
Heathen
deity..........Jer. 44:15-30
Mystical
Babylon........Rev. 18:7

B. *Names of:*
Of Sheba ......1 Kin. 10:1
Vashti ....Esth. 1:9
Esther ....Esth. 5:3
Of Heaven.....Jer. 7:18
Of the South...Matt. 12:42

Quench—*to extinguish*

A. *Applied literally to:*
Fire...........Num. 11:2
Thirst.........Ps. 104:11

B. *Applied figuratively to:*
Love..........Song 8:7
God's wrath ...2 Kin. 22:17
Spirit ....1 Thess. 5:19
Persecution....Heb. 11:34

Question—*an inquiry*

Asked by:

Wicked ....Matt. 22:16-40
John 18:33-38
Sincere ....Matt. 18:1-6
Acts 1:6
Jesus...........Matt. 22:41-45

Quietness—*noiselessness*

A. *Descriptive of:*
People.........Judg. 18:7, 27
City ....2 Kin. 11:20
Nation.........2 Chr. 14:1, 5
Earth..........Is. 14:7

B. *Realization of:*
Predicted ......Is. 32:17, 18
Comes from
God...........1 Chr. 22:9
Preferred ......Prov. 17:1
To be sought ..1 Thess. 4:11
Undeniable ....Acts 19:36
Commanded ...2 Thess. 3:12
Obtainable.....Ps. 131:2
Very
valuable.......1 Pet. 3:4
Rewarded......Is. 30:15

Quirinius

Roman governor of
Syria ....Luke 2:1-4

Quitters, quitting

Unworthy........Luke 9:62
Believers should {Gal. 6:9
not............... {2 Thess. 3:13
Press on ....Phil. 3:12-14
Continue........2 Tim. 3:14

Quiver—*a case for carrying arrows*

Used by:

Hunters..........Gen. 27:3
Soldiers ....Job 39:23
Is. 22:6

Figurative of:

Children ....Ps. 127:5
Messiah..........Is. 49:2

Quotations

A. *Introduced by:*
"The Holy
Spirit" ....Acts 28:25
"As it is
written" ......Rom. 15:9
"The
Scripture".....Gal. 3:8
Old Testament
writer.........Rom. 10:5-20

B. *Purposes of:*
Cite
fulfillment.....Matt. 1:22, 23
Confirm a
truth..........Matt. 4:4
Prove a
doctrine.......Rom. 4:5-8
Show the true
meaning ......Acts 2:25-36

R

Raamah—*trembling*

Son of Cush......Gen. 10:6, 7
Father of Sheba and
Dedan............Gen. 10:7
Noted traders .....Ezek. 27:22

Raamiah—*Yahweh has thundered*

Postexilic chief....Neh. 7:7
Same as
Reelaiah.........Ezra 2:2

Raamses, Rameses—*Ra (Egyptian sun god) created him*

Treasure city built by Hebrew
slaves ....Ex. 1:11

Rabbah, Rabbath—*great*

1. Town of
Judah.........Josh. 15:60
2. Capital of
Ammon.......Amos 1:14
Bedstead of Og
here ....Deut. 3:11
On Gad's
boundary .....Josh. 13:25
Besieged by
Joab ....2 Sam. 12:26
Defeated and enslaved by
David........2 Sam. 12:29-31
Destruction of,
foretold ....Jer. 49:2, 3

Rabbi, Rabboni—*my master*

A. *Applied to:*
John the
Baptist........John 3:26
Jesus Christ ...John 3:2
John 1:38, 49

B. *Significance of:*
Coveted title...Matt. 23:6, 7
Forbidden by
Christ.........Matt. 23:8
Expressive of imperfect
faith ....Mark 14:45
John 20:16

Rabbith—*multitude*

Frontier town of
Issachar..........Josh. 19:20

Rabboni—*Aramaic form of Rabbi*

Mary addresses Christ
as ....John 20:16

Rabmag—*head of the Magi*

Title applied to Nergal-Sar-
ezer ....Jer. 39:3, 13

Rabsaris—*head chamberlain*

Title applied to:

Assyrian officials sent by Sennacherib ....2 Kin. 18:17
Babylonian Nebu-
shasban ....Jer. 39:13
Babylonian
prince...........Jer. 39:3

Rabshakeh—*Head of the cupbearers*

Sent ....2 Kin. 18:17
King of Assyria
sent..............Is. 36:2
And told him the
words of ....Is. 36:22
Hear all the
words ....2 Kin. 19:4

Raca—*a term of insult*

Use of, forbidden by
Christ ....Matt. 5:21, 22

Race, Christian

Requirements of:

Discipline ....1 Cor. 9:24-27
Patience ....Eccl. 9:11
Steadfastness .....Gal. 5:7

Race, human

Unity of..........Gen. 3:20
Divisions of......Gen. 10:1-32
Scattering of......Gen. 11:1-9
Bounds of.......Acts 17:26
Depravity of.......Rom. 1:18-32
Salvation of......John 3:16

Rachal—*trader*

City in Judah....1 Sam. 30:29

Rachel—*ewe*

Laban's younger daughter; Jacob's
favorite wife......Gen. 29:28-30
Supports her husband's
position..........Gen. 31:14-16
Mother of Joseph and
Benjamin........Gen. 30:22-25
Prophecy
concerning, ⎰Jer. 31:15
quoted ....⎱Matt. 2:18

Rachel, tomb of

At Bethlehem—first mention
of in Bible.......Gen. 35:19, 20

Racial relations

Salvation is ⎰Eph. 2:11-22
for all ....⎱Eph. 3:7-9
All are same in
Christ ....Col. 3:9-11

Raddai—*Yahweh has subdued*

One of David's
brothers..........1 Chr. 2:14

Radiance in life

Caused by:

Wisdom............Prov. 4:7-9
Soul winning......Dan. 12:3
Transfiguration ...Matt. 17:2
Beholding the ⎰Ps. 34:5
Lord.............⎱2 Cor. 3:7-18

Rafters—*timbers used to support a roof*

Made of fir........Song 1:17

Ragau (see Reu)

Rage—*raving and violent madness; fury*

A. *Descriptive of:*
    Sea............Luke 8:24
    Anger ....Dan. 3:13
    Nations........Ps. 2:1
B. *Caused by:*
    Insane
    madness ......2 Chr. 16:7-10

Supposed
insult ....2 Kin. 5:11, 12
Jealousy.......Prov. 6:34
Insolence against
God..........2 Kin. 19:27, 28

Rags—*tattered and spoiled clothing*

Used as
cushions ....Jer. 38:11-13
Reward of
drowsiness ......Prov. 23:21
Man's righteousness
like..............Is. 64:6

Rahab (I)—*violence*

Prostitute living in
Jericho.........Josh. 2:1
Concealed Joshua's
spies ....Josh. 2:1-24
Spared by invading
Israelites ....Josh. 6:17-25
Included among the
faithful..........Heb. 11:31
Cited as an
example.........James 2:25
Ancestress of
Christ ....Matt. 1:5

Rahab (II)—*pride, arrogance*

Used figuratively of
Egypt...........Ps. 87:4
Translated "the
proud" ....Job 9:13

Raham—*pity*

Descendant of
Caleb.............1 Chr. 2:44

Rain—*water falling from clouds*

A. *Features concerning:*
    Sent by God ...Jer. 14:22
    Sent on all
    mankind......Matt. 5:45
    Sign of God's
    goodness......Deut. 28:12
    Controlled by
    God's ⎰Job 28:26
    decrees ......⎱Job 37:6
    Withheld because of
    sin............Deut. 11:17
    Sent as a result of
    judgment .....Gen. 7:4
    Former and
    latter ....Jer. 5:24
    To be prayed
    for............1 Kin. 8:35, 36
B. *Figurative of:*
    God's Word....Is. 55:10, 11

Spiritual
blessing . . . . Ps. 72:6
Righteous-
ness. . . . . Hos. 10:12
Final
judgment . . . . . Matt. 7:24-27
Hell . . . . Ps. 11:6
Earth's
ingathering . . . James 5:7

Rainbow

Appears after the
flood . . . . Gen. 9:12, 13
Sign of God's
covenant. . . . . Gen. 9:16, 17
On angel's head . . . Rev. 10:1
Over God's
throne. . . . . Rev. 4:3

Raisins—*dried grapes*

Nourishing food . . . 1 Sam. 25:18
Provided for
David . . . . 2 Sam. 16:1

Rakem—*variegated*

Manassite . . . . 1 Chr. 7:16

Rakkath—*bank, shore*

Fortified city of
Naphtali. . . . . Josh. 19:32, 35

Rakkon—*shore*

Danite village . . . . . Josh. 19:40, 46

Ram (I)—*high, exalted*

1. Ancestor of
   David . . . . Ruth 4:19
   Ancestor of
   Christ. . . . . Matt. 1:3, 4
2. Man of
   Judah . . . . 1 Chr. 2:25, 27

Ram (II)—*a male sheep*

Used as food . . . . . Gen. 31:38
Used in
offerings. . . . . Gen. 22:13
Appointed for certain
offerings. . . . . Lev. 5:15
Skin of, used as
coverings. . . . . Ex. 26:14
Horns of, used as
trumpets . . . . Josh. 6:4-13

Ram (III)—*an instrument of war*

Used to destroy gates and
walls . . . . Ezek. 4:2

Ramah

1. Town of
   Asher . . . . Josh. 19:24, 29
2. City of
   Naphtali . . . . . Josh. 19:32, 36
3. Benjamite city near
   Jerusalem . . . . Josh. 18:21, 25
   Deborah's palm near
   here . . . . Judg. 4:5
   Fortress built . . 1 Kin. 15:17-22
   Gathering of
   captives. . . . . . . Jer. 40:1
   Reinhabited after
   exile . . . . Ezra 2:26
   Probable site of Rachel's
   tomb. . . . . 1 Sam. 10:2
   Samuel's head-
   quarters. . . . . . 1 Sam. 7:15, 17
   David flees
   to . . . . 1 Sam. 19:18-23
4. Town called Ramoth
   Gilead . . . . 2 Kin. 8:28, 29

Ramathaim Zophim

Home of
Elkanah . . . . 1 Sam. 1:1
Also called
"Ramah" . . . . 1 Sam. 1:19

See Ramah 4

Ramathite—*an inhabitant of Ramah*

Shimei called. . . . . . 1 Chr. 27:27

Ramath Mizpah—*a town in Palestine*

An inheritance of
Gad . . . . Josh. 13:24-26

Ramoth—*high places*

1. Town of Issachar; possibly
   same as Remeth and
   Jarmuth . . . . . . Josh. 19:21
   Josh. 21:28, 29
   1 Chr. 6:73
2. Town of the south; see Ramah
3. Town of
   Gilead . . . . Deut. 4:43
4. A son of
   Bani . . . . Ezra 10:29

Ramoth Gilead

City of   ⎧ Deut. 4:43
refuge east   ⎨ Josh. 20:8
of Jordan . . . ⎩ 1 Chr. 6:80
Site of Ahab's fatal conflict with
Syrians. . . . . 1 Kin. 22:1-39

Rampart—*a city's outer fortification*

Around:

Certain cities......2 Sam. 20:15

Ransom—*to redeem by a payment*

A. *Of man, for:*

Israelites ......Ex. 30:12-16
Murderer,
forbidden .....Num. 35:31, 32
Brother,
impossible.....Ps. 49:7, 8

B. *Of Christ:*

For all........Matt. 20:28
From grave....Hos. 13:14
From Satan....Jer. 31:11
Cause of joy...Is. 35:10

Rapacity—*seizing others' goods; covetous*

Descriptive of
Satan ....1 Pet. 5:8
Characteristic of false
teachers.........Luke 20:45-47

Rape—*forced sexual relations*

A. *Features concerning:*

Death penalty
for............Deut. 22:25-27
Captives subjected
to............Is. 13:16

B. *Example of:*

Tamar by   { 2 Sam. 13:6-29,
Amnon   { 32, 33

Rapha, Raphah—*he (God) has healed*

1. Benjamin's fifth
   son ....1 Chr. 8:1, 2
   But not
   listed.........Gen. 46:21
2. Descendant of
   Jonathan......1 Chr. 8:37
   Called Rephaiah
   in............1 Chr. 9:43
3. Same word translated
   "giant"........2 Sam. 21:16-20

Raphu—*cured*

Benjamite........Num. 13:9

Rapture, the—*translation of saved at Christ's return*

Not all   { 1 Cor. 15:51
will   { 1 Thess. 4:15,
sleep ....{ 17
Dead in   { 1 Cor. 15:52
Christ will   { 1 Thess. 4:13, 14,
rise............{ 16

Living to be
transformed......1 Cor. 15:51-53
Saints caught
up...............1 Thess. 4:16, 17

Rashness—*ill-advised and hasty action*

Examples of:

Moses' killing the
Egyptian ....Ex. 2:11, 12
Jephthah's vow ...Judg. 11:30-39
Israel's vow against the
Benjamites ......Judg. 21:1-6
Josiah's war against
Necho...........2 Chr. 35:20-24
Peter's cutting off the ear of
Malchus........John 18:10

Rationing—*limits prescribed for necessities*

By Joseph, to save
Egypt ....Gen. 41:35-57

Raven—*a flesh-eating bird*

A. *Characteristics of:*

Unclean for
food ....Lev. 11:15
Solitary in
habit.........Is. 34:11
Flesh-eating ...Prov. 30:17
Black ....Song 5:11

B. *Special features concerning:*

First creature sent from the
ark ....Gen. 8:7
Elijah fed by..1 Kin. 17:4-7
Fed by God....Luke 12:24

Razor—*a sharp instrument used for cutting off hair*

Forbidden to:

Nazirites ......Num. 6:1-5
Samson ....Judg. 13:5
Mentioned in Hannah's
vow ....1 Sam. 1:11
Used by barbers...Ezek. 5:1

See Hair; Knife

Readiness—*being prepared for action*

A. *Descriptive of:*

Being
prepared ......Matt. 22:4, 8
Being
responsive ....2 Cor. 8:11, 19

B. *Objects of:*

Willing
people ......Luke 1:17

Passover.......Luke 22:12, 13
Lord's return ..Matt. 24:44
Preaching the
Gospel.......Rom. 1:15

Reading the Bible

A. *Blessings of:*
Brings
repentance....2 Kin. 22:8-20
Reminds us of
duties.........Neh. 8:12, 13
Produces
reformation ...Neh. 13:1-3
Gives knowledge of
prophecy......Rev. 1:3

B. *Reactions to:*
Responsive-
ness..........Ex. 24:7
Rejection......Jer. 36:21-28
Rebellion ......Luke 4:16-30
Request for more
light ....Acts 8:29-35
Research ......Acts 17:10, 11

Reaiah—*Yahweh has provided for*

1. Reubenite ....1 Chr. 5:5
2. Founder of Nethinim
family.........Ezra 2:47
3. Calebite
family.........1 Chr. 4:2

Real property

A. *Characteristic features of:*
Property
desired........Gen. 23:4
Price
stipulated .....Gen. 33:19
Posts erected ..Deut. 19:14
Posterity remem-
bered ....Num. 33:54
Publicity
required.......Ruth 4:1-4
Proof docu-
mented ....Jer. 32:10-17

B. *Unusual examples of:*
Monopoly of land
established ....Gen. 47:20
Sale as a prophetic
proof.........Jer. 32:6-44
Mark of beast
required.......Rev. 13:16, 17

Reaping

A. *Provisions concerning:*
Areas
restricted .....Lev. 19:9, 10

Times
restricted .....Lev. 25:1-11
Sin hinders ....Jer. 12:13

B. *Figurative of:*
Harvest of
souls.........John 4:35-38
Trust in God...Matt. 6:26
Gospel age.....Amos 9:13-15
Injustice......Matt. 25:26
Payment for
services ....1 Cor. 9:11
Blessings .....2 Cor. 9:6
Reward for righteous-
ness..........Gal. 6:8, 9
Punishment
for sin ....Hos. 10:13
Judgment on the
world ....Rev. 14:14-16
Final
judgment .....Matt. 13:30-43

Reason—*the faculty by which we think*

A. *Faculty of:*
Makes men
sane ....Dan. 4:36
Prepares for
salvation......Is. 1:18
Makes men
guilty ....Mark 11:31-33

B. *Inadequacy of:*
Biased against the
truth.........Mark 2:6-8
Gospel not
explained   {1 Cor. 1:18-31
by .... {1 Cor. 2:1-14

Reba—*fourth part*

Midianite chief slain by
Israelites ....Num. 31:8
Josh. 13:21

Rebekah, Rebecca—*loops of a rope*

Daughter of
Bethuel..........Gen. 22:20-23
Becomes Isaac's
wife.............Gen. 24:15-67
Mother of Esau and
Jacob ....Gen. 25:21-28
Poses as Isaac's
sister...........Gen. 26:6-11
Disturbed by Esau's
marriages ....Gen. 26:34, 35
Causes Jacob to deceive
Isaac...........Gen. 27:1-29
Urges Jacob to leave
home............Gen. 27:42-46

Burial of, in
Machpelah ......Gen. 49:29-31
Mentioned by
Paul.............Rom. 9:10

Rebellion—*active opposition to
authority*

A. *Against:*
God ....Dan. 9:5, 9
God's word ....Num. 20:24
Davidic
kingship ......1 Kin. 12:19
Constituted
priesthood ....Num. 17:1-10
Spirit.........Is. 63:10

B. *Evil of:*
Keeps from
blessings ....Num. 20:24
Increases sin..Job 34:37
Needs to be
confessed .....Dan. 9:4-12
Characterizes a
people ....Is. 65:2

See Insurrection

Rebuilding Jerusalem

Permitted by
proclamation .....Ezra 1:1-4
Opposed ....Ezra 4:1-6
Neh. 4:1-3
Temple............Ezra 5:1, 2
Ezra 6:14, 15
Walls ....Neh. 6:15, 16

Rebuke—*to reprimand sharply*

Jesus' power to restrain:

Sea ....Matt. 8:26
Demons............Matt. 17:18
Fever ....Luke 4:39
Peter..............Mark 8:33

Rebuke for sin

A. *Manner of:*
Before all ......1 Tim. 5:20
With long-
suffering ......2 Tim. 4:2
Sharply........Titus 2:15
With all
authority......Titus 2:15

B. *Examples of:*
Isaac by
Abimelech ....Gen. 26:6-11
Laban by
Jacob ....Gen. 31:36-42
Saul by
Samuel ....1 Sam. 13:13

Ahab by
Elijah ....1 Kin. 21:20
Judah by
Zechariah.....2 Chr. 24:20
Israel by
Ezra ....Ezra 10:10, 11
David by
God...........Ps. 39:11
Peter by Paul ..Gal. 2:11-14
Christians by
God...........Heb. 12:5
Church by
Christ.........Rev. 3:19

Receive—*to take into one's possession*

A. *Good things:*
Word.........James 1:21
Holy Spirit.....Acts 2:38
Christ Jesus ...Col. 2:6
Forgiveness ...Acts 26:18
Petitions.......1 John 3:22
Reward........1 Cor. 3:8, 14

B. *Evil things:*
Punishment....Rom. 1:27
Beast's mark...Rev. 13:16
Reward for unrighteous-
ness..........2 Pet. 2:13

Rechab—*rider*

1. Assassin of Ish-
bosheth.......2 Sam. 4:2, 6
2. Father of Jehonadab,
founder of the
Rechabites....2 Kin. 10:15-23
Related to the
Kenites ....1 Chr. 2:55
3. Postexilic
ruler ....Neh. 3:14

Rechabites—*descendants of Rechab*

Kenite clan fathered by Rechab
and believing in the simple
life ....Jer. 35:1-19

Rechah—*softness*

Place in Judah ...1 Chr. 4:12

Reciprocation—*mutual interchange*

Gentiles to Jews ..Rom. 15:27
Students to
teachers..........Gal. 6:6

Recompense—*to pay back in kind*

A. *On the righteous:*
Even now .....Prov. 11:31
According to one's righteous-
ness...........Ps. 18:20, 24

Eagerly
expected......Heb. 10:35

B. *On the unrighteous:*
Justly
deserved......Rom. 1:27
Belongs to God
only..........Heb. 10:30
Will surely
come..........Jer. 51:56
To the next
generation....Jer. 32:18
Fully at the second
advent........2 Thess. 1:6

Reconciliation—*making peace between enemies*

A. *Effected on men while:*
Helpless......Rom. 5:6
Sinners.......Rom. 5:8
Enemies of
God..........Rom. 5:10
God-haters....Col. 1:21

B. *Accomplished by:*
God in
Christ........2 Cor. 5:18
Christ's
death........Rom. 5:10
Christ's
blood........Eph. 2:13

C. *Productive of:*
Peace with
God..........Rom. 5:1
Access to
God..........Rom. 5:2
Union of Jews and
Gentiles......Eph. 2:14

Recorder—*high court official*

Records events....2 Sam. 8:16
Represents the
king..............2 Kin. 18:18
Repairs the
Temple..........2 Chr. 34:8

Recover—*to restore lost things*

A. *Of sickness:*
By remedy.....2 Kin. 20:7
By a miracle...2 Kin. 5:3-14
Sought from
idols..........2 Kin. 1:2-17

B. *Of physical things:*
Defeat in
war............2 Chr. 13:19, 20
Conquered
territory......2 Sam. 8:3
Captured
people........Jer. 41:16

Recreation—*relaxation and restoration*

Among children,
natural..........Zech. 8:5
Among adults, sometimes
boring...........Eccl. 2:1-11
Lord's place in....Jer. 33:11
Of the wicked,
evil..............Judg. 16:25

Red—*being red or ruddy*

Blood............2 Kin. 3:22
Wine.............Prov. 23:31
Complexion......Lam. 4:7

Red dragon—*another name for Satan*

Seen in John's
vision............Rev. 12:3-17

Redemption—*deliverance by sacrifice*

A. *Defined as deliverance from:*
Curse of the
Law..........Gal. 3:13
Bondage of the
Law..........Gal. 4:5
Iniquity........Titus 2:14
Destruction....Ps. 103:4
Death.........Hos. 13:14
Grave.........Ps. 49:15
Aimless
conduct......1 Pet. 1:18
Present evil
world.........Gal. 1:4

B. *Accomplished by:*
God's power...Deut. 7:8
Christ's
blood........Eph. 1:7
God's grace....Rom. 3:24, 25

C. *Benefits of:*
Forgiveness....Col. 1:14
Justification...Rom. 3:24
Adoption.....Gal. 4:4, 5
God's
possession...1 Cor. 6:20
God's people...Titus 2:14
Purification....Titus 2:14
Sealing.......Eph. 4:30
Inheritance....Heb. 9:15
Heaven's
glory.........Rev. 14:3, 4

Red heifer (see Heifer)

Red horse—*symbol of war*

Seen in John's
vision..........Rev. 6:4

Red Sea—*sea of reeds*

Locusts
destroyed........Ex. 10:19
Divided by God ...Ex. 14:21
Crossed by
Israel............Ex. 14:22, 29
Egyptians
drowned.........Ex. 15:4, 21
Boundary of promised
land..............Ex. 23:31
Israelites camp
by......Num. 33:10, 11
Ships built on .....1 Kin. 9:26

Reed—*tall grass growing in marshes*

Figurative of:

Weakness.........Is. 36:6
Instability.........Matt. 11:7
Davidic line.......Is. 42:3

Refining, spiritual

By afflictions......Is. 48:10
By fire ....Zech. 13:9
For a purpose.....John 15:2
More than
gold..............1 Pet. 1:7

Reflection—*contemplation on*

Past..............Mark 14:72
Present........Luke 14:31-33
Future ....Acts 21:12-14

Reformations, religious

Manifested by or in:

Recovery of the
Law..............2 Kin. 22:8-20
Resolving to follow the
Lord ....Ezra 10:1-17
Religious zeal for the
Lord ....Neh. 13:11-31
Restoration of
judges............2 Chr. 19:1-11

Refresh—*to renew; to restore*

Spiritual:

In the spirit ....1 Cor. 16:18
In the heart.......Philem. 7, 20
Often needed......2 Tim. 1:16
Mutual............Rom. 15:32
Special times......Acts 3:19
Refused...........Is. 28:12

Refuge—*a shelter against harm*

Divine:

In the Lord ....Ps. 142:5
From storms .....Is. 4:5, 6

Time of trouble ...Ps. 9:9
Place of
protection........Ps. 91:9, 10
Always ready .....Ps. 46:1

Refuge, cities of (see Cities, Levitical)

Refuse—*to reject or decline*

A. *Of things, physical:*
Marriage.......Ex. 22:17
Passage........Num. 20:21
King...........1 Sam. 16:7
Display ....Esth. 1:12
Leader.........Acts 7:35
Martyrdom ....Acts 25:11
Fables ....1 Tim. 4:7
Adoption ......Heb. 11:24-26

B. *Of things, spiritual:*
Hardness of
heart..........Ex. 7:14
Disobed-
ience..........Ex. 16:28
Obedience .....1 Sam. 8:19
Messiah ....Ps. 118:22
Salvation ......Is. 8:6
Shame.........Jer. 3:3
Repentance...Hos. 11:5
Healing ....Jer. 15:18
God ....Heb. 12:25

Refuse Gate—*a gate of Jerusalem*

Nehemiah viewed city
from.............Neh. 2:13
Wall dedicated
near..............Neh. 12:31

Regem—*friend*

Calebite...........1 Chr. 2:47

Regem-Melech—*friend of the king*

Sent in deputation to
Zechariah ....Zech. 7:2

Regeneration (see Born again; New
birth)

Register—*a record of genealogies*

Priests not
recorded in.......Ezra 2:62
Excluded from
priesthood........Neh. 7:63-65
Those
recorded in.......Neh. 7:5-62

Rehabiah—*Yahweh is wide*

Grandson of
Moses............1 Chr. 23:17

Rehob—*open place*

1. Two cities of
   Asher.........Josh. 19:24, 28
   One assigned to
   Levites.........Josh. 21:31
   Delayed conquest of
   one ....Judg. 1:31
2. Northern city visited by
   Joshua's
   spies...........Num. 13:21
   Defeated by
   David.........2 Sam. 10:8
3. Father of
   Hadadezer ....2 Sam. 8:3, 12
4. Signer of the
   covenant......Neh. 10:11

Rehoboam—*the people are enlarged*

Son and successor of
Solomon ....1 Kin. 11:43
Refuses reformatory
measures.........1 Kin. 12:1-15
Ten tribes revolt
from ....1 Kin. 12:16-24
Temporary prosperity
of ....2 Chr. 11:5-23
Lapses into
idolatry ....1 Kin. 14:21-24
Kingdom of, invaded by
Egypt ....1 Kin. 14:25-28
Reigns 17 years ...1 Kin. 14:21
Death of ....1 Kin. 14:29-31
In Christ's
genealogy ....Matt. 1:7

Rehoboth—*broad places, streets*

1. Name of a well dug by
   Isaac.........Gen. 26:22
2. City "by the
   river" ....Gen. 36:37
3. Built by
   Asshur.........Gen. 10:11

Rehum—*beloved*

1. Persian
   officer.........Ezra 4:8-23
2. Postexilic
   returnee .....Ezra 2:2
3. Priest who returns with
   Zerubbabel....Neh. 12:3, 7
   Same as
   Harim.........Neh. 12:15
4. Signer of the
   covenant.........Neh. 10:25
5. Postexilic
   Levite.........Neh. 3:17

Rei—*friendly*

One of David's faithful
officers ....1 Kin. 1:8

Reign—*to rule over*

A. *Descriptive of the rule of:*
   Man ....Gen. 36:31
   God ....Ps. 47:8
   Christ ....Rev. 20:4, 6
   Believers.......Rev. 5:10
   Sin ....Rom. 5:21
   Death ....Rom. 5:14, 17
   Grace.........Rom. 5:21

B. *Of Christ's rule:*
   Predicted ....Is. 32:1
   Described......Jer. 23:5, 6
   Announced ....Luke 1:31-33
   Rejected.......Luke 19:14, 27
   Fulfilled ....Rom. 15:12
   Enthroned ....1 Cor. 15:25
   Eternal ....Rev. 11:15-17

Reject—*to refuse; to disown*

A. *Man's rejection of:*
   God ....1 Sam. 8:7
   God's Word....1 Sam. 15:23, 26
   God's
   knowledge ....Hos. 4:6
   Christ ....Mark 8:31

B. *God's rejection of man, as:*
   Unbeliever.....John 12:48
   Divisive......Titus 3:10
   Unfruitful .....Heb. 6:8
   Reprobate .....Heb. 12:17

Rejoice—*to be glad*

A. *Kinds of:*
   Gloating.......Mic. 7:8
   Vindictive .....Rev. 18:20
   Marital ....Prov. 5:18
   Defiant ....Is. 8:6
   Prophetic......John 8:56
   Future.........Phil. 2:16
   Rewarded......Ps. 126:6

B. *Caused by:*
   God's
   blessing.......Ex. 18:9
   God's Word....Jer. 15:16
   Assurance ....Luke 10:20
   Salvation ....Luke 15:6-10
   Persecution....Acts 5:41
   Reunion of
   believers.......Phil. 2:28
   Exaltation ....James 1:9
   Christ's
   return.........1 Pet. 4:13

C. *Sphere of, in:*
God's
salvation......Ps. 21:1
God's
protection.....Ps. 63:7
God's
blessings......Ps. 106:5
Lord Himself..Hab. 3:18

D. *Agents of:*
Heart..........1 Chr. 16:10
Soul...........Ps. 35:9
Earth..........Ps. 97:1
God's people...Ps. 118:24
Believing
spirit.........Luke 1:47

Rekem—*friendship*

1. Midianite king slain by
Moses........Num. 31:8
2. Descendant of
Caleb.........1 Chr. 2:43, 44
3. City of
Benjamin.....Josh. 18:27

Relapse—*to turn back to sin again*

Danger of,
explained.........Heb. 6:4-6

Relatives—*those of near kin*

A. *Good derived from:*
Encourage-
ment..........Esth. 4:12-17
Salvation......John 1:40-42

B. *Evil derived from:*
Strife..........Gen. 31:1-42
Persecution....Mark 13:12
Jealousy.......Gen. 37:3-11

Relief—*thorough service*

In early church...Acts 4:32-37
Determined to
send.............Acts 11:29
Fulfilled at Christ's
return............2 Thess. 1:7

Religion, false

Characterized by:

Apostasy..........2 Thess. 2:3, 4
Backsliding......Jer. 5:23-31
Ceremonialism....Mark 7:3-13
Display..........Matt. 6:5
Ease.............1 Kin. 12:27-31
Formalism........2 Tim. 3:5

Remain—*continue; abide*

Used of:

God's
faithfulness.......2 Tim. 2:13

One's earthly
calling...........1 Cor. 7:20, 24

Remaliah—*whom Yahweh has adored*

Father of Pekah...2 Kin. 15:25

Remedy—*a cure*

Without..........Prov. 6:15
Right kind.......1 John 1:7

Remember—*to call to mind again*

Aids to:

Rainbow..........Gen. 9:15, 16
Covenant........Ex. 2:24
Passover.........Ex. 13:3
Sabbath..........Ex. 20:8
Offering..........Num. 5:15
Son (child).......2 Sam. 18:18
Prophet's
presence.........1 Kin. 17:18
Book.............Mal. 3:16
Lord's Supper....Luke 22:19
Epistle...........2 Pet. 3:1

See Memories

Remeth—*a high place*

Frontier town of
Issachar..........Josh. 19:21

Remission—*forgiveness*

A. *Based upon:*
Christ's
death.........Matt. 26:28
Faith in
Christ.........Acts 10:43
Repentance....Mark 1:4

B. *Significance of:*
Shows God's righ-
teousness.....Rom. 3:23-26
Makes salvation
real..........Luke 1:77
Must be
preached......Luke 24:47

Remnant—*what is left over*

A. *Used literally of:*
Cloth left
over..........Ex. 26:12
Race left
remaining.....Deut. 3:11
Nation still
surviving......Amos 1:8

B. *Used spiritually of the faithful
Israel:*
Punished......Is. 1:9
Protected......Is. 37:31-33

Scattered ..... Ezek. 5:10
Gathered ...... Is. 10:20-22
Repentant .... Jer. 31:7-9
Forgiven....... Mic. 7:18
Saved......... Jer. 23:3-8
             Rom. 9:27
Blessing ...... Mic. 5:7, 8
Holy.......... Zeph. 3:12, 13
Elected .... Rom. 11:5

Remorse—*distress arising from guilt*

Of a renegade.... Matt. 27:3-5
Of a disciple....... Luke 22:62
In flame .... Luke 16:24

Remphan—*a name for Kiyyan*

Worshiped by
Israelites .... Acts 7:41-43

Rend—*to tear apart by force*

Figurative of
repentance ..... Joel 2:13

Renewal of strength

A. *Sources of:*
Holy Spirit..... Titus 3:5
Wait for the
   Lord .... Is. 40:31
Cleansing from
   sin............ Ps. 51:10

B. *Objects of:*
Youth-
   fulness........ Ps. 103:5
Peoples........ Is. 41:1-3
Inward man ... 2 Cor. 4:16
New man...... Col. 3:10
Mind .... Rom. 12:2

Renown—*of great reputation*

Man .... Gen. 6:4
City............. Ezek. 26:17
God............. Dan. 9:15
Plant............ Ezek. 34:29

Renunciation—*giving up the right to do something*

Blessings of:

True discipleship .. Luke 14:33
True reward ...... Mark 10:28-31
Future reward .... Luke 18:28-30

Repentance

A. *Described as:*
"Turned" ..... Acts 9:35
"Repent" ..... Acts 8:22
"Return" ..... 1 Sam. 7:3
"Conver-
   sion"........... Acts 15:3

B. *Kinds of:*
National .... Joel 3:5-18
Internal .... Ps. 51:10-13
Unavailing..... Heb. 12:16, 17
True........... Acts 9:1-20
Unreal........ Ex. 9:27-35

C. *Derived from gift of:*
God .... Acts 11:18
Christ .... Acts 5:31
Spirit .... Zech. 12:10

D. *Things leading to:*
God's long-
   suffering ..... 2 Pet. 3:9
God's
   goodness...... Rom. 2:4
Conviction of
   sin............ Acts 2:37, 38

E. *Productive of:*
Life............ Acts 11:18
Remission of
   sins .... Mark 1:4
New spirit ..... Ezek. 18:31
New heart ..... Ezek. 18:31
Joy .... Luke 15:7, 10

F. *Signs of:*
Reformation of
   life........... Matt. 3:8
Restitution .... Luke 19:8
Godly sorrow .. 2 Cor. 7:9, 10

See Conversion

Rephael—*God has healed*

Levite porter...... 1 Chr. 26:7

Rephah—*riches*

Ancestor of
Joshua .... 1 Chr. 7:25-27

Rephaiah—*Yahweh has healed*

1. Man of
   Issachar ...... 1 Chr. 7:2
2. Descendant of
   Jonathan...... 1 Chr. 9:43
   Called
   Raphah .... 1 Chr. 8:37
3. Simeonite
   prince........ 1 Chr. 4:42, 43
4. Postexilic
   ruler .... Neh. 3:9
5. Descendant of
   David......... 1 Chr. 3:21

Rephaim—*giants*

1. Early race of giants in
   Palestine...... Gen. 14:5

Among doomed
nations.......Gen. 15:20
See Giants
2. Valley near
Jerusalem....2 Sam. 23:13, 14
Very fertile ....Is. 17:5
Scene of Philistine
defeats........2 Sam. 5:18-22

Rephidim—*rests*

Israelite camp.....Num. 33:12-15
Moses struck
rock........Ex. 17:1-7
Amalek defeated ..Ex. 17:8-16

Report—*a transmitted account of something*

A. *Kinds of:*
True..........1 Kin. 10:6
Good ....Prov. 15:30
False ....Ex. 23:1
Defaming.....Jer. 20:10
Slanderous....Rom. 3:8
Evil..........2 Cor. 6:8

B. *Good, obtained by:*
Fear ....Deut. 2:25

Reproach—*something imputed to the discredit of others*

A. *Objects of:*
God ....2 Kin. 19:4-23
God's people..Neh. 6:13
Messiah ......Rom. 15:3
Christians ....Luke 6:22

B. *Agents of:*
Enemies......Neh. 4:4
Foolish ....Ps. 74:22
Scorner.......Prov. 22:10
Satan ....1 Tim. 3:7
1 Tim. 5:14, 15

C. *Evil causes of:*
Unbelief......Jer. 6:10
Idolatry.......Ezek. 22:4
Breaking God's
Law.........Num. 15:30, 31
Sin ....Prov. 14:34

D. *Good causes of:*
Faith in God's
promises .....Heb. 11:24-26
Living for
Christ.........1 Pet. 4:14
Suffering for
Christ.........Heb. 13:13

E. *Of God's people:*
Permitted by
God..........Jer. 15:15

Reprobate—*rejected after testing*

A. *Causes of:*
Not having
Christ........2 Cor. 13:3-5
Rejecting the
faith ....2 Tim. 3:8
Spiritual
barrenness ....Heb. 6:7, 8
Lack of
discipline......1 Cor. 9:24-27
Rejection by the
Lord ....Jer. 6:30

B. *Consequences of, given up to:*
Evil...........Rom. 1:24-32
Delusion.......2 Thess. 2:11, 12
Blindness......Matt. 13:13-15
Destruction....2 Pet. 2:9-22

Reproof—*a cutting rebuke for misconduct*

A. *Sources of:*
God ....Ps. 50:8, 21
Backslidings ...Jer. 2:19
God's Word....2 Tim. 3:16
John the
Baptist........Luke 3:16, 19

B. *Examples of:*
Samuel ....1 Sam. 13:13
Daniel ....Dan. 5:22, 23
John the
Baptist........Matt. 3:7-12
Stephen ......Acts 7:51
Paul ....Gal. 2:11

Reptiles of the Bible

A. *Features concerning:*
Created by
God..........Gen. 1:24, 25
Made to praise
God..........Ps. 148:7, 10
Placed under man's
power........Gen. 1:26
Classified as
unclean ....Lev. 11:31-43
Seen in a
vision........Acts 10:11-14
Worshiped by
pagans.......Rom. 1:23
Likeness of,
forbidden .....Deut. 4:16, 18
Portrayed on
walls.........Ezek. 8:10

B. *List of:*
Asp...........Rom. 3:13
Chameleon ...Lev. 11:30
Frog..........Rev. 16:13
Gecko ....Lev. 11:30

Leviathan......Job 41:1, 2
Lizard ....Lev. 11:30
Scorpion......Deut. 8:15
Serpents......Matt. 10:16
Snail..........Ps. 58:8
Viper ....Acts 28:3

Reputation—*public esteem; fame*

A. *Good:*
Wonderful
asset..........Prov. 22:1
Based on
integrity ......2 Cor. 8:18-24
Hated by
wicked.........Dan. 6:4-8
Required of church
officials ......Acts 6:3
Worthy of
trust ....Acts 16:2

B. *Dangers of:*
Universal
praise.........Luke 6:26
Flattering
speech ....Rom. 16:18
Worldly
friendship.....James 4:4
Worldly
praise.........1 John 4:5, 6
Undue deference
toward........Gal. 2:6

Resen—*fortress*

City built by
Asshur ....Gen. 10:11, 12

Reservoirs—*where water is stored*

Family cisterns....Is. 36:16
Garden pools......Eccl. 2:6

Resh

Letter of the Hebrew
alphabet..........Ps. 119:153-160

Resheph—*home*

Descendant of
Ephraim..........1 Chr. 7:23-25

Residue—*a remnant*

A. *Used literally of:*
Survivors......Jer. 8:3

B. *Used spiritually of:*
Faithful
remnant ......Is. 28:5
Promised
seed ....Zech. 8:11-13

Resignation—*patient submission to*

Disquieting
problem ....Josh. 22:9-34
Tragic death ......2 Sam. 19:1-8
God's
chastening ......Job 2:10
Cross ....Mark 14:36
Sufferings ahead ..Acts 21:11-14
Pain ....2 Cor. 12:7-10
Want ....Phil. 4:11, 12

Resist—*to stand against*

A. *Of evil things:*
Sin ....Heb. 12:4
Adversaries....Luke 21:15
Proud.........James 4:6

B. *Of good things:*
God's will......Rom. 9:19
Holy Spirit....Acts 7:51
Truth......2 Tim. 3:8
Wisdom ......Acts 6:10
Constituted
authority......Rom. 13:2

Respect—*honor manifested toward the worthy*

A. *Wrong kind:*
Favoring the
wealthy......James 2:3, 9

B. *Right kind:*
Rejects the
proud.........Ps. 40:4
Toward
parents ......Heb. 12:9
Toward
husbands .....Eph. 5:33
Toward
Christ.........Matt. 21:37

C. *On God's part:*
Regards the
lowly ....Ps. 138:6
Honors His
covenant......2 Kin. 13:23
Makes God
just...........1 Pet. 1:17

Responsibility—*accountability for one's actions*

A. *Shifting of, by:*
Blaming
another ....Gen. 3:12
Claiming
innocency.....Matt. 27:24
Blaming a
people ....Ex. 32:21-24

B. *Cannot be excused by:*
Ignorance ..... Acts 17:30, 31
Unbelief .... John 3:18-20
Previous
good .... Ex. 33:12, 13
One's
ancestors ..... Matt. 3:9, 10

C. *Is increased by:*
Sight .... John 9:39-41
Privilege ...... John 15:22, 24
Opportunity ... Matt. 11:20-24
Continuance
in sin .... Matt. 23:31-35
Rejection ..... Matt. 10:11-15

Rest—*peace and quiet*

A. *Descriptive of:*
Physical
relaxation ..... Gen. 18:4
Sinful
laziness .... Matt. 26:45
Confidence .... Hab. 3:16-19
Completion of
salvation ..... Heb. 4:3, 8-11

B. *Need of:*
Recognized in God's
Law .... Ex. 20:10, 11
Recognized by
Christ .... Mark 6:31
Longed after .. Ps. 55:6
Provided for .. Rev. 6:11
Enjoyed after { Job 3:13, 17
death .... { Rev. 14:13

C. *Source of, in:*
Christ .... Matt. 11:28, 29
Trust .... Ps. 37:7
Returning to
God .... Is. 30:15

D. *Disturbance of, by:*
Sin .... Is. 57:20
Rebellion ..... Is. 28:12
Persecution .... Acts 9:23
Anxiety .... 2 Cor. 2:13

See Quietness

Restitution—*restoring*

Of damaged
property .... Ex. 22:3-12

Restoration—*renewal of something to
its former state*

A. *Miraculous, from:*
Death .... 2 Kin. 8:1, 5
Dried hand .... 1 Kin. 13:4, 6
Withered
hand .... Mark 3:5

Blindness ...... Mark 8:25
Curse .... Acts 3:21

B. *Natural of:*
Man's wife ..... Gen. 20:7, 14
Man's
position .... Gen. 40:13, 21
Land .... 2 Sam. 9:7
Visit .... Heb. 13:19

C. *Spiritual:*
Joy .... Ps. 51:11, 12
Recovery ..... Jer. 30:17
God's
blessings ..... Joel 2:25
Christ .... Is. 49:6

Restoration of Israel

Promised in the
prophets .... Is. 11:11
Seen in John's
ministry .... Matt. 17:11
Anticipated by
Caiaphas .... John 11:49-52
Questioned by the
disciples .... Acts 1:6
Realized at
Pentecost .... Joel 2:28-32
Fulfilled in the
Church .... Eph. 2:11-22
Perfected in
Heaven .... Heb. 12:22-28

Restraints, divine

On:

Man's wrath ..... Ps. 76:10
Man's designs .... Gen. 11:6, 7
Natural forces ... Gen. 8:2
Child bearing ..... Gen. 16:2
Wicked .... 2 Kin. 19:28
Antichrist .... 2 Thess. 2:3-7

Resurrection—*arising from the dead*

A. *Doctrine of:*
Looked for in
faith .... Job 19:25-27
Taught in Old { Is. 26:19
Testament ... { Dan. 12:2, 3, 13
Denied by { Matt. 22:23-28
Sadducees .... { Acts 23:6, 8
Affirmed { John 5:28, 29
by { John 6:39, 40,
Christ .... { 44
Illustrated by
Lazarus .... John 11:23-44
Explained away by false
teachers .... 2 Tim. 2:18
Questioned by
some .... 1 Cor. 15:12

Mocked at by
heathen.......Acts 17:32
Proclaimed by
Paul.........Acts 24:14, 15

B. *Accomplished by:*
God's power ...Matt. 22:28, 29
Christ.........John 5:28, 29
Holy Spirit.....Rom. 8:11

C. *Proof of, based on:*
God's power ...1 Cor. 6:14
Union with
Christ.........Rom. 8:11
Christ's
resurrection...1 Cor. 15:12-56

D. *Time of, at:*
Last day.......John 6:39-44
Christ's
return.........1 Thess. 4:13-18
Last trumpet...1 Cor. 15:51-55

E. *Nature of:*
Incorruptible ...1 Cor. 15:42, 54
Glorious ....1 Cor. 15:43
Spiritual ....1 Cor. 15:44
Transform-
ing...........1 Cor. 15:51
Like angels ...Matt. 22:30
Like Christ ....Phil. 3:21

F. *Of the wicked:*
Predicted ......Dan. 12:2
Described......John 5:28, 29
Simulta-
neous.........Acts 24:15

Resurrection of Christ

A. *Features concerning:*
Foretold in ⎧Ps. 16:10, 11
the Psalms ...⎩Acts 13:34, 35
Presented in ⎧Is. 53:10-12
prophecy....⎩1 Cor. 15:4
Announced ⎧Mark 9:9, 10
by Christ.....⎩John 2:19-22
Proclaimed by ⎧Acts 2:32
the apostles ..⎩Acts 3:15

B. *Accomplished by:*
God's power ...Acts 2:24
Christ's
power.........John 10:18
Spirit's
power.........Rom. 8:11

C. *Proven by:*
Empty tomb ...John 20:1-9
Angelic
testimony .....Matt. 28:5-7
His enemies...Matt. 28:11-15

Many
infallible ⎧John 20:20, 27
proofs.........⎩Acts 1:3
Apostolic ⎧Acts 1:22
preaching ....⎩Acts 4:33
LORD's Day
(first day of ⎧John 20:1, 19
the week)....⎩1 Cor. 16:2

D. *Purposes of:*
Fulfill
Scripture......Luke 24:45, 46
Forgive sins ...1 Cor. 15:17
Justify the ⎧Rom. 4:25
sinner........⎩Rom. 8:34
Give hope ....1 Cor. 15:18, 19
Make faith
real...........1 Cor. 15:14-17
Prove His ⎧Ps. 2:7
Sonship......⎩Rom. 1:4
Set Him on David's
throne ....Acts 2:30-32
Insure His ⎧Acts 4:10, 11
exaltation ....⎩Phil. 2:9, 10
Guarantee the coming
judgment ....Acts 17:31
Seal the believer's
resur- ⎧Acts 26:23
rection.......⎩1 Cor. 15:20, 23

E. *Appearances of, to:*
Mary
Magdalene ....Mark 16:9
Other
women........Matt. 28:9
Two disciples ...Luke 24:13-15
Simon Peter ...Luke 24:34
Ten apostles ...John 20:19, 24
Eleven
apostles.......John 20:26
Apostles at Sea of
Tiberias......John 21:1
Apostles in
Galilee.......Matt. 28:16, 17
500 brethren ...1 Cor. 15:6
All the ⎧Luke 24:51
apostles......⎩Acts 1:9
Paul...........1 Cor. 15:8
James ....1 Cor. 15:7

Resurrections of the Bible

Widow's son ......1 Kin. 17:17-22
Shunammite's
son...............2 Kin. 4:32-35
Unnamed man ...2 Kin. 13:20, 21
Jairus' daughter...Matt. 9:23-25
Widow's only
son...........Luke 7:11-15
Lazarus of
Bethany..........John 11:43, 44

Many saints......Matt. 27:52, 53
Dorcas...........Acts 9:36-40
In symbolism .....Rev. 11:8, 11

Resurrection, spiritual

A. *Accomplished by power of:*
God ....Eph. 1:19
Christ ....Eph. 5:14
Holy Spirit.....Ezek. 11:19

B. *Features concerning:*
Takes place
now..........John 5:25
Gives eternal
life...........John 5:24
Delivers from spiritual
death ....Rom. 6:4, 13
Changes life ...Is. 32:15
Issues in
immortality ...John 11:25, 26
Delivers from Satan's
power.........Acts 26:18
Realized in new
life...........Phil. 3:10, 11
Called "first" ..Rev. 20:5, 6

Retaliation—*returning like for like*

Forbidden.........Luke 9:54-56
Return good, not
evil...............Prov. 25:21, 22
God's
responsibility .....Prov. 20:22
Christ's teaching
on................Matt. 5:39-44

Retribution—*merited punishment for evil done*

A. *Expressed by:*
God's wrath ...Rom. 1:18
Lamb's
wrath.........Rev. 6:16, 17
Vengeance.....Jude 7
Punishment...2 Thess. 1:6-9
Corruption.....2 Pet. 2:9-22

B. *Due to the sinner's:*
Sin ....Rom. 2:1-9
Evil works.....Ex. 32:34
Persecution of the
righteous ....2 Thess. 1:6
Rejection of
Christ.........Heb. 10:29, 30

C. *Deliverance from, by:*
Christ ....1 Thess. 1:10
God's appoint-
ment..........1 Thess. 5:9

Return

Descriptive of:

Going back
home............Gen. 31:3, 13
Repentance ......2 Chr. 6:24, 38
Vengeance or
retribution ......1 Kin. 2:33, 44
Christ's advent...Acts 15:16
Death............Gen. 3:19

Reu—*friend*

Descendant of
Shem............Gen. 11:10-21
Luke 3:35

Reuben—*behold a son*

Jacob's eldest
son..............Gen. 29:31, 32
Guilty of misconduct; loses preeminence.......Gen. 35:22
Proposes plan to save Joseph's
life ....Gen. 37:21-29
Offers sons as
pledge...........Gen. 42:37
Father of four
sons.............Gen. 46:8, 9
Pronounced
unstable.........Gen. 49:3, 4
Descendants of....Num. 26:5-11

Reubenites—*descendants of Reuben*

Divided into four tribal
families..........Num. 26:5-11
Elizur, warrior ....Num. 1:5
Census of, at
Sinai ....Num. 1:18-21
Census of, at
conquest ....Num. 26:7
Place of, in
march............Num. 2:10
Seek inheritance east of
Jordan ....Num. 32:1-42
Join in war against
Canaanites......Josh. 1:12-18
Altar erected by,
misunderstood....Josh. 22:10-34
Criticized by
Deborah.........Judg. 5:15, 16
Enslaved by
Assyria..........2 Kin. 15:29

Reuel—*friend of God*

1. Son of Esau ...Gen. 36:2-4
2. Moses' father-in-
law ....Ex. 2:18
3. Benjamite .....1 Chr. 9:8

4. Gadite leader ..Num. 2:14
   Called Deuel...Num. 7:42, 47

Reumah—*exalted*

Nahor's
concubine ....Gen. 22:24

Revelation—*an uncovering of
something hidden*

A. *Source of:*
   God ....Dan. 2:28-47
   Christ ....John 1:18
   The Spirit......1 Cor. 2:10
   Not in man ....Matt. 16:17

B. *Objects of:*
   God ....Matt. 11:25, 27
   Christ ....2 Thess. 1:7
   Man of sin ....2 Thess. 2:3, 6, 8

C. *Instruments of:*
   Prophets.......1 Pet. 1:10-12
   Daniel ....Dan. 10:1
   Christ ....Heb. 1:1, 2
   Apostles ....1 Cor. 2:10
   Paul ....Gal. 1:16

D. *Of the first advent:*
   Predicted ......Is. 40:5
   Revealed ......Is. 53:1
   Rejected.......John 12:38-41
   Of God's righteous-
   ness...........Is. 56:1
   Of peace and {Jer. 33:6-8
   truth.........{Eph. 2:11-17

E. *Time of the second advent:*
   Uncovering ....Matt. 10:26
   Judgment......Luke 17:26-30
   Victory ....2 Thess. 2:3, 6, 8
   Glory ....1 Pet. 5:1
   Resurrection...Rom. 8:18, 19
   Reward........1 Cor. 3:13, 14
   Glorification ...1 John 3:2
   Grace..........1 Pet. 1:5, 13
   Joy ....1 Pet. 4:13

F. *Of divine truth, characteristics
   of:*
   God-
   originated.....Dan. 2:47
   Verbal.........Heb. 1:1
   In the created
   world ....Ps. 19:1, 2
   Illuminative ...Eph. 1:17
   Now
   revealed.......Rom. 16:26
   Truth communi-
   cating.........Eph. 3:3, 4

Revelation, the—*a book of the New
   Testament*

Vision of the Son of
Man..............Rev. 1:9-20
Message to the seven
churches ....Rev. 2:1-3:22
The book of seven
seals ....Rev. 4:1-6:17
The judgment.....Rev. 7:1-9:21
The two beasts....Rev. 13
Babylon   {Rev. 17:1-
doomed ....{ 18:24
The marriage
supper............Rev. 19:6-10
The judgment of the
wicked ....Rev. 20:11-15
New heaven and new
earth.............Rev. 21:1-8
The new
Jerusalem ....Rev. 21:9-22:5
Christ's coming ...Rev. 22:6-21

Revenge—*to take vengeance*

A. *Manifestation of:*
   Belongs to
   God............Rev. 18:20
   Performed by
   rulers ....Rom. 13:4
   Righteously
   allowed ....1 Kin. 20:42
   Pleaded for ....Jer. 11:20
   Disallowed among
   men............Prov. 20:22
   Forbidden to
   disciples.......Luke 9:54, 55

B. *Antidotes of:*
   Overcome by
   kindness ....1 Sam. 25:30-34
   Exhibit love....Luke 6:35
   Bless ....Rom. 12:14
   Forbear
   wrath.........Rom. 12:19
   Manifest
   forbearance ....Matt. 5:38-41
   Flee from ......Gen. 27:41-45

C. *Examples of:*
   Simeon and
   Levi............Gen. 34:25
   Joseph.........Gen. 42:9-24
   Samson........Judg. 16:28-30
   Joab...........2 Sam. 3:27, 30
   Jezebel ....1 Kin. 19:2
   Ahab ....1 Kin. 22:26, 27
   Haman ....Esth. 3:8-15
   Philistines .....Ezek. 25:15-17
   Herodias.......Mark 6:19-24
   Jews...........Acts 7:54, 59

Reverence—*a feeling of deep respect, love, awe and esteem*

Manifested toward:

God...............Ps. 89:7
God's house.......Lev. 19:30
Kings.............1 Kin. 1:31

Revile—*to speak of another abusively*

Christ,
  object of ....Matt. 27:39
Christ, submissive
  under ....1 Pet. 2:23
Christians,
  objects of ....Matt. 5:11
Right attitude
  toward ....1 Cor. 4:12
Punishment of ....1 Cor. 6:10
False teachers....2 Pet. 2:10-12

Revival—*renewed zeal to obey God*

Conditions for:

Humility ....2 Chr. 7:14
Prayer ....2 Chr. 7:14
                  James 5:16
Broken heart......Ps. 34:18
Confession........Ps. 66:18
Repentance ....2 Cor. 7:10
Turning from   {2 Chr. 7:14
  sin ....{2 Tim. 2:19
Complete   {Acts 9:5, 6
  surrender........{Rom. 12:1, 2

Revive—*to live again more vigorously*

A. *Descriptive of:*
  Renewed
    strength .....Gen. 45:27
  Refreshment...Judg. 15:19
  Restoration....Neh. 4:2
  Resurrection...1 Kin. 17:22
  Spiritual
    renewal.......Ps. 71:20

B. *Of the Spirit:*
  Given to the
    humble ......Is. 57:15
  Source of joy ..Ps. 85:6
  Possible even in
    trouble........Ps. 138:7
  Source of   {Hos. 6:2, 3
    fruitfulness...{Hos. 14:7

C. *Accomplished by:*
  God ....1 Tim. 6:13
  Christ ....1 Cor. 15:45
  Holy Spirit...John 6:63
  God's Word...Ps. 119:25, 50
  God's
    precepts......Ps. 119:93

Reward of the righteous

A. *Described as:*
  Sure ....Prov. 11:18
  Full...........Ruth 2:12
  Remem-
    bered ....2 Chr. 15:7
  Great ....Matt. 5:12
  Open ....Matt. 6:4, 6, 18

B. *Obtained by:*
  Keeping God's command-
    ments.........Ps. 19:11
  Sowing righteous-
    ness..........Prov. 11:18
  Fearing God's command-
    ments.........Prov. 13:13
  Feeding an
    enemy ....Prov. 25:21, 22
  Simple
    service.......Matt. 6:1
  Grace through
    faith ....Rom. 4:4, 5, 16
  Faithful
    service........Col. 3:23, 24
  Seeking God
    diligently......Heb. 11:6

C. *At Christ's return:*
  After the
    resurrection...Rev. 11:18
  Tested by
    fire............1 Cor. 3:8-14
  According to
    works.........Rev. 22:12

See Crowns of Christians; Hire; Wages

Reward of the wicked

A. *Visited upon:*
  Now...........Ps. 91:8
  At the
    judgment .....2 Tim. 4:14

B. *Measure of:*
  By
    retribution ....Rev. 18:6
  According to the
    wickedness....2 Sam. 3:39
  Plentifully .....Ps. 31:23

Rezeph—*glowing stone*

Place destroyed by the
  Assyrians.........2 Kin. 19:12

Rezin

1. King of Damascus; joins Pekah
   against
   Ahaz..........2 Kin. 15:37

Confederacy of, inspires Isaiah's
great messianic
prophecy......Is. 7:1–9:12
2. Head of a Nethinim
family........Ezra 2:48

Rezon—*prince*

Son of Eliadah; establishes Syrian
kingdom ....1 Kin. 11:23-25

Rhegium—*a city of southern Italy*

Paul's ship
arrived at ....Acts 28:13

Rhesa

Ancestor of
Christ ....Luke 3:27

Rhoda—*rose bush*

Servant girl ......Acts 12:13-16

Rhodes—*an island off the southwest
coast of Asia Minor*

Paul's ship
passes by........Acts 21:1

Rib

Eve formed of
Adam's...........Gen. 2:22

Ribai—*Yahweh strives*

One of David's mighty
men.............2 Sam. 23:29

Riblah—*fertility*

1. Town on Israel's eastern
border ....Num. 34:11
2. Town in the land of
Hamath.......2 Kin. 23:33
Headquarters of:
Pharaoh
Necho ....2 Kin. 23:31-35
Nebuchad- { 2 Kin. 25:6, 20,
nezzar .... { 21
Zedekiah blinded
here ....Jer. 39:5-7

Rich—*wealthy*

A. *Spiritual handicaps of:*
Selfishly
satisfied.......Luke 6:24
Reluctant to leave
riches........Luke 18:22-25

Forgetful of
God..........Luke 12:15-21
Indifferent to others'
needs ....Luke 16:19-31
Easily
tempted.......1 Tim. 6:9
Hindered
spiritually ....Matt. 19:23, 24
Misplaced
trust ....Prov. 11:28

B. *Applied, spiritually, to:*
God ....Eph. 2:4
Christ ....Rom. 10:12
Christians .....James 2:5
True riches ...2 Cor. 8:9
Good works ...1 Tim. 6:18
Worldly
people ....Jer. 5:27, 28
Self-
righteous ....Hos. 12:8
Synagogue of
Satan ....Rev. 2:9

Riches, earthly

A. *Described as:*
Spiritually
valueless.....Ps. 49:6, 7
Inferior.......Heb. 11:26
Fleeting ......Prov. 23:5
Unsatisfying ...Eccl. 4:8
Hurtful ....Eccl. 5:13, 14
Deceitful .....Matt. 13:22
Choking ......Luke 8:14
Uncertain......1 Tim. 6:17
Corrupted ....James 5:2

B. *Proper attitude toward:*
Not to:
Put first ......1 Kin. 3:11, 13
Be trusted ....Ps. 52:7
Set heart
upon........Ps. 62:10
Be desired ....Prov. 30:8
Not forever ...Prov. 27:24
Use in giving ..2 Cor. 8:2
Remember God's
supply ....Phil. 4:19

Riches, management of

Reflects spiritual
attitude ....Luke 16:10-12
Demands budget ..Luke 14:28-30

Riches, spiritual

Source of, in:

God's Law ....Ps. 119:14
Divine wisdom ....Prov. 3:13, 14

Unselfish service . . Prov. 13:7
Reverential fear . . . Prov. 22:4
Fulfillment . . . . Rom. 11:12
Christ . . . . Col. 1:27
Assurance . . . . Col. 2:2
Christ's Word . . . . . Col. 3:16

Riddle—*a hidden saying solved by guessing*

Samson's
famous . . . . Judg. 14:12-19
Classed as a
parable . . . . Ezek. 17:2
Avoided by God . . . Num. 12:8

Ridicule (see Mocking)

Right—*that which is just and fair*

A. *Things that are:*
God's Law . . . . . Ps. 19:8
God's Word . . . . Ps. 33:4
God's Way . . . . . Ps. 107:7
Thoughts of the
righteous . . . . . Prov. 12:5
Work of the
pure . . . . Prov. 21:8
Obedience to
God . . . . Acts 4:19, 20
Obedience to
parents . . . . Eph. 6:1

B. *Things that are not:*
False riches . . . . Jer. 17:11
Injustice to the
poor . . . . Is. 10:2
Man's way . . . . . Prov. 21:2
Man's heart . . . . Ps. 78:37

Righteous—*that which is upright*

A. *Applied to:*
God . . . . John 17:25
Christ . . . . 1 John 2:1
Messiah . . . . Is. 53:11
Christians . . . . . Matt. 25:37, 46

B. *Blessings of:*
Prayers of,
heard . . . . Prov. 15:29
Safely
guarded . . . . . . Prov. 18:10
Bold as a
lion . . . . Prov. 28:1
Shine forth . . . . Matt. 13:43

Righteousness—*uprightness before God*

A. *Kinds of:*
Created . . . . Eph. 4:24
Legal . . . . Phil. 3:6

Personal . . . . Phil. 3:9
Imputed . . . . Phil. 3:9
Experi-
mental . . . . Heb. 5:13
Actual . . . . Heb. 11:33
Real . . . . 1 John 2:29

B. *Of Christ, He:*
Is the
believer's . . . . Jer. 33:16
Loves . . . . Heb. 1:9
Judges with . . . . Is. 11:4
Is girded
with . . . . Is. 11:5
Brings in . . . . . . Is. 46:13
Fulfills all . . . . . Matt. 3:15
Confers upon
believers . . . . . Is. 61:10

Rimmon—*pomegranate*

1. Benjamite . . . . . 2 Sam. 4:2-9
2. Rock near
Gibeah . . . . Judg. 20:45-47
Benjamites hide
here . . . . Judg. 21:13-23
3. Town in south
Judah . . . . Josh. 15:1, 32
Assigned to
Simeon . . . . Josh. 19:7, 8
Mentioned in
prophecy . . . . . . Zech. 14:10
Called En
Rimmon . . . . . . Neh. 11:29
4. Syrian God (meaning
"thunderer") worshiped by
Naaman . . . . . . 2 Kin. 5:18
5. City of
Zebulun . . . . . . Josh. 19:13
Levitical city . . . 1 Chr. 6:77
Called
Dimnah . . . . . . Josh. 21:35

Rimmon Perez—*pomegranate of breach*

Israelite camp . . . . . Num. 33:19, 20

Ring

A. *Article of furniture, for:*
Poles of the
ark . . . . Ex. 25:12-15
Curtains . . . . Ex. 26:29
Priest's
ephod . . . . Ex. 28:23-28
Incense altar . . . Ex. 30:4

B. *Article of apparel:*
Symbol of
authority . . . . . . Gen. 41:42
Sealing royal
documents . . . . Esth. 3:12
Gifts . . . . Ex. 35:22

Feminine
adornment....Is. 3:16, 21
Expressive of
position.......Luke 15:22
Sign of social
status.........James 2:2

Ringleader—*the leader of a mob*

Paul contemptuously
called ....Acts 24:5

Rinnah—*ringing cry*

Son of Shimon ....1 Chr. 4:20

Riot—*an unruly mob*

Pacified by town
clerk ....Acts 19:20-41

Riphath—*descendants of Gomer*

Son of Gomer.....Gen. 10:3
Called Diphath....1 Chr. 1:6

Rise, risen, rising, raised

A. *Of resurrection:*
Christ's........Mark 8:31
Believers'
(spiritually) ...Col. 2:12
Believers'
(physically) ...John 11:23, 24

B. *Of Christ's resurrection:*
Predicted .....Mark 14:28
Fulfilled ....Matt. 28:6, 7
Remem-
bered ....John 2:22
Evidenced ....John 21:14
Preached .....1 Cor. 15:11-15
Misunder-
stood ....Mark 9:9, 10

Rissah—*ruin; rain*

Israelite camp....Num. 33:21, 22

Rithmah—*broom plant*

Israelite camp.....Num. 33:18, 19

Rivalry—*competition*

Between man and
neighbor ....Eccl. 4:4

River—*a large stream of water*

A. *Uses of:*
Water ....Jer. 2:18
Irrigation ......Gen. 2:10
Bathing........Ex. 2:5
Baptisms......Matt. 3:6
Healing........2 Kin. 5:10

B. *List of:*
Abanah........2 Kin. 5:12
Arnon ....Josh. 12:1
Chebar ....Ezek. 10:15, 20
Euphrates .....Gen. 2:14
Gihon ....Gen. 2:13
Gozan ....2 Kin. 17:6
Hiddekel.......Gen. 2:14
Jabbok ....Deut. 2:37
Jordan.........Josh. 3:8
Kanah ....Josh. 16:8
Kishon ....Judg. 5:21
Nile (Sihor) ...Jer. 2:18
Pharpar........2 Kin. 5:12
Pishon.........Gen. 2:11
Ulai ....Dan. 8:2, 16

C. *Figurative of:*
Prosperity of
saints ....Ps. 1:3
Affliction ......Ps. 124:4
Christ ....Is. 32:1, 2
God's
presence ......Is. 33:21
Peace..........Is. 66:12
Holy Spirit.....John 7:38, 39

Rizia—*delight*

Asherite ....1 Chr. 7:39

Rizpah—*glowing coal*

Saul's concubine taken
by Abner.........2 Sam. 3:6-8
Sons of, killed.....2 Sam. 21:8, 9
Grief-stricken, cares
for corpses ....2 Sam. 21:10-14

Road (see Highway)

Rob, robbery

A. *Used literally of:*
Plundering.....1 Sam. 23:1
Taking from the
poor ....Prov. 22:22
Robbers ....Judg. 9:25

B. *Used figuratively of:*
Dishonest
riches.........Ps. 62:10
Holding back from
God...........Mal. 3:8, 9
False
teachers ......John 10:1, 8
Taking
wages.........2 Cor. 11:8

Rock

A. *Used for:*
Altars ....Judg. 6:20, 26

Idol worship...Is. 57:5
Protection.....1 Sam. 13:6
Shade.........Is. 32:2
Inscriptions....Job 19:24
Executions.....2 Chr. 25:12
Foundations....Matt. 7:24, 25
Shelter.......Job 24:8
Tomb.........Matt. 27:60

B. *Miracles connected with:*
Water from....Ex. 17:6
Fire from.....Judg. 6:21
Broken by
wind..........1 Kin. 19:11
Split at Christ's
death.........Matt. 27:51

C. *Figurative of Christ, as:*
Refuge........Is. 32:2
Foundation of the
Church......Matt. 16:18
Source of
blessings......1 Cor. 10:4
Stone of
stumbling....Is. 8:14
Foundation of
faith.........Matt. 7:24, 25

Rock of Escaping

Cliff on the Wilderness of
Maon............1 Sam. 23:28

Rod—*a staff or stick*

A. *Used for:*
Sign of
authority......Ex. 4:17, 20
Egyptians'
staffs.........Ex. 7:12
Punishment....Ex. 21:20
Club...........1 Sam. 14:27
Correction of
children.......Prov. 13:24

B. *Figurative of:*
Christ.........Is. 11:1
Christ's rule ..Ps. 2:9
Authority......Is. 14:5, 29
The Gospel ....Ps. 110:2

Roebuck—*the deer, gazelle*

In Solomon's
provisions..........1 Kin. 4:23

Rogelim—*spies*

Town in Gilead ...2 Sam. 17:27

Rohgah—*tumult*

Asherite ....1 Chr. 7:34

Romamti-Ezer—*I have raised up help*

Son of Heman ....1 Chr. 25:4, 31

Roman

1. Inhabitant of
Rome.........Acts 2:10
2. Official agent of the Roman
government...John 11:46-48
3. Person possessing Roman
citizenship...Acts 16:21-38

Romans, the Epistle to the—*a book of the New Testament*

The power of the
Gospel ....Rom. 1:16
The pagans
condemned......Rom. 1:17-32
The Jews
condemned......Rom. 2:1-9
The advantages of
the Jews......Rom. 3:1-8
None righteous....Rom. 3:9-20
Righteousness through
faith.............Rom. 3:21-31
Abraham
justified ....Rom. 4
The second
Adam.........Rom. 5:12-21
On baptism ......Rom. 6
The pull of sin ....Rom. 7
The spiritual life ..Rom. 8
The destiny of the
Jews ....Rom. 9–11
Life as worship....Rom. 12:1, 2
Serving the
body ....Rom. 12:3-21
Bearing with one
another ....Rom. 14, 15
Greetings ....Rom. 16:1-24

Rome—*the chief city of Italy*

Jews expelled
from ....Acts 18:2
Paul:
Writes to Christians
of ....Rom. 1:7
Desires to go
to ....Acts 19:21
Comes to ......Acts 28:14
Imprisoned in ....Acts 28:16

Rooster crowing

Announced the
dawn............Mark 13:35
Reminded Peter...Matt. 26:34, 74

Root—*the part of a plant underground*

Used figuratively of:

Material
foundation ....Jer. 12:2
Remnant..........Judg. 5:14

National
existence . . . . .Is. 14:30
National source . . .Rom. 11:16-18
Source of evil . . . . .1 Tim. 6:10
Judgment and
destruction . . . . . . .1 Kin. 14:15
Restoration . . . . . . .2 Kin. 19:30
Spiritual life . . . . . .Hos. 14:5
Spiritual
foundation . . . . . . .Eph. 3:17
Messiah . . . . .Is. 11:1, 10

Rose—*a beautiful flower*

Of Sharon . . . . .Song 2:1
Desert shall
blossom . . . . .Is. 35:1

Rosh—*head, chief*

1. Benjamin's
   son . . . . .Gen. 46:21
2. Northern people connected with
   Meshech and
   Tubal . . . . .Ezek. 38:2

Rot—*to decay*

A. *Used literally of:*
   Sickness . . . . . . .Num. 5:21-27
   Hardwood
   trees . . . . .Is. 40:20

B. *Used figuratively of:*
   Wicked . . . . .Prov. 10:7
   Foolish wife . . .Prov. 12:4

Rowing—*to navigate a boat with oars*

Against odds . . . . .Jon. 1:13
With much
labor . . . . .Mark 6:48

Royal—*belonging to a king*

A. *Used literally of:*
   King's
   children . . . . . . .2 Kin. 11:1
   Robes of
   royalty . . . . .Esth. 6:8
   City of a
   king . . . . .2 Sam. 12:26

B. *Used spiritually of:*
   True Israel . . . . .Is. 62:3
   True Church . . .1 Pet. 2:9

Ruby—*a valuable gem (red pearl)*

Very valuable . . . .Prov. 3:15
Wisdom more valuable
than . . . . .Job 28:18
Good wife above price
of . . . . .Prov. 31:10
Reddish color . . . . .Lam. 4:7

Rudder—*a steering apparatus*

Literally . . . . .Acts 27:40
Figuratively . . . . . .James 3:4

Rudeness—*discourtesy*

Shown toward:

Christ . . . . .Matt. 26:67, 68
Paul . . . . .Acts 23:2

Rue—*a pungent perennial shrub*

Tithed by
Pharisees . . . . .Luke 11:42

Rufus—*red-haired*

1. Son of Simeon of
   Cyrene . . . . .Mark 15:21
2. Christian of
   Rome . . . . .Rom. 16:13
   Probably the same as 1.

Rule—*to govern*

A. *Of natural things:*
   Sun and
   moon . . . . .Gen. 1:16, 18
   Sea . . . . .Ps. 89:9

B. *Among men:*
   Man over
   woman . . . . .Gen. 3:16
   King over
   people . . . . . . .Ezra 4:20
   Diligent over the
   lazy . . . . .Prov. 12:24
   Servant over a
   son . . . . .Prov. 17:2
   Rich over
   poor . . . . .Prov. 22:7
   Servants over a
   people . . . . .Neh. 5:15

C. *Of the Messiah:*
   Promised . . . . . .Zech. 6:13
   Victorious . . . . .Ps. 110:2
   Announced . . . .Matt. 2:6
   Established . . . .Rev. 12:5
   Described . . . . .Rev. 2:27

Ruler—*one who governs*

A. *Good characteristics of:*
   Upholding the
   good . . . . .Rom. 13:3
   Believing . . . . . .Matt. 9:18, 23
   Chosen by
   God . . . . .2 Sam. 7:8

B. *Bad characteristics of:*
   Men-pleasers . . .John 12:42, 43
   Ignorant . . . . . . .Acts 3:17
   Hostile . . . . .Acts 4:26

Loving
bribes.........Hos. 4:18

C. *Respect toward:*
Commanded...Ex. 22:28
Illustrated.....Acts 23:5

Ruler of this world

Satan thus
called............John 14:30
To be cast out....John 12:31
Is judged.........John 16:11
Source of evil....Eph. 2:2

Rumah—*high place*

Residence of
Pedaiah......2 Kin. 23:36

Run—*to move swiftly*

A. *Used literally of:*
Man...........Num. 11:27
Water.........Ps. 105:41
Race...........1 Cor. 9:24

B. *Used figuratively of:*
Eagerness in:
Evil..........Prov. 1:16
Good.........Ps. 119:32
Joy of
salvation......Ps. 23:5
Christian life...1 Cor. 9:26

Rush—*a cylindrical, often hollow marsh plant*

Cut off from Israel; rendered
"bulrush".........Is. 9:14
Signifying
restoration.......Is. 35:7

Rust—*corrosion of metals*

Destruction of earthly
treasures.........Matt. 6:19, 20
Of gold and
silver..............James 5:3

Ruth—*female companion*

Moabitess.........Ruth 1:4
Follows Naomi....Ruth 1:6-18
Marries Boaz......Ruth 4:9-13
Ancestress of   ⎰Ruth 4:13, 21,
Christ............⎱   22

Ruth, the Book of—*a book of the Old Testament*

Naomi's
misfortunes......Ruth 1:1-14
Ruth's loyalty....Ruth 1:14-22
The favor of
Boaz............Ruth 2:1-23
Boaz redeems.....Ruth 3:8–4:12

The generations of
Ruth.............Ruth 4:13-22

S

Sabachthani—*hast thou forsaken me?*

Christ's cry on the
cross.............Matt. 27:46

Sabaoth—*hosts*

God as Lord of....Rom. 9:29
                      James 5:4

Sabbath—*rest*

A. *History of:*
Instituted at
creation.......Gen. 2:2, 3
Observed before
Sinai..........Ex. 16:22-30
Commanded at
Sinai..........Ex. 20:8-11
Repeated at Canaan's
entry......Deut. 5:12-15
References
to.............2 Kin. 4:23
Proper observance of,
described......Is. 56:2-7
Postexilic Jews encouraged to
keep.........Neh. 10:31
Perversion of, condemned by
Christ.........Luke 13:14-17
Christ teaches
on.............Mark 6:2
Paul preached
on.............Acts 13:14

B. *Features concerning:*
Commemorative of
creation.......Ex. 20:8-11
Seventh day during the Old
Testament....Deut. 5:14
Observance of, a perpetual
covenant.....Ex. 31:16, 17
Made for man's
good.........Mark 2:27
Christ's Lordship
over.........Luke 6:5

C. *Regulations concerning:*
Work prohibited
on.............Lev. 23:3
Cattle must rest
on.............Ex. 20:10
Business forbidden
on.............Jer. 17:21, 22
To last from evening until
evening.......Lev. 23:32

Worship on....Ezek. 46:3
Works of mercy
on ....Matt. 12:12
Necessities lawful
on ....Luke 13:15, 16

See First day of the week

Sabbath day's journey—*about 3,100 feet*

Between Mt. Olivet and
Jerusalem ....Acts 1:12

Sabbatical year—*a rest every seventh
year*

A. *Purpose of:*
Rest the land ..Ex. 23:10, 11
Emancipate
slaves.........Ex. 21:2-6
Remit debts....Deut. 15:1-6

B. *Allusions to, in history, in:*
Time of the
judges ....Ruth 4:1-10
Preexilic
times ....Jer. 32:6-16
Postexilic
times ....Neh. 10:31

C. *Spiritual significance of:*
Punishment for non-
observance....Lev. 26:33-35
Illustrative of
spiritual   (Is. 61:1-3
release.......(Luke 4:18-21
Figurative of spiritual
rest ....Heb. 4:1-11

See Jubilee, Year of

Sabeans—*descendants of Sheba*

Job's property attacked
by...............Job 1:13-15
Subject to Israel ..Is. 45:14

See Sheba 4, 5, 6

Sabtah

Son of Cush and grandson of
Ham ....Gen. 10:7

Sabtechah

Son of Cush and grandson of
Ham ....Gen. 10:7

Sacar—*hired*

1. Ahiam's
father.........1 Chr. 11:35
Called
Sharar ....2 Sam. 23:33
2. Family of
gatekeepers ...1 Chr. 26:4

Sachiah—*fame of Yahweh*

Benjamite........1 Chr. 8:10

Sackcloth—*a coarse fabric made of
goat's hair*

A. *Worn by:*
Kings.........2 Kin. 6:30
Prophets.......Is. 20:2
People........Luke 10:13
Women......Is. 32:11

B. *Expressive of:*
Sorrow ....Gen. 37:34
Repentance....Joel 1:8, 13
Subjection.....1 Kin. 20:31, 32
Fasting ....Is. 58:5
Protest ....Esth. 4:1-4

C. *Symbolic of:*
Severe
judgment .....Is. 50:3
God's
judgment .....Rev. 6:12

Sacrament (see Baptism, Christian;
Lord's Supper)

Sacred places

Chosen by God ...Deut. 12:11
Not to trust in ....John 4:20-24

Sacrifice, sacrifices

A. *Requirements of:*
Upon altar
only ....Ex. 20:24
Clean
animals ....Gen. 8:20
To God
alone ....Ex. 22:20
Perfect
animals ....Lev. 22:19
At place divinely
established....Deut. 12:5, 6
By appointed
priests ....1 Sam. 2:28
In faith........Gen. 4:4
In obedience...1 Sam. 15:22

B. *Perversion of, in offering:*
To demons....1 Cor. 10:20
To idols.......2 Chr. 34:25
Defective
animals ....Mal. 1:13, 14
Without
respect........1 Sam. 2:29

C. *Inadequacy of:*
Could not
atone for   (Ps. 40:6
sins ....(Heb. 10:1-4

Limited to legal
purification ...Heb. 9:13, 22

D. *Figurative of:*
Christ's
sacrifice.......1 Cor. 5:7
Prayer ....Ps. 141:2
Worship ....1 Pet. 2:5
Righ-
teousness .....Ps. 51:19

E. *Of Christ to:*
Redeem from the
curse.........Gal. 3:13
Secure our
redemption....Matt. 20:28
Reconcile God and
man ....Rom. 5:10

Sacrilege—*profaning holy things*

A. *Done by:*
Defaming God's
name ....2 Kin. 18:28-35
Profaning the
Sabbath.......Neh. 13:15-21
Debauching holy
things.........John 2:14-16

B. *Those guilty of:*
People ....1 Sam. 6:19
Pagans ....Dan. 5:1-4
Priests.........Lev. 10:1-7
Pharisees ......Matt. 23:16-22

Saddle—*cloth or leather seat for a rider*

Balaam's ....Num. 22:21

Sadducees—*followers of Zadok*

Rejected by
John ....Matt. 3:7
Tested Jesus .....Matt. 16:1-12
Silenced by
Jesus............Matt. 22:23-34
Disturbed by teaching of
resurrection ......Acts 4:1, 2
Opposed
apostles ....Acts 5:17-40

Safe, safety—*dwelling without fear or harm*

A. *False means of:*
Wickedness...Job 21:7-9, 17
Folly ....Job 5:2-4
False hope....1 Thess. 5:3

B. *True means of:*
LORD ....Ps. 4:8
LORD's
protection.....Deut. 33:12

Apostolic
admonition....Phil. 3:1

Saffron—*a variety of crocus; used as a perfume or medicine*

Figurative of the
bride ....Song 4:14

Sail—*an expanse of material used to catch the wind and propel a sailing ship*

Figurative of:

Enemies'
weakness.........Is. 33:23
The pride of
Tyre.............Ezek. 27:7

Sailors—*mariners; seamen*

Skilled ....1 Kin. 9:27
Fearful............Jon. 1:5
Cry bitterly ......Ezek. 27:8-36
Storm-tossed.....Acts 27:18-31

Saints—*God's redeemed people*

A. *Descriptive of:*
Old Testament
believers .....Matt. 27:52
Christians .....Acts 9:32, 41
Christian
martyrs ....Rev. 16:6
Present with Christ at His
return.........1 Thess. 3:13

B. *Their weaknesses, subject to:*
Needs ....Rom. 12:13
              2 Cor. 9:1, 12
Persecution....Dan. 7:21, 25

C. *Their duty to:*
Keep God's
Word ....Jude 3
Grow
spiritually.....Eph. 4:12
Avoid evil .....Eph. 5:3
Judge world ...1 Cor. 6:1, 2
Pray for
others.........Eph. 6:18
Minister to
others.........Heb. 6:10

D. *God's protection of, He:*
Forsakes them
not ....Ps. 37:28
Gathers
them..........Ps. 50:5
Keeps them....1 Sam. 2:9
Counts them
precious.......Ps. 116:15

Intercedes for
them..........Rom. 8:27
Will glorify
them..........2 Thess. 1:10

Salamis—*a town of Cyprus*

Paul preaches
here..............Acts 13:4, 5

Salcah—*wandering*

City in Bashan ....Deut. 3:10

Salem—*peace*

Jerusalem's original
name.........Gen. 14:18
Used poetically....Ps. 76:2

Salim—*completeness*

Place near
Aenon...........John 3:23

Sallai—*rejecter*

1. Benjamite
   chief........Neh. 11:8
2. Priestly
   family.........Neh. 12:20
   Called Sallu....Neh. 12:7

Sallu—*contempt*

Benjamite
family...........1 Chr. 9:7

See Sallai 2

Salma—*clothing*

Son of Hur........1 Chr. 2:50, 51

Salmon

Father of Boaz ....Ruth 4:20, 21
Ancestor of
Christ ....Matt. 1:4, 5

Salome—*feminine of Solomon*

1. Among ministering
   women........Mark 15:40, 41
   Visits empty
   tomb..........Mark 16:1
2. Herodias' daughter (not
   named in the
   Bible) ....Matt. 14:6-11

Salt

A. *Uses of:*
   Seasoning:
   Food ....Job 6:6
   Sacrifice ......Lev. 2:13

Everlasting
covenant......Num. 18:19
Rubbed on infants at
birth ....Ezek. 16:4
Making land unpro-
ductive........Judg. 9:45

B. *Miracles connected with:*
   Lot's wife becomes pillar
   of..........Gen. 19:26
   Elisha purified water
   with ....2 Kin. 2:19-22

C. *Figurative of:*
   God's everlasting
   covenant......Num. 18:19
   Barrenness and
   desolation....Deut. 29:23
   Good
   influence......Matt. 5:13
   Peace in the
   heart..........Mark 9:50
   Wise speech ...Col. 4:6
   Final
   judgment .....Mark 9:49
   Reprobation ...Ezek. 47:9, 11

Salt, City of

City in the wilderness of
Judah ....Josh. 15:62

Salt Sea

Old Testament
name for the ⎰ Gen. 14:3
Dead Sea........⎱ Num. 34:3, 12

Salt, Valley of—*a valley south of the Dead Sea*

Site of:

David's victory....2 Sam. 8:13
Amaziah's
victory ....2 Kin. 14:7

Salu—*restored*

Simeonite prince ..Num. 25:14

Salvation

A. *Descriptive of:*
   National
   deliverance....Ex. 14:13
   Deliverance from
   enemies.......2 Chr. 20:17
   Messiah ....Matt. 1:21

B. *Source of, in:*
   God's grace....Eph. 2:5, 8
   God's love .....Rom. 5:8
   God's mercy ...Titus 3:5

Christ alone ...Acts 4:12
Cross..........1 Cor. 1:18

C. *History of:*
Promised to
Adam.........Gen. 3:15
Announced to
Abram.......Gen. 12:1-3
Revealed to the
prophets .....1 Pet. 1:10-12
Longed for by the
saints ....Ps. 119:81, 174
Promised to
Gentiles.......Is. 45:21, 22
To be realized by the
Messiah.......Is. 59:16, 17
Seen in Christ's
birth.......Luke 1:69, 77
Christ, the
author ....Heb. 5:9
Appeared to all
men.......Titus 2:11
Proclaimed to
Israel ....Zech. 9:9
Accomplished on the
cross..........John 3:14, 15
Preached through the
Gospel ....Eph. 1:13
Rejected by
Israel.........Acts 13:26-46
Extended to
Gentiles.......Acts 28:28
This age, day
of.............2 Cor. 6:2
God's long-suffering
in.............2 Pet. 3:9
Final, nearer each
day ....Rom. 13:11
Consummated in the second
advent ....Heb. 9:28
Praise for, in
heaven.......Rev. 7:10

D. *Requirements of:*
Confession....Acts 2:21
Repentance....Mark 1:15
Faith ....John 3:14-18
Regenera-
tion...........John 3:3-8
Holy
Scripture......2 Tim. 3:15

E. *Negative blessings of,*
deliverance from:
Sin ....Matt. 1:21
Satan's
power........Heb. 2:14, 15
Wrath ....Rom. 5:9
Eternal
death ....John 3:16, 17

F. *Positive blessings of:*
Chosen to .....2 Thess. 2:13
Appointed to ..1 Thess. 5:9
Kept unto .....1 Pet. 1:5
Rejoiced in ....1 Pet. 4:13
To be worked
out ....Phil. 2:12

G. *Temporal aspects of:*
Past ....Eph. 2:8
Present........1 Cor. 1:18
Future.........Heb. 9:28

Samaria—*watch tower*

1. Capital of
Israel ....1 Kin. 16:24-29
Israel's "crown of
pride".........Is. 28:1
Besieged twice by
Ben-Hadad....1 Kin. 20:1-22
Miraculously
saved ....2 Kin. 6:8-23
Worshipers of Baal
destroyed .....2 Kin. 10:1-28
Threatened
with divine   {Is. 28:1-4
judgment......{Amos 3:11, 12
Repopulated with
foreigners.....2 Kin. 17:24-41
2. Name of Northern
Kingdom......1 Kin. 21:1
3. District of Palestine in Christ's
time ....Luke 17:11-19
Preaching in, forbidden by
Christ.........Matt. 10:5
Gospel
preached.....Acts 1:8
Churches established
there..........Acts 9:31
Paul preached
there..........Acts 15:3

Samaritans—*inhabitants of Samaria*

Made of mixed
races.............2 Kin. 17:24-41
Seek alliance with
Jews ....Ezra 4:1-4
Christ and the woman
of ....John 4:5-42
Story of "the good
Samaritan".......Luke 10:30-37
Beliefs of.........John 4:25
Converts among ..Acts 8:5-25

Samek

Letter of the Hebrew
alphabet..........Ps. 119:113-120

Samgar-Nebo—*be gracious, Nebo*

Prince of Nebuchad-
nezzar............Jer. 39:3

Samlah—*a garment*

Edomite king .....Gen. 36:36, 37

Samos—*an island off the coast of Lydia*

Visited by Paul....Acts 20:15

Samothrace—*an island in the Aegean Sea*

Visited by Paul....Acts 16:11

Samson—*sunlike*

A. *Life of:*
   Birth of,
   predicted......Judg. 13:2-23
   God's Spirit moves
   him...........Judg. 13:24, 25
   Desired a Philistine
   wife...........Judg. 14:1-9
   Propounded a
   riddle ....Judg. 14:10-14
   Betrayed, kills 30
   men...........Judg. 14:15-20
   Enticed by Delilah, loses
   strength ......Judg. 16:4-20
   Blinded and
   bound.........Judg. 16:21
   Destroyed
   over 3,000 in ⎧Judg. 16:22-31
   his death.....⎩Heb. 11:32

B. *Contrasts of his life:*
   Parents' concern; his
   unconcern .....Judg. 13:8
   Obedient, victorious;
   disobedient,
   defeated ......Judg. 15:14
   Seeks revenge; is
   revenged......Judg. 15:1-8
   Spirit-moved; animated by
   lust ....Judg. 15:14
   Physically strong; morally
   weak..........Judg. 16:3, 12
   Greater victory in
   death than in ⎧Judg. 16:29, 30
   life..........⎩Heb. 11:32

Samuel—*name of God (a godly name)*

A. *Life of:*
   Born in answer to Hannah's
   prayer ....1 Sam. 1:5-21
   Dedicated to God before his
   birth..........1 Sam. 1:11, 22
   Brought to
   Shiloh.........1 Sam. 1:24-28

His mother praised God
for............1 Sam. 2:1-10
Received a revelation
concerning Eli's
house.........1 Sam. 3:1-19
Recognized as a
prophet ....1 Sam. 3:20, 21
Became a circuit
judge ....1 Sam. 7:15-17
Organized
porter   ⎧1 Chr. 9:22
service......⎩1 Chr. 26:28
Called Israel to
repentance....1 Sam. 7:3-6
Anointed Saul as
king ....1 Sam. 10:1
Lamented in
death ....1 Sam. 25:1

B. *Character of:*
   Inspired as a
   writer.........1 Chr. 29:29
   Inspired as a
   prophet ....Acts 3:24
   Diligent as a
   judge ....1 Sam. 7:15-17
   Faithful to
   God...........Heb. 11:32-34
   Industrious in
   service........1 Chr. 9:22
   Devout in
   life...........Jer. 15:1
   Powerful in
   prayer ....Ps. 99:6
   Remembered in
   death ....1 Sam. 25:1

Samuel, the Books of—*books of the Old Testament*

A. *1 Samuel:*
   Birth of
   Samuel ....1 Sam. 1:19-28
   Hannah's
   song ....1 Sam. 2:1-10
   The ark
   captured ......1 Sam. 4:1-11
   The ark
   returned ......1 Sam. 6:1-21
   Saul chosen as
   king ....1 Sam. 9:1-27
   Saul
   anointed ......1 Sam. 10:1-27
   Saul against the
   Philistines.....1 Sam. 13:1-4
   Saul is
   rejected.......1 Sam. 15:10-31
   David is
   anointed ......1 Sam. 16:1-13

David and
Goliath ....1 Sam. 17:23-58
Jonathan's
love ....1 Sam. 19:1-7
Saul against
David.........1 Sam. 23:6-29
David spares { 1 Sam. 24:1-8
Saul.   { 1 Sam. 26:1-16
The medium of En
Dor ....1 Sam. 28:7-25
David against the
Amalekites....1 Sam. 30:1-31
Death of
Saul ....1 Sam. 31:1-13

B. *2 Samuel:*
David's
lament........2 Sam. 1:17-27
David anointed as
king ....2 Sam. 2:1-7
The ark in
Zion ....2 Sam. 6:1-19
David plans the
Temple........2 Sam. 7:1-29
The kingdom
expands ....2 Sam. 8:1-18
David and Bath-
sheba ....2 Sam. 11:1-27
Nathan rebukes
David ....2 Sam. 12:1-12
David
repents.......2 Sam. 12:13, 14
David's child
dies ....2 Sam. 12:15-23
Amnon and
Tamar ....2 Sam. 13:1-19
The mighty
men...........2 Sam. 23:8-39
David takes a
census ....2 Sam. 24:1-25

Sanballat—*Sin (the moon-god) has
given life*

Influential
Samaritan ....Neh. 2:10
Opposes Nehemiah's
plans ....Neh. 4:7, 8
Seeks to assassinate
Nehemiah ....Neh. 6:1-4
Fails in
intimidation .....Neh. 6:5-14
His daughter marries Eliashib, the
high priest.......Neh. 13:4, 28

Sanctification—*growing in holiness*

Produced by:

God...............1 Thess. 5:23
Christ............Heb. 2:11

Holy Spirit ....1 Pet. 1:2
Truth ....John 17:17, 19
Christ's blood .....Heb. 9:14
Prayer ....1 Tim. 4:4, 5

See Godliness; Holiness of Christians;
Piety

Sanctimoniousness—*assumed and
pretended holiness*

Condemned by
Christ ....Matt. 6:5

Sanctuary (see Holy of Holies;
Tabernacle)

Sand

Figurative uses of:

One's posterity ....Gen. 22:17
Weight.............Job 6:3
Large number of
people............Josh. 11:4
God's thoughts toward
us................Ps. 139:17, 18

Sandals, Shoe—*leather strapped to the
feet*

A. *Characteristics of:*
Worn on the
feet ....1 Kin. 2:5
Tied by a
strap..........Gen. 14:23
Some considered
worthless .....Amos 2:6
Used for dress
occasions .....Luke 15:22
Worn as
adornment ....Song 7:1
Worn out after a
journey ....Josh. 9:5, 13
Preserved super-
naturally......Deut. 29:5
Worn by Christ's
disciples......Mark 6:9

B. *Symbolism of:*
Taking on—readiness for a
journey ......Ex. 12:11
Putting off—
reverence   { Ex. 3:5
before God ... { Josh. 5:15
Want of—
mourning .....2 Sam. 15:30
Giving to another—
manner of attestation
in Israel.......Ruth 4:7, 8
To unloose another's—act of
homage ....Luke 3:16

C. *Figurative of:*
Protection and
provision......Deut. 33:25
Preparation for
service........Eph. 6:15
Alertness ......Is. 5:27

Sanitation and hygiene

A. *Laws relating to:*
Dead bodies ...Lev. 11:24-40
Contagion .....Num. 9:6, 10
Leprosy........Lev. 13:2-59
Menstrua-
tion...........Lev. 15:19-30
Women in
childbirth .....Lev. 12:2-8
Man's
discharge .....Lev. 15:2-18

B. *Provisions for health:*
Washing.......Deut. 23:10, 11
Burning ....Num. 31:19-23
Isolation.......Lev. 13:2-5,
31-33
Destruction....Lev. 14:39-45
Covering
excrement ....Deut. 23:12, 13

Sanity, spiritual

Young men
urged to.........Titus 2:6
Accomplished by
Christ ....Luke 8:35
Illustrated by Paul's
change ....Acts 26:11, 25

Sansannah—*palm branch*

Town in south
Judah ....Josh. 15:31

Sap—*the living fluid of woody plants*

Lord's trees full
of ....Ps. 104:16

Saph—*basin*

Philistine giant....2 Sam. 21:18
Called Sippai......1 Chr. 20:4

Sapphira—*beautiful*

Wife of Ananias...Acts 5:1
Struck dead for
lying ....Acts 5:1-11

Sapphire—*a precious stone*

Worn by high
priest.............Ex. 28:18
John's vision ......Rev. 21:19

Sarah, Sarai—*princess*

Wife of Abram ....Gen. 11:29-31
Abraham's
half sister ....Gen. 20:11-13
Represented as Abram's
sister ....Gen. 12:10-20
Barren ....Gen. 11:30
Gave Abram her
maid ....Gen. 16:1-3
Promised a   { Gen. 17:15-21
son..............{ Rom. 9:9
Gave birth to
Isaac ....Gen. 21:1-8

Saraph—*burning*

Descendant of
Judah ....1 Chr. 4:22

Sarcasm—*a biting taunt, mock*

A. *Purposes of, to:*
Recall
injustice ......Judg. 9:7-19
Remind of duty
neglected .....1 Sam. 26:15
Mock
idolaters .....1 Kin. 18:27
Deflate pride...1 Kin. 20:10, 11
Warn of
defeat.........2 Kin. 14:8-12

B. *Uttered by:*
Friend ....Job 11:2-12
Enemies ....Neh. 4:2, 3
Persecutors ...Matt. 27:28, 29
Apostle...:....Acts 23:1-5
God ....Jer. 25:27

Sardis—*the chief city of Lydia in Asia Minor*

One of the seven
churches ....Rev. 1:11

Sardites

Descendants of
Sered.............Num. 26:26

Sardius—*a precious stone*

Used in
"breastplate" .....Ex. 28:15-17
In the garden of
Eden ....Ezek. 28:13
Worn by Priest....Ex. 28:17

Sardonyx—*a precious stone*

In John's vision ...Rev. 21:19, 20

Sargon—*the constituted king*

King of Assyria ...Is. 20:1

Sarid—*survivor*

Village of
Zebulun ....Josh. 19:10, 12

Sarsechim

Prince of Nebuchad-
nezzar.............Jer. 39:3

Satan—*adversary*

A. *Names of* (see Devil)

B. *Designs of, to:*
Undo God's
work ....Mark 4:15
Make men turn away from
God ....Job 2:4, 5
Instigate evil .. John 13:2, 27
Secure men's (Luke 4:6-8
worship ...... (2 Thess. 2:3, 4

C. *Character of:*
Deceiver ....Rev. 12:9
Father of lies ..John 8:44
Adversary .....1 Pet. 5:8

D. *Methods of:*
Disguises
himself.........2 Cor. 11:14
Insinuates
doubt ....Gen. 3:1
Misuses
Scripture......Matt. 4:6
Uses
schemes ......2 Cor. 2:11
Afflicts
believers ......Luke 13:16

E. *Judgment upon:*
Bound ....Mark 3:27
Cast out ....John 12:31
Judged ....John 16:11
Bruised ....Rom. 16:20
Assigned to
hell ....Matt. 25:41

Satiate(d)—*to be satisfied*

Scorners and fools
shall be...........Prov. 1:22, 31
The sword
shall be.......Jer. 46:10
Israel was not.....Ezek. 16:28

Satire—*exposing problems to ridicule*

Jesus' devastating
use of ....Matt. 23:1-33

Satisfaction—*that which completely
fulfills*

A. *Of physical things:*
Sexual
pleasures......Prov. 5:19
Bread of
heaven........Ps. 105:40
Long life........Ps. 91:16

B. *Of spiritual things, God's:*
Mercy ....Ps. 90:14
Presence........Ps. 17:15

C. *Of things empty of:*
Labor..........Is. 55:2
Sinful ways....Ezek. 16:28, 29
Persecution....Job 19:22

Satrap—*protector of the land*

Officials appointed over the
kingdom ....Dan. 6:1

Saul—*asked* (of God)

1. Son of Kish; first king of
Israel ....1 Sam. 9:1, 2
Seeks his father's
donkeys........1 Sam. 9:3-14
Meets
Samuel ....1 Sam. 9:16-27
Anointed as
king ....1 Sam. 10:1-16
Victories and
family.........1 Sam. 14:47-52
Fights against Philistines;
becomes
jealous of   (1 Sam. 17:1-58
David........(1 Sam. 18:6-13
Promises his daughter to
David.........1 Sam. 18:14-30
Seeks to murder
David ....1 Sam. 19:1-24
Pursues
David ....1 Sam. 23:1-28
His life spared by
David ....1 Sam. 26:1-25
Defeated, commits
suicide........1 Sam. 31:1-6
Burial of.......1 Sam. 31:7-13
David's lament
over ....2 Sam. 1:17-27
Sin of,
exposed.......2 Sam. 21:1-9
2. King of
Edom ....Gen. 36:37

Savior—*one who saves*

Applied to:

God...............Ps. 106:21
Christ.............2 Tim. 1:10

Savior, Jesus as

A. *Characteristics of:*
Only............Acts 4:10, 12
Complete ......Col. 2:10
Powerful.......Col. 1:12-18
Authorita-
tive ....John 10:18
Universal .....1 Tim. 4:10

B. *Announcement of, by:*
Prophets.......Is. 42:6, 7
Angels.........Matt. 1:20, 21
John the
Baptist.......John 1:29
Christ.........John 12:44-50
Peter ....Acts 5:31
Paul...........1 Tim. 1:15
John...........1 John 4:14

C. *Office of, involves His:*
Becoming
man ....Heb. 2:14
Perfect righ-
teousness .....Heb. 5:8, 9
Perfect
obedience.....Rom. 5:19, 20
Dying for us ...1 Pet. 1:18-20

D. *Saves us from:*
Wrath ....Rom. 5:9
Sin ....John 1:29
Death ....John 11:25, 26

Saw—*a toothed tool for cutting*

Stones ....1 Kin. 7:9
Wood............Is. 10:15
For torture........1 Chr. 20:3

Scab

Disqualifies an
offering ....Lev. 22:21, 22
Priest observes....Lev. 13:6-8
Israel threatened
with.............Deut. 28:27

Scabbard—*a sheath*

For God's Word...Jer. 47:6

Scandal—*something disgraceful in*

Priesthood ....1 Sam. 2:22-24
Family ....2 Sam. 13:1-22

Scapegoat—*a goat of departure*

Bears sin away...Lev. 16:8-22
Typical of Christ ..Is. 53:6, 11, 12

Scarlet—*a brilliant crimson*

A. *Literal uses of, for:*
Tabernacle.....Ex. 26:1, 31, 36

Identifica-
tion...........Gen. 38:28, 30

B. *Symbolic uses of:*
Royalty........Matt. 27:28
Prosperity ....2 Sam. 1:24
Conquest .....Nah. 2:3
Deep sin.......Is. 1:18

Scatter—*to disperse abroad*

A. *Applied to:*
Nations........Gen. 11:8, 9
Christians .....Acts 8:1, 4

B. *Caused by:*
Sin ....1 Kin. 14:15, 16
Persecution....Acts 11:19

Scepter—*a royal staff*

Sign of
authority.........Esth. 4:11
Of Judah's tribe ...Gen. 49:10
Promise
concerning .....Num. 24:17
Fulfilled in
Christ ....Heb. 1:8

Sceva

Jewish priest at
Ephesus.........Acts 19:14

Schemes of Satan

Known by
Christians ....2 Cor. 2:11
Warnings   (2 Cor. 11:3,
against ....(13-15
Armor provided
against ....Eph. 6:11
World falls
before...........Rev. 13:1-18

Schism—*a division within a body*

Prohibition
concerning ....1 Cor. 12:25
Translated "pulls
away".............Matt. 9:16

Scholars—*men reputed for learning*

Numbered by
David ....1 Chr. 25:1, 7, 8
God's judgment
against ....Mal. 2:12
Moses, an
expert...........Acts 7:22
Gamaliel,
famous as ....Acts 5:34

School—*an institution of learning*

Home ....Deut. 6:6-10
Temple............1 Chr. 25:7, 8

In Ephesus........Acts 19:1, 9
Levites, teachers
of ....2 Chr. 17:7-9
Best subjects of ...Is. 50:4

Schoolmaster—*a tutor*

Applied to the Mosaic
Law..............Gal. 3:24, 25

Science—*exact knowledge*

A. *Implied reference to:*
  Architecture ...2 Chr. 2:1-18
  Astronomy ....Gen. 15:5
  Biology ....Ps. 139:13-16
  Engineering....Gen. 6:14-16
  Medicine ....Ps. 103:3
  Meteorology ...Job 38:22-38
  Surveying .....Ezek. 40:5, 6

B. *Significance of, to:*
  Manifest God's
   existence......Ps. 19:1-6
  Prove God's
   prophecies ....Jer. 25:12
  Illustrate heaven's
   glory..........Rev. 21:9-23
  Point to Christ as
   source of......Col. 2, 3

Scoffers

Wicked ....Prov. 9:7
Unwilling to take
 rebuke ....Prov. 9:7, 8
Incorrigible ......Prov. 15:12
Abomination .....Prov. 24:9

Scorners—*arrogant disdainers of others*

Classified among
 Fools.............Prov. 1:22

Scorpion—*an eight-legged creature
having a poisonous tail*

A. *Used literally of:*
  Desert
   creatures......Deut. 8:15
  Poisonous
   creatures......Luke 10:19

B. *Used figuratively of:*
  Heavy
   burdens.......1 Kin. 12:11
  Agents of
   antichrist .....Rev. 9:3, 5, 10

Scourging—*punishment by whipping;
flogging*

For immorality....Lev. 19:20
Forty blows ......Deut. 25:1-3

Of Christ.........Matt. 27:26
                  Mark 15:15
                  John 19:1
Of Christians......Matt. 10:17
Thirty-nine
 lashes ....2 Cor. 11:24
Of apostles........Acts 5:40
                  Gal. 6:17

Scribe's knife—*a knife used to sharpen
reed pens*

Used by Jehoiakim on Jeremiah's
 scroll.............Jer. 36:23-28

Scribes—*experts in legal matters*

A. *Employment of:*
  Transcribers of legal
   contracts......Jer. 32:12
  Keepers of
   records........Jer. 36:25, 26
  Advisers in state
   affairs.........1 Chr. 27:32
  Custodians of draft
   records........2 Kin. 25:19
  Collectors of temple
   revenue.......2 Kin. 12:10
  Teacher of the
   Law..........Ezra 7:6, 10, 12

B. *Characteristics of, in New
  Testament times, their:*
  Righteousness
   external.......Matt. 5:20
  Teaching without
   authority .....Matt. 7:29

C. *Their attitude toward Christ:*
  Accusing Him of
   blasphemy ....Mark 2:6, 7
  Seeking to
   accuse ....Luke 6:7
  Questioning His
   authority......Luke 20:1, 2

D. *Christ's attitude toward:*
  Exposes
   them..........Matt. 23:13-36
  Condemns
   them..........Luke 20:46, 47
  Calls them
   hypocrites.....Matt. 15:1-9

Scriptures—*God's revelation*

A. *Called:*
  Word of God ..Heb. 4:12
  Word of
   truth..........James 1:18
  Oracles of
   God...........Rom. 3:2

Word ....James 1:21-23
Holy
 Scriptures.....Rom. 1:2
Sword of the
 Spirit ....Eph. 6:17
Scriptures of the
 prophets .....Rom. 16:26

B. *Described as:*
Author-
 itative.........1 Pet. 4:11
Inspired ....2 Tim. 3:16
Effectual in
 life.............1 Thess. 2:13
Truth..........Ps. 119:160
Perfect ....Ps. 19:7
Sharp..........Heb. 4:12
Pure...........Prov. 30:5

C. *Inspiration of, proved by:*
External
 evidence .....Heb. 2:1-4
Internal
 nature ....2 Tim. 3:16, 17
Infallibility.....John 10:35
Fulfillment of
 prophecy......John 5:39, 45-47

D. *Understanding of, by:*
Spirit's
 illumination...1 Cor. 2:10-14
Searching.....John 5:39
Reasoning .....Acts 17:2
Comparing ....2 Pet. 1:20, 21
Human help ...Acts 17:10-12

E. *Proper uses of:*
Regener-
 ation...........1 Pet. 1:23
Salvation .....2 Tim. 3:15
Producing
 life.............John 20:31
Searching our
 hearts.........Heb. 4:12
Spiritual
 growth........Acts 20:32
Sanctifi-
 cation.........John 17:17
Illumination ...Ps. 119:105
Keeping from
 sin ....Ps. 119:9, 11
Defeating
 Satan ....Eph. 6:16, 17
Proving
 truth..........Acts 18:28

F. *Misuses of, by:*
Satan..........Matt. 4:6
Hypocrites.....Matt. 22:23-29
False
 teachers .....2 Cor. 2:17
Unlearned .....2 Pet. 3:16

G. *Positive attitudes toward:*
Let dwell in
 richly ....Col. 3:16
Search daily ...Acts 17:11
Hide in the
 heart..........Ps. 119:11
Love...........Ps. 119:97, 113,
 167
Delight in......Ps. 1:2
Receive with
 meekness .....James 1:21
Teach to
 children.......Deut. 11:19
Obey ....James 1:22
Read ....Deut. 17:19

H. *Negative attitudes toward, not
 to:*
Add to or subtract
 from ....Deut. 4:2
Handle
 deceitfully ....2 Cor. 4:2
Twist..........2 Pet. 3:16
Invalidating by
 traditions .....Mark 7:9-13

I. *Fulfillment of, cited to show:*
Christ's:
 Mission.......Luke 4:16-21
 Death.........Luke 24:27,
 44-47
 Rejection .....Acts 28:25-29
 Resurrec-
 tion..........Acts 2:24-31
Spirit's
 descent ....John 14:16-21
Faith ....Rom. 4:3

J. *Distortion of:*
Condemned.....Prov. 30:5, 6
 Rev. 22:18-20
Predicted ......2 Tim. 4:3, 4

K. *Memorization of:*
Keeps from
 sin ....Ps. 119:11
Gives under-
 standing ......Ps. 119:130
Facilitates
 prayer ....John 15:7

Scriptures, devotional readings

A. *For personal needs:*
Comfort ....Ps. 43:1-5
 Rom. 8:26-28
Courage ....Ps. 46:1-11
 2 Cor. 4:7-18
Direction ......Heb. 4:16
 James 1:5, 6

Peace..........Ps. 4:1-8
                Phil. 4:4-7
Relief..........Ps. 91:1-16
                2 Cor. 12:8-10
Rest ....Matt. 11:28-30
                Rom. 8:31-39
Temptation ....Ps. 1:1-6
                1 Cor. 10:6-13
                James 1:12-16

B. *For Instruction:*
   Sermon on the
     mount ....Matt. 5:1-7:29
   Prayer..........Matt. 6:5-15
                Phil. 4:6, 7
   Golden rule....Matt. 7:12
   Great com-
     mandment ....Matt. 22:36-40
   Salvation .....John 3:1-36
   Good
     shepherd.....John 10:1-18
   Spiritual   ⎰John 15:1-17
     fruit..........⎱Gal. 5:22, 23
   Guilt ....Rom. 8:1
   Righ-
     teousness .....Rom. 3:19-28
   Justification ...Rom. 5:1-21
   Christian   ⎰Rom. 12:1-21
     service.......⎱Rom. 13:1-14
   Stewardship ...2 Cor. 8:1-24
                2 Cor. 9:1-15
   Love..........1 Cor. 13:1-13
   Regenera-
     tion..........Eph. 2:1-10
   Christ's
     exaltation.....Phil. 2:5-11
   Resurrection...1 Thess. 4:13-18
   Judgment.......Rev. 20:10-15
   New heaven   ⎰Rev. 21:1-27
     and earth ....⎱Rev. 22:1-5

Scriptures, distortion of

Condemned ......Prov. 30:5, 6
Turning unto
  fables ....2 Tim. 4:3, 4
By unlearned......2 Pet. 3:15-17
God will punish ...Rev. 22:18-20

Scroll—*a papyrus or leather roll* (book)

Applied to the
  heavens ....Is. 34:4
Sky split apart
  like a............Rev. 6:14
Called a book .....Ps. 40:7
State documents written
  on................Ezra 6:2
Scripture written
  on................Is. 8:1

Scum—*the residue of dirt*

Used
  figuratively.......Ezek. 24:6-12

Scythians—*natives of Scythia*

In the Christian
  church ....Col. 3:11

Sea—*a large body of water*

A. *Described as:*
   Created by
     God............Acts 4:24
   Deep ....Ps. 68:22
   Turbulent and
     dangerous.....Ps. 89:9
   All rivers run
     into..........Eccl. 1:7
   Bound by God's
     decree ....Jer. 5:22
   Manifesting God's
     works.........Ps. 104:24, 25

B. *List of, in the Bible:*
   Great Sea (Mediter-
     ranean) ....Ezek. 47:10
   Salt or Dead
     Sea ....Gen. 14:3
   Red Sea ......Ex. 10:19
   Sea of Galilee (Chin-
     nereth).......Num. 34:11
   Adriatic........Acts 27:27

C. *Figurative of:*
   Extension of the
     Gospel ....Is. 11:9
   Righ-
     teousness .....Is. 48:18
   False
     teachers ......Jude 13

Seagull

Listed as
  unclean ....Lev. 11:13, 16

Sea, cast metal

Vessel in the
  Temple..........1 Kin. 7:23

Sea of glass

Before the throne of
  God ....Rev. 4:6

Seal—*instrument used to authenticate ownership*

A. *Used literally to:*
   Guarantee business
     deals..........Jer. 32:11-14

Ratify
covenants.....Neh. 10:1
Insure a
prophecy......Dan. 9:24
Protect
books.........Rev. 5:2, 5, 9
Lock doors ....Matt. 27:66

B. *Used figuratively of:*
Ownership of
married ⎰
love..........⎱Song 4:12
Song 8:6
Hidden
things.........Is. 29:11
God's witness to
Christ........John 6:27
Believer's
security......2 Cor. 1:22
Assurance .....Eph. 4:30
God's ownership of His
people ......Rev. 7:3-8

Seamstress—*a dressmaker*

Dorcas known
as................Acts 9:36-42

Search—*to make intensive investigation*

A. *Applied literally to:*
Lost article ....Gen. 31:34-37
Records........Ezra 4:15, 19
Child ....Matt. 2:8
Scriptures ....John 5:39
Enemy.........1 Sam. 23:23

B. *Applied figuratively to:*
Man's heart....Ps. 139:1, 23
Under-
standing ......Prov. 2:4
Conscience ....Prov. 20:27
Self-examin-
ation..........Judg. 5:16

Season—*a period of time*

A. *Descriptive of:*
Period of the
year ....Gen. 1:14
Revealed
times ....1 Thess. 5:1
Right time.....Deut. 11:14

B. *Of the year:*
Guaranteed by
God............Gen. 8:22
Proof of God's
providence....Acts 14:17
Indicated by the
moon ....Ps. 104:19

Seat—*a place of authority*

A. *Descriptive of:*
Inner court ....Ezek. 8:3
Assembly ......Matt. 23:6

B. *Figurative of:*
God's throne...Job 23:3
Association with
evil ....Ps. 1:1
Satanic
power.........Rev. 13:2

Seba

Cush's oldest
son..............Gen. 10:7
See Sabeans

Secacah—*thicket*

Village of Judah...Josh. 15:1, 61

Sechu—*observatory*

Village near
Ramah ....1 Sam. 19:22

Second

A. *Descriptive of:*
Next in order ..Gen. 1:8
Repetition .....1 Kin. 18:34
Second
advent ....Heb. 9:28

B. *Used figuratively and spiritually
of:*
Christ ....1 Cor. 15:47
Finality........Titus 3:10
New
covenant......Heb. 8:7
Death ....Rev. 2:11

Second chance

None in hell.......Luke 16:23-31

Second coming of Christ

A. *Described as:*
Day of:
The Lord .....1 Thess. 5:2
Lord Jesus....1 Cor. 5:5
God ....2 Pet. 3:12
That Day .....2 Thess. 1:10
Last day......John 12:48

B. *Purposes of, to:*
Fulfill His
Word ....John 14:3
Raise the
dead ....1 Thess. 4:13-18
Destroy
death ....1 Cor. 15:25, 26

Gather the
elect .... Matt. 24:31
Judge the
world .... Matt. 25:32-46
Glorify
believers ..... Col. 3:4
Reward God's
people .... Matt. 16:27

C. *Time of:*
Unknown to
us............ Matt. 24:27, 36
After the Gospel's proclamation
to all.......... Matt. 24:14
After the rise of
antichrist ..... 2 Thess. 2:2, 3
At the last
trumpet....... 1 Cor. 15:51, 52
In days like
Noah's........ Matt. 24:37-47

D. *Manner of:*
In the clouds .. Matt. 24:30
In flaming
fire............ 2 Thess. 1:7, 8
With the
angels........ Matt. 25:31
As a thief..... 1 Thess. 5:2, 3
In His glory.... Matt. 25:31

E. *Believer's attitude toward, to:*
Wait for ...... 1 Cor. 1:7
Look for ...... Titus 2:13
Be ready for ... Matt. 24:42-51
Love.......... 2 Tim. 4:8
Be busy until .. Luke 19:13-18
Pray for ...... Rev. 22:20

Secret disciples

Among Jewish
leaders .... John 12:42
Fearful of Jewish
disfavor .... John 19:38

Secret prayer

Commended by
Christ........... Matt. 6:6
Practiced by:
Christ............ Mark 1:35
Peter............ Acts 10:9

Secret things

Known by God.... Deut. 29:29
See Mystery

Secrets—*things unknown to others*

To be kept .... Prov. 25:9
Sign of
faithfulness....... Prov. 11:13

To those who expose,
condemned....... Prov. 20:19

Sects of Christ's time

Pharisees .... Acts 15:5
                 Acts 26:5
Sadducees .... Acts 5:17
Herodians........ Matt. 22:16
Christians described
as .... Acts 24:5, 14

Secundus—*second*

Thessalonian
Christian .... Acts 20:4

Security of the saints

A. *Expressed by:*
"Shall never
perish"........ John 10:28
"None of them is
lost" .... John 17:12
"Kept by the power of
God".......... 1 Pet. 1:5

B. *Guaranteed by:*
Spirit's
sealing .... 2 Cor. 1:21, 22
Christ's
intercession ... Rom. 8:34-39
God's power ... Jude 24

See Assurance

Sedition—*attack upon an established government*

Miriam and Aaron, against
Moses............ Num. 12:1-13

Seducers—*those who lead others astray*

A. *Agents of:*
Evil leaders .... 2 Kin. 21:9

B. *Characteristics of:*
Lead to evil.... Rev. 2:20
Preach false
message....... Ezek. 13:9, 10

Seed—*the essential element of transmitting life*

A. *Descriptive of:*
One's
ancestry ...... Gen. 12:7
Messianic
line .... Gen. 21:12
Christ .... Gal. 3:16, 19

B. *Figurative of true believers:*
Born of God ... 1 Pet. 1:23
Abraham's true
children .... Gal. 3:29

Children of
promise .... Rom. 9:7, 8
Including Israel's
faithful .... Rom. 9:29

C. *Sowing of, figurative of:*
God's Word .... Matt. 13:3, 32
Spiritual
blessings ...... 1 Cor. 9:11
Christ's
death .... John 12:24
Christian's
body .... 1 Cor. 15:36-49

Seeking—*trying to obtain*

A. *Things of the world:*
Worldly
things .... Matt. 6:32
One's life ..... Luke 17:33
One's selfish
interest .... Phil. 2:21

B. *Things of the Spirit:*
True wisdom .. Prov. 2:4
God's
kingdom ...... Matt. 6:33
Another's
benefit .... 2 Cor. 12:14
Peace .... 1 Pet. 3:11
Heavenly
country ...... Heb. 11:14

Seers—*prophets*

Amos .... Amos 7:12
Asaph .... 2 Chr. 29:30
Gad .... 2 Sam. 24:11
Heman .... 1 Chr. 25:5
Samuel .... 1 Sam. 9:19
Zadok .... 2 Sam. 15:27
Iddo .... 2 Chr. 9:29
Hanani .... 2 Chr. 16:7
Jeduthun ...... 2 Chr. 35:15

Segub—*exalted*

1. Son of Hiel .... 1 Kin. 16:34
2. Son of
Hezron .... 1 Chr. 2:21, 22

Seir—*hairy; shaggy*

1. Mt. Seir .... Gen. 14:6
Home of
Esau .... Gen. 32:3
Mountain range of
Edom .... Gen. 36:21
Horites dispossessed by Esau's
descendants ... Deut. 2:12
Refuge of Amalekite
remnant ...... 1 Chr. 4:42, 43
Desolation of .. Ezek. 35:15

2. Landmark on Judah's
boundary ..... Josh. 15:10

Seirah—*rough*

Ehud's refuge ..... Judg. 3:26

Seize—*to take or keep fast, hold*

Let darkness ...... Job 3:6
Let us kill him
and .... Matt. 21:38

Sela

Place in Edom .... 2 Kin. 14:7

Selah

Musical term found in
Psalms .... Ps. 3:2
Found in .... Hab. 3:3, 9, 13

Seled—*exultation*

Judahite .... 1 Chr. 2:30

Seleucia—*a city on the seacoast of
Syria*

Paul and Barnabas embark
from .... Acts 13:4

Self-abasement

Jacob, before
Esau .... Gen. 33:3-10
Moses, before
God .... Ex. 3:11
Roman, before
Christ .... Luke 7:7-9
Christ, true example
of .... Phil. 2:5-8

Self-acceptance—*having the proper
attitude toward oneself*

A. *Based on, by Christians:*
Planned before birth by
God .... Ps. 139:13-16
Workmanship ʃ Ps. 138:8
of God .... ⎨ Eph. 2:10
Christ has provided
life .... John 10:10
God desires man's
fellowship ..... John 17:3
God's love ..... Rom. 5:8
Living epistle of
God .... 2 Cor. 3:2
Complete in
Christ .... Col. 2:10
Chosen by
God .... 1 Pet. 2:9

B. *Hindered by, false attitudes:*
Looking on outward
appearance .... 1 Sam. 16:7

Questioning God's
direction ...... Is. 45:9
Doubting God's
grace .... 2 Cor. 12:9, 10

Self-condemnation

Caused by one's:

Heart .... 1 John 3:20
Conscience .... John 8:7-9
Sins .... 2 Sam. 24:17
Mouth .... Job 9:20
Evil works .... Matt. 23:31

Self-control

A. *Origin of:*
Brought about by
Christ .... Luke 8:35
Christian
grace .... 2 Pet. 1:6

B. *Elements involved in:*
Ruling one's
spirit .... Prov. 16:32
Soberness ...... Rom. 12:3
Control of the
body .... 1 Cor. 9:27

C. *Hindered by:*
Fleshly lusts .. 1 Pet. 2:11
Tongue .... Ps. 39:1, 2
Drink .... Prov. 23:29-35
Sexual sins ... 1 Thess. 4:3, 4
Unclean
spirit .... Mark 5:2-16
Self-expres-
sionism .... Prov. 25:28

Self-deception

A. *Factors contributing to:*
Scoffers .... 2 Pet. 3:3, 4
Worldliness .... Matt. 24:48-51
False
teaching ...... 1 Thess. 5:3

B. *Examples of:*
Babylon .... Is. 47:7-11
Jewish
women .... Jer. 44:16-19
Jewish
leaders .... John 8:33, 41

Self-denial

A. *Expressed by:*
"Denying" ..... Titus 2:12
"No longer should
live" .... 1 Pet. 4:2
"Does not
forsake" ...... Luke 14:33
"Take his
cross" .... Matt. 10:38

"Crucified the
flesh" .... Gal. 5:24
"Put off" ...... Eph. 4:22
"Put to
death" .... Col. 3:5

B. *Objects of:*
Appetite .... Prov. 23:2
Sinful
pleasures ..... Heb. 11:25, 26
Worldly
ambitions ..... Matt. 16:24-26

C. *Willingness to, manifested by:*
Judah .... Gen. 44:33
Moses .... Ex. 32:32
Paul .... Acts 20:22-24

D. *Commended as:*
Christian
duty .... Rom. 12:1, 2
Rewardable .... Luke 18:28-30

Self-exaltation

A. *Manifested by:*
Satan .... Is. 14:12-15
Antichrist ...... 2 Thess. 2:4
Wicked .... Ps. 73:9

B. *Evils of, seen in:*
Self-
abasement .... Matt. 23:12
Pride .... Prov. 16:18

C. *Antidotes of:*
Humility .... Prov. 15:33
Christ's
example ...... Phil. 2:5-8

See Pride

Self-examination

A. *Purposes of, to:*
Test one's
faith .... 2 Cor. 13:5
Prepare for the Lord's
Supper .... 1 Cor. 11:28-32
Prove one's
work .... Gal. 6:4
Test all
things .... 1 Thess. 5:21

B. *Means of:*
God Himself ... Ps. 26:2
God's Word .... Heb. 4:12
Christ's
example .... Heb. 12:1, 2

Selfishness—*loving one's self first*

A. *Exemplified in:*
Self-love ...... 2 Tim. 3:2
Self-seeking ... Phil. 2:21

B. *Avoidance of, by:*
Seeking the good of
others. . . . . . . .1 Cor. 10:24
Putting Christ
first. . . . . .Phil. 1:21, 22
Manifesting
love. . . . . .1 Cor. 13:5

C. *Examples of:*
Nabal. . . . . .1 Sam. 25:3, 11
Haman . . . . . . .Esth. 6:6
James and
John . . . . .Mark 10:35-37
Jewish
people . . . . . . .John 6:26
Solomon. . . . . .Eccl. 2:10, 11
Rich fool . . . . .Luke 12:16-21
Rich man . . . . .Luke 16:19-25

D. *Consequences of:*
Poverty. . . . . . .Prov. 23:21
Sin . . . . .Rom. 13:13, 14
Loss of
spirituality . . . .Gal. 5:16, 17

Self-righteousness

A. *Described as:*
Objection-
able. . . . . .Deut. 9:4-6
Self-
condemned . . .Job 9:20
Unprofitable . . .Is. 57:12
Like filthy
rags. . . . . .Is. 64:6
Offensive . . . . .Is. 65:5
External . . . . . .Matt. 23:25-28
One-sided. . . . .Luke 11:42
Boastful . . . . . .Luke 18:11, 12
Insufficient . . . .Phil. 3:4-9

B. *Condemned because it:*
Cannot make
pure . . . . .Prov. 30:12
Cannot save . . .Matt. 5:20
Rejects God's righ-
teousness . . . . .Rom. 10:3

C. *Examples of:*
Saul . . . . .1 Sam. 15:13-21
Young man. . . .Matt. 19:16-20
Lawyer . . . . . . .Luke 10:25, 29
Pharisees . . . . .Luke 11:39

Self-will—*stubbornness*

A. *Manifested in:*
Presumption . . .Num. 14:40-45
Unbelief . . . . . .2 Kin. 17:14
Evil heart. . . . . .Jer. 7:24
Disobeying
parents . . . . . . .Deut. 21:18-20

Pride . . . . .Neh. 9:16, 29
Stubborn-
ness. . . . . .Is. 48:4-8
Rejecting God's
messengers . . .Jer. 44:16
Resisting God's
Spirit . . . . .Acts 7:51
False
teaching . . . . . .2 Pet. 2:10

B. *Sin of, among Christians:*
Illustrated . . . . .Acts 15:36-40
Warned
against. . . . . . . .Heb. 3:7-12

C. *Examples of:*
Simeon and
Levi. . . . . .Gen. 49:5, 6
Israelites . . . . . .Ex. 32:9
Saul. . . . . .1 Sam. 15:19-23
David. . . . . .2 Sam. 24:4

See Pride

Semachiah—*Yahweh supports*

Levite porter . . . . . .1 Chr. 26:7

Semei—*Greek form of Shimei*

In Christ's
ancestry. . . . . .Luke 3:26

Senaah—*thorny*

Family of ⎰Ezra 2:35
returnees . . . .⎱Neh. 7:38

Seneh—*thorn bush*

Sharp rock between Michmash and
Gibeah . . . . .1 Sam. 14:4, 5

Senir—*mount of light*

Amorite name of Mount
Hermon . . . . .Deut. 3:9
Noted for firs . . . . .Ezek. 27:5

Sennacherib—*Sin* (moon-god)
multiplied brothers

Assyrian king (705–681 B.C.);
son and successor of
Sargon II. . . . . .2 Kin. 18:13
Death of, by
assassination . . . . .2 Kin. 19:36, 37

Senses—*the faculties of feeling*

Described
figuratively. . . . . . .Eccl. 12:3-6
Used by Isaac . . . . .Gen. 27:21-27
Impaired in
Barzillai . . . . .2 Sam. 19:32-35

Use of, as
evidence ....John 20:26-29
Proper use of .....Heb. 5:14

Senses, spiritual

Taste ....Ps. 34:8
Sight............Eph. 1:18
Hearing.........Gal. 3:2

Sensual—*fleshly*

Descriptive of:

Unregenerate ....Jude 19
Worldly
wisdom.........James 3:15
Same as
"natural".......1 Cor. 2:14
Rebellious against
God ....Rom. 8:7

Sensualist—*one who satisfies the
physical senses*

Illustrated by:

Nabal............1 Sam. 25:36
Rich fool.........Luke 12:16-21

Senuah (see Hassenuah)

Seorim—*barley*

Name of a priestly
course............1 Chr. 24:1-8

Separating courtyard—*the Temple yard*

Of Ezekiel's
Temple..........Ezek. 41:12

Separation—*setting apart from
something*

A. *As a good act from:*
Unclean ....Lev. 15:31
Evil workers ...Num. 16:21
Heathen
filthiness......Ezra 6:21
Pagan intermar-
riages.........Ezra 9:1, 2
Foreigners .....Neh. 13:3
Wine ....Num. 6:2-6

B. *As an evil act by:*
False
teachers ......Luke 6:22
Separatists.....Jude 19
Whisperers ....Prov. 16:28
Gossipers ......Prov. 17:9

C. *As descriptive of:*
God's
judgment .....Deut. 29:21
God's
sovereignty ...Deut. 32:8

Israel's
uniqueness....Lev. 20:24
Choice of the
Levites........Num. 8:14
Nazirite vow...Num. 6:2-6
Christian
obedience .....2 Cor. 6:17
Union with
Christ.........Rom. 8:35, 39
Christ's
purity.........Heb. 7:26
Final
separation.....Matt. 25:32

Sephar—*numbering*

Place on Joktan's
boundary........Gen. 10:30

Sepharad

Place inhabited by
exiles............Obad. 20

Sepharvaim—*an Assyrian city*

People of, sent to
Samaria ....2 Kin. 17:24, 31

Serah—*abundance*

Daughter of
Asher ....Gen. 46:17
Called Sarah .....Num. 26:46

Seraiah—*Yahweh has prevailed*

1. David's
secretary......2 Sam. 8:17
Called Sheva, ⎧2 Sam. 20:25
Shisha, and   ⎨1 Kin. 4:3
Shavsha......⎩1 Chr. 18:16
2. Son of
Tanhumeth ...2 Kin. 25:23
3. Son of
Kenaz.........1 Chr. 4:13, 14
4. Simeonite.....1 Chr. 4:35
5. Chief priest ...Jer. 52:24, 27
6. Postexilic
leader.........Neh. 12:1, 12
7. Signer of the
covenant......Neh. 10:2
8. Postexilic
priest ....Neh. 11:11
9. Officer of King
Jehoiakim.....Jer. 36:26
10. Prince of Judah; carries
Jeremiah's prophecy to
Babylon.......Jer. 51:59, 61

Seraphim—*burning ones*

Type of angels ....Is. 6:1, 2

Sered—*deliverance*

Son of Zebulun; founder of
Sardites .... Gen. 46:14

Sergius Paulus

Roman proconsul of Cyprus
converted by
Paul.............. Acts 13:7-12

Sermon on the Mount

Preached by
Christ .... Matt. 5—7
Those blessed ..... Matt. 5:3-12
Salt and light ..... Matt. 5:13-16
The law fulfilled... Matt. 5:17-20
On anger.......... Matt. 5:21-26
On adultery and
divorce .... Matt. 5:27-32
Oaths............. Matt. 5:33-37
Love your
enemies.......... Matt. 5:38-48
The religious { Matt. 6:1-4
life .... { Matt. 6:5-15
How to pray ...... Matt. 6:16-18
Undivided
devotion.......... Matt. 6:19-34
Judging others .... Matt. 7:1-6
Encouragement to
pray.............. Matt. 7:7-12
Entering the
kingdom .... Matt. 7:13-23
Two
foundations ...... Matt. 7:24-27

Serpents

A. *Characteristics of:*
Pierced by
God............ Job 26:13
Cunning........ Gen. 3:1
Some
poisonous..... Num. 21:6
Live on rocks, walls,
etc. .... Prov. 30:19
Cursed by
God............ Gen. 3:14, 15

B. *Miracles connected with:*
Aaron's rod turned
into........... Ex. 7:9, 15
Israelites
cured by { Num. 21:6-9
looking at.... { John 3:14, 15
Power over, given to
apostles....... Mark 16:18
Healing from bite
of............. Acts 28:3-6

C. *Figurative of:*
Intoxication .... Prov. 23:31, 32
Wisdom .... Matt. 10:16
Malice......... Ps. 58:3, 4
Unexpected
evil .... Eccl. 10:8
Enemies .... Is. 14:29
Christ......... John 3:14-16
Satan......... Rev. 20:2
Dan's
treachery ..... Gen. 49:17
Sting of wine .. Prov. 23:31, 32
Wickedness of
sinners........ Ps. 58:3, 4

Serug—*branch*

Descendant of
Shem............. Gen. 11:20-23
In Christ's
ancestry.......... Luke 3:35

Servant—*one who serves others*

A. *Descriptive of:*
Slave .... Gen. 9:25
Social
inferior........ Gen. 19:2
Worshiper of
God........... 1 Sam. 3:9
Messenger of
God........... Josh. 1:2
Messiah .... Is. 42:1
Follower of
Christ......... 2 Tim. 2:24

B. *Applied distinctively to:*
Prophets........ Zech. 1:6
Messiah .... Zech. 3:8
Moses .... Mal. 4:4
Christians ..... Acts 2:18
Glorified
saints .... Rev. 22:3

See Slave

Service to God

A. *Requirements of:*
Fear........... Ps. 2:11
Upright
walking....... Ps. 101:6
Absolute
loyalty .... Matt. 6:24
Regener-
ation......... Rom. 7:6
Serve the
Lord.......... Rom. 12:11
Humility....... Acts 20:19
Love.......... Gal. 5:13

B. *Rewards of:*
Divine honor . .John 12:26
Acceptance before
God.............Rom. 14:18
Inheritance....Col. 3:24
Eternal
blessed-   (Rev. 7:15
ness.......... {Rev. 22:3

Seth—*appointed*

Third son of
Adam ....Gen. 4:25
In Christ's
ancestry.........Luke 3:38

Sethur—*hidden*

Asherite spy .....Num. 13:2, 13

Setting—*woven together*

For precious stones worn by the
high priest........Ex. 28:11
Corded chains on
filigree ....Ex. 28:13, 14
Same Hebrew word translated
"woven" ....Ps. 45:13

Seven—*one more than six*

A. *Of social customs:*
Serving for a
wife............Gen. 29:20, 27
Bowing........Gen. 33:3
Mourning......Gen. 50:10
Feast ....Judg. 14:12, 17
Fasting ....1 Sam. 31:13

B. *Of things:*
Days ....Gen. 2:3
Weeks.........Dan. 9:25
Months........Lev. 23:24-44
Years..........Gen. 41:1-57
Nations........Deut. 7:1
Ways..........Deut. 28:7
Women........Is. 4:1
Brethren......Mark 12:20-22
Spirits ....Matt. 12:45
Men ....Acts 6:3-5
Churches .....Rev. 1:4, 20

C. *Of rituals:*
Victims of
sacrifices......Lev. 23:18
Sprinkling of
blood ....Lev. 4:6
Sprinkling of
oil ....Lev. 14:16
Passover......Ex. 12:15
Consecra-
tion...........Ex. 29:30, 35
Defilement....Lev. 12:2
Convocation..Lev. 23:24-44
Jubilee........Lev. 25:8

D. *Miracles:*
Plagues........Ex. 7:25
Jericho's fall ...Josh. 6:4, 8, 13
Naaman's
baths ....2 Kin. 5:10
Loaves........Matt. 15:34
Baskets........Matt. 15:37

E. *Of symbols:*
Purification...Ps. 12:6
Worship ......Ps. 119:164
Gospel light...Is. 30:26
Churches .....Rev. 1:4
Seals ....Rev. 5:1
Angels........Rev. 8:2
Heads and
crowns........Rev. 13:1
Plagues.......Rev. 15:6
Bowls.........Rev. 15:7
Kings.........Rev. 17:10

Seven sayings from the cross

1. "Father, forgive
   them"........Luke 23:34
2. "Today you will be with Me in
   Paradise" .....Luke 23:43
3. "Woman, behold your
   son" ....John 19:26
4. "My God, My
   God"..........Matt. 27:46
5. "I thirst" .....John 19:28
6. "It is
   finished"......John 19:30
7. "Father, into Your
   hands".........Luke 23:46

Seventy

Elders appointed . .Ex. 24:1, 9
Years in
Babylon ....Dan. 9:2
Weeks in prophetic
vision ....Dan. 9:24
In forgiveness.....Matt. 18:22
Disciples sent
forth ....Luke 10:1

Sexes—*male and female*

A. *Creation of:*
By God ....Gen. 1:27
For:
Union ....Gen. 2:23-25
Helpfulness ...Gen. 2:18
Procreation ...Gen. 4:1
Sexual
needs ....Prov. 5:17-19

B. *Regulations concerning:*
Distinctive clothing
for ....Deut. 22:5

Subordination
of............1 Cor. 11:3-16
Equality in
Christ........Gal. 3:28
Different functions
of............1 Tim. 2:8-15
Love
between ......Eph. 5:22-33

Sexual love

Good and ⎰Gen. 1:27, 28
holy.............⎱Gen. 2:24, 25
For procreation ...Gen. 4:1
In marriage only ..Prov. 5:15-20
Expression of ⎰Song 1:12-15
love ....⎱Song 3:1-5
Mutual responsi-
bility ....1 Cor. 7:3-5

Sexual perversion

A. *Types of:*
Adultery.......Deut. 22:22-29
Prostitution....Deut. 23:17
Incest ....Lev. 18:6-18
Homosex-
uality ....Rom. 1:26, 27
Mankind with
beasts.........Deut. 27:21

B. *Judgment upon:*
Defilement.....Lev. 18:22-28
Destruction....1 Cor. 5:1-5
Death ....Lev. 20:13-16

Shaalbim, Shaalabbin—*jackals*

Amorite city assigned to
Danites...........Josh. 19:42
Subdued by house of
Joseph ....Judg. 1:35

Shaalbonite—*an inhabitant of Shaalbim*

Eliahba called.....2 Sam. 23:32

Shaalim—*district of foxes*

Mentioned in Saul's
pursuit ....1 Sam. 9:4

Shaaph—*friendship*

1. Descendant of
Caleb ....1 Chr. 2:47
2. Son of Caleb...1 Chr. 2:49

Shaaraim, Sharaim—*double gate*

1. Village in
Judah........Josh. 15:36
2. City of
Simeon ......1 Chr. 4:31

Shaashgaz

Persian eunuch ...Esth. 2:14

Shabbethai—*Sabbath-born*

Postexilic Levite ..Ezra 10:15
Interprets the
law..............Neh. 8:7, 8

Shadow

A. *Used literally of:*
Man ....Acts 5:15
Mountain.....Judg. 9:36
Sundial ....2 Kin. 20:9-11

B. *Used figuratively of:*
Protection .....Ps. 91:1
Brevity ....Ps. 102:11
Change........James 1:17
Death ....Matt. 4:16
Types..........Col. 2:17
Old Testament
period.........Heb. 10:1

Shadrach

Hananiah's Babylonian
name.............Dan. 1:3, 7
Cast into the fiery
furnace...........Dan. 3:1-28

Shageh—*wandering*

Father of one of David's mighty
men.............1 Chr. 11:34

Shaharaim—*double dawn*

Benjamite.........1 Chr. 8:8-11

Shahazimah—*heights*

Town of
Issachar..........Josh. 19:17, 22

Shake—*to move violently*

A. *Descriptive of:*
Thunder.......Ps. 77:18
Earthquakes...Acts 4:31
Fear..........Matt. 28:4

B. *Used figuratively of:*
Fear...........Is. 14:16
Second
advent ....Heb. 12:26, 27
Rejection ......Luke 9:5
Acts 18:6

Shalim—*district of foxes*

Mentioned in Saul's
pursuit ....1 Sam. 9:4

Shalisha—*a third part*

Mentioned in Saul's
pursuit ....1 Sam. 9:4

Shallecheth—*a casting out*

Gate of Solomon's
temple ....1 Chr. 26:16

Shallum—*recompense*

1. King of
   Israel ....2 Kin. 15:10-15
2. Husband of
   Huldah........2 Kin. 22:14
3. Judahite ....1 Chr. 2:40, 41
4. Simeonite......1 Chr. 4:25
5. Father of
   Hilkiah........1 Chr. 6:12, 13
6. Naphtali's
   son ....1 Chr. 7:13
7. Family of
   porters........Ezra 2:42
8. Father of
   Jehizkiah .....2 Chr. 28:12
9. One who divorced his foreign
   wife...........Ezra 10:24
10. Another who divorced his
    foreign wife...Ezra 10:42
11. Son of
    Hallohesh.....Neh. 3:12
12. Jeremiah's
    uncle ....Jer. 32:7
13. Father of
    Maaseiah .....Jer. 35:4

Shalmai—*Yahweh is recompenser*

Head of a family of
Nethinim.........Ezra 2:46

Shalman

Contraction of
Shalmaneser .....Hos. 10:14

Shalmaneser—*Shulmanu (a god) is chief*

Assyrian king .....2 Kin. 17:3

Shama—*He (God) has heard*

Son of Hotham....1 Chr. 11:44

Shamariah—*Yahweh has kept*

Son of
Rehoboam.......2 Chr. 11:18, 19

Shame—*a feeling of guilt*

A. *Caused by:*
   Rape ....2 Sam. 13:13

Defeat ....2 Chr. 32:21
Folly ....Prov. 3:35
Idleness ......Prov. 10:5
Pride ....Prov. 11:2
A wicked
wife..........Prov. 12:4
Lying..........Prov. 13:5
Stub-
bornness......Prov. 13:18
Haste in
speech ....Prov. 18:13
Mistreatment of
parents ....Prov. 19:26
Evil
companions...Prov. 28:7
Juvenile
delinquency...Prov. 29:15
Nakedness....Is. 47:3
Idolatry........Jer. 2:26, 27
Impropriety...1 Cor. 11:6
Lust ....Phil. 3:19

B. *Of the unregenerate:*
   Hardened in ...Jer. 8:12
   Pleasure
   in .... {Rom. 1:26, 27,
                   32
   Vessels of.....Rom. 9:21
   Glory in ......Phil. 3:19
   Like foam .....Jude 13

C. *In the Christian life, of:*
   Unregenerate's
   life............Rom. 6:21
   Sinful things...Eph. 5:12
   Improper
   behavior .....1 Cor. 11:14, 22
   Christ ....Rom. 1:16

Shamer (see Shemer)

Shamgar—*cupbearer*

Judge of Israel; struck down 600
Philistines ....Judg. 3:31

Shamhuth—*desolation*

Commander in David's
army ....1 Chr. 27:8

Shamir—*a sharp point*

1. Town in
   Judah.........Josh. 15:1, 48
2. Town in
   Ephraim ......Judg. 10:1
3. Levite ....1 Chr. 24:24

Shamma—*astonishment*

Asherite ....1 Chr. 7:36, 37

Shammah—*waste*

1. Son of Reuel...Gen. 36:13, 17

2. Son of Jesse ...1 Sam. 16:9
Called
Shimea ....1 Chr. 2:13
3. One of David's mighty
men..........2 Sam. 23:11
Also called Shammoth the
Harorite.......1 Chr. 11:27

Shammai—*celebrated*

1. Grandson of
Jerahmeel....1 Chr. 2:28, 32
2. Descendant of
Caleb ....1 Chr. 2:44, 45
3. Descendant of
Judah........1 Chr. 4:17

Shammoth—*waste*

One of David's mighty
men..............1 Chr. 11:27

Shammua—*renowned*

1. Reubenite
spy ....Num. 13:2-4
2. Son of David ..2 Sam. 5:13, 14
3. Levite ....Neh. 11:17
4. Postexilic
priest ....Neh. 12:1, 18

Shamsherai—*sunlike*

Son of Jeroham ...1 Chr. 8:26

Shapham—*youthful*

Gadite ....1 Chr. 5:12

Shaphan—*prudent, shy*

Scribe under
Josiah ....2 Kin. 22:3
Takes book of the Law to
Josiah ....2 Kin. 22:8-10
Is sent to Huldah for
interpretation ....2 Kin. 22:14
Assists in repairs of
temple ....2 Chr. 34:8
Father of notable (Jer. 36:10-12,
son..............(25

Shaphat—*he has judged*

1. Simeonite
spy ....Num. 13:2-5
2. Son of
Shemaiah .....1 Chr. 3:22
3. Gadite chief ...1 Chr. 5:11, 12
4. One of David's
herdsmen .....1 Chr. 27:29
5. Father of the prophet
Elisha.......1 Kin. 19:16, 19

Shaphir—*glittering*

Town of Judah....Mic. 1:11

Sharai—*Yahweh is deliverer*

Divorced his foreign
wife.............Ezra 10:34, 40

Sharar—*firm*

Father of Ahiam ..2 Sam. 23:33

Sharers

Of sins............1 Tim. 5:22

See Partake

Sharezer, Sherezer—*protect the king*

1. Son of Sennach-
erib ....Is. 37:38
2. Sent to Zechariah concerning
fasting ....Zech. 7:1-3

Sharon—*plain*

1. Coastal plain between Joppa
and Mt.
Carmel........1 Chr. 27:29
Famed for
roses.........Song 2:1
Inhabitants turn to the
Lord ....Acts 9:35
2. Pasture east of the
Jordan ....1 Chr. 5:16

Sharonite—*an inhabitant of Sharon*

Shitrai ....1 Chr. 27:29

Sharp—*having a keen edge; biting*

A. *Descriptive of:*
Stone..........Ex. 4:25
Knives.........Josh. 5:2, 3
Share..........1 Sam. 13:20, 21
Rocks ....1 Sam. 14:4
Arrows ....Is. 5:28

B. *Used to compare a sword with:*
Tongue........Ps. 57:4
Adulteress ....Prov. 5:4
Mouth.........Is. 49:2
God's Word....Heb. 4:12

C. *Figurative of:*
Deceitfulness ..Ps. 52:2
Falsehood .....Prov. 25:18
Contention ....Acts 15:39
Severe
rebuke ......2 Cor. 13:10
Christ's
conquest......Rev. 14:14-18

Sharuhen—*abode of pleasure*

Town of Judah assigned to
Simeon...........Josh. 19:1, 6
Called (Josh. 15:36
Shaaraim........(1 Chr. 4:31

Shashai—*whitish*

Divorced his foreign
wife ....Ezra 10:34, 40

Shashak—*assaulter*

Benjamite.........1 Chr. 8:14, 25

Shaul—*asked* (of God)

1. Son of
   Simeon ....Gen. 46:10
   Founder of a tribal
   family.........Num. 26:13
2. Kohathite
   Levite.........1 Chr. 6:24

Shave—*to cut off the hair*

A. Used worthily to express:
   Accommo-
   dation........Gen. 41:14
   Cleansing......Lev. 14:8, 9
   Commit-
   ment..........Deut. 21:12
   Mourning......Job 1:18-20
   Sorrow ....Jer. 41:5

B. Used unworthily to express:
   Defeat of a
   Nazirite.......Judg. 16:19
   Contempt......2 Sam. 10:4
   Unnatural-
   ness...........1 Cor. 11:5, 6

Shaveh—*plain*

Valley near Salem; Abram meets
king of Sodom
here..............Gen. 14:17, 18

Shaveh-kiriathaim—*plain of Kiriathaim*

Plain near Kiriathaim inhabited by
Emim ....Gen. 14:5

Shavsha, Shisha—*nobility*

David's
secretary.........1 Chr. 18:14, 16
Serves under Solomon
also ....1 Kin. 4:3

Sheal—*asking*

Divorced his foreign
wife ....Ezra 10:29

Shealtiel—*I have asked God*

Son of King Jeconiah and father of
Zerubbabel ....1 Chr. 3:17

Sheariah—*Yahweh has esteemed*

Descendant of
Saul..............1 Chr. 9:44

Shear-Jashub—*a remnant shall return*

Symbolic name given to Isaiah's
son...............Is. 7:3

Sheba—*seven; an oath*

1. City in territory assigned to
   Simeon ...Josh. 19:1, 2
2. Benjamite insur-
   rectionist .....2 Sam. 20:1-22
3. Descendant of Cush through
   Raamah......Gen. 10:7
4. Descendant of
   Shem ....Gen. 10:28
5. Grandson of Abraham and
   Keturah.......Gen. 25:3
6. Gadite chief ...1 Chr. 5:13
7. Land of, occupied by Sabeans,
   famous   (Job 1:15
   traders.......(Ps. 72:10
   Queen of, visits Solomon;
   marvels at his
   wisdom ....1 Kin. 10:1-13
   Mentioned by
   Christ.........Matt. 12:42

Shebah—*seven; an oath*

Name given to a well and town
(Beersheba) ......Gen. 26:31-33

Shebaniah—*Yahweh has returned me*

1. Levite
   trumpeter.....1 Chr. 15:24
2. Levite; offers prayer and signs
   covenant......Neh. 9:4, 5
3. Levite who signs
   covenant......Neh. 10:12
4. Priest who signs
   covenant......Neh. 10:4

Shebarim—*breakings*

Place near Ai .....Josh. 7:5

Shebat

Eleventh month of the Hebrew
year..............Zech. 1:7

Sheber—*breaking*

Son of Caleb ......1 Chr. 2:48

Shebna—*perhaps an abbreviation of Shebaniah*

Treasurer under
Hezekiah.........Is. 22:15
Demoted to position of
scribe ....2 Kin. 19:2
Man of pride and luxury; replaced
by Eliakim ......Is. 22:19-21

Shebuel—*God is renown*

1. Son of
   Gershom......1 Chr. 23:16
2. Son of
   Heman........1 Chr. 25:4

Shecaniah, Shechaniah—*Yahweh has dwelt*

1. Descendant of
   Zerubbabel...1 Chr. 3:21, 22
2. Postexilic
   returnee......Ezra 8:5
3. Descendant of
   Aaron.........1 Chr. 24:11
4. Priest.........2 Chr. 31:15
5. Divorced his foreign
   wife..........Ezra 10:2, 3
6. Father of
   Shemaiah.....Neh. 3:29
   Probably same as number 1
7. Postexilic
   priest........Neh. 12:3, 7
8. Father-in-law of
   Tobiah........Neh. 6:18

Shechem—*shoulder*

1. Son of Hamor; seduces Dinah, Jacob's
   daughter......Gen. 34:1-31
2. Son of Gilead; founder of a
   tribal family...Num. 26:31
3. Son of
   Shemida ......1 Chr. 7:19
4. Ancient city of
   Ephraim ......Gen. 33:18
   Abram camps
   near..........Gen. 12:6
   Jacob buys ground
   here ....Gen. 33:18, 19
   Hivites,
   inhabit........Gen. 34:2
   Inhabitants of, slaughtered by
   Simeon and
   Levi..........Gen. 34:25-29
   Pastures
   near ....Gen. 37:12, 13
   Becomes city of
   refuge.........Josh. 20:7
   Joseph buried
   here ....Josh. 24:32
   Joshua's farewell address
   here ....Josh. 24:1, 25
   Center of idol-
   worship.......Judg. 9:1, 4-7
   Town
   destroyed .....Judg. 9:23, 45
   Jeroboam made king
   here ....1 Kin. 12:1-19

Name of, used
poetically .....Ps. 108:7

Shed—*to pour out*

A. *Descriptive of:*
   Blood..........Gen. 9:6
   Holy Spirit.....Titus 3:6

B. *As applied to blood, indicative of:*
   Justifiable
   execution .....Gen. 9:6
   Unjustifiable
   murder........Gen. 37:22
   Unacceptable
   sacrifice......Lev. 17:1-5
   Attempted   {1 Sam. 25:31,
   vengeance ...{   34
   Unpardon-
   able...........2 Kin. 24:4
   Abomina-
   tion...........Prov. 6:16, 17
   Heinous
   crime ....Is. 59:7
   New
   covenant......Matt. 26:28

Shedeur—*shedder of light*

Reubenite leader ..Num. 1:5

Sheep—*a domesticated animal*

A. *Characteristics of:*
   Domesti-
   cated ....2 Sam. 12:3
   Gentle.........Jer. 11:19
   Defenseless ...Mic. 5:8
   Needful of
   care...........Ezek. 34:5

B. *Uses of, for:*
   Food ....1 Sam. 25:18
   Milk...........1 Cor. 9:7
   Clothing.......Prov. 31:13
   Presents ....2 Sam. 17:29
   Tribute ....2 Kin. 3:4
   Sacrifice ......Gen. 4:4

C. *Uses of, in Levitical system as:*
   Burnt
   offering ....Lev. 1:10
   Sin offering....Lev. 4:32
   Trespass
   offering ....Lev. 5:15
   Peace
   offering ....Lev. 22:21

D. *Needs of, for:*
   Protection .....Job 30:1
   Shepherd ......John 10:4, 27
   Fold ....John 10:1

Pastures.......Ex. 3:1
Water.........Gen. 29:8-10
Rest...........Ps. 23:1, 2
Shearing.......1 Sam. 25:2, 11

E. *Figurative of:*
Innocent ......2 Sam. 24:17
Wicked........Ps. 49:14
Jewish
people ....Ps. 74:1
Backsliders ....Jer. 50:6
Lost sinners ...Matt. 9:36
Christians .....John 10:1-16
Christ ....John 1:29
Saved.........Matt. 26:31-34
Church.........Acts 20:28

See Lamb; Lamb of God

Sheepbreeder

Mesha, king of
Moab............2 Kin. 3:4

Sheepfold—*shelter*

Enclosure for
flocks ....Num. 32:16
Entrance to, only by
Christ ....John 10:1

Sheep Gate—*a gate of the restored Jerusalem*

Repaired ....Neh. 3:32
Dedicated.........Neh. 12:38, 39

Sheepshearers

Employed by
Judah ....Gen. 38:12
Many employed by
Nabal ....1 Sam. 25:7, 11
Used
figuratively.......Is. 53:7

Sheerah—*blood-relationship*

Daughter of Ephraim; builder of
cities ....1 Chr. 7:24

Sheets

Large piece of
cloth ....Acts 11:5

Shehariah—*Yahweh is the dawn*

Benjamite.........1 Chr. 8:26

Shekel—*a Jewish measure (approximately .533 oz.)*

A. *As a weight:*
Standard of,
defined........Ex. 30:13

Used in
weighing......Josh. 7:21

See Weights

B. *As money:*
Used in
currency......1 Sam. 9:8
Fines paid in...Deut. 22:19, 29
Revenues of the sanctuary paid
in............Neh. 10:32

Shekinah—*a word expressing the glory and presence of God*

A. *As indicative of God's presence:*
In nature ....Ps. 18:7-15
In the exodus from
Egypt ....Ex. 13:21, 22
At Sinai ....Ex. 24:16-18
In tabernacle ..Ex. 40:34-38
Upon the mercy
seat...........Ex. 25:22
In the   ⎧ Num. 9:15-23
wilderness ...⎨ Num. 10:11-36
In the
Temple........2 Chr. 7:1-3

B. *Illustrated by Christ in His:*
Divine
nature ....Col. 2:9
Incarnation ...Luke 1:35
Nativity ......Luke 2:9
Manifestation ⎧Hag. 2:9
to Israel......⎨Zech. 2:5
Transfigur-
ation..........2 Pet. 1:17
Ascension .....Acts 1:9
Transforming
us by His   ⎧2 Cor. 3:18
Spirit ....⎨2 Cor. 4:6
Return........Matt. 24:44
Eternal habitation with
saints ....Rev. 21:3

C. *Accompanied by:*
Angels.........Is. 6:1-4
Cloud.........Num. 9:15-23
Fire...........Heb. 12:18-21
Earthquake....Hag. 2:21

Shelah—*sprout; request*

1. Son of
Arphaxad .....1 Chr. 1:18
Called Salah ...Luke 3:35
2. Son of Judah ..Gen. 38:1-26
Founder of the
Shelanites.....Num. 26:20
3. Pool at
Jerusalem .....Neh. 3:15

Shelemiah—*friend of Yahweh*

1. Father of
   Hananiah .....Neh. 3:30
2. Postexilic
   priest ....Neh. 13:13
3. Father of
   Irijah ....Jer. 37:13
4. Porter ....1 Chr. 26:14
   Called Meshele-
   miah........1 Chr. 9:21
5. Ancestor of
   Jehudi ....Jer. 36:14
6. Son of
   Abdeel ....Jer. 36:26
7. Father of
   Jehucal ......Jer. 37:3

Sheleph—*drawn out*

Son of Joktan; head of a
tribe. ....1 Chr. 1:20

Shelesh—*might*

Asherite ....1 Chr. 7:35

Shelomi—*at peace*

Father of an Asherite
prince ....Num. 34:27

Shelomith, Shelomoth—*peaceful*

1. Daughter of Dibri; her son
   executed ......Lev. 24:10-23
2. Chief Levite   {1 Chr. 23:18
   of Moses .....{1 Chr. 24:22
3. Gershonites in David's
   time ....1 Chr. 23:9
4. Descendant of Moses, had
   charge of
   treasures....1 Chr. 26:25
5. Son or daughter of King
   Rehoboam ....2 Chr. 11:20
6. Daughter of
   Zerubbabel...1 Chr. 3:19
7. Family who went with
   Ezra ....Ezra 8:10

Shelumiel—*at peace with God*

Simeonite
warrior..........Num. 1:6

Shem—*name; renown*

Oldest son of
Noah.............Gen. 5:32
Escapes the
flood ....Gen. 7:13
Receives a
blessing ....Gen. 9:23, 26
Ancestor of Semitic
people...........Gen. 10:22-32
Ancestor of:
Abram ....Gen. 11:10-26
Jesus............Luke 3:36

Shema—*report; rumor*

1. Reubenite ....1 Chr. 5:8
2. Benjamite
   head ....1 Chr. 8:12, 13
3. Ezra's
   attendant .....Neh. 8:4
4. City of
   Judah.........Josh. 15:26
5. Son of
   Hebron ......1 Chr. 2:43

Shemaah—*fame*

Father of two of David's
warriors..........1 Chr. 12:3

Shemaiah—*Jehovah has heard*

1. Father of
   Shimri ....1 Chr. 4:37
2. Reubenite ....1 Chr. 5:4
3. Levite who helped move the
   ark ....1 Chr. 15:8, 12
4. Scribe in David's
   time ....1 Chr. 24:6
5. Son of
   Obed-Edom ...1 Chr. 26:4, 6, 7
6. Prophet of
   Judah.........1 Kin. 12:22-24
   Explains Shishak's invasion as
   divine
   punishment ...2 Chr. 12:5-8
   Records Rehoboam's
   reign.........2 Chr. 12:15
7. Levite teacher under Jehoshaphat ....2 Chr. 17:8
8. Levite in Hezekiah's
   reign..........2 Chr. 29:14, 15
9. Levite
   treasurer......2 Chr. 31:14, 15
10. Officer of Levites in Josiah's
    reign..........2 Chr. 35:9
11. Father of
    Urijah ....Jer. 26:20
12. False
    prophet ....Jer. 29:24-28
13. Father of
    Delaiah ....Jer. 36:12
14. Descendant of
    David.........1 Chr. 3:22
15. Keeper of the East Gate to
    Nehemiah.....Neh. 3:29
16. Merarite Levite living in
    Jerusalem.....1 Chr. 9:14

17. Son of
    Adonikam.....Ezra 8:13
18. Leading man under
    Ezra..........Ezra 8:16
19. Priest who divorced his foreign
    wife..........Ezra 10:21
20. Man who divorced his foreign
    wife..........Ezra 10:31
21. Prophet hired by
    Sanballat......Neh. 6:10-14
22. Priest who signs
    covenant......Neh. 10:1,8
23. Participant in dedication
    service......Neh. 12:34
24. Postexilic
    priest.........Neh. 12:35
25. Levite
    musician.....Neh. 12:36

Shemariah—*Jehovah keeps*

1. Mighty man of
   Benjamin......1 Chr. 12:5
2. Son of
   Rehoboam....2 Chr. 11:18, 19
3. Divorced his foreign
   wife..........Ezra 10:31, 32

Shemeber—*splendor of heroism*

King of Zeboiim...Gen. 14:2

Shemed—*destruction*

Son of Elpaal.....1 Chr. 8:12

Shemer, Shamer—*guard*

1. Sells Omri hill on which
   Samaria is
   built..........1 Kin. 16:23, 24
2. Levite.........1 Chr. 6:46
3. Asherite.......1 Chr. 7:30, 34

Shemida, Shemidah—*fame of knowing*

Descendant of Manasseh;
founder of the
Shemidaites.....Num. 26:29, 32

Sheminith—*eighth*

Musical term......1 Chr. 15:21

Shemiramoth—*fame of the highest*

1. Levite musician in David's
   time...........1 Chr. 15:18, 20
2. Levite teacher under Jehoshaphat.......2 Chr. 17:8

Shemuel—*name of God*

1. Grandson of
   Issachar......1 Chr. 7:1, 2

2. Representative of
   Simeon.......Num. 34:20

Shen—*tooth; a pointed rock*

Rock west of
Jerusalem........1 Sam. 7:12

Shenazzar

Son of Jeconiah...1 Chr. 3:18

Shepham—*nakedness*

Place near the Sea of
Galilee...........Num. 34:11

Shephatiah—*Yahweh judges*

1. Benjamite
   warrior.......1 Chr. 12:5
2. Son of David..2 Sam. 3:4
3. Simeonite
   chief..........1 Chr. 27:16
4. Son of King Jeho-
   shaphat.......2 Chr. 21:2
5. Opponent of
   Jeremiah......Jer. 38:1
6. Descendant of
   Judah.........Neh. 11:4
7. Servant of Solomon whose
   descendants return from
   exile..........Ezra 2:57

Shepher—*beauty*

Israelite
encampment.....Num. 33:23

Shepherd—*one who cares for the sheep*

A. *Duties of, toward his flock:*
   Defend........1 Sam. 17:34-36
   Water.........Gen. 29:2-10
   Give rest to....Jer. 33:12
   Know..........John 10:3-5
   Number.......Jer. 33:13
   Secure pasture
   for............1 Chr. 4:39-41
   Search for the ⎰Ezek. 34:12-16
   lost..........⎱Luke 15:4, 5

B. *Good, described as:*
   Faithful........Gen. 31:38-40
   Fearless.......1 Sam. 17:34-36
   Unselfish.....Luke 15:3-6
   Considerate....Gen. 33:13, 14
   Believing.....Luke 2:8-20

C. *Bad, described as:*
   Unfaithful.....Ezek. 34:1-10
   Cowardly.....John 10:12, 13
   Selfish.........Is. 56:11, 12
   Ruthless.......Ex. 2:17, 19
   Unbelieving....Jer. 50:6

D. *Descriptive of:*

God	Ps. 78:52, 53
Christ	Heb. 13:20
Joshua	Num. 27:16-23
David	2 Sam. 5:2
Judges	1 Chr. 17:6
National leaders	Jer. 49:19
Cyrus	Is. 44:28
Jewish leaders	Matt. 9:36
Church elders	1 Pet. 5:2

Shepherd, Jesus the good

A. *Described prophetically in His:*

Prophetic position (teaching)	Is. 40:10, 11
Priestly position (sacrifice)	Zech. 13:7 / Matt. 26:31
Kingly position (ruling)	Ezek. 37:24 / Matt. 2:6

B. *Described typically as:*

Good	John 10:11, 14
Chief	1 Pet. 5:4
Great	Heb. 13:20
One	John 10:16
Gentle	Is. 40:11
One who separates	Matt. 25:31-46

Shepho—*unconcern*

Son of Shobal ..... Gen. 36:23

Sherebiah—*Yahweh has sent burning heat*

1. Levite family returning with Ezra .... Ezra 8:18
2. Levite who assists Ezra ...... Neh. 8:7

Sheresh—*root*

Grandson of Manasseh .... 1 Chr. 7:16

Sheshach—*probably a cryptogram*

Symbolic of Babylon ...... Jer. 25:26

Sheshai—*whitish*

Descendant of Anak .... Num. 13:22
Driven out by Caleb .... Josh. 15:14
Destroyed by Judah .... Judg. 1:10

Sheshan—*whitish*

Jerahmeelite ..... 1 Chr. 2:31-35

Sheshbazzar—*sin (the moon god) protect the father*

Prince of Judah ... Ezra 1:8, 11

Shethar—*star*

Persian prince ..... Esth. 1:14

Shethar-Boznai—*starry splendor*

Official of Persia .. Ezra 5:3, 6

Sheva—*self-satisfying*

1. Son of Caleb ... 1 Chr. 2:43, 49
2. David's scribe .... 2 Sam. 20:25

Shibboleth—*stream or ear of corn*

Password .... Judg. 12:5, 6

Shicron—*drunkenness*

Town of Judah .... Josh. 15:11

Shield—*a protective armor*

A. *Uses of:*

Protection	2 Chr. 14:8
Treasures in war	1 Kin. 14:25, 26
Riches	2 Chr. 32:27
Ornamenting public buildings	1 Kin. 10:17

B. *Figurative of:*

God's:

Protection	Ps. 33:20
Favor	Ps. 5:12
Salvation	Ps. 18:35
Truth	Ps. 91:4
Faith	Eph. 6:16
Rulers	Ps. 47:9

Shiggaion

Plural form:

Shigionoth .... Hab. 3:1

Shihor—*black; turbid*

Name given to the Nile .... Is. 23:3
Israel's southwestern border ...... Josh. 13:3

Shihor Libnath—*turbid stream of Libnath*

Small river in Asher's territory .... Josh. 19:26

Shilhi—*Yahweh has sent*

Father of
Azubah ....1 Kin. 22:42

Shilhim—*missiles*

Town in south
Judah ....Josh. 15:1, 32

Shillem—*compensation*

Son of Napthali ...Gen. 46:24

Shiloah—*sent*

A pool of Jerusalem, figurative of
God's
protection ....Is. 8:6

See Siloam

Shiloh

1. Town of
   Ephraim ......Judg. 21:19
   Center of religious
   worship ....Judg. 18:31
   Canaan divided
   here ....Josh. 18:1, 10
   Benjamites seize women
   here ....Judg. 21:19-23
   Ark of the covenant taken
   from ....1 Sam. 4:3-11
   Site of Eli's
   judgeship ...1 Sam. 4:12-18
   Home of
   Ahijah ....1 Kin. 14:2, 4
   Punishment given
   to ....Jer. 7:12-15
2. Messianic
   title ....Gen. 49:10

Shiloni—*a Shilonite*

Father of
Zechariah ....Neh. 11:5

Shilonite

Native of Shiloh...1 Kin. 11:29

Shilshah—*might*

Asherite ....1 Chr. 7:36, 37

Shimea, Shimeah—*He (God) has heard*

1. Gershonite
   Levite.........1 Chr. 6:39
2. Merarite
   Levite.........1 Chr. 6:30
3. Brother of
   David.........2 Sam. 13:3
4. Son of David ..1 Chr. 3:1, 5

5. Benjamite .....1 Chr. 8:1, 32
   Called
   Shimeam......1 Chr. 9:38

Shimeath—*report*

Ammonitess.......2 Kin. 12:21

Shimeathites

Family of
scribes ....1 Chr. 2:55

Shimei, Shimi—*renowned*

1. Son of
   Gershon ......Ex. 6:17
2. Son of
   Merari ....1 Chr. 6:29
3. Simeonite......1 Chr. 4:24-27
4. Levite ....1 Chr. 6:42
5. Benjamite family
   head...........1 Chr. 8:21
6. Gershonite family
   head...........1 Chr. 23:7, 9
7. Levite musician in David's
   time ....1 Chr. 25:3, 17
8. Overseer of vineyards under
   David.........1 Chr. 27:27
9. Benjamite; insults
   David.........2 Sam. 16:5-13
   Pardoned, but
   confined .....2 Sam. 19:16-23
   Breaks parole; executed by
   Solomon ...1 Kin. 2:39-46
10. Faithful follower of
    Solomon .....1 Kin. 1:8
11. Levite; assists in
    purification ...2 Chr. 29:14-16
12. Levite treasurer in Hezekiah's
    reign.........2 Chr. 31:12, 13
13. Benjamite ancestor of
    Mordecai......Esth. 2:5
14. Brother of
    Zerubbabel....1 Chr. 3:19

Shimeon—*hearing*

Divorced his foreign
wife ....Ezra 10:31

Shimon—*trier*

Judahite family ...1 Chr. 4:1, 20

Shimrath—*guarding*

Benjamite.........1 Chr. 8:21

Shimri—*vigilant*

1. Father of
   Jediael ......1 Chr. 11:45
2. Merarite
   Levite.........1 Chr. 26:10

3. Levite; assists in
purification ...2 Chr. 29:13

Shimrith—*vigilant*

Moabitess.........2 Chr. 24:26

Shimron—*watching*

1. Son of
Issachar ......Gen. 46:13
2. Town of
Zebulun.......Josh. 11:1

Shimron Meron—*guard of lashing*

Town conquered by
Joshua ....Josh. 12:20

Shimshai—*sunny*

Scribe opposing the
Jews ....Ezra 4:8-24

Shin

Letter of the Hebrew
alphabet..........Ps. 119:161-168

Shinab—*king of Admah*

Fought against
Chedorlaomer ....Gen. 14:1, 12

Shinar—*the region around Babylon*

Original home of Noah's
sons..............Gen. 10:10
Tower built here ..Gen. 11:2-9
Amraphel, king
of ....Gen. 14:1, 9
Home of the remnant
Jews ....Is. 11:11

Shine—*to radiate with light*

A. *Used literally of:*
Sun.............Job 31:26
Moon............Job 25:5
Star ....Joel 3:15
Earth ....Ezek. 43:2
Moses' face ...Ex. 34:29-35
Christ's face ...Matt. 17:2
Angels..........Acts 12:7
Glorified
Christ..........Acts 9:3
Christ's
return.........Luke 17:24

B. *Applied figuratively to:*
God's
blessing ....Num. 6:25
God's Word....2 Pet. 1:19
Christ's first   (Is. 9:2
advent ....{John 1:5
Gospel..........2 Cor. 4:4
Believer's life ..Matt. 5:16

Regeneration ..2 Cor. 4:6
Believer's   (Dan. 12:3
glory.........{Matt. 13:43

Shion—*ruin*

Town of
Issachar..........Josh. 19:19

Shiphi—*abundant*

Simeonite.........1 Chr. 4:37

Shiphmite—*a native of Shiphmoth*

Zabdi called.......1 Chr. 27:27

Shiphrah—*beauty*

Hebrew midwife...Ex. 1:15

Shiphtan—*judicial*

Ephraimite........Num. 34:24

Ships—*vessels designed for use on water*

A. *Uses of:*
Fishing ....John 21:3-8
Travel ....Jon. 1:3
Cargoes ....Acts 27:3, 10, 38
War ....Num. 24:24
Commerce.....Ps. 107:23

B. *Parts of:*
Figurehead ....Acts 28:11
Skiff...........Acts 27:16-32
Anchor ....Acts 27:29, 40
Rudder ....Acts 27:40
Cables.........Acts 27:17
Ropes ....Acts 27:32
Sails...........Is. 33:23
Oars...........Ezek. 27:6

C. *Notable ones:*
Ark............Gen. 7:17, 18
Jonah's ....Jon. 1:3, 4
Of Tarshish ...Is. 23:1, 14
Paul's.........Acts 27:1-44

Shipwreck—*a wreck of a sea-going vessel*

Paul in three .....2 Cor. 11:25
Figurative of
apostasy..........1 Tim. 1:19

Shisha—*distinction*

Father of Solomon's
scribes ....1 Kin. 4:3
Called Shavsha....1 Chr. 18:16

Shitrai—*Yahweh is deciding*

Sharonite overseer of David's
herds..............1 Chr. 27:29

Shiza—*splendor*

Reubenite.........1 Chr. 11:42

Shoa—*rich*

Race or tribe against
Israel............Ezek. 23:23

Shobab—*returning*

1. Son of Caleb...1 Chr. 2:18
2. Son of David ..2 Sam. 5:14

Shobach—*expansion*

Commander of the Syrian
army.............2 Sam. 10:16-18
Spelled
Shophach ....1 Chr. 19:16, 18

Shobai—*glorious*

Head of a family of
porters ....Ezra 2:42

Shobal—*flowing*

1. Son of Seir; a Horite
chief ....Gen. 36:20-29
2. Judahite, son of Caleb
and ancestor of the
people of Kirjath
Jearim..........1 Chr. 2:50, 52

Shobek—*forsaking*

Signer of Nehemiah's sealed
covenant..........Neh. 10:24

Shobi—*Yahweh is glorious*

Ammonite who
brings food to   {2 Sam. 17:27,
David ....{ 28

Shoe (see Sandals)

Shoham—*beryl or onyx*

Merarite Levite ...1 Chr. 24:27

Shomer—*keeper, watchman*

Asherite ....1 Chr. 7:30, 32

Short—*not long; brief*

A. *Descriptive of:*
Life............Ps. 89:47
Time of the devil on
earth.........Rev. 12:12
Gospel age......1 Cor. 7:29

B. *Expressive of God's:*
Power ....Is. 50:2
Plan ....Rev. 22:6
Provision ......Is. 59:1, 2
Tribulation ....Matt. 24:21, 22

Short measure

Abomination......Mic. 6:10

Shoulder

A. *Of men, used for:*
Burdens ....Is. 46:7
Supporting
clothes........Ex. 12:34

B. *Figurative of:*
Notable
persons ......Ezek. 24:4, 5
Destruction....Ezek. 29:7
Servitude ......Is. 10:27
Rebellion .....Zech. 7:11
Messianic
authority......Is. 9:6
Security ......Deut. 33:12
Twelve tribes ..Ex. 28:10-12

Shout, Shouted

A. *Occasions of, in:*
Conquest ......Josh. 6:5, 16, 20
Choosing a
king ....1 Sam. 10:24
Sound of
singing........Ex. 32:17, 18
Laying foundation of the
Temple........Ezek. 3:11-13

B. *In spiritual things:*
At creation ....Job 38:7
In the Messiah's
arrival ....Zech. 9:9

Shovel

1. Used for removing
ashes ....Ex. 27:3
2. Winnowing
tool...........Is. 30:24

Showbread—*bread of your face*

A. *Provisions concerning:*
Provided by the
people ....Lev. 24:8
Prepared by the
Levites........1 Chr. 9:32
Presented to the
Lord ....Lev. 24:7, 8
Provided for   {Lev. 24:9
priests only ..{Matt. 12:4, 5

B. *Table of:*
Placed in   {Ex. 26:35
Holy Place ...{Heb. 9:2
Made of
acacia........Ex. 25:23-28
Carried by: Kohathite
Levites........Num. 4:4, 7, 15
High priest ....Num. 4:7, 8, 16

C. *Symbolic of:*
Twelve tribes . . Ex. 28:10-12
Christ . . . . John 6:48
Church . . . . 1 Cor. 10:17

Showers—*sudden outpourings*

A. *Used literally of rain:*
Withheld . . . . . Jer. 3:3
Predicted . . . . . Luke 12:54
Requested . . . . . Zech. 10:1
Blessing . . . . . . Ps. 65:10

B. *Used figuratively of:*
God's Word . . . . Deut. 32:2
God's wrath . . . Ezek. 13:11, 13
Messiah's
advent . . . . Ps. 72:6
Gospel . . . . Ezek. 34:25, 26
Remnant . . . . . . Mic. 5:7

Shroud—*to cover or shelter*

Used
figuratively . . . . Ezek. 31:3

Shua, Shuah, Shuhah—*prosperity*

1. Son of Abraham by
Keturah . . . . . . Gen. 25:1, 2
2. Father of Judah's
wife . . . . Gen. 38:2, 12
3. Descendant of
Judah . . . . 1 Chr. 4:1, 11
4. Daughter of
Heber . . . . 1 Chr. 7:32

Shual—*jackal*

1. Asherite . . . . . . 1 Chr. 7:30, 36
2. Region raided by a Philistine
company . . . . . 1 Sam. 13:17

Shubael, Shebuel

1. Levite, son of
Amram . . . . . . 1 Chr. 24:20
2. Levite, son of
Heman . . . . 1 Chr. 25:4

Shuham—*depression*

Son of Dan . . . . . . Num. 26:42
Called Hushim . . . . Gen. 46:23
Head of the
Shuhamites . . . . . . Num. 26:42, 43

Shuhite—*a descendant of Shua*

Bildad called; a descendant
of Abraham   (Gen. 25:1-4
by Keturah . . . . . . (Job 2:11

Shulamite—*a native of Shulam*

Shepherd's
sweetheart . . . . . . Song 6:13

Shumathites

Family of Kirjath
Jearim . . . . 1 Chr. 2:53

Shunammite—*a native of Shunem*

1. Abishag, David's nurse
called . . . . 1 Kin. 1:3, 15
2. Woman who cared for
Elisha . . . . 2 Kin. 4:8-12

Shunem—*uneven*

Border town of
Issachar . . . . Josh. 19:18

Shuni—*fortunate*

Son of Gad . . . . Gen. 46:16

Shuppim—*serpent*

Levite porter . . . . . . 1 Chr. 26:16

Shur—*fortification*

Wilderness in south
Palestine . . . . Gen. 16:7
Israel went from Red Sea
to . . . . Ex. 15:22
On Egypt's
border . . . . 1 Sam. 15:7
Hagar flees to . . . . . Gen. 16:7

Shushan—*a city of Elam*

Residence of Persian
monarchs . . . . Esth. 1:2
Located on river
Ulai . . . . Dan. 8:2
Court of Ahasuerus
here . . . . Esth. 1:2, 5

Shut—*to close securely*

A. *Applied literally to:*
Ark . . . . Gen. 7:16
Door . . . . Gen. 19:6, 10
Animals . . . . . . Dan. 6:22
Court . . . . Jer. 33:1
Prison . . . . Acts 26:10

B. *Applied figuratively to:*
God's
mercies . . . . . . Ps. 77:9
Finality of
salvation . . . . . Matt. 25:10
Union with
Christ . . . . Song 4:12
Spiritual
blindness . . . . . Is. 6:10
Awe . . . . Is. 52:15
Heaven's
glory . . . . Is. 60:11
God's Word . . . . Jer. 20:9

Vision ....Dan. 12:4
Secret prayer ..Matt. 6:6
Christ's
sovereignty ...Rev. 3:7, 8

Shuthelah

1. Son of Ephraim; head of a
   family........Num. 26:35, 36
2. Ephraimite.....1 Chr. 7:20, 21

Shuttle—a weaving tool

Our days swifter
than.............Job 7:6

Siaha, Sia—assembly

Family of
returning   ⎰Ezra 2:43, 44
Nethinim........⎱Neh. 7:47

Sibbechai

One of David's mighty
men.........1 Chr. 11:29
Slays a Philistine
giant ....2 Sam. 21:18
Commander of a
division ....1 Chr. 27:11

Sibmah, Shibmah—balsam

Town of Reuben ..Num. 32:3, 38
Famous for
wines ....Is. 16:8, 9

Sibraim—double hope

Place in north
Palestine ....Ezek. 47:16

Sick, Sickness—the state of being
unwell

A. Caused by:
   Age...........Gen. 48:1, 10
   Accident .....2 Kin. 1:2
   Wine ....Hos. 7:5
   Sins ....Mic. 6:13
   Despondency ..Prov. 13:12
   Prophetic
   visions ....Dan. 8:27
   Love..........Song 2:5
   God's
   judgment .....2 Chr. 21:14-19
   God's
   sovereignty ...John 11:4

B. Healing of, by:
   Figs ....2 Kin. 20:7
   Miracle ....1 Kin. 17:17-23

Prayer........James 5:14, 15
God's mercy ...Phil. 2:25-30

See Diseases; Healing

Sickle—an instrument for cutting grain

Literally..........Deut. 16:9
Figuratively......Mark 4:29
                Rev. 14:14-19

Siddim, Vale of

Valley of bitumen pits near the
Dead Sea....Gen. 14:3, 8, 10

Sidon, Zidon—fishery

Canaanite city 20 miles north of
Tyre.............Gen. 10:15, 19
Israel's northern
boundary........Josh. 19:28
Canaanites not expelled
from ....Judg. 1:31
Israelites oppressed
by..............Judg. 10:12
Gods of, entice
Israelites ....1 Kin. 11:5, 33
Judgments pronounced
on................Is. 23:12
Israelites sold as slaves
by..............Joel 3:4-6
People from, hear
Jesus............Luke 6:17
Visited by Jesus...Matt. 15:21
Paul visits at......Acts 27:3

Siege of a city—a military blockage

A. Methods employed in:
   Supplies cut
   off ....2 Kin. 19:24
   Ambushes
   laid ....Judg. 9:34
   Battering rams
   used ....Ezek. 4:2
   Arrows shot ...2 Kin. 19:32

B. Suffering of:
   Famine ....2 Kin. 6:26-29
   Pestilence......Jer. 21:6

C. Examples of:
   Jericho ....Josh. 6:2-20
   Jerusalem......2 Kin. 24:10, 11

See War

Sieve, sift—screen

Used figuratively of:

God's judgment ...Amos 9:9
Satan's
temptation ....Luke 22:31

Sign—*an outward token having spiritual significance*

A. *Descriptive of:*
Heavenly
bodies.........Gen. 1:14
Rainbow.......Gen. 9:12-17
Circumcision..Gen. 17:11
Bloodshed ....Ex. 12:13
God's
wonders .....Ps. 65:8
Covenant......Rom. 4:11
Miracles ......Deut. 26:8
Memorial .....Num. 16:38
Symbolic act..Is. 8:18
Witness........Is. 19:19, 20
Outward
display ....John 4:48

B. *Purposes of, to:*
Authenticate ⎰Deut. 13:1
a prophecy...⎱1 Sam. 2:31, 34
Strengthen ⎰Judg. 6:17
faith ....⎱Is. 7:11
Recall God's
blessings ......Josh. 24:15-17
Confirm God's ⎰2 Kin. 19:28, 29
Word ....⎱Heb. 2:4
Insure a ⎰2 Kin. 20:5,
promise ......⎱ 9-11
Confirm a
prophecy......1 Kin. 13:3-5

C. *Concerning Christ in His:*
Nativity ......Luke 2:12
Ministry ......John 20:30
Acts 2:22
Resurrection...Matt. 12:38-40

D. *Value of:*
Discounted as
such ....Matt. 16:1-4
Demanded unneces-
sarily ....John 6:30
Demonstrated by
apostles.......Acts 5:12
Displayed by
Paul ....Rom. 15:19

E. *In prophecy, concerning:*
Christ's first ⎰Is. 7:11, 14
advent ....⎱Matt. 1:21-23
Second
advent ....Matt. 24:3, 30
Antichrist......2 Thess. 2:9
End............Rev. 15:1

F. *As assurance of:*
Presence.......Ex. 3:12
Judgment upon
sin ....Num. 17:10

Goodness......Ps. 86:17
Genuineness...2 Thess. 3:17

See Token

Signify—*to make known by signs*

A. *Concerning men:*
Peter's death...John 21:19

B. *Concerning predicted events:*
Christ's
Death........John 12:33
Gospel age.....Rev. 1:1

Sihon—*bold*

Amorite king residing at
Heshbon ....Num. 21:26-30
Victorious over
Moabites........Num. 21:26-30
Ruler of five Midianite
princes ....Josh. 13:21
Refused Israel's request for
passage ....Deut. 2:26-28
Defeated by
Israel............Num. 21:21-32
Territory of, assigned to Reuben
and Gad.......Num. 32:1-38
Victory over, long
celebrated.......Deut. 31:4

Silas, Silvanus—*wooded*

Leader in the Jerusalem
church ....Acts 15:22
Christian
prophet ....Acts 15:32
Sent on a
mission..........Acts 15:22-35
Became Paul's
companion ......Acts 15:36-41
Roman citizen ....Acts 16:25-39
Paul commended his work at
Corinth ....2 Cor. 1:19
Called Silvanus....1 Thess. 1:1
Associated in Paul's
writings ....2 Thess. 1:1
Peter's helper ....1 Pet. 5:12

Silence—*the lack of noise*

A. *Kinds of:*
Will of ⎰1 Pet. 2:15
God..........⎱Rev. 8:1
Troubled........Jer. 20:9

B. *Virtue of:*
Suitable time
for ....Eccl. 3:7
Commanded...1 Cor. 14:34
Sign of
prudence......Prov. 21:23

Sign of
wisdom . . . . . . .Prov. 17:28

C. *Forbidden to God's:*
Watchmen. . . . .Is. 62:6
Messengers . . .Acts 5:27-42
Praisers. . . . . . . .Ps. 30:12

D. *Considered as:*
Blessing . . . . . . .Zech. 2:13
Curse. . . . . .1 Sam. 2:9
Judgment. . . . . .Jer. 8:14

E. *Of God:*
Broken in
judgment . . . . .Ps. 50:3
Misunderstood by
men. . . . . .Ps. 50:21, 23

F. *Of Christ:*
Predicted . . . . . .Is. 53:7
Before:
Sinners . . . . . . .John 8:6
High priest . . .Matt. 26:62, 63
Pilate . . . . .Matt. 27:14
Herod . . . . .Luke 23:9

Silk—*a clothing material derived from
the silkworm*

Sign of:

Luxury. . . . . .Ezek. 16:10, 13
Wantonness. . . . . . .Rev. 18:12

Silla—*twig; basket*

Quarter of suburb of
Jerusalem . . . . .2 Kin. 12:20

Siloam—*sent*

Tower of, kills 18
people. . . . . .Luke 13:4
Blind man washes
in . . . . .John 9:1-11

Silver—*a precious metal*

A. *Features concerning:*
Mined from the
earth. . . . . .Job 28:1
Melted by
fire. . . . . .Ezek. 22:22
Sign of
wealth . . . . .Gen. 13:2
Used as
money . . . . .Gen. 23:15, 16
Article of
commerce. . . . .Ezek. 27:12
Given as
presents. . . . . . .1 Kin. 10:25

Used in:
Tabernacle. . . .Ex. 38:19
Temple . . . . . . .2 Kin. 12:13
Christ sold for
30 pieces of . .{Zech. 11:12
{Matt. 26:15
Peter devoid
of . . . . .Acts 3:6

B. *Figurative of:*
God's Word. . . .Ps. 12:6
God's people. . .Zech. 13:9
Under-
standing . . . . . .Prov. 3:13, 14
Degen-
eration. . . . . . . .Is. 1:22
Rejection . . . . . .Jer. 6:30

Silversmith—*a worker in silver*

Demetrius, an
Ephesian . . . . .Acts 19:24-41

Simeon—*hearing*

1. Son of Jacob by
Leah . . . . .Gen. 29:32, 33
Joined Levi in massacre of
Shechemites . .Gen. 34:25-31
Held as hostage by
Joseph . . . . .Gen. 42:24, 36
Denounced by
Jacob . . . . .Gen. 34:30
Sons of . . . . .Gen. 46:10
2. Tribe of, descendants of Jacob's
son . . . . .Gen. 46:10
Number of, at first
census . . . . .Num. 1:23
Number of, at second
census . . . . .Num. 26:12-14
Position of, on Mt.
Gerizim . . . . . . .Deut. 27:12
Inheritance of, within
Judah's . . . . . . .Josh. 19:1-9
With Judah, fought
Canaanites. . . .Judg. 1:1, 3, 17
Victory over Ham and
Amalekites. . . .1 Chr. 4:24-43
Recognized in Ezekiel's
vision . . . . .Ezek. 48:24-33
3. Ancestor of
Christ. . . . . .Luke 3:30
4. Righteous man; blessed the
child Jesus . . . .Luke 2:25-35
5. Christian prophet at
Antioch. . . . . . . .Acts 13:1

Similitude—*likeness of two things*

A. *Expressive of:*
Physical . . . . . . .2 Chr. 4:3
Typical . . . . .Rom. 5:14

Literary
(simile) ....Ps. 144:12
Spiritual ....James 3:9

B. *Expressed by:*
"Like" ....James 1:6
"As" ....1 Pet. 2:5
"Likeness" ....Rom. 6:5
"Liken" ....Matt. 7:24, 26

Simon—*hearing*

1. Simon Peter ...Matt. 4:18
   See Peter
2. One of the Twelve; called "the
   Canaanite" ....Matt. 10:4
3. One of Jesus'
   brothers .....Matt. 13:55
4. The leper ......Matt. 26:6
5. Pharisee ......Luke 7:36-40
6. Man of
   Cyrene ....Matt. 27:32
7. Father of Judas
   Iscariot .....John 6:71
8. Sorcerer ....Acts 8:9-24
9. Tanner in
   Joppa ....Acts 9:43

Simple, the

Enlightened by (Ps. 19:7
God's Word .....(Ps. 119:105
Able to
understand ....Prov. 1:4
Receptive of
correction ....Prov. 19:25
Void of
understanding ....Prov. 7:7
Easily tempted ....Prov. 9:4, 16
Gullible ....Prov. 14:15
Inherit folly ......Prov. 14:18
Unmindful of
danger ....Prov. 22:3
The LORD
preserves ....Ps. 116:6

Simplicity—*that which is in its purest form*

A. *Necessary in:*
Prayer ....Matt. 6:5-15
Dress ....1 Pet. 3:3-5
Conduct ....2 Cor. 1:12
Giving ....Rom. 12:8
Preaching .....1 Thess. 2:3-7

B. *Purposes of, to:*
Avoid outward
display ....Matt. 6:1-4
Defeat Satan ..2 Cor. 11:3, 4
Remain pure in an evil
world ....Rom. 16:19

Sin—*disobedience of God's Law*

A. *Defined as:*
Trans-
gression ....1 John 3:4
Unrighteous-
ness ....1 John 5:17
Omission of known
duty ....James 4:17
Not from
faith ....Rom. 14:23
Thought of
foolishness ....Prov. 24:9

B. *Sources of, in:*
Satan ....John 8:44
Man's heart ....Matt. 15:19, 20
Lust ....James 1:15
Adam's transgres-
sion ....Rom. 5:12, 16
Natural birth ..Ps. 51:5

C. *Kinds of:*
National ....Prov. 14:34
Personal ....Josh. 7:20
Secret ....Ps. 90:8
Presump-
tuous ....Ps. 19:13
Open ....1 Tim. 5:24
Shameless .....Is. 3:9
Youthful ....Ps. 25:7
Public ....2 Sam. 24:10, 17
Unforgive- (Matt. 12:21, 32
able ....(John 8:24
Of ignorance ..Lev. 4:2
Willfully ......Heb. 10:26

D. *Consequences of, among the unregenerate:*
Blindness ......John 9:41
                2 Cor. 4:3, 4
Servitude ......John 8:34
Irreconcil-
able ....1 Tim. 3:1-7
Death ....Rom. 6:23

E. *God's attitude toward:*
Withholds men
from ....Gen. 20:6
Punishes for ..Ex. 32:34
Provides a fountain
for ....Zech. 13:1
Blots out .....Is. 44:22
Casts away ....Mic. 7:19
Forgives ....Ex. 34:7
Remembers no
more ....Jer. 31:34

F. *Christ's relationship to:*
Free of ....1 John 3:5
Knew no ......2 Cor. 5:21

Makes men conscious
of............John 15:22, 24
Died for our ...1 Cor. 15:3
As an offering {Is. 53:10
for...........{Heb. 9:28
Substitu- {Is. 53:5, 6
tionary.......{Matt. 26:28
Takes it
away........John 1:29
Saves His people
from ....Matt. 1:21
Has power to
forgive.......Matt. 9:6
Makes propitiation
for ....Heb. 2:17
Purges our.....Heb. 1:3
Cleanses us
from ....1 John 1:7, 9
Washes us
from ....Rev. 1:5

G. *Regenerate must:*
Acknowl-
edge ....Ps. 32:5
Confess....Ps. 51:3, 4
Be sorry for....Ps. 38:18
Not serve......Rom. 6:6
Not obey ......Rom. 6:6, 12
Subdue ....Rom. 6:14-22
Lay aside ......Heb. 12:1
Resist.........Heb. 12:4
Keep from .....Ps. 19:13

H. *Helps against:*
Use God's
Word ....Ps. 119:11
Guard the
tongue.......Ps. 39:1
Walk in the
Spirit ......Rom. 8:1-14
Avoid evil
companions ...1 Tim. 5:22
Confess to the
Lord ....1 John 1:8, 9
Exercise love ..1 Pet. 4:8
Go to the
Advocate .....1 John 2:1

Sin—*wrongdoing; transgression*

1. Wilderness between the Red
Sea and
Sinai.......Ex. 16:1
2. City of Egypt ..Ezek. 30:15, 16

Sinai

Mountain (same as Horeb) where
the Law was
given............Ex. 19:1-25

Used allegorically by
Paul.............Gal. 4:24, 25

See Horeb

Sincerity—*freedom from deceit;
genuineness*

A. *Descriptive of:*
God's Word....1 Pet. 2:2
Faith ....1 Tim. 1:5
Believer's
love.........2 Cor. 8:8, 24

B. *Should characterize:*
Young men....Titus 2:6, 7
Worship ....John 4:23, 24
Preaching.....2 Cor. 2:17
Believer's life ..2 Cor. 1:12
Public
relationships ..Judg. 9:16, 19

C. *Examples of:*
Nathanael .....John 1:47
Christ ....1 Pet. 2:22
Paul ....1 Thess. 2:3-5

Singed—*burnt hair*

Miraculously saved from
being.............Dan. 3:27

Singers—*those who make music with
voice*

Leaders of ....1 Chr. 25:2-6
Under teachers....1 Chr. 15:22, 27
Mixed............2 Chr. 35:15, 25

Singing—*uttering words in musical
tones*

A. *Descriptive of:*
Birds ....Ps. 104:12
Trees..........1 Chr. 16:33
Believers.......Eph. 5:19
Redeemed .....Rev. 5:9
Morning
stars ....Job 38:7

B. *Occasions of:*
Times of:
Victory......Ex. 15:1, 21
Revelry.......Ex. 32:18
Imprison-
ment.........Acts 16:25
Joy ....James 5:13
Lord's
Supper.......Matt. 26:30

C. *Manner of, with:*
Thanks-
giving.........Ps. 147:7

Joy . . . . Ps. 27:6
Gladness . . . . Jer. 31:7
Spirit . . . . 1 Cor. 14:15
Grace . . . . Col. 3:16

D. *Objects of:*
  God's:
   Power . . . . . . Ps. 59:16
   Mercies . . . . . . Ps. 89:1
   Righteous-
    ness . . . . Ps. 51:14
  New song . . . . . Rev. 14:3

Sinim, Sinites—*people in the far east*

1. Canaanite
   people . . . . Gen. 10:15-18
2. Distant land from which people
   will return . . . . Is. 49:7-12

Sink—*to go down under something soft*

Used literally of:

Stone . . . . 1 Sam. 17:49
Army . . . . Ex. 15:4, 5, 10
Boat . . . . Luke 5:7
Man . . . . Matt. 14:30

Sinlessness (see Holiness of Christ;
  Perfection)

Sinners—*those who are unregenerate*

A. *Descriptive of:*
  Wicked city . . . . Gen. 13:13
  Race . . . . 1 Sam. 15:18
  Wicked
   Israelites . . . . . . Amos 9:8, 10
  Jewish
   people . . . . Matt. 26:45, 47
  Man under   (Luke 5:8
   conviction . . . (Luke 18:13
  Human race . . . Rom. 5:8, 19

B. *Characteristics of:*
  Hostile to
   God . . . . Jude 15
  Scheme
   wickedly . . . . . . Ps. 26:9, 10
  Easily
   ensnared . . . . . Eccl. 7:26
  Righteous enticed
   by . . . . Prov. 1:10
  Law made
   for . . . . 1 Tim. 1:9
  Conscious of
   sin . . . . Luke 18:13
  Able to
   repent . . . . Luke 15:7, 10
  Conversion
   of . . . . James 5:20

In need of
 cleansing . . . . . James 4:8
C. *Punishment of:*
  Pursued by
   evil . . . . Prov. 13:21
  Overthrown by
   evil . . . . Prov. 13:6
  Wealth of, acquired by the
   just . . . . Prov. 13:22
  Sorrow given
   to . . . . Ezek. 18:20
  Will be
   punished . . . . . Prov. 11:31
  Will be
   consumed . . . . Ps. 104:35
D. *Christ's relationship to:*
  Came to call . . . Luke 5:32
  Friend of . . . . . . Luke 7:34
  Receives
   such . . . . Luke 15:1, 2
  Endures hostility
   from . . . . Heb. 12:3
  Separate
   from . . . . Heb. 7:26

Sion—*elevated*

Name given to all or part of Mt.
 Hermon . . . . Deut. 4:48

See Zion

Siphmoth—*fruitful*

David shares spoils
 with . . . . 1 Sam. 30:26-28

Sippai—*Yahweh is preserver*

Philistine giant . . . . 1 Chr. 20:4
Called Saph . . . . . . 2 Sam. 21:18

Sirah—*turning aside*

Well near
 Hebron . . . . 2 Sam. 3:26

Sirion—*coat of mail*

Sidonian name for Mt.
 Hermon . . . . Deut. 3:9

Sisera—*meditation*

1. Canaanite commander of
   Jabin's army; slain by
   Jael . . . . Judg. 4:2-22
2. Ancestor of postexilic
   Nethinim . . . . . . Ezra 2:43, 53

Sismai—*Yahweh is distinguished*

Judahite . . . . 1 Chr. 2:40

Sister

A. *Descriptive of:*
Female
relative ...... Gen. 24:30-60
Women of the same
tribe .... Num. 25:18

B. *Features concerning:*
Protected by:
Brothers ...... Gen. 34:13-31
Laws .... Lev. 18:9-13, 18
Friction
between ..... Luke 10:39, 40
Loved by
Jesus .... John 11:5

C. *Figurative of:*
Samaria and
Jerusalem ..... Ezek. 23:1-49
Christian ..... Matt. 12:50
Christian
woman ...... Rom. 16:1
Church .... 2 John 13

Sistrum—*a musical instrument*

A part of
worship .... 2 Sam. 6:5

Sit

A. *Descriptive of:*
Man .... Gen. 18:1
Judge .... Ex. 18:13, 14
Priest .... Zech. 6:13
King .... Deut. 17:15, 18
God .... Ps. 2:4
Messiah .... Ps. 110:1

B. *Purposes of, to:*
Eat .... Matt. 26:20, 21
Rest .... John 4:6
Mourn .... Neh. 1:4
Teach .... Matt. 26:55
Transact
business ...... Matt. 9:9
Beg .... Luke 18:35
Learn .... Mark 5:15
Ride .... Matt. 21:5
Worship ...... Acts 2:2

C. *Figurative of Christ's:*
Session .... Heb. 1:3
Rule .... Matt. 19:28
Judgment ..... Matt. 25:31

Sitnah—*enmity*

Well dug by Isaac near
Gerar .... Gen. 26:21

Sivan

Third month of the Jewish
and Babylonian
year .... Esth. 8:9

Skeptical—*characterized by doubts*

Thomas, the
doubter .... John 20:24-28

Skilled—*those possessing special abilities*

A. *Required of:*
Soldiers .... 1 Chr. 5:18
Craftsmen ..... 2 Chr. 2:7, 14
Musicians ...... 2 Chr. 34:12

B. *Obtained by:*
Spirit's help .... Ex. 31:2-5
God's Word .... Ps. 119:98-100
Lᴏʀᴅ's help .... Ps. 144:1

Skins—*the outer covering of a body*

A. *Of animals, used for:*
Clothing .... Gen. 3:21
Deception ..... Gen. 27:16
Coverings ..... Ex. 26:14
Bottles .... Josh. 9:4

B. *Of man:*
Diseased .... Lev. 13:1-46
Sign of race ... Jer. 13:23
Seal of death .. Job 19:26

Skull—*skeleton of the head*

Abimelech's crushed by a
woman .... Judg. 9:53
Jezebel's left by
dogs .... 2 Kin. 9:30-37
They brought Him to a place
called .... Mark 15:22
Another name for
Golgotha .... Matt. 27:33

See Golgotha

Sky—*the expanse of the heaven*

A. *Place of:*
Stars .... Heb. 11:12
Expansion ..... Job 37:18
Weather
changes ...... Matt. 16:2, 3
Thunder ...... Ps. 77:17

B. *Figurative of:*
God's abode ... Ps. 18:11
Righ-
teousness ..... Is. 45:8
Ultimate
judgment ..... Jer. 51:9

Slander—*a malicious statement*

A. *Described as:*
Destructive ....Prov. 11:9
Deceitful ......Ps. 52:2
Deluding ......Prov. 10:18
Devouring .....Prov. 16:27-30

B. *Hurled against:*
Joseph.........Gen. 39:14-19
David..........2 Sam. 10:3
Jews...........Ezra 4:7-16
Christ ....Matt. 26:59-61
Paul ....Acts 24:5, 6
Stephen ....Acts 6:11
Christians .....1 Pet. 2:12

C. *Hurled against the righteous by:*
Devil ....Job 1:9-11
Revilers ......1 Pet. 3:16
Hypocrites.....Prov. 11:9
False leaders...3 John 9, 10

D. *Charged against Christ as:*
Winebibber ....Matt. 11:19
Blasphemer ....Matt. 9:3
Demonized ....John 8:48, 52
Rebel ....Luke 23:5
Insur-
rectionist ....Luke 23:2

E. *Christians:*
Warned
against........Titus 3:1, 2
Must endure ...Matt. 5:11, 12
Must lay
aside..........Eph. 4:31

Slave, slavery—*a state of bondage*

A. *Acquired by:*
Purchase ......Gen. 17:12
Voluntary
service........Ex. 21:5-6
Birth ....Ex. 21:2-4
Capture ......Deut. 20:11-14
Debt...........2 Kin. 4:1
Arrest ....Ex. 22:2, 3
Inheritance ...Lev. 25:46
Gift...........Gen. 29:24, 29

B. *Rights of:*
Sabbath rest ...Ex. 20:10
Share in religious
feasts ....Deut. 12:12, 18
Membership in
covenant......Gen. 17:10-14
Refuge for
fugitive ......Deut. 23:15, 16
Murder of,
punishable ...Ex. 21:12
Freedom of, if
maimed .....Ex. 21:26, 27

Entitled to
justice ....Job 31:13-15

C. *Privileges of:*
Entrusted with
missions ......Gen. 24:1-14
Advice of,
heeded........1 Sam. 9:5-10
Marriage in master's
house ....1 Chr. 2:34, 35
Rule over
sons ....Prov. 17:2
May become
heir...........Gen. 15:1-4
May secure
freedom.......Ex. 21:2-6

D. *State of, under Christianity:*
Union "in
Christ".......Gal. 3:28
Treatment of with
justice ....Eph. 6:9
Duties of, as pleasing
God...........Eph. 6:5-8

Sleep—*a state of complete or partial
unconsciousness*

A. *Descriptive of:*
Slumber ......Prov. 6:4, 10
Desolation .....Jer. 51:39, 57
Unregen-
eracy ....1 Thess. 5:6, 7
Death ....John 11:11-14
Spiritual
indifference ...Matt. 25:5
Prophetic
vision.........Dan. 8:18

B. *Beneficial:*
When given   (Ps. 3:5
by God.......(Ps. 127:2
While trusting
God...........Ps. 4:8
While obeying
parents ....Prov. 6:20-22
When following
wisdom ....Prov. 3:21-24
To the working
man ....Eccl. 5:12
After duty is
done ....Ps. 132:1-5
During a pleasant
dream.........Jer. 31:23-26

C. *Condemned:*
When
excessive......Prov. 6:9-11
During
harvest ....Prov. 10:5
In times of
danger ....Matt. 26:45-47

D. *Inability to:*
Caused by
worry.........Dan. 2:1
Produced by
insomnia......Esth. 6:1
Brought on by
overwork......Gen. 31:40

Sling—*an instrument for throwing stones*

A. *Used by:*
Warriors.......Judg. 20:16
David.....1 Sam. 17:40-50

B. *Figurative of:*
God's
punishment...1 Sam. 25:29
Foolishness....Prov. 26:8

Slothfulness, sluggard—*laziness*

A. *Sources of, in:*
Excessive
sleep.........Prov. 6:9-11
Laziness.......Prov. 19:15, 24
Indifference....Judg. 18:9
Desires........Prov. 21:25
Fearful imagina-
tions..........Prov. 22:13

B. *Way of:*
Brings
hunger.......Prov. 19:15
Leads to
poverty.......Prov. 20:4
Produces
waste........Prov. 18:9
Causes decay..Eccl. 10:18
Results in forced
labor..........Prov. 12:24

C. *Antidotes of, in:*
Faithfulness...Matt. 25:26-30
Fervent spirit..Rom. 12:11
Following the
faithful......Heb. 6:12

Small—*little in size; few in number*

A. *Applied to God's:*
Choice.........Num. 16:5, 9
Faithful
remnant......Is. 1:9

B. *Applied to man's:*
Sin...........Ezek. 16:20
Unconcern....Zech. 4:10

Smith—*a metal worker*

Blacksmith.......1 Sam. 13:19, 20
Worker in iron....Is. 44:12
Tubal-Cain, first...Gen. 4:22

Demetrius,
silversmith.......Acts 19:24-27
Alexander,
coppersmith......2 Tim. 4:14

Smoke

A. *Resulting from:*
Destruction....Gen. 19:28
God's
presence......Is. 6:4
God's
vengeance....Is. 34:8-10
Babylon's
end..........Rev. 14:8-11
World's end...Is. 51:6

B. *Figurative of:*
Our life........Ps. 102:3
Spiritual
distress......Ps. 119:83
Something
offensive......Is. 65:5
Spirit's
advent.......Joel 2:29, 30

Smyrna—*a city of Iona in Asia Minor*

One of the seven
churches.........Rev. 1:11

Snail

Creature with a spiral
tail...............Ps. 58:8

Snake charmer

Alluded to........Ps. 58:4, 5

Snares—*traps*

A. *Uses of:*
Catch birds....Prov. 7:23

B. *Figurative of:*
Pagan
nations.......Josh. 23:12, 13
Idols.........Judg. 2:3
God's represen-
tative.........Ex. 10:7
Words.........Prov. 6:2
Wicked
works.........Ps. 9:16
Fear of man...Prov. 29:25
Immoral
woman......Eccl. 7:26
Christ.........Is. 8:14, 15
Sudden
destruction....Luke 21:34, 35
Riches.........1 Tim. 6:9, 10
Devil's trap....2 Tim. 2:26

Sneezed

Seven times.......2 Kin. 4:35

Snow—*frozen crystallized flakes of water*

A. *Characteristics of:*
Comes in
winter ....Prov. 26:1
Sent by God ...Job 37:6
Waters the
earth..........Is. 55:10
Melts with
heat ....Job 6:16, 17
Notable event
during ....2 Sam. 23:20

B. *Whiteness illustrative of:*
Leprosy.........Ex. 4:6
Converted ⎰Ps. 51:7
sinner ⎱Is. 1:18
Nazirite's
purity.........Lam. 4:7
Angel..........Matt. 28:3
Risen Christ ...Rev. 1:14

So

Egyptian king.....2 Kin. 17:4

Soap

Figuratively in ....Mal. 3:2

Sober, sobriety

A. *Described as:*
Sanity ....2 Cor. 5:13
Soberness (not
drunk).........1 Tim. 3:2, 11
Temperate
nature ....Titus 1:8
Humble
mind.........Rom. 12:3
Moral
rectitude......Titus 2:12
Self- ⎰1 Cor. 7:9
control........⎱Gal. 5:23

B. *Incentives to, found in:*
Lord's return ..1 Thess. 5:1-7
Nearness of the
end ....1 Pet. 4:7
Satan's
attacks........1 Cor. 7:5

C. *Required of:*
Christians .....1 Thess. 5:6, 8
Church
officers........1 Tim. 3:2, 3
Wives of church
officers........1 Tim. 3:11
Aged men .....Titus 2:2

Young
women.......Titus 2:4
Young men ...Titus 2:6
Women.......1 Tim. 2:9
Children ......1 Tim. 2:15
Evangelists ...2 Tim. 4:5

See Temperance

Sociability—*friendly relations in social gatherings*

A. *Manifested in:*
Family life.....John 12:1-9
National life ...Neh. 8:9-18
Church life ....Acts 2:46

B. *Christian's kind, governed by:*
No fellowship with
evil ....2 Cor. 6:14-18
Righteous
living ....Titus 2:12
Honesty in all
things.........Col. 3:9-14

Socialism (see Communism, Christian)

Socoh, Sochoh—*thorn*

1. Town in south
Judah.........Josh. 15:1, 35
Where David killed
Goliath ....1 Sam. 17:1, 49
2. Town in Judah's hill
country ....Josh. 15:1, 48

Sodi—*an acquaintance*

Father of the Zebulunite
spy...............Num. 13:10

Sodom—*burnt*

A. *History of:*
Located in Jordan
plain ....Gen. 13:10
Became Lot's
residence......Gen. 13:11-13
Wickedness of,
notorious .....Gen. 13:13
Plundered by Chedor-
laomer........Gen. 14:9-24
Abraham interceded
for ....Gen. 18:16-33
Destroyed by
God..........Gen. 19:1-28
Lot sent out
of.............Gen. 19:29, 30

B. *Destruction of, illustrative of:*
God's wrath ...Deut. 29:23
Sudden
destruction....Lam. 4:6

Total
destruction....Jer. 49:18
Future
judgment .....Matt. 11:23, 24
Example to the
ungodly.......2 Pet. 2:6

C. *Sin of, illustrative of:*
Shame-
lessness.......Is. 3:9
Obduracy.....Jer. 23:14
Unnatural-
ness..........Jude 7

D. *Figurative of:*
Wickedness....Deut. 32:32
Jerusalem......Is. 1:9, 10
Judah.........Ezek. 16:46-63

Sodomite—*a male cult prostitute*

Prohibition of .....Deut. 23:17, 18
Prevalence of, under
Rehoboam.......1 Kin. 14:24
Asa's removal of ..1 Kin. 15:11, 12
Jehoshaphat's riddance
of ....1 Kin. 22:46
Josiah's reforms
against ....2 Kin. 23:7
Result of
unbelief ....Rom. 1:27

Soil—*dirt*

It was planted in
good ....Ezek. 17:8
Uzziah loved it....2 Chr. 26:10

Sojourn, sojourner

A. *Descriptive of:*
Abram in
Egypt.........Gen. 12:10
Jacob with
Laban......Gen. 32:4
Israel in
Egypt.......Gen. 47:4
Stranger.......Ex. 12:48, 49
Wandering
Levite.......Deut. 18:6
Naomi in
Moab......Ruth 1:1
Remnant in
Egypt.......Jer. 42:15-22
Jews in
captivity ......Ezra 1:4

B. *Characterized by:*
Simplicity of
living ....Heb. 11:9
Being among
enemies.......2 Kin. 8:1, 2

Lord's
blessing ......Gen. 26:2, 3

C. *Figurative of:*
Christian in the
world ....1 Pet. 1:17

See Foreigners; Strangers

Sold

Descriptive of:

Purchase..........Matt. 26:9
Slavery......Ps. 105:17
Bondage to sin ....Rom. 7:14

Soldiers—*military agents of a nation*

A. *Good characteristics of:*
Obedience .....Matt. 8:9
Devotion ......Acts 10:7
Subduing
riots ....Acts 21:31-35
Guarding
prisoners......Acts 12:4-6

B. *Bad charcteristics of:*
Cowardice .....Deut. 20:8
Discontent and
violence......Luke 3:14
Rashness ......Acts 27:42
Bribery ....Matt. 28:12
Irreligion .....John 19:2, 3, 23

C. *Figurative of:*
Christians .....2 Tim. 2:4
Christian
workers.......Phil. 2:25
Spiritual
armor.........Eph. 6:10-18

Solitude—*aloneness*

For:

Adam, not good...Gen. 2:18
Prayer, good .....Matt. 6:6
Matt. 14:23
Rest, necessary....Mark 6:30, 31

Solomon—*peace*

A. *Life of:*
David's son by Bath-
sheba ....2 Sam. 12:24
Name of,
significant.....1 Chr. 22:9
Anointed over
opposition.....1 Kin. 1:5-48
Spared
Adonijah......1 Kin. 1:49-53
Received dying instruction from
David.......1 Kin. 2:1-10
Purged his kingdom of corrupt
leaders........1 Kin. 2:11-46

Prayer of, for
wisdom .... 1 Kin. 3:1-15
Organized his
kingdom ...... 1 Kin. 4:1-28
Fame of, world
wide .... 1 Kin. 4:29-34
Built the
Temple........ 1 Kin. 5-6
Dedicated the
Temple........ 1 Kin. 8:22-66
Built personal
palace......... 1 Kin. 7:1-12
LORD reappeared
to............. 1 Kin. 9:1-9
Strengthened his
kingdom ...... 1 Kin. 9:10-28
Received queen of
Sheba......... 1 Kin. 10:1-13
Encouraged
commerce...... 1 Kin. 10:14-29
Falls into polygamy and
idolatry ...... 1 Kin. 11:1-8
God warned
him .... 1 Kin. 11:9-13
Adversaries arise against
him .... 1 Kin. 11:14-40
Reign and
death .... 1 Kin. 11:41-43

B. *Good features of:*
Chooses an understanding
heart .... 1 Kin. 3:5-9
Exhibited sound
judgment ..... 1 Kin. 3:16-28
Excels in
wisdom ...... 1 Kin. 4:29-34
Great writer ... 1 Kin. 4:32
Writer of
Psalms........ Ps. 72 (Title)

C. *Bad features of:*
Loves luxury .. Eccl. 2:1-11
Marries
pagans .... 1 Kin. 11:1-3
Turns to
idolatry .... 1 Kin. 11:4-8
Enslaves
Israel .... 1 Kin. 12:1-4

Son

A. *Descriptive of:*
Male child ..... Gen. 4:25, 26
Half brothers .. Gen. 25:9
Grandson...... Gen. 29:5
Disciple....... Prov. 7:1
One possessing a certain
character ... 1 Sam. 2:12
One destined to a certain
end .... John 17:12

Messiah .... Is. 7:14
Angels........ Job 1:6

B. *Characteristics of, sometimes:*
Jealous .... Judg. 9:2, 18
Quite
different ..... Gen. 9:18-27
Disloyal .... Luke 15:25-30
Unlike their
father........ 2 Sam. 13:30-39
Spiritually
different ..... Gen. 25:22-34

C. *Admonitions addressed to,
concerning:*
Instruction .... Prov. 1:8
Sinners .... Prov. 1:10-19
Wisdom ...... Prov. 3:13-35
Correction.... Prov. 3:11, 12
Immorality ... Prov. 5:1-23
Life's
dangers ...... Prov. 6:1-35

Son-in-law—*a daughter's husband*

Sinful............ Gen. 19:14
Believing........ Mark 1:29, 30

Son of God—*a title indicating Christ's deity*

A. *Descriptive of Christ as:*
Eternally   { Ps. 2:7
begotten ..... { Heb. 1:5
Messianic
King .... Ps. 89:26, 27
Virgin-born .... Luke 1:31-35
Trinity-
member....... Matt. 28:19
Priest-king..... Heb. 1:8
Heb. 5:5, 6

B. *Witnesses of, by:*
Father......... Matt. 17:5
Demons ...... Mark 5:7
Satan......... Matt. 4:3, 6
Men .... Matt. 16:16
Christ
Himself ..... John 9:35-37
His
resurrection... Rom. 1:1-4
Christians ..... Acts 2:36
Scriptures ..... John 20:31
Inner
witness .... 1 John 5:10-13

C. *Significance of, as indicating:*
Cost of man's reconcilia-
tion............ Rom. 5:6-11
Greatness of God's
love............ John 3:16

Sin of
unbelief.......Heb. 10:28, 29
Worship due
Christ.......Rev. 4:11
Dignity of
human   {Rom. 8:3
nature ....{Heb. 2:14
Humanity of
Christ.......Gal. 4:4
Pattern of
glorifi-   {Rom. 8:29
cation.......{Phil. 3:21
Destruction of
Satan ....1 John 3:8
Uniqueness of
Christ.......Heb. 1:5-9

D. *Belief in Christ as:*
Derived from the
Scriptures.....John 20:31
Necessary for eternal
life............John 3:18, 36
Source of eternal
life............John 6:40
Foundation of the
faith ....Acts 9:20
Affirmation of
deity ....1 John 2:23, 24
Illustrated .....John 11:14-44

E. *Powers of Christ as, to:*
Have life in
Himself ....John 5:26
Reveal the
Father ....Matt. 11:27
Glorify the
Father ....John 17:1
Do the Father's
works.........John 5:19, 20
Redeem men...Gal. 4:4, 5
Give freedom ..John 8:36
Raise the
dead ....John 5:21, 25
Judge men.....John 5:22

Son of Man—*a self-designation of Christ*

A. *Title of, applied to:*
Ezekiel ......Ezek. 2:1, 3, 6
Daniel ....Dan. 8:17
Messiah ....Dan. 7:13
Christ:
By Himself....Matt. 8:20
By only Stephen
elsewhere ....Acts 7:56
In John's
vision ....Rev. 1:13

B. *As indicative of Christ's:*
Self-
designation ...Matt. 16:13

Humanity......Matt. 11:19
Messiahship ...Luke 18:31
Lordship.......Matt. 12:8
Sovereignty....Matt. 13:41
Obedience .....Phil. 2:8
Suffering......Mark 9:12
Death ....Matt. 12:40
Resurrection...Matt. 17:9-23
Regal power...Matt. 16:28
Return........Matt. 24:27-37
Glorification ...Heb. 2:6-10

C. *Christ's powers as, to:*
Forgive sins ...Matt. 9:6
Save men......Luke 19:10
Redeem men...Matt. 20:28
Rule His
Church ....Col. 1:17, 18
Reward men...Matt. 16:27
Matt. 19:28

Song of Solomon—*a book of the Old Testament*

The bride and the
bridegroom......Song 1
Song of the
bride ....Song 2:8–3:5
Song of the
bridegroom......Song 4:1-15
The bride
meditates........Song 4:16–6:3
The bridegroom
appeals..........Song 6:4–7:9
Lovers united ....Song 7:10–8:14

Songs

A. *Described as:*
New ....Rev. 5:9
Spiritual ......Eph. 5:19

B. *Uses of, as:*
Witness........Deut. 31:19-22
Torment........Ps. 137:3
March ....Num. 21:17, 18
Processional ...1 Chr. 13:7, 8

C. *Expressive of:*
Triumph.......Judg. 5:12
Physical joy ...Gen. 31:27
Spiritual joy ...Ps. 119:54
Deliverance ...Ps. 32:7
Hypocrisy .....Amos 5:23
Derision ....Ps. 69:12

D. *Figurative of:*
Passover
(the Lord's   {Is. 30:29
Supper) ......{Matt. 26:26-30
Messiah's
advent........Is. 42:10
Gospel age.....Is. 26:1, 2

Song writer

Solomon, famous
as . . . . 1 Kin. 4:32

Sonship of believers

A. *Evidences of, seen in:*
New nature . . . 1 John 3:9-12
Possession of the
Spirit . . . . Rom. 8:15-17
Chastise-
ment . . . . Heb. 12:5-8

B. *Blessedness of, manifested in:*
Regener-
ation . . . . John 1:12
Adoption . . . . . Gal. 4:5, 6
Glorification . . . Rom. 8:19-21

Soothsayer—*a diviner, fortune teller*

Among
Philistines . . . . Is. 2:6
At Babylon . . . . Dan. 2:27
At Philippi . . . . . . Acts 16:12, 16
Unable to
interpret . . . . Dan. 4:7
Forbidden in
Israel . . . . Mic. 5:12

See Divination

Sopater—*of sound parentage*

One of Paul's
companions . . . . . . Acts 20:4

Sophereth—*writer, scribe*

Descendants of Solomon's
servants . . . . Neh. 7:57

Sorcerers—*supposed possessors of
supernatural powers*

A. *Prevalence of, in:*
Assyria . . . . Nah. 3:4, 5
Egypt . . . . Ex. 7:11
Babylon . . . . . Is. 47:9-13
Palestine . . . . . . Acts 8:9-24
Last days . . . . . Rev. 9:21

B. *Punishment of, described:*
Legally . . . . Deut. 18:10-12
Prophetically . . Mal. 3:5
Symbolically . . Rev. 21:8

See Divination; Magic, magician

Sorcery—*the practice of magic*

Forbidden in
Israel . . . . Deut. 18:10
Condemned by the
prophets . . . . Mic. 5:12

Practiced by
Manasseh . . . . 2 Chr. 33:6
Work of the
flesh . . . . Gal. 5:20

Sore

Result of plague . . . Lev. 13:42, 43

Sorek—*a choice vine*

Valley, home of
Delilah . . . . Judg. 16:4

Sorrow—*grief*

A. *Kinds of:*
Hypocritical . . . Matt. 14:9
Unfruitful . . . . . Matt. 19:22
Temporary . . . . . John 16:6, 20-22
Continual . . . . . . Rom. 9:2
Fruitful . . . . 2 Cor. 7:8-11
Christian . . . . . . 1 Thess. 4:13

B. *Caused by:*
Sin . . . . Gen. 3:16, 17
Death . . . . John 11:33-36
Drunkenness . . Prov. 23:29-35
Love of
money . . . . 1 Tim. 6:10
Apostasy . . . . . . Ps. 16:4
Persecution . . . Esth. 9:22
Hardship of
life . . . . Ps. 90:10
Knowledge . . . . Eccl. 1:18
Distressing
news . . . . Acts 20:37, 38

C. *Of the righteous:*
Not like the
world's . . . . 1 Thess. 4:13
Sometimes
intense . . . . Ps. 18:4, 5
Seen in the
face . . . . Neh. 2:2-4
None in God's
blessings . . . . . Prov. 10:22
Shown in
repentance . . . . 2 Cor. 7:10
To be
removed . . . . . . Is. 25:8
None in
heaven . . . . Rev. 21:4
Shall flee
away . . . . Is. 51:11

See Grief

Sosipater—*saving a father*

Kinsman of Paul . . Rom. 16:21

Sosthenes—*of sound strength*

1. Ruler of the synagogue at
   Corinth ......Acts 18:17
2. Paul's Christian
   brother ....1 Cor. 1:1

Sotai—*Yahweh is turning aside*

Head of a family of
   servants.........Ezra 2:55

Soul—*the immaterial part of man*

A. *Descriptive of:*
   People.........Acts 2:41, 43
   Sinner ....James 5:20
   Emotional
      life.............1 Sam. 18:1, 3
   Spiritual life ..Ps. 42:1, 2, 4
   Disembodied ⎰Rev. 6:9
      state ⎱Rev. 20:4

B. *Characteristics of:*
   Belongs to
      God............Ezek. 18:3, 4
   Possesses
      immortality ...Matt. 10:28
   Most vital
      asset..........Matt. 16:26
   Leaves body at
      death ....Gen. 35:18

C. *Abilities of, able to:*
   Believe ....Heb. 10:39
   Love God......Luke 10:27
   Sin ....Mic. 6:7
   Prosper........3 John 2
   Survive
      death ....Matt. 10:28

D. *Duties of, to:*
   Keep itself .....Deut. 4:9
   Seek the
      LORD..........Deut. 4:29
   Love the
      LORD..........Deut. 6:5
   Serve the
      LORD..........Deut. 10:12
   Store God's
      Word ....Deut. 11:18
   Keep God's
      Law ....Deut. 26:16
   Obey God......Deut. 30:2, 6, 10
   Get wisdom....Prov. 19:8

E. *Enemies of, seen in:*
   Fleshly lusts ...1 Pet. 2:11
   Evil environ-
      ment..........2 Pet. 2:8
   Sin ....Lev. 5:4, 15, 17
   Adultery.......Prov. 6:32
   Evil men.......Prov. 22:24, 25
   Ignorance .....Prov. 8:36
   Hell ....Prov. 23:14

F. *Of the righteous:*
   Kept by God...Ps. 121:7
   Vexed by sin ..2 Pet. 2:8
   Subject to
      authorities ....Rom. 13:1
   Purified by
      obedience .....1 Pet. 1:22
   Not allowed to
      famish ....Prov. 10:3
   Restored.......Ps. 23:1, 3
   Enriched.......Prov. 11:25
   Satisfied ....Prov. 13:25
   Reign with
      Christ.........Rev. 20:4

G. *Of the wicked:*
   Desires evil ....Prov. 21:10
   Delights in abomina-
      tions..........Is. 66:3
   Has nothing ...Prov. 13:4
   Required.......Luke 12:19, 20
   To be
      punished......Rom. 2:9

Soul winning

Importance of.....James 5:20
Christ's
   command ....Matt. 4:19
Our reward ......Dan. 12:3

Sound (see Sober)

Sound doctrine

A. *Manifested in:*
   Heart's
      prayer ....Ps. 119:80
   Speech ....2 Tim. 1:13
   Righteous
      living ....1 Tim. 1:10

B. *Need of:*
   For
      exhortation ...Titus 1:9
   For the faith ...Titus 1:13
   Denied by
      some..........2 Tim. 4:3

Sour grapes—*not yet mature*

Used
   proverbially ......Jer. 31:29, 30

Sowing—*scattering seed*

A. *Restrictions upon, regarding:*
   Sabbath year ..Lev. 25:3-22
   Mingled seed ..Lev. 19:19
   Weather.......Eccl. 11:4, 6

B. *Figurative of evil things:*

Iniquity........Job 4:8
Wind ....Hos. 8:7
Discord........Prov. 6:14, 19
Strife..........Prov. 16:28
False
teaching ......Matt. 13:25, 39
Sin ....Gal. 6:7, 8

C. *Figurative of good things:*

God's Word.....Is. 55:10
Reward........2 Cor. 9:6, 10
Gospel.........Matt. 13:3, 4, 37
Gospel
messengers ...John 4:36, 37
Resurrection...1 Cor. 15:36-44
Eternal life ....Gal. 6:7-9

Spain—*a country in southwest Europe*

Paul desires to
visit ....Rom. 15:24, 28

Sparrow—*a small bird*

Value of ....Matt. 10:29, 31

Spearmen—*infantry men with spears*

One of, pierces Christ's
side ....John 19:34
Paul's military
escort ....Acts 23:23, 24

Special—*something separated to one's own use*

A. *Applied literally to:*

Israel (God's   {Ex. 19:5
own).........   {Deut. 7:6
Treasure (Solomon's
own).........Eccl. 2:8
Translated:
"Jewels"....Mal. 3:17

B. *Applied figuratively to:*

True Israel.....Ps. 135:4
Christian ......Titus 2:14
True church ...1 Pet. 2:9

Speck—*a small particle*

Used in contrast to a
beam.............Matt. 7:3, 5

Speckled

Spotted (of
goats)............Gen. 30:32-39
Colored (of
birds) ....Jer. 12:9

Speech—*the intelligible utterance of the mouth*

A. *Of the wicked, consisting of:*

Lies ....Ps. 58:3
Cursing........Ps. 59:12
Enticements ...Prov. 7:21
Blasphemies ...Dan. 7:25
Earthly
things........John 3:31
Deception .....Rom. 16:18

B. *Of the righteous, consisting of:*

God's righ-
teousness ...Ps. 35:28
Wisdom ....1 Cor. 2:6, 7
God's Word...Ps. 119:172
Truth...........Eph. 4:25
Mystery of
Christ.........Col. 4:3, 4
Sound
doctrine.......Titus 2:1, 8

Speed—*to hasten*

"Let him make"...Is. 5:19
"They shall come
with"..............Is. 5:26

Spending—*paying out money or service for things*

A. *Wastefully, on:*

Harlots........Luke 15:30
Physicians .....Mark 5:26

B. *Wisely:*

In Christ's
service ....2 Cor. 12:15

Spices—*aromatic vegetable compounds*

A. *Uses of:*

Food ....Song 8:2
Incense........Ex. 30:34-38
Fragrance .....Song 4:10

B. *Features concerning:*

Used as
presents.......Gen. 43:11
Objects of
commerce.....Gen. 37:25
Tokens of royal
favor..........1 Kin. 10:2
Stored in the
temple ....1 Chr. 9:29
Sign of
wealth ....2 Kin. 20:13

Spider

Web of, figurative of:

Insecurity..........Is. 59:5
Godless ....Job 8:14

Spies—*secret agents of a foreign government*

A. *Purpose of, to:*
Search out
Canaan .... Num. 13:1-33
Prepare for
invasion....... Josh. 2:1-21
Search out new
land.......... Judg. 18:2-17
Make false
charges .... Luke 20:20

B. *Men accused of, falsely:*
Jacob's sons ... Gen. 42:9-34
David's
servants....... 2 Sam. 10:3

Spikenard

Used as a
perfume........ Song 1:12
Mary uses it in
anointing ⎰ Mark 14:3
Jesus.......... ⎱ John 12:3

Spill—*to flow forth*

Water.......... 2 Sam. 14:14
Wine.......... Luke 5:37

Spinning—*twisting fibers together to form cloth*

Work done by
women.......... Ex. 35:25
Sign of industry... Prov. 31:19
As an
illustration .... Matt. 6:28

Spirit—*an immaterial being*

A. *Descriptive of:*
Holy Spirit..... Gen. 1:2
Angels......... Heb. 1:7, 14
Man's immaterial
nature .... 1 Cor. 2:11
Evil........... 1 Sam. 16:14-23
Believer's immaterial
nature .... 1 Cor. 5:3, 5
Controlling
influence...... Is. 29:10
Inward
reality .... Rom. 2:29
Disembodied ⎰ Heb. 12:23
state .... ⎱ 1 Pet. 3:19

B. *Characteristics of, in man:*
Center of
emotions...... 1 Kin. 21:5
Source of
passions....... Ezek. 3:14

Cause of volitions
(will)......... Prov. 16:32
Subject to
divine ⎰ Deut. 2:30
influence..... ⎱ Is. 19:14
Leaves body ⎰ Eccl. 12:7
at death...... ⎱ James 2:26

See Soul

Spirit, Holy (see Holy Spirit)

Spirit of Christ

A. *Descriptive of the Holy Spirit as:*
Dwelling in Old Testament
prophets ...... 1 Pet. 1:10-11
Sent by God ... Gal. 4:6
Given to
believers ...... Rom. 8:9
Supplying
believers ...... Phil. 1:19
Produces
boldness ...... Acts 4:29-31
Commanded... Eph. 5:18

B. *Christ's human spirit (consciousness), of His:*
Perception..... Mark 2:8
Emotions ...... Mark 8:12
Life........... Luke 23:46

Spirits, discerning

A. *Described as:*
Spiritual gift... 1 Cor. 12:10
Necessary ..... 1 Thess. 5:19-21

B. *Tests of:*
Christ's:
Deity .... 1 Cor. 12:3
Humanity..... 1 John 4:1-6
Christian
fellowship..... 1 John 2:18, 19

Spiritual—*the holy or immaterial*

A. *Applied to:*
Gifts........... 1 Cor. 12:1
Law.......... Rom. 7:14
Things........ Rom. 15:27
Christians ..... 1 Cor. 3:1
Resurrected
body .... 1 Cor. 15:44-46
Evil forces..... Eph. 6:12

B. *Designating, Christians:*
Ideal state ..... 1 Cor. 3:1
Discernment... 1 Cor. 2:13-15
Duty .... Gal. 6:1
Manner of
life............ Col. 3:16

Spiritual gifts (see Gifts, spiritual)

Spiritually—*a holy frame of mind*

Source of ....Gal. 5:22-26
Expression of .....1 Cor. 13:1-13
Growth in........2 Pet. 1:4-11
Enemies of........1 John 2:15-17

Spite—*an injury prompted by contempt*

Inflicted upon
Christ ....Matt. 22:6

Spitting, spittle

A. *Symbolic of:*
Contempt......Num. 12:14
Rejection ......Matt. 26:67
Uncleanness ...Lev. 15:8

B. *Miraculous uses of, to heal:*
Dumb man ....Mark 7:33-35
Blind man .....Mark 8:23-25
Man born
blind ....John 9:6, 7

Spoil—*loot or plunder*

Cattle............Josh. 8:2
Silver and Gold ...Nah. 2:9

See Plunder

Spokesman—*one who speaks for others*

Aaron deputed to
be ....Ex. 4:14-16

Sponge—*a very absorbent sea fossil*

Full of vinegar, offered to
Christ ....Matt. 27:48

Spot, spotless

A. *Descriptive of:*
Blemish on the
face...........Job 11:15
Imperfection of the
body ....Song 4:7
Mixed colors...Gen. 30:32-39
Leopard's
spots..........Jer. 13:23

B. *Figuratively ("spotless") of:*
False
teachers ......2 Pet. 2:13
Christ's
death ....1 Pet. 1:19
Believer's
perfection.....2 Pet. 3:14
Glorified
Church ......Eph. 5:27
Obedience .....1 Tim. 6:14

Springtime—*the season of nature's rebirth*

Symbolically
described........Song 2:11-13

Sprinkle

A. *Used literally of:*
Water ....Num. 8:7
Oil.............Lev. 14:16

B. *Of blood, used in:*
Passover......Ex. 12:21, 22
Sinaitic ⎰Ex. 24:8
covenant.....⎱Heb. 9:19, 21
Sin offering....Lev. 4:6
New
covenant....Heb. 12:24

C. *Used figuratively of:*
Regener-
ation........Heb. 10:22
Purification....1 Pet. 1:2

Square—*having four equal sides*

Altar..............Ex. 27:1
Breastplate.......Ex. 39:8, 9
City of God ......Rev. 21:16

Stab—*to pierce with a knife*

Asahel by Abner ..2 Sam. 2:22, 23
Abner by Joab ....2 Sam. 3:27
Amasa by Joab....2 Sam. 20:10

Stachys—*head of grain*

One whom Paul
loved.............Rom. 16:9

Staff—*a long stick or rod*

A traveler's
support...........Gen. 32:10
Denotes food
support...........Lev. 26:26
A military
weapon ....Is. 10:24

Stairs, winding

Part of Solomon's
Temple...........1 Kin. 6:8

Stalls—*quarters for animals*

40,000 in Solomon's
time..............1 Kin. 4:26

Stammerer—*one who stutters*

Used of judicial
punishment ......Is. 28:11
Of the Gospel
age...............Is. 32:1, 4

Stars

A. *Features concerning:*
Created by
God..........Gen. 1:16
Ordained by
God..........Ps. 8:3
Set in the
expanse......Gen. 1:17
Follow fixed
ordinances....Jer. 31:35, 36
Named by
God..........Ps. 147:4
Established
forever........Ps. 148:3, 6
Of vast
numbers......Gen. 15:5
Manifest God's
power.........Is. 40:26
Of different
proportions ..1 Cor. 15:41
Very high......Job 22:12

B. *Worship of:*
Forbidden .....Deut. 4:19
Punished.....Deut. 17:3-7
Introduced by
Manasseh.....2 Kin. 21:3
Condemned
by the   {Jer. 8:2
prophets ..... {Zeph. 1:4, 5

C. *List of, in Bible:*
Arcturus......Job 9:9
Mazzaroth.....Job 38:32
Orion..........Job 9:9
Pleiades ....Job 9:9
Chambers of the
south ....Job 9:9
Of Beth-
lehem.........Matt. 2:2, 9, 10

D. *Figurative of:*
Christ's:
First advent ..Num. 24:17
Second
advent.......Rev. 22:16
Angels........Rev. 1:16, 20
Judgment.....Ezek. 32:7
False
security ......Obad. 4
Glorified
saints ....Dan. 12:3
Apostates .....Jude 13

State—*established government*

A. *Agents of:*
Under God's   {Dan. 4:17, 25
control.......   {John 19:10, 11
Sometimes
evil ....Mark 6:14-29

Sometimes
good..........Neh. 2:1-9
Protectors of the
Law..........Rom. 13:1-4

B. *Duties of Christians to:*
Pray for ....1 Tim. 2:1, 2
Pay taxes to ...Matt. 22:17-21
Be subject to ..Rom. 13:5, 6
Resist (when
evil) ....Acts 4:17-21

Stature—*the natural height of the body*

A. *Used physically of:*
Giants.........Num. 13:32
Sabeans ....Is. 45:14

B. *Significance of:*
Normal, in human
growth........Luke 2:52
Cannot be
changed ......Matt. 6:27
Not indicative of
greatness .....1 Sam. 16:7
In spiritual
things.........Eph. 4:13

Statute of limitation

Recognized in the
Law..............Deut. 15:1-5, 9

Steadfastness—*firm, persistent and determined in one's endeavors*

A. *In human things, following:*
Person.........Ruth 1:18
Leader........Jer. 35:1-19
Principle......Dan. 1:8

B. *In spiritual things:*
Enduring chastise-
ment..........Heb. 12:7
Bearing
persecution ...Rom. 8:35-37
Maintaining perse-
verance......Heb. 3:6, 14
Stability of
faith ....Col. 2:5
Persevering in
service........1 Cor. 15:58
Resisting
Satan ....1 Pet. 5:9
Defending Christian
liberty ....Gal. 5:1

C. *Elements of, seen in:*
Having a
goal...........Phil. 3:12-14
Discipline......1 Cor. 9:25-27
Run the race ..Heb. 12:1, 2

Never give
up ....Rev. 3:10, 21

Stealing—*taking another's property*

Common on
earth.............Matt. 6:19
Forbidden in:
Law..............Ex. 20:15
Gospel ....Rom. 13:9
Christians not to
do................Eph. 4:28
Excludes from
heaven ....1 Cor. 6:9, 10
None in heaven ...Matt. 6:20

Stephanas—*crowned*

Corinthian
Christian ....1 Cor. 1:16
First convert of
Achaia ....1 Cor. 16:15
Visits Paul ....1 Cor. 16:17

Stephen—*wreath or crown*

One of the seven
deacons ....Acts 6:1-8
Accused falsely by
Jews ....Acts 6:9-15
Spoke before the Jewish
Sanhedrin ....Acts 7:2-53
Became first Christian
martyr ....Acts 7:54-60
Saul (Paul) instigated in death
of ....Acts 7:58

Stew—*a thick vegetable soup*

Price of Esau's
birthright.......Gen. 25:29-34
Eaten by Elisha's
disciples..........2 Kin. 4:38-41
Ordinary food....Hag. 2:12

Steward, stewardship—*a trust granted for profitable use*

A. *Descriptive of:*
One over Joseph's
household.....Gen. 43:19
Curator or
guardian ......Matt. 20:8
Manager.......Luke 16:2, 3
Management of entrusted
duties.........1 Cor. 9:17

B. *Duties of, to:*
Expend
monies........Rom. 16:23
Serve wisely ...Luke 12:42

C. *Of spiritual things, based on:*
Lord's
ownership....{Ps. 24:1, 2
{Rom. 14:8
Our
redemption....1 Cor. 6:20
Gifts
bestowed {Matt. 25:14, 15
upon us......{1 Pet. 4:10
Offices given {Eph. 3:2-10
to us......{Titus 1:7
Faithful in responsi-
bilities ....Luke 16:1-3

Stewardship, personal financial

Basic principles:

Settling
accounts ....Rom. 14:12
God's
ownership.......{Ps. 24:1
{Rom. 14:7, 8
Finances {Matt. 19:16-22
and {Luke 16:10-13
spirituality {1 Cor. 6:20
inseparable....{2 Cor. 8:3-8
Needs will be {Matt. 6:24-34
provided........{Phil. 4:19
Content with {Ps. 37:25
what God {1 Tim. 6:6-10
provides.......{Heb. 13:5
Righteousness...{Prov. 16:8
{Rom. 12:17
Avoid debt......{Prov. 22:7
{Rom. 13:8
Do not {Prov. 6:1-5
co-sign ....{Prov. 22:26
Inheritance {Prov. 17:2
uncertain......{Prov. 20:21
Proper priority ....Matt. 6:19-21, 33
Prosperity {Deut. 29:9
is from {Ps. 1:1-3
God ....{3 John 2
Saving ....Prov. 21:20
Laziness {Prov. 24:30, 31
condemned.....{Heb. 6:12
Giving {Prov. 3:9, 10
is {Mal. 3:10-12
encouraged......{2 Cor. 9:6-8

Sticks—*pieces of wood*

Gathering on Sabbath
condemned.....Num. 15:32-35
Necessary.........1 Kin. 17:10-12
Miracle
producing ....2 Kin. 6:6
Two become
one............Ezek. 37:16-22
Viper in bundle
of ....Acts 28:3

Stiff-necked—*rebellious; unteachable*

A. *Indicative of Israel's rebelliousness at:*
- Sinai..........Ex. 32:9
- Conquest......Deut. 9:6, 13
- Captivity......2 Chr. 36:13
- Christ's first advent.......Acts 7:51

B. *Remedies of, seen in:*
- Circumcision (regeneration).......Deut. 10:16
- Yield to God...2 Chr. 30:8

Still

A. *Indicative of:*
- God's voice....1 Kin. 19:12
- God's presence......Ps. 139:18
- Fright.........Ex. 15:16
- Fixed character.....Rev. 22:11
- Peace..........Jer. 47:6
- Quietness......Num. 13:30

B. *Accomplished by:*
- God...........Ps. 107:29
- Christ.........Mark 4:39
- Submission....Ps. 46:10
- Communion....Ps. 4:4

Stink, stench—*a foul smell*

A. *Caused by:*
- Dead fish......Ex. 7:18, 21
- Corpse.........John 11:39
- Wounds........Ps. 38:5

B. *Figurative of:*
- Hell............Is. 34:3, 4

Stir up

A. *Of strife, etc., by:*
- Wrath.........Prov. 15:18
- Hatred.........Prov. 10:12
- Grievous words.........Prov. 15:1
- Unbelief.......Acts 13:50
- Agitators......Acts 6:12
- Kings.........Dan. 11:2, 25

B. *Of good things:*
- Generosity.....Ex. 35:21, 26
- Repentance....Is. 64:7
- Ministry.......2 Tim. 1:6
- Memory.......2 Pet. 1:13

C. *Of God's sovereignty in:*
- Fulfilling His Word { 2 Chr. 36:22 / Ezra 1:1
- Accomplishing His purpose { Is. 13:17 / Hag. 1:14

Stocks—*blocks of wood*

- Instrument of punishment......Acts 16:19, 24
- Punishment.......Job 33:11

Stoics—*pertaining to a colonnade or porch*

- Sect of philosophers founded by Zeno around 308 B.C..........Acts 17:18

Stones—*rocks*

A. *Natural uses of:*
- Weighing......Lev. 19:36
- Knives.........Ex. 4:25
- Weapons......1 Sam. 17:40-50
- Holding water.........Ex. 7:19
- Covering wells..........Gen. 29:2
- Covering tombs.........Matt. 27:60
- Landmarks....Deut. 19:14
- Writing inscriptions...Ex. 24:12
- Buildings.......Matt. 24:1, 2
- Missiles........Ex. 21:18

B. *Religious uses of:*
- Altars.........Ex. 20:25
- Grave.........Josh. 7:26
- Memorial......Josh. 4:20
- Witness........Josh. 24:26, 27
- Inscriptions....Deut. 27:4, 8
- Idolatry........Lev. 26:1

C. *Figurative of:*
- Reprobation...1 Sam. 25:37
- Contempt......2 Sam. 16:6, 13
- Christ's rejection......Ps. 118:22
- Christ as foundation....Is. 28:16
- Desolation.....Jer. 51:26
- Unregeneracy.........Ezek. 11:19
- Christ's advent.......Dan. 2:34, 35
- Conscience....Hab. 2:11
- Insensibility...Zech. 7:12
- Gentiles.......Matt. 3:9
- Christ as Head.........Matt. 21:42-44
- Good works...1 Cor. 3:12
- Christians.....1 Pet. 2:5

Spirit's
witness . . . . Rev. 2:17

See Rock

Stones, precious

Agate	Ex. 28:19
Amethyst	Rev. 21:20
Beryl	Rev. 21:20
Chalcedony	Rev. 21:19
Chrysolite	Rev. 21:20
Crystal	Rev. 22:1
Diamond	Jer. 17:1
Emerald	Ex. 28:17
Jasper	Rev. 4:3
Jacinth	Ex. 28:19
Onyx	Gen. 2:12
Ruby	Prov. 3:15
Sapphire	Job 28:6, 16
Sardius	Rev. 4:3
Sardonyx	Rev. 21:20
Topaz	Job 28:17

Stoning—a means of executing criminals

A. *Punishment inflicted for:*
Sacrificing
children . . . . . Lev. 20:2-5
Divination . . . . . Lev. 20:27
Blasphemy . . . . . Lev. 24:15-23
Sabbath-
breaking . . . . . Num. 15:32-36
Apostasy . . . . . Deut. 13:1-10
Idolatry . . . . Deut. 17:2-7
Juvenile
rebellion . . . . . Deut. 21:18-21
Adultery . . . . . . Deut. 22:22

B. *Examples of:*
Achan . . . . Josh. 7:20-26
Adoram . . . . . . 1 Kin. 12:18
Naboth . . . . . . 1 Kin. 21:13
Zechariah . . . 2 Chr. 24:20, 21
Stephen . . . . . . Acts 7:59
Paul . . . . Acts 14:19
Prophets . . . . . . Heb. 11:37

Stool

Birthstool . . . . Ex. 1:16

Storehouses—places for storing things

A. *Descriptive of:*
Barns . . . . Deut. 28:8
Warehouses . . . Gen. 41:56
Temple . . . . Mal. 3:10

B. *Used for storing:*
Grain . . . . 2 Chr. 32:28
The tithe . . . . . Mal. 3:10

Stork—a large, long-legged, migratory bird

Nesting of . . . . Ps. 104:17
Migration of . . . . . . Jer. 8:7
Ceremonially
unclean . . . . Lev. 11:19

Storm—a violent upheaval of nature

A. *Described as:*
Grievous . . . . . . Ex. 9:23-25
Sent by God . . Josh. 10:11
Destructive . . . . Matt. 7:27

B. *Effects of, upon:*
Israelites . . . . . Ex. 19:16, 19
Philistines . . . . . 1 Sam. 7:10
Mariners . . . . . . Jon. 1:4-14
Animals . . . . . . Ps. 29:3-9
Disciples . . . . . . Mark 4:37-41
Soldiers and
sailors . . . .
Acts 27:14-44
Nature . . . . Ps. 29:3, 5, 8

Strangers—foreigners living among the Jews

A. *Descriptive of:*
Non-Jews . . . . . . Ex. 12:48
Foreigners . . . . . Matt. 17:25
Transients . . . . . Luke 24:18

B. *Positive laws, to:*
Love them . . . . . Lev. 19:34
Relieve them . . Lev. 25:35
Provide for
them . . . . Deut. 10:18
Share in left-
overs . . . . Deut. 24:19-22
Treat fairly . . . . Deut. 24:14, 17
Share in religious
festivals . . . . . . Deut. 16:11, 14
Hear the law . . . Deut. 31:12

See Foreigners; Sojourn, sojourners

Strategem—a plan designed to deceive an enemy

Joshua's famous . . Josh. 8:1-22
Gibeonites'
trickery . . . . Josh. 9:2-27
Hushai's
successful . . . . 2 Sam. 17:6-14

Straw—the stalk of wheat or barley

Used for animals . . Gen. 24:25, 32
Used in making
bricks . . . . Ex. 5:7-18
Eaten by a lion . . . . Is. 11:7
Something
worthless . . . . Job 41:27-29

Stray animals

Must be
returned.........Ex. 23:4
Saul's pursuit of...1 Sam. 9:3-5

Streets—*principal thoroughfares*

A. *Uses of:*
Display ....Matt. 6:5
Teaching ......Luke 13:26
Parades........Esth. 6:9, 11
Procla-
mations.......Neh. 8:3-5

B. *Dangers of, from:*
Fighting ....Josh. 2:19
Prostitutes.....Prov. 7:6-23
Wicked ....Ps. 55:11
Assault ....Judg. 19:15-26

Strength, strengthen—*resident power*

A. *Kinds of:*
Physical ....Prov. 20:29
Constitu-
tional ....Ps. 90:10
Hereditary ......Gen. 49:3
Angelic ....Ps. 103:20
Military ....Dan. 2:37
Spiritual ....Ps. 138:3
Superhuman...Judg. 16:5, 6, 19
Divine.........Is. 63:1

B. *Dissipation of, by:*
Iniquity........Ps. 31:10
Hunger........1 Sam. 28:20, 22
Sexual
looseness......Prov. 31:3
Age............Ps. 71:9
Visions ....Dan. 10:8, 16, 17

C. *Increase of:*
From:
God ....Is. 41:10
Christ ....2 Tim. 4:17
Spirit ....Eph. 3:16
Brothers......Luke 22:32
By:
Wisdom ......Eccl. 7:19
Waiting on the
Lord.........Is. 40:31
Lord's grace ..2 Cor. 12:9

Strife—*conflicts between people*

A. *Sources of, in:*
Hatred........Prov. 10:12
Perverse-
ness.........Prov. 16:28
Transgres-
sion..........Prov. 17:19
Scorner........Prov. 22:10
Anger ....Prov. 29:22
Flesh ....Gal. 5:19-21

B. *Actual causes of, seen in:*
Self-seeking ...Luke 22:24
Dispute between
men...........Gen. 13:7-11
Contentious
man ....Prov. 26:21
Being carnal ..1 Cor. 3:3
Disputes.......1 Tim. 6:4

C. *Avoidance of, by:*
Being slow to
anger ....Prov. 15:18
Simplicity of
life ....Prov. 17:1

See Contention; Quarrel

Strike—*afflict; attack*

A. *Descriptive of:*
Plagues........Ex. 3:20
Miracle........Ex. 17:5, 6
God's punish-
ments.........Deut. 28:22-28
Death ....2 Sam. 4:6, 7
Fear ....Dan. 5:6
Smeared
blood ....Ex. 12:7, 22
Slapping ....John 18:22

B. *Of divine punishment, upon:*
Christ ....Is. 53:4, 8
Sinners ....Prov. 7:23
World ....Ps. 110:5
Rebellious .....Is. 14:6
Israel..........Is. 30:26
Philistines .....1 Sam. 5:6, 9
Pagan nation ..2 Chr. 14:12
King's house...2 Chr. 21:5-19

C. *Used messianically of Christ's:*
Scourging .....Is. 50:6
Bearing our
sins...........Is. 53:4
Death ....Zech. 13:7
Judgment......Is. 11:4

Stripes—*used in scourging*

Limit of.........Deut. 25:1-4
Because of sin....Ps. 89:32
Upon the
Messiah,   ⎰Is. 53:5
healing..........⎱1 Pet. 2:24
Uselessness of, on a
fool ....Prov. 17:10
Paul's experience ⎰Acts 16:23, 33
with.............⎱2 Cor. 11:23

Striving, spiritual

To enter the strait
gate...........Luke 13:24
Against sin.......Heb. 12:4
With divine help ..Col. 1:29
In prayer ....Rom. 15:30
For the faith of the
Gospel ....Phil. 1:27

Stroke—*a blow*

With an ax.......Deut. 19:5
With a sword .....Esth. 9:5

Strong drink (see Drunkenness)

Stronghold—*fortress*

David captured....2 Sam. 5:7, 9
The LORD is ......Nah. 1:7

Studs—*ornaments*

Of silver ....Song 1:11

Study—*intensive intellectual effort*

Of the   (Acts 17:10, 11
Scriptures ......(2 Tim. 3:16, 17

Stumble—*to trip on some obstacle*

A. *Occasions of, found in:*
Strong drink....Is. 28:7
God's Word....1 Pet. 2:8
Christ ....Rom. 9:32, 33
Christ
crucified ......1 Cor. 1:23
Christian
liberty ....1 Cor. 8:9

B. *Avoidance of, by:*
Following
wisdom ....Prov. 3:21, 23

See Offend, offense

Suah—*sweepings*

Asherite ....1 Chr. 7:36

Subjection—*the state of being under another's control*

A. *Of domestic and civil relationships:*
Servants to
masters ....1 Pet. 2:18
Citizens to
government...Rom. 13:1-6
Children to
parents ....1 Tim. 3:4
Wives to
husbands .....Eph. 5:24
Younger to
elder ....1 Pet. 5:5

B. *Of spiritual relationships:*
Creation to
sin ....Rom. 8:20, 21
Demons to the
disciples.......Luke 10:17, 20
Believers to the
Gospel ....2 Cor. 9:13
Christians to one
another ....1 Pet. 5:5
Christians to
God...........Heb. 12:9
Creation to
Christ.........Heb. 2:5, 8
Church to
Christ.........Eph. 5:24
Christ to
God...........1 Cor. 15:28

Subjugation—*the state of being subdued by force*

Physical force.....1 Sam. 13:19-23
Spiritual power....Mark 5:1-15

Submission—*humble obedience to another's will*

Each other........Eph. 5:21
Husbands ....Eph. 5:22
Rulers............1 Pet. 2:13
Elders............1 Pet. 5:5
Christian leaders ..Heb. 13:17
God...............James 4:7

Substitution—*replacing one person or thing for another*

Ram for the
man.............Gen. 22:13
Offering for the
offerer...........Lev. 16:21, 22
Levites for the first-
born............Num. 3:12-45
Christ for the   (Is. 53:4-6
sinner ....(1 Pet. 2:24

Success—*accomplishment of goals in life*

A. *Rules of:*
Put God first...Matt. 6:32-34
Follow the
Book..........Josh. 1:7-9
Seek the
goal...........Phil. 3:13, 14
Never give
up ....Gal. 6:9
Do all for
Christ.........Phil. 1:20, 21

B. *Hindrances of, seen in:*

Disobedience	Heb. 4:6, 11
Enemies	Neh. 4:1-23
Sluggishness	Prov. 24:30-34
Love of the world	Matt. 16:26

Succoth—*booths*

1. Place east of the Jordan .... Judg. 8:4, 5

   Jacob's residence here .... Gen. 33:17
2. Israel's first camp .... Ex. 12:37

Succoth Benoth—*tabernacles of girls*

Idol set up in Samaria by Babylonians ...... 2 Kin. 17:30

Suchathites

Descendants of Caleb............ 1 Chr. 2:42, 55

Suck—*to give milk to offspring*

Characteristics of:

True among animals...........	1 Sam. 7:9
Normal for human mothers...........	Job 3:12
Figurative of Israel's restoration	Is. 60:16
Figurative of wicked	Job 20:16

Suffering—*afflicted; in pain*

Need prayer in .... James 5:13

Suffering for Christ

Necessary in Christian living............	1 Cor. 12:26 / Phil. 1:29
Blessed privilege	Acts 5:41
Never in vain	Gal. 3:4
After Christ's example.........	Phil. 3:10 / 1 Pet. 2:20, 21
Of short duration...........	1 Pet. 5:10
Not comparable to heaven's glory	Rom. 8:18 / 1 Pet. 4:13

Sufferings of Christ

A. *Features concerning:*

Predicted	1 Pet. 1:11
Announced	Mark 9:12
Explained.....	Luke 24:26, 46
Fulfilled	Acts 3:18
Witnessed	1 Pet. 5:1
Proclaimed	Acts 17:2, 3

B. *Benefits of, to Christ:*

Preparation for priesthood	Heb. 2:17, 18
Learned obedience.....	Heb. 5:8
Way to glory ..	Heb. 2:9, 10

C. *Benefits of, to Christians:*

Brought to God...........	1 Pet. 3:18
Our: Sins atoned...	Heb. 9:26-28
Example......	1 Pet. 2:21-23
Fellowship....	Phil. 3:10
Consolation....	2 Cor. 1:5-7

Suicide—*self-murder*

A. *Thought of, induced by:*

Life's weariness	Job 3:20-23
Life's vanity ...	Eccl. 2:17
Anger	Jon. 4:3, 8, 9

B. *Brought on by:*

Hopelessness..........	Judg. 16:29, 30
Sin	1 Kin. 16:18, 19
Disappointment...........	2 Sam. 17:23
Betrayal of Christ..........	Matt. 27:3-5

C. *Other features concerning:*

Desired by some..........	Rev. 9:6
Attempted but prevented.....	Acts 16:27, 28
Imputed to Christ........	John 8:22
Satan tempts Christ to.....	Luke 4:9

D. *Principles prohibiting, found in:*

Body's sacredness ...	1 Cor. 6:19
Prohibition against murder........	Ex. 20:13
Faith's expectancy....	2 Tim. 4:6-8, 18

Sukkiim

African people in Shishak's army .... 2 Chr. 12:3

Summer

Made by God	Ps. 74:17
Sign of God's covenant	Gen. 8:22

Time of:
Fruit harvest.....2 Sam. 16:1, 2
Sowing and
harvest..........Prov. 6:6-8
Figurative of:
Industry..........Prov. 10:5
Opportunity......Jer. 8:20
Preceded by
spring ....Matt. 24:32

Sun

A. *Characteristics of:*
Created by
God...........Gen. 1:14, 16
Under God's
control.......{Ps. 104:19
            {Matt. 5:45
Made to rule...Gen. 1:16
Necessary for
fruit ....Deut. 33:14
Given for
light ....Jer. 31:35
Made for God's
glory..........Ps. 148:3
Causes:
Scorching.....Jon. 4:8
Sunstroke ....2 Kin. 4:18, 19

B. *Miracles connected with:*
Stands still.....Josh. 10:12, 13
Shadows of, turned
back ....2 Kin. 20:9-11
Darkening of, at
crucifixion ....Luke 23:44-49
Going down at
noon..........Amos 8:9

C. *Worship of:*
Forbidden .....Deut. 4:19
By Manasseh ..2 Kin. 21:3, 5
By Jews ....Jer. 8:2

D. *Figurative of:*
God's
presence ......Ps. 84:11
Earth's sphere of
action.........Eccl. 1:3, 9, 14
God's Law.....Ps. 19:4-7
Future glory...Matt. 13:43
Christ's glory ..Matt. 17:2

Sunday (see First day of week)

Sundial—*an instrument for telling time*
Miracle of.........Is. 38:8

Sunstroke—*stricken by sun's heat*
Child dies of ......2 Kin. 4:18-20

Superstition—*gullible ideas based on
fancy or fear*

A. *Causes of, in wrong views of:*
God ....1 Kin. 20:23
Holy objects ...1 Sam. 4:3
God's
providence ....Jer. 44:15-19

B. *Manifestations of, in:*
Seeking illogical
causes ....Acts 28:4
Ignorance of the true
God...........Acts 17:22
Perverting true
religion ....Mark 7:1-16

Supper (see Lord's Supper)

Sur—*turning aside, entrance*

Name given to a
gate...............2 Kin. 11:6
Called "Gate of the
Foundation"......2 Chr. 23:5

Sure—*something trustworthy*

A. *Descriptive of divine things:*
God's law......Ps. 19:7
New
covenant......Acts 13:34
God's:
Prophecies.....2 Pet. 1:19
Promises.......Rom. 4:16

B. *Applied to the believer's:*
Calling and
election ....2 Pet. 1:10
Faith ....John 6:69
Dedication.....Neh. 9:38
Confidence in God's
Word ....Luke 1:1
Reward.......Prov. 11:18

Surety—*one who guarantees another's
debt*

A. *Descriptive of:*
Guarantee .....Gen. 43:9
Our Lord ......Heb. 7:22

B. *Features concerning:*
Risks involved
in..............Prov. 11:15
Warning
against........Prov. 6:1-5

Surname—*a family name*

A. *Descriptive of:*
Simon Peter ...Acts 10:5, 32
John Mark.....Acts 12:12, 25
Judas
Iscariot ....Luke 22:3

Judas
Barsabas......Acts 15:22
Joses
Barnabas......Acts 4:36
James and John
Boanerges.....Mark 3:17

B. *Figurative of God's:*
Call of
Gentiles.......Is. 44:5
Sovereignty over
kings ....Is. 45:4

Susanna—*lily*

Believing woman ministering to
Christ ....Luke 8:2, 3

Susi—*horseman*

Mannassite spy ...Num. 13:11

Suspicion—*doubt of another's intent*

A. *Kinds of:*
Unjustified.....Josh. 22:9-31
Pretended .....Gen. 42:7-12
Unsuspected...John 13:21-28

B. *Objects of:*
Esau by
Jacob.........Gen. 32:3-12
Jeremiah by
officials ....Jer. 37:12-15
Jews by
Haman........Esth. 3:8, 9
Mary by
Joseph ....Matt. 1:18-25
Peter by a
damsel ....Matt. 26:69-74

Sustenance—*means of sustaining life*

Israel by the
Lord ....Neh. 9:21
Elijah by ravens and a
widow........1 Kin. 17:1-9
Believer by the
Lord ....Ps. 3:5

Swaddling—*bandages, wrappings*

Figurative of
Jerusalem ......Ezek. 16:3, 4
Jesus wrapped
in ....Luke 2:7

Swallow—*a long-winged, migratory bird*

Nesting in the
sanctuary ....Ps. 84:3
Noted for
chattering.......Is. 38:14

Swallow—*to engulf; to overwhelm*

A. *Applied miraculously to:*
Aaron's rod....Ex. 7:12
Red Sea ......Ex. 15:12
Earth.........Num. 16:30-34
Great fish......Jon. 1:17

B. *Applied figuratively to:*
God's
judgments ....Ps. 21:9
Conquest ......Jer. 51:34, 44
Captivity ......Hos. 8:7, 8
Sorrow ....2 Cor. 2:7
Resurrection...Is. 25:8

Swearing—*taking an oath*

A. *Kinds of:*
Proclama-
tory...........Ex. 17:16
Protective ....Gen. 21:23
Personal......1 Sam. 20:17
Purificatory...Neh. 13:25-30
Promissory ...Luke 1:73
Prohibited ....James 5:12

B. *Of God, objects of:*
God's
purpose ....Is. 14:24, 25
God's
covenant......Is. 54:9, 10
Messianic
priesthood ....Heb. 7:21

See Oaths

Sweat—*perspiration*

Penalty of man's
sin ....Gen. 3:18, 19
Cause of,
avoided ....Ezek. 44:18
Of Jesus, in
prayer...........Luke 22:44

Sweet—*that which is pleasing to the taste*

A. *Descriptive, literally, of:*
Water ....Ex. 15:25
Honey.........Judg. 14:18
Incense........Ex. 25:6

B. *Descriptive, figuratively, of:*
God's Law.....Ps. 19:10
God's Word....Ps. 119:103
Spiritual
fellowship.....Ps. 55:14
Meditation.....Ps. 104:34
Pleasant
words........Prov. 16:24
Sleep..........Prov. 3:24
Christians .....2 Cor. 2:15

Christian
service .... Eph. 5:2

Swim—*to propel oneself in water by natural means*

Miraculously, of
iron .... 2 Kin. 6:6
Naturally, of
people .... Acts 27:42, 43
Figuratively, of
tears .... Ps. 6:6

Swine—*hogs*

A. *Features concerning:*
Classed as
unclean .... Lev. 11:7, 8
Eating of,
abominable ... Is. 65:4
Caring of, a
degradation ... Luke 15:16
Herd of,
drowned ..... Matt. 8:30-32

B. *Figurative of:*
Abominable
things .... Is. 65:4
False
teachers ..... 2 Pet. 2:22
Indiscrete
woman .... Prov. 11:22
Reprobate ..... Matt. 7:6

Sword—*a weapon of war*

A. *Described as:*
Having hilt and
blade .... Judg. 3:22
Worn in a
sheath .... 1 Sam. 17:51
Fastened at the
waist .... 2 Sam. 20:8

B. *Used for:*
Defense .... Luke 22:36, 38
Fighting in
war .... Josh. 6:21
Executing
criminals ...... 1 Sam. 15:33
Suicide .... Acts 16:27

C. *Figurative of:*
Divine
retribution .... Deut. 32:41
Divine
victory .... Josh. 5:13
God's
judgment ..... 1 Chr. 21:12
An
adulteress ..... Prov. 5:3, 4
Anguish of
soul .... Luke 2:35

State .... Rom. 13:4
God's Word ... Eph. 6:17

Sycamore—*a fig-bearing tree* (not the same as the American sycamore)

Overseers appointed
to care for .... 1 Chr. 27:28
Abundant in
Palestine .... 1 Kin. 10:27
Amos, a gatherer
of .... Amos 7:14
Zacchaeus climbs
up .... Luke 19:4

Sychar

City of Samaria; Jesus talks to
woman near ...... John 4:5-39

Syene—*seven*

An Egyptian   {Ezek. 29:10
city .... {Ezek. 30:6

Symbols—*a thing or act representing something spiritual*

A. *Of things:*
Names .... Is. 7:3, 14
Numbers ...... Rev. 13:18
Garments ...... Zech. 3:3-9
Metals .... 1 Cor. 3:12
Animals .... Dan. 7:1-8

B. *Of acts (gestures):*
Tearing:
Mantle .... 1 Sam. 15:27, 28
Garment ...... 1 Kin. 11:30-32
Curtain ...... Matt. 27:51
Wearing a
yoke .... Jer. 27:2-12
Buying a
field .... Jer. 32:6-15
Piercing the
ear .... Ex. 21:6
Surrendering the
shoe .... Ruth 4:7
Going naked ... Is. 20:2, 3

C. *Of spiritual truths:*
Bow—God's
covenant ...... Gen. 9:12, 13
Circumcision—
God's   {Gen. 17:1-14
covenant ..... {Rom. 4:11
Passover—   {Ex. 12:3-28
Christ .... {1 Cor. 5:7
Rock—Christ .. 1 Cor. 10:4
Blood sprinkled—
Christ's   {Ex. 12:21, 22
blood .... {1 Pet. 1:18, 19

Bronze
serpent—
Christ........ { Num. 21:8, 9 / John 3:14
Lamb—
Christ.........John 1:29
Bread and wine—
the new
covenant..... { Matt. 26:26-28 / 1 Cor. 11:23-29

Sympathy—*a fellow-feeling for another person*

A. *Manifested in:*
Bearing
others'
burdens...... { Gal. 6:2 / Heb. 13:3
Expressing
sorrow........John 11:19-33
Offering help in
need...........Luke 10:33-35
Helping the
weak..........Acts 20:35

B. *Expressed by:*
Servant for a
prophet.......Jer. 38:7-13
King for a
king...........2 Sam. 10:2
A maid for a
general........2 Kin. 5:1-4
Old man for a
king...........2 Sam. 19:31-39
Pagan for a
Jew...........Dan. 6:18-23

Synagogue—*a Jewish assembly*

A. *Organization of:*
Under elders...Luke 7:3-5
Ruler in
charge........Mark 5:22
Attendant......Luke 4:17, 20
Chief seats of,
coveted.......Matt. 23:6
Expulsion
from..........John 9:22, 34

B. *Purposes of, for:*
Prayer.........Matt. 6:5
Reading
Scripture......Acts 13:15
Hearing
expositions....Acts 13:14, 15
Discipline......Acts 9:2

C. *Christ's relation to:*
Teaches often
in.............John 18:20
Worships in....Luke 4:16-21
Performs miracles
in.............Matt. 12:9, 10

Expelled
from..........Luke 4:22-30

Syntyche—*fortunate*

Philippian woman exhorted by
Paul.............Phil. 4:2

Syracuse—*a city of Sicily*

Visited by Paul....Acts 28:12

Syria—*the high land*

News of Jesus went
into.............Matt. 4:24
Governed by
Romans.........Luke 2:2
Gospel preached
to...............Acts 15:23, 41

Syria, Syrians—*the Aramaeans*

Descendants of Aram, Shem's
son.............Gen. 10:22
Related to the
Hebrews........Deut. 26:5
Intermarriage of, with
Hebrews.........Gen. 24:4, 10-67
Called Syrians.....2 Sam. 10:11
Speak Aramaic....Dan. 2:4
Idolatrous.........2 Kin. 5:18
Subdued by
David...........2 Sam. 8:11-13
Elijah anointed king
over............1 Kin. 19:15
Army of, routed...2 Kin. 7:5-7
Joined Israel against
Jerusalem.......2 Kin. 16:5
Taken captive by
Assyria..........2 Kin. 16:9
Destruction of,
foretold.........Is. 17:1-3
Governed by
Romans.........Luke 2:2
Gospel preached
to...............Acts 15:23, 41

Syro-Phoenician—*an inhabitant of Phoenicia*

Daughter of, freed of
demon..........Mark 7:25-31

Syrtis Sands

Endangers Paul's
ship.............Acts 27:17

System—*an orderly method of procedure in*

Orderly writing...Luke 1:3
Governing
people...........Ex. 18:13-27

Church
government ......Acts 6:1-7
Priestly ministry ..Luke 1:8, 9
Giving ....1 Cor. 16:1, 2

T

Taanach, Tanach—*sandy*

Canaanite city conquered by
Joshua ....Josh. 12:21
Assigned to
Manasseh ......Josh. 17:11
Assigned to Kohathite
Levites ....Josh. 21:25
Canaanites not expelled
from ....Josh. 17:12, 13
Site of Canaanite
defeat ....Judg. 5:19-22

Taanath Shiloh—*approach to Shiloh*

City of Ephraim ...Josh. 16:5, 6

Tabbaoth—*rings*

Ancestor of a Nethinim
family ....Ezra 2:43

Tabbath—*extension*

Refuge of
Midianites ....Judg. 7:22

Tabeel—*God is good*

Persian official ....Ezra 4:7
Father of a puppet king
put forth by Rezin and
Pekah ....Is. 7:1, 6

Taberah—*burning*

Israelite camp; fire destroys many
here ....Num. 11:1-3

Tabernacle

A. *Descriptive of:*
Moses' administrative
office..........Ex. 33:7-11
Structure erected at
Sinai..........Ex. 40:2, 35-38
Portable shrine containing an
idol ....Acts 7:43
Tent prepared for the ark by
David ....1 Chr. 16:1-43
Heavenly
prototype ....{ Heb. 8:2, 5
{ Heb. 9:11, 24
Holy city ......Rev. 21:3

B. *Sinaitic, constructed:*
By divine
revelation ....{ Ex. 25:8
{ Heb. 8:5
By craftsmen inspired by the
Spirit ....Ex. 31:1-11
Out of contributions willingly
supplied.......Ex. 25:1-9
For the manifestation
of God's
glory..........{ Ex. 25:8
{ Ex. 29:42, 43
In two parts—holy place
and
Most Holy ...{ Ex. 26:33, 34
{ Heb. 9:2-7
With surrounding
court...........Ex. 40:8
Within a year's
time ....Ex. 40:2, 17

C. *History of:*
Set up at
Sinai..........Ex. 40:1-38
Sanctified and
dedicated .....Ex. 40:9-16
Moved by priests and
Levites........Num. 4:1-49
Camped at
Gilgal ....Josh. 5:10, 11
Set up at
Shiloh.........Josh. 18:1
Israel's
center of   { Judg. 18:31
worship......{ 1 Sam. 1:3, 9,
{ 24
Ark of, taken by
Philistines.....1 Sam. 4:1-22
Worship not { 1 Sam. 7:1, 2,
confined to...{ 15-17
Located at Nob during Saul's
reign..........1 Sam. 21:1-6
Moved to
Gibeon ....1 Kin. 3:4
Ark of, brought to Jerusalem by
David ....2 Sam. 6:17
Brought to the Temple by
Solomon ......1 Kin. 8:1, 4, 5

D. *Typology of, seen in:*
Christ ....John 1:14
God's
household.....Eph. 2:19
Believer........1 Cor. 6:19
Heaven........Heb. 9:23, 24

E. *Typology of, seen in Christ:*
Candlestick—His enlightening
us..............Rev. 1:13
Sacred bread—His sustaining
us..............John 6:27-59

Altar of incense—His
intercession
for us . . . . {John 17:1-26
Heb. 7:25
Veil—His
flesh . . . . Heb. 10:20
Ark (wood and gold)—His
humanity and
deity . . . . John 1:14

Tabernacle, Feast of (see Feasts, Hebrew)

Table

A. *Descriptive of:*
Article of
furniture . . . . . . Matt. 15:27
For
showbread . . . . Heb. 9:2

B. *Figurative of:*
God's
provision . . . . . . Ps. 23:5
Intimate
fellowship . . . . . Luke 22:30
Lord's
Supper . . . . 1 Cor. 10:21

Tablet

A. *Descriptive of:*
Small writing
board . . . . Luke 1:63
Stone slabs . . . . Ex. 24:12

B. *Figurative of:*
Christian's
heart . . . . 2 Cor. 3:3
Human heart . . Prov. 3:3

Tabor—*mountain height*

1. Mountain on borders of
Zebulun and
Issachar . . . . . . Josh. 19:12, 22
Great among
mountains . . . . Jer. 46:18
Scene of rally
against
Sisera . . . . {Judg. 4:6, 12,
14
2. Town of
Zebulun . . . . . . 1 Chr. 6:77
3. Terebinth of, near
Ramah . . . . 1 Sam. 10:3

Tabrimmon—*Rimmon is good*

Father of
Ben-Hadad . . . . . . 1 Kin. 15:18

Tachmonite—*wise*

Descriptive of one of David's
heroes . . . . 2 Sam. 23:8

Same as Hachmonite
in . . . . 1 Chr. 11:11

Tackle—*ropes, cord, line*

Ship's ropes . . . . Is. 33:23
All of a ship's removable
gear . . . . Acts 27:19

Tactfulness—*the knack of knowing the right thing to do or say*

A. *Manifested in:*
Appeasing
hatred . . . . {Gen. 32:4, 5,
13-21
Settling
disputes . . . . 1 Kin. 3:24-28
Obtaining
one's
wishes . . . . {Esth. 5:1-8
Esth. 7:1-6

B. *Illustrated by Christ, in:*
Rebuking a
Pharisee . . . . . . Luke 7:39-50
Teaching
humility . . . . . . Mark 10:35-45
Forgiving a
sinner . . . . John 8:1-11
Rebuking His
disciples . . . . . . John 21:15-23

Tadmor—*palm tree*

Trading center near
Damascus . . . . 2 Chr. 8:4
A desert town . . . . . 1 Kin. 9:18

Tahan—*encampment*

Ephraimite;
founder of the
Tahanites
{Num. 26:35
1 Chr. 7:25

Tahath—*station*

1. Kohathite
Levite . . . . 1 Chr. 6:24
2, 3. Two descendants of
Ephraim . . . . . . 1 Chr. 7:20
4. Israelite encamp-
ment . . . . Num. 33:26, 27

Tahpanhes, Tehaphnehes

City of Egypt;
refuge of fleeing
Jews
{Jer. 2:16
Jer. 44:1
Ezek. 30:18

Tahpenes—*royal wife*

Egyptian queen . . . 1 Kin. 11:19, 20

Tahrea—*flight*

Descendant of
Saul . . . . 1 Chr. 9:41
Called Tarea . . . . . . 1 Chr. 8:33, 35

Tahtim Hodshi

Place visited by census-taking
Joab............2 Sam. 24:6

Tailoring—*the art of making clothes*

For Aaron's
garments........Ex. 39:1

Tale

Nonsensical talk ..Luke 24:11

Talebearer—*one who gossips*

Reveals secrets....Prov. 11:13
Injures
character........Prov. 18:8
Creates strife......Prov. 26:20

Talent—*see Jewish measures*

Of gold ....Ex. 37:24
Of silver ......2 Kin. 5:5, 22, 23
Of bronze........Ex. 38:29
Of iron........1 Chr. 29:7
Parable of........Matt. 25:14-30

Talitha, cumi—*"Damsel, arise"*

Jairus' daughter thus
addressed ....Mark 5:41

Talk—*verbal communication between persons*

A. *Described as:*
   Divine.........Ex. 33:9
   Deceitful ......Job 13:7
   Proud..........1 Sam. 2:3
   Trouble-
   making ....Prov. 24:2
   Idle...........Titus 1:10
   Foolish ....Eph. 5:4
B. *Of good things, God's:*
   Law.........Deut. 6:7
   Judgment......Ps. 37:30, 31
   Righ-
   teousness .....Ps. 71:24
   Power ....Ps. 145:11

Talmai—*plowman*

1. Son of Anak driven out by
   Caleb.........Josh. 15:14
2. King of Geshur whose
   daughter, Maacah, becomes
   David's wife..2 Sam. 3:3

Talmon—*oppressor, violent*

Levite porter......1 Chr. 9:17
Descendants of, return from
exile.............Ezra 2:42

Members of, become temple
porters ....Neh. 11:19

Tamah—*combat*

Family of
Nethinim........Ezra 2:53

Tamar—*palm tree*

1. Wife of Er and mother of Perez
   and Zerah.....Gen. 38:6-30
   Ancestress of tribal
   families ......Num. 26:20, 21
2. Absalom's
   sister.........2 Sam. 13:1-32
3. Absalom's
   daughter......2 Sam. 14:27
4. Place south of the Dead
   Sea ....Ezek. 47:19

Tamarisk tree

Planted by
Abraham.........Gen. 21:33
Saul was under ...1 Sam. 22:6

Tambourine—*a musical instrument*

A part of
worship ....2 Sam. 6:5

Tammuz—*a Babylonian god*

Mourned by women of
Jerusalem ....Ezek. 8:14

Tanhumeth—*consolation*

Father of
Seraiah..........2 Kin. 25:23

Tanner (Simon, the)—*dresser of hides*

Peter lodges
with.............Acts 10:5, 6, 32

Tapestry—*hand-woven coverings*

Symbolic of:

Licentiousness ....Prov. 7:16
Diligence.........Prov. 31:22

Taphath—*a drop*

Daughter of
Solomon ....1 Kin. 4:11

Tappuah—*apple*

1. Town of
   Judah ......Josh. 15:1, 34
2. Town of
   Ephraim ....Josh. 16:8, 9
3. Son of
   Hebron ....1 Chr. 2:43

Taralah—*power of God*

City of
Benjamin.........Josh. 18:21, 27

Tares—*the bearded darnel*

Sown among
wheat............Matt. 13:24-40

Tarpelites

People transported to Samaria by
the Assyrians.....Ezra 4:9

Tarry—*to delay*

Divine visitation . . Hab. 2:3
Spirit's coming....Luke 24:49
Christ's return ....Heb. 10:37

Tarshish, Tharshish

1. Son of Javan and great
   grandson of
   Noah ....Gen. 10:4
2. City at a great distance from
   Palestine......Jon. 1:3
   Ships of, noted in
   commerce....Ps. 48:7
3. Benjamite .....1 Chr. 7:10
4. Persian
   prince.........Esth. 1:14

Tarsus—*the capital of the Roman
province of Cilicia*

Paul's birthplace . . Acts 21:39
Saul sent to.......Acts 9:30
Visited by
Barnabas.........Acts 11:25

Tartak—*hero of darkness*

Deity worshiped by the
Avites............2 Kin. 17:31

Tartan—*the title of Assyria's
commander*

Sent to fight against
Jerusalem ....2 Kin. 18:17

Taskmaster—*a foreman*

Over sons of
Israel.............Ex. 1:11

Tassel

On Israelites'
garments.........Num. 15:38-40

Taste

A. *Of divine things:*
   God's Word....Ps. 119:103

Lord...........Ps. 34:8
Heavenly gift . . Heb. 6:4

B. *Of material things:*
   Honey.........1 Sam. 14:29, 43
   Manna.........Ex. 16:31
   Food ....1 Sam. 14:24
   Wine ....John 2:9
   Vinegar......Matt. 27:34
   Death ....Heb. 2:9

Tattenai

Persian governor opposing the
Jews ....Ezra 5:3, 6

Tattooing—*marking the skin indelibly*

Forbidden by
God..............Lev. 19:28

Tau

Letter in the Hebrew
alphabet..........Ps. 119:169-176

Taunt—*a scornful glee*

Goliath against   (1 Sam. 17:43,
David .... (44
David against
Abner............1 Sam. 26:14-16
Rabshakeh against the
Jews ....2 Kin. 18:28-35
Soldiers and people against
Christ ....Matt. 27:28-41

Taxes—*money, goods, or labor paid to a
government*

A. *Derived from:*
   People's
   possessions....1 Sam. 8:10-18
   Poor...........Amos 5:11

B. *Paid by:*
   Forced labor...Deut. 20:11
   Foreigners.....1 Chr. 22:2
   All people....2 Sam. 8:6, 14
   Forced labor...1 Kin. 5:13-17
   All except
   Levites........Ezra 7:24
   Christians ....Rom. 13:6, 7

C. *Used for:*
   Sanctuary .....Ex. 30:11-16
   King's
   household....1 Kin. 4:7-19
   Tribute to foreign
   nations.......2 Kin. 15:17-22
   Authorities ....Rom. 13:6, 7

D. *Abuses of:*
Lead to
rebellion ......1 Kin. 12:1-19
Burden people with
debts..........Neh. 5:1-13
Bring enslave-
ment..........Neh. 9:36, 37

Tax collectors—*Jews engaged in tax collecting*

A. *Features concerning:*
Collector of { Matt. 9:9
taxes......... { Luke 5:27
Often guilty of
extortion......Luke 3:12, 13
Classed with
lowest { Matt. 9:10, 11
sinners....... { Matt. 21:31, 32
Do not even, do the
same..........Matt. 5:46
Thomas and Matthew,
the.............Matt. 10:3
"Thank You that I am
not" ....Luke 18:11
As a heathen
and a ....Matt. 18:17

B. *Spiritual attitude of:*
Often conscien-
tious..........Luke 19:2, 8
Often
hospitable.....Luke 5:29
Received John's
beliefs.........Matt. 21:32
Listened to
Jesus..........Luke 15:1
Conscious of their
sins ....Luke 18:13, 14
Many sat with
Him...........Mark 2:15
Why do ye eat
with ....Luke 5:30
A friend of....Matt. 11:19
Luke 7:34

Teacher—*the Greek equivalent of the Hebrew word "rabbi" (meaning "my master")*

Instructed in
song ....1 Chr. 25:1
Come from God...John 3:2
To the Gentiles ...2 Tim. 1:11

Teaching, teachers

A. *Those capable of:*
Parents........Deut. 11:19
Levites ....Lev. 10:11
Ancestors......Jer. 9:14
Disciples......Matt. 28:19, 20
Older women ...Titus 2:3
Nature.........1 Cor. 11:14

B. *Significance of:*
Combined with
preaching .....Matt. 4:23
Divine
calling ....Eph. 4:11
Necessary for
bishops ....1 Tim. 3:2
Necessary for the Lord's bond-
servants.......2 Tim. 2:24-26
From house to
house.........Acts 20:20
By sharing.....Gal. 6:6
Not granted to women to teach
men...........1 Tim. 2:12

C. *Authority of, in divine things:*
Derived from
Christ.........Matt. 28:19, 20
Empowered by the
Spirit ....John 14:26
Taught by the
LORD...........Is. 54:13
Originates in
revelation .....Gal. 1:12

D. *Objects of, in divine things, concerning:*
God's way .....Ps. 27:11
God's path ....Ps. 25:4, 5
God's Law .....Ps. 119:12, 26, 66
God's will .....Ps. 143:10
Holiness ....Titus 2:12
Spiritual
truths ....Heb. 8:11, 12

E. *Perversion of, by:*
False
prophets ......Is. 9:15
False priests ...Mic. 3:11
Traditional-
ists............Matt. 15:9
False
teachers ......1 Tim. 4:1-3
Judaizers ......Acts 15:1
False
believers ......2 Tim. 4:3, 4

Tear, Torn

A. *Used literally of:*
Garments......Ezra 9:3, 5
Clothing.......Esth. 4:1
Rocks ....Matt. 27:51
Flesh ....Matt. 7:6

B. *Used figuratively of:*
Destruction....Hos. 13:8

Dissolution of the old
economy......Mark 15:38

Tears

A. *Kinds of:*
Agonizing .....Ps. 6:6
Rewarded.....Ps. 126:5
Repentant .....Luke 7:38, 44
Insincere ......Heb. 12:17
Intense ......Heb. 5:6-8
Woman's ......Esth. 8:3

B. *Caused by:*
Remorse......Gen. 27:34
Approaching
death ....2 Kin. 20:1-5
Oppression......Eccl. 4:1
Defeat.........Is. 16:9
Affliction and
anguish ......2 Cor. 2:4
Christian
service......Acts 20:19, 31

Tebah—*slaughter*

Son of Nahor .....Gen. 22:24

Tebaliah—*Yahweh has immersed*

Merarite
Korahite ......1 Chr. 26:11

Tebeth—*the name of the Hebrew tenth month*

Esther becomes queen
in ....Esth. 2:16, 17

Teeth, tooth

A. *Used for:*
Eating ....Num. 11:33
Showing
hatred ....Acts 7:54

B. *Figurative of:*
Destruction....Job 4:10
Holding on to
life............Job 13:14
God's
chastening ....Job 16:9
Escaped with the "skin of my
teeth"......Job 19:20
Judgment......Ps. 3:7
Hatred.........Ps. 35:16
Persecution....Ps. 57:4
Corporate
guilt ......Jer. 31:29, 30
Greediness.....Dan. 7:5, 7, 19
Starvation .....Amos 4:6
Hired
prophets ......Mic. 3:5
Remorse......Matt. 13:42, 50

Tehinnah—*grace*

Judahite ....1 Chr. 4:12

Tekel—*weighed*

Descriptive of Babylon's
judgment........Dan. 5:25

Tekoa, Tekoah—*firm, settlement*

Asshur the father { 1 Chr. 2:24
of ....{ 1 Chr. 4:5
Fortress city of
Judah ....2 Chr. 20:20
Home of a wise { 2 Sam. 14:2, 4,
woman..........{ 9
Fortified by
Rehoboam.......2 Chr. 11:6
Home of Amos....Amos 1:1

Tekoite—*an inhabitant of Tekoa*

Ikkesh thus
called ....2 Sam. 23:26
Among postexilic
workmen.........Neh. 3:5, 27

Tel Abib—*hill of grain*

Place in
Babylonia ....Ezek. 3:15

Telah—*fracture*

Ephraimite........1 Chr. 7:25

Telaim—*little lambs*

Saul assembles his army
here..............1 Sam. 15:4

Telassar—*hill of Assur*

City of
Mesopotamia.....2 Kin. 19:12
Children of Eden
in ....Is. 37:12

Telem—*a lamb*

1. Town in south
Judah.........Josh. 15:24
2. Divorced his foreign
wife..........Ezra 10:24

Tel Harsha—*mound of the craftman's work*

Babylonian
town ....Neh. 7:61

Tel Melah—*hill of salt*

Place in
Babylonia ....Ezra 2:59

Tema—*sunburnt*

Son of Ishmael....Gen. 25:15
Descendants of
Abraham.........1 Chr. 1:30
Troops of ....Job 6:19
Remote from
Palestine ....Jer. 25:23
On trade route through
Arabia.........Is. 21:13, 14

Teman—*the south*

1. Grandson of Esau; duke of
   Edom ....Gen. 36:11, 15
2. Another duke of
   Edom ....Gen. 36:42
3. Tribe in northeast
   Edom ....Gen. 36:34
   Judgment pronounced
   against........Amos 1:12
   God appears
   from ....Hab. 3:3

Temanite—*an inhabitant of Teman*

Job's friend,
Eliphaz..........Job 42:7, 9

Temeni—*fortunate*

Son of Ashur......1 Chr. 4:5, 6

Temperance

A. *Needed in:*
   Eating ....Prov. 23:1-3
   Sexual
   appetites......1 Cor. 7:1-9
   All things......1 Cor. 9:25-27
B. *Helped by:*
   Self-control....Prov. 16:32
   God's Spirit....Gal. 5:23
   Spiritual
   growth........2 Pet. 1:6
C. *In the use of wine, total
   recommended by:*
   Solomon.......Prov. 23:31-35
   Angel.........Judg. 13:3-5
   Nazirite vow...Num. 6:2, 3
   First, among
   Rechabites....Jer. 35:1-10

See Self-control; Sober, sobriety

Tempests—*terrible storms*

A. *Literal uses of:*
   At Sinai ....Heb. 12:18-21
   Jonah's ship tossed
   by ....Jon. 1:4-15
   Calmed by
   Christ.........Matt. 8:23-27

Paul's ship destroyed
by ....Acts 27:14-20

B. *Figurative of:*
   Destructive-
   ness........Is. 28:2
   God's wrath ...Jer. 30:23
   God's
   chastening ....Job 9:17
   Furious
   troubles.......Ps. 55:8
   God's
   judgments ....Ps. 83:15
   Hell's
   torments......Ps. 11:6
   Raging destructive-
   ness.........2 Pet. 2:17
   Destruction by
   war ....Amos 1:14

Temple, Herod's

Zechariah received
vision in..........Luke 1:5-22
Infant Jesus greeted here by
Simeon and
Anna............Luke 2:22-39
Jesus visited
at 12 ....Luke 2:42-52
Jesus visited and
cleansed.........John 2:15-17
Construction of,
specified.........John 2:19, 20
Jesus taught in....John 8:20
Jesus cleansed
again............Matt. 21:12-16
Jesus spoke parables
in ....Matt. 21:23-46
Jesus exposes Pharisees
in ....Matt. 23:1-39
Destruction of,
foretold ....Matt. 24:1, 2
Veil of, torn at {Matt. 27:51
Christ's death ... {Heb. 10:20
Christians worshiped
here.............Acts 2:46
Apostles taught
here.............Acts 3:1-26
Stephen's teaching on the
true.............Acts 7:46-50
Paul accused of
profaning........Acts 21:20-30

Temple, Solomon's

A. *Features regarding:*
   Site of, on Mt.
   Moriah........2 Sam. 24:18-25

Conceived by
David........2 Sam. 7:1-3
Building of, forbidden to
David.......1 Chr. 22:5-16
David promised a greater
house........2 Sam. 7:4-29
Pattern of, given to Solomon by
David........1 Chr. 28:1-21
Provisions for, given to
Solomon....1 Chr. 29:1-19
Supplies furnished by
Hiram........1 Kin. 5:1-18
Construction of, by
Solomon.....2 Chr. 3-4
Dedication of, by
Solomon.....2 Chr. 6
Seven years in
building.......1 Kin. 6:38
No noise in
building.......1 Kin. 6:7
Date of   { 1 Kin. 6:1, 37,
building.....{   38
Workmen employed
in..........1 Kin. 5:15-17

B. *History of:*
Ark brought
into...........1 Kin. 8:1-9
Filled with God's
glory........1 Kin. 8:10, 11
Treasures taken
away.........1 Kin. 14:25, 26
Repaired by
Jehoash.......2 Kin. 12:4-14
Treasures of, given to
Arameans by
Jehoash.....2 Kin. 12:17, 18
Treasures of, given to Assyrians
by Ahaz.....2 Kin. 16:14, 18
Worship of, restored by
Hezekiah.....2 Chr. 29:3-35
Treasures of, given by Hezekiah
to Assyrians...2 Kin. 18:13-16
Desecrated by Manasseh's
idolatry.......2 Kin. 21:4-7
Repaired and purified by
Josiah.........2 Kin. 23:4-12
Plundered and burned by
Babylonians...2 Kin. 25:9-17

Temple, spiritual

A. *Descriptive of:*
Christ's body ..John 2:19, 21
Believer's
body..........1 Cor. 6:19
True Church...1 Cor. 3:16, 17

Apostate
church.......2 Thess. 2:4

B. *Believers as, described as:*
Indwelt by
God...........2 Cor. 6:16
Indwelt by
Christ........Eph. 3:17, 18
Indwelt by the
Spirit.........Eph. 2:21, 22
Priests.........1 Pet. 2:5
Offering spiritual
sacrifices......Heb. 13:15, 16

Temple, Zerubbabel's

By the order of
Cyrus............Ezra 1:1-4
Temple vessels restored
for...............Ezra 1:7-11
Worship of,
restored..........Ezra 3:3-13
Work of rebuilding
hindered..........Ezra 4:1-24
Building of,
completed........Ezra 6:13-18
Inferiority of......Ezra 3:12

Temple tax

Levied yearly upon all
Jews............Matt. 17:24-27

Temporal—*for a short time*

Things that are
seen..............2 Cor. 4:18

Temporal blessings

A. *Consisting of:*
Rain...........Matt. 5:45
Seedtime and
harvest.......Gen. 8:22
Food and
raiment.......Luke 12:22-31
Prosperity......Deut. 8:7-18
Children........Ps. 127:3-5
Preservation of
life...........2 Tim. 4:16-18
Providential   { Gen. 24:12-14,
guidance.....{   42-44

B. *God's supply of:*
Promised.......Prov. 3:9, 10
Provided.......Neh. 9:15
Prayed for.....Matt. 6:11
Acknowl-
edged.........Ps. 23:1-5
Explained......Deut. 8:2, 3
Contingent
upon   { Mal. 3:7-11
obedience....{ Matt. 6:25-34

Object of
praise ....Ps. 103:1-5

Temptation—*a testing designed to strengthen or corrupt*

A. *Of God:*
Forbidden .....Matt. 4:7
By Israel.......Ps. 78:18-56
Heb. 3:9
Not possible ...James 1:13

B. *Of Christ:*
By:
The devil .....Matt. 4:1-10
Jewish
leaders.......Matt. 16:1
His disciples ..Matt. 16:23
Like us, but without
sin ....Heb. 4:15
Design of .....Heb. 2:18

C. *Of Satan, against:*
Job ....Job 1:6-12
David.........1 Chr. 21:1
Joshua........Zech. 3:1-5
Jesus ....Luke 4:1-13
Ananias and
Sapphira .....Acts 5:1-3
Christians .....1 Cor. 7:5

D. *Of Christians:*
By:
Lust ....James 1:13-15
Riches ....1 Tim. 6:9
Liability to...Gal. 6:1
Warnings
against.......Matt. 26:41
Prayer
against.......Matt. 6:13
Limitation
of............1 Cor. 10:13
Deliverance
from ....2 Pet. 2:9

Temptress—*female tempter*

Eve ....Gen. 3:6
Potiphar's wife ....Gen. 39:1-19
Delilah............Judg. 16:6-20
Jezebel...........1 Kin. 21:7
Job's wife.........Job 2:9
Adulteress ....Prov. 7:5-27
Herodias' daughter
(Salome) ....Mark 6:22-29

Ten Commandments

A. *Features concerning:*
Given at
Sinai..........Ex. 20:1-17

Written on
stone ....Ex. 24:12
Written by
God...........Ex. 31:18
First stones
broken........Ex. 32:19
Another copy
given ....Ex. 34:1
Put in the
ark ....Deut. 10:1-5
Called a
covenant......Ex. 34:28
Given in a different
form ....Deut. 5:6-21
The greatest ⌠Matt. 22:35-40
of these ......⌡Rom. 13:8-10

B. *Allusions to, in Scripture:*
First ....Acts 17:23
Second ....1 Kin. 18:17-40
Third ....Matt. 5:33-37
Fourth.........Jer. 17:21-27
Fifth...........Deut. 21:18-21
Eph. 6:1-3
Sixth ....Num. 35:16-21
Seventh ....Num. 5:12-31
Matt. 5:27-32
Eighth.........Matt. 19:18
Ninth..........Deut. 19:16-21
Tenth..........Rom. 7:7

Tender—*soft; compassionate*

A. *Used of physical things:*
Animal ....Gen. 18:7
Grass..........2 Sam. 23:4
Son............Prov. 4:3
Women........Deut. 28:56

B. *Used of spiritual things:*
Messiah ....Is. 53:2
Compassion ...Eph. 4:32
God's mercy ...Luke 1:78
Man's heart....2 Kin. 22:19
Christ's
return.........Matt. 24:32
Babylon's
destruction....Is. 47:1

Tenderness—*expressing a feeling or sympathy*

Shown toward the
young ....Gen. 33:13
Expressed toward an
enemy...........1 Sam. 30:11-15
Illustrated by a
Samaritan.......Luke 10:33-36
Manifested by a
father ....Luke 15:11-24

Tens of the Bible

A. *Descriptive of:*

Brothers .... Gen. 42:3
Cubits .... Ex. 26:16
Pillars and
  sockets ...... Ex. 27:12
Command-
  ments .... Ex. 34:28
Shekels .... Num. 7:14
Years .... Ruth 1:4
Loaves .... 1 Sam. 17:17
Tribes .... 1 Kin. 11:31, 35
Degrees .... 2 Kin. 20:9-11
Virgins .... Matt. 25:1-13
Talents .... Matt. 25:28
Lepers .... Luke 17:11-19
Pieces of
  money .... Luke 19:12-27
Horns .... Rev. 12:3

B. *Expressive of:*

Repre-
  sentation ..... Ruth 4:2
Intensity ...... Num. 14:22
Sufficiency .... Neh. 4:12
Magnitude ...... Dan. 1:20
Remnant .... Amos 5:3
Completion ..... Dan. 7:7, 20, 24
Perfection ..... Luke 19:16-24

Tentmaker

The occupation of:

Aquila and
  Priscilla ...... Acts 18:2, 3
Paul .... Acts 18:2, 3

Tents—*movable habitations*

A. *Used by:*

People .... 1 Chr. 17:5
Shepherds ...... Is. 38:12
Armies .... 1 Sam. 13:2
Rechabites ..... Jer. 35:7, 10
Women .... Gen. 24:67
Maidservants ... Gen. 31:33

B. *Features concerning:*

Fastened by
  cords .... Is. 54:2
Door
  provided ...... Gen. 18:1
Used for the
  ark .... 2 Sam. 7:1-6

C. *Figurative of:*

Shortness of ⎰ Is. 38:12
  life .... ⎱ 2 Cor. 5:1
Heavens .... Is. 40:22
Enlarge .... Is. 54:2

Terah—*duration; wandering*

1. Father of
   Abram .... Gen. 11:26
   Idolater ...... Josh. 24:2
   Dies in
     Haran ...... Gen. 11:25-32
2. Israelite encamp-
   ment .... Num. 33:1, 27

Teraphim—*household idols*

Laban's, stolen by
  Rachel .... Gen. 31:19-35
Used in idolatry ... Hos. 3:4

Terebinth tree

A. *Uses of:*

Landmarks ..... Judg. 6:11, 19
Burial place .... Gen. 35:8

B. *Figurative of:*

Judgment ...... Is. 1:29, 30

Teresh—*dry*

King's official ..... Esth. 2:21

Terrestrial—*belonging to the earth*

Spoken of
  bodies .... 1 Cor. 15:40

Terror—*extreme fear*

A. *Caused by:*

Lord's
  presence ...... Heb. 12:21
Fear .... Job 9:34
Death .... Job 24:17
War .... Ezek. 21:12
Fright .... Luke 24:37
Persecutors .... 1 Pet. 3:14

B. *Sent as means of:*

Protection ..... Gen. 35:5
Punishment .... Lev. 26:16

C. *Safeguards against, found in:*

God's
  promise ...... Ps. 91:5
God's plan ..... Luke 21:9

Tertius—*third*

Paul's scribe ...... Rom. 16:22

Tertullus—*diminutive of Tertius*

Orator who accuses
  Paul .... Acts 24:1-8

Test—*something that manifests a person's real character*

A. *Kinds of:*

Given to
  Solomon ...... 1 Kin. 10:1-3

Physical ....1 Sam. 17:38, 39
Supernatural...Ex. 7—11
Spiritual ....Dan. 6:1-28
National ....Ex. 32:1-35

B. *Purposes of, to:*
Test
obedience .... { Gen. 3:1-8
               { Gen. 22:1-18
Learn God's
will ....Judg. 6:36-40
Accept good
diet ....Dan. 1:12-16
Refute Satan's
claims.........Job 1:6-22
Destroy
idolatry ....1 Kin. 18:22-24

C. *Descriptive of:*
Testing
physically .... { 1 Sam. 17:39
                { Luke 14:19
Testing
morally ....John 6:6
Showing something to be
true...........Gen. 42:15, 16

D. *Objects of, among Christians:*
Faith ....2 Cor. 13:5
Abilities ....1 Tim. 3:10

Testament—*a will or covenant*

Descriptive of a person's
will...............Heb. 9:15-17

Testimony—*witness borne in behalf of something*

A. *Necessary elements of, seen in:*
Verbal
expression ....2 Sam. 1:16
Witnesses......Neh. 13:15
            John 8:17

B. *Means of:*
Prophets.......Acts 10:42, 43
Friends ....3 John 12
Jews...........Acts 22:12
Messengers....Acts 20:21, 24
Song ....Deut. 31:21
Our sins ....Is. 59:12

C. *Reaction to:*
Believed ....2 Thess. 1:10
Confirmed .....1 Cor. 1:6

D. *Purpose of, to:*
Establish the
Gospel ....Acts 10:42
Prove Jesus was the
Christ..........Acts 18:5
Lead to
repentance....Acts 20:21
Qualify for
office...........1 Tim. 3:7

Tests of Faith

By:

Difficult
demands ....Gen. 12:1, 2
Severe trials ......Job 1:6-22
Prosperity of the
wicked ....Ps. 73:1-28
Hardships........2 Cor. 11:21-33

Teth

Letter in the Hebrew
alphabet..........Ps. 119:65-72

Tetrarch—*a ruler over a fourth part of a kingdom*

Applied to Herod
Antipas...........Matt. 14:1

Thaddaeus—*breast*

One of the twelve
disciples.........Mark 3:18

Thahash—*porpoise, dolphin*

Son of Nahor .....Gen. 22:24

Thankfulness—*gratitude for blessings*

A. *Described as:*
Spiritual
sacrifice.......Ps. 116:17
Duty ....2 Thess. 2:13
Unceasing .....Eph. 1:16
Spontaneous ....Phil. 1:3
In Christ's
name ....Eph. 5:20
God's will......1 Thess. 5:18
Heaven's
theme.........Rev. 7:12

B. *Expressed for:*
Food ....John 6:11, 23
Wisdom ....Dan. 2:23
Converts ......1 Thess. 1:2
Prayer
answered .....John 11:41
Victory ....1 Cor. 15:57
Salvation ......2 Cor. 9:15
Lord's
Supper........1 Cor. 11:24
Changed
lives ....1 Thess. 2:13

C. *Expressed by:*
Healed
Samaritan.....Luke 17:12-19
Righteous .....Ps. 140:13

Theater—*a place of public assembly*

Paul kept from
entering..........Acts 19:29-31

Thebez—*brightness*

Fortified city near
Shechem ....Judg. 9:50-55

Theft, thief—*the act and agent of
stealing*

A. *Kinds of:*
Imputed ....Gen. 44:1-17
Improbable ....Matt. 28:11-13
Real ....Acts 5:1-3

B. *Characteristics of:*
Done often at
night..........Jer. 49:9
Comes unexpect-
edly...........Luke 12:39
Purpose of, to
steal ....John 10:10
Window used
by ....John 10:1

C. *Objects of:*
Idol............Gen. 31:19-35
Food ....Prov. 6:30
Traveler ......Luke 10:30, 36
Money........John 12:6

D. *Evil of:*
Condemned....Ex. 22:1-12
Punished .....Josh. 7:21-26
Inconsistent with
truth..........Jer. 7:9, 10
Defiles a
man ....Matt. 15:19, 20
Excludes from
heaven........1 Cor. 6:10
Not to be among
Christians.....Eph. 4:28

See Stealing

Theocracy—*government by God*

Evident under
Moses............Ex. 19:3-6
Continued under
Joshua ....Josh. 1:1-8
Rejected by
Israel............1 Sam. 8:4-9
To be restored ....Is. 2:2-4
                  Is. 9:6, 7

Theophany—*an appearance of God*

A. *Of God:*
At Sinai ....Ex. 24:9-12
In the
tabernacle ....Ex. 40:34-38
In the
Temple........1 Kin. 8:10, 11
To Isaiah ......Is. 6:1-9

B. *Of Christ as "the angel," to:*
Abraham .....Gen. 18:1-8

Jacob..........Gen. 31:11, 13
Moses ....Ex. 3:1-11
Joshua..........Josh. 5:13-15
Israel...........Judg. 2:1-5
Gideon ....Judg. 6:11-24
Manoah ....Judg. 13:2-25
Paul ....Acts 27:23, 24

C. *Of Christ, as incarnate, in:*
Old
Testament ....1 Cor. 10:4, 9
Nativity ....John 1:14, 18
His:
Resurrected
form ....John 20:26-29
Ascended
form ....Acts 7:55, 56
Return in
glory.........Rev. 1:7, 8
Glorified
form ....Matt. 17:1-9

Theophilus—*beloved of God*

Luke addresses   ⎰ Luke 1:3
his writings to... ⎱ Acts 1:1

Thessalonians, the Epistles to the—
books of the New Testament

A. *1 Thessalonians:*
Commen-
dation.........1 Thess. 1:2-10
Paul's apostolic
ministry.......1 Thess. 2:1-20
Timothy as
envoy.........1 Thess. 3:1-10
The quiet   ⎰ 1 Thess. 4:11,
life............⎱   12
The second
coming........1 Thess. 4:13-18
Sons of light, not
darkness ......1 Thess. 5:4-7
Christian
conduct.......1 Thess. 5:12-24

B. *2 Thessalonians:*
Encouragement in
suffering ......2 Thess. 1:3-12
The man of
sin............2 Thess. 2:3-10
Stead-
fastness.......2 Thess. 2:15-17
Maintaining
order..........2 Thess. 3:1-15

Thessalonica—*an important city of
Macedonia (modern Salonika)*

Paul preaches in ..Acts 17:1-13
Paul writes letters to
churches of.......1 Thess. 1:1

Theudas—*God-giving*

Leader of an unsuccessful
revolt . . . . Acts 5:36

Thirst—*a craving for water*

A. *Caused by:*
Wilderness
drought . . . . Ex. 17:3
Unbelief . . . . . . Deut. 28:47, 48
Siege . . . . 2 Chr. 32:11
Travels . . . . 2 Cor. 11:27
Extreme pain . . John 19:28
Flame . . . . Luke 16:24

B. *Figurative of:*
Salvation . . . . . . Is. 55:1
Righ-
teousness . . . . . Matt. 5:6
Holy Spirit . . . . . John 7:37-39
Serving
Christ . . . . Matt. 25:35-42

C. *Satisfaction of:*
By a miracle . . Neh. 9:15, 20
Longed for . . . . . Ps. 63:1
In Christ
alone . . . . John 6:35
Final
invitation . . . . Rev. 22:17
Perfectly {Is. 49:10
fulfilled . . . . {Rev. 7:16

Thirty heroes, the

Served David . . . . . 1 Chr. 12:1-40

Thirty pieces of silver—*bribe of Judas*

Price of slave . . . . Ex. 21:32
Given to Judas . . . . Matt. 26:14-16
Buys field . . . . . . Matt. 27:3-10

Thistle—*spiny weeds*

Obnoxious among
wheat . . . . Job 31:40

Thomas—*twin*

Apostle of
Christ . . . . Matt. 10:3
Ready to die with
Christ . . . . John 11:16
In need of
instruction . . . . . . John 14:1-6
Not present when Christ
appears . . . . John 20:19-24
States terms of
belief . . . . John 20:25
Christ appears
again and {John 20:26-29
convinces him . . . {John 21:1, 2

In the upper
room . . . . Acts 1:13

Thongs—*leather straps*

Used to bind
Paul . . . . Acts 22:25

Thorn—*a plant with sharp projections
on its stems*

A. *Used literally of:*
Earth's
produce . . . . Gen. 3:18
Land under
judgment . . . . . Is. 34:13
Christ's
crown . . . . John 19:2

B. *Used figuratively of:*
Unbelief . . . . Is. 32:13-15
Judgments . . . . . Hos. 2:6
Pain . . . . Prov. 26:9
False
prophets . . . . . . Matt. 7:15, 16
Agent of
Satan . . . . 2 Cor. 12:7
Barrenness . . . . . Matt. 13:7, 22

Thought—*the reasoning of the mind*

A. *Of the wicked, described as:*
Evil . . . . Gen. 6:5
Abominable . . . . Prov. 15:26
Sinful . . . . Is. 59:7
Devoid of
God . . . . Ps. 10:4
Futile . . . . Rom. 1:21
Known by
God . . . . 1 Cor. 3:20
In need of
repentance . . . . Acts 8:22

B. *Of the believer:*
Compre-
hended by {1 Chr. 28:9
God . . . . {Ps. 139:2
Captivated by
Christ . . . . 2 Cor. 10:5
Criticized by God's
Word . . . . Heb. 4:12
In need of examin-
ation . . . . Ps. 139:23

C. *Of God:*
Not like
man's . . . . Is. 55:8, 9
To believer,
good . . . . Ps. 139:17

Thousand years

As one day . . . . 2 Pet. 3:8
Millennial reign . . . Rev. 20:1-7

Thread

Refused by
  Abram ....Gen. 14:23
Tied to hand .....Gen. 38:28
Lips like scarlet ...Song 4:3

Threatenings—*menacing actions or words against another*

A. *Purposes of, to:*
  Silence a
    prophet ....1 Kin. 19:1, 2
  Hinder a
    work..........Neh. 6:1-14
  Hinder the
    Gospel.........Acts 4:17, 21

B. *Exemplified by:*
  Jehoram against
    Elisha........2 Kin. 6:31
  Jews against
    Christians.....Acts 4:29
  Saul against
    Christians.....Acts 9:1

Threshing—*separating kernels of grain by force*

A. *Characteristics of:*
  Done by a
    stick ....Is. 28:27
  By cartwheels
    also...........Is. 28:27, 28
  By the feet of
    cattle ....Hos. 10:11

B. *Figurative of:*
  God's
    judgments ....Jer. 51:33
  Minister's
    labor..........1 Cor. 9:9, 10

Threshold

Will shake ....Amos 9:1
Descriptive of Nineveh's
  fall ....Zeph. 2:14

Throat—*the front part of the neck*

Glutton's
  warning ....Prov. 23:2
Thirsty one ......Ps. 69:3
Source of evil .....Ps. 5:9

Throne—*the seat and symbol of regal authority*

A. *Of men:*
  Under God's
    sovereignty ...Dan. 5:18-21
  Established on righ-
    teousness .....Prov. 16:12
  Upheld by
    mercy.........Prov. 20:28
  Subject to:
    Succession....2 Chr. 6:10, 16
  Termin-
    ation.........Jer. 22:4-30

B. *Of God:*
  Resplendent in
    glory.........Is. 6:1-3
  Relentless in
    power.........Dan. 2:44
  Ruling over   { Dan. 4:25, 34,
    all ....{ 35
  Righteous in
    execution .....Ps. 9:4, 7, 8
  Regal throughout
    eternity ....Rev. 22:1, 3

C. *Of Christ:*
  Based upon the Davidic
    covenant .....2 Sam. 7:12-16
  Of eternal   { Ps. 89:4, 29, 36
    duration .....{ Dan. 7:13, 14
  Explained in its
    nature ....Is. 9:6, 7
  Symbolized in its
    functions......Zech. 6:12, 13
  Promised to
    Christ.........Luke 1:31-33
  Christ rises to
    possess........Heb. 8:1
  Christ now   { Eph. 1:20-22
    rules from....{ 1 Pet. 3:20-22
  Shares with the
    Godhead......Rev. 5:12-14
  Shares with   { Luke 22:30
    believers .....{ Rev. 3:21
  Judges men
    from ....Matt. 25:31

Thumb—*first of man's fingers*

Anointing of, as an act of
  consecration......Lev. 8:23, 24
As an act of   { Lev. 14:14, 17,
  purification......{ 25, 28
Cutting off, an act of
  subjugation ......Judg. 1:6, 7

Thunder—*the sound produced by lightning*

A. *Supernaturally brought:*
  Upon the
    Egyptians .....Ex. 9:22-34
  At Sinai ....Ex. 19:16
  Against the
    Philistines.....1 Sam. 7:10
  At David's   { 2 Sam. 22:14,
    deliverance...{ 15

B. *Figurative of:*
God's:
Power ....Job 26:14
Control........Ps. 104:7
Majesty........Rev. 4:5
Visitations of
judgment .....Rev. 11:19

Thyatira—*an important town in the Roman province of Asia*

Residence of
Lydia.............Acts 16:14
One of the seven
churches ....Rev. 2:18-24
Sea of Galilee
called ....John 6:1, 23

Thyine—*a small cone-bearing tree*

Wood of, used for
furniture ....Rev. 18:12

Tibhath—*slaughter*

Town in the kingdom of
Zobah.............1 Chr. 18:8

Tibni—*intelligent*

Son of Ginath.....1 Kin. 16:21, 22

Tidal—*splendor*

King allied with
Chedorlaomer ....Gen. 14:1, 9

Tidings

A. *Descriptive of:*
Joyful ....Gen. 29:13
Good ....1 Kin. 1:42
B. *Of salvation:*
Out of Zion...Is. 40:9
By a person....Is. 41:27
By an angel....Luke 2:8-18
See News

Tiglath-Pileser—*my trust is in the god Ninib*

Powerful Assyrian king who
invades
Samaria ....2 Kin. 15:29

Tikvah—*hope*

1. Father-in-law of
Huldah........2 Kin. 22:14
Called
Tokhath ......2 Chr. 34:22
2. Father-in-law of
Jahaziah ......Ezra 10:15

Tile

Earthen roof .....Luke 5:19

Tiller—*a farmer*

Man's first job ...Gen. 2:5
Sin's handicap
on................Gen. 4:12
Industry in,
commended ......Prov. 12:11

Tilon—*scorn*

Son of Shimon ...1 Chr. 4:20

Timaeus—*highly prized*

Father of
Bartimaeus......Mark 10:46

Timbrel—*a small hand drum*

Used in:

Entertainment ....Gen. 31:27
Worship ....Ps. 81:1-4

Time—*the period between two eternities*

A. *Computation of, by:*
Years..........Gen. 15:13
Months........1 Chr. 27:1
Weeks.........Dan. 10:2
Days ....Gen. 8:3
Moments .....Ex. 33:5
Sundial ....2 Kin. 20:9-11
B. *Events of, dated by:*
Succession of
families ......Gen. 5:1-32
Lives of great
men........Gen. 7:6, 11
Succession of
kings ....1 Kin. 11:42, 43
Earthquakes ....Amos 1:1
Important events (the
exodus).......1 Kin. 6:1
Important
emperors......Luke 3:1
C. *Periods of, stated in years:*
Bondage in
Egypt.........Acts 7:6
Wilderness
wanderings ...Deut. 1:3
Judges........Judg. 11:26
Captivity .....Dan. 9:2
Seventy weeks (490
years)........Dan. 9:24-27
D. *Sequence of prophetic events in, indicated by:*
"The time is fulfilled" (Christ's
advent) ....Mark 1:15

"The fullness of the time"
(Christ's
advent) ....Gal. 4:4
"The times of the Gentiles" (the
Gospel age) ...Luke 21:24
"The day of salvation" (the
Gospel age) ...2 Cor. 6:2
"In the last days" (the Gospel
age)...........Acts 2:17
"In the last days"
(the time before
Christ's
return).......$\left\{\begin{array}{l} 2 \text{ Tim. } 3:1 \\ 2 \text{ Pet. } 3:3 \end{array}\right.$
"The last day"
(Christ's
return)........$\left\{\begin{array}{l} \text{John } 6:39, 54 \\ \text{John } 12:48 \end{array}\right.$
"New heavens"
(eternity) .....2 Pet. 3:13

E. *Importance of, indicated by:*
Shortness of
life............Ps. 89:47
Making the most of
it............Eph. 5:16
Purpose of, for
salvation......2 Pet. 3:9, 15
Uncertainty
of............Luke 12:16-23
Our goal,
eternity......$\left\{\begin{array}{l} \text{Heb. } 11:10, \\ 13-16 \end{array}\right.$
God's plan in ..Acts 14:15-17

F. *For everything:*
To give birth, to
die............Eccl. 3:1-8, 17

Timidity—*lack of courage*

Nicodemus........John 3:1, 2
Joseph of
Arimathea........John 19:38
Certain people ....John 9:18-23

Timna, Timnah—*restraint*

1. Concubine of
Eliphaz ....Gen. 36:12, 22
2. Duke of
Edom ....Gen. 36:40

Timnah—*allotted portion*

1. Town of
Judah.........Josh. 15:10
Assigned to
Dan...........Josh. 19:40, 43
Captured by
Philistines.....2 Chr. 28:18
2. Town in Judah's hill
country.........Josh. 15:57

Timnath Serah—*extra portion*

Village in Ephraim's hill
country ....Josh. 19:50

Place of Joshua's
burial ....Josh. 24:29, 30
Called Timnath
Heres ....Judg. 2:9

Timnite—*an inhabitant of Timnah*

Samson thus
called ....Judg. 15:6

Timon—*deeming worthy*

One of the seven
deacons ....Acts 6:1-5

Timothy, the Epistles to—*books of the
New Testament*

A. *1 Timothy:*
Toward true
doctrine.......1 Tim. 1:3-7
Paul's
ministry.......1 Tim. 1:12-17
Christ, the
Mediator......1 Tim. 2:5, 6
Instructions to
women........1 Tim. 2:9-15
Church
officials ....1 Tim. 3:1-13
The good
minister.......1 Tim. 4:6-16
Fight the good
fight ....1 Tim. 6:11-21

B. *2 Timothy:*
Call to responsi-
bility..........2 Tim. 1:6-18
Call for
strength ......2 Tim. 2:1-13
Against
apostasy ......2 Tim. 3:1-9
The Scriptures called
inspired ....2 Tim. 3:14-17
Charge to
Timothy ......2 Tim. 4:1-8
Paul's personal
concerns......2 Tim. 4:9-18

Timothy—*revere God*

A. *Life of:*
Of mixed
parentage .....Acts 16:1, 3
Faith of, from
childhood ....$\left\{\begin{array}{l} 2 \text{ Tim. } 1:5 \\ 2 \text{ Tim. } 3:15 \end{array}\right.$
Becomes Paul's
companion....Acts 16:1-3
Ordained by the
presbytery ...1 Tim. 4:14
Left behind at
Troas.........Acts 17:14
Sent by Paul
to Thessa-
lonica........$\left\{\begin{array}{l} 1 \text{ Thess. } 3:1, 2, \\ 6 \end{array}\right.$

Rejoined Paul at
Corinth.......Acts 18:1-5
Preached Christ to
Corinthians...2 Cor. 1:19
Sent by Paul into
Macedonia....Acts 19:22
Sent by Paul to
Corinth.......1 Cor. 4:17
Returned with Paul to
Jerusalem.....Acts 20:1-5
With Paul in ⎰Phil. 1:1
Rome ⎱Phil. 2:19, 23
Set free........Heb. 13:23
Left at Ephesus by
Paul ....1 Tim. 1:3
Paul summoned
him to ⎰2 Tim. 4:9, 11,
Rome.......⎱ 21

B. *Character of:*
Devout from
childhood.....2 Tim. 3:15
Faithful in
service.......Phil. 2:22
Beloved by
Paul......1 Tim. 1:2, 18
Follows Paul's
way..........1 Cor. 4:17
In need of
instruction....1 Tim. 4:12-16
Of sickly
nature........1 Tim. 5:23
Urged to remain
faithful.......1 Tim. 6:20, 21
Emotional.....2 Tim. 1:4

Tin—*a metal obtained by smelting*

Used in early
times............Num. 31:22
Brought from
Tarshish.........Ezek. 27:12

Tiphsah—*passage; crossing*

1. Place designating Solomon's
northern
boundary.....1 Kin. 4:24
2. Unidentified town attacked by
Mena* .....2 Kin. 15:16

Tiras

Son of Japheth....Gen. 10:2

Tirathites

Family of
scribes...........1 Chr. 2:55

Tirhakah—*the king of Cush (Nubia)*

Opposes
Sennacherib......2 Kin. 19:9

Tirhanah—*kindness*

Son of Caleb......1 Chr. 2:42, 48

Tiria—*foundation*

Son of Jehaleleel..1 Chr. 4:16

Tirzah—*delight*

1. Zelophehad's youngest
daughter......Num. 26:33
2. Town near
Samaria.......Josh. 12:24
Seat of Jeroboam's
rule...........1 Kin. 14:17
Israel's kings rule here down to
Omri..........1 Kin. 16:6-23
Famous for its
beauty.......Song 6:4

Tishbite—*an inhabitant of Tishbeh*

Elijah thus
called............1 Kin. 17:1

Tithes—*the tenth of one's income*

Given by Abraham to
Melchizedek......Heb. 7:1, 2, 6
Promised by
Jacob.............Gen. 28:22
Belongs to the
LORD............Lev. 27:30-33
Given to Levites..Num. 18:21-24
Given by Levites to
priests............Num. 18:25-28
Taken to
Temple..........Deut. 12:5-19
Rules regarding..Deut. 14:22-29
Honesty in,
required..........Deut. 26:13-15
Of animals, every
tenth............Lev. 27:32, 33
Recognition of, by
Jews.............Neh. 13:5, 12
Promise
regarding.........Mal. 3:7-12
Pharisaic legalism on,
condemned.......Luke 18:9-14

Titles—*appellations of honor*

Condemned by
Christ.............Matt. 23:1-10

Tittle—*a mark distinguishing similar
letters*

Figurative of minute
requirements.....Matt. 5:18

See Jot

Titus

Greek Christian and Paul's
companion .... Titus 1:4
Sent by Paul to
Corinth .... 2 Cor. 7:13, 14
Organized Corinthian relief
fund............. 2 Cor. 8:6-23
Met Paul in
Macedonia .... 2 Cor. 7:6, 7
Accompanied Paul to
Crete............ Titus 1:5
Sent by Paul to
Dalmatia .... 2 Tim. 4:10

Titus, the Epistle to—*a book of the New Testament*

Qualifications of an
elder .... Titus 1:5-9
Against false
teachings........ Titus 1:10-16
Domestic life..... Titus 2:1-10
Godly living...... Titus 3:3-8

Tizite

Description of Joha, David's
mighty man ...... 1 Chr. 11:45

Tob—*good*

Jephthah's refuge east of the
Jordan .... Judg. 11:3, 5

Tobadonijah—*good is Lord Yahweh*

Levite teacher..... 2 Chr. 17:7, 8

Tobiah—*Yahweh is good*

1. Founder of a postexilic
   family......... Ezra 2:60
2. Ammonite servant; ridiculed the
   Jews.......... Neh. 2:10

Tobijah—*Yahweh is good*

1. Levite
   teacher .... 2 Chr. 17:7, 8
2. Came from
   Babylon....... Zech. 6:10, 14

Tochen—*a measure*

Town of Simeon .. 1 Chr. 4:32

Toe—*the terminal part of the foot*

Aaron's,
anointed .... Ex. 29:20
Of captives,
amputated....... Judg. 1:6, 7
Of an image....... Dan. 2:41, 42

Togarmah

Northern country inhabited by
descendants of
Gomer .... Gen. 10:3

Toi

King of Hamath; sends embassy to
salute David...... 2 Sam. 8:9-12

Token—*a visible sign*

Guarantee .... Josh. 2:12, 18,
21

See Sign

Tola—*worm; scarlet*

1. Son of Issachar and family
   head.......... Gen. 46:13
2. Son of Puah; a judge of
   Israel .... Judg. 10:1

Tolad—*begetter*

Simeonite town ... 1 Chr. 4:29
Called Eltolad..... Josh. 19:4

Tolerance—*an attitude of patience toward opposing views*

A. *Approved in dealing with:*
   Disputes among
   brothers....... Mark 9:38-40
   Weaker
   brother .... Rom. 14:1-23
   Repentant
   brother .... 2 Cor. 2:4-11

B. *Condemned in dealing with:*
   Sin .... 1 Cor. 5:1-13
   Evil........... 2 Cor. 6:14-18
   Sin in
   ourselves...... Mark 9:43-48
   Error .... 2 John 10, 11

Tomb—*a place of burial*

John's body placed
in .... Mark 6:25-29
Christ's body
placed in Joseph's (Matt. 27:57-60
\ John 19:41, 42
Figurative of
hypocrisy........ Matt. 23:27

Tongue—*the organ of speech*

A. *Descriptive of:*
   Speech .... Ex. 4:10
   The physical
   organ .... Judg. 7:5
   Externalism.... 1 John 3:18
   People or
   race........... Is. 66:18

Spiritual gift...1 Cor. 12:10-30
Submission ....Is. 45:23

B. *Kinds of:*
Backbiting.....Prov. 25:23
As of fire ......Acts 2:3
Deceitful .....Mic. 6:12
Double ....1 Tim. 3:8
False ....Ps. 120:3
Flattering......Prov. 6:24
Gentle ....Prov. 25:15
Just ....Prov. 10:20
Lying..........Prov. 21:6
Muttering ....Is. 59:3
New...........Mark 16:17
Perverse ......Prov. 17:20
Sharpened .....Ps. 140:3
Slow..........Ex. 4:10
Stammering ...Is. 33:19
Wholesome ...Prov. 15:4
Wise..........Prov. 15:2

C. *Characteristics of:*
Small but
important .....James 3:5
Untameable....James 3:6-8
Source of
trouble........Prov. 21:23
Means of sin...Ps. 39:1
Known by
God...........Ps. 139:4

D. *Proper employment of, in:*
Speaking:
God's righteous-
ness..........Ps. 35:28
Wisdom ......Ps. 37:30
God's Word...Ps. 119:172
Singing
praises ....Ps. 126:2
Kindness ......Prov. 31:26
Confessing
Christ.........Phil. 2:11

See Slander

Tongues, speaking in

A. *At Pentecost:*
Opposite of
Babel ....Gen. 11:6-9
Sign of the Spirit's
coming........Acts 2:3, 4
External manifesta-
tion...........Acts 2:4-6
Meaning of, interpreted by
Peter..........Acts 2:14-40

B. *At Corinth:*
Spiritual gift { 1 Cor. 12:8-10,
(last rank) ...   28-30

Interpreter of,
required.......1 Cor. 14:27, 28
Love superior
to.............1 Cor. 13:1-13
Subject to
abuse ....1 Cor. 14:22-26

Tools of the Bible

Anvil ....Is. 41:7
Awl..............Deut. 15:17
Axe.............1 Chr. 20:3
Bellows ....Jer. 6:29
Brickkiln.........2 Sam. 12:31
Compass.........Is. 44:13
Refining pot......Prov. 17:3
Fleshhook........1 Sam. 2:13
Fork ....Ex. 27:3
Furnace..........Prov. 17:3
Goad............1 Sam. 13:21
Engraving tool ...Ex. 32:4
Hammer.........Ps. 74:6
Inkhorn..........Ezek. 9:2
Knife ....Gen. 22:6
Mattock ....1 Sam. 13:21
Ox goad ....Judg. 3:31
Firepans ....Ex. 27:3
Plane ....Is. 44:13
Plowshare.......Is. 2:4
Plumb line ....Amos 7:8
Pruning hook ....Is. 2:4
Razor ....Num. 6:5
Saw.............2 Sam. 12:31
Shovel ....Ex. 27:3
Sickle...........Deut. 16:9
Wheel...........Eccl. 12:6

Topaz—*a precious stone*

Used in
breastplate ......Ex. 39:10
Of great value.....Job 28:19
In Eden..........Ezek. 28:13
In New
Jerusalem ....Rev. 21:2, 20

Tophel—*lime; cement*

Israelite camp.....Deut. 1:1

Tophet—*altar*

Place of human sacrifice
in the valley of
Hinnom ....Jer. 7:31, 32

Torment—*to suffer unbearable pain*

A. *Kinds of:*
Physical ....Matt. 8:6
Eternal ....Rev. 20:10
Internal ....2 Pet. 2:7, 8

B. *Means of:*
Official . . . . Matt. 18:34
Persecutors . . . . Heb. 11:35
Fear . . . . 1 John 4:18
Flame . . . . Luke 16:23-25
God . . . . Rev. 14:9-11
Human soul . . . Job 19:2

Touch—*contact between two things*

A. *Kinds of:*
Unclean . . . . . . Lev. 5:2, 3
Angelic . . . . 1 Kin. 19:5, 7
Queenly . . . . . . Esth. 5:2
Cleansing . . . . . Is. 6:7
Healing . . . . Matt. 8:3
Sexual . . . . 1 Cor. 7:1
Satanic . . . . John 5:18

B. *Purposes of, to:*
Purify . . . . Is. 6:7
Strengthen . . . . Dan. 10:10-18
Harm . . . . Zech. 2:8
Heal . . . . Mark 5:27-31
Receive a
blessing . . . . . . Mark 10:13
Restore to
life . . . . Luke 7:14
Manifest
faith . . . . Luke 7:39-50

Towel—*a cloth used in drying*

Used by Christ . . . . John 13:4, 5

Tower of the Ovens—*a tower of Jerusalem*

Rebuilt by
Nehemiah . . . . Neh. 3:11

Tower of the Hundred

Restored by
Eliashib . . . . Neh. 3:1

Towers

A. *Purposes of, for:*
Protection . . . . . Matt. 21:33
Watchmen . . . . . 2 Kin. 9:17
Safeguarding
people . . . . 2 Chr. 26:10, 15

B. *Partial list of:*
Babel . . . . Gen. 11:4, 9
David . . . . Song 4:4
Lebanon . . . . . . Song 7:4
Penuel . . . . Judg. 8:17
Shechem . . . . . Judg. 9:40, 47, 49
Siloam . . . . Luke 13:4

Trachonitis—*hilly land*

Volcanic region southeast of
Damascus . . . . Luke 3:1

Trade and transportation

A. *Objects of, such as:*
Gold . . . . 1 Kin. 9:28
Timber . . . . 1 Kin. 5:6, 8, 9
Hardwood . . . . 1 Kin. 10:11, 12
Spices . . . . 1 Kin. 10:10, 15
Property . . . . . . Ruth 4:3, 4
Slaves . . . . Joel 3:6

B. *Means of, by:*
Wagons . . . . . . Gen. 46:5, 6
Cows . . . . 1 Sam. 6:7, 8
Rafts . . . . 1 Kin. 5:7-9
Camels . . . . 1 Kin. 10:1, 2
Donkeys . . . . . . Num. 22:21-33
Horses . . . . 1 Kin. 20:20
Caravans . . . . . Gen. 37:25-36

C. *Centers of, in:*
Tyre . . . . Ezek. 27:1-36
Jerusalem . . . . . Neh. 13:15-21

Trades and crafts

Baker . . . . Gen. 40:1
Brick makers . . . . . Ex. 5:7
Carpenter . . . . Is. 41:7
Engineers . . . . Gen. 11:3, 4
Farmers . . . . Ps. 104:13-15
Fishermen . . . . Matt. 4:18-22
Lawyers . . . . Luke 5:17
Millers . . . . Ex. 11:5
Physician . . . . Col. 4:14
Smiths . . . . Is. 44:12

Traditions—*precepts passed down from past generations*

A. *Jewish, described as:*
Commandments of
men . . . . Matt. 15:9
Rejection of God's
Word . . . . Mark 7:8, 9
Productive of
hypocrisy . . . . . Mark 7:6, 7
Inconsistent with
Christ . . . . Col. 2:8

B. *Christian described as:*
Inspired by the
Spirit . . . . John 15:26, 27
Handed down by
apostles . . . . . . 2 Thess. 3:6, 7
Based on eyewit-
nesses . . . . 2 Pet. 1:16, 19
Classed as   (1 Tim. 5:18
Scripture . . . . . (2 Pet. 3:16
Once for all
delivered . . . . . . Jude 3
Consisting of fundamental
truths . . . . 1 Cor. 15:1-3
Originating   (Matt. 28:20
with Christ . . . (1 Cor. 11:1-23

Traffic, spiritual

Buying the truth . . Prov. 23:23
Value of wisdom . . Prov. 2:2-4
Above gold in
value. . . . . Ps. 119:72, 127
Without price . . . . . Is. 55:1
True gold, from
Christ . . . . Rev. 3:18

Train

Trailing robe . . . . . . Is. 6:1

Traitor—one who betrays a trust

Descriptive of:
Judas . . . . Luke 6:16
End-time people . . 2 Tim. 3:4

Trance—a somnolent state

Peter's on a
housetop . . . . Acts 10:10

Transfiguration—a radical change in appearance of

Moses. . . . . Ex. 34:29-35
Christ, on a high
mountain. . . . . Matt. 17:1-13
Christ,
remembered . . . . . . 2 Pet. 1:16-18
Stephen. . . . . Acts 6:15

Transgression—a violation of God's Law

A. Described as:
Personal . . . . 1 Tim. 2:14
Public . . . . Rom. 5:14
Political . . . . Esth. 3:3
Pre-
meditated . . . . Josh. 7:11-25

B. Caused by:
Law . . . . Rom. 4:15
Sin . . . . 1 John 3:4
Wine . . . . Hab. 2:5
Idolatry. . . . . 1 Chr. 5:25
Inter-
marriage . . . . . Ezra 10:10, 13
Fear of the
people . . . . 1 Sam. 15:24

C. Productive of:
Power-
lessness . . . . Judg. 2:20-23
Unfaith-
fulness. . . . . 1 Chr. 9:1
Death . . . . 1 Chr. 10:13
Destruction . . . . . Ps. 37:38
Curse. . . . . Is. 24:5, 6

D. Punishment of, by:
Defeat . . . . 2 Chr. 12:1-5
Disease . . . . 2 Chr. 26:16-21
Captivity . . . . Neh. 1:8
Affliction . . . . . . Ps. 107:17
Death in hell. . . Is. 66:24

E. Reaction to, by:
Further dis-
obedience . . . . . Num. 14:41-45
Covering up . . . Job 31:33
Repentance . . . . Ezra 9:4-7

F. Forgiveness of:
Difficult . . . . Josh. 24:19
Out of God's
mercy. . . . . Ex. 34:7
By:
Confession. . . Ps. 32:1, 5
Removal. . . . . Ps. 103:12
Blotting out . . Is. 44:22

G. Christ's relation to:
Wounded for
our . . . . Is. 53:5
Stricken for
our . . . . Is. 53:8
Make intercession
for . . . . Is. 53:12
Provided a Redeemer
for . . . . Rom. 11:26, 27
Died for our . . . Heb. 9:15

See Sin

Transitory—passing quickly away

A. Descriptive of man's:
Life. . . . . Ps. 39:4, 5
Pleasures . . . . . . Is. 47:8, 9
Plans . . . . Luke 12:16-21

B. Caused by:
World's passing
away. . . . . 1 John 2:15-17
Our
mortality. . . . . Ps. 90:3-12
Impending future
world . . . . 2 Cor. 4:17, 18

Translations—physical transportation to heaven

Enoch. . . . . Heb. 11:5
Elijah . . . . 2 Kin. 2:1-11
Christians. . . . . 1 Thess. 4:16, 17

Travail—the labor pains of childbirth

A. Descriptive of:
Anguish . . . . Is. 53:11

B. Of a woman's, described as:
Fearful . . . . Ps. 48:6

Painful . . . . Is. 13:8
Hazardous . . . . . Gen. 35:16-19
Joyful
afterwards . . . . John 16:21

C. *Figurative of:*
New Israel . . . . Is. 66:7, 8
Messiah's
birth . . . . Mic. 4:9, 10
Redemption . . . Mic. 5:3
New birth . . . . Gal. 4:19
Creation's
rebirth . . . . . . Rom. 8:22

Treachery—*pretending friendship in order to betray*

A. *Manifested by:*
Woman . . . . Judg. 4:18-21
People . . . . Josh. 9:3-15
King . . . . 2 Sam. 11:14, 15
Son . . . . 2 Sam. 13:28, 29
Enemy . . . . Esth. 3:8-15
Disciple . . . . . . Matt. 26:47-50

B. *Accompanied by:*
Deceit . . . . Gen. 34:13-31
Soothing
words . . . . Judg. 9:1-5
Professed
favor . . . . 1 Sam. 18:17-19
Pretense . . . . . Dan. 6:1-8

Treason—*betrayal of one's country*

A. *Instances of:*
Rahab against
Jericho . . . . Josh. 2:1-24
Israelites against
Rehoboam . . . . 1 Kin. 12:16-19
Absalom against
David . . . . 2 Sam. 15:1-14
Sheba against
David . . . . 2 Sam. 20:1-22
Athaliah
against   {2 Kin. 11
Judah   {2 Chr. 22:10-12

B. *Characterized by:*
Conspiracy . . . . 1 Kin. 16:9-11, 20
Giving   {1 Sam. 30:15,
secrets . . . . . . {16
Falling out . . . . 2 Sam. 3:6-21
Jealousy . . . . . Num. 12:1-11

See Conspiracy; Treachery

Treasure—*something valuable stored away*

A. *Descriptive of:*
Places for storing
archives . . . . . . Ezra 5:17

B. *Figurative of:*
Earth's productive
capacity . . . . . . Ps. 17:14
Wisdom . . . . Prov. 2:4
People of
God . . . . Ex. 19:5
Man's spiritual
possibilities . . . Matt. 12:35
New life in
Christ . . . . 2 Cor. 4:6, 7
Christ as the divine
depository . . . . Col. 2:3, 9
Future
rewards . . . . . . Matt. 6:19, 20

Treasurer—*a custodian of public funds*

Under:

David, Ahijah . . . . . 1 Chr. 26:20
Solomon, Jehiel . . . 1 Chr. 29:7, 8
Hezekiah,
Shebna . . . . Is. 22:15
Cyrus,
Mithredath . . . . . . Ezra 1:8
Candace, the Ethiopian
eunuch . . . . Acts 8:27
At Corinth,
Erastus . . . . Rom. 16:23

Treasury
Gifts for temple kept
here . . . . Luke 21:1
Storehouses . . . 1 Kin. 7:51

Tree

A. *Characteristics of:*
Created by
God . . . . Gen. 1:11, 12
Of fixed
varieties . . . . . . Gen. 1:12, 29
Can be
grafted . . . . Rom. 11:24
Subject to God's
judgments . . . . Hag. 2:17, 19

B. *Used for:*
Shade . . . . Gen. 18:4
Burial sites . . . . Gen. 35:8
Food . . . . Deut. 20:19, 20
Cross . . . . Acts 5:30
Buildings . . . . . 1 Kin. 5:10
Idolatry . . . . Is. 44:14, 17
Fuel . . . . Is. 44:15, 16, 19

C. *List of, in Bible:*
Acacia . . . . Ex. 36:20
Almond . . . . . . Gen. 30:37
Aloe . . . . Ps. 45:8
Broom . . . . 1 Kin. 19:4, 5
Cedar . . . . 1 Kin. 10:27

Chestnut ......Gen. 30:37
Cypress........Is. 44:14
Fig ....Deut. 8:8
Fir..............2 Sam. 6:5
Mulberry ......2 Sam. 5:23
Myrtle.........Is. 41:19
Oak ....Is. 44:14
Olive ....Judg. 9:9
Palm ....Ex. 15:27
Pomegranate ..Deut. 8:8
Poplar ....Hos. 4:13
Sycamore......Amos 7:14
Terebinth......Hos. 4:13
Willow ....Is. 44:4

D. *Figurative of:*
Righteous .....Ps. 1:1-3
Believer's life ..Prov. 11:30
Wisdom ....Prov. 3:18
Basic
character .....Matt. 7:17-19
Continued
prosperity......Is. 65:22
Judgment......Luke 23:31
Eternal life ....Rev. 22:14
Covenant......Rom. 11:24

Tree of life

In Eden ....Gen. 2:9
In New
Jerusalem ....Rev. 22:1, 2

Tremble—*to shake with fear*

A. *Expressive of:*
Deep
concern.......Gen. 27:33
Fear...........Mark 16:8
Filial trust ....Is. 66:2, 5
Appre-
hension ....1 Sam. 16:4
Infirmity.......Eccl. 12:3
Obedience .....Phil. 2:12

B. *Applied to:*
People.........Dan. 6:26
Earth..........Ps. 97:4
Nations........Is. 64:2
Heart..........Deut. 28:65
Flesh..........Ps. 119:120
Servants.......Eph. 6:5
Christians .....1 Cor. 2:3

C. *Caused by:*
Physical
change........Luke 8:47
Earthquake....Acts 16:29

Trials—*hardships that try our faith*

A. *Characteristics of:*
Some very
severe.........2 Cor. 1:8-10

Cause of, sometimes
unknown .....Job 1:7-22
Sometimes
physical.......2 Cor. 12:7-10
Endurable ....1 Cor. 10:13
Rewardable....Matt. 5:10-12

B. *Design of, to:*
Test faith .....Gen. 22:1-18
Purify   {Mal. 3:3, 4
faith ....{1 Pet. 1:6-9
Increase
patience ......James 1:3, 4, 12
Bring us to a better
place..........Ps. 66:10-12
Chasten us ....Is. 48:10
Glorify God....1 Pet. 4:12-16

Tribes of Israel

Twelve in
number ....Gen. 49:28
Descended from Jacob's
sons..............Gen. 35:22-26
Jacob forecasted future
of ....Gen. 49:3-27
Moses foretold future
of ....Deut. 33:6-29
Numbered ....Num. 1:44-46
Camped by
standards........Num. 2:2-31
Canaan divided
among ....Josh. 15–19
Names of,
engraven ....Ex. 39:14
United until Rehoboam's
rebellion..........1 Kin. 12:16-20
Returned after
exile...............Ezra 8:35
Typical of
Christians ....James 1:1

Tribulation—*a state or time of great
affliction*

A. *Descriptive of:*
Afflictions .....1 Sam. 10:19
Persecutions...1 Thess. 3:4
Severe
testings ......Rev. 2:10, 22

B. *Christian's attitude toward:*
Must expect ...Acts 14:22
Glory in ......Rom. 5:3
Overcome .....Rom. 8:35-37
Patient in......Rom. 12:12
Joyful in ......2 Cor. 7:4
Don't lose
heart.........Eph. 3:13

Tribute—*a tax imposed upon a subjugated nation*

Imposed by
Jews ....Ezra 4:20
Imposed upon
Jews ....Ezra 4:13
Israelites..........2 Kin. 23:33
Christ settles question
concerning ......Matt. 22:17-21
Paul's admonition
concerning ......Rom. 13:6, 7

Trickery—*use of guile or deceit*

By Gibeonites .....Josh. 9:3-16
By Saul ....1 Sam. 28:7-10
By Amnon ....2 Sam. 13:1-33
Christians, beware
of ....Eph. 4:14

Trinity, the

A. *Revealed in the Old Testament:*
   At Creation....Gen. 1:1-3, 26
   In the personality
   of the   (Is. 40:13
   Spirit ....(Is. 48:16
   By:
   Divine
   angel ....Judg. 13:8-23
   Personification of
   Wisdom......Prov. 8:22-31
   Threefold
   "Holy" ....Is. 6:3
   Aaronic bene-
   diction ......Num. 6:24-27

B. *Revealed in the New
   Testament:*
   At Christ's
   baptism ......Matt. 3:16, 17
   In:
   Christ's   (John 14:26
   teaching ....(John 15:26
   Baptismal
   formula ......Matt. 28:19
   Apostolic bene-
   diction ....2 Cor. 13:14
   Apostolic
   teaching ....Gal. 4:4-6

Triumphal entrance—*Jesus' entry into Jerusalem on the last week of His earthly ministry*

Prophesied........Zech. 9:9
Fulfilled..........Matt. 21:2-11

Troas—*a seaport city near Troy*

Paul received vision
here..............Acts 16:8-11

Trogyllium—*a seaport city of Asia Minor*

Paul's ship tarried
here..............Acts 20:15

Troops—*a group of soldiers*

Place in fortified
cities.............2 Chr. 17:2
Come together and
camp............Job 19:12
"Daughter of
troops".........Mic. 5:1

Trophimus—*nourishing*

One of Paul's
companions ......Acts 20:4

Trouble—*that which causes concern or distress*

A. *Kinds of:*
   Physical, of
   nature ....Ps. 46:3
   Mental.........Dan. 5:9
   Spiritual, of the
   wicked........Is. 57:20
   Spiritual, of the
   righteous .....Ps. 77:3
   National.......Jer. 30:7
   Domestic......Prov. 11:29

B. *Caused by:*
   Misdeeds of
   sons ....Gen. 34:30
   Mysterious
   dream.........Dan. 2:1, 3
   Unexpected
   news..........1 Sam. 28:21
   Sin ....Josh. 7:25
   Evil   (1 Sam. 16:14,
   spirits.......(15
   Enemies ....Ezra 4:4
   Physical
   malady........Job 4:5
   God's:
   Withdrawal...Ps. 30:7
   Wrath ......Ps. 78:49
   Our sins ......Ps. 38:4-6
   Mouth.........Prov. 21:23
   Angel
   visitant ......Luke 1:12, 29
   Wars, etc .....Mark 13:7
   Trials.........2 Cor. 7:5
   Afflicted ......2 Thess. 1:7

C. *God's help to His saints in, to:*
   Hide...........Ps. 27:5
   Deliver ....Ps. 50:15
                  2 Cor. 1:8-10

Help............Ps. 46:1
Attend.........Ps. 91:15
Revive.........Ps. 138:7

Truce—*a temporary cessation of warfare*

With good
results............2 Sam. 2:25-31

True—*that which agrees with the facts*

A. *Applied to:*
God ....John 17:3
Christ ....Rev. 3:7, 14
God's
Judgments ....Rev. 16:7
Believer's
heart..........2 Cor. 6:8
Worshipers ....John 4:23

B. *Proof of:*
Given by
men............John 5:32
Based upon
testimony .....John 8:13-18
Recognized by
men............John 10:41

See Truth

Trumpet—*a wind musical instrument*

A. *Features concerning:*
Instrument of
music.........1 Chr. 13:8
Made of ram's
horn..........Josh. 6:4

B. *Uses of, in Israel, to:*
Signal God's
presence ......Ex. 19:16, 19
Regulate
marchings ....Num. 10:2, 5, 6
Call
assemblies ....Num. 10:2, 3, 7
Announce a
feast ....Lev. 23:23-25
Gather the
nation ....Judg. 3:27
Alert against an
enemy ....Neh. 4:18, 20
Herald a new
king ....1 Kin. 1:34-41
Hail a religious
event ....1 Chr. 13:8
Assist in
worship ....Neh. 12:35-41

C. *Uses of, at Christ's return, to:*
Herald Christ's
coming........Matt. 24:31

Signal
prophetic   ⎰Rev. 8:2, 6, 13
events .... ⎱Rev. 9:14
Raise the
dead ....1 Thess. 4:16

Trust—*to put one's confidence in*

A. *Not to be placed in:*
Weapons ......Ps. 44:6
Wealth ....Ps. 49:6, 7
Leaders........Ps. 146:3
Man ....Jer. 17:5
Works.........Jer. 48:7
One's own righ-
teousness .....Ezek. 33:13

B. *To be placed in:*
God's:
Name.........Ps. 33:21
Word.........Ps. 119:42
Christ ....Matt. 12:17-21

C. *Benefits of:*
Joy ....Ps. 5:11
Deliverance....Ps. 22:4, 5
Triumph.......Ps. 25:2, 3
God's
goodness......Ps. 31:19
Mercy ....Ps. 32:10
Provision .....Ps. 37:3, 5
Blessedness ...Ps. 40:4
Safety ....Ps. 56:4, 11
Usefulness ....Ps. 73:28
Guidance .....Prov. 3:5, 6
Inheritance ....Is. 57:13

Truth—*that which agrees with final reality*

A. *Ascribed to:*
God's Law ....Ps. 119:142-160
Christ ....John 14:6
Holy Spirit.....John 14:17
God's Word....John 17:17, 19
Gospel........Gal. 2:5, 14

B. *Effects of, to:*
Make free .....John 8:31, 32
Sanctify ....John 17:17-19
Purify ....1 Pet. 1:22
Establish.......Eph. 4:15

C. *Wrong attitudes toward, to:*
Change into a
lie............Rom. 1:25
Disobey........Rom. 2:8
Walk contrary
to............Gal. 2:14
Love not.......2 Thess. 2:10
Believe not ....2 Thess. 2:12
Be destitute
of.............1 Tim. 6:5

Never come
to............2 Tim. 3:7
Resist.........2 Tim. 3:8
Turn from ....2 Tim. 4:4

D. *Right attitudes toward, to:*
Speak ....Eph. 4:25
Walk in........3 John 3, 4
Declare ....Acts 26:25
Worship in.....John 4:23, 24
Come to.......1 Tim. 2:4
Believe and
know ....1 Tim. 4:3
Handle
accurately ....2 Tim. 2:15
Obey ....1 Pet. 1:22
Be
established....2 Pet. 1:12

Truthfulness—*abiding by the truth*

Commanded .....Ps. 15:2
Exemplified by
Levi.............Mal. 2:6
Should characterize
Christians ....Eph. 4:25

Tryphena—*delicate*

Woman at Rome commended by
Paul............Rom. 16:12

Tryphosa—*dainty*

Woman at Rome commended by
Paul............Rom. 16:12

Tsadde

Letter of the Hebrew
alphabet..........Ps. 119:137-144

Tubal

1. Son of
   Japheth ....Gen. 10:2
2. Tribe associated with Javan and
   Meshech ......Is. 66:19
   In Gog's
   army.........Ezek. 38:2, 3
   Punishment
   of............Ezek. 32:26, 27

Tubal-Cain—*Tubal, the smith*

Son of Lamech....Gen. 4:19-22

Tumors

Threatened as a
curse..............Deut. 28:27
Inflicted upon
Philistines ....1 Sam. 5:6-12

Tumult—*a confused uproar*

Against:

God.............Is. 37:29
Christ............Matt. 27:24
Paul............Acts 19:29, 40
Paul pleads
innocent of......Acts 24:18

Tunic—*an outer garment*

Makers of:

God—for man.....Gen. 3:21
Jacob—for
Joseph ....Gen. 37:3
Dorcas—for
wearing ....Acts 9:39

Turban—*a headdress*

Worn by the high
priest.............Ex. 28:36-39
Inscription "Holiness to the Lord"
worn on..........Ex. 39:28-31
Worn by Aaron
for anointing
and on Day of ⎧Lev. 8:9
Atonement ⎩Lev. 16:4
Uncovering of,
forbidden.........Lev. 21:10-12
Removal of, because of
sin ....Ezek. 21:26
Symbolic restoration
of ....Zech. 3:5

Turtledove—*a dove or pigeon*

Migratory bird ....Song 2:12
Term of
affection ....Ps. 74:19
Offering of the ⎧Lev. 12:2, 6-8
poor.............⎩Luke 2:24

Twelve

Angels ....Rev. 21:12
Apostles ....Rev. 21:14
Baskets ....John 6:13
Bronze bulls ......Jer. 52:20
Brothers ....Gen. 42:32
Cakes.............Lev. 24:5
Cities ....1 Chr. 6:63
Cubits ....1 Kin. 7:15
Foundations ......Rev. 21:14
Fruits ....Rev. 22:2
Gates ....Rev. 21:12
Golden pans ......Num. 7:86
Governors ....1 Kin. 4:7
Hours............John 11:9
Legions of
angels............Matt. 26:53
Lions ....1 Kin. 10:20

Male goats........Ezra 8:35
Men ....Josh. 3:12
Months ....Dan. 4:29
Officers ....1 Kin. 4:7
Oxen..............2 Chr. 4:15
Patriarchs.........Acts 7:8
Pieces.............1 Kin. 11:30
Pillars.............Ex. 24:4
Princes............Gen. 17:20
Rods..............Num. 17:2
Silver bowls.......Num. 7:84
Sons of Jacob.....Gen. 35:22
Springs ....Num. 33:9
Stars..............Rev. 12:1
Stones ....1 Kin. 18:31
Thousand ....2 Sam. 17:1
Thrones...........Matt. 19:28
Tribes.............Luke 22:30
Wells ....Ex. 15:27
Years of age ......Luke 2:42

Twins of the Bible

Esau and Jacob ...Gen. 25:24-26
Perez and Zerah ..Gen. 38:27-30

Two

Lights.............Gen. 1:16
Tablets of stone ...Ex. 34:1, 4
Goats.............Lev. 16:7, 8
Spies.............Josh. 2:1, 4
Wives.............1 Sam. 1:2
Evils ....Jer. 2:13
Masters...........Matt. 6:24
Witnesses.........Matt. 18:16
People agreeing ...Matt. 18:19, 20
Command-
ments ....Matt. 22:40
Thieves...........Matt. 27:38
Covenants ....Gal. 4:24
Become one.......Eph. 5:31
Hard pressed from both
directions ....Phil. 1:23

Tychicus—chance happening

Asian Christian and
companion ....Acts 20:4
Carried Paul's letter to
Colossians........Col. 4:7
Carried letter to
Ephesians ....Eph. 6:21, 22
Accompanied Onesimus to his
master ....Col. 4:7
Later sent to Ephesus by
Paul.............2 Tim. 4:12

Types, typology—divine illustration of truth

May be:

Ceremony—
Passover ....1 Cor. 5:7
Event—wilderness
journeys ....1 Cor. 10:1-11
Institution—
priesthood........Heb. 9:11
Person—Adam ....Rom. 5:14
Thing—veil ....Heb. 10:20

Tyrannus—tyrant

Paul teaches in his
school............Acts 19:9

Tyre—a seaport city 25 miles south of Sidon

Ancient city......Josh. 19:29
Noted for
commerce........Ezek. 27:1-36
King of, helped
Solomon ....1 Kin. 5:1-10
Denounced by
prophets.........Joel 3:4-6
Fall of, predicted ..Ezek. 26:1-21
Jesus visited ......Matt. 15:21-28

U

Ucal—I am strong

Proverbs addressed
to ....Prov. 30:1

Uel—will of God

Divorced his foreign
wife ....Ezra 10:34

Ulai—a river of Elam near Shushan

Scene of Daniel's
visions ....Dan. 8:2-16

Ulam—first; leader

Manassite.........1 Chr. 7:16, 17

Ulla—burden

Descendant of
Asher ....1 Chr. 7:30, 39

Ummah—association

Asherite town.....Josh. 19:24, 30

Unbelief

A. Caused by:
Sin ....John 16:9

Satan..........John 8:43-47
Evil heart......Heb. 3:12
Honor from one
another........John 5:44
Not belonging to
Christ.........John 10:26
Judicial
blindness......John 12:37-40

B. *Manifested in:*
Questioning   ⎰Gen. 3:1-6
God's Word..   ⎱2 Pet. 3:4, 5
Turning from
God...........Heb. 3:12
Questioning God's
power.........Ps. 78:19, 20
Hating God's
messengers ...Acts 7:54, 57
Resisting the
Spirit ....Acts 7:51, 52
Discounting
evidence ......John 12:37
Opposing the
Gospel........1 Thess. 2:14-16
Rejecting   ⎰John 12:48
Christ.......⎱John 16:9

C. *Consequences of, seen in:*
Hindering
miracles......Matt. 13:58
Exclusion from
blessings ......Heb. 3:15-19
Condemna-
tion...........John 3:18, 19
Rejection ......Rom. 11:20
Judgment.......John 12:48
Death ....John 8:24, 25
Destruction....2 Thess. 1:8, 9
God's wrath ....John 3:36

D. *Those guilty, described as:*
Stiffnecked ....Acts 7:51
Uncircum-
cised ....Jer. 6:10
Blinded........Eph. 4:18
Rebels ....Num. 17:10

Unbelievers—*those who reject Christ*

Condemnation
of ....Mark 16:16
Intermarriage with Christians,
forbidden.........2 Cor. 6:14, 15

Uncertainties—*things which may or
may not happen*

A. *Caused by:*
Unknown
future.........Prov. 27:1
Divine
Providence....James 4:13-17

Our lack of
knowledge ....John 21:18-23

B. *Need not affect our:*
Assurance .....1 Cor. 9:26
Trust in God...Rom. 4:19-21
Plans ....Acts 21:11-15

Uncharitableness—*a critical spirit*

Condemning   ⎰Matt. 7:1-4
others...........⎱James 4:11, 12
Passing false
judgments........Luke 7:39
Assuming superior
holiness ....John 8:1-11
Not forgiving   ⎰Luke 15:25-32
readily ....⎱2 Cor. 2:6-11
Imputing evil to
others............1 Sam. 1:14-17

Uncircumcised—*not circumcised*

A. *Descriptive of:*
Gentiles ....Gal. 2:7
Unregenerate
state ....Col. 2:13
Unregenerate Jews and
Gentiles......Jer. 9:25, 26

B. *State of, in the Old Testament,
excludes from:*
Passover......Ex. 12:48
Land ....Josh. 5:6, 7
Sanctuary ....Ezek. 44:7, 9
Holy city .....Is. 52:1

C. *State of, in the New Testament:*
Has no spiritual
value ....Gal. 5:6
Need not be
changed ......1 Cor. 7:18, 19
Explained.....Rom. 2:25-29

Unclean—*that which is defiled*

A. *Descriptive of:*
Men and   ⎰Lev. 15:1-33
women.......⎱Deut. 23:10
Not of the
Lord ....Is. 52:1
Person.........Eph. 5:5
Sons of
Israel ....Lev. 16:16

B. *Transformation of, by:*
Purification ....Is. 6:5-7
Separation.....2 Cor. 6:17
Knowledge in
Jesus.........Rom. 14:14
Prayer.........1 Tim. 4:3-5

See Clean; Pollute; Sanitation and
hygiene

Unconditional surrender

Required by
Christ ....Luke 14:26, 27
As sacrifice ....Rom. 12:1

Undefiled—*untainted*

Such persons are
blessed ....Ps. 119:1
Christ is ....Heb. 7:26
Describes marriage
act ....Heb. 13:4
Applied to true
religion...........James 1:27
Our inheritance thus
called ....1 Pet. 1:4

Understanding—*knowing things in their
right relationship*

A. *Means of, by:*
   God's:
     Gift............1 Kin. 3:9-12
     Revelation....Rom. 1:20
     Word.........Ps. 119:104, 130
   Books ....Dan. 9:2, 23
   Holy Spirit.....Ex. 31:3
   Christ ....1 John 5:20
   Prayer.........Ps. 119:34-125
   Faith ....Heb. 11:3
   Enlightening...Eph. 1:18
   Interpre-
     tation ....Neh. 8:2-13
   Explanation....Luke 24:45
   Reproof........Prov. 15:32
   Later event ....Ps. 73:17

B. *Limitations on, by:*
   Unbelief ....John 8:43
   Unregen-
     eracy ....Eph. 4:18
   Spiritual
     blindness......Is. 6:9, 10
   Judicial
     punishment ...Is. 44:18, 19
   Difficulties.....2 Pet. 3:16

Unfruitfulness—*not producing good
fruit*

A. *Caused by:*
   Unfaithful-
     ness............Is. 5:1-7
   Worldliness....James 4:1-4
   Negligence.....Luke 19:20-27

B. *Punished by:*
   God's
     judgments ....Matt. 3:10
   Rejection:
     Now ....John 15:2, 4, 6
     Hereafter .....Heb. 6:8

Ungodliness, ungodly—*the morally
corrupt*

A. *Described as:*
   Prospering in the
     world ....Ps. 73:12
   Growing
     worse.........2 Tim. 2:16
   Perverting God's
     grace ....Jude 4
   Abounding in the last
     days ....Jude 18
   Christ died
     for ....Rom. 5:6

B. *Judgments upon, by:*
   Flood...........2 Pet. 2:5, 6
   Law ....1 Tim. 1:9
   God's decree...Jude 4
   God's
     revelation.....Rom. 1:18
   Christ's
     return.........Jude 14, 15
   World's end....2 Pet. 3:7
   Final
     judgment .....Ps. 1:4-6

Unintentionally—*without premeditation*

Concerning an innocent
killer ....Josh. 20:3-5

Union

Of:

Godhead.........John 17:21, 22
Christ and
  believers ....John 15:1-7
God and man .....Acts 17:28, 29
Mankind..........Acts 17:26
Satan and the
  unsaved..........John 8:44
Believers in
  prayer............Matt. 18:19, 20

See Oneness

Union with Christ

A. *Compared to:*
   Head and the
     body...........Eph. 4:15, 16
   Marriage
     bond..........Eph. 5:23, 30
   Building ....Eph. 2:21, 22
   Parts of the
     body...........1 Cor. 12:12, 27
   Vine and
     branches......John 15:4, 5
   Food and the
     body..........John 6:56, 57

B. *Illustrated in the "togethers":*
Crucified ...... Rom. 6:6
Buried .... Rom. 6:4
Made alive.... Eph. 2:5
Sitting .... Eph. 2:6
Suffering ...... Rom. 8:17
Reigning....... 2 Tim. 2:12
Glorified ...... Rom. 8:17

C. *Manifested in, oneness:*
Of mind ...... 1 Cor. 2:16
Of spirit ...... 1 Cor. 6:17
In suffering.... Phil. 3:10
In worship.... 1 Cor. 10:16, 17
In ministry .... 2 Cor. 5:18-21

Unity of believers

A. *Based upon:*
Indwelling { 1 Cor. 3:16, 17
Spirit { 1 Cor. 6:19
New birth ..... 2 Cor. 5:17
Union with
Christ........ 2 Cor. 13:5

B. *Expressed by oneness of:*
Mind .... 1 Pet. 3:8
Unity of
Spirit .... Ps. 133:1-3
Faith .... Eph. 4:4-6
Fellowship..... Acts 2:42-47
Concern ...... 1 Cor. 12:25, 26

C. *Consistent with such
differences as:*
Physical .... 1 Pet. 3:1-7
Social......... Eph. 6:5-9
Mental........ 1 Cor. 1:26-29

Unjust

Described as:

Abomination...... Prov. 29:27
Recipient of God's
blessings....... Matt. 5:45
Christ died for .... 1 Pet. 3:18

Unknown god

Altar to .... Acts 17:22, 23

Unleavened bread

Used in the { Ex. 12:8-20
passover........ { Mark 14:1, 12
Typical of
Christians ...... 1 Cor. 5:7, 8

Unmercifulness—*lacking mercy*

Shown by Simeon and
Levi............ Gen. 34:25-31
By Pharaoh ...... Ex. 5:4-19
By creditor........ Matt. 18:28-30

Unni—*answering is with Yahweh*

Levite musician ... 1 Chr. 15:18

Unpardonable sin

Sin not { Matt. 12:31, 32
forgivable .... { Luke 12:10

Unrest—*a state of agitation*

Of the nations .... Luke 21:25, 26
Of the wicked..... Is. 57:20
Remedy given by
Christ............ Matt. 11:28
Available to
Christians .... Phil. 4:7

Unrighteousness—*wickedness*

A. *Attitude toward, by the wicked,
they:*
Suppress the truth
in .... Rom. 1:18
Are filled
with .... Rom. 1:29
Obey it .... Rom. 2:8
Love the wages
of............. 2 Pet. 2:15
Take pleasure
in............. 2 Thess. 2:12
Receive the wages
of............. 2 Pet. 2:13
Shall not inherit the
kingdom ...... 1 Cor. 6:9

B. *Relation of believers toward:*
They are cleansed
from .... 1 John 1:9
God is merciful toward
their .... Heb. 8:12
Must not fellowship
with .... 2 Cor. 6:14
All the world
guilty .... Rom. 3:1-20

Unselfishness—*not putting self first*

A. *Christ, an example of, in His:*
Mission .... John 6:38
Suffering ...... Matt. 26:39, 42
Concern .... John 19:26, 27
Death .... Phil. 2:5-8

B. *In the believer, prompted by:*
Christ's
example....... Phil. 2:3-8
Love........... 1 Cor. 13:4, 5
Concern ...... 1 Cor. 10:23-33
Christian
service........ Phil. 2:25-30
Sacrifice ...... Rev. 12:11

C. *Examples of:*
Abram.........Gen. 13:8-12
Moses ....Num. 14:12-29
Gideon ....Judg. 8:22, 23
Jonathan .....1 Sam. 18:4
David.........1 Chr. 21:17
Nehemiah .....Neh. 5:14-19
Daniel ....Dan. 5:17
Christians ....Acts 4:34, 35
Paul...........1 Cor. 9:19-23
Onesiphorus ...2 Tim. 1:16-18

Unspeakable

God's Gift.........2 Cor. 9:15

Untempered mortar—*whitewash*

Figurative of false
prophets.........Ezek. 13:10, 14

Unwittingly—*without premeditation*

Concerning an innocent
killer ....Josh. 20:3-5

Unworldliness—*a heavenly frame of mind*

A. *Negatively expressed in, not:*
Loving the
world ....1 John 2:15-17
Fellowshiping with
evil ....2 Cor. 6:14-18
Mixing in worldly
affairs.........2 Tim. 2:4

B. *Positively expressed in:*
Seeking God's kingdom
first............Matt. 6:33, 34
Living for
Jesus..........Gal. 2:20
Becoming a living
sacrifice.......Rom. 12:1, 2
Having a heavenly
mind...........Col. 3:1, 2
Looking for
Jesus..........Titus 2:11-15
Looking to
Jesus..........Heb. 12:1, 2

Unworthiness—*not being fit; lacking merit*

A. *Caused by a sense of:*
Failure........Gen. 32:10
Social
difference .... { 1 Sam. 18:18,
                23
Sin ....Luke 15:19, 21
Inferiority .....John 1:27

B. *Examples of:*
Moses ....Ex. 4:10
Centurion .....Matt. 8:8
Peter ....Luke 5:8
Paul...........1 Cor. 15:9

Upharsin—*and divided*

Interpreted by
Daniel...........Dan. 5:5, 25, 28

Uphaz

Unidentified place of fine
gold ....Jer. 10:9

Upper room—*chamber, usually built on a roof*

Ahaziah fell
from ....2 Kin. 1:2
Ahaz's ....2 Kin. 23:12
Disciples prepared for
Christ ....Mark 14:14-16
Dorcas placed in ..Acts 9:36, 37
Paul preached in ..Acts 20:7, 8

Uprightness—*character approved by God*

A. *Descriptive of:*
God's nature...Is. 26:7
Man's state....Eccl. 7:29
Devout ....Job 1:1, 8

B. *Of God, manifested in His:*
Works.........Ps. 111:8
Judgments.....Ps. 119:137
Delights ....1 Chr. 29:17

C. *Blessings of, for saints:*
Temporal
blessings ......Ps. 84:11
Lord's
blessings ......Ps. 11:7
Prosperity .....Prov. 14:11
Deliverance....Prov. 11:3, 6, 11
Salvation ......Ps. 7:10
God's
presence ......Ps. 140:13
Light in
darkness ......Ps. 112:4
Answered
prayer ....Prov. 15:8
Righteous-
ness...........Ps. 36:10
Joy ....Ps. 32:11
Glory..........Ps. 64:10
Final
dominion .....Ps. 49:14

D. *Attitude of wicked toward, they:*
Are devoid
of.............Hab. 2:4

Leave the path
of............Prov. 2:13
Hate..........Prov. 29:10
Persecute......Ps. 37:14
Laugh to
scorn ....Job 12:4

Ur—*flame*

Father of
Eliphal ....1 Chr. 11:35
Called Ahasbai ....2 Sam. 23:34

Ur of the Chaldeans

City of Abram's {Gen. 11:28-31
early life.   {Gen. 15:7
Located in Mesopotamia by
Stephen ....Acts 7:2, 4

Urbanus—*polite*

Christian...........Rom. 16:9

Uri—*an abbreviation of Urijah*

1. Father of
   Bezaleel.......1 Chr. 2:20
2. Father of
   Geber.........1 Kin. 4:19
3. Divorced his foreign
   wife.........Ezra 10:24

Uriah—*Yahweh is light*

1. Hittite and one of David's
   warriors......2 Sam. 23:39
   Condemned to death by
   David........2 Sam. 11:1-27
2. Priest..........Ezra 8:33

Uriel—*God is light*

1. Kohathite
   Levite.........1 Chr. 6:22, 24
2. Man of
   Gibeah.......2 Chr. 13:2

Urijah—*Yahweh is light*

1. High priest in Ahaz'
   time ....2 Kin. 16:10-16
2. Postexilic
   priest ....Neh. 3:4, 21
3. Prophet in Jeremiah's
   time ....Jer. 26:20-23
4. Stands with
   Ezra ....Neh. 8:4

Urim and Thummim—*lights and perfections*

Placed in the breastplate of the
high priest........Ex. 28:30
Method of   {Num. 27:21
consulting God ..{1 Sam. 14:3-37

Use of, confined to
priests...........Deut. 33:8
Answer by,
refused...........1 Sam. 28:6

Usurpation—*seizing authority illegally*

A. *Methods of, by:*
   Intrigue ......2 Sam. 15:1-12
   Defying God's
   Law............1 Sam. 13:8-14
   Changing God's
   worship.......2 Kin. 16:10-17
   Conspiracy ....1 Kin. 15:27, 28
   Assuming dictatorial
   rights ....3 John 9, 10

B. *Consequences of, seen in:*
   Defeat and
   death ....2 Kin. 11:1-6
   Another
   conspiracy ....2 Kin. 15:10-15
   Defeat and conditional
   forgiveness....1 Kin. 1:5-53

C. *Spirit of, manifested in:*
   Man's trans-
   gression......Gen. 3:1-7
   Satan's fall ....Is. 14:12-14
   Woman's
   weakness ....1 Tim. 2:12
   Antichrist's {2 Thess. 2:3, 4
   desire ....{Rev. 13:1-18

Utensils, kitchen

Bowls............Amos 6:6
Platter ....Matt. 14:11
Jar...............1 Kin. 17:12
Cup and dish....Matt. 23:25
Fleshhooks.......1 Sam. 2:13, 14
Iron pan........Ezek. 4:3
Kettle (pot) ....1 Sam. 2:14
Kneading bowls ..Ex. 8:3
Millstones........Is. 47:2
Pan ....Lev. 2:5

Uthai—*Yahweh is help*

1. Judahite ....1 Chr. 9:4
2. Postexilic
   returnee ......Ezra 8:14

Uz—*firmness*

1. Descendant of
   Shem ....Gen. 10:23
2. Descendant of
   Seir..........Gen. 36:28
3. Place in south Edom; residence
   of Job........Job 1:1

Uzai—*hoped for*

Father of Palal ....Neh. 3:25

Uzal

Son of Joktan.....Gen. 10:27

Uzza, Uzzah—*strength*

1. Son of
   Shimei.......1 Chr. 6:29
2. Descendant of
   Ehud..........1 Chr. 8:7
3. Head of a returning Temple
   servant
   family........Ezra 2:49
4. Name of a
   garden........2 Kin. 21:18, 26
5. Son of Abinadab struck down
   for touching the ark of the
   covenant......2 Sam. 6:3-11

Uzzen Sheerah—*top of Sherah*

Town built by Sherah, Ephraim's
daughter.........1 Chr. 7:24

Uzzi—*my strength*

1. Descendant of
   Aaron..........1 Chr. 6:5, 51
2. Descendant of
   Issachar......1 Chr. 7:1-3
3. Son of Bela....1 Chr. 7:7
4. Levite
   overseer.....Neh. 11:22
5. Postexilic
   priest.........Neh. 12:19, 42

Uzzia—*my strength is Yahweh*

One of David's mighty
men..............1 Chr. 11:44

Uzziah—*my strength is Yahweh*

1. Kohathite
   Levite.........1 Chr. 6:24
2. Father of
   Jehonathan...1 Chr. 27:25
3. King of
   Judah, called { 2 Kin. 14:21
   Azariah....... { 2 Kin. 15:1-7
   Reigned 52
   years..........2 Kin. 15:1, 2
   Reigned
   righteously....2 Chr. 26:4, 5
   Conquered the
   Philistines.....2 Chr. 26:6-8
   Strengthened
   Jerusalem.....2 Chr. 26:9
   Developed
   agriculture....2 Chr. 26:10
   Usurped priestly function;
   stricken with
   leprosy........2 Chr. 26:16-21

Life of, written by
Isaiah........2 Chr. 26:22, 23
Earthquake in the days
of............Amos 1:1
Death of, time of Isaiah's
vision.........Is. 6:1
4. Priest who divorced his foreign
   wife..........Ezra 10:19, 21
5. Judahite......Neh. 11:4

Uzziel—*God is my strength*

1. Levite, son of Kohath and
   family head...Ex. 6:18, 22
2. Son of Bela...1 Chr. 7:7
3. Simeonite
   captain........1 Chr. 4:41-43
4. Levite
   musician......1 Chr. 25:3, 4
5. Levite assisting in Hezekiah's
   reforms......2 Chr. 29:14-19
6. Goldsmith working on
   Jerusalem's
   wall..........Neh. 3:8

V

Vagabond—*an aimless wanderer*

Curse on Cain....Gen. 4:12, 14
Curse upon the
wicked..........Ps. 109:10

Vail (see Veil, the sacred; Veil,
woman's)

Vain—*empty; useless*

A. *Applied to physical things:*
   Beauty........Prov. 31:30
   Life...........Eccl. 6:12
   Adornment....Jer. 4:30
   Healing.......Jer. 46:11
   Protection....1 Sam. 25:21
   Safety........Ps. 33:17
   World's
   creation......Is. 45:18, 19

B. *Applied to spiritual things:*
   Idolatry.......Acts 14:15
   Serving God...Mal. 3:14
   Babblings.....2 Tim. 2:16

C. *Applied to possibilities:*
   God's grace....1 Cor. 15:10
   Christ's
   death.........Gal. 2:21
   Scriptures.....James 4:5
   Faith..........1 Cor. 15:2-17
   Worship.......Is. 45:19

Labor............1 Thess. 3:5
Reception......1 Thess. 2:1, 2
Sufferings .....Gal. 3:4

See Futile

Vajezatha—*son of the atmosphere*

One of Haman's
sons.............Esth. 9:9

Valley Gate

Entrance into
Jerusalem ....Neh. 2:13

Valley of Dry Bones

Vision of
Ezekiel...........Ezek. 37:1-14

Valley, the King's

A valley near
Jerusalem ....Gen. 14:17-20
Site of Absalom's
monument ......2 Sam. 18:18

Vaniah—*Yahweh is praise*

Divorced his foreign
wife..............Ezra 10:36

Various—*of all kinds*

Colors ....Ezek. 17:3
Diseases ....Luke 4:40
Doctrines ....Heb. 13:9
Lusts ....Titus 3:3
Miracles ....Heb. 2:4
Times ....Heb. 1:1
Trials ....James 1:2
Washings ....Heb. 9:10

Vashti—*beautiful woman*

Queen of Ahasuerus, deposed and
divorced..........Esth. 1:9-22

Veal

Prepared for King
Saul..............1 Sam. 28:21-25

Vegetables—*plants grown for food*

Part of God's
creation...........Gen. 1:11, 12
Controversy
regarding.........Rom. 14:1-23
Preferred by
Daniel............Dan. 1:12, 16

Veil, the sacred

A. *Features regarding:*
Made by divine
command .....Ex. 26:31, 32
Used to separate the holy and
Most Holy ....Ex. 26:33
Means of concealing the divine
person ....Ex. 40:3
In the Temple
also...........2 Chr. 3:14
Rent at Christ's
death ....Matt. 27:51

B. *Entrance through:*
By the high priest
alone ....Heb. 9:6, 7
On Day of Atonement
only ....Heb. 9:7
Taking blood ..Heb. 9:7

C. *Figurative of:*
Old Testament dispensa-
tion...........Heb. 9:8
Christ's flesh...Heb. 10:20
Access now into God's
presence ......Heb. 10:19-22

Veil, woman's

A. *Literal uses of:*
For modesty ...Gen. 24:65
For
adornment ....Is. 3:19
To conceal
identity ....Gen. 38:14
To soften the divine glory
of God ....Ex. 34:33-35

B. *Figurative of:*
Coming of the
Lord ....Is. 25:7
Turning to the
Lord ....2 Cor. 3:14-16

Vengeance—*retribution as a
punishment*

A. *Belonging to God, as:*
Judgment upon
sin............Jer. 11:20-23
Right not to
be taken by   ⎰Ezek. 25:12-17
man..........⎱Heb. 10:30
Set time ....Jer. 46:9, 10

B. *Visitation of, by God, at:*
Nation's fall ...Jer. 51:6, 11, 36
Christ's first
coming........Is. 35:4-10
Jerusalem's
destruction....Luke 21:22
Sodom's
destruction....Jude 7
Christ's
return.........2 Thess. 1:8

See Revenge

Venison—*the flesh of deer*

Isaac's favorite
dish . . . . Gen. 27:1-33

Ventriloquism—*appearing to speak
from another source*

From the dust . . . . . Is. 29:4

Verdict—*a judicial decision*

Unjustly
rendered . . . . Luke 23:13-26
Pronounced by
hypocrites . . . . John 8:1-11

Vermilion—*a brilliant red color*

Ceiling painted
with . . . . Jer. 22:14

Vessels—*hollow utensils for holding
things*

A. *Made of:*
Wood or
stone . . . . Ex. 7:19
Gold and
silver . . . . Dan. 5:2
Clay . . . . Rom. 9:21
Bronze . . . . Ezra 8:27

B. *Of the tabernacle:*
Under care of
Levites . . . . Num. 3:31, 32
Carried away into
Babylon . . . . 2 Chr. 36:18
Belshazzar uses in
feast . . . . Dan. 5:1-4
Returned to
Jerusalem . . . . . Ezra 1:7-11

C. *Figurative of:*
Mankind . . . . Rom. 9:21-23
Human
weakness . . . . . 2 Cor. 4:7
Believers . . . . . . 2 Tim. 2:20, 21
Person's body or
wife . . . . 1 Thess. 4:4
Chosen
person . . . . Acts 9:15

Vex—*to irritate*

Caused by
nagging . . . . Judg. 16:16

See Harass; Distress

Vicarious suffering of Christ

A. *Expressed in Old Testament, by:*
Types . . . . Gen. 22:7, 8, 13
Explicit   {Is. 53:1-12
prophecies . . .{Acts 8:32-35

B. *Expressed in the New
Testament, by:*
John the
Baptist . . . . John 1:29
Christ
Himself . . . . . . Mark 10:45
Peter . . . . 1 Pet. 1:18, 19
John . . . . 1 John 3:16
Paul . . . . Gal. 2:20
Hebrews . . . . . . Heb. 2:9, 17

Victory—*attaining the mastery over*

A. *Of Christ:*
Promised . . . . . . Ps. 110:1-7
Accompanied by
suffering . . . . . Is. 53:10-12
By
resurrection . . . Acts 2:29-36
By His
return . . . . Rev. 19:11-21

B. *Of Christians:*
Through
Christ . . . . Phil. 4:13
By the Holy   {Gal. 5:16, 17, 22,
Spirit . . . . . . {25
Over:
Flesh . . . . Gal. 5:16-21
World . . . . 1 John 5:4
Satan . . . . James 4:7

Vigor in old age

Moses at 120 . . . . . Deut. 34:7
Caleb at 85 . . . . . Josh. 14:10-13
Jehoiada at 130 . . 2 Chr. 24:15, 16

Vileness—*the state of physical or moral
corruption*

Used of:

Something insignifi-
cant . . . . Job 40:4
Human
corruption . . . . Judg. 19:24

See Rotten; Filthy

Village—*a settlement*

Of the
Samaritans . . . . . . Luke 9:52

Vine, vineyard

A. *Features regarding:*
Grown by
Noah . . . . Gen. 9:20
Native of
Palestine . . . . . Deut. 6:11
Reaping of, by
poor . . . . 2 Kin. 25:12

Fruit of, God's
gift .... Ps. 107:37
Pruning of,
necessary ..... Lev. 25:3, 4
Dead branches
burned .... John 15:5, 6

B. *Enemies of:*
Hail and
frost .... Ps. 78:47
Foxes .... Song 2:15
Boars .... Ps. 80:13
Thieves ...... Jer. 49:9
Stones .... Is. 5:2
Sloth .... Prov. 24:30, 31

C. *Laws concerning:*
Care of, exempts from military
service ...... Deut. 20:6
Diverse seed forbidden
in .... Deut. 22:9
Neighbors may
eat .... Deut. 23:24
No cultivation of, during
Sabbatical
year .... Ex. 23:11
Second gathering of,
forbidden ..... Lev. 19:10
New, five years'
waiting ...... Lev. 19:23-25
Nazirites forbidden to eat
of .... Num. 6:3, 4
Rechabites forbidden to
plant .... Jer. 35:7-9
Not to be
mortgaged ... Neh. 5:3, 4

D. *Figurative of:*
Jewish
nation ...... Is. 5:1-7
Growth in
grace .... Hos. 14:7
Purifying
afflictions .... John 15:1, 2
Peacefulness ... 1 Kin. 4:25
Worthless-
ness .... John 15:2, 6
Fruitful wife .. Ps. 128:3
God's
kingdom ..... Matt. 20:1-16

Vinedresser

Poor made to be .. 2 Kin. 25:12

Vinegar—*wine or strong drink
fermented*

Figurative of
agitation .... Prov. 25:20
Hard on teeth ..... Prov. 10:26
Forbidden to
Nazirites .... Num. 6:3

Offered to Christ in
mockery .... Ps. 69:21

Viper—*a deadly snake*

Figurative of spiritual
transformation ... Is. 11:8
Figurative of Dan's
treachery .... Gen. 49:17
Jewish leaders compared
to .... Matt. 3:7
Paul bit by .... Acts 28:3-5

Virgin—*a woman untouched sexually*

Penalty for seduction
of .... Deut. 22:28, 29
Parable of ten ..... Matt. 25:1-13
Specifications
regarding .... 1 Cor. 7:28-38
Christ born of .... Luke 1:26-35
Figurative of
Christians .... Rev. 14:4

Virgin conception

Prophesied .... Is. 7:14
Christ conceived {Matt. 1:18
of Holy Spirit ... {Luke 1:26-35
Born of virgin ..... Matt. 1:19-25

Visions—*divine revelations*

A. *Characteristics of:*
Under-
standable ..... Dan. 7:15-19
Authenticated by divine
glory .... Ezek. 8:1-4
Personal and
phenomenal .. Dan. 10:7-9
Prophetic ...... Dan. 9:23-27
Dated and
localized ..... Ezek. 1:1-3
Causes trembling and
dread .... Dan. 10:7-17
Meaning of,
interpreted .... Dan. 9:21-24
Absence of,
tragic .... Prov. 29:18
Performances of,
sure .... Ezek. 12:21-28
Proof of
messianic {Joel 2:28
times .... {Acts 2:17
Imitated by false
prophets ...... Jer. 14:14

B. *Productive of:*
Guidance ...... Gen. 46:2-5
Direction ..... Acts 16:9, 10
Encourage-
ment .... Acts 18:9, 10
Warning .... Is. 21:2-6

Judgment......1 Sam. 3:15-18
Action for the
Lord ....Acts 26:19, 20

C. *Objects of, revealed in:*
Israel's
future........Gen. 15:1-21
Succession of world
empires ....Dan. 7:1-8
Ram.........Dan. 8:1-7, 20
Expanding
river ....Ezek. 47:1-12
Throne of
God..........Rev. 4:1-11

Visit, visitation—*to go to see a person*

Descriptive of:

Going to a
person............Acts 15:36
God's care ....Ps. 65:9
God's purposed
time.............Luke 19:44

Visitors

Moses and
Elijah ....Matt. 17:3

Voice of God, the

A. *Importance of:*
Must be
obeyed........Gen. 3:1-19
Disobedience to,
judged........Jer. 42:5-22
Obedience to, the essence of
true religion...1 Sam. 15:19-24
Obedience to,
rewarded......Gen. 22:6-18
Sign of the
covenant......Josh. 24:24, 25

B. *Heard by:*
Adam..........Gen. 3:9, 10
Moses ....Ex. 19:19
Israel..........Deut. 5:22-26
Samuel ....1 Sam. 3:1-14
Elijah ....1 Kin. 19:12, 13
Isaiah ....Is. 6:8-10
Ezekiel ....Ezek. 1:24, 25
Ezek. 2:1
Christ ....Mark 1:11
Peter, James, and
John..........Matt. 17:1, 5
Paul...........Acts 9:4, 7
John...........Rev. 1:10-15

Vomit—*to throw up*

A. *Used literally of:*
Dog ....Prov. 26:11

One who eats in
excess ....Prov. 25:16
Drunken
man ....Is. 19:14
Great fish .....Jon. 2:10

B. *Used figuratively of:*
False
teaching ......2 Pet. 2:22
Judgment......Jer. 48:25, 26
Riches.........Job 20:15

Vophsi—*rich*

Naphtalite spy ....Num. 13:14

Vow—*a voluntary pledge to fulfill an agreement*

A. *Objects of one's:*
Life............Num. 6:1-21
Children.......1 Sam. 1:11-28
Possessions ...Gen. 28:22
Gifts..........Ps. 76:11

B. *Features concerning:*
Must be
voluntary .....Deut. 23:21, 22
Must be
uttered.......Deut. 23:23
Once made,
binding ......Eccl. 5:4, 5
Benefits of, sometimes
included ......Gen. 28:20-22
Invalidity of,
specified .....Num. 30:1-16
Abuse of,
condemned ...Matt. 15:4-6
Rashness in,
condemned ...Prov. 20:25
Perfection in,
required.......Lev. 22:18-25
Wickedness of
some..........Jer. 44:25

Voyage—*an extended trip*

Paul's to Rome....Acts 27:10

Vulture—*a carrion-eating bird of prey*

Classed as
unclean ....Lev. 11:13, 18

W

Wafers—*thin cakes of flour*

Often made with
honey ....Ex. 16:31

Used in various offerings........ { Ex. 29:2 / Lev. 2:4

Wages, hire—*payments for work performed*

A. *Principles governing payment of:*
Must be paid promptly....Deut. 24:14, 15
Withholding of, forbidden .....James 5:4

B. *Paid to such classes as:*
Soldiers .....2 Sam. 10:6
Fishermen .....Mark 1:20
Shepherds .....John 10:12, 13
Masons and carpenters ....2 Chr. 24:12
Farm laborers.......Matt. 20:1-16
Male prostitutes ....Deut. 23:18
Nurses.........Ex. 2:9
Ministers .....1 Cor. 9:4-14
Teachers.......Gal. 6:6, 7
Gospel messengers ...Luke 10:7

C. *Figurative of:*
Spiritual death ....Rom. 6:23
Unrighteous-ness.....2 Pet. 2:15
Reward.......John 4:36

See Hire

Wailing—*crying out in constant mourning*

A. *Caused by:*
King's decree ..Esth. 4:3
City's destruction....Ezek. 27:31, 32
God's judgment .....Amos 5:16, 17
Girl's death ....Mark 5:38-42
Christ's return.........Rev. 1:7
Hell's torments ....Matt. 13:42, 50

B. *Performed by:*
Women........Jer. 9:17-20
Prophets......Mic. 1:8
Merchants.....Rev. 18:15, 19

See Mourning

Waist

A. *Used literally of:*
Hips ....Gen. 37:34
Ex. 28:42

B. *Used figuratively of:*
Source of knowledge ....Eph. 6:14

Waiting on the Lord

A. *Agents of:*
Creatures......Ps. 145:15
Creation......Rom. 8:19, 23
Gentiles ......Is. 51:5
Christians .....1 Cor. 1:7

B. *Manner of:*
With the soul...........Ps. 62:1, 5
With quietness......Lam. 3:25, 26
With patience ......Ps. 40:1
With courage......Ps. 27:14
All the day ....Ps. 25:5
Continually....Hos. 12:6
With great hope ....Ps. 130:5, 6
With crying....Ps. 69:3

C. *Objects of God's:*
Salvation .....Is. 25:9
Law ....Is. 42:4
Protection ....Ps. 33:20
Pardon ....Ps. 39:7, 8
Food ....Ps. 104:27
Kingdom ......Mark 15:43
Holy Spirit.....Acts 1:4
Son............1 Thess. 1:10

D. *Blessings attending, described as:*
Spiritual renewal.......Is. 40:31
Not be ashamed ......Ps. 69:6
Inherit the land...........Ps. 37:9, 34
Something unusual.......Is. 64:4
Unusual blessing ......Luke 12:36, 37

Walk of believers

A. *Stated negatively, not:*
In darkness....John 8:12
After the flesh ....Rom. 8:1, 4
As Gentiles ....Eph. 4:17
In craftiness ...2 Cor. 4:2
In sin..........Col. 3:5-7
In disorder....2 Thess. 3:6, 11

B. *Stated positively:*
In the light ....1 John 1:7

In the truth....3 John 3, 4
In Christ ....Col. 2:6
In the Spirit ...Gal. 5:16, 25
In love ....Eph. 5:2
As children of
light.........Eph. 5:8
As Christ
walked........1 John 2:6
After His command-
ments.........2 John 6
By faith........2 Cor. 5:7
In good
works.........Eph. 2:10
Worthy........Eph. 4:1
Worthy of the
Lord..........Col. 1:10
Worthy of
God...........1 Thess. 2:12
Circum-
spectly.......Eph. 5:15
In wisdom.....Col. 4:5
Pleasing God ..1 Thess. 4:1

Wall—*a rampart or partition*

A. *Used for:*
Shooting arrows
from..........2 Sam. 11:24
Observation ...2 Sam. 18:24

B. *Unusual events connected with:*
Woman lives
on............Josh. 2:15
Jericho's, falls by
faith.........Josh. 6:5, 20
Saul's body   (1 Sam. 31:10,
fastened to...(11
Woman
throws stone (2 Sam. 11:20,
from..........(21
27,000 killed
by............1 Kin. 20:30
Son sacrificed
on............2 Kin. 3:27
Warning inscribed
on............Dan. 5:5, 25-28
Paul escapes
through.......Acts 9:25

C. *Figurative of:*
Defense........1 Sam. 25:16
Protection .....Ezra 9:9
Great power ...Ps. 18:29
Peacefulness...Ps. 122:7
Self-
sufficiency ....Prov. 18:11
Powerless......Prov. 25:28
Salvation ......Is. 26:1
God's
kingdom ......Is. 56:5
Heaven........Is. 60:18-21

Spiritual
leaders........Is. 62:6
God's
messengers ....Jer. 1:18, 19
Protection .....Zech. 2:5
Hypocrisy .....Acts 23:3
Ceremonial
law ....Eph. 2:14
New
Jerusalem.....Rev. 21:12-19

D. *Of Jerusalem:*
Built by
Solomon ......1 Kin. 3:1
Broken down by
Jehoash.......2 Kin. 14:13
Destroyed by Babylon-
ians...........2 Chr. 36:19
Seen at night by
Nehemiah.....Neh. 2:12-18
Rebuilt by
returnees .....Neh. 6:1, 6, 15
Dedication of ..Neh. 12:27-47

Wallow—*to roll about in an ungainly
manner*

Blood ....2 Sam. 20:12
Vomit..........Jer. 48:26
Ashes..........Jer. 6:26
On the ground ...Mark 9:20
Mire ....2 Pet. 2:22

Wandering—*roaming about*

A. *Descriptive of:*
Hagar's
travels ....Gen. 21:14
Israel's wilderness
travels ....Num. 32:13
God's
pilgrims.......Heb. 11:37, 38
Captivity ......Hos. 9:17
Joseph in the
field..........Gen. 37:15
Early Saints ...Heb. 11:38

B. *Figurative of:*
Apostasy ......Ps. 119:10
Dissatis-
faction........Prov. 27:8
Hopelessness ..Jude 13

Wanderer—*one who moves about
aimlessly*

Curse on Cain ....Gen. 4:12, 14
Curse on the
wicked ....Ps. 109:10
Professional exorcists
called ....Acts 19:13

Want—*to lack*

A. *Caused by:*
Hastiness ......Prov. 21:5
Greed..........Prov. 22:16
Sloth ....Prov. 24:30-34
Debauchery....Dan. 5:27

B. *Provision against, by:*
Trusting the
LORD..........Ps. 23:1
God's plan .....Jer. 33:17, 18

See Lack

Wantonness—*lustful behavior*

In suggestive
movements......Is. 3:16
Characteristic of doctrinal
laxity.............2 Pet. 2:18
Unbecoming to a
Christian ....Rom. 13:13

War—*armed conflicts between nations*

A. *Caused by:*
Sin ....James 4:1, 2
God's
judgments .....2 Sam. 12:10
God's decree...Ex. 17:16

B. *Regulations concerning:*
Consultation of:
Urim ....1 Sam. 28:6
Ephod ....1 Sam. 30:7, 8
Prophets......1 Kin. 22:7-28
Troops
mustered......Judg. 3:27
Some
dismissed ....Deut. 20:5-8
Spies
dispatched ....Num. 13:17
Ark brought
in.............1 Sam. 4:4-6
Sacrifice
offered........1 Sam. 7:8, 9
Speech
delivered......2 Chr. 20:20-22
Demand made for
surrender .....Deut. 20:10
Trumpet
sounded.......Num. 10:9

C. *Methods of attack, by:*
Ambush ....Josh. 8:3-26
Surprise
attack......Judg. 7:16-22
Personal combat of
champions ....1 Sam. 17:1-51
Divided
tactics ....2 Sam. 10:9-14

Massed
formation .....1 Kin. 22:31-33
Battle cry......Jer. 4:19

D. *Captives of:*
Sometimes
eliminated ....Josh. 6:21
Made
servants.......2 Sam. 8:2
Ruled over.....2 Sam. 5:2
Deported ......2 Kin. 17:6

See Siege of a city

Wardrobe—*one's clothing*

Woman's.........Is. 3:18-23
Directions
concerning .....1 Pet. 3:3-5
Keeper of ....2 Kin. 22:14

Wares

Sold in Tyrus .....Ezek. 27:1-27

Warfare, spiritual

A. *Enemies combatted:*
World ....James 4:1-4
Flesh ....1 Pet. 4:1-4
Devil ....1 Pet. 5:8
Invisible foes ..Eph. 6:12

B. *Conquest over, by:*
God's Word....Eph. 6:17
God's armor ..Eph. 6:10-17
Faith ....1 John 5:4, 5
Christ's
promise ....John 16:33

C. *Soldiers of, must:*
Avoid worldly entangle-
ments.........2 Tim. 2:4
Pray...........Eph. 6:18
Deny self ......1 Cor. 9:25-27
Endure
hardness ......2 Tim. 2:3, 10
Be self-
controlled.....1 Thess. 5:6
Be alert........1 Cor. 16:13
Wear armor ...Eph. 6:11

Warning—*to caution one concerning his action*

A. *Means of, by:*
God's Word....Ps. 19:9-11
Prophet........Ezek. 3:17-27
Messenger.....Acts 20:31
Dream.........Matt. 2:12, 22
Angel..........Acts 10:22
God ....Heb. 11:7

B. *Reactions to:*

Obeyed . . . . Jon. 3:1-10
Accepted . . . . . . Heb. 11:7
Ignored . . . . 2 Sam. 2:20-23
Rejected . . . . Gen. 2:16, 17
Scoffed at . . . . . Gen. 19:14
Disobeyed . . . . . Num. 14:40-45

C. *Disobedience to, brings:*

Judgment . . . . . . Jude 6, 7
Torments . . . . . . Luke 16:23-28
Destruction . . . . Prov. 29:1

Wash—*to cleanse something with a liquid*

A. *Kinds of:*

Ceremonial . . . . Ex. 30:18-20
Miraculous . . . . John 9:7, 11, 15
Demonstra-
tive . . . . John 13:5-14
Symbolic . . . . . Matt. 27:24
Typical . . . . Ps. 51:2, 7
Spiritual . . . . . . Acts 22:16
Regenerative . . Titus 3:5

B. *Materials used:*

Water . . . . Gen. 24:32
Tears . . . . Luke 7:38, 44
Snow . . . . Job 9:30
Wine . . . . Gen. 49:11
Blood . . . . Ps. 58:10

C. *Objects of:*

Hands . . . . Matt. 27:24
Face . . . . Gen. 43:31
Feet . . . . Gen. 18:4
Body . . . . 2 Sam. 11:2
Clothes . . . . 2 Sam. 19:24

See Purification

Washpot

Moab described as
God's . . . . Ps. 60:6-8

Waste—*a state of ruin*

A. *Objects of:*

Cities . . . . Ezek. 19:7
Nations . . . . Nah. 3:7
Possessions . . . . Luke 15:13
Temple . . . . Is. 64:11

B. *Caused by:*

God's
judgments . . . . Amos 7:9
God's hatred . . Mal. 1:3
Squandering . . . Luke 15:11-32

C. *State of:*

Lamented . . . . . . Neh. 2:3, 17
To be
corrected . . . . . Is. 61:4

Watch—*to attend to, guard*

The LORD . . . . Gen. 31:49
As guards . . . . 2 Kin. 11:4-7

Watches of day, night—*period of time*

Jesus walks on
water . . . . Matt. 14:25
Time of coming . . . Matt. 24:43
Luke 12:37, 38

Watchmen, spiritual

Set by God . . . . Is. 62:6
Message to . . . . Is. 21:11, 12
Responsibility of . . Ezek. 33:1-9
Some are
faithful . . . . Ezek. 3:17-21
Some are
faithless . . . . Is. 56:10
In vain without the
LORD . . . . Ps. 127:1
Leaders in the
church . . . . Heb. 13:17

Water

A. *Described as:*

Living . . . . Jer. 2:13
Cold . . . . Jer. 18:14
Still . . . . Ps. 23:2
Deep . . . . Ps. 69:2, 14
Pools . . . . Ps. 107:35
Mighty . . . . Is. 28:2

B. *God's control over, He:*

Creates . . . . Gen. 1:2, 6, 7
Gives . . . . Ps. 104:13
Blesses the earth
with . . . . Is. 55:10
Withholds . . . . . Is. 50:2
Reveals His wonders
in . . . . Ps. 107:23-32
Sets bounds
to . . . . Ps. 104:5-9

C. *Miracles connected with:*

Changed into
blood . . . . Ex. 7:17-25
Divided . . . . Ex. 14:21-29
Bitter made
sweet . . . . Ex. 15:22-25
From a rock . . . Ex. 17:1-7
Jordan
divided . . . . Josh. 3:14-17
Consumed by
fire . . . . 1 Kin. 18:38
Valley, full of . . 2 Kin. 3:16-24
Axe floats on . . 2 Kin. 6:5-7
Christ walks
on . . . . Mark 6:49-52

Changed into
wine . . . . John 2:1-11
Healing of . . . . . 2 Kin. 2:19-22

D. *Normal uses of, for:*
Drinking. . . . . . Gen. 24:43
Washing. . . . . . Gen. 18:4
Animals . . . . . . Ps. 42:1
Vegetation. . . . Deut. 11:10, 11
Sea creatures . . . Ps. 104:25, 26

E. *Special uses of, for:*
Cleansing. . . . . Ex. 30:18-20
               Ex. 40:7-32
Purification. . . . Ex. 19:10
Baptism . . . . . . Acts 8:36-39
Sanctifi-
cation. . . . . Eph. 5:26
Business . . . . . . Ps. 107:23

F. *Figurative of:*
Instability . . . . . Gen. 49:4
Cowardice . . . . Josh. 7:5
Spiritual
growth. . . . . . Ps. 1:3
Peace. . . . . Ps. 23:2
Afflictions . . . . Is. 43:2
Persecution . . Ps. 124:4, 5
Adultery . . . . . Prov. 9:17
Universal
Gospel . . . . . . Is. 11:9
Salvation . . . . . Is. 55:1
Gospel age . . Is. 41:17-20
Holy Spirit . . Ezek. 47:1-12
Eternal life . . . Rev. 22:17
Christ . . . . John 4:10-15
Regeneration . . John 7:37, 38

G. *Cure for:*
Doubting
commander . . . 2 Kin. 5:1-15
Afflicted . . . . . . John 5:1-7
Blind man . . . . John 9:6-11

H. *Used for a test:*
By Gideon . . . . Judg. 7:4-7

I. *Conduit:*
Hezekiah
builds . . . . 2 Kin. 20:20

Water and blood

From Christ. . . . . . John 19:34

Water Gate—*a gate of Jerusalem*

Law is read . . . . . . Neh. 8:1, 2

Waterproofing—*making vessels watertight*

By means of:
Pitch. . . . . Gen. 6:14

Asphalt and
pitch . . . . Ex. 2:3

Waw

Letter in the Hebrew
alphabet. . . . . Ps. 119:41-48

Wax—*beeswax*

Figurative of
persecution. . . . . . Ps. 22:14
Of the wicked before
God . . . . Ps. 68:2
Of the
mountains. . . . . . . Ps. 97:5

Way (see Highway; Path)

Way, Christ as

Leading to
Father. . . . . John 14:6

Way, God's

Right . . . . Hos. 14:9
Just. . . . . Dan. 4:37
True . . . . Rev. 15:3
Higher than
man's . . . . Is. 55:8, 9
Unsearchable . . . . . Rom. 11:33

Waymarks—*roadmarkings*

Give direction. . . . . Jer. 31:21

Ways of God's people

A. *With reference to God's way, to:*
Understand . . . . Ps. 119:27
Pray for direction
in . . . . Ex. 33:13
Walk in. . . . . . . Deut. 8:6
Remember. . . . . Deut. 8:2
Known . . . . Ps. 67:2
Teach to trans-
gressors . . . . . Ps. 51:13
Rejoice in . . . . . Ps. 119:14

B. *God's attitude toward, He:*
Knows. . . . . Ps. 1:6
Are acquainted
with . . . . Ps. 139:3
Delights in. . . . . Ps. 37:23
Leads us in . . . . Ps. 139:24
Teaches . . . . . . Ps. 25:9, 12
Makes
known . . . . Ps. 103:7
Makes
perfect. . . . . . . Ps. 18:32
Blesses . . . . Prov. 8:32

C. *With reference to our way:*

Acknowledge Him
in . . . . Prov. 3:6
Commit to the
LORD. . . . . Ps. 37:5
Makes
prosperous . . . . Josh. 1:8
All before
God. . . . . Ps. 119:168
Teach me. . . . . . Ps. 143:8

Ways of man

Described as:

Perverse before
God . . . . Num. 22:32
Hard . . . . Prov. 13:15
Abomination . . . . . Prov. 15:9
Not good. . . . . Prov. 16:29
Dark . . . . Prov. 2:13

Weak, weakness

A. *Kinds of:*

Political . . . . 2 Sam. 3:1
Physical . . . . . . Judg. 16:7, 17
          2 Cor. 11:30
Spiritual . . . . Is. 35:3
Moral. . . . . 2 Sam. 3:39
          Rom. 8:26

B. *Caused by:*

Fasting. . . . . Ps. 109:24
Discourage-
ment. . . . . Neh. 6:9
Sin . . . . 1 Cor. 11:26-30
Discouraging
preaching . . . . Jer. 38:4
Conscientious
doubts . . . . Rom. 14:1-23

C. *Victory over, by:*

Christ . . . . 2 Cor. 13:3, 4
Grace. . . . . 2 Cor. 12:9, 10
Faith . . . . Heb. 11:33, 34

D. *Our duty toward, to:*

Bear. . . . . Rom. 15:1
Support. . . . . . . Acts 20:35
          1 Cor. 9:22
Not become a stumbling
block . . . . 1 Cor. 8:9

E. *Our duties with reference to:*

Pleasure in . . . . 2 Cor. 12:10
Help those afflicted
with . . . . Rom. 15:1

Wealth—*riches*

A. *Descriptive of:*

Material
possessions. . . . Gen. 34:29

B. *Advantages of:*

Given by
God. . . . . Deut. 8:18, 19
Source of
security . . . . . . Prov. 18:11
Adds friends . . . Prov. 19:4

C. *Disadvantages of:*

Produces self-
sufficiency . . . . Deut. 8:17
Leads to
conceit. . . . . . . Job 31:25
Subject to
loss . . . . Prov. 13:11
Lost by
dissipation . . . . Prov. 5:8-10
Cannot save . . . Ps. 49:6, 7
Must be left to
others. . . . . Ps. 49:10

See Riches, earthly

Wean—*to accustom a child to independance from the mother's milk*

Celebrated . . . . Gen. 21:8
Figurative of spiritual
rest . . . . Ps. 131:2

Weapons, spiritual

Against:

World—faith . . . . . 1 John 5:4
Satan—armor of
God . . . . Eph. 6:11-17
Flesh—the Spirit . . Gal. 5:16-25

Weary—*to become tired*

A. *Caused by:*

Journeys. . . . . . John 4:6
Ritualism . . . . . Is. 1:14
Study. . . . . Eccl. 12:12
Anxiety. . . . . . . Gen. 27:46
Words . . . . Mal. 2:17
Not speaking . . Jer. 20:9
Too frequent
visits. . . . . Prov. 25:17

B. *Overcome by:*

Waiting on the
LORD. . . . . Is. 40:30, 31
Appropriate
word. . . . . Is. 50:4
God's
promise . . . . . . Is. 28:12
Persevering
faith . . . . Gal. 6:9
Promised
ruler . . . . Is. 32:1, 2
Looking to
Jesus. . . . . Heb. 12:2, 3

Weather

Proverb
concerning . . . . .Job 37:9-11
Under divine
control . . . . . . .1 Sam. 12:16-19
Signs of. . . . . .Luke 12:54-57

Weaving—*uniting threads to produce cloth*

Men endowed in art
of . . . . .Ex. 35:35
Performed by worthy
women. . . . . .Prov. 31:13, 19
Figurative of life's
shortness. . . . . . . .Job 7:6

See Spinning

Wedding (See Marriage)

Wedge of gold

Stolen by Achan . .Josh. 7:20, 21

Weeds

Wrapped around Jonah's
head . . . . .Jon. 2:5

Week—*seven days*

Origin of, early. . . .Gen. 2:1-3
Used in dating
events. . . . . .Gen. 7:4, 10
One, length of
mourning . . . . .Gen. 50:10
Part of ceremonial
Law . . . . .Ex. 13:6, 7
Seventy, prophecy
of . . . . .Dan. 9:24
Christ arose on first day
of . . . . .Matt. 28:1
Christians
worship on first   (Acts 20:7
day of. . . . . 1 Cor. 16:2

See Pentecost

Weeks of years

Seven. . . . . .Lev. 25:8
Seventy. . . . . .Jer. 25:11
              Dan. 9:2

Weeping—*intense crying*

A. *Kinds of:*
  Rebellious . . . . .Num. 11:4-20
  Hypocritical . . .Judg. 14:16, 17
  Sincere . . . . . . .1 Sam. 20:41
  Exhausting . . .1 Sam. 30:4
  Secret . . . . .Jer. 13:17
  Permanent. . . .Matt. 8:12
  Bitterly . . . . . . .Matt. 26:75

  Divine. . . . . . . .John 11:35
  Sympathetic . . .Rom. 12:15

B. *Caused by:*
  Despair. . . . . . .Gen. 21:16
  Death . . . . .Gen. 50:1
  Love. . . . . .Gen. 29:11
  Joy of
  reunion . . . . . .Gen. 33:4
  Loss of child. . .Gen. 37:35
  Restraint of
  joy. . . . . .Gen. 42:24
  Hearing God's
  Word . . . : . . . . .Neh. 8:9

C. *Passing away of:*
  After a child's
  death . . . . .2 Sam. 12:21-23
  In the
  morning . . . . . .Ps. 30:5
  In eternity. . . . .Is. 65:19
  After seeing the
  Lord . . . . .John 20:11-18

Weights and measures

A. *Monies of the Bible:*
  Bekah . . . . .Ex. 38:26
  Gerahs . . . . . . .Ex. 30:13
  Mite. . . . . .Mark 12:42
  Pence. . . . . .Matt. 18:28
  Daric. . . . . .1 Chr. 29:7
  Drachma . . . . . .Ezra 2:69
  Pieces of
  silver . . . . .Matt. 26:15
  Shekel. . . . . . . .Ex. 30:24
  Shekels of
  gold. . . . . .1 Chr. 21:25
  Shekels of
  silver . . . . .2 Sam. 24:24
  Silver. . . . . .2 Chr. 21:3
  Talents . . . . . . .Matt. 18:24
  Talents of
  bronze . . . . . . .1 Chr. 29:7
  Talents of
  gold. . . . . .1 Chr. 29:4
  Talents of
  iron. . . . . .1 Chr. 29:7
  Talents of
  silver . . . . .1 Chr. 29:4

B. *Distance or length
  measurements:*
  Acre. . . . . .1 Sam. 14:14
  Cubit. . . . . .Gen. 6:15
  Fathom . . . . . . .Acts 27:28
  Finger . . . . .Jer. 52:21
  Miles . . . . .Luke 24:13
  Hand-
  breadth . . . . . .Ex. 25:25
  Measuring
  rod. . . . . .Ezek. 40:3

Pace............2 Sam. 6:13
Span............Ex. 28:16
Sabbath day's
journey ......Acts 1:12

C. *Liquid measures:*
Bath..........1 Kin. 7:26
Kor...........Ezek. 45:14
Gallons ....John 2:6
Hin...........Ex. 29:40
Homer ....Ezek. 45:11
Kab...........2 Kin. 6:25
Log...........Lev. 14:10

D. *Dry measures:*
Kab...........2 Kin. 6:25
Ephah ....Ex. 16:36
Homer ....Lev. 27:16
Log...........Lev. 14:10
Omer ....Ex. 16:16
Gerah ....Ex. 30:13
Mina ....1 Kin. 10:17

E. *Weight measures:*
Beka..........Ex. 38:26
Shekel ....2 Sam. 14:26
Talents ....Ex. 38:27

Welcome—*to receive with gladness*

A. *Extended to:*
Returning
brother ......Gen. 33:1-11
Father........Gen. 46:29-34
Hero..........1 Sam. 18:6, 7
Prodigal son .. Luke 15:20-32
Messiah ......Matt. 21:6-10

B. *Circumstances attending:*
Courtesies
offered ....Gen. 18:1-8
Discourtesies
shown ....2 Sam. 10:1-5
Fear
expressed ....1 Sam. 16:4, 5
Fellowship
denied ....2 John 10, 11

Wells—*pits dug for water*

A. *Features concerning:*
Women come
to, for ⎰Gen. 24:13, 14
water ⎱John 4:7
Surrounded by
trees ....Gen. 49:22
Often very
deep ....John 4:11
Covered with large
stone ....Gen. 29:2, 3
Sometimes cause
strife.........Gen. 21:25

B. *Names of:*
Beer ....Num. 21:16-18
Beer
Lahai Roi .....Gen. 16:14
Beersheba ....Gen. 21:30, 31
Beeroth.......Deut. 10:6
Esek..........Gen. 26:20
Jacob.........John 4:6
Rehoboth .....Gen. 26:22
Sitnah ....Gen. 26:21

C. *Figurative of:*
Salvation ......Is. 12:3
False
teaching ......2 Pet. 2:17
One's wife ....Prov. 5:15
The Holy
Spirit ....John 4:10

Whale

Created by God ...Gen. 1:21

See Great Fish

Wheat—*a cereal grass used for food*

A. *Features concerning:*
Grown in
Egypt.........Ex. 9:32
Grown in
Palestine......1 Kin. 5:11
Made into
bread ....Ex. 29:2
Used in trade ..Ezek. 27:17
Harvested ....Ruth 2:23
Threshed .....Judg. 6:11
Gathered .....Matt. 3:12
Harvesting of,
celebrated....Ex. 34:22

B. *Figurative of:*
Spiritual
blessings .....Ps. 81:16
Christians .....Matt. 3:12
Christ's
death ....John 12:24
Resurrection ..1 Cor. 15:37

Wheel—*a circular frame*

A. *Used on:*
Carts ....Is. 28:27, 28
Threshing
instrument ...Prov. 20:26
Chariots.......Nah. 3:2
Jehovah's
throne ....Ezek. 10:1-22

B. *Figurative of:*
Future
things.........Ezek. 1:15-28
Punishment....Prov. 20:26

Cycle of nature
("course").....James 3:6
God's
sovereignty ...Ezek. 10:9-19

Whelp—*offspring of certain animals*

Figurative of:

Judah.............Gen. 49:9
Dan..............Deut. 33:22
Babylonians......Jer. 51:38

Whirlwind—*a great storm or tempest*

A. *Used literally of:*
Elijah's
translation ....2 Kin. 2:1
Its fury........Is. 17:13

B. *Used figuratively of:*
Sudden
destruction....Prov. 1:27
Suddenness....Is. 5:28
God's anger...Jer. 23:19
God's might ...Nah. 1:3

Whisperer—*a gossiper*

Separates chief
friends ....Prov. 16:28

Whistle—*meaning to call, allure, or
entice*

Applied to:

Nations ....Is. 5:26
Egypt and
Assyria...........Is. 7:18
Israel ....Zech. 10:8

White (see Colors)

Whore, Whoredom (see Adultery;
Harlot)

Wicked, the

A. *Satan as "the wicked one"*
Unregenerate belong
to.............Matt. 13:38
Snatches away the good
seed ....Matt. 13:19
World lies in...1 John 5:19
Christians can ⌠Eph. 6:16
overcome ....⌡1 John 2:13

B. *Descriptive of:*
Sodomites .....Gen. 13:13
Egyptians......Ex. 9:27
Athaliah.......2 Chr. 24:7
Haman ....Esth. 7:6
Jews...........Matt. 12:38, 45
Apostates......1 Cor. 5:13

C. *State of, described as:*
Desiring evil ...Prov. 21:10
Have no
peace ....Is. 48:22
Pours out
evil ....Prov. 15:28
Refusing
judgment .....Prov. 21:7
Cruel in their
mercies ....Prov. 12:10
Like the troubled
sea...........Is. 57:20
Far from
God..........Prov. 15:29
Offering abominable
sacrifice......Prov. 15:8
Way is like
darkness ......Prov. 4:19

D. *God's attitude toward:*
Will not
justify ....Ex. 23:7
Will punish ....Ps. 75:8
Will
overthrow.....Prov. 21:12
Their thoughts abominable
to.............Prov. 15:26
God hates .....Ps. 11:5
Made for the day of
doom ....Prov. 16:4

E. *Punishment of:*
Shortened
life............Prov. 10:27
Soon
destroyed ....Ps. 37:35, 36
Driven away...Prov. 14:32
Slain by evil ...Ps. 34:21
His lamp put
out ....Job 21:17
His triumph
short..........Ps. 37:10
His name put out
forever.......Ps. 9:5
Silent in the
grave ....Ps. 31:17
God rains fire
on ....Ps. 11:6
Cast into hell ..Ps. 9:17
Consumed .....Ps. 37:20
Will die........Prov. 11:7
In the resurrection,
judgment .....Acts 24:15

F. *Attitude of believers toward:*
Wonder about their
prosperity.....Ps. 73:3
Concerned about their
triumph.......Ps. 94:3, 4

Will not sit
with .... Ps. 26:5
Must not
envy .... Prov. 24:19
Will triumph
over .... Ps. 58:10

Wickedness—*all forms of evil*

A. *Man's relationship to:*
Not profited
by .... Prov. 10:2
Not established
by .... Prov. 12:3
Sells himself
to .... 1 Kin. 21:25
Strengthens himself
in .... Ps. 52:7
Refuses to turn
from .... Jer. 44:5
Inside
mankind .... Luke 11:39
Among all .... Jer. 44:9
Will fall by .... Prov. 11:5
Driven away .... Prov. 14:32

B. *God's punishment of, seen in:*
Driving out other
nations .... Deut. 9:4, 5
Shiloh's
destruction .... Jer. 7:12
Judah's
punishment .... Jer. 1:16
Destruction of food
supply .... Ps. 107:33, 34
Causing the
flood .... Gen. 6:5-7
Death of
men .... Judg. 9:56
Destroying
men .... Ps. 94:23

C. *Attitude of the righteous
toward:*
Wash heart
of .... Jer. 4:14
Struggle
against .... Eph. 6:12
Fear to
commit .... Gen. 39:9
Not to dwell
in .... Ps. 84:10
Pray for end
of .... Ps. 7:9
Confession
of .... 1 Kin. 8:47

Wick-trimmers

Used for trimming wicks in
lamps .... Ex. 37:23

Trays used to catch snuff of
lamps .... Ex. 25:38

Widow—*a woman who has outlived her
husband*

A. *Provision of, for:*
Remarriage .... Rom. 7:3
Food .... Deut. 24:19-21
Protection .... Is. 1:17, 23
Vows of .... Num. 30:9
Raiment .... Deut. 24:17

B. *Mistreatment of, by:*
Children .... 1 Tim. 5:4
Neglect .... Acts 6:1
Scribes .... Mark 12:40
Creditors .... 2 Kin. 4:1
Princes .... Is. 1:23
Judges .... Is. 10:1, 2

C. *Protection of, by:*
God .... Ex. 22:22-24
Law .... Deut. 24:17
Pure religion .... James 1:27
Honor .... 1 Tim. 5:3

D. *Examples of:*
Naomi .... Ruth 1:20, 21
Woman of
Tekoa .... 2 Sam. 14:4, 5
Woman of
Zarephath .... 1 Kin. 17:9, 10
Anna .... Luke 2:36, 37
"A certain poor
widow" .... Luke 21:2, 3

Wife—*a married woman*

A. *Described as:*
"A helper comparable to
him" .... Gen. 2:18, 20
"The crown to her
husband" .... Prov. 12:4
"A good
thing" .... Prov. 18:22
"The weaker
vessel" .... 1 Pet. 3:7
"The wife of your
youth" .... Mal. 2:14, 15
"Your
companion" .... Mal. 2:14

B. *Duties of, to:*
Submit to
husband .... 1 Pet. 3:5, 6
Reverence her
husband .... Eph. 5:33
Love her
husband .... Titus 2:4
Learn from her
husband .... 1 Cor. 14:34, 35

Be
trustworthy...Prov. 31:11, 12
Love her
children......Titus 2:4
Be chaste......Titus 2:5
Be home-
makers........Titus 2:5

C. *Duties of husband toward, to:*
Love...........Eph. 5:25, 28
Honor..........1 Pet. 3:7
Provide for ....1 Tim. 5:8
Instruct........1 Cor. 14:35
Protect........1 Sam. 30:1-19
Not divorce....1 Cor. 7:11

D. *Relationship with her husband,*
to be:
Exclusive......Prov. 5:15-17, 20
Satisfying......Prov. 5:18, 19
Mutually
agreeable ....1 Cor. 7:1-5
Undefiled.....Heb. 13:4

E. *Special temptations of:*
Disobedience ..Gen. 3:1-19
Unfaithful-
ness..........John 4:17, 18
Conten-
tiousness......Prov. 19:13
Assertion of
authority......1 Tim. 2:11-15

F. *Types of:*
Disobedient—
Eve...........Gen. 3:1-8
Obedient—
Sarah.........1 Pet. 3:5, 6
Worldly—
Lot's.........Gen. 19:26
Humble—
Manoah's.....Judg. 13:22, 23
Prayerful—
Hannah.......1 Sam. 1:1-15
Prudent— { 1 Sam. 25:3,
Abigail...... 14-35
Criticizing—
Michal.......2 Sam. 6:15, 16
Unscrupulous—
Jezebel........1 Kin. 21:5-15
Modest—
Vashti ....Esth. 1:11, 12
Foolish—
Job's wife.....Job 2:7-10
Cruel—
Herodias ......Matt. 14:3-12
Righteous—
Elizabeth......Luke 1:5, 6

Lying—
Sapphira......Acts 5:1-10

Wilderness—*a desolate place*

A. *Descriptive of:*
Israel's
wanderings ...Ex. 16:1
Desolate
place..........Matt. 3:1, 3
Desolation.....Jer. 22:6

B. *Characterized by:*
Wild
creatures......Deut. 8:15
No water ......Deut. 8:15
"Great and
terrible".......Deut. 1:19
Uninhabited ...Ps. 107:4, 5

C. *Israel's journey in,*
characterized by:
God's
provision......Deut. 2:7
God's
guidance......Ps. 78:52
God's mighty
acts...........Ps. 78:15, 16
Israel's provoking
God...........Ps. 78:17-19, 40
Israel's sin.....Heb. 3:7-19
Testings ....Deut. 8:2

D. *Significant events in:*
Hagar's flight ..Gen. 16:6-8
Israel's
journeys ......Ps. 136:16
John's
preaching .....Matt. 3:1-12
Jesus'
temptation....Matt. 4:1
Jesus'
miracle.......Matt. 15:33-38
Moses'
serpent........John 3:14

Wild ox

Of great
strength.........Num. 23:22
Very wild and
ferocious.........Job 39:9-12
Frisky in youth ...Ps. 29:6

Willingness

A. *On God's part, to:*
Exercise
mercy.........2 Kin. 8:18, 19
Rule
sovereignly....Dan. 4:17

Save men......1 Tim. 2:4
2 Pet. 3:9

B. *On Christ's part, to:*
Do God's will ..Heb. 10:7, 9
Submit to the
Father ....John 8:28, 29
Reveal the
Father ....Matt. 11:27
Heal people....Matt. 8:2, 3
Die ....Mark 14:36

C. *On man's part, to:*
Do Satan's
will ....John 8:44
Refuse
salvation......John 5:40
Pervert the
truth.........2 Pet. 3:5
Follow evil.....Mark 15:15
Persecute the
righteous .....Matt. 2:13

D. *On the believer's part, to:*
Be saved......Rev. 22:17
Follow
Christ........Matt. 16:24
Live godly ....2 Tim. 3:12
Give ....2 Cor. 8:3-12
Die ....2 Cor. 5:8

Will of God

A. *Defined in terms of:*
Salvation .....2 Pet. 3:9
Salvation of
children.......Matt. 18:14
Belief in
Christ........Matt. 12:50
Everlasting
life..........John 6:39, 40
Thanks-
giving........1 Thess. 5:18
Sanctifi-
cation.........1 Thess. 4:3

B. *Characteristics of:*
Can be:
Known ......Rom. 2:18
Proved.......Rom. 12:2
Done ....Matt. 6:10
Sovereign over:
Nations......Dan. 4:35
Individuals ..Acts 21:14

C. *God's power in doing, seen in:*
Predestina-
tion..........Rom. 9:18-23
Sovereignty....Dan. 4:35
Man's
salvation......1 Tim. 2:4

Believer's
salvation......James 1:18
Redemption ..Gal. 1:4

D. *Believer's relationship to, seen in his:*
Calling ....1 Cor. 1:1
Regeneration ..James 1:18
Sanctifica-
tion...........Heb. 10:10
Trans-
formation .....Rom. 12:2
Instruction .....Ps. 143:10
Prayers.......1 John 5:14
Submission ....Acts 21:14
Whole life .....1 Pet. 4:2
Daily work ....Eph. 6:6
Travels ....Rom. 1:10
Plans ....James 4:13-15
Suffering ......1 Pet. 3:17
Perfection .....Col. 4:12

Will of man (see Freedom; Liberty, spiritual)

Willow—*a tree*

Booths made of ...Lev. 23:40, 42
Grows beside
brooks ....Job 40:22
Harps hung on ....Ps. 137:2

See Poplar tree

Wind—*movement of the air*

A. *Characteristics of:*
Movement of,
significant.....Luke 12:54, 55
Cannot be
seen ....John 3:8
Sometimes
destructive....Job 1:19
Dries the
earth.........Gen. 8:1
Often accompanies
rain...........1 Kin. 18:44, 45
Makes sea
rough........Ps. 107:25
Drives ships ...Acts 27:7, 13-18
Drives chaff
away..........Ps. 1:4
Possesses
weight ....Job 28:25

B. *God's relation to, He:*
Creates........Amos 4:13
Sends.........Ps. 147:18
Brings out of His
treasuries .....Ps. 135:7

Gathers........Prov. 30:4
Controls........Ps. 107:25

C. *Directions of, from:*
East ....Jer. 18:17
West ....Ex. 10:19
North...........Prov. 25:23
South...........Acts 27:13
All directions .. Ezek. 37:9

D. *Miracles connected with:*
Flood subsided
by ....Gen. 8:1
Locust brought and taken
by ....Ex. 10:13, 19
Red Sea divided
by ....Ex. 14:21
Quail brought
by ....Num. 11:31
Rain brought
by ....1 Kin. 18:44, 45
Mountains broken
by ....1 Kin. 19:11
Jonah's ship tossed
by ....Jon. 1:4
Christ calms .. Matt. 8:26

E. *Figurative of:*
Empty
speech ....Job 8:2
Empty
boasting ......Prov. 25:14
Vanity..........Eccl. 5:16
Calamity ......Is. 32:2
God's
discipline......Hos. 13:15
God's
judgment .....Jer. 22:22
Dispersion .....Ezek. 5:10
Ruin............Hos. 8:7
Holy Spirit.....Acts 2:2
False
teaching ......Eph. 4:14

Windows of Heaven

Descriptive of:

Judgment rendered
"opened".........Gen. 7:11
Unbelief ....2 Kin. 7:2, 19
Blessings..........Mal. 3:10

Vine

A. *Kinds of:*
New............Luke 5:37-39
Old ....Luke 5:39
Fermented.....Num. 6:3
Refined........Is. 25:6

B. *Features concerning:*
Made from
grapes ....Gen. 40:11
Mixed ....Prov. 23:30
Kept in
bottles ....Jer. 13:12
Kept in
wineskins .....Matt. 9:17

C. *Used by:*
Noah ....Gen. 9:20, 21
Melchizedek .. Gen. 14:18
Isaac ....Gen. 27:25
Esther ....Esth. 5:6
Jesus ....John 2:1-11
Timothy ....1 Tim. 5:23

D. *Uses of, as:*
Offering ....Lev. 23:13
Drink...........Gen. 27:25
Festive drink .. Esth. 1:7
Disinfectant ... Luke 10:34
Drug ....Mark 15:23
Medicine ......1 Tim. 5:23

E. *Evil effects of:*
Leads to
violence.......Prov. 4:17
Mocks a man .. Prov. 20:1
Make poor.....Prov. 23:20, 21
Bites like a
serpent........Prov. 23:31, 32
Impairs the
judgment ......Prov. 31:4, 5
Inflames the
passions.......Is. 5:11
Enslaves the
heart..........Hos. 4:11

F. *Intoxication from, falsely
charged to:*
Hannah........1 Sam. 1:12-16
Jesus ....Matt. 11:19
Apostles ....Acts 2:13

G. *Uses of, in:*
Offering ....Num. 15:4-10
Miracle........John 2:1-10
Lord's
Supper........Matt. 26:27-29

H. *Figurative of:*
God's wrath ... Ps. 75:8
Wisdom's
blessings ......Prov. 9:2, 5
Gospel.........Is. 55:1
Christ's
blood ....Matt. 26:27-29
Fornication .... Rev. 17:2

See Drunkenness; Temperance

Wings—*the locomotive appendages on flying creatures*

A. *Used literally of:*
Flying
creatures......Gen. 1:21
Cherubim......Ex. 25:20

B. *Used figuratively of:*
God's mercy...Ps. 57:1
Protection .....Luke 13:34

Winking the eye

Hate ....Ps. 35:19
Evil................Prov. 6:12, 13

Winnow—*to toss about*

A. *Used literally of:*
Fork for winnowing
grain...........Is. 30:24

B. *Used figuratively of judgments:*
God's...........Is. 30:24
Nation's ....Jer. 51:2
Christ's........Matt. 3:12

Winter—*the cold season of the year*

Made by God .....Ps. 74:17
Continuance of,
guaranteed......Gen. 8:22
Time of snow .....2 Sam. 23:20
Hazards of travel
during...........2 Tim. 4:21

Wipe—*to clean or dry*

A. *Used literally of:*
Dust removal ..Luke 10:11
Feet dried .....John 13:5

B. *Used figuratively of:*
Jerusalem's
destruction....2 Kin. 21:13
Tears
removed ......Rev. 7:17

Wisdom—*knowledge guided by understanding*

A. *Sources of, in:*
Spirit ....Ex. 31:3
Lord............Ex. 36:1, 2
God's Law....Deut. 4:6
Fear of the
LORD..........Prov. 9:10
Righteous ......Prov. 10:31

B. *Ascribed to:*
Workmen.....Ex. 36:2
Women ....Prov. 31:26
Bezaleel ......Ex. 31:2-5
Joseph........Acts 7:9, 10

Moses ....Acts 7:22
Joshua........Deut. 34:9
Hiram ....1 Kin. 7:13, 14
Solomon.......1 Kin. 3:16-28
Children of
Issachar ......1 Chr. 12:32
Ezra...........Ezra 7:25
Daniel.........Dan. 1:17
Magi ....Matt. 2:1-12
Stephen.......Acts 6:3, 10
Paul...........2 Pet. 3:15

C. *Described as:*
Discerning.....Gen. 41:33
Technical
skill...........Ex. 28:3
Common
sense ....2 Sam. 20:14-22
Mechanical
skill..........1 Kin. 7:14
Understand-
ing............Prov. 10:13, 23
Military
ability........Is. 10:13
Commercial
industry......Ezek. 28:3-5

D. *Value of:*
Gives
happiness ....Prov. 3:13
Benefits of,
many ....Prov. 4:5-10
Keeps from
evil ....Prov. 5:1-6
Better than
rubies.........Prov. 8:11
Above gold in
value ....Prov. 16:16
Should be
acquired ......Prov. 23:23
Excels folly ...Eccl. 2:13
Gives life ......Eccl. 7:12
Makes
strong ....Eccl. 7:19
Better than
weapons .....Eccl. 9:18
Insures
stability.......Is. 33:6
Produces good
fruit ....James 3:17

E. *Limitations of:*
Cannot save
us.............1 Cor. 1:19-21
Cause of self-
glory.........Jer. 9:23
Can pervert....Is. 47:10
Nothing, without
God...........Jer. 8:9
Can corrupt ...Ezek. 28:17

Of this world,
foolishness....1 Cor. 3:19
Earthly,
sensual.......James 3:15
Gospel not preached
in.............1 Cor. 2:1-5

F. *Of believers:*
Given by
Christ........Luke 21:15
Gift of the
Spirit ....1 Cor. 12:8
Given by
God...........Eph. 1:17
Prayed for .....Col. 1:9
Means of
instruction ....Col. 1:28
Lack of, ask
for ....James 1:5

Wisdom of Christ

Predicted ....Is. 11:1, 2
Incarnated.......1 Cor. 1:24
Realized ....Luke 2:52
Displayed ....Matt. 13:54
Perfected ....Col. 2:3
Imputed ....1 Cor. 1:30

Wisdom of God

A. *Described as:*
Universal ......Dan. 2:20
Infinite ....Ps. 147:5
Unsearch-
able............Is. 40:28
Mighty ....Job 36:5
Perfect ....Job 37:16

B. *Manifested in:*
Creation.......Ps. 104:24
Nature.........Job 38:34-41
Sovereignty...Dan. 2:20, 21
The Church....Eph. 3:10

Witchcraft—*the practice of sorcery*

Forbidden in
Israel.............Deut. 18:9-14
Used by Jezebel..2 Kin. 9:22
Condemned by the
prophets..........Mic. 5:12
Practiced by
Manasseh ....2 Chr. 33:6
Suppressed by
Saul..............1 Sam. 28:3, 9
Work of the
flesh..............Gal. 5:20

See Divination

Wither—*to dry up*

A. *Caused by:*
God's
judgment .....Is. 40:7, 24
Christ's
judgment .....Matt. 21:19, 20
No root........Matt. 13:6
Heat..........James 1:11

B. *Applied literally to:*
Ear of grain...Gen. 41:23
Gourd ....Jon. 4:7
Man's hand....Luke 6:6, 8

Witnessing—*bearing testimony to something*

A. *Elements of, seen in:*
Public
transaction....Ruth 4:1-11
Signing a
document .....Jer. 32:10-12
Calling
witnesses .....Lev. 5:1
Requiring two
witnesses .....1 Tim. 5:19
Rejection of false
witnesses .....Prov. 24:28

B. *Material means of, by:*
Heap stones ...Gen. 31:44-52
Song ....Deut. 31:19-21
Altar ....Josh. 22:26-34
Works.........John 10:25
Sign
(miracles) .....Heb. 2:4

C. *Spiritual means of, by:*
God's Law ....Deut. 31:26
Gospel.........Matt. 24:14
Father ....John 5:37
Conscience ....Rom. 2:15
Holy Spirit.....Rom. 8:16

D. *To Christ as object, by:*
John the
Baptist........John 1:7, 8, 15
His works .....John 5:36
Father ....John 8:18
Himself........John 8:18
Holy Spirit.....John 15:26, 27
His disciples ...John 15:27
Prophets.......Acts 10:43

E. *Of Christians to Christ:*
Chosen ....Acts 10:41
Commis-
sioned ....Acts 1:8
Empowered....Acts 4:33
Confirmed ....Heb. 2:3, 4

F. *Objects of Christ's:*
Resurrection...Acts 2:32

Saviorhood ....Acts 5:31, 32
Life............Acts 1:21, 22
Mission.......Acts 10:41-43
Sufferings ....1 Pet. 5:1

See Testimony

Wizard (see Witchcraft)

Wolf—*a dog-like animal*

A. *Characteristics of:*
Ravenous......Gen. 49:27
Nocturnal ......Jer. 5:6
Sheep-eating...John 10:12

B. *Figurative of:*
False
prophets ......Matt. 7:15
Gospel trans-
formation .....Is. 11:6

Woman—*the female sex*

A. *Described as:*
Beautiful ......2 Sam. 11:2
Wise...........2 Sam. 20:16
Widow ....1 Kin. 17:9, 10
Evil............Prov. 6:24
Foolish ....Job 2:10
Gracious.......Prov. 11:16
Excellent ......Prov. 12:4
Contentious ...Prov. 21:19
Adulterous.....Prov. 30:20
Prominent .....Acts 17:12
Gullible........2 Tim. 3:6
Holy...........1 Pet. 3:5

B. *Work of:*
Kneading
meal ....Gen. 18:6
Drawing {Gen. 24:11, 13,
water 15
Tending
sheep ....Gen. 29:6
Making cloth ..Prov. 31:13, 19
Caring for the {Prov. 31:27
household .....{1 Tim. 5:14

C. *Rights of, to:*
Marry ....1 Cor. 7:36
Hold
property ......Num. 27:6-11
Make vows ....Num. 30:3-9

D. *Position of, in relation to man:*
Created from
man ....Gen. 2:21-25
Made to help
man ....Gen. 2:18, 20
Glory of man ..1 Cor. 11:7-9
Becomes subject to
man ....Gen. 3:16

Weaker than
man ....1 Pet. 3:7

E. *Position of, in spiritual things:*
Insight of,
noted ....Judg. 13:23
Prayer of,
answered .....1 Sam. 1:9-28
Understanding of,
rewarded......1 Sam. 25:3-42
Faith of, brings
salvation .....Luke 7:37-50
Made equal in
Christ.........Gal. 3:28
Labor of,
commended...Phil. 4:2, 3
Faith of,
transmitted ...2 Tim. 1:5

F. *Good traits of:*
Obedience ....1 Pet. 3:5-7
Concern for
children.......Ex. 2:2-10
Loyalty........Ruth 1:14-18
Desire for
children.......1 Sam. 1:9-28
Modesty.......Esth. 1:10-12
Industry.......Prov. 31:10-31
Complete
devotion .....Luke 7:38-50
Tenderness ....John 11:20-35

G. *Bad traits of:*
Inciting to
evil ....Gen. 3:6, 7
Crafty ....Prov. 7:10
Fond of
adornments ...Is. 3:16-24
Self-
indulgent .....Is. 32:9, 11
Easily led into
idolatry ....Jer. 7:18
Led away......2 Tim. 3:6

H. *Prohibitions concerning, not to:*
Wear man's
clothing.......Deut. 22:5
Have head
shaved........1 Cor. 11:5-15
Usurp
authority......1 Tim. 2:11-15
Be unchaste ..1 Pet. 3:1-7

Womb—*the uterus*

A. *God's control over, to:*
Close ....Gen. 20:18
Open ....Gen. 29:31
Fashion us in ..Job 31:15
Separate and
call ....Gal. 1:15

Cause to
conceive ..... Luke 1:31
Make alive .... Rom. 4:19-21

B. *Babe inside:*
Grows mysteri-
ously .... Eccl. 11:5
Known by
God .... Ps. 139:13-16
Deformed ...... Acts 3:2
Leaps .... Luke 1:41, 44

C. *Man coming from:*
Different ...... Gen. 25:23, 24
Consecrated .. Judg. 13:5, 7
Naked .... Job 1:21
Helpless ...... Ps. 22:9, 10
Sustained ..... Ps. 71:6
Estranged ..... Ps. 58:3

Women of the Bible, named

Abi, wife of
Ahaz .... 2 Kin. 18:1, 2
Abigail
(1) wife of
Nabal .... 1 Sam. 25:3
(2) sister of
David .... 1 Chr. 2:15, 16
Abihail, wife of
Abishur .... 1 Chr. 2:29
Abijah, wife of
Hezron .... 1 Chr. 2:24
Abishag, nurse of
David .... 1 Kin. 1:1-3
Abital, David's
wife .... 2 Sam. 3:1, 4
Achsah, daughter of
Caleb .... Josh. 15:16
Adah
(1) a wife of
Lamech .... Gen. 4:19
(2) Canaanite wife of
Esau .... Gen. 36:2
Ahinoam
(1) wife of Saul .. 1 Sam. 14:50
(2) a
Jezreelitess .... 1 Sam. 25:43
Aholah .... Ezek. 23:4
Anah, daughter of
Zibeon .... Gen. 36:2
Anna, an aged
widow .... Luke 2:36, 37
Apphia, a Christian of
Colosse .... Philem. 2
Asenath, wife of
Joseph .... Gen. 41:45
Atarah, wife of
Jerahmeel .... 1 Chr. 2:26

Athaliah, mother of
Ahaziah .... 2 Kin. 8:26
Azubah
(1) first wife of
Caleb .... 1 Chr. 2:18
(2) daughter of
Shilhi .... 1 Kin. 22:42
Baara, wife of
Shaharaim .... 1 Chr. 8:8
Basemath
(1) daughter of
Elon .... Gen. 26:34
(2) a third wife of
Esau .... Gen. 36:2-3
Bathsheba, wife of
David .... 2 Sam. 11:3, 27
Bernice, sister of
Agrippa .... Acts 25:13
Bilhah, Rachel's
handmaid .... Gen. 29:29
Bithiah, daughter of a
Pharaoh .... 1 Chr. 4:17
Candace, a
queen .... Acts 8:27
Chloe, woman of
Corinth .... 1 Cor. 1:11
Claudia, Christian of
Rome .... 2 Tim. 4:21
Cozbi, Midianite
slain .... Num. 25:15-18
Damaris, woman of
Athens .... Acts 17:34
Deborah
(1) Rebekah's
nurse .... Gen. 35:8
(2) judge .... Judg. 4:4
Delilah, Philistine
woman .... Judg. 16:4, 5
Dinah, daughter of
Jacob .... Gen. 30:19, 21
Dorcas, called
Tabitha .... Acts 9:36
Drusilla, wife of
Felix .... Acts 24:24
Eglah, one of David's
wives .... 2 Sam. 3:5
Elizabeth, mother of John the
Baptist .... Luke 1:5, 13
Elisheba, wife of
Aaron .... Ex. 6:23
Ephah, concubine of
Caleb .... 1 Chr. 2:46
Ephrath, mother of
Hur .... 1 Chr. 2:19
Esther, a Jewess who became
queen of Persia ... Esth. 2:16, 17
Eunice, mother of
Timothy .... 2 Tim. 1:5

Euodias, a colaborer with
Paul.............Phil. 4:2

Eve, first
woman...........Gen. 3:20

Gomer, wife of
Hosea............Hos. 1:2, 3

Hagar, Sarai's
maid ....Gen. 16:1

Haggith, wife of
David............2 Sam. 3:2, 4

Hammoleketh, mother of
Ishod.............1 Chr. 7:18

Hamutal, daughter of
Jeremiah.........2 Kin. 23:31

Hannah, mother of
Samuel...........1 Sam. 1:20

Hazelelponi, in genealogies of
Judah............1 Chr. 4:1-3

Helah, one of the wives of
Ashhur...........1 Chr. 4:5

Hephzibah, mother of
Manasseh.........2 Kin. 21:1

Herodias, sister-in-law of
Herod............Matt. 14:3-6

Hodesh, wife of
Shaharaim ....1 Chr. 8:8, 9

Hoglah, a daughter of
Zelophehad......Num. 26:33

Huldah, a
prophetess.......2 Kin. 22:14

Hushim, a
Moabitess ....1 Chr. 8:8-11

Iscah, daughter of
Haran............Gen. 11:29

Jael, wife of
Heber ....Judg. 4:17

Jecholiah, wife of
Amaziah ....2 Kin. 15:1, 2

Jedidah, mother of
Josiah............2 Kin. 22:1

Jehoaddan, wife of
Joash............2 Kin. 14:1, 2

Jehosheba, daughter of
Joram............2 Kin. 11:2

Jemimah, Job's
daughter.........Job 42:12, 14

Jerioth, wife of
Caleb.............1 Chr. 2:18

Jerusha, daughter of
Zadok............2 Kin. 15:33

Jezebel, wife of
Ahab.............1 Kin. 16:30, 31

Joanna, wife of
Chuza...........Luke 8:3

Jochebed, mother of
Moses............Ex. 6:20

Judith, daughter of
Beeri ....Gen. 26:34

Julia, Christian woman of
Rome ....Rom. 16:15

Keren-Happuch, Job's
daughter ....Job 42:14

Keturah, second wife of
Abraham.........Gen. 25:1

Keziah, daughter of
Job...............Job 42:14

Leah, wife of
Jacob ....Gen. 29:21-25

Lois, grandmother of
Timothy..........2 Tim. 1:5

Lo-Ruhamah, daughter of
Gomer ....Hos. 1:3-6

Lydia, first Christian
convert in
Europe ....Acts 16:14

Maachah
(1) daughter of
Nahor...........Gen. 22:23, 24
(2) daughter of
Talmai ....2 Sam. 3:3
(3) daughter of
Abishalom.......1 Kin. 15:2
(4) mother of
Asa ....1 Kin. 15:9, 10
(5) concubine of
Caleb............1 Chr. 2:48
(6) wife of
Machir ....1 Chr. 7:16
(7) wife of
Jehiel ....1 Chr. 8:29

Mahalath
(1) wife of
Esau ....Gen. 28:9
(2) granddaughter of
David ....2 Chr. 11:18

Mahlah, daughter of
Zelophehad......Num. 26:33

Mara, another name for
Naomi...........Ruth 1:20

Martha, friend of
Christ ....Luke 10:38-41

Mary
(1) mother of
Jesus............Matt. 1:16
(2) Mary
Magdalene .....Matt. 27:56-61
(3) Mary, sister of
Martha..........Luke 10:38, 39
(4) Mary, wife of
Clopas ....John 19:25
(5) Mary, mother of
Mark............Acts 12:12
(6) a Christian at
Rome ....Rom. 16:6

Matred, mother-in-law of
Hadar ....Gen. 36:39

Mehetabel, daughter of
Matred...........Gen. 36:39

Merab, King Saul's eldest
daughter........1 Sam. 14:49

Meshullemeth, wife of
Manasseh........2 Kin. 21:18, 19

Michal, daughter of King
Saul.............1 Sam. 14:49

Milcah
(1) daughter of
Haran............Gen. 11:29
(2) daughter of
Zelophehad......Num. 26:33

Miriam
(1) sister of
Moses...........Ex. 15:20
(2) disputed daughter of
Ezra.............1 Chr. 4:17

Naamah
(1) daughter of
Lamech.........Gen. 4:19-22
(2) wife of
Solomon........1 Kin. 14:21

Naarah, one of the wives of
Ashur.............1 Chr. 4:5

Naomi, wife of
Elimelech........Ruth 1:2

Nehushta, daughter of
Elnathan..........2 Kin. 24:8

Noadiah, a false
prophetess.......Neh. 6:14

Noah, daughter of
Zelophehad......Num. 26:33

Oholah...........Ezek. 23:4

Oholibah.........Ezek. 23:4

Orpah, sister-in-law of
Ruth..............Ruth 1:4

Peninnah, one of
the wives of
Elkanah.........1 Sam. 1:1, 2

Persis, convert of early
Church...........Rom. 16:12

Phoebe, a
deaconess.......Rom. 16:1-2

Priscilla, wife of
Aquila...........Acts 18:2

Puah, a midwife..Ex. 1:15

Rachel, wife of
Jacob............Gen. 29:28

Rahab, aid to Israel's
spies............Josh. 2:1-3

Reumah, mother of
Tebah...........Gen. 22:24

Rhoda, a damsel ..Acts 12:13

Rizpah, concubine of
Saul..............2 Sam. 3:7

Ruth, daughter-in-law of
Naomi............Ruth 1:3, 4

Salome, wife of { Matt. 27:56
Zebedee........ { Mark 15:40

Sapphira, wife of
Ananias..........Acts 5:1

Sarah, (Sarai) wife
of Abraham
(Abram).........Gen. 11:29

Serah, daughter of
Asher............Gen. 46:17

Sheerah, daughter of
Beriah...........1 Chr. 7:23, 24

Shelomith
(1) daughter of
Dibri............Lev. 24:11
(2) daughter of
Zerubbabel......1 Chr. 3:19

Shimeath, mother of
Zabad...........2 Chr. 24:26

Shimrith, mother of
Jehozabad.......2 Chr. 24:26

Shiphrah, a
midwife.........Ex. 1:15

Shua, daughter of
Heber...........1 Chr. 7:32

Susanna, ministered to
Jesus...........Luke 8:3

Syntyche, convert of Church at
Philippi..........Phil. 4:2

Tabitha, same as
Dorcas..........Acts 9:36

Tahpenes, queen of
Egypt...........1 Kin. 11:19

Tamar
(1) daughter-in-law of
Judah...........Gen. 38:6
(2) a daughter of
David...........2 Sam. 13:1
(3) daughter of
Absalom.........2 Sam. 14:27

Taphath, one of Solomon's
daughters.......1 Kin. 4:11

Timna, concubine of
Eliphaz.........Gen. 36:12

Tirzah, one of daughters of
Zelophehad......Num. 26:33

Tryphena convert at
Rome...........Rom. 16:12

Tryphosa, convert at
Rome...........Rom. 16:12

Vashti, wife of
Ahasuerus.......Esth. 1:9

Zebudah, mother of
Jehoiakim.......2 Kin. 23:36

Zeresh, wife of
Haman..........Esth. 5:10

Zeruah, a widow..1 Kin. 11:26

Zeruiah, mother of
Joab.............2 Sam. 17:25

Zibiah, mother of
Jehoash . . . . 2 Kin. 12:1
Zillah, wife of
Lamech . . . . Gen. 4:19
Zilpah, Leah's
handmaid . . . . Gen. 29:24
Zipporah, wife of
Moses . . . . Ex. 2:21

Wonderful—*full of wonder*

A. *Ascribed to:*
Human love . . 2 Sam. 1:26
LORD's
works . . . . Ps. 78:4
Mysterious
things . . . . Prov. 30:18
Lord's Law . . . Ps. 119:18
Lord's
testimonies . . . Ps. 119:129
Lord's
knowledge . . . Ps. 139:6
Our being . . . . . Ps. 139:14
Messiah's
name . . . . Is. 9:6

B. *Descriptive of the Lord's work,
as:*
Numerous . . . . . Ps. 40:5
Transmitted . . . Ps. 78:4
Remem-
bered . . . . Ps. 111:4
Praised . . . . Is. 25:1

Wonders—*miraculous works*

A. *Performed by:*
God . . . . Heb. 2:4
Moses and
Aaron . . . . Ex. 11:10
Christ . . . . Acts 2:22
Apostles . . . . . . Acts 2:43
Jesus' name . . . Acts 4:30
Stephen . . . . . . Acts 6:8
Paul and
Barnabas . . . . . . Acts 14:3
Paul . . . . 2 Cor. 12:12

B. *Places of:*
Egypt . . . . Acts 7:36
Land of Ham . . Ps. 105:27
Canaan . . . . Josh. 3:5
Deep . . . . Ps. 107:24
Heaven . . . . Dan. 6:27
Among the
peoples . . . . . Ps. 77:14

C. *Described as:*
Numerous . . . . . Ex. 11:9
Great . . . . Acts 6:8
Mighty . . . . Dan. 4:3

D. *Man's reactions to:*
Did not
remember . . . . . Neh. 9:17
Forgetful of . . . Ps. 78:11, 12
Not under-
standing . . . . . Ps. 106:7
Not believing . . Ps. 78:32
Inquiring
about . . . . Jer. 21:2

E. *Believer's attitude toward, to:*
Remember . . . . . 1 Chr. 16:9, 12
Declare . . . . Ps. 71:17
Give thanks
for . . . . Ps. 136:1, 4
Consider . . . . . . Job 37:14

Wood

A. *Descriptive of:*
Part of a tree . . Num. 19:6
Forest . . . . Josh. 17:15, 18

B. *Place of:*
Animals . . . . 2 Kin. 2:24
Fortresses . . . . . 2 Chr. 27:4

C. *Used for:*
Fire . . . . 1 Kin. 18:23-38
Carts . . . . 1 Sam. 6:14
Weapons . . . . . Num. 35:18
Ships . . . . Gen. 6:14
Palanquin . . . . . Song 3:9
Musical
instruments . . 1 Kin. 10:12
Buildings . . . . . 1 Kin. 6:15-33
Tabernacle
furniture . . . . . Ex. 25:9-28
Platform . . . . . . Neh. 8:4
Gods . . . . Is. 37:19

Woodcutters

Gibeonites . . . . . . Josh. 9:17-27
Classed with "water
carriers" . . . . . . Josh. 9:21, 23
Sent to Solomon . . 2 Chr. 2:10

Woof—*the threads crossing the warp
of a woven garment*

Inspection of, for
leprosy . . . . Lev. 13:48-59

Wool—*the soft hair of sheep*

Inspection of, for
leprosy . . . . Lev. 13:47-59
Mixture of,
forbidden . . . . Deut. 22:11
Used as a test . . . . Judg. 6:37
Valuable article of
trade . . . . Ezek. 27:18

Figurative of
whiteness ....Is. 1:18

Word of God

A. Called:
Book of the
Law...........Neh. 8:3
Law of the
LORD...........Ps. 1:2
Scriptures .....John 5:39
Holy
Scriptures.....Rom. 1:2
Word of God ..Heb. 4:12
Word...........James 1:21-23
Word of life...Phil. 2:16
Book...........Rev. 22:19

B. Descriptive of:
Old Testament
Law............Mark 7:13
God's revealed
plan............Rom. 9:6
God's completed
revelation.....Col. 1:25-27
Christ's
message.......Luke 5:1
Christian
Gospel........Acts 4:31

C. Described as:
Pure...........Ps. 19:8
Restraining ....Ps. 119:11
Perfect ....Ps. 19:7
Sure...........Ps. 111:7, 8
Truth..........Ps. 119:142, 151,
                160
Enduring ......Is. 40:8
Effectual.......Is. 55:11
Sanctifying ....Eph. 5:26
Harmonious ...Acts 15:15
Inspired ....2 Pet. 1:21
Living and
active.........Heb. 4:12

D. Compared to:
Lamp...........Ps. 119:105
Fire.............Jer. 5:14
Hammer.......Jer. 23:29
Seed...........Matt. 13:18-23
Sword..........Eph. 6:17

E. Agency of, to:
Heal...........Ps. 107:20
Make free .....John 8:32
Illuminate .....Ps. 119:130
Bear witness...John 20:31
Produce faith..Rom. 10:17
Make wise.....2 Tim. 3:15-17
Exhort.........2 Tim. 4:2
Rejoice the
heart..........Jer. 15:16

Create the
world ....Heb. 11:3
Regenerate ....James 1:18
Destroy the
world ....2 Pet. 3:5-7

F. Proper attitude toward, to:
Stand in awe
of.............Ps. 119:161
Tremble at.....Is. 66:2, 5
Speak
faithfully......Jer. 23:28
Search.........Acts 17:11
Speak boldly...Acts 4:29, 31
Preach.........Acts 8:25
Receive........Acts 11:1
Glorify.........Acts 13:48
Teach ....Acts 18:11
Obey...........1 Pet. 3:1
Handle
accurately ....2 Tim. 2:15
Do.............James 1:22, 23
Suffer for......Rev. 1:9

G. In the believer's life, as:
Restraint ......Ps. 119:9, 11
Guide..........Ps. 119:133
Source of
joy............ Ps. 119:47, 97, 162
Standard of
conduct.......Titus 2:5
Source of new
life............1 Pet. 1:23
Spiritual
food ....1 Pet. 2:2

H. Prohibitions concerning, not to be:
Preached in man's
wisdom ....1 Cor. 2:4, 13
Used
deceitfully ....2 Cor. 4:2
Altered ....Rev. 22:18, 19

Words—intelligible sounds or signs

A. Described as:
Acceptable....Eccl. 12:10
Lying and
corrupt ....Dan. 2:9
Persuasive .....1 Cor. 2:4
Easy...........1 Cor. 14:9, 19
Inexpressible ..2 Cor. 12:4
Empty.........Eph. 5:6
Flattering......1 Thess. 2:5
Wholesome ...1 Tim. 6:3

B. Power of, to:
Stir up wrath ..Prov. 15:1
Wound ....Prov. 26:22
Sustain ....Is. 50:4

Determine
destiny........Matt. 12:36, 37

Work, Christ's

A. *Defined as:*
Doing God's
will ....John 4:34
Limited in
time ....John 9:4
Incompar-
able...........John 15:24
Initiated by
God............John 14:10
Finished in the
cross..........John 17:4

B. *Design of, to:*
Attest His
mission ....John 5:36
Encourage
faith ....John 14:11, 12
Judge men.....John 15:24

Work, the Christian's

A. *Agency of, by:*
God ....Phil. 2:13
Spirit ....1 Cor. 12:11
God's Word....1 Thess. 2:13
Faith ....Gal. 5:6

B. *Characteristics of:*
Designed for God's
glory...........Matt. 5:16
Divinely
called ....Acts 13:2
Produces eventual
glory...........2 Cor. 4:17
Subject to examin-
ation...........Gal. 6:4
Final perfection
in..............Heb. 13:21

C. *God's regard for, will:*
Reward........Jer. 31:16
Perfect ....Phil. 1:6
Not forget .....Heb. 6:10

See Labor, spiritual

Work, physical

Required of
Christians ....2 Thess. 3:7-14
Nehemiah's zeal...Neh. 6:1-4
Paul's example....Acts 18:1-3

See Labor, physical

Works, God's

A. *Described as:*
Perfect ....Deut. 32:4

Awesome......Ps. 66:3
Incompar-
able...........Ps. 86:8
Honorable and
glorious.......Ps. 111:3
Marvelous .....Ps. 139:14
Righteous .....Ps. 145:17
Unusual ......Is. 28:21
Great and
marvelous.....Rev. 15:3

B. *Manifested in:*
Creation ....Gen. 1:1-3
Heavens.......Ps. 8:3
Deeps ....Ps. 107:24
Regenerate
people ....Is. 19:25

C. *God's attitude toward:*
Rejoice in .....Ps. 104:31
Made known to His
people ....Ps. 111:6
His mercies
over ....Ps. 145:9
Glorified in ....Is. 60:21

D. *Believer's attitude toward, to:*
Consider.......Ps. 8:3
Behold.........Ps. 46:8
Meditate.......Ps. 77:12
Meditate
upon ....Ps. 143:5
Triumph in ....Ps. 92:4
Declare........Ps. 107:22
Praise God
for............Ps. 145:4, 10
Pray for revival
of.............Hab. 3:2

E. *Unbeliever's attitude toward:*
Not
regarding .....Ps. 28:5
Forgetting.....Ps. 78:11
Not believed...Acts 13:41

Works, good

A. *Considered negatively, they
cannot:*
Justify.........Rom. 4:2-6
Determine God's
election ....Rom. 9:11
Secure righteous-
ness...........Rom. 9:31, 32
Substitute for
grace ....Rom. 11:6

B. *Considered positively:*
Reward for ....1 Cor. 3:13-15
Created for ....Eph. 2:10
Prepared for ...2 Tim. 2:21
Equipped for...2 Tim. 3:17

Works, Satan's (see Satan)

Works, the unbeliever's

A. *Described as:*
Wicked.......Col. 1:21
Done in
darkness....Is. 29:15
Abominable...Ps. 14:1
Deceitful......Prov. 11:18
Evil............John 7:7
Unfruitful.....Eph. 5:11

B. *God's attitude toward, will:*
Never forget...Amos 8:7
Reward.......Prov. 24:12
Bring to
judgment.....Rev. 20:12, 13

C. *Believer's relation to:*
Cast off......Rom. 13:12
Have no fellowship
with........Eph. 5:11
Be delivered
from.........2 Tim. 4:18

World

A. *God's relation to, as:*
Maker........Jer. 10:12
Possessor......Ps. 24:1
Redeemer.....John 3:16
Judge..........Ps. 96:13

B. *Christ's relation to, as:*
Maker........John 1:10
Sin-bearer.....John 1:29
Savior.........John 12:47
Life...........John 6:33, 51
Light..........John 8:12
Judge..........Acts 17:31
Overcomer.....John 16:33
Reconciler.....2 Cor. 5:19

C. *Christian's relation to:*
Light of.......Matt. 5:14
Not of........John 17:14, 16
Chosen out
of............John 15:19
Tribulation
in.............John 16:33
Sent into by
Christ.........John 17:18
Not conformed
to............Rom. 12:2
Crucified to....Gal. 6:14
To live
soberly........Titus 2:12
Unspotted
from.........James 1:27
Overcomers
of............1 John 5:4, 5

Denying desires
of.............Titus 2:12

D. *Dangers of, arising from:*
Wisdom.......1 Cor. 3:19
Love of.......2 Tim. 4:10
Friendship.....James 4:4
Corruptions....2 Pet. 1:4
Lusts..........1 John 2:15-17
False
prophets......1 John 4:1
Deceivers.....2 John 7

E. *In the plan of redemption:*
Elect chosen
before.........Eph. 1:4
Revelation made
before.........Matt. 13:35
Sin's entrance
into...........Rom. 5:12
Its guilt before
God...........Rom. 3:19
Original revelation
to.............Rom. 1:20
God's love
for............John 3:16
Christ's mission
to.............John 12:47
Spirit's conviction
of.............John 16:8
Gospel preached
in.............Matt. 24:14
Reconciliation
of.............2 Cor. 5:19
Destruction
of.............2 Pet. 3:7
Final judgment
of.............Acts 17:31
Satan
deceives.......Rev. 12:9

Worm—*a soft-bodied, slender, creeping animal*

A. *Ravages of:*
On bread......Ex. 16:15, 20
On plants.....Jon. 4:7
On the body...Acts 12:23
In the grave...Job 24:19, 20
In hell.........Mark 9:44-48

B. *Figurative of:*
Insignifi-
cance.........Job 25:6
Messiah.......Ps. 22:6

Wormwood—*a bitter-tasting plant*

Figurative of
idolatry..........Deut. 29:18
Of adultery.......Prov. 5:4

Of God's
judgments........Jer. 9:15
Symbol of doom ..Rev. 8:11

Worry (see Cares, worldly)

Worship—*an act of reverence*

A. *Of God:*
Defined.......John 4:20-24
Commanded...1 Chr. 16:29
Corrupted .....Rom. 1:25
Perverted ....2 Kin. 21:3, 21
Debated ....1 Kin. 18:21-39

B. *Of Christ, by:*
Angels.........Heb. 1:6
Magi ....Matt. 2:1-2, 11
Men ....John 9:30-38
Women ....Matt. 15:25
Disciples......Matt. 28:17
Heavenly
choir.........Rev. 4:10, 11

C. *Of wrong objects, such as:*
Heavenly
host..........Deut. 17:3
Other gods....Ex. 34:14
Demons ....Deut. 32:17
Creatures......Rom. 1:25
Images ......Dan. 3:5-18
Man ....Acts 10:25, 26
Antichrist......Rev. 13:4-13

D. *Of wrong objects, by:*
Israel..........2 Kin. 21:3, 21
Pagans ....Rom. 1:25
Professing
Christians.....Col. 2:18
World ....2 Thess. 2:3-12

Worthiness—*acceptableness for some benefit*

A. *Of Christ:*
For more
glory.........Heb. 3:3
To open the
book..........Rev. 5:2, 4
To receive
worship.......Rev. 5:9-14

B. *Of believers, for:*
Provisions.....Matt. 10:10
Discipleship....Matt. 10:37
Their calling...Eph. 4:1
Suffering .....Acts 5:41
Their walk....Col. 1:10
Honor ....1 Tim. 6:1
Kingdom ......2 Thess. 1:5

Worthless—*useless, despicable*

Sacrifice ....Is. 1:13
Religion..........James 1:26

Vile things ....1 Sam. 15:9

See Futile

Wound—*to injure*

A. *Of physical injury, by:*
God ....Deut. 32:39
Battle.........1 Sam. 31:3
Adultery ....Prov. 6:32, 33
Robbers ......Luke 10:30, 34
Evil spirit.....Acts 19:16

B. *Of spiritual injury, by:*
God's
punishment ...Jer. 30:14
Drunkenness ..Prov. 23:29, 30
Adultery ......Prov. 6:32, 33
Sin ....Is. 1:6

Wrappings—*clothes for the dead*

Lazarus attired
in ....John 11:43, 44

Wrath of God

A. *Described as:*
Anger ....Num. 32:10-13
Prolonged .....Ps. 90:9
Great.........Zech. 7:12
Willing ....Rom. 9:22
Revealed ......Rom. 1:18
Stored up.....Rom. 2:5-8
Abiding........John 3:36
Accom-
plished........Rev. 6:16, 17

B. *Caused by:*
Apostasy ......2 Chr. 34:24, 25
Sympathy with
evil ....Lev. 10:1-6
Unfaithful-
ness.........Josh. 22:20
Provocations ..2 Kin. 23:26
Fellowship with
evil ....2 Chr. 19:2
Mockery......2 Chr. 36:16
Idolatry........Ps. 78:58, 59
Inter-
marriage ......Ezra 10:10-14
Profaning the
Sabbath.......Neh. 13:18
Speaking against
God...........Ps. 78:19-21

C. *Effects of, seen in:*
Egypt's
destruction....Ex. 15:4, 7
Great plague...Num. 11:33
Israel's
wanderings ...Num. 32:10-13
Withholding of
rain...........Deut. 11:17

Destruction of a
people ....1 Sam. 28:18
Trouble........Ps. 90:7
Man's death ...Ps. 90:9
Jerusalem's
destruction....Luke 21:23, 24
Punishments of
hell ....Rev. 14:10
Final
judgments ....Rev. 19:15
Israel's
captivity ......2 Chr. 36:16, 17

D. *Deliverance from, by:*
Atonement ....Num. 16:46
Keeping an
oath ....Josh. 9:19, 20
Humbling
oneself........2 Chr. 32:26
Intercession ...Ps. 106:23
Christ ....Rom. 5:8, 9
God's appoint-
ment.........1 Thess. 5:9

Wrestling

Sisters ....Gen. 30:8
Jacob.............Gen. 32:24-30
Christians.........Eph. 6:12

Write, writing, written

A. *Purposes of, to:*
Record God's
Word ....Ex. 24:4, 12
Record
history.......Luke 1:3
Record
dictation ......Jer. 36:2, 27, 28
Make legal....Deut. 24:1-4
Issue orders ...Esth. 8:5, 8, 10
Insure a
covenant......Neh. 9:38
Indicate
name ....Luke 1:63
Indicate the
saved ....Rev. 20:15
Establish
inspiration ....Rev. 22:18, 19

B. *Unusual:*
By God's
finger ....Ex. 31:18
Destroyed and
restored......Jer. 36:21-32
On a wall......Dan. 5:5-29
On the
ground.......John 8:6, 8
On the cross...John 19:19-22
In hearts ......Rom. 2:15

C. *Of the Bible as written,
involving its:*
Authority......Acts 24:14
Determination of
events ......Heb. 10:7-10
Fulfillment.....Luke 21:22
Messianic
character .....Luke 24:44, 46
Saving
purpose ......John 20:31
Harmony ......Acts 15:15
Spiritual aim...Rom. 15:4
Finality ....Rev. 22:18, 19

D. *Figurative of:*
God's real
people ....Rev. 20:12, 15
Indelible
character .....2 Cor. 3:2, 3
Innate
knowledge ....Rom. 2:15

Y

Yah—*a poetic form of Yahweh*

Found only in poetry and in proper
names............Ps. 68:4

Years, thousand

In God's sight, one
day...............2 Pet. 3:8
Time of Satan's
bondage.......Rev. 20:2-7

Yield—*to produce; to surrender*

A. *Used literally of:*
Plants ....Gen. 1:11-29
Earth..........Ps. 67:6
God's
servants......Dan. 3:28

B. *Used figuratively of:*
Discipline......Heb. 12:11
Spiritual
fruit ....Mark 4:8

Yod

Tenth letter of the Hebrew
alphabet..........Ps. 119:73-80

Yoke—*a frame uniting animals for
work*

A. *Used literally on:*
Animals ....Deut. 21:3
Captives.......Jer. 28:10-14
Slaves ....1 Tim. 6:1

B. *Used figuratively of:*
Oppression.....Deut. 28:48
Hard service ... 1 Kin. 12:4-14
Submission .... Jer. 27:8
Bondage to
sin .... Lam. 1:14
Discipleship....Matt. 11:29, 30
Legalistic
ordinances ....Gal. 5:1
Marriage.......2 Cor. 6:14

Young men

A. *Characteristics of, seen in:*
Unwise
counsel ...... 1 Kin. 12:8-14
Godly fervor ... 1 John 2:13, 14
Passion .... Prov. 7:7-23
Strength....... Prov. 20:29
Impatience ....Luke 15:12, 13

B. *Special needs of:*
God's Word....Ps. 119:9
Knowledge and
discretion ....Prov. 1:4
Encourage-
ment..........Is. 40:30, 31
Full
surrender .....Matt. 19:20-22
Soberness.....Titus 2:6
Counsel ...... 1 John 2:13, 14

Youth—*the early age of life*

A. *Evils of, seen in:*
Sin .... Ps. 25:7
Lusts .... 2 Tim. 2:22
Enticements ...Prov. 1:10-16
Self-will ...... Luke 15:12, 13

B. *Good of, seen in:*
Enthusiasm....1 Sam. 17:26-51
Children...... Ps. 127:3, 4
Hardships.....Lam. 3:27
Godly
example....... 1 Tim. 4:12

Z

Zaanan—*rich in flocks*

Town in west
Judah ....Mic. 1:11

Zaanannim

Border point of
Naphtali..........Josh. 19:32, 33

Zaavan—*unquiet*

Son of Ezer ...... Gen. 36:27

Zabad—*gift*

1. Descendant of
Judah ....1 Chr. 2:3, 36
2. Ephraimite.....1 Chr. 7:20, 21
3. One of Joash's
murderers......2 Chr. 24:26
Called
Jozachar......2 Kin. 12:21
4. Son of Zattu .. Ezra 10:27
5. Son of
Hashum.......Ezra 10:33
6. Son of Nebo ...Ezra 10:43

Zabbai—(God) *has given*

1. Man who divorced his foreign
wife...........Ezra 10:28
2. Father of
Baruch........Neh. 3:20

Zabbud—*given* (by God)

Postexilic
returnee.........Ezra 8:14

Zabdi—(God) *has given*

1. Achan's
grandfather ...Josh. 7:1, 17, 18
2. Benjamite ....1 Chr. 8:1, 19
3. One of David's
officers........1 Chr. 27:27

Zabdiel—*God has given*

1. Father of
Jashobeam ....1 Chr. 27:2
2. Postexilic
official ....Neh. 11:14

Zabud—*bestowed*

Son of Nathan ... 1 Kin. 4:5

Zaccai—*probably a contraction of*
'"*Zechariah*"

Head of a postexilic
family ....Ezra 2:9

Zacchaeus—*pure*

Wealthy tax-gatherer converted to
Christ ....Luke 19:1-10

Zaccur, Zacchur—*remembered*

1. Father of the Reubenite
spy ....Num. 13:2, 4
2. Simeonite......1 Chr. 4:24, 26
3. Merarite
Levite.........1 Chr. 24:27
4. Asaphite
Levite.........1 Chr. 25:2, 10

5. Signer of the
   covenant......Neh. 10:1, 12
6. A treasurer under
   Nehemiah......Neh. 13:13

Zacharias

Father of John the
Baptist ....Luke 1:5-17

Zadok—*righteous*

1. Descendant of
   Aaron........1 Chr. 24:1-3
   Co-priest with
   Abiathar ......2 Sam. 20:25
   Loyal to
   David........2 Sam. 15:24-29
   Gently rebuked by
   David........2 Sam. 19:11-14
   Remained aloof from Adonijah's
   usurpation ....1 Kin. 1:8-26
   Commanded by David to anoint
   Solomon .....1 Kin. 1:32-45
   Replaces
   Abiathar ......1 Kin. 2:35
   Sons of,
   faithful......Ezek. 48:11
2. Priest, the son or grandson of
   Ahitub........1 Chr. 6:12
3. Jotham's maternal
   grandfather ....2 Kin. 15:33
4. Postexilic workman, son of
   Baana........Neh. 3:4
5. Postexilic workman, son of
   Immer ......Neh. 3:29
6. Ancestor of
   Christ........Matt. 1:14

Zaham—*foul*

Son of
Rehoboam........2 Chr. 11:18, 19

Zair—*little*

Battle camp in
Edom ....2 Kin. 8:21

Zalaph—*caper-plant*

Father of
Hanum ....Neh. 3:30

Zalmon—*dark*

1. One of David's mighty
   men...........2 Sam. 23:28
2. Mount near
   Shechem......Judg. 9:48

Zalmonah—*shady*

Israelite camp....Num. 33:41, 42

Zalmunna—*deprived of shade*

Midianite king ....Judg. 8:4-21

Zamzummmim—*murmurers*

Race of giants.....Deut. 2:20, 21
Same as the
Zuzim......Gen. 14:5

Zanoah—*rejected*

1. Town in south
   Judah.........Josh. 15:1, 34
2. Town of
   Judah.........Josh. 15:56

Zaphnath-Paaneah—*revealer of secrets*

Name given to Joseph by
Pharaoh..........Gen. 41:45

Zaphon—*concealed*

Town of Gad east of the
Jordan ....Josh. 13:24, 27

Zarephath

Town of Sidon
where Elijah   {1 Kin. 17:8-24
restores widow's
son.............   {Luke 4:26

Zaretan—*cooling*

Town near   {Josh. 3:16
Jezreel   {1 Kin. 4:12
Hiram worked
near..............1 Kin. 7:46

Zattu—*lovely*

Founder of a postexilic
family............Ezra 2:2, 8
Members of,
divorced foreign   {Ezra 10:18, 19,
wives............. {   27
Signs covenant....Neh. 10:1, 14

Zayin

Letter of the Hebrew
alphabet..........Ps. 119:49-56

Zaza—*projection*

Jerahmeelite ......1 Chr. 2:33

Zeal—*intense enthusiasm for something*

A. *Kinds of:*
   Divine..........Is. 9:7
   Glorious ....Is. 63:15
   Wrathful ......Ezek. 5:13

Stirring........2 Cor. 9:2
Intense......2 Cor. 7:11
Boastful......Phil. 3:4, 6
Ignorant......Rom. 10:2, 3
Righteous......John 2:15-17
Sinful........2 Sam. 21:1, 2

B. *Manifested in concern for:*
Lord's sake......Num. 25:11, 13
Others'
salvation......Rom. 10:1
Missionary
work........Rom. 15:18-25
Reformation of
character......2 Cor. 7:11
Desire for spiritual
gifts........1 Cor. 14:12
Doing good
works........Titus 2:14

C. *Illustrated in Paul's life by his:*
Desire to
reach the ⎰Rom. 9:1-3
Jews........⎱Rom. 10:1
Determination to evangelize
all ....1 Cor. 9:19-23
Willingness to lose all things for
Christ........Phil. 3:4-16
Plan to minister to unreached
places........Rom. 1:14, 15
Support of
himself........2 Cor. 11:7-12

D. *Examples of:*
Moses........Ex. 32:19-35
Phinehas......Num. 25:7-13
Joshua........Josh. 24:14-16
Gideon........Judg. 6:11-32
David........1 Sam. 17:26-51
Elijah........1 Kin. 19:10
Jehu........2 Kin. 9:1-37
Josiah........2 Kin. 22:1-20
Ezra........Ezra 7:10
Nehemiah......Neh. 4:1-23
Peter and
John........Acts 4:8-20
Timothy........Phil. 2:19-22
Epaphro-
ditus........Phil. 2:25-30
Epaphras......Col. 4:12, 13

Zealot—*zealous one*

Applied to Simon, the Canaanite; a
party of fanatical
Jews ....Luke 6:15

Zebadiah—*Yahweh has bestowed*

1, 2. Two ⎰1 Chr. 8:1, 15,
Benjamites...⎱ 17

3. Benjamite warrior among
David's mighty
men......1 Chr. 12:1-7
4. One of David's com-
manders ......1 Chr. 27:7
5. Korahite
Levite........1 Chr. 26:1, 2
6. Levite teacher under Jehoshaphat......2 Chr. 17:8
7. Officer of Jehosha-
phat......2 Chr. 19:11
8. Postexilic
returnee ......Ezra 8:8
9. Priest who put away his foreign
wife..........Ezra 10:20

Zebah—*victim; sacrifice*

King of Midian killed by
Gideon........Judg. 8:4-28

Zebaim—*gazelles*

Native place of Solomon's
slaves ....Ezra 2:55, 57

Zebedee—*Yahweh is gift*

Galilean fisherman; father of James
and John........Matt. 4:21, 22

Zebina—*purchased*

Priest who put away his foreign
wife..........Ezra 10:43

Zeboim—*hyenas*

1. One of five cities destroyed with
Sodom and
Gomorrah.....Gen. 10:19
2. Valley in
Benjamin ......1 Sam. 13:16-18
3. City of
Judah........Neh. 11:34

Zebudah—*given*

Mother of
Jehoiakim........2 Kin. 23:36

Zebul—*hesitation*

Ruler of Shechem; exposes Gaal's
revolt ....Judg. 9:26-41

Zebulun—*dwelling*

1. Sixth son of Leah and
Jacob........Gen. 30:19, 20
2. Descendants of 1; a tribe of
Israel ....Num. 2:7
Predictions
concerning....Gen. 49:13
First numbering
of............Num. 1:30, 31

Second numbering
of............Num. 26:27
Representatives
of............Num. 1:9
Territory of....Josh. 19:10-16
Warriors of, fight with
Deborah......Judg. 5:14, 18
Warriors of, aid
Gideon.......Judg. 6:34, 35
Judge Elon, member
of............Judg. 12:11, 12
Warriors of, in David's
army.........1 Chr. 12:33, 40
Some of, respond to Hezekiah's
reforms......2 Chr. 30:10-18
Christ visits   (Is. 9:1
land of....... (Matt. 4:13-15
Those sealed
of............Rev. 7:8

Zebulunites—*natives of Zebulun*

Descendants of Jacob's
son..............Num. 26:27
Elon thus called...Judg. 12:11, 12

Zechariah—*Yahweh remembers*

1. Benjamite.....1 Chr. 9:35, 37
2. Levite porter and
   counselor....1 Chr. 9:21, 22
3. Levite musician in David's
   reign.........1 Chr. 15:18, 20
4. Priestly
   trumpeter....1 Chr. 15:24
5. Kohathite
   Levite........1 Chr. 24:25
6. Merarite Levite in David's
   reign.......1 Chr. 26:10, 11
7. Manassite....1 Chr. 27:21
8. Teaching prince under Jehoshaphat........2 Chr. 17:7
9. Asaphite
   Levite........2 Chr. 20:14
10. Son of King Jehosha-
    phat........2 Chr. 21:2-4
11. Son of Jehoiada
    killed in the   (2 Chr. 24:20-22
    Temple........ (Matt. 23:35
12. Prophet in Uzziah's
    reign........2 Chr. 26:5
13. King of Israel;
    last ruler of Jehu's
    dynasty.......2 Kin. 15:8-12
14. Reubenite
    chief..........1 Chr. 5:7
15. Faithful man in Isaiah's
    time..........Is. 8:2
16. Grandfather of
    Hezekiah......2 Kin. 18:1, 2

17. Levite during Hezekiah's
    reign.........2 Chr. 29:13
18. Kohathite Levite employed as
    overseer......2 Chr. 34:12
19. Temple ruler during Josiah's
    reign.........2 Chr. 35:8
20. Postexilic
    returnee......Ezra 8:3
21. Son of Bebai...Ezra 8:11
22. Man sent by Ezra to secure
    Levites......Ezra 8:15, 16
23. One of Ezra's
    assistants.....Neh. 8:4
24. Jew who divorced his foreign
    wife...........Ezra 10:26
25. Levite
    trumpeter.....Neh. 12:35, 36
26. Priest in dedication
    ceremony.....Neh. 12:41
27. Man of Judah, family of
    Perez.........Neh. 11:4
28. Man of Judah, son of a
    Shilonite.....Neh. 11:5
29. Postexilic
    priest........Neh. 11:12
30. Postexilic
    prophet and   (Ezra 5:1
    priest........ (Zech. 1:1, 7

Zechariah, the Book of—*a book of the
Old Testament*

Call to
repentance......Zech. 1:2-6
The visions........Zech. 1:7—6:15
Against insincerity and
disobedience......Zech. 7:1-14
Restoration of
Jerusalem.......Zech. 8:1-23
Against nations...Zech. 9:1-8
The King comes...Zech. 9:9-17
Parable of
shepherds.......Zech. 11:4-17
Jerusalem
spoiled..........Zech. 14:1-6
Jerusalem
restored.........Zech. 14:7-21

Zecher—*memorial*

Benjamite.........1 Chr. 8:31

Zedad—*siding*

Place on Palestine's north
boundary........Num. 34:8
                 Ezek. 47:15

Zedekiah, Zidkijah—*Yahweh is righteousness*

1. False prophet who counsels Ahab unwisely ......1 Kin. 22:6-24
2. Immoral prophet killed by Nebuchadnezzar ....Jer. 29:21-23
3. Prince under King Jehoiakim.....Jer. 36:12
4. Son of Jeconiah ......1 Chr. 3:16
5. Last king of Judah; uncle and successor of Jehoiachin ....2 Kin. 24:17, 18
   Reigns wickedly for 11 years.....2 Chr. 36:11-13
   Rebels against Jeremiah .....2 Chr. 36:12
   Rebels against Nebuchadnezzar ....Jer. 52:3
   Makes alliance with Egypt ....Ezek. 17:11-21
   Rebellion of, denounced by Jeremiah .....Jer. 34:1-22
   Consults with { Jer. 37:15-21
   Jeremiah .....{ Jer. 38:14-28
   Imprisons Jeremiah .....Jer. 38:1-13
   Captured, blinded, taken to { Jer. 39:1-14
   Babylon ....{ 2 Kin. 25:1-7
6. High official who signs the covenant.....Neh. 10:1

Zeeb—*wolf*

Midianite prince slain by Gideon's men ....Judg. 7:25

Zelah—*rib*

Towns assigned to Benjamin........Josh. 18:28
Burial place of Kish, Saul, and Jonathan ....2 Sam. 21:14

Zelek—*cleft*

One of David's mighty men .....2 Sam. 23:37

Zelophehad—*shadow of the fear*

Manassite whose five daughters secure female rights .....Num. 27:1-7

Zelzah—*sun protection*

Town in south Benjamin near Rachel's tomb ....1 Sam. 10:2

Zemaraim—*double mount forest*

1. Town of Benjamin near Jericho........Josh. 18:22
2. Mountain in Ephraim ......2 Chr. 13:4

Zemarites

Tribe of Canaanites ....Gen. 10:18

Zemirah—*song*

Grandson of Benjamin.....1 Chr. 7:6, 8

Zenan—*place of flocks*

Town in Judah....Josh. 15:21, 37

Zenas—*gift of Zeus*

Christian lawyer ..Titus 3:13

Zephaniah—*hidden of Yahweh*

1. Ancestor of Samuel ......1 Chr. 6:33, 36
2. Author of Zephaniah ....Zeph. 1:1
3. Priest and friend of Jeremiah during Zedekiah's reign.........Jer. 21:1
4. Father of a certain Josiah in Zechariah's time ....Zech. 6:10

Zephaniah, the Book of—*a book of the Old Testament*

Coming judgment.........Zeph. 1:2-18
Call to repentance ......Zeph. 2:1-3
The nations judged ....Zeph. 2:4-15
Jerusalem is blessed ....Zeph. 3:9-20

Zephath—*watchtower*

Canaanite town destroyed by Simeon and Judah ....Judg. 1:17
See Hormah

Zephathah

Valley near Mareshah ....2 Chr. 14:10

Zepho, Zephi—*watch*

Grandson of Esau and a chief of { Gen. 36:15, 19
Edom ....{ 1 Chr. 1:36

Zephon—*watching*

Son of Gad and tribal
head ....Num. 26:15
Called Ziphion ....Gen. 46:16

Zer—*rock*

City assigned to
Naphtali.........Josh. 19:32, 35

Zerah—*dawning*

1. Son of Reuel
   and duke of ⎰ Gen. 36:17, 19
   Edom ....⎱ 1 Chr. 1:44
2. Son of Judah ..Num. 26:20
   Ancestor of
   Achan ....Josh. 7:1-18
3. Son of Simeon and tribal
   head ....Num. 26:12, 13
   Called Zohar..Gen. 46:10
4. Gershomite ⎰ 1 Chr. 6:20, 21,
   Levite........⎱ 41
5. Ethiopian general defeated by
   King Asa......2 Chr. 14:8-15

Zerahiah—*Yahweh is appearing*

1. Ancestor of
   Ezra ....Ezra 7:1, 4, 5
2. Son of Pahath-
   Moab ....Ezra 8:4

Zered—*willow bush*

Brook and valley crossed by
Israel.............Num. 21:12

Zereda, Zeredah—*the fortress*

1. City of Ephraim; birthplace of
   Jeroboam .....1 Kin. 11:26
2. City in the Jordan
   valley ....2 Chr. 4:17
   Same as Zaretan
   in ....1 Kin. 7:46

Zererah

Town in the Jordan
valley ....Judg. 7:22
Same as Zaretan ..1 Kin. 7:46

Zeresh—*golden*

Wife of Haman....Esth. 5:10, 14

Zereth—*splendor*

Judahite ....1 Chr. 4:5-7

Zereth Shahar—*the splendor of dawn*

City of Reuben....Josh. 13:19

Zeror—*bundle*

Benjamite.........1 Sam. 9:1

Zeruah—*smitten; leprous*

Mother of King
Jeroboam I ....1 Kin. 11:26

Zerubbabel—*seed of Babel*

Descendant of
David ....1 Chr. 3:19
Leader of Jewish
exiles............Neh. 7:6, 7
Restores worship in
Jerusalem ....Ezra 3:1-8
Rebuilds the
Temple...........Zech. 4:1-14
Prophecy
concerning ......Hag. 2:23
Ancestor of ⎰ Matt. 1:12, 13
Christ ....⎱ Luke 3:27

Zeruiah—*balm*

Mother of Joab....2 Sam. 17:25

Zetham—*olive tree*

Gershonite
Levite ....1 Chr. 23:7, 8

Zethan—*olive tree*

Benjamite.........1 Chr. 7:6, 10

Zethar—*sacrifice*

One of the seven chamberlains of
King Ahasuerus ..Esth. 1:10

Zia—*the trembler*

Gadite ....1 Chr. 5:11, 13

Ziba—*plant*

Saul's servant.....2 Sam. 9:9
Befriends David ...2 Sam. 16:1-4
Accused of deception by
Mephibosheth ....2 Sam. 19:17-30

Zibeon—*hyena*

Son of Seir and a clan
chief ....Gen. 36:20, 21

Zibia—*gazelle*

Benjamite and household
head ....1 Chr. 8:8, 9

Zibiah—*gazelle*

Mother of King
Jehoash ....2 Kin. 12:1

Zichri—*famous*

1. Kohathite
   Levite.........Ex. 6:21

2, 3, 4. Three Benjamites... $\left\{\begin{array}{l}\text{1 Chr. 8:19, 23,} \\ \text{27}\end{array}\right.$
5. Son of Asaph..1 Chr. 9:15
6. Descendant of Moses........1 Chr. 26:25
7. Reubenite .....1 Chr. 27:16
8. Judahite ......2 Chr. 17:16
9. Mighty man in Pekah's army........2 Chr. 28:7
10. Benjamite .....Neh. 11:9
11. Postexilic priest ....Neh. 12:17

Ziddim—*sides*

City of Naphtali...Josh. 19:35

Ziha

Head of a Nethinim family...........Ezra 2:43

Ziklag—*winding*

City on the border of Judah ....Josh. 15:1, 31
Assigned to Simeon...........Josh. 19:1, 5
Held by David.....1 Sam. 27:6
Overthrown by Amalekites.......1 Sam. 30:1-31
Occupied by returnees........Neh. 11:28

Zillah—*shadow*

One of Lamech's wives............Gen. 4:19-23

Zillethai—*shadow of Yahweh*

1. Benjamite .....1 Chr. 8:20
2. Manassite captain........1 Chr. 12:20

Zilpah—*a drop*

Leah's maid.......Gen. 29:24
Mother of Gad and Asher........Gen. 30:9-13

Zimmah—*counsel*

Gershonite Levite...........$\left\{\begin{array}{l}\text{1 Chr. 6:20, 42,} \\ \text{43}\end{array}\right.$

Zimran—*antelope*

Son of Abraham and Keturah..........Gen. 25:1, 2

Zimri—*pertaining to an antelope*

1. Grandson of Judah.........1 Chr. 2:3-6

Called Zabdi...Josh. 7:1-18
2. Simeonite prince slain by Phinehas......Num. 25:6-14
3. Benjamite .....1 Chr. 8:1, 36
4. King of Israel for seven days ....1 Kin. 16:8-20
5. Place or people otherwise unknown ....Jer. 25:25

Zin—*low land*

Wilderness through which the Israelites passed............Num. 20:1
Border of Judah and Edom ....Josh. 15:1-3

Zina—*abundance*

Son of Shimei.....1 Chr. 23:10

Zion—*fortress*

A. Used literally of:
Jebusite fortress captured by David.........2 Sam. 5:6-9
Place from which Solomon brings the ark ....2 Chr. 5:2
Area occupied by the Temple.......Is. 8:18
B. Used figuratively of:
Israel as a people of God............2 Kin. 19:21
God's spiritual kingdom ......Ps. 125:1
Eternal city....Heb. 12:22, 28
Heaven........Rev. 14:1

Zior—*smallness*

Town of Judah....Josh. 15:54

Ziph—*refining place*

1. Town in south Judah.........Josh. 15:24
2. City in the hill country of Judah.........Josh. 15:55
David hides from Saul in wilderness here..........$\left\{\begin{array}{l}\text{1 Sam. 23:14,} \\ \text{15}\end{array}\right.$
3. Son of Jehaleleel .....1 Chr. 4:16

Ziphah—*lent*

Son of Jehaleleel ..1 Chr. 4:16

Ziphites—*inhabitants of Ziph*

Betray David......1 Sam. 23:19-24

Ziphron—*beautiful top*

Place in north
Palestine ....Num. 34:9

Zippor—*sparrow*

Father of Balak ...Num. 22:4, 10

Zipporah—*bird*

Daughter of Jethro; wife of
Moses ....Ex. 18:1, 2

Zithri—*my protection*

Grandson of
Kohath...........Ex. 6:18, 22

Ziv—*splendor, bloom*

Second month of the Jewish
year..............1 Kin. 6:1

Ziz—*brightness*

Pass leading from Dead Sea to
Jerusalem ....2 Chr. 20:16

Ziza—*brightness*
1. Simeonite
   leader........ { 1 Chr. 4:24, 37, 38
2. Son of
   Rehoboam ....2 Chr. 11:18-20

Zizah

Gershonite
Levite .... { 1 Chr. 23:7, 10, 11

See Zina

Zoan

City in Lower
Egypt ....Num. 13:22
Places of God's
miracles ....Ps. 78:12, 43
Princes resided
at ....Is. 30:2, 4
Object of God's
wrath ....Ezek. 30:14

Zoar—*little*

Ancient city of Canaan originally
named Bela.......Gen. 14:2, 8
Spared destruction at Lot's
request...........Gen. 19:20-23
Seen by Moses from Mt.
Pisgah...........Deut. 34:1-3
Object of prophetic
doom............Is. 15:5

Zobah

Syrian kingdom; wars against
Saul.............1 Sam. 14:47

Zobebah—*the affable*

Judahite ....1 Chr. 4:1, 8

Zohar—*gray*
1. Father of Ephron the
   Hittite ....Gen. 23:8
2. Son of
   Simeon ......Gen. 46:10

Zoheleth—*serpent*

Stone near
En-rogel..........1 Kin. 1:9

Zoheth—*proud*

Descendant of
Judah ....1 Chr. 4:1, 20

Zophah—*pot-bellied jug*

Asherite ....{ 1 Chr. 7:30, 35, 36

Zophar—*chirper*

Naamathite and friend of
Job...............Job 2:11

Zophim—*watchers*

Field on the top of Mt.
Pisgah...........Num. 23:14

Zorah, Zareah, Zoreah—*hornet*

Town of Judah....Josh. 15:1, 33
Inhabited by
Danites..........Josh. 19:40, 41
Place of Samson's
birth and
burial ....{ Judg. 13:24, 25 Judg. 16:30, 31
Inhabited by
returnees........Neh. 11:25, 29

Zorathite

Native of Zorah...1 Chr. 4:2
Descendants of
Caleb.............1 Chr. 2:50, 53

Zorite

Same as
Zorathite.........1 Chr. 2:54

Zuar—*small, little*

Father of
Nethanel . . . . Num. 1:8

Zuph—*honeycomb*

1. Ancestor of
   Samuel . . . . 1 Chr. 6:33, 35
2. Region in
   Judah . . . . 1 Sam. 9:4-6

Zur—*rock*

1. A Midianite
   leader . . . . Num. 25:15, 18
2. Son of Jehiel . . . 1 Chr. 8:30

Zuriel—*God is a rock*

Merarite Levite . . . Num. 3:35

Zurishaddai—*the Almighty is a rock*

Father of
Shelumiel . . . . Num. 7:36, 41

Zuzim—*prominent; giant*

Tribe east of the
Jordan . . . . Gen. 14:5
Probably same as
Zamzummims . . . . Deut. 2:20

Nelson's Quick-Reference™ Series

Nelson's Quick-Reference™ Bible Concordance
Gives you easy access to over 40,000 key Bible references that are most often sought. Save time and avoid the tedium that goes with wading through long lists of references less sought after. Keyed to the New King James Version, but useful with any.
400 pages / 0-8407-6907-5 / available now

Nelson's Quick-Reference™ Bible Dictionary
More like a "mini-encyclopedia" than a standard dictionary, this compact reference offers an A-Z way to discover fascinating details about the Bible—its characters, history, setting, and doctrines.
784 pages / 0-8407-6906-7 / available now

Nelson's Quick-Reference™ Bible Handbook
Helps you read each of the Bible's 66 books, plus those of the Apocrypha. Offers book introductions, brief summaries, historical and faith-and-life highlights, at-a-glance charts, and detailed teaching outlines. Suggests individual reading plans and schedules for group study.
416 pages / 0-8407-6904-0 / available now

Nelson's Quick-Reference™
Bible Questions and Answers
Learning is fun, lively, and exciting with the over 6,000 questions and answers covering the whole Bible. Variety keeps interest high—short answer, true/false, multiple choice, fill in the blank, and sentence completion.
384 pages / 0-8407-6905-9 / available now

Nelson's Quick-Reference™
Introduction to the Bible
Introduces the Bible as a whole and describes all its parts from an historical and evangelical theological perspective. Explore the fascinating variety in Scripture—story and

song, poetry and prophecy, and more. Discover its divinely revealed answers to the most important questions of life.

384 pages / 0-8407-3206-6 / available now

Nelson's Quick-Reference™
Bible People and Places

From Aaron to Zurishaddain, and from Dan to Beersheba, quickly identify each person and place in the Bible—and many key events. One list, arranged from A to Z, gives brief descriptions and Scripture references, and tells what the names mean, how to say them, and which refer to the same person or place. Variant spellings make this guide useful with any translation.

384 pages / 0-8407-6912-1 / available now

Nelson's Quick-Reference™
Chapter-by-Chapter Bible Commentary

By Warren W. Wiersbe. Supplement your Bible reading with this devotional commentary that spotlights the spiritual and practical truths of Scripture. Drawn from Wiersbe's over forty-five years of study, reflection, and teaching on Scripture, these succinct comments are organized and expressed memorably—a heart-provoking aid to your personal devotions.

864 pages / 0-7852-8235-1 / available now

Nelson's Quick-Reference™
The Life of Christ

By Howard F. Vos. Survey the works and words of the most influential life ever lived—Jesus of Nazareth, the Christ of God. Understand Him in His context by discovering the historical, political, and religious settings in which He lived; and by exploring the Gospels' account of His message, miracles, and complete ministry—the lives He touched and changed by His living, dying, and rising again!

320 pages / 0-8407-3363-1 / available now

Nelson's Quick-Reference™
Introduction to Church History

By Howard F. Vos. Trace the story of the followers of Jesus—from the Upper Room at Pentecost to the ends of the earth as the Christian churches girdle the globe today. Meet the leaders and events that helped spread the Gospel and strengthen the churches. Through this, the most up-to-date introduction to contemporary Christianity worldwide, explore the trends that shape our churches even today.

416 pages / 0-7852-8420-8 / available now

Nelson's Quick-Reference™ Bible Maps and Charts

Make any Bible a study Bible with this unique collection of maps, book charts, and other visuals that present clear information about Bible people, events, and teachings in ways that heighten your interest, retention, and understanding in Bible study. Seeing it helps you believe it!

approx 300 pages / 0-8407-6908-3 / April, 1994